British and Irish Poets

British and Irish Poets

A Biographical Dictionary, 449–2006

WILLIAM STEWART

Foreword by Steven Barfield

McFarland & Company, Inc., Publishers

Jefferson, North Carolina, and London

LIBRARY OF CONGRESS CATALOGUING-IN-PUBLICATION DATA

British and Irish poets : a biographical
dictionary, 449–2006 / compiled by William Stewart ;
foreword by Steven Barfield.
p.   cm.
Includes bibliographical references and index.

ISBN-13: 978-0-7864-2891-5
illustrated case binding : 50# alkaline paper ∞

1. Poets, English — Biography — Dictionaries.
2. Poets, Irish — Biography — Dictionaries.
3. English poetry — Bio-bibliography — Dictionaries.
4. English poetry — Irish authors — Bio-bibliography — Dictionaries.
5. English poetry — Welsh authors — Bio-bibliography — Dictionaries.
6. English poetry — Scottish authors — Bio-bibliography — Dictionaries.
I. Stewart, William, 1927–   II. Barfield, Steven.

PR502.B67   2007   821.09 — dc22   2006102416
                         [B]

British Library cataloguing data are available

On the cover *(left to right, top to bottom):* The Venerable Bede (Morse Library,
Beloit College), William Shakespeare (Clipart.com), Robert Burns (Clipart.com),
Lady Mary Wroth (James A. Cannavino Library, Marist College), Alexander Pope
(National Portrait Gallery, London), John Keats (National Portrait Gallery,
London), Elizabeth Barrett Browning (Library of Congress), Dylan Thomas
(John Mitchell), W.H. Auden (California Institute of Technology), Percy Bysshe
Shelley, from *Finden's Landscape & Portrait Illustrations to the Life and Works of
Lord Byron, Volume 2* (London: John Murray, 1832), William Butler Yeats
(George Eastman House, Rochester, NY), Seamus Heaney (University of Leeds)

Manufactured in the United States of America

*McFarland & Company, Inc., Publishers
Box 611, Jefferson, North Carolina 28640
www.mcfarlandpub.com*

Table of Contents

Foreword

by Steven Barfield

The 1500 hundred year history of poetry written in English is extremely rich and diverse; so much so, in fact, that some may find the very variety and wealth of poetry intimidating. As William Stewart suggests in his preface, it is a resource that is very much part of "our" own history, present and future, albeit one that is encountered through the words left for us by individuals struggling to transform lived experience into the successful nerve and sinew of poetry. Robert Frost remarked that "Poetry is a way of taking life by the throat," while another American poet, Emily Dickinson, said, "If I feel physically as if the top of my head were taken off, I know that is poetry." Such passionate comments tell us something about why poetry matters and why we as readers continue to care about it.

Cleanth Brooks and Robert Penn Warren, in 1938, produced their famous anthology, *Understanding Poetry: An Anthology for College Students.* They made the claim in their prefatory "Letter to the Teacher" that "this book has been conceived on the assumption that if poetry is worth teaching at all it is worth teaching as poetry. The temptation to make a substitute for the poem as the object of study is usually overpowering." Yet, while it is true that there is no substitute for reading actual poetry with due attention and appropriate care, there are many readers and students of poetry who desire or need to know something more about the life and careers of the poets and the different times and societies in which they created their work. For these readers and students in particular, Stewart's book will act as an invaluable one-volume map to help locate the men and women behind the poetry, as well as providing a companion where readers can find further sources of information and discover additional poems by the poets whose work interests them.

One of the strengths of Stewart's book is that it can guide the reader who comes across an individual, stray poem that comes to inhabit their own imagination, to find other poems by the poets and to explore the work of their near contemporaries. Stewart is generous and wideranging in his choice of the poets whose essential details he records in this book, mixing the familiar names with the forgotten and obscure, representing women and men from all walks of life and fully reflecting the current "internationalization" of poetry written in English by poets from across the world. Finally, two appendices, bibliography and index of the book further encourage the reader to seek out the poetic voices they might not yet be acquainted with, but who may become valuable to them in the future.

Steven Barfield is Senior Lecturer in English Literature at the University of Westminster, United Kingdom.

Preface

Poets of any nation are representatives of a time and an age, and what they write about reflects the values, attitudes, experiences, hopes and dreams of that slice of time. Thus poets and their poems are an essential part of history, for on looking back through their poems we glimpse cultural, national, social, economic, religious and military history. In the works of British and Irish poets, we witness the rise and fall of monarchs and the rise and decline of the British Empire, and the birth of nations who have won their independence, such as Ireland and America and the African states, and many other countries

Through the poems of Britain and Ireland we can trace an intricate weaving of the threads that make Scotland, England, Ireland and Wales what they are in the first years of the 21st century. Through the poems in the 1500-year period of this book we can trace the struggle for personal and national independence; of a rugged insistence to keep alive dialects and languages that were perhaps destined for obscurity; and a determination to embrace change, as we become a multiracial, multicultural society.

We can revel in the pride of great achievements and victories and feel the disgrace of the evil acts and tyranny portrayed by some poems, or lose ourselves in the sights, sounds and smells evoked by others. The poets of the 21st century write different poetry from their poetic ancestors, yet what they have to say and how they say it is no less important, and in years to come will form an important slice of current society. And throughout poetry we can look toward the fu-ture. Those are the things that make poetry more than just a pleasant read; they are part and parcel of our very life.

The Structure of the Book

Each entry is made up of:

1. A short biography:
2. Some of the poet's main publications:
3. Some of the poems' titles (but no verses);
4. A list of sources in which the poems appear.

The poems chosen say something about the poet and his or her range of interests. The aim of each entry is to give information; to stimulate curiosity and provide resources for further study. Some of the poets are well known, the names of others have long-since passed out of the current usage; and others, particularly those who write in the vernacular, or in Scots, Gaelic, Irish or Welsh, deserve to be known to a wider audience.

The Sources

The Sources list for each entry refers to books and Internet links that were used in the writing of the entry, where more information can be found including many of the poems.

The main sources used throughout this book are:

1. *Dictionary of National Biography*. Electronic Edition, 1.1. Oxford University Press, 1997.

2. *Encyclopædia Britannica Ultimate Reference Suite* DVD, 2006.

3. *English Poetry: Author Search.* Chadwyck-Healey Ltd., 1995. (http://www.lib.utexas.edu:8080/search/epoetry/author.html).

4. *Microsoft Encarta* 2006 [DVD]. Microsoft Corporation, 2006.

5. *Poemhunter* (www.poemhunter.com).

6. Stanford University libraries and Academic Information Resources. (http://library.stanford.edu).

7. *The Columbia Granger's Index to Poetry.* 11th ed. (http://www.columbiagrangers.org).

8. *The Columbia Granger's World of Poetry*, Columbia University Press, 2005. (http://www.columbiagrangers. org).

9. *The Oxford Companion to English Literature.* 6th edition. Margaret Drabble, ed. Oxford University Press, 2000.

10. *Wikipedia, the Free Encyclopedia* (http://en. wikipedia.org/wiki/Wikipedia).

In addition to those quoted, other Internet links are listed in the Sources relevant to each poet.

THE POETS

ABBOT, JOHN B.D. (fl. 1623)

English poet and divine who embraced the Catholic religion and retired to the convent of St. John the Baptist at Antwerp. There, in 1623, he wrote *Jesus Praefigured or a Poem of the Holy Name of Jesus* (in five books). The work is dedicated to Charles, Prince of Wales (later Charles I, 1625–49). A second dedication is to Señora Doña Maria de Austria, the daughter of Philip III of Spain. He also wrote a long poem, "To the High and Mightie Prince, Charles, Prince of Wales, Duke of Cornwall, Earle of Chester." *The Sad Condition of a Distracted Kingdome* was published in 1645 and *Devovt Rhapsodies* in 1647. His poem "The Fable of Philo the Jew" is an imaginary conversation between God and the angels about creation.

Sources: *Dictionary of National Biography.* Electronic Edition 1.1. Oxford University Press, 1997. *Chadwyck-Healey English Poetry Database: Jacobean and Caroline Poetry 1603–1660* (http://library.stanford.edu/depts/hasrg/hdis/engpo.html). *Oldpoetry* (www.oldpoetry.com). *Stanford University Libraries and Academic Information Resources* (http://library.stanford.edu).

ABERCROMBIE, LASCELLES (1881–1938)

English poet, journalist and dramatist, associated with Georgian poetry. (The Georgians were a group of poets who gained a large popular readership during the early years of George V's reign, 1910–1936. Their poetry tried to maintain the romantic tradition of an earlier age in order to combat the values of Modernism.) Abercrombie had a distinguished academic career in literature at the universities of Liverpool, Leeds and Oxford between 1919 and 1938. He published many poems and collections of poems between 1908 and 1931. *Interludes and Poems* appeared in 1908, the same year that he began to write for the *Liverpool Courier.* His work is included in a five volumes series titled *Georgian Poetry* (1912–1922) edited by Sir Edward Howard Marsh. He and several others formed the Georgian journal *New Numbers,* a vehicle where much of his best work appeared, with that of Rupert Brooke, John Drinkwater and Wilfrid Gibson. His "Witchcraft: New Style," published in *Georgian Poetry* 1918–1919, beautifully creates an atmosphere of a public house. Some of his poems: "The Box," "Emblems of Love," "From Vashti," "Hymn to Love," "The Sale of Saint Thomas."

Sources: *Biography of Lascelles Abercrombie* (http://www.paralumun.com/bioabercrombie.htm). *Dictionary of National Biography.* Electronic Edition 1.1. Oxford University Press, 1997. *Encyclopædia Britannica Ultimate Reference Suite DVD, 2006. Poemhunter* (www.poemhunter.com). *The Columbia Granger's Index to Poetry.* 11th ed. *The Columbia Granger's World of Poetry,* Columbia University Press, 2005 (http://www.columbiagrangers.org). *The Georgian Poets: Abercrombie, Brooke, Drinkwater, Lascelles, Thomas (Writers and Their Works).* Rennie Parker. Northcote House Educational Publishers, Tavistock, England, 1998. *The Literary Encyclopedia* (www.LitEncyc.com). *The National Portrait Gallery* (www.npg.org.uk). *The Oxford Companion to English Literature.* 6th edition. Margaret Drabble, ed. Oxford University Press, 2000.

ABSE, DANNIE (1923–)

Welsh poet, playwright, essayist, novelist and medical doctor who integrated both his Welsh and Jewish heritages into his poetry. He was editor of the literary magazine *Poetry and Poverty* from 1949 to 1954. His first book of verse, *After Every Green* (1948), has been followed by many other individual poems and collections. His *Tenants of the House* (1957) addresses moral and political concerns in parable form. One of the themes he explores in *Poems, Golders Green* (1962) is of being a Welshman and Jew in London. He has also published novels and works for the theatre. His autobiography, *A Poet in the Family* (1974), captures the feelings of difference of a Jewish boy growing up in South Wales and the only Jewish student in a Roman Catholic grammar school. "He is a lyric poet of depth, whose imaginative reach can be both adventurous and demanding" (foreword to *White Coat, Purple Coat: Collected Poems 1948–1988*. New York: Persea Books, 1991). The first line of the closing stanza of "Presences" reminds us, "The future's future is another place...."

Sources: *Dannie Abse Selected Poems*. Canto Publications. ISBN: 1903515009: Compact Disk. *Encyclopædia Britannica Ultimate Reference Suite DVD, 2006. The Columbia Granger's Index to Poetry*. 11th ed. *The Columbia Granger's World of Poetry*. Columbia University Press, 2005 (http://www.columbiagrangers.org). *The National Portrait Gallery* (www.npg.org.uk). *The Oxford Companion to English Literature*. 6th edition. Margaret Drabble, ed. Oxford University Press, 2000.

ACKROYD, PETER (1949–)

Born in London, he was educated at St. Benedict's School, Ealing, and graduated M.A. from Clare College, Cambridge (1971), and was a Mellon Fellow at Yale University (1971–1973). He worked at *The Spectator* magazine between 1973 and 1977 and became joint managing editor and film critic in 1978. He was nominated a fellow of the Royal Society in 1984 and is currently a regular radio broadcaster and book critic. In 1986 he became the principal book reviewer for *The Times* newspaper. He was made a Commander of the Order of the British Empire in 2003 and has won nine major literary prizes and awards. His poetry career started with *London Lickpenny* (1973) and *The Diversions of Purley* (1987). He is better known for his fiction and non-fiction publications, including biographies, of which the latest are *Turner* (2005) and *Newton* (2006). *The Last Testament of Oscar Wilde* (1983) is a reconstruction through the eyes of Wilde of his last years living in poverty in Paris. *London: The Biography* (2000) is a discussion of London through the ages. Some of his poems: "All These," "And the Children," "It Would Be Easy," "The Day."

Sources: *Contemporary Writers in the UK* (www.contemporarywriters.com). *Encyclopædia Britannica Ultimate Reference Suite DVD, 2006. Microsoft Encarta* 2006 (DVD). Microsoft Corporation, 2006. *P.E.N. New Poetry*. Robert Nye, ed. Quartet Books, 1986. *The Columbia Granger's Index to Poetry*. 11th ed. *The Columbia Granger's World of Poetry*. Columbia University Press, 2005 (http://www.columbiagrangers.org). *The National Portrait Gallery* (www.npg.org.uk). *The Oxford Companion to English Literature*. 6th edition. Margaret Drabble, ed. Oxford University Press, 2000. *Who's Who*. London: A & C Black, 2005. *Wikipedia, the Free Encyclopedia* (http://en.wikipedia.org/wiki/Wikipedia).

ADAMS, SARAH FLOWER (1805–1848)

English poet, actress (playing Lady Macbeth in 1837), and Unitarian hymn-writer. She was one of the earliest feminists and contributed 13 hymns to the Unitarian *Hymns and Anthems*, published in 1841, and contributed to the first illustrated government report on Children in the Mines, 1842. Her hymn "Nearer My God to Thee" is supposed to have been the hymn the band on the RMS *Titanic* played as it sank after hitting an iceberg on 14 April 1912, although this is disputed. Her poem "The Mourners Came at Break of Day" tells the story of the women who visited the tomb of Jesus on Easter Sunday and joy of the Resurrection. Her poem "Summer Recollection" evokes feelings of a balmy summer's day, with bees gathering nectar from the lime trees and contented cows lying on the lush grass, chewing the cud. Some of her other poems: "He Sendeth Sun, He Sendeth Shower," "Love! Thou Makest All Things Even," "Part in Peace: Is Day Before Us?"

Sources: *Dictionary of National Biography*. Electronic Edition 1.1. Oxford University Press, 1997. *The Columbia Granger's Index to Poetry*. 11th ed. *The Columbia Granger's World of Poetry*. Columbia University Press, 2005 (http://www.columbiagrangers.org). *The National Portrait Gallery* (www.npg.org.uk). *Poemhunter* (www.poemhunter.com). *The Oxford Companion to English Literature*. 6th edition. Margaret Drabble, ed. Oxford University Press, 2000.

ADAMSON, HENRY (d. 1639)

A Scottish poet, native of Perth, and son of Provost James Adamson, who was dean of guild in Perth at the time of the Gowrie conspiracy — an attempt on the life of King James VI at Gowrie House in Perth. Although educated for the Church, Adamson was a Latin poet of consequence. His elegy, *The Muses Threnodie or Mirthfull Mourning on the Death of Master Gall* (1638), a work of nine books, gives an account of the history and surroundings of Perth. Perth is famous for its golf, and he makes reference to it in his poem. "First Muse" is a pastoral poem set around the Scottish rivers of Earn and Tay, bringing in classical references to Venus and Phoebe.

Sources: *Dictionary of National Biography*. Electronic Edition 1.1. Oxford University Press, 1997. *Oldpoetry* (www.oldpoetry.com). *Significant and Famous Scots* (http://www.electricscotland.com/history/other/adamson_henry.htm).

ADCOCK, KAREN FLEUR (1934–)

Born in Papakura, Auckland, New Zealand, Adcock came to England with her parents in 1939 and was educated there. She returned to New Zealand in 1947 and graduated B.A. in classics from Victoria University, Wellington, in 1954. She lectured on classics at the University of Otago in Dunedin, New Zealand, and was then librarian at the Alexander

Turnbull Library, Wellington. On returning to England in 1963, she took two creative writing fellowships, and in 1908 she became a freelance writer, producing her own poetry, translating and editing collections, and delivering talks on poetry for the BBC. She has received nine major awards both in New Zealand and in Britain and received the Order of the British Empire in 1996. Some of her publications: *The Eye of the Hurricane*, 1964. *High Tide in the Garden*, 1971. *The Inner Harbor*, 1979. *Selected Poems*, 1983. *The Virgin and the Nightingale: Medieval Latin Poems*, 1983 (translations). *The Incident Book*, 1986. *Time-Zones*, 1991. *Looking Back*, 1997. *Poems 1960–2000*, 2000. Some of her poems: "A House in Byzantium," "Advice to a Discarded Lover," "Against Coupling," "Night-piece," "Wife to Husband."

Sources: *Biography of Fleur Adcock* (www.english. emory.edu/Bahri/Adcock.html). *Microsoft Encarta* 2006 (DVD). Microsoft Corporation, 2006. *Encyclopædia Britannica Ultimate Reference Suite DVD, 2006. Fleur Adcock* (www.contemporarywriters.com/authors/?p=auth161). *The National Portrait Gallery* (www.npg.org.uk). *New Zealand Love Poems*. Lauris Edmond, ed. Oxford University Press, 2000. *The Greek Anthology and Other Ancient Epigrams*. Peter Jay, ed. Penguin Books, 1981. *The Norton Anthology of Literature by Women: The Tradition in English*. Sandra M. Gilbert and Susan Guber, eds. W.W. Norton, 1985. *The Oxford Companion to English Literature*. 6th edition. Margaret Drabble, ed. Oxford University Press, 2000. *The Penguin Book of New Zealand Verse*. Ian Wedde and Harvey McQueen, eds. Penguin, 1985. *Who's Who*. London: A & C Black, 2005.

ADDISON, JOSEPH (1672–1719)

Essayist, poet, dramatist and statesman; the son of a clergyman, born at Milston, Wiltshire, and educated at Charterhouse School, Queen's College, and Magdalen College, Oxford, from where he graduated in 1693. He was a major contributor to *The Tatler* and founded the *Spectator* in 1711. His tragedy *Cato* was published in 1713. Two of his longer poems are "An Account of the Greatest English Poets" and "A Letter from Italy." At least six hymns are credited to him. He is buried in the South Transept of Westminster Abbey. Joseph Haydn set "The Spacious Firmament on High" to an adaptation of his own "The Heavens Are Telling" from *The Creation*. This music can be found online at http://www.cyber hymnal.org/htm/s/p/spacious.htm. Some of his other poems: "How Are Thy Servants Blest, O Lord!" "Hymn," "Ode."

Sources: *Encyclopædia Britannica Ultimate Reference Suite DVD, 2006. Oldpoetry* (www.oldpoetry.com). *Poemhunter* (www.poemhunter.com). *Samuel Johnson's Lives of the English Poets, 1779–1781* (http://www2.hn.psu.edu/ Faculty/KKemmerer/poetspreface.htm). *The Columbia Granger's Index to Poetry*. 11th ed. *The Columbia Granger's World of Poetry*. Columbia University Press, 2005 (http:// www.columbiagrangers.org). *The National Portrait Gallery* (www.npg.org.uk). *The Oxford Companion to English Literature*. 6th edition. Margaret Drabble, ed. Oxford University Press, 2000. *The Poetical Works of Joseph Addison*. John Bell. Apollo Press, 1778. *Westminster Abbey Official Guide* (no date).

AE (GEORGE WILLIAM RUSSELL) (1867–1935)

Irish poet, mystic, painter, economist, and journalist, better known by his pseudonym "AE" (AEon). He was editor of *The Irish Homestead* (1904–23) and *The Irish Statesman* (1923–30). He published his volume of poems *Homeward: Songs by the Way* in 1894 and two volumes of *Collected Poems* in 1913 and 1926. *The Candle of Vision* (1918) is the best guide to his religious beliefs. In 1934 he published a poem of Celtic mythology, *The House of the Titans*. Some of his other poems have allusions to mythical Celtic figures. Explanations of these can be found at http://www.bartleby.com/253/1001.html. When he spoke of the political upheavals of the time he was ignored. After the death of his wife in 1932, Russell moved to England—first to London in 1933 and then to Bournemouth, where he died. His poem "A Memory" reflects his realization that life is frail. Some of his other poems: "By the Margin of the Great Deep," "Immortality," "Krishna," "Self-Discipline," "The Great Breath," "The Man to the Angel."

Sources: *Collected Poems, by AE,* London: Macmillan, 1913 and 2001. *Dictionary of National Biography*. Electronic Edition 1.1. Oxford University Press, 1997. *Encyclopædia Britannica Ultimate Reference Suite DVD, 2006. John Burns Library, Boston College, Massachusetts* (www.bc.edu/li braries/centers/burns). *Poemhunter* (www.poemhunter. com). *PoetryConnection.net* (www.poetryconnection.net). *The Columbia Granger's Index to Poetry*. 11th ed. *The Columbia Granger's World of Poetry*. Columbia University Press, 2005 (http://www.columbiagrangers.org). *The National Portrait Gallery* (www.npg.org.uk). *The Oxford Companion to English Literature*. 6th edition. Margaret Drabble, ed. Oxford University Press, 2000.

AGARD, JOHN (1949–)

Playwright, poet, short story and children's writer born in Guyana, he worked as sub-editor and feature writer for the *Guyana Sunday Chronicle* newspaper. He came to England in 1977, where he became a lecturer for the Commonwealth Institute, traveling to schools throughout the U.K. to promote a better understanding of Caribbean culture. In 1993 he was appointed writer in residence at the South Bank Centre, London, and became poet in residence at the BBC in London. He won the Paul Hamlyn Award for Poetry in 1997 and has traveled extensively throughout the world performing his poetry. He co-edited "A Caribbean Dozen" (1994) with his partner, Grace Nichols (see entry for other joint collections). He has won several literary awards. Some of his other poetry publications: *Man to Pan*, 1982 (winner of the Casa de las Américas Prize). *Limbo Dancer in Dark Glasses*, 1983. *Mangoes and Bullets: Selected and New Poems 1972–84*, 1985. *Weblines*, 2000. *Half-caste and Other Poems*, 2005. Some of his poems: "Ask Mummy Ask Daddy," "By All Means Bless," "For Bob Marley," "Listen Mr. Oxford Don," "New Shoes," "Wind and River Romance."

Sources: *British Council Arts* (http://www.contemporarywriters.com). *Caribbean Poetry Now.* Stewart Brown, ed. Edward Arnold, 1992. *Other: British and Irish Poetry since 1970.* Richard Caddel and Peter Quartermain, eds. Wesleyan University Press, 1999. *Poetry by John Agard* (http://www.humboldt.edu/~me2/engl240b/student_projects/agard/poetry.htm). *The Columbia Granger's Index to Poetry.* 11th ed. *The Columbia Granger's World of Poetry.* Columbia University Press, 2005 (http://www.columbiagrangers.org). *The Heinemann Book of Caribbean Poetry.* Stewart Brown and Ian McDonald, eds. Heinemann, 1992. *The National Portrait Gallery* (www.npg.org.uk). *The Oxford Companion to English Literature.* 6th edition. Margaret Drabble, ed. Oxford University Press, 2000. *The Oxford Treasury of Children's Poems.* Michael Harrison and Christopher Stuart-Clark, eds. Oxford University Press, 1988. *Wheel and Come Again: An Anthology of Reggae Poetry.* Kwame Dawes, ed. Goose Lane Editions, 1998.

AGBABI, PATIENCE (1965–)

Agbabi, one of the "Next Generation" poets, was born in London to Nigerian parents and fostered from birth by a white family. She lived in Sussex and North Wales and graduated from Oxford University. In her debut poetry collection, *R A W*, published by Gecko Press in 1995, Agbabi uses a rap style and won the 1997 Excelle Literary Award. Her work appears in numerous journals and anthologies. "Her strength is a punchy, polyvocal delivery which juxtaposes rap with fluctuating metres and intonations without ever losing the thread," writes *The Weekly Journal* (from the book blurb). Some lines from "Ufo Woman" in *Transformatrix* (her second collection, Payback Press, 2000) vividly portray the sense of not belonging (she was asked if her color washed off). She was featured on National Poetry Day in October 2000. Agbabi has read at key literature festivals in the U.K. and at music festivals. She has also worked extensively for The British Council, delivering her work in Europe and Africa. "The London Eye" is one of her poems on the London underground trains.

Sources: *Canongate Books Ltd.* (www.canongate.net). *Contemporary Writers in the UK* (www.contemporarywriters.com). *New Internationalist magazine on-line* (www.newint.org/issue326/mix.htm). *Poetrybooks.co.uk* (www.poetrybooks.co.uk).

AIRD, THOMAS (1802–1876)

Scottish poet, editor of the *Edinburgh Weekly Journal* and the *Dumfriesshire and Galloway Herald*, a post he held for twenty-eight years. His philosophy was "Christian Universalism": the belief that everything in heaven and on earth ultimately will be reconciled back to the Creator through the work of Jesus Christ, his Son. In plain language, no one is going to be endlessly tortured as was commonly taught. He was born in Bowden in the house now known as "Aird's Cottage." While at the local parish school of Bowden, Roxburghshire, Aird showed such promise that he gained a place Edinburgh University. Resisting pressure to enter the Church of Scotland, Aird devoted himself at Edinburgh to literature. He was a prolific writer; many of his poems relate to Scottish life and ways, others have a definite religious theme, and still others relate to nature. His book *Old Bachelor in the Scottish Village*, a prose description of Scottish character with descriptive sketches of the seasons, gained great popularity in Scotland and reached a second edition in 1857. His book *Songs of the Season* consists of twelve songs, all of which relate to nature. He published fifteen books of poems covering a broad range of themes. One of his most tender poems is "My Mother's Grave," in which he longs to be able to turn the clock back.

Sources: *Bowden, the Village. The Scottish Borders* (www.bowden.bordernet.co.uk). *Dictionary of National Biography.* Electronic Edition 1.1. Oxford University Press, 1997. *English Poetry: Author Search.* Chadwyck-Healey Ltd., 1995 (http://www.lib.utexas.edu:8080/search/epoetry/author.html). *Oldpoetry* (www.oldpoetry.com). *A Victorian Anthology, 1837–1895.* Edmund Clarence Stedman, ed. Cambridge: Riverside Press, 1895. *English Poetry Bibliography: Thomas Aird.* The University of Chicago (www.lib.uchicago.edu/efts/EngPo/ENGPO.bib.html).

AKENSIDE, MARK (1721–1770)

Northumbrian poet and physician from a Presbyterian family. He published his first poem, "The Virtuoso," in *Gentleman's Magazine* at the age of sixteen and went on to publish over sixty poems in his short life. Although sent to Edinburgh by the Presbyterians of Newcastle in 1739 to study for the ministry, he decided on medicine and qualified at Leiden, Holland, in 1744. He published *The Pleasures of Imagination* in 1744 (in three books and 2000 lines). He was editor of the magazine *Museum*, to which he contributed a large number of essays in prose. He died of a fever, it is said, in the bed in which John Milton (see entry) died, a bed which a friend had given to Akenside nine years before. In "Ode XII: On Recovering from a Fit of Sickness, In the Country," he reminisces about his favorite place, called Goulder's Hill. Some of his other poems:

"Amoret," "The Complaint," "For a Column at Runnymede," "Hymn to Science," "Ode IX, To Curio," "Ode on a Sermon Against Glory," "Ode to the Country Gentlemen of England," "The Nightingale."

Sources: *Dictionary of National Biography.* Electronic Edition 1.1. Oxford University Press, 1997. *Encyclopædia Britannica Ultimate Reference Suite DVD, 2006. English Poetry: Author Search.* Chadwyck-Healey Ltd., 1995 (http://www.lib.utexas.edu:8080/search/epoetry/author. html). *Mark Akenside, James Macpherson, Edward Young.* S.H. Clark, ed. Fyfield Books, 1994. *Oldpoetry* (www.old-poetry.com). *Poemhunter* (www.poemhunter.com). *Samuel Johnson's Lives of the English Poets, 1779–1781* (http://www2. hn.psu.edu/Faculty/KKemmerer/poets/preface.htm). *The Columbia Granger's Index to Poetry.* 11th ed. *The Columbia Granger's World of Poetry.* Columbia University Press, 2005 (http://www.columbiagrangers.org). *The Literary Encyclopedia* (www.LitEncyc.com). *The National Portrait Gallery* (www.npg.org.uk). *The Oxford Companion to English Literature.* 6th edition. Margaret Drabble, ed. Oxford University Press, 2000. *The Poetical Works of Mark Akenside and John Dyer.* Robert Aris Willmott, ed. George Routledge and Co., 1855.

ALABASTER, WILLIAM (1567–1640)

Dr. Johnson compared Alabaster's tragic poem "Roxana" (1632) with the later poems of John Milton. Because of his pamphlet *Seven Motives,* outlining the reasons for his conversion to Roman Catholicism, he was imprisoned in the Tower of London. And following another publication, he was sentenced by the Spanish Inquisition to five years in prison. On escaping to England and reconverting to Protestantism, he was once more in favor with King James I, who named him doctor of divinity at Cambridge in 1614. Alabaster became chaplain to the king in 1618. "Though all forsake thee, Lord, yet I will die"—based on Matthew 26:34—taps into how Peter might have felt at the trial of Christ when he denied Him.

Sources: *Dictionary of National Biography.* Electronic Edition 1.1. Oxford University Press, 1997. *Encyclopædia Britannica Ultimate Reference Suite DVD, 2006. Oldpoetry* (www.oldpoetry.com). *Sonnet Central* (www.sonnets.org). *The Columbia Granger's Index to Poetry.* 11th ed. *The Columbia Granger's World of Poetry.* Columbia University Press, 2005 (http://www.columbiagrangers.org). *The Oxford Companion to English Literature.* 6th edition. Margaret Drabble, ed. Oxford University Press, 2000.

ALDINGTON, RICHARD EDWARD GODFREY (1892–1962)

With his wife, Hilda Doolittle (although the marriage didn't last), he edited *The Egoist,* the main channel for the Imagism movement, which was a revolt against Romanticism. His novel *Death of a Hero* (1929), an anti-war book, became an international best-seller. He spent time as a Hollywood script writer, but tiring of that, he returned to France. He published his autobiography, *Life for Life's Sake,* in 1941, and helped to translate the *Larousse Encyclopedia of Mythology.* He had a passion for truth and spoke out forcefully against hypocrisy or suppression. This led him into conflict with the establishment when in his biography *Lawrence of Arabia* (1955) he exposed Lawrence as a self-pitying and lying fraud. In "The Lover"—taken from his collection *Images of War* (1919)—he speaks of death as a lover, and how he awaits the one love from whom there is no escape. Some of his other poems: "At the British Museum," "Bombardment," "Childhood," "Daisy," "Epilogue," "Goodbye!" "Images," "Lemures," "Prelude," "Round-Pond," "The Faun Sees Snow for the First Time," "The Poplar."

Sources: *Dictionary of National Biography.* Electronic Edition 1.1. Oxford University Press, 1997. *Encyclopædia Britannica Ultimate Reference Suite DVD, 2006. Modern British Poetry.* 7th rev. ed. Louis Untermeyer, ed. Harcourt, Brace, 1962. *Poemhunter* (www.poemhunter.com). *The Columbia Granger's Index to Poetry.* 11th ed. *The Columbia Granger's World of Poetry.* Columbia University Press, 2005 (http://www.columbiagrangers.org). *The National Portrait Gallery* (www.npg.org.uk). *The Oxford Companion to English Literature.* 6th edition. Margaret Drabble, ed. Oxford University Press, 2000. *Westminster Abbey Official Guide* (no date).

ALED, TUDUR (fl. 1480–1525)

Aled was a Welsh poet and Franciscan friar whose bardic name derived from the river Aled, which flows through his native Llansannan in Denbighshire. He was a bardic teacher and chief bard of the first Eisteddfod, held in 1525. Aled is said to be a gifted, ardent, and skillful poet; many of his poems are written in Welsh. His wide range of poetry uses imagery and ornamentation and his poems contain a great deal of references to the origins of Welsh, Norman or English families. In his work, the Welsh bardic tradition of the Middle Ages reached its climax, but changes in society led to an inevitable decline in the bardic craft of Wales, though it has seen a revival in recent years. Aled wrote several poems describing his love of a Welsh Cob stallion called "The Abbot of Aberconwy."

Sources: *Dictionary of National Biography.* Electronic Edition 1.1. Oxford University Press, 1997. *Encyclopædia Britannica Ultimate Reference Suite DVD, 2006. Go Britannia! Wales: Welsh Literature—Poets of the Gentry* (www.britannia.com). *Horses in Literature* (http://www.aptt2.org.uk/w3d/macador/horselit.html).

ALEXANDER, CECIL FRANCES HUMPHREYS (1818–1895)

Alexander was the wife of William Alexander, bishop of Derry and Raphoe, later the Anglican primate for Ireland. She and her sister founded a school for the deaf, and she set up the Girls' Friendly Society in Londonderry in 1877. She wrote about 400 hymns, as well as many poems. Four of her best known hymns are included in the current Methodist Hymn Book—*Hymns and Psalms*: "All Things Bright and Beautiful"; "Once in David's Royal City"; "There is a Green Hill Far Away"; and "Jesus Calls Us O'er the Tumult." By twenty-first century standards, some of her hymns could be classified as sentimental; however, they all contain the Gospel. She was encouraged in her writing by John Keble, who edited her *Hymns for Little Children* (1848), which went to 69 editions. She wrote poems and published in *Dublin University Magazine*. The second verse of "All Things Bright and Beautiful" (although omitted from modern hymnbooks) contains a telling comment on the social order of the Victorian Age: rich and poor, high and lowly, are all estates ordained by God.

Sources: *Cecil Frances Alexander—Hymn Writer* (www.ulsterhistory.co.uk). *Dictionary of National Biography*. Electronic Edition 1.1. Oxford University Press, 1997. *Methodist Hymns and Psalms*. London: Methodist Publishing House 1983. *Oldpoetry* (www.oldpoetry.com). *The Columbia Granger's Index to Poetry*. 11th ed. *The Columbia Granger's World of Poetry*. Columbia University Press, 2005 (http://www.columbiagrangers.org).

ALEXANDER, SIR WILLIAM, EARL OF STIRLING (?1567–1640)

Scottish poet and politician who held various government offices, including secretary of state for Scotland in 1626. He was tutor of Prince Henry of Scotland (1594–1612) and went to England on the accession of James I (also James VI of Scotland). He was an early developer of British colonization of Nova Scotia; he brought many British settlers to "New Scotland." In 1630, King Charles I rewarded his service by making him the Earl of Stirling. "Elegy IV: On the Death of Prince Henry" mourns the death of his pupil. His main publications: *To Aurora*, 1604, a collection of songs and love sonnets dedicated to James VI (included in *The Golden Treasury*, Francis T. Palgrave, ed. 1875. *Doomsday*, 1614. *An Encouragement to Colonies*, 1624. *Four Monarchicke*, 1664–67.

Sources: *Dictionary of National Biography*. Electronic Edition 1.1. Oxford University Press, 1997. *Encyclopædia Britannica Ultimate Reference Suite DVD, 2006. Founding of New Scotland (Nova Scotia)* (www.chebucto.ns.ca/Heritage). *Oldpoetry* (www.oldpoetry.com). *The Columbia Granger's Index to Poetry*. 11th ed. *The Columbia Granger's World of Poetry*. Columbia University Press, 2005 (http://www.columbiagrangers.org). *The Oxford Companion to English Literature*. 6th edition. Margaret Drabble, ed. Oxford University Press, 2000. *The Poetical Works of Sir*

William Alexander Volume 2. Maurice Ogle & Co., 1872. *Virtual American Biographies* (www.famousamericans.net).

ALEYN, CHARLES (d. 1640)

Aleyn was educated at Sidney Sussex College, Cambridge, and became a master in Thomas Farnaby's celebrated school in St. Giles, Cripplegate, London. Subsequently he was private tutor to Sir Edward Sherburne, commissary-general and clerk of the ordnance, author as well as poet. Sidney College claims that he was a pioneering newspaper editor and translator of *Aesop's Fables*. Aleyn was buried in the churchyard of St. Andrew's, Holborn. His main publications: *The Battailes of Crescey and Poictiers*, 1631, reprinted in 1633. *The Historie of Henrie of that name the Seventh King of England*, 1638. *The History of Eurialus and Lucretia*, 1639. *The Battailes of Crescey and Poictiers* describes in detail the sights and sounds and the horrors of combat.

Sources: *Dictionary of National Biography*. Electronic Edition 1.1. Oxford University Press, 1997. *SETIS: The Scholarly Electronic Text and Image Service* (http://setis.library.usyd.edu.au). *Sidney Sussex College Cambridge* (www.sid.cam.ac.uk).

ALFRED (AELFRED), KING OF THE WEST SAXONS (849–899)

The great king of Wessex (871–899), a Saxon kingdom in southwestern England. He prevented England from falling to the Danes by defeating them at the Battle of Edington (Wiltshire) in 878 and recapturing London in 886. Famous as these victories are, his patronage of learning has earned him equal respect. He is remembered as "the darling of the English," and "England's schoolmaster." Compilation of the *Anglo-Saxon Chronicle* began during his reign. He encouraged the best scholars to the monasteries and bestowed upon them some of them highest ecclesiastical honors. He gladly received all strangers who brought with them any knowledge or any useful art. He was buried at Hyde Abbey, Winchester. One of Alfred's poems is "The Proverbs of Alfred." A quotation attributed to him runs, "I desire to leave to the men that come after me a remembrance of me in good works."

Sources: Bartleby.com has a useful bibliography: *Alfred and the Old English Prose of his Reign. Dictionary of National Biography*. Electronic Edition 1.1. Oxford University Press, 1997. *Encyclopædia Britannica Ultimate Reference Suite DVD, 2006. Encyclopedia of Britain*. Bamber Gascoigne. London: Macmillan, 1994. *The Columbia Granger's Index to Poetry*. 11th ed. *The Columbia Granger's World of Poetry*. Columbia University Press, 2005 (http://www.columbiagrangers.org). *The National Portrait Gallery* (www.npg.org.uk). *The Oxford Companion to English Literature*. 6th edition. Margaret Drabble, ed. Oxford University Press, 2000.

ALLINGHAM, WILLIAM (1824–1889)

Irish poet who through hard work and dedication improved his education to become a customs official. Around 1844 he contributed to Leigh Hunt's *Journal*, then in 1847 he met Leigh Hunt, who introduced him to other poets and writers. He was sub-editor, then editor, of *Fraser's Magazine*. His main works are: *Poems, with a Dedication to Leigh Hunt*, 1850. *Day and Night Songs*, 1855 (illustrated by Dante Rossetti). *The Ballad Book* for the *Golden Treasury* series, 1864 (editor). *Laurence Bloomfield in Ireland*, 1864 (an enlightening social document of the era). *Varieties in Prose*, 1893 (three volumes published posthumously). Allingham's poetry is lyrical and descriptive and full of color. Two contrasting poems are "Autumnal Sonnet" and "The Fairies" (included in many children's anthologies). The symbolism of the former is of approaching autumn of life; the latter, often used in training for singers because of its vowel sounds and contrasting consonants, encourages the singer to rush along with the fairies and little men dressed in green jackets and red caps. Some of his other poems: "A Day-Dream's Reflection," "A Dream," "A Gravestone," "A Memory."

Sources: *County Donegal on the Internet* (www.dun-na-ngall.com). *Dictionary of National Biography.* Electronic Edition 1.1. Oxford University Press, 1997. *English Poetry: Author Search.* Chadwyck-Healey Ltd., 1995 (http://www.lib.utexas.edu:8080/search/epoetry/author.html). *Poemhunter* (www.poemhunter.com). *Poetry Archive, William Allingham* (www.poetry-archive.com). *Sonnet Central* (www.sonnets.org). *The Columbia Granger's Index to Poetry.* 11th ed. *The Columbia Granger's World of Poetry.* Columbia University Press, 2005 (http://www.columbiagrangers.org). *The Family Album of Favorite Poems.* Ernest P. Edward, ed. Grosset and Dunlap, 1959. *The National Portrait Gallery* (www.npg.org.uk). *The Oxford Companion to English Literature.* 6th edition. Margaret Drabble, ed. Oxford University Press, 2000.

ALLOTT, KENNETH (1912–1973)

Welsh born Allott was educated in Newcastle, where he was known as "Speedy" because he spoke so quickly. He worked as a reviewer for the *Morning Post* and with Geoffrey Grigson on *New Verse*. He was regarded by many as one of the most promising poets of the day; Francis Scarfe devoted a whole chapter to him in *Auden and After*. Allott became general editor of the *Pelican Book of English Prose* (1956) and of the *Oxford History of English Literature*, and was a leading authority on Victorian literature and edited many poetic selections. Some of his poems: "Aunt Sally Speaks," "Cheshire Cat," "Departure Platform," "Lament for a Cricket Eleven," "Offering," "Prize for Good Conduct," "The Statue."

Sources: *Oldpoetry* (www.oldpoetry.com). *The Columbia Granger's Index to Poetry.* 11th ed. *The Columbia Granger's World of Poetry.* Columbia University Press, 2005 (http://www.columbiagrangers.org). *Biography of Kenneth Allott; Wikipedia, the Free Encyclopedia* (http://en.wikipedia.org/wiki/Wikipedia).

ALVAREZ, ALFRED (1929–)

Born in London, he suffered the loss of both his parents through suicide when he was a child. He studied English at Corpus Christi College, Oxford, graduated B.A. (1952) and M.A. (1956) and was made an honorary fellow in 2001. He studied at Princeton University, New Jersey, from 1953 to 1954 on a Proctor Visiting Fellowship, and was Visiting Fellow of Rockefeller Foundation, New York (1955–1956). He returned to Princeton as lecturer in creative writing from 1957 to 1958. He has also lectured in New Mexico. He turned to creative writing in 1966 and is possibly best known for *The Savage God: A Study of Suicide* (1971). *Where Did It All Go Right?* (1999) is his autobiography. East London University awarded him an honorary doctor of literature in 1998. Jared Harris played Alvarez in the 2003 film *Sylvia*, about the troubled relationship between Sylvia Plath and Ted Hughes (see entries). Some of his poetry publications: *The New Poetry*, 1962. *Lost,* 1968. *Apparition*, 1971. *Autumn to Autumn, and Selected Poems, 1953–1976*, 1978. Some of his poems: "Cemetery in New Mexico," "Dying," "Lost," "Operation," "The Fortunate Fall."

Sources: *Encyclopædia Britannica Ultimate Reference Suite DVD, 2006. The New Modern Poetry: British and American Poetry since World War II.* M.L. Rosenthal, ed. Macmillan, 1967. *The Oxford Companion to English Literature.* 6th edition. Margaret Drabble, ed. Oxford University Press, 2000. *Voices within the Ark: The Modern Jewish Poets.* Howard Schwartz, and Anthony Rudolf, ed. Avon Books, 1980. *Who's Who.* London: A & C Black, 2005

ALVES, ROBERT (1745–1794)

Born in Elgin, Scotland, of humble stock, Alves showed promise at Elgin grammar school, then took a degree in philosophy a Marischal College, Aberdeen. His "Elegy on Time" gained him the approval and friendship of Dr. Beattie, professor at Marischal College. He was a teacher in a parish school, a tutor, and headmaster of the Banff grammar school, a post he held from 1773 until 1779, when, on account of a disappointment in love, he migrated to Edinburgh. There he taught the classics and several modern languages. His main works are: *Ode to Britannia*, 1780 (which praises the Scottish soldiers in the campaign in the Carolinas). *Poems*, 1782. *Edinburgh,* 1789 (describing the social conditions of the capital). *Weeping Bard*, 1789 (an autobiographical poem). *Sketches of the History of*

Literature, containing Lives and Characters of the most eminent Writers in different languages, ancient and modern, and critical remarks on their works: Together with several Literary Essays, 1794 (published posthumously by Dr. Alexander Chapman). *The Banks of Esk,* 1801 (a defense of Scotland and Scotsmen, against English critics, also published posthumously).

Sources: *Dictionary of National Biography.* Electronic Edition 1.1. Oxford University Press, 1997. *Significant and Famous Scots* (http://www.electricscotland.com/history/other/alves_robert.htm).

ALVI, MONIZA (1954–)

Born in Lahore, Pakistan — her parents moved to England when she was an infant — she grew up in Hertfordshire and was educated at the universities of York and London. After a long career as a secondary school teacher, she now tutors for the Open College of the Arts and lives in London with her husband and daughter. In 2002 she received a Cholmondeley Award for her poetry. Her poetry publications: *Peacock Luggage,* 1992 (with Peter Daniels). *The Country at My Shoulder,* 1993 (short listed for the T.S. Eliot Prize and Whitbread Poetry Award, which led to her being selected for the Poetry Society's New Generation Poets promotion). Some of her publications: *A Bowl of Warm Air,* 1996. *Carrying My Wife,* 2000. *Souls,* 2002. *How the Stone Found its Voice,* 2005 (inspired by Rudyard Kipling's *Just So Stories* [see entry]). Some of her poems: "And If," "Backgrounds," "Grand Hotel," "Presents from My Aunts in Pakistan," "The Wedding," "Throwing Out My Father's Dictionary."

Sources: *Anthology of Twentieth-Century British and Irish Poetry.* Keith Tuma, ed. Oxford University Press. 2001. *British Council Arts* (http://www.contemporarywriters.com). *Making for Planet Alice: New Women Poets.* Maura Dooley, ed. Bloodaxe Books, 1997. *New Blood,* Neil Astley, ed. Bloodaxe Books, 1999. *The Columbia Granger's Index to Poetry.* 11th ed. *The Columbia Granger's World of Poetry.* Columbia University Press, 2005 (http://www.columbiagrangers.org). *Wikipedia, the Free Encyclopedia* (http://en.wikipedia.org/wiki/Wikipedia).

AMHURST, NICHOLAS (1697–1742)

Satirical poet, political pamphleteer, and editor of the political journal *The Craftsman,* founded in 1726, to which he contributed under the pseudonym of "Caleb D'Anvers of Gray's Inn." While at St. John's College, Oxford, he published "Epistle from a Student at Oxford to the Chevalier; Protestant Popery" and "Strephon's Revenge; a Satire on the Oxford Toasts." He was expelled from Oxford in 1719; some said it was because of his outspoken views and his libertinism and misconduct, others that it was political. His *Terræ Filius* (1721) was severe satire

of Oxford University. In 1737 he was imprisoned for a few days for "suspected libel," for publishing in *The Craftsman* a letter purporting to come from Colley Cibber, then poet laureate. Robert Southey, in *Specimens of the Later English Poets, with preliminary notices,* 3 Volumes (1807), lists thirteen poems by Amhurst. His other poetical publications (in addition to several other works): *Poems on Several Occasions,* 1723. *A Collection of Poems,* 1731. "The Bowling Green" (a translation of Addison's Latin poem "Sphaeristerium") is a description of the skill of bowling.

Sources: *Aberdeen Studies in Scottish Philosophy* (www.abdn.ac.uk). *Biography of Nicholas Amhurst: Online Classic Encyclopedia — Love to Know* (http://www.19.1911encyclopedia.org). *Dictionary of National Biography.* Electronic Edition 1.1. Oxford University Press, 1997. *Encyclopædia Britannica Ultimate Reference Suite DVD, 2006. English Poetry: Author Search.* Chadwyck-Healey Ltd., 1995 (http://www.lib.utexas.edu:8080/search/epoetry/author.html). *Every-day Boo, The Death of Nicholas Amhurst* (http://www.uab.edu/english/hone/etexts/edb/day-pages/117-april27.html). *From Steele and Addison to Pope and Swift.* Vol. 9 (http://www.bartleby.com/219/0700.html). *The Cambridge History of English and American Literature in 18 Volumes,* 1907–21. New York: Putnam, 1907–1921. *The National Portrait Gallery* (www.npg.org.uk). *The Nature and Purpose of Poetry; Nature* (http://www.ourcivilisation.com/smartboard/shop/poet18/nature.htm).

AMIS, SIR KINGSLEY (1922–1995)

London-born, he was educated at the City of London School and St. John's College, Oxford. Although probably best known for his novels — his first novel, *Lucky Jim,* was made into a film in 1957 — he published six volumes of poetry. Because of his disgruntled anti-hero Jim Dixon in *Lucky Jim* (and some of his other anti-heroes), Amis was grouped with the "Angry Young Men," who expressed similar social discontent. It has also been rumored that Amis wrote part of Ian Fleming's last book, *The Man with the Golden Gun.* Amis was one of the group sometimes called "The Movement" whose poems began appearing in 1956 in the anthology *New Lines.* Their poems were anti-romantic, witty, rational, and sardonic in tone. His collections of poems are: *Bright November,* 1947. *A Frame of Mind,* 1953. *Poems: Fantasy Portraits,* 1954. *A Case of Samples: Poems 1946–1956,* 1956. "Ode to Me" is a celebration of reaching the age of fifty and looking forward to more. Some of his other poems: "Acts of Kindness," "A Bookshop Idyll," "Departure," "Drinking Song," "Farewell Blues," "Letter to Elizabeth," "Mightier than the Pen," "Swansea Bay," "The Value of Suffering."

Sources: *Biography of Sir Kingsley Amis* (www.kirjasto.sci.fi/amis.htm). *Encyclopædia Britannica Ultimate Reference Suite DVD, 2006. The Columbia Granger's Index to Poetry.* 11th ed. *The Columbia Granger's World of Poetry.*

Columbia University Press, 2005 (http://www.columbia grangers.org). *The National Portrait Gallery* (www.npg. org.uk). *The Oxford Companion to English Literature*. 6th edition. Margaret Drabble, ed. Oxford University Press, 2000. *Wikipedia, the Free Encyclopedia* (http://en. wikipedia.org/wiki/Wikipedia).

ANDERSON, ALEXANDER (1845–1909)

Scottish labor poet who wrote under the pseudonym of "Surfaceman." Anderson was born in Dumfriesshire and became a surfaceman, one who kept the railway bed in repair. Of limited formal education, he spent his leisure in self-culture, mastering German, French, Spanish, and Latin sufficiently to read many of the poets and playwrights. His first poem was published in *The People's Friend* of Dundee in 1870. He published *A Song of Labor and Other Poems* (1873) and *The Two Angels and Other Poems* (1875). His work appeared in *Good Words, Chamber's Journal, Cassell's Magazine*, the *Contemporary Review*, and *Songs of the Rail* (1878; 3rd edit. 1881). Between 1880 and his death he was assistant librarian in Edinburgh University, secretary to the Edinburgh Philosophical Institution, and acting chief librarian at the university. His poetry (over 200 poems) shows great sensitivity to the nature of people, similar to that of Robert Burns. Some of his poems: "A Song of the Laborer," "Cuddle Doon," "Jenny wi' the Airn [iron] Teeth," "Langsyne, When Life Was Bonnie." "Killed on the Telegraph Wire" is a tender story of a bird killed on the telegraph wires, "bleeding his little life away."

Sources: Alexander Anderson, *Dundee Advertiser*, 6th January, 1896, Dundee Public Library (http://www.dun deecity.gov.uk/library/main.htm). *Dictionary of National Biography*. Electronic Edition 1.1. Oxford University Press, 1997. *English Poetry: Author Search*. Chadwyck-Healey Ltd., 1995 (http://www.lib.utexas.edu:8080/search/epo etry/author.html). *Significant and Famous Scots* (http://www.electricscotland.com/history/other/anderson_alexander.htm). *The Columbia Granger's Index to Poetry*. 11th ed. *The Columbia Granger's World of Poetry*. Columbia University Press, 2005 (http://www.columbiagrangers.org).

ANEIRIN (6th CENTURY)

This Welsh bard was the son of Caw ab Geraint, lord of Cwm Cawlwyd, a chief of the Otadini or Gododin, a tribe occupying the sea coast south of the Firth of Forth, Scotland, lying between the walls of Septimius Severus and Antoninus Pius. Aneirin appears to have been educated at St. Cadoc's College at Llancarvan, Glamorganshire, and afterwards to have entered the bardic order. He wrote the *Book of Aneirin*, containing a long poem called "Y Gododdin," which concerns the ill-fated expedition of the Britons to recapture the fortress at Catraeth (Catt-

erick, Yorkshire) from the Saxons in 603, from which battle he fled, and for a short time was a prisoner. The poem — a series of odes to the heroism of various participants in the siege — describes the hardships he underwent when in captivity. The work served as a model for later Welsh poets and exerted great influence on early Romantic poetry. Parts of the Gododdin: "Men went to Gododdin, laughter-loving / to Cattraeth's vale in glitt'ring row / Youth / Lord of Gododdin will be praised in song / When a crowd of cares."

Sources: *Dictionary of National Biography*. Electronic Edition 1.1. Oxford University Press, 1997. *Encyclopædia Britannica Ultimate Reference Suite DVD, 2006*. *Microsoft Encarta 2006* (DVD). Microsoft Corporation, 2006. *The Book of Aneurin* (with English translation) (http://www.maryjones.us/ctexts/aindex.html). *The Columbia Granger's Index to Poetry*. 11th ed. *The Columbia Granger's World of Poetry*. Columbia University Press, 2005 (http://www.columbiagrangers.org). *The Oxford Book of Welsh Verse in English*. Gwyn Jones, ed. Oxford University Press, 1977. *The Oxford Companion to English Literature*. 6th edition. Margaret Drabble, ed. Oxford University Press, 2000. *Wikipedia, the Free Encyclopedia* (http://en.wikipedia. org/wiki/Wikipedia).

ANNAND, JAMES KING (1908–1993)

When Annand graduated from Edinburgh University, he became a schoolteacher and poet, translating work from German and medieval Latin into Scots. He was a supporter of the Scots Language Society and a life-long champion of the Scots language. Among his several volumes of poetry are a collection of three books of verse for children called *Bairn Rhymes*, which are illustrated with line drawings by Dennis Carabine. Mercat Press republished *Bairn Rhymes: Scots Verse for Children* in 1998 (ISBN 187364485X). These poems are said to be among the best writing for children in any language. "Yule" captures the excitement of trying to find a stocking to hang up on Christmas Eve. Some of his other poems: "Arctic Convoy," "Heron," "I Winna Let On," "Mavis," "What Finer Hills?"

Sources: *The Flag in the Wind Features — Scots Language: YULE*, by John K. Annand (www.scotsindependent.org/features/scots/yule.htm). Scots Language Resource Centre (http://scotsyett.com/scotsoun.htm). *Significant and Famous Scots* (http://www.electricscotland.com/history/other/annand_james.htm). *The Columbia Granger's Index to Poetry*. 11th ed. *The Columbia Granger's World of Poetry*, Columbia University Press, 2005 (http://www.columbiagrangers.org).

ANSTEY, CHRISTOPHER (1724–1805)

Educated at Eton College, Anstey took his bachelor's degree at King's College, Cambridge, in 1746. In 1766 he began publishing the famous series of letters in rhyme entitled *The New Bath Guide* (later illustrated by George Cruikshank in 1830), a series of poetical episodes humorously depicting contemporary life and the amusements, customs and activities of those who resorted to Bath for the purposes of health, fashion or society. *The New Bath Guide* shows how the amiable but socially challenged Blunderhead family managed to survive the season in Bath. This work was widely read in its time. Its success was instantaneous, and although he wrote many more poems, he never repeated the success of *The New Bath Guide*. "Here is Bath in 18th century color, crowded with fops, gamblers, charlatans, quacks and social climbers" (Anstey, Christopher, *The New Bath Guide*, Broadcast Books, Bristol, ISBN 1 874092. www.broadcastbooks.co.uk). Letter VI, page 63, describes the scene where Mr. B finds his daughter, Tabitha, in bed with two lusty lovers.

Sources: *Dictionary of National Biography*. Electronic Edition 1.1. Oxford University Press, 1997. *Encyclopædia Britannica Ultimate Reference Suite DVD, 2006. English Poetry: Author Search*. Chadwyck-Healey Ltd., 1995 (http://www.lib.utexas.edu:8080/search/epoetry/author.html). *The Columbia Granger's Index to Poetry*. 11th ed. *The Columbia Granger's World of Poetry*. Columbia University Press, 2005 (http://www.columbiagrangers.org). *The National Portrait Gallery* (www.npg.org.uk). *The Oxford Companion to English Literature*. 6th edition. Margaret Drabble, ed. Oxford University Press, 2000. *Westminster Abbey Official Guide* (no date).

ARBUCKLE, JAMES (1700–?1734)

Born in Belfast and educated at Glasgow University, Arbuckle's political views and activities conflicted with the university's Calvinistic philosophy. He published a number of poems and became part of the circle of the Edinburgh poet-bookseller Allan Ramsay. He moved to Dublin in 1724–25 and was involved in the "Molesworth Circle," a group that met for literary and scientific discussion at the country house of Viscount Robert Molesworth (1656–1725). For two years he was the principal writer of the *Dublin Weekly Journal* of 1723–25. His "Snuff" is a mock-heroic poem containing some curious information respecting snuff-taking and snuff-boxes of the time. He contributed to the *Edinburgh Miscellany* of 1721, and in the same year he produced a poem titled "Glotta" describing the scenery about the Clyde in winter and the "sport" of golf.

Sources: *Dictionary of National Biography*. Electronic Edition 1.1. Oxford University Press, 1997. *The Glasgow Story* (www.theglasgowstory.com). *The Oxford Companion to English Literature*. 6th edition. Margaret Drabble, ed. Oxford University Press, 2000.

ARMITAGE, SIMON (1963–)

Born in Huddersfield, England, Armitage studied geography at Portsmouth Polytechnic, gained a postgraduate qualification in social work at Manchester University, then worked as a probation officer in Oldham, Lancashire. His poetry is exciting, combining humor with realism and critical seriousness. He has been short listed for major literature prizes and won the *Sunday Times* Young Writer of the Year Award in 1993, and was poet in residence for the New Millennium Experience Company in 1999. *Mister Heracles* (2000), an adaptation of Euripides' *Heracles*, was commissioned by the West Yorkshire Playhouse. He has worked extensively in film, radio and television. *The Dead Sea Poems* (2001) is a collection in which questions of belief and trust, of identity and knowledge, are mingled with more mundane considerations, such as the problems of owning a dog and the vicissitudes of the job market. His "Poem" is a poignant reminder that what we do is sometimes not appreciated by others.

Sources: British Council (www.contemporarywriters. com). Poemhunter (www.poemhunter.com). *The Columbia Granger's Index to Poetry*. 11th ed. *The Columbia Granger's World of Poetry*. Columbia University Press, 2005 (http://www.columbiagrangers.org). *The Oxford Companion to English Literature*. 6th edition. Margaret Drabble, ed. Oxford University Press, 2000.

ARMSTRONG, EDMUND JOHN (1841–1865)

Dublin poet whose life was cut short by illness. His early experience of a burst blood vessel in the lung cut short his study at Trinity College, Dublin. After traveling in Europe he returned to his course and in 1864 was elected president of the Undergraduate Philosophical Society, Trinity College, Dublin. He was buried at Monkstown, Co. Dublin. Friends published the volume *Poems by the Late Edmund J. Armstrong* in 1865, which included two long poems, "The Prisoner of Mount Saint Michael," a romantic tale of passion and crime, and the idyllic "Ovoca," partly dramatic, partly narrative, as well as many lyrical pieces which demonstrated his genius. A new edition appeared in 1877, *The Poetical Works of Edmund J. Armstrong*, edited by G.F. Armstrong, Longmans, Green, and Co. Longman also published, in 1877, *Essays and Sketches by Edmund J. Armstrong*.

Sources: *A Dictionary of Irish Biography*. Henry Boylan, ed. Dublin: Gill and Macmillan, 1998. *Dictionary of National Biography*. Electronic Edition 1.1. Oxford University Press, 1997.

ARMSTRONG, JOHN (1709–1779)

Scottish doctor, poet and essayist, from Roxburghshire, the son of a clergyman. After qualifying from Edinburgh in 1732 he practiced in London. In 1746 he was appointed physician to the London Soldiers Hospital, and from 1760 to 1763 was physician to the forces in Germany during the Seven Years' War. In 1735 he published a satirical pamphlet, *Essay for abridging the Study of Physick*. In 1736 his sex manual for newlyweds, *The Oeconomy of Love*, was published anonymously. *Winter* was published in 1770. His most renowned work, *The Art of Preserving Health*, published in four books in 1744, was immediately popular and remains his best known work. Some of his other poems: "Advice to Lovers," "Causes of Old Age," "Diet," "Madness," "The Advantages of Washing," "The Dangers of Sexual Excess," "Urban Pollution."

Sources: *Dictionary of National Biography*. Electronic Edition 1.1. Oxford University Press, 1997. *Significant and Famous Scots* (http://www.electricscotland.com/history/other/armstrong_john.htm). *The Columbia Granger's Index to Poetry*. 11th ed. *The Columbia Granger's World of Poetry*, Columbia University Press, 2005 (http://www.columbiagrangers.org). *The National Portrait Gallery* (www.npg.org.uk). *The Oxford Companion to English Literature*. 6th edition. Margaret Drabble, ed. Oxford University Press, 2000.

ARNOLD, SIR EDWIN (1832–1904)

Kentish poet and journalist, graduated from University College, Oxford (where he won the Newdigate prize for poetry), in 1854. He served as principal of the government college in Poona, Bombay, and returned to England in 1861 to join the staff of the *Daily Telegraph*. On the death of Thornton Leigh Hunt in 1873, Arnold was appointed editor of the newspaper. He won fame for his blank-verse epic *The Light of Asia* (1879), dealing with the life of Buddha. The poem was attacked for its alleged distortion of Buddhist doctrine and for its tolerant attitude toward a non-Christian religion. Besides other volumes of poetry, he wrote a number of picturesque travel books and translated *The Bhagavad Gita* and the *Kama Sutra*. Some of his poems: "After Death in Arabia," "Almond Blossom," "Darien," "Destiny," "He and She," "The Deva's Song," "To a Pair of Egyptian Slippers."

Sources: *Dictionary of National Biography*. Electronic Edition 1.1. Oxford University Press, 1997. *Encyclopædia Britannica Ultimate Reference Suite DVD, 2006. English Poetry: Author Search*. Chadwyck-Healey Ltd., 1995 (http://www.lib.utexas.edu:8080/search/epoetry/author.html). *The Columbia Granger's Index to Poetry*. 11th ed. *The Columbia Granger's World of Poetry*, Columbia University Press, 2005 (http://www.columbiagrangers.org). *The National Portrait Gallery* (www.npg.org.uk). *The Oxford Companion to English Literature*. 6th edition. Margaret Drabble, ed. Oxford University Press, 2000.

ARNOLD, MATTHEW (1822–1888)

English Victorian poet, literary and social critic, the eldest son of Dr. Thomas Arnold, famous as headmaster of Rugby School. His poem "Alaric at Rome" won him a place at Rugby, and from there he went to Balliol College, Oxford. In 1847 he was appointed private secretary to the Marquis of Lansdowne. Later he became inspector for schools, a post he held for 35 years, during which time he strove to improve education in England. In 1857 he was elected professor of poetry at Oxford. In his later years Arnold turned more to writing essays on literary, educational and social topics. He is noted especially for his attacks on the contemporary tastes and manners of the "Barbarians" (the aristocracy), the "Philistines" (the commercial middle class), and the "Populace." There is a bust of him in Poets' Corner, Westminster Abbey. Some of his poems: "Absence," "At Some Lone Alehouse," "Bacchanalia; or, The New Age," "Below the Surface-Stream," "Growing Old," "Lines Written in Kensington Gardens," "The Buried Life."

Sources: *Dictionary of National Biography*. Electronic Edition 1.1. Oxford University Press, 1997. *Encyclopædia Britannica Ultimate Reference Suite DVD, 2006. English Poetry: Author Search*. Chadwyck-Healey Ltd., 1995 (http://www.lib.utexas.edu:8080/search/epoetry/author.html). *The Academy of American Poets* (http://www.poets.org/index.cfm). *The Columbia Granger's Index to Poetry*. 11th ed. *The Columbia Granger's World of Poetry*, Columbia University Press, 2005 (http://www.columbiagrangers.org). *The National Portrait Gallery* (www.npg.org.uk). *The Oxford Companion to English Literature*. 6th edition. Margaret Drabble, ed. Oxford University Press, 2000. *Westminster Abbey Official Guide* (no date).

ASHE, THOMAS (1836–1889)

Irish poet and novelist who, while working in Bordeaux, suffered a short imprisonment for wounding in a duel a gentleman whose sister he had seduced. Returning to Dublin, he was appointed secretary to the Diocesan and Endowed Schools Commission, but, getting into debt, resigned his office and retired to Switzerland. He then spent several years in foreign travel, living — according to his *Memoirs and Confessions* (3 vols., 1815) — in freedom and experiencing a somewhat varied fortune. Between 1806 and his death, he published (along with *Memoirs*) several travel books and novels. As a poet he does not rank high; however, his poems do show a descriptive tenderness. Some of his poems: "A Machine Hand," "A Vision of Children," "A Word to the West End," "Corpse-bearing," "Marian," "The Brook," "The City Clerk," "To Two Bereaved."

Sources: *Dictionary of National Biography*. Electronic Edition 1.1. Oxford University Press, 1997. *The Columbia Granger's Index to Poetry*. 11th ed. *The Columbia Granger's World of Poetry*, Columbia University Press, 2005 (http://www.columbiagrangers.org).

ASKEW, ANNE (1521–1546)

Forced by her father to marry at the age of fifteen, Askew rebelled, refused to take her husband's name, left the marital home and moved to London, where she gave sermons and distributed Protestant books. Because such books had been banned she was arrested and imprisoned in the Tower of London, where she was tortured in an attempt to force her to name other Protestants. Not even the promise of a king's pardon could induce Askew to name names. Found guilty of being a Protestant, she was condemned to be burned at the stake for preaching against the doctrine of transubstantiation. A full account of her life and death can be found in *Book of Martyrs* by John Foxe (1563). While in Newgate prison, Askew wrote a 56 line ballad that reflects the words of Stephen the Martyr in Acts 7:59–60. Another ballad attributed to her is "Martyrdom — I Am a Woman Poor and Blind," in which she rejoices that her spirit will rise from the ashes at the Resurrection of the Dead.

Sources: *Dictionary of National Biography.* Electronic Edition 1.1. Oxford University Press, 1997. *The Columbia Granger's Index to Poetry.* 11th ed. *The Columbia Granger's World of Poetry,* Columbia University Press, 2005 (http://www.columbiagrangers.org).

ASKHAM, JOHN (1825–1894)

Born the youngest of seven at Wellingborough, Northamptonshire, to a shoemaker father, Askham received very little education and at the age of ten he started work with his father. He found time and means to educate himself, and at the age of twenty-five, he published his verses in local newspapers and then as volumes, financed by subscriptions. He is buried in Wellingborough cemetery. His publications are: *Sonnets on the Months and Other Poems,* 1863. *Descriptive Poems, Miscellaneous Pieces and Miscellaneous Sonnets,* 1866. *Judith and Other Poems, and a Centenary of Sonnets,* 1868. *Poems and Sonnets,* 1875. *Sketches in Prose and Verse,* 1893. Askham's poem "Work While it is Day" vividly demonstrates his philosophy of working while it is day — when he is strong and his blood is young, and the hours are too precious to waste — possibly reflecting the phrase from John 9:4 "the night cometh when no man can work."

Sources: *Dictionary of National Biography.* Electronic Edition 1.1. Oxford University Press, 1997.

ASQUITH, HERBERT ASHLEY (1881–1947)

Herbert Asquith was the second son of the first Earl of Oxford and Asquith, Herbert Henry Asquith, British prime minister (1908–1916), and often times people would get them confused with each other.

Asquith was a poet, novelist and lawyer. He married his wife, Cynthia, also a writer, in 1910. Asquith served as a captain in the Royal Artillery in France during World War I. Some of his poems: "A Ship Sails Up to Bideford," "Birthday Gifts," "The Elephant," "In Praise of Young Girls," "Nightfall," "Skating," "The Mare," "The Volunteer." "The Hairy Dog," although written about a shaggy dog, can also be viewed as an analogy to humans. The dog's ears and eyes are buried beneath layers of hair and seldom are seen, yet there is beauty if only we could look beneath the surface.

Sources: *Oldpoetry* (www.oldpoetry.com). *The Columbia Granger's Index to Poetry.* 11th ed. The Columbia Granger's World of Poetry. Columbia University Press, 2005 (http://www.columbiagrangers.org).

ASTELL, MARY (1666–1731)

Mary Astell, "the first English feminist," daughter of a merchant at Newcastle-upon-Tyne, settled in London. She advocated female education and vehemently condemned the inequalities of marriage. This brought her into conflict with the Divine Right of Kings and the views of the Church of England. Her major works are: *A Serious Proposal to the Ladies* (which ran to four editions by 1701 and proposed that education for women would make a greater contribution to the upbringing of children and, therefore, to the nation), 1694. *Reflections on Marriage,* 1700 (see entry for Chudleigh, Lady Mary). *The Christian Religion, as professed by a Daughter of the Church of England,* 1705. *Occasional Communion,* 1705. *In Emulation of Mr. Cowleys Poem Call'd the Motto* characterizes her religious beliefs — she does not wish to be rich or great, or to be admired, but to be true. She cannot be a Peter or a Paul and although her sex denies her what men may achieve, she can obey her Lord. She ends her poem by saying that although she may not suffer the martyr's fire, at least she can martyr her desires.

Sources: *Dictionary of National Biography.* Electronic Edition 1.1. Oxford University Press, 1997. *The Columbia Granger's Index to Poetry.* 11th ed. *The Columbia Granger's World of Poetry,* Columbia University Press, 2005 (http://www.columbiagrangers.org). *The Literary Encyclopedia* (www.LitEncyc.com). *The Oxford Companion to English Literature.* 6th edition. Margaret Drabble, ed. Oxford University Press, 2000.

ATHERSTONE, EDWIN (1788–1872)

The DNB says that Atherstone was a "voluminous writer in verse and prose." Born in Nottingham to a working family, the thirteenth of fifteen children, he was educated at Fulneck Moravian School in Yorkshire. He taught music at a Franciscan school in Taunton and later moved from Bath to London, where he dealt in and collected paintings, running two art galleries. In addition to poems he wrote several plays. His published poems: *The Last Days of Herculaneum*, 1821. *Abradates and Panthea*, 1821. *Midsummer Day's Dream*, 1824. *The Fall of Nineveh*, 1868 (thirty books). *The Sea-Kings in England*, 1830 (an epic poem dealing with the times of Alfred the Great). *The Handwriting on the Wall*, 1858. *Israel in Egypt*, 1861 (a poem of nearly twenty thousand lines).

Sources: *Dictionary of National Biography*. Electronic Edition 1.1. Oxford University Press, 1997. *English Poetry: Author Search*. Chadwyck-Healey Ltd., 1995 (http://www.lib.utexas.edu:8080/search/epoetry/author.html). *Stanford University Libraries and Academic Information Resources* (http://library.stanford.edu). *The Life and Work of Edwin Atherstone: The Corvey Poets Project at the University of Nebraska* (http://www.unl.edu/Corvey/html/Projects/Corvey%20Poets/PoetsIndex.htm).

AUDEN, WYSTAN HUGH (1907–1973)

A Yorkshire man who moved to the USA in 1939 and became an American citizen in 1946, Auden taught in several American universities. He returned to England in 1956, when he was elected professor of poetry at Oxford University. After graduating from Christ Church, Oxford, in 1928, and a year in Berlin, he became a schoolteacher noted for his caring and wisdom. His poem "Spain" (1937) was influenced by his experiences of driving an ambulance in Spain for the Republican side. He died in Vienna and was buried in Kirchstetten, and is commemorated by a stone in Poets' Corner, Westminster Abbey. Auden's work ranges from rigorous traditional to original yet intricate, as well as the technical forms. He was also partly responsible for re-introducing Anglo-Saxon accentual meter (fixed number of stresses per line or stanza regardless of the number of syllables that are present) to English poetry. Some of his poems: "A New Age," "As I Walked Out One Evening," "Give Me a Doctor," "In Memory of W.B. Yeats," "Old People's Home," "The Fall of Rome," "The Unknown Citizen," "We Too Had Known Golden Hours."

Sources: *Dictionary of National Biography*. Electronic Edition 1.1. Oxford University Press, 1997. *Encyclopædia Britannica Ultimate Reference Suite DVD*, 2006. *Poemhunter* (www.poemhunter.com). *The Columbia Granger's Index to Poetry*. 11th ed. *The Columbia Granger's World of Poetry*, Columbia University Press, 2005 (http://www.columbiagrangers.org). *The National Portrait Gallery* (www.npg.org.uk). *The Oxford Companion to English Literature*. 6th edition. Margaret Drabble, ed. Oxford University Press, 2000. *Westminster Abbey Official Guide* (no date).

AUSTEN, JANE (1775–1817)

The daughter of a clergyman and the youngest of seven children, Austen lived most of her life at Steventon near Basingstoke. She eventually settled in to a cottage at Chawton (now a museum) about a mile from Alton, Hampshire, until 1871, when due to ill health she moved to Winchester, where she died. She is buried in Winchester Cathedral, and a tablet commemorates her in Poets' Corner in Westminster Abbey. Her novels portray life with humor and gentle irony. Her poems are varied in subject and her humor is evident. Part of her final poem, "Written at Winchester on Tuesday the 15th July 1817," written 3 days before she died, seems to be an analogy of her departure. Some of her other poems: "Happy the Lab'rer," "I've a Pain in My Head," "Miss Lloyd has now went to Miss Green," "Mock Panegyric on a Young Friend," "My Dearest Frank, I Wish You Joy," "Ode to Pity," "Of a Ministry Pitiful, Angry, Mean," "Oh! Mr. Best You're Very Bad," "See They Come, Post Haste from Thanet," "This Little Bag."

Sources: *Dictionary of National Biography*. Electronic Edition 1.1. Oxford University Press, 1997. *Encyclopædia Britannica Ultimate Reference Suite DVD*, 2006. *Poemhunter* (www.poemhunter.com). *The Columbia Granger's Index to Poetry*. 11th ed. *The Columbia Granger's World of Poetry*, Columbia University Press, 2005 (http://www.columbiagrangers.org). *The National Portrait Gallery* (www.npg.org.uk). *The Oxford Companion to English Literature*. 6th edition. Margaret Drabble, ed. Oxford University Press, 2000. *Westminster Abbey Official Guide* (no date).

AUSTIN, ALFRED (1835–1913)

Yorkshire poet laureate. He abandoned law for literature, though his first efforts at prose and poetry were not very successful. He was journalist and special correspondent abroad, and from 1883 to 1895, editor of the *National Review*, the first four years jointly with William John Courthope. He maintained that for a poem to be great it had to an epic or dramatic romance on a theme combining love, patriotism, and religion. Between 1871 and 1908 he published twenty volumes of verse; his poems are a mixture of good and bad. He seems never to have come out from under the shadow of Scott and Byron. Some of his poems: "Agatha," "At His Grave," "Is Life worth living?" "Love's Blindness," "The Haymakers' Song."

Sources: *Dictionary of National Biography*. Electronic Edition 1.1. Oxford University Press, 1997. *Encyclopædia Britannica Ultimate Reference Suite DVD*, 2006. *English Poetry: Author Search*. Chadwyck-Healey Ltd., 1995 (http://www.lib.utexas.edu:8080/search/epoetry/author.html). *Great Books Online* (www.bartleby.com). *Poemhunter* (www.poemhunter.com). *The Columbia Granger's Index to Poetry*. 11th ed. *The Columbia Granger's World of Poetry*, Columbia University Press, 2005 (http://www.columbiagrangers.org). *The National Portrait Gallery* (www.npg.org.uk). *The Oxford Companion to English Literature*. 6th edition. Margaret Drabble, ed. Oxford University Press, 2000.

AYRES, PAM (1947–)

English writer of humorous poetry and entertainer who has appeared on television and national radio, reciting her poems in broad Oxfordshire dialect. Born in Oxfordshire, Ayres worked in the Civil Service for MI5, the Security Service, and served in the Women's Royal Air Force. In 1975 the television talent show *Opportunity Knocks* gave her publicity. She has published several books of poems, toured in a one-woman stage show, hosted her own TV show and performed her stage show for Her Majesty, the Queen. She was identified as the fifth best-selling poet in Britain during 1998 and 1999 and was awarded the Member of the British Empire for services to literature and entertainment in 2004. Her poems are mostly concerned with the details of everyday life. "I Wish I'd Looked After Me Teeth" was voted in the Top 10 of a BBC poll to find the nation's "100 Favorite Comic Poems."

Sources: *Make 'em Laugh* (www.monologues.co.uk). *Wikipedia, the Free Encyclopedia* (http://en.wikipedia.org/wiki/Wikipedia).

AYTON (AYTOUN), SIR ROBERT (1570–1638)

Descended from a noble Norman, the family was given the lands of Aytoun in Berwickshire by King Robert Bruce. Ayton was one of the earliest Scottish poets to use standard English as opposed to the Scottish vernacular, although he did write in Latin, Greek, and French. He graduated from the University of St. Andrews in 1588 and studied civil law at the University of Paris. He was knighted in 1612 by James I and held various lucrative offices during the reigns of James I and Charles I. He is buried in the South Ambulatory of Westminster Abbey near Henry VII Chapel. A poem ascribed to Ayton, "Old Long Syne," could have been the inspiration for the more famous "Auld Lang Syne" by Robert Burns. Ayton was never reckoned to be a great poet; however, many of his poems are refined, tender and romantic, often with a hint of unrequited love. Some of his poems: "When Thou Did Thinke I Did Not Love," "To His Forsaken Mistress," "To an Inconstant One."

Sources: *Dictionary of National Biography.* Electronic Edition 1.1. Oxford University Press, 1997. *Encyclopædia Britannica Ultimate Reference Suite DVD, 2006. English Poetry: Author Search.* Chadwyck-Healey Ltd., 1995 (http://www.lib.utexas.edu:8080/search/epoetry/author.html). *Poemhunter* (www.poemhunter.com). *Significant and Famous Scots* (http://www.electricscotland.com/history/other/ayton_robert.htm). *The Columbia Granger's Index to Poetry.* 11th ed. *The Columbia Granger's World of Poetry,* Columbia University Press, 2005 (http://www.columbiagrangers.org). *Westminster Abbey Official Guide* (no date).

AYTOUN, WILLIAM EDMOND-STOUNE (1813–1865)

Scottish poet, novelist, journalist, lawyer, and sheriff of Orkney, famous for parodies and light verse. Sir Robert Ayton (see above) was one of his ancestors. Educated at Edinburgh University and in Germany, in 1840 he was called to the Scottish bar. In 1844 he joined the staff of *Blackwoods Edinburgh Magazine*, to which he contributed political, humorous and satirical items. He was a highly popular professor of rhetoric and *belles lettres* at Edinburgh University, where he wrote fiction and political essays and translated Goethe. A prolific poet, his main publications are: *Poland, Homer, and Other Poems,* 1832. *Lays of the Cavaliers,* 1848. *Lays of the Scottish Cavaliers,* 1849. *Bothwell,* 1856 (a poetical monologue in six parts, dealing with the relations between the hero and Mary Queen of Scots). Some of his other poems: "Blind Old Milton," "The Execution of Montrose," "The Massacre of MacPherson," "The Refusal of Charon."

Sources: *Dictionary of National Biography.* Electronic Edition 1.1. Oxford University Press, 1997. *Encyclopædia Britannica Ultimate Reference Suite DVD, 2006. Poem hunter* (www.poemhunter.com). *Scotland's Lawyer Poets, Sir Robert Aytoun* (http://www.wvu.edu/~lawfac/jelkins/lp-2001/intro/scots.html). *The Columbia Granger's Index to Poetry.* 11th ed. *The Columbia Granger's World of Poetry,* Columbia University Press, 2005 (http://www.columbiagrangers.org). *The National Portrait Gallery* (www.npg.org.uk). *The Oxford Companion to English Literature.* 6th edition. Margaret Drabble, ed. Oxford University Press, 2000.

BACON, SIR FRANCIS, VISCOUNT ST. ALBANS (1561–1626)

Bacon is more remembered for his position as Lord Chancellor of England (1618–21) and for his non-fiction than for his poetry. His public life came to an end in 1621 when he was charged with taking bribes as judge and spent a few days in the Tower of London. Some of his publications are: *The Proficience and Advancement of Learning,* 1605. *Novum Organum,* 1620 (an English translation can be found at www.luminarium.org/sevenlit/bacon). *History of Henry the Seventh,* 1621. *The New Atlantis,* 1626 (describing a Utopian community). *Sylva Sylvarum,* 1627 (a miscellaneous collection of observations and experiments in natural history). *Translation of Certain Psalms into English Verse,* 1624. His *Essays* (1597–1625) are reckoned to be the most original of all his works. Some of his poems: "Guiltless Heart," "Sing a New Song" (appears to be inspired by Psalm 150), "Help Lord" (a plea that Truth and Right will prevail), "The Life of Man" (the world is but a bubble and the life of man is less than a hand span).

Sources: *Dictionary of National Biography.* Electronic Edition 1.1. Oxford University Press, 1997. *Encyclopædia Britannica Ultimate Reference Suite DVD,* 2006. *Poems of Sir Frances Bacon* (www.shakespeare-oxford.com). *The Columbia Granger's Index to Poetry.* 11th ed. *The Columbia Granger's World of Poetry,* Columbia University Press, 2005 (http://www.columbiagrangers.org). *The National Portrait Gallery* (www.npg.org.uk). *The New Oxford Book of Sixteenth Century Verse.* Emrys Jones, ed. Oxford University Press, 2002. *The Oxford Companion to English Literature.* 6th edition. Margaret Drabble, ed. Oxford University Press, 2000.

BAILEY, THOMAS, and PHILIP JAMES (1785–1902)

Thomas, the father, 1785–1856

He was born at Nottingham and educated mainly at Gilling, North Yorkshire. His main occupation was as a silk-hosier at Nottingham. From 1836 to 1843 he served on the town council, then from 1845 he was proprietor and editor of the *Nottingham Mercury,* one of the chief papers of the town. This venture folded in 1852 because of his liberal views on the 1851 Ecclesiastical Titles Bill (which barred Catholics from holding ecclesiastical titles, and the land that went with them). He died at his mansion in the village of Basford, near Nottingham, where he had lived for many years, engaged in literary pursuits and in the formation of a choice collection of books and engravings. Some of his poetry publications: *What is Life? and Other Poems,* 1820. *The Carnival of Death,* 1822. *Ireton,* 1827. *Recreations in Retirement,* 1836. *The Advent of Charity and Other Poems,* 1851. Some of his other publications: *Annals of Nottinghamshire: A New and Popular History of the County of Nottingham, Including the Borough,* 1852–1855 (4 volumes). *Handbook to Nottingham Castle,* 1854. *Handbook to Newstead Abbey,* 1855. *Records of Longevity,* 1857.

Philip James, the son, 1816–1902

He attended Glasgow University but left without graduating, and in 1835 moved to London and was called to the bar in 1840. At a young age he learned Byron's "Childe Harold" by heart. In 1836 he returned to Basford to work on his own translation of Goethe's *Faust,* published in 1839. It was an immediate success and was praised by many poets, including Tennyson. The influence of Byron is apparent in its 22 scenes and 8103 lines. It passed through several editions, both in England and America, where thirty unauthorized editions appeared before 1889. By 1889 the final version reached nearly 40,000 lines, with an introduction and 52 scenes. He died after an attack of influenza and was buried in Nottingham Cemetery. Some of his other publications: *The Angel World, and Other Poems,* 1850.

The Mystic, and Other Poems, 1855. *The Universal Hymn,* 1867. *Festus Birthday Book,* 1882. *Beauties of Festus,* 1884. *Causa Britannica, a Poem in Latin Hexameters with English Paraphrase,* 1883. Some of his other poems: "Helen's Song," "I Loved Her for That She Was Beautiful," "Nottingham Castle, an Ode," "We Live in Deeds."

Sources: *Poems That Touch the Heart.* A.L. Alexander, ed. Doubleday, 1956. An extract of *Festus* can be found at (http://www.fullbooks.com/Library-of-the-Worlds-Best-Literaturex23537.html). *Dictionary of National Biography.* Electronic Edition 1.1. Oxford University Press, 1997. *Great Books Online* (www.bartleby.com). *The National Portrait Gallery* (www.npg.org.uk). *New Catholic Dictionary: Ecclesiastical Titles Act* (http://www.catholic-forum.com/saints/ncd02922.htm). *Oldpoetry* (www.oldpoetry.com). *The New Oxford Book of Victorian Verse.* Christopher Ricks, ed. Oxford University Press, 2002. *The Oxford Book of English Mystical Verse, 13th-20th Centuries.* D.H.S. Nicholson and A.H. Lee, eds. Oxford University Press, 1916. *The Oxford Companion to English Literature.* 6th edition. Margaret Drabble, ed. Oxford University Press, 2000. *Wikipedia, the Free* Encyclopedia (http://en.wikipedia.org/wiki/Wikipedia).

BAILLIE, LADY GRISEL (1665–1746)

Songwriter born at Redbraes Castle (Scottish Borders); the heroine of Joanna Baillie's poem "The Legend of Lady Griseld Baillie." She concealed her covenanting father, Sir Patrick Hume (1641–1724), in the church vaults in the border town of Polwarth (1684). After Robert Baillie's execution, Sir Patrick Hume (later Earl Marchmont) fled to Holland. When it was safe to return to Scotland, Lady Grisel married George Baillie, the son of Robert Baillie. Her *The Household Book of Lady Grisell Baillie* (edited by R. Scott-Moncrieff, Edinburgh, 1911) gives a remarkable insight into household management in the 18th century. She was the first deaconess of the Church of Scotland and the Deaconess Hospital in Edinburgh, now the headquarters of Lothian Health. The poem "And Werena My Heart Licht I Wad Dee" was possibly written at a time when she was parted from her lover in Holland.

Sources: *Dictionary of National Biography.* Electronic Edition 1.1. Oxford University Press, 1997. *Early Modern Women Poets (1520–1700).* Jane Stevenson and Peter Davidson, ed. Oxford University Press, 2001. *Encyclopædia Britannica Ultimate Reference Suite DVD,* 2006. *The Columbia Granger's Index to Poetry.* 11th ed. *The Columbia Granger's World of Poetry,* Columbia University Press, 2005 (http://www.columbiagrangers.org). *The Literary Encyclopedia* (www.LitEncyc.com).

BAILLIE, JOANNA (1762–1857 or 1762–1851)

A Scottish poet descended from the patriot William Wallace, who lived most of her life in England. Of her many publications, the early ones are:

Fugitive Verses, 1790 (anonymously, with a second edition in 1842). *Plays on the Passions*, 1798 (containing *Basil*, a tragedy on love; the *Trial*, a comedy on the same subject; and *De Monfort*, a tragedy on hatred). *Collection of Poems*, 1823. She wrote 27 dramatic plays, poems, songs and several hymns. "The Legend of Lady Griseld Baillie" portrays the courage of Grisel, who acted as courier between her father, Sir Patrick Hume and his friend, Robert Baillie, imprisoned, accused of complicity in the 1683 Rye House plot to assassinate King Charles II, because of his pro–Roman Catholic policies. Robert Baillie, a covenanter, was hanged in 1684. "The Legend of Lady Griseld Baillie" tells of a time when Scotland struggled to be free from Catholic dominance. "The Outlaw's Song" portrays the feelings of a man outlawed from home and hearth and family with no place of his own, when the very birds of the air have a place to rest.

Sources: *Dictionary of National Biography*. Electronic Edition 1.1. Oxford University Press, 1997. *Encyclopædia Britannica Ultimate Reference Suite DVD*, 2006. *English Poetry: Author Search*. Chadwyck-Healey Ltd., 1995 (http://www.lib.utexas.edu:8080/search/epoetry/author. html). *Poemhunter* (www.poemhunter.com). *The Columbia Granger's Index to Poetry*. 11th ed. *The Columbia Granger's World of Poetry*, Columbia University Press, 2005 (http://www.columbiagrangers.org). *The National Portrait Gallery* (www.npg.org.uk). *The New Penguin Book of Scottish Verse*. Robert Crawford and Mick Imlah, eds. Penguin Books, 2000. *The Oxford Companion to English Literature*. 6th edition. Margaret Drabble, ed. Oxford University Press, 2000.

BAKER, HENRY (1698–1774)

London-born naturalist, author, minor poet and Fellow of the Royal Society whose fame rests on his accumulating a fortune based on his method for teaching deaf children. In 1728 (under the name of Henry Stonecastle) he and Daniel Defoe (whose daughter he married) set up the *Universal Spectator and Weekly Journal*, a copy of which is in the Bodleian Library, Oxford. He wrote *The Microscope Made Easy* (1743) and *Employment for the Microscope* (1753). He is credited with introducing the Alpine strawberry and the rhubarb plant into England. His poem collections: *Invocation of Health*, 1723. *Original Poems*, 1723, reprinted in 1725. *The Universe, a Poem intended to restrain the Pride of Man*, 1727. *Medulla Poetarum Romanorum*, 1737 (a selection from the Roman poets, with translations). Some of his other poems: "The Declaimer," "Kitty's Dream," "Love," "The Rapture."

Sources: *Dictionary of National Biography*. Electronic Edition 1.1. Oxford University Press, 1997. *English Poetry: Author Search*. Chadwyck-Healey Ltd., 1995 (http://www. lib.utexas.edu:8080/search/epoetry/author.html). *Stan-*

ford University Libraries and Academic Information Resources (http://library.stanford.edu). *The Columbia Granger's Index to Poetry*. 11th ed. *The Columbia Granger's World of Poetry*, Columbia University Press, 2005 (http://www.columbiagrangers.org). *The National Portrait Gallery* (www.npg.org.uk). *The New Oxford Book of Eighteenth Century Verse*. Roger Lonsdale, ed. Oxford University Press 2003.

BAKER, SIR HENRY WILLIAMS (1821–1877)

London-born hymn writer, the son of Vice-admiral Sir Henry Loraine Baker, who served with distinction at Guadaloupe in 1815. Young Henry attended Trinity College at Cambridge, was ordained in 1844, and spent most of his career as vicar of Monkland Priory Church in Herefordshire. He assumed the baronetcy in 1859. From 1860 to 1877 he was editor-in-chief of the Anglican *Hymns Ancient and Modern*. He held the doctrine of the celibacy of the clergy, and at his death the baronetcy devolved on a kinsman. He was the author of *Daily Prayers for the Use of Those Who Have to Work Hard*, as well as of *Daily Text-book* and of some tracts on religious subjects. He wrote twenty-three hymns, translated nine and composed two hymn tunes. Seven of his hymns are in the current *Ancient and Modern* hymnbook. One of his best-known hymns is the paraphrase of Psalm 23, "The King of Love My Shepherd Is."

Sources: *Dictionary of National Biography*. Electronic Edition 1.1. Oxford University Press, 1997. *Hymns Ancient and Modern New Standard*, 1987. *The Cyber Hymnal* (http://www.cyberhymnal.org/index.htm).

BAKEWELL, JOHN (1721–1819)

Born in Brailsford, Derbyshire, he experienced a religious conversion at the age of 18, and in 1744 (the year of the first Methodist Conference) he began to preach and soon became an ardent evangelist. He moved to London shortly after, where he met John and Charles Wesley, Augustus Toplady, and other notable preachers. He spent many years of his life preaching for the Wesleyans, and he was buried in the Wesleyan Cemetery, City Road Chapel, London. Although he wrote only three hymns, the one that is probably in every hymnbook is "Hail, Thou Once Despised Jesus." This worshipful and strongly doctrinal hymn text presents a vivid contrast between the shame and suffering of Christ's earthly life and the greatness of His eternal glorification, where the Redeemed join with the angles to sing Emmanuel's praise.

Sources: *Hymn Devotionals* (http://our.homewithgod. com/ewerluvd/hymndevotionals/5_13.htm). *The Cyber Hymnal* (http://www.cyberhymnal.org/index.htm).

BALDWIN, WILLIAM (c. 1515–1563)

A west-country poet who studied logic and philosophy at Oxford, then became a proofreader to

Edward Whitchurch, the Protestant publisher from Camberwell, London. His *A Treatise of Morall Phylosophie, Contayning the Sayinges of the Wyse*, was published in 1547, and *Canticles or Balades of Salomon, phraselyke declared in Englyshe Metres*, in 1549. During the reigns of Edward VI (1547–1553) and Queen Mary (1553–1558) he was employed to prepare theatrical exhibitions for the court. In 1559 he superintended the publication of the *Mirror for Magistrates* (see also Niccols, Richard, and Ferrers, George), contributing four poems of his own: "The Story of Richard, Earl of Cambridge, being put to death at Southampton," "How Thomas Montague, Earl of Salisbury, in the midst of his glory was by chance slain by a Piece of Ordnance," "Story of William de la Pole, Duke of Suffolk, being punished for abusing his King and causing the Destruction of good Duke Humphrey," and "The Story of Jack Cade naming himself Mortimer, and his Rebelling against the King." In 1560 he published a poetical, "The Funeralles of King Edward the Sixt; wherein are declared the Causers and Causes of his Death."

Sources: *Dictionary of National Biography.* Electronic Edition 1.1. Oxford University Press, 1997. *English Poetry: Author Search.* Chadwyck-Healey Ltd., 1995 (http://www.lib.utexas.edu:8080/search/epoetry/author.html). *The Oxford Companion to English Literature.* 6th edition. Margaret Drabble, ed. Oxford University Press, 2000.

BAMFORD, SAMUEL (1788–1872)

Lancashire weaver, poet, and journalist who campaigned for the reform of working-class conditions. In 1819 he was imprisoned for taking part in a meeting in St. Peter's Fields Manchester that led to the "Peterloo Massacre," where mounted troops dispersed the peaceful. About 500 people were injured and 11 killed. Bamford's publications include: *An Account of the Arrest and Imprisonment of Samuel Bamford, Middleton, on Suspicion of High Treason*, 1817. *The Weaver Boy, or Miscellaneous Poetry*, 1819. *Homely Rhymes*, 1843. *Passages in the Life of a Radical*, 1840–4. *Tawk o'Seawth Lankeshur, by Samhul Beamfort*, 1850 (local dialect). *Life of Amos Ogden*, 1853. *The Dialect of South Lancashire, or Tim Bobbin's Tummus and Meary, with his Rhymes, with Glossary*, 1854. *Early Days*, 1849, 1859. Some of his other poems: "The Bard's Reformation," "Farewell to My Cottage," "Homely Rhymes on Bad Times," "The Landowner," "Touch Him!" "God help the poor" (gives wonderful insight into what it was like to be poor in England in 1819 a child with pale lips and frozen red hands).

Sources: *Dictionary of National Biography.* Electronic Edition 1.1. Oxford University Press, 1997. *Encyclopædia Britannica Ultimate Reference Suite DVD*, 2006. *Modern History Sourcebook: Samuel Bamford (1788–1872): Passages in the Life of a Radical-on the Peterloo Massacre, 1819* (www.fordham.edu/halsall/mod/1819bamford.html). *The Columbia Granger's Index to Poetry.* 11th ed. *The Columbia Granger's World of Poetry*, Columbia University Press, 2005 (http://www.columbiagrangers.org). *The Oxford Companion to English Literature.* 6th edition. Margaret Drabble, ed. Oxford University Press, 2000. *The Poorhouse Fugitives: Self-Taught Poets and Poetry in Victorian Britain.* Brian Maidment, ed. Carcanet, 1987.

BAMPFYLDE, JOHN CODRINGTON (1754–1796)

The second son of Sir Richard Warwick Bampfylde, of Poltimore, Devonshire, educated at Cambridge University. He had every opportunity, but in London he lost his sense of direction. He fell in love with and proposed to Miss Palmer, niece of Sir Joshua Reynolds, to whom, in 1778, he dedicated *Sixteen Sonnets*. Angered at Sir Joshua's refusal — Joshua virtually threw him out — he broke one of Sir Joshua's windows and was sent to Newgate prison. Although his mother secured his release, he thereafter lived in squalor and spent some years in a private mental asylum before he died of tuberculosis. Some of his poems: "On Christmas," "On Hearing That Torture Was Suppressed Throughout the Austrian Dominions," "On a Frightful Dream" (reads as an expression of his experience in the asylum), "On a Wet Summer," "To the Evening," "To the Redbreast," "Written at a Farm."

Sources: *A Century of Sonnets: The Romantic-Era Revival, 1750–1850.* Paula R. Feldman and Daniel Robinson, ed. Oxford University Press, 1999. *Dictionary of National Biography.* Electronic Edition 1.1. Oxford University Press, 1997. *English Poetry: Author Search.* Chadwyck-Healey Ltd., 1995 (http://www.lib.utexas.edu:8080/search/epoetry/author.html). *The National Portrait Gallery* (www.npg.org.uk). *Oldpoetry* (www.oldpoetry.com). *Stanford University Libraries and Academic Information Resources* (http://library.stanford.edu). *The Columbia Granger's Index to Poetry.* 11th ed. *The Columbia Granger's World of Poetry*, Columbia University Press, 2005 (http://www.columbiagrangers.org).

BANIM BROTHERS, MICHAEL (1796–1874) and JOHN (1798–1842)

Irish brothers who collaborated in many writing novels and dramas. They were born in Kilkenny to a prosperous businessman who ensured that his sons had a good education. Michael studied law, but had to take over the family business; John studied art at the academy of the Royal Dublin Society. While Michael carried on the business, John became a teacher of drawing in Kilkenny, falling into emotional distress over the death of a woman he loved. Now living in Dublin, he turned away from art and devoted himself to writing poetry. In 1824 the brothers started publishing a series of novels, *Tales, by the*

O'Hara Family, which some say were on a par with Scott's *Waverley Novels*. The Banims may be justly called the first national novelists of Ireland, and John Banim has been called "the Scott of Ireland." John moved to London and worked in journalism, and over the years the brothers continued to cooperate on their novels. Ill health plagued John; nevertheless, he labored on, suffering crippling pain, and at the age of twenty-eight he looked forty. He tottered as he walked, and he died in his hometown. Illness afflicted Michael also, and, like his brother, he carried on writing. Michael lived to a good age, and when he died Benjamin Disraeli granted his widow a pension from the civil list. Although it is their novels for which they are famous, John also wrote a few poems. "The Celt's Paradise" is one. Another, "The Irish Mother in the Penal Days," is a vivid portrayal of the suffering endured in the struggle for Catholic emancipation. Some of their other poems: "Chaunt of the Cholera," "Song. As We Are Men and Irishmen," "Song. Yes! Discord's Hand to the Last It Was," "The Clare Election," "The Irish Mother to Her Child," "The Irish Peasant to His Child," "The Irish Priests' Song," "The Irish Soldier," "The New Reformation," "The Peasant's Unarmed Police," "The Reconciliation," "The Shamrock and the Lily."

Sources: *An Anthology of Irish Verse: The Poetry of Ireland from Mythological Times to the Present*. Padraic Colum, Padraic ed. Kilkenny Press, 1948. *Bibliography of 19th-c. Irish Literature* (http://info.wlu.ca/~wwweng/faculty/jwright/irish/biblio-main.htm). *Catholic Encyclopedia* (http://www.newadvent.org). *Dictionary of National Biography*. Electronic Edition 1.1. Oxford University Press, 1997. *Encyclopædia Britannica Ultimate Reference Suite DVD*, 2006. *English Poetry: Author Search*. Chadwyck-Healey Ltd., 1995 (http://www.lib.utexas.edu:8080/search/epoetry/author.html). *Stanford University Libraries and Academic Information Resources* (http://library.stanford.edu). *The Columbia Granger's Index to Poetry*. 11th ed. *The Columbia Granger's World of Poetry*, Columbia University Press, 2005 (http://www.columbiagrangers.org). *The Oxford Companion to English Literature*. 6th edition. Margaret Drabble, ed. Oxford University Press, 2000.

BARBAULD, ANNA LETITIA (1743–1825)

Daughter of John Aikin, D.D., she could read with ease before the age of three years. She so mastered French, Italian, Latin and Greek that in 1753, she became a classics tutor at a dissenting academy in Warrington, Lancashire. Aikin married the Rev. Rochemont Barbauld (from an exiled French Protestant family). The Barbaulds moved to London, where she lived the rest of her life. Her husband committed suicide in 1808. Mrs. Barbauld wrote over 200 poems and some twenty hymns, which include: *Poems*, 1773 (with four editions in the first year). *Miscellaneous Pieces in Prose*, 1773 (in collaboration with her brother). *Hymns in Prose for Children*, 1781. *The British Novelists*, 1810, in 50 volumes (edited). *Epistle to William Wilberforce, Esq., on the Rejection of the Bill for Abolishing the Slave Trade*, 1791. Some of her other poems: "A Summer Evening's Meditation," "Hymn to Content," "Ode to Spring," "On A Lady's Writing," "On the Backwardness of the Spring 1771," "Ovid to His Wife," "The Caterpillar," "The Rights of Women."

Sources: *Dictionary of National Biography*. Electronic Edition 1.1. Oxford University Press, 1997. *Encyclopædia Britannica Ultimate Reference Suite DVD*, 2006. *Poem hunter* (www.poemhunter.com). *The Columbia Granger's Index to Poetry*. 11th ed. *The Columbia Granger's World of Poetry*, Columbia University Press, 2005 (http://www.columbiagrangers.org). *The Cyber Hymnal* (http://www.cyberhymnal.org/index.htm). *The National Portrait Gallery* (www.npg.org.uk). *The Online Books Page* (http://digital.library.upenn.edu/books). *The Oxford Companion to English Literature*. 6th edition. Margaret Drabble, ed. Oxford University Press, 2000. *The Poems of Anna Letitia Barbauld*. William McCarthy and Elizabeth Kraft, ed. University of Georgia Press, 1994.

BARBER MARY (1690–1757)

Irish poet whose poetic name was Sapphira, began writing poetry for the purpose of stimulating her children's lessons. Her "The Widow Gordon's Petition" raised money to support an officer's widow left penniless and with a blind child. A friendship sprang up between Mrs. Barber and Jonathan Swift, who introduced her to his influential friends in England — where she finally settled. *Poems on Several Occasions* (1734), which went through three editions, was criticized by some as being dull. She survived ill health and slanderous reports about forgery and in 1737 cooperated with Swift to publish his *Polite Conversations*, which was presented as a successful play at the theatre in Dublin. In 1755 a selection from her *Poems* was published in two volumes of *Poems by the Most Eminent Ladies*. G. Colman and B. Thornton, eds. Northern Kentucky University, 2003. Some of her other poems: "To a Lady," "Written for My Son ... at His First Putting on Breeches," "Written for My Son ... Upon His Master's First Bringing in a Rod."

Sources: *British Literature 1640–1789* (www.blackwellpublishing.com/contents.asp?ref=063121769X). *Dictionary of National Biography*. Electronic Edition 1.1. Oxford University Press, 1997. *English Poetry: Author Search*. Chadwyck-Healey Ltd., 1995 (http://www.lib.utexas.edu:8080/search/epoetry/author.html). *Eighteenth Century Women Poets: An Oxford Anthology*. Roger Lonsdale, ed. Oxford University Press, 1989. *Poemhunter* (www.poemhunter.com). *The Columbia Granger's Index to Poetry*. 11th ed. *The Columbia Granger's World of Poetry*, Columbia University Press, 2005 (http://www.columbiagrangers.

org). *The Poetry of Mary Barber*. Bernard Tucker, ed. The Edwin Mellen Press, 1992.

BARBOUR, JOHN (?1316–1395)

Archdeacon of Aberdeen and author of a Scottish national epic of 13,000 lines, *The Bruce*, which celebrates the story of the War of Independence and the deeds of King Robert of Scotland and James Douglas at the Battle of Bannockburn, 1314. Barbour helped in the negotiations for ransoming King David II, who had been a prisoner in England after his capture in the Battle of Neville's Cross (1346). He enjoyed royal favor and in 1388 was given a life pension from Robert II. "Bruce's address to his captains before Bannockburn" is written in broad Scots. It is a poem of praise for the gallant Scots who preferred death to slavery. A translation by Archie Duncan can be found at www2.arts.gla.ac.uk/SESLL/STELLA/STARN/poetry/BRUS/intro.htm.

Sources: Canongate Books Ltd (www.canongate.net). *Dictionary of National Biography*. Electronic Edition 1.1. Oxford University Press, 1997. *Encyclopædia Britannica Ultimate Reference Suite DVD*, 2006. *Great Books Online* (www.bartleby.com). *Oldpoetry* (www.oldpoetry.com). *The Columbia Granger's Index to Poetry*. 11th ed. *The Columbia Granger's World of Poetry*, Columbia University Press, 2005 (http://www.columbiagrangers.org). *The Oxford Companion to English Literature*. 6th edition. Margaret Drabble, ed. Oxford University Press, 2000.

BARCLAY, ALEXANDER (?1475–1552)

Barclay was chaplain at the College of St. Mary Ottery, Devon, then a Benedictine monk at Ely — where he probably wrote his eclogues. Later he became a Franciscan friar of Canterbury, and in 1552, rector of All Hallows, London. His poem "The Ship of Fools" (1509) was a translation — not literal, but an adaptation to suit English conditions — from "Das Narrenschiff" (1494), a poem by the German humanist, moralist and satirist Sebastian Brant, in which more than 100 fools are gathered on a ship bound for Narragonia, the fools' paradise. His poem "Geographers" is a salutary reminder to people not to get above themselves. All knowledge, he says, is of little value if we do not know ourselves or how we should conduct ourselves. Some of his other poems: "Eating in Hall," "Here Beginneth the Castle of Labour," "Preachment for Preachers," "Star of the Sea," "The Life of Saint George," "The Mirror of Good Manners," "The Tudor Rose," "Winter."

Sources: *Dictionary of National Biography*. Electronic Edition 1.1. Oxford University Press, 1997. *Encyclopædia Britannica Ultimate Reference Suite DVD*, 2006. *English Poetry: Author Search*. Chadwyck-Healey Ltd., 1995 (http://www.lib.utexas.edu:8080/search/epoetry/author.html). *Great Books Online* (www.bartleby.com). *The Columbia Granger's Index to Poetry*. 11th ed. *The Columbia Granger's World of Poetry*, Columbia University Press, 2005

(http://www.columbiagrangers.org). *The Oxford Book of Late Medieval Verse and Prose*. Douglas Gray, ed. Clarendon Press, 1985. *The Oxford Companion to English Literature*. 6th edition. Margaret Drabble, ed. Oxford University Press, 2000.

BARDWELL, LELAND (1928–)

Born in India of Irish parents, Bardwell was brought to Ireland at two years old, grew up in Leixlip, County Kildare, and was educated in Dublin and London. She has written six novels, including *Different Kinds of Love* (1994), which has been translated into German as *Zeit vertreibt Liebe*. Her plays include *Thursday* and *Open Ended Prescription*. She has also broadcast radio plays, including *The Revenge of Constance* and *Just Another Killing*. Her musical, *Edith Piaf*, toured Ireland. She is a member of Aosdána and lives in County Sligo. Her short story collection, *Different Kinds of Love* (1986), has been translated into German and French. Some of her poetry publications: *The Mad Cyclist*, 1970. *The Fly and the Bedbug*, 1984. *Dostoevsky's Grave, New and Selected Poems*, 1991. *The White Beach, New and Selected Poems 1960–1988*, 1998. *The Noise of Masonry Settling*, 2006.

Sources: *Short Biography and Works of Leland Bardwell* (http://www.artscouncil.ie/aosdana/biogs/literature/lelandbardwell.html). *Irish Writers, Books by Leland Bardwell* (http://www.kennysirishbookshop.ie/categories/irish writers/bardwellleland.shtml).

BARING, MAURICE (1874–1945)

Fellow of the Royal Society of Literature, Baring was one of the family of Baring's Bank. Educated at Eton College, he left Trinity College, Cambridge, without graduating. Baring was a brilliant linguist with a varied career as a diplomat, journalist and war correspondent in Russia and the Balkans. During World War I he served with the Royal Flying Corps. He was appointed to the Order of the British Empire in 1918 and as officer of the Legion of Honor in 1935. In addition to his autobiography, *The Puppet Show of Memory* (1922), he published several other novels and collections of stories, two non-fiction books and a book of great ghost stories. A painting of Baring, G.K. Chesterton, and Hilaire Belloc (1932) by James Gunn is shown on the National Portrait Gallery website. "The Dying Reservist" is a memorial to his many friends killed in World War I, where he speaks of the pain of their not hearing the song of the harvest home. Some of his other poems: "Ballad," "I Dare Not Pray to Thee," "Julian Grenfell" (see entry), "Moan in the Form of a Ballade."

Sources: *Dictionary of National Biography*. Electronic Edition 1.1. Oxford University Press, 1997. *Encyclopædia Britannica Ultimate Reference Suite DVD*, 2006. *The*

National Portrait Gallery (www.npg.org.uk). *The Columbia Granger's Index to Poetry.* 11th ed. *The Columbia Granger's World of Poetry,* Columbia University Press, 2005 (http://www.columbiagrangers.org). *The Home Book of Verse.* Burton Egbert Stevenson, ed. New York: Henry Holt and Company 1953. *The Oxford Companion to English Literature.* 6th edition. Margaret Drabble, ed. Oxford University Press, 2000.

BARING-GOULD, SABINE (1824–1924)

The Rev. Baring-Gould was an historian, author, hymn writer, and collector of folk songs. He was an accomplished linguist and after attending schools in Germany and France and after graduating from Clare College, Cambridge, in 1856, he entered the ministry. He wrote over 100 books, including 30 novels and several hymns. His main publications: *Book of Were-Wolves,* 1865. *Curious Myths of the Middle Ages,* 1866, 1868. *The Origin and Development of Religious Belief,* 1869–1870 (2 volumes). *Lives of the Saints,* 1907 (16-volumes). *The History of the Evangelical Revival,* 1920. Two of his hymns are in most current hymn books: "Now the Day is Over," the child's evening hymn, to which he composed the popular tune Eudoxia, and the rousing hymn "Onward, Christian Soldiers." Some of his other poems: "Daily, Daily, Sing the Praises," "The Olive Tree."

Sources: *Dictionary of National Biography.* Electronic Edition 1.1. Oxford University Press, 1997. *Poemhunter* (www.poemhunter.com). *Sabine Baring-Gould Biography and the folk songs of South-West England* (www.btinternet.com/~greenjack). *The Columbia Granger's Index to Poetry.* 11th ed. *The Columbia Granger's World of Poetry,* Columbia University Press, 2005 (http://www.columbiagrangers.org). *The Cyber Hymnal* (http://www.cyberhymnal.org/index.htm). *The National Portrait Gallery* (www.npg.org.uk). *The Oxford Companion to English Literature.* 6th edition. Margaret Drabble, ed. Oxford University Press, 2000.

BARKER, GEORGE GRANVILLE (1913–1991)

Poet, novelist and artist, Barker was born in Loughton, Essex, England, of Irish and English parentage. At the age of twenty he published the novel *Alanna Autumnal,* and *Thirty Preliminary Poems.* He was visiting professor of English literature at the Imperial Tohoku University in Japan in 1939 and taught in several American universities. He lived in Rome from 1960 to 1965 and settled at Bintry House in Norfolk, England, where he lived with his novelist wife Elspeth Barker. Elizabeth Smart's famous prose poem "By Grand Central Station I Sat Down and Wept" was inspired by her affair with Barker. In her semi-autobiographical novel *Come and Tell me Some Lies,* Raffaella Barker (his daughter) writes about the chaotic life at Bintry

House. His poems include "Sonnet to My Mother;" in spite of all her failings he still loves his mother. Some of his other poems: "Circular from America," "Grandfather, Grandfather," "January Jumps About," "Summer Song," "True Confession."

Sources: *Encyclopædia Britannica Ultimate Reference Suite DVD,* 2006. *Poets' Graves, George Barker* (www.poetsgraves.co.uk/barker.htm). *The Columbia Granger's Index to Poetry.* 11th ed. *The Columbia Granger's World of Poetry,* Columbia University Press, 2005 (http://www.columbiagrangers.org). *The Life and Work of George Barker: Poets' Graves* (www.poetsgraves.co.uk/barker.htm). *The National Portrait Gallery* (www.npg.org.uk). *The Oxford Book of Sonnets.* John Fuller, ed. Oxford University Press, 2000. *The Oxford Companion to English Literature.* 6th edition. Margaret Drabble, ed. Oxford University Press, 2000.

BARKER, JANE (1652–?1727)

Novelist, convert to Roman Catholicism, political poet, and alleged Jacobite spy, she wrote prolifically on a variety of subjects. She was born at Wilsthorpe, Lincolnshire, the daughter of Thomas, a former Royalist soldier. Many of her male relations died young, fighting against James Scott, Protestant Duke of Monmouth at Sedgemoor ("The Pitchfork Rebellion") (1685). A staunch Jacobite, after the 1688 Revolution she followed the Stuart family into exile. Back in England, and with failing eyesight, her late years were spent in Richmond and at Wilsthorpe, under the patronage of the Countess of Exeter. *A Patch-Work Screen for the Ladies* (1723) and *The Lining of the Patch-Work Screen* (1726) include realistic stories and romances interspersed with poems, hymns, odes, recipes, and religious and philosophical reflections. Her long poem "On the Death of My Brother" portrays her grief and may reflect all her other losses. Some of her other poems: "A Bacchanalian Song," "A Virgin Life," "The Complaint," "The Contract with the muses writ on the bark of a shady ash-tree," "The Necessity of Fate," "To My Friends Who Praised My Poems," "To My Young Lover."

Sources: *British Women Writers: An Anthology from the Fourteenth Century to the Present.* Dale Spender and Janet Todd, eds. Peter Bedrick Books. 1989. *Dictionary of National Biography.* Electronic Edition 1.1. Oxford University Press, 1997. *English Poetry: Author Search.* Chadwyck-Healey Ltd., 1995 (http://www.lib.utexas.edu:8080/search/epoetry/author.html). *The Columbia Granger's Index to Poetry.* 11th ed. *The Columbia Granger's World of Poetry,* Columbia University Press, 2005 (http://www.columbiagrangers.org).

BARKER, LES (1947–)

Les Barker, from Manchester, England, is most well known for his comic poetry and parodies of popular songs. He worked as an accountant before he began playing folk music venues with "The Mrs.

Ackroyd Band" (named after his mongrel dog, Mrs. Ackroyd). He has toured solo around the world and published dozens of books and many albums. His books are a mixture of monologues and comic songs, with a few serious songs. Barker created several characters, such as "Jason and the Arguments," "Cosmo the Fairly Accurate Knife Thrower" and "Captain Indecisive." The titles of some of his poems indicate his turn of phrase and his obvious love of dogs: "A Cardi and Bloke," "Al Satians to Crewe," "An Infinite Number of Occasional Tables," "Collie flowers," "Endurance," "First They Came for the Mime Artists," "Get a Dog and Barker Yourself," "Irritable Bow-Wow Syndrome," "Camel Ye Faithful," "Reign of Terrier," "Royders of the Lost Ack," "Spaniel in the Lion's Den," "The Beagle has Landed," "Up the Creek Without a Poodle," "Wolfhound Amadeus Mozart."

Sources: *Les Barker Books* (www.waterbug.com). *Poems and Writings from Les Barker* (www.blodtandsmidigt. com/LesBarker/LesBarker.html)

BARNES, BARNABE (?1569–1609)

Elizabethan poet, son of Richard Barnes, bishop of Durham. In 1591 he joined the expedition to Normandy led by the Earl of Essex. In 1593 he published his sonnet sequence *Parthenophil and Parthenophe*, and *Sonnettes, Madrigals, Elegies, and Odes*; *A Divine Century of Spiritual* (1595), *Four Books of Offices* (1606) in prose, along with two plays and several other works. His imagery is imaginative and expressive, and his madrigals, although few, prove him to have been a born singer. Some of his poems: "A Blast of Wind, a Momentary Breath," "An Ode," "Asclepiad," "Carmen Anacreontivm," "Content," "God's Virtue," "No More Lewd Lays," "Oh Whether Shall My Troubled Muse Incline?" "The Life of Man," "Then, First with Locks Dishevelled, and Bare," "To the Beautiful Lady the Lady Brigett Manners," "Vulcan in Lemnos Isle."

Sources: *Dictionary of National Biography.* Electronic Edition 1.1. Oxford University Press, 1997. *Encyclopædia Britannica Ultimate Reference Suite DVD,* 2006. *English Poetry: Author Search.* Chadwyck-Healey Ltd., 1995 (http://www.lib.utexas.edu:8080/search/epoetry/author. html). *Poemhunter* (www.poemhunter.com). *The Columbia Granger's Index to Poetry.* 11th ed. *The Columbia Granger's World of Poetry,* Columbia University Press, 2005 (http://www.columbiagrangers.org). *The Elizabethan Sonnet* (www.sonnets.org). *The New Oxford Book of Sixteenth Century Verse.* Emrys Jones, ed. Oxford University Press, 2002. *The Oxford Companion to English Literature.* 6th edition. Margaret Drabble, ed. Oxford University Press, 2000.

BARNES, WILLIAM (1801–1886)

An ordained priest, schoolmaster, poet and author, known as the Dorsetshire Burns. He campaigned for the purification of the English language by getting rid of all foreign influences. His poems both in the local dialect and in English tell of life and labor in rural southwestern England. His first Dorset dialect poems were published in the *Dorset County Chronicle* (1833–34). His books, many of them concerned with education, history and language, include: *Poems of Rural Life*— two series, 1844 and 1862. *Hwomely Rhymes*, 1859. *Poems of Rural Life in Common English*, 1868. *Anglo-Saxon primer*, 1878. *An Outline of English Speech-Craft*, 1878. He was a regular contributor to the *Gentleman's Magazine, Retrospective Review,* and *Macmillan's Magazine.* His sense of humor is displayed in "The Bachelor," where the sentiment is take all your riches but give me a good wife. Some of his other poems: "Mater Dolorosa," "The Broken Heart," "The Castle Ruins," "The Surprise," "The Wife A-Lost," "Tokens," "Woak Hill," "Zummer an' Winter."

Sources: *Dictionary of National Biography.* Electronic Edition 1.1. Oxford University Press, 1997. *Encyclopædia Britannica Ultimate Reference Suite DVD,* 2006. *English Poetry: Author Search.* Chadwyck-Healey Ltd., 1995 (http://www.lib.utexas.edu:8080/search/epoetry/author.html). *Poemhunter* (www.poemhunter.com). *The Columbia Granger's Index to Poetry.* 11th ed. *The Columbia Granger's World of Poetry,* Columbia University Press, 2005 (http://www.columbiagrangers.org). *The Dorset Page* (www.thedorsetpage.com). *The National Portrait Gallery* (www.npg.org.uk). *The New Oxford Book of Victorian Verse.* Christopher Ricks, ed. Oxford University Press 2002. *The Oxford Companion to English Literature.* 6th edition. Margaret Drabble, ed. Oxford University Press, 2000.

BARNFIELD, RICHARD (1574–1629)

Elizabethan poet, born at Norbury, Shropshire, he graduated from Brasenose College, Oxford, in 1592. He formed an intimate friendship with the poets Thomas Watson and later Michael Drayton. In 1594 he published his first volume, *The Affectionate Shepherd,* a pastoral based on the second eclogue of Virgil, describing the love of Daphne for Ganymede. Early in 1595 he published another volume, *Cynthia,* also addressed to Ganymede. Some of the poems attributed to Shakespeare are thought to have been composed by Barnfield. He has the distinction of being the only Elizabethan poet, other than Shakespeare, to have addressed love sonnets to a man, as in *The Affectionate Shepherd,* in which he finds it sad that it is not the done thing to "love a lovely lad." Some of his other poems: "A Comparison of the Life of Man," "A Shepherd's Complaint," "Against the Dispraisers of Poetry," "As It Fell Upon a Day," "Cherry-lipped Adonis...," "Daphnis to Ganymede," "The Complaint of Chastity," "The Nightingale," "To His Friend Master R.L., in Praise of Music and Poetry."

Sources: *Dictionary of National Biography.* Electronic Edition 1.1. Oxford University Press, 1997. *Elizabethan Lyrics.* Norman Ault, ed. William Sloane Associates, 1949. *English Poetry: Author Search.* Chadwyck-Healey Ltd., 1995 (http://www.lib.utexas.edu:8080/search/epoetry/author. html). *The Columbia Granger's Index to Poetry.* 11th ed. *The Columbia Granger's World of Poetry,* Columbia University Press, 2005 (http://www.columbiagrangers.org). *The Elizabethan Sonnet* (www.sonnets.org). *The National Portrait Gallery* (www.npg.org.uk). *The Oxford Companion to English Literature.* 6th edition. Margaret Drabble, ed. Oxford University Press, 2000.

BARRY, SEBASTIAN (1955–)

Irish playwright, novelist and poet, born in Dublin to Francis and Joan Barry and graduated from Trinity College, Dublin, in 1977. He has lived in France, Switzerland, England, Greece, Italy, and Iowa. He became an honorary writing fellow at the University of Iowa and now lives in County Wicklow, Ireland. His early plays include *Boss Grady's Boys* (1990), which opened in 1988 and won the BBC/Stewart Parker Award. *The Steward of Christendom* first played in 1995 and opened in January 1997 at the Majestic Theater, Broadway. It won the Christopher Ewart-Biggs Memorial Prize, the Ireland/America Literary Prize, the Critics' Circle Award for Best New Play, and the Writers' Guild Award (Best Fringe Play). His poetry collections: *The Water-Colorist,* 1983. *The Rhetorical Town,* 1985. *Fanny Hawke Goes to the Mainland Forever,* 1987. *The Pinkening Boy: New Poems,* 2004. Some of his poems: "An Ending," "Cassibus Impositis Venor," "Christ-in-the-Woods," "Sketch from the Great Bull Wall," "The February Town," "The Indian River," "The Pardon of Assisi," "The Return," "The Room of Rhetoric," "The Winter Jacket," "The Wounds," "The Wrong Shoes."

Sources: *1996–1998 Broadway Premieres. The Steward of Christendom* (http://www.infoplease.com/ipea/A0152816. html). *Sebastian Barry* (http://www.contemporarywriters. com/authors/?p=auth02B11P375512626533). *British Council Arts* (http://www.contemporarywriters.com). *The Columbia Granger's Index to Poetry.* 11th ed. *The Columbia Granger's World of Poetry,* Columbia University Press, 2005 (http://www.columbiagrangers.org). *The Inherited Boundaries: Younger Poets of the Republic of Ireland.* Sebastian Barry, ed. The Dolmen Press, 1986. *The Oxford Companion to English Literature.* 6th edition. Margaret Drabble, ed. Oxford University Press, 2000. *The Steward of Christendom, Details of the Play* (http://www.glue.umd.edu/~sschreib/au tumn_02/investigations/steward.html).

BARTON, BERNARD (1784–1849)

Barton, known as the "Quaker Poet," was born at Carlisle and educated by Quakers. When his wife died in childbirth he became a tutor to a Liverpool merchant, but soon returned to his home in Woodbridge, Suffolk, to work in a bank, where he re-

mained until he died. He wrote 10 books of poems, many of which became hymns. A prolific poet, his works include: *Metrical Effusions,* 1812. *Convict's Appeal,* 1818 (dedicated to James Montgomery [see entry]), is a protest in verse against the severity of the criminal code. *Devotional Verses,* 1826. *Household Verses,* 1849. Some of his other poems: "A Call to Build the Lord's House," "Bruce and the Spider," "Comfort in a Cloudy Day," "Getting to the Watch-Tower," "Hope in Conflict," "Lamp of our Feet" (possibly inspired by Psalm 119:105), "Not Ours the Vows" (which maybe his heart's expression after the death of his wife), "Pride Reproved," "The Famine of the Word," "The Frailty of Man's Goodness," "The Lukewarm Threatened," "The Three Faithful, in the Fiery Furnace," "Walking in the Light."

Sources: *Best Loved Story Poems.* Walter E. Thwing, ed. Garden City, 1941. *Dictionary of National Biography.* Electronic Edition 1.1. Oxford University Press, 1997. *English Poetry: Author Search.* Chadwyck-Healey Ltd., 1995 (http://www.lib.utexas.edu:8080/search/epoetry/author. html). *Poemhunter* (www.poemhunter.com). *The Columbia Granger's Index to Poetry.* 11th ed. *The Columbia Granger's World of Poetry,* Columbia University Press, 2005 (http://www.columbiagrangers.org). *The Cyber Hymnal* (http://www.cyberhymnal.org/index.htm). *The National Portrait Gallery* (www.npg.org.uk).

BAYLISS, JOHN CLIFFORD (1919–1978)

Bayliss, born in Gloucestershire, graduated from St. Catherine's College, Cambridge, where he is listed as one of their famous alumni. He was a civil servant, then served in the Royal Air Force in India. He edited *The Fortune Anthology* (1942) with Nicholas Moore and Douglas Newton, *New Road* (1943 and 1944) with Alex Comfort, and *A Romantic Miscellany* (1946) with Derek Stanford. His collection *The White Knight and Other Poems* was published in 1944. He contributed in the war years to *Poetry London* and *Poetry Quarterly* and later to *Poetry Review.* He was also published in *Air Force Poetry* (1944), in *Poetry of the Forties* (Penguin Books) (1968), and *Surrealist Poetry in English* (Penguin Books) (1992). He is sometimes associated with the New Apocalyptics, perhaps because of his poem "Apocalypse and Resurrection;" he is also called a surrealist or New Romantic. Some of his other poems: "October," "Reported Missing," "Seven Dreams."

Sources: *English and American Surrealist Poetry.* Edward B. Germain, ed. Penguin Books, 1978. *The Columbia Granger's Index to Poetry.* 11th ed. *The Columbia Granger's World of Poetry,* Columbia University Press, 2005 (http://www.columbiagrangers.org). *Wikipedia, the Free Encyclopedia* (http://en.wikipedia.org/wiki/Wikipedia).

BAYLY, NATHANIEL THOMAS HAYNES (1797–1839)

A versatile songwriter, novelist, dramatist and ballet writer. He seemed destined for either the law or the church, but by his teens it was obvious that literature was his forte. He wrote hundreds of poems and popular songs, which were set to music by Sir Henry Bishop and other eminent composers; Bayly wrote the music for some of them. He also wrote several novels and a number of farces. Among the best known of his songs are "The Mistletoe Bough;" "Oh, No, We Never Mention Her;" "She Wore a Wreath of Roses," and "I'd be a Butterfly." Some of his other poems: "A Novel of High Life," "A Trip to Portsmouth," "Caraboo," "Condolence," "Gaily the Troubadour," "Inconstancy," "Lines Written in the Vale of Llangollen, in Wales," "Long, Long Ago," "Love and Science," "Oh! Love is Born in Youthful Days," "Oh! Where Do Fairies Hide Their Heads?" "Out, John," "To a Tell-Tale," "To Laura," "To Rosa," "We Met."

Sources: *A Short Biographical Dictionary of English Literature* (www.blackmask.com/thatway/books164c/shobio. htm). *Dictionary of National Biography.* Electronic Edition 1.1. Oxford University Press, 1997. *English Poetry: Author Search.* Chadwyck-Healey Ltd., 1995 (http://www.lib. utexas.edu:8080/search/epoetry/author.html). *The Columbia Granger's Index to Poetry.* 11th ed. *The Columbia Granger's World of Poetry,* Columbia University Press, 2005 (http://www.columbiagrangers.org). *The Home Book of Verse.* Burton Egbert Stevenson, ed. New York: Henry Holt and Company 1953. *The Oxford Companion to English Literature.* 6th edition. Margaret Drabble, ed. Oxford University Press, 2000.

BEATTIE, GEORGE (1786–1823)

Beattie, a Scottish lawyer poet, is best known for his popular, long, comic poem "John O'Arnha: a Tale" about the Montrose town officer of the day. Thwarted in love, Beattie shot himself on the beach at St. Cyrus, near Montrose. He had the gift of humor and conversation, evident in his poems. "John O'Arnha," first published in the *Montrose Review* in 1815, then later published in a separate form, bears some resemblance to "Tam o' Shanter" by Robert Burns. It is full of rollicking humor and vivid descriptions. Other poems are "Murderit Mynstrell," 1818 — written when a boy — charmingly simple in character; the "Bark," 1819; and the "Dream," 1820. He also wrote several small lyrics.

Sources: *Angus Authors, Angus Council* (www.angus. gov.uk/history/features/authors.htm). *Dictionary of National Biography.* Electronic Edition 1.1. Oxford University Press, 1997. For a full text of *John O'Arnha,* see www. scotstext.org/roughs/ george_beattie/john_o_arnha.asp.

BEATTIE, JAMES (1735–1803)

Poet, essayist, and moral philosopher. After graduating from Marischal College, Aberdeen, he be-

came a schoolmaster and eventually professor of moral philosophy and logic at his old college. He achieved fame with his "Essay on the Nature and Immutability of Truth," which defended Christianity against the philosophy of David Hume (1770). The poems he wrote about natural beauty influenced other poets such as Robert Burns, Sir Walter Scott, and Lord Byron. Success was tinged with sadness: his wife became insane and his sons, one of whom was a promising poet, died young. Beattie became ill and never recovered his health. His major poetical publications are: *Poems on Several Subjects,* 1766. *The Minstrel,* 1771–1772 (2 volumes). *Essays on Poetry,* 1778. Some of his other poems: "An Epitaph," "Edwin, the Minstrel," "Elegy (Tir'd with the busy crouds)," "Law," "Nature and the Poets," "The Hares, a Fable," "The Hermit," "The Judgment of Paris," "The Question," "The Wolf and Shepherds, a Fable," "The Youth of a Poet," "To Mr. Alexander Ross."

Sources: *Dictionary of National Biography.* Electronic Edition 1.1. Oxford University Press, 1997. *Encyclopædia Britannica Ultimate Reference Suite DVD,* 2006. *English Poetry: Author Search.* Chadwyck-Healey Ltd., 1995 (http://www.lib.utexas.edu:8080/search/epoetry/author. html). *Representative Poetry Online, John Askham* (http:// rpo.library.utoronto.ca/poet/371.html). *Significant and Famous Scots* (http://www.electricscotland.com/history/ other/beattie_james.htm). *The Columbia Granger's Index to Poetry.* 11th ed. *The Columbia Granger's World of Poetry,* Columbia University Press, 2005 (http://www.columbia grangers.org). *The National Portrait Gallery* (www.npg. org.uk). *The New Oxford Book of Eighteenth Century Verse.* Roger Lonsdale, ed. Oxford University Press, 2003. *The Oxford Companion to English Literature.* 6th edition. Margaret Drabble, ed. Oxford University Press, 2000.

BEAUMONT BROTHERS, SIR JOHN and FRANCIS (1583–1627)

John, the elder, 1583–1627

From Leicestershire, on the death of his father in 1598, John had to leave university, and like his brother, he preferred literature to law. In 1602 he published anonymously "Metamorphosis of Tobacco," a mock-heroic poem. "Of His Dear Son, Gervase" pours out his grief over his son's death at age seven. Some of his other poems: "A Description of Love," "Bosworth Field," "Epitaph upon My Dear Brother, Francis Beaumont," "Thou Who Art Our Author and Our End," "Of Sir Philip Sidney," "Of True Liberty," "Richard III's Speech," "The Assumption," "To His Late Majesty Concerning the True Form of English Poetry," "Upon a Funeral."

Francis, the younger, 1584–1616

Thrown off course by the premature death of his father, Francis failed to graduate from Oxford, and fared no better at law. His collaboration with John Fletcher—who apparently replaced Shakespeare around 1609 as chief dramatist of the King's Men—lasted seven years and produced 54 plays. Among those were three masterpieces: *The Maides Tragedy*, *Philaster*, and *A King and No King*. He collaborated with John Fletcher in writing the *Faithful Shepherdess* (?1610). Beaumont's first play, the prose comedy *The Woman Hater* (1605), was written for the popular children's company Boys of St. Paul's. The brothers are buried together in Poets' Corner, Westminster Abbey. Some of his poems: "Aspatia's Song," "Away, Delights," "Bridal Song," "Lay a Garland on My Hearse," "On the Tombs in Westminster Abbey," "The Author to the Reader," "The Glance," "The Indifferent," "The Month of May," "To the True Patroness of all Poetry, Calliope," "True Beauty."

Sources: *An Anthology of Catholic Poets.* Joyce Kilmer, ed. Fredonia Books, 2003. *Dictionary of National Biography.* Electronic Edition 1.1. Oxford University Press, 1997. *Encyclopædia Britannica Ultimate Reference Suite DVD,* 2006. *English Poetry: Author Search.* Chadwyck-Healey Ltd., 1995 (http://www.lib.utexas.edu:8080/search/epoetry/author.html). *The Life and Works of Francis Beaumont* (www.luminarium.org/sevenlit/beaumont). *Stanford University libraries and Academic Information Resources* (http://library.stanford.edu). *The Columbia Granger's Index to Poetry.* 11th ed. *The Columbia Granger's World of Poetry,* Columbia University Press, 2005 (http://www.columbiagrangers.org). *The National Portrait Gallery* (www.npg.org.uk). *The New Oxford Book of Seventeenth Century Verse.* Alastair Fowler, ed. Oxford University Press, 2004. *The Oxford Book of English Verse, 1250–1918.* Sir Arthur Quiller-Couch, ed (New edition, revised and enlarged, Oxford University Press, 1939. *The Oxford Companion to English Literature.* 6th edition. Margaret Drabble, ed. Oxford University Press, 2000. *Westminster Abbey Official Guide* (no date).

BEAUMONT, JOSEPH (1616–1699)

Born at Hadleigh, Leicestershire, educated at the local grammar school and Peterhouse College, Cambridge, Beaumont had a brilliant career. When in 1644 he was one of the royalist fellows ejected from Cambridge, he retired to his old home at Hadleigh, where he started to write his epic poem (some 30,000 lines) "Psyche" (1648). The poem represents the passage of the soul through the various temptations and assaults of life into eternal happiness. At the Restoration, Beaumont was made one of the king's chaplains in 1660. His appointment to master of Jesus College, Cambridge, was overshadowed by the death of his wife. In 1674 he was appointed professor of divinity to Cambridge University. "Whit Sunday" speaks of the Holy Spirit descending as the Eternal Dove. Many of his poems relate to the various disciples and Saints or to religious feast days of the Church. Some of his other poems: "Anniversar-

ium Baptismi," "Biothanatos," "Christmas Day," "Civill Warr," "David's Elegy upon Jonathan," "House and Home," "Morning Hymn," "Purification of the Blessed Virgin," "The Ascension," "The Candle," "The Cheat," "The Garden," "The Hourglass."

Sources: *Dictionary of National Biography.* Electronic Edition 1.1. Oxford University Press, 1997. *English Poetry: Author Search.* Chadwyck-Healey Ltd., 1995 (http://www.lib.utexas.edu:8080/search/epoetry/author.html). *Great Books Online* (www.bartleby.com). *Stanford University libraries and Academic Information Resources* (http://library.stanford.edu). *The Columbia Granger's Index to Poetry.* 11th ed. *The Columbia Granger's World of Poetry,* Columbia University Press, 2005 (http://www.columbiagrangers.org). *The Complete Poems of Dr. Joseph Beaumont.* 2 Volumes, Alexander B. Grosart, ed. Edinburgh University Press, 1880. *The Oxford Book of Christian Verse.* Donald Davie, ed. Oxford University Press, 2003.

BECKETT, SAMUEL BARCLAY (1906–1989)

Irish author, critic, poet and playwright, a graduate of Trinity College, Dublin and winner of the 1969 Nobel Prize for Literature. It is said that Beckett was an unhappy boy who grew into an unhappy young man, one who would not allow anyone to penetrate his solitude. His origins are in Huguenot stock, and he settled down in Paris in 1937, where he suffered a perforated lung when he was stabbed in the street. During World War II, he joined the underground movement and fought for the resistance. Most of his major works, including his poems, were originally written in French. Some of his poems: "Alba," "Ascension," "Cascando," "Dieppe," "Dortmunder," "Echo's Bones," "Roundelay," "Something There," "Waiting for Godot."

Sources: *Beckett Shorts: Selected Poems, Calder Publications* (www.calderpublications.com/books/0714543055.html). *Collected Poems by Samuel Beckett, 1930–1978.* John Calder Pub. 1999. *Encyclopædia Britannica Ultimate Reference Suite DVD,* 2006. *The Columbia Granger's Index to Poetry.* 11th ed (http://www.columbiagrangers.org). *The National Portrait Gallery* (www.npg.org.uk). *The Oxford Companion to English Literature.* 6th edition. Margaret Drabble, ed. Oxford University Press, 2000.

BEDDOES, THOMAS LOVELL (1803–1849)

Gifted poet of the late Romantic Elizabethan revival period, educated at Charterhouse School and Oxford University. He qualified as a doctor in Germany in 1832 and lived the rest of his life on the Continent. The death of his father when he was five years old may have contributed to his obsession with death in his life and work. His life ended with his committing suicide by poisoning. His major works are: *Bride's Tragedy*, 1822. *Death's Jest-Book* or *Fool's*

Tragedy, 1850. Many of his other poems do not reflect his preoccupation with death, rather they are tender and poignant. One such is "Dream-Pedlary" (1835), in which he poses the question: If there were dreams to sell, what would you buy? Some of his other poems: "A Beautiful Night," "A Fantastic Simile," "A Lake," "Ballad of Human Life," "Death's Jest Book," "Doomsday," "Lines Written in Switzerland," "Lines, Written at Geneva, July, 1824," "Lord Alcohol," "Song of Thanatos," "Song of the Stygian Naiades," "Sonnet: To Tartar, a Terrier Beauty," "The Lily of the Valley," "The Tree of Life."

Sources: Carcaent Books (www.carcanet.co.uk). *Confucius to Cummings: An Anthology of Poetry.* Ezra Pound and Marcella Spann, ed. New Directions Publishing Corporation, 1964. *Dictionary of National Biography.* Electronic Edition 1.1. Oxford University Press, 1997. *Encyclopædia Britannica Ultimate Reference Suite DVD,* 2006. *English Poetry: Author Search.* Chadwyck-Healey Ltd., 1995 (http://www.lib.utexas.edu:8080/search/epoetry/author.html). *Oldpoetry* (www.oldpoetry.com). *Oxford Book of English Verse.* Christopher Ricks, ed. Oxford University Press, 1999. *The Columbia Granger's Index to Poetry.* 11th ed. *The Columbia Granger's World of Poetry,* Columbia University Press, 2005 (http://www.columbiagrangers.org). *The Oxford Companion to English Literature.* 6th edition. Margaret Drabble, ed. Oxford University Press, 2000.

BEDE (BAEDA or BEDA), SAINT, THE VENERABLE (673–735)

Anglo-Saxon monk whose *Historia Ecclesiastica Gentis Anglorum (History of the English Church and People)* (1731) chronicled the occupation of England by the Romans and the centuries after they departed. He gives accounts of early English saints and tells the story of Caedmon and the creation of *Caedmon's Hymn.* He wrote many other biblical commentaries. The Monastery of St. Peter at Wearmouth (near Sunderland, Durham) was his home. His remains are entombed in the Galilee Chapel of Durham Cathedral. His Feast Day is 25 May. Most of what he wrote is in Latin. Some of those that have been translated into English: "Bede's Death Song" (a modern English translation is held at http://eir.library.utoronto.ca/rpo/display/poet20.html); "A Sparrow's Flight"; "Hymn" (six stanzas, available in English).

Sources: *A Little Book of Comfort.* Anthony Guest. Harper Collins 1993. *Dictionary of National Biography.* Electronic Edition 1.1. Oxford University Press, 1997. *Encyclopædia Britannica Ultimate Reference Suite DVD,* 2006. *Encyclopedia of Britain.* Bamber Gascoigne. London, Macmillan, 1994. *Medieval Sourcebook: Bede: Ecclesiastical History of England* (English translation) (www.fordham.edu/halsall/basis/bede-book1.html). *The Anglo-Saxon World: An Anthology.* Kevin Crossley-Holland, ed. Oxford University Press, 1982. *The Columbia Granger's Index to Poetry.* 11th ed. *The Columbia Granger's World of Poetry,*

Columbia University Press, 2005 (http://www.columbiagrangers.org). *The Oxford Companion to English Literature.* 6th edition. Margaret Drabble, ed. Oxford University Press, 2000.

BEECHING, HENRY CHARLES (1859–1919)

He was born in London to a family of ship-owners and bankers from Bexhill, Sussex. Graduating from Balliol College, Oxford, in 1883, he was ordained into the Anglican Church. He held various church positions: curate of St. Matthew's, Mossley Hill, Liverpool; curate of Yattendon, Berkshire; chaplain of Lincoln's Inn; and professor of pastoral theology at King's College, London. His last appointment, in 1911, was dean of Norwich cathedral. He died of heart failure and his ashes were buried in the Cathedral. As an undergraduate he contributed to *Waifs and Strays,* an undergraduate periodical, and went on to write books on doctrine and essays. In 1895 *Love in a Garden and Other Poems* was published, followed in 1898 by *Pages from a Private Diary*— having previously been published in the *Cornhill Magazine.* With John William MacKail and Bowyer Nichols (see entries) he published *Mensae Secundae,* 1879, *Love in Idleness,* 1883, and *Love's Looking-glass,* 1891. Some of his other poems: "A Song of the Three Kings," "First Snow," "From the Window in December," "Going Down Hill on a Bicycle," "Knowledge after Death," "Prayers," "The Blackbird," "The Dry Lake."

Sources: *A Sacrifice of Praise: An Anthology of Christian Poetry in English from Caedmon to the Mid-Twentieth Century.* James H. Trott, ed. Cumberland House Publishing, 1999. *Dictionary of National Biography.* Electronic Edition 1.1. Oxford University Press, 1997. *The New Oxford Book of Children's Verse.* Neil Philip, ed. Oxford University Press, 1996. *The Oxford Book of Victorian Verse.* Quiller-Couch, ed. Oxford University Press, 1971.

BEEDOME, THOMAS (d. ?1641)

Though little is known of his life, he is the author of a little volume of verses, songs, epistles, epigrams, elegies, and devotional poems, published posthumously in 1641 under the title *Poems Divine and Humane,* edited by Henry Glapthorne (see entry). The chief poem is entitled "The Jealous Lover, or the Constant Maid." "The Choyce" tells of his love for a maiden who might not be beautiful, or who may even be deformed; what matters is her soul that is beautiful. The phrase that keeps repeating is, "What care I?" Some of his other poems: "The Broken Heart," "The Petition," "The Question and Answer," "To the Noble Sir Francis Drake."

Sources: *Dictionary of National Biography.* Electronic Edition 1.1. Oxford University Press, 1997. *The Oxford Book of Short Poems.* P.J. Kavanagh and James Michie, eds.

Oxford University Press, 1985. *Stanford University Libraries and Academic Information Resources* (http://library.stanford.edu). *The Columbia Granger's Index to Poetry*. 11th ed. *The Columbia Granger's World of Poetry*, Columbia University Press, 2005 (http://www.columbiagrangers.org).

BEER, PATRICIA (1919–1999)

She was born in Exmouth, Devon (her birth date varies with the anthology); her father was a railways clerk and her mother a schoolteacher, both of whom belonged to Plymouth Brethren. She describes her strict upbringing in her memoir of childhood, *Mrs. Beer's House* (1968). She graduated with a first-class degree in English from Exeter University and a B.Litt. from St. Hugh's College, Oxford. She taught English literature in Italy and at Goldsmith's College, London, then left teaching in 1968 to become a full-time writer living with her husband, John Damien Parsons, at Up Ottery, near Honiton in Devon, where she died. Devon is a major presence in her poetry. She edited several significant anthologies, broadcast, and contributed to literary reviews. Her historical novel *Moon's Ottery* (1978) is set in Elizabethan times. Some of her other poetry publications: *The Survivors*, 1963. *Just Like the Resurrection*, 1967. *The Estuary*, 1971. *Driving West*, 1975. *Selected Poems*, 1979. *Collected Poems*, 1988. Some of her poems: "Ballad of the Underpass," "Jane Austen," "Lion Hunts," "The Christmas Tree," "Victorian Trains," "Waterloo."

Sources: Carcanet Press (http://www.carcanet.co.uk). *Peace and War: A Collection of Poems*. Michael Harrison, and Christopher Stuart-Clark, ed. Oxford University Press, 1989. *Poet with a Wry Line on Dissenters and Devon. Obituary by John Mullan, Thursday, August 19, 1999. The Guardian* (http://www.guardian.co.uk/obituaries/story/0,269137,00.html). *The Columbia Granger's Index to Poetry*. 11th ed. *The Columbia Granger's World of Poetry*, Columbia University Press, 2005 (http://www.columbiagrangers.org). *The Faber Book of English History in Verse*. Kenneth Baker, ed. Faber and Faber, 1988. *The Harvill Book of Twentieth-Century Poetry in English*. Michael Schmidt, ed. The Harvill Press, 1999. *The National Portrait Gallery* (www.npg.org.uk). *The Oxford Book of Christmas Poems*. Michael Harrison and Christopher Stuart-Clark, eds. Oxford University Press, 1983. *The Oxford Companion to English Literature*. 6th edition. Margaret Drabble, ed. Oxford University Press, 2000. *Wikipedia, the Free Encyclopedia* (http://en.wikipedia.org/wiki/Wikipedia).

BEHN, APHRA (1640–1689)

Behn (formerly Johnson), a dramatist, novelist, and poet, is said to have been the first Englishwoman known to earn her living by writing. However, this could be challenged by Emelia Lanier (see entry), whose poem "Salve Deus Rex Judaeorum" ("Eve's Apology in Defence of Women") was published in 1611. Unrewarded for her time as a Jacobite spy in Holland and briefly imprisoned for debt, she began to write to support herself. Between 1670 and 1688 her output of plays, poetry and novels was prodigious. She published *Poems on Several Occasions* (1684), and *Miscellany*, another collection of poems, in 1685. She is buried in the East Walk Cloisters of Westminster Abbey. One of her shorter poems — "And Forgive Us Our Trespasses" — reveals her keen religious belief. Some of her other poems: "A Thousand Martyrs I Have Made," "In Imitation of Horace," "On the Death of E. Waller, Esq.," "Silvio's Complaint: A Song," "Song from Abdelazar," "The Disappointment," "The Dream. A Song," "The Invitation: A Song," "To My Lady Morland at Tunbrige," "To the Fair Clarinda," "'Twas There, I Saw My Rival Take."

Sources: *BBC: Historic Figures — Aphra Ben* (www.bbc.co.uk/history/historic_figures/behn_aphra.shtml). *Dictionary of National Biography*. Electronic Edition 1.1. Oxford University Press, 1997. *Encyclopædia Britannica Ultimate Reference Suite DVD*, 2006. *English Poetry: Author Search*. Chadwyck-Healey Ltd., 1995 (http://www.lib.utexas.edu:8080/search/epoetry/author.html). *Everyman's Book of English Verse*. John Wain, ed. J.M Dent, 1981. *The Aphra Behn Page* (www.lit-arts.net/Behn/begin-ab.htm). *The Columbia Granger's Index to Poetry*. 11th ed. *The Columbia Granger's World of Poetry*, Columbia University Press, 2005 (http://www.columbiagrangers.org). *The National Portrait Gallery* (www.npg.org.uk). *The Oxford Companion to English Literature*. 6th edition. Margaret Drabble, ed. Oxford University Press, 2000. *Westminster Abbey Official Guide* (no date).

BELL, MARTIN (1918–1978)

Born in Southampton, a graduate of Southampton University, and founding member of "The Group." He was a member of the Communist Party of Great Britain. He was a Gregory Fellow at Leeds University 1967 to 1969, and part-time lecturer at Leeds College of Art; he also wrote under the pseudonym "Titus Oates." His first successful poem was a translation of Gérard de Nerval's sonnet "El Desdichado," written while serving with the Royal Engineers in Italy during the war. His *Collected Poems 1937–1966* (1967) celebrates famous people and satirizes patriotism and religions. Some of his other poems: "David Guest," "Ode to Groucho," "Reasons for Refusal," "Senilio Passes, Singing," "Senilio's Weather Saw," "Winter Coming On."

Sources: *Dictionary of National Biography*. Electronic Edition 1.1. Oxford University Press, 1997. *The Columbia Granger's Index to Poetry*. 11th ed. *The Columbia Granger's World of Poetry*, Columbia University Press, 2005 (http://www.columbiagrangers.org). *The Faber Book of War Poetry*. Kenneth Baker, ed. Faber and Faber, 1996. *The Martin Bell Papers*. The University of Tulsa, McFarlin Library, Department of Special Collections (www.lib.utulsa.edu/Speccoll/bellm00.htm). *The Oxford Companion to English*

Literature. 6th edition. Margaret Drabble, ed. Oxford University Press, 2000.

BELLENDEN, JOHN (1533–?1587)

Bellenden (several different spellings) was a Scottish writer and poet, educated at St. Andrews University, who took his medical degree at the Sorbonne, Paris. His 1536 translation from Latin into the Scottish vernacular of Hector Boece's *The History and Chronicle of Scotland* had a profound influence on Scottish national feeling. Among other stories, it relates Macbeth's meeting with the witches. Bellenden also translated the first five books of Livy's *Roman History.* His opposition to the Reformation put him out of favor with King James V (1512–1542) and he went into exile. He wrote poems to preface his translations, and one other, "A Starscape," is set among the various stars in the night sky.

Sources: *An Anthology of Catholic Poets.* Joyce Kilmer, ed. Fredonia Books, 2003. *Dictionary of National Biography.* Electronic Edition 1.1. Oxford University Press, 1997. *Encyclopædia Britannica Ultimate Reference Suite DVD,* 2006. *Significant and Famous Scots* (http://www.electric scotland.com/history/other/bellenden_william.htm). *The Columbia Granger's Index to Poetry.* 11th ed. *The Columbia Granger's World of Poetry,* Columbia University Press, 2005 (http://www.columbiagrangers.org). *The Oxford Companion to English Literature.* 6th edition. Margaret Drabble, ed. Oxford University Press, 2000.

BELLERBY, FRANCES (1899–1975)

Frances Parker was the daughter of an Anglo-Catholic curate in East Bristol and was educated at Mortimer House School, Clifton. She worked as a kennel-maid, taught English, Latin and games, was a private tutor, and was on the staff of the *Bristol Times and Mirror.* In 1929 she married the economist Professor John Rotherford Bellerby (1896–1977). Her novel, *Shadowy Bricks*— which describes her and her husband's vision of education — was published in 1932. The couple separated in 1942, and Frances settled in Cornwall and later in Devon, producing poetry and short stories. During the 1950s she was diagnosed with breast cancer, but she survived another twenty years, though in poor physical and mental health. Her papers are now held by the library of Exeter University. Her poetry publications: *The Brightening Cloud and Other Poems,* 1949. *The Stone Angel and the Stone Man: Poems,* 1958. *First Known and Other Poems,* 1975. *Stuttering Water,* 1970. *Selected Poems,* 1987. Some of her poems: "A Clear Shell," "An Inconclusive Evening," "Invalided Home," "It is Not Likely Now," "The Old Ones," "War Casualty in April."

Sources: *Chaos of the Night: Women's Poetry and Verse of the Second World War.* Catherine W. Reilly, ed. Virago Press, 1984. *Enitharmon Press* (http://www.enitharmon.co.

uk). *Shades of Green.* Anne Harvey, ed. Greenwillow Books, 1991. *The Chatto Book of Modern Poetry 1915–1955.* Cecil Day Lewis and John Lehmann, eds. Chatto & Windus, 1966. *The Columbia Granger's Index to Poetry.* 11th ed. *The Columbia Granger's World of Poetry,* Columbia University Press, 2005 (http://www.columbiagrangers.org). *The Faber Book of 20th Century German Poems.* Michael Hofmann, Faber & Faber, 2005. *University of Exeter Library* (http://www.library.ex.ac.uk/special/Guides/archives/081–90/082_01.html). *Wikipedia, the Free Encyclopedia* (http://en.wikipedia.org/wiki/Wikipedia).

BELLOC, JOSEPH HILAIRE PIERRE RENE (1870–1953)

Sussex poet, historian, biographer, journalist and essayist, most remembered for his endearing children's poetry. He graduated with first-class honors in history from Balliol College, Oxford. Born in France, he took British nationality in 1902. He was a journalist and editor of the *Morning Post* and a member of Parliament for Salford, Lancashire. His essays show contempt for the political, literary and social establishments of his day. His first book of poems, *The Bad Child's Book of Beasts and Verses and Sonnets,* was published in 1896; thereafter his output was enormous. One of his comic poems is "Henry King, Who Chewed Bits of String, and Was Early Cut Off in Dreadful Agonies." Some of his other poems: "Franklin Hyde," "George," "Godolphin Horne," "Ha'nacker Mill," "In a Boat," "On a General Election," "The Early Morning," "The Elephant," "The Frog," "The Hippopotamus," "The Justice of the Peace," "The Lion," "The Llama," "The Scorpion," "The South Country," "West Sussex Drinking Song."

Sources: *Dictionary of National Biography.* Electronic Edition 1.1. Oxford University Press, 1997. *Encyclopædia Britannica Ultimate Reference Suite DVD,* 2006. *Modern British Poetry.* Louis Untermeyer, ed. Harcourt, Brace, 7th rev. ed., 1962. *The Columbia Granger's Index to Poetry.* 11th ed. *The Columbia Granger's World of Poetry,* Columbia University Press, 2005 (http://www.columbiagrangers.org). *The National Portrait Gallery* (www.npg.org.uk). *The Oxford Companion to English Literature.* 6th edition. Margaret Drabble, ed. Oxford University Press, 2000.

BENSON, ARTHUR CHRISTOPHER (1862–1925)

Benson was the son of a former Archbishop of Canterbury. He was a schoolmaster at Eton College, but resigned in 1903 with the idea of concentrating on his writing and went to live at Cambridge. In collaboration with Viscount Esher (1907) he published, in three volumes, *Selections from the Correspondence of Queen Victoria.* He was elected master of Magdalene College, Cambridge, in 1915. The following year, under the pseudonym "Christopher Carr," Benson published the imaginary *Memoirs of*

Arthur Hamilton. Three volumes of poems and one of essays soon followed. He wrote the nationalistic "Land of Hope and Glory," set to music by Sir Edward Elgar (from the trio of his *Pomp and Circumstance No. 1*), which is traditionally sung (accompanied by flag waving) at the last night of the Proms from the Royal Albert Hall, London. Some of his other poems: "Amen," "Burnham Beeches," "By the Cage," "Knapweed," "Lord Vyet," "Prelude," "S. Vincent De Paul," "The Ant-Heap," "The Ash-Heap," "The Monotone," "The Phoenix," "The Pinewood," "The Shadow," "The Soul of a Cat."

Sources: *Dictionary of National Biography.* Electronic Edition 1.1. Oxford University Press, 1997. *English Poetry: Author Search.* Chadwyck-Healey Ltd., 1995 (http://www.lib.utexas.edu:8080/search/epoetry/author.html). *The Columbia Granger's Index to Poetry.* 11th ed. *The Columbia Granger's World of Poetry,* Columbia University Press, 2005 (http://www.columbiagrangers.org). *The New Oxford Book of Victorian Verse.* Christopher Ricks, ed. Oxford University Press, 2002. *The Oxford Companion to English Literature.* 6th edition. Margaret Drabble, ed. Oxford University Press, 2000.

BENTLEY, EDMUND CLERIHEW (1875–1956)

London-born and educated at Merton College, Oxford, he studied law but abandoned it for journalism, which he practiced for most of his life. By the end of 1899 he was a regular contributor to the *Speaker,* the Liberal weekly. He is remembered as the inventor of the clerihew, a light verse in lines usually of varying length, rhyming aabb, and usually dealing with a person named in the initial rhyme. In addition to his poetry, he is the author of *Trent's Last Case* (1913), published as one of Nelson's two-shilling novels, a classic detective story that challenges the infallibility of Sherlock Holmes and is said to have heralded the demise of that famous detective. Some of his clerihews: "'Dear me!' exclaimed Homer," "After dinner Erasmus," "Ballade of Liquid Refreshment," "Dr. Clifford," "George III," "J.S. Mill," "Liszt," "'No, sir,' said General Sherman," "The Art of Biography," "The Intrepid Ricardo," "The Younger Van Eyck," "Wynkyn de Worde."

Sources: *Dictionary of National Biography.* Electronic Edition 1.1. Oxford University Press, 1997. *Encyclopædia Britannica Ultimate Reference Suite DVD,* 2006. *The Columbia Granger's Index to Poetry.* 11th ed. *The Columbia Granger's World of Poetry,* Columbia University Press, 2005 (http://www.columbiagrangers.org). *The Faber Book of Comic Verse.* Michael Roberts, and Janet Adam Smith, ed. Faber & Faber, 1978. *The National Portrait Gallery* (www.npg.org.uk). *The Oxford Companion to English Literature.* 6th edition. Margaret Drabble, ed. Oxford University Press, 2000.

BERRIDGE, JOHN (1716–1793)

Berridge, an evangelical clergyman of Kingston, Nottinghamshire, graduated from Clare Hall, Cambridge, in 1734. In 1775 he became vicar of Everton, Bedfordshire, where he spent the rest of his life. He was friendly with John Wesley and George Whitefield and he became known as the "the pedlar of the Gospel." When ordered by the bishop to stop his itinerant preaching, Berridge quoted Mark 16:15: "Go into all the world and preach the gospel to every creature," and he carried on. His works were numerous and include: *A Collection of Divine Songs,* 1760 (mainly a collection of Charles Wesley's hymns). *Sion's Songs: or Hymns Composed for the Use of Them That Love and Follow the Lord Jesus Christ in Sincerity. Sion's* (342 hymns, some of which had previously appeared in the *Gospel Magazine* under the signature of "Old Everton," and others that were adapted from Charles Wesley), 1785 and 1815. Some of his other hymns: "Happy Saints Who Dwell in Light," "Since Jesus Freely Did Appear," "The Means of Grace Are in My Hand."

Sources: *Dictionary of National Biography.* Electronic Edition 1.1. Oxford University Press, 1997. *The Cyber Hymnal* (http://www.cyberhymnal.org/index.htm). *The Reformed University Fellowship (RUF) Hymnbook* (http://igracemusic.com/igracemusic/hymnbook).

BERRY, JAMES (1924–)

Born in Jamaica, he showed promise as an author from a young age. From 1941 to 1945 he worked in America but, finding the discrimination against black people intolerable, he returned to Jamaica. From 1948 to 1977 he worked in England for British Telecom as an overseas telegraph operator, attending evening classes to further his education. The award of a C. Day Lewis Fellowship allowed him to write full-time. He now lives in Brighton, Sussex, and divides his time between the U.K. and Jamaica. He has won several prizes for his poetry and was awarded the Order of the British Empire in 1990. An active campaigner on the part of black people, he helps to promote young black writers in particular. In his poems, he uses a mixture of standard English and Creole, the language of Jamaica. Two of the anthologies he has edited are *Bluefoot Traveler: An Anthology of West Indian Poets of Britain* (1976) and *News for Babylon* (1984). Some of his poems: "Back to Hometown Kingston," "Benediction," "Fantasy of an African Boy," "Sounds of a Dreamer," "Spirits of Movement," "Thinking Back on Yard Time."

Sources: *100 Poems on the Underground.* Gerald Benson, Judith Cherniak and Cicely Herb, eds. Cassell, 1991. *Around the World in 80 Poems.* James Berry. Illustrated by Katherine Lucas. Macmillan Children's Books, 2004. *Biography and Works of James Berry. C4 — BookBox* (http://

www.channel4.com/learning/microsites/B/bookbox/authors/berry/). *Caribbean Poetry Now.* Stewart Brown, ed. Edward Arnold, 1992. *Microsoft Encarta 2006* (DVD). Microsoft Corporation, 2006. *Only One of Me: Selected Poems of James Berry.* Macmillan Children's Books, 2004. *The Columbia Granger's Index to Poetry.* 11th ed. *The Columbia Granger's World of Poetry,* Columbia University Press, 2005 (http://www.columbiagrangers.org). *The Heinemann Book of Caribbean Poetry.* Stewart Brown and Ian McDonald, eds. Heinemann, 1992. *The New British Poetry, 1968–1988.* Gillian Allnutt, Fred D'Aguiar and Ken Edwards, ed. Grafton Books, 1989. *The Oxford Companion to English Literature.* 6th edition. Margaret Drabble, ed. Oxford University Press, 2000. *The Penguin Book of Caribbean Verse in English.* Paula Burnett, ed. Penguin Books, 1986. *Wheel and Come Again: An Anthology of Reggae Poetry.* Kwame Dawes, ed. Goose Lane Editions, 1998.

BESANT, SIR WALTER (1836–1901)

Born in Portsmouth and educated at King's College London and Christ's College, Cambridge, Besant is better known for his novels and philanthropy than for his poetry. Much of his boyhood is described by him in his novel *By Celia's Arbor.* He was professor at the Royal College, Mauritius, and secretary to the Palestine Exploration Fund (1868–1886), a society founded in 1864 for the systematic exploration of Palestine. His collaboration with James Rice, editor of *Once a Week,* which lasted until Rice's death (1882), produced several best-selling novels. He published *Early French Poetry* in 1969. His novel *All Sorts and Conditions of Men* (1882) was based on his impressions of the East London slums. He founded the "Society of Authors" in 1884. Some of his poems: "May Day," "Faith and Freedom," "The Day is Coming," "To Daphne."

Sources: *A Century of Humorous Verse, 1850–1950.* Roger Lancelyn Green, ed. E.P. Dutton (Everyman's Library), 1959. *Dictionary of National Biography.* Electronic Edition 1.1. Oxford University Press, 1997. *Encyclopædia Britannica Ultimate Reference Suite DVD,* 2006. *The Columbia Granger's Index to Poetry.* 11th ed (http://www.columbiagrangers.org). *The Home Book of Verse.* Burton Egbert Stevenson, ed. New York: Henry Holt and Company, 1953. *The National Portrait Gallery* (www.npg.org.uk). *The Oxford Companion to English Literature.* 6th edition. Margaret Drabble, ed. Oxford University Press, 2000.

BETJEMAN, SIR JOHN (1906–1984)

Broadcaster, television presenter and poet laureate known for writing about the recent past in such a way as to make it accessible and familiar. The only child of a London furniture manufacturer, he was educated at Marlborough College, Wiltshire, and Magdalen College, Oxford, which he left without graduating. He was a schoolmaster, assistant editor of the *Architectural Review* in 1930, and film critic of the *London Evening Standard* in 1933. His writings on Victorian architecture paved the way for the founding of the Victorian Society. His first poems were published in *London Mercury* in 1930; his first collection, *Mount Zion,* was published in 1931, and *Collected Poems* followed in 1958. He went on to publish many more collections of poems, as well as his blank verse autobiography, *Summoned by Bells,* in 1960. Betjeman wrote non-fiction books, including several guidebooks to English counties. He was knighted in 1969 and is buried in Poets' Corner of Westminster Abbey. His many poems are witty and sometimes satirical. Some of his poems: "A Bay in Anglesey," "Blame the Vicar," "Cornish Cliffs," "Diary of a Church Mouse," "The Cottage Hospital," "The Olympic Girl," "Winter Seascape."

Sources: *Dictionary of National Biography.* Electronic Edition 1.1. Oxford University Press, 1997. *Encyclopædia Britannica Ultimate Reference Suite DVD,* 2006. *John Betjeman Home Page* (www.johnbetjeman.com). *The Collected Poems of John Betjeman.* Birkenhead, Earl of, ed. John Murray, 1979, reissued 1990. *The Columbia Granger's Index to Poetry.* 11th ed. *The Columbia Granger's World of Poetry,* Columbia University Press, 2005 (http://www.columbia grangers.org). *The National Portrait Gallery* (www.npg.org.uk). *The Oxford Companion to English Literature.* 6th edition. Margaret Drabble, ed. Oxford University Press, 2000. *Westminster Abbey Official Guide* (no date).

BEWICK, ELIZABETH (1919–)

Born in Seaham Harbour, County Durham, she had a long career in librarianship, interrupted by service in the Women's Royal Naval Service (W.R.N.S.) mostly in and around Portsmouth. She then spent a year at University College, London, after which she specialized in library work with children and spent the next 12 years working in the metropolitan boroughs of St. Pancras, St. Marylebone and Islington, before moving to Hampshire in 1961 to set up the School Library Service in that county. Bewick lives in Winchester, has lectured and written reviews, and has been an external examiner for the Library Association. For many years she ran poetry readings in the deanery under the auspices of the Winchester Cathedral Players. In 1994 she received the "Southampton City Writers" annual award for her contributions to poetry. Her publications (all written after she retired): *Comfort Me with Apples and Other Poems,* 1987. *Heartsease: Poems,* 1991. *Making a Roux,* 2000. Some of her poems: "A Question of Carelessness," "Black My Beginning," "Heartsease," "Love-in-idleness," "Monkey-faces," "Oranges at Christmas Time," "Step-mothers," "Three-faces-under-a-hood," "Too Many Levels," "Trinities," "Wild Pansy."

Sources: *Oranges At Christmas Time by Elizabeth Bewick* (http://books.guardian.co.uk/departments/poetry/story/0,1669221,00.html). *Making a Roux, book by Eliza-*

beth Bewick (http://www.peterloopoets.com/html/stock list_17.html). *Heartsease by Elizabeth Bewick* (http://www. peterloopoets.com/html/stocklist_18.html). *The Columbia Granger's Index to Poetry.* 11th ed. *The Columbia Granger's World of Poetry,* Columbia University Press, 2005 (http://www.columbiagrangers.org).

BICKERSTAFFE, ISAAC (?1733–?1812)

Irish playwright and poet, said to have been a page to Lord Chesterfield, the lord lieutenant of Ireland and to have become an officer in the royal marines, but was dismissed under discreditable (and unspecified) circumstances. His success came in London around 1755 with the writing of several comedies and opera librettos. He collaborated with Thomas Arne to produce the first comic opera, *Love in a Village,* produced at Covent Garden (1762). Between 1760 and 1771 Bickerstaffe produced many pieces for the stage, including *The Maide of the Mill* (1765). Suspected of a gay relationship, he fled to France; the rest of his life (and death) is obscure. He left behind him some amusing poems. Part of his *Love in a Village* (act I, sc. 5) about the jolly miller who lived on the River Dee is well known. Some of his other poems: "An Expostulation," "The Recruiting Serjeant."

Sources: *Dictionary of National Biography.* Electronic Edition 1.1. Oxford University Press, 1997. *Encyclopædia Britannica Ultimate Reference Suite DVD,* 2006. *Great Books Online* (www.bartleby.com). *List of Irish Poets and Dramatists* (www.answers.com/topic/list-of-irish-dramatists). *The Columbia Granger's Index to Poetry.* 11th ed. *The Columbia Granger's World of Poetry,* Columbia University Press, 2005 (http://www.columbiagrangers.org). *The Faber Book of Comic Verse.* Michael Roberts and Janet Adam Smith, eds. Faber & Faber 1978. *The Oxford Companion to English Literature.* 6th edition. Margaret Drabble, ed. Oxford University Press, 2000.

BICKERSTETH, EDWARD HENRY (1825–1906)

Born in Islington, London, Bickersteth was the son of the Rev. Edward Bickersteth, assistant secretary to the Church Missionary Society. At Trinity College, Cambridge, he won several prizes for poetry. He was vicar of Christ Church, Hampstead, for thirty years and was appointed Bishop of Exeter in 1885. He toured India, Palestine and Japan, mainly to encourage missionary work. *Yesterday, To-day, and For Ever: A Poem in Twelve Books,* in blank verse, culminating in the Apocalypse, was published in 1866. He edited three hymnals and was a voluminous writer of hymns as well as dozens of poems. Some of his hymns appear in different hymnbooks; three are in *Sankey's Sacred Songs and Solos:* "Come Ye Ourselves Apart," "Peace, Perfect Peace," and "Till He Come," which is associated with the Communion service. Some of his other poems: "A Mother to Her

Son on His Birthday," "Confirmation," "Conversion of Saint Paul," "Easter Day—Morning Prayer," "The Epiphany," "Good Friday," "Holy Communion," "Holy Matrimony," "A Marriage Hymn," "God, the Rock of Ages," "Saint Andrew's Day," "Whitsunday."

Sources: *Dictionary of National Biography.* Electronic Edition 1.1. Oxford University Press, 1997. *English Poetry: Author Search.* Chadwyck-Healey Ltd., 1995 (http://www.lib.utexas.edu:8080/search/epoetry/author.html). *Yesterday, Today and Forever: A Poem, in Twelve Books.* New York: Robert Carter and Brothers, 1875. *Stanford University Libraries and Academic Information Resources* (http://library.stanford.edu). *The Columbia Granger's Index to Poetry.* 11th ed. *The Columbia Granger's World of Poetry,* Columbia University Press, 2005 (http://www.columbiagrangers.org). *The Cyber Hymnal* (http://www.cyberhymnal.org/index.htm.

BIGG, JOHN STANYAN (1828–1865)

Born at Ulverston in the Lake District and educated there and in Warwickshire, Bigg showed great literary promise at an early age; he used to recite the *Arabian Nights* to his friends, who paid him for the entertainment. He was editor for many years of the *Ulverston Advertiser* (he became proprietor in 1860) and for some years editor of the Irish paper *Downshire Protestant.* Bigg belonged to the "Spasmodic School," a derogatory term applied to certain poets by Professor Aytoun in his spasmodic tragedy *Firmilian* (1854). Some of his poems: "An Irish Picture," "Hartley Pit Catastrophe," "Night and the Soul," "Only a Little House," "Remorse," "Shifting Scenes and Other Poems," "Spring and Summer," "The Huguenot's Doom," "The Sea-King."

Sources: *Dictionary of National Biography.* Electronic Edition 1.1. Oxford University Press, 1997. *English Poetry: Author Search.* Chadwyck-Healey Ltd., 1995 (http://www.lib.utexas.edu:8080/search/epoetry/author.html). *The Columbia Granger's Index to Poetry.* 11th ed. *The Columbia Granger's World of Poetry,* Columbia University Press, 2005 (http://www.columbiagrangers.org). *The New Oxford Book of Victorian Verse.* Christopher Ricks, ed. Oxford University Press, 1987.

BINYON, (ROBERT) LAURENCE (1869–1943)

English poet, dramatist, and art historian. The son of a clergyman, of Quaker stock, he was educated at St. Paul's School and Trinity College, Oxford, and, in 1890, was awarded the Newdigate prize his poem "Persephone." He was in charge of Oriental prints and drawings at the British Museum, London, and his first book on Oriental art, *Painting in the Far East* (1908), was a classic. His best-known dramas are *Atilla* (1907) and *Arthur* (1923), set to music by Edward Elgar. He is one commemorated by a stone in Poets' Corner of Westminster Abbey, to

"The Poets of the First World War." (The dates given there are 1869–1945.) One of his many poems, "For the Fallen" (1914), is quoted at the Act of Remembrance on Armistice Day and ends "We will remember them." Some of his other poems: "In the High Leaves of a Walnut," "In the Shadow of a Broken House," "Invocation to Youth," "Men of Verdun," "Nothing is Enough!" "The Anvil," "The Apple Boughs," "The Arras Road," "The Bathers," "The Bowl of Water," "The Children Dancing," "The Healers," "The Zeppelin."

Sources: *A Treasury of War Poetry—The Fallen* (www. geocities.com/-bblair/fallen_twp.htm). *Collected Poems Laurence Binyon: Volume 2.* Macmillan and Co., Limited, 1931. *Dictionary of National Biography.* Electronic Edition 1.1. Oxford University Press, 1997. *Encyclopædia Britannica Ultimate Reference Suite DVD*, 2006. *English Poetry: Author Search.* Chadwyck-Healey Ltd., 1995 (http://www. lib.utexas.edu:8080/search/epoetry/author.html). *The Columbia Granger's Index to Poetry.* 11th ed. *The Columbia Granger's World of Poetry,* Columbia University Press, 2005 (http://www.columbiagrangers.org). *The National Portrait Gallery* (www.npg.org.uk). *The Oxford Companion to English Literature.* 6th edition. Margaret Drabble, ed. Oxford University Press, 2000. *Westminster Abbey Official Guide* (no date).

BISSET, JAMES (1762–1832)

Born in the Scottish city of Perth, he was educated at a school where the fee for him and his sister together was a penny a week and enough peat every Monday morning during winter to keep the fire. His love of art and literature was fostered in early childhood by reading copies of the *Gentleman's Magazine* and old books from a second-hand bookstall. At fifteen he became an artist's apprentice at Birmingham, and by 1785 he was gaining a reputation as a painter of miniatures. Although he composed many poems he will be longest remembered for his unique, superbly engraved *Poetic Survey round Birmingham* (1800). *The Patriotic Clarion, or Britain's Call to Glory, original Songs written on the threatened Invasion* (1803) was dedicated by permission to the Duke of York. In 1804 he published *Critical Essays on the Dramatic Essays of the Young Roscius. A Picturesque Guide to Leamington* was published in 1814. He died and was buried at Leamington, Warwickshire. Some of his poem: "Flights of Fancy," "Ramble of the Gods through Birmingham," "Songs of Peace," "The Orphan Boy," "Theatrum Oceani."

Sources: *Dictionary of National Biography.* Electronic Edition 1.1. Oxford University Press, 1997. *The Columbia Granger's Index to Poetry.* 11th ed. *The Columbia Granger's World of Poetry,* Columbia University Press, 2005 (http://www.columbiagrangers.org). *The New Oxford Book of Eighteenth Century Verse.* Roger Lonsdale, ed. Oxford University Press, 1984.

BLACKIE, JOHN STUART (1809–1895)

Born in Glasgow, he was educated at Marischal College, Aberdeen, and at Edinburgh University with the idea of taking law, then a further three years of theology at Aberdeen University. From there he studied in Germany and Italy, where he turned from the idea of either the Church or law and became a student of Greek. From 1839 to 1850 he was professor of humanities at Marischal College, and from 1851 to 1882, professor of Greek at Edinburgh University. His inaugural lecture was on "Classical Literature in its relation to the Nineteenth Century." He was instrumental in establishing the Chair of Celtic Studies at Edinburgh. His public funeral service was in St. Giles's Cathedral, Edinburgh, and he was buried in the Dean Cemetery. Some of his publications: *Lays and Legends of Ancient Greece*, 1857. *Lyrical Poems*, 1860. *Lays of the Highlands and Islands*, 1872. *Songs of Religion and Life*, 1876. *A Song of Heroes*, 1890. Some of his poems: "A Boat Song," "All Creatures, Praise," "Ben Dorain," "How Small is Man," "MacCrimmon's Lament," "The Old Soldier of the Gareloch Head."

Sources: *Dictionary of National Biography.* Electronic Edition 1.1. Oxford University Press, 1997. *English Poetry: Author Search.* Chadwyck-Healey Ltd., 1995 (http://www. lib.utexas.edu:8080/search/epoetry/author.html). *Lyra Celtica: An Anthology of Representative Celtic Poetry.* E.A. Sharp & J. Matthay, ed. John Grant, 1924. *The National Portrait Gallery* (www.npg.org.uk). *Poems and Songs Gaelic and English.* Mary Mackellar. Maclachlan & Stewart, 1880. *Poems of the Scottish Hills: An Anthology.* Hamish Brown, ed. Aberdeen University Press, 1982. *Stanford University Libraries and Academic Information Resources* (http://library.stanford.edu). *The Columbia Granger's Index to Poetry.* 11th ed. *The Columbia Granger's World of Poetry,* Columbia University Press, 2005 (http://www.columbia grangers.org). *Unity Hymns and Chorals.* William Channing Gannett, ed. Unity Publishing Company, 1911.

BLACKLOCK, THOMAS (1721–1791)

Born at Annan, Dumfriesshire, and though his parents were poor, young Thomas was well educated despite having lost his sight at six months old by an attack of smallpox. He acquired a little Latin and at the age of twelve attempted to write poetry. When his father was killed when Thomas was nineteen, he was patronized by Dr. Stevenson, an eminent physician at Edinburgh, who supported him entirely at the grammar school for four years. Blacklock contributed ten songs to the *Scots Musical Museum* (six volumes that appeared between 1787 and 1803, produced by James Johnson, with poems mainly by Robert Burns. It was re-issued by Folklore Associates, Hatboro, Pennsylvania, in 1962), four of them to which he composed the melody. His other works included an "Essay towards Universal Etymology" and some theological papers. In his closing years he became deaf as well as blind and suffered long periods of dejection. His major works: *A Collection of Original Poems,* 1760. *The Graham: An Heroic Ballad. In Four Cantos,* 1774. *Poems by the Late Reverend Dr. Thomas Blacklock: Together with an Essay on the Education of the Blind,* 1793.

Sources: *Dictionary of National Biography.* Electronic Edition 1.1. Oxford University Press, 1997. *English Poetry: Author Search.* Chadwyck-Healey Ltd., 1995 (http://www.lib.utexas.edu:8080/search/epoetry/author.html). *Significant and Famous Scots* (http://www.electricscotland.com/history/other/blacklock_thomas.htm). *Stanford University libraries and Academic Information Resources* (http://library.stanford.edu). *The Burns Encyclopedia* (www.robertburns.org/encyclopedia). *The Oxford Companion to English Literature.* 6th edition. Margaret Drabble, ed. Oxford University Press, 2000.

BLACKMORE, SIR RICHARD (1654–1729)

The son of an attorney at law, born at Corsham, Wiltshire, he was educated at Westminster School and graduated B.A. (1674) and M.A. (1676) from St. Edmund Hall, Oxford. After a period as a schoolmaster, he took a medical degree at Padua. On his return to England he was admitted fellow of the Royal College of Physicians, and later was one of the Queen Anne's physicians. Between 1695 and 1697 he published *Prince Arthur, an Heroick Poem* in twelve books. His "Satyr against Wit" (1700) aroused a storm of protest from the writers he attacked for their grossness and irreligion. He retired to Boxted, Essex, in 1722 and died there. Some of his other publications: *A Paraphrase on the Book of Job,* 1700. *Eliza,* 1705. *Creation: A Philosophical Poem,* 1712. *A Collection of Poems on Various Subjects,* 1718. *A New Version of the Psalms of David,* 1721. *Redemption,* 1722. *Alfred,* 1723. Some of his poems: "An Ode to the Divine Being," "Creation," "Our Saviour and His Twelve Apostles," "Possibilities," "The Nature of Man," "The Story of Don Carlos, Prince of Spain," "To Colon."

Sources: *Dictionary of National Biography.* Electronic Edition 1.1. Oxford University Press, 1997. *Eighteenth-Century English Verse.* Dennis Davison, ed. Penguin Books, 1988. *English Poetry: Author Search.* Chadwyck-Healey Ltd., 1995 (http://www.lib.utexas.edu:8080/search/epoetry/author.html). *Poetry.* Jill P. Baumgaertner, ed. Harcourt, Brace, Jovanovich, 1990. *Samuel Johnson's Lives of the English Poets, 1779–1781* (http://www2.hn.psu.edu/Faculty/KKemmerer/poets/preface.htm). *Stanford University Libraries and Academic Information Resources* (http://library.stanford.edu). *The Columbia Granger's Index to Poetry.* 11th ed. *The Columbia Granger's World of Poetry,* Columbia University Press, 2005 (http://www.columbiagrangers.org). *The Faber Book of Useful Verse.* Simon Brett, ed. Faber & Faber, 1981. *The Oxford Companion to English Literature.* 6th edition. Margaret Drabble, ed. Oxford University Press, 2000.

BLACKMORE, RICHARD DODDRIDGE (1825–1900)

Novelist, barrister, minor poet, and author of the hugely successful novel *Lorna Doone* (1869). The son of a clergyman, he was educated mainly at Blundell's School, Tiverton, Devon, to which county the family moved when Mrs. Blackmore died of typhus fever three months after Richard was born. He was head-boy for some time, and won a scholarship to Oxford and graduated in 1847. Due to epilepsy — brought about by the ill-treatment of the big boys at Blundell's, it is said — he gave up law, taught classics, then a legacy enabled him to retire to the country to write and grow fruit. He published thirteen other novels and a collection of poems, *Fringilla, Some Tales in Verse* (1895) plus a number of short stories, poems and translations from the classics. One poem, "Dominus Illuminatio Mea," brings comfort to the dying soul whose trust is in the Lord (*The New Oxford Book of English Verse 1250–1950.* H. Gardiner, ed. Oxford University Press, 1972, has the whole poem). "Yes," a love poem, is in *The Home Book of Verse* (Burton Egbert Stevenson, ed. New York: Henry Holt and Company 1953).

Sources: *Dictionary of National Biography.* Electronic Edition 1.1. Oxford University Press, 1997. *Encyclopædia Britannica Ultimate Reference Suite DVD,* 2006. *The Columbia Granger's Index to Poetry.* 11th ed. *The Columbia Granger's World of Poetry,* Columbia University Press, 2005 (http://www.columbiagrangers.org). *The Oxford Companion to English Literature.* 6th edition. Margaret Drabble, ed. Oxford University Press, 2000.

BLACKWOOD, HELEN SELINA, COUNTESS OF DUFFERIN (1807–1867)

The eldest daughter of Tom Sheridan (younger son of Richard Brinsley Sheridan) and his wife, Caroline Henrietta; afterwards successively Mrs. Blackwood, Lady Dufferin, and Countess of Gifford, songwriter and poet. She married Commander Price Blackwood at the age of seventeen. Although the youngest son of Hans, Lord Dufferin, owing to the death of his two brothers in 1839 he succeeded to the title and estate in Ireland of Baron Dufferin and Clandeboye. He died in 1841 on board a ship off Belfast, aged 47, owing to an accidental overdose of morphia. Lady Dufferin dedicated herself to the education of her only son and to writing. Her chief poems are: "The Charming Woman," "The Mother's Lament," "The Irish Emigrant" (which tells the story of a young man saying goodbye in a graveyard to his wife, Mary, who died in childbirth, as he prepares to leave Ireland to find work in a far-off land).

Sources: *Dictionary of National Biography.* Electronic Edition 1.1. Oxford University Press, 1997. *English Poetry,* Second Edition (http://collections.chadwyck.co.uk/mar keting/home_ep2.jsp). *The Columbia Granger's Index to Poetry.* 11th ed. *The Columbia Granger's World of Poetry,* Columbia University Press, 2005 (http://www.columbia grangers.org). *The Oxford Anthology of English Poetry, Vol. II: Blake to Heaney.* John Wain, ed. Oxford University Press, 1990.

BLAIR, ROBERT (1699–1746)

Born in Edinburgh and educated at Edinburgh University and in Holland, Blair followed his father and grandfather into the Church, and was ordained at Athelstaneford (East Lothian) and licensed to preach in 1729. He is thought to have been a member of the Athenian Society, a small literary club in Edinburgh that published in 1720 the *Edinburgh Miscellany.* Although anonymous, Blair seems to have contributed two brief paraphrases of Scripture. In 1728 he wrote "Poem Dedicated to the Memory of William Law" (professor of philosophy in Edinburgh, whose daughter Isabella, he married in 1738). His major poem "The Grave" (1743) expressed his feelings on bereavement and death and was one of the first of the Romantic Movement in English literature. It is believed to have influenced Thomas Gray's "Elegy in a Country Churchyard" (1751). It was the first and (some say) the best of a whole series of mortuary (or graveyard) poems, containing seven hundred and sixty-seven lines of blank verse. William Blake (see entry) produced twelve illustrations for the 1808 edition. Some of his other poems: "A New Dawn," "Law," "Ode," translated from the Latin of Florentius Volusenus.

Sources: *A Little Book of Comfort.* Anthony Guest, ed. HarperCollins, 1993. *Dictionary of National Biography.* Electronic Edition 1.1. Oxford University Press, 1997. *Overview of Rev. Robert Blair* (http://www.geo.ed.ac.uk/ scotgaz/people/famousfirst2017.html). *The Columbia Granger's Index to Poetry.* 11th ed. *The Columbia Granger's World of Poetry,* Columbia University Press, 2005 (http:// www.columbiagrangers.org). *The Oxford Anthology of English Poetry. Vol. I: Spenser to Crabbe.* John Wain, ed. Oxford University Press, 1990. *The Oxford Book of Death.* D.J. Enright, ed. Oxford University Press, 1987. *The Works of the British Poets, Vol. 33 (Blair, Glynn, Boyce, Shaw, Lovibond, and Penrose).* J. Sharpe, 1808.

BLAKE, WILLIAM (1757–1827)

London-born poet, painter and engraver who had a childhood vision of angels and the prophet Ezekiel. It was possibly this early experience that led him in later life to join the Swedenborgian New Church. He wrote and illuminated many books. In 1791 he designed and engraved six plates to *Original Stories for Children,* by Mary Wollstonecraft, and some to *Elements of Morality* translated by her from the German. His poem "Everlasting Gospel" attacks the traditional views of Jesus. At his death it was generally held that he was gifted but insane. A bust was erected to him in Poets' Corner of Westminster Abbey in 1957 (see also, Young, Edward). His main books of poems or songs are: *Poetical Sketches,* 1783. *Songs of Innocence,* 1789. *Songs of Experience,* 1794. His poem "Jerusalem" (1804), set to music by Sir Hubert Parry (1848–1918), is better known than his children's hymn "Little Lamb, Who Made Thee?" Some of his other poems: "America: A Prophecy," "Auguries of Innocence," "The Book of Thel," "Gnomic Verses," "An Island in the Moon," "Songs of Experience," "All Religions Are One," "An Ancient Proverb."

Sources: *Dictionary of National Biography.* Electronic Edition 1.1. Oxford University Press, 1997. *Encyclopædia Britannica Ultimate Reference Suite DVD,* 2006. *English Poetry: Author Search.* Chadwyck-Healey Ltd., 1995 (http://www.lib.utexas.edu:8080/search/epoetry/author. html). *The Columbia Granger's Index to Poetry.* 11th ed. *The Columbia Granger's World of Poetry,* Columbia University Press, 2005 (http://www.columbiagrangers.org). *The Complete Poems of William Blake.* Alicia Ostriker, ed. Penguin Books, 1977. *The National Portrait Gallery* (www.npg.org. uk). *The Norton Anthology of English Literature.* 7th ed. Vol. 2, M.H. Abrams, ed. W.W. Norton, 2000. *The Oxford Companion to English Literature.* 6th edition. Margaret Drabble, ed. Oxford University Press, 2000. *Westminster Abbey Official Guide* (no date).

BLAMIRE, SUSANNA (1747–1794)

Blamire, "The Muse of Cumberland" who wrote in standard English, her native Cumberland dialect, and in Scots, never published during her lifetime; her poems and songs were written to entrain her family and friends. *The Poetical Works of Miss Susanna Blamire* was published in 1842. She was included in *The Songstresses of Scotland* (Strahan 1871). Her poem "Stocklewath; or, The Cumbrian Village" (1,156 lines) was written sometime after Goldsmith's "The Deserted Village" (1770). In 1994, she was commemorated by a memorial tablet in Carlisle Cathedral, Cumberland. In the same year, the Lakeland Dialect Society published a bicentenary tribute to her. Some of her other poems: "A North Country Village," "And Ye Shall Walk in Silk Attire, also known as The Siller Croun [The Silver Crown]" (in which a suitor tempts the maiden with silver, but she remains true to her Donald), "Auld Robin Forbes," "The Banks of Yarrow," "The Loss of the Roebuck," "The Sailor Lad's Return," "The Soldier's Return," "The Village Club," "'Tis for Glory We Fight," "Wey, Ned, Man!"

Sources: *Dictionary of National Biography.* Electronic Edition 1.1. Oxford University Press, 1997. *Eighteenth*

Century Women Poets: An Oxford Anthology. Roger Lonsdale, ed. Oxford University Press, 1989. *English Poetry: Author Search.* Chadwyck-Healey Ltd., 1995 (http://www.lib.utexas.edu:8080/search/epoetry/author.html). *The Columbia Granger's Index to Poetry.* 11th ed. *The Columbia Granger's World of Poetry,* Columbia University Press, 2005 (http://www.columbiagrangers.org). *The Oxford Companion to English Literature.* 6th edition. Margaret Drabble, ed. Oxford University Press, 2000.

BLANCHARD, SAMUEL LAMAN (1804–1845)

Born in Great Yarmouth but brought up in East London. When his father refused help for his Samuel to attend university, he became a clerk, a task he found distasteful, so he determined to try the stage. He contributed dramatic sketches to the *Drama* and for a little while joined a traveling troop of actors. For three years he was secretary to the Zoological Society. In 1828 he published *Lyric Offerings,* a collection of verse, which he dedicated to Charles Lamb, and contributed prose and verse to the *Monthly Magazine,* for which he became acting editor in 1831. He then edited the *True Sun* (a daily liberal paper), the *Court Journal,* the *Courier,* and *George Cruikshank's Omnibus,* a monthly magazine to which he contributed several poems. Some of his poems are: "Hidden Joys," "Infancy Asleep," "Lines Written on the First Page of Mulberry Leaves," "Love Seeking a Lodging," "Nell Gwynne's Looking-glass," "Science and Good-Humour," "The Mother's Hope," "Today," "Wishes of Youth," "Yesterday" (a melancholy poem).

Sources: *Dictionary of National Biography.* Electronic Edition 1.1. Oxford University Press, 1997. *English Poetry: Author Search.* Chadwyck-Healey Ltd., 1995 (http://www.lib.utexas.edu:8080/search/epoetry/author.html). *Oldpoetry* (www.oldpoetry.com). *The Columbia Granger's Index to Poetry.* 11th ed. *The Columbia Granger's World of Poetry,* Columbia University Press, 2005 (http://www.columbiagrangers.org). *The Home Book of Verse,* Burton Egbert Stevenson. New York: Henry Holt and Company 1953. *The National Portrait Gallery* (www.npg.org.uk).

BLIND, MATHILDE (1841–1896)

Born Cohen, the daughter of a German Jewish banker, she adopted the name Blind when her mother married Karl Blind. Because of his involvement in the Baden insurrection (1848–49), the family was expelled and took refuge in London, where Mathilde was educated. Her cosmopolitan work was influenced by her independent character; she traveled in Switzerland by herself at the age of eighteen and had a continuing association with European countries. She also wrote under the pseudonym "Claude Lake." Visits to Scotland inspired her with two remarkable poems: "The Prophecy of St. Oran" (1881) and "The Heather on Fire" (1886)—a denun-

ciation of the Highland Clearances. Her most ambitious work, *The Ascent of Man* (1888), was based on Darwin's The *Origin of Species* (1859). Some of her publications: *Ode to Schiller,* 1859 (which was recited at Bradford on occasion of the dramatist's centenary). *Dramas in Miniature,* 1891. *Songs and Sonnets,* 1893. *Birds of Passage: Songs of the Orient and Occident,* 1895. Some of her other poems: "Love in Exile," "Anne Hathaway's Cottage," "Apple-Gathering," "The Robin Redbreast," "A Highland Village," "Manchester by Night," "The Music-Lesson," "A Winter Landscape."

Sources: *A Treasury of Jewish Poetry.* Nathan Ausubel, and Maryann Ausubel, ed. Crown, 1957. *Dictionary of National Biography.* Electronic Edition 1.1. Oxford University Press, 1997. *Iona: A History of the Island.* M. McNeil. Blackie and Son Ltd., 1920. *Poemhunter* (www.poemhunter.com). *Sonnets Central* (www.sonnets.org/blind.htm). *The Columbia Granger's Index to Poetry.* 11th ed. *The Columbia Granger's World of Poetry,* Columbia University Press, 2005 (http://www.columbiagrangers.org). *The Literary Encyclopedia* (www.LitEncyc.com). *The Oxford Companion to English Literature.* 6th edition. Margaret Drabble, ed. Oxford University Press, 2000.

BLOOM, VALERIE (1956–)

Born in Clarendon, Jamaica, she came to England in 1979 and graduated in English with African and Caribbean studies from the University of Kent, and in 1995 she was awarded an honorary master's degree by the same university. She lives in Kent with her husband and three children and spends her time writing, performing, conducting writing courses and visiting schools and colleges. She writes poetry both in English and the Jamaican patois for readers of all ages. She has had residencies in England, Ireland, Northern Ireland and Wales, and has performed widely in the Caribbean and at the Edinburgh World of Music Art and Dance (WOMAD) and Hay on Wye Festivals. Her collection *Fruit* won Américas Honor Award (U.S.) and the Nestlé Smarties Book Prize (Bronze, 1997). Some of her recent poetry publications: *On a Camel to the Moon and Other Poems About Journeys,* 2001 (illustrator, Garry Parsons). *Hot Like Fire,* 2002. *Surprising Joy,* 2003 (children). *Whoop an' Shout!* 2003 (illustrator, David Dean) (children). *On Good Form: Poetry Made Simple,* 2006. Some of her poems: "For Michael," "Life in Uncle Sam's Backyard," "Sun-a-shine, Rain-a-fall," "Wat a Rain."

Sources: *A Twist in the Tale.* Valerie Bloom, ed. Macmillan Children's Books, 2005. *Ain't I a Woman! A Book of Women's Poetry from Around the World.* Illona Linthwaite, ed. Peter Bedrick Books, 1988. *British Council Arts* (http://www.contemporarywriters.com). *Caribbean Poetry Now.* Stewart Brown, ed. Edward Arnold, 1992. *One River, Many Creeks: Poems from All Around the World.*

Valerie Bloom, ed. Macmillan Children's Books, 2003. *The Columbia Granger's Index to Poetry.* 11th ed. *The Columbia Granger's World of Poetry,* Columbia University Press, 2005 (http://www.columbiagrangers.org). *The Faber Book of Vernacular Verse.* Tom Paulin, Faber & Faber, 1990. *The New British Poetry, 1968–1988.* Gillian Allnutt, Fred D'Aguiar and Ken Edwards, ed. Grafton Books, 1989. *The New Oxford Book of Children's Verse.* Neil Philip, ed. Oxford University Press, 1996. *The Penguin Book of Caribbean Verse in English.* Paula Burnett, ed. Penguin Books, 1986. *Valerie Bloom's Home Page* (http://www.valbloom.co.uk/).*Watchers and Seekers: Creative Writing by Black Women in Britain.* Rhonda Cobham, and Merle Collins, ed. Peter Bedrick Books, 1988.

BLUNDEN, EDMUND CHARLES (1896–1974)

Born in London to parents who were both schoolteachers, he spent most of his young life in the village of Yalding in Kent. He was educated at Cleave's Grammar School and Christ's Hospital, Horsham, Sussex (the school moved from London in 1902.) Commissioned in 1915, Blunden fought in France and Belgium with the Royal Sussex Regiment and was awarded the Military Cross in 1916. After the war he was a journalist for the *Athenaeum.* He taught in Japan and Hong Kong and served with the U.K. liaison mission in Tokyo from 1947 to 1950. He was a tutor at Oxford and served on the staff of *The Times Literary Supplement.* He was awarded numerous honors and was appointed Commander of the British Empire in 1951. His war poetry is reckoned to be the best of its kind, and he is one of the poets commemorated by a tablet in Poets' Corner of Westminster Abbey, to "The Poets of the First World War." Some of his poems: "1916 Seen from 1921," "Behind the Line," "Flanders Now," "January Full Moon, Ypres," "The Aftermath," "The Blind Lead the Blind."

Sources: *Dictionary of National Biography.* Electronic Edition 1.1. Oxford University Press, 1997. *Encyclopædia Britannica Ultimate Reference Suite DVD,* 2006. *Minds at War, The Poetry and Experience of the First World War.* David Roberts. Saxon Books, 1999, 2003 (www.warpoetry.co.uk/minds_p1.html). *The Columbia Granger's Index to Poetry.* 11th ed. *The Columbia Granger's World of Poetry,* Columbia University Press, 2005 (http://www.columbiagrangers.org). *The Oxford Companion to English Literature.* 6th edition. Margaret Drabble, ed. Oxford University Press, 2000. *The Poems of Edmund Blunden, 1914–1930.* Cobden-Sanderson, 1930. *Westminster Abbey Official Guide* (no date).

BLUNT, WILFRID SCAWEN (1840–1922)

Blunt was a Sussex traveler and politician, born into wealth and best known for his support for Egyptian, Indian and Irish independence, which earned him a spell in an Irish jail. His *Ideas about India* (1885) and *The Future of Islam* (1882) made him unpopular with the British government. He spent part of every year in Egypt, dressing as an Arab, speaking the Bedouin dialect, and arbitrating in tribal disputes. He was buried, according to his wishes, in the woods of his estate without religious rites. His many poems, including "The Love Sonnets of Proteus" and "The Wind and the Whirlwind," are vivid, genuine, versatile and spontaneous. His sense of justice is caught in the poem "The Deeds That Might Have Been." Some of his other poems: "Ambition," "As to His Choice of Her," "Assassins," "Coronation Ode (1911)," "Farewell to Juliet," "Fear Has Cast Out Love," "Gibraltar," "Honor Dishonored," "Mockery of Life," "Sea Lavender," "St. Valentine's Day," "The Falcon," "The Morte d'Arthur," "The Sinner-Saint," "To One Now Estranged," "Written at Sea."

Sources: *A Treasury of Great Poems: English and American.* Louis Untermeyer, ed. Simon and Schuster, 1955. *Dictionary of National Biography.* Electronic Edition 1.1. Oxford University Press, 1997. *Encyclopædia Britannica Ultimate Reference Suite DVD,* 2006. *English Poetry: Author Search.* Chadwyck-Healey Ltd., 1995 (http://www.lib.utexas.edu:8080/search/epoetry/author.html). *Poems of Wilfrid Scawen Blunt.* Macmillan and Co., 1923. *The Columbia Granger's Index to Poetry.* 11th ed. *The Columbia Granger's World of Poetry,* Columbia University Press, 2005 (http://www.columbiagrangers.org). *The National Portrait Gallery* (www.npg.org.uk). *The Oxford Companion to English Literature.* 6th edition. Margaret Drabble, ed. Oxford University Press, 2000.

BOLAND, EAVAN AISLING (1944–)

Born in Dublin, she was educated wherever her father's diplomatic career took him, including London and New York. After graduating from Trinity College, Cambridge, in 1966, where she read Latin and English, she became a freelance lecturer and a journalist and critic for *The Irish Times.* She has taught at several universities and is writer in residence at Trinity College, Dublin, and at the National Maternity Hospital, Dublin. She is also professor of English at Stanford University in Palo Alto, California. Her experiences as a wife and mother have influenced her to write about the beauty and importance of all things common — of flowers, and fabrics, of colors and cosmetics. Some of her publications: *23 Poems,* 1962. *New Territory* 1967. *The War Horse,* 1975. *In Her Own Image,* 1980. *Night Feed,* 1982. *Outside History: Selected Poems, 1980–1990,* 1990. *In a Time of Violence,* 1994. *An Origin Like Water: Collected Poems, 1967–1987,* 1996. *After Every War,* 2004 (translations from German-speaking women poets). Some of her poems: "An Irish Childhood in England: 1951," "Child of Our Time," "Nights of Childhood," "The Achill

Woman," "The Emigrant Irish," "The Pomegranate."

Sources: *A Look in the Mirror and Other Poems.* Padraic Fallon & Eavan Boland, ed. Carcanet Press. 2003. *Americans' Favorite Poems: The Favorite Poem Project Anthology.* Robert Pinsky and Maggie Dietz, ed. W.W. Norton, 2000. *Anthology of Twentieth-Century British and Irish Poetry.* Keith Tuma, ed. Oxford University Press, 2001. *Bitter Harvest: An Anthology of Contemporary Irish Verse.* John Montague, ed. Scribner's, 1989. *Contemporary Irish Poetry: An Anthology.* Anthony Bradley, ed. University of California Press (New and rev. ed., 1988). *Encyclopædia Britannica Ultimate Reference Suite DVD,* 2006. *Modern Irish Poetry.* Patrick Crotty, ed. The Blackstaff Press, 1995. *The Body Electric: America's Best Poetry from the American Poetry Review.* Stephen Berg, David Bonanno, and Arthur Vogelsang, ed. W.W. Norton, 2000. *The Columbia Granger's Index to Poetry.* 11th ed. *The Columbia Granger's World of Poetry,* Columbia University Press, 2005 (http://www.columbiagrangers.org). *The Making of a Poem: A Norton Anthology of Poetic Forms.* Mark Strand and Eavan Boland, ed. W.W. Norton, 2000. *The Oxford Companion to English Literature.* 6th edition. Margaret Drabble, ed. Oxford University Press, 2000. *Wikipedia, the Free* Encyclopedia (http://en.wikipedia.org/wiki/Wikipedia).

BOLD, HENRY (1627–1683)

The fourth son of Captain William Bold of Newstead in Hampshire, he was educated at Winchester School, then at New College Oxford from 1645 until he was dislodged in 1648 by the parliamentary forces. He moved to London, where he died and was buried at West Twyford near Acton, West London. Little else is known about him, except his books — which are now rare — and his many poems and songs. His works were quoted by such people as the book collector Sir George Henry Freeling (1789–1841). Some of his publications: *St. George's Day, Sacred to the Coronation of his Most Excellent Majesty Charles II,* 1661. *On the Thunder Happening After the Solemnity of the Coronation of Charles II,* 1661. *Poems Lyrique, Macaronique, Heroique,* 1664. *Latine Songs,* 1685. *Poems,* 1664. *Wit a Sporting in a Pleasant Grove,* 1657. Some of his poems/songs: "At General Monk's Coming to London," "Idle Sinner," "Let's Wet the Whistle of the Muse," "Love, Let Me Have My Mistress Such," "Proud [Venus now at last] Resigned," "Thou Glorious Envy, of the Nation," "Why Dost Thou Say I Am Forsworn."

Sources: *Dictionary of National Biography.* Electronic Edition 1.1. Oxford University Press, 1997. *English Poetry: Author Search.* Chadwyck-Healey Ltd., 1995 (http://www.lib.utexas.edu:8080/search/epoetry/author.html). *Stanford University libraries and Academic Information Resources* (http://library.stanford.edu). *Poemhunter* (www.poemhunter.com). *The Gambit Book of Love Poems.* Geoffrey Grigson, ed. Gambit, 1973. *The New Oxford Book of Seventeenth Century Verse.* Alistair Fowler, ed. Oxford University Press, 1991.

BOLTON (BOULTON), EDMUND (?1575–?1633)

Catholic historian and poet, born in Leicestershire, educated at Trinity Hall, Cambridge, then studied law in London. The last years of his life were mostly spent in debtors' prisons, either the "Fleet" (referred to in Dickens' *Pickwick Papers*) or in the "Marshalsea" (Dickens, *Little Dorrit*). His main publications are: *A Pastoral Ode* and three other pieces in *England's Helicon,* a collection of sonnets, 1600. *The Roman Histories of Lucius Iulius Florus,* a translation under the pseudonym of "Philanactophil," and dedicated to the Duke of Buckingham (a distant relative), 1618. *Life of King Henry II,* written (date unknown) for *Speed's Chronicle,* but rejected because of his pro-Catholic sympathies. *Hypercritica,* a short critical treatise of contemporary authors, 1618. Some of his other poems: "A Palinode," "Carol," "The Elements of Armories," "The Shepheard's Song," "To Favonius."

Sources: *Catholic Encyclopedia* (http://www.newadvent.org). *Dictionary of National Biography.* Electronic Edition 1.1. Oxford University Press, 1997. *England's Helico* (www.shakespeares-sonnets.com/Helicon.htm). *Encyclopedia of Britain.* Bamber Gascoigne. London, Macmillan, 1994. *Great Books Online,* www.bartleby.com. *The Columbia Granger's Index to Poetry.* 11th ed. *The Columbia Granger's World of Poetry,* Columbia University Press, 2005 (http://www.columbiagrangers.org). *The New Oxford Book of Christian Verse.* Donald Davie, ed. Oxford University Press, 1981. *The New Oxford Book of Sixteenth Century Verse.* Emrys Jones, ed. Oxford University Press, 2002

BONAR, HORATIUS (1808–1889)

Scottish Presbyterian, evangelical minister, who for many years was in charge of the Chalmers Memorial Church in Edinburgh. He was awarded the honorary degree of D.D. from Aberdeen University in 1853. He wrote several evangelistic books; *God's Way of Peace* (1862) was reprinted in 1993 as *The Everlasting Righteousness.* He also wrote more than 600 hymns and published several volumes of hymns, particularly *Hymns of Faith and Hope* (three series, 1857–1866). He was dubbed "the prince of Scottish hymn writers." The current Methodist hymnbook, *Psalms and Hymns,* includes seven of Bonar's hymns. Possibly the one hymn in every hymnbook is "I Heard the Voice of Jesus Say, 'Come unto Me and rest....'" Some of his other poems and hymns: "A Churchyard by the Sea," "Be True," "Beyond the Smiling and the Weeping," "Blessing, and Honor," "For the Coming of the Bridegroom," "Life a Span," "Love is of God," "My Old Letters," "My Prayer," "Shepherd's Plain," "Sunrise," "The Flight of Time," "This Do in Remembrance of Me."

Sources: *Dictionary of National Biography.* Electronic Edition 1.1. Oxford University Press, 1997. *Encyclopædia Britannica Ultimate Reference Suite DVD,* 2006. *English*

Poetry: Author Search. Chadwyck-Healey Ltd., 1995 (http://www.lib.utexas.edu:8080/search/epoetry/author.html). *Reformed University Fellowship, Hymnbook Online.* Hymn Resource, Belmont University (http://igracemusic.com/igracemusic/hymnbook/home.html). *The Columbia Granger's Index to Poetry.* 11th ed. *The Columbia Granger's World of Poetry,* Columbia University Press, 2005 (http://www.columbiagrangers.org). *The Speaker's Treasury of 400 Quotable Poems.* Croft M. Pentz, ed. Zondervan, 1963.

BOSWELL, JAMES (1740–1795)

The son of Lord Alexander Boswell of Auchinleck, of Ayrshire, he studied at Edinburgh, Glasgow and Holland and practiced law in Scotland and England. He achieved literary fame with *Account of Corsica* (1768). He formed a friendship with Samuel Johnson; Johnson and he toured Scotland which, in 1785, resulted in his *Journal of a Tour of the Hebrides with Samuel Johnson.* The *Life of Samuel Johnson* was published in 1791, by which time Boswell was suffering from alcoholism, gambling addiction, and venereal disease. Although he was not a great poet, his main works are: *Ode to Tragedy,* 1761. *Elegy Upon the Death of a Young Lady,* 1761. Contributions to *Collections of Original Poems by Mr. Blacklock and Other Scotch Gentlemen,* Vol. II, 1762. The first lines of three of his untitled poems read: "Five winter days at Mannheim shall I be / Here am I, sitting in a German inn / Ye who with fortune ever are at strife."

Sources: *Dictionary of National Biography.* Electronic Edition 1.1. Oxford University Press, 1997. *Encyclopædia Britannica Ultimate Reference Suite DVD,* 2006. *Encyclopedia of Britain.* Bamber Gascoigne. London, Macmillan, 1994. *The Columbia Granger's Index to Poetry.* 11th ed. *The Columbia Granger's World of Poetry,* Columbia University Press, 2005 (http://www.columbiagrangers.org). *The National Portrait Gallery* (www.npg.org.uk). *The Oxford Book of Travel Verse.* Kevin Holland-Crossley, ed. Oxford University Press, 1986. *The Oxford Companion to English Literature.* 6th edition. Margaret Drabble, ed. Oxford University Press, 2000.

BOTTOMLEY, GORDON (1874–1948)

Bottomley was one of the Georgian poets, born in Yorkshire. He was a semi-invalid for most of his life, yet his poetic output was prolific. His first volume of poems, *The Mickle Drede,* was published in 1896, and he was included in *Georgian Poetry* by E. Marsh, 1912. He believed passionately that industrialization had massacred the beauty of English countryside. His work is heavily marked by strains of medievalism and the Bible. His main publications are: *A Hymn of Touch,* 1905. *Babel: The Gate of God,* 1907. *A Hymn of Imagination,* 1912. *King Lear's Wife,* 1915 (verse drama). In his poem "To Iron Founders and Others" he addresses factory owners and accuses them of making machines to make more machines,

and in the process destroying every blade of grass and driving the birds out of sight. Some of his other poems: "A Song of Apple-Gathering," "Ardvorlich's Wife," "At the North Cape" (dedicated to Lascelles Abercrombie, 1938), "Atlantis," "Midnight Fires," "The Embarkation," "The End of the World," "The Maid of Arc," "The Sower," "The Viaduct."

Sources: *Dictionary of National Biography.* Electronic Edition 1.1. Oxford University Press, 1997. *Poems and Plays of Gordon Bottomley.* Claude Colleer Abbott, ed. The Bodley Head, 1953. *The Columbia Granger's Index to Poetry.* 11th ed. *The Columbia Granger's World of Poetry,* Columbia University Press, 2005 (http://www.columbiagrangers.org). *The Literary Encyclopedia* (www.LitEncyc.com). *The Oxford Book of English Verse.* Christopher Ricks, ed. Oxford University Press, 1999. *The Oxford Companion to English Literature.* 6th edition. Margaret Drabble, ed. Oxford University Press, 2000.

BOURDILLON, FRANCIS WILLIAM (1852–1921)

Sussex-born and educated at Worcester College, Oxford, he was a royal tutor at Cumberland Lodge. His poem "The Night Has a Thousand Eyes" secured his fame. He also edited poems and chronicles from Old French; his edition and translation of *Aucassin and Nicolette* (written by an anonymous troubadour of the thirteenth century) was published in 1887. In 1906 the Bibliographical Society published his study "The Early Editions of the Roman de la Rose." Some of his other publications: *Among the Flowers, and Other Poems,* 1878. *Young Maids and Old China: Verses,* 1888. *Where Lilies Live and Waters Wind Away: Verses,* 1889. *Ailes d'Alouette,* 1890. *A Lost God,* London, 1891. *Sursum Corda,* 1893. *Minuscula: Lyrics of Nature, Art and Love,* 1897. *Through the Gateway,* 1900. *Preludes and Romances,* 1908. *Christmas Roses for Nineteen-Hundred and Fourteen,* 1914. *Easter Lilies for nineteen hundred and fifteen,* 1915. *Gerard and Isabel: A Romance in Form of Cantefable,* 1921. Some of his poems: "A Violinist," "Eurydice," "Night," "Old and Young," "On the South Downs," "The Chantry of the Cherubim," "The Debt Unpayable," "Where Runs the River."

Sources: *English Poetry: Author Search.* Chadwyck-Healey Ltd., 1995 (http://www.lib.utexas.edu:8080/search/epoetry/author.html). *Legends: Paladins and Princes: The Tale of Aucassin and Nicolette* (http://www.legends.dm.net/paladins/aucassin.html). *Poemhunter* (www.poemhunter.com). *The Columbia Granger's Index to Poetry.* 11th ed. *The Columbia Granger's World of Poetry,* Columbia University Press, 2005 (http://www.columbiagrangers.org). *The Home Book of Verse.* Burton Egbert Stevenson, ed. New York: Henry Holt and Company 1953.

BOURKE, EVA (CURRENT)

Born in Germany, she has lived in Ireland for many years and now lives in Galway. She studied

German literature, history of art and educational psychology at Munich University and has translated poetry into and from German. She has written in the *West in the Connacht Tribune,* supporting the work of young Irish poets, and by way of the Galway writers' workshop. Bourke has lectured extensively on contemporary Irish poetry in the USA, Germany, Austria and Hungary. Her poems have appeared in major literary journals in Ireland, in British and American magazines as well as in Swedish, Dutch, French and Italian translations in Europe and Canada. In 1997 she represented Ireland during the *Festival Poesie Franco/Anglaise* in Paris. In 2002 she translated an English language version of Elisabeth Borchers' *Winter on White Paper.* She is also the editor of *In Green Ink,* a major dual language English-German anthology of Irish poetry (1996). She has received a number of awards and bursaries from The Arts Council. Some of her publications: *Gonella,* 1985. *Litany for the Pig,* 1989. *Spring in Henry Street,* 1996. *Travels with Gandolfo,* 2000. *The Latitude of Naples.* 2005.

Sources: *Biography of Eva Bourke, Aosdana* (http://www.artscouncil.ie/aosdana/biogs/literature/evabourke.html). *Biography and Works of Eva Bourke, Dedalus* (http://www.dedaluspress.com/poets/bourke.html).

BOURNE, VINCENT (1695–1747)

"Vinny" Bourne, a Latin poet, was educated at Westminster School and Trinity College, Cambridge, and became a lifelong master at Westminster School. He was also housekeeper and deputy sergeant-at-arms to the House of Commons. His major works are *Carmina Comitialia* (editor), which contains some verses of his own, 1721; and *Poemata, Latine partim reddita, partim scripta,* 1734, 2nd ed. 1735, 3rd ed. 1743. William Cowper (a pupil of Bourne's at Westminster) translated several of his pieces into English, and said this of him: "I love the memory of Vinny Bourne. I think him a better Latin poet than Tibullus, Propertius, Ausonius, or any of the writers in his way except Ovid, and not at all inferior to him" (DNB). Charles Lamb (see entry) had a high opinion of Bourne and included nine translations of Bourne's poems among his *Miscellaneous Poems.* An edition of Bourne's poems was published in 1840. He was obviously fond of nature, for many of his poems are about animals or birds. Some of his poems: "Epitaph on a Dog," "Invitation to the Redbreast," "Sparrows Self-Domesticated," "The Jackdaw," "The Silk Worm," "The Snail."

Sources: *Dictionary of National Biography.* Electronic Edition 1.1. Oxford University Press, 1997. *The Columbia Granger's Index to Poetry.* 11th ed. *The Columbia Granger's World of Poetry,* Columbia University Press, 2005 (http://www.columbiagrangers.org). *The Poetical Works of William Cowper.* H.S. Milford, ed. Oxford University Press, 1926. *The Works of Charles and Mary Lamb. Vol. 5.* G.P. Putnam's Sons, 1903.

BOWLES, WILLIAM LISLE (1762–1850)

Northampton-born Anglican clergyman, poet and critic. Educated at Westminster School and Trinity College, Oxford. His poem of 1783, "Calpe Obsessa, or the Siege of Gibraltar," won him the chancellor's prize for Latin verse. He took Holy Orders and had several church appointments in Wiltshire and Gloucestershire; his final appointment was Bremhill, in Wiltshire, where he remained until near his death. Some of his principal works: *Fourteen Sonnets,* which by 1794 had been enlarged to 27 sonnets and 13 other poems, 1789. *The Battle of the Nile,* 1799. *The Missionary of the Andes,* 1815. *The Grave of the Last Saxon,* 1822. *St. John in Patmos,* 1833. Bourne influenced the work of many poets, including Samuel Taylor Coleridge. He was not without his critics, who rose to defend Alexander Pope against Bourne when he attacked Pope's morals and poetic principles, a controversy that dragged on for seven years. Some of his other poems: "At Dover Cliffs," "Distant View of England from the Sea," "Hope," "In Age," "In Youth," "Netley Abbey," "The Butterfly and the Bee," "Time and Grief," "To a Friend."

Sources: *Dictionary of National Biography.* Electronic Edition 1.1. Oxford University Press, 1997. *Encyclopædia Britannica Ultimate Reference Suite DVD,* 2006. *English Poetry: Author Search.* Chadwyck-Healey Ltd., 1995 (http://www.lib.utexas.edu:8080/search/epoetry/author. html). *The Columbia Granger's Index to Poetry.* 11th ed. *The Columbia Granger's World of Poetry,* Columbia University Press, 2005 (http://www.columbiagrangers.org). *The National Portrait Gallery* (www.npg.org.uk). *The Oxford Companion to English Literature.* 6th edition. Margaret Drabble, ed. Oxford University Press, 2000. *The Sonnet: An Anthology.* Robert M. Bender and Charles L. Squier, eds. Washington Square Press, 1987.

BOWRING, SIR JOHN (1792–1872)

Devonian author and statesman from a cloth trading, Unitarian family. He had a distinguished diplomatic career, was twice a member of Parliament, and was knighted in 1854. He was fluent, sources say, in over 20 languages and could speak many more. In 1822, caught by the French for carrying dispatches to the Portuguese ministers announcing the intended invasion of the peninsula, he was arrested, spent two weeks in prison and was condemned to perpetual exile from France. He became co-editor of the *Westminster Review* in 1825. In 1828 Bowring was appointed a commissioner for the reform of public accounts. He translated a vast amount of poetry and the folklore of almost every European country, and was a prolific hymn-writer. A sample of his poetic works includes: *Matins and Vespers* (1823, 4th ed. 1851). *Hymns,* 1825. *Servian Popular Poetry,* 1827. Some of his other poems/hymns: "Blessings of Instruction," "God is Love," "In the Cross of Christ I Glory," "Mourn Not as Those Without Hope," "Retirement," "The Beauties of Creation," "The Minstrel Harp of Poetry," "To a Mother on the Death of a Child," "Wednesday Evening."

Sources: *Dictionary of National Biography.* Electronic Edition 1.1. Oxford University Press, 1997. *Dictionary of Unitarian & Universalist Biography: Sir John Bowring* (www.uua.org/uuhs/duub/articles/sirjohnbowring.html). *Encyclopædia Britannica Ultimate Reference Suite DVD,* 2006. *English Poetry: Author Search.* Chadwyck-Healey Ltd., 1995 (http://www.lib.utexas.edu:8080/search/epo etry/author.html). *The Columbia Granger's Index to Poetry.* 11th ed. *The Columbia Granger's World of Poetry,* Columbia University Press, 2005 (http://www.columbiagrangers. org). *The Home Book of Verse.* Burton Egbert Stevenson, ed. New York: Henry Holt and Company, 1953. *The National Portrait Gallery* (www.npg.org.uk).

BOYSE, SAMUEL (1708–1749)

Born in Dublin, the son of a dissenting minister, Boyse's studies at Glasgow University were interrupted by a premature marriage and he returned to Ireland. When his father died in 1728, Boyse went to Edinburgh and later moved to England. However, he seems to have been unable to manage his financial affairs, and being constantly in debt, he wrote begging letters to several of his father's friends. It is reported that by 1740 he was so destitute that everything he had — clothing and sheets — were in the pawn shop and his only covering was a blanket. He died in that state. Some of his major publications: *Translations and Poems,* 1731. *The Tears of the Muses,* 1736. *Translations and Poems,* 1738. *The Deity: A Poem,* 1739. *Albion's Triumph,* 1743. *The Friend of Liberty,* 1751. *Poems on Several Occasions,* 1757. Some of his poems: "On Platonic Love," "Retirement: A Poem," "The Force of Love: A Pastoral Essay," "The Tears of the Muses," "The Triumphs of Nature," "Written in the Ancient Palace of Falkland, Sept. 1735."

Sources: *Dictionary of National Biography.* Electronic Edition 1.1. Oxford University Press, 1997. *English Poetry: Author Search.* Chadwyck-Healey Ltd., 1995 (http://www. lib.utexas.edu:8080/search/epoetry/author.html). *SETIS: The Scholarly Electronic Text and Image Service* (http://setis. library.usyd.edu.au/). *The Columbia Granger's Index to Poetry.* 11th ed. *The Columbia Granger's World of Poetry,* Columbia University Press, 2005 (http://www.columbia grangers.org). *The Oxford Book of Garden Verse.* John Dixon Hunt, ed. Oxford University Press, 1993.

BRADY, NICHOLAS (1659–1726)

Born at Bandon, County Cork, son of Major Nicholas Brady, who served in the king's army in the rebellion. Educated Westminster School, Christ Church Oxford, and Trinity College, Dublin, he became an Anglican clergyman. During the Revolution he supported the cause of William, Prince of Orange, and during his time as vicar in Cork, he prevented the burning of the town of Bandon, ordered by James II. He was vicar of St. Catherine Cree Church, London, and chaplain to King William II and Queen Anne. He also operated a school in Richmond, Surrey. A few of his main publications: *The Rape,* or the *Innocent Impostors,* 1692 (a tragedy). *Ode for St. Cecilia's Day,* 1692 (set to music by Henry Purcell). *New Version of the Psalms of David,* 1696 (with Nahum Tate). *Virgil's Aeneid,* 1726 (a blank-verse translation).

Sources: *Dictionary of National Biography.* Electronic Edition 1.1. Oxford University Press, 1997. *Encyclopædia Britannica Ultimate Reference Suite DVD,* 2006. *The Columbia Granger's Index to Poetry.* 11th ed. The Columbia Granger's World of Poetry, Columbia University Press, 2005 (http://www.columbiagrangers.org).

BRAMSTON, JAMES (?1694–1744)

Born into a family of lawyers of considerable standing, Bramston's father was Francis Bramston, fourth son of Sir Moundeford Bramston, master in chancery, who in his turn was younger son of Sir John Bramston the elder, lord chief justice of the king's bench. He was educated at Westminster School and Christ Church, Oxford, but he chose the Church instead of law and was vicar of two parishes in Sussex: Lurgashall then Harting. In 1729 he published *Art of Politicks,* an imitation of the *Ars Poetica* of Horace, followed by *The Man of Taste* (1731). Both satires abound with contemporary references to life in the 18th century and were reprinted in Vol. I. of Dodsley's *Poems by Several Hands* (6 volumes, 1770). He also wrote some Latin poems and parodied John Phillips's "Splendid Shilling" in "The Crooked Sixpence." Some of his other poems: "The Art of Politicks," "Time's Changes."

Sources: *Dictionary of National Biography.* Electronic Edition 1.1. Oxford University Press, 1997. *English Poetry: Author Search.* Chadwyck-Healey Ltd., 1995 (http://www. lib.utexas.edu:8080/search/epoetry/author.html). *Great Books Online.* www.bartleby.com. *The Columbia Granger's Index to Poetry.* 11th ed. *The Columbia Granger's World of Poetry,* Columbia University Press, 2005 (http://www.co lumbiagrangers.org). *The Faber Book of Comic Verse.* Michael Roberts, and Janet Adam Smith, ed. Faber and Faber, 1978. *The New Oxford Book of Eighteenth Century Verse.* Roger Lonsdale, ed. Oxford University Press, 1984. *The Oxford Book of Eighteenth Century Verse.* David Nichol Smith, ed. Oxford University Press, 1926.

BRATHWAITE, RICHARD (?1588–1673)

Born in Burneside, near Kendal in the Lake District, he was the son of a barrister and educated at

Oriel College, Oxford, and at Pembroke College, Cambridge, where he studied law. In 1638, on moving to London, he devoted himself to poetry and dramatic writing. After his brother died, he lived at Burneside and became captain of a company of foot in the trained bands. It is said that he served on the royalist side in the civil war. He was later deputy-lieutenant of the county of Westmoreland and justice of the peace. He wrote many satires. Some of his publications: *The Golden Fleece,* 1611 (a collection of poems). *The Poet's Willow,* 614 (a moral treatise). *The Prodigals Teares,* 1614. *The Shepheards Tale,* 1621 (a collection of pastorals). *The English Gentleman,* 1630. *The English Gentlewoman,* 1631. *The Psalmes of David,* 1638. *Astræa's Tears,* 1641. *The Honest Ghost,* 1658. *The Captive Captain,* 1665. Some of his poems: "Nature's Embassy," "Of Maids' Inconstancy," "The Church Ape," "The City Ape," "The Country Ape," "The Court Ape," "The Judiciall Ape," "The Nightingale," "The Politicall Ape," "Vandunk's Four Humours, in Quality and Quantity."

Sources: *Dictionary of National Biography.* Electronic Edition 1.1. Oxford University Press, 1997. *English Poetry: Author Search.* Chadwyck-Healey Ltd., 1995 (http://www.lib.utexas.edu:8080/search/epoetry/author.html). *The Columbia Granger's Index to Poetry.* 11th ed. *The Columbia Granger's World of Poetry,* Columbia University Press, 2005 (http://www.columbiagrangers.org). *The National Portrait Gallery* (www.npg.org.uk). *The New Oxford Book of Seventeenth Century Verse.* Alastair Fowler, ed. Oxford University Press, 2004. *The Penguin Book of Bird Poetry.* Peggy Munsterberg, ed. Penguin Books, 1984.

BRETON, NICHOLAS (?1545–?1626)

The details of his life are scant, but he was born into a wealthy family. His father died when Nicholas was 14, and his mother married the poet George Gascoigne (see entry). Breton (pronounced Britton) was educated at Oriel College, Oxford (so it is thought), but settled in London, where he spent most of his life. He was a satirical, religious, romance, and pastoral writer in both prose and verse and became the author of over 50 books and poems. Among his patrons were King James I and Mary Herbert, Countess of Pembroke. His finest lyrics are included in *England's Helicon* (see Edmund Bolton) and in his collection the *Passionate Shepheard.*Some of his poems: "A Passionate Soñett made by the Kinge of Scots," "A Solemne Long Enduring Passion," "Amoris Lachrimae: For the Death of Sir Philip Sidney," "An Assurance," "An Epitaph upon Poet Spencer," "Aspiration," "Beauty," "Faithful unto death," "Heart-Pain," "Love Rejected," "Sir Phillipp Sydney's Epitaph," "Sweete Penelope," "The Countesse of Penbrook's Passion," "The Honor of Valor," "The Nightingale and Phillis," "The Pilgrimage to Paradise," "What is Hell?"

Sources: *Dictionary of National Biography.* Electronic Edition 1.1. Oxford University Press, 1997. *Encyclopædia Britannica Ultimate Reference Suite DVD,* 2006. *English Poetry: Author Search.* Chadwyck-Healey Ltd., 1995 (http://www.lib.utexas.edu:8080/search/epoetry/author.html). *Oldpoetry* (www.oldpoetry.com). *The Columbia Granger's Index to Poetry.* 11th ed. *The Columbia Granger's World of Poetry,* Columbia University Press, 2005 (http://www.columbiagrangers.org). *The New Oxford Book of Sixteenth Century Verse.* Emrys Jones, ed. Oxford University Press, 2002. *The New Penguin Book of English Verse.* Paul Keegan, ed. Penguin Books, 2000. *The Oxford Companion to English Literature.* 6th edition. Margaret Drabble, ed. Oxford University Press, 2000. *The Works in Verse and Prose of Nicholas Breton.* Rev. Alexander B. Grosart, ed. Edinburgh University Press, 1879.

BRETT, REGINALD BALIOL, 2nd VISCOUNT ESHER (1852–1930)

Educated at Eton College College and Trinity College, Cambridge, he succeeded his father in 1899. He became liberal member of Parliament for Falmouth in 1880. He refused several lucrative and influential posts and instead made reforming the army his priority. He was deputy governor, then governor, of Windsor Castle. He and A.C. Benson edited Queen Victoria's papers, *The Correspondence of Queen Victoria* (1907). He may not have been great poet, but some lines of "At Swindon" show a tender poignancy as he reminisces about the ten years since they last spoke, but the tears remain just as hot.

Sources: *Dictionary of National Biography.* Electronic Edition 1.1. Oxford University Press, 1997. *Great Books Online,* www.bartleby.com. *The Columbia Granger's Index to Poetry.* 11th ed. *The Columbia Granger's World of Poetry,* Columbia University Press, 2005 (http://www.columbiagrangers.org). *The Penguin Book of Homosexual Verse.* Stephen Coote, ed. Penguin Books, 1983.

BRIDGES, ROBERT SEYMOUR (1844–1930)

Born to a prosperous Suffolk family, Bridges was educated at Eton College and Corpus Christi, Oxford. He practiced medicine until 1882; after that he devoted himself almost entirely to poetry. He was adviser to the Oxford University Press on style and linguistics. He was appointed poet laureate in 1913 and was one of the founders of the "Society for Pure English." His published works of poems, plays, hymns, and anthologies include: *Eros and Psyche,* 1885. *Shorter Poems,* 1890 and 1894. *New Poems,* 1899. *The Spirit of Man,* 1916. *New Verse,* 1925. *The Testament of Beauty,* 1929. Two of his hymns: "All Praise Be to God," "Rejoice, O Land, in God Thy Might." Of his several hymn translations, probably the best known is "When Morning Gilds the Skies." His 1918 poem "To the United States of America" commemorates the American soldiers who were killed during World War I, where they joined with free men everywhere to win freedom. He ends with what sounds like prophecy — that we will create new world and not just patch up the old one.

Sources: *Dictionary of National Biography.* Electronic Edition 1.1. Oxford University Press, 1997. *English Poetry: Author Search.* Chadwyck-Healey Ltd., 1995 (http://www.lib.utexas.edu:8080/search/epoetry/author.html). *Oldpoetry* (www.oldpoetry.com). *The Columbia Granger's Index to Poetry.* 11th ed. *The Columbia Granger's World of Poetry,* Columbia University Press, 2005 (http://www.columbiagrangers.org). *The Cyber Hymnal* (http://www.cyberhymnal.org/index.htm). *The National Portrait Gallery* (www.npg.org.uk). *The Norton Anthology of Modern Poetry.* 2nd ed. Richard Ellmann, and Robert O'Clair, ed. W.W. Norton, 1988. *The Oxford Companion to English Literature.* 6th edition. Margaret Drabble, ed. Oxford University Press, 2000.

BRITTAIN, VERA (1892–1970)

Newcastle-born feminist, poet and novelist, from a wealthy background. World War I interrupted her study at Somerville College, Oxford, and she joined the Voluntary Aid Detachment (V.A.D.) and nursed in France. After the War, back at Oxford, she became associated with the peace movement, to which she was committed for the rest of her life. She was an honorary life president of the Society of Women Writers and Journalists, a vice-president of the National Peace Council, and a fellow of the Royal Society of Literature. Brittain's diaries were posthumously published as *Chronicle of Youth* (1981). Her main works are: *Verses of a V.A.D.,* 1919. *The Dark Tide,* 1923 (a controversial novel of sexism in Oxford). *Testament of Youth,* 1933 (the story of her experiences in France). *Testament of Experience,* 1957 (a memoir). A few lines of her poem "Perhaps" could be expressing something of the horror of war when her brother was killed. She expresses the darkness of soul where the sun does not shine, where the skies are grey and living is in vain.

Sources: *Books and Writers, Biograpy of Vera Brittain* (http://www.kirjasto.sci.fi/britta.htm). *Dictionary of National Biography.* Electronic Edition 1.1. Oxford University Press, 1997. *Oldpoetry* (www.oldpoetry.com). *Scars upon My Heart: Women's Poetry and Verse of the First World War.* Catherine W Reilly, ed. Virago Press, 1981. *The Columbia Granger's Index to Poetry.* 11th ed. *The Columbia Granger's World of Poetry,* Columbia University Press, 2005 (http://www.columbiagrangers.org). *The Oxford Companion to English Literature.* 6th edition. Margaret Drabble, ed. Oxford University Press, 2000. *The Superfluous Woman, poem by Vera Brittain* (1920) (http://www.aftermathww1.com/brittain.asp).

BROME, ALEXANDER (1620–1666)

Royalist attorney in the lord mayor's court and in the court of king's bench, and poet who opposed the Rump Parliament in England (or Long Parliament, called by Charles I, which lasted from 1640 to 1660). After the Restoration (of Charles II in 1666), Brome concentrated on writing. His gaiety and wit won him the title of the "English Anacreon." His "Songs and Poems" were collected in 1661 with commendatory verses by Izaak Walton and others and a dedication to Sir J. Robinson, lieutenant of the Tower. A second edition in 1664 is prefixed by a letter signed "R.B." (probably the initials of Richard Brathwaite, see entry). He was a contributor to, and editor of, translations of Horace published in 1666. Some of his other publications: *Songs and Other Poems,* 1661. *The Cunning Lovers,* a comedy, 1654. Some of his poems: "Against Mourning," "Love, Drink, and Debt," "On the Death of King Charles," "Plain Dealing," "The Answer to the Curse Against Ale," "The Clown," "The Prisoners," "The Resolve," "The Riddle."

Sources: *Dictionary of National Biography.* Electronic Edition 1.1. Oxford University Press, 1997. *Encyclopædia Britannica Ultimate Reference Suite DVD,* 2006. *Encyclopedia of Britain.* Bamber Gascoigne. London: Macmillan, 1994. *The Columbia Granger's Index to Poetry.* 11th ed. *The Columbia Granger's World of Poetry,* Columbia University Press, 2005 (http://www.columbiagrangers.org). *The National Portrait Gallery* (www.npg.org.uk). *The New Oxford Book of Seventeenth Century Verse.* Alastair Fowler, ed. Oxford University Press, 2004. *The Oxford Book of English Verse.* Christopher Ricks, ed. Oxford University Press, 1999. *The Oxford Companion to English Literature.* 6th edition. Margaret Drabble, ed. Oxford University Press, 2000. *The Penguin Book of Renaissance Verse 1509–1659.* David Norbrook, ed. Penguin Books, 1992.

BRONTË FAMILY: CHARLOTTE (1816–1855), EMILY (1818–1848), ANNE (1820–1849)

The Brontë sisters and their brother, Branwell, were born to Patrick Brontë, the Irish-born rector of Haworth in Yorkshire. The girls have all become household names for their contribution to English literature, through novels as well as poetry. Sadly, Branwell's life ended in heartache, addicted to alcohol and opium and having had an affair with his employer's wife. When their mother died in 1821, Charlotte and Emily were sent to join their elder sisters, Maria and Elizabeth, at the Cowan Bridge School in Lancashire for the daughters of clergy. The fees were low, the food unattractive, and the discipline harsh. It was upon this bleak school that Charlotte based "Lowood" in her novel *Jane Eyre.* Charlotte and Emily were brought home after their sisters died, and at Haworth the girls, encouraged by Branwell, developed the imaginary kingdoms of Angria and Gondal. All three girls took a succession of unsatisfactory jobs as governesses or teachers and dreamed of opening a school together, which their aunt had agreed to finance. Prospectuses were issued, but no pupils were attracted to distant Haworth. Charlotte married her father's curate in 1854 in Haworth church. The sisters' first venture into poetry, *Poems by Currer, Ellis and Action Bell* (to which Anne contributed 21 poems) was not a success (Currer, Ellis and Action Bell are pseudonyms). The venture cost the sisters about £50 and only two copies were sold. Charlotte was the first in print with *Jane Eyre* (1847). It was followed by Emily's *Wuthering Heights* (1847), Anne's *Agnes Grey* (1847), and Anne's *Tenant of Wildfall Hall* (1848). Extreme interest forced the sisters into revealing their identities. Although the sisters are famous for their novels, they were all substantial poets. Some of Anne's poems: "A Reminiscence," "He Doeth All Things Well," "The Arbour," "The Captive Dove," "The Doubter's Prayer." Some of Charlotte's poems: "Home-Sickness," "Master and Pupil," "On the Death of Anne Brontë," "On the Death of Emily Jane Brontë," "The Fairies' Farewell." Some of Emily's poems: "A Day Dream," "A Little While, a Little While," "And When Thy Heart is Resting," "Harp of Wild and Dream Like Strain," "How Still, How Happy! Those Are Words," "Ladybird! Ladybird!" "Dream, Where Art Thou Now?" "The Evening Sun," "The Evening Sun was Sinking Down," "The Prisoner," "The Two Children," "When Days of Beauty Deck the Earth."

Sources: *Dictionary of National Biography.* Electronic Edition 1.1. Oxford University Press, 1997. *Encyclopædia Britannica Ultimate Reference Suite DVD,* 2006. *English Poetry: Author Search.* Chadwyck-Healey Ltd., 1995 (http://www.lib.utexas.edu:8080/search/epoetry/author.html). *Everyman's Book of Victorian Verse.* J.R. Watson, ed. J.M. Dent, 1982. *Encyclopedia of Britain.* Bamber Gascoigne. London, Macmillan, 1994. *Gladly Learn and Gladly Teach: Poems of the School Experience.* Helen Plotz, ed. Greenwillow Books, 1981. *Selected Poems of Bronte Sisters* (www.web-books.com/Classics/Poetry/Anthology/Bronte). *The Brontes* (www.bronte-country.com/brontes.html). *The Columbia Granger's Index to Poetry.* 11th ed. *The Columbia Granger's World of Poetry,* Columbia University Press, 2005 (http://www.columbiagrangers.org). *The National Portrait Gallery* (www.npg.org.uk). *The New Oxford Book of Victorian Verse.* Christopher Ricks, ed. Oxford University Press, 1987. *The Oxford Companion to English Literature.* 6th edition. Margaret Drabble, ed. Oxford University Press, 2000. *Westminster Abbey Official Guide* (no date).

BROOKE, RUPERT CHAWNER (1887–1915)

From Rugby (where his father taught classics) Brooke went to King's College, Cambridge, in 1906 and became a member of the Apostles, an intellectual society founded during the 1820s with Ten-

nyson and Arthur Hallam among its members. He studied in Germany and traveled in Italy, the United States, Canada, and the South Seas. He was already an established and prolific poet before he wrote his war poetry; *Poems* was published in 1911. On the outbreak of World War I he joined the Royal Naval Volunteer Reserve, and on the way to the Dardanelles he died of septicemia on a hospital ship and was buried in an olive grove on the island of Skyros. His best-known work is the wartime sonnet sequence *1914 and Other Poems* (1915), which brought him posthumous fame. One of his most popular sonnets, "The Soldier," begins with the familiar line: "If I should die, think only this of me." Brooke began writing poetry at age nine and composed some prize-winning verse in "The Pyramids" and "The Bastille" while at Rugby School. Some of his other poems: "Beauty and Beauty," "Clouds," "Dawn," "Dining-Room Tea," "Doubts," "The Hill," "The Life Beyond," "The Vision of the Archangels."

Sources: *Dictionary of National Biography.* Electronic Edition 1.1. Oxford University Press, 1997. *Encyclopædia Britannica Ultimate Reference Suite DVD,* 2006. *The Collected Poems of Rupert Brooke.* Kessinger Publishing Co. 2005. *The Columbia Granger's Index to Poetry.* 11th ed. *The Columbia Granger's World of Poetry,* Columbia University Press, 2005 (http://www.columbiagrangers.org). *The National Portrait Gallery* (www.npg.org.uk). *The Oxford Companion to English Literature.* 6th edition. Margaret Drabble, ed. Oxford University Press, 2000. *Westminster Abbey Official Guide* (no date).

BROOME, WILLIAM (1689–1745)

Broome was from a poor background but through benefit he attend Eton College and St. John's College, Cambridge, and was the rector of several churches in Suffolk and Norfolk. With John Ozell and William Oldisworth he translated the *Iliad* (1712). He collaborated with Alexander Pope and Elijah Fenton to translate Homer's *Odyssey* (1713 to 1725); he translated eight of the books. He also made translations from the Greek of Anacreon. His own *Poems on Several Occasions* was published in 1727. The Samuel Johnson website lists several poems: "An Epistle to My Friend Mr. Elijah Fenton, Author of Mariamne, a Tragedy," "Melancholy: An Ode, Occasion'd by the Death of a Beloved Daughter," "On the Death of My Dear Friend, Dr. Elijah Fenton," "Prologue to Mr. Fenton's Excellent Tragedy Mariamne," "To Mr. A. Pope, Who Corrected My Verses." Some of his other poems: "Chap. 43 of Ecclesiasticus," "Courage in Love," "From the Eleventh Book of the Iliads of Homer, in Milton's Style," "The Battle of the Gods and Titans," "The Coquette," "The Rose-Bud," "The Widow and Virgin Sisters."

Sources: *Dictionary of National Biography.* Electronic Edition 1.1. Oxford University Press, 1997. *Eighteenth Century Women Poets: An Oxford Anthology.* Roger Lonsdale, ed. Oxford University Press, 1989. *Encyclopædia Britannica Ultimate Reference Suite DVD,* 2006. *Samuel Johnson's Lives of the English Poets* (1747) (http://www2.hn.psu.edu/ Faculty/KKemmerer/poets/preface.htm). *The Columbia Granger's Index to Poetry.* 11th ed. *The Columbia Granger's World of Poetry,* Columbia University Press, 2005 (http:// www.columbiagrangers.org). *The Oxford Book of English Verse.* Christopher Ricks, ed. Oxford University Press, 1999. *The Poetical Works of William Broome.* C. Cooke, 1796.

BROWN, GEORGE MACKAY
(1917–1996)

Known as "The Bard of Orkney," Brown was an Orcadian through and through. The sixth and youngest child of a Gaelic-speaking part-time tailor and postman, he attended Stromness Academy, New Battle Abbey, and Edinburgh University, where he read English, then did postgraduate work on Gerard Manley Hopkins. After overcoming tuberculosis, he devoted his life to writing. For forty years he published short stories, essays, children's books and poems in anthologies and in thirteen collections of his own. The composer Sir Peter Maxwell Davies set over thirty pieces of Brown's work to music. His tales are steeped in Norse and island folklore. His first novel, *Greenvoe* (a voe is a bay) (1972) remained in print for many years. He was awarded the Order of the British Empire in 1974. His autobiography — *For the Islands I Sing*— was published posthumously in 1997. Orkney poet Edwin Muir encouraged Brown and published his first collection of poetry, *The Storm,* in 1954. His poems evoke strong feelings of a past that is dead and gone. Some of his poems: "Beachcomber," "Dead Fires," "Haddock Fishermen," "Hamnavoe Market," "Island School," "Press-Gang," "Runes from a Holy Island," "Taxman."

Sources: *BBC—Writing Scotland* (www.bbc.co.uk/scot land/arts/writingscotland / learning_journeys/place/ george_mackay_brown). Canongate Publishers (www. canongate.net). *Encyclopædia Britannica Ultimate Reference Suite DVD,* 2006. *George Mackay Brown site index* (www.georgemackaybrown.co.uk/gmb/siteindex.htm). *Significant and Famous Scots* (http://www.electricscotland. com/history/other/brown_georgem.htm). *The Columbia Granger's Index to Poetry.* 11th ed. *The Columbia Granger's World of Poetry,* Columbia University Press, 2005 (http:// www.columbiagrangers.org). *The National Portrait Gallery* (www.npg.org.uk). *The New Penguin Book of Scottish Verse.* Robert Crawford and Mick Imlah, ed. Penguin Books, 2000. *The Oxford Book of Contemporary Verse, 1945–1980.* D.J. Enright, ed. Oxford University Press, 1980. *The Oxford Companion to English Literature.* 6th edition. Margaret Drabble, ed. Oxford University Press, 2000.

BROWN, THOMAS (TOM)
(1663–1704)

A native of Shropshire, Brown is mainly known for his satirical writing and as author of the poem "Dr. Fell." His intemperate behavior at Christ Church, Oxford, brought him into conflict with the dean, one Dr. Fell. Leaving Oxford without a degree and in need of money, he worked in a school at Kingston-on-Thames and later was headmaster of the grammar school there. After three years he settled down to writing satirical poems and pamphlets and translating Greek, Latin, French, and Spanish authors. He is buried in the East Walk of Westminster Abbey. A collected edition of his works, published in 1707–1778, contains essays, poems, satires, epigrams, original letters and translations. The story goes that his threatened expulsion from Oxford was stayed when the dean challenged him to an impromptu translation of Latin epigram. His result is "Dr. Fell," with its well-known opening line: "I do not love thee, Dr. Fell." Some of his other poems: "Oaths," "To That Most Senseless Scoundrel, the Author of Legion's Humble Address to the Lords," "The Cavalcade, and Disbanding the Royal Regiment," "England's Triumph for Their Conquest in Flanders, in the Year 1694."

Sources: *Dictionary of National Biography.* Electronic Edition 1.1. Oxford University Press, 1997. *Encyclopædia Britannica Ultimate Reference Suite DVD,* 2006. *English Poetry: Author Search.* Chadwyck-Healey Ltd., 1995 (http://www.lib.utexas.edu:8080/search/epoetry/author. html). *Folksinger's Wordbook.* Irwin Silber and Fred Silber, eds. Oak Publications, 1973. *I Saw Esau: The Schoolchild's Pocket Book.* Iona Opie and Peter Opie, eds. 1947; American reissue, Candlewick Press, 1992. *The Columbia Granger's Index to Poetry.* 11th ed. *The Columbia Granger's World of Poetry,* Columbia University Press, 2005 (http://www.columbiagrangers.org). *The Faber Book of Comic Verse.* Michael Roberts and Janet Adam Smith, eds. 1978. *The Faber Book of Epigrams and Epitaphs.* Geoffrey Grigson, ed. Faber & Faber, 1977. *The Oxford Companion to English Literature.* 6th edition. Margaret Drabble, ed. Oxford University Press, 2000. *The Remains of Mr. Tho. Brown, Serious and Comical, in Prose and Verse.* Printed for Sam. Briscoe, etc., 1720. *Westminster Abbey Official Guide* (no date).

BROWN, THOMAS EDWARD
(1830–1897)

Born on the Isle of Man, the son of a vicar, educated on the island and at Christ Church, Oxford, he became a Fellow at Oriel College. He was a master at Clifton College, Bristol, for nearly thirty years and died there from a brain hemorrhage while giving an address to the boys. He was buried at Redland Green, Bristol. A portrait by Sir William Richmond is in the library at Clifton College and another is in the Newbolt Room. He was a prolific poet on a wide rang of topics, many of them in the Manx dialect and dealing with Manx life. The first of his tales in verse, "Betsy Lee," appeared in *Macmillan's Magazine* for April 1873. His poem "My Garden" is familiar with its opening line: "A Garden Is a Lovesome Thing, God wot!" Some of his other poems: "Between Our Folding Lips," "Braddan Vicarage," "Dartmoor: Sunset at Chagford," "I Bended Unto Me," "Roman Women," "The Bristol Channel," "The Voices of Nature," "Vespers," "Wesley in Heaven," "When Love Meets Love."

Sources: *Dictionary of National Biography.* Electronic Edition 1.1. Oxford University Press, 1997. *English Poetry: Author Search.* Chadwyck-Healey Ltd., 1995 (http://www. lib.utexas.edu:8080/search/epoetry/author.html). *Life and Works of T.E. Brown* (www.isle-of-man.com/manxnote book/people/writers/teb.htm). *The Collected Poems of T.E. Brown,* Macmillan & Co., Ltd (1909). *The Columbia Granger's Index to Poetry.* 11th ed. *The Columbia Granger's World of Poetry,* Columbia University Press, 2005 (http:// www.columbiagrangers.org). *The Faber Book of Poems and Places.* Geoffrey Grigson, ed. Faber & Faber, 1980. *The New Oxford Book of Victorian Verse.* Christopher Ricks, ed. Oxford University Press, 2002. *The Oxford Book of English Verse.* Christopher Ricks, ed. Oxford University Press, 1999. *The Oxford Companion to English Literature.* 6th edition. Margaret Drabble, ed. Oxford University Press, 2000.

BROWNE, ISAAC HAWKINS (1705–1760)

Born at Burton upon Trent to a wealthy clergyman, he was educated at Westminster School and Trinity College, Cambridge. A brilliant scholar, he became a mediocre lawyer and was twice a member of Parliament for Wenlock in Shropshire, but is reputed never to have opened his mouth in the House. Some time before 1744 he wrote "Design and Beauty," a poem of some length addressed to Highmore the painter. He published his Latin poem "De Animi Immortalitate" ("The Immortality of the Soul") in 1754. His son published an edition of his poems in 1768. His complete ode, "A Pipe of Tobacco," is available on the Granger website. Some of his lighter poems are witty and were well received at the time. Dr. Johnson found his poems pleasing. Some of his other poems: "A letter from a Captain in Country Quarters to his Corinna in Town," "An Epitaph: In Imitation of Dryden," "From Cælia to Cloe," "On a Fit of the Gout," "On Design and Beauty," "On the Author's Birth-Day," "The Fire Side, a Pastoral Soliloquy," "The Foundling Hospital for Wit."

Sources: *A Collection of Poems in Six Volumes. By Several Hands. With Notes.* London: Printed for J. Dodsley, 1782 (www.muohio.edu/anthologies/dodsley.htm). *Dictionary of National Biography.* Electronic Edition 1.1. Oxford University Press, 1997. *English Poetry: Author Search.* Chadwyck-Healey Ltd., 1995 (http://www.lib.utexas.edu: 8080/search/epoetry/author.html). *Stanford University libraries and Academic Information Resources* (http://library. stanford.edu). *The Columbia Granger's Index to Poetry.* 11th ed. *The Columbia Granger's World of Poetry,* Columbia University Press, 2005 (http://www.columbiagrangers. org). *The National Portrait Gallery* (www.npg.org.uk). *The New Oxford Book of Eighteenth-century Verse.* Roger Lonsdale, ed. Oxford University Press, 1984.

BROWNE, SIR THOMAS (1605–1882)

London-born physician, poet and author, from a Cheshire family. Educated at Winchester College and Pembroke College, Oxford, he received his medical degree from Leiden, Holland, and lived and died in Norfolk. His famous treatise *Religio Medici* was published in 1642. He was knighted by Charles II in 1671. Much of what he wrote was published posthumously. His *Miscellany Tracts* (1684) dealt with such disparate subjects as plants mentioned in Scripture; the fish eaten by Jesus with his disciples after his resurrection from the dead; fishes, birds, and insects; hawks and falconry; cymbals; artificial hills, mounts, or burrows in England; and answers of the Oracle of Apollo at Delphos to Croesus, King of Lydia. He was not a major poet, and many of his poems are of a religious nature. Some of his poems: "A Colloquy with God," "If Thou Could'st Empty All Thyself of Self," "Lars: A Pastoral of Norway," "For a Toe, Such as the Funeral Pyre," "Signs of Spring."

Sources: *A Sacrifice of Praise: An Anthology of Christian Poetry in English from Caedmon to the Mid-Twentieth Century.* James H. Trott, ed. Cumberland House Publishing, 1999. *Dictionary of National Biography.* Electronic Edition 1.1. Oxford University Press, 1997. *Encyclopædia Britannica Ultimate Reference Suite DVD,* 2006. *Poemhunter* (www.poemhunter.com). *The Columbia Granger's Index to Poetry.* 11th ed. *The Columbia Granger's World of Poetry,* Columbia University Press, 2005 (http://www.columbia grangers.org). *The Faber Book of Epigrams and Epitaphs.* Geoffrey Grigson, ed. Faber & Faber, 1977. *The National Portrait Gallery* (www.npg.org.uk). *The New Oxford Book of Seventeenth Century Verse.* Alastair Fowler, ed. Oxford University Press, 2004. *The Oxford Companion to English Literature.* 6th edition. Margaret Drabble, ed. Oxford University Press, 2000.

BROWNE, SIR WILLIAM (1692–1774)

Born in the county of Durham, the son of a physician, Browne took his medical degree at Cambridge in 1721. In 1726 he became a fellow of the College of Physicians, was closely involved with the group thereafter and in 1736 he became a fellow. He was knighted in 1748. He supported the argument that only people with degrees from Oxford or Cambridge should be allowed to practice medicine. This barred Scottish graduates, and a group of protesters forced his resignation as president of the Royal College. In his will he left three gold medals worth five guineas each to be given to undergraduates at Cambridge for Greek and Latin odes and epigrams. Most of his many writings — which included an unfinished version of the Book of Job — are in Latin. His "Epigram" — satirizing both Whigs and Tories — was written on the occasion of the presentation of Bishop Moore's library to the university of Cambridge by King George I.

Sources: *Dictionary of National Biography.* Electronic Edition 1.1. Oxford University Press, 1997. *The Columbia Granger's Index to Poetry.* 11th ed. *The Columbia Granger's World of Poetry,* Columbia University Press, 2005 (http://www.columbiagrangers.org). *The Faber Book of Comic Verse.* Michael Roberts and Janet Adam Smith, eds. Faber and Faber, 1978. *The National Portrait Gallery* (www.npg.org.uk).

BROWNE, WILLIAM (1591–?1643)

Born in Tavistock, Devon, he graduated from Exeter College, Oxford. In 1613 while studying law at the Inner Temple, London, Browne published the first book of *Britannia's Pastorals* (a narrative poem in three books, reminiscent of Spenser's *Faerie Queene*). He then collaborated with friends on *The Shepherd's Pipe* (1614), and wrote the *Inner Temple Masque* (performed January 1615). He dedicated the second book of *Britannia's Pastorals* (1616) to the earl of Pembroke, in whose service he remained for the rest of his life; the third book was published posthumously. One of his best known poems, "On the Countess Dowager of Pembroke," is a tribute to his patron on her funeral. His love of his native Devon is expressed in "A Devonshire Walk." Some of his other poems: "A Hapless Shepherd on a Daye," "A Sigh from Oxford," "A Welcome," "Fairest, When I Am Gone, as Now the Glass," "Memory," "Ode," "Praise of Spenser," "Sing Soft, Ye Pretty Birds, While Cælia Sleeps," "Song," "The Inner Temple Masque," "The Rose," "The Siren's Song," "Thirsis' Praise of His Mistress," "Venus and Adonis," "Visions."

Sources: *Dictionary of National Biography.* Electronic Edition 1.1. Oxford University Press, 1997. *Encyclopædia Britannica Ultimate Reference Suite DVD,* 2006. *English Poetry: Author Search.* Chadwyck-Healey Ltd., 1995 (http://www.lib.utexas.edu:8080/search/epoetry/author.html). *Poemhunter* (www.poemhunter.com). *Poems of William Browne.* Gordon Goodwin. 1894. *The Columbia Granger's Index to Poetry.* 11th ed. *The Columbia Granger's World of Poetry,* Columbia University Press, 2005 (http://www.columbiagrangers.org). *The Oxford Anthology of English Literature Vol. I.* Frank Kermode, and John Hollander, ed. Oxford University Press, 1973. *The Oxford Book of English Verse.* Christopher Ricks, ed. Oxford University Press, 1999. *The Oxford Companion to English Literature.* 6th edition. Margaret Drabble, ed. Oxford University Press, 2000.

BROWNING, ELIZABETH BARRETT and ROBERT (1806–1889)

Elizabeth Barrett, 1806–1861

The daughter of a despotic father who owed his wealth to plantations in Jamaica, Elizabeth spent her childhood in Worcestershire, but illness struck when she was fifteen and left her an invalid. The family finally settled in Wimpole Street, London. Robert Browning, admiring her poetry, wrote to her; they met and fell in love. When her father refused his consent, they eloped and were married in Italy in 1846. Their only child, Robert, was born in 1849. Elizabeth was a prolific poet and in 1848 she wrote "The Runaway Slave at Pilgrim's Point," a protest against slavery in the United States. Her *Sonnets from the Portuguese* (1850) (Portuguese was Robert's pet name for his wife) record her reluctance to marry. Her most ambitious work, *Aurora Leigh* (1857) is a long blank-verse poem telling the complicated and melodramatic love story of a young girl and a misguided philanthropist. Some of her other poems: "A Child Asleep," "Adequacy," "De Profundis," "The Cry of the Children," "The Exile's Return," "The House of Clouds," "The King's Gift," "The Mediator," "The Young Queen."

Robert, 1812–1889

The son of a Bank of England clerk, his education was mainly his father's library. Browning's elopement with Elizabeth Barrett in 1846 gave rise to the 1943 film *The Barretts of Wimpole Street.* He was a prolific poet noted for his dramatic monologues and his psychological insight into human nature. He died in Italy and is buried in Poets' Corner, Westminster Abbey. *The Ring and the Book* in 1868–1869 is the story of a Roman murder trial in 12 books. His work was noticed by many influential poets, and *The Monthly Repository* published several of his poems. Between 1841 and 1846 Browning published *Bells and Pomegranates,* which included "How They Brought the Good News from Ghent to Aix." Other well-known poems are: "The Pied Piper of Hamelin" and "Home Thoughts from Abroad," a poem written possibly in the heat of Italy, and its well-known first line: "Oh, to be in England now that April's there." Some of his other poems: "A Death in the Desert," "Belief and Unbelief," "Epigram on School Days," "Italy of the South," "Lines on Swinburne," "The Boy and the Angel," "The First-Born of Egypt."

Sources: *A Century of Sonnets: The Romantic-Era Revival 1750–1850.* Paula R. Feldman and Daniel Robinson, ed. Oxford University Press, 1999. *Bread and Roses: An Anthology of Nineteenth- and Twentieth-Century Poetry by Women Writers.* Diana Scott, ed. Virago Press, 1982.

Dictionary of National Biography. Electronic Edition 1.1. Oxford University Press, 1997. *Encyclopædia Britannica Ultimate Reference Suite DVD,* 2006. *English Poetry: Author Search.* Chadwyck-Healey Ltd., 1995 (http://www.lib.utexas.edu:8080/search/epoetry/author.html). *Selected Poems of Robert Browning.* Daniel Karlin, ed. Penguin Books, 1989. *The Columbia Granger's Index to Poetry.* 11th ed. *The Columbia Granger's World of Poetry,* Columbia University Press, 2005 (http://www.columbiagrangers.org). *The Complete Poetical Works of Mrs. Browning (Elizabeth Barrett Browning).* Harriet Waters Preston, ed. Houghton Mifflin, 1900. *The Family Book of Verse.* Lewis Gannett, ed. Harper & Row, 1961. *The National Portrait Gallery* (www.npg.org.uk). *The Oxford Companion to English Literature.* 6th edition. Margaret Drabble, ed. Oxford University Press, 2000. *Westminster Abbey Official Guide* (no date).

BROWNJOHN, ALAN CHARLES (1931–)

Poet, novelist and critic born in London and educated at Brockley County School and Merton College, Oxford, where he read modern history. Brownjohn worked as a schoolteacher between 1957 and 1965 and lectured at Battersea College of Education and South Bank Polytechnic until he left to become a full-time freelance writer in 1979. He has lectured in poetry and creative writing and is a regular broadcaster, reviewer and contributor to journals, including the *Times Literary Supplement, Encounter* and the *Sunday Times.* He has served on the Arts Council literature panel, was a Labor councilor and a candidate for Parliament. His work is mainly in collections; his first, *The Railings,* was published in 1961. One of his collections for children, *Brownjohn's Beast,* was published in 1970. His poem "Ruse" evokes happy memories of the children's game "hide and seek." Some of his other poems: "Cat," "Class Incident from Graves," "Cure," "Elephant," "In a Convent Garden," "In This City," "Ostrich," "Pitman's Common Sense Arithmetic, 1917," "Seven Activities for a Young Child," "The Train."

Sources: *Alan Brownjohn (An Interview)* (http://lidiavianu.esential.ro/alan_brownjohn.htm). *British Council Arts* (http://www.contemporarywriters.com). *Cat Will Rhyme with Hat: A Book of Poems.* Jean Chapman, ed. Scribner's, 1986. *The Columbia Granger's Index to Poetry.* 11th ed. *The Columbia Granger's World of Poetry,* Columbia University Press, 2005 (http://www.columbiagrangers.org). *The New Oxford Book of Children's Verse.* Neil Philip, ed. Oxford University Press, 1996. *The Oxford Book of Twentieth-Century English Verse.* Philip Larkin, ed. Oxford University Press, 1973. *The Oxford Companion to English Literature.* 6th edition. Margaret Drabble, ed. Oxford University Press, 2000. *The Oxford Treasury of Children's Poems.* Michael Harrison and Christopher Stuart-Clark, eds. Oxford University Press, 1988. *Who's Who.* London: A & C Black, 2005.

BRUCE, GEORGE (1909–2002)

Bruce was born in Fraserburgh, Aberdeenshire, to a fishing family. After graduating from Aberdeen University, he taught English before starting on a long career with the BBC. He was arts producer for over 24 years and literary critic for the *Sunday Times.* He retired from the BBC in 1970, immediately published his *Collected Poems* and continued to publish many books over the next thirty years. On reaching the age of ninety, he jokingly remarked that he was just getting into his stride. His fifth collection, *Pursuit: Poems 1986–1998,* won him the Saltire Literary Award in 1999. "Cliff Face Erosion"—which Bruce considered to be his finest poem, possibly a metaphor for his own life—was his response to a photograph by Orlando Gualtieri of an eroding cliff face near Fraserburgh. Some of his other poems: "Kinnaird Head," "My House," "Sumburgh Heid," "The Fisherman," "The Singers," "Tom on the Beach."

Sources: *An Interview with George Bruce, by Mallie Boman: August 21, 2001* (http://www.wooster.edu/artful dodge/interviews/bruce.htm). *Biography of George Bruce* (http://www.nls.uk/writestuff/heads/wee-bruce.html). *The Columbia Granger's Index to Poetry.* 11th ed. *The Columbia Granger's World of Poetry,* Columbia University Press, 2005 (http://www.columbiagrangers.org).

BRUCE, MICHAEL (1746–1767)

The "Gentle poet of Lochleven" was born in Kinross-shire, Scotland. His schooling was often interrupted by the need to herd cattle or help his father, a weaver. By the age of fifteen he knew Greek and Latin and his family and neighbors clubbed together to send him to Edinburgh University. In 1766 he took charge of a Burgher school at Forest Hill, near Clackmannan (Burghers were a breakaway from the Presbyterian Church). While there he wrote "Lochleven," a poem recalling his childhood memories. Ill with tuberculosis, he returned home and wrote his "Elegy to Spring" shortly before he died. His birthplace is maintained as a museum by the Michael Bruce Memorial Trust. He also wrote several hymns. There was a dispute about one of his poems, "Ode to the Cuckoo," whether he or John Logan (see entry) wrote it. Eight hymns are credited to him. The most well-known is the rousing "Behold! The Mountain of the Lord," sung to the tune "Glasgow." Some of his other poems: "Ode: To a Fountain," "Sir James the Ross: An Historical Ballad," "The Eagle, Crow, and Shepherd: A Fable," "The Last Day," "Vernal Ode."

Sources: *A Book of Scottish Verse.* Maurice Lindsay and R.L. Mackie, eds. St. Martin's Press, 1983. *Biography of Michael Bruce. LoveToKnow Online Classic Encyclopedia* (http://34.1911encyclopedia.org). *Dictionary of National*

Biography. Electronic Edition 1.1. Oxford University Press, 1997. *Encyclopædia Britannica Ultimate Reference Suite DVD,* 2006. *English Poetry: Author Search.* Chadwyck-Healey Ltd., 1995 (http://www.lib.utexas.edu:8080/search/epoetry/author.html). *The Columbia Granger's Index to Poetry.* 11th ed. *The Columbia Granger's World of Poetry,* Columbia University Press, 2005 (http://www.columbiagrangers.org). *The Cyber Hymnal* (http://www.cyberhymnal.org/index.htm). *The New Oxford Book of Eighteenth-century Verse.* Roger Lonsdale, ed. Oxford University Press, 1984.

BRYDGES, SIR SAMUEL EGERTON (1762–1837)

Born between Canterbury and Dover, the second son of Edward Brydges, and educated at Maidstone School, Canterbury, and Queen's College, Cambridge, he was called to the bar but never practiced. He seemed to live under the delusion that he was a great writer, but his published volumes of poems failed to arouse much enthusiasm. His novels *Mary de Clifford* (1792) and *Arthur Fitz-Albini* (1798) were fairly popular. He tried unsuccessfully to get the House of Lords to establish his claim to the title Baron Chandos. He was elected member of Parliament for Maidstone in 1812 and from 1813 to 1822 was involved in running Lee Priory Press, which published rare editions of Elizabethan works. From 1818 he lived abroad. Some of his other publications are: *Poems,* 1807. *Select Poems,* 1814. *Occasional Poems,* 1814. Some of his poems: "Dedication to a Novel, 1799," "Elegy, from a Novel, 1802," "Human Fate," "Lines Written Immediately After Parting from a Lady," "Moral Axioms," "On Dreams, October 15, 1782," "Poets and Modern Poetry," "The Gamekeeper's Return at Night," "To Miss M —," "Verses," "Upon Ancient Mansions."

Sources: *Dictionary of National Biography.* Electronic Edition 1.1. Oxford University Press, 1997. *Encyclopædia Britannica Ultimate Reference Suite DVD,* 2006. *English Poetry: Author Search.* Chadwyck-Healey Ltd., 1995 (http://www.lib.utexas.edu:8080/search/epoetry/author.html). *Poetry Page — Brydges* (http://www.geocities.com/Athens/Olympus/2601/brydges.html). *SETIS — The Scholarly Electronic Text and Image Service-English Poetry Collection* (http://setis.library.usyd.edu.au/poetry/browse/b-epdtoc.html). *Sweet Little Anger, by Sir Samuel Egerton Brydges.* *Angelic Poetry* (www.sarahsarchangels.com/poems/poems3.html). *The Burns Encyclopedia* (www.robertburns.org/encyclopedia). *The Columbia Granger's Index to Poetry.* 11th ed. *The Columbia Granger's World of Poetry,* Columbia University Press, 2005 (http://www.columbiagrangers.org). *The National Portrait Gallery* (www.npg.org.uk). *The Oxford Companion to English Literature.* 6th edition. Margaret Drabble, ed. Oxford University Press, 2000. *The Sonnet: An Anthology.* Robert M. Bender and Charles L. Squier, eds. Washington Square Press, 1987.

BUCHAN, JOHN, 1st BARON TWEEDSMUIR (1875–1940)

Born in Perth, the son of a Calvinist Presbyterian minister, he was educated at the universities of Glasgow and Oxford. He had a varied career: government official; publishing, editing and journalism; member of Parliament for the Scottish universities, 1927–35; and high commissioner to the General Assembly of the Church of Scotland and governor-general of Canada from 1935. His autobiography, *Memory Hold-the-Door,* was published in 1940. He died of a brain hemorrhage shortly after signing Canada's entry into the Second World War. Although better known for his thrillers — *Prester John* (1910); *Thirty-Nine Steps* (1915) *Greenmantle* (1916) (the list of his published books numbers well over a hundred) — and for his biographies, he was also a poet. *The Gipsy's Song to the Lady Cassilis* invites you to meander with him. Some of his other poems: "From the Pentlands," "The Kirk Bell," "Leap in the Smoke," "On Leave."

Sources: *Biography of John Buchan: John Buchan Society* (www.johnbuchansociety.co.uk). *Dictionary of National Biography.* Electronic Edition 1.1. Oxford University Press, 1997. *Encyclopædia Britannica Ultimate Reference Suite DVD,* 2006. *Never Such Innocence: A New Anthology of Great War Verse.* Martin Stephen, ed. Buchan and Enright, 1988. *Oldpoetry* (www.oldpoetry.com). *The Columbia Granger's Index to Poetry.* 11th ed. *The Columbia Granger's World of Poetry,* Columbia University Press, 2005 (http://www.columbiagrangers.org). *The National Portrait Gallery* (www.npg.org.uk). *The Oxford Companion to English Literature.* 6th edition. Margaret Drabble, ed. Oxford University Press, 2000.

BUCHANAN, DUGALD 1716–1768

A Gaelic poet, "the Cowper of the highlands" was born at the mill of Ardoch in the valley of Strathtyre and parish of Balquihidder, Perthshire. When the Society for Propagating Christian Knowledge was established in Scotland, Buchanan was appointed schoolmaster and catechist at Kinloch Rannoch in the parish of Fortingale. He assisted the Rev. James Stewart of Killin in translating the New Testament into Gaelic. He was interred at Little Leny in the parish of Callander, the burial place of the Buchanans of Leny and Cambusmore. His poems are reckoned to be equal to any in the Gaelic language for style, matter, and the harmony of their versification. His poems: "Am Bruadar [The Dream]," "An Claigeann [The Skull]," "An Geamhradh [The Winter]," "Laoidhibh Spioradail [Spiritual Hymns]," "Latha a'Bhreitheanis [The Day of Judgment]."

Sources: *Dictionary of National Biography.* Electronic Edition 1.1. Oxford University Press, 1997. *The Columbia Granger's Index to Poetry.* 11th ed. *The Columbia Granger's*

World of Poetry, Columbia University Press, 2005 (http://www.columbiagrangers.org).

BUCHANAN, ROBERT WILLIAMS (1841–1901)

Although born in Staffordshire, Buchanan was brought up mainly in Glasgow and attended university there. His atheist father instilled into him hostility to religion, something that colored his whole life. In London, Buchanan had advice from many leading writers. His early successes came in: *The Rathboy,* a play (co-authored with Charles Gibbon and performed at the Standard Theatre) in 1861; and *Undertones,* his first book of poems, 1863. Success followed success with more collections of poems published; his total output was impressive, and although he wrote some excellent material, he is more often remembered for his scurrilous attacks on Swinburne in the *Spectator* of 1866. By 1874 he was living in relative affluent seclusion in Oban and died bankrupt and with few friends. "A Poem to David" (from *North Coast, and Other Poems,* 1867–1868) (to David Gray, another poet) seems to echo his loneliness and his contempt for praise and opinion. Some of his other poems: "The Ballad of Judas Iscariot," "The Blind Linnet," "The Churchyard," "The Faëry Reaper," "The Little Herd-Boy's Song," "The Starling," "The Wanderers."

Sources: *Dictionary of National Biography.* Electronic Edition 1.1. Oxford University Press, 1997. *English Poetry: Author Search.* Chadwyck-Healey Ltd., 1995 (http://www.lib.utexas.edu:8080/search/epoetry/author.html). *Fellow Mortals: An Anthology of Animal Verse.* Roy Fuller, ed. Macdonald and Evans, 1981. *Selected Poems by Robert Buchanan* (www.victorianweb.org/authors/buchanan). *The Book of a Thousand Poems: A Family Treasury.* J. Murray Macbain, ed. Peter Bedrick Books, 1983. *The Columbia Granger's Index to Poetry.* 11th ed. *The Columbia Granger's World of Poetry,* Columbia University Press, 2005 (http://www.columbiagrangers.org). *The Home Book of Verse.* Burton Egbert Stevenson, ed. New York: Henry Holt and Company, 1953. *The Literary Encyclopedia* (www.LitEncyc.com).

BUNTING, BASIL (1900–1985)

Born on Tyneside, the son of a physician. In 1918 he spent six months in prison for refusing military conscription on Quaker principles. Working in Paris in the early 1920s, he was sub-editor of the *Transatlantic Review.* By 1925 he was earning his living as music critic for *Outlook* and other magazines in London. During World War II he abandoned his pacifist principles, joined the Royal Air Force, was sent to Iran and stayed on after the war, first in the diplomatic service, then as a journalist, before being expelled by Mossadegh in the early 1950s. His success in Britain came in 1966 when his semi-autobiographical poem "Briggflatts" (named after a Quaker settlement in Cumbria) was published in 1971. He was made an honorary D.Litt. of the University of Newcastle, and he was president of the Poetry Society (1972–1976) and of Northern Arts (1973–1976). Some of his poems: "Against the Tricks of Time," "At Briggflatts Meetinghouse," "Attis: Or, Something Missing," "Birthday Greeting," "Chorus of Furies," "Envoi to the Reader," "Fishermen," "Hymn to Alias Thor," "The Passport Officer," "The Pious Cat," "What the Chairman Told Tom."

Sources: *Basil Bunting Poetry Centre* (www.dur.ac.uk/basil_bunting_poetry.centre). *Dictionary of National Biography.* Electronic Edition 1.1. Oxford University Press, 1997. *The Columbia Granger's Index to Poetry.* 11th ed. *The Columbia Granger's World of Poetry,* Columbia University Press, 2005 (http://www.columbiagrangers.org). *The Complete Poems of Basil Bunting.* Richard Caddel, ed. Oxford University Press, 1994. *The Literary Encyclopedia* (www.LitEncyc.com). *The National Portrait Gallery* (www.npg.org.uk). *The Oxford Companion to English Literature.* 6th edition. Margaret Drabble, ed. Oxford University Press, 2000.

BUNYAN, JOHN (1628–1688)

Bunyan's father, a traveling mender of pots and pans from the village of Elstow, Bedfordshire, though poor, ensured his son had an education. John followed his father's trade until he joined the parliamentary army during the English Civil War (1642–1651). In 1648 he experienced a religious conversion and became a powerful preacher and writer. After the Restoration, he was jailed for eleven years because he did not have a license to preach. *Grace Abounding to the Chief of Sinners* (1666) is his spiritual autobiography. *The Pilgrim's Progress* (1678) — rich in imagery and symbolism, an allegory of the Christian's journey through life — was popular then, and still is. A window in Westminster Abbey was dedicated to Bunyan in 1912. He wrote many other books and poems. Some of his poems: "Christian Loses His Burden," "My Little Bird," "Neither Hook nor Line," "Of Beauty," "Of the Boy and Butterfly," "Of the Cuckoo," "The Author's Apology for His Book," "The Pilgrim Song [He who would valiant be]," "Upon Death," "Upon Fly-blows," "Upon the Snail," "Upon the Horse and His Rider."

Sources: *A Literature of Sports.* Tom Dodge, ed. D.C. Heath and Company, 1980. *Dictionary of National Biography.* Electronic Edition 1.1. Oxford University Press, 1997. *Encyclopædia Britannica Ultimate Reference Suite DVD,* 2006. *English Poetry: Author Search.* Chadwyck-Healey Ltd., 1995 (http://www.lib.utexas.edu:8080/search/epoetry/author.html). *Everyman's Book of English Verse.* John Wain, ed. J.M. Dent, 1981. *The Columbia Granger's Index to Poetry.* 11th ed. *The Columbia Granger's World of Poetry,* Columbia University Press, 2005 (http://www.columbiagrangers.org). *The National Portrait Gallery* (www.npg.

org.uk). *The New Oxford Book of Seventeenth Century Verse.* Alastair Fowler, ed. Oxford University Press, 2004. *The Penguin Book of Bird Poetry.* Peggy Munsterberg, ed. Penguin Books (1984) *Westminster Abbey Official Guide* (no date).

BURNAND, SIR FRANCIS COWLEY (1836–1917)

Burnand was the only son of Francis Burnand, a London stockbroker of French-Swiss origin; his mother, Emma Cowley, was a descendant of Hannah Cowley (see entry). Educated at Eton College and Trinity College, Cambridge, he studied for the Church, then was called to the bar, which he abandoned for the stage and dramatic writing. In all he wrote more than 100 farces, burlesque librettos of opera, and adaptations from the French; two of his burlesques were *Black-Eyed Susan* (1866) and *The Colonel* (1881). He wrote the libretto for Gilbert and Sullivan's *Cox and Box, or the Long Lost Brother,* performed in 1867. He was editor of *Punch* from 1880 until 1906, and his series *Happy Thoughts* ran from 1863 to 1864. He was knighted in 1902. Though not a great poet, his humor shows through in *His Heart Was True to Poll* ('His' refers to a man called William Kidd). Some of his other poems: "Fishing for Sticklebacks, with Rod and Line," "Oh, My Geraldine," "Tubby or Not Tubby — There's the Rub."

Sources: *Dictionary of National Biography.* Electronic Edition 1.1. Oxford University Press, 1997. *Gilbert and Sullivan Archive Arthur Sullivan Major Works* (http://math.boisestate.edu/gas/other_sullivan/html/othersul.html). *New Catholic Dictionary* (www.catholic-forum.com/saints/ncd01507.htm). *Pith and Vinegar: An Anthology of Short Humorous Poetry.* William Cole, ed. Simon & Schuster, 1969. *The Brand-X Anthology of Poetry.* William Zaranka, ed. Apple-Wood Books, 1981. *The Columbia Granger's Index to Poetry.* 11th ed. *The Columbia Granger's World of Poetry,* Columbia University Press, 2005 (http://www.columbiagrangers.org). *The National Portrait Gallery* (www.npg.org.uk). *The Oxford Companion to English Literature.* 6th edition. Margaret Drabble, ed. Oxford University Press, 2000.

BURNS, JAMES DRUMMOND (1823–1864)

Born in Edinburgh and educated at the charitable Heriot's Hospital, he was a brilliant student. His early religious impressions derive from the New Greyfriars church (famed in the book *Greyfriars' Bobby* by Eleanor Atkinson, first published in 1912). He was ordained in 1841 and took the Free Church at Dunblane, Perthshire. Ill health took him to a church in Madeira from 1847 until 1853, after which he settled in Hampstead, London. His ministry was successful and influential. He was one of the examining board of the English Presbyterian Theological College. His published books of poems: *The Vision*

of Prophecy, and Other Poems, 1854. *The Heavenly Jerusalem, or Glimpses within the Gates,* 1856. *The Evening Hymns,* 1857. Though not a great poet, Burns' "Hushed Was the Evening Hymn" has remained a firm children's favorite. It tells the story of young Samuel in the temple with Eli in I Samuel 3. Some of his poems: "Boaz and the Reapers," "Discovery of the North-West Passage," "My First Birthday in a Foreign Land," "The Bay of Barcelona," "The Dial and Fountain," "The Grave of Doddridge at Lisbon," "The Picture of a Martyrdom."

Sources: *Dictionary of National Biography.* Electronic Edition 1.1. Oxford University Press, 1997. *English Poetry: Author Search.* Chadwyck-Healey Ltd., 1995 (http://www.lib.utexas.edu:8080/search/epoetry/author.html). *Stanford University Libraries and Academic Information Resources* (http://library.stanford.edu). *The Cyber Hymnal* (http://www.cyberhymnal.org/index.htm).

BURNS, ROBERT (1759–1796)

Scotland's national poet. One of seven children, Burns was born January 25 in a small thatched cottage at Alloway, near Ayr (now a museum). Scots all over the world celebrate Burns Night on that date. William Burns, a stern Calvinist farmer, ensured that Robert received a sound education in English, including classic authors from Shakespeare onward, and a knowledge of French and mathematics. His spare time was occupied on his father's ailing farm as laborer and ploughman. His father died in 1784, saved from the embarrassment of Robert's satirical attacks on the kirk, and from his love affairs, which resulted in many illegitimate children. Yet it was these relationships that produced the warmest, richest, most tender and most sensuous love songs that any poet has written, songs such as: "Auld Lang Syne," "Scots Wha Hae," "Comin' thro' the Rye," and "Mary of Argyle." A Burns memorial was erected in Poets' Corner of Westminster Abbey in 1885. Some of his other poems: "A Red, Red Rose," "Allan Water," "Flow Gently, Sweet Afton," "Grace After Dinner," "Mary Morison," "Ode [for General Washington's Birthday]," "To a Mouse," "To a Haggis."

Sources: *Dictionary of National Biography.* Electronic Edition 1.1. Oxford University Press, 1997. *Encyclopædia Britannica Ultimate Reference Suite DVD,* 2006. *English Poetry: Author Search.* Chadwyck-Healey Ltd., 1995 (http://www.lib.utexas.edu:8080/search/epoetry/author.html). *The Burns Encyclopedia* (www.robertburns.org/encyclopedia). *The Columbia Granger's Index to Poetry.* 11th ed. *The Columbia Granger's World of Poetry,* Columbia University Press, 2005 (http://www.columbiagrangers.org). *The National Portrait Gallery* (www.npg.org.uk). *The New Oxford Book of Eighteenth Century Verse.* Roger Lonsdale, ed. Oxford University Press, 1984. *The Oxford Companion to English Literature.* 6th edition. Margaret Drabble, ed. Oxford University Press, 2000.

BURNSIDE, JOHN (1955–)

Scottish poet and novelist Burside was born in Dunfermline, Fifeshire. He studied English and European languages at Cambridge College of Arts and Technology. A former computer software engineer, he has been a freelance writer since 1996. He is a former writer in residence at Dundee University and now teaches at St. Andrews University. In addition to his poetry, he has published several novels, and his memoir, *A Lie About My Father,* was published in 2006. *Burning Elvis* (2000) is a collection of short stories. He has won ten major literary awards and prizes. In 2005 *The Good Neighbor* was short listed for the Forward Poetry Prize (Best Poetry Collection of the Year). Some of his poetry publications: *The Hoop,* 1998. *Common Knowledge,* 1991. *Feast Days,* 1992. *The Myth of the Twin,* 1994. *Swimming in the Flood,* 1995. *A Normal Skin,* 1997. *The Mercy Boys,* 1999. *The Good Neighbour,* 2005. Some of his poems: "Autobiography," "Dundee," "Homage to Kare Kivijarvi," "Septuagesima," "Swimming in the Flood."

Sources: *British Council Arts* (http://www.contemporarywriters.com). *Emergency Kit: Poems for Strange Times.* Jo Shapcott and Matthew Sweeney, ed. Faber and Faber, 1996. *Biography of John Burnside* (http://www.nls.uk/writestuff/heads/wee-burnside.html). *Penguin Modern Poets, Book 9.* John Burnside, Robert Crawford, Kathleen Jamie, ed. Penguin Books, 1996. *Septuagesima, Poem by John Burnside* (http://www.thepoem.co.uk/poems/burnside.htm). *The Columbia Granger's Index to Poetry.* 11th ed. *The Columbia Granger's World of Poetry,* Columbia University Press, 2005 (http://www.columbiagrangers.org). *The New Penguin Book of Scottish Verse.* Robert Crawford and Mick Imlah, eds. Penguin Books, 2000. *The Oxford Companion to English Literature.* 6th edition. Margaret Drabble, ed. Oxford University Press, 2000.

BURRELL, LADY SOPHIA (?1750–1802)

The daughter of Charles Raymond (knighted in 1774) of Valentines, Essex, she married William Burrell, member of Parliament for Haslemere in 1773. In 1787 her husband's health failed and they retired to Deepdene, Sussex, where she concentrated on her writing. Sir William died in 1796 and Lady Sophia married the Rev. William Clay in 1797. They retired to West Cowes, Isle of Wight, where she died. Her major publications: *Comala,* 1784. *Thymriad,* 1794. *Telemachus,* 1794. *Maximian,* 1800 (tragedy). *Theodora,* 1800 (tragedy). Some of her poems: "Chloe and Myra," "Epigram on Two Ladies," "The Picture of a Fine Gentleman," "The School for Satire," "Verses to a Lady, on Her Saying She Preferred Commonalty to an Irish Peerage."

Sources: *Dictionary of National Biography.* Electronic Edition 1.1. Oxford University Press, 1997. *Eighteenth Cen-*

tury Women Poets: An Oxford Anthology. Roger Lonsdale, ed. Oxford University Press, 1989. *The Columbia Granger's Index to Poetry.* 11th ed. *The Columbia Granger's World of Poetry,* Columbia University Press, 2005 (http://www.columbiagrangers.org).

BURTON, SIR RICHARD FRANCIS (1821–1890)

Burton studied at Trinity College, Oxford, became a talented linguist and had a colorful life: intrepid traveler, linguist, scholar, soldier, anthropologist, and a prolific and gifted writer. He published 43 volumes on his explorations and almost 30 volumes of translations, including the unexpurgated translations of the *Kama Sutra* (1883) and *The Arabian Nights* (1885–1888). He was the first European to discover Lake Tanganyika. He also entered the forbidden Muslim cities of Mecca and Medina. He mapped new trade routes, identified and catalogued valuable natural resources, and analyzed the political, religious, and economic systems in foreign countries. His *City of the Saints* (1861) is an account of the Mormon settlement at Utah. Some of his poems: "An Unpraised Picture," "Black Sheep," "Extras," "In Sleep," "Love is Strong," "On a Ferry Boat," "The First Song," "The Forefather," "The Glorious Game," "The Polar Quest."

Sources: *Dictionary of National Biography.* Electronic Edition 1.1. Oxford University Press, 1997. *Encyclopædia Britannica Ultimate Reference Suite DVD,* 2006. *The Columbia Granger's Index to Poetry.* 11th ed. The Columbia Granger's World of Poetry, Columbia University Press, 2005 (http://www.columbiagrangers.org). *The Home Book of Verse.* Burton Egbert Stevenson, ed. New York: Henry Holt and Company, 1953. *The National Portrait Gallery* (www.npg.org.uk). *The Oxford Companion to English Literature.* 6th edition. Margaret Drabble, ed. Oxford University Press, 2000. *The Sir Richard Burton Society* (www.pages.drexel.edu/~garsonkw/burton.html).

BUSH, DUNCAN (1946–)

The biographical detail on this poet is scant. He was born in Cardiff and now divides his time between homes in Luxembourg and the upper Swansea Valley of south Wales. He has published translations of Mallarmé, Baudelaire, Pavese and Pierre de la Prée. *The Genre of Silence* (1991) is a mixture of history and fiction of the life of the Russian poet Victor Bal, who "disappeared" under Stalinism. Bush's central concerns are the nature of work, the impact of industry on its environs, and the fate of modern man at the centre of a complicated web of social, political and personal forces. Some of his poetry publications: *Aquarium,* 1983. *Black Faces, Red Mouths: Poems on the Mining Communities and 1984–85 Strike,* 1985. *Salt: Poems,* 1985. *Masks,* 1994 (winner of the Welsh Book of the Year Award). *The Hook,*

1997 (brings together *Aquarium* and *Salt*). *Midway*, 1998 (largely biographical, he explores the second half of the 20th century). Some of his poems: "Drainlayer," "Living in Real Times," "Pneumoconiosis," "Summer 1984," "The Hook," "The Sunday the Power Went Off."

Sources: *Anglo-Welsh Poetry, 1480–1980*. Raymond Garlick and Roland Mathias, ed. Poetry Wales Press, 1984. *Anglo-Welsh Poetry, 1480–1990*. Raymond Garlick and Roland Mathias, ed. Poetry Wales Press, 1993. *Books by Duncan Bush: Results — enCompass Culture* (http://www.encompassculture.com/results/?qs=Duncan%20Bush). *The Columbia Granger's Index to Poetry*. 11th ed. *The Columbia Granger's World of Poetry*, Columbia University Press, 2005 (http://www.columbiagrangers.org). *Poems by Duncan Bush: Transcript (English)* (http://www.transcript-review.org/sub.cfm?lan=en&id=2991). *Twentieth Century Anglo-Welsh Poetry*. Dannie Abse. Seren Books/Dufour Editions, 1997.

BUTLER, SAMUEL (1612–1680)

Butler, the son of a farmer, was born at Strensham in Worcestershire and educated at the King's School, Worcester. He was secretary to the Countess of Kent and steward to Richard Vaughan, Earl of Carberry at Ludlow Castle. His poem *Hudibras* (1662–63) — satirizing Cromwellians and the Presbyterian church — was reckoned to be the most memorable and popular burlesque poem in the English language, and secured Butler's place in poetic history. It may well have been this that led to his being employed as secretary to the Duke of Buckingham. He was awarded a pension by Charles II, although it said that he died in poverty. A monument is erected to Butler in Poets' Corner of Westminster Abbey. Some of his other poems: "Arms and the Man," "Godly Casuistry," "Independent Squire," "On William Prynne," "Presbyterian Church Government," "Satire upon the Licentious Age of Charles II," "The Argument," "The Metaphysical Sectarian."

Sources: *Dictionary of National Biography*. Electronic Edition 1.1. Oxford University Press, 1997. *Oldpoetry* (www.oldpoetry.com). *The Columbia Anthology of British Poetry*. Carl Woodring, and James Shapiro, ed. Columbia University Press, 1995. *The Columbia Granger's Index to Poetry*. 11th ed. *The Columbia Granger's World of Poetry*, Columbia University Press, 2005 (http://www.columbiagrangers.org). *The National Portrait Gallery* (www.npg.org.uk). *The New Oxford Book of Seventeenth Century Verse*. Alastair Fowler, ed. Oxford University Press (2004). *The Oxford Companion to English Literature*. 6th edition. Margaret Drabble, ed. Oxford University Press, 2000. *The Penguin Book of Light Verse*. Gavin Ewart, ed. Penguin Books, 1980. To read the whole of *Hudibras* online (http://www.exclassics.com/hudibras/hbintro.htm). *Westminster Abbey Official Guide* (no date).

BUTLER, SAMUEL (1835–1902)

Coming from a family of eminent clergyman and educated at Shrewsbury and St. John's College,

Cambridge, Butler rebelled and made a small fortune as a sheep farmer in New Zealand. On his return to England he engaged himself in art (some of his paintings were exhibited at the Royal Academy in 1868–1876), music (he composed several works in collaboration with Henry Festings Jones and produced some musical compositions), and literature. His 1872 satire *Erewhon* (an anagram of "nowhere") describes a country in which manners and laws were the reverse of those in England and brought Butler immediate literary fame; *Erewhon Revisited* was published in 1901. *The Fair Haven* (1872) is an ironic attack on the Resurrection. His only novel — semibiographical *The Way of All Flesh* (1903) — is ranked among the great English novels. A trip to Canada in 1874–1875 inspired the poem "A Psalm of Montreal," a lament that the statue of beautiful Discobolus had been stowed away in some lumber room. Some of his other poems: "A Ballad in Two Parts," "A Prayer," "From Thomson's Autumn," "Hudibras's Elegy," "Prologue to the Queen of Aragon," "Satire (Upon Marriage)."

Sources: *Dictionary of National Biography*. Electronic Edition 1.1. Oxford University Press, 1997. *Great Books Online*, www.bartleby.com. *The Columbia Granger's Index to Poetry*. 11th ed. *The Columbia Granger's World of Poetry*, Columbia University Press, 2005 (http://www.columbiagrangers.org). *The Faber Book of Comic Verse*. Michael Roberts and Janet Adam Smith, eds. Faber & Faber, 1978. *The National Portrait Gallery* (www.npg.org.uk). *The Oxford Book of Satirical Verse*. Geoffrey Grigson, ed. Oxford University Press, 1980. *The Oxford Companion to English Literature*. 6th edition. Margaret Drabble, ed. Oxford University Press, 2000. *Works of the British Poets, Vol. 6: The Poetical Works of Samuel Butler, Vol. 3, including the Poems of John Phillips*. Thomas Park, ed. J. Sharpe, 1808.

BYROM, JOHN (1692–1763)

Born near Manchester, John Byrom was educated at Chester, Merchant Taylors' School, Manchester, and Trinity College, Cambridge, where he was elected fellow in 1714. He earned his living by teaching his own method of shorthand or "tychygraphy," which marked a stage in the development of shorthand. He was elected a fellow of the Royal Society in 1724 and contributed two papers on shorthand. The death of his elder and unmarried brother in 1740 relieved him from the necessity of teaching shorthand. His popular pastoral poem *Colin and Phoebe* appeared in *The Spectator* (October 1714), and his collected *Miscellaneous Poems* were published in 1773. Byrom also wrote some forceful hymns, the most famous of which is the Christmas hymn "Christians Awake, Salute the Happy Morn." Some of his other poems: "A Full and True Account of a Horrid and Barbarous Robbery," "Contentment; or, The Happy Workman's Song," "Epigram on the

Feuds between Handel and Bononcini, where he likens their differences to those between Tweedledum and Tweedledee!" "Jacobite Toast," "My Dog Tray," "My Spirit Longeth for Thee," "On the Origin of Evil," "On Two Monopolists," "Tom the Porter."

Sources: *Dictionary of National Biography.* Electronic Edition 1.1. Oxford University Press, 1997. *Encyclopædia Britannica Ultimate Reference Suite DVD,* 2006. *English Poetry: Author Search.* Chadwyck-Healey Ltd., 1995 (http://www.lib.utexas.edu:8080/search/epoetry/author.html). *The Columbia Granger's Index to Poetry.* 11th ed. *The Columbia Granger's World of Poetry,* Columbia University Press, 2005 (http://www.columbiagrangers.org). *The Cyber Hymnal* (http://www.cyberhymnal.org/index.htm). *The Faber Book of Comic Verse.* Michael Roberts, and Janet Adam Smith, ed. Faber & Faber, 1978. *The National Portrait Gallery* (www.npg.org.uk). *The New Oxford Book of Eighteenth Century Verse.* Roger Lonsdale, ed. Oxford University Press, 1984. *The Oxford Book of Satirical Verse.* Geoffrey Grigson, ed. Oxford University Press, 1980. *The Oxford Companion to English Literature.* 6th edition. Margaret Drabble, ed. Oxford University Press, 2000.

BYRON, GEORGE GORDON, SIXTH LORD (1788–1824)

Educated at Harrow and Trinity College, Cambridge, Lord Byron inherited the title at the age of ten. By twenty-four he was among the most famous poets in England. Some say that his club foot influenced his character and drove him to excesses. His marriage in 1815 was not a happy one. Pursued by scandal and rumor, he left England and spent most of his short life in Italy, often in the company of Percy and Mary Shelley. He died of fever helping freedom fighters in Greece, and a commemorative stone is in Poets' Corner of Westminster Abbey. He wrote passionate poems; his long poems included *Childe Harolde's Pilgrimage* in four cantos; he wrote short poems, challenging poems, and romantic poems, for example, *She Walks in Beauty* ('She' is Byron's cousin, Mrs. Wilmot.) Some of his other poems: "The Adieu," "At Thirty Years," "Beppo: A Venetian Story," "The Bride of Abydos," "By the Rivers of Babylon We Sat Down and Wept," "Elegy on Newstead Abbey," "The Age of Bronze," "The Butterfly," "The Chain I Gave," "The Destruction of Sennacherib," "When We Two Parted."

Sources: *Dictionary of National Biography.* Electronic Edition 1.1. Oxford University Press, 1997. *Encyclopædia Britannica Ultimate Reference Suite DVD,* 2006. *English Poetry: Author Search.* Chadwyck-Healey Ltd., 1995 (http://www.lib.utexas.edu:8080/search/epoetry/author.html). *Encyclopedia of Britain.* Bamber Gascoigne. London: Macmillan, 1994. *The Columbia Granger's Index to Poetry.* 11th ed. *The Columbia Granger's World of Poetry,* Columbia University Press, 2005 (http://www.columbiagrangers.org). *The National Portrait Gallery* (www.npg.

org.uk). *The New Oxford Book of Romantic Period Verse.* Jerome J. McGann. Oxford University Press, 1993. *The Oxford Companion to English Literature.* 6th edition. Margaret Drabble, ed. Oxford University Press, 2000. *The Poems of Byron.* Paul E. More, ed. Houghton Mifflin, 1933. *Westminster Abbey Official Guide* (no date).

CAEDMON (fl. 658–680)

Little is known about Saint Caedmon the great Anglo-Saxon poet (the name is thought to be Celtic) other than what Bede records. Caedmon, an illiterate Northumbrian herdsman, had a vision in which he learned a hymn, which he recited perfectly when he awoke. He became a monk at Streaneshalch monastery (Whitby) during the rule of the Abbess Hild (between 658 and 680), when he was already an old man. The monks instructed him in the Bible, which he turned into sung verse, thus making Scripture accessible to the laity. A stone is set in the floor of Poets' Corner, Westminster Abbey. Some of his poems: Caedmon's *Hymn, Christ and Satan* (the fallen angels; Christ's descent into hell after his death, and the temptation of Christ by Satan), *Daniel* (the Book of Daniel), *Exodus* (the flight of the Israelites), *Genesis* (the Creation).

Sources: *An Anthology of Catholic Poets.* Shane Leslie, ed. Macmillan, 1952. *Dictionary of National Biography.* Electronic Edition, 1.1. Oxford University Press, 1997. *Encyclopædia Britannica Ultimate Reference Suite DVD,* 2006. *Encyclopedia of Britain.* Bamber Gascoigne. London: Macmillan, 1994. *The Columbia Granger's Index to Poetry.* 11th ed. *The Columbia Granger's World of Poetry,* Columbia University Press, 2005 (http://www.columbiagrangers.org). *The Oxford Companion to English Literature.* 6th edition. Margaret Drabble, ed. Oxford University Press, 2000. *Westminster Abbey Official Guide* (no date).

CALVERLEY, CHARLES STUART (1831–1884)

Calverley (born Blayds, who assumed the family name of Calverley from 1852) was a brilliant student at Harrow, Balliol College, Oxford, and Christ's College, Cambridge, although his pranks and disregard for discipline caused his dismissal from Oxford. He won the chancellor's prize for Latin verse at both universities, as well as several other prizes for both Latin and Greek. At Cambridge he won the Craven scholarship in 1854, the Camden medal in 1853 and 1855, the Browne medal (for a Greek ode) in 1855, and the members' prize for a Latin essay in 1856. He became a barrister, but owing to a skating accident, was prevented from a professional career. During the last years of his life he was an invalid, suffering from Bright's Disease (kidneys). His main publications: *Verses and Translations,* 1862. *Translations,* 1866. *Fly Leaves,* 1872. *Theocritus,* 1869. Some of his poems: "April: or, The New Hat," "Australia," "Charades," "In the Gloaming," "Lines Suggested by the Fourteenth of February," "Ode to Tobacco," "The Bottling of the Wasp," "The Cat," "The Cuckoo," "The Poet and the Fly."

Sources: *Charles Stuart Calverley, Martley's "Lost" Poet* (http://www.martley.org.uk/people/lostpoet.htm). *Dictionary of National Biography.* Electronic Edition, 1.1. Oxford University Press, 1997. *English Poetry: Author Search.* Chadwyck-Healey Ltd., 1995 (http://www.lib.utexas.edu:8080/search/epoetry/author.html). *Poemhunter* (www.poemhunter.com). *The Columbia Granger's Index to Poetry.* 11th ed. *The Columbia Granger's World of Poetry,* Columbia University Press, 2005 (http://www.columbiagrangers.org). *The Complete Works of C.S. Calverley.* G. Bell and Sons, 1926. *The Home Book of Verse.* Burton Egbert Stevenson, ed. New York: Henry Holt and Company, 1953. *The Oxford Companion to English Literature.* 6th edition. Margaret Drabble, ed. Oxford University Press, 2000.

CAMERON, JOHN NORMAN (1905–1953)

Scottish poet, born in India and educated in Edinburgh and at Oriel College, Oxford. After spending time as an education officer in Nigeria, then in advertising in London, he worked in government propaganda with British forces during World War II and until 1947. He was the friend of W.H. Auden, Robert Graves, and Dylan Thomas (see entries). He published poetry before the war, mainly in *New Verse.* His collected poems were published posthumously in 1957. His poems are often built on a parable and a single image. *Nostalgia for Death* shows the seriousness that is often present in what appears as fun, where he pokes fun at the seriousness of personality idiosyncrasies. Some of his other poems: "A Visit to the Dead," "For the Fly-Leaf of a School-Book," "Forgive Me, Sire," "The Compassionate Fool," "The Disused Temple," "The Unfinished Race," "The Verdict," "Three Love Poems."

Sources: *Golden Treasury of the Best Songs & Lyrical Poems in the English Language.* Francis Turner Palgrave, ed. Oxford University Press (1964, Sixth edition, updated by John Press, 1994). *Norman Cameron: His Life, Work and Letters* (http://www.greenex.co.uk/cameron.html). *The Columbia Granger's Index to Poetry.* 11th ed. *The Columbia Granger's World of Poetry,* Columbia University Press, 2005 (http://www.columbiagrangers.org). *The Oxford Book of Twentieth-Century English Verse.* Philip Larkin, ed. Oxford University Press, 1973. *The Oxford Companion to English Literature.* 6th edition. Margaret Drabble, ed. Oxford University Press, 2000.

CAMPBELL, JOSEPH (1879–1944)

Born in County Down, Ireland, he was educated at St. Malachi's College, Belfast, and worked for his father before becoming a teacher of English. In 1904 he helped found the Ulster Literary Theatre; his own play, *Little Cowherd of Slainge,* was performed in 1905. Before the First World War he lived in London, where he was secretary of the Irish Literary Society. During the Easter Rising (1916) he served as an intelligence officer and was later interned for seventeen months during the Irish Civil War (1922–1923). In 1925 he set up the School of Irish Studies at Fordham University, New York. From 1939 until his death he lived in Glencree, County Wicklow. He wrote as Seosamh Mac Cathmhaoil (also Seosamh MacCathmhaoil). His poems were set to music by Arnold Bax and Ivor Gurney. Some of his poetry publications: *Songs of Uladh,* 1904. *The Garden of the Bees,* 1905. *The Man-Child,* 1907. *The Gilly of Christ,* 1907. *The Mountainy Singer,* 1909. Some of his poems: "Butterfly in the Fields," "Go, Ploughman, Plough," "The Blind Man at the Fair," "The Hills of Cualann."

Sources: *A Book of Animal Poems.* William Cole, ed. Viking, 1973. *An Anthology of Irish Literature.* David H. Greene, ed. H. Modern Library, 1954. *Biography of Joseph Campbell: Ulster History Circle* (http://www.ulsterhistory.co.uk/josephcampbell.htm). *The Book of Irish Verse: An Anthology of Irish Poetry from the Sixth Century to the Present.* John Montague, ed. Macmillan, 1974. *The Columbia Granger's Index to Poetry.* 11th ed. *The Columbia Granger's World of Poetry,* Columbia University Press, 2005 (http://www.columbiagrangers.org). *The Oxford Book of Irish Verse: XVIIth Century–XXth Century.* Donagh MacDonagh, and Leenox Robinson, ed. Oxford University Press, 1958. *The Oxford Book of Twentieth-Century English Verse.* Philip Larkin, ed. Oxford University Press, 1973. *The Oxford Companion to English Literature.* 6th edition. Margaret Drabble, ed. Oxford University Press, 2000. *Wikipedia, the Free Encyclopedia* (http://en.wikipedia.org/wiki/Wikipedia).

CAMPBELL, THOMAS (1774–1844)

Scottish poet whose family suffered financially in the American War of Independence (1775–1781). While at Glasgow grammar school and Glasgow University, Campbell proved himself an able classical scholar and won numerous prizes. Needing to earn a living, he worked as a tutor, after which he settled in Edinburgh and engaged himself in literary work. Interested in education, he had a hand in the founding of University College, London. He edited *The New Monthly Review* (1820–1831) and served as Rector of Glasgow University (1827–29). He had long interest in justice for Poland and when he was buried in Poets' Corner of Westminster Abbey, a Polish noble scattered upon his coffin a handful of earth from the grave of Kosciusko. His main works are: *Pleasures of Hope,* 1799. *Gertrude of Wyoming,* 1809. *Specimens of the British Poets,* 1819 (seven volumes). *Theodoric,* 1824. *Pilgrim of Glencoe,* 1842. And his war poems: "Ye Mariners of England," "The Battle of the Baltic," "Hohenlinden." Some of his other poems: "Ben Lomond," "Dirge of Wallace," "Gertrude of Wyoming," "Lines on Poland," "On Slavery," "The Soldier's Dream."

Sources: *Dictionary of National Biography*. Electronic Edition, 1.1. Oxford University Press, 1997. *Encyclopædia Britannica Ultimate Reference Suite DVD*, 2006. *English Poetry: Author Search*. Chadwyck-Healey Ltd., 1995 (http://www.lib.utexas.edu:8080/search/epoetry/author.html). *The Columbia Granger's Index to Poetry*. 11th ed. *The Columbia Granger's World of Poetry*, Columbia University Press, 2005 (http://www.columbiagrangers.org). *The Complete Poetical Works of Thomas Campbell*. J. Logie Robertson, ed. Oxford University Press, 1907. *The Cyber Hymnal* (http://www.cyberhymnal.org/index.htm). *The National Portrait Gallery* (www.npg.org.uk). *The Oxford Book of English Verse*. Christopher Ricks, ed. Oxford University Press, 1999. *The Oxford Companion to English Literature*. 6th edition. Margaret Drabble, ed. Oxford University Press, 2000. *Westminster Abbey Official Guide* (no date).

CAMPION, THOMAS (1567–1620)

Physician, poet, composer of masques, outstanding songwriter, literary theorist, and brilliant lutenist. Educated at Cambridge University (1581–1584), he studied law in London, but he was never called to the bar. He also qualified as a doctor, possibly in France, and practiced medicine from 1606 until his death. He deplored the use of rhymed, accentual meters, insisting instead that timing and sound duration are the fundamental elements in verse structure. *The Selected Songs,* edited by W.H. Auden, was published in 1972. His major works are: Five sets of verses appearing anonymously in Sidney's *Astrophel and Stella,* 1591. *Poemata* (Latin epigrams), 1595. *A Booke of Ayres* (with Philip Rosseter) 1601. Four more *Bookes of Ayres,* 1613–1617. *Songs of Mourning* (when Prince Henry died), 1612. Some of his vast output is in Latin; many are epigrams. Some of his other poems: "A Hymn in Praise of Neptune," "A Lamentation," "Beauty, Since You So Much Desire," "First Love," "Lord Hay's Mask," "My Life's Delight," "Rose-Cheeked Laura, Come," "The Entertainment," "To the Most Sacred King James," "To the World."

Sources: *Encyclopædia Britannica Ultimate Reference Suite DVD*, 2006. *English Poetry: Author Search*. Chadwyck-Healey Ltd., 1995 (http://www.lib.utexas.edu:8080/search/epoetry/author.html). *The Columbia Granger's Index to Poetry*. 11th ed. *The Columbia Granger's World of Poetry*, Columbia University Press, 2005 (http://www.columbiagrangers.org). *The Literary Encyclopedia* (www.LitEncyc.com). *The Oxford Companion to English Literature*. 6th edition. Margaret Drabble, ed. Oxford University Press, 2000. *The Works of Thomas Campion*. Walter R. Davis, ed. New York: W.W. Norton, 1969.

CANNAN, MAY WEDDERBURN (1893–1973)

She was born at Oxford, where her father was dean of Trinity College. In 1911 she joined the Voluntary Aid Detachment, and when war broke out she spent some time nursing in Rouen. Returning to England, she helped her father run the Clarendon Press, which included publishing material for the War Propaganda Bureau. Her first poems were published in *The Scotsman* in 1908. Her major publications: *In War Time*, 1917. *The Lonely Generation* (memoirs), 1934. *Grey Ghosts and Voices* (her autobiography, published posthumously, 1976. *The Tears of War: The Story of a Young Poet and a War Hero*, May Wedderburn Cannan and Bevil Brian Quiller-Couch, Cavalier Paperbacks, 2002. ISBN: 1899470190. CavalierPaperbacks.co.uk. Some of her other poems: "Lamplight," "Love, 1916," "Rouen," "Since They Have Died."

Sources: *Poemhunter* (www.poemhunter.com). *Scars Upon My Heart: Women's Poetry and Verse of the First World War*. Catherine W Reilly, ed. Virago Press, 1981. *The Columbia Granger's Index to Poetry*. 11th ed. *The Columbia Granger's World of Poetry,* Columbia University Press, 2005 (http://www.columbiagrangers.org). *The Wedderburn Book* (Vol. 1, p. 317), published privately by Alexander Wedderburn, 1898.

CANNING, GEORGE (1770–1827)

British statesman born into an Anglo-Irish family, he is known for his liberal policies as foreign secretary (1807–1809, 1822–1827) and as prime minister for a short period during 1827. In order to support the family after her husband died, his beautiful mother became an actress, something that did not fit comfortably with eighteenth century English society. Educated at Eton College and after graduating from Christ Church, Oxford (1791), he came under the influence of the prime minister, William Pitt (the "Younger"), and was elected member of Parliament for Newtown, Isle of Wight, in 1793. Canning and Viscount Castlereagh were at loggerheads and ended up fighting a duel; Canning was wounded in the thigh. They both resigned, and when Castelreagh committed suicide in 1822, Canning became foreign secretary. He is buried in the North Transept of Westminster Abbey. His *Poems* were published in 1823, and he collaborated with others to produce several long poems. Some of his poems: "All the Talents," "Blue and Buff," "Elijah's Mantle," "New Morality," "The Rovers, or, The Double Arrangement," "The Grand Consulation," "The Pilgrimage to Mecca," "The Slavery of Greece," "The Traitor's Epitaph."

Sources: *Dictionary of National Biography*. Electronic Edition, 1.1. Oxford University Press, 1997. *Encyclopædia Britannica Ultimate Reference Suite DVD*, 2006. *English Poetry: Author Search*. Chadwyck-Healey Ltd., 1995 (http://www.lib.utexas.edu:8080/search/epoetry/author.html). *Encyclopedia of Britain*. Bamber Gascoigne. London: Macmillan, 1994. *The Columbia Granger's Index to Poetry*.

11th ed. *The Columbia Granger's World of Poetry*, Columbia University Press, 2005 (http://www.columbiagrangers.org). *The National Portrait Gallery* (www.npg.org.uk). *The Oxford Companion to English Literature*. 6th edition. Margaret Drabble, ed. Oxford University Press, 2000. *Poetry of the Anti-Jacobin*. William Gifford, ed. J. Wright, pub., 1801. *Westminster Abbey Official Guide* (no date).

CANTON, WILLIAM (1845–1926)

Canton was born in China. His father, a colonial civil servant, died in Jamaica when William was nine. Educated in France, he started studying for the Catholic priesthood but early in adult life converted to Protestantism. From 1867 he engaged in teaching and journalism in London and, from 1876 to 1898, worked for newspapers in Glasgow. He moved back to London and became sub-editor of *The Contemporary Review* and editor of *The Sunday Magazine*. He published non-fiction as well as verse. His major works: *The Invisible Playmate: A Story of the Unseen*, 1894 (commemorating his daughter, who died young). *W.V. Her Book*, 1896. *A Child's Book of Saints*, 1898. *In memory of W.V.*, 1901. *A history of the British and Foreign Bible Society*, 1904–1910 (5 volumes). *Poems*, 1927. Some of his other poems: "A Child's Prayer," "A New Poet," "Bethlehem," "Carol," "Day-Dreams," "Easter Dawn," "John Calvin's Dream," "Laus Infantium," "Life and Death," "The Crow," "The Door in Heaven," "The Shepherd."

Sources: *Dictionary of National Biography*. Electronic Edition, 1.1. Oxford University Press, 1997. *English Poetry: Author Search*. Chadwyck-Healey Ltd., 1995 (http://www.lib.utexas.edu:8080/search/epoetry/author.html). *Our Holidays in Poetry*. Mildred P. Harrington and Josephine H. Thomas, eds. H.W. Wilson, 1929. *Penguin poetry anthologies* (http://encyclopedia.thefreedictionary.com/Penguin%20poetry%20anthologies). *The Book of a Thousand Poems: A Family Treasury*. J. Murray Macbain, ed. Peter Bedrick Books, 1983. *The Columbia Granger's Index to Poetry*. 11th ed. *The Columbia Granger's World of Poetry*, Columbia University Press, 2005 (http://www.columbiagrangers.org).

CARBERY, ETHNA (ANNA MACMANUS) (1866–1902)

Ethna Carbery is the pen name of the Belfast poet Anna MacManus, the wife of the novelist Séamus MacManus. She began publishing in her teens, and her writings were popular with the early Sinn Féin movement. She contributed to most of the Irish magazines and newspapers of her time: the *Nation, United Ireland, Harper's Magazine, New York Criterion, The Century*, and other American periodicals. Her posthumous publications are: *The Four Winds of Eirinn*, 1902 (a book of poetry, finished and edited by her husband; it went to nine editions within a year). *The Passionate Hearts*, 1903 (a collection of

short stories). *In the Celtic Past*, 1904. Some of her poems: "Hills o' My Heart," "On an Island," "The Heathery Hill," "The King of Ireland's Cairn," "The Love-Talker," "The Shadow House of Lugh."

Sources: All the poems of Ethna Carber can be found online at http://www.thehypertexts.com/Ethna_Carbery_Poet_Poetry_Picture_Bio.htm. *An Anthology of Irish Verse: The Poetry of Ireland from Mythological Times to the Present*. Padraic Colum, ed. Liveright, 1948. *A Celebration of Women Writers: Mrs. Seumas Macmanus (Anna Johnston)*. http://digital.library.upenn.edu/women/carberry/macmanus.html). *The Columbia Granger's Index to Poetry*. 11th ed. *The Columbia Granger's World of Poetry*, Columbia University Press, 2005 (http://www.columbiagrangers.org). *The Home Book of Verse*. Burton Egbert Stevenson, ed. New York: Henry Holt and Company, 1953. *The Women Poets in English: An Anthology*. Ann Stanford, ed. McGraw-Hill, 1972.

CAREW, RICHARD (1555–1620)

Carew is best known for his long poem *Survey of Cornwall* (1602; modern edition, 1953). He had estates in Cornwall and through his marriage he inherited a part of the Coswarth property in Cheshire. A genius, he was admitted to Christ Church, Oxford, at the age of eleven years; a skilled linguist, he was proficient in Greek, Italian, German, French, and Spanish. He was a justice of the peace, high sheriff of Cornwall, member of Parliament for Saltash, and deputy-lieutenant of Cornwall serving under Sir Walter Raleigh, as colonel of the regiment, charged with protecting Cawsand Bay. He was an active member of the Society of Antiquaries, and he also translated several texts. His last work was *The Excellencie of the English Tongue* (1614). Some of his other poems: "A Herrings Tale," "River Lynher," "The Recovery of Jerusalem."

Sources: *Dictionary of National Biography*. Electronic Edition, 1.1. Oxford University Press, 1997. *The Columbia Granger's Index to Poetry*. 11th ed. *The Columbia Granger's World of Poetry*, Columbia University Press, 2005 (http://www.columbiagrangers.org). *The Faber Book of Poems and Places*. Geoffrey Grigson, ed. Faber & Faber, 1980. *Representative Poetry Online* (http://eir.library.utoronto.ca/rpo/display/poet371.html). *Wikipedia, the Free Encyclopedia* (http://en.wikipedia.org/wiki/Wikipedia).

CAREW, THOMAS (?1595–?1639)

English cavalier poet and songwriter of light-hearted lyrics in praise of love, strongly influenced by John Donne and Ben Jonson. A lawyer's son, he was educated at Oxford University (which college is uncertain) and trained in law. He spent several years in the diplomatic service in Europe and in America before being appointed to the household of King Charles I, who had a high opinion of his wit and abilities and rewarded him with an estate. His masque, *Coelum Britannicum*, was performed by the king and his gentlemen in 1634. He translated a number of the Psalms and is said to have died regretting a life of libertinism. His elegy for John Donne was published with Donne's poems in 1633. His own poems were published a few weeks after his death. Some of his poems: "A Beautiful Mistress," "A Lady's Prayer to Cupid," "A Rapture," "Epitaph on the Lady Mary Villiers," "Good Counsel to a Young Maid," "In the Person of a Lady to Her Inconstant Servant," "On Sight of a Gentlewoman's Face in the Water," "The Carver, To His Mistress," "To Ben Jonson."

Sources: *Dictionary of National Biography.* Electronic Edition, 1.1. Oxford University Press, 1997. *Encyclopædia Britannica Ultimate Reference Suite DVD,* 2006. *English Poetry: Author Search.* Chadwyck-Healey Ltd., 1995 (http://www.lib.utexas.edu:8080/search/epoetry/author.html). *Erotic Literature: Twenty-four Centuries of Sensual Writing.* Jane Mills, ed. HarperCollins, 1993. *The Cavalier Poets: An Anthology.* Thomas Crofts, ed. Dover Publications, 1995. *The Columbia Granger's Index to Poetry.* 11th ed. *The Columbia Granger's World of Poetry,* Columbia University Press, 2005 (http://www.columbiagrangers.org). *The New Oxford Book of Seventeenth Century Verse.* Alastair Fowler, ed. Oxford University Press, 2004. *The Oxford Companion to English Literature.* 6th edition. Margaret Drabble, ed. Oxford University Press, 2000. *Wikipedia, the Free Encyclopedia* (http://en.wikipedia.org/wiki/Wikipedia).

CAREY, HENRY (?1693–1743)

Carey's life and death are shrouded in mystery, but he is thought to have been the illegitimate son or grandson of George Savile, the first marquis of Halifax. Apparently he lived in poverty and committed suicide; a benefit performance for his widow and four small children was given at Drury Lane on 17 November 1743. He wrote the ballad "Sally in Our Alley" for a musical burlesque with the impossible title *Chrononhotonthologos.* His burlesque, *The Dragon of Wantley,* had a longer first run than John Gay's *The Beggar's Opera.* Of his theatre work, the best is said to be *The Honest Yorkshire-Man* (1735) (linking him with Yorkshire). His son's claim that Carey was the author of "God Save the King" has been disputed. The DNB has a complete list of Carey's works. Carey is the man who gave the nickname "Namby Pamby" to the English language in his poem by that name. Some of his other poems: "A Drinking-Song," "A Lilliputian Ode on Their Majesties' Accession," "Roger and Dolly," "Sally Sweetbread," "The Author's Quietus," "The Huntsman's Rouse," "The Maid's Husband."

Sources: *Dictionary of National Biography.* Electronic Edition, 1.1. Oxford University Press, 1997. *Encyclopædia Britannica Ultimate Reference Suite DVD,* 2006. *The Columbia Granger's Index to Poetry.* 11th ed. *The Columbia Granger's World of Poetry,* Columbia University Press, 2005 (http://www.columbiagrangers.org). *Faber Book of Nonsense Verse.* Geoffrey Grigson, ed. Faber & Faber, 1979. *The National Portrait Gallery* (www.npg.org.uk). *The New Oxford Book of English Verse, 1250–1950.* Helen Gardner, ed. Oxford University Press, 1972. *The Oxford Book of English Verse.* Christopher Ricks, ed. Oxford University Press, 1999. *The Oxford Companion to English Literature.* 6th edition. Margaret Drabble, ed. Oxford University Press, 2000. *The Oxford Nursery Rhyme Book.* Iona Opie and Peter Opie, eds. Oxford University Press, 1955.

CARKESSE, JAMES (fl. 1679)

Little is known of this poet, who was educated at Westminster School and in 1652 was elected to a scholarship at Christ Church, Oxford. He was a clerk in Samuel Pepys's office at the Admiralty. It seems probable that he joined the Roman catholic church before 1679, in which year he published *Lucida Intervalla: containing divers miscellaneous Poems written at Finsbury and Bethlem by the Doctor's Patient Extraordinary.* It seems, from what Carkesse said, that he wrote poetry to prove that was not insane, but the doctor in charge of Bethlem hospital (Bedlam), Thomas Allen, insisted that if Carkesse stopped writing poetry he would then be fit to be discharged. Copies of *Lucida Intervalla* are held in many university libraries around the world. Some of his poems: "His Petition to Mr. Speaker," "His Rule of Behaviour: If You Are Civil, I Am Sober," "On the Doctors' Telling Him that till He Left off Making Verses He Was Not Fit to be Discharged."

Sources: *Dictionary of National Biography.* Electronic Edition, 1.1. Oxford University Press, 1997. *Lucida Intervalla by James Carkasse.* The Augustan Reprint Society, 1679. *Microsoft Encarta* 2006 (DVD). Microsoft Corporation, 2006. *Notes on the history of mental health care* (http://www.mind.org.uk/Information/Factsheets/History+of+mental+health/Notes+on+the+History+of+Mental+Health+Care.htm). *Patterns of Madness in the Eighteenth Century: A Reader.* Allan Ingram, ed. Liverpool University Press, 1998. *The Chatto Book of Nonsense Poetry.* Hugh Haughton, ed. Chatto & Windus, 1988. *The New Oxford Book of Seventeenth Century Verse.* Alastair Fowler, ed. Oxford University Press, 1991.

CARNEGIE, JAMES, 9th EARL OF SOUTHESK (1827–1905)

Carnegie succeeded his father as sixth baronet of Pittarow at Kinnaird Castle, Brechin, Scotland. They lost the 5th earldom in 1715 when they supported the Jacobite uprising. James successfully had it restored in 1869. He explored the Rockies and the source of the Athabasca and Saskatchewan rivers, and in 1860 was made a fellow of the Geographical Society. He was honorary doctor of the universities of St. Andrews and Aberdeen. He was a collector of gems and Assyrian, Hittite, Babylonian, and Persian antiquities. His main publications are:

Saskatchewan and the Rocky Mountains, 1875. *Herminius: A Romance*, 1882. *Suomira, A Fantasy*, 1899. *Jonas Fisher: a Poem in Brown and White*, 1875. One of his poems, *The Flitch of Dunmow*, tells he story of one of Britain's oldest and most popular ceremonies of the Town of Dunmow in Essex. The Dunmow Flitch Trials exist to award a flitch (side) of bacon to married couples (who may come from anywhere in the world) if they can satisfy the judge and jury of 6 maidens and 6 bachelors that in "twelvemonth and a day" they have "not wisht themselves unmarried again."

Sources: *Clan Carnegie* (http://www.electricscotland.com/webclans/atoc/carnegi2.html). *Dictionary of National Biography*. Electronic Edition, 1.1. Oxford University Press, 1997. *Encyclopedia of Britain*. Bamber Gascoigne. London: Macmillan, 1994. *The Columbia Granger's Index to Poetry*. 11th ed. *The Columbia Granger's World of Poetry*, Columbia University Press, 2005 (http://www.columbiagrangers.org). *The Official Dunmow Flitch Trials Committee website* (www.dunmowflitchtrials.co.uk).

CARR, SIR JOHN (1732–1807)

Born in County Durham, of farming stock and educated at St. Paul's School, London, Carr became headmaster of Hertford grammar school. Because he lacked a university education he was turned down as head of St. Paul's School. Marischal College, Aberdeen, awarded him the degree of LL.D. From 1805 till death he was honorary canon at Lincoln Cathedral. His main publications are: The third volume of *The Life and Opinions of Tristram Shandy, Gentleman*, 1760 (Laurence Sterne's comic novel, in nine volumes). *Filial Piety*, 1763 (a mock-heroic poem). *Extract of a Private Letter to a Critic*, 1764. *Epponina*, 1765 (a dramatic essay addressed to ladies). Translations from *Lucian*, 1773 (volume 2 in 1779 was followed by three more between 1779 and 1798). *Poems*, 1809. Some of his poems: "Bankruptcy Rendered Easy," "Derwent; an Ode," "Epigram on the Grave of Robespierre," "Farewell Lines to Bristol Hot Wells," "An Indian Massacre-Song," "Memories of Childhood," "Sonnet upon a Swedish Cottage."

Sources: *Dictionary of National Biography*. Electronic Edition, 1.1. Oxford University Press, 1997. *Oldpoetry* (www.oldpoetry.com). *The Columbia Granger's Index to Poetry*. 11th ed. *The Columbia Granger's World of Poetry*, Columbia University Press, 2005 (http://www.columbia-grangers.org). *The Life and Opinion of Tristram Shandy*. Laurence Sterne, 1995, The Folio Society. *The New Oxford Book of Eighteenth-Century Verse*. Roger Lonsdale, ed. Oxford University Press, 1984. *Tristram Shandy Online* (http://www.gifu-u.ac.jp/~masaru/TS/contents.html).

CARROLL, LEWIS (1832–1898)

Lewis Carroll is the pen name of Charles Lutwidge Dodgson, author and mathematician. Born at Daresbury, near Warrington — where his father was the minister and afterwards archdeacon of Richmond and one of the canons of Ripon Cathedral — he was educated at Rugby and Christ Church, Oxford, where he was lecturer in mathematics from 1855 to 1881. In 1861 he was ordained deacon, but never took priest's orders, partly perhaps from shyness, and partly from a constitutional stammer that prevented reading aloud. He wrote *Alice's Adventures in Wonderland* (1865) for Alice Liddell (afterwards Mrs. Reginald Hargreaves), the second daughter of Dean Liddell of Oxford. *Through the Looking Glass and What Alice Found There* was published in 1887. Both books were illustrated by Mr. (afterwards Sir) John Tenniel. Among his many other books was *Euclid and his Modern Rivals* (1879). Some of his poems: "A Long Tale," "A Mouse's Tale," "Disillusioned," "Four Riddles," "Limerick," "Solitude," "The Baker's Tale," "The Valley of the Shadow of Death," "You Are Old Father William." Mrs. Hargreaves died in 1934 at the age of 82 and is buried in the churchyard at Lyndhurst, Hampshire.

Sources: *Dictionary of National Biography*. Electronic Edition, 1.1. Oxford University Press, 1997. *Encyclopædia Britannica Ultimate Reference Suite DVD*, 2006. *The Faber Book of Comic Verse*. Michael Roberts and Janet Adam Smith, eds. Faber & Faber, 1978. *The Humorous Verse of Lewis Carroll*. Amereon Ltd., 1960. *The National Portrait Gallery* (www.npg.org.uk). *The Oxford Companion to English Literature*. 6th edition. Margaret Drabble, ed. Oxford University Press, 2000. *Westminster Abbey Official Guide* (no date).

CARSON, CIARAN GERARD (1948–)

Poet and novelist Carson was born in Belfast, Northern Ireland, where he still lives. After graduating from Queen's University, Belfast, he was traditional arts officer (1976–1994), then literary officer for the Arts Council of Northern Ireland until 1998. From 1998 to 2003 he was a freelance writer. Then he became the director of The Seamus Heaney (see entry) Centre of Poetry at Queen's University, Belfast. He is also an accomplished musician and the author of *Last Night's Fun: About Time, Food and Music* (1996), a study of Irish traditional music. His awards and prizes: Eric Gregory Award, 1978. Alice Hunt Bartlett Award, 1987. Irish Times Irish Literature Prize for Poetry, 1990. T.S. Eliot Prize, 1993. Yorkshire Post Book Award (Book of the Year), 1997. Cholmondeley Award, 2003. Forward Poetry Prize (Best Poetry Collection of the Year), 2003. Some of his publications: *The Irish for No*, 1987. *The New Estate and Other Poems*, 1988. *Belfast Confetti*, 1990. *First Language: Poems*, 1993. *Breaking News*, 2003. Some of his poems: "Asylum," "Bagpipe Music," "Calvin Klein's Obsession," "Last Orders," "Metamorphoses of Ovid (43 B.C.–A.D. 17)," "Night Patrol," "The Bomb Disposal."

Sources: *British Council Arts* (http://www.contemporarywriters.com). *Ireland in Poetry.* Charles Sullivan, ed. Harry N. Abrams, 1990. *Modern Irish Poetry.* Patrick Crotty, ed. The Blackstaff Press, 1995. *Poetry with an Edge.* Neil Astley, ed. Bloodaxe Books, 1988. *Poets from the North of Ireland.* Frank Ormsby, ed. The Blackstaff Press, 1990. *The Faber Book of Drink, Drinkers and Drinking.* Simon Rae, ed. Faber & Faber, 1991. *The Oxford Companion to English Literature.* 6th edition. Margaret Drabble, ed. Oxford University Press, 2000. *Who's Who.* London: A & C Black, 2005.

CARTER, ANGELA OLIVE (1940–1992)

Carter, formerly Stalker, author, poet and essayist, is known for her macabre use of symbolism, myths, legends and fairy tales in her books. Born in Eastbourne, Sussex, she studied medieval literature at Bristol University. Her main prose publications are: *Shadow Dance*, 1966. *The Magic Toyshop*, 1967 (filmed 1986). *Several Perceptions*, 1968. *The Infernal Desire Machines of Doctor Hoffman*, 1972. *The Passion of New Eve*, 1977. *Wise Children*, 1991. She also wrote short stories and five books on philosophy and edited five volumes, including *The Virago Book of Fairy Tales* (1990). Poem collections: *Unicorn*, 1966. *Five Quiet Shouters. My Cat in Her First Spring*, 1966.

Sources: *Encyclopædia Britannica Ultimate Reference Suite DVD*, 2006. *My Cat in Her First Spring: Sixties Press—Poetry* (http://www.sixtiespress.co.uk/poetry.htm). *The Angela Carter Unofficial Web Site* (http://perso.wanadoo.fr/andrew.milne/page%201.htm). *The National Portrait Gallery* (www.npg.org.uk). *The Oxford Companion to English Literature.* 6th edition. Margaret Drabble, ed. Oxford University Press, 2000.

CARTER, ELIZABETH (1717–1806)

Born in Deal, Kent, the daughter of a clergyman, she was one of the Blue Stocking Circle of intelligent, learned and sociable women who flourished in London in the second half of the 18th century. Her mother died when Elizabeth was young and her father supervised her education. She learned Latin, Greek, and Hebrew and many European languages. From 1734, under the pen-name "Eliza," she wrote poems regularly for the *Gentleman's Magazine.* Her main publications: *Poems on Particular Occasions*; 1738, 1762; 1766; 1776; 1777. *Sir Isaac Newton's Philosphy Explain'd for the Use of the Ladies*, 1739 (translated from the Italian). *All the works of Epictetus which are now extant*, 1758. In 1807 her nephew, Montagu Pennington, published her memoirs, in which were included the new edition of her poems, some miscellaneous essays in prose, and other writings. Some of her poems: "Ancreon Ode XXX," "Epitaph on a Young Lady," "In Diem Natalem, 1735," "Ode to Melancholy," "Ode to Wisdom," "Ode, to a Lady in London," "To a Gentleman, on His Intending to Cut Down a Grove to Enlarge His Prospect."

Sources: *Dictionary of National Biography.* Electronic Edition, 1.1. Oxford University Press, 1997. *Women Writing Before 1800: Elizabeth Carter* (1717–1806) (http://www.18thcenturyarchive.org/women/Carter/default.htm). *Encyclopædia Britannica Ultimate Reference Suite DVD*, 2006. *English Poetry: Author Search.* Chadwyck-Healey Ltd., 1995 (http://www.lib.utexas.edu:8080/search/epoetry/author.html). *The Bluestockings: Bibliography* (http://bartleby.school.aol.com/221/1500.html). *The Columbia Granger's Index to Poetry.* 11th ed. *The Columbia Granger's World of Poetry*, Columbia University Press, 2005 (http://www.columbiagrangers.org). *The Literary Encyclopedia* (www.LitEncyc.com). *The National Portrait Gallery* (www.npg.org.uk). *The Oxford Companion to English Literature.* 6th edition. Margaret Drabble, ed. Oxford University Press, 2000.

CARTWRIGHT, WILLIAM (1611–1643)

Brought up in Gloucestershire, Cartwright attended Westminster School as a king's scholar and in 1668 went to Christ Church, Oxford, then took holy orders. He was junior proctor of Oxford University in 1643. Accomplished in Greek, Latin, French and Italian, he was an excellent orator and an admirable poet. Cartwright's plays and poems were published in one volume by Humphrey Moseley in 1651. His successful play *The Royal Slave* was played before Charles I in 1636 and again at Hampton Court on command of the Queen. The king wore black on the day of Cartwright's funeral, so highly did he hold him in his esteem, and he was mourned by many great men of the day. Some of his poems: "A Dream Broke," "Beauty and Denial," "The Dead Sparrow," "Falsehood," "Francis and Saint Benedight," "Love But One," "A New Year's Gift," "No Platonic [or Platonique] Love," "On a Gentlewomans Silkhood," "On the Queen's Return from the Low Countries," "The Chambermaids Posset," "To Chloe Who for His Sake Wished Herself Younger," "Upon the Dramatick Poems of Mr. John Fletcher."

Sources: *Ben Jonson and the Cavalier Poets.* Hugh MacLaen, ed. New York: W.W. Norton & Company, 1974. *Dictionary of National Biography.* Electronic Edition, 1.1. Oxford University Press, 1997. *Encyclopædia Britannica Ultimate Reference Suite DVD*, 2006. *English Poetry: Author Search.* Chadwyck-Healey Ltd., 1995 (http://www.lib.utexas.edu:8080/search/epoetry/author.html). *The Columbia Granger's Index to Poetry.* 11th ed. *The Columbia Granger's World of Poetry*, Columbia University Press, 2005 (http://www.columbiagrangers.org). *The Gift of Great Poetry.* Lucien Stryk, ed. Regnery Gateway, 1992. *The Oxford Book of English Verse.* Christopher Ricks, ed. Oxford University Press, 1999. *The Oxford Companion to English Literature.* 6th edition. Margaret Drabble, ed. Oxford University Press, 2000.

CARY, ELIZABETH, VISCOUNTESS FALKLAND (circa. 1585–1639)

Born in Oxfordshire, the daughter of Sir Lawrence Tanfield, lord chief baron of the exchequer, she married Sir Henry Cary, lord deputy of Ireland (created first viscount Falkland in 1620) when she was fifteen. She taught herself French, Spanish, Italian, Latin, and Hebrew. She converted to the Catholic faith at the age of nineteen, but kept it secret for twenty years. When she declared her faith, this caused a rift between her and her husband, and they were given a Privy Council separation around 1625. She wrote the verse drama *The Tragedie of Mariam* (1613), the first known play in English by a woman. Possibly autobiographical, it is the story of a dictatorial husband and a non-compliant wife, a theme that is echoed in her poems. Some of her other poems: "Chorus," "To My Noble Friend, Mr. George Sandys," "To the Author," "To the Queenes Most Excellent Majestie."

Sources: *Dictionary of National Biography.* Electronic Edition, 1.1. Oxford University Press, 1997. *Early Modern Women Poets (1520–1700).* Jane Stevenson and Peter Davidson, ed. Oxford University Press, 2001. *The Columbia Granger's Index to Poetry.* 11th ed. *The Columbia Granger's World of Poetry,* Columbia University Press, 2005 (http://www.columbiagrangers.org). *The National Portrait Gallery* (www.npg.org.uk). *The Oxford Companion to English Literature.* 6th edition. Margaret Drabble, ed. Oxford University Press, 2000.

CARYLL, LORD JOHN (1625–1711)

Caryll came from an old-established Roman Catholic family from West Harting in Sussex. He was temporarily the English agent at the court of Rome before becoming secretary to Mary of Modena, the second wife of James II, in 1686. He followed James into exile, where he died and was buried in the church of the English Dominicans at Paris. He was a minor poet and author of a few plays during the reign of Charles II: *The English Princess, or the Death of Richard III*, 1666 (tragedy); and *Sir Salomon, or the Cautious Coxcomb,* 1671 (comedy). He played a part in the translation of Ovid's *Epistles* (1680) and in the collection of *Miscellany Poems* by Dryden (1683). He translated the "First Eclogue" of Virgil, and in 1700 he published anonymously *The Psalmes of David, translated from the Vulgat.* In his long and vicious poem "The Hypocrite, Written upon the Lord Shaftesbury in the Year 1678," he compares Shaftesbury with the inconsistent wind or to a changeable woman. "Naboth's Vineyard," in which he refers to wealth and power as "siren charms," is based on the story of Naboth in 1 Kings 21:7–29.

Sources: *Anthology of Poems on Affairs of State: Augustan Satirical Verse, 1660–1714.* George de F. Lord, ed. Yale University Press, 1975. *Dictionary of National Biography.* Electronic Edition, 1.1. Oxford University Press, 1997. *The Columbia Granger's Index to Poetry.* 11th ed. *The Columbia Granger's World of Poetry,* Columbia University Press, 2005

(http://www.columbiagrangers.org). *The Oxford Companion to English Literature.* 6th edition. Margaret Drabble, ed. Oxford University Press, 2000.

CASEMENT, SIR ROGER (1864–1916)

Born in Dublin the son of a Protestant father and Catholic mother, Casement served for many years as a distinguished diplomat. His criticism of how the native workers were treated forced the Belgian government to overhaul its administration of the Congo in 1908. He was knighted in 1911, left the diplomatic service due to in ill health, and retired to Dublin. In 1913 he helped form the Irish National Volunteers. In July 1914 he visited New York to drum up support for the organization. When war broke out, he hoped for German assistance in gaining Irish independence from Britain. Although he traveled to Germany, his hope for having German troops sent to Ireland did not materialize. When he returned to Ireland in April 1916 he was arrested, charged with treason and of being involved in the Easter Uprising, convicted on 29 June 1916, taken to Pentonville Prison in London and hanged on 3 August 1916. Some of his poems: "Forest Thoughts," "Fragment," "In the Streets of Catania," "Lost Youth."

Sources: *BBC—History—Roger Casement: Secrets of the Black Diaries* (http://www.bbc.co.uk/history/society_culture/protest_reform/casement_04.shtml). *Dictionary of National Biography.* Electronic Edition, 1.1. Oxford University Press, 1997. *Encyclopædia Britannica Ultimate Reference Suite DVD,* 2006. *First World War.com—Who's Who—Sir Roger Casement* (http://www.firstworldwar.com/bio/casement.htm). *The Columbia Granger's Index to Poetry.* 11th ed. *The Columbia Granger's World of Poetry,* Columbia University Press, 2005 (http://www.columbiagrangers.org). *The National Portrait Gallery* (www.npg.org.uk). *Treasury of Irish Religious Verse.* Patrick Murray, ed. Crossroad, 1986.

CASTILLO, JOHN (1792–1845)

Irish-born of Roman Catholic parents, Castillo (the Bard of the Dales) was brought up near Whitby, Yorkshire, and practiced the trade of a journeyman stone mason in the Cleveland area of northeast England. He joined the Wesleyan Methodist Society in 1818 and was a popular and energetic revivalist preacher in the North Riding. Most of what he wrote is of a religious nature and written in the Cleveland dialect. His popular (very long) poem "Awd Isaac" occupied the first place in his volume of poems, *Awd Isaac, The Steeplechase, and Other Poems* (1831). A complete edition of his poems was published in 1850. His other main publications: *A Specimen of the Bilsdale Dialect,* 1831. *The Bard of the Dales,* 1858. *The Lucky Dream* is a long poem written in dialect and tells the story of being welcomed as a king by a friend on a freezing night on the moors. Some of his other poems: "Intemperance," "Merry Christmas as Kept in England," "On Friendship," "The Broken Guide Post," "The Leisure Hour," "To a Fox Taken in a Trap," "To a Withered Flower!" "Wisdom: The Traveller's Consolation."

Sources: *Dictionary of National Biography.* Electronic Edition, 1.1. Oxford University Press, 1997. *English Poetry: Author Search.* Chadwyck-Healey Ltd., 1995 (http://www.lib.utexas.edu:8080/search/epoetry/author.html). *Yorkshire Dialect Poems edited by FW Moorman* (http://www.hyphenologist.co.uk/songs/ydp.html).

CASWALL, EDWARD (1814–1878)

Hampshire-born clergyman, he was educated at Marlborough College and Brasenose College, Oxford. Ordained as an Anglican priest in 1840, he converted to Roman Catholicism in 1847, and when his wife died in 1851 he joined the Oratory of St. Philip Neri under Dr. (afterwards Cardinal) Newman. His writing career started while at Oxford, when he published two pamphlets under the pen name "Scriblerus Redivivus": *Pluck Examination Papers* (1836); *A new Art, teaching how to be plucked, being a treatise after the fashion of Aristotle* (1837). Later, *Sermons on the Seen and Unseen* (1846). Besides poems (mainly sacred), he wrote several hymns and translated others, many of which are included in most modern hymnbooks. His translation from St. Bernard, "Jesus, The Very Thought of Thee," is one of the finest. "*See Amid the Winter's Snow*" is a popular Christmas carol. "The Good Shepherd" is set to a German melody. Some of his other poems: "Associations with Places," "Autumn," "Before Our Lady in the Temple," "Captive Linnet," "Lines Written on Leaving Oxford," "The Dependence of all Things on God," "The Angels," "The Third Degree of Humility."

Sources: *Catholic Encyclopedia* (http://www.newadvent.org). *Dictionary of National Biography.* Electronic Edition, 1.1. Oxford University Press, 1997. *Encyclopædia Britannica Ultimate Reference Suite DVD*, 2006. *English Poetry: Author Search.* Chadwyck-Healey Ltd., 1995 (http://www.lib.utexas.edu:8080/search/epoetry/author.html). *Poems by Edward Caswall.* Thomas Richardson and Son, 1861. *The Cyber Hymnal* (http://www.cyberhymnal.org/index.htm). *The National Portrait Gallery* (www.npg.org.uk).

CAUSLEY, CHARLES (1917–2003)

Prize-winning poet, playwright, broadcaster and children's author. Born in Cornwall, he lived and worked for most of his life there as a teacher, apart from service in the Royal Navy from 1940 to 1946. His early life was influenced by watching his father die of tuberculosis as a result of the First World War, and the presence of shell-shocked war veterans in his home town. After the war, having trained as a teacher, he returned to Launceston grammar school. He was awarded an honorary doctorate from Exeter University and appointed commander of the British Empire in 1986. Some of his publications: *Hands to Dance*, 1951 (revised and enlarged in 1979 as *Hands to Dance and Skylark*; short stories of his military service). *Farewell, Aggie Weston*, 1951 (poems; Agnes Weston was a founder of sailors' hostels). *Survivor's Leave*, 1953 (poems). Some of his poems: "Armistice Day," "For an Ex-Far East Prisoner of War," "H.M.S. Glory at Sydney," "Loss of an Oil Tanker," "On Seeing a Poet of the First World War on the Station at Abbeville," "Song of the Dying Gunner A.A.1," "Ten Types of Hospital Visitor."

Sources: *Life and Works of Charles Causley* (http://pedia.newsfilter.co.uk/wikipedia/c/ch/charles_causley.html). *Most Unfashionable Poet Alive: Charles Causley. A Review by Dana Gioia* (http://www.danagioia.net/essays/ecausley.htm). *Obituary of Charles Causley: Telegraph News* (www.opinion.telegraph.co.uk/). *Poetry of the World Wars.* Michael Foss, ed. Peter Bedrick Books, 1990. *The Biography and Burial of Charles Causley* (www.poetsgraves.co.uk/causley.htm). *The Columbia Granger's Index to Poetry.* 11th ed. *The Columbia Granger's World of Poetry*, Columbia University Press, 2005 (http://www.columbiagrangers.org). *The Naked Astronaut: Poems on Birth and Birthdays.* Ren Graziani, ed. Faber and Faber, 1983. *The National Portrait Gallery* (www.npg.org.uk). *The Oxford Book of Christmas Poems.* Michael Harrison and Christopher Stuart-Clark, eds. Oxford University Press, 1983. *The Oxford Companion to English Literature.* 6th edition. Margaret Drabble, ed. Oxford University Press, 2000. *Tongues of Fire: An Anthology of Religious and Poetic Experience.* Karen Armstrong, ed. Penguin Books, 1987.

CAVENDISH, MARGARET, DUCHESS OF NEWCASTLE (1623–1673)

Her father (Sir Thomas Lucas) supported Charles I during the Civil War, and in 1644 Margaret was forced into exile in France as Queen Henrietta's maid of honor; she married Sir William Cavendish in 1645 as his second wife. After the Restoration he was created 1st Duke of Newcastle in 1665. Her first volume of poetry, *Poems and Fancies*, published in 1653, made her a literary celebrity. She went on to publish more poetry, plays, romances, biographies, and a biography of her husband. She was criticized for being a woman writer and for her outlandish, sometimes masculine, clothes. A monument was erected to the Duke and Duchess in the North Transept of Westminster Abbey. The opening lines of "The Ruine of this Island" have a prophetic ring: that England will rue the day when She becomes too proud to pray. Some of her other poems: "Nature's Cook," "Of Cold Winds," "Of the Theme of Love," "The Claspe," "The Common Fate of Books," "The Fort or Castle of Hope," "The Pastime of the Queen of Fairies," "The Soul's Garment."

Sources: *Dictionary of National Biography.* Electronic Edition, 1.1. Oxford University Press, 1997. *English Poetry: Author Search.* Chadwyck-Healey Ltd., 1995 (http://www.lib.utexas.edu:8080/search/epoetry/author.html). *The Columbia Granger's Index to Poetry.* 11th ed. *The Columbia Granger's World of Poetry,* Columbia University Press, 2005 (http://www.columbiagrangers.org). *The National Portrait Gallery* (www.npg.org.uk). *The Oxford Companion to English Literature.* 6th edition. Margaret Drabble, ed. Oxford University Press, 2000. *The Penguin Book of Renaissance Verse 1509–1659.* David Norbrook, ed. Penguin Books, 1992. *Westminster Abbey Official Guide* (no date).

CAWTHORN, JAMES (1719–1761)

The son of an upholsterer, he was educated at the grammar schools of Sheffield and Kirkby Lonsdale. After graduating from Clare Hall, Cambridge, he became a teacher, eventually becoming headmaster of Tonbridge grammar school, Kent. He was thrown from his horse and killed and was buried in Tonbridge church, where a marble slab with a Latin epitaph was put up for him. Verses were printed to his memory by Lord Eardley in the *Gentleman's Magazine,* xxxi, 232. His "Abelard and Heloise" was published in the *Poetical Calendar* in 1746 and his volume *Poems* was published in 1771. His literary career started at school when he published a periodical, *The Tea-Table.* He is known to have published the *Perjured Lovers* while at Sheffield, and soon afterward, "Meditation" in the *Gentleman's Magazine.* His poems were not collected until 1771, when they were published by subscription. His paraphrase of Job 38 was published in Volume 6 of the *Gentleman's Magazine* (1736). Some of his other poems: "Of Taste; an Essay," "The Englishman at the Table," "Wit and Learning." (Wit is the name of the cheeky child of Greek mythology who played all sorts of pranks on his elders).

Sources: *Dictionary of National Biography.* Electronic Edition, 1.1. Oxford University Press, 1997. *Eighteenth-Century English Verse.* Dennis Davison, ed. Penguin Books, 1988. *English Poetry: Author Search.* Chadwyck-Healey Ltd., 1995 (http://www.lib.utexas.edu:8080/search/epoetry/author.html). *Gentleman's Magazine* (http://etext.lib.virginia.edu/etcbin/browse-gm2?id=2GM1736). *The Columbia Granger's Index to Poetry.* 11th ed. *The Columbia Granger's World of Poetry,* Columbia University Press, 2005 (http://www.columbiagrangers.org). *The New Oxford Book of Eighteenth Century Verse.* Roger Lonsdale, ed. Oxford University Press, 1984. *The Oxford Book of Comic Verse.* John Gross, ed. Oxford University Press, 1994. *The Oxford Book of English Verse.* Christopher Ricks, ed. Oxford University Press, 1999.

CENNICK, JOHN (1718–1755)

Born in Reading, Berkshire, to Church of England parents, at a young age he became linked to the Methodists in the very early days of the movement and gave up a career as a surveyor. John Wesley appointed him a teacher at Kingswood School, Bristol, and it was there where he preached his first public sermon on June 14, 1739. Because of doctrinal differences, he left the Wesleys and aligned himself with George Whitefield. Later still he joined the Moravian Brethren and was ordained by them in 1749. He is buried in the Moravian Burial Ground, Chelsea, England. He published several volumes of sermons and four collections of hymns: *Sacred Hymns for the Children of God in the Day of their Pilgrimage,* 1741, *Sacred Hymns for the Use of Religious Societies,* 1743, *A Collection of Sacred Hymns,* 1749, and *Hymns for the Honor of Jesus Christ.* 1754. Some of his hymns: "Be Present at Our Table, Lord," Children of the Heavenly King," "Ere I Sleep, for Every Favor," "Lo, He Comes with Clouds Descending," "We Sing to Thee, Thou Son of God," "We Thank Thee, Lord."

Sources: *Dictionary of National Biography.* Electronic Edition, 1.1. Oxford University Press, 1997. *Papers of John Cennick — Collection 150* (www.wheaton.edu/bgc/archives/GUIDES/150.htm). *The Cyber Hymnal* (http://www.cyberhymnal.org/index.htm). *The National Portrait Gallery* (www.npg.org.uk). *The Reformed University Fellowship (RUF) Hymnbook* (http://igracemusic.com/igracemusic/hymnbook).

CHALKHILL, JOHN (fl. 1600)

Not much is known of this minor poet, except that he was at Trinity College, Cambridge, in 1610, and is the author several poems. Izaac Walton's *Compleat Angler* (1653–1655) contains two of Chalkhill's poems: "Condon's Song" (referred to as "O, The Sweet Contentment") and "The Angler" (referred to as "O, the Gallant Fisher's Life"). Thirty years later Chalkhill published *Thealma and Clearchus, A Pastoral History in smooth and easie Verse* (1683), edited by Izaac Walton. Walton, in his preface, says of Chalkhill, "And I have also this truth to say of the author, that he was in his time a man generally known and as well belov'd; for he was humble and obliging in his behaviour, a gentleman, a scholar, very innocent and prudent: and indeed his whole life was useful, quiet, and virtuous" (DNB).

Sources: *Dictionary of National Biography.* Electronic Edition, 1.1. Oxford University Press, 1997. *The Columbia Granger's Index to Poetry.* 11th ed. *The Columbia Granger's World of Poetry,* Columbia University Press, 2005 (http://www.columbiagrangers.org). *The Home Book of Verse.* Burton Egbert Stevenson, ed. New York: Henry Holt and Company, 1953. *The Oxford Book of Seventeenth Century Verse.* H.J.C. Grierson and G. Bullough, eds. Oxford University Press, 1934. *The Oxford Companion to English Literature.* 6th edition. Margaret Drabble, ed. Oxford University Press, 2000.

CHAPMAN, GEORGE (?1559–1634)

Born near Hitchin, Hertfordshire, it is thought he attended Oxford University, Cambridge or both, but whichever, he was an excellent Greek and Latin scholar. William Browne, in the second book of *Britannia's Pastorals*, styles Chapman "The Learned Shepheard of Faire Hitching Hill" (DNB). By 1585 he was working in London for the wealthy commoner Sir Ralph Sadler and probably served as a volunteer in the Netherlands. His Homer translations inspired the sonnet of John Keats, *On First Looking into Chapman's Homer* (1815). His main publications: *The Shadow of Night, Two Poeticall Hymnes*, 1593. *Ovids Banquet of Sence*, 1595. *All Fools*, 1605. *Eastward Ho!* 1605 (written with Ben Jonson and John Marston. The authors were imprisoned because James I found the play offensive to his fellow Scots). *Bussy D'Ambois*, 1607. *The Conspiracy and Tragedy of Byron*, 1608. *Iliad* (translation) 1612. *Odyssey*, 1614–1615 (translation). Some of his poems: "Bridal Song," "Certain Ancient Greek Epigrams," "Complimentary Sonnets," "For Good Men," "Helen and the Elders," "Of Friendship," "Of Great Men," "The Amorous Zodiac," "Winter."

Sources: *Chapman's Homer: The Iliad*. Steven Shankman, ed. Princeton University Press, 1956. *Dictionary of National Biography*. Electronic Edition, 1.1. Oxford University Press, 1997. *Encyclopædia Britannica Ultimate Reference Suite DVD*, 2006. *English Poetry: Author Search*. Chadwyck-Healey Ltd., 1995 (http://www.lib.utexas.edu:8080/search/epoetry/author.html), *I–V*. W.H. Auden, and Norman Holmes Pearson, ed. Viking Press, 1950. *The Columbia Granger's Index to Poetry*. 11th ed. *The Columbia Granger's World of Poetry*, Columbia University Press, 2005 (http://www.columbiagrangers.org). *The New Oxford Book of English Verse, 1250–1950*. Helen Gardner, ed. Oxford University Press, 1972. *The Oxford Companion to English Literature*. 6th edition. Margaret Drabble, ed. Oxford University Press, 2000.

CHATTERTON, THOMAS (1752–1770)

Born in Bristol to a poor schoolmaster, he was considered a dull boy at school, but by the age of eight he was a pupil at Colston's Hospital, the bluecoat school at Bristol. He left the school at fifteen and was apprenticed to a Bristol attorney, but finding his position intolerable, with his master dismissive of him and his poetry, he went to London. Despair set in at his not being able to make a decent living. Half-starved, he ended his life with arsenic. His first poem, "On the Last Epiphany, or Christ coming to Judgment," was published in *Felix Farley's Bristol Journal* in 1763. Soon after that he paraphrased the ninth chapter of Job and several chapters of Isaiah. His poems were written in an imitation of medieval style and he invented an entire medieval setting to go with them. He even composed "historical" documents and made hundreds of drawings, including maps, to lend authenticity. Some of his other poems: "An African Song," "A Hymn for Christmas Day,"

"Minstrel's Song," "A New Song," "Chatterton's Will," "The Advice," "The Methodist."

Sources: *Dictionary of National Biography*. Electronic Edition, 1.1. Oxford University Press, 1997. *Encyclopædia Britannica Ultimate Reference Suite DVD*, 2006. *English Poetry: Author Search*. Chadwyck-Healey Ltd., 1995 (http://www.lib.utexas.edu:8080/search/epoetry/author.html). Many of Chatterton's poems are at Oldpoetry (www.oldpoetry.com). *The Columbia Granger's Index to Poetry*. 11th ed. *The Columbia Granger's World of Poetry*, Columbia University Press, 2005 (http://www.columbiagrangers.org). *The London Book of English Verse*. Herbert Read, and Barbara Dobree, ed. MacMillan, 1952. *The National Portrait Gallery* (www.npg.org.uk). *The New Oxford Book of English Verse, 1250–1950*. Helen Gardner, ed. Oxford University Press, 1972. *The Oxford Companion to English Literature*. 6th edition. Margaret Drabble, ed. Oxford University Press, 2000.

CHAUCER, GEOFFREY (?1340–1400)

Little is known about Chaucer's life but that he was the son of a rich London wine merchant and that he was a page in the household of Prince Lionel, later duke of Clarence, for many years. In 1359–60 he was with the army of Edward III in France, where he was captured by the French but ransomed. He married a lady-in-waiting to Philippa of Hainault, Edward III's queen. Between 1370 and 1378, Chaucer was frequently on diplomatic missions to the Continent. From 1374 on he held several official positions, and in 1386 he was knight of the shire for Kent. He was the greatest English poet before Shakespeare and first great poet to be buried in the South Transept of Westminster Abbey in what became known as Poets' Corner. His main works: *The Book of the Duchess*, 1369. *The House of Fame*, 1370 (circa). *Troilus and Criseyde*, 1385 (circa). *The Canterbury Tales* (post 1387). Some of his other poems: "The Complaint of Chaucer to His Empty Purse," "The Complaint unto Pity," "The Hous of Fame," "The Parlement of Foules," "To Rosamounde," "Womanly Noblesse."

Sources: *Dictionary of National Biography*. Electronic Edition, 1.1. Oxford University Press, 1997. *Encyclopædia Britannica Ultimate Reference Suite DVD*, 2006. *English Poetry: Author Search*. Chadwyck-Healey Ltd., 1995 (http://www.lib.utexas.edu:8080/search/epoetry/author.html). *Poemhunter* (www.poemhunter.com). *The Columbia Granger's Index to Poetry*. 11th ed. *The Columbia Granger's World of Poetry*, Columbia University Press, 2005 (http://www.columbiagrangers.org). *The National Portrait Gallery* (www.npg.org.uk). *The Oxford Companion to English Literature*. 6th edition. Margaret Drabble, ed. Oxford University Press, 2000. *The Riverside Chaucer*. F.N. Robinson, ed. Houghton Mifflin, 1987. *Westminster Abbey Official Guide* (no date).

CHESTER, SIR ROBERT (?1566–?1640)

Not much is known about this poet. His wife was Anne Capell, daughter of Sir Henry Capell of Essex;

they had one child, Sir Edward, and he was knighted in 1603. His long poem, *Love's Marty: or, Rosalin's Complaint, allegorically shadowing the truth of Love in the constant Fate of the Phenix and Turtle,* was published in 1601. The Phoenix and the Turtle — an allegorical poem on the mystical nature of love by William Shakespeare, was appended to Chester's *Love's Martyr.* Two other poems are credited to him: "The Authour's request to the Phenix," "To the Kind Reader" (which, in 1611, was reissued as *The Anuals of Great Brittaine*; parts of the poem are thought to relate to Queen Elizabeth and the Earl of Essex). Some of his poems (many of them short): "A poore sheapheards profecye," "And if my loue shall be releeu'd by thee," "Diana in thy bosome plast her bower," "I haue no loue, but you my Doue," "Seeing that my hart made choise of thee," and "Though death from life my bodie part."

Sources: *Dictionary of National Biography.* Electronic Edition, 1.1. Oxford University Press, 1997. *Elizabethan Lyrics.* Norman Ault, ed. William Sloane Associates, 1949. *English Poetry: Author Search.* Chadwyck-Healey Ltd., 1995 (http://www.lib.utexas.edu:8080/search/epoetry/author.html). *The Columbia Granger's Index to Poetry.* 11th ed. *The Columbia Granger's World of Poetry,* Columbia University Press, 2005 (http://www.columbiagrangers.org). *The complete Love's Martyr,* is on http://phoenixandturtle.net/loves_martyr.htm.

CHESTERFIELD, PHILIP DORMER STANHOPE, 4TH EARL OF (1694–1773)

Educated privately, then at Trinity Hall, Cambridge, he became a member of Parliament, distinguished statesman, diplomat and ambassador to the Hague. In 1715 he was appointed gentleman of the bedchamber to George, prince of Wales (later George II). He negotiated the marriage of William, prince of Orange, with Anne, princess royal of England. He was the patron of many struggling authors. Dickens caricatured him as Sir John Chester in *Barnaby Rudge* (1841). He is the author of several literary criticisms. Some of his poems: "Advice to a Lady in Autumn," "On Lord Ila's Improvements, near Hounslow Heath," "On Miss Eleanor Ambrose, a Celebrated Beauty in Dublin," "Verses Written in a Lady's Sherlock 'Upon Death.'"

Sources: *Dictionary of National Biography.* Electronic Edition, 1.1. Oxford University Press, 1997. *Encyclopædia Britannica Ultimate Reference Suite DVD,* 2006. *The Columbia Granger's Index to Poetry.* 11th ed. *The Columbia Granger's World of Poetry,* Columbia University Press, 2005 (http://www.columbiagrangers.org). *The Faber Book of Useful Verse.* Simon Brett, ed. Faber and Faber, 1981. *The National Portrait Gallery* (www.npg.org.uk). *The Oxford Companion to English Literature.* 6th edition. Margaret Drabble, ed. Oxford University Press, 2000.

CHESTERTON, GILBERT KEITH (1874–1936)

Born in London, the elder son of Edward Chesterton, head of a Kensington firm of auctioneers and estate agents, he was educated at St. Paul's School. He attended the Slade School of Art, studied English literature at London University, and became a journalist. He was received into the Roman Catholic Church in 1922. The friendship he and Hillaire Belloc developed earned them the nickname of "Chesterbelloc." His novel *The Napoleon of Notting Hill* (1904) was a statement against imperialism, sparked by the Boer War. In addition to his prolific poetry output, he was a literary critic of many well-known writers and the author of many short stories and of the *Father Brown* detective series. His volume of verse, *The Wild Knight* — illustrated by the author — was published in 1900. Some of his poems: "A Broad Minded Bishop Rebukes the Verminous St. Francis," "'A Thank-You' for Coming to Tea," "A Vision of Edens," "A Wedding in War-Time," "Absent Friends," "Advice to a Young Man on Writing Verses," "The Babe Unborn," "The Ballad of the White Horse," "The Donkey," "The Secret People."

Sources: *Collected Works of G.K. Chesterton.* Aidan Mackey, ed. Ignatius, 1994. *Dictionary of National Biography.* Electronic Edition, 1.1. Oxford University Press, 1997. *Encyclopædia Britannica Ultimate Reference Suite DVD,* 2006. *The Columbia Granger's Index to Poetry.* 11th ed. *The Columbia Granger's World of Poetry,* Columbia University Press, 2005 (http://www.columbiagrangers.org). *The National Portrait Gallery* (www.npg.org.uk). *The Oxford Companion to English Literature.* 6th edition. Margaret Drabble, ed. Oxford University Press, 2000.

CHILDISH, BILLY (1959–)

Born in Chatham, Kent, he left school at 16, worked as an apprentice stonemason at the Naval Dockyard at Chatham, then spent time at St. Martin's School of Art to study painting. In spite of suffering from dyslexia, he has published over 40 collections of his poetry, recorded over 100 full-length independent LPs, produced over 2,500 paintings and has become a cult figure in America, Europe and Japan. In his poems and in his novel (one of three) *My Fault* (Virgin Books, 2005), he details his love life and childhood sexual abuse. In 2000 he formed the musical group the Buff Medways, named after a type of poultry bred in his home town. He continues to live and work in Chatham. Some of his publications: *The Medway Poets,* 1980. *Poetry Like Dirt,* 1983. *Poems From the Barrier Block,* 1984. *Poems of Laughter and Violence, Selected Poetry 1981–86,* 1992. *In 5 minits you'll know me, Selected poems 1985—1995.* 1997. Some of his poems and lyrics: "A

Terrible Thing," "Carreer Opportunities," "Girl from '62," "I Am the Strange Hero of Hunger," "The Strangest Thing."

Sources: *Three Poems by Billy Childish* (http://www.3ammagazine.com/poetry/2002_jun/three_poems.html). *Biography of Billy Childish: The Poets, Part 1, Billy Childish* (http://www.bbc.co.uk/radio4/arts/heardallaboutit_poets1.shtml). *The Billy Childish Home Page* (http://www.theebillychildish.com/index.htm). *Wikipedia, the Free Encyclopedia* (http://en.wikipedia.org/wiki/Wikipedia).

CHUDLEIGH, LADY MARY (1656–1710)

An early feminist who was inspired by Mary Astell (see entry), often referred to as "the first English feminist." From Devonshire, she married Sir George Chudleigh but the marriage was not happy. She found pleasure in reading and writing poetry, and was one of the women who formed part of the literary circle centered around Dryden. She corresponded with Mary Astell, and her poem, "The Ladies' Defence" (1701), according to *The Oxford Companion to English Literature*, was in response to Astell's poem "Some Reflections on Marriage." *The Dictionary of National Biography* says that it was a response "to a sermon on 'Conjugal Duty' preached by Mr. Sprint." In her poem "To the Ladies," she draws attention to the status of the "wife," who differs from a servant only in name. It refers to her marriage ceremony as a "fatal knot" and says the word "obey" makes the man supreme. Her other publications are: *Poems on Several Occasions*, 1703. *Essays upon several Subjects*, 1710. *Poems*, 1713 and 1722 (posthumous editions). Some of her other poems: "Solitude," "The Offering: Part One," "The Resolve," "The Wish," "To Almystrea."

Sources: *Biography of Mary Lee Chudleigh; Sunshine for Women* (http://www.pinn.net/~sunshine/march99/chudle.html). *Dictionary of National Biography*. Electronic Edition, 1.1. Oxford University Press, 1997. *English Poetry: Author Search*. Chadwyck-Healey Ltd., 1995 (http://www.lib.utexas.edu:8080/search/epoetry/author.html). *Poemhunter* (www.poemhunter.com). *The Columbia Granger's Index to Poetry*. 11th ed. *The Columbia Granger's World of Poetry*, Columbia University Press, 2005 (http://www.columbiagrangers.org). *The Oxford Companion to English Literature*. 6th edition. Margaret Drabble, ed. Oxford University Press, 2000. *The Poems and Prose of Mary, Lady Chudleigh*. Margaret J.M. Ezell, ed. Oxford University Press, 1993.

CHURCHILL, CHARLES (1731–1764)

London-born Churchill, the son of a clergyman, was educated at Westminster School, although it is uncertain that he went to Cambridge University. He was ordained more from necessity than conviction or desire and succeeded his father as curate of St. John's Westminster in 1758. His fortunes changed with the publication of his satire *The Rosciad*, influenced by Dryden, and published at his own risk in 1761. He resigned his clerical position in 1763 and his pen became something to be feared in literary circles. Some of his other publications, mainly satires: *The Apology*, 1761. *The Prophecy of Famine*, 1762. *The Author*, 1763. *The Epistle to William Hogarth*, 1763. *The Duellist*, 1764 (a defense of his friend John Wilkes, wounded in a duel, *The Times*, 1764). The epitaph on his gravestone is "Life to the last enjoyed, here Churchill lies," lines from his poem "The Candidate." Some of his other poems: "Character of a Critic," "Dedication," "European Crimes," "Independence," "Night; an Epistle to Robert Lloyd," "The Ghost," "The Journey," "The Pains of Education."

Sources: *Dictionary of National Biography*. Electronic Edition, 1.1. Oxford University Press, 1997. *Encyclopædia Britannica Ultimate Reference Suite DVD*, 2006. *English Poetry: Author Search*. Chadwyck-Healey Ltd., 1995 (http://www.lib.utexas.edu:8080/search/epoetry/author.html). *Poems of Charles Churchill*. Barnes and Noble, 1933. *The Columbia Granger's Index to Poetry*. 11th ed. *The Columbia Granger's World of Poetry*, Columbia University Press, 2005 (http://www.columbiagrangers.org). *The National Portrait Gallery* (www.npg.org.uk). *The Oxford Book of Satirical Verse*. Geoffrey Grigson, ed. Oxford University Press, 1980. *The Oxford Companion to English Literature*. 6th edition. Margaret Drabble, ed. Oxford University Press, 2000.

CHURCHYARD, THOMAS (?1520–1604)

Born at Shrewsbury, in his youth Churchyard was attached to the household of Henry Howard, Earl of Surrey. He was a soldier and was taken prisoner several times and served under Lord Grey at the siege of Leith in 1560. In a poem entitled "A tragicall discours of the vnhappie mans life" (printed in *The Firste Part of Churchyardes Chippes* (1575), he gives a long account of his adventures. He issued a number of broadsheets, tracts and small volumes in verse and prose, several containing autobiographic pieces. *Generall Rehearsall of Warres (Churchyard's Choise)* (1579) reviews the deeds of the soldiers and sailors of England from the time of Henry VIII. His descriptions of the sieges of Leith and Edinburgh are among the best of his narrative poems. Possibly his most noteworthy publication is *The Worthines of Wales* (1587), a long chorographical poem of historical interest. He also translated three books of Ovid's *Tristia*. He was buried at St. Margaret's, Westminster. Some of his other poems: "A Farewell to a Fondling," "A Fayned Fancy betweene the Spider and the Gowte," "A Musicall Consort," "A Tale of a Friar and a Shoemaker's Wife."

Sources: *Dictionary of National Biography*. Electronic Edition, 1.1. Oxford University Press, 1997. *English Poetry:*

Author Search. Chadwyck-Healey Ltd., 1995 (http://www. lib.utexas.edu:8080/search/epoetry/author.html). *Great Books Online* (www.bartleby.com). *The Columbia Granger's Index to Poetry.* 11th ed. *The Columbia Granger's World of Poetry,* Columbia University Press, 2005 (http://www. columbiagrangers.org). *The Oxford Companion to English Literature.* 6th edition. Margaret Drabble, ed. Oxford University Press, 2000. *The Penguin Book of Renaissance Verse 1509–1659.* David Norbrook, ed. Penguin Books, 1992.

CIBBER, COLLEY (1671–1757)

Cibber's father was Caius Cibber, the sculptor. Although his parents hoped he would be a clergyman, he turned to the stage in 1690 and became a popular comedian, wrote or adapted some thirty plays, and became manager of Drury Lane Theatre. His appointment as poet laureate in 1730 was not a popular choice. Alexander Pope satirized him as the "Dunce" in his mock-epic poem *Dunciad* (1743). Cibber's first play, *Love's Last Shift* (1696), is regarded as the first sentimental comedy. In 1700 he produced his popular adaptation of Shakespeare's *Richard III.* His final stage appearance was in his own adaptation of Shakespeare's *King John* in 1745. His autobiography, *An Apology for the Life of Mr. Colley Cibber,* was published in 1740. His poem "The Blind Boy" was set to music by Schubert. It paints the picture of a boy, though asking "What is light," also says that he will not bemoan what he cannot have, yet when he sings he is a king.

Sources: *Dictionary of National Biography.* Electronic Edition, 1.1. Oxford University Press, 1997. *Encyclopædia Britannica Ultimate Reference Suite DVD,* 2006. *Great Books Online* (www.bartleby.com). *Colley Cibber, Texts Set to Music* (http://www.recmusic.org/lieder/c/cibber). *The Columbia Granger's Index to Poetry.* 11th ed. *The Columbia Granger's World of Poetry,* Columbia University Press, 2005 (http://www.columbiagrangers.org). *The National Portrait Gallery* (www.npg.org.uk). *The New Oxford Book of Eighteenth-Century Verse.* Roger Lonsdale, ed. Oxford University Press, 1984. *The Oxford Companion to English Literature.* 6th edition. Margaret Drabble, ed. Oxford University Press, 2000.

CLANCHY, KATE (1965–)

Born in Glasgow, Scotland, she was educated in Edinburgh and Oxford. She lived in London's East End for several years before moving to Oxford, where she now works as a teacher, journalist and freelance writer. Her poetry features regularly in magazines and in *The Scotsman,* the *New Statesman* and *Poetry Review.* She also writes for radio and broadcasts on the World Service and BBC Radio 3 and 4. She teaches creative writing at the Arvon Foundation (with centers in various parts of Britain), and was poet in residence for the Red Cross in the U.K. as part of the Poetry Society's Poetry Places scheme. She was a member of the new Images writ-

ers' exchange to Australia, organized by the British Council and the Arts Council of England. Her collection *Slattern* (1995) won four major literary awards and *Samarkand* (1999) won the 1999 Scottish Arts Council Book Award. Some of her poems: "Deadman's Shoes," "For a Wedding," "Foreign," "Love," "On Breast-Feeding," "One Night When We Paused Half-Way," "Poem for a Man with No Sense of Smell," "Recognition," "Rejoice in the Lamb."

Sources: *All the Poems You Need to Say Hello by Kate Clanchy.* Picador, 2004. *British Council Arts* (http://www. contemporarywriters.com). Kate Clanchy, Poem for a Man with No Sense of Smell (http://www.thepoem.co.uk/ poems/clanchy.htm). *Making for Planet Alice: New Women Poets.* Maura Dooley, ed. Bloodaxe Books, 1997. *Newborn, by Kate Clanchy*—poems covering pregnancy, birth and caring for a new baby. Picador, 2005. *The Columbia Granger's Index to Poetry.* 11th ed. *The Columbia Granger's World of Poetry,* Columbia University Press, 2005 (http://www.columbiagrangers.org). *The Oxford Companion to English Literature.* 6th edition. Margaret Drabble, ed. Oxford University Press, 2000.

CLANVOW, SIR JOHN (circa 1341–1391)

Clanvow, born possibly near Hereford, was a soldier who fought several campaigns in France. He was knight bachelor to the Earl of Hereford and entered the service of Edward III on Hereford's death in 1373. Then later he was in the service of Richard II and held political offices in England and abroad. He was one of the group of "chamber knights," the most trusted executants of the royal will. He died near Istanbul. Clanvow wrote a religious tract in prose, "The Two Ways," in which he condemns luxury and worldliness and exhorts his readers to obey the commandments and to love God. His main work is "The Cuckoo and the Nightingale or The Book of Cupid God of Love." In the poem Clanvow praises the God of Love, who can make the high even higher, yet bring down the low down to the grave, and hard hearts he can make free. It is love that makes the birds sing in the trees and the branches bust into bud and bloom.

Sources: *Dictionary of National Biography.* Electronic Edition, 1.1. Oxford University Press, 1997. *Encyclopædia Britannica Ultimate Reference Suite DVD,* 2006. *The Columbia Granger's Index to Poetry.* 11th ed. *The Columbia Granger's World of Poetry,* Columbia University Press, 2005 (http://www.columbiagrangers.org). *The Oxford Companion to English Literature.* 6th edition. Margaret Drabble, ed. Oxford University Press, 2000. *The Penguin Book of Bird Poetry.* Peggy Munsterberg, ed. 1984.

CLARE, JOHN (1793–1864)

Born into a poor farming family near Peterborough, Northamptonshire, Clare went to work at the age of seven. The son of a ballad singer, he wrote his first poems on his mother's sugar bags. Clare wrote about everything in the countryside: birds, animals, flowers, people, the months and seasons. By the mid-nineteenth century, the fashion for rural poetry waned, so did Clare's popularity. In 1837 he was committed to an asylum in Essex. He escaped in July 1841 and walked the 80 miles home, eating grass by the roadside. At the end of 1841 he was certified insane and spent the rest of his life at St. Andrew's Asylum, Northampton, writing some of his best poetry. A limestone and slate tablet commemorates him in Poets' Corner, Westminster Abbey. His main publications: *Poems Descriptive of Rural Life and Scenery,* 1820. *The Village Minstrel,* 1821. *The Shepherd's Calendar: With Village Stories, and Other Poems,* 1827. *The Rural Muse,* 1835. Some of his other poems: "Autumn," "Badger," "Early Nightingale," "Little Trotty Wagtail," "Secret Love," "The Beanfield," "The Firetail's Nest."

Sources: *Dictionary of National Biography.* Electronic Edition, 1.1. Oxford University Press, 1997. *Encyclopædia Britannica Ultimate Reference Suite DVD,* 2006. *English Poetry: Author Search.* Chadwyck-Healey Ltd., 1995 (http://www.lib.utexas.edu:8080/search/epoetry/author. html). *Saturday's Children: Poems of Work.* Helen Plotz, ed. Greenwillow Books, 1982. *The Columbia Granger's Index to Poetry.* 11th ed. *The Columbia Granger's World of Poetry,* Columbia University Press, 2005 (http://www.co lumbiagrangers.org). *The National Portrait Gallery* (www. npg.org.uk). *The Oxford Book of Nineteenth-Century English Verse.* John Hayward, ed. Oxford University Press, 1964; reprinted, with corrections, 1965. *The Oxford Companion to English Literature.* 6th edition. Margaret Drabble, ed. Oxford University Press, 2000. *Westminster Abbey Official Guide* (no date).

CLARIS, JOHN CHALK (?1797–1866)

Born at Canterbury, where his father was a bookseller and publisher, he was educated at the King's School, Canterbury. He became editor of the *Kent Herald* in Canterbury around 1826 and remained in this post until 1865. He supported the cause of reform and wrote enthusiastically in favor of Catholic emancipation; he also campaigned for parliamentary reform (the Great Reform Act was passed in 1832). The following poetical works were published under the name of "Arthur Brooke" (DNB): *Juvenile Pieces,* 1816. *Poems,* 1817. *Durovernum: The Curse of Chatterton, and Other Poems,* 1818. *Thoughts and Feelings,* 1820. *Retrospection,* 1821. *Elegy on the Death of Percy Bysshe Shelley,* 1822. Five of his poems are available at *Oldpotery.com:* "A Lament," "Night Thought," "Sonnet. To —," "To a Friend."

Sources: *Dictionary of National Biography.* Electronic Edition, 1.1. Oxford University Press, 1997. *Oldpoetry* (www.oldpoetry.com).

CLARKE, AUSTIN (1896–1974)

Considered one of the most important Irish poets to come along after W.B. Yeats, he was born in Dublin and was educated at Belvedere College and then University College Dublin (UCD). He graduated in 1916, earned an M.A. in 1917 and was appointed as a lecturer in UCD in the same year. His early poetry was heavily indebted to poets associated with the Irish Literary Renaissance, such as W.B. Yeats and George Russell (AE). From 1922 to 1937, when he returned to Dublin, Clarke worked as a journalist and book reviewer in England. From 1929 to 1955 he concentrated on writing verse plays and working with the Dublin Verse Speaking Society and the Lyric Theatre Company, which he helped found. He received numerous awards, including Ireland's highest literary honor, the Gregory Medal. He published three novels, memoirs, and literary criticism, and had several of his plays broadcast on the radio. Some of his poems: "A Statue for Dublin Bay," "A Vision of Mars," "Civil War," "Old-Fashioned Pilgrimage," "Rousseau," "The Tantalus," "The Vengeance of Fionn," "The Young Woman of Beare," "Three Poems about Children."

Sources: *Anthology of Twentieth-Century British and Irish Poetry.* Keith Tuma, ed. Oxford University Press, 2001. *Austin Clarke: His Life and Works.* Austin Clarke. Humanities Press, 1974. *Collected Poems of Austin Clarke.* Liam Miller, ed. The Dolmen Press, 1974. *Biography of Austin Clarke* (http://homepage.eircom.net/~splash/ Clarke.html). *Irish Poetry: An Interpretive Anthology from Before Swift to Yeats and After.* W.J. McCormack, ed. New York University Press, 2000. *The Columbia Granger's Index to Poetry.* 11th ed. *The Columbia Granger's World of Poetry,* Columbia University Press, 2005 (http://www.columbia-grangers.org). *The New Oxford Book of Irish Verse.* Thomas Kinsella, ed. Oxford University Press, 1986. *The Oxford Companion to English Literature.* 6th edition. Margaret Drabble, ed. Oxford University Press, 2000.

CLARKE, GILLIAN (1937–)

Welsh poet and playwright, she read English at University College, Cardiff, then worked for the BBC in London, but now lives in Talgarreg in Dyfed, a strongly Welsh-speaking area. She runs various creative writing courses up to master's level. She has given poetry readings and lectures in Europe and the United States and her work has been translated into many languages. She was assistant editor of *The Anglo-Welsh Review* in 1971 and editor from 1975 to 1984. Her poems were first published in *Poetry Wales* in 1970. Her work taps into Welsh myth and legend and her own sense of womanhood. Some of her main publications: *Letter from a Far Country,* 1982. *Selected Poems,* 1985. *Letting in the Rumour,* 1989. *The King of Britain's Daughter,* 1993. *Collected Poems,* 1997. Clarke says "On the Train" was written in

October 1999 while traveling home to Wales the day after the Paddington rail crash (from her website). Some of her other poems: "Baby-Sitting," "Border," "East Moors," "Foghorns," "Glass," "Letter from a Far Country," "St. Thomas's Day," "Suicide on Pentwyn Bridge," "The Hare," "The Water-Diviner."

Sources: *CREW Welsh Writers Online* (http://www. swan.ac.uk/english/crew/index.htm). *Gillian Clarke Welcome Page* (http://www.gillianclarke.co.uk). *Parents: An Anthology of Poems by Women Writers.* Myra Schneider and Dilys Wood, eds. Enitharmon Press, 2000. *The Columbia Granger's Index to Poetry.* 11th ed. *The Columbia Granger's World of Poetry,* Columbia University Press, 2005 (http://www.columbiagrangers.org). *The Harvill Book of Twentieth-Century Poetry in English.* Michael Schmidt, ed. The Harvill Press, 1999. *The New Exeter Book of Riddles.* Kevin Crossley-Holland and Lawrence Sail, eds. Enitharmon Press, 1999. *The Oxford Companion to English Literature.* 6th edition. Margaret Drabble, ed. Oxford University Press, 2000.

CLELAND, WILLIAM (1661–1689)

Cleland was known as "the troubadour of the Covenanters." At just eighteen, having spent three years at St. Andrews University, he was a captain in the covenanting army and later lieutenant-colonel of the Cameronian regiment raised by the earl of Angus. He was present at the 1679 battles of Drumclog and Bothwell Bridge, between the Covenanters and the troops of John Graham of Claverhouse (later Viscount Dundee), the arch persecutor of the Covenanters. At the battle of Dunkeld in 1689, between the Cameronians and the government troops, Cleland died a heroic death by a Highland bullet in the liver and another in the head within an hour of the first assault. He was the author of *A Collection of Several Poems and Verses Composed Upon Various Occasions*, which appeared posthumously in 1697. Two of the poems: "A Mock Poem," "An Acrostic Upon His Name," "An Answer to a Letter, from a Soldier Comrade, While in the Camp," "Hello, My Fancy," "How Mean a Thing is it to Stay," "O'er Hills, O'er Mountains, Scrogie Woods," "The Highland Host" (a satirical attack on the Highland troops and their leaders).

Sources: *Come Hither.* Walter de la Mare, ed. Knopf, 1957; Dover Publications, 1995. *Dictionary of National Biography.* Electronic Edition, 1.1. Oxford University Press, 1997. *English Poetry: Author Search.* Chadwyck-Healey Ltd., 1995 (http://www.lib.utexas.edu:8080/search/epoetry/author.html). *Significant and Famous Scots* (http://www.electricscotland.com/history/other/cleland_william.htm). *The Battle of Dunkeld* (http://www.clan-cameron.org/battles/1689_b.html). *The Columbia Granger's Index to Poetry.* 11th ed. *The Columbia Granger's World of Poetry,* Columbia University Press, 2005 (http://www.columbiagrangers.org).

CLERK, SIR JOHN, OF PENICUIK (1676–1755)

The eldest son of Sir John Clerk of Penicuik (south of Edinburgh), he was educated at the universities of Glasgow and Leiden. He studied music under the composer and violinist Arcangelo Corelli in Rome. He became highly a proficient violin and harpsichord player and in his lifetime composed five cantatas for solo voice, strings and continuo. However, music for a man of his social standing could only be a hobby, so he studied for law, and was called to the bar in 1700. He was one of the commissioners for the Treaty of Union (Scotland and England) in 1707, was returned to the first parliament of Great Britain in the same year, and succeeded to the title in 1722. A renowned collector of valuable antiques, he became a fellow of the Society of Antiquaries in 1725 and of the Royal Society in 1728. He was patron to the poet Allan Ramsay (see entry). Clerk's son and successor, Sir James Clerk, erected an obelisk to his father's memory at Penicuik. Some of his poems: "Fane Wald I Luve," "Merry May the Maid Be," "The Country Seat," "The Miller."

Sources: *Biography of Sir John Clerk, Concerto Caledonia* (http://www.concal.org/clerk.htm). *Biography of Sir John Clerk, Scotland's People* (http://www.scotlandspeople.gov.uk/content/help/index.aspx?1089). *Five Cantos by Sir John Clerk, Musica Scotica* (http://www.musicascotica.org.uk/fivecantatas.htm). *The Cherry-Tree.* Geoffrey Grigson, ed. Phoenix House, 1959. *The Home Book of Verse.* Burton Egbert Stevenson, ed. New York: Henry Holt and Company, 1953. *The Oxford Book of Garden Verse.* John Dixon Hunt, ed. Oxford University Press, 1993. *The Oxford Book of Scottish Verse.* John MacQueen and Tom Scott, eds. Oxford University Press, 1966.

CLERKE, ELLEN MARY (1840–1906)

Clerke was the elder sister of the more famous Agnes Mary Clerke (1842–1907), historian of astronomy, although Ellen Mary was also an authority on the subject. She was born at Skibbereen, County Cork, Ireland. The sisters were companions through life and shared a taste for music, literature, and science. A gifted and accomplished writer, for twenty years Ellen Mary wrote a weekly leader for the London *Tablet*, the Roman Catholic magazine. She lived in Italy for seven years and she devoted much of her time to verse translations of Italian poetry and writing stories for periodicals in Florence. She died after a short illness at her home in South Kensington, London. Her main publications are: *The Flying Dutchman and Other Poems*, 1881. *Fable and Song in Italy*, 1899 (essays, studies and specimens of Italian poetry translated into English). Some of her translations: *Virgin Pure* (Gambara, Veronica, 1485–1550). *Oh, Mystery, Faith Alone Can Comprehend*

(Gambara, Veronica, 1485–1550). *Colloquy between Christ, Our Lady and the Angel* (da Todi, Jacopone, 1228–1306). *Hymn of Alessandro Manzoni* (Manzoni, Alessandro, 1785–1873). *Two Ballads of Our Lady* (Dunbar, William, c. 1465–c. 1530).

Sources: *Carmina Mariana: An English Anthology in Verse in Honour of or in Relation to the Blessed Virgin Mary.* Orby Shipley, ed. Burns and Oates, 1894. *Catholic Encyclopedia* (http://www.newadvent.org). *Dictionary of National Biography.* Electronic Edition, 1.1. Oxford University Press, 1997. *Great Books Online.* www.bartleby.com.

CLEVELAND, JOHN (1613–1658)

A cavalier poet, born at Loughborough, Leicestershire, son of a clergyman, and educated at Christ's College, Cambridge. One of his orations, addressed to Charles I when on a visit to Cambridge in 1641, gratified the king, who called for him, gave him his hand to kiss, and commanded a copy to be sent after him to Huntingdon. A staunch Royalist opposed to Cromwell, Cleveland as judge advocate spent three months in prison when the Parliamentarians took charge. When Charles I surrendered to the Scots and was then handed to the English, Cleveland wrote a scathing attack on the Scots' betrayal in his satire, "The Rebel Scot." His works were highly popular, going through many editions between 1647 and 1700. Some of his poems: "An Elegy on Ben Jonson," "Anacreon," "Epitaph on the Earl of Strafford," "On the Memory of Mr. Edward King, Drown'd in the Irish Seas," "Parting with a Friend on the Way," "The Author's Mock-Song to Mark Anthony," "The King's Disguise," "The Scots Apostasie," "To the State of Love," "Upon the King's Return from Scotland."

Sources: *Dictionary of National Biography.* Electronic Edition, 1.1. Oxford University Press, 1997. *Encyclopædia Britannica Ultimate Reference Suite DVD,* 2006. *English Poetry: Author Search.* Chadwyck-Healey Ltd., 1995 (http://www.lib.utexas.edu:8080/search/epoetry/author.html). *Oldpoetry* (www.oldpoetry.com). *The Anchor Anthology of Seventeenth-Century Verse, Vol. II.* Louis L. Martz and Richard S. Sylvester, ed. Doubleday Anchor Books, 1969. *The Columbia Granger's Index to Poetry.* 11th ed. *The Columbia Granger's World of Poetry,* Columbia University Press, 2005 (http://www.columbiagrangers.org). *The National Portrait Gallery* (www.npg.org.uk). *The New Oxford Book of Seventeenth Century Verse.* Alastair Fowler, ed. Oxford University Press (2004). *The Oxford Companion to English Literature.* 6th edition. Margaret Drabble, ed. Oxford University Press, 2000.

CLIVE, CAROLINE ARCHER (1801–1873)

Born in London, the daughter of Edmund Meysey-Wigley of Shakenhurst, Worcestershire, sometime member of Parliament for Worcester. She married, in 1840, the Rev. Archer Clive, for many years member of Parliament for Hereford, and later chancellor of Hereford Cathedral. She was lame from childhood, a fact that is reflected in some of her writings. She died from burns received when her dress caught fire. She wrote under the pseudonym of V. Some of her publications: *IX Poems,* 1841, and a larger edition, 1840. *I Watched the Heavens,* 1842. *The Queen's Ball,* 1847. *The Valley of the Rea,* 1851. *The Morlas,* 1853. *Paul Ferroll,* 1855 (a novel). *Poems* 1856. *Year after Year,* 1858. *Why Paul Ferroll Killed His Wife,* 1860. *Poems,* 1872. Some of her poems: "A Last Day," "August 1865," "'Death, Death! Oh! Amiable, Lovely Death!' Shakespeare," "Epitaph for a Young Lady," "Old Age," "The Crab Tree," "The First Morning of 1860," "The Queen's Ball," "Translation from Tasso," "Written in Health," "Written in Illness."

Sources: *Dictionary of National Biography.* Electronic Edition, 1.1. Oxford University Press, 1997. *Oldpoetry* (www.oldpoetry.com). *Poems by Caroline Clive.* Longmans, Green, and Co., 1872. *The Columbia Granger's Index to Poetry.* 11th ed. *The Columbia Granger's World of Poetry,* Columbia University Press, 2005 (http://www.columbiagrangers.org). *The Oxford Companion to English Literature.* 6th edition. Margaret Drabble, ed. Oxford University Press, 2000.

CLOUGH, ARTHUR HUGH (1819–1861)

The son of a prosperous Liverpool cotton merchant, he spent some of his early years in South Carolina. He was educated at Rugby School under Thomas Arnold and at Balliol College, Oxford. In 1842 he was elected to a fellowship at Oriel College. He spent some time in France and Italy, then became the head of University Hall, London, in 1849. After two years he gave up and sailed to Boston, Massachusetts, in 1852 in the same ship with Thackeray and Lowell Emerson. There he worked in education but returned to England after one year. While traveling in Italy he contracted malaria, from which he died, leaving much of his work to be published posthumously. His main (often very long) poems are: *The Bothie of Toper-na-Vuolich,* 1848 (a novel in verse). *Amours de Voyage,* 1858. *Poems,* 1862. *Dipsychus,* 1865. Some of his other poems: "A Highland Glen near Loch Ericht," "Genesis XXIV," "Seven Sonnets," "That out of sight is out of mind," "The mighty ocean rolls and raves," "When Israel Came Out of Egypt," "Where lies the land to which the ship would go?"

Sources: *Dictionary of National Biography.* Electronic Edition, 1.1. Oxford University Press, 1997. *Encyclopædia Britannica Ultimate Reference Suite DVD,* 2006. *English*

Poetry: Author Search. Chadwyck-Healey Ltd., 1995 (http://www.lib.utexas.edu:8080/search/epoetry/author.html). *The Columbia Granger's Index to Poetry.* 11th ed. *The Columbia Granger's World of Poetry,* Columbia University Press, 2005 (http://www.columbiagrangers.org). *The National Portrait Gallery* (www.npg.org.uk). *The Oxford Companion to English Literature.* 6th edition. Margaret Drabble, ed. Oxford University Press, 2000. *The Poems of Arthur Hugh Clough.* H.F. Lowry, A.L.P. Norrington and F.L. Mulhauser, eds. Clarendon Press, 1951.

CLUYSENAAR, ANNE (1936–)

She was born Belgium, daughter of the painter John Cluysenaar, and came to England in 1939. Her education was at Trinity College, Dublin and Edinburgh University. For over twenty years, she taught literature, linguistics and stylistics in a number of British universities. She played a key role in the introduction of creative writing as a university subject at Lancaster and Birmingham universities (late sixties and early seventies), and Sheffield City Polytechnic (late seventies and eighties), where she also initiated and edited the magazine *Sheaf.* She was founding director of the Verbal Arts Association, 1983 (now absorbed into the National Association for Writers in Education, NAWE). She helped to develop and taught "In the Practice and Teaching of Creative Writing" at the University of Wales, Cardiff. Now retired from full-time teaching, she continues to undertake commissions and writing or mixed-media workshops. Cluysenaar and her husband Walt run a smallholding near Usk, South Wales. She is a fellow of the Welsh Academy. Her poetry publications include: *Nodes* (1971), *Double Helix* (1982) and *Timeslips* (1992). Some of her poems: "Cauldron Rituals," "Dark Mothers," "Poems of Memory."

Sources: *Parents: An Anthology of Poems by Women Writers.* Myra Schneider and Dilys Wood, eds. Enitharmon Press, 2000. *The Columbia Granger's Index to Poetry.* 11th ed. *The Columbia Granger's World of Poetry,* Columbia University Press, 2005 (http://www.columbiagrangers.org). *The Oxford Companion to English Literature.* 6th edition. Margaret Drabble, ed. Oxford University Press, 2000. *The Virago Book of Love Poetry.* Wendy Mulford, ed. Virago Press, 1990.

COBBING, BOB (1920–2002)

Born in Enfield, Middlesex, he trained as an accountant, then as a teacher. In the mid–1950s he was involved with the Hendon Experimental Art Club and the Hendon-based magazine *And,* then later, with the setting up of the Writers Forum in 1963. He left teaching to manage *Better Books* on Charing Cross Road, London. In the early 1970s the Poetry Society allowed Cobbing to use its facilities and his own equipment to allow anyone to print their own book of poetry. He was co-founder of the Association of Little Presses. Much of his later work consists of visual texts, anything that was readable as a sign on the page. His obituary was written by Robert Sheppard in the *Guardian,* Monday, 7 October 2002. Some of his publications: *A B C D Sound Poem Sequence,* 1965. *So Six Sound Poems,* 1968. *Etcetera: A New Collection of Found and Sound Poems,* 1970. *Chronology Sound Poetry,* 1974. *Cygnet Ring Collected Poems,* 1977. *Concerning Concrete Poetry,* 1978. *Vowels Consequences Collected Poems.* 1985. Some of his poems: "Alphabet of Fishes," "Beethoven Today," "Bird Bee," "Hymn to the Sacred Mushroom," "Worm."

Sources: *Anthology of Twentieth-Century British and Irish Poetry.* Keith Tuma, ed. Oxford University Press, 2001. *Bob Cobbing Publications: Bob Cobbing Author Page* (http://wings.buffalo.edu/epc/authors/cobbing/cobbing-pub.html). For an example of Cobbing's work see (http://www.artpool.hu/kepkolteszet/Cobbing.html). *The Columbia Granger's Index to Poetry.* 11th ed. *The Columbia Granger's World of Poetry,* Columbia University Press, 2005 (http://www.columbiagrangers.org). *The New British Poetry, 1968–88.* Gillian Allnutt, Fred D'Aguiar and Ken Edwards, eds. Grafton Books, 1989. *Wikipedia, the Free Encyclopedia* (http://en.wikipedia.org/wiki/Wikipedia).

COFFEY, BRIAN (1905–1995)

Born in Dublin (his father was professor of anatomy and the first President of University College, Dublin), Coffey studied arts and the sciences at University College, Dublin. In France he studied physical chemistry under Jean Baptiste Perrin, who won the Nobel Prize for Physics in 1926, and philosophy at the Catholique de Paris with the French philosopher Jacques Maritain. He worked in Paris and taught philosophy at St. Louis University, Missouri; he returned in 1954 to Europe, where he worked as a teacher of mathematics in England until his retirement. In 1934 he began contributing reviews (and one poem) to the *Criterion*; his interest in French poetry dates from this period. After the war he was appointed an assistant professor at St. Louis University, Missouri, supervising postgraduates in the philosophy of science and mathematical logic. In 1973, he retired from teaching to Southampton. Some of his poetry publications: *Three Poems,* 1933. *Selected Poems,* 1971. *Poems and Versions 1929–1990,* 1991. Some of his poems: "Cold," "For What for Whom Unwanted," "Headrock," "Missouri Sequence," "The Nicest Phantasies Are Shared," "The Prayers."

Sources: *Biography of Bob Coffey* (http://www.answers.com/topic/brian-coffey). *Contemporary Irish Poetry: An Anthology.* Anthony Bradley, ed. University of California Press. New and rev. ed., 1988. *Fred Beake: The Poetry of Brian Coffey* (http://www.dgdclynx.plus.com/lynx/lynx14.html). *The Missouri Sequence by Brian Coffey* (http://indigo.ie/~tjac/Poets/Brian_Coffey/brian_coffey.htm).

COKAYNE, SIR ASTON (1608–1684)

Born into a long line of English aristocrats, whose seat was at Ashbourne in Derbyshire, he was educated at Chenie school, Buckinghamshire, and at Trinity College, Cambridge. Through marriage with the heiress of the family of Herthull, he acquired large estates in several midland counties, including the lordship of Pooley (in Polesworth), Warwickshire. His life was uneventful; he toured France and Italy, then he seems to have settled down to running his estate and writing poetry. He died almost penniless. His main publications are: *Dianea*, 1654 (a translation from Italian by Gio. Francisco Loredano). *The Obstinate Lady,* 1657 (comedy). *Small Poems of Divers Sorts,* 1658. *A Chain of Golden Poems,* 1659 (a reissue of his poems with additions, and another reissue in 1662). *Choice Poems,* 1669 (the final reissue). Some of his other poems: "Epitaph on a Great Sleeper," "Funeral Elegy on the Death of His Very Good Friend, Mr. Michael Drayton," "Lady, in Your Applause Verse Goes," "Of a Mistress," "Of Lycoris," "To Lesbia," "To My Noble Cousin Colonel Ralph Sneyde," "To Plautia," "To Thalia."

Sources: *Dictionary of National Biography.* Electronic Edition, 1.1. Oxford University Press, 1997. *English Poetry: Author Search.* Chadwyck-Healey Ltd., 1995 (http://www.lib.utexas.edu:8080/search/epoetry/author.html). *Stanford University Libraries and Academic Information Resources* (http://library.stanford.edu). *The Columbia Granger's Index to Poetry.* 11th ed. *The Columbia Granger's World of Poetry,* Columbia University Press, 2005 (http://www.columbia grangers.org). *The Faber Book of Epigrams and Epitaphs.* Geoffrey Grigson, ed. Faber & Faber, 1977.

COLERIDGE, HARTLEY (1796–1849)

The eldest son of Samuel Taylor Coleridge, born at Clevedon, Somersetshire, he is the subject of two poems by his father: "Frost at Midnight" and "The Nightingale." After his parents separated he was brought up in the household of Robert Southey and was educated principally at Ambleside school, where, it is reported, he never played, but passed the time he could spare from school tasks in reading, walking, dreaming, or relating his dreams to others. He went on to Merton College, Oxford, but forfeited his Oxford Oriel Fellowship through intemperance. His foray into teaching was not successful and he turned to the Lake District, where he remained for the rest of his life. His poems, particularly his sonnets, are strongly influenced by Wordsworth, who dedicated his poem "Six Years Old" to him. Some of his poems: "A Brother's Love to His Sister," "Butter's Etymological Spelling Book," "Chaucer," "Dedicatory Sonnet to S.T. Coleridge," "Early Death," "Full Well I Know," "He Lived amidst th' Untrodden Ways" (possibly inspired by Wordsworth' *She Dwelt Among the Untrodden Ways*), "Long Time a Child," "Prayer," "The Birth-Day," "To Wordsworth."

Sources: *Dictionary of National Biography.* Electronic Edition, 1.1. Oxford University Press, 1997. *Encyclopædia Britannica Ultimate Reference Suite DVD,* 2006. *English Poetry: Author Search.* Chadwyck-Healey Ltd., 1995 (http://www.lib.utexas.edu:8080/search/epoetry/author. html). *English Poetry: A Poetic Record, from Chaucer to Yeats.* David Hopkins, ed. Routledge, 1990. *Hartley Coleridge* (http://www.sonnets.org/coleridgeh.htm#010). *Poems, 1833 of Coleridge, Hartley.* Woodstock Books, 1990. *The Columbia Granger's Index to Poetry.* 11th ed. *The Columbia Granger's World of Poetry,* Columbia University Press, 2005 (http://www.columbiagrangers.org). *The Oxford Companion to English Literature.* 6th edition. Margaret Drabble, ed. Oxford University Press, 2000.

COLERIDGE, MARY ELIZABETH (1861–1907)

The daughter of Arthur Duke Coleridge, grandnephew of Samuel Taylor, Coleridge was born in South Kensington, London. Steeped in literature and history from early childhood, at her own request she was taught Hebrew, Italian, French, German, and Greek. At twenty she began to write essays for the *Monthly Packet,* *Merry England,* and other periodicals. She also wrote a critical preface to Canon Dixon's *Last Poems* (1905). She devoted much time to teaching working women in her own home and gave lessons on English literature at the Working Women's College. Just before she died she finished a short *Life of Holman Hunt,* undertaken at the painter's request and published soon after her death. Two of her novels: *The King with Two Faces,* 1897 (a story based on Swedish history that would earn her the admiration of the Swedish Foreign Minister and would run to several editions), and *The Lady on the Drawing-room Floor,* 1906. Her main poetry publications: *Fancy's Following,* 1896. *Fancy's Guerdon,* 1897. *Gathered Leaves,* 1910. Some of her poems: "Affection," "Astrology," "Christ's Friends," "Deep Calleth unto Deep," "The Nurse's Lament," "Youth's Dying."

Sources: *Dictionary of National Biography.* Electronic Edition, 1.1. Oxford University Press, 1997. *English Poetry: Author Search.* Chadwyck-Healey Ltd., 1995 (http://www.lib.utexas.edu:8080/search/epoetry/author.html). *The Collected Poems of Mary Coleridge.* Theresa Whistler. Rupert Hart-Davis, 1954. *The Columbia Granger's Index to Poetry.* 11th ed. *The Columbia Granger's World of Poetry,* Columbia University Press, 2005 (http://www.columbiagrangers. org). *The Oxford Companion to English Literature.* 6th edition. Margaret Drabble, ed. Oxford University Press, 2000.

COLERIDGE, SAMUEL TAYLOR and SARA (1772–1852)

Samuel, the father, 1772–1834

Born in Ottery St. Mary, Devonshire, the youngest son of a clergyman and master of the grammar school, Samuel was a bright and imaginative child who had read the *Arabian Nights* before the age of five. Educated at Christ's Hospital School, London (now situated at Horsham, Sussex), he was a good scholar and before his fifteenth year had translated the eight hymns of Synesius from Greek into English. He went on to Jesus College, Cambridge, but fired by French revolutionary politics, he enlisted in the 15th Light Dragoons under the name of Comberbache. He was bought out by his brother under the "insanity" clause and left Cambridge without graduating, then studied philosophy at Göttingen University. His later life was marred by opium addiction and unsatisfactory friendships with Southey and Wordsworth. At times he was close to suicide. His *Lyrical Ballads* (1798), written with William Wordsworth, started the English Romantic movement. He is commemorated by a bust in Poets' Corner of Westminster Abbey. Some of his poems: "Anthem for the Children of Christ's Hospital," "Destruction of the Bastille," "Frost at Midnight," "Kubla Khan," "The Dungeon," "The Foster-Mother's Tale," "The Nightingale," "The Rime of the Ancient Mariner."

Sara, the daughter, 1802–1852

Sara grew up mainly in the company of the families of Wordsworth and Southey in the Lake District. Widely read, she was fluent in six languages. A poet in her own right, she was also the editor of her father's works. She married her cousin, Henry Nelson Coleridge, and spent the rest of her life in London. Much information is contained in her *Memoir and Letters* published by her daughter in 1873. Along with Dora Wordsworth and Edith Southey, she is one of the three maidens celebrated in Wordsworth's *Trias* (1828). Her two major translations: *Latin Account of the Abipones* (from Martin Dobrizhoffer in three volumes), 1992, and *Memoirs* (of the Chevalier Bayard), 1825. Her major poetry publications: *Pretty Lessons in Verse for Good Children*, 1834. *Phantasmion*, 1837 (a fairy story with lyrics, set in the Lake country). Some of her other poems: "Blest is the tarn which towering cliffs o'ershade," "Father! No Amaranths E'er Shall Wreathe My Brow," "Sleep, My Babe," "The Child," "The Garden Year," "The Months," "The Mother," "The Storm," "Trees."

Sources: *Dictionary of National Biography.* Electronic Edition, 1.1. Oxford University Press, 1997. *Encyclopædia Britannica Ultimate Reference Suite DVD,* 2006. *English Poetry: Author Search.* Chadwyck-Healey Ltd., 1995 (http://www.lib.utexas.edu:8080/search/epoetry/author.html). *Oldpoetry* (www.oldpoetry.com). *The Columbia Granger's Index to Poetry.* 11th ed. *The Columbia Granger's World of Poetry,* Columbia University Press, 2005 (http://www.columbiagrangers.org). *The Major Works of Samuel Taylor Coleridge.* H.J. Jackson, ed. Oxford University Press, 2000. *The National Portrait Gallery* (www.npg.org.uk). *The Oxford Book of Regency Verse 1798–1837.* H.S. Milford, ed. Oxford University Press, 1928. *The Oxford Companion to English Literature.* 6th edition. Margaret Drabble, ed. Oxford University Press, 2000. *The Random House Book of Poetry for Children.* Jack Prelutsky, ed. The Random House Group, 1983. *Westminster Abbey Official Guide* (no date).

COLES, VINCENT STUCKEY STRATTON (1845–1929)

The son of the Rev. James Stratton Coles, rector of Shepton Beauchamp, Somerset, he was educated at Eton College and Balliol College, Oxford, then took Holy Orders in 1869 to become curate of Wantage, near Oxford. He succeeded his father as rector of Shepton Beauchamp (where he is buried) in 1872, but resigned in 1884 to become one of the librarians of Pusey House, Oxford, and was principal from 1897 until 1909, when he resigned from ill health (Pusey House is the center of Catholic worship, teaching and practice and a place of scholarship and learning in the University of Oxford and for the wider Church). From 1910 to 1920 he was warden of the community of the Epiphany at Truro. His major publications: *Pastoral Work in Country Districts,* 1906 (being lectures delivered at Cambridge in Lent 1905). *Lenten Meditations,* 1899 (4th ed. 1905). *Advent Meditations,* 1899 (new edition 1901). Some of his hymns (a few of them are in the current *Hymns Ancient and Modern*): "Almighty Father, Lord Most High," "Lamb of God, Whose Love Divine," "Shepherd of the Sheep," "We Pray Thee, Heavenly Father."

Sources: *Dictionary of National Biography.* Electronic Edition, 1.1. Oxford University Press, 1997. *The Cyber Hymnal* (http://www.cyberhymnal.org/index.htm).

COLLIER, MARY (1688–?1762)

Born near Midhurst, Sussex, of poor parents, she had little education. When her parents died she moved to Petersfield, Hampshire, where she supported herself by washing clothes, brewing, and other types of manual work. She retired to a garret in Alton where she died. *Poems on Several Occasions* was published in 1762. In her poem "The Woman's Labor: An Epistle to Mr. Stephen Duck" (see entry) (1739)—an angry response to his comments in praise of men and the idleness of rural women—she spoke up for the common woman and railed against the women's double-shift during the work day. She describes the seasonal drudgery common to working-class women trying to earn an honest living, how women reap the harvest as well as men, then come home to start work again and are so worked that they have little time to dream.

Sources: *Dictionary of National Biography*. Electronic Edition, 1.1. Oxford University Press, 1997. For a translation of *Early Modern Notes: The Woman's Labor*, see (http://www.earlymodernweb.org.uk/emn/index.php/archives/2005/03/the-womans-labour/). *Mary Collier* (http://www.pinn.net/~sunshine/march99/collierhtml). *The Columbia Granger's Index to Poetry*. 11th ed. *The Columbia Granger's World of Poetry*, Columbia University Press, 2005 (http://www.columbiagrangers.org).

COLLINS, JOHN (?1742–1808)

Actor, poet, orator, and musical entertainer, he was born, raised and educated in Bath, the son of a tailor. His work as a stay maker did not suit his personality and he was drawn to the stage at an early age, and by twenty he had appeared at a theatre in Smock Alley, Dublin, as young Mirabel in the *Inconstant*. He toured local taverns of England and Ireland, delivering lectures from *The Brush*, a collection of pleasant old theatrical stories (date unknown) with humorous songs all written by himself. *Scripscrapologia*, a collection of poems encompassing a great range of different topics and original poems from *The Brush*, was published in 1793. "Tomorrow" was included in Palgrave's *Golden Treasury* (1964) and some of his pieces were included in Frederick Locker-Lampson's (see entry) *Lyra Elegantiarum* (1867). Some of his other poems: "Ben Block, "Paternal Love and Filial Piety," "The Chapter of King," "The Desponding Negro" (an anti-slavery poem), "The Golden Days of Good Queen Bess," "The Golden Farmer," "The Hibernian Fisherman."

Sources: *Dictionary of National Biography*. Electronic Edition, 1.1. Oxford University Press, 1997. *English Poetry: Author Search*. Chadwyck-Healey Ltd., 1995 (http://www.lib.utexas.edu:8080/search/epoetry/author.html). *Golden Treasury of the Best Songs & Lyrical Poems in the English Language*. Francis Turner Palgrave, ed. Oxford University Press (1964, Sixth edition, updated by John Press, 1994). *Lyra Elegantiarum*. Frederick Locker Lampson. London: Ward, Lock & Co., 1867. *The Columbia Granger's Index to Poetry*. 11th ed. *The Columbia Granger's World of Poetry*, Columbia University Press, 2005 (http://www.columbiagrangers.org). *The Faber Book of Useful Verse*. Simon Brett, ed. Faber & Faber, 1981.

COLLINS, WILLIAM (1721–1759)

A pre-Romantic poet of many odes, the son of a hatter from Chichester, Sussex, Collins was educated at Winchester College and Magdalen College, Oxford, where he published his *Persian Eclogues* (1742). Dr. Samuel Johnson says of him, "About this time I fell into his company. His appearance was de-

cent and manly; his knowledge considerable, his views extensive, his conversation elegant, and his disposition cheerful." Johnson ends his entry with, "As men are often esteemed who cannot be loved, so the poetry of Collins may sometimes extort praise when it gives little pleasure" (DNB). More modern poets have not been so harsh. Suffering from depression, Collins isolated himself at Chichester and died neglected and forgotten by his literary friends. Some of his poems: "A Fidele," "An Ode on the Popular Superstitions of the Highlands of Scotland," "Captain Molly," "How Sleep the Brave," "Ode on the Poetical Character," "Ode to Evening," "Ode to Fear," "Ode to Mercy," "Ode to Pity," "Ode to Simplicity," "The Lookout."

Sources: *Dictionary of National Biography*. Electronic Edition, 1.1. Oxford University Press, 1997. *Encyclopædia Britannica Ultimate Reference Suite DVD*, 2006. *English Poetry: Author Search*. Chadwyck-Healey Ltd., 1995 (http://www.lib.utexas.edu:8080/search/epoetry/author.html). *Samuel Johnson's Lives of the English Poets*, 1779–1781 (http://www2.hn.psu.edu/Faculty/KKemmerer/poets/preface.htm). *The National Portrait Gallery* (www.npg.org.uk). *The New Oxford Book of Eighteenth-Century Verse*. Roger Lonsdale, ed. Oxford University Press, 1984. *The New Oxford Book of English Verse, 1250–1950*. Helen Gardner, ed. Oxford University Press, 1972. *The Oxford Companion to English Literature*. 6th edition. Margaret Drabble, ed. Oxford University Press, 2000.

COLMAN, GEORGE (1762–1836)

The son of George Colman (1732–1794), dramatist and manager of the Haymarket Theatre, London, he was educated at Westminster School, Christ Church College, Oxford, and King's College, Aberdeen. He entered into a secret marriage at Gretna Green with a small-time actress; eventually they did marry with his father's blessing, in 1784. Upon the death of his father in 1794 Colman purchased the Haymarket patent. His comic operas, farces, melodramas, scurrilous satiric verse, and sentimental comedies made him a lot of money, which he wasted through extravagance. From 1824 until his death he was examiner (censor) of plays, a task he performed with tyrannical zeal, cutting all references to "God" "heaven" and "providence," and would not even allow a lover to address his mistress as an "angel." He died in London and was buried beside his father under the vaults in Kensington Church. Some of his poems: "Address at Drury Lane," "Bluebeard," "Hero and Leander," "London Rurality," "My Nightgown and Slippers," "Paddy O'Raffarty's Song to an Old Coquette," "Song: Judy O'Flannikin," "The Lady of the Wreck," "The Maid of the Moor, or, The Water-Fiends."

Sources: *Broad Grins, My Nightgown and Slippers and Other Humorous Works, Prose and Poetical of George Colman* *the Younger.* George B. Buckstone, ed. John Camden Hotten, 1872. *Dictionary of National Biography.* Electronic Edition, 1.1. Oxford University Press, 1997. *Encyclopædia Britannica Ultimate Reference Suite DVD,* 2006. *The National Portrait Gallery* (www.npg.org.uk). *The Columbia Granger's Index to Poetry.* 11th ed. *The Columbia Granger's World of Poetry,* Columbia University Press, 2005 (http://www.columbiagrangers.org). *The New Oxford Book of Eighteenth-Century Verse.* Roger Lonsdale, ed. Oxford University Press, 1984. *The Oxford Companion to English Literature.* 6th edition. Margaret Drabble, ed. Oxford University Press, 2000.

COLMAN, WALTER (d. 1645)

Colman, of noble birth and wealthy parents, entered the Franciscan Order at the English College at Douai in France in 1625. He was imprisoned in London when he refused to take the Oath of Allegiance (denying the authority of the Pope) but was released on intervention of friends. When persecution of the Catholics broke out in 1641 he, with several others, was tried at the Old Bailey and condemned to be hung, drawn and quartered. Although that execution was stayed, he died a lingering death in Newgate prison. He is known for only one poem of great rarity, "La Dance Machabre," or "Deaths Duell." The dedication to Henrietta Maria, consort of King Charles I, is in French. In it he comments that death levels both master and slave; there is no difference in rank.

Sources: *Catholic Encyclopedia* (http://www.newadvent.org). *Dictionary of National Biography.* Electronic Edition, 1.1. Oxford University Press, 1997. *The National Portrait Gallery* (www.npg.org.uk).

COLUM, PADRAIC (1881–1972)

He was born in Longford in the northwest of Ireland, where his father was workhouse master. From 1898 to 1904 he worked as a clerk in the Irish Railway Clearing House in Dublin and left to become a full-time writer. *The Saxon Shillin* (1902) won a competition for a play to discourage young Irishmen from joining the British army. He went on to write other plays but seems to have been drawn to poetry. He married in 1912, and in 1914 the couple sailed to America. For some time in the 1930s they lived in France, where Colum renewed his friendship with James Joyce (see entry). Colum taught comparative literature at Columbia University, became a U.S. citizen in 1945, and died in Enfield, Connecticut. Some of his poetry publications: *Wild Earth,* 1907. *The King of Ireland's Son,* 1916. *Dramatic Legends,* 1922. *Creatures,* 1927. *Irish Elegies,* 1958. Some of his poems: "A Drover," "Across the Door," "The Ballad of Downal Baun," "The Book of Kells," "The Fire Bringer," "The Stations of the Cross," "The Wall of China."

Sources: *An Anthology of Revolutionary Poetry.* Marcus Graham, ed. The Active Press, 1929. *Biography of Padraic Colum* (http://www.irelandseye.com/aarticles/history/people/writers/pcolum.shtm). *Encyclopædia Britannica Ultimate Reference Suite DVD,* 2006. *Ireland in Poetry.* Charles Sullivan, ed. Harry N. Abrams, 1990. *Microsoft Encarta 2006* (DVD). Microsoft Corporation, 2006. *Roofs of Gold: Poems to Read Aloud.* Padraic Colum, ed. Macmillan, 1964. *Sung Under the Silver Umbrella.* Association for Childhood Education International, ed. Macmillan, 1935. *The Columbia Granger's Index to Poetry.* 11th ed. *The Columbia Granger's World of Poetry,* Columbia University Press, 2005 (http://www.columbiagrangers.org). *The Golden Book of Catholic Poetry.* Alfred Noyes, ed. J.B. Lippincott, 1946. *The Home Book of Verse.* Burton Egbert Stevenson, ed. New York: Henry Holt and Company, 1953. *The Oxford Companion to English Literature.* 6th edition. Margaret Drabble, ed. Oxford University Press, 2000.

COLUMBA, SAINT (fl. 543–615)

Born in Tyrconnell, now County Donegal, Ireland. His father — grandson of Conall Gulban, from whom the northwest of Ulster takes its name of Tirconaill, and great-grandson of Niall Naighiallach, king of Ireland from 379 to 405 — was chief of a mountainous district in the northwest of Ireland. Columba (known in Ireland and the western isles as Columcille) is credited with the main role in the conversion of Scotland to Christianity. He and his 12 disciples erected a church and a monastery on the island of Iona, Inner Hebrides, Scotland (c. 563) as their springboard for the conversion of Scotland, in the time of Aidan MacGabrain of Dunadd, king of Dalriada. Columba died at Iona. His feast day is June 9. Restoration of the abbey buildings began in 1938 when Rev. George F. MacLeod established the Iona Community. Several books and Latin hymns are attributed to Columba. Some of his poems: "A Boat Song," "An Invocation," "Farewell to Ireland," "On a Dead Scholar," "Prayer to the Virgin," "St. Columcille the Scribe," "The Boyhood of Christ," "The Maker on High."

Sources: *An Anthology of World Poetry.* Mark Van Doren, ed. Reynal & Hitchcock, Inc., 1936. *Catholic Encyclopedia* (http://www.newadvent.org). *Dictionary of National Biography.* Electronic Edition, 1.1. Oxford University Press, 1997. *Encyclopædia Britannica Ultimate Reference Suite DVD,* 2006. *Isle of Iona, Scotland* (http://www.isle-of-iona.com). *Iona: A history of the Island.* M. McNeil. Blackie and Son Ltd., 1920, republished 1973. *The Columbia Granger's Index to Poetry.* 11th ed. *The Columbia Granger's World of Poetry,* Columbia University Press, 2005 (http://www.columbiagrangers.org). *The New Oxford Book of Irish Verse.* Thomas Kinsella, ed. Oxford University Press, 1986. *The New Penguin Book of Scottish Verse.* Robert Crawford and Mick Imlah, ed. Penguin Books, 2000. *The Oxford Companion to English Literature.* 6th edition. Margaret Drabble, ed. Oxford University Press, 2000.

COLVIN, IAN DUNCAN (1877–1938)

Journalist, biographer, and poet, he was born at Inverness, son of a Free Church minister. Educated at Crieff Academy and Inverness College, he studied rhetoric and English literature at Edinburgh University, where he won the gold medal for history and literature. He worked for the *Allahabad Pioneer* in London and in India, and for the *Cape Times*. In 1909 he became lead writer of the *Morning Post* in London, writing leading articles for the next twenty-eight years. He wrote political verse and tales under the pseudonym "Rip van Winkle" and was a fierce critic of whatever government was in power. He denounced the 1921 Irish "treaty," was hostile toward the Indian Round Table Conference of 1931, and he supported General Franco during he Spanish Civil War. Some of his publications: *South and East Africa*, 1910. *The Cape of Adventure*, 1912. *The Germans in England 1066–1598*, 1915. *The Unseen Hand in English History*, 1817. *The Safety of the Nation*, 1919. *The Life of General Dyer*, 1929. *The Life of Lord Carson*, Vol. II, 1934. *The Life of Lord Carson*, Vol. III, 1936. Two of his poems: "The Flying Dutchman," "Tristan da Cunha."

Sources: *Dictionary of National Biography*. Electronic Edition, 1.1. Oxford University Press, 1997. *The Columbia Granger's Index to Poetry*. 11th ed. *The Columbia Granger's World of Poetry*, Columbia University Press, 2005 (http://www.columbiagrangers.org). *The Penguin Book of Southern African Verse*. Stephen Gray, ed. Penguin Books, 1989.

COMFORT, ALEX (1920–2000)

Physician and physicist, he is best known for his popular *Joy of Sex* books and his work on aging. Educated at home by his parents in London, he nearly killed himself at age 14 while constructing a bomb. He went on to Trinity College Cambridge and taught and did research both in London and in the United States. A noted anarchist and pacifist, he was active in the nuclear disarmament movement. In a famous wartime opinion piece he called for the prosecution as war criminals of Allied leaders who directed saturation bombing of Germany. Some of his publications: *The Silver River*, 1938 (a diary of his travels in the South Atlantic). *No Such Liberty*, 1941 (novel). *Authority and Delinquency in the Modern State*, 1950. *The Biology of Senescence*, 1956. *The Process of Aging*, 1964. Some of his poems: "After Shakespeare," "After You, Madam," "Fear of the Earth," "Haste to the Wedding," "Letter to an American Visitor," "Notes for My Son," "Song for the Heroes," "The Atoll in the Mind," "The Song of Lazarus."

Sources: *Encyclopædia Britannica Ultimate Reference Suite DVD*, 2006. *Erotic Poetry: The Lyrics, Ballads, Idylls,* *and Epics of Love— Classical to Contemporary*. William Cole, ed. Random House, 1963. *The Columbia Granger's Index to Poetry*. 11th ed. *The Columbia Granger's World of Poetry,* Columbia University Press, 2005 (http://www.columbiagrangers.org). *The Joy of Sex & The Joy of Cooking Compared* (http://www.goodbyemag.com/mar00/comfort.html). *The National Portrait Gallery* (www.npg.org.uk). *The New British Poets: An Anthology*. Kenneth Rexroth, ed. New Directions, 1949.

CONDER, JOSIAH (1789–1855)

A London bookseller, blinded in one eye through smallpox, he won two silver medals for his essays to the *Monthly Preceptor* at the age of ten. He inherited his father's business in 1813. Largely self-educated, he became proprietor of the periodical the *Eclectic Review* from 1814 until 1837. *On Protestant Nonconformity* (two volumes) was published in 1818. His *Congregational Hymn-Book* sold 90,000 copies in its first seven years. In 1810 he published an anonymous volume, *The Associate Minstrels,* to which Ann and Jane Taylor (see The Taylor Sisters) and others contributed. Around 1824 he started on the series of 30 volumes of the *Modern Traveler* (1825–1829), this by a man who had never left England. From 1832 he was editor for 23 years of the *Patriot* newspaper, which represented the principles of evangelical nonconformists. Some of his other publications: *The Withered Oak*, 1805. *The Star in the East, with Other Poems Chiefly Religious and Domestic*, 1824. *Sacred Poems, Domestic Poems, and Miscellaneous Poems*, 1824. *The Choir and the Oratory*, 1836. *The Last Night of Slavery*, 1837. *Hymns of Praise, Prayer, and Devout Meditation*, 1856. His best-known hymn is probably "Day by day the manna fell..."

Sources: *Dictionary of National Biography*. Electronic Edition, 1.1. Oxford University Press, 1997. *English Poetry: Author Search*. Chadwyck-Healey Ltd., 1995 (http://www.lib.utexas.edu:8080/search/epoetry/author.html). *The Columbia Granger's Index to Poetry*. 11th ed. *The Columbia Granger's World of Poetry,* Columbia University Press, 2005 (http://www.columbiagrangers.org). *The Cyber Hymnal* (http://www.cyberhymnal.org/index.htm). *The National Portrait Gallery* (www.npg.org.uk).

CONGREVE, WILLIAM (1670–1729)

Congreve, the most prominent writer of Restoration comedies, was born at Bardsey, near Leeds, and educated at Trinity College, Dublin. He abandoned law for literature. His first comedy, *The Old Bachelor* (1693) established him as a dramatist, and in the opinion of Dryden, Congreve was the equal of Shakespeare. His comedy *Double Dealer* (1693) met with some opposition and some ladies were scandalized; Queen Mary, however, came to see it. Jeremy Collier, a clergyman, in his pamphlet, *A View of the Immorality and Profaneness of the English Stage,* accused Congreve and others of licentiousness. Congreve seems to have lost heart; his health suffered, and his literary output dried up. His body lay in state in the Jerusalem Chamber of Westminster Abbey, and Henrietta, Duchess of Marlborough, erected a monument to him in the South Aisle of Westminster Abbey with an inscription of her own writing. Some of his other publications: *Love for Love*, 1695 (comedy). *The Mourning Bride*, 1697 (tragedy). *Incognita* 1692 (novel). *Semele*, 1707 (opera). Some of his poems: "A Nymph and a Swain," "False Though She Be," "Jack Frenchman's Defeat," "The Way of the World."

Sources: *Dictionary of National Biography.* Electronic Edition, 1.1. Oxford University Press, 1997. *Encyclopædia Britannica Ultimate Reference Suite DVD*, 2006. *English Poetry: Author Search.* Chadwyck-Healey Ltd., 1995 (http://www.lib.utexas.edu:8080/search/epoetry/author. html). *The Columbia Granger's Index to Poetry.* 11th ed. *The Columbia Granger's World of Poetry*, Columbia University Press, 2005 (http://www.columbiagrangers.org). *The National Portrait Gallery* (www.npg.org.uk). *The Oxford Anthology of English Poetry. Vol. I: Spenser to Crabbe.* John Wain, ed. Oxford University Press, 1990. *The Oxford Companion to English Literature.* 6th edition. Margaret Drabble, ed. Oxford University Press, 2000. *Westminster Abbey Official Guide* (no date).

CONQUEST, (GEORGE) ROBERT (ACWORTH) (1917–)

Born at Malvern, Worcestershire, the son of a wealthy American father and English mother, he was educated at Winchester College, the University of Grenoble, and graduated M.A. in 1972 from Magdalen College, Oxford. He was awarded a doctor of literature degree in 1975. After the war, in which he served in the Oxford and Buckingham Light Infantry, he joined the Foreign Office, was present in Bulgaria when the communists overthrew the government, then worked in the Information Research Department specializing in the Soviet Union. He became literary editor of the *Spectator* in 1963 and is the author of twenty books on the Soviet Union, including the classic *The Great Terror* (Macmillan, 1968). He was awarded the Order of the British Empire in 1995 and Companion of the Order of St. Michael and St. George in 1996. He is a research fellow at the Hoover Institution, Stanford University, California. Some of his poems: "747 (London–Chicago)," "Adriatic," "Aids to Composition," "Appalachian Convalescence," "Bagpipes at the Biltmore," "Guided Missiles Experimental Range," "On the Danube," "Seal Rocks: San Francisco," "The Agents."

Sources: *English and American Surrealist Poetry.* Edward B. Germain, ed. Penguin Books, 1978. *Robert Conquest, Biography* (http://www.spartacus.schoolnet.co.uk/HIS conquest.htm),. *Biography of Robert Conquest* (http://www-hoover.stanford.edu/bios/conquest.html). *New Lines: Poets of the 1950s: An Anthology.* Robert Conquest, ed. Macmillan, 1956 (http://homepages.wmich.edu/~cooneys/tchg/wby/new-lines.html). *Poems on Poetry: The Mirror's Garland.* Robert Wallace and James G. Taaffe, eds. E.P. Dutton, 1963. *The Columbia Granger's Index to Poetry.* 11th ed. *The Columbia Granger's World of Poetry*, Columbia University Press, 2005 (http://www.columbiagrangers.org). *The Oxford Companion to English Literature.* 6th edition. Margaret Drabble, ed. Oxford University Press, 2000. *Who's Who.* London: A & C Black, 2005.

CONRAN, ANTHONY (1931–)

Poet, translator and critic, he was born in India, where his father was a railway engineer. Brought back to Wales for health reasons, he was raised by grandparents in Colwyn Bay and graduated in English and philosophy from the University College of North Wales, Bangor. From 1957 to 1982 he was research fellow and tutor in the English Department at Bangor. His early work was as the translator of *The Penguin Book of Welsh Verse*, 1967, extended and reissued as *Welsh Verse* in 1986. In *The Peacemakers* (1997) he translated a selection of poems by Waldo Williams (see entry). He wrote an experimental drama, *Branwen* (performed 1989), and several critical essays on Anglo-Welsh poetry (*see also* Nigel Jenkins). Some of his poetry publications: *Formal Poems*, 1960. *Poems 1951–67*, 1974. *Spirit Level*, 1974. *Life Fund*, 1979. *Eros Proposes a Toast*, 1998. *Theatre of Flowers*, 1998. *Blodeuwedd*, 1988. *All Hallows: Symphony in 3 Movements*, 1995. Some of his poems: "Death of a Species," "Elegy for the Welsh Dead, in the Falkland Islands," "Fledgling," "The Spoils of Annwn," "Thirteen Ways of Looking at a Hoover."

Sources: *A Brief History of Wales — Ch. 26 — Continued Concern* (http://www.peternwilliams.com/wales/wal26. html). *Anglo-Welsh Poetry, 1480–1980.* Raymond Garlick and Roland Mathias, ed. Poetry Wales Press, 1984. *Anglo-Welsh Poetry, 1480–1990.* Raymond Garlick and Roland Mathias, ed. Poetry Wales Press, 1993. *CREW Welsh Writers Online* (http://www.swan.ac.uk/english/crew/index. htm). *Go Britannia, Wales: Welsh Literature — 20th Century, Pt. III* (http://www.britannia.com/wales/lit/lit18.html). *Thirteen Ways of Looking at Tony Conran.* Nigel Jenkins, ed. Welsh Union of Writers, 1995. *Twentieth Century Anglo-Welsh Poetry.* Dannie Abse, ed. Seren Books / Dufour Editions, 1997. *World Poetry: An Anthology of Verse from Antiquity to Our Time.* Katharine Washburn and John S. Major, eds. 1338, 1998.

CONSTABLE, HENRY (1562–1613)

The son of Sir Robert Constable of Newark, Nottinghamshire, he was educated at St. John's College, Cambridge, but migrated to Paris where, being of the Catholic faith, he was more accepted. He served as the Pope's representative in Edinburgh in 1599, but when he returned to England he was imprisoned in the Tower of London in 1604, though released the same year. He died at Liege. His *Diana*— a book of 23 sonnets — was published in 1592 and is possibly the same book of poems he is said to have presented to King James in July 1600. He contributed four pastorals to *England's Helicon* (1600). His work is considered to have had an important influence on the development of the sonnet. Some of his poems: "Diaphenia," "Love's Franciscan," "Gracious Shepherd," "To His Flocks," "To Our Blessed Lady," "To Saint Margaret," "To Saint Mary Magdalen," "To the Marquess of Piscat's Soul."

Sources: *Dictionary of National Biography.* Electronic Edition, 1.1. Oxford University Press, 1997. *English Poetry: Author Search.* Chadwyck-Healey Ltd., 1995 (http://www.lib.utexas.edu:8080/search/epoetry/author.html). *The Anchor Anthology of Seventeenth-Century Verse, Vol. II.* Louis L. Martz and Richard S. Sylvester, ed. Doubleday Anchor Books, 1969. *The Columbia Granger's Index to Poetry.* 11th ed. *The Columbia Granger's World of Poetry,* Columbia University Press, 2005 (http://www.columbiagrangers.org). *The Golden Book of Catholic Poetry.* Alfred Noyes, ed. J.B. Lippincott, 1946. *The Oxford Book of Christian Verse.* Lord David Cecil, ed. Oxford University Press, 1940. *The Oxford Companion to English Literature.* 6th edition. Margaret Drabble, ed. Oxford University Press, 2000.

CONSTANTINE, DAVID (1944–)

English writer, poet and translator, fellow in German of Queen's College, Oxford. Born in Salford, Lancashire, he read modern languages at Wadham College, Oxford, and lectured in German at Durham from 1969 to 1981 and at Oxford from 1981 to 2000. He has won many prestigious awards and published translations of poetry and prose by German, French and Greek writers. Himself wheelchair dependent following a diving accident in 1982, he co-founded in 1990 Motivation, a charity that works to improve the quality of life of people with mobility impairment. His main publications: *Watching for Dolphins*, 1983. *Selected Poems*, 1991. *Caspar Hauser*, 1994. *Selected Poems of Friedeirch Holderlin*, 1996. *The Pelt of Wasps*, 1998. *Something for the Ghosts*, 2002. Some of his poems: "A Brightness to Cast Shadows," "Atlantis," "Birdsong," "Christ to Lazarus," "Heroes Meet Again in the Underworld" (translation of Homer), "Mary Magdalene and the Sun," "Shoes in the Charity Shop," "The Drowned," "The Trees Here," "You Are Distant, You Are Already Leaving."

Sources: *Biography of David Constantine, and his Poem, Dominion Poetry Review* (http://www.poetrysociety.org.uk/review/pr91-2/constant.htm). Carcanet Press (http://www.carcanet.co.uk). *Some Contemporary Poets of Britain and Ireland: An Anthology.* Michael Schmidt, ed. Carcanet Press, 1983. *The Columbia Granger's Index to Poetry.* 11th ed. *The Columbia Granger's World of Poetry,* Columbia University Press, 2005 (http://www.columbiagrangers.org). *The*

Oxford Companion to English Literature. 6th edition. Margaret Drabble, ed. Oxford University Press, 2000.

COOK, ELIZA (1818–1889)

From a humble background — her father was a London brazier — and largely self-educated, encouraged by her mother, she wrote some remarkably lasting and often quoted poetry. While living near Horsham, Sussex, when her father retired, she began writing poetry; some of her most enduring poems such as "I'm Afloat" and the "Star of Glengarry" were written at a young age. She wrote for various magazines and was praised in the *Literary Gazette*. She conducted *Eliza Cook's Journal* from 1849–1854, until ill health caused her to give up. Her sympathetic poem "Poor Hood" led to the erection of a monument in Kensal Green Cemetery, West London, to the genius Thomas Hood. Her main publications: *Lays of a Wild Harp*, 1835. *Old Arm Chair*, 1836 (published in the *Weekly Dispatch*). *Melaia and Other Poems*, 1838 (American edition, 1844). *New Echoes and Other Poems*, 1864. Some of her other poems: "A Home in the Heart," "A Song for Ragged Schools," "Away from the Revel," "Old Dobbin," "The Bonnie Scot," "The Englishman," "The Indian Hunter," "The Mouse and the Cake," "The Old Arm-Chair," "The Old Clock."

Sources: *Dictionary of National Biography.* Electronic Edition, 1.1. Oxford University Press, 1997. *English Poetry: Author Search.* Chadwyck-Healey Ltd., 1995 (http://www.lib.utexas.edu:8080/search/epoetry/author.html). *Great Books Online.* www.bartleby.com. *The Columbia Granger's Index to Poetry.* 11th ed. *The Columbia Granger's World of Poetry,* Columbia University Press, 2005 (http://www.columbiagrangers.org). *The Fireside Book of Humorous Poetry.* William Cole, ed. Simon and Schuster, 1959. *The National Portrait Gallery* (www.npg.org.uk). *The Oxford Companion to English Literature.* 6th edition. Margaret Drabble, ed. Oxford University Press, 2000.

COOPER, THOMAS (1805–1892)

Born at Leicester, he returned to Gainsborough with his widowed mother, who eked out a meager living as a dyer and by making and selling work boxes. Thomas attended the local Bluecoat School, and at fifteen became a shoemaker and at twenty-three opened his own school; he taught himself six languages, including Greek, Latin, and Hebrew. He was involved in the Chartist movement, was a lay preacher, and started writing for the *Stamford Mercury* in 1836. His ambition took him to London in 1839, where he became a journalist and writer. Following a Chartist speech in Hanley, Staffordshire, which caused a riot, he was imprisoned for two years on a charge of sedition and conspiracy. He wrote novels, poetry and his autobiography, *The Life of Thomas Cooper* (1872), as well as many books and tracts on Christian belief. Among his many works is *Paradise of Martyrs* (1873), and while in prison he wrote *Purgatory of Suicides* (1845), a political epic in ten books, written in Spenserian stanzas. Cooper's *Poetical Works* were published in London, 1877. Some of his poems: "Chartist Song," "The Old Man's Song," "The Swineherd of Stow," "The Woodman's Song."

Sources: *Dictionary of National Biography.* Electronic Edition, 1.1. Oxford University Press, 1997. *English Poetry: Author Search.* Chadwyck-Healey Ltd., 1995 (http://www.lib.utexas.edu:8080/search/epoetry/author.html). *Stanford University Libraries and Academic Information Resources* (http://library.stanford.edu). *The Columbia Granger's Index to Poetry.* 11th ed. *The Columbia Granger's World of Poetry,* Columbia University Press, 2005 (http://www.columbiagrangers.org). *The Poorhouse Fugitives: Self-Taught Poets and Poetry in Victorian Britain.* Brian Maidment, ed. Carcanet, 1987.

COPE, WENDY (1945–)

Born in Erith, Kent, and educated at Farringtrons School in Chislehurst, Kent, she read history at St. Hilda's College, Oxford, trained as a teacher at Westminster College of Education, Oxford, and taught in primary schools in London. She was arts and reviews editor for *Contact,* the Inner London Education Authority magazine, and continued to teach part time before becoming a freelance writer in 1986. She was television critic for *The Spectator* magazine until 1990. She is a fellow of the Royal Society of Literature. Prizes and awards: Michael Braude Award for Light Verse (American Academy of 1987 Cholmondeley Award), 1995. The Whitbread Poetry Award, short listed for her collection *If I Don't Know,* 2001. Some of her major poetry collections: *Making Cocoa for Kingsley Amis,* 1988. *Twiddling Your Thumbs,* 1986. *The River Girl,* 1991. *From Serious Concerns,* 1992. *Big Orchard Book of Funny Poems,* 2000 (editor). *Heaven on Earth: 101 Happy Poems,* 2001 (editor). Some of her poems: "Emily Dickinson," "Engineers' Corner," "English Weather," "Giving Up Smoking," "Men are Like Bloody Buses," "Strugnell's Sonnets," "Waste Land Limericks."

Sources: *A Poem a Day,* Karen McCosker and Nicholas Albery, eds. Steer Forth Press, 1996. *Poems of Wendy Cope* (http://www.arlindo-correia.com/050900.html). *The Columbia Granger's Index to Poetry.* 11th ed. *The Columbia Granger's World of Poetry,* Columbia University Press, 2005 (http://www.columbiagrangers.org). *The Norton Introduction to Literature.* 7th edition. Jerome Beaty and J. Paul Hunter, eds. W.W. Norton, 1998. *The Oxford Companion to English Literature.* 6th edition. Margaret Drabble, ed. Oxford University Press, 2000. *Who's Who.* London: A & C Black, 2005.

COPPARD, ALFRED EDGAR (1878–1957)

The son of a poor tailor, he lived in Folkestone, Kent, and Brighton, Sussex. Detesting injustice and cruelty, he became prominent in the peace movement. By 1907 he was clerk in the Eagle Ironworks at Oxford, which he left in 1919 to become a full-time writer, supplementing his income by prize money from his athletic prowess. He was greatly encouraged when an American periodical paid him fifty pounds for a story of a few thousand words. Between his 1921 short story *Adam and Eve and Pinch Me* and his 2001 *Short Stories,* he published twenty-eight books of short stories or poems. The first part of his autobiography, *It's Me O Lord,* was published posthumously in 1957. His first collection of poems, *Hips and Haws* (1922, republished 2004, Kessinger Publishing Co., ISBN 1–4179–5513–9) was followed by many others. Some of his poems: "Epitaph," "Forester's Song," "Mendacity," "The Apostate," "The Horse," "The Unfortunate Miller."

Sources: *Dictionary of National Biography.* Electronic Edition, 1.1. Oxford University Press, 1997. *Encyclopædia Britannica Ultimate Reference Suite DVD,* 2006. *The Columbia Granger's Index to Poetry.* 11th ed (http://www.columbiagrangers.org). *The National Portrait Gallery* (www.npg.org.uk). *The Oxford Book of Modern Verse, 1892–1935.* William Butler Yeats, ed. Oxford University Press, 1936. *The Oxford Companion to English Literature.* 6th edition. Margaret Drabble, ed. Oxford University Press, 2000.

CORBET, RICHARD (1582–1635)

The son of a gardener, educated at Westminster School and Pembroke College, Oxford, he then took holy orders. He was chaplain to James I and later appointed bishop of Oxford, then of Norwich. He was appointed to the vicarage of Stewkley, Berkshire, in 1620, a position he held till his death. He was strongly opposed to the puritans, and frequently admonished his clergy for puritan practices. He contributed generously to the rebuilding of St. Paul's in 1634, was renowned for his joviality, wit and his love of practical jokes, and was often seen in the company of Ben Jonson. Two notable collections: *Certain Elegant Poems,* 1647. *Poetica Stromata,* 1648. Some of his poems: "An Elegy Upon the Death of His Own Father," "An Epitaph on Doctor Donne, Dean of St. Paul's," "Certain True Words Spoken Concerning One Benet Corbett after Her Death," "Fairies Farewell," "Great Tom," "Iter Boreale," "Like to the Thundering Tone," "On Mr. Francis Beaumont (Then Newly Dead)," "The Distracted Puritan," "To His Son, Vincent Corbet" (on his third birthday).

Sources: *Dictionary of National Biography.* Electronic Edition, 1.1. Oxford University Press, 1997. *English Poetry:*

Author Search. Chadwyck-Healey Ltd., 1995 (http://www.lib.utexas.edu:8080/search/epoetry/author.html). *The Anchor Anthology of Seventeenth-Century Verse, Vol. II.* Louis L. Martz and Richard S. Sylvester, ed. Doubleday Anchor Books, 1969. *The Columbia Granger's Index to Poetry.* 11th ed. *The Columbia Granger's World of Poetry,* Columbia University Press, 2005 (http://www.columbiagrangers.org). *The Oxford Companion to English Literature.* 6th edition. Margaret Drabble, ed. Oxford University Press, 2000.

CORMAC, KING OF CASHEL (836–908)

The chief bishop of Leth Mogha, Ireland, descended from one of the ancient Irish clans, he received a sound education in verse composition and the art of penmanship. The Rock of Cashel (meaning fortress), to which the town Cashel (County Tipperary) owes its origin, is an isolated elevation of stratified limestone, rising abruptly from a broad and fertile plain called the Golden Vein. Although most of Cormac's writings are in Gaelic, his *Instructions of King Cormac*—full of sound common sense — has been translated by Kuno Meyer and can be found in full at http://www.wildideas.net/cathbad/pagan/cormac.html.

Sources: *Catholic Encyclopedia* (http://www.newadvent.org). *Dictionary of National Biography.* Electronic Edition, 1.1. Oxford University Press, 1997. *The Columbia Granger's Index to Poetry.* 11th ed. *The Columbia Granger's World of Poetry,* Columbia University Press, 2005 (http://www.columbiagrangers.org).

CORNFORD, FRANCES CROFTS DARWIN and (RUPERT) JOHN (1886–1960)

Frances Crofts Darwin Cornford, the mother, 1886–1960

The mother was the only child of Sir Francis Darwin, son of Charles Darwin. She was born in Cambridge (her father was lecturer in botany), educated privately and spent almost all her life there. She married Francis Macdonald Cornford, professor of ancient philosophy at Cambridge University. From the age of seventeen she suffered from bouts of severe depression. She started writing poetry at sixteen and subsequently published a sufficient body of poetry to entitle her to a distinguished place among the minor poets of the "Georgian" period and later years. Rupert Brooke was one of her closest friends and she was always eager to profit by criticism from him and others. One of her early books was a "morality" play, *Death and the Princess* (1912). Her *Collected Poems* appeared in 1954, and she was awarded the Queen's Medal for Poetry in 1959. Although best known for her comic poem "To a Fat Lady Seen from the Train," her "A Child's Dream" better conveys her feelings. Some of her other poems: "A Wasted Day," "All Souls' Night," "Autumn Morning at Cambridge," "In France," "Preëxistence," "Spring Morning," "Village before Sunset," "The Watch," "Weekend Stroll."

(Rupert) John Cornford, the son, 1915–1936

John, the eldest son, was educated at Trinity College, Cambridge, and the London School of Economics. He became a member of the Communist Party. When the Spanish Civil War broke out in 1936, he was one of the first to enlist against Franco and died at the battle of Lopera soon after he wrote his most famous poem, "Heart of the Heartless World." His body was never recovered. He despised Georgian poetry, which his mother embraced; from an early age his own poetry was influenced by Robert Graves, T.S. Eliot, and W.H. Auden (see entries). His poems and prose pieces were published in *John Cornford: A Memoir* (edited by Pat Sloan) in 1938. His main poems: "A Letter From Aragon, 1936," "Poems from Spain, 1936," "The Last Mile to Huesca, 1936."

Sources: *Dictionary of National Biography.* Electronic Edition, 1.1. Oxford University Press, 1997. *John Cornford: A Letter from Aragon (1936)* (http://www.spartacus.schoolnet.co.uk/SPcornford.htm). *The Columbia Granger's Index to Poetry.* 11th ed. *The Columbia Granger's World of Poetry,* Columbia University Press, 2005 (http://www.columbiagrangers.org). *The Home Book of Modern Verse.* Burton Egbert Stevenson, ed. Henry Holt, 1953. *The National Portrait Gallery* (www.npg.org.uk). *The Oxford Book of Twentieth-Century English Verse.* Philip Larkin, ed. Oxford University Press, 1973. *The Oxford Book of War Poetry.* Jon Stallworthy, Oxford University Press, 1984. *The Oxford Companion to English Literature.* 6th edition. Margaret Drabble, ed. Oxford University Press, 2000.

CORY, WILLIAM JOHNSON (1823–1892)

Born Johnson, he changed his name in 1870 on inheriting an estate at Halsdon, Devon. He was educated at Eton College, where he was elected king's scholar in 1831 and Newcastle scholar in 1841, and at King's College, Cambridge, where he gained the chancellor's medal for an English poem on Plato in 1843 and the Craven Scholarship in 1844. His reputation was that he was the most brilliant Eton tutor of his day. Between 1861 and 1865 Cory was a leading figure in opening King's College, Cambridge, previously an exclusive foundation, and in the introduction of mathematics and natural science into its course of study. He left Eton after twenty-six years in 1872 and retired to Hampstead, London. Some of his publications are: *Ionica,* 1858 (published anonymously; a new enlarged edition reissued in 1891 contains the translation of the epigram of Heraclitus). *Lucretilis*, 1871. *Nuces*, 1869–70 (a series of lessons on the new Latin primer). Cory will forever be remembered for "The Eton Boating Song," first performed on 4 June 1863. Some of his other poems: "A Ballad for a Boy," "The Bride's Song," "Parting."

Sources: *Biography.ms* (http://www.biography.ms). *Dictionary of National Biography*. Electronic Edition, 1.1. Oxford University Press, 1997. *Oldpoetry* (www.oldpoetry. com). *The Columbia Granger's Index to Poetry*. 11th ed. *The Columbia Granger's World of Poetry*, Columbia University Press, 2005 (http://www.columbiagrangers.org). *The Oxford Book of Children's Verse*. Iona Opie and Peter Opie, eds. Oxford University Press, 1973. *The Oxford Companion to English Literature*. 6th edition. Margaret Drabble, ed. Oxford University Press, 2000.

COTTON, CHARLES (1630–1687)

Cotton was born at Beresford in Staffordshire. His father, also Charles, who married well and came into estates in Derbyshire and Staffordshire, was a friend of many great poets, among them Ben Jonson and John Donne. Although there is no evidence of a university education, Cotton's classical achievements were impressive, as was his knowledge of French and Italian literature; he had traveled in those countries. Although a staunch Royalist, neither he nor his father appears to have suffered at the hands of the Commonwealth soldiers. In 1649 he contributed an elegy on Henry, lord Hastings, to Richard Brome's *Lachrymæ Musarum*. He also contributed to Izaac Walton's *Compleat Angler* (1653–1655). No collection of Cotton's poems was published until after his death, but they had been passed among his friends in manuscript. Some of his publications: *Scarronides*, 1664 (a mock-heroic burlesque of Virgi). *Horace*, 1671 (a translation of Corneille's). *The Moral Philosophy of the Stoics*, 1667 (a translation from the French by Du Vair). Some of his poems: "Evening," "Ode to Cupid," "On Tobacco," "The Angler's Ballad," "The New Year," "To Mr. Izaak Walton."

Sources: *Dictionary of National Biography*. Electronic Edition, 1.1. Oxford University Press, 1997. *Encyclopædia Britannica Ultimate Reference Suite DVD*, 2006. *English Poetry: Author Search*. Chadwyck-Healey Ltd., 1995 (http://www.lib.utexas.edu:8080/search/epoetry/author. html). *Oldpoetry* (www.oldpoetry.com). *The Columbia Granger's Index to Poetry*. 11th ed. *The Columbia Granger's World of Poetry*, Columbia University Press, 2005 (http:// www.columbiagrangers.org). *The Golden Treasury of Longer Poems*. Ernest Rhys, ed. E.P. Dutton, 1949. *The Oxford Book of Garden Verse*. John Dixon Hunt, ed. Oxford University Press, 1993. *The Oxford Book of Sonnets*. John Fuller, ed. Oxford University Press, 2000. *The Oxford Companion to English Literature*. 6th edition. Margaret Drabble, ed. Oxford University Press, 2000.

COTTON, NATHANIEL (1705–1788)

Born in London, the son of a merchant, he studied medicine in Holland and was practicing in St. Albans around 1740, where he remained until his death. He kept Collegium Insanorum, a private asylum, in which the poet Cowper was confined during one period of eighteen months from 1763 to 1765. Cowper said of Cotton: "I was not only treated with kindness by him while I was ill ... and attended with the utmost diligence ... I could open my mind upon the subject without reserve, I could hardly have found a fitter person for the purpose" (DNB). Cotton published *Observations on a Particular Kind of Scarlet Fever That Lately Prevailed In and About St. Albans* (1749). His major poetical publications are: *Visions in Verse, for the Entertainment and Instruction of Younger Minds*, 1751, and a seventh (enlarged) edition, 1767. *Various Pieces in Prose and Verse, Many of Which Were Never Before Published*, published by his son, 1791. Some of his poems: "Death and the Rake," "The Bee, the Ant, and the Sparrow," "The Lamb and the Pig," "The Night Piece," "To a Child of Five Years Old" and "Tomorrow."

Sources: *Dictionary of National Biography*. Electronic Edition, 1.1. Oxford University Press, 1997. *English Poetry: Author Search*. Chadwyck-Healey Ltd., 1995 (http://www. lib.utexas.edu:8080/search/epoetry/author.html). *The Columbia Granger's Index to Poetry*. 11th ed. *The Columbia Granger's World of Poetry*, Columbia University Press, 2005 (http://www.columbiagrangers.org). *The Oxford Book of Children's Verse*. Iona Opie and Peter Opie, eds. Oxford University Press, 1973.

COTTON, ROGER (?1550–1650)

Born in Whitchurch, Shropshire, and was probably educated in the free school there. He had five brothers, most of whom were patrons of literature; Allen, the youngest, became lord mayor of London and was knighted. Roger settled in London and carried on the business of a draper in Canning Street, having been admitted a member of the Drapers' Company. He became friends with Hugh Broughton, the Christian teacher and preacher, and it is said that Roger read he Bible twelve times in a year. He wrote several religious books with long titles (which have been abbreviated): *A Direction to the waters of lyfe*, 1592, A third edition. *A Direct Way, whereby the plainest man may be guided to the Waters of Life*, 1610. *An Armor of Proofe, brought from the Tower of Dauid, to fight against Spannyardes, and all enimies of the trueth*, 1592. *A Spirituall Song: Setting downe the treacherous practises of the wicked, against the children of God*, 1596. Some of his poems: "A Description of Old Rome," "G.W. in Praise of This Book," "P.K. in Commendation of This Work," "Spiritual Song."

Sources: *Dictionary of National Biography.* Electronic Edition, 1.1. Oxford University Press, 1997. *English Poetry: Author Search.* Chadwyck-Healey Ltd., 1995 (http://www. lib.utexas.edu:8080/search/epoetry/author.html). *Oldpoetry* (www.oldpoetry.com).

COURTHOPE, WILLIAM JOHN (1842–1917)

Born in South Malling vicarage, near Lewes, Sussex, he attended Harrow School, Corpus Christi College, Oxford, and New College, Oxford. He won the Newdigate prize in 1864, and chancellor's prize for an English essay on *The Genius of Spenser.* Trained in law, in 1887 he became a civil service commissioner, and as senior commissioner, a post he held from 1892 until his retirement in 1907, he did much to humanize the examinations for the higher appointments. He became professor of poetry at Oxford and was made an honorary fellow of New College, Oxford, in 1896. Between 1871 and 1889 he published five volumes (out of ten) of the works of Alexander Pope. His principal publications: *History of English Poetry*, 1895–1910. *The Chancellor's Garden*, 1888. *Life in Poetry, Law in Taste*, 1901 (his professorial lectures). *Ludibria Lunae*, 1869 (a satirical burlesque of women's rights). *Paradise of Birds*, 1870. Translations of *Martial's Epigrams*, 1914. *The Country Town and Other Poems*, 1920. Some of his poems: "Bird Catcher's Song," "Dodoism," "Hop-Picking," "In Memory of Arthur Eden," "The Chancellor's Garden," "The Trail of the Bird."

Sources: *Dictionary of National Biography.* Electronic Edition, 1.1. Oxford University Press, 1997. *Encyclopædia Britannica Ultimate Reference Suite DVD*, 2006. *English Poetry: Author Search.* Chadwyck-Healey Ltd., 1995 (http://www.lib.utexas.edu:8080/search/epoetry/author. html). *Great Books Online.* www.bartleby.com. *Other Men's Flowers.* A.P. Wavell, ed. Jonathan Cape, 1990. *Stanford University Libraries and Academic Information Resources* (http://library.stanford.edu). *The Columbia Granger's Index to Poetry.* 11th ed. *The Columbia Granger's World of Poetry*, Columbia University Press, 2005 (http://www.columbia-grangers.org). *The Oxford Companion to English Literature.* 6th edition. Margaret Drabble, ed. Oxford University Press, 2000.

COUSIN, ANNE ROSS (1824–1906)

Born in Hull (her father, David Ross Cundell, M.D., was an assistant surgeon of the 33rd regiment at Waterloo) in 1847, she married William Cousin, a Presbyterian minister. She wrote several hymns, but the best known is "The Sands of Time are Sinking." It is adapted from her poem of nineteen stanzas, *In Immanuel's Land* (written at Irvine, Ayrshire, in 1854). It appeared first in *The Christian Treasury* (1857) under the heading "Last Words of Samuel Rutherford." The hymn uses stanzas 1, 5, 13, and 17. In 1910 a stained-glass window to her memory was placed in St. Aidan's United Free Church, Melrose, where her husband was once minister. Some of her other hymns and poems: "In the Songless Night, the Daylight Dreary," "King Eternal, King Immortal," "Lord, Mine Must Be a Spotless Dress," "Christ, What Burdens Bowed Thy Head," "Now is the Time," "Thou That on the Billow," "The Sands of Time Are Sinking," "To Thee and to Thy Christ, O God," "To Thy Father and Thy Mother," "When We Reach Our Peaceful Dwelling."

Sources: *A Sacrifice of Praise: An Anthology of Christian Poetry in English from Caedmon to the Mid-Twentieth Century.* James H. Trott, ed. Cumberland House Publishing, 1999. *Dictionary of National Biography.* Electronic Edition, 1.1. Oxford University Press, 1997. *Last Words, the Complete, The Sands of Time Are Sinking* (http://www.puritansermons.com/poetry/ruth18.htm). *The Columbia Granger's Index to Poetry.* 11th ed. *The Columbia Granger's World of Poetry*, Columbia University Press, 2005 (http://www.columbiagrangers.org). *The Cyber Hymnal* (http://www.cyberhymnal.org/index.htm).

COWARD, SIR NOEL PEIRCE (1899–1973)

Born at Teddington, Middlesex, the son of Arthur Sabin Coward, a clerk. Both father and mother were musical and keen theatre-goers. At an early age he could play accurately by ear numbers from the show he had seen that day. When he was twelve, he played Prince Mussel in *The Goldfish* as one of a "Star Cast of Wonder Children." He sold his first song at the age of sixteen; his first West End play, *I'll Leave It to You*, was performed in 1917. He became a rich celebrity, beloved both at home and in the United States. He was knighted in 1970 and received a special Tony Award for lifetime achievement in that same year. He died of a heart attack on his estate in Jamaica and is commemorated by a floor stone in the nave of Westminster Abbey. Some of his publications: *Bitter Sweet*, 1929. *Blithe Spirit*, a play, 1941. *In Which We Serve*, 1942. *The Happy Breed*, 1943. *Brief Encounter*, 1945. Some of his poems: "Don't Let's Be Beastly to the Germans," "London Pride," "Mad Dogs and Englishmen," "Mrs. Worthington."

Sources: *Dictionary of National Biography.* Electronic Edition, 1.1. Oxford University Press, 1997. *Encyclopædia Britannica Ultimate Reference Suite DVD*, 2006. *Reading Lyrics.* Robert Gottlieb and Robert Kimball, ed. Pantheon Books, 2000. *The Columbia Granger's Index to Poetry.* 11th ed. *The Columbia Granger's World of Poetry*, Columbia University Press, 2005 (http://www.columbiagrangers. org). *Biography of Noel Coward. The Knitting Circle: Theatre* (http://myweb.lsbu.ac.uk/~stafflag/noelcoward.html). *The National Portrait Gallery* (www.npg.org.uk). *The Oxford Companion to English Literature.* 6th edition. Margaret Drabble, ed. Oxford University Press, 2000. *Westminster Abbey Official Guide* (no date).

COWLEY, ABRAHAM (1618–1667)

The son of a London stationer, he was educated at Westminster School and Trinity College, Cambridge, where he and Richard Crashaw became friends. After Crashaw's death Cowley wrote an elegy addressing him as "poet and saint." A supporter of the Royalists in the English Civil War, he moved to Oxford, where he wrote the satire *The Puritan and the Papist* (1643). In 1644 he went into exile in Paris as secretary to Lord Jermyn, Queen Henrietta Maria's chamberlain. When he returned to England, he was imprisoned briefly as a Royalist spy. His greatest contribution to posterity was adapting the difficult style of the Greek lyric poet Pindar to the English ode. He is buried near Chaucer and Spenser in Poets' Corner of Westminster Abbey. Charles II declared that he had not left a better man behind him in England. His main publications: *Pyramus and Thisbe*, 1628. *Constantius and Philetus*, 1630. *Poetical Blossoms*, 1633. *The Mistress*, 1647. *Ode Upon the Blessed Restoration*, 1660. *Verses upon several occasions*, 1663. Some of his poems: "Beauty," "David and Jonathan," "Music and Poetry," "The Country-Mouse," "The Duel," "The Grasshopper."

Sources: *Dictionary of National Biography.* Electronic Edition, 1.1. Oxford University Press, 1997. *Encyclopædia Britannica Ultimate Reference Suite DVD,* 2006. *English Poetry: Author Search.* Chadwyck-Healey Ltd., 1995 (http://www.lib.utexas.edu:8080/search/epoetry/author.html). *Jacobean and Caroline Poetry: An Anthology.* T.G.S. Cain, ed. Methuen, 1981. *Samuel Johnson's Lives of the English Poets,* 1779–1781 (http://www2.hn.psu.edu/Faculty/KKemmerer/poets/preface.htm). *The Columbia Granger's Index to Poetry.* 11th ed. *The Columbia Granger's World of Poetry,* Columbia University Press, 2005 (http://www.columbiagrangers.org). *The National Portrait Gallery* (www.npg.org.uk). *The Oxford Companion to English Literature.* 6th edition. Margaret Drabble, ed. Oxford University Press, 2000. *Westminster Abbey Official Guide* (no date).

COWLEY, HANNAH (1743–1809)

Born in Tiverton, Devonshire, the daughter of Philip Parkhouse, a bookseller, she married a captain in the East India Company's service. Challenged by her husband to write a better play than the one they had just seen, she produced *The Runaway*, performed at Drury Lane in 1776. She experienced great anxiety about the performances of her plays, and this involved her in newspaper warfare with Hannah More, whom she taxed with plagiarism. She also quarreled with the managers of Drury Lane and Covent Garden by alleging that they had misused her manuscripts. Some of her main publications: *Albina, Countess Raimond*, 1779 (tragedy). *The Belle's Stratagem,* 1780 (comedy). *The Maid of Arragon,* 1780 (two volumes, poetry). *Which Is the Man?* 1782 (comedy). *A Bold Stroke for a Husband*, 1783 (comedy). *The Scottish Village, or Pitcairn Green,* 1787 (poetry). *A Day in Turkey, or the Russian Slaves,* 1792 (comedy). *The Town Before You,* 1795 (comedy). *The Siege of Acre,* 1799 (four volumes). Some of her other poems: "A Charity Hymn," "Elegy on a Field of Battle," "The Death of Chatterton," "The Lame Youth."

Sources: *Dictionary of National Biography.* Electronic Edition, 1.1. Oxford University Press, 1997. *Eighteenth Century Women Poets: An Oxford Anthology.* Roger Lonsdale, ed. Oxford University Press, 1989. *The Columbia Granger's Index to Poetry.* 11th ed. *The Columbia Granger's World of Poetry,* Columbia University Press, 2005 (http://www.columbiagrangers.org). *The National Portrait Gallery* (www.npg.org.uk). *The Oxford Companion to English Literature.* 6th edition. Margaret Drabble, ed. Oxford University Press, 2000.

COWPER, WILLIAM (1731–1800)

William Cowper (pronounced "Cooper") was the son of the rector of Great Berkhamsted, Hertfordshire, and chaplain to King George II. Educated at Westminster School, he was called to the bar in 1745, but never practiced. He suffered throughout his life from severe (possibly manic) depression and during one of his periods of hospitalization he experienced a profound religious conversion. He and George Herbert share a commemorative window in St. George's Chapel, Westminster Abbey. His poems are of everyday life—hedgerows, ditches, rivers, haystacks, and hares. Also a prolific hymn-writer, one of his best-known is "God Moves in a Mysterious Way." He collaborated with John Newton to write the hymn "Light Shining Out of Darkness." Between 1765 and 1773 at the village of Olney, Buckinghamshire, Cowper, and John Newton (who was curate there) published the *Olney Hymns.* Cowper's poem "Against Slavery" is an example of how he spoke up for the poor and the downtrodden. Some of his other poems: "Abuse of the Gospel," "How to Grow Cucumbers," "R.S.S. Written in a Fit of Illness," "The Bee and the Pine-Apple," "The Castaway," "The Retired Cat," "The Sower."

Sources: *Dictionary of National Biography.* Electronic Edition, 1.1. Oxford University Press, 1997. *Encyclopædia Britannica Ultimate Reference Suite DVD,* 2006. *English Poetry: Author Search.* Chadwyck-Healey Ltd., 1995 (http://www.lib.utexas.edu:8080/search/epoetry/author.html). *Poet's Corner Bookshelf* (http://www.theotherpages.org/poems/olney.html). *The Columbia Granger's Index to Poetry.* 11th ed. *The Columbia Granger's World of Poetry,* Columbia University Press, 2005 (http://www.columbiagrangers.org). *The Cyber Hymnal* (http://www.cyberhymnal.org/index.htm). *The Oxford Companion to English Literature.* 6th edition. Margaret Drabble, ed. Oxford University Press, 2000. *The Poetical Works of William Cowper.* 3rd edition. H.S. Milford, ed. Oxford University Press, 1926. *Westminster Abbey Official Guide* (no date).

CRABBE, GEORGE (1754–1832)

Born in the village of Aldeburgh, Suffolk, where his father worked as a customs official. He was chiefly self-educated, largely through his father's *Martin's Philosophical Magazine*, which he bought for the mathematical part; the poems he handed over to the son. He was apprenticed to a surgeon at fourteen. At twenty-four he moved to London to become a writer. Edmund Burke befriended him and helped him get his poem "The Library" published in 1781. He took holy orders and became curate of Aldeburgh in 1781, then chaplain to the Duke of Rutland at Belvoir Castle in 1782. He practiced medicine and helped the poor of his various parishes. Many of his poems are long and contain within them sketches of people taken from the Register of Births, Marriage, and Deaths. Some of his publications: *Inebriety*, 1775. *The Candidate*, 1780. *The Village*, 1783. *Newspaper*, 1785. *Poems*, 1807. *The Parish Register*, 1807. *The Borough*, 1810. *Tales of the Hall*, 1819. Some of his other poems: "Phoebe Dawson," "Resurrection," "Sir Eustace Grey," "Tales," "The Ancient Mansion," "The Whistling Boy," "The World of Dreams."

Sources: *Dictionary of National Biography*. Electronic Edition, 1.1. Oxford University Press, 1997. *Encyclopædia Britannica Ultimate Reference Suite DVD, 2006. English Poetry: Author Search*. Chadwyck-Healey Ltd., 1995 (http://www.lib.utexas.edu:8080/search/epoetry/author. html). *The Columbia Granger's Index to Poetry*. 11th ed. *The Columbia Granger's World of Poetry*, Columbia University Press, 2005 (http://www.columbiagrangers.org). *The National Portrait Gallery* (www.npg.org.uk). *The Oxford Companion to English Literature*. 6th edition. Margaret Drabble, ed. Oxford University Press, 2000. *The Poetical Works of Crabbe, Heber, and Pollok*. Lippincott, Grambo. 1854.

CRAIG, ALEXANDER (?1567–1627)

Minor Scottish poet, born at Banff and educated at St. Andrews University. When James VI became king of England, Craig migrated to London and published *The Poetical Essayes of Alexander Craige, Scots-Britane* (1604). For this flattery of the king and queen he was granted a pension and returned to Scotland. His other known publications are: *The Amorose Songes, and Sonets*, 1606 (dedicated to Queen Anne; a copy of which is held at Rutgers University, New Brunswick, New Jersey). *The Poetical Recreations*, 1609 (dedicated to the Earl of Dunbar). *Poeticall Recreations*, 1623 (consisting chiefly of epigrams). *The Pilgrime and Heremite*, 1631. He contributed some verses to *The Famous Historie of the Renowned and Valiant Prince Robert, surnamed the Bruce, King of Scotland* (1615). Some of his poems: "Appellation to the Lion," "The Pilgrime and Heremite," "To Cynthia," "To Erantina," "To Kala," "To Pandora," "To Penelope."

Sources: *Alexander Craig, Two Sonnets* (www.sonnets. org/craig.htm). *Dictionary of National Biography*. Electronic Edition, 1.1. Oxford University Press, 1997. *English Poetry: Author Search*. Chadwyck-Healey Ltd., 1995 (http://www.lib.utexas.edu:8080/search/epoetry/author. html). *Oldpoetry* (www.oldpoetry.com). *Stanford University Libraries and Academic Information Resources* (http://library.stanford.edu).

CRAIK, DINAH MARIA MULOCK (1826–1887)

The daughter of Thomas Mulock, a Nonconformist clergyman from Stoke-upon-Trent, Staffordshire, she came to London in about 1846. There she met some influential people who encouraged her in her writing stories for children, of which *Cola Monti* (1849) was the best known. In 1865 she married George Lillie Craik, a partner in the Macmillan publishing company, and lived at Shortlands, Bromley, Kent. She wrote the Christmas carol "God Rest Ye, Merry Gentlemen." Some of her publications: *The Ogilvies*, 1849 (three-volume novel). *Olive*, 1850 (novel). *Alice Learmont*, 1852 (fairy story). *John Halifax, Gentleman*, 1857 (novel). *The Head of the Family*, 1851 (novel). *Avillion and Other Tales*, 1853 (short stories). *John Halifax, Gentleman*, 1857 (novel). *The Little Lame Prince*, 1875 (novel). *Poems of Thirty Years, New and Old*, 1881. Some of her poems: "A Hymn for Christmas Morning," "Four Years," "Green Things Growing," "Highland Cattle," "Philip, My King," "Rothesay Bay," "The Aurora on the Clyde," "The Blackbird," "The Canary in His Cage," "Westward Ho!"

Sources: *Dictionary of National Biography*. Electronic Edition, 1.1. Oxford University Press, 1997. *Dinah Maria Mulock Craik, 18 Sonnets* (www.sonnets.org/craik.htm). *Oldpoetry* (www.oldpoetry.com). *Poems, by the Author of "A Life for a Life" (Dinah Maria Mulock Craik)*. Ticknor & Fields, 1860. *The Best Loved Poems of the American People*. Hazel Felleman, ed. Doubleday, 1936. *The Columbia Granger's Index to Poetry*. 11th ed. *The Columbia Granger's World of Poetry*, Columbia University Press, 2005 (http://www.columbiagrangers.org). *The National Portrait Gallery* (www.npg.org.uk). *The Oxford Companion to English Literature*. 6th edition. Margaret Drabble, ed. Oxford University Press, 2000.

CRASHAW, RICHARD (?1613–1649)

His father, William, was one of the Puritan clergymen officiating at the execution of Mary Queen of Scots in 1587. Orphaned from the age of fourteen, Richard was educated at Charterhouse School and Pembroke College, Cambridge, and was one of the group known as the Metaphysical Poets. He had Roman Catholic leanings and fled to France in 1644, where he became a Catholic sometime around 1645, and died of a fever in Rome. Although he wrote secular poetry in Latin and Greek as well as in English, his fame rests mostly on his intense religious poetry. His *Steps to the Temple* (1646) refers to George Herbert's *The Temple* (1633). His English religious poems were republished in Paris in 1652 under the title *Carmen Deo Nostro* (*Hymn to Our Lord*). Some of his other poems: "And He Answered Them Nothing" (probably inspired by the trial of Jesus before Pilate as recorded in Matthew 27:12), "Delights of the Muses," "Hymn for New Year's Day," "The Flaming Heart," "The Shepherd's Hymn," "To Pontius Washing His Hands," "Upon the Death of a Friend."

Sources: *Dictionary of National Biography.* Electronic Edition, 1.1. Oxford University Press, 1997. *Encyclopædia Britannica Ultimate Reference Suite DVD, 2006. English Poetry: Author Search.* Chadwyck-Healey Ltd., 1995 (http://www.lib.utexas.edu:8080/search/epoetry/author.html). *Richard Crashaw* (http://www.luminarium.org/sevenlit/crashaw/). *The Columbia Granger's Index to Poetry.* 11th ed. *The Columbia Granger's World of Poetry,* Columbia University Press, 2005 (http://www.columbiagrangers.org). *The Complete Poetry of Richard Crashaw.* George Walton Williams, ed. New York University Press, 1972. *The Oxford Companion to English Literature.* 6th edition. Margaret Drabble, ed. Oxford University Press, 2000.

CRAWFORD, ROBERT (1959–)

Scottish poet, born in Belshill, Lanarkshire, he received his M.A. from Glasgow University and his doctorate of philosophy from Oxford. After teaching at the universities of Oxford and Glasgow, in 1989 he started teaching at St. Andrews, where he is currently professor of modern Scottish literature and head of the School of English. He has served as a judge for the T.S. Eliot Prize, the National Poetry Competition, and other awards. Teaching interests include Scottish literature, modern and contemporary poetry, T.S. Eliot, and creative writing. He lives in St. Andrews, near the sea, and is a fellow of the Royal Society of Edinburgh. He has published several volumes of literary criticism on Scottish literature and poetry. His awards: Eric Gregory, 1988. Scottish Arts Council Book, 1993 and 1999. Some of his poetry publications: *A Scottish Assembly*, 1990. *Sharawaggi*, 1990 (with W.N. Herbert, see entry). *The Tip of My Tongue*, 2003. *Selected Poems*, 2005. Some of his poems: "At Landsdowne Kirk," "Blue Song," "Doun the Burn, Davie," "Downtown Sunday," "Scotland in the 1890s," "The Herr-Knit Bunnet," "To Henry Darnley, King of Scots."

Sources: *British Council Arts* (http://www.contemporarywriters.com). *Golden Treasury of the Best Songs & Lyrical Poems in the English Language.* Francis Turner Palgrave, ed. Oxford University Press (1964, Sixth edition, updated by John Press, 1994). *Professor Robert Crawford (Head of School)* (http://www.st-andrews.ac.uk/english/crawford/home.html). *Outsiders: Poems about Rebels, Exiles, and Renegades.* Laure-Anne Bosselaar, ed. Milkweed Editions,

1999. *Penguin Modern Poets, Book 9.* John Burnside, Robert Crawford, and Kathleen Jamie, ed. Penguin Books, 1996. *The Columbia Granger's Index to Poetry.* 11th ed. *The Columbia Granger's World of Poetry,* Columbia University Press, 2005 (http://www.columbiagrangers.org). *The New Penguin Book of Scottish Verse.* Robert Crawford and Mick Imlah, ed. Penguin Books, 2000. *The Oxford Companion to English Literature.* 6th edition. Margaret Drabble, ed. Oxford University Press, 2000. *The Penguin Book of Poetry from Britain and Ireland Since 1945.* Robert Crawford, and Simon Armitage, ed. Penguin Books, 1998. *The Scottish Collection of Verse to 1800.* Eileen Dunlop and Kamm Antony, eds. Richard Drew, 1985.

CREECH, THOMAS (1659–1700)

Born at Blandford, Dorset, of humble parentage, he received his classical training from Thomas Curgenven, rector of Folke in Dorset, master of Sherborne School. Educated at Wadham College, Oxford, under the tuition of Robert Pitt, he earned a B.A. in 1680, M.A. in 1683, and B.D. in 1696 and was elected a fellow in 1683. For two years (1694–1696) he was the headmaster of Sherborne School, but he then returned to Oxford, where his strange behavior caused concern. He suffered from depression and hanged himself. He was famed for his translations of Plutarch, Virgil and Ovid. His other translations and poems: *Lucretius*, 1682. *Horace*, 1684. *Idylls of Theocritus*, 1684. *The Thirteenth Satire of Juvenal*, 1693. *The Astronomicon of Manilius*, 1697. Some of his other poems: "De Rerum Natura" ("On the Nature of Things") (Lucretius), "Eclogues [of Virgil]," "Idylls [of Theocritus]," "To Mr. Dryden, on *Religio Laici*."

Sources: *Biography of Thomas Creech* (http://68.1911encyclopedia.org/c/cr/creech_thomas.htm). *Dictionary of National Biography.* Electronic Edition, 1.1. Oxford University Press, 1997. *Love to Know Encyclopedia* (http://www.1911encyclopedia.org/). *The Columbia Granger's Index to Poetry.* 11th ed. *The Columbia Granger's World of Poetry,* Columbia University Press, 2005 (http://www.columbiagrangers.org).

CREWDSON, JANE (1809–1863)

Cornish-born Jane Fox married Thomas Dillworth Crewdson, a Manchester manufacturer, in 1836. She composed her poetry and hymns during periods of ill health and contributed several hymns to Squire Lovell's *Selection of Scriptural Poetry*, 1848. Her main publications are: *Aunt Jane's Verses for Children*, 1851. *Lays of the Reformation*, 1860. *A Little While, and Other Poems,* 1864. Some of her hymns and poems: "Tis Not the Cross I Have to Bear," "A Little While," "Give to the Lord Thy Heart," "Gratitude," "How Tenderly Thy Hand is Laid," "I've Found a Joy in Sorrow," "Looking unto Jesus," "Lord, We Know That Thou Art Near Us," "For the Peace Which Floweth as a River," "Savior, I Have

Naught to Plead," "Thou Whose Bounty Fills My Cup," "One Touch from Thee," "The Followers of the Son of God," "There is No Sorrow, Lord, Too Light," "Though Gloom May Veil Our Troubled Skies."

Sources: *Dictionary of National Biography.* Electronic Edition, 1.1. Oxford University Press, 1997. *Hymn Writers of the Church* (http://www.ccel.org/ccel/nutter/hymnwriters.html3). *The Cyber Hymnal* (http://www.cyberhymnal.org/index.htm).

CRIPPS, ARTHUR SHEARLY (1869–1952)

Cripps spent 50 years as an Anglican priest in what is now Zimbabwe. Born in Tunbridge Wells, Kent, England, he studied modern history at Oxford and joined the Christian Social Union, whose members exposed exploiting employers. He was ordained as an Anglican priest in 1893 and served as assistant curate at Ickleham in Sussex. In 1897, inspired by Olive Schreiner's book *Trooper Peter Halket of Mashonaland* (1897) in which she attacks Cecil Rhodes and his Chartered Company, he joined the Society for the Propagation of the Gospel in Zimbabwe (Mashonaland). His book *Africa for Africans* was published in 1927. Some of his other publications: *Primavera*, 1890 (poetry). *Titania and Other Poems*, 1900. *The Black Christ*, 1902 (poetry). *Lyra Evangelistica: Missionary Verses of Mashonaland*, 1909. *Lake and War: African Land and Water Verses*, 1917. *Africa: Verses*, 1939. Some of his poems: "An Easter Hymn," "Les Belles Roses sans Mercie," "Missa Viatoris."

Sources: *Biography of Arthur Shearly Cripps, Zimbabwe, Anglican priest* (http://www.dacb.org/stories/zimbabwe/cripps_arthur.html). *The Dust Diaries*, Sheers, Owen. Houghton Mifflin, 2004 (http://www.houghtonmifflinbooks.com/booksellers/press_release/sheers/). *The Oxford Book of Victorian Verse.* Arthur Quiller-Couch, ed. Oxford University Press, 1971. *Literary map of Africa, Southern Africa — Zimbabwe* (http://web.udl.es/usuaris/m0163949/zimbabwe.htm).

CRISTALL, ANNE BATTEN (b. 1769)

Cristall was born in Penzance but the family moved to London when she was young. Her brother was Joshua Cristall, the celebrated water-colorist whose portrait is in the National Art Gallery. She became a schoolteacher and by the late 1780s she had become a friend of Mary Wollstonecraft. The poet George Dyer (see entry) took a personal interest in her and in 1797 introduced her to Robert Southey (see entry). There is no record of her death. Her *Poetical Sketches*, twenty-four poems of accomplished if melancholic pieces, some of them with several parts, were published in 1795. Some of her poems: "Before Twilight. Eyezion," "Elegy on a

Young Lady," "Ode on Truth: Addressed to George Dyer," "The Blind Man," "The Snow-Fiend," "The Triumph of Superstition, Raphael and Ianthe," "Verses Written in the Spring," "Written in Devonshire, Near the Dart," "Written When the Mind Was Oppressed."

Sources: *Dictionary of National Biography.* Electronic Edition, 1.1. Oxford University Press, 1997. *Poetical Sketches of Anne Batten: All Her Poems* (http://etext.lib.virginia.edu/toc/modeng/public/CriSket:html). *Romantic Women Poets: An Anthology.* Duncan Wu, ed. Blackwell Publishers, 1997.

CROLY, GEORGE (1780-1860)

Irish clergyman, ordained in 1804, and a distinguished classical scholar, he was educated at Trinity College, Dublin. After several appointments, around 1810, accompanied by his widowed mother and his sisters, he settled in London. In 1835 he became rector of St. Stephen's, Walbrook, London (built by Christopher Wren, 1672 to 1687, after the Great Fire of 1666, and situated close to the Bank of England). He was dramatic critic to the *New Times* and a regular contributor to the *Literary Gazette* and *Blackwood's Magazine*. He became principal lead writer to the *Britannia* newspaper. In addition to his poems he wrote several hymns. Some of his principal publications: *Paris*, 1815 (inspired by Byron's *Childe Harold*). *The Angel of the World*, 1817. *Catiline*, 1822 (tragedy). *May Fair*, 1827 (satire). *Salathiel*, 1829 (romance). Marston, (novel), 1846. *The Modern Orlando*, 1846 (poem). *Scenes from Scripture and Other Poems*, 1851. *Psalms and Hymns for Public Worship*, 1854. Some of his poems and hymns: "A Supplication," "Be Still, Be Still, Impatient Soul," "Behold Me, Lord, and If Thou Find," "Death and Resurrection," "Domestic Love," "Lift Up Your Heads, Ye Gates of Light."

Sources: *Dictionary of National Biography.* Electronic Edition, 1.1. Oxford University Press, 1997. *English Poetry: Author Search.* Chadwyck-Healey Ltd., 1995 (http://www.lib.utexas.edu:8080/search/epoetry/author.html). *England's Thousand Best Churches.* S. Jenkins. Allen Lane, 1999. *The Columbia Granger's Index to Poetry.* 11th ed. *The Columbia Granger's World of Poetry*, Columbia University Press, 2005 (http://www.columbiagrangers.org). *The National Portrait Gallery* (www.npg.org.uk). *The Oxford Companion to English Literature.* 6th edition. Margaret Drabble, ed. Oxford University Press, 2000. *The World's Great Religious Poetry.* Caroline Miles Hill, ed. Macmillan, 1954.

CROMPTON, HUGH (circa 1657)

From what can be deduced, Crompton was from Lancashire and from a well-to-do family who fell into financial difficulties, forcing Crompton to earn his living, which he seems to have done by his poetry. Sometime before 1687 he emigrated to Ireland. It seems that his education was cut short when his father's business failed. Hugh occupied his spare time writing poetry. His known publications: *The Glory of Women*, 1652. *Pierides*, 1657. *Poems*, 1657. Some of his poems: "A Walk in a Summer-morning," "Epigram LXVII: Time, the Interpreter," "Epigram VII: Winifred," "Loves Gain," "The Country Girl," "The Cruel Boy," "The Evil Temper," "To the Executioner."

Sources: Dictionary of National Biography. Electronic Edition, 1.1. Oxford University Press, 1997. *English Poetry: Author Search.* Chadwyck-Healey Ltd., 1995 (http://www.lib.utexas.edu:8080/search/epoetry/author.html). *Stanford University Libraries and Academic Information Resources* (http://library.stanford.edu). *The National Portrait Gallery* (www.npg.org.uk). *The New Oxford Book of Seventeenth Century Verse.* Alastair Fowler, ed. Oxford University Press (2004).

CROSLAND, THOMAS WILLIAM HODGSON (1865–1924)

Born in Leeds, an anti-Scottish Tory and monarchist, he was a Fleet Street reviewer, critic, and editor for *The Outlook, The Academy*, and the *Penny Illustrated Paper*. He launched a bitter attack on Oscar Wilde's "De Profundis" (written about his experience in Reading Jail for homosexuality [1896–1897]). Himself a sufferer from diabetes and heart problems, Crosland's poems reveal a keen feeling for disadvantaged. His major poetical publications: *The Absent-minded Mule, and Other Occasional Verses*, 1899. *The Finer Spirit, and Other Poems*, 1900. *Outlook Odes*, 1902. *Sonnets*, 1912. *War Poems by X*, 1916. *The Collected Poems of T.W.H. Crosland*, 1917. *Last Poems*, 1928. *Antarctic*. Some of his poems: "Charing Cross," "Killed," "Marching On," "Recipe," "Slain," "The 'Student,'" "The Baby in the Ward," "The Eagle: The Good Conceit," "The Rhyme of the Beast," "The White Feather Legion," "Titanic."

Sources: English Poetry: Author Search. Chadwyck-Healey Ltd., 1995 (http://www.lib.utexas.edu:8080/search/epoetry/author.html). *Oscar Wilde's Last Stand.* Philip Hoare. Arcade Publishing. 1998. *Representative Poetry Online* (http://eir.library.utoronto.ca/). *The Columbia Granger's Index to Poetry.* 11th ed. *The Columbia Granger's World of Poetry*, Columbia University Press, 2005 (http://www.columbiagrangers.org). *The Oxford Book of War Poetry.* Jon Stallworthy, Oxford University Press, 1984.

CROSSLEY-HOLLAND, KEVIN (1941–)

Born in Mursley, North Buckinghamshire, he grew up in Whiteleaf, a village in the Chiltern hills of western England, and now lives in Norfolk, England. While studying at Oxford University, he developed a passion for Anglo-Saxon literature and has lectured in Anglo-Saxon literature in England and in America, where he was professor of humanities and fine arts at the University of St. Thomas, Minnesota (1991–1995). At the beginning of his writing career he worked as a poetry, fiction and children's book editor for Macmillan, later becoming editorial director at Victor Gollancz. He is well-known for his reinterpretations of medieval legends; his Arthurian trilogy — set in the Welsh Marches in the Middle Ages — has been published in 23 languages. He has also written libretti for two operas with the composer Nicola LeFanu. He has published several poetry collections, the last one being *Once Upon a Poem* (2005), and translated, among others, *The Battle of Maldon and Other Old English Poems* (1965) and *Beowulf* (1968). Some of his poems: "Book Moth," "Fish in River," "Postcards from Kodai," "Riddle," "They're Marked Men," "Weathercock," "Wild Swan."

Sources: An Anthology of Old English Poetry. Charles W. Kennedy, ed. Oxford University Press, 1960. *British Council Arts* (http://www.contemporarywriters.com). *Biography of Kevin Crossley-Holland* (http://www.ncbf.org.uk/03/crossley-holland/crossley-holland.html). *The Columbia Granger's Index to Poetry.* 11th ed. *The Columbia Granger's World of Poetry*, Columbia University Press, 2005 (http://www.columbiagrangers.org). *The Kingfisher Book of Children's Poetry.* Michael Rosen, ed. Kingfisher Books, 1985. *The New Exeter Book of Riddles.* Kevin Crossley-Holland and Lawrence Sail, ed. Enitharmon Press, 1999. *The Oxford Book of Travel Verse.* Kevin Crossley-Holland, ed. Oxford University Press, 1986. *The Oxford Companion to English Literature.* 6th edition. Margaret Drabble, ed. Oxford University Press, 2000. *The Rattle Bag: An Anthology of Poetry.* Seamus Heaney, and Ted Hughes, ed. Faber and Faber, 1982. *Who's Who.* London: A & C Black, 2005.

CROSSMAN, SAMUEL (?1624–1684)

A clergyman, educated at Pembroke College, Cambridge, from where he graduated in 1660. He was ejected from the rectory of Little Henny in Essex in 1662 because he wanted to have the Book of Common Prayer adapted to suit Puritans as well as Anglicans. Subsequently he conformed and became one of the king's chaplains, was appointed to a post in Bristol, and succeeded to the deanery of Bristol in 1683. After his death a broadsheet appeared under the title *The Last Testimony and Declaration of the Rev. Samuel Crossman, D.D., and Dean of Bristol, setting forth his dutiful and true affection to the Church of England, as by law established.* In 1664 he published *The Young Man's Meditation, or Some Few Sacred Poems upon Select Subjects, and Scriptures.* Some of these poems have been set to music as hymns; one such is "My Song is Love Unknown," which appears in many current hymnbooks. Some of his other hymns and poems: "I Said Sometimes with Tears," "Farewell, Poor World, I Must Be Gone," "Jerusalem on High," "My Life's a Shade, My Days," "Sweet Place."

Sources: *Dictionary of National Biography*. Electronic Edition, 1.1. Oxford University Press, 1997. *English Poetry: Author Search*. Chadwyck-Healey Ltd., 1995 (http://www.lib.utexas.edu:8080/search/epoetry/author.html). *The Columbia Granger's Index to Poetry*. 11th ed. *The Columbia Granger's World of Poetry*, Columbia University Press, 2005 (http://www.columbiagrangers.org). *The Cyber Hymnal* (http://www.cyberhymnal.org/index.htm).

CROWE, WILLIAM (1745–1829)

Clergyman poet who spent his childhood at Winchester, Hampshire, where his father was a carpenter, and where William was a chorister in Winchester College chapel. He was admitted as fellow of New College, Oxford, in 1767, became a tutor, and was elected the public orator of New College in 1784. He was rector for Alton Barnes in Wiltshire. Somewhat eccentric, he was often observed walking from Alton Barnes to his college at Oxford with his coat and a few articles of underclothing flung over a stick and with his boots covered with dust. *Lewesdon Hill* (1788) is a long poem about a hill in the western part of Dorset, on the edge of the parish of Broadwindsor. Some of his other publications: *Poems of William Collins, with notes, and Dr. Johnson's Life, corrected and enlarged*, 1828. *Notes and Queries*, 1853 (a Latin ode on the death of his son who died in battle in 1815). Some of his poems: "Ode to the King of France," "On the Death of Captain Cook," "On the Increase of Human Life," "Succession," "The British Theatre," "To a Lady, Fortune-Telling with Cards."

Sources: *Dictionary of National Biography*. Electronic Edition, 1.1. Oxford University Press, 1997. *English Poetry: Author Search*. Chadwyck-Healey Ltd., 1995 (http://www.lib.utexas.edu:8080/search/epoetry/author.html). *The Columbia Granger's World of Poetry*, Columbia University Press, 2005 (http://www.columbiagrangers.org). *The National Portrait Gallery* (www.npg.org.uk). *William Crowe, Lewesdon Hill, 1788* (http://www.arts.ualberta.ca/~dmiall/Tintern/Crowe.htm).

CROWLEY, EDWARD ALEXANDER (ALEISTER) (1875–1947)

He was born in Leamington Spa, Warwickshire, the son of a wealthy brewer turned Plymouth Brethren, and educated at Trinity College, Cambridge, but left in 1898 without graduating. He was a mountaineer of repute and won a reputation as an explorer and big-game hunter. He belonged to the London's Hermetic Order of the Golden Dawn (see also W.B. Yeats). *The Book of the Law* (1904) was a prose poem he claimed to have been dictated to him by some super intelligence. He has been dubbed "wickedest man in the world" and the "Great Beast 666" (from the Book of Revelation). He died at Hastings and was cremated at Brighton. Apprecia-

tion for his poetry was overshadowed by his bizarre personal life, which today would pass almost unnoticed. Some of his other poetry publications: *Songs of the Spirit*, 1898. *Aceldama: A Place to Bury Strangers In*, 1898. *Songs for Italy*, 1923. *Little Poems in Prose*, 1928. *Ahab: And Other Poems*, 1974. Some of his poems: "A Birthday," "A Saint's Damnation," "Lyric of Love to Leah," "Pan to Artemis," "The Lesbian Hell," "The Two Mice."

Sources: *Dictionary of National Biography*. Electronic Edition, 1.1. Oxford University Press, 1997. *English Poetry: Author Search*. Chadwyck-Healey Ltd., 1995 (http://www.lib.utexas.edu:8080/search/epoetry/author.html). *Biography of Aleister Crowley* (http://skepdic.com/crowley.html). *Biography, poems and picture of Aleister Crowley* (http://www.love-poems.me.uk/biography_crowley_aleister.htm). *Aleister Crowley, Poems & Miscellaneous* (http://www.poeforward.com/poetrycorner/crowley/poems.htm). *The National Portrait Gallery* (www.npg.org.uk). *Poemhunter* (www.poemhunter.com). *The Book of the Law: Liber AL vel Legis, sub figura CCXX* (http://www.sacred-texts.com/oto/engccxx.htm). *The Columbia Granger's Index to Poetry*. 11th ed. *The Columbia Granger's World of Poetry*, Columbia University Press, 2005 (http://www.columbiagrangers.org). *The Oxford Companion to English Literature*. 6th edition. Margaret Drabble, ed. Oxford University Press, 2000. *The Penguin Book of Homosexual Verse*. Stephen Coote, ed. Penguin Books, 1983. *Thelma Texts in the Internet Sacred Text Archive* (http://www.sacred-texts.com/oto/index.htm). *Wikipedia, the Free Encyclopedia* (http://en.wikipedia.org/wiki/Wikipedia).

CROZIER, ANDREW (1943–)

He has an M.A. from Cambridge University and a Ph.D. from Essex University, and is affiliated with the School of English and American Studies at the University of Sussex, Brighton. His many books of poetry are collected in *All Where Each Is* (Allardyce, Barnett, 1985). He is closely associated with the British Poetry Revival — the general name given to a loose poetic movement in Britain that took place in the 1960s and 1970s, a modernist-inspired reaction to the movement's more conservative approach to British poetry. His collected poems, *All Where Each Is*, was published in 1985. With Jeremy Prynne (see entry) he was co-editor of the important revival magazine *The English Intelligencer*. He was co-editor with Tim Longville of *A Various Art* (Carcanet, 1987), and in 1995, he edited Carl Rakosi's *Poems 1923–1941* for the Sun and Moon Press. Some of his poems: "Birds in Sunlight," "Clouds and Windows," "Driftwood and Seacoal," "Evaporation of a Dream," "February Evenings," "High Zero," "The Advance of Happiness," "Utamaro Variations," "Winter Intimacies."

Sources: *Andrew Crozier, Writing by Numbers: A Preview* (http://jacketmagazine.com/11/lopez-by-crozier.html). *Other Men's Flowers*. A.P. Wavell, ed. Jonathan Cape, 1990.

The Columbia Granger's Index to Poetry. 11th ed. *The Columbia Granger's World of Poetry,* Columbia University Press, 2005 (http://www.columbiagrangers.org). *The New British Poetry, 1968–88.* Gillian Allnutt, Fred D'Aguiar and Ken Edwards, ed. Grafton Books, 1989. *University of Delaware: Special Collections Department. Archive of the Park 1. Andrew Crozier* (http://www.lib.udel.edu/ud/spec/findaids/thepark.htm). *Wikipedia, the Free Encyclopedia* (http://en.wikipedia.org/wiki/Wikipedia).

CUNNINGHAM, ALLAN (1784–1842)

A stone mason poet from Dumfriesshire who became clerk of works to the London sculptor Francis Chantery (1781–1841). Cunningham was inspired by hearing Burns recite "Tam o' Shanter" and by his friendship with James Hogg, "the Ettrick Shepherd" (see entry). His biographies of Sir Walter Scott and Robert Burns helped to popularize these poets. His *Lives of the Most Eminent British Painters, Sculptors, and Architects* ran to six volumes (1829–1833). Many of his poems were included as songs in Cromek's *Remains of Nithsdale and Galloway Song* (1810). Two of his poems were set to music by Peter Warlock (pseudonym of Philip Heseltine): "Gone were but the winter cold" and "The spring of the year." His other main publications are: *Sir Marmaduke Maxwell,* 1822. *Traditional Tales of the English and Scottish Peasantry,* 1822 (two volumes). *The Songs of Scotland, Ancient and Modern,* 1825 (four volumes, which includes "A Wet Sheet and a Flowing Sea," said to be one of the best sea songs). Some of his other poems: "Gone Were but the Winter Cold," "The Maid I Love," "The Poet's Bridal-Day Song," "The Sun Rises Bright in France."

Sources: *Come Hither.* Walter de la Mare, ed. Knopf, 1957; Dover Publications, 1995. *Dictionary of National Biography.* Electronic Edition, 1.1. Oxford University Press, 1997. *Encyclopædia Britannica Ultimate Reference Suite DVD,* 2006. *English Poetry: Author Search.* Chadwyck-Healey Ltd., 1995 (http://www.lib.utexas.edu:8080/search/epoetry/author.html). *Significant and Famous Scots* (http://www.electricscotland.com/history/other/cleland_william.htm). *The Burns Encyclopedia* (www.robertburns.org/encyclopedia). *The Columbia Granger's Index to Poetry.* 11th ed. *The Columbia Granger's World of Poetry,* Columbia University Press, 2005 (http://www.columbiagrangers.org). *The National Portrait Gallery* (www.npg.org.uk). *The Oxford Companion to English Literature.* 6th edition. Margaret Drabble, ed. Oxford University Press, 2000.

CURRY, NEIL (1937–)

Born in Newcastle upon Tyne, he now lives at Ulverston in the Lake District. After reading English at Bristol University, he taught at the University of Guelph, Ontario, Canada, and at secondary schools in England. His verse translations of Euripides, published by Methuen and Cambridge University Press,

and in the USA by Doubleday, have been performed in many countries. Some publications are: *Ships in Bottles,* 1998 (a Poetry Book Society recommendation). *Walking to Santiago,* 1992 (inspired by the poet's 500-mile journey along the Pilgrim Road from the Pyrenees to Santiago de Compostela). *The Bending of the Bow: The Closing Books of the Odyssey,* 1993 (translated by Curry and illustrated by Jim Dine). *The Road to the Gunpowder House,* 2003. *Christopher Smart,* 2005 (Smart [see entry] composed many of his poems while locked away in a madhouse, then ending his days in a debtor's jail (quote from the book blurb). Some of his poems: "Anne Hathaway Composes Her 18th Sonnet," "Dandelion," "Galapagos," "Gardens," "In a Calendar of Saints," "John Clare and the Acts of Enclosure," "Memorial to the Vicars of Urswick," "St. Kilda," "Swallows and Tortoises."

Sources: *Curry, Neil & Dine, Jim—The Bending of the Bow* (http://www.inpressbooks.co.uk/bending_of_the_bow_the_by_curry_neil_dine_jim_i079.aspx). *P.E.N. New Poetry I.* Robert Nye, ed. Quartet Books, 1986. *Shades of Green.* Anne Harvey, ed. Greenwillow Books, 1991. *The Columbia Granger's Index to Poetry.* 11th ed. *The Columbia Granger's World of Poetry,* Columbia University Press, 2005 (http://www.columbiagrangers.org). *The New Lake Poets.* William Scammell, ed. Bloodaxe Books, 1991. *The Oxford Book of Garden Verse.* John Dixon Hunt, ed. Oxford University Press, 1993.

CURTIS, TONY (1946–)

Not to be confused with the Irish poet (see entry). Born in Carmarthen, West Wales, he read English at the University College of Swansea, then earned a master of fine arts degree at Goddard College, Vermont, USA. In 1994 he was made professor of poetry at the University of Glamorgan and director of the M.A. in writing. Some of his early poems, together with those of Nigel Jenkins and Duncan Bush (see entries), are to be found in the volume *Three Young Anglo-Welsh Poets* (1974). He has lectured in the USA, Canada, Europe, Eastern Europe, the Far East and in Ireland. In 2000 he was made a fellow of the Royal Society of Literature. Some of his poetry publications: *The Last Candles,* 1989. *Taken for Pearls,* 1994. *War Voices,* 1995. *Heaven's Gate,* 2001. *The Book of Winter Cures: New and Selected Poems,* 2002. *Considering Cassandra—Poems and a Story,* 2003. Some of his poems: "Brigitte Bardot in Grangetown," "Games with My Daughter," "Land Army Photographs," "Neighbour's Pear Tree," "Pembrokeshire Buzzards," "The Last Letter," "To My Father," "We Can Say That."

Sources: *A Welsh American Portfolio* (http://www.wiu.edu/foliopress/welsh/pages/pcurtis.htm 0). *Anglo-Welsh Poetry, 1480–1980.* Raymond Garlick and Roland Mathias, ed. Poetry Wales Press, 1984. *Anglo-Welsh Poetry,*

1480–1990. Raymond Garlick and Roland Mathias, ed. Poetry Wales Press, 1993. *CREW Welsh Writers Online* (http://www.swan.ac.uk/english/crew/index.htm). *The Columbia Granger's Index to Poetry.* 11th ed. *The Columbia Granger's World of Poetry,* Columbia University Press, 2005 (http://www.columbiagrangers.org). *The Oxford Companion to English Literature.* 6th edition. Margaret Drabble, ed. Oxford University Press, 2000. *Twentieth Century Anglo-Welsh Poetry.* Dannie Abse, ed. Seren Books / Dufour Editions, 1997.

CURTIS, TONY (1955–)

Tony Curtis is often confused with the Welsh poet (see entry). Born in Dublin, he studied literature at Essex University and Trinity College, Dublin. He edited "Pickings and Cuttings," quotations by Dennis O'Driscoll (see entry) in the literary journal *Poetry Ireland Review* and published "As The Poet Said" in *Poetry Ireland* (1997). He was awarded the National Poetry Prize in 1993 for his poem "The Dowser and the Child." In 2003 he was awarded the Varuna House Exchange Fellowship to Australia. In addition to his own poems, he has translated from several other poets. He now lives in North County Dublin and is a member of Aosdána. Some of his poetry publications: *The Shifting of Stones,* 1986. *Behind the Green Curtain,* 1988. *Three Songs of Home,* 1994. *What Darkness Covers,* 2003. *New & Selected Poems,* 2006. Some of his translations: *A Shoal of Silver Angelfish* (Koster, Edward B., 1861–1937). *Cold Landscape* (Peaux, Augusta, 1859–1944). *Fever Tune* (Van de Woestijne, Karel, 1878–1929). *Landscape* (Van Ostaijen, Paul, 1896–1928). *Lonely Night* (Boutens, P.C., 1870–1943). *Shower* (Winkler Prins, Jacob, 1849–1904).

Sources: *Aosdána—An Irish Affiliation of Artists* (http://www.irishwriters-online.com/tonycurtis.html). *The Columbia Granger's Index to Poetry.* 11th ed. *The Columbia Granger's World of Poetry,* Columbia University Press, 2005 (http://www.columbiagrangers.org). *Tony Curtis in De Brakke Hond* (http://www.brakkehond.be/bio.asp?au=Tony+Curtis). *Turning Tides: Modern Dutch and Flemish Verse in English Versions by Irish Poets.* Peter van de Kamp, ed. Story Line Press, 1994.

CUTTS, JOHN, BARON CUTTS OF GOWRAN (1661–1707)

Lieutenant-general, son of an Essex squire, entered Catharine Hall, Cambridge, at the age of fifteen, but did not graduate. A passage in Addison's *Musae Anglicanæ; History of Anglo-Latin Poetry* (2 volumes, 1691–1699) is said to refer to Cutts having been the first to plant the imperialist flag on the walls of Buda in the war against the Turks in 1686. He fought on the side of William of Orange at the Battle of the Boyne (1690) and at both Sieges of Limerick (1690 and 1691). He was given the honorary degree of LL.D. by Cambridge University in 1690 and appointed governor of the Isle of Wight in 1693. Many of his poems are songs set to music. He died in poverty in Dublin. Some of his poems and songs: "Farewel to Love," "La Muse de Cavalier," "On the Death of the Queen," "Poetical Exercises," "The Innocent Gazer," "The Original and Excellence of the Muses," "The Tyranny of Phillis," "To a Lady, Who Desired Me Not to Be in Love with Her," "To Her Royal Highness the Princess of Orange," "Wisdom."

Sources: *Dictionary of National Biography.* Electronic Edition, 1.1. Oxford University Press, 1997. *English Poetry: Author Search.* Chadwyck-Healey Ltd., 1995 (http://www.lib.utexas.edu:8080/search/epoetry/author.html). *Sieges of Limerick* (http://members.tripod.com/Preachan/sieges1.html). *Stanford University libraries and Academic Information Resources* (http://library.stanford.edu). *The Columbia Granger's Index to Poetry.* 11th ed. *The Columbia Granger's World of Poetry,* Columbia University Press, 2005 (http://www.columbiagrangers.org). *The National Portrait Gallery* (www.npg.org.uk).

CYNDDELW BRYDYDD MAWR (?1157–?1195)

Cynddelw Brydydd Mawr (English translation "Cynddelw the Great Poet") was an outstanding Welsh poet of the 12th century. He was court bard to Madog ap Maredudd, the last prince of the entire Kingdom of Powys (died 1160), and then to Madog's enemy Owain Gwynedd, prince of Gwynedd (died 1170). His poems — composed in the Welsh bardic tradition — include a small amount of religious verse and a large number of eulogies to the chief princes throughout Wales. Cynddelw seems, therefore, to have been the chief bard of all of Wales. Some of his poems: "Elegy on Madog," "In Praise of Owain Gwynedd," "Petition for Reconciliation," "Poem on His Death-Bed."

Sources: *Encyclopædia Britannica Ultimate Reference Suite DVD,* 2006. *Gwaith Cynddelw Brydydd Mawr: Volume 1.* Nerys Ann Jones and Ann Parry Owen, ed. University of Wales Press, 1991. Volumes 2, 1995. *The Columbia Granger's Index to Poetry.* 11th ed. *The Columbia Granger's World of Poetry,* Columbia University Press, 2005 (http://www.columbiagrangers.org). *The Oxford Book of Welsh Verse in English.* Gwyn Jones, ed. Oxford University Press, 1977. *University of Wales, Centre for Advanced Welsh & Celtic Studies* (http://www.wales.ac.uk/newpages/EXTERNAL/E4156.asp). *Wikipedia, the Free Encyclopedia* (http://en.wikipedia.org/wiki/Wikipedia).

DABYDEEN, DAVID (1955–)

Born in Berbice, Guyana, he has lived in England since 1969. After graduating with B.A. honors in English from Cambridge University, he gained a Ph.D. in 18th century literature and art at University College, London, in 1982, and was awarded a research fellowship at Wolfson College, Oxford. He is director of the Centre for Caribbean Studies and professor at the Centre for British Comparative Cultural Studies at Warwick University. He is also Guyana's ambassador-at-large and a member of UNESCO's executive board. The Royal Society of Literature made him a fellow, the second West Indian writer (the other being the novelist V.S. Naipaul) and the only Guyanese writer to receive the title. He has received five literary awards, the last one being the 2004 Raja Rao Award for Literature (India). His long poem "Turner" was inspired by the painting "Slave Traders" by William Turner (1775–1851). Some of his other poetry publications: 1*Slave Song*, 1984 (republished 2005). *Coolie Odyssey*1, 1988. *Turner: New and Selected Poems*, 1994. Some of his poems: "Catching Crabs," "Coolie Mother," "Coolie Son," "Men and Women," "Miranda," "Two Cultures."

Sources: *Anthology of Twentieth-Century British and Irish Poetry.* Keith Tuma, ed. Oxford University Press, 2001. *British Council Arts* (http://www.contemporarywriters.com). *The Heinemann Book of Caribbean Poetry.* Stewart Brown, and Ian McDonald, ed. Heinemann, 1992. *The New British Poetry, 1968–88.* Gillian Allnutt, Fred D'Aguiar and Ken Edwards, ed. Grafton Books, 1989. *The Oxford Companion to English Literature.* 6th edition. Margaret Drabble, ed. Oxford University Press, 2000. *The Penguin Book of Caribbean Verse in English.* Paula Burnett, ed. Penguin Books, 1986. *Under Another Sky: An Anthology of Commonwealth Poetry Prize Winners.* Alastair Niven, ed. Carcanet, 1987. *Wikipedia, the Free Encyclopedia.* (http://en.wikipedia.org/wiki/Wikipedia).

D'AGUIAR, FRED (1960–)

Poet, novelist and playwright, he was born in London to Guyanese parents, lived in Guyana with his grandparents in Airy Hall, a little town about 40 miles away from Georgetown, until he was 12, then returned to England. He trained as a psychiatric nurse before reading African and Caribbean studies at the University of Kent, Canterbury, graduating in 1985. His first collection of poetry, *Mama Dot* (1985), established his reputation as one of the finest British poets of his generation. That and *Airy Hall* (1989) won him the Guyana Poetry Prize in 1989, the first of many awards. His novel *The Longest Memory* (1994), which tells the story of an eighteenth-century slave, was adapted for television and televised by Channel 4 in the U.K. He was Judith E. Wilson Fellow at Cambridge University England (1989–1990); visiting writer at Amherst College, Massachusetts, USA (1992–1994); and assistant professor of English at Bates College, Lewiston, Maine, USA (1994–1995). He is currently professor of English and creative writing at the University of Miami. Some of his poems: "Airy Hall Icongraphy," "Airy Hall's Exits," "GDR," "Langston," "Letter to England," "On Duty," "Sound Bite."

Sources: *Biography of Fred D'aguiar* (http://www.humboldt.edu/~me2/engl240b/student_projects/daguiar/daguiarbio.htm). *British Council Arts* (http://www.contemporarywriters.com). *Caribbean Poetry Now.* Stewart Brown, ed. Edward Arnold, 1992. *Other British and Irish Poetry Since 1970.* Richard Caddel and Peter Quartermain. ed. Wesleyan University Press, 1999. *The Columbia Granger's Index to Poetry.* 11th ed. *The Columbia Granger's World of Poetry,* Columbia University Press, 2005 (http://www.columbiagrangers.org). *The Heinemann Book of Caribbean Poetry.* Stewart Brown, and Ian McDonald, ed. Heinemann, 1992. *The Oxford Companion to English Literature.* 6th edition. Margaret Drabble, ed. Oxford University Press, 2000. *The Penguin Book of Caribbean Verse in English.* Paula Burnett, ed. Penguin Books, 1986. *Wheel and Come Again: An Anthology of Reggae Poetry.* Kwame Dawes, ed. Goose Lane Editions, 1998.

DALTON, AMANDA (1957–)

She was born in Coventry, Warwickshire, worked in Leicestershire comprehensive schools and as a youth theater leader, then she was a deputy head teacher for five years. She organized writers' courses for four years for the Arvon Foundation at Lumb Bank in West Yorkshire. She also writes plays for stage and radio and is now education director at the Royal Exchange Theatre, Manchester. *How to Disappear,* her first poetry book, was published in 1999 and was short listed for the Forward prize for best first collection in 1999. Her radio version of *Room of Leaves* (a section of *How to Disappear*) was broadcast on BBC Radio 4 in autumn 1998 and has been short listed for a Prix Italia award for radio drama. In 2004 she was named in "Next Generation Poets" as one of the 20 most exciting poets. Some of her poems: "Almost Bird," "In Love," "Kitchen Beast," "Nest," "The Dad-Baby."

Sources: *Amada Dalton, Books: Special Reports. Guardian Unlimited* (http://books.guardian.co.uk/nextgenerationpoets). *New Blood.* Neil Astley, ed. Bloodaxe Books, 1999. *The Columbia Granger's Index to Poetry.* 11th ed. *The Columbia Granger's World of Poetry,* Columbia University Press, 2005 (http://www.columbiagrangers.org). *Biography and poems of Amanda Dalton. The Poetry Book Society* (http://www.poetrybooks.co.uk/PBS/pbs_dalton_amanda.asp).

DALTON, JOHN (1709–1763)

Born at Dean in Cumberland, the son of the rector, he was educated locally and at Queen's College, Oxford, graduating in 1730. He was tutor to the son of the Duke of Somerset, then after earning his M.A. in 1734, he was an assistant preacher at St. James's, Westminster, and took the degrees of B.D. and D.D. in 1750. While employed as tutor, he adapted Milton's masque of *Comus* for the stage, set to music by Dr. Arne and performed in 1738, a work that ran for many years. In 1750 he put on a benefit performance at Drury Lane Theatre for Mrs. Elizabeth

Foster, a granddaughter of Milton, for which Dr. Johnson wrote a new prologue, which was spoken by David Garrick. In addition to several published sermons, he wrote *Descriptive Poem, Addressed to Two Ladies at Their Return from Viewing the Mines, near Whitehaven.* One poem is "Agape the Sooty Collier Stands." The poet contrasts a miner, face blackened with coal dust, with the two ladies as goddesses whose presence soothes the collier's aching body.

Sources: *Dictionary of National Biography.* Electronic Edition 1.1. Oxford University Press, 1997. *The Columbia Granger's Index to Poetry.* 11th ed. *The Columbia Granger's World of Poetry,* Columbia University Press, 2005 (http://www.columbiagrangers.org).

DANIEL, SAMUEL (1562–1619)

One of the Renaissance poets and dramatists, thought to have been born near Taunton, Somerset. He left Magdalen Hall, Oxford, without graduating and was later employed as tutor to William Herbert, the future Earl of Pembroke at Wilton House, near Salisbury, and then to Lady Anne Clifford at Skipton Castle in Yorkshire. Sir Philip Sidney included twenty-seven of Daniel's sonnets in the 1591 edition of *Astrophel and Stella*; this brought Daniel into the limelight. He is mentioned by name in Spenser's "Colin Clouts Come Home Againe." There is a tradition that he succeeded Spenser as poet laureate. Early in the reign of James I he was often at court and wrote masques for the queen. Towards the end of his life, he retired to his farm in Somerset. Some of his poems: "A Description of Beauty," "A Panegyrike Congratulatorie to the Kings Most Excellent Majestie," "Delia: Contayning Certaine [50] Sonnets," "Hymen's Triumph," "The Complaint of Rosamond," "The Tragedie of Cleopatra," "To Her Sacred Majestie," "To the Lady Margaret, Countess of Cumberland."

Sources: *Dictionary of National Biography.* Electronic Edition 1.1. Oxford University Press, 1997. *The Complete Life and Works of Samuel Daniel* (http://www.luminarium.org/renlit/daniel.htm). *The Complete Works in Verse and Prose of Samuel Daniel.* Alexander B. Grosart, ed. Russell & Russell, 1963. *The National Portrait Gallery* (www.npg.org.uk). *The New Oxford Book of English Verse, 1250–1950.* Helen Gardner, ed. Oxford University Press, 1972. *The Oxford Companion to English Literature.* 6th edition. Margaret Drabble, ed. Oxford University Press, 2000.

DARBY, JOHN NELSON (1800–1882)

Founder of the Darbyites. Born in London, educated at Westminster School and at Trinity College, Dublin, he graduated in 1819 as gold medalist. He tried law and the Church but resigned because of dissatisfaction with the Anglican establishment. He and like-minded friends, meeting in Plymouth, formed the Plymouth Brethren in 1831. Darby trav-

eled worldwide "spreading the word." In 1834 the group commenced a magazine called *The Christian Witness.* Today's fundamentalist churches owe much to his doctrines. He was a prolific writer and the Darby Bible is a translation by him. Some of his hymns: "And is it So," "Hark! Ten Thousand Voices Crying," "Lord, Thy Love's Unbounded," "Rest of the Saints Above," "Rise, My Soul, Thy God Directs Thee," "This World is a Wilderness Wide," "Though Faint, Yet Pursuing, We Go on Our Way."

Sources: *Dictionary of National Biography.* Electronic Edition 1.1. Oxford University Press, 1997. *Encyclopædia Britannica Ultimate Reference Suite DVD,* 2006. *The Cyber Hymnal* (http://www.cyberhymnal.org/index.htm).

DARLEY, GEORGE (1795–1846)

Born in Dublin, and after leaving Trinity College, Dublin, he chose to be a writer, which caused him to be estranged from his family. In London in 1821 he was critic for the *London Magazine* (under the signature of John Lacy) and other journals, and dramatic reviewer of the *Athenæum.* In his own day, Darley's greatest successes were his popular scientific treatises on geometry, algebra, and trigonometry, though his early literary works were less successful. However, in more recent times his unfinished lyrical epic *Nepenthe* (1835), regarded as unreadable at the time with its imagery and symbolism, has become more popular. He suffered from a life-long serious stammer, which seems to have caused him to be reclusive. His main publications: *The Errors of Ecstacie,* 1822. *Lilian of the Vale,* 1826. *Sylvia, or the May Queen,* 1827. *Thomas à Becket,* 1840. *Ethelstan,* 1841. Some of his poems: "Compassion," "Maid Marian's Song," "Nepenthe," "On the Death of a Recluse," "Sylvia; or, The May Queen," "The Elfin Pedlar," "The Enchanted Spring," "The Fallen Star," "The Nightingale and the Thorn."

Sources: *Dictionary of National Biography.* Electronic Edition 1.1. Oxford University Press, 1997. *Encyclopædia Britannica Ultimate Reference Suite DVD,* 2006. *English Poetry: Author Search.* Chadwyck-Healey Ltd., 1995 (http://www.lib.utexas.edu:8080/search/epoetry/author.html). *The Book of a Thousand Poems: A Family Treasury.* J. Murray Macbain, ed. Peter Bedrick Books, 1983. *The Book of Irish Verse: An Anthology of Irish Poetry from the Sixth Century to the Present.* John Montague, ed. Macmillan, 1974. *The Columbia Granger's Index to Poetry.* 11th ed. *The Columbia Granger's World of Poetry,* Columbia University Press, 2005 (http://www.columbiagrangers.org). *The Oxford Companion to English Literature.* 6th edition. Margaret Drabble, ed. Oxford University Press, 2000.

DARWIN, ERASMUS (1731–1802)

One of the leading intellectuals of eighteenth century England, Erasmus Darwin was a man with a remarkable array of interests and pursuits. The grandfather of Charles Darwin was a respected physician, a well known poet, philosopher, botanist, and naturalist. He was educated at St. John's College, Cambridge (1750–54), and at Edinburgh, where he studied medicine and established a successful practice in Litchfield, Staffordshire. Later he moved to Derby, where, in 1784, he founded the Philosophical Society and opened a dispensary at Lichfield. He advanced his own concepts of evolution, which were similar to those of J.B. Lamarck. Throughout, Darwin seems to have struggled between his profession and his poetic aspirations, at one time determining to give up poetry. His major publications: *A Plan for the Conduct of Female Education in Boarding Schools*, 1797. *Zoonomia, or, The Laws of Organic Life*, 1798. *Phytologia, or the Philosophy of Agriculture and Gardening*, 1800. Some of his poems: "Kew," "Nightmare," "Remembrance," "The Action of Invisible Ink," "The Botanic Garden," "The Economy of Vegetation," "The Golden Age," "The Temple of Nature; or, The Origin of Society."

Sources: *Dictionary of National Biography.* Electronic Edition 1.1. Oxford University Press, 1997. *Encyclopædia Britannica Ultimate Reference Suite DVD, 2006. English Poetry: Author Search.* Chadwyck-Healey Ltd., 1995 (http://www.lib.utexas.edu:8080/search/epoetry/author.html). *The Columbia Granger's Index to Poetry.* 11th ed. *The Columbia Granger's World of Poetry,* Columbia University Press, 2005 (http://www.columbiagrangers.org). *The National Portrait Gallery* (www.npg.org.uk). *The New Oxford Book of Romantic Period Verse.* Jerome J. McGann. Oxford University Press, 1993. *The Oxford Companion to English Literature.* 6th edition. Margaret Drabble, ed. Oxford University Press, 2000.

DARYUSH, ELIZABETH (1887–1977)

She followed her poet laureate father, Robert Bridges, into poetry, but did not follow his style. Her poems are often critical of the upper classes and the social injustice and human suffering their privilege levies upon others. She married Ali Akbar Daryush, an Iranian whom she had met when he was studying at Oxford University. Later he became a diplomat in his own country and she spent four years in Iran, but spent most of her life in Boar's Hill outside Oxford. Her poetry, although largely neglected, has been compared to that of Thomas Hardy. Her main publications: *Verses*, 1930. *Verses, Third Book*, 1933. *The Last Man, and Other Poems*, 1936. *Collected Poems*, 1976. Some of her poems: "Anger Lay by Me All Night Long," "Armistice," "Autumn, Dark Wanderer," "Eyes That Queenly Sit," "Farewell for a While," "Flanders Fields," "For a Survivor of the Mesopotamian Campaign," "Forbidden Love," "Fresh Spring," "Unknown Warrior," "War Tribunal."

Sources: *Chaos of the Night: Women's Poetry and Verse of the Second World War.* Catherine W. Reilly, ed. Virago

Press, 1984. *Oldpoetry* (www.oldpoetry.com). *The Columbia Granger's Index to Poetry.* 11th ed. *The Columbia Granger's World of Poetry,* Columbia University Press, 2005 (http://www.columbiagrangers.org). *The Oxford Companion to English Literature.* 6th edition. Margaret Drabble, ed. Oxford University Press, 2000.

D'AVENANT, SIR WILLIAM (1606–1668)

Born in Oxford, he was the son of John D'Avenant, mayor of Oxford, although it was rumored that he was the natural son of William Shakespeare. His first play, *The Cruell Brother*, was performed in 1627. A severe case of syphilis (in which he lost his nose, and almost his life) interrupted his writing career for three years. He was poet laureate after Ben Jonson in 1638. During the English Civil War he was a staunch royalist and was knighted for his bravery in 1643. In 1650, on his way to Maryland as governor, he was arrested by a man of war and spent the next two years in prison in Cowes Castle, on the Isle of Wight. At the Restoration Davenant opened the Duke's Theatre — which was later amalgamated with King's Company in Drury Lane — and became a successful theater manager and playwright. D'Avenant ("Sweet Swan of Isis") was buried in Poets' Corner of Westminster Abbey. Some of his poems: "Aubade," "Gondibert," "Ladies in Arms," "Praise and Prayer," "The Coquet," "To a Mistress Dying," "Weep No More for What is Past."

Sources: *Dictionary of National Biography.* Electronic Edition 1.1. Oxford University Press, 1997. *English Poetry: Author Search.* Chadwyck-Healey Ltd., 1995 (http://www.lib.utexas.edu:8080/search/epoetry/author.html). *Poemhunter* (www.poemhunter.com). *The Columbia Granger's Index to Poetry.* 11th ed. *The Columbia Granger's World of Poetry,* Columbia University Press, 2005 (http://www.columbiagrangers.org). *The Faber Book of English Verse.* John Hayward, ed. Faber & Faber, 1958. *The Oxford Companion to English Literature.* 6th edition. Margaret Drabble, ed. Oxford University Press, 2000. *Westminster Abbey Official Guide* (no date).

DAVIDSON, JOHN (1857–1909)

Scottish poet, novelist and dramatist, he was born at Barrhead, Renfrewshire, the son of a clergyman. He taught in various schools in Scotland from 1872 to 1899, a job he loathed; then he moved to London, determined to earn a living solely by his writing. He wrote for the *Speaker* and the *Glasgow Herald*, but struggled financially, supporting his own family and a mentally ill brother whose passage he paid to Australia. He became increasingly dependent on his friends for support and in 1906 was granted Civil List pension and a year later moved to Penzance. He became mentally unbalanced, paranoid, and angry, and drowned himself the sea near

Penzance, blaming his despair on debt and bad health. His body was found on the seashore months later; he was buried at sea. Some of his publications: *Perfervid*, 1890. *In a Music Hall and Other Poems*, 1891. *Fleet Street Eclogues*, 1893. *Ballads and Songs*, 1894. *Fleet Street Eclogues*, 1896. *New Ballads*, 1897. *The Last Ballad*, 1899. Some of his poems: "A Ballad of Hell," "Imagination," "In Romney Marsh," "Song of a Train," "The Last Rose," "Thirty Bob a Week," "War Song."

Sources: *Dictionary of National Biography.* Electronic Edition 1.1. Oxford University Press, 1997. *Encyclopædia Britannica Ultimate Reference Suite DVD, 2006. English Poetry: Author Search.* Chadwyck-Healey Ltd., 1995 (http://www.lib.utexas.edu:8080/search/epoetry/author.html). *Oldpoetry* (www.oldpoetry.com). *Poemhunter* (www.poemhunter.com). *The Columbia Granger's Index to Poetry.* 11th ed. *The Columbia Granger's World of Poetry,* Columbia University Press, 2005 (http://www.columbia grangers.org). *The Oxford Companion to English Literature.* 6th edition. Margaret Drabble, ed. Oxford University Press, 2000.

DAVIE, DONALD ALFRED (1922–1995)

Born in Barnsley, Yorkshire, the son of a Baptist shopkeeper, he was educated at the local grammar school. After five years' service in the Royal Navy during World War II, he graduated in 1947 and gained a doctorate in 1951 both from Cambridge University. Based at Murmansk during the war, he learned to read Polish and Russian poetry and translated widely in both languages throughout his life. He taught literature at Trinity College, Dublin, and in several English universities until 1968, then at Stanford and Vanderbilt universities. From the mid 1940s, he was a key figure in the "Movement." He retired to Exeter, Devon, in 1988, where he died. Some of his publications: *Purity of Diction in English Verse*, 1952. *New and Selected Poems*, 1961. *Collected Poems*, 1993. *Poems and Melodramas*, 1995. *New Collected Poems*, 2002. Some of his poems: "1945," "Across the Bay," "After the Calamitous Convoy (July 1942)," "Barnsley Cricket Club," "Chernobyl: A Disaster," "Hawkshead and Dachau in a Christmas Glass," "Ordinary God," "The Elect," "The Forests of Lithuania," "The Fountain of Arethusa," "The North Sea, in a Snowstorm."

Sources: *Collected Poems of Donald Davie.* Neil Powell, ed. Carcanet, 2002. *Encyclopædia Britannica Ultimate Reference Suite DVD, 2006. Biography of Donald Alfred Davie. Talk Poetry* (http://www.talkpoetry.com/pages/brief/brief.php?id=9&PHPSESSID=). *The Columbia Granger's Index to Poetry.* 11th ed. *The Columbia Granger's World of Poetry,* Columbia University Press, 2005 (http://www.columbia-grangers.org). *The Oxford Companion to English Literature.* 6th edition. Margaret Drabble, ed. Oxford University Press, 2000.

DAVIES, GRAHAME (1964–)

Poet, editor, novelist and literary critic, he was born and brought up in Coedpoeth near Wrexham in northeast Wales. After graduating in English literature from Cambridge University, he was a journalist with the Thomson organization at Newcastle-upon-Tyne and worked on newspapers in south Wales from 1985 until 1991. Since then he has worked for BBC Wales and is currently the executive producer of BBC Wales' Welsh-language New Media Services. In 1997, he was awarded a doctorate by the University of Wales. His first volume of poetry, *Adennill Tir* (1997), won the Harri Webb Memorial Prize, and in 1998, he was second to Emyr Lewis in the competition for the National Eisteddfod Crown. In 2000, he co-edited *Oxygen*, a bilingual anthology of Welsh poets under age 45. His second volume of poetry, *Cadwyni Rhyddid* (2001) won the Wales Arts Council's 2002 Book of the Year award at the Hay on Wye Festival of Literature, with a prize of £3,000. Some of his poems in English: "Grau," "Red," "Rough Guide," "Valley Villanelle." Some of his Welch poems: "Llwyd," "Tywyllwch," "Villanelle y Cymoedd," "Y Mynyddoedd."

Sources: *Life and Work of Grahame Davies* (http://www.grahamedavies.com/english_about.shtml). *New Media and the Welsh Language* (http://spruce.flint.umich.edu/~ellisjs/Grahame%20Davies.pdf).

DAVIES, IDRIS (1905–1953)

Idris Davies, born in Rhymney in Monmouthshire, is possibly Wales's greatest poet of the twentieth century. He started work in the mines at fourteen, but after taking a correspondence course, he went to Loughborough College and the Nottingham University and qualified as a teacher. He worked in London and in several places in Wales before finally becoming a teacher in the Rhymney Valley in 1947. But only six years later he died of cancer. Although his poetry is concerned with the plight of the valleys of South Wales and denounces oppression and exploitation, it also affirms life, solidarity of community, the possibility of enjoyment amid the bleakness, and hope for a better future. His main publications: *Gwalia Deserta*, 1938. *Tonypandy and Other Poems*, 1945. *The Angry Summer*, 1953. Some of his poems: "Consider Famous Men, Dai Bach," "High Summer on the Mountains," "Hywel and Blodwen," "In Gardens in the Rhondda," "The Lay Preacher Ponders."

Sources: *Anglo-Welsh Poetry, 1480–1980.* Raymond Garlick and Roland Mathias, ed. Poetry Wales Press, 1984. *Idris Davies: A Carol for the Coalfield* (http://www.nhi.clara.net/bs0057.htm). *The Columbia Granger's Index to Poetry.* 11th ed. *The Columbia Granger's World of Poetry,* Columbia University Press, 2005 (http://www.columbia

grangers.org). *The Complete Works of Idris Davies*. Daffyd Johnston, ed. University of Wales Press, 1994. *The Oxford Companion to English Literature*. 6th edition. Margaret Drabble, ed. Oxford University Press, 2000. *Twentieth Century Anglo-Welsh Poetry*. Dannie Abse, ed. Seren Books / Dufour Editions, 1997.

DAVIES, JOHN OF HEREFORD (?1565–1618)

Born at Hereford and believed to have been educated at Oxford University, he was a writing master who became a prolific poet. He lived in Oxford, where he taught penmanship to pupils from all the noblest families, though from 1608 Davies was living in London. When his first wife died she was buried in the church of St. Dunstan, where he erected a monument to her with memorial verses by him. Although he married again, he was buried beside his first wife. His major publications (some of the long titles have been shortened): *Mirum in Modum*, 1602. *Microcosmos*, 1603. *A Request to the City of Hereford*, 1605. *Humours Heau'n on Earth*, 1605. *The Holy Roode*, 1609. *Wittes Pilgrimage*, 1610/1611. *The Scourge of Folly*, 1610/1611. Some of his other poems: "A Blind Man Cannot See the Default of His Eyes," "Against Amorous Andrugio," "An Acknowledgement of Gods Gifts," "The Complaint of a Sinner," "To the Printer," "To the Sacred Queene of England's Most Excellent Majestie," "To the World," "Too Much Honie Breakes the Belly," "Yee Have Made a Mocke of the Counsell of the Poore."

Sources: *Dictionary of National Biography*. Electronic Edition 1.1. Oxford University Press, 1997. *Encyclopædia Britannica Ultimate Reference Suite DVD*, 2006. *English Poetry: Author Search*. Chadwyck-Healey Ltd., 1995 (http://www.lib.utexas.edu:8080/search/epoetry/author. html). *The Columbia Granger's Index to Poetry*. 11th ed. *The Columbia Granger's World of Poetry*, Columbia University Press, 2005 (http://www.columbiagrangers.org). *The Complete Works of John Davies of Hereford*. AMS Press, 1967. *The Oxford Companion to English Literature*. 6th edition. Margaret Drabble, ed. Oxford University Press, 2000.

DAVIES, SIR JOHN (1569–1626)

Born at Tisbury, Wiltshire, educated at Winchester College and the Queen's College Oxford (or possibly New College, Oxford), he graduated in 1590 and was called to the bar in 1595. He was disbarred in 1598 for hitting Richard Martin over the head with a cudgel because he had criticized his poem "Orchestra." He was reinstated to the bar in 1601 and became member of Parliament for Corfe Castle, Dorset. His poem "Nosce Teipsum" endeared him to King James I, who knighted him and appointed him solicitor general for Ireland in 1603 and attorney general for Ireland in 1606. He died before he could take up his appointment of lord chief justice of England. His main publications: *Orchestra. or, A Poem[e] of Da[u]ncing*, 1596. *Astraea* (acrostic poems, all of which spelled out "Elizabetha Regina"), 1599. *Yet Other Twelve Wonders of the World, a Lottery*, 1608 (set to music by John Maynard in 1611). *A Contention Betwixt a Wife, a Widow and a Maid*, 1608. Some of his other poems: "A Poem of Dancing," "Epigrams," "Meditations of a Gull," "Of Tobacco," "Sonnets to Philomel," "The Gulling; Sonnets."

Sources: *Dictionary of National Biography*. Electronic Edition 1.1. Oxford University Press, 1997. *Elizabethan Sonnets*. Maurice Evans, ed. J.M. Dent, 1977. *Encyclopædia Britannica Ultimate Reference Suite DVD*, 2006. *English Poetry: Author Search*. Chadwyck-Healey Ltd., 1995 (http://www.lib.utexas.edu:8080/search/epoetry/author. html). *The Columbia Granger's Index to Poetry*. 11th ed. *The Columbia Granger's World of Poetry*, Columbia University Press, 2005 (http://www.columbiagrangers.org). *The New Oxford Book of Sixteenth Century Verse*. Emrys Jones, ed. Oxford University Press, 1991. *The Oxford Companion to English Literature*. 6th edition. Margaret Drabble, ed. Oxford University Press, 2000.

DAVIES, SNEYD (1709–1769)

Born in Kingsland, Herefordshire, where his father was the rector, he was educated at Eton College and King's College, Cambridge, where he became a fellow. He was a distinguished scholar and wrote poetry from an early age. When his father died in 1732, Davies took over his father's living at Kingsland, and became almost a recluse, finding comfort in his writing. However, he collaborated with Timothy Thomas, nearby rector of Presteigne, in translating into Latin Alexander Pope's poem "Essay on Man" (1733–1734). Frederick Cornwallis, archbishop of Canterbury (an old Etonian with Davies) appointed Davies archdeacon of Derby in 1755. Davies's poems were never collected. They are to be found in Dodsley's collection (1775), Vols. V and VI; and in Nichols's collection (1780), Vols. VI and VII. Two of his poems: "A Voyage to Tintern Abbey," "A Scene [after Hunting] at Swallowfield in Berkshire."

Sources: *Dictionary of National Biography*. Electronic Edition 1.1. Oxford University Press, 1997. *Great Books Online* (www.bartleby.com). *The Columbia Granger's Index to Poetry*. 11th ed. *The Columbia Granger's World of Poetry*, Columbia University Press, 2005 (http://www.columbia grangers.org). *The National Portrait Gallery* (www.npg. org.uk). *The New Oxford Book of Eighteenth Century Verse*. Roger Lonsdale, ed. Oxford University Press, 1984.

DAVIES, WILLIAM HENRY (1871–1940)

Born at his paternal grandfather's public house, Church House Tavern, Newport, Monmouthshire, Wales, to a poor family, he was apprenticed to a picture framer at age 14. He moved to London at the age of twenty, living in poverty. In 1893, having come into a small inheritance, he spent six years globe trotting. In 1896, while boarding a moving train Renfrew, Ontario, he slipped and suffered a traumatic amputation of his right leg at the knee. He returned to London and devoted himself to writing. In 1912, Edward Marsh selected several of his poems for inclusion in the first volume of his successful *Georgian Poetry*. Davies wrote twenty volumes in all, including several novels, and most sold well. His favorite topics were the things he knew best — city poverty and rural contentment. The opening lines of *Leisure* are the well known: "What is this life if, full of care/ We have no time to stand and stare." His main publications: *The Soul's Destroyer*, 1905. *Autobiography of a Super-Tramp*, 1908. *Complete Poems*, 1963. *Young Emma*, 1980 (the story of his courtship). Some of his poems: "Ambition," "The Inquest," "The Power of Silence," "The Villain."

Sources: *Dictionary of National Biography.* Electronic Edition 1.1. Oxford University Press, 1997. *Modern British Poetry*. 7th rev. ed. Louis Untermeyer, ed. Harcourt, Brace, 1962. *The Columbia Granger's Index to Poetry*. 11th ed. *The Columbia Granger's World of Poetry*, Columbia University Press, 2005 (http://www.columbiagrangers.org). *The Oxford Companion to English Literature.* 6th edition. Margaret Drabble, ed. Oxford University Press, 2000.

DAVIS, DAVID (1745–1827)

Welsh poet from Goitreisaf, near Lampeter, Cardiganshire. Born Jacob, he and his brothers adopted the name Davis. He was known by his bardic name as Dafydd ab Ieuan Rhydderch (Evan Roderick). Educated at Leominster, Llanbydder, and Llangeler, along with the grammar school at Carmarthen, in 1764 he became a divinity student at the Carmarthen (Presbyterian) Academy under Samuel Thomas. He was appointed co-pastor at Llwyn-rhyd-owen, Cardiganshire, in 1769, where he received Presbyterian ordination in 1773. For thirty years he ran Castell Howell Farm in the Vale of Cletwr as a school, where he was known as Dafis Castellhywel. For many years candidates for Anglican orders were ordained direct from the school. He was distinguished as one of the most successful classical teachers in the principality. He was buried in the churchyard of Llanwenog, Cardiganshire, where a monument with an inscription in Welsh is erected to his memory. He wrote in Welsh and his *Telyn Dewi (Harp of David)* — a collection of his poetical pieces in Welsh, Latin, and English — was edited by his eldest son, the Rev. David Davis (1824).

Sources: *Dictionary of National Biography.* Electronic Edition 1.1. Oxford University Press, 1997. *Genuki: Theological Colleges in Wales* (http://www.genuki.org.uk/big/wal/TheoColl.html).

DAVIS, THOMAS OSBORNE (1814–1845)

Irish lawyer, poet and politician, born at Mallow, County Cork, whose father, a surgeon in the royal artillery, died in 1814 on his way to join Wellington's forces on the Continent. He graduated from Trinity College, Dublin, in 1836, and in 1837 published an anonymous pamphlet on the *Reform of the Lords, By a Graduate of Dublin University.* He became a supporter of the nationalists. In 1842 he helped found the immensely popular *Nation* newspaper, to which he contributed stirring nationalistic poems. He died of fever and was buried at Mount Jerome Cemetery, Dublin, where a marble statue by Hogan was erected over his grave. Though a Protestant and brought up as a Tory, one of his chief objects was to break down the fierce antagonism between the Roman Catholics and the Protestants of his country. Some of his poems: "A Ballad of Freedom," "A Rally for Ireland," "Lament for the Death of Eoghan Ruadh O'Neill," "Song of the Volunteers of 1782," "The Exile," "The Girl I Left Behind Me," "The Irish Hurrah," "This Native Land," "Tipperary," "We Must Not Fail."

Sources: *An Anthology of Revolutionary Poetry.* Marcus Graham, ed. The Active Press, 1929. *Dictionary of National Biography.* Electronic Edition 1.1. Oxford University Press, 1997. *English Poetry: Author Search.* Chadwyck-Healey Ltd., 1995 (http://www.lib.utexas.edu:8080/search/epoetry/author.html). *The Columbia Granger's Index to Poetry.* 11th ed. *The Columbia Granger's World of Poetry,* Columbia University Press, 2005 (http://www.columbiagrangers.org). *The Poems of Thomas Davis.* D. & J. Sadlier & Co., 1866.

DAVISON, FRANCIS and WALTER (?1575–?1619)

Francis, the elder brother, ?1575–1619

Son of William Davison, secretary of state to Queen Elizabeth, who was Elizabeth's scapegoat in the matter of the execution of Mary Queen of Scots. In 1593, Davison was admitted as a member of Gray's Inn Court and in December 1594 was among the contributors to the *Gray's Inn Masque*, for which he wrote some speeches. In 1595, accompanied by his tutor, Edward Smyth, he started on his travels and by the autumn of 1596 they were in Florence. Some of his publications (with shortened titles): *Answer to Mrs. Mary Cornwallis*, 1600. *A Poetical Rapsody*, 1602; 2nd ed., 1608; 3rd. ed., 1611; and 4th ed., 1621. It includes "The Lie," attributed to Sir Walter Raleigh; the song "In Praise of a Beggar's Life," quoted in *The Compleat Angler* (1653–1655), as well as poems by many notable poets. The *Rapsody* was edited by Sir Egerton Brydges in 1814 and by Sir Harris Nicolas in 1826.

The brothers contributed a large number of

poems: eclogues, sonnets, odes, elegies, madrigals and epigrams, translations from Horace, Martial, Petrarch, and Jodelle. Some of Francis's other poems: "Are Women Fair?" "Bought," "Her Commendation," "His Farewell to His Unkind and Unconstant Mistress," "Madrigal," "To Cupid."

Walter, the youngest brother, 1581–?1608

Walter was born in London and entered King's College, Cambridge, in 1596, but left without graduating. About 1602 he was a soldier in the Low Countries. It is assumed that he died there. He contributed some poems to *A Poetical Rapsody*, written, so Francis says, when Walter was eighteen. Two of Walter's poems: "At Her Fair Hands," "To His Lady, Who Had Vowed Virginity."

Sources: *A Poetical Rapsody* (http://www.bartleby.com/214/0609.html). *Dictionary of National Biography.* Electronic Edition 1.1. Oxford University Press, 1997. *The Columbia Granger's Index to Poetry.* 11th ed. *The Columbia Granger's World of Poetry,* Columbia University Press, 2005 (http://www.columbiagrangers.org). *The Home Book of Modern Verse.* Burton Egbert Stevenson, ed. Henry Holt, 1953. *The Oxford Companion to English Literature.* 6th edition. Margaret Drabble, ed. Oxford University Press, 2000.

DAY-LEWIS, CECIL (1904–1972)

Born at Ballintubbert, County Laois, Ireland, the only child of the Rev. Frank Cecil Day-Lewis, Church of Ireland curate, he lived most of his life in England. He was educated at Sherborne School and Dorset and Wadham College, Oxford, where he became associated with a group of left-wing poets led by W.H. Auden, with whom he edited *Oxford Poetry* (1927). Lewis was a member of the Communist party from 1935 to 1938 and wrote for the *Left Review.* His early poetry focuses on social themes. His collection of essays is noteworthy. He wrote detective stories under the pseudonym of "Nicholas Blake." He was professor of poetry at Oxford from 1951 to 1956 and poet laureate of Great Britain from 1967 to 1972. He is buried at Stinsford in Dorset, only a few feet from Thomas Hardy's grave. Some of his publications: *Transitional Poem,* 1929. *A Hope for Poetry,* 1934. Translation of *Virgil's Aeneid,* 1952. *The Buried Day,* 1960 (autobiography). Some of his poems: "Do Not Expect Again a Phoenix Hour," "Flight to Italy," "From Feathers to Iron," "Dreams, O Destinations," "Overtures to Death," "Sheepdog Trials in Hyde Park."

Sources: *Chief Modern Poets of Britain and America.* 5th edition. Gerald DeWitt Sanders and John Herbert Nelson, eds., Macmillan, 1970. *Dictionary of National Biography.* Electronic Edition 1.1. Oxford University Press, 1997. *The Columbia Granger's Index to Poetry.* 11th ed. *The Columbia Granger's World of Poetry,* Columbia University Press, 2005 (http://www.columbiagrangers.org). *The Na-tional Portrait Gallery* (www.npg.org.uk). *The Oxford Book of Twentieth-Century English Verse.* Philip Larkin, ed. Oxford University Press, 1973. *The Oxford Companion to English Literature.* 6th edition. Margaret Drabble, ed. Oxford University Press, 2000.

DEANE, SEAMUS (1940–)

Born in Derry, Ireland, he was educated at Queen's University, Belfast, and gained his Ph.D. at Cambridge University. He taught literature at University College in Dublin for many years and is currently professor of Irish studies at the University of Notre Dame. He is also director of the Field Day Theater and Publishing Company. He has written on Irish studies, including the poets Jonathan Swift and James Joyce (see entries), but his focus is on Irish literary modernism. He is the author of *Celtic Revivals: Essays in Modern Irish Literature* 1880–1980 (1985); *A Short History of Irish Literature* (1986); and *The French Enlightenment and Revolution in England 1789–1832* (1988). His awards include the Æ Award (1973), and he was short listed for the Booker Prize for his novel *Reading in the Dark* (1996). He lives in Dublin. His poetry publications: *Gradual Wars,* 1972. *Rumours,* 1977. *History Lessons,* 1983. *Selected Poems,* 1988. Some of his poems: "A Burial," "Derry," "Fording the River," "Guerillas," "Reading Paradise Lost in Protestant Ulster 1984," "Roots," "The Brethren."

Sources: *Bitter Harvest: An Anthology of Contemporary Irish Verse.* John Montague, ed. Scribner's, 1989. *Contemporary Irish Poetry: An Anthology.* Anthony Bradley, ed. University of California Press. New and rev. ed., 1988. *Department of English, University of Notre Dame, Faculty Bios* (http://www.nd.edu/~english/Faculty-Bios.html). *Ireland in Poetrt.* Charles Sullivan, ed. Harry N. Abrams, 1990. *Poets from the North of Ireland.* Frank Ormsby, ed. The Blackstaff Press, 1990. *Biography of Seamus Deane, Reading Group Centre* (http://www.randomhouse.com/vintage/read/reading/deane.html). *The Columbia Granger's Index to Poetry.* 11th ed. *The Columbia Granger's World of Poetry,* Columbia University Press, 2005 (http://www.columbiagrangers.org). *The Field Day Anthology of Irish Writing.* Seamus Deane, ed. Faber and Faber, 1991. *The Oxford Companion to English Literature.* 6th edition. Margaret Drabble, ed. Oxford University Press, 2000. *Wikipedia, the Free Encyclopedia* (http://en.wikipedia.org/wiki/Wikipedia).

DECK, JAMES GEORGE (1807–1884)

Born in Bury St. Edmunds, Suffolk, he received a military training in Paris under one of Napoleon's generals and served as an officer in the 14th Madras Native Infantry of the East India Company from 1824 to 1826. On a trip to England he experienced a profound religious conversion and resigned his commission with the intention of becoming a clergyman. Instead he and his wife joined the Plymouth

Brethren and Deck became an evangelist in the West of England. He wrote religious poetry that was used in the movement's earliest hymn books. Having suffered a stroke and partial paralysis, Deck and his family emigrated to New Zealand in 1853. Within three months his wife died and later, with his second wife, the family moved to Wellington. His preaching tours had a significant impact on the development of the Brethren movement in New Zealand. Some of his hymns: "Abba, Father! We Approach Thee," "Jesus, Thy Name I Love," "Lamb of God! Our Souls Adore Thee," "Lamb of God, Still Keep Me," "Savior! Hasten Thine Appearing."

Sources: *Biography of James George Deck. Dictionary of New Zealand* (http://www.dnzb.govt.nz/dnzb/default.asp?Find_Quick.asp?PersonEssay=1D8). *Hymns by James George Deck* (http://www.stempublishing.com/hymns/authors/deck). *Oldpoetry* (www.oldpoetry.com). *The Cyber Hymnal* (http://www.cyberhymnal.org/index.htm).

DEELEY, PATRICK (1953–)

Originally from Loughrea, County Galway, Ireland, he has spent more than half his life teaching in Dublin, where at present he is principal of a large primary school. He also runs a workshop in Ballyfermot, specializing in children's poetry. Among his fiction for children are *The Lost Orchard* (2000), *My Dog Lively*, illustrated by Martin Fagan (2001), and *Snobby Cat*, illustrated by Tatyana Feeney (2005). Some of his collections: *Intimate Strangers*, 1986. *Names for Love*, 1990. *Turane: The Hidden Village*, 1995. *Decoding Samara*, 2000. Some of his poems: "By Cruagh Wood," "Elegy," "Rathgar Pastoral," "Woodman," "Yard Sticks."

Sources: *Biography of Patrick Deeley*. Dedalus Press (http://www.dedaluspress.com/poets/deeley.html). *The Irish Poets Library* (http://www.irishcultureandcustoms.com/Poetry/1Libr3.html). *Elegy, by Patrick Deeley* (http://www.stingingfly.org/issue4/4deeley.htm).

DEFOE, DANIEL (1660–1731)

Born in London, the son of a butcher, he became a hosiery merchant, traveling widely on the Continent. He took part in the Monmouth Rebellion (1685) and in 1688 joined the advancing forces of William III. He was popular with the king after the publication of his poem "The True Born Englishman" (1701). He served two prison sentences: one for his pamphlet *The Shortest Way with the Dissenters* (1702) attacking the Anglican Church, and the other for an attack in his newspaper, *The Review*, on the Whig opposition. He was a secret agent for the Tory government, gathering information and testing the political climate. Defoe is considered to be the founder of British journalism and the first true novelist. Some of his publications: *Robinson Crusoe*, 1719. *Captain Singleton*, 1720. *Journal of the Plague Year*, 1722. *Captain Jack*, 1722. *Moll Flanders*, 1722. *Roxanda*, 1724. *Tour Through the Whole Island of Great Britain*, 1724–1727. *London the Most Flourishing City in the Universe*, 1728. Some of his other poems: "Hymn to the Pillory" (written while in Newgate Prison), "Reformation of Manners," "The Spanish Descent," "The Vision."

Sources: *Anthology of Poems on Affairs of State: Augustan Satirical Verse, 1660–1714*. George de F. Lord, ed. Yale University Press, 1975. *Biography of Daniel Defoe* (http://www.spartacus.schoolnet.co.uk/Jdefoe.htm). *Dictionary of National Biography*. Electronic Edition 1.1. Oxford University Press, 1997. *Encyclopædia Britannica Ultimate Reference Suite DVD*, 2006. *English Poetry: Author Search*. Chadwyck-Healey Ltd., 1995 (http://www.lib.utexas.edu:8080/search/epoetry/author.html). *The Columbia Granger's Index to Poetry*. 11th ed. *The Columbia Granger's World of Poetry*, Columbia University Press, 2005 (http://www.columbiagrangers.org). *The Oxford Book of Travel Verse*. Kevin Crossley-Holland, ed. Oxford University Press, 1986. *The Oxford Companion to English Literature*. 6th edition. Margaret Drabble, ed. Oxford University Press, 2000.

DEKKER, THOMAS (?1570–1632)

Little is known about Dekkers's life, other than he lived in London and by 1598 he was writing for the Admiral's Men, an acting company. He and Ben Jonson were antagonists in what became known as the "war of the poets" or the "war of the theatre." Although successful, he was in the debtors' prison from 1613 to 1619. He was partly responsible for devising the street entertainment to celebrate the entry of James I into London in 1603 and provided the lord mayor's pageant in 1612. A prolific writer, he had part in some 50 plays. His plays and his numerous tracts afford valuable insights into the social life of Elizabethan and Jacobean times. Some of his publications: *The Shoemakers Holiday*, 1600. *Satiromastix*, 1601 (a play attacking his rival Ben Jonson). *The Wonderfull Yeare*, 1603 (about the plague). *The Belman of London*, 1608 (about roguery and crime). *The Guls Horne-Booke*, 1609 (behavior in the London theaters). *The Honest Whore, Part 2*1, 1630. Some of his other poems: "Beauty, Arise!" "Folly's Song," "Golden Slumbers" (lullaby), "Old Fortunatus," "The Happy Heart," "The Witch of Edmonton."

Sources: *Dictionary of National Biography*. Electronic Edition 1.1. Oxford University Press, 1997. *Encyclopædia Britannica Ultimate Reference Suite DVD*, 2006. *The Columbia Granger's Index to Poetry*. 11th ed. *The Columbia Granger's World of Poetry*, Columbia University Press, 2005 (http://www.columbiagrangers.org). *The New Oxford Book of Sixteenth Century Verse*. Emrys Jones, ed. Oxford University Press, 1991. *The Oxford Book of the Supernatural*. D.J. Enright, ed. Oxford University Press, 1994. *The Oxford Companion to English Literature*. 6th edition. Margaret Drabble, ed. Oxford University Press, 2000. *The*

Penguin Book of Renaissance Verse 1509–1659. David Norbrook, ed. Penguin Books, 1992. *Life and Work of Thomas Dekker* (http://www.luminarium.org/sevenlit/dekker/).

de La MARE, WALTER JOHN (1873–1956)

Born at Charlton, Kent, the son of an official in the Bank of England, he was educated at St. Paul's Cathedral Choristers' School. On leaving school at fifteen he worked in the London office of the Anglo-American Oil Company until 1908. He received honorary degrees from the universities of Oxford, Cambridge, London, St. Andrews, and Bristol, and was an honorary fellow of Keble College, Oxford. He was made a Companion of Honor in 1948 and received the Order of Merit in 1953. His ashes are buried in the crypt of St. Paul's Cathedral, where there is a memorial plaque. Some of his publications: *Songs of Childhood,* 1902 (poetry collection under the pseudonym Walter Ramal). *Henry Brocken,* 1904 (novel). *Poems,* 1906. *The Listeners,* 1912 (poetry). *Peacock Pie,* 1913 (poems for children). *Memoirs of a Midget,* 1921 (children's novel). *Crossings,* 1922 (a fairy play). *Collected Poems: The Burning Glass,* 1945. *Collected Rhymes and Verses,* 1970. Some of his poems: "Alas, Alack!" "An Abandoned Church," "As Lucy Went A-Walking," "How Sleep the Brave," "The Mocking Fairy," "The Traveler," "Tom's Little Dog," "Winter Dusk."

Sources: *Collected Poems of Walter De La Mare.* Henry Holt, 1941. *Dictionary of National Biography.* Electronic Edition 1.1. Oxford University Press, 1997. *Encyclopædia Britannica Ultimate Reference Suite DVD,* 2006. *Poemhunter* (www.poemhunter.com). *Selected Poems of Walter De La Mare.* Faber and Faber, 1973. *The Columbia Granger's Index to Poetry.* 11th ed. *The Columbia Granger's World of Poetry,* Columbia University Press, 2005 (http://www.columbiagrangers.org). *The Oxford Companion to English Literature.* 6th edition. Margaret Drabble, ed. Oxford University Press, 2000.

DELANTY, GREG (1958–)

Irish poet, born in Cork, he attended University College in Cork, where he was the contemporary of, among others, Maurice Riordan, Theo Dorgan, Sean Dunne (see entries) and other poets. He now lives for most of the year in America, where he teaches at St. Michael's College, Vermont. He became an American citizen in 1994. His poems have appeared in American, Irish, English, Australian, Japanese and Argentinean anthologies, including the *Norton Introduction to Poetry* (1981) and *Contemporary Poets of New England,* Middlebury College Press (2002). With Nuala Ni Dhomhnaill (see entry), he edited *Jumping Off Shadows: Selected Contemporary Irish Poetry* (1995). He has won many awards, including the Patrick Kavanagh Award (1983); the Alan Dowling Poetry Fellowship (1986); the Austin Clarke Centenary Poetry Award (1996); and the National Poetry Competition (Poetry Society of England) (1999). Some of his publications: *Cast in the Fire,* 1986. *Southward,* 1992. *American Wake,* 1995. *The Hellbox,* 1998. *The Blind Stitch,* 2001. *The Ship of Birth,* 2003. *Collected Poems 1986–2006,* 2006. Some of his poems: "About Time," "Bran at the Island of Women," "Seagulls," "The Gift," "Thrust & Parry."

Sources: *Bitter Harvest: An Anthology of Contemporary Irish Verse.* John Montague, ed. Scribner's, 1989. Carcanet press (http://www.carcanet.co.uk). *Biography of Greg Delanty* (http://64.233.179.104/search?q=cache:zr8WCedIK4gJ:64.78.63.75/downloads/Greg_Delanty.doc+Greg+Delanty&hl=en&ct=clnk&cd=5). *Biography of Greg Delanty* (http://www.irishwriters-online.com/gregdelanty.html). *Life and Work of Greg Delanty* (http://www.munsterlit.ie/Conwriters/greg_delanty.htm). *The Columbia Granger's Index to Poetry.* 11th ed. *The Columbia Granger's World of Poetry,* Columbia University Press, 2005 (http://www.columbiagrangers.org). *Turning Tides: Modern Dutch and Flemish Verse in English Versions by Irish Poets.* Peter van de Kamp, ed. Story Line Press, 1994. *World Poetry: An Anthology of Verse from Antiquity to Our Time.* Katharine Washburn and John S. Major, eds. Publisher, 1338, 1998.

DENHAM, SIR JOHN (1615–1669)

Born in Dublin, the son of an Irish judge, educated in London at Trinity College, Oxford, he studied law at Lincoln's Inn. He inherited the family mansion at Egham, Surrey, but squandered a small fortune on gambling. He was knighted by Charles II and elected to the Royal Society. At the beginning of the civil wars, as a Royalist and sheriff of Surrey, the king made him governor of Farnham Castle, Surrey, which he lost to the parliamentary forces and he ended up in prison. After the Restoration in 1660, he was made surveyor-general of works, and was member of Parliament for Old Sarum, Hampshire, from 1661 till his death. He is buried in Poets' Corner of Westminster Abbey. Some of his publications: *The Sophy,* 1642 (a tragedy). *Cooper's Hill,* 1642. *The Destruction of Troy,* 1645. *Anatomy of Play,* 1651. *Session of the Poets,* 1697. *Psalms of David, fitted to the Tunes used in Churches,* 1744. Some of his poems: "An Elegie upon the Death of the Lord Hastings," "On Mr. Abraham Cowley, His Death and Burial Amongst the Ancient Poets," "The Grasse-Hopper," "The Passion of Dido for Aeneas."

Sources: *Ben Jonson and the Cavalier Poets.* Hugh MacLaen, ed. New York: W.W. Norton & Company, 1974. *Dictionary of National Biography.* Electronic Edition 1.1. Oxford University Press, 1997. *Encyclopædia Britannica Ultimate Reference Suite DVD,* 2006. *English Poetry: Author Search.* Chadwyck-Healey Ltd., 1995 (http://www.lib.utexas.edu:8080/search/epoetry/author.html). *Stanford University libraries and Academic Information Resources* (http://library.stanford.edu). *The Columbia Granger's Index to Poetry.* 11th ed. *The Columbia Granger's World of Poetry,* Columbia University Press, 2005 (http://www.columbia grangers.org). *The National Portrait Gallery* (www.npg.org.uk). *The Oxford Companion to English Literature.* 6th edition. Margaret Drabble, ed. Oxford University Press, 2000. *Westminster Abbey Official Guide* (no date).

DENNY, SIR EDWARD (1796–1889)

The eldest son of Sir Edward, the 3rd baronet of Tralee Castle, County Kerry, Ireland, he was high sheriff for County Kerry. His mother (a descendant of Edward I) died in 1828, and he succeeded to his father's tile in 1831. He owned a good part of Tralee, but he was a caring landlord who kept the rents at an affordable level. He gave liberally to poor relations and to the development of the Plymouth Brethren. He lived quietly in a cottage in Islington, London, where he devoted his time to the study of the prophetic books of the Bible and wrote on the subject of prophecy. He was buried in the Paddington Cemetery, London. Some of his publications: *A Selection of Hymns* (London: Central Tract Depot), 1939. *Hymns and Poems,* 1848, 3rd edition 1870. Some of his hymns and poems: "Bride of the Lamb, Awake, Awake," "Children of Light, Arise and Shine," "Dear Lord, Amid the Throng That Pressed," "Hope of Our Hearts, O Lord, Appear," "Joy to the Ransomed Earth," "Sweet Feast of Love Divine," "While in Sweet Communion Feeding."

Sources: *Biography of Sir Edward Denny, 1796–1889* (Spiritual Songsters) (http://www.stempublishing.com/hymns/biographies/denny.html). *The Columbia Granger's Index to Poetry.* 11th ed. *The Columbia Granger's World of Poetry,* Columbia University Press, 2005 (http://www.columbiagrangers.org). *The Cyber Hymnal* (http://www.cyberhymnal.org/index.htm). *The Speaker's Treasury of 400 Quotable Poems.* Croft M. Pentz, ed. Zondervan, 1963.

DERMODY, THOMAS (1775–1802)

Born in Ennis, the county town of County Clare, he was educated at his father's school. He ran away to Dublin where the Rev. Gilbert Austin, principal of a school near Dublin, made a selection of Dermody's poems and published the book at his own expense in 1792. Despite all efforts he sank into squalor, saved by his enlisting in the Army, where he rose through the ranks to lieutenant. He served abroad with distinction, was wounded, and, returning with his regiment to England, was placed on half-pay. Sadly, he relapsed to his former habits and died in poverty near Sydenham, Kent, and was buried in Lewisham churchyard. Some of his publications: *The Rights of Justice, or Rational Liberty,* 1793 (on the French Revolution). *The Reform,* 1793. *Poems Moral and Descriptive,* 1800. *Poems on various Subjects,* 1802. *The Harp of Erin, or the Poetical Works of the Late Thomas Dermody,* 1807 (2 volumes). Some of his poems: "An Epistle Nugatory," "Sonnet, to Miss Brooke," "The Petition of Tom Dermody to the Three Fates in Council Sitting," "To Miss Sidney and Miss Olivia Owenson."

Sources: *An Anthology of Irish Verse: The Poetry of Ireland from Mythological Times to the Present.* Padraic Colum, ed. Liveright, 1948. *Bibliography of 19th-c. Irish Literature* (http://info.wlu.ca/~wwweng/faculty/jwright/irish/bibliomain.htm). *Dictionary of National Biography.* Electronic Edition 1.1. Oxford University Press, 1997. *English Poetry: Author Search.* Chadwyck-Healey Ltd., 1995 (http://www.lib.utexas.edu:8080/search/epoetry/author.html). *The Columbia Granger's Index to Poetry.* 11th ed. *The Columbia Granger's World of Poetry,* Columbia University Press, 2005 (http://www.columbiagrangers.org).

De STEIN, SIR EDWARD SINAUER (1887–1965)

Born in London, the son of Baroness Clara de Stein, and Sigmund Sinauer, who took his wife's name. After Eton College, and Magdalen College, Oxford, he became a lawyer. During World War I he served as an officer in the King's Royal Rifle Corps, then formed the De Stein merchant bank. During World War II he was director of finance at the Ministry of Supply, for which he was knighted in 1946. He was a philanthropist and founded and fully endowed a boys' club near Shepherd's Bush. He bought Lindisfarne Castle on Holy Island, where he acted as a philanthropist to the islanders and gave the castle to the National Trust. He was chairman of the British Red Cross finance committee from 1949 to 1963. He created a remarkable water-garden at his fishing cottage at Fulling Mills near Easton on the River Itchen, Hampshire, where he died. He left a large sum to form the Easton Trust to found hostels where boys from schools for the maladjusted could be helped to enter normal life. Two of his poems: "Chloe," "Elegy on the Death of Bingo Our Trench Dog."

Sources: *Dictionary of National Biography.* Electronic Edition 1.1. Oxford University Press, 1997. *Never Such Innocence: A New Anthology of Great War Verse.* Martin Stephen, ed. Buchan and Enright, 1988. *The Columbia Granger's Index to Poetry.* 11th ed. *The Columbia Granger's World of Poetry,* Columbia University Press, 2005 (http://www.columbiagrangers.org).

De VERE, SIR AUBREY and AUBREY THOMAS (1788–1902)

Irish father and son poets from Curragh Chase, County Limerick, related to the earls of Oxford.

Sir Aubrey, the father, (1788–1846)

Born Hunt, Sir Aubrey took the name De Vere on succeeding to the title in 1818. His sonnets were highly praised by Wordsworth. His main publications:

Julian the Apostate, a Dramatic Poem, 1822, republished 1858. *The Duke of Mercia, an Historical Drama, the Lamentations of Ireland, and Other Poems,* 1823, republished 1858. *The Song of Faith, Devout Exercises and Sonnets,* 1842, republished 1875. *Mary Tudor, an Historical Drama,* 1847, republished 1884. Some of his poems: "Reality," "The Children Band," "The Opening of the Tomb of Charlemagne," "The Right Use of Prayer," "The Rock of Cashel," "Waterloo."

Aubrey Thomas, the son (1814–1902)

Aubrey was educated privately in Ireland and at Trinity College, Dublin, where he won a prize for a theological essay. He developed a particular friendship with William Wordsworth and visited him at Rydal Mount, Ambleside, Cumbria. When he returned to Ireland at the beginning of 1846 after a few years, the country was in the grip of the "potato famine." He threw himself energetically into the work of the relief committees. In 1851 he was received into the Roman Catholic Church in the archbishop's chapel at Avignon, and in 1854 he was appointed as professor of political and social science in the new Dublin Catholic University. He was buried in the churchyard at Askeaton, County Limerick. Some of his publications: *The Waldenses and Other Poems,* 1842. *The Search after Proserpine and Other Poems,* 1843. *English Misrule and Irish Misdeeds,* 1848. *May Carols Hymns to the Virgin and Saints,* 1881, 3rd edition, 1857. *Constitutional and Unconstitutional Political Action,* 1882. *Inisfail, a Lyrical Chronicle of Ireland,* 1862 (six centuries of Irish recorded history). *The Infant Bridal and Other Poems,* 1864. *The Legends of St. Patrick,* 1872. *Alexander the Great* 1874, (verse drama). *St. Thomas of Canterbury,* 1876 (verse drama). *Recollections,* 1897. Some of his other poems: "A Year of Sorrow," "Autumnal Ode," "Coleridge," "Feast of the Most Holy Trinity," "Florence MacCarthy's Farewell to His English Lover," "The Foray of Queen Meave," "The Song: Little Black Rose," "The Wedding of the Clans."

Sources: *A Sacrifice of Praise: An Anthology of Christian Poetry in English from Caedmon to the Mid-Twentieth Century.* James H. Trott, ed. Cumberland House Publishing, 1999. *An Anthology of Irish Literature.* David H. Greene, ed. H. Modern Library, 1954. *Dictionary of National Biography.* Electronic Edition 1.1. Oxford University Press, 1997. *English Poetry: Author Search.* Chadwyck-Healey Ltd., 1995 (http://www.lib.utexas.edu:8080/search/epoetry/author.html). *The Columbia Granger's Index to Poetry.* 11th ed. *The Columbia Granger's World of Poetry,* Columbia University Press, 2005 (http://www.columbiagrangers.org). *The Golden Book of Catholic Poetry.* Alfred Noyes, ed. J.B. Lippincott, 1946. *The National Portrait Gallery* (www.npg.org.uk). *The New Oxford Book of English Verse, 1250–1950.* Helen Gardner, ed. Oxford University Press, 1972. *The Oxford Book of Nineteenth-Century English Verse.* John Hayward, ed. Oxford University Press, 1964; reprinted, with corrections, 1965. *The Oxford Companion to English Literature.* 6th edition. Margaret Drabble, ed. Oxford University Press, 2000.

De VERE, EDWARD, 17th EARL OF OXFORD (1550–1604)

Born at Castle Hedingham, Essex, he succeeded to the title at the age eight and was a royal ward under the care of William Cecil (later Lord Burghley). At his majority he regained control of his estates and married Anne Cecil, daughter of Lord Burghley. He studied at Queens' College, Cambridge, and St. John's College, Cambridge, before receiving legal training at Gray's Inn. He was a notable patron of writers and was also patron of the "Oxford's Men," an acting company. He flirted with Catholicism but in late 1580 he denounced a group of Catholic friends to the queen, accusing them of treasonous activities and asking her mercy for his own errors. In the 20th century he emerged the strongest candidate proposed for the authorship of some of Shakespeare's plays. Some of his poems: "A Louer Reiected Complaineth," "Fayre Fooles," "Greife of Minde," "His Good Name Being Blemished, He Bewaileth," "His Mynde Not Quietly Setled He Writeth Thus," "Loue Thy Choyse," "The Complaint of a Louer, Wearing Blacke and Tawnie."

Sources: *Dictionary of National Biography.* Electronic Edition 1.1. Oxford University Press, 1997. *Edward de Vere, Earl of Oxford* (http://www.luminarium.org/renlit/devere.htm). *Encyclopædia Britannica Ultimate Reference Suite DVD,* 2006. *English Poetry: Author Search.* Chadwyck-Healey Ltd., 1995 (http://www.lib.utexas.edu:8080/search/epoetry/author.html). *The Columbia Granger's Index to Poetry.* 11th ed. *The Columbia Granger's World of Poetry,* Columbia University Press, 2005 (http://www.columbiagrangers.org). *The New Oxford Book of Sixteenth Century Verse.* Emrys Jones, ed. Oxford University Press, 1991. *The Oxford Companion to English Literature.* 6th edition. Margaret Drabble, ed. Oxford University Press, 2000.

DEVLIN, DENIS (1908–1959)

Born in Greenock, Scotland, of Irish parents, he was educated at Belvedere College, Dublin, and University College, Dublin (UCD), where he read modern languages. From 1926 to 1927 he was at a seminarian for the Roman Catholic priesthood at Clonliffe College, Dublin. He abandoned the priesthood and read literature at Munich University from 1930 to 1933 and studied at Sorbonne, Paris, then returned to UCD to complete his M.A. thesis on Montaigne. He entered the Irish diplomatic service in 1935 and served in Italy, New York, Washington, London, and Turkey. Since his death, there have been two *Collected Poems* published; the first in 1964, edited by Coffey, and the second in 1989 edited by J.C.C. Mays. Some of his publications: *First Poems*, 1930. *Intercessions*, 1937. *Lough Derg and Other Poems*, 1946. *Exile*, 1949. *The Heavenly Foreigner*, 1950. *Memoirs of a Turcoman Diplomat*, 1959. Some of his poems: "Ank'hor Vat," "Ascension," "Encounter," "Liffey Bridge," "Regrets," "The Colours of Love," "The Passion of Christ," "Welcome My World," "Where the Light," "Wishes for Her."

Sources: *An Anthology of Irish Verse: The Poetry of Ireland from Mythological Times to the Present.* Padraic Colum, ed. Liveright, 1948. *Contemporary Irish Poetry: An Anthology.* Anthony Bradley, ed. University of California Press. New and rev. ed., 1988. *Biography of Denis Devlin* (http://www.irishwriters-online.com/denisdevlin.html). *University College Dublin Archives, Denis Devlin* (http://www.ucd.ie/archives/html/collections/devlin-dennis.html). *The Columbia Granger's Index to Poetry.* 11th ed. *The Columbia Granger's World of Poetry,* Columbia University Press, 2005 (http://www.columbiagrangers.org). *Wikipedia, the Free Encyclopedia.* (http://en.wikipedia.org/wiki/Wikipedia).

DIAPER, WILLIAM (1685–1717)

Born in Bridgwater, Somerset, he studied at Balliol College, Oxford, graduated in 1702, and remained as a scholar until 1705. He was ordained deacon in Wells in 1709 and was curate in Brent in the same diocese. He was also curate at Crick, Northamptonshire, and at Dean, near Basingstoke, Hampshire. Jonathan Swift introduced Diaper to his circle where Henry St. John, first Viscount Bolingbroke, and Sir William Wyndham became his patrons. Diaper struggled on in poverty, and when Queen Anne died, his patrons lost their influence and his situation worsened. His death is obscure. Some of his publications: *Nereides: Or, Sea-Eclogues, Callipædia and Dryades*, 1712. *An Imitation of the Seventeenth Epistle of the First Book of Horace*, 1714. *Halieutica*, 1722 (translation of Oppian, the 2nd century Greek poet; Diaper completed two of the five books). Some of his other poems: "A Letter from a Gentleman in Lincolnshire to His Friend," "Brent; a Poem to Thomas Palmer Esq.," "Dryades: A Poem," "To Mr. Congreve."

Sources: *Dictionary of National Biography.* Electronic Edition 1.1. Oxford University Press, 1997. *English Poetry: Author Search.* Chadwyck-Healey Ltd., 1995 (http://www.lib.utexas.edu:8080/search/epoetry/author.html). *Life of William Diaper by John Nichols* (http://athena.english.vt.edu/~drad/NereidesBio.html). *Oldpoetry* (www.oldpoetry.com). *The Columbia Granger's Index to Poetry.* 11th ed. *The Columbia Granger's World of Poetry,* Columbia University Press, 2005 (http://www.columbiagrangers.org). *The New Oxford Book of Eighteenth Century Verse.* Roger Lonsdale, ed. Oxford University Press, 1984. *The Oxford Companion to English Literature.* 6th edition. Margaret Drabble, ed. Oxford University Press, 2000.

DICKENS, CHARLES HUFFHAM (1812–1870)

He was born at 387 Mile End Terrace, Commercial Road, Landport, Portsea, Portsmouth, Hampshire. His father was a clerk in the navy pay office at Portsmouth dockyard before moving to Chatham, Kent, around 1816. The father spent some time in the debtors' prison, the "Marshalsea," described in *Little Dorrit.* Dickens was a reporter on the *Morning Chronicle* and edited two journals: *Household Words* and *All the Year Round.* He is reckoned to be the greatest novelist of Victorian England, and his novels, which are wonderful social documents of the time, appealed to a wide range of readers. He was also vocal in support for the abolition of slavery. He wrote poems, short stories and some twenty novels, several of which have been made into films. He died suddenly, leaving unfinished his last novel, *The Mystery of Edwin Drood*, and is buried in Poets' Corner of Westminster Abbey. Some of his poems: "A Child's Hymn," "Gabriel Grub's Song," "George Edmunds' Song," "Joe Gargery's Epitaph on His Father," "Lucy's Song," "Squire Norton's Song," "The Cannibals' Grace before Meat," "The Ivy Green," "The Song of the Wreck."

Sources: *Dictionary of National Biography.* Electronic Edition 1.1. Oxford University Press, 1997. *Encyclopædia Britannica Ultimate Reference Suite DVD, 2006. Faber Book of Nonsense Verse.* Geoffrey Grigson, ed. Faber & Faber, 1979. *Encyclopedia of Britain.* Bamber Gascoigne. London: Macmillan, 1994. *The Columbia Granger's Index to Poetry.* 11th ed. *The Columbia Granger's World of Poetry,* Columbia University Press, 2005 (http://www.columbiagrangers.org). *The Faber Book of Vernacular Verse.* Tom Paulin, Faber & Faber, 1990. *The National Portrait Gallery* (www.npg.org.uk). *The Oxford Companion to English Literature.* 6th edition. Margaret Drabble, ed. Oxford University Press, 2000. *The Poems and Verse of Charles Dickens.* F.G. Kitton, ed. New York: Harper & Brothers, 1903. *Westminster Abbey Official Guide* (no date).

DILLON, WENTWORTH, 4TH EARL OF ROSCOMMON (1633–1685)

Born in Roscommon County, in Ireland, brought up a Protestant, he was educated in Yorkshire and at the Protestant University in Caen, Normandy. His lands and titles were given back after the Restoration, and he took his seat in the Irish parliament by proxy on 10 July 1661. He was involved in disputes about land in England and in Ireland. He was awarded two honorary degrees: one from Cambridge in 1680 and one from Oxford in 1683. The earl had no children and the title consequently devolved on his uncle. Two of his publications: *Art of Poetry*, 1640 (a translation of Horace, with editions in 1684 and 1709). *Essay on Translated Verse*, 1684, enlarged 1685. Some of his poems: "A Paraphrase of *The Prayer of Jere-*

miah," "A Prospect of Death," "An Ode on Solitude," "On Mr. Dryden's *Religio Laici*," "On the Death of a Lady's Dog," "Paraphrase on Psalm 148," "Song on a Young Lady who Sung Finely," "The Ghost of the Old House of Commons."

Sources: *County Roscommon, IrelandGenWeb Project* (http://www.rootsweb.com/~irlrosco/). *Dictionary of National Biography*. Electronic Edition 1.1. Oxford University Press, 1997. *English Poetry: Author Search*. Chadwyck-Healey Ltd., 1995 (http://www.lib.utexas.edu:8080/search/epoetry/author.html). *English Poetry: A Poetic Record, from Chaucer to Yeats*. David Hopkins, ed. Routledge, 1990. *The Columbia Granger's Index to Poetry*. 11th ed. *The Columbia Granger's World of Poetry*, Columbia University Press, 2005 (http://www.columbiagrangers.org). *The National Portrait Gallery* (www.npg.org.uk). *The Oxford Companion to English Literature*. 6th edition. Margaret Drabble, ed. Oxford University Press, 2000.

DIXON, RICHARD WATSON (1833–1900)

Historian, pre-Raphaelite poet and clergyman, born at Islington, Birmingham, the son of a distinguished Wesleyan preacher. Educated at King Edward's School, Birmingham, he graduated from Pembroke College, Oxford, in 1857 and was ordained in 1858. He was second master at Carlisle High School from 1863 to 1868 and minor canon and honorary librarian of Carlisle Cathedral from 1868 to 1875. He received the honorary degree of D.D. from Oxford in 1899. He died at Warkworth, Northumberland. Some of his publications: *The Close of the Tenth Century of the Christian Era*, 1858 (the Arnold essay prize). *Christ's Company*, 1861 (poems). *St. John in Patmos*, 1863 (the Cramer prize for a sacred poem). *Historical Odes*, 1863. *Odes and Eclogues*, 1884. *Lyrical Poems*, 1886. *History of the Church of England from the Abolition of the Roman Jurisdiction*, 1878–1902 (covering the period from 1529 to 1570). He completed six volumes, two of which were published posthumously. Some of his poems: "Humanity," "Love's Consolation," "Rapture: an Ode," "Song: The Feathers of the Willow," "The Judgment of the May," "The Wizard's Funeral," "Winter Will Follow."

Sources: *Dictionary of National Biography*. Electronic Edition 1.1. Oxford University Press, 1997. *English Poetry: Author Search*. Chadwyck-Healey Ltd., 1995 (http://www.lib.utexas.edu:8080/search/epoetry/author.html). *Oldpoetry* (www.oldpoetry.com). *The Collected Poems of Canon Richard Watson Dixon (1833–1900)*. Peter Lang Publishing, 1989. *The Columbia Granger's Index to Poetry*. 11th ed. *The Columbia Granger's World of Poetry*, Columbia University Press, 2005 (http://www.columbiagrangers.org). *The Oxford Companion to English Literature*. 6th edition. Margaret Drabble, ed. Oxford University Press, 2000. *Wikipedia, the Free Encyclopedia*. (http://en.wikipedia.org/wiki/Wikipedia).

DOBELL, SYDNEY THOMPSON (1824–1874)

Born at Cranbrook, Kent, he was one of the so-called Spasmodic school of poets. His father was a wine merchant, his mother the daughter of the political reformer Samuel Thompson. The family moved to Cheltenham when Dobell was twelve years old. He was educated privately and never attended either school or university. His political views, particularly reform, are expressed in many of his poems and he had an interest in the cause of oppressed nationalities. Although not a rich man, he was always ready to help needy men of letters, and it was through his exertions that David Gray's poems were published. From about 1857 his health began to fail; he spent most winters abroad and wrote very little. He was buried at Painswick, Gloucester. Some of his publications: *The Roman*, 1850 (a long dramatic poem, which appeared under the pseudonym of Sydney Yendys, a palindrome). *Balder*, 1854. *A Series of Sonnets on the Crimean War*, 1855 (with Alexander Smith, see entry). *England in Time of War*, 1856. Some of his other poems: "A Shower in War Time," "America, II," "Grass from the Battle-field," "Sonnet: The Army Surgeon."

Sources: *Dictionary of National Biography*. Electronic Edition 1.1. Oxford University Press, 1997. *Encyclopædia Britannica Ultimate Reference Suite DVD*, 2006. *English Poetry: Author Search*. Chadwyck-Healey Ltd., 1995 (http://www.lib.utexas.edu:8080/search/epoetry/author.html). *Patriotic Poems America Loves*. Jean Anne Vincent, ed. Doubleday, 1968. *The Columbia Granger's Index to Poetry*. 11th ed. *The Columbia Granger's World of Poetry*, Columbia University Press, 2005 (http://www.columbiagrangers.org). *The Oxford Book of Victorian Verse*. Arthur Quiller-Couch, ed. Oxford University Press, 1971. *The Oxford Companion to English Literature*. 6th edition. Margaret Drabble, ed. Oxford University Press, 2000. *Wikipedia, the Free Encyclopedia*. (http://en.wikipedia.org/wiki/Wikipedia).

DOBSON, HENRY AUSTIN (1840–1921)

Born at Plymouth, Devon, the son of a civil engineer, he had a mixed education — Beaumaris grammar school, North Wales, at Coventry, at Strasbourg, and then in France. He worked for the Board of Trade from 1856 to 1901 and was awarded a civil list pension in 1904. In addition to his many poems he wrote several non-fiction books, biographies and memoirs and a series of Eighteenth Century Vignettes (1892–1894–1896). In all, he edited more than fifty volumes. Although not a great poet, his poems are delightful and easy to read. He published a 300 page bibliography of his works before he retired, which makes clear that his mind was principally applied to literature. He died at Ealing, London.

Some of his publications: *A City Flower*, 1864. *Incognita*, 1866. *Une Marquise*, 1868. *The Story of Rosina*, 1869. *Vignettes in Rhyme*, 1873. *The Civil Service Handbook of English Literature*, 1874. *Proverbs in Porcelain*, 1877. *A Paladin of Philanthrop*, 1899 and 1901. Some of his poems: "A Garden Song," "In After Days," "On the Future of Poetry," "The Cradle," "The Ladies of St. James's," "With Pipe and Flute."

Sources: *Dictionary of National Biography*. Electronic Edition 1.1. Oxford University Press, 1997. *Encyclopædia Britannica Ultimate Reference Suite DVD*, 2006. *English Poetry: Author Search*. Chadwyck-Healey Ltd., 1995 (http://www.lib.utexas.edu:8080/search/epoetry/author.html). *Poemhunter* (www.poemhunter.com). *The Columbia Granger's Index to Poetry*. 11th ed. *The Columbia Granger's World of Poetry*, Columbia University Press, 2005 (http://www.columbiagrangers.org). *The National Portrait Gallery* (www.npg.org.uk). *The Oxford Companion to English Literature*. 6th edition. Margaret Drabble, ed. Oxford University Press, 2000.

DODDRIDGE, PHILIP (1702–1751)

London-born, Non-conformist clergyman, the son of prosperous businessman. He was educated at Kingston-on-Thames and at St. Albans, where he was taught by the Presbyterian minister Samuel Clarke. The Duchess of Bedford heard of him and offered to see him through university after his father died. As a non-conformist he declined, and entered John Jennings' non-conformist academy at Kibworth, Leicestershire, in 1719. He set up a charity school at Northampton in 1737 and was influential in the foundation of the county infirmary in 1743. Never in good health, he died while in Portugal and was buried in the English cemetery at Lisbon. Besides a New Testament commentary and other theological works, he wrote over 400 hymns. Some of his publications: *The Rise and Progress of Religion in the Soul*, 1745. *The Family Expositor*, 1739–1756. *Some Remarkable Passages in the Life of the honourable Colonel James Gardiner*, 1747 (the philanderer referred to in Walter Scott's *Waverly*). Some of his hymns and poems: "Christ's Resurrection and Ascension," "Hark, the Glad Sound! the Saviour Comes," "Live While You Live," "God of Bethel" (*see* Logan, John), "Ye Golden Lamps of Heaven, Farewell."

Sources: *A Sacrifice of Praise: An Anthology of Christian Poetry in English from Caedmon to the Mid-Twentieth Century*. James H. Trott, ed. Cumberland House Publishing, 1999. *A World Treasury of Oral Poetry*. Ruth Finnegan, ed. Indiana University Press, 1978. *Dictionary of National Biography*. Electronic Edition 1.1. Oxford University Press, 1997. *Christian History Institute, Philip Doddridge* (http://chi.gospelcom.net/DAILYF/2003/10/daily-10-26-2003.shtml). *The Columbia Granger's Index to Poetry*. 11th ed. *The Columbia Granger's World of Poetry*, Columbia University Press, 2005 (http://www.columbiagrangers.

org). *The Cyber Hymnal* (http://www.cyberhymnal.org/index.htm). *The National Portrait Gallery* (www.npg.org.uk). *The Oxford Companion to English Literature*. 6th edition. Margaret Drabble, ed. Oxford University Press, 2000.

DODSLEY, ROBERT 1703–1764

Born near Mansfield, Nottinghamshire, the son of a schoolmaster, nothing is known of his education. While in the service of the Hon. Mrs. Lowther he started writing poetry, and with the profits from his writings, with his brother James, he opened a bookseller's shop in London in 1735. He published Pope's First *Epistle of the Second Book of Horace Imitated* in 1737 and went on to publish the works of many famous and influential people. In 1758 he co-founded with Edmund Burke *The Annual Register*. He is buried at Durham, where he died on a visit to a friend. In addition to his poetry he published many dramas. Some of his publications: *Servitude*, 1729 (a poem, with an introduction by Daniel Defoe). *The Footman's Friendly Advice to his Brethren of the Livery*, 1731. *A Muse in Livery, or The Footman's Miscellany*, 1732. *The Toy-shop*, 1732 (a dramatic satire). *Sir John Cockle at Court*, 1738. *A Collection of Poems by Several Hands*, 1748–1758 (6 volumes). Some of his other poems: "Agriculture," "The Footman: An Epistle to My Friend," "The Progress of Love," "The Stolen Kiss."

Sources: *Dictionary of National Biography*. Electronic Edition 1.1. Oxford University Press, 1997. *English Poetry: Author Search*. Chadwyck-Healey Ltd., 1995 (http://www.lib.utexas.edu:8080/search/epoetry/author.html). *Biography of Robert Dodsley, with links. Infoplease* (http://www.infoplease.com/ce6/people/A0815765.html). *Robert Dodsley—The Famous Bookseller and Publisher of London* (http://www.fzc.dk/Boswell/People/people.php?id=30). *The Columbia Granger's Index to Poetry*. 11th ed. *The Columbia Granger's World of Poetry*, Columbia University Press, 2005 (http://www.columbiagrangers.org). *The National Portrait Gallery* (www.npg.org.uk). *The New Oxford Book of Eighteenth Century Verse*. Roger Lonsdale, ed. Oxford University Press (2003. *The Oxford Companion to English Literature*. 6th edition. Margaret Drabble, ed. Oxford University Press, 2000.

DOLBEN, DIGBY AUGUSTUS STEWART MACKWORTH (1848–1867)

Born in Guernsey, he was brought up at Finedon Hall in Northamptonshire, and educated at Eton College, where Robert Bridges was his mentor. His staunch, almost violently anti-Catholic, Protestant parents were shocked by his outward confession to the Roman Catholic faith. He was sent down from Eton in 1863 for a few months for having made a forbidden visit to a Jesuit house. Before he was sixteen, he became a lay member of an irregular order of English Benedictines under the leadership of

"Father Ignatius" and loved to wear a monk's habit and cowl and walk barefoot. He formed a romantic attachment to another pupil and wrote love letters to several male friends. Before he could go up to Oxford, he drowned in the River Welland near Luffenham, Leicestershire, trying to save the life of Walter Prichard, his tutor's young son. Robert Bridges edited a partial edition *Poems* of his verse in 1911. Some of his poems: "A Letter," "A Poem Without a Name I & II," "A Sea Song," "A Song of Eighteen," "The Pilgrim and the Knight."

Sources: *Dictionary of National Biography.* Electronic Edition 1.1. Oxford University Press, 1997. *English Poetry: Author Search.* Chadwyck-Healey Ltd., 1995 (http://www.lib.utexas.edu:8080/search/epoetry/author.html). *List of famous Old Etonians born in the 19th century* (http://www.1-electric.com/articles/List_of_famous_Old_Etonians_born_in_the_19th_century). *Oldpoetry* (www.oldpoetry.com). *Stanford University libraries and Academic Information Resources* (http://library.stanford.edu).

DOMETT, ALFRED (1811–1887)

Born at Camberwell Grove, Surrey, and after leaving St. John's College, Cambridge, without a degree, he was admitted to the bar, then emigrated to New Zealand in 1842. His attempt at farming was not a success so he concentrated on journalism and became editor of the *Nelson Examiner* in 1843. He was involved for many years with the dispute about the administration of Maori land and was elected from Nelson to the House of Representatives in 1855. He was prime minister for one year from 1862 to 1863. He retired to England in 1871 and was made a companion of the order of St. Michael and St. George in 1880. Encouraged by Robert Browning, he published (1872) his long poem *Ranolf and Amohia, a South-Sea Day Dream,* about Maori life, with a second edition in 1883. He was also the author of the official publications: *Narrative of the Wairoan Massacre* (1843). *Petition to the House of Commons for the recall of Governor Fitzroy* (1845). *Ordinances of New Zealand Classified* (1850). Some of his other poems: "A Christmas Hymn," "A Glee for Winter," "A Maori Girl's Song," "An Invitation."

Sources: *Dictionary of National Biography.* Electronic Edition 1.1. Oxford University Press, 1997. *Encyclopædia Britannica Ultimate Reference Suite DVD,* 2006. *The Columbia Granger's Index to Poetry.* 11th ed. *The Columbia Granger's World of Poetry,* Columbia University Press, 2005 (http://www.columbiagrangers.org). *The Oxford Book of Travel Verse.* Kevin Crossley-Holland, ed. Oxford University Press, 1986. *The Oxford Companion to English Literature.* 6th edition. Margaret Drabble, ed. Oxford University Press, 2000.

DONNE, JOHN (1573–1631)

Born in London of Roman Catholic parents, his father, a prosperous merchant, died when Donne was four, and his mother remarried. He was educated at Hart Hall (now Hertford College), Oxford, but because he would not swear allegiance to the Protestant Queen Elizabeth, he was barred from taking a degree. Although trained in law, he never practiced, and from 1597 to 1602 he was secretary to Sir Thomas Egerton. Around 1601 he fell into disgrace by secretly marrying Anne More, Lady Egerton's niece, for which he was imprisoned, lost his job, and lived the next ten years in poverty. He embraced Protestantism and took holy orders and was ordained in 1615, became dean of St. Paul's in 1621, and was reckoned to be foremost preacher in the England of his day. He was a widower for fourteen years before he died of stomach cancer. He was the author of many religious works as well as being a voluminous poet. Some of his poems: "A Litany," "Community," "Elegies," "Holy Sonnets," "The Broken Heart," "The Dissolution," "The Flea," "To Mr. George Herbert," "Woman's Constancy."

Sources: *Dictionary of National Biography.* Electronic Edition 1.1. Oxford University Press, 1997. *Encyclopædia Britannica Ultimate Reference Suite DVD,* 2006. *English Poetry: Author Search.* Chadwyck-Healey Ltd., 1995 (http://www.lib.utexas.edu:8080/search/epoetry/author.html). *Stanford University libraries and Academic Information Resources* (http://library.stanford.edu). *The Columbia Granger's Index to Poetry.* 11th ed. *The Columbia Granger's World of Poetry,* Columbia University Press, 2005 (http://www.columbiagrangers.org). *The Complete English Poems of John Donne.* A.J. Smith, ed. Penguin Books, 1971. *The National Portrait Gallery* (www.npg.org.uk). *The Oxford Companion to English Literature.* 6th edition. Margaret Drabble, ed. Oxford University Press, 2000.

DOOLEY, MAURA (1957–)

Born in Truro, Cornwall, she grew up in Bristol, gained her B.A. from York University and her postgraduate certificate of education at Bristol University. She lives in London and is lecturer in creative writing at Goldsmiths College, University of London. She helped coordinate experimental workshops for performing arts labs, creating new plays for younger audiences, and was part of a creative team developing educational new films for Jim Henson Productions. She also directed the literature program at the South Bank Centre. She chairs the board of the Poetry Book Society, is on the council of management of the Arvon Foundation and is on the advisory board of the journal *Modern Poetry in Translation.* She won the Eric Gregory Award in 1987. Some of her poetry publications: *Ivy Leaves and Arrows,* 1986. *Turbulence,* 1988. *Northern Stories,* 1990. *Explaining Magnetism,* 1991. *Kissing a Bone,* 1996. *Sound Barrier: Poems 1982–2002,* 2002. Some of her poems: "At Les Deux Magots," "Does It Go Like This?" "Letters from Yorkshire," "Mansize," "Six

Filled the Woodshed with Soft Cries," "Up on the Roof," "What Every Woman Should Carry."

Sources: *Goldsmith's College, University of London* (http://www.goldsmiths.ac.uk/departments/english-comparative-literature/staff/m-dooley.php). *Love's Witness: Five Centuries of Love Poetry by Women.* Jill Hollis, ed. Carroll and Graf, Inc., 1993. *Making for Planet Alice: New Women Poets.* Maura Dooley, ed. Bloodaxe Books, 1997. *New Blood,* Neil Astley, ed. Bloodaxe Books, 1999. *Poetry with an Edge.* Neil Astley, ed. Bloodaxe Books, 1988. *Singing Brink: Anthology of Poetry from Lumb Bank.* Maura Dooley & David Hunter, ed. Arvon Press, 1988. *The Columbia Granger's Index to Poetry.* 11th ed. *The Columbia Granger's World of Poetry,* Columbia University Press, 2005 (http://www.columbiagrangers.org). *The Honey Gatherers: An Anthology of Love Poems.* Maura Dooley, ed. Bloodaxe Books, 2003.

DORGAN, THEO (1953–)

Born in Cork, he graduated with a B.A. in English and philosophy and an M.A. in English from University College, Cork, where he was tutor and lecturer, then literature officer with Triskel Arts Centre, Cork. From 1986 to 1989 he was a co-director of the Cork Film Festival. He is a member of Aosdána and the Irish Arts Council. He co-edited *The Great Book of Ireland* (1991) and co-edited essays by various authors on the legacy of the 1916 Easter Rising. He has also published a selection of poems in Italian, *La Case ai Margini del Mundo* (1999), and a Spanish translation of *Sappho's Daughter*, titled *La Hija de Safo* (2001). A former director of Poetry Ireland (Éigse Éireann), he has worked extensively as a broadcaster of literary programs on both radio and television. Some of his poetry publications: *Slow Air,* 1975. *A Moscow Quartet,* 1989. *The Ordinary House of Love,* 1991. *Rosa Mundi,* 1995. *Sappho's Daughter,* 1998. Some of his poems: "A Futile Poem," "A Stroll to Parfondeval," "If Only," "Kilmainham, Easter," "Message About the Times," "Silver Talk," "Song of the Alpine Hunter," "Theatre."

Sources: *A Poem a Day.* Karen McCosker, and Nicholas Albery, ed. Steer Forth Press, 1996. *Biography of Theo Dorgan* (http://www.irishwriters-online.com/theodorgan.html). *The Great Book of Gaelic.* Malcolm Maclean & Theo Dorgan, ed. Canongate Books, 2002. *Turning Tides: Modern Dutch and Flemish Verse in English Versions by Irish Poets.* Peter van de Kamp, ed. Story Line Press, 1994. *Two poems by Theo Dorgan* (http://www.munsterlit.ie/Conwrit ers/poems_by_theo.htm).

DOUGHTY, CHARLES MONTAGU (1843–1926)

Born at Suffolk, the son of a clergyman landowner, he was educated at both Caius College and Downing College, Cambridge, where he read geology. His paper on the Jostedal-Brae glaciers in Norway, read at the 1864 meeting of the British As-

sociation, was a summation of nine months alone in Norway studying glacier action. From a deep interest in sixteenth-century literature and a study of Teutonic languages, he determined that his life-work would be poetry in the style of Chaucer and Spenser. *Travels in Arabia Deserta* (1888) relates his experiences of several years in Arabia, where he lived like an Arab and spoke the language; Edward Garnett published the abridged version *Wanderings in Arabia* in 1908. He was an honorary doctor of letters of both Oxford and Cambridge universities and an honorary fellow of the British Academy. He died at Sissinghurst, Kent. Some of his poetry publications: *Under Arms,* 1900. *The Dawn in Britain,* 1906/1907 (six volumes). *Adam Cast Forth,* 1908. *The Cliffs,* 1908. *The Titans,* 1916. *The Clouds,* 1912. *Mansoul,* 1920.

Sources: *Dictionary of National Biography.* Electronic Edition 1.1. Oxford University Press, 1997. *Encyclopædia Britannica Ultimate Reference Suite DVD,* 2006. *English Poetry: Author Search.* Chadwyck-Healey Ltd., 1995 (http://www.lib.utexas.edu:8080/search/epoetry/author.html). *Poets of the English Language.* Vol. V. W.H. Auden and Norman Holmes Pearson, ed. Viking Press, 1950. *Stanford University libraries and Academic Information Resources* (http://library.stanford.edu). *The Columbia Granger's Index to Poetry.* 11th ed. *The Columbia Granger's World of Poetry,* Columbia University Press, 2005 (http://www.columbiagrangers.org). *The National Portrait Gallery* (www.npg.org.uk). *The Oxford Companion to English Literature.* 6th edition. Margaret Drabble, ed. Oxford University Press, 2000.

DOUGLAS, LORD ALFRED BRUCE (1870–1945)

Son of the Marquess of Queensberry, born in Worcestershire and educated at Winchester College and Magdalen College, Oxford. He and Oscar Wilde formed a gay relationship, which led to the famous trial and imprisonment of Oscar Wilde in 1895 (see entry). Douglas was the editor of a literary journal, *The Academy,* from 1907 to 1910. Winston Churchill brought a libel case against Douglas in 1923 because Douglas claimed that Churchill had been part of a conspiracy to kill Lord Kitchener. He was found guilty and sentenced to six months in prison. While in prison, he wrote his last major poetic work, "In Excelsis." He became a Roman Catholic in 1911 and died at Lancing, Sussex. Some of his publications: *Collected Poems,* 1919. *The Complete Poems of Lord Alfred Douglas,* 1928. *The Autobiography of Lord Alfred Douglas,* 1931. *Sonnets,* 1935. *Oscar Wilde: A Summing Up,* 1940. Some of his poems: "Apologia," "Lighten Our Darkness," "Ode to My Soul," "Rejected," "The City of the Soul," "The Dead Poet," "The Green River," "The Hen," "The Witch," "Two Loves."

Sources: *Aesthetes and Decadents of the 1890s.* Karl Beckson, ed. Academy Chicago Publishers, 1981. *"Autobiography" of Lord Alfred Douglas.* Reprint Services Corporation, 1994. *Dictionary of National Biography.* Electronic Edition 1.1. Oxford University Press, 1997. *The Columbia Granger's Index to Poetry.* 11th ed. *The Columbia Granger's World of Poetry,* Columbia University Press, 2005 (http://www.columbiagrangers.org). *The Home Book of Modern Verse.* Burton Egbert Stevenson, ed. Henry Holt, 1953. *The National Portrait Gallery* (www.npg.org.uk). *The Unofficial Website of Lord Alfred "Bosie" Douglas* (http://www.geocities.com/starparty1/bosie). *Wikipedia, the Free Encyclopedia* (http://en.wikipedia.org/wiki/Wikipedia).

DOUGLAS, GAWIN (GAVIN) (?1474–1522)

Born (possibly) at the castle of Tantallon in East Lothian, the son of Archibald Douglas, 5th Earl of Angus — known as "Archibald Bell-the-Cat" — he was educated at St. Andrews University and possibly Paris. He held various church appointments and was made Bishop of Dunkeld (Perth and Kinross) in 1515. Eleven months after the Battle of Flodden (1513) — where James IV was killed — his uncle, the 6th Earl of Angus, married Margaret, the royal widow. In the ensuing power struggle, because of his allegiance to the queen, he was imprisoned by the regent, the Duke of Albany, for a year and only released on the intervention of the pope. He was banished in 1521 to England, where he died of plague. His three posthumously published works: *The Palice of Honor,* circa 1535. *King Hart,* 1786. *The Æneid,* 1553 (the earliest translation into English, or rather, into colloquial Scots). Some of his shorter poems: "Conscience," "Heir the Translatour of This Buk Makis Mensioun of Thre of Hys Pryncipall Warkis," "Heyr Begynnys the Proloug of Virgyll Prynce of Latyn Poetis," "Winter."

Sources: *Dictionary of National Biography.* Electronic Edition 1.1. Oxford University Press, 1997. *Encyclopædia Britannica Ultimate Reference Suite DVD,* 2006. *English Poetry: Author Search.* Chadwyck-Healey Ltd., 1995 (http://www.lib.utexas.edu:8080/search/epoetry/author.html). *Oldpoetry* (www.oldpoetry.com). *The Columbia Granger's Index to Poetry.* 11th ed. *The Columbia Granger's World of Poetry,* Columbia University Press, 2005 (http://www.columbiagrangers.org). *The Oxford Companion to English Literature.* 6th edition. Margaret Drabble, ed. Oxford University Press, 2000. *The Palis of Honoure: Introduction.* Gavin Douglas. David Parkinson, ed. Kalamazoo, Michigan: Medieval Institute Publications, 1992 (http://www.lib.rochester.edu/camelot/teams/palisint.htm). *The Poetical Works of Gavin Douglas.* John Small, ed. William Paterson Publisher, 1874. *The Shorter Poems of Gavin Douglas.* 2nd edition. P. Bawcutt, ed. Scottish Text Society, 2003.

DOUGLAS, KEITH CASTELLAIN (1920–1944)

Born at Royal Tunbridge Wells, Kent, his father was a World War I Army officer who left the family when his son was seven. Educated at Edgeborough School, Guildford, and at Christ's Hospital, Sussex, Douglas early revealed talents as artist, poet, and sportsman. He went up to Merton College, Oxford, in 1938, where he was greatly influenced by his tutor, Edmund Blunden, soldier-poet of WWI (see entry). His education at Oxford was cut short by the outbreak of war. He enlisted in 1940 and by 1941 he was serving as a tank commander in North Africa, where some of his most powerful poems were written. He survived being wounded by a mine in January 1943 but was killed at the Normandy landing, outside the village of St. Pierre. His posthumous publications: *Alamein to Zem-Zem,* 1946. *Collected Poems,* 1951 (edited by J. Waller and G.S. Fraser). *Douglas' Selected Poems,* 1964 (edited by Ted Hughes). *Complete Poems,* 1979 (edited by Desmond Graham). Some of his poems: "Behavior of Fish in an Egyptian Tea Garden," "Cairo Jag," "Desert Flowers," "Simplify Me When I'm Dead," "The Offensive," "Waterloo."

Sources: *Dictionary of National Biography.* Electronic Edition 1.1. Oxford University Press, 1997. *Encyclopædia Britannica Ultimate Reference Suite DVD,* 2006. *First Lines, Poems Written in Youth, from Herbert to Heaney.* Jon Stallworthy, ed. Carcanet, 1987. *The Columbia Granger's Index to Poetry.* 11th ed. *The Columbia Granger's World of Poetry,* Columbia University Press, 2005 (http://www.columbiagrangers.org). *The Complete Poems of Keith Douglas.* Introduction by Ted Hughes, Faber and Faber, 2000. *The Oxford Book of War Poetry.* Jon Stallworthy, Oxford University Press, 1984. *The Oxford Companion to English Literature.* 6th edition. Margaret Drabble, ed. Oxford University Press, 2000.

DOUGLAS, NEIL (1750–1823)

Scottish poet about whose early life little is known. He was educated at Glasgow University and became a nonconformist preacher. *Sermons on Important Subjects, With Some Essays in Poetry* was published in 1789. This contained an ode referring to the illness and recovery of King George III. A master of the Gaelic language, he went on a preaching tour of Argyllshire in 1797. In 1817 he was charged with sedition; the case was laughed out of court. He died in Glasgow. In *A Monitory Address to Great Britain*1 (published in 1792 under the pseudonym "Britannicus"), he urges the king to abolish the slave trade as being anti-Christian, to do away with dueling and church patronage, and to issue a proclamation against vice. Some of his other publications: *The Lady's Scull,* 1794. *King David's Psalms,* 1815 (translations and paraphrases, intended to be sung.). Some of his poems: "Lavinia" (based upon the Book of Ruth), "Britain's Guilt, Danger, and Duty," "Thoughts on Modern Politics" (a poem on the slave trade), "The Royal Penitent, or true Repentance exemplified in David, King of Israel" (a poem in two parts).

Sources: *Dictionary of National Biography*. Electronic Edition 1.1. Oxford University Press, 1997.

DOWDEN, EDWARD (1843–1913)

Born in Cork, the son of an Irish merchant and landowner, he was educated at Queen's College, Cork, and Trinity College, Dublin, from where he graduated in 1863. He was appointed professor of English literature at Trinity in 1867 — a post he held till his death — and lectured at Oxford (1890–1893) and Cambridge (1893–1896). His critical strength was his ability to get inside the writer's mind rather than creating a record of personal impressions or opinions. In politics, he disliked Irish nationalism and fought vigorously against home rule. He was eager to help and encourage young men; house became an intellectual center. He died in Dublin. Some of his publications: *Shakespeare: A Critical Study of His Mind and Art*, 1875. *Southey: A Critical Study of His Mind and Art*, 1880. *The Life of Percy Bysshe Shelley*, 1886. *Introduction to Shakespeare*, 1893. *Robert Browning*, 1904. *A Woman's Reliquary*, 1913 (a book of poems written for his second wife, Elizabeth Dickinson). Some of his poems: "A Peach," "Brother Death," "Burdens," "Communion," "In the Cathedral Close," "In the Garden," "Love's Lord," "New Hymns for Solitude."

Sources: *A Treasury of Poems for Worship and Devotion*. Charles L. Wallis, ed. Harper, 1959. *Dictionary of National Biography*. Electronic Edition 1.1. Oxford University Press, 1997. *Encyclopædia Britannica Ultimate Reference Suite DVD*, 2006. *English Poetry: Author Search*. Chadwyck-Healey Ltd., 1995 (http://www.lib.utexas.edu:8080/search/epoetry/author.html). *Poetry Archive, Edward Dowden* (http://www.poetry-archive.com/d/dowden_edward_bibliography.html). *Poems of Edward Dowden*. (http://www.sonnets.org/dowden.htm). *The Columbia Granger's Index to Poetry*. 11th ed. *The Columbia Granger's World of Poetry*, Columbia University Press, 2005 (http://www.columbiagrangers.org). *The Home Book of Modern Verse*. Burton Egbert Stevenson, ed. Henry Holt, 1953. *The Oxford Companion to English Literature*. 6th edition. Margaret Drabble, ed. Oxford University Press, 2000.

DOWLAND, JOHN (1563–1626)

It is unknown whether this composer, virtuoso lutenist, and skilled singer — one of the most famous musicians of his time, with a music degree from Oxford University in 1588 — was English or Irish. He is known to have gone to Paris in 1580 in the service of Sir Henry Cobham, the ambassador to the French court. Disappointed that his Catholic faith excluded him from the post of court lutenist in 1594, he traveled on the Continent, visiting German and Italian courts where he was warmly received. He composed around 90 works for solo lute, many in dance form. His songs are harmonized tunes, not madrigals. His main publications: *First Booke of Songes*, 1597. *Second Booke of Songs*, 1600. *Third and Last Booke of Songs*, 1603. *Lachrimae, or Seaven Teares*, 1604. *Varietie of Lute-lessons*, 1610. *In Darkness Let Me Dwell*, 1610. *From Silent Night*, 1612. *Lasso vita mia*, 1612. *A Pilgrimes Solace*, 1612. Some of his poems: "Awake Sweet Loue Thou Art Returnd," "Away with These Selfe Louing Lads," "Come Away, Come Sweet Loue," "Wilt Thou Vnkind Thus Reaue Me of My Harte."

Sources: *Dictionary of National Biography*. Electronic Edition 1.1. Oxford University Press, 1997. *Encyclopædia Britannica Ultimate Reference Suite DVD*, 2006. *English Poetry: Author Search*. Chadwyck-Healey Ltd., 1995 (http://www.lib.utexas.edu:8080/search/epoetry/author.html). *The Columbia Granger's Index to Poetry*. 11th ed. *The Columbia Granger's World of Poetry*, Columbia University Press, 2005 (http://www.columbiagrangers.org). *The New Oxford Book of Sixteenth Century Verse*. Emrys Jones, ed. Oxford University Press, 1991. *The Oxford Companion to English Literature*. 6th edition. Margaret Drabble, ed. Oxford University Press, 2000.

DOWNMAN, HUGH (1740–1809)

Born at Exeter, Devon, and educated at Exeter Grammar School and Balliol College, Oxford, from where he graduated B.A. in 1763. He was an ordained minister, studied medicine at Edinburgh, and earned an M.A. at Jesus College, Cambridge, in 1770, then practiced medicine in Exeter. Several times he had to withdraw from practice because of ill health. Besides many poems, he published a number of plays, helped to translate an edition of Voltaire's works, and founded a literary society with 12 members in Exeter in 1796. His best known poem, and the one relevant to infant care, was published between 1774 and 1776, *Infancy or the management of children: a poem in three books*. Seven editions were published during his lifetime. He stressed two important principles: health is the greatest blessing a person can have, and a person's future depends on the management during the first years of life. His other main publications: *The Land of the Muses*, 1768 (a poem in the manner of Spenser). *Poems to Thespia*, 1781. *The Death Song of Ragnar Lodbrach*, 1781. *Poems*, 1791.

Sources: *Dictionary of National Biography*. Electronic Edition 1.1. Oxford University Press, 1997. *English Poetry: Author Search*. Chadwyck-Healey Ltd., 1995 (http://www.lib.utexas.edu:8080/search/epoetry/author.html). *Hugh Downman, MD (1740–1809) of Exeter and his poem on infant care* (http://fn.bmjjournals.com/cgi/content/full/88/3/F253).

DOWSON, ERNEST CHRISTOPHER (1867–1900)

Born in Kent to prosperous parents, he entered Queen's College, Oxford, but left in 1888 when his father fell on hard times. He is one of the most gifted of the circle of English poets of the 1890s known as the Decadents, all members of the Rhymers' Club. In 1891 he met Adelaide Foltinowicz, a girl aged 12, the inspiration for his best-known poem, "Non Sum Qualis Eram Bonae sub Regno Cynarae." After she refused his offer of marriage Dowson sunk into a life of dissolution and strong drink. Within months, in 1894, both his parents died: his father of tuberculosis, his mother of suicide, and he discovered the symptoms of his own tuberculosis. He then moved to Brittany but was found destitute by a friend who brought him home to London, where he died. Some of his publications: *Dilemmas*, 1895 (short stories). *Verses*, 1896. *Decorations*, 1899 (poetry). Some of his poems: "Breton Afternoon," "Carthusians," "From the Icelandic," "My Lady April," "Nuns of the Perpetual Adoration," "The Passing of Tennyson," "To a Lost Love," "Yvonne of Brittany."

Sources: *Dictionary of National Biography*. Electronic Edition 1.1. Oxford University Press, 1997. *Encyclopædia Britannica Ultimate Reference Suite DVD*, 2006. *English Poetry: Author Search*. Chadwyck-Healey Ltd., 1995 (http://www.lib.utexas.edu:8080/search/epoetry/author.html). *The Columbia Granger's Index to Poetry*. 11th ed. *The Columbia Granger's World of Poetry*, Columbia University Press, 2005 (http://www.columbiagrangers.org). *The National Portrait Gallery* (www.npg.org.uk). *The Oxford Companion to English Literature*. 6th edition. Margaret Drabble, ed. Oxford University Press, 2000. *The Poems of Ernest Dowson*. Arthur Symons Dodd, ed. Mead and Company, 1922.

DOYLE, SIR ARTHUR IGNATIUS CONAN (1859–1930)

Scottish author and poet, Doyle was born in Edinburgh and educated at Stonyhurst Jesuit School in Lancashire, England, followed by an another year of schooling in Austria. He qualified as a doctor from Edinburgh University in 1885 and practiced at Southsea, Portsmouth, from 1882 to 1890. The insights he derived from the observation skills of his medical professor, Joseph Bell, inspired him in his legendary detective novels of Sherlock Holmes. He also wrote non-fiction: *The Great Boer War* (1900). *The British Campaign in France and Flanders*, 6 volumes (1916–20). *The Crime of the Congo* (1909). He was knighted in 1902 for his medical services during the South African (Boer) War. He was interested in spiritualism and psychic research. He died at Crowborough, Sussex, and in 1930, thousands filled London's Royal Albert Hall for a séance during which Estelle Roberts, the spiritualist medium, claimed to have contacted Sir Arthur. He is buried in the church yard at Minstead in the New Forest, Hampshire. Some of his poems: "A Hunting Morning," "A Parable," "A Tragedy," "Cremona," "H.M.S. Foudroy-

ant," "Pennarby Mine," "The Old Huntsman," "The Passing," "Ware Holes."

Sources: *Arthur Conan Doyle: Poems* (http://www.poetry-archive.com/d/doyle_arthur_conan.html). *Dictionary of National Biography*. Electronic Edition 1.1. Oxford University Press, 1997. *Encyclopædia Britannica Ultimate Reference Suite DVD*, 2006. *The Columbia Granger's Index to Poetry*. 11th ed. *The Columbia Granger's World of Poetry*, Columbia University Press, 2005 (http://www.columbia grangers.org). *The Home Book of Modern Verse*. Burton Egbert Stevenson, ed. Henry Holt, 1953. *The National Portrait Gallery* (www.npg.org.uk). *The Oxford Companion to English Literature*. 6th edition. Margaret Drabble, ed. Oxford University Press, 2000. *Wikipedia, the Free Encyclopedia*. (http://en.wikipedia.org/wiki/Wikipedia).

DOYLE, SIR FRANCIS HASTINGS CHARLES (1810–1888)

Yorkshire born, he belonged to a military family which produced several distinguished officers. Educated at Eton College under John Keate, he graduated from Christ Church, Oxford, in 1832, then became a lawyer and was called to the bar in 1837. He succeeded to the baronetcy in 1839. He became the assistant-solicitor of the excise in 1845, receiver-general of customs from 1846 to 1869, then commissioner of customs until 1883. He was fellow of All Souls, Oxford, and followed Matthew Arnold as professor of poetry at Oxford from 1867 to 1877. His poetry uses the ballad form to describe modern events, particularly deeds of bravery. Some of his publications: *Miscellaneous Verses*, 1834, second edition with additions, 1840. *The Two Destinies*, 1844. *Oedipus, King of Thebes*, 1849. *The Duke's Funeral*, 1852. *The Return of the Guards and Other Poems*, 1866. *Robin Hood's Bay: An Ode addressed to the English People*, 1878. Some of his poems: "Mehrab Khan," "Private of the Buffs, or, The British Soldier in China," "The Catholic," "The Crusader's Return," "The Death of Hector," "The Loss of the Birkenhead," "The Old Cavalier," "The Red Thread of Honor."

Sources: *Dictionary of National Biography*. Electronic Edition 1.1. Oxford University Press, 1997. *English Poetry: Author Search*. Chadwyck-Healey Ltd., 1995 (http://www.lib.utexas.edu:8080/search/epoetry/author.html). *The Columbia Granger's Index to Poetry*. 11th ed. *The Columbia Granger's World of Poetry*, Columbia University Press, 2005 (http://www.columbiagrangers.org). *The National Portrait Gallery* (www.npg.org.uk). *The Oxford Companion to English Literature*. 6th edition. Margaret Drabble, ed. Oxford University Press, 2000. *Wikipedia, the Free Encyclopedia*. (http://en.wikipedia.org/wiki/Wikipedia).

DRANE, (MOTHER) AUGUSTA THEODOSIA (1823–1894)

She was born to Protestant parents at Bromley St. Leonard's, Middlesex; her father was a partner in an

East India mercantile house. At the age of fourteen the family moved to Babbicombe, Devonshire. She converted to Roman Catholicism and entered the Third Order of St. Dominic at Clifton, Bristol, in 1853, taking the name of Sister Francis Raphael. In 1860, at the convent of Stone, Staffordshire, she was appointed mistress of novices, and in 1863, mistress of studies, and prioress in 1872. On the death of Mother Imelda Poole in 1881, she became provincial, thus taking charge of the whole congregation and the convents of Stoke-on-Trent, Bow, and St. Mary Church, a post she held until two weeks before her death. Some of her publications: *Catholic Legends and Stories*, 1855. *Historical Tales*, 1862. *Tales and Traditions*, 1862. *History of England for Family Use*, 1862. *Christian Schools and Scholars*, 1867. *Songs in the Night, and Other Poems*, 1876. *History of St. Catherine of Siena*, 1880. *The Spirit of the Dominican Order*, 1896. Two of her poems: "Forgotten Among the Lilies," "What the Soul Desires."

Sources: *Memoir of Mother Francis Raphael, O.S.D., Augusta Theodosia Drane*. B. Wilberforce, O.P., London, 1895. *Catholic Encyclopedia* (http://www.newadvent.org). *Dictionary of National Biography*. Electronic Edition 1.1. Oxford University Press, 1997. *Poems by Augusta Theodosia Drane: Poetry Archive* (www.poetry-archive.com). *The Oxford Book of English Mystical Verse, 13th–20th Centuries*. D.H.S. Nicholson and A.H. Lee, ed. Oxford University Press, 1916.

DRAYCOTT, JANE (1954–)

Jane Draycott studied in London and Bristol, where she took a postgraduate degree in medieval English literature. She has worked as a teacher in London, Tanzania and Strasbourg, and lectured in creative writing at the universities of Reading and Oxford and online for the Trace Online Writing Centre, part of Nottingham Trent University. She now lives in Oxfordshire and teaches at the universities of Oxford and Lancaster. She is currently resident writer at Henley's River and Rowing Museum, and is also Royal Literary Fund Fellow at Oxford Brookes University. In 2002 she won the Keats Shelley Prize, and in 2004, she was named as one of the Next Generation poets. She is a mentor on the Crossing Borders creative writing scheme, set up by the British Council and Lancaster University. Her poetry publications: *Prince Rupert's Drop*, 1994. *No Theatre*, 1996. *Christina the Astonishing*, 1998. *The Night Tree*, 2004. *Tideway*, 2002. Some of her poems: "Circus," "Eldorado," "Search," "What Matters."

Sources: *A Little Book of Comfort*. Anthony Guest, ed. HarperCollins, 1993. *Biography of Jane Draycott, The Poetry Book Society*, (http://www.poetrybooks.co.uk/PBS/pbs_draycott_jane.asp). *Biography and Poems of Jane Draycott, Poetry Workshop* (http://www.btinternet.com/~car-

penter/clock11.htm). *The Columbia Granger's Index to Poetry*. 11th ed. *The Columbia Granger's World of Poetry*, Columbia University Press, 2005 (http://www.columbia-grangers.org). *The Oxford Book of Sonnets*. John Fuller, ed. Oxford University Press, 2000. *Wikipedia, the Free Encyclopedia*. (http://en.wikipedia.org/wiki/Wikipedia).

DRAYTON, MICHAEL (1563–1631)

It is conjectured that Drayton was born at Hartshill, near Atherstone, Warwickshire, and that he was in the service of Sir Henry Goodere of Powlesworth, Warwickshire, who seems to have played a part in Drayton's education. Just as little is known about his birth, little is known about his life, apart from his voluminous publications. When James I ascended the throne in 1603, Drayton acclaimed the accession in verse, but was indiscreet not to mention the departed Queen Elizabeth. This breach of etiquette cost him a place at court. He was buried in Poets' Corner of Westminster Abbey, where a monument was erected to him by the Countess of Dorset. Some of his publications: *Harmonie of the Church*, 1591. *Idea, the Shepherd's Garland*, 1593. *Peirs Gaveston*, 1593. *Idea's Mirror*, 1594. *Matilda*, 1594. *Endymion and Phoebe*, 1595. *Robert, Duke of Normandy*, 1596. *England's Heroical Epistles*, 1597. *Poems Lyric and Pastoral*, 1606. *Poly-Olbion*, 1612–1622. Some of his poems: "Baron's War," "The Battle of Agincourt," "The Fairy Palace," "The Moone-Calfe," "The Owle," "To the Virginian Voyage," "Wrestlers."

Sources: *Dictionary of National Biography*. Electronic Edition 1.1. Oxford University Press, 1997. *Encyclopædia Britannica Ultimate Reference Suite DVD*, 2006. *English Poetry: Author Search*. Chadwyck-Healey Ltd., 1995 (http://www.lib.utexas.edu:8080/search/epoetry/author.html). *The National Portrait Gallery* (www.npg.org.uk). *Poets of the English Language. Volumes I–V.* W.H. Auden and Norman Holmes Pearson, eds. Viking Press, 1950. *The Oxford Companion to English Literature*. 6th edition. Margaret Drabble, ed. Oxford University Press, 2000. *The Cherry-Tree*. Geoffrey Grigson, ed. Phoenix House, 1959. *The Columbia Granger's Index to Poetry*. 11th ed. *The Columbia Granger's World of Poetry*, Columbia University Press, 2005 (http://www.columbiagrangers.org). *Westminster Abbey Official Guide* (no date).

DRENNAN, WILLIAM (1754–1820)

Irish-born son of a Belfast Presbyterian minister who qualified as a doctor from Edinburgh University in 1778, then settled in Newry, Northern Ireland. There he became interested in politics and literature, and his letters to the press signed "Orellana, the Irish Helot" attracted much attention. He moved to Dublin in 1789, where he was involved in the famous society of the United Irishmen, for which he was tried for sedition in 1794 and acquitted. The 1798 rebellion brought his political career to a close;

in 1800 he married an English lady of some wealth, and in 1807 left Dublin for good and settled in Belfast. He founded the Belfast Academical Institution and started the *Belfast Magazine*. At his funeral his coffin was carried by six Protestants and six Catholics. He is chiefly remembered for his poem *Erin* (1795), in which he penned the first reference in print to Ireland as "the emerald isle." Some of his publications: *Fugitive Pieces*, 1815. *Electra*, 1817 (a translation of Sophocles). Some of his other poems: "Glendalloch, and Other Poems," "The Wail of the Women after the Battle," "The Wake of William Orr."

Sources: *1798 Ireland: History and Links* (http://home-pages.iol.ie/~fagann/1798/). *19th Century British and Irish Authors. The Victorian Literary Studies Archive, William Drennan* (http://www.lang.nagoya-u.ac.jp/~matsuoka/19th-authors.html). *Dictionary of National Biography*. Electronic Edition 1.1. Oxford University Press, 1997. *The Columbia Granger's Index to Poetry*. 11th ed. *The Columbia Granger's World of Poetry*, Columbia University Press, 2005 (http://www.columbiagrangers.org).

DRINKWATER, JOHN (1882–1937)

Born at Leytonstone, Essex, the son of a schoolmaster turned actor, theatrical manager, and playwright, he grew up in Oxfordshire and worked as an insurance clerk with the Northern Assurance Company. Later, in Birmingham, and dissatisfied with his work, he met (Sir) Barry Jackson and in 1907 they founded the Pilgrim Players, an amateur dramatic society that developed into the Birmingham Repertory Theatre Company, with Drinkwater as the manager (1913). A prolific poet as well as playwright, he was one of the group of poets associated with the Gloucestershire village of Dymock. His work appeared in *Georgian Poetry* (1912–1922). He also wrote stories for children and produced several critical studies. Some of his publications: *Poems*, 1903. *Abraham Lincoln*, 1918 (which had a year's run at the Hammersmith Lyric Theatre). *Mary Stuart*, 1921. *Oliver Cromwell*, 1921. *Robert E. Lee*, 1923. *The Collected Poems*, 1923. *Bird in Hand*, 1927 (a comedy, successful on both sides of the Atlantic). *Summer Harvest*, 1933 (poetry collection). Some of his poems: "Christmas Eve," "David and Jonathan," "Fairford Nightingales," "John Keats," "Rupert Brooke," "The Cotswold Farmers."

Sources: *Dictionary of National Biography*. Electronic Edition 1.1. Oxford University Press, 1997. *Encyclopædia Britannica Ultimate Reference Suite DVD*, 2006. *Poems by John Drinkwater: Poets' Corner Bookshelf* (http://www.theotherpages.org/poems/gp2_4a.html). *The Collected Poems of John Drinkwater (1917–1922)*. Sidgwick and Jackson Limited, 1923. *The Columbia Granger's Index to Poetry*. 11th ed. *The Columbia Granger's World of Poetry*, Columbia University Press, 2005 (http://www.columbiagrangers.

org). *The National Portrait Gallery* (www.npg.org.uk). *The Oxford Companion to English Literature*. 6th edition. Margaret Drabble, ed. Oxford University Press, 2000. *Wikipedia, the Free Encyclopedia*. (http://en.wikipedia.org/wiki/Wikipedia).

DRUMMOND, WILLIAM HAMILTON (1778–1865)

Born in Larne, County Antrim, the son of Naval surgeon, he was educated at Belfast Academy. He studied in his spare time for the ministry, was ordained in 1800, and was given a church in Belfast. He ran a boarding school in Belfast, where one of his pupils was Thomas Romney Robinson, the astronomer. He was a founding member of the Belfast Literary Society (1801), and a member of the Royal Irish Academy, where for many years he was the librarian, with an interest in Celtic literature. He was granted a degree of doctor of divinity from Marischal College, Aberdeen, in 1810. He was buried at Harold's Cross Cemetery near Dublin. Some of his poetry: *Juvenile Poems*, 1795. *Hibernia*, 1797. *The Man of Age*, 1798. *The First Book of T. Lucretius Carus: Of the Nature of Things*, 1808 (translation). *The Giants' Causeway*, 1811. *Who Are the Happy?* 1818 (a poem on the Christian beatitudes, with other poems on sacred subjects). *Clontarf*, 1822. *Bruce's Invasion of Ireland*, 1826. *Battle of Trafalgar*, 1835. *The Pleasures of Benevolence*, 1835. *Ancient Irish Minstrelsy*, 1852.

Sources: *Dictionary of National Biography*. Electronic Edition 1.1. Oxford University Press, 1997. *English Poetry, Second Edition Bibliography* (http://collections.chadwyck.co.uk/html/ep2/bibliography/d.htm).

DRUMMOND, WILLIAM, OF HAWTHORNDEN (1585–1649)

He was born at Castle Hawthornden near Edinburgh, the son of a wealthy landowner. From 1500 he was gentleman-usher to King James VI. Educated at the Edinburgh High School, he graduated from Edinburgh University in 1605 and then spent two years in France studying law (he inherited the estate in 1610.) Interested in science, his patent for converting salt water into sweet was granted in 1627. He wrote in English, rather than in Scots, for which he was severely criticized. He adapted and translated poems from French, Italian, and Spanish. The execution of Charles I is said to have hastened Drummond's death. Some of his publications: *Tears on the Death of Meliades*, 1613. *Poems*, 1616 (including 41 sonnets). *Forth Feasting*, 1617 (a celebration of King James' visit to Scotland). *A Midnight's Trance*, 1619. *A Cypresse Grove* 1623, (a meditation on death, second edition, 1630). *A Pastorall Elegie*, 1638. *The History of Scotland*, 1655. Some of his poems: "Her Passing," "On Mary Magdalene," "Phoebus Arise," "Summons to Love," "To His Lute," "To Sir William Alexander," "To the Nightingale."

Sources: *Dictionary of National Biography*. Electronic Edition 1.1. Oxford University Press, 1997. *Encyclopædia Britannica Ultimate Reference Suite DVD*, 2006. *William Drummond of Hawthornden, Poems* (http://www.sonnets.org/drummond.htm). *Poemhunter* (www.poemhunter.com). *The Columbia Granger's Index to Poetry*. 11th ed. *The Columbia Granger's World of Poetry*, Columbia University Press, 2005 (http://www.columbiagrangers.org). *The National Portrait Gallery* (www.npg.org.uk). *The New Oxford Book of Seventeenth Century Verse*. Alastair Fowler, ed. Oxford University Press, 2004. *The Oxford Book of Christian Verse*. Lord David Cecil, ed. Oxford University Press, 1940. *The Oxford Companion to English Literature*. 6th edition. Margaret Drabble, ed. Oxford University Press, 2000.

DRYDEN, JOHN (1631–1700)

Born in Northamptonshire, where his father was a justice of the peace, he was educated at Westminster School and graduated from Trinity College, Cambridge, in 1654. After Cambridge he worked as a hack-writer for Herringman, a London bookseller. He married Lady Elizabeth Howard in 1663 and they had four children. He was elected a member of the Royal Society in 1662. He excelled at drama, criticism, satire and lyric. He translated, among others, Virgil, Plutrach, and Chaucer. His change of religion is reflected in his two poems, "Religio Laici," 1682 (in favor of Anglicanism) and "The Hind and the Panther," 1687 (in favor of Catholicism). He was buried by the side of Chaucer and Cowley in the Poets' Corner of Westminster Abbey. Some of his publications: *Heroic Stanzas*, 1659 (on the death of Oliver Cromwell). *Astraea Redux*, 1660 (on the Restoration). *Annus Mirabilis*, 1667. *All for Love*, 1678. *Absalom and Achitophel*, 1681 and 1682. *Fables Ancient and Modern*, 1700. Some of his other poems: "A Song for St. Cecilia's Day," "An Ode, on the Death of Mr. Henry Purcell," "Hidden Flame," "Lines on Milton."

Sources: *Dictionary of National Biography*. Electronic Edition 1.1. Oxford University Press, 1997. *Dryden, Poems and Prose*. Douglas Grant, ed. Penguin Books, 1955, repr. 1985. *Encyclopædia Britannica Ultimate Reference Suite DVD*, 2006. *English Poetry: Author Search*. Chadwyck-Healey Ltd., 1995 (http://www.lib.utexas.edu:8080/search/epoetry/author.html). *Poemhunter* (www.poemhunter.com). *The Columbia Granger's Index to Poetry*. 11th ed. *The Columbia Granger's World of Poetry*, Columbia University Press, 2005 (http://www.columbiagrangers.org). *The New Oxford Book of English Verse, 1250–1950*. Helen Gardner, ed. Oxford University Press, 1972. *The Oxford Anthology of English Poetry, Vol. I: Spenser to Crabbe*. John Wain, ed. Oxford University Press, 1990. *The Oxford Companion to English Literature*. 6th edition. Margaret Drab-

ble, ed. Oxford University Press, 2000. *The Poems of John Dryden, Vol. 2, 1682–1685*. Paul Hammond, ed. Longman, 1995. *The Poetical Works of Dryden*. George R. Noyes, ed. Houghton Mifflin Company, 1950. *The Works of John Dryden* (www.luminarium.org/eightlit/dryden/drydenbib.htm). *The Works of John Dryden*. NTC/Contemporary Publishing Company, 1999. *Westminster Abbey Official Guide* (no date).

DUCK, STEPHEN (1705–1756)

Born to poor parents at Charlton in Wiltshire, he had little education and started his working life as an agricultural laborer at fourteen. With the aid of a dictionary he educated himself to read *Paradise Lost*, the *Spectator*, L'Estrange's translation of *Seneca's Morals*, and works by Shakespeare, Dryden, and Virgil. He was given a pension by Queen Caroline, who made him a yeoman of the guard, and in 1735, keeper of the queen's library at Richmond, called Merlin's Cave. He was ordained as a priest in 1746, and in 1752 was appointed to the rectory of Byfleet, Surrey. He fell out of favor and eventually drowned himself. He burned his early attempts at poetry but persevered and was encouraged by a fellow clergyman by the name of Stanley to write "Thresher's Labor" (1737), a poem that ensured his fame, the more so when Mary Collier (see entry) wrote her angry response, "The Woman's Labor: an Epistle to Mr. Stephen Duck" in 1739. Two of his other publications: *Poems on Several Subjects*, 1730. *Cæsar's Camp on St. George's Hill*, 1755. Two of his other poems: "On Mites, to a Lady," "On Richmond Park."

Sources: *Dictionary of National Biography*. Electronic Edition 1.1. Oxford University Press, 1997. *Duck, Stephen. The Thresher's Labor / Stephen Duck and the Woman's Labour / Mary Collier, introduction by Moira Ferguson*. Los Angeles: Williams Andrews Clark Memorial Library, University of California, 1985. *English Poetry: Author Search*. Chadwyck-Healey Ltd., 1995 (http://www.lib.utexas.edu:8080/search/epoetry/author.html). *The Columbia Granger's Index to Poetry*. 11th ed. *The Columbia Granger's World of Poetry*, Columbia University Press, 2005 (http://www.columbiagrangers.org). *The National Portrait Gallery* (www.npg.org.uk). *The New Oxford Book of Eighteenth Century Verse*. Roger Lonsdale, ed. Oxford University Press, 2003. *The Oxford Companion to English Literature*. 6th edition. Margaret Drabble, ed. Oxford University Press, 2000.

DUFFY, CAROL ANN (1955–)

Born in Glasgow, she was brought up and educated in Stafford. After graduating from Liverpool University in 1977, she worked for Granada Television before becoming a freelance writer in London. From 1982 to 1984 she worked in East End schools on a C. Day Lewis Fellowship. In 1996 she started lecturing in poetry at Manchester Metropolitan

University. Her plays have been performed at the Liverpool Playhouse and the Almeida Theatre in London. She became a commander of the British Empire in 2002 and a fellow of the Royal Society of Literature in 1999. She won the Eric Gregory Award, 1984, the Dylan Thomas Award, 1989, the Cholmondeley Award, and the Lannan Literary Award from the Lannan Foundation (USA), 1995. Some of her publications: *Standing Female Nude*, 1985. *Selling Manhattan,* 1987. *The Other Country*, 1990. *Mean Time*, 1993. *The World's Wife,* 1999. *Feminine Gospels*, 2002. *The Good Child's Guide to Rock N Roll*, 2003. *Out of Fashion*, 2004. Some of her other poems: "In Mrs. Tilscher's Class," "Never Go Back," "September, 1997," "Stealing," "Talent," "War Photographer."

Sources: *Biography and Works of Carol Ann Duffy* (http://www.contemporarywriters.com/authors/?p=auth 104). *Life and Works of Carol Ann Duffy: Knitting Circle* (http://myweb.lsbu.ac.uk/~stafflag/carolannduffy.html). *The Columbia Granger's Index to Poetry.* 11th ed. *The Columbia Granger's World of Poetry,* Columbia University Press, 2005 (http://www.columbiagrangers.org). *Who's Who.* London: A & C Black, 2005.

DUFFY, KATHERINE (1962–)

Irish poet born in Dundalk, County Louth, she now lives in Dublin. After working for many years as a librarian, she now works as a parliamentary translator in the Houses of the Oireachtas (the Parliament of Ireland). She writes fiction in both English and Irish, and her award-winning novel for teenagers, *Splanctha!,* was published by Cló Iar-Chonnachta in 1997. A selection of work from her 1998 collection, *The Erratic Behaviour of Tides,* together with some more recent pieces, was included in the anthology *Breaking the Skin: Twenty-first Century Irish Poets* (Black Mountain Press, Belfast in 2002).

Sources: *Biography of Katherine Duffy, Dedalus* (http://www.dedaluspress.com/poets/duffy.html). *Poem by Katherine Duffy* (http://www.brakkehond.be/76/duffy1e.html). *Poems by Katherine Duffy* (http://homepage.tinet.ie/~johndeane/page19.html).

DUHIG, IAN (1954–)

Born in London of Irish parents, Duhig was educated at Catholic schools which he left at sixteen. After several years of menial and manual work, he took exams at night school and went to Leeds University. After that he worked with homeless people for fifteen years in projects in London, Yorkshire and Northern Ireland until his job was made redundant. Since then he has taught and written in whatever combinations made him a living. While involved in social work, he encouraged people, whether homeless or suffering from addiction, to help themselves

through poetry. He made recording of his poetry at the Audio Workshop, London, which was produced by Richard Carrington in 2003. He has won the National Poetry Competition twice, and also the Forward Prize for Best Poem. His poetry publications: *The Bradford Count,* 1991. *The Mersey Goldfish. Nominies,* 1994 and 1998. *The Lammas Hireling,* 2003. Some of his poems: "Clare's Jig," "Fred," "From the Irish," "I Prayed to the Ghost of Carrie," "Margin Prayer from an Ancient Psalter," "No Derry Slubberdegullion with College Airs," "The First Second," "The Frog."

Sources: *Modern Irish Poetry.* Patrick Crotty, ed. The Blackstaff Press, 1995. *New Blood,* Neil Astley, ed. Bloodaxe Books, 1999. *The Bloodaxe Book of 20th Century Poetry, from Britain and Ireland.* Edna Longley, ed. Bloodaxe Books, 2000. *The Columbia Granger's Index to Poetry.* 11th ed. *The Columbia Granger's World of Poetry,* Columbia University Press, 2005 (http://www.columbiagrangers. org). *The Oxford Companion to English Literature.* 6th edition. Margaret Drabble, ed. Oxford University Press, 2000.

DUKE, RICHARD (1658–1711)

Born in London, he was educated at Westminster School and Trinity College, Cambridge, and was awarded his M.A. in 1682. He took holy orders and became rector of Blaby in Leicestershire in 1687. He was chaplain to Queen Anne and to Dr. Jonathan Trelawney, bishop of Winchester. He died at his residence in Witney, Oxfordshire. A small volume of fifteen sermons was published in 1714. *Poems upon Several Occasions* (1717), was published in conjunction with those of Roscommon, including the fragmentary beginning of *The Review.* Samuel Johnson's praise of Duke was mixed with derision of his qualities. Some of his poems: "A Panegyric upon [Titus] Oates," "Floriana a pastoral upon the death of Her Grace the Duchess of Southampton," "Funeral Tears," "Funeral Tears Upon the Death of Captain William Bedloe," "Idylls of Theocritus," "On the Death of King Charles the Second and the Inauguration of King James the Second," "On the Marriage of George Prince of Denmark and the Lady Anne," "The Fifth Elegy of the First Book of Ovid," "To Caelia."

Sources: *Anthology of Poems on Affairs of State: Augustan Satirical Verse, 1660–1714.* George de F. Lord, ed. Yale University Press, 1975. *Dictionary of National Biography.* Electronic Edition 1.1. Oxford University Press, 1997. *English Poetry: Author Search.* Chadwyck-Healey Ltd., 1995 (http://www.lib.utexas.edu:8080/search/epoetry/author.html). *Samuel Johnson's Lives of the English Poets, 1779–1781* (http://www2.hn.psu.edu/Faculty/KKemmerer/poets/preface.htm). *The Columbia Granger's Index to Poetry.* 11th ed. *The Columbia Granger's World of Poetry,* Columbia University Press, 2005 (http://www.columbiagrangers.org). *The Oxford Book of Classical Verse in Translation.* Adrian Poole, and Jeremy Maule, ed. 1995.

DUNBAR, WILLIAM (?1465–?1513)

One of the "Scottish Chaucerians," probably a native of East Lothian and thought to be related to the Earls of March. He graduated M.A. from St. Andrews University in 1479 and joined the order of Franciscan friars. On one of his begging trips he survived being shipwrecked on the coast of Denmark. He was with the ambassadors sent to the court of Henry VII to negotiate the marriage of his daughter Margaret Tudor to James IV, for whom he became the court poet, and from whom he received a pension. He distinguished himself in royal service and possibly died with his king in the Battle of Flodden in 1513. Some of his poems: "A Ballat of the Abbot of Tungland," "Ballad of Our Lady," "Flyting of Dunbar and Kennedie," "In Honour of the City of London," "The Ballad of Kynd Kittok," "The Dance of the Sevin Deidly Synnis," "The Goldyn Targe," "The Quenis Progress at Aberdeen," "The Thrissill and the Rois" (written in honor of the royal marriage), "Tua Mariit Wemen and the Wedo."

Sources: *Dictionary of National Biography.* Electronic Edition 1.1. Oxford University Press, 1997. *Encyclopædia Britannica Ultimate Reference Suite DVD,* 2006. *English Poetry: Author Search.* Chadwyck-Healey Ltd., 1995 (http://www.lib.utexas.edu:8080/search/epoetry/author.html). *First Scottish Books (Chepman & Myller Prints)— Digital Library* (http://www.nls.uk/digitallibrary/chepman/page.htm). *Great Books Online* (www.bartleby.com). *The Columbia Granger's Index to Poetry.* 11th ed. *The Columbia Granger's World of Poetry,* Columbia University Press, 2005 (http://www.columbiagrangers.org). *The Oxford Book of Light Verse.* W.H. Auden, ed. Oxford University Press, 1938. *The Oxford Companion to English Literature.* 6th edition. Margaret Drabble, ed. Oxford University Press, 2000. *The Poems of William Dunbar. 2 Vols.* Priscilla Bawcutt, ed. Assoc. for Scottish Lit. Studies. 1998.

DUNMORE, HELEN (1952–)

Born in Yorkshire, she graduated in English from York University, then taught in Finland for two years. She has worked as a writer, reader and performer, taught poetry and creative writing courses for the Arvon Foundation, and taken part in the Poetry Society's Writer in Schools program. She has also taught at the University of Glamorgan, the University of Bristol's Continuing Education Department and for the Open College of the Arts. She also reviews for *The Times* and *The Observer,* contributes to arts programs on BBC Radio, and has been a judge for the T.S. Eliot Prize and the Whitbread Book of the Year award. Her novel *Zennor in Darkness* (1993) won the McKitterick Prize, and *A Spell of Winter* (1995) won the first Orange Prize for Fiction. She was awarded honorary doctorate of literature from the universities of Glamorgan (1998) and Exeter (2001). She has published seven collections of poetry; the first was *The Apple Fall* 1983; the last was *Snollygoster and Other Poems* (2001). Some of her poems: "Seal Run," "The Bride's Nights in a Strange Village," "The Horse Landscape," "The Parachute Packers," "The Sea Skater," "Wild Strawberries."

Sources: *Golden Treasury of the Best Songs & Lyrical Poems in the English Language.* Francis Turner Palgrave, ed. Oxford University Press (1964, Sixth edition, updated by John Press, 1994). *Poetry with an Edge.* Neil Astley, ed. Bloodaxe Books, 1988. *Shades of Green.* Anne Harvey, ed. Greenwillow Books, 1991. *The Columbia Granger's Index to Poetry.* 11th ed. *The Columbia Granger's World of Poetry,* Columbia University Press, 2005 (http://www.columbiagrangers.org). *The Oxford Companion to English Literature.* 6th edition. Margaret Drabble, ed. Oxford University Press, 2000. *The Virago Book of Love Poetry.* Wendy Mulford, ed. Virago Press, 1990. *Who's Who.* London: A & C Black, 2005.

DUNN, DOUGLAS EAGLESHAM (1942–)

Professor of English and director of the Scottish Studies Institute at St. Andrew's University, he was born in Inchinnan, Renfrewshire. Educated at the Scottish School of Librarianship, he worked as a librarian in Scotland and Akron, Ohio, before reading English at Hull University. He holds honorary doctorates from the universities of Dundee (law) and Hull (literature), and has won several prestigious literary awards. He has edited various anthologies and critical works, written several television and radio plays, and published short stories. He became fellow of the Royal Society of Literature in 1981 and was appointed an officer of the Order of the British Empire in 2003. Some of his poetry publications: *Terry Street,* 1969. *Love or Nothing,* 1974. *St. Kilda's Parliament 1879–1979,* 1981. *Elegies,* 1985. *Boyfriends and Girlfriends,* 1995. *The Donkey's Ears,* 2000. *The Year's Afternoon,* 2000. *New Selected Poems 1964–2000,* 2002. Some of his poems: "After the War," "Friendship of Young Poets," "Love Poem," "The Clothes Pit," "The Drying-Green," "The Harp of Renfrewshire," "War Blinded."

Sources: *Biography and Bibliography of Douglas Dunn* (http://www.arlindo-correia.com/020305.html). *Encyclopædia Britannica Ultimate Reference Suite DVD,* 2006. *The Columbia Granger's Index to Poetry.* 11th ed. *The Columbia Granger's World of Poetry,* Columbia University Press, 2005 (http://www.columbiagrangers.org). *The National Portrait Gallery* (www.npg.org.uk). *The Norton Anthology of Poetry.* 4th ed. Margaret Ferguson, Mary Jo Salter and Jon Stal, eds. W.W. Norton, 1996. *The Oxford Book of Contemporary Verse, 1945–1980.* D.J. Enright, ed. Oxford University Press, 1980. *The Oxford Companion to English Literature.* 6th edition. Margaret Drabble, ed. Oxford University Press, 2000. *Who's Who.* London: A & C Black, 2005.

DUNNE, SEÁN (1956–1995)

Irish poet, from Waterford City, he studied English at University College, Cork, where he was a contemporary of Thomas McCarthy and Theo Dorgan (see entries). He detailed his student political activities in his memoir *The Road to Silence: An Irish Spiritual Odyssey* (1995). After college he settled in Cork, where he worked in the city library and continued to write and publish poems. Around the time first book, *Against the Storm: Poems,* was published in 1985, he began working as a freelance journalist and joined the *Cork Examiner* daily newspaper, where he became a prominent columnist. Among the anthologies he edited are *Poets of Munster* (1985), *The Cork Anthology* (1993) and *Something Understood: A Spiritual Anthology* (1995). He published two other poetry collections: *The Sheltered Nest* (1992) and *Time and the Island* (1996), as well as a memoir, *In My Father's House* (1991, republished, 2000). His *Collected* was published by the Gallery Press in 2005. He died suddenly in Cork, where he had spent his adult life. Some of his poems: "Autumn," "Quatrain," "Refugees at Cobh," "Requiescat," "Sydney Place," "Throwing the Beads," "Time, Please," "Tristitia Ante."

Sources: *Bitter Harvest, an Anthology of Contemporary Irish Verse.* John Montague, ed. Scribner's, 1989. *Biography of Seán Dunne* (http://www.gallerypress.com/Authors/Sdunne/sdunne.html). *Biography of Seán Dunne, Irish Writers Online* (http://www.irishwriters-online.com/seandunne.html). *Life and Works of Seán Dunne* (http://www.munsterlit.ie/Conwriters/sean_dunne.htm). *Modern Irish Poetry.* Patrick Crotty, ed. The Blackstaff Press, 1995. *The Columbia Granger's Index to Poetry.* 11th ed. *The Columbia Granger's World of Poetry,* Columbia University Press, 2005 (http://www.columbiagrangers.org). *Turning Tides: Modern Dutch and Flemish Verse in English Versions by Irish Poets.* Peter van de Kamp, ed. Story Line Press, 1994.

DUNSANY, EDWARD JOHN MORETON DRAZ PLUNKETT, 18TH BARON (1878–1957)

Born in London of Anglo-Irish parents, he was educated at Eton College and the military academy Sandhurst. He joined the Coldstream Guards and served in the South African War (African themes appear much in his writing) and World War I (as a captain in the Royal Inniskilling Fusiliers). He was wounded and taken prisoner by the rebels in the Easter week rebellion in Dublin in 1916. His experiences of escaping from the Germans in Greece, where he went as Byron professor of English literature in 1939, are recorded in his poem "A Journey" (1943). Unsuccessful at politics, he devoted himself increasingly to literature — lyric poetry, short stories, and short plays. He was a popular lecturer and broadcaster and was an honorary doctor of literature of Dublin (1940). He died in Dublin. In more than 50 verse plays, novels, short stories and memoirs, he combined imaginative power with intellectual ingenuity to create a credible world of fantasy. Some of his other poems: "On the Safe Side," "Songs From an Evil Wood," "The Deserted Kingdom," "The Memory," "There is No Wrath in the Stars."

Sources: *Dictionary of National Biography.* Electronic Edition 1.1. Oxford University Press, 1997. *Encyclopædia Britannica Ultimate Reference Suite DVD,* 2006. *The Columbia Granger's Index to Poetry.* 11th ed. *The Columbia Granger's World of Poetry,* Columbia University Press, 2005 (http://www.columbiagrangers.org). *The Home Book of Modern Verse.* Burton Egbert Stevenson, ed. Henry Holt, 1953. *The National Portrait Gallery* (www.npg.org.uk). *The Oxford Companion to English Literature.* 6th edition. Margaret Drabble, ed. Oxford University Press, 2000. Note: Inniskilling is the correct spelling for the regiment. Enniskillen Castle is the home of the Regimental Museum.

DURCAN, PAUL (1944–)

Dublin poet, a member of Aosdána, he studied archaeology and medieval history at University College, Cork. He has been outspoken in his condemnation of sectarian violence in Northern Ireland from the 1970s onward. His poems are often topical, as in his long narrative poem *Six Nuns die in Convent Inferno,* based on a fire in a Dublin convent in 1986. His 1985 collection, *The Berlin Wall Café,* relates the painful breakdown of his own marriage, and *Daddy, Daddy* (1990) addresses the relationship with his father. He has won four prestigious literary awards. Some of his other publications: *Westport in the Light of Asia Minor,* 1975. *The Selected Paul Durcan,* 1982. *Going Home to Russia,* 1987. *A Snail in My Prime: New and Selected Poems,* 1993. *Greetings to Our Friends in Brazil,* 1999. *Cries of an Irish Caveman,* 2001. Some of his other poems: "10.30 A.M. Mass, June 16, 1985," "Around the Corner from Francis Bacon," "In Memory of Those Murdered in the Dublin Massacre," "Ireland 1972," "Ireland 1977," "The Pietà's Over," "The Turkish Carpet," "The Weeping Headstones of the Isaac Becketts."

Sources: *Bitter Harvest, an Anthology of Contemporary Irish Verse.* John Montague, ed. Scribner's, 1989. *Biography of Paul Durcan* (http://www.irishwriters-online.com/pauldurcan.html). *Modern Irish Poetry.* Patrick Crotty, ed. The Blackstaff Press, 1995. *Life and Work of Paul Durcan* (http://www.contemporarywriters.com/authors/?p=auth01J17P482412620204). *The Columbia Granger's Index to Poetry.* 11th ed. *The Columbia Granger's World of Poetry,* Columbia University Press, 2005 (http://www.columbiagrangers.org). *The Oxford Companion to English Literature.* 6th edition. Margaret Drabble, ed. Oxford University Press, 2000. *Wikipedia, the Free Encyclopedia.* (http://en.wikipedia.org/wiki/Wikipedia).

D'URFEY, THOMAS (1653–1723)

Generally known as "Tom Durfey," he was born at Exeter, of Huguenot descent, and remained a Protestant until he died. He was writing in the reigns of four monarchs: Charles II, James II, William and Mary, and Queen Anne. His output of tales, satires, melodramas and farces was enormous, and many of his songs were set to music by Henry Purcell, Thomas Farmer, and Dr. John Blow, and were highly popular. Although troubled by a stammer in speech, he sang his own songs in public. He was buried at St. James's Church, Piccadilly, at the expense of the Earl of Dorset. Some of his publications: *Madam Fickle, or, the Witty False One*, 1677. *New Collection of Songs and Poems*, 1683. *A Fool's Preferment*, 1688. *Hymn to Piety, to My Dear Mother*, 1698. *Songs Compleat by Tom D'Urfey*. 1720 (six volumes). Some of his other poems: "A Shepherd Kept Sheep on a Hill So High," "Bright Was the Morning," "Chloe Divine," "The Bath, or, The Western Lass," "The Crown's Far Too Weighty," "The Fisherman's Song," "The Winchester Wedding."

Sources: *Dictionary of National Biography.* Electronic Edition 1.1. Oxford University Press, 1997. *English Poetry: Author Search.* Chadwyck-Healey Ltd., 1995 (http://www.lib.utexas.edu:8080/search/epoetry/author.html). *The Columbia Granger's Index to Poetry.* 11th ed. *The Columbia Granger's World of Poetry,* Columbia University Press, 2005 (http://www.columbiagrangers.org). *The Common Muse, an Anthology of Popular British Ballad Poetry, XVth–XXth Century.* Vivian de Sola Pinto and Allan Edwin Rodway, eds. Philosophical Library, 1957. *The Contemplator's Short Biography of Thomas D'Urfey* (http://www.contemplator.com/history/durfey.html). *The Oxford Book of Seventeenth Century Verse.* H.J.C. Grierson and G. Bullough, eds. Oxford University Press, 1934. *The Oxford Companion to English Literature.* 6th edition. Margaret Drabble, ed. Oxford University Press, 2000. *Thomas d'Urfey, texts set to music* (http://www.recmusic.org/lieder/u/durfey/). *Thomas Durfey and the Restoration Drama: The Work of a Forgotten Writer.* John McVeagh. Ashgate Publishing, Limited, 2000.

DURRELL, LAWRENCE GEORGE (1912–1990)

Anglo-Irish novelist, playwright and poet, born in Darjeeling, India, the son of a British civil engineer (his brother Gerald, 1925–1995, was the zoologist and owner of a zoo on Jersey, Channel Islands.) Educated in India and England, he worked for a time as a jazz pianist in a London nightclub, and started his writing career in Paris in the 1930s. The family moved to Corfu in 1935, and during World War II he served as press attaché to the British embassies in Cairo and Alexandria. After the war he held various diplomatic and teaching jobs. He finally settled in France, where he lived for the rest of his life. He wrote verse plays and farcical short stories but is best known for *The Alexandria Quartet*, a series of four interconnected novels (1957–60). Some of his poetry publications: *A Private Country*, 1943. *Cities, Plains and People*, 1946. *On Seeming to Presume*, 1948. *The Tree of Idleness*, 1955. *Collected poems*, 1960. Some of his poems: "A Ballad of the Good Lord Nelson," "A Water-Color of Venice," "Acropolis," "Alexandria," "Eight Aspects of Melissa," "Paphos," "Salamis," "Sarajevo."

Sources: *Encyclopædia Britannica Ultimate Reference Suite DVD,* 2006. *Erotic Poetry: The Lyrics, Ballads, Idyls, and Epics of Love—Classical to Contemporary.* William Cole, ed. Random House, 1963. *Biography of Lawrence Durrell.* (http://www.kirjasto.sci.fi/durrell.htm). *The Columbia Granger's Index to Poetry.* 11th ed. *The Columbia Granger's World of Poetry,* Columbia University Press, 2005 (http://www.columbiagrangers.org). *The National Portrait Gallery* (www.npg.org.uk). *The New Yorker Book of Poems.* The New Yorker editors. Viking Press, 1969. *The Oxford Companion to English Literature.* 6th edition. Margaret Drabble, ed. Oxford University Press, 2000. *Who's Who.* London: A & C Black, 2005.

DYER, SIR EDWARD (1543–1607)

Born at Sharpham Park, Somersetshire, he was educated at Oxford University, at either Balliol College or at Broadgates Hall (Pembroke College), but did not graduate. His patron at the court of Queen Elizabeth, in 1571, was the Earl of Leicester. He suffered poor health, attributed to falling into disfavor with the queen. Whatever the reason, the queen forgave him and sent him on two diplomatic missions to deal with land owing to the queen: to the Low Countries in 1584 and to Denmark in 1589. He was knighted in 1596 and appointed to the chancellorship of the order of the Garter. His most famous poem (some authorities doubt that it is his), "My Mynde to Me a Kingdome Is," was set to music by William Byrd (*Psalmes, Sonets, and Songs of Sadness and Piety,* 1588). "The Lowest Trees Have Tops" was set to music by John Dowland in 1603. Some of his other poems: "Coridon to His Phillis," "Cynthia," "The Shepherd's Conceit of Prometheus," "A Lady Forsaken, Complayneth," "Fancy, Farewell," "I Would It Were Not As It Is," "Where One Would Be."

Sources: *Dictionary of National Biography.* Electronic Edition 1.1. Oxford University Press, 1997. *Encyclopædia Britannica Ultimate Reference Suite DVD,* 2006. *English Poetry: Author Search.* Chadwyck-Healey Ltd., 1995 (http://www.lib.utexas.edu:8080/search/epoetry/author.html). *The Columbia Granger's Index to Poetry.* 11th ed. *The Columbia Granger's World of Poetry,* Columbia University Press, 2005 (http://www.columbiagrangers.org). *The New Oxford Book of Sixteenth Century Verse.* Emrys Jones, ed. Oxford University Press, 1991. *The Oxford Companion to English Literature.* 6th edition. Margaret Drabble, ed. Oxford University Press, 2000.

DYER, GEORGE (1755–1841)

Born in London, he was educated at Christ's Hospital from 1762 to 1774 and was for a long time at the head of school. He graduated from Emmanuel College, Cambridge, in 1778, then worked at two schools and returned to Cambridge, where he was tutor in the family of Robert Robinson, a minister of a dissenting congregation. In 1792 he went to London, where he made friends with Charles Lamb, and was employed in such literary tasks as making indexes and correcting the press. Dyer became totally blind; he died in London. In addition to his poetry, which included many odes, he published works on various social issues. Some of his poetry: *Poems, Consisting of Odes and Elegies*, 1792. *The Poet's Fate, a Poetical Dialogue*, 1797. *Poems*, 1801. *Poems and Critical Essays*, 1802. *Poetics, or a Series of Poems and Disquisitions on Poetry*, 1812. Some of his poems: "In Deep Distress, I Cried to God," "On Taking Leave of Arthur Aikin," "On Visiting the Tomb of David Hume," "Poetic Sympathies," "The Poet's Fate," "The Redress," "To Gilbert Wakefield."

Sources: *Dictionary of National Biography*. Electronic Edition 1.1. Oxford University Press, 1997. *English Poetry: Author Search*. Chadwyck-Healey Ltd., 1995 (http://www.lib.utexas.edu:8080/search/epoetry/author.html). *Poems, by George Dyer*. Longman and Rees, 1801. *Romanticism*. Duncan Wu, ed. Blackwell, 1994. *The Columbia Granger's Index to Poetry*. 11th ed. *The Columbia Granger's World of Poetry*, Columbia University Press, 2005 (http://www.columbia grangers.org). *The National Portrait Gallery* (www.npg.org.uk). *The Oxford Companion to English Literature*. 6th edition. Margaret Drabble, ed. Oxford University Press, 2000.

DYER, JOHN (1699–1758)

Born in Aberglasney, Carmarthenshire, Wales, he was educated at Westminster School. He started in his solicitor father's office, and on the death of his father he gave up the business to study art and became an itinerant painter. Having caught malaria in the Campagna, and not being successful as painter, in 1741 he took holy orders and became vicar of Catthorpe in Leicestershire. In 1751 he was appointed by Lord Hardwicke as chancellor to Belchford in Lincolnshire. He had two more livings: Coningsby (where he died, probably of tuberculosis) and Kirkby-on-Bane, both in Lincolnshire. He was made bachelor of laws of Cambridge University by royal mandate in 1752. Some of his publications: *Grongar Hill*, 1726. *The Ruins of Rome*, 1740. *The Fleece*, 1757. Some of his poems: "A Night Prospect," "An Epistle to a Famous Painter," "An Epistle to a Friend in Town," "On the Destruction of Lisbon, 1756," "Paraphrase of Part of Chapter 7 of Ecclesiastes," "The Country Walk," "To Aurelia," "To His Son," "Written at St. Peter's."

Sources: *A Treasury of Great Poems: English and American*. Louis Untermeyer, ed. Simon and Schuster, 1955. *Dictionary of National Biography*. Electronic Edition 1.1. Oxford University Press, 1997. *Encyclopædia Britannica Ultimate Reference Suite DVD*, 2006. *English Poetry: Author Search*. Chadwyck-Healey Ltd., 1995 (http://www.lib.utexas.edu:8080/search/epoetry/author.html). *Samuel Johnson's Lives of the English Poets*, 1779–1781 (http://www2.hn.psu.edu/Faculty/KKemmerer/poets/preface.htm). *The Columbia Granger's Index to Poetry*. 11th ed. *The Columbia Granger's World of Poetry*, Columbia University Press, 2005 (http://www.columbiagrangers.org). *The Oxford Companion to English Literature*. 6th edition. Margaret Drabble, ed. Oxford University Press, 2000. *The Poetical Works of Mark Akenside and John Dyer*. Robert Aris Willmott, ed. George Routledge and Co., 1855.

EDWARDS, THOMAS (1699–1757)

Born possibly at Pitshanger, Middlesex, and educated privately, in 1721 Edwards followed his father and grandfather into law at Lincoln's Inn. He inherited the Pitshanger estate at an early age and gave up law to concentrate on literature, then bought an estate at Turrick, Ellesborough, where he resided from 1740 till his death. He was elected fellow of the Society of Antiquaries in 1745. His main publication is *A Supplement to Mr. Warburton's Edition of Shakspear, Being the Canons of Criticism, and Glossary: Collected from the Notes in That Celebrated Work, and Proper to Be Bound Up with It* (second edition, 1748). He wrote some fifty sonnets as well as other poems. Some of his poems: "Sonnet on a Family Picture," "To His Grace Thomas, Archbishop of Canterbury," "To Shakespeare," "To the Author of Clarissa," "To the Editor of Mr. Pope's Works," "Tongue-Doughty Pedant," "Sonnet, Young, Fair, and Good!" "Sonnet, Peace to Thy Ashes," "Sonnet, on a Family-Picture," "Sonnet, Thou, Who Successive in That Honor'd Seat."

Sources: *A Century of Sonnets: The Romantic-Era Revival 1750–1850*. Paula R. Feldman and Daniel Robinson, eds. Oxford University Press, 1999. *Dictionary of National Biography*. Electronic Edition 1.1. Oxford University Press, 1997. *English Poetry: Author Search*. Chadwyck-Healey Ltd., 1995 (http://www.lib.utexas.edu:8080/search/epoetry/author.html). *Seventeenth and Early Eighteenth Century Sonnets* (www.sonnets.org/edwards.htm). *The Columbia Granger's Index to Poetry*. 11th ed. *The Columbia Granger's World of Poetry*, Columbia University Press, 2005 (http://www.columbiagrangers.org). *The Oxford Book of Sonnets*. John Fuller, ed. Oxford University Press, 2000. *The Sonnet: An Anthology*. Robert M. Bender and Charles L. Squier, ed. Washington Square Press, 1987. *The Sonnets of Thomas Edwards (1765–1780)*. Los Angeles: William Andrews Clark Memorial Library, University of California, 1974.

EGAN, DESMOND (1936–)

Irish poet born in Athlone, County Westmeath, he founded the Goldsmith Press in 1972 and edited the literary magazine *Era*. He has been awarded the U.S. National Poetry award for his *Collected Poems* (1983). He lives in County Kildare. Many of his poems are translations from Dutch poets. His other poetry publications: *Midland*, 1972. *Leaves*, 1974. *Siege!* 1976. *Athlone?* 1980. *Seeing Double*, 1983. *A Song for My Father*, 1989. *Selected Poems*, 1992. *Elegies*, 1996. *Famine*, 1997. *Music* 2000. Some of his translations: *At a Grave* (Martinus Nijhoff, 1894–1953). *Autumn Wind* (Adrian Roland Holst, 1888–1976). Columbus (J. Slauerhoff, 1898–1936). *Evening* (Willem Kloos, 1859–1938). *Honeysuckle* (J.C. Bloem, 1887–1966). *The Empty Room* (Hans Andreus, 1926–1977). *X-Rays* (I.K. Bonset, 1883–1931).

Sources: *Biography of Desmond Egan* (http://www.irishwriters-online.com/desmondegan.html). *Selected Poems of Desmond Egan* (http://mek.oszk.hu/00200/00271/html/index_ir.htm). *The Columbia Granger's Index to Poetry*. 11th ed. *The Columbia Granger's World of Poetry*, Columbia University Press, 2005 (http://www.columbiagrangers.org). *Turning Tides: Modern Dutch and Flemish Verse in English Versions by Irish Poets*. Peter van de Kamp, ed. Story Line Press, 1994.

EGERTON, SARAH FYGE (1670–1723)

Born in London, one of the six daughters of a physician, she wrote her most important feminist poem, "The Female Advocate," at the age of fourteen. An expanded edition was published in 1687 and again in 1707. Her father, objecting to her poetry, sent her to relatives in Shenley, Buckinghamshire, around 1687, then she was forced into marriage with Edward Field, an attorney who died in the mid–1690s, leaving her well-off. Her later poems talk about the growing love between her and Field and her grief at his death. She then married her second cousin, the Reverend Thomas Egerton, a much older widower with grown children. By 1703 the two were embroiled in a suit and counter-suit for divorce, but remained married until he died in 1720. *Poems on Several Occasions* was published in 1703, with a second edition in 1706. Some of her other poems: "On My Leaving London, June the 29," "On My Wedding Day," "Repulse to Alcander," "The Emulation," "To Marina," "To One Who Said I Must Not Love," "To Orabella, Marry'd to an Old Man," "To Philaster."

Sources: *Dictionary of National Biography*. Electronic Edition 1.1. Oxford University Press, 1997. *Early Modern Women Poets (1520–1700)*. Jane Stevenson and Peter Davidson, ed. Oxford University Press, 2001. *Eighteenth Century Women Poets: An Oxford Anthology*. Roger Lonsdale, ed. Oxford University Press, 1989. *English Poetry: Author Search*. Chadwyck-Healey Ltd., 1995 (http://www.lib.utexas.edu:8080/search/epoetry/author.html). *Poetry by English Women: Elizabethan to Victorian*, R.E. Pritchard, ed. Continuum, 1990. *Sarah Fyge Field Egerton* (http://

www.pinn.net/~sunshine/whm2000/eger2.html). *The Columbia Granger's Index to Poetry*. 11th ed. *The Columbia Granger's World of Poetry*, Columbia University Press, 2005 (http://www.columbiagrangers.org).

ELFYN, MENNA (1951–)

Welsh-speaking poet, born near Swansea, she is a fellow of the Royal Society of Literature and a member of Yr Academi Gymreig (the Welsh Arts Council for Wales). Since 1998 she has been writing director of the M.A. creative writing program at Trinity College, Carmarthen, and poet laureate for the Children of Wales since 2002. Although she writes in Welsh, her work has been translated into 15 languages; her English language translators include Tony Conran and Gillian Clarke (see entries). Her first bi-lingual book of poetry, *Eucalyptus: Detholiad O Gerddi/Selected Poems 1978–1994*, was published in 1995 and was followed by *Cell Angel* (1996) and *Cusan Dyn Dall/Blind Man's Kiss* (2001). Her two books of children's poetry are *Ffwl Yn Y Dwr: Casgliad O Gerddi I Bobl Ifanc* (1999) and *Caneri Pinc ar Dywod Euraid* (2003). She has also written stage plays, adaptations and scripts for television, radio plays, textbooks and libretti, and co-wrote *The Garden of Light* (1999) for the New York Philharmonic Orchestra. Some of her poems: "Baggage Carousel," "Bags," "Litany on Beginning a Burial," "Stone Poem," "The Theology of Hair."

Sources: *An Introduction — Crossing Borders* (Menna Elfyn) (http://www.mennaelfyn.co.uk/pages/Erthyglau/Winter%20Words%20-%20Menna%20Elfyn.htm). *British Council Arts* (http://www.contemporarywriters.com). *The Bloodaxe Book of Modern Welsh Poetry*. Menna Elfyn and John Rowland, eds. Bloodaxe Books, 2003. *The Royal Literary Fund* (http://www.rlf.org.uk/fellowship scheme/profile.cfm?fellow=24&menu=3).

ELIOT, GEORGE (1819–1880)

George Eliot, the pseudonym of Mary Ann or Marian Cross (formerly, Evans) — said to be one of the greatest novelists in England's history — was born in Warwickshire. Her father was overseer to Arbury Hall, the Newdigate family's seven thousand acre estate. Religious as a child, she underwent a crisis of faith, accelerated by her translation in 1846 of *Life of Jesus*, by Dr. David Friedrich Strauss (1835), in which he questioned the divinity of Jesus. After her father died in 1849, she became assistant editor for the London *Westminster Review*. She became a social outcast and was cut off by her family for living with George Henry Lewes (who was already married and remained so). Lewes encouraged Eliot to write and her first of many novels, *Adam Bede*, was published in 1859. She ceased writing when Lewes died in 1878. She married John Walter Cross, her financial adviser, in 1880, and died seven months later. She also wrote short stories and poems. Some of her poems: "Armgart," "Brother and Sister," "Roses," "Stradivarius," "The Choir Invisible," "The Death of Moses," "The Legend of Jubal," "The Spanish Gypsy," "Two Lovers."

Sources: *Collected Poems of George Eliot*. Lucien Jenkins, ed. Skoob Books Publication Ltd., 1989. *Dictionary of National Biography*. Electronic Edition 1.1. Oxford University Press, 1997. *Encyclopædia Britannica Ultimate Reference Suite DVD*, 2006. *The Columbia Granger's Index to Poetry*. 11th ed. *The Columbia Granger's World of Poetry*, Columbia University Press, 2005 (http://www.columbia grangers.org). *The National Portrait Gallery* (www.npg.org.uk). *The Oxford Companion to English Literature*. 6th edition. Margaret Drabble, ed. Oxford University Press, 2000. *Westminster Abbey Official Guide* (no date).

ELIOT, T(HOMAS) S(TEARNS) (1888–1965)

Born in St. Louis, Missouri, he was educated at Harvard, the Sorbonne and Merton College, Oxford; he became a British citizen in 1927. He worked briefly as a schoolteacher, then from 1917 to 1925, he worked at Lloyds Bank in London. In the 1920s, he suffered from ill health and at times was close to breakdown. He became a director in the publishing firm of Faber and Faber, and took responsibility for his firm's selection of poets. In 1927 he became a member of the Anglican Church; many of his poems reflect his spiritual journey. In 1948 he was awarded the Nobel Prize for Literature and the Order of Merit. He is commemorated by a memorial stone in Poets' Corner of Westminster Abbey. His first work *Prufrock and Other Observations* was published in 1917. *Collected Poems 1909–1962* was published in 1963. The musical *Cats* was inspired by his *Old Possum's Book of Cats*. Some of his other poems: "Ash Wednesday," "Boston Evening Transcript," "Four Quartets," "Journey of the Magi," "Murder in the Cathedral," "Ode on Independence Day, July 4th 1918," "Sweeney Agonistes," "The Rock."

Sources: *Collected Poems 1909–1962 of T.S. Eliot*. Harcourt Brace, 1963; reprinted 1991. *Dictionary of National Biography*. Electronic Edition 1.1. Oxford University Press, 1997. *Modern American Poetry* (http://www.english.uiuc.edu/maps/index.htm). *The Columbia Granger's Index to Poetry*. 11th ed. *The Columbia Granger's World of Poetry*, Columbia University Press, 2005 (http://www.columbia grangers.org). *The Oxford Companion to English Literature*. 6th edition. Margaret Drabble, ed. Oxford University Press, 2000.

ELIZABETH I (1533–1603)

"Good Queen Bess" was born at Greenwich, London, the daughter of Henry VIII and Anne Boleyn. The last of the Tudor monarchs, she reigned as queen of England and Ireland from 1558 to 1603. The kingdom she inherited was torn between the Puri-tans who had prospered under Edward VI and the Catholics who had benefited under Mary. England was losing possessions in France, and France supported Mary Stuart's claim to the English throne. Eventually Elizabeth had Mary (Queen of Scots, Elizabeth's cousin, a pawn in the hands of her unscrupulous nobles) imprisoned and executed in 1587. The Elizabethan Age saw massive expansion in commerce and the arts. Literature blossomed through the works of Spenser, Marlowe and Shakespeare (see entries). Francis Drake and Walter Raleigh (see entry) were instrumental in expanding English influence in the New World. She died at Richmond and is buried in Henry VII Chapel of Westminster Abbey. She was succeeded by Mary Stuart's son, James VI of Scotland. Some of her poems: "Doubt of Future Foes," "On Fortune," "On Monsieur's Departure," "The Queen's Answer," "When I Was Fair and Young," "Written on a Wall at Woodstock."

Sources: *Britannia* (http://www.britannia.com/history/monarchs/mon45.html). *Dictionary of National Biography*. Electronic Edition 1.1. Oxford University Press, 1997. *Encyclopædia Britannica Ultimate Reference Suite DVD*, 2006. *English Poetry: Author Search*. Chadwyck-Healey Ltd., 1995 (http://www.lib.utexas.edu:8080/search/epoetry/author.html). *Encyclopedia of Britain*. Bamber Gascoigne. London: Macmillan, 1994. *The Columbia Granger's Index to Poetry*. 11th ed. *The Columbia Granger's World of Poetry*, Columbia University Press, 2005 (http://www.columbiagrangers.org). *The National Portrait Gallery* (www.npg.org.uk). *The Norton Anthology of Poetry*. 4th ed. Margaret Ferguson, Mary Jo Salter and Jon Stal, eds. W.W. Norton, 1996. *The Oxford Companion to English Literature*. 6th edition. Margaret Drabble, ed. Oxford University Press, 2000. *The Penguin Book of Women Poets*. Carol Cosman, Joan Keefe and Kathleen Weaver, eds. Penguin Books, 1978. *Westminster Abbey Official Guide* (no date).

ELLERTON, JOHN (1826–1893)

Born in Clerkenwell, London, he was educated privately and at King William's College, Isle of Man. At Trinity College, Cambridge (1848), he placed second in the chancellor's medal competition with a poem titled "The Death of Baldur" about the Norse god of peace. After ordination in 1850 he served in Sussex, Shropshire, London and Essex, and was heavily involved in social concerns. He was consultant on the supplement to *Hymns Ancient and Modern*, published in 1889. He died in Torquay, Devon, of a stroke. Some of his publications: *Hymns for Schools and Bible Classes*, 1859. *Church Hymns*, 1871 (co-editor). *Notes and Illustrations of Church Hymns*, 1881. *The Children's Hymn Book*, 1881 (with Mrs. Carey Brock). *London Mission Hymn Book*, 1884 (with W. Walsham How and Edward H. Bickersteth, bishop of Exeter). *Hymns, Original and Translated*, 1888. *Manual of Parochial Work*, 1892 (editor). Some of his hymns/poems: "From East to West, from Shore to Shore," "Hail to the Lord Who Comes," "Savior, Again to Thy Dear Name!" "Shine Thou Upon Us, Lord," "The Day Thou Gavest, Lord, is Ended."

Sources: *Dictionary of National Biography.* Electronic Edition 1.1. Oxford University Press, 1997. *Everyman's Book of Victorian Verse.* J.R. Watson, ed. J.M. Dent, 1982. *The Columbia Granger's Index to Poetry.* 11th ed. *The Columbia Granger's World of Poetry,* Columbia University Press, 2005 (http://www.columbiagrangers.org). *The Cyber Hymnal* (http://www.cyberhymnal.org/index.htm). *The World's Great Religious Poetry.* Caroline Miles Hill, ed. Macmillan, 1954.

ELLIOT, JANE (JEAN) (1727–1805)

The daughter of Sir Gilbert Elliot, second baronet of Minto, was born at Minto House, the family seat in Teviotdale. It is difficult to sort fact from myth, but it is reported that when she was about nineteen, she entertained a party of Jacobites, giving her father time to escape. Another story is that she composed "Flowers of Flodden" as response to her brother Gilbert's challenge that she couldn't write a ballad about Flodden. Although there is doubt about the authenticity of the work, Burns insisted that it was a modern composition, and when Sir Walter Scott wrote his *Border Minstrelsy* he inserted it (in 1803) as "by a lady of family in Roxburghshire" (DNB). She wrote "The Lament" to commemorate the 10,000 Scots who died in the Battle of Flodden in 1513, and by tradition, it is now sung only at funerals. After the death of her father in 1766 (her brother Gilbert inherited the title), she moved with her mother and sisters to Edinburgh, where she spent most of the second half of her life. After her mother and sisters had died, she lived alone in the house in Brown Square, Edinburgh. She died either at Minto House or at Mount Teviot, the residence of her younger brother, Admiral John Elliot.

Sources: *Dictionary of National Biography.* Electronic Edition 1.1. Oxford University Press, 1997. *The Columbia Granger's Index to Poetry.* 11th ed. *The Columbia Granger's World of Poetry,* Columbia University Press, 2005 (http://www.columbiagrangers.org). *The Oxford Companion to English Literature.* 6th edition. Margaret Drabble, ed. Oxford University Press, 2000. *The Scottish Collection of Verse to 1800.* Eileen Dunlop and Kamm Antony, eds. Richard Drew, 1985.

ELLIOTT, CHARLOTTE (1789–1871)

Elliott lived the first 32 years of her life in Clapham, London. Following a serious illness that left her a permanent invalid, she spent the remainder of her life in Brighton, Sussex, with intervals at Torquay, Devon, and on the Continent. In 1836 she became editor of the *Yearly Remembrancer,* in which she included (anonymously) her most well-known poem, "Just as I Am Without One Plea," which for many years remained an anonymous poem. It was later set to music and is included in almost every hymnbook throughout the world. She went on to write over 150 poems; many of them appeared in *Hymns for a Week* (1839), of which forty thousand copies were sold. She is buried at St. Andrew's Church, Hove, Sussex. Some of her other publications: *The Invalid's Hymn Book,* 1834. *Hours of Sorrow,* 1836. *Thoughts in Verse on Sacred Subjects,* 1869. *Selections from the Poems of Charlotte Elliott,* 1873. *Leaves from the Unpublished Journals, Letters, and Poems,* 1874. Some of her other hymns/poems: "I Want That Adorning Divine," "My God and Father, While I Stray," "The Hour of Prayer," "Watch and Pray."

Sources: *Biography of Miss Charlotte Elliott, 1789–1871 (Spiritual Songsters)* (http://www.stempublishing.com/hymns/biographies/elliott.html). *Dictionary of National Biography.* Electronic Edition 1.1. Oxford University Press, 1997. *English Poetry: Author Search.* Chadwyck-Healey Ltd., 1995 (http://www.lib.utexas.edu:8080/search/epoetry/author.html). *Stanford University libraries and Academic Information Resources* (http://library.stanford.edu). *The Columbia Granger's Index to Poetry.* 11th ed. *The Columbia Granger's World of Poetry,* Columbia University Press, 2005 (http://www.columbiagrangers.org). *The Cyber Hymnal* (http://www.cyberhymnal.org/index.htm). *The Speaker's Treasury of 400 Quotable Poems.* Croft M. Pentz, ed. Zondervan, 1963.

ELLIOTT, EBENEZER (1781–1849)

"The Corn-Law Rhymer" was born at the New Foundry, Masborough, parish of Rotherham, Yorkshire. His forebears had the reputation of being border raiders, stealing from both the English and the Scots. When seventeen he wrote his first poem, "Vernal Walk," dedicated to Miss Austen. He became a master founder in Sheffield and in his leisure hours he studied botany, collected plants and flowers, and developed a great love for nature. His fortunes were mixed; he gained, he lost; his life work became the repeal of the iniquitous Corn Laws, for which he blamed his misfortunes and upon which he focused his poetry. He died at Great Houghton near Barnsley, having lived to see the hated "bread tax" abolished in 1849. A bronze statue to his memory was erected in the market-place of Sheffield in 1854. Some of his publications: *Night, a Descriptive Poem,* 1818. *The Village Patriarch,* 1829. *Corn Law Rhymes,* 1831. *Poems,* 1834. *More Prose and Verse,* 1850. Some of his other poems: "British Rural Cottages in 1842," "England in 1844," "The Cornlaw Catechism," "The Splendid Village," "The Year of Seeds."

Sources: *Dictionary of National Biography.* Electronic Edition 1.1. Oxford University Press, 1997. *English Poetry:*

Author Search. Chadwyck-Healey Ltd., 1995 (http://www. lib.utexas.edu:8080/search/epoetry/author.html). *More Verse and Prose by the Cornlaw Rhymer, Ebenezer Elliot.* Charles Fox, 1850. *The Columbia Granger's Index to Poetry.* 11th ed. *The Columbia Granger's World of Poetry,* Columbia University Press, 2005 (http://www.columbiagrangers.org). *The National Portrait Gallery* (www.npg.org.uk). *The New Oxford Book of Romantic Period Verse.* Jerome J. McGann. Oxford University Press, 1993. *The Oxford Book of Satirical Verse.* Geoffrey Grigson, ed. Oxford University Press, 1980. *The Oxford Companion to English Literature.* 6th edition. Margaret Drabble, ed. Oxford University Press, 2000. *Tygers of Wrath: Poems of Hate, Anger, and Invective.* X.J. Kennedy, ed. University of Georgia Press, 1981.

ELTON, SIR CHARLES ABRAHAM (1778–1853)

Born at Bristol, the only son of the Rev. Sir Abraham Elton, fifth baronet. Educated at Eton College, he was commissioned into the army at the age of fifteen and served in Holland under the Duke of York. He was afterwards lieutenant-colonel of the Somersetshire militia. He married in 1804 and had five sons and eight daughters. The two eldest sons were drowned in 1819 while bathing near Weston-super-Mare. He inherited the title in 1842 and lived in retirement at Clevedon Court, Bristol. He died at Bath. Some of his publications: *Poems,* 1804. *Tales of Romance, and Other Poems, Including Selections from Propertius,* 1810. *Specimens of the Classical Poets in a Chronological Series from Homer to Tryphiodorus, Translated into English Verse,* 1814. *Remains of Hesiod, translated—with notes,* 1815. *Appeal to Scripture and Tradition in Defence of the Unitarian Faith,* 1818. *The Brothers, a Monody and Other Poems,* 1820 (referring to the death of his sons). Some of his poems: "Archilochos," "The Birth of the Muses," "The Creation of Woman," "The Goddess Hecate," "The Inspiration of Wine."

Sources: *Dictionary of National Biography.* Electronic Edition 1.1. Oxford University Press, 1997. *The Columbia Granger's Index to Poetry.* 11th ed. *The Columbia Granger's World of Poetry,* Columbia University Press, 2005 (http://www.columbiagrangers.org). *The Greek Poets.* Nathan Haskell Dole, ed. Crowell, 1904.

ELYS, EDMUND (fl. 1707)

Born at Haccombe, Devon, the son of a clergyman, he was educated at Exeter and Balliol College, Oxford, with an M.A. in 1658. In 1659 he succeeded his father to the rectory of East Allington, Devon. During the Civil Wars he was suspected of being a Royalist sympathizer and imprisoned in Exeter by Major Blackmore. Further misfortune befell him when, in 1677, his living was confiscated and he sought refuge in London, where he was imprisoned for not swearing allegiance to King William III. Deprived of his rectory, he retired to Totnes, Devon, suffering from severe asthma. He wrote many pamphlets in support of the Quakers, though he was not a Quaker himself. Although not a great poet, his works give an insight into his life and times. Some of his publications: *An Alphabet of Elegiack Groans,* 1656. *Anglia Rediviva,* 1660. *The Bishops Downefall,* 1642. *Dia Poemata,* 1655. *Divine poems,* 1659. *The Quiet Soul,* 1659. *Miscellanea,* 1662. *A Vindication of the Honor of King Charles I,* 1691. *A Refutation of Some of the False Conceits in Mr. Locke's Essay Concerning Human Understanding,* 1697.

Sources: *A New Canon of English Poetry.* James Reeves, and Martin Seymour-Smith, ed. Barnes and Noble, 1967. *Dictionary of National Biography.* Electronic Edition 1.1. Oxford University Press, 1997. *Early English Books Online Text Creation Partnership* (http://www.lib.umich.edu/tcp/eebo/texts/letterE.html). *English Poetry: Author Search.* Chadwyck-Healey Ltd., 1995 (http://www.lib.utexas.edu:8080/search/epoetry/author.html). *John Locke Bibliography—Name/Title Index—E* (http://www.libraries.psu.edu/tas/locke/ne.html). *SETIS: The Scholarly Electronic Text and Image Service* (http://setis.library.usyd.edu.au). *The Columbia Granger's Index to Poetry.* 11th ed. *The Columbia Granger's World of Poetry,* Columbia University Press, 2005 (http://www.columbiagrangers.org).

EMPSON, SIR WILLIAM (1906–1984)

Born at Yokefleet Hall, Howden, Yorkshire, son of an Army officer, he was educated at Winchester College and studied mathematics and English at Magdalene College, Cambridge. His first book, *Seven Types of Ambiguity* (1930), established his reputation as a critic. He left Cambridge under a cloud, for sexual impropriety—entertaining a lady in his rooms. He was professor of English literature at Tokyo University from 1931 to 1934, and at Peking National University from 1937 to 1939. Blessed with a remarkable memory, he could write out the complete texts of many of the classics. During the war years he worked for the propaganda department of the BBC. From 1947 to 1952, he returned to his post at Peking National University, then was professor of English at Sheffield University from 1953 until his retirement in 1971. He was knighted in 1979 and had honorary degrees from the universities of East Anglia, Bristol, Sheffield, and Cambridge. He died in London. Some of his poems: "China," "Chinese Ballad," "Autumn on Nan-Yueh," "Aubade," "Bacchus," "Homage to the British Museum," "Missing Dates," "The Death of the King's Canary," "This Last Pain."

Sources: *Dictionary of National Biography.* Electronic Edition 1.1. Oxford University Press, 1997. *Encyclopædia Britannica Ultimate Reference Suite DVD,* 2006. *Poemhunter* (www.poemhunter.com). *Portraits of Poets,* Sebastian Barker, ed., Carcanet, 1986. *The Columbia Granger's Index to Poetry.* 11th ed. *The Columbia Granger's World of Poetry,* Columbia University Press, 2005 (http://www.co

lumbiagrangers.org). *The National Portrait Gallery* (www.npg.org.uk). *The Oxford Companion to English Literature*. 6th edition. Margaret Drabble, ed. Oxford University Press, 2000. *The Poetry Anthology, 1912–1977.* Daryl Hine and Joseph Parisi, eds. Houghton Mifflin, 1978.

ENRIGHT, DENNIS JOSEPH (1920–2002)

D.J. Enright was born at Royal Leamington Spa, Warwickshire, and graduated M.A. from Downing College, Cambridge. From 1947 to 1959 he taught English in Japan, Germany, Thailand, and Singapore. He was joint editor of *Encounter* in London (1970–1972) and from 1975 to 1980 was honorary professor at Warwick University. His autobiography, *Memoirs of a Mendicant Professor* (1969), relates his years abroad, as do his four novels and his poems. *Joke Shop* (1976) and *Wild Ghost Chase* (1978) are two books for children. He also published volumes of literary criticism: *Figures of Speech* (1965), *A Mania for Sentences* (1983), *Fair of Speech: The Uses of Euphemism* (1985), and *The Alluring Problem* (1986). Not drawn into sentimentalism, his poems express his dismay and distress at squalor, poverty, cruelty, and suffering. His first collection of poems, *The Laughing Hyena and Other Poems* (1953), was followed by several others, the last being *Collected Poems: 1948–1998* (1998). Some of his poems: "A Child's Guide to Welfare," "After Brecht," "Apocalypse," "Better Be Kind to Them Now," "Paradise Illustrated," "The Egyptian Cat," "The Last Democrat," "The Monuments of Hiroshima."

Sources: *Don't Forget to Fly: A Cycle of Modern Poems.* Paul B. Janeczko, ed. Bradbury Press, 1981. *Encyclopædia Britannica Ultimate Reference Suite DVD,* 2006. *Microsoft Encarta* 2006 (DVD). Microsoft Corporation, 2006. *Never Such Innocence: A New Anthology of Great War Verse.* Martin Stephen, ed. Buchan and Enright, 1988. *Pet Poems.* Robert Fisher, ed. Faber and Faber, 1989. *The Antaeus Anthology.* Daniel Halpern, ed. Bantam Books, 1986. *The New Modern Poetry: British and American Poetry Since World War II.* M.L. Rosenthal, ed. Macmillan, 1967. *The Oxford Book of Comic Verse.* John Gross, ed. Oxford University Press, 1994. *The Oxford Book of Contemporary Verse, 1945–1980.* D.J. Enright, ed. Oxford University Press, 1980. *The Oxford Book of Friendship.* D.J. Enright and David Rawlinson, eds. Oxford University Press, 1991. *The Oxford Companion to English Literature.* 6th edition. Margaret Drabble, ed. Oxford University Press, 2000. *Wikipedia, the Free Encyclopedia.* (http://en.wikipedia.org/wiki/Wikipedia).

ERCELDOUNE, THOMAS OF LEARMONT (fl. ?1220–?1297)

Also known as Thomas the Rhymer, he is credited with The "Ballad of Thomas the Rhymer" and the metrical romance "Tristrem and the Hunters" (which Sir Walter Scott included in his *Minstrelsy of the Scot-*tish Border* in 1802). Thomas lived in Erceldoune, Berwickshire, present day Earlstoun. The "Ballad" describes how the fairy Queen of Elfland, grateful for his love, gave him the gift of prophesy, with the condition that she would summon him one day. He disappeared after walking out of his tower house and was never seen again. According to legend, he will return again to Scotland's aid in the hour of her greatest need. As a seer he ranks with Merlin, and has been called "The Nostradamus of Scotland." Belief in his predictions were even consulted before the Jacobite uprisings of 1715 and 1745. His prophecies included the death of King Alexander III in 1296, the succession of Robert the Bruce to the throne in 1306, the disastrous Scots defeat at Flodden in 1513, the defeat of Mary Queen of Scots' forces at the Battle of Pinkie in 1567, and the Union of the Crowns in 1603.

Sources: *Britannia Biographies* (http://www.britannia.com/bios/rhymer.html). *Dictionary of National Biography.* Electronic Edition 1.1. Oxford University Press, 1997. *Encyclopædia Britannica Ultimate Reference Suite DVD,* 2006. *Scotch Myth—Thomas the Rhymer* (http://www.firstfoot.com/scotchmyth/thomastherhymer.htm). *The Ballad of Thomas the Rhymer* (http://www.cowdenknowes.com/rhymer.htm). *The Columbia Granger's Index to Poetry.* 11th ed. *The Columbia Granger's World of Poetry,* Columbia University Press, 2005 (http://www.columbiagrangers.org). *The Oxford Book of Scottish Verse.* John MacQueen and Tom Scott, ed. Oxford University Press, 1966. *The Oxford Companion to English Literature.* 6th edition. Margaret Drabble, ed. Oxford University Press, 2000.

ERSKINE, RALPH (1685–1752)

Scottish cleric born at Monilaws, Northumberland. While at Edinburgh University he narrowly escaped a fire in the Parliament Close, where he lodged. He was licensed in 1709 by Dunfermline presbytery and ordained in 1711. He was one of the "twelve apostles" of 1721, arraigned by the synod of Fife for non-compliance with the act of 1720, regarding the Marrow doctrine (a complex issue to do with justification). He refused to comply and he and many others joined the secession from the Church of Scotland. He was buried at Dunfermline; a statue of him was erected in front of the Queen Anne Street Church. Some of his publications: *Song of Solomon,* 1738. *Book of Lamentations,* 1750 (a paraphrase). *Job's Hymns,* 1753. *Scripture Songs,* 1754. *Gospel Sonnets,* 1762 (25th edition, 1797). *Gospel Sonnets,* 1797. Some of his poems: "A Fourfold Exercise for the Believer," "A Song of Praise [Isaiah 25:1–12]," "Benefits Accruing to Believers from Christ," "Christ the Believer's Sweet Nourishment," "Earth Despicable, Heaven Desirable," "Smoking Spiritualized," "The Believer's Faith and Hope Encouraged," "The Believer's Riddle," "The Free Gospel-Call [Isaiah 55:1–3]."

Sources: *A Sacrifice of Praise: An Anthology of Christian Poetry in English from Caedmon to the Mid-Twentieth Century.* James H. Trott, ed. Cumberland House Publishing, 1999. *Dictionary of National Biography.* Electronic Edition 1.1. Oxford University Press, 1997. *Ralph Erskine's Marvelous Ministry by G. Ella* (http://www.puritansermons.com/erskine/erskin19.htm). *Some Sidelights on Ralph Erskine by Alasdair B. Gordon* (http://www.puritansermons.com/erskine/erskin16.htm). *The Columbia Granger's Index to Poetry.* 11th ed. *The Columbia Granger's World of Poetry,* Columbia University Press, 2005 (http://www.columbiagrangers.org).

ERSKINE, THOMAS, 1ST BARON ERSKINE (1750–1823)

Born in Edinburgh, the youngest son the tenth earl of Buchan, he attended the grammar school at St. Andrews. He served in the Navy under Sir David Lindsay, and in the Army under John, Duke of Argyll. Around 1772 he published an anonymous and widely read pamphlet, *Abuses in the Army.* He went to Trinity College, Cambridge, in 1776 and received an honorary M.A. degree in 1778. He was called to the bar in 1778, and his struggling existence changed when he became a successful defense attorney in several high profile cases: a libel suite brought by Lord Sandwich against Captain Baillie, and the court-marital of Admiral Lord Keppel for incompetence in the engagement off Ushant against the French fleet. He was created Baron Erskine of Restormel, and Lord Chancellor in 1806. He was buried at the family burial place, Uphall, Linlithgow. *The Poetical Works of the Right Honorable, Thomas, Lord Erskine* was published in 1823. Some of his poems: "French and English," "James Alan Park," "On Scott's Poem 'The Field of Waterloo,'" "On Tom Moore's Translation of Anacreon," "Petition of Peter."

Sources: *Dictionary of National Biography.* Electronic Edition 1.1. Oxford University Press, 1997. *Encyclopædia Britannica Ultimate Reference Suite DVD,* 2006. *English Poetry: Author Search.* Chadwyck-Healey Ltd., 1995 (http://www.lib.utexas.edu:8080/search/epoetry/author.html). *The Columbia Granger's Index to Poetry.* 11th ed. *The Columbia Granger's World of Poetry,* Columbia University Press, 2005 (http://www.columbiagrangers.org). *The Faber Book of Epigrams and Epitaphs.* Geoffrey Grigson, ed. Faber & Faber, 1977. *The Humorous Poetry of the English Language.* J. Parton, ed. Mason Brothers, 1857. *The National Portrait Gallery* (www.npg.org.uk).

ESSEX, ROBERT DEVEREUX, 2nd EARL OF (1567–1601)

Born at Netherwood, Herefordshire, the son of the first Earl of Essex, he inherited the title in 1576 under the guardianship of Lord Burghley. He had some education at Trinity College, Cambridge, but there is nothing outstanding about this. Essex was a cousin of Elizabeth on his mother's side, and when he was presented at court, he quickly became the queen's favorite and, rumored, her lover. It is said Elizabeth was always anxious when he was away on his (often successful) military campaigns. He was made privy councillor in 1593 and in 1594 uncovered an alleged plot against the queen's life by her physician, Roderigo Lopez. However close the relationship, he was wayward and self-willed and this eventually led to his loss of favor, and after a disastrous campaign in Ireland, Elizabeth deprived him of his office for deserting his post. He was executed for treason in trying to stir up a rebellion. Some of his poems: "A Passion of My Lord of Essex," "Change Thy Mind Since She Doth Change," "Happy Were He," "To Plead My Faith."

Sources: *Britannia Biographies* (http://www.britannia.com/bios/rhymer.html). *Dictionary of National Biography.* Electronic Edition 1.1. Oxford University Press, 1997. *Elizabethan Lyrics.* Norman Ault, ed. William Sloane Associates, 1949. *Encyclopædia Britannica Ultimate Reference Suite DVD,* 2006. *Great Books Online* (www.bartleby.com). *The Columbia Granger's Index to Poetry.* 11th ed. *The Columbia Granger's World of Poetry,* Columbia University Press, 2005 (http://www.columbiagrangers.org). *The Oxford Companion to English Literature.* 6th edition. Margaret Drabble, ed. Oxford University Press, 2000. *Westminster Abbey Official Guide* (no date).

ETHEREGE, SIR GEORGE (1635–1691)

Born at Maidenhead, Berkshire, little is known of his education, although he was at Cambridge University for a short time. He lived several years in France then was apprenticed to an attorney in 1653. Between 1668 and 1671 he was secretary to the English ambassador to Turkey, Sir Daniel Harvey. In June 1676 he and John Wilmot, 2nd Earl of Rochester (and some others), engaged in a drunken brawl at Epsom, in which one of the group was killed. About 1680 he married a rich widow and was knighted. From 1685 to 1688 he was envoy to Ratisbon (Regensburg) for James II. When King James was deposed in 1688, Etherege, a staunch Jacobite, followed his king into exile to Paris, and he died there. Three of his comedies, some written in rhyme, are *The Comical Revenge, or Love in a Tub,* 1664; *She Wou'd If She Could,* 1667; and *The Man of Mode, or Sir Fopling Flutter,* 1676. Some of his poems: "Chloris, 'Tis Not in Your Power," "Ephelia to Bajazet," "Letter to Lord Middleton," "Silvia," "To a Very Young Lady."

Sources: *Anthology of Poems on Affairs of State: Augustan Satirical Verse, 1660–1714.* George de F. Lord, ed. Yale University Press, 1975. *Dictionary of National Biography.* Electronic Edition 1.1. Oxford University Press, 1997. *Encyclopædia Britannica Ultimate Reference Suite DVD,* 2006. *English Poetry: Author Search.* Chadwyck-Healey Ltd., 1995 (http://www.lib.utexas.edu:8080/search/epoetry/author. html). *The Columbia Granger's Index to Poetry.* 11th ed. *The Columbia Granger's World of Poetry,* Columbia University Press, 2005 (http://www.columbiagrangers.org). *The Oxford Book of Seventeenth Century Verse.* H.J.C. Grierson and G. Bullough, eds. Oxford University Press, 1934. *The Oxford Companion to English Literature.* 6th edition. Margaret Drabble, ed. Oxford University Press, 2000.

EUSDEN, LAURENCE (1688–1730)

Son of the Rev. Laurence Eusden, rector of Spofforth, Yorkshire, educated at St. Peter's School, York, he graduated M.A. from Trinity College, Cambridge, in 1708. Following a flattering poem (some said sycophantic), "A Poem on the Marriage of His Grace the Duke of Newcastle" (1917), he was appointed poet laureate and lord chamberlain, an appointment ridiculed by Thomas Cooke in *Battle of the Poets* (1725). Around 1725, he took holy orders and was appointed chaplain to Richard, Lord Willoughby de Broke, and took the rectory of Coningsby in Lincolnshire, where he remained until he died. Some of his other publications: *Poetical Miscellanies,* 1714. *To Her Royal Highness on the Birth of the Prince,* 1718. *Ode for the Birthday,* 1723. *An Ode for the New-Year,* 1720. *The Origin of the Knights of the Bath, a Poem,* 1725. *Hero and Leander,* 1750. Some of his other poems: "A Poem, Sacred to the Immortal Memory of the Late King," "Medea" (on Euripides), "Poem, on the Happy Succession, and Coronation of His Present Majesty," "To a Lady, That Wept at the Hearing Cato Read."

Sources: *Dictionary of National Biography.* Electronic Edition 1.1. Oxford University Press, 1997. *Encyclopædia Britannica Ultimate Reference Suite DVD,* 2006. *English Poetry: Author Search.* Chadwyck-Healey Ltd., 1995 (http://www.lib.utexas.edu:8080/search/epoetry/author.html). *Lawrence Eusden and Colley Cibber, Poet Laureate, exhibition* (http://www.library.otago.ac.nz/Exhibitions/poet_laureate/pl_eusdenandcibber.html). *Oldpoetry* (www.oldpoetry.com). *Selected Writings of the Laureate Dunces, Nahum Tate, Laurence Eusden, and Colley Cibber.* The Edwin Mellen Press, 1999. *The Columbia Granger's Index to Poetry.* 11th ed. *The Columbia Granger's World of Poetry,* Columbia University Press, 2005 (http://www.columbiagrangers.org). *The Oxford Book of Classical Verse in Translation.* Adrian Poole and Jeremy Maule, eds. 1995. *The Oxford Companion to English Literature.* 6th edition. Margaret Drabble, ed. Oxford University Press, 2000.

EVANS, ELLIS HUMPHREY (1887–1917)

One the "Heroes of Wales" whose bardic name was Hedd Wyn or "White Peace," he was born in Penlan, Trawsfynydd, where his roots went back generations, and worked as a shepherd on his father's farm. By the age of 28 he had won four eisteddfod chairs for his poetry. Conscripted into the 15th bat-

talion of the Royal Welsh Fusiliers in 1917, he was sent to the Western Front, where he was killed on July 31, 1917, during the battle for Pilckem Ridge, Ypres. Buried initially on the battlefield, following the armistice, his body was moved to Artillery Wood Cemetery, Boezinge, Belgium, where the inscription reads "Y Prifardd Hedd Wyn" (The Principle Bard, Hedd Wyn). At the 1917 National Eisteddfod, he was posthumously awarded the chair for his poem "Yr Arwr" (The Hero), which describes the realities of war for both the soldiers and their families back home. Following the announcement of his win and revelation of the author's identity, the chair itself was draped in black in memorial of Wyn. A Welsh-language film, *Wynn Hedd,* based on his life, was produced in 1992 and was made available on video.

Sources: *Family Trees of the Famous: Hedd Wyn (Ellis Humphrey Evans)* (http://www.s4c.co.uk/helachau/e_family_humphrey.shtml). *First World War.com — Prose & Poetry — Hedd Wyn.* http://www.firstworldwar.com/poetsandprose/wyn.htm). *Hedd Wyn (Ellis Humphrey Evans) / 100 Welsh Heroes / 100 Arwyr Cymru* (http://www.100welshheroes.com/en/biography/heddwyn). *Hellfire Corner — The Great War — At the Going Down of the Sun* (http://www.hellfire-corner.demon.co.uk/jacky4.htm). *Text of Yr Eneiniogby Hedd Wwn* (http://cy.wikisource.org/wiki/Yr_Arwr). *The Oxford Book of Welsh Verse in English.* Gwyn Jones, ed. Oxford University Press, 1977. *Two of Ellis Humphrey Evans's poems in Welsh* (http://www.webexcel.ndirect.co.uk/gwarnant/beirdd/modern/hedd.htm).

EWART, GAVIN BUCHANAN (1916–1995)

Born in London and educated at Christ's College, Cambridge, he saw active service in World War II, after which he worked in publishing, with the British Council, and in advertising. He became a full-time writer in 1971, though his first poem, "Phallus in Wonderland," was published at the age of 17. His work is humorous and irreverent and erotic; W.H. Smith's bookshops banned *The Pleasures of the Flesh* (1966). He also wrote children's poems as well as poetry on serious subjects, and edited numerous anthologies, including the 1980 *Penguin Book of Light Verse.* Some of his other publications: *Poems and Songs,* 1939. *Londoners,* 1964. *The Gavin Ewart Show,* 1971. *No Fool Like an Old Fool,* 1976. *All My Little Ones,* 1978. *The Collected Ewart: 1933–1980,* 1980. *The Ewart Quarto,* 1984. *The Learned Hippopotamus,* 1986 (for children). *Penultimate Poems,* 1989. *Caterpillar Stew,* 1990 (for children). *Collected Poems: 1980–1990,* 1991. Some of his other poems: "A Dialogue Between the Head and Heart," "A 14-Year-Old Convalescent Cat in the Winter," "Bánk the Palatine," "John Betjeman's Brighton," "North American Haiku," "Psychoanalysis."

Sources: *Encyclopædia Britannica Ultimate Reference*

Suite DVD, 2006. *Biography of Gavin Ewart* (http://www.arlindo-correia.com/051100.html). *In Quest of the Miracle Stag: The Poetry of Hungary.* Adam Makkai, ed. Atlantic-Centaur, Corvina, 1996. *The Chatto Book of Love Poetry.* John Fuller, ed. Chatto and Windus, 1990. *The Columbia Granger's Index to Poetry.* 11th ed. *The Columbia Granger's World of Poetry,* Columbia University Press, 2005 (http://www.columbiagrangers.org). *The National Portrait Gallery* (www.npg.org.uk). *The Oxford Book of Short Poems.* P.J. Kavanagh and James Michie, eds. Oxford University Press, 1985. *The Oxford Companion to English Literature.* 6th edition. Margaret Drabble, ed. Oxford University Press, 2000. *The War Poets: An Anthology of the War Poetry of the 20th Century.* Oscar Williams, ed. John Day, 1945.

FAINLIGHT, RUTH (1931–)

Born in New York City to an English-born father and a Ukrainian mother, she has lived in England since 1946. She was poet in residence at Vanderbilt University, Nashville, Tennessee, in 1985 and 1990, and writing tutor (for libretti) at the Performing Arts Labs, International Opera and Music Theatre Labs in the U.K. in 1997–1999. She has written librettos for stage and radio. Many of her own poems are translated into Portuguese, French and Spanish, and she has translated the work of the Portuguese poet Sophia de Mello Breyner Andresen (1919–). Fainlight is also the poetry editor of the journal *European Judaism.* She lives in London and is married to the writer Alan Sillitoe (see entry). She has received three literary awards. Some of her poetry publications: *Cages,* 1966. *To See the Matter Clearly,* 1968. *Sibyls and Others,* 1980. *Fifteen to Infinity,* 1983. *The Knot,* 1990. *This Time of Year,* 1994. *Selected Poems,* 1995. *Sugar-Paper Blue,* 1997. *Burning Wire,* 2002. Some of her poems: "Another Full Moon," "Archive Film Material," "God's Language," "Lilith," "The Future," "The Vampire Housewife."

Sources: *Biography of Ruth Fainlight* (http://www.arlindo-correia.com/081004.html). *Bread and Roses: An Anthology of Nineteenth- and Twentieth-Century Poetry by Women Writers.* Diana Scott, ed. Virago Press, 1982. *British Council Arts* (http://www.contemporarywriters.com). *Holocaust Poetry.* Hilda Schiff, ed. HarperCollins, 1995. *The Carnegie Mellon Anthology of Poetry.* Gerald Costanzo and Jim Daniels, eds. Carnegie Mellon University Press, 1993. *The Columbia Granger's Index to Poetry.* 11th ed. *The Columbia Granger's World of Poetry,* Columbia University Press, 2005 (http://www.columbiagrangers.org). *The Life and Work of Ruth Fainlight* (http://www.writersartists.net/rf2.htm). *The Oxford Companion to English Literature.* 6th edition. Margaret Drabble, ed. Oxford University Press, 2000. *The Poetry Anthology, 1912–1977.* Daryl Hine and Joseph Parisi, eds. Houghton Mifflin, 1978. *Voices Within the Ark: The Modern Jewish Poets.* Howard Schwartz and Anthony Rudolf, eds. Avon Books, 1980.

FAIRFAX, THOMAS, 3RD BARON FAIRFAX OF CAMERON (1612–1671)

He was born at Denton, Yorkshire, son of Ferdinando, second Lord Fairfax, and educated at St. John's College, Cambridge. From 1629 to 1631 he fought with the Dutch against the Spanish; he participated in the Bishops' Wars (1639 and 1640) against the Scots (an attempt by Charles II to impose on the Scots a new *Book of Common Prayer*). He was knighted in January 1640 and succeeded to his father's title in 1648. He distinguished himself as Parliamentarian general during the Civil Wars and was seriously wounded in the siege of Helmsley Castle, Yorkshire (September 1644). He was largely responsible for the defeat of Charles I at Naseby, Northamptonshire (June 14, 1645), although he actively sought to prevent the death of Charles I. He was one of the members of Parliament who invited Charles II to become monarch. So incensed was he at the desecration of Cromwell's remains that he retired from politics. Some of his poems: "On the Fatal Day January 30, 1648," "Shortness of Life," "Upon the New Building at Appleton."

Sources: *Dictionary of National Biography.* Electronic Edition 1.1. Oxford University Press, 1997. *Encyclopædia Britannica Ultimate Reference Suite DVD,* 2006. *The Bodleian Library, Oxford* (http://search.ox.ac.uk/). *The Columbia Granger's Index to Poetry.* 11th ed. *The Columbia Granger's World of Poetry,* Columbia University Press, 2005 (http://www.columbiagrangers.org). *The National Portrait Gallery* (www.npg.org.uk). *The New Oxford Book of Sixteenth Century Verse.* Emrys Jones, ed. Oxford University Press, 1991.

FALCONER, WILLIAM (1732–1769)

Born in Edinburgh, the son of a poor barber, he became a merchant seaman. Although poorly educated, he understood French, Spanish, Italian, and German. He was second mate on board a ship in the Levant trade when, on a voyage from Alexandria to Venice, it was wrecked off Greece. His major poem *The Shipwreck* (1762) (dedicated to the Duke of York, then rear-admiral) is an autobiographical narrative of that event of 1749, in which Falconer was one of three survivors. The Duke advised him to enter the Royal Navy. He did, and sailed on the *Royal George* under Sir Charles Hardy in November 1762 and as purser on the frigate *Glory* and other ships. He died at sea when the *Aurora* was shipwrecked off the Cape of Good Hope on the way to India. Some of his other publications: *Demagogue,* 1764 (a political satire). *The Universal Marine Dictionary,* 1769. Some of his other poems: "An Address to Miranda," "Description of a Ninety Gun Ship," "High o'er the Poop the Audacious Seas Aspire," "The Fond Lover," "The Midshipman," "The Shipwreck."

Sources: *Dictionary of National Biography*. Electronic Edition 1.1. Oxford University Press, 1997. *English Poetry: Author Search*. Chadwyck-Healey Ltd., 1995 (http://www.lib.utexas.edu:8080/search/epoetry/author.html). *The Columbia Granger's Index to Poetry*. 11th ed. *The Columbia Granger's World of Poetry*, Columbia University Press, 2005 (http://www.columbiagrangers.org). *The Eternal Sea: An Anthology of Sea Poetry*. W.M. Williamson, ed. Coward-McCann, 1946. *The Oxford Book of the Sea*. Jonathan Raban, ed. Oxford University Press, 1992. *The Oxford Companion to English Literature*. 6th edition. Margaret Drabble, ed. Oxford University Press, 2000. *William Falconer's Dictionary of the Marine* (http://southseas.nla.gov.au/refs/falc/title.html).

FALLON, PADRAIC (1905–1974)

Irish poet, born in Athenry, County Galway, but moved Dublin while he was in his teens, where his first poems were published in the *Irish Statesman* by 'Æ' (George Russell) (see entry, under AE). He worked as a customs official for over forty years in Wexford and moved back to Dublin in 1963, and then to Cornwall in 1967 before returning to Kinsale, County Cork. He died in Aylesford, Kent, and is buried in Kinsale. Fallon wrote short stories and literary journalism; his verse plays *Diarmuid and Grainne* (1950) and *The Vision of Mac Conglinne* (1953) were broadcast on Radio Éireann. His play *Sweet Love Till Morn* was staged by the Abbey Theatre, Dublin, in 1971. The screenplay *The Fenians* was directed for television by James Plunkett in 1966. His *Collected Poems* was published by Dolmen Press a few months before his death. In 1990 Carcanet published a new *Collected Poems*, adding previously unpublished work. His biography, *A Hymn of the Dawn*, was published by Lilliput Press in 2003. His poems include: "A Bit of Brass," "Assumption," "Dardanelles 1916," "Homeric Hymn to Hermes," "Painting of My Father," "Three Houses," "Yeats at Athenry Perhaps."

Sources: *A Hymn of the Dawn*; part autobiographical book by Padraic Fallon. Published by the Lilliput Press (http://www.lilliputpress.ie/listbook.html?oid=2733039). *A Look in the Mirror and Other Poems*. Padraic Fallon and Eavan Boland, eds. Carcanet Press. 2003. *Biography of Padraic Fallon* (http://www.irishwriters-online.com/padraicfallon.html). Carcanet Press (http://www.carcanet.co.uk). *Contemporary Irish Poetry: An Anthology*. Anthony Bradley, ed. University of California Press. New and rev. ed., 1988. *Dylan Thomas's Choice: An Anthology of Verse Spoken by Dylan Thomas*. Ralph Maud and Aneirin Talfan Davies, eds. New Directions, 1963. *Modern Irish Poetry*. Patrick Crotty, ed. The Blackstaff Press, 1995. *The Book of Irish Verse: An Anthology of Irish Poetry from the Sixth Century to the Present*. John Montague, ed. Macmillan, 1974. *The Columbia Granger's Index to Poetry*. 11th ed. *The Columbia Granger's World of Poetry*, Columbia University Press, 2005 (http://www.columbiagrangers.org). *The Penguin Book of Contemporary Irish Poetry*. Peter Fallon and Derek Mahon, eds. Penguin Books, 1990. *World Poetry: An Anthology of Verse from Antiquity to Our Time*. Katharine Washburn and John S. Major, eds. Publisher, 1338, 1998.

FANE, JULIAN HENRY CHARLES (1827–1870)

The fifth son of the eleventh earl of Westmorland, born at Florence, educated at Harrow School, Fane graduated M.A. from Trinity College, Cambridge, in 1851. He was a member of the "Cambridge Apostles," an elite intellectual secret society founded in 1820 by George Tomlinson. In 1850 he won the chancellor's medal for English verse for his poem "The Death of Adelaide, Queen Dowager." His article "Heinrich Heine, Poet and Humorist" was included in the first *Saturday Review*, 3 November 1855. An accomplished musician, he set many of Heine's verses to music. Between 1856 and 1868 he was on diplomatic service in Paris, Russia, Austria and Luxembourg. He never recovered from the premature death of his wife and died a year later. Some of his other publications: *A Complete Collection of the English Poems Which Have Obtained the Chancellor's Gold Medal in the University of Cambridge*, 1850. *Poems*, 1852. *Poems by Heinrich Heine, Translated by Julian Fane*, 1854. *Ad Matrem*, 1857. *Tannhäuser, or the Battle of the Bards*, 1861 (under the pseudonym "Neville Temple" with Edward Lytton under the pseudonym "Edward Trevor").

Sources: *Dictionary of National Biography*. Electronic Edition 1.1. Oxford University Press, 1997. *English Poetry. Second Edition Bibliography* (http://collections.chadwyck.co.uk/html/ep2/bibliography/d.htm). *English Poetry: Author Search*. Chadwyck-Healey Ltd., 1995 (http://www.lib.utexas.edu:8080/search/epoetry/author.html). *The Columbia Granger's Index to Poetry*. 11th ed. *The Columbia Granger's World of Poetry*, Columbia University Press, 2005 (http://www.columbiagrangers.org). *The Home Book of Modern Verse*. Burton Egbert Stevenson, ed. Henry Holt, 1953.

FANE, MILDMAY, 2nd EARL OF WESTMORLAND (1602–1665)

The eldest son of Francis Fane, the first earl (his mother was Lady Mary Mildmay, daughter of Queen Elizabeth's treasurer), he was educated at Emmanuel College, Cambridge (founded by his grandfather, Sir Walter Mildmay). Between 1620 and 1628 he was in Parliament three times. Created a knight of the Bath at the coronation of Charles I, he sided with the king on the outbreak of the Civil War. He was arrested by Parliament, imprisoned for several months in the Tower of London, and released only after paying a large fine. And at the Restoration his property was returned to him and he was appointed Lord Lieutenant of Northamptonshire. In addition to his collection of 137 poems, *Otia Sacra* (sacred meditations), published in 1648, he translated many of the works of several classical poets. Some of his poems: "16–December 1641," "3 Graces," "A Dedication of My First Son," "At Newmarket Horse Race," "Epitaph of Sir Foulk Hunkes," "Humane Science Handmaid to Divine," "In Praise of Fidelia," "The Yong Man and Christ," "The Yong Protector Unprotected."

Sources: *Dictionary of National Biography.* Electronic Edition 1.1. Oxford University Press, 1997. *Early Modern Literary Studies* (http://www.shu.ac.uk/emls/09-1/mcraerev.html). *English Poetry: Author Search.* Chadwyck-Healey Ltd., 1995 (http://www.lib.utexas.edu:8080/search/epoetry/author.html). *Life of Mildmay Fane, 2nd Earl of Westmorland* (http://www.luminarium.org/sevenlit/fane/fanebio.htm). *The Columbia Granger's Index to Poetry.* 11th ed. *The Columbia Granger's World of Poetry*, Columbia University Press, 2005 (http://www.columbiagrangers.org). *The National Portrait Gallery* (www.npg.org.uk). *The Poetry of Mildmay Fane, Second Earl of Westmorland.* Tom Cain, ed. Manchester University Press, 2001.

FANSHAWE, CATHERINE MARIA (1765–1834)

Born in Chipstead, Surrey, Fanshawe was the daughter of a clerk in the household of George III. She seems to have suffered from some deformity, although it is not clear what. After the death of her parents she lived with her three sisters (all of whom predeceased her) at Richmond, Surrey, and became part of a circle of people interested in literature, art, and science. Though all were good artists, Catherine was the only one who wrote poetry. Sir Walter Scott thought her poetry beautiful, and several of her poems were published in Joanna Baillie's *Collection of Poems* (1823). Her poem "A Riddle on the Letter H" was long thought to have been by Byron (it was in at least two editions of his works). Some of her other poems: "Charade," "Enigma," "Fragment in Imitation of Wordsworth," "Liberty," "Memorials," "Speech of the Member for Odium, " "The Country Cat Docketed by Miss Fanshawe," "Then Welcome Lawns, and Welcome Shades," "When Last We Parted."

Sources: *Dictionary of National Biography.* Electronic Edition 1.1. Oxford University Press, 1997. *English Poetry: Author Search.* Chadwyck-Healey Ltd., 1995 (http://www.lib.utexas.edu:8080/search/epoetry/author.html). *Faber Book of Nonsense Verse.* Geoffrey Grigson, ed. Faber and Faber, 1979. *Love's Witness: Five Centuries of Love Poetry by Women.* Jill Hollis, ed. Carroll and Graf, Inc., 1993. *The Columbia Granger's Index to Poetry.* 11th ed. *The Columbia Granger's World of Poetry*, Columbia University Press, 2005 (http://www.columbiagrangers.org). *The National Portrait Gallery* (www.npg.org.uk). *The Oxford Book of Comic Verse.* John Gross, ed. Oxford University Press, 1994.

FANSHAWE, SIR RICHARD (1608–1666)

Born at Ware Park, Hertfordshire, the fifth son of Sir Henry Fanshawe, he was educated at Thomas Farnaby's school in Cripplegate, London, then at Jesus College, Cambridge. He studied languages in Europe and in 1635 became secretary to Lord Aston, English ambassador to Spain. He supported Charles in the Civil War, and his journey to Spain in 1650 to seek assistance, though unsuccessful, resulted in his being knighted. He was taken prisoner at the Battle of Worcester and after the Restoration was appointed ambassador to Portugal and later to Spain, where he died. Some of his poetical works: *The Pastor Fido* (*The Faithfull Shepheard*), 1647 (translated from the poem of the Italian Baptista). *A selection from Horace*, 1652. *Os Lusíadas*, 1655 (a translation from the Portuguese poem of Luis Vaz de Camões of 1572, which documents the voyages of Vasco da Gama of 1498). He also translated Francis Beaumont and John Fletcher's *Faithful Shepherdess* (?1610) into Latin. Some of his poems: "A Nightingale," "That Louelie Mouth, Which Doth to Taste Invite," "The Praise of the Winde," "Vpon the Report of Fowre Kings Dead at Once."

Sources: *Dictionary of National Biography.* Electronic Edition 1.1. Oxford University Press, 1997. *Encyclopædia Britannica.* Electronic Edition, 2005. *English Poetry: Author Search.* Chadwyck-Healey Ltd., 1995 (http://www.lib.utexas.edu:8080/search/epoetry/author.html). *The Columbia Granger's Index to Poetry.* 11th ed. *The Columbia Granger's World of Poetry*, Columbia University Press, 2005 (http://www.columbiagrangers.org). *The National Portrait Gallery* (www.npg.org.uk). *The Oxford Companion to English Literature.* 6th edition. Margaret Drabble, ed. Oxford University Press, 2000. *Vasco Da Gama: 1498, North Park University* (http://campus.northpark.edu/history/WebChron/WestEurope/DaGama.html).

FANTHORPE, U.A. (URSULA ASKHAM) (1929–)

Born in Kent, she was educated at St. Anne's College, Oxford, and the University of London Institute of Education. She became an English teacher, then from 1962-70 was head of English at Cheltenham Ladies' College. She holds honorary doctorates from the University of West England and the University of Gloucestershire, and was awarded Hawthornden Fellowships between 1987 and 1997. In 1989 she became a full-time writer; in 1994 she was the first woman to be nominated for the post of Oxford professor of poetry, and in 1999 was a leading contender for the post of poet laureate. In 2001 she was made commander of the British Empire for services to poetry, and was also awarded the 2003 Queen's Gold Medal for Poetry. She lives in Gloucestershire. Her first collection, *Side Effects* (1978), reflects her experiences working as a school counselor and a hospital clerk. Some of her recent poetry publications: *Consequences*, 2000. *Christmas Poems*, 2002. *Queuing for the Sun*, 2003. *Collected Poems*, 2004. *Collected Poems*, 2005. Some of her poems: "At the Ferry," "Fanfare," "Father in the Railway Buffet," "From the Third Storey," "Our Dog Chasing Swifts."

Sources: *Ain't I a Woman! A Book of Women's Poetry From Around the World.* Illona Linthwaite, ed. Peter Bedrick Books, 1988. *British Council Arts* (http://www.contemporarywriters.com). *Microsoft Encarta* 2006 (DVD). Microsoft Corporation, 2006. *Naming the Waves: Contemporary Lesbian Poetry.* Christian McEwen, ed. The Crossing Press, 1989. *Parents: An Anthology of Poems by Women Writers.* Myra Schneider and Dilys Wood, ed. Enitharmon Press, 2000. *The Columbia Granger's Index to Poetry.* 11th ed. *The Columbia Granger's World of Poetry,* Columbia University Press, 2005 (http://www.columbiagrangers.org). *The Faber Book of 20th Century Women's Poetry.* Fleur Adcock, ed. Faber and Faber, 1987. *The New Exeter Book of Riddles.* Kevin Crossley-Holland and Lawrence Sail, eds. Enitharmon Press, 1999. *The Norton Anthology of Poetry.* 4th ed. Margaret Ferguson, Mary Jo Salter and Jon Stal, eds. W.W. Norton, 1996. *The Oxford Book of Christmas Poems.* Michael Harrison and Christopher Stuart-Clark, eds. Oxford University Press, 1983. *The Oxford Companion to English Literature.* 6th edition. Margaret Drabble, ed. Oxford University Press, 2000. *The Virago Book of Love Poetry.* Wendy Mulford, ed. Virago Press, 1990.

FARJEON, ELEANOR (1881–1965)

She was born in Hampstead, London, the daughter of the novelist Benjamin Leopold Farjeon, and granddaughter of the American actor Joseph Jefferson. Although lacking in formal education, she absorbed literature like a sponge from her father's vast library. When her father died leaving no money, Eleanor turned to writing. She and Philip Edward Thomas (see entry) became friends and how they helped each other to develop as poets is described in his *The Last Four Years* (1958). Following the death of Thomas she spent four formative years, 1917 to 1921, near Amberley, Sussex, out of which was born the romantic fantasy *Martin Pippin in the Apple-Orchard* (1921). Although not written for children, it rapidly became popular with young people. Throughout the twenties she regularly wrote poems and verses for the *Daily Herald* and for *Time and Tide: Pan Worship*, 1908. Other major publications: *Nursery Rhymes of London Town*, 1916. *The Children's Bells*, 1957. *Silver-Sand and Snow*, 1951. Some of her poems: "Light the Lamps Up, Lamplighter!" "Morning Has Broken" (set to an old Gaelic tune, it has become a popular hymn), "Ode to a Fat Cat," "The Flower-Seller," "Window Boxes."

Sources: *Dictionary of National Biography.* Electronic

Edition 1.1. Oxford University Press, 1997. *Earth Prayers from Around the World: 365 Prayers, Poems, and Invocations for Honoring the Earth.* Elizabeth Roberts and Elais Amidon, eds. Harper Collins, 1991. *Encyclopædia Britannica Ultimate Reference Suite DVD*, 2006. *Piping Down the Valley Wild: Poetry for the Young of All Ages*, Nancy Larrick, ed. Delacorte Press, 1968. *The Columbia Granger's Index to Poetry.* 11th ed. *The Columbia Granger's World of Poetry*, Columbia University Press, 2005 (http://www.columbiagrangers.org). *The Cyber Hymnal* (http://www.cyberhymnal.org/index.htm). *The Oxford Companion to English Literature.* 6th edition. Margaret Drabble, ed. Oxford University Press, 2000.

FARLEY, PAUL (1965–)

Born in Liverpool, England, he studied at the Chelsea School of Art. He was writer in residence at the Wordsworth Trust, Grasmere, from 2000 to 2002, and currently lectures in creative writing at the University of Lancaster. He also writes radio drama, and his play, *When Louis Met George*, was broadcast on BBC Radio 4 in March 2003. In 2004, he was named as one of the Poetry Book Society's "Next Generation" poets. He won the Arvon Poetry Competition in 1996 and his first collection of poetry, *The Boy from the Chemist is Here to See You* (1998), won the Forward Poetry Prize for Best First Collection. It was short listed for the Whitbread Poetry Award and won a Somerset Maugham Award. He was named *Sunday Times* Young Writer of the Year in 1999. His other publications: *The Ice Age*, 2002. *Paul Farley Reading From his Poems*, 2005. Some of his poems: "A Minute's Silence," "A Tunnel," "Duel," "Liverpool Disappears for a Billionth of a Second," "Monopoly," "The Lapse," "Treacle."

Sources: *British Council Arts* (http://www.contemporarywriters.com). *Poems by Paul Farley* (http://www.poetryarchive.org/poetryarchive/singlePoet.do?poetId=27). *The National Portrait Gallery* (www.npg.org.uk).

FAWCETT, JOHN (1740–1817)

Born at Lidget Green, near Bradford, Yorkshire, he was converted under the ministry of George Whitefield at the age of 16. He first joined the Methodists, then was ordained a Baptist minister at Wainsgate near Hebden Bridge, Yorkshire. Although invited to London to succeed the celebrated Dr. J. Gill as pastor of Carter's Lane, he felt unable to leave the congregation of Wainsgate. Out of this experience he wrote his well-known hymn "Blest Be the Tie That Binds." In 1777 a new chapel was built for him at Hebden Bridge. About the same time he opened a school at Breasley Hall, and he received the degree of doctor of divinity from an American college. In 1811 he published his *Devotional Commentary on the Holy Scriptures*, a large two volume work. Some of his poetic publications: *Poetic Essays*,

1767. *The Christian's Humble Plea*, 1772. *The Death of Euminio, a Divine Poem*, 1779. *The Reign of Death*, 1780. Some of his other many hymns/poems: "How Precious is the Book Divine," "Lord, Dismiss Us with Thy Blessing," "Afflicted Saint, to Christ Draw Near," "Thy Presence, Gracious God, Afford."

Sources: *Biography of John Fawcett* (Spiritual Songsters) (http://www.stempublishing.com/hymns/biographies/fawcett.html). *Dictionary of National Biography.* Electronic Edition 1.1. Oxford University Press, 1997. *The Cyber Hymnal* (http://www.cyberhymnal.org/index.htm). *The National Portrait Gallery* (www.npg.org.uk).

FAWKES, FRANCIS (1720–1777)

Born in Warmsworth, Yorkshire, where his father was rector, and educated in Bury, Lancashire, and Jesus College, Cambridge, he graduated M.A. in 1745. He was ordained in the Anglican Church and was chaplain to the Princess Dowager of Wales. It was said that he was too fond of the gay social life to be considered for any serious post. However, he was a fine translator, possibly on a par with Alexander Pope. Although always poor, his cheerful good humor drew many friends to him. Some of his publications: *Bramham Park*, 1745. *Partridge-Shooting, an Eclogue*, 1757. *The Works of Anacreon, Sappho, Bion, Moschus and Musæus. Translated from the original Greek*, 11760, 2nd edition, 1789. *Original Poems and Translations*, 1761. *The Complete Family Bible*, 1761. *The Poetical Calendar*, 1763. *The Idylliums of Theocritus, Translated from the Greek*, 1767. *The Works of Horace in English Verse, by Mr. Duncombe and Other Hands*, 1767. *The Argonautics of Apollonius Rhodius*, 1780. Some of his poems: "The Brown Jug" (which was extremely popular), "The Power of Love," "Hymn to Venus."

Sources: *An Antidote Against Melancholy.* Pratt Manufacturing Company, 1884. *Dictionary of National Biography.* Electronic Edition 1.1. Oxford University Press, 1997. *English Poetry.* Second Edition Bibliography (http://collections.chadwyck.co.uk/html/ep2/bibliography/d.htm). *The Columbia Granger's Index to Poetry.* 11th ed. *The Columbia Granger's World of Poetry*, Columbia University Press, 2005 (http://www.columbiagrangers.org). *The Oxford Book of Classical Verse in Translation.* Adrian Poole, and Jeremy Maule, ed. 1995.

FEAVER, VICKI (1943–)

Born in Nottingham, she graduated in music and English from Durham University and University College, London, and now lives in Scotland. She is a former tutor of creative writing and is emeritus professor at Chichester University, Sussex. She was awarded a Hawthornden Fellowship (1993) and a Cholmondeley Award (1999). She is the author of two poetry collections: *Close Relatives* (1981) and *The Handless Maiden* (1994), which won the Heinemann Award and was short listed for the Forward Poetry Prize for Best Poetry Collection of the Year. She has also published essays on the process of writing and on twentieth century women poets. Her work is included in several contemporary poetry anthologies, including *Penguin Modern Poets 2* (1995), with Carol Ann Duffy and Eavan Boland (see entries); *After Ovid* (1996), an anthology of several translations of Ovid's *Metamorphoses*; and *The Penguin Book of Poetry from Britain and Ireland Since 1945* (1998). Some of her poems: "Coat," "Hemingway's Hat," "Judith," "Lily Pond," "Marigolds," "Oi Yoi Yoi," "The River God," "Without you, I prefer the nights."

Sources: *British Council Arts* (http://www.contemporarywriters.com). *Emergency Kit: Poems for Strange Times.* Jo Shapcott and Matthew Sweeney, ed. Faber and Faber, 1996. *Love's Witness: Five Centuries of Love Poetry by Women.* Jill Hollis, ed. Carroll and Graf, Inc., 1993. *Poetry Archive* (www.poetry-archive.com). *The Columbia Granger's Index to Poetry.* 11th ed. *The Columbia Granger's World of Poetry*, Columbia University Press, 2005 (http://www.columbiagrangers.org). *The New Exeter Book of Riddles.* Kevin Crossley-Holland and Lawrence Sail, eds. Enitharmon Press, 1999. *The Oxford Companion to English Literature.* 6th edition. Margaret Drabble, ed. Oxford University Press, 2000. *Vicci Bentley interviews Vicki Feaver* (http://www.poetrymagazines.org.uk/magazine/record.asp?id=390 0). *Voices in the Gallery.* Dannie Abse and Joan Abse, eds. Tate Gallery, 1986.

FEINSTEIN, ELAINE BARBARA (1930–)

She was born in Bootle, Lancashire, graduated M.A. from Newnham College, Cambridge, and was awarded an honorary doctorate from the University of Leicester in 1999. She has been an editor for Cambridge University Press (1960–1962); lecturer in English at Bishop's Stortford Training College (1963–1966); assistant lecturer in English literature at the University of Essex (1967–1970); and a journalist. She contributes to many periodicals, including the *Times Literary Supplement*, and was writer in residence for the British Council in Singapore and Tromsoe, Norway. Her later work has been influenced by the Russian poet Marina Tsvetayeva (1892–1941), which she translated from the Russian. Three of her awards have been for her translations. She has written a number of plays for television and published fourteen novels, several biographies, and fourteen collections of poetry. Her first volume of poetry, *In a Green Eye*, was published in 1966. The last *Collected Poems and Translations* was published in 2003. Some of her poems: "A Quiet War in Leicester," "Against Winter," "Annus Mirabilis 1989," "How Did They Kill My Grandmother?" "Insomnia," "Night Thoughts," "Poem of the End," "Under Stone."

Sources: *British Council Arts* (http://www.contemporarywriters.com). *Holocaust Poetry*. Hilda Schiff, ed. HarperCollins, 1995. *Portraits of Poets*, Sebastian Barker, ed., Carcanet, 1986. *Selected Poems of Marina Tsvetaeva*. Elaine Feinstein, ed. Penguin Books, 1993. *The Columbia Granger's Index to Poetry*. 11th ed. *The Columbia Granger's World of Poetry*, Columbia University Press, 2005 (http://www.columbiagrangers.org). *The Elaine Feinstein Page* (http://www.elainefeinstein.com/). *The Faber Book of War Poetry*. Kenneth Baker, ed. Faber and Faber, 1996. *The Oxford Book of English Verse*. Christopher Ricks, ed. Oxford University Press, 1999. *The Oxford Companion to English Literature*. 6th edition. Margaret Drabble, ed. Oxford University Press, 2000. *Voices Within the Ark: The Modern Jewish Poets*. Howard Schwartz, and Anthony Rudolf, ed. Avon Books, 1980. *Who's Who*. London: A & C Black, 2005.

FENTON, ELIJAH (1683–1730)

Born at Shelton, Staffordshire, he graduated from Jesus College, Cambridge, in 1704. His refusal to swear the Oath of Allegiance barred him from being ordained in the Church of England. For a time he was headmaster of the grammar school at Sevenoaks, Kent, and secretary to the Earl of Orrery. From 1714 to 1720 he was tutor to Lord Broghill, the earl's son. He spent the rest of his short life in the service of Lady Trumbull as auditor of accounts. He assisted Alexander Pope and William Broome (see entries) in their translation of the *Odyssey*. Samuel Johnson says of Fenton: "He was never named but with praise and fondness, as a man in the highest degree amiable and excellent." Some of his publications: *Oxford and Cambridge Miscellany Poems*, 1708. *An Ode Addressed to the Savoir Vivre Club*, 1710. *To the Queen, on Her Majesty's Birth-day*, 1712. *Poems on Several Occasions*, 1717. *Life of Milton*, 1720. *Marianne*, 1723. Some of his poems: "An Ode to the Sun, for the New Year," "The Fair Nun," "To a Lady Sitting before Her Glass," "To Mr. Pope."

Sources: *A Short Biographical Dictionary of English Literature* (http://classiclit.about.com/library/bl-etexts/jcousin/bl-jcousin-bio-f.htm). *A Treasury of Minor British Poetry*. J. Churton Collins, ed. Edward Arnold, 1896. *Dictionary of National Biography*. Electronic Edition 1.1. Oxford University Press, 1997. *Encyclopædia Britannica*. Electronic Edition, 2005. *English Poetry: Author Search*. Chadwyck-Healey Ltd., 1995 (http://www.lib.utexas.edu:8080/search/epoetry/author.html). *Oldpoetry* (www.oldpoetry.com). *Samuel Johnson's Lives of the English Poets*, 1779–1781 (http://www2.hn.psu.edu/Faculty/KKemmerer/poets/preface.htm). *The Columbia Granger's Index to Poetry*. 11th ed. *The Columbia Granger's World of Poetry*, Columbia University Press, 2005 (http://www.columbiagrangers.org).

FENTON, JAMES MARTIN (1949–)

Born in Lincoln, England, he studied psychology and philosophy at Magdalen College, Oxford, graduating in 1970. He had a distinguished career as a journalist, as a freelancer and working for the main newspapers. He contributed regularly to the *New York Review of Books*. He translated the lyrics of Verdi's opera *Rigoletto*, setting the action in the 1950s New York Mafia world. He won the Newdigate Prize for his first poetry cycle, *Our Western Furniture,* in 1968, and the 1984 Geoffrey Faber Memorial Prize for his poetry. His poem "A German Requiem" (1981) won the Southern Arts Literature Award for Poetry. He was professor of poetry at Oxford University from 1994 to 1999. Some of his other publications: *Put Thou Thy Tears Into My Bottle*, 1969. *Children in Exile: Poems 1968–1984*, 1985. *The Snap Revolution*, 1986. *All the Wrong Places: Adrift in the Politics of the Pacific Rim*, 1988. *Out of Danger*, 1994. *An Introduction to English Poetry*, 2002. Some of his other poems: "Cambodia," "Dead Soldiers," "Exempla," "Out of Danger," "Terminal Moraine," "The Memory of War."

Sources: *Against Forgetting: Twentieth-Century Poetry of Witness*. Carolyn Forché, ed. W.W. Norton, 1993. *Biography of James Fenton, with Links* (http://www.bedfordstmartins.com/litlinks/poetry/fenton.htm). *The Bloodaxe Book of 20th Century Poetry, from Britain and Ireland*. Edna Longley, ed. Bloodaxe Books, 2000. *The Columbia Granger's Index to Poetry*. 11th ed. *The Columbia Granger's World of Poetry*, Columbia University Press, 2005 (http://www.columbiagrangers.org). *The National Portrait Gallery* (www.npg.org.uk). *The Oxford Companion to English Literature*. 6th edition. Margaret Drabble, ed. Oxford University Press, 2000. *Who's Who*. London: A & C Black, 2005. *Wikipedia, the Free Encyclopedia* (http://en.wikipedia.org/wiki/Wikipedia).

FERGUSON, SIR SAMUEL (1810–1886)

Born in Belfast, and educated at Belfast Academical Institution and Trinity College, Dublin, he studied at Lincoln's Inn, London, before being called to the Irish bar in 1838. He wrote many papers for the Royal Irish Academy, becoming its president in 1882. He founded the Protestant Repeal Association and sought to restore an Irish parliament. He became deputy keeper of the public records of Ireland in 1867 and was knighted in 1878. He is an influential figure in Irish poetry, drawing heavily on Irish mythology for his poems such as "The Tain Quest" and "The Death of Dermid Lays of the Western Gael." He wrote the love song "The Lark in the Clear Air." His poem "At the Polo-Ground" expressed his deep concern at the murders of the chief secretary and under-secretary of the paper *The Nation* in Phoenix Park, Dublin, 1882. Some of his other publications: *Lays of the Western Gael*, 1865. *Congal, an Epic Poem in Five Books*, 1872. *Ogham Inscriptions in Ireland, Wales and Scotland*, 1887. Some of his poems: "Cashel of Munster," "Cean

Dubh Deelish," "The Fair Hills of Ireland," "The Fairy Thorn," "The Forging of the Anchor."

Sources: *Dictionary of National Biography.* Electronic Edition 1.1. Oxford University Press, 1997. *Encyclopædia Britannica.* Electronic Edition, 2005. *English Poetry: Author Search.* Chadwyck-Healey Ltd., 1995 (http://www.lib.utexas.edu:8080/search/epoetry/author.html). *Famous Irish Lives—Sir Samuel Ferguson* (http://www.irelandseye.com/irish/people/famous/sfergson.shtm). *Poemhunter* (www.poemhunter.com). *The Columbia Granger's Index to Poetry.* 11th ed. *The Columbia Granger's World of Poetry,* Columbia University Press, 2005 (http://www.columbiagrangers.org). *The Oxford Companion to English Literature.* 6th edition. Margaret Drabble, ed. Oxford University Press, 2000.

FERGUSSON, ROBERT (1750–1774)

Born and died in Edinburgh, he was one of the leading figures of the 18th-century revival of Scots vernacular writing and the chief forerunner of Robert Burns. Although entered at St. Andrews University, his father's death forced him leave without graduating, and he worked as a clerk for the rest of his short life. Toward the end he suffered from fits of depression and religious guilt. After falling down stairs and sustaining a severe head injury, then developing manic depression, he was confined in the public asylum, where he died. A plain gravestone with a poetical epitaph by Robert Burns was placed at his head in 1789. He wrote three songs, set to familiar Scottish airs, for the singer Tenducci, to be sung in the opera *Artaxerxes.* Some of his poems: "A Saturday's Expedition," "Against Repining at Fortune," "Auld Reikie, a Poem [Edinburgh]," "Decay of Friendship," "Drinking Song," "Elegy on John Hogg," "Epitaph on General Wolfe," "Leith Races," "The Amputation, a Burlesque Elegy," "The Complaint," "The Rivers of Scotland, an Ode," "To My Auld Breeks."

Sources: *Dictionary of National Biography.* Electronic Edition 1.1. Oxford University Press, 1997. *Encyclopædia Britannica Ultimate Reference Suite DVD,* 2006. *English Poetry: Author Search.* Chadwyck-Healey Ltd., 1995 (http://www.lib.utexas.edu:8080/search/epoetry/author.html). *The Columbia Granger's Index to Poetry.* 11th ed. *The Columbia Granger's World of Poetry,* Columbia University Press, 2005 (http://www.columbiagrangers.org). *The Oxford Companion to English Literature.* 6th edition. Margaret Drabble, ed. Oxford University Press, 2000. *The Poetical Works of Robert Fergusson.* Chapman and Lang, 1800.

FERRERS, GEORGE (?1500–1579)

Born in St. Albans, Hertfordshire, he studied canon law at Cambridge and graduated B.A. in 1531. In 1534 he published an English translation of the Magna Carta and other important statutes. He was member of Parliament for Plymouth three times between 1542 and 1553. He served in some capacity in the court of Henry VIII and attended Henry VIII in his military expeditions against Scotland and France. Henry left him a small legacy in appreciation of his services. He is also served with Edward VI (1547–1553) against the Scots in 1548. He cooperated with William Baldwin (see entry) in inventing the series of historical poems *Mirror for Magistrates* (see also Richard Niccols), 1559. Ferrers contributed the opening poem, on the fall of Robert Tresilian (a judge who was executed for treason in 1388), a poem dealing with the murder of Thomas of Woodstock (Earl of Buckingham and Duke of Gloucester, murdered in Calais in 1397 on behalf of his nephew, King Richard II), and a poem on the death of Richard II (who died in 1400 in suspicious circumstances as a prisoner in Pontefract Castle, West Yorkshire).

Sources: *Dictionary of National Biography.* Electronic Edition 1.1. Oxford University Press, 1997.

FINCH, ANNE, COUNTESS OF WINCHILSEA (1661–1720)

The daughter of Sir William Kingsmill, she married Colonel Heneage Finch in 1684; he became the 4th earl of Winchilsea in 1712. Orphaned when young, she was possibly reared by her uncle. Finch was gentleman of the bedchamber to James II when Duke of York, and his niece Anne was maid of honor to Mary of Modena the duchess. She was a friend of many other poets; her poem "The Spleen: A Pindaric Poem" inspired Nicholas Rowe (see entry) to compose "An Epistle to Flavia" in her honor. In Alexander Pope's *Miscellanies* (1727), he included "An Impromptu to Lady Winchilsea." Her nature poetry was greatly admired by Wordsworth. The only collected edition of her poems, *A New Miscellany of Original Poems,* was published in 1713, containing a tragedy never acted, called *Aristomenes, or the Royal Shepherd.* Some of her other poems: "A Nocturnal Reverie," "A Pastoral Dialogue between Two Shepherdesses," "A Song on the South Sea," "Ardelia's Answer to Ephelia," "Caesar and Brutus," "Enquiry after Peace: A Fragment," "The Greater Trial," "The Hog, the Sheep and Goat, Carrying to a Fair," "The Petition for an Absolute Retreat."

Sources: *A Treasury of Great Poems: English and American.* Louis Untermeyer, ed. Simon and Schuster, 1955. *Dictionary of National Biography.* Electronic Edition 1.1. Oxford University Press, 1997. *English Poetry: Author Search.* Chadwyck-Healey Ltd., 1995 (http://www.lib.utexas.edu:8080/search/epoetry/author.html). *The Columbia Granger's Index to Poetry.* 11th ed. *The Columbia Granger's World of Poetry,* Columbia University Press, 2005 (http://www.columbiagrangers.org). *The Oxford Companion to English Literature.* 6th edition. Margaret Drabble, ed. Oxford University Press, 2000. *The National Portrait*

Gallery (www.npg.org.uk). *Selected Poems of Anne Finch, Countess of Winchilsea.* Denys Thompson, ed. Carcanet Press, 1987. *The Women Poets in English: An Anthology.* Ann Stanford, ed. McGraw-Hill, 1972.

FINCH, PETER (1947–)

Welsh poet, living in Cardiff, he is an avant-garde poet whose output is prodigious. He has published some twenty-five volumes of poetry, a collection of short stories, numerous reviews and critical essays, as well as a highly acclaimed, comprehensive guide to *The Poetry Business* (1994). His writing is "not recommended for the poetically conservative, strictly for addicts, masochists and freewheeling bohemians who like to shake a leg in suburbia" (*The Independent on Sunday*). He exhibited visual poetry internationally and toured with sound poet Bob Cobbing (see entry). He is much in demand as a reader as well as a lecturer at festivals and venues up and down the country. He compiles the poetry section of Macmillan's annual *Writer's Handbook* and the self-publishing section for A&C Black's *Writers' & Artists' Yearbook.* Some of his publications: *Pieces of the Universe,* 1969. *Connecting Tubes,* 1980. *Selected Poems,* 1987. *Poems for Ghosts,* 1991. *Five Hundred Cobbings,* 1994. Some of his poems: "A Welsh Wordscape," "How Callum Innes Paints," "Marks the English Left on the Map," "The Computer's First Proverbs," "The Tattoo," "Why Do You Want to Be English?"

Sources: *Anglo-Welsh Poetry, 1480–1980.* Raymond Garlick and Roland Mathias, ed. Poetry Wales Press, 1984. *Anglo-Welsh Poetry, 1480–1990.* Raymond Garlick and Roland Mathias, ed. Poetry Wales Press, 1993. *Biography and Works of Peter Finch* (http://www.peterfinch.co.uk/). *Other British and Irish Poetry Since 1970.* Richard Caddel and Peter Quartermain, ed. Wesleyan University Press, 1999. *The Art of Noise: Peter Finch Sounds Off Claire Powell* (http://www.peterfinch.co.uk/noise.htm). *The Columbia Granger's Index to Poetry.* 11th ed. *The Columbia Granger's World of Poetry,* Columbia University Press, 2005 (http://www.columbiagrangers.org). *The New British Poetry, 1968–88.* Gillian Allnutt, Fred D'Aguiar and Ken Edwards, eds. Grafton Books, 1989. *Twentieth Century Anglo-Welsh Poetry.* Dannie Abse, ed. Seren Books / Dufour Editions, 1997.

FINLAY, IAN HAMILTON (1925–)

Born in Nassau, he was educated in Scotland and in the Orkney Islands, and was in the Army from 1944 to 1947. After the war he worked as a shepherd and became known in the 1950s as a writer of plays, short stories and poetry and as a broadcaster. With Jessie McGuffie he founded the Wild Hawthorn Press in 1961, and soon established himself as Britain's leading concrete poet — poetry that deals with the visual aspect of the poem. As a sculptor his designs have been executed as stone-carvings, as constructed objects and even in the form of neon light-

ing. He devotes a lot of time to his garden, Little Sparta, at Dunsyre near Edinburgh. He was made honorary professor at Dundee University in 1999 and a commander of the British Empire in 2002. Some of his publications: *The Sea Bed and Other Stories,* 1958. *The Dancers Inherit the Party,* 1960. *Rapel,* 1963 (his first collection of concrete poetry). Some of his poems: "Bedtime," "Orkney Interior," "Orkney Lyrics," "The Boat's Blueprint," "The Cloud's Anchor," "The Horizon of Holland."

Sources: *A Book of Scottish Verse.* Maurice Lindsay and R.L. Mackie, eds. St. Martin's Press, 1983. *Ian Hamilton Finlay Artist and Art: The-artists.org* (http://www.the-artists.org/ArtistView.cfm?id=8A01F432-BBCF-11D4-A93500D0B7069B40). *The Grove Dictionary of Art* (http://www.artnet.com/library/02/0283/T028352.asp). *The National Portrait Gallery* (www.npg.org.uk). *The New Penguin Book of Scottish Verse.* Robert Crawford and Mick Imlah, eds. Penguin Books, 2000. *The Oxford Companion to English Literature.* 6th edition. Margaret Drabble, ed. Oxford University Press, 2000. *Who's Who.* London: A & C Black, 2005. *Wikipedia, the Free Encyclopedia* (http://en.wikipedia.org/wiki/Wikipedia).

FINLAY, JOHN (1782–1810)

Scottish poet, born of humble parents at Glasgow. Educated in one of the academies at Glasgow and at Glasgow University, he proved to be a distinguished student, thought to border on genius. In 1802 he published *Wallace, or the Vale of Ellerslie, and Other Poems,* with a second edition with some additions in 1804. In 1808 he published *Scottish Historical and Romantic Ballads, Chiefly Ancient, with Explanatory Notes and a Glossary;* Sir Walter Scott greatly admired the beauty of the Scottish ballads. He also published an edition of Robert Blair's *The Grave,* wrote a life of Cervantes, and superintended an edition of Adam Smith's *Wealth of Nations.* His life was cut short by a sudden illness at Moffat, where he is buried. At his death he was collecting materials for a continuation of *Warton's History of Poetry* (1774–1781).

Sources: *Dictionary of National Biography.* Electronic Edition 1.1. Oxford University Press, 1997. *Historical Perspective for Moffat* (Dumfries and Galloway) (http://www.geo.ed.ac.uk/scotgaz/towns/townhistory358.html). *The Columbia Granger's Index to Poetry.* 11th ed. *The Columbia Granger's World of Poetry,* Columbia University Press, 2005 (http://www.columbiagrangers.org).

FISHER, ALLEN (1944–)

Born in London, he started writing poetry in his early twenties and has become a successful poet, painter, publisher, teacher and performer associated with the British Poetry Revival. His early long project *Place* was published in a series of books and pamphlets in the 1970s. He has been working on a project called *Gravity as a consequence of shape* since 1982, which was completed in 2005. He is head of art at the University of Surrey, Roehampton. He has exhibited widely and his work is represented in the Tate Gallery, the Living Museum, Iceland, and City Gallery, York. He is the editor of the Hereford based *Spanner*— a magazine that focuses on particular authors or subjects in each issue, which has published many of the revival poets. He has published over 100 books of poetry, graphics and art documentation. Two of his books are: *The Apocalyptic Sonnets* (1978) and *Poetry for Schools* (1980). Some of his poems: "Emergent Manner," "Four Novels," "Mummers' Strut," "Murder One," "Stepping Out," "The Ditchley Portrait," "The Gardener's Preface."

Sources: *Biography and Works of Allen Fisher* (http://epc.buffalo.edu/authors/fisher/bio.html) and at (http://www.soton.ac.uk/~bepc/poets/fisher.htm). *Anthology of Twentieth-Century British and Irish Poetry.* Keith Tuma, ed. Oxford University Press, 2001. *Spanner (Magazine) Home Page* (http://www.shadoof.net/spanner/). *The Columbia Granger's Index to Poetry.* 11th ed. *The Columbia Granger's World of Poetry,* Columbia University Press, 2005 (http://www.columbiagrangers.org). *The New British Poetry, 1968–88.* Gillian Allnutt, Fred D'Aguiar and Ken Edwards, ed. Grafton Books, 1989. *Wikipedia, the Free Encyclopedia* (http://en.wikipedia.org/wiki/Wikipedia).

FISHER, ROY (1930–)

He was born in Handsworth, Birmingham, and studied at Birmingham University. From 1963 until 1971 he was head of English and drama at Bordesley College of Education, Birmingham. He then joined the Department of American Studies at Keele University, Staffordshire, where he stayed until 1982, after which he worked as a freelance writer and musician. As a jazz pianist, he married jazz with poetry and was one of the first British poets to be associated with the Black Mountain School of jazz poetry, which started in North Carolina in the early 1950s. He was thus one of the key figures in the British Poetry Revival. Some of his publications: *City,* 1962 (admired in the United States but almost ignored in Britain). *Poems 1955–1980,* 1981. *A Furnace,* 1986. *Poems 1955–1987,* 1988. *The Dow Low Drop,* 1996. Some of his poems: "Commuter," "Diversions," "Five Morning Poems from a Picture by Manet," "Five Pilgrims in the Prologue to the Canterbury Tales," "Handsworth Liberties," "Inscriptions for Bluebeard's Castle," "Matrix," "Studies," "The Billiard Table," "The Open Poem and the Closed Poem."

Sources: *Biography of Roy Fisher: Literary Heritage* (http://www3.shropshire-cc.gov.uk/fisher.htm). *Poems, 1955–1987 of Roy Fisher.* Oxford University Press, 1988. *The Columbia Granger's Index to Poetry.* 11th ed. *The Columbia Granger's World of Poetry,* Columbia University Press, 2005 (http://www.columbiagrangers.org). *The Ox-*

ford Companion to English Literature. 6th edition. Margaret Drabble, ed. Oxford University Press, 2000. *Wikipedia, the Free Encyclopedia* (http://en.wikipedia.org/wiki/Wikipedia).

FITCHETT, JOHN (1776–1838)

He was born in Liverpool, Merseyside, the son of a wine merchant. His parents having died before he was ten, he was raised by an uncle, a lawyer, in Warrington, Lancashire, and attended the local grammar school. He became a highly successful partner in his uncle's law firm. He died unmarried at Warrington and was buried at Winwick Church. His large and choice library was left to his nephew, John Fitchett Marsh. His first published work, "Bewsey, a Poem" (1796) achieved considerable success; *Minor Poems, Composed at Various Times* was published in 1836. He labored for over forty years on what is believed to be the longest poem ever composed––in the form of a romantic epic poem, covering the antiquities, physical features, religion, and civil and religious condition of England in the time of King Alfred the Great. It was first published for private circulation between 1808 and 1834. He rewrote part of it but died before completing the revision. His friend Robert Roscoe finished it by adding 2,585 lines, the entire work ran to more than 131,000 lines. The work —*King Alfred, a Poem*— was published by Pickering in 1841–1842.

Sources: A copy of *King flAlfred* is held at the Cornell University Library, New York (http://cdl.library.cornell.edu/cgi-bin/moa/sgml/moa-idx?notisid=ABR0102-0001-229). *Dictionary of National Biography.* Electronic Edition 1.1. Oxford University Press, 1997.

FITZGERALD, EDWARD (1809–1883)

He was born at Bredfield House, near Woodbridge, Suffolk, into a wealthy family. After King Edward the Sixth's Grammar School, Bury St. Edmunds, he went to Trinity College, Cambridge, from where he graduated in 1830. Lord Tennyson (see entry) dedicated to him his poem "Tiresias," though Fitzgerald died just before it was published. He was buried at Boulge, Suffolk. Fitzgerald never took up a profession but turned his energies into writing. In 1849, he published the biography of the Quaker poet Bernard Barton (see entry). He is renowned for his translation (1859) from the Persian of *Rubáiyát of Omar Khayyám,* the astronomer poet of Persia. Some of his other publications: *Euphranor, a Dialogue on Youth,* 1851. *Six Dramas of Calderon, freely translated by Edward Fitzgerald,* 1853. *Polonius: a Collection of Wise Saws and Modern Instances,* 1852 (with a preface on proverbs and aphorisms). *Agamemnon of Æschylus,* 1876 (translation). *Tales of the Hall,* 1882 (with an introduction,

Readings in Crabbe (see entry, Crabbe, George). Some of his other poems: "Agamemnon," "Chivalry at a Discount," "Some We Loved," "The Meadows in Spring," "The Three Arrows."

Sources: *Dictionary of National Biography*. Electronic Edition 1.1. Oxford University Press, 1997. *Encyclopædia Britannica Ultimate Reference Suite DVD*, 2006. *English Poetry: Author Search*. Chadwyck-Healey Ltd., 1995 (http://www.lib.utexas.edu:8080/search/epoetry/author.html). *Poemhunter* (www.poemhunter.com). *The Columbia Granger's Index to Poetry*. 11th ed. *The Columbia Granger's World of Poetry*, Columbia University Press, 2005 (http://www.columbiagrangers.org). *The Home Book of Modern Verse*. Burton Egbert Stevenson, ed. Henry Holt, 1953. *The National Portrait Gallery* (www.npg.org.uk). *The Oxford Companion to English Literature*. 6th edition. Margaret Drabble, ed. Oxford University Press, 2000. *Unauthorized Versions: Poems and Their Parodies*. Kenneth Baker, ed. Faber and Faber, 1990.

FLATMAN, THOMAS (1637–1688)

Born in London, his education was at Winchester College and New College, Oxford, though he left without a degree in 1657 to take up law at Inner Temple. He was created M.A. of Cambridge by the king's letters of December 1666. He became a successful miniature painter as well as poet. Alexander Pope imitated Flatman's ode "A Thought of Death" in his own "The Dying Christian to His Soul." The Duke of Ormonde was so pleased with the ode on the death of his son, the Earl of Ossory (published in 1680), that he sent the poet a diamond ring. Some of his other publications: *A Panegyric to Charles the Second*, 1660. *Poems and Songs*, 1686 (4th edition). *A Song for St. Cecilia's Day*, 1686. Some of his other poems: "An Appeal to Cats in the Business of Love," "Castabella Going to Sea," "De Rerum Natura [On the Nature of Things]" (translation of Lucretius), "Death," "On Marriage," "On the Death of the Earl of Rochester," "The Advice," "The Batchelor's Song," "The Defiance," "The Sad Day," "To His Sacred Majesty King James II."

Sources: *Dictionary of National Biography*. Electronic Edition 1.1. Oxford University Press, 1997. *English Poetry: Author Search*. Chadwyck-Healey Ltd., 1995 (http://www.lib.utexas.edu:8080/search/epoetry/author.html). *Stanford University Libraries and Academic Information Resources* (http://library.stanford.edu). *The Columbia Granger's Index to Poetry*. 11th ed. *The Columbia Granger's World of Poetry*, Columbia University Press, 2005 (http://www.columbiagrangers.org). *The Oxford Book of Marriage*. Helge Rubenstein, ed. Oxford University Press, 1990. *The Oxford Companion to English Literature*. 6th edition. Margaret Drabble, ed. Oxford University Press, 2000. *The Poetry of Cats*. Samuel Carr, ed. Viking Press, 1974.

FLECKER, HERMAN JAMES ELROY (1884–1915)

Born at Lewisham, London, he was educated at Dean Close School, Cheltenham, where his father, the Rev. William Herman Flecker, D.D., was headmaster, then at Uppingham, Rutland. He studied classics at Trinity College, Oxford, and Oriental languages at Caius College, Cambridge. In 1910 he was appointed vice consul to Istanbul, where he contracted tuberculosis, thereafter spending much of his short life in and out of hospitals in England and Switzerland. He died in a sanatorium in Switzerland and was buried at Cheltenham. He claimed to be a disciple of the French Parnassian school — the desire to create something of beauty. Some of his publications: *The Bridge of Fire*, 1907. *Thirty-six Poems*, 1910. *Forty-two Poems*, 1911. *The Golden Journey to Samarkand*, 1913. *The Old Ships*, 1915. *Collected Prose*, 1920. *Hassan*, 1922 (a play). *Don Juan*, 1925 (a play). Some of his poems: "Ballad of the Londoner," "Gates of Damascus," "God Save the King" (see Carey, Henry), "Ode to the Glory of Greece," "Pavlova in London," "To a Poet a Thousand Years Hence," "The Welsh Sea."

Sources: *Dance in Poetry: An International Anthology of Poems on Dance*. Alkis Raftis, ed. Princeton Book Company, 1991. *Dictionary of National Biography*. Electronic Edition 1.1. Oxford University Press, 1997. *The Columbia Granger's Index to Poetry*. 11th ed. *The Columbia Granger's World of Poetry*, Columbia University Press, 2005 (http://www.columbiagrangers.org). *The Home Book of Modern Verse*. Burton Egbert Stevenson, ed. Henry Holt, 1953. *The Oxford Book of Twentieth-Century English Verse*. Philip Larkin, ed. Oxford University Press, 1973. *The Oxford Companion to English Literature*. 6th edition. Margaret Drabble, ed. Oxford University Press, 2000.

FLECKNOE, RICHARD (d. 1678?)

Although it is not certain, it is thought he was a Jesuit priest of Irish extraction. He traveled extensively between 1640 and 1648, visiting the Low Countries; Rome, Istanbul, Portugal and Brazil. He was known by the nickname of "Langbaine" because of his long, lean frame. John Dryden (see entry) lampooned him in his hostile *MacFlecknoe* (1682); however, Robert Southey and Charles Lamb (see entries) praised his work. He wrote many plays as well as poetry. There is no record of the circumstances of his death. Some of his publications (with shortened titles): *Hierothalamium...*, 1626. *The Affections of a Pious Soule...*, 1640. *Miscellania, or Poems of All Sorts...*, 1653. *Love's Dominion*, 1654 (a play). *Relation of Ten Years' Travels in Europe, Asia, Affrique, and America*, 1654. *Ariadne*, 1654 (possibly the first English opera). *The Diarium or Journal...*, 1656. *Sketches in Enigmatical Characters...*, 1658. *The Mar-*

riage of Oceanus and Britannia, 1659. *Sir William Davenant's Voyage to the Other World*, 1668. *Poems in Epigrams of All Sorts*, 1670. Some of his poems: "Invocation of Silence," "On the Death of Our Lord," "The Ant."

Sources: *Dictionary of National Biography.* Electronic Edition 1.1. Oxford University Press, 1997. *Encyclopædia Britannica Ultimate Reference Suite DVD*, 2006. *Songs from the British Drama.* Edward Bliss Reed, ed. Yale University Press, 1925. *The Columbia Granger's Index to Poetry.* 11th ed. *The Columbia Granger's World of Poetry,* Columbia University Press, 2005 (http://www.columbiagrangers.org). *The New Oxford Book of Seventeenth Century Verse.* Alastair Fowler, ed. Oxford University Press, 1991. *The Oxford Companion to English Literature.* 6th edition. Margaret Drabble, ed. Oxford University Press, 2000. *Treasury of Irish Religious Verse.* Patrick Murray, ed. Crossroad, 1986.

FLETCHER, GILES, and sons PHINEAS and GILES (?1549–1650)

Giles, the elder, ?1549–1611

His place of birth is disputed, but he was a native of Kent and was educated at Eton College and at King's College, Cambridge, where he studied civil law. He was created doctor of laws in 1581 and was member of Parliament for Winchelsea in 1585. He was employed on diplomatic service in Scotland, Germany, Holland, Russia and Denmark, and became a trusted servant of Queen Elizabeth. In 1591 he published *Of the Russe Common Wealth*, a comprehensive account of Russian geography, government, law, methods of warfare, church, and manners. He died in London and was buried there. The Sonnet cycle *Licia or Poems of Love* in 52 parts is available at http://members.aol.com/ericblomqu/fletcher.htm. Some of his poems: "Cruell Fayre Love, I Justly Do Complaine," "For If Alone Thou Thinke to Waft My Love," "If That I Dye (Fayre Lycia) with Disdaine," "Lyke Memnons Rocke Toucht, with the Rising Sunne," "My Griefe Begunne (Faire Saint) When First I Saw," "Sweet, I Protest, and Seale It with an Oath."

Phineas, 1582–1650

The elder son was born at Cranbrook, Kent, where his grandfather was rector. Like his father, he was educated at Eton College and at King's College, Cambridge, graduating M.A. in 1607–8. From 1616 to 1621 he was chaplain to Sir Henry Willoughby at Risley, Derbyshire, then rector of Hilgay, Norfolk, where he lived for the rest of his life. He antagonized some people with his attack on Roman Catholicism in *Locustæ vel Pietas Jesuitica: The Locusts or Apollyonists*, published in 1627. Some of his publications: *Sicelides*, 1614 (a pastoral play). *Brittain's Ida*, 1627. *The Way to Blessedness, a Treatise — on the First Psalm*, 1632. *Joy in Tribulation, a Consolation for Afflicted*

Spirits, 1632. *The Purple Island or the Isle of Man*, 1633 (an allegory of the human body). *Sylva Poetica Auctore P.F.*, 1633 (a collection of Latin poems and eclogues). *A Father's Testament*, 1670. Some of his poems: "Against a Rich Man Despising Poverty," "Piscatorie Eclogues," "The Divine Wooer," "To a Girl" (translation from Asclepiades), "To My Soul."

Giles, the younger, ?1588–1623

Believed to have been educated at Westminster School, he read classics at Trinity College, Cambridge, and graduated in 1606. After his ordination he held a college position and was known for his sermons at the Church of St. Mary the Great. Around 1618 he became rector of Alderton, Suffolk. Little else is known of his life, but the religious nature of his poetry and his use of imagery is said to have inspired John Milton's *Paradise Lost* (1667). He started writing poetry while at Cambridge, with "Canto upon the death of Eliza" (1603), published in a volume of academic verse. His major work, *Christ's Victorie and Triumph in Heaven and Earth over and after Death*, followed in 1610. He published a prose tract, *The Reward of the Faithfull: The Labour of the Faithfull: the Ground of Our Faith*, in 1623. Some of his other poems: "A Canto Upon the Death of Eliza," "A Description of Encolpius," "Christ's Triumph After Death," "Christ's Victory in Heaven," "Christ's Victory on Earth," "Upon the Most Lamented Departure of the Right Hopeful, and Blessed Prince Henry Prince of Wales."

Sources: *A Sacrifice of Praise: An Anthology of Christian Poetry in English from Caedmon to the Mid-Twentieth Century.* James H. Trott, ed. Cumberland House Publishing, 1999. *Dictionary of National Biography.* Electronic Edition 1.1. Oxford University Press, 1997. *Encyclopædia Britannica Ultimate Reference Suite DVD*, 2006. *English Poetry: Author Search.* Chadwyck-Healey Ltd., 1995 (http://www.lib.utexas.edu:8080/search/epoetry/author.html). *Giles and Phineas Fletcher: Poetical Works.* Frederick S. Boas, ed. (Cambridge: Cambridge University Press, 1908. *Jacobean and Caroline Poetry: An Anthology.* T.G.S. Cain, ed. Methuen, 1981. *Stanford University Libraries and Academic Information Resources* (http://library.stanford.edu). *The Columbia Granger's Index to Poetry.* 11th ed. *The Columbia Granger's World of Poetry,* Columbia University Press, 2005 (http://www.columbiagrangers.org). *The New Oxford Book of Seventeenth Century Verse.* Alastair Fowler, ed. Oxford University Press, 1991. *The New Oxford Book of Christian Verse.* Donald Davie, ed. Oxford University Press, 1981. *The Oxford Companion to English Literature.* 6th edition. Margaret Drabble, ed. Oxford University Press, 2000. *The Sonnet: An Anthology.* Robert M. Bender and Charles L. Squier, eds. Washington Square Press, 1987. *The World's Great Religious Poetry.* Caroline Miles Hill, ed. Macmillan, 1954.

FLETCHER, JOHN (1579–1625)

The nephew of Giles Fletcher, The Elder (see entry), he was born in Rye, Sussex, where his father was the vicar. He later became bishop of Bristol then of London, and was queen's chaplain at the trial and execution of Mary Queen of Scots in 1587. John was educated at Corpus Christi College, Cambridge. He died in the London plague that killed some 40,000 others and was buried at St. Saviour's, Southwark. He is best known as a dramatist and for his collaboration with Francis Beaumont and Philip Massinger (see entries). He began writing for the Shakespeare's King's Men when they moved to Blackfriars in 1610; when Shakespeare retired, Fletcher became the company's chief dramatist. Between 1609 and 1625 he wrote 21 plays and collaborated on as many more. The masterpieces of the Beaumont and Fletcher collaboration are *Philaster, The Maides Tragedy* and *A King and No King*. One of Fletcher's own best plays is *The Faithfull Shepheardesse*. Some of his poems: "Beggar's Bush," "Come Hither, You, That Love," "Fletcher's Lament for His Friend," "Take, Oh, Take Those Lips Away," "The Chances," "The Little French Lawyer," "The Mad Lover."

Sources: *Dictionary of National Biography*. Electronic Edition 1.1. Oxford University Press, 1997. *Encyclopædia Britannica Ultimate Reference Suite DVD*, 2006. *English Lyric Poems, 1500–1900*. C. Day Lewis, ed. Appleton-Century-Crofts, 1961. *Friendship Poems*. Peter Washington, ed. Alfred A. Knopf, 1995. *Poemhunter* (www.poemhunter.com). *The Columbia Granger's Index to Poetry*. 11th ed. *The Columbia Granger's World of Poetry*, Columbia University Press, 2005 (http://www.columbiagrangers.org). *The Gambit Book of Love Poems*. Geoffrey Grigson, ed. Gambit, 1973. *The Oxford Companion to English Literature*. 6th edition. Margaret Drabble, ed. Oxford University Press, 2000.

FLETCHER, ROBERT (fl. 1586)

He appears to have come from Warwickshire and graduated B.A. (1564) and M.A. (1567) from Merton College, Oxford. On account of some misdemeanor he was asked to leave and renounce his fellowship. He became a schoolmaster at Taunton, Somerset, and afterwards a preacher, though there is no record of his being ordained. He wrote many epigrams and short poems. His known publications: *An Introduction to the Looue of God* (shortened title), 1581. *The Song of Solomon*, 1586. *The Nine English Worthies* 1606 (from Henry I [1100–35] to Prince Henry [1594–1612], son of James I; a brief life of each monarch in prose is followed by an epitaph in verse, except in the last case, where the life is wholly in verse). Some of his poems: "A Sing-song on Clarinda's Wedding," "Degenerate Love and Choyce," "May Day," "The Engagement Stated," "The Model of the New Religion," "The Myrtle Grove," "Upon the Death of John Selden," "Some of His Epigrams: 24, in Candidum," "31, Ad Rufinum," "44, in Sextum," "60, De Curiatio," "75, in Lupercum," "78, in Uarum," "95, in Nævolum."

Sources: *Dictionary of National Biography*. Electronic Edition 1.1. Oxford University Press, 1997. See his poems and epigrams in *English Poetry: Author Search*. Chadwyck-Healey Ltd., 1995 (http://www.lib.utexas.edu:8080/search/epoetry/author.html).

FLOWER, ROBIN ERNEST WILLIAM (1881–1946)

Born in Leeds of Irish descent and educated at Leeds Grammar School, he entered Pembroke College, Oxford, as a classical scholar in 1900 and was appointed to the British Museum in the department of manuscripts in 1906. He studied Irish and worked in Ireland with the Norwegian philologist Professor Carl J.S. Marstrander, absorbing the Irish language and traditions. He completed the catalogue of Irish manuscripts, started by Standish Hayes O'Grady, for the British Museum in 1926; it was a work of the great importance. From 1939 he was in charge of the British Museum manuscripts at the National Library of Wales, Aberystwyth. He lectured in Celtic at University College, London, and at Yale and other American universities. He received the honorary degrees of D.Litt. Celt. from the National University of Ireland (1927), and D.Litt. from Dublin (1937). He was appointed commander of the British Empire in 1945. He died in London. Some of his publications: *The Islandman*, 1934 (a translation of Tomás Ó Crohan's autobiography). *The Western Island*, 1944. *The Irish Tradition*, 1947. Some of his poems: "Pangur Ban," "Say Not That Beauty," "Troy."

Sources: *Anglo-Saxonists — 20th Century* (http://www.u.arizona.edu/~ctb/20ef.html#rflower). *Dictionary of National Biography*. Electronic Edition 1.1. Oxford University Press, 1997. *Seven Centuries of Poetry: Chaucer to Dylan Thomas*. A.N. Jeffares, ed. Longmans, Green, 1955. *The Columbia Granger's Index to Poetry*. 11th ed. *The Columbia Granger's World of Poetry*, Columbia University Press, 2005 (http://www.columbiagrangers.org). *The Triumphant Cat*. Walter Payne, ed. Carrol and Graf, 1993.

FLYNN, LEONTIA (1974–)

Irish poet from Belfast, she has recently completed a Ph.D. at Queen's College, Belfast, on Medbh McGuckian (see entry). She was awarded an Eric Gregory Award in 2001, and her first collection, *These Days* (2004), was short listed for the Forward Prize Best First Collection. It also won the Felix Dennis Prize for Best First Collection in 2004; only two other female poets have won this category — Kate Clanchy (1996) and Jane Duran (1995). *These Days* also won the Whitbread Prize in 2004. The Poetry Book Society included her in the 'Next Generation' poets. Three of her poems: "Atlantic Avenue," "Leaving Belfast," "Mangles."

Sources: *Biography of Leontia Flynn, Results — enCom-*

pass Culture (http://www.encompassculture.com/results/ ?qs=Leontia%20Flynn). *British Council Arts* (http://www. contemporarywriters.com). *Next Generation Poets: Lancaster University News* (http://domino.lancs.ac.uk/info/ lunews.nsf/Tx/1219B3BD2A8CB66F80256EBA00374FB D). *The Review of Contemporary Poetry—Titles and Poets.* The Boho Press (http://www.bohopress.co.uk/detail. asp?seq=40). The Scottish Poetry Library (http://www. spl.org.uk/poets_a-z/flynn.html). Whitbread Prize Book Awards 2005 (http://www.lmsbooks.co.uk/Whitbread Prize.htm).

FORD, JOHN (?1586–1640)

Born in Ilsington, Devon, he was educated at Exeter College, Oxford, before studying law at the Middle Temple in 1602. He became one of England's major dramatists of the Caroline period, whose tragedies — some eighteen — are of a high order. Not much is know of him apart from his poems and dramas. He collaborated with Thomas Dekker (see entry) on the play *The Witch of Edmonton* (1621). There is evidence of some collaboration with other dramatists — Thomas Middleton, John Fletcher, and Francis Beaumont (see entries) and William Rowley. His own plays are concerned with the qualities of human nature such as dignity, courage and endurance under suffering, or a noble and virtuous heroine who is torn between her true love and an unhappy forced marriage. Some of his plays: *The Lover's Melancholy*, 1629. *Love's Sacrifice*, 1633. *'Tis Pity She's a Whore*, 1633. *The Broken Heart*, 1633. *Perkin Warbeck*, 1634. *The Lady's Trial*, 1639. Some of his poems: "Beauty's Beauty," "Can You Paint a Thought?" "Minutes are numbered by the fall of Sands," "Of This Ingenious Comedy."

Sources: *Biography of John Ford, and Links* (http:// www.bn23.com/portal/Arts/Literature/Drama/17th_ Century/Ford__John). *Dictionary of National Biography.* Electronic Edition 1.1. Oxford University Press, 1997. *Dictionary of National Biography.* Electronic Edition 1.1. Oxford University Press, 1997. *Encyclopædia Britannica Ultimate Reference Suite DVD, 2006. Poets of the English Language.* Vol. V. W.H. Auden and Norman Holmes Pearson, eds. Viking Press, 1950. *The Oxford Book of Death.* D.J. Enright, ed. Oxford University Press, 1987. *The Oxford Companion to English Literature.* 6th edition. Margaret Drabble, ed. Oxford University Press, 2000.

FORD, THOMAS (?1580–1648)

He was a court musician from 1611 to 1625; firstly to Henry, Prince of Wales (Henry was the first child of James VI of Scotland); then to Charles, as prince then as king. His most important work was *Musicke of Sundrie Kindes*, in two books (1607). The first contained eleven songs, some of them very well known. His love song "There is a Lady Sweet and Kind" is in the repertoire of almost every male ballad singer. The second book contained eighteen

pieces. An anthem in five parts, "Let God Arise," was printed in the Musical Antiquarian Society's publication for 1845. To Sir William Leighton's *Tears and Lamentacions of a Sorrowfull Soule* (1614) Ford contributed the anthems "Almighty God, Which Hast Me Brought" and "Not Unto Us." He contributed three sacred canons to John Hilton's *Catch That Catch Can* (1652): "I Am So Weary, O Lord," "I Lift My Heart to Thee," and "Look Down, O Lord." He was buried on the in St. Margaret's, Westminster. Some of his other poems: "Faire, Sweet Cruell," "Goe Passions to the Cruell Faire," "How Shall I Then Discribe My Loue," "Shut Not Sweet Brest."

Sources: *Dictionary of National Biography.* Electronic Edition 1.1. Oxford University Press, 1997. *English Poetry: Author Search.* Chadwyck-Healey Ltd., 1995 (http://www. lib.utexas.edu:8080/search/epoetry/author.html). *Here of a Sunday Morning, HOASM: Thomas Ford* (http://www. hoasm.org/IVM/Ford.html). *The Columbia Granger's Index to Poetry.* 11th ed. *The Columbia Granger's World of Poetry,* Columbia University Press, 2005 (http://www. columbiagrangers.org). *The New Oxford Book of Seventeenth Century Verse.* Alastair Fowler, ed. Oxford University Press, 1991.

FORREST, WILLIAM (fl. 1581)

A Catholic priest who was educated at Christ Church, Oxford, Forrest was present at the discussions held at Oxford in 1530 when Henry VIII desired to procure the judgment of the university in the matter of a divorce. He appears to have attended the funeral of Queen Catherine of Arragon at Peterborough in 1536. In 1551 he issued a paraphrased copy of some of the *Psalms.* Soon after Mary Tudor came to the throne in 1553, he wrote "A New Ballade of the Marigolde," a long poem on her accession, upon which she appointed him one of her chaplains. "Of his career after the death of his royal mistress nothing certain is known. He was probably protected by Thomas Howard, duke of Norfolk, to whom he dedicated his *History of Joseph* shortly before the duke's execution in 1572" (DNB). Some of his poems: "Te Deum, Lauding God Specially with Prayer Therin, for Our Quene Mary," "The Pater Noster to Gods Glory," "The Prologe to the Queenis Maiestee," "Theophilus," "To the Queenys Majestie."

Sources: *An Anthology of Catholic Poets.* Joyce Kilmer, ed. Fredonia Books, 2003. *Dictionary of National Biography.* Electronic Edition 1.1. Oxford University Press, 1997. *English Poetry: Author Search.* Chadwyck-Healey Ltd., 1995 (http://www.lib.utexas.edu:8080/search/epoetry/author. html). *The Columbia Granger's Index to Poetry.* 11th ed. *The Columbia Granger's World of Poetry,* Columbia University Press, 2005 (http://www.columbiagrangers.org). *The Common Muse, an Anthology of Popular British Ballad Poetry, XVth–XXth Century.* Vivian de Sola Pinto and Allan Edwin Rodway, eds. Philosophical Library, 1957.

FOWLER, WILLIAM (1560–1612)

This Scottish poet was the son of Thomas Fowler, executor to the Countess of Lennox, Arabella Stuart's grandmother. He was at one time pastor of Hawick, having been driven from France by the Jesuits. In 1581 (while living in Edinburgh) he published *An Answer to the Calumnious Letter and erroneous propositiouns of an apostat named M. Jo. Hammiltoun,* setting out his allegations of the errors of Roman Catholicism. He was a prominent burgess of Edinburgh and about 1590 became secretary to Queen Anne, the wife of James VI, whom he accompanied to England in 1603. Two of his sonnets, addressed to Arabella Stuart, were included in *Progresses of James I* by John Nichols (1828). In September 1609 a grant was made to him of two thousand acres in Ulster. Fowler's sister married John Drummond, first laird of Hawthornden, who was mother of William Drummond (see entry). Some of his poems: "Grieve not, faire flower of colour, sight, and scent," "If When I Die," "In Orkney," "Ship-broken Men Whom Stormy Seas Sore Toss," "The Tarantula of Love" (seventy-two sonnets in the Italian style), "The Triumphs of Petrarch" (translation).

Sources: *Dictionary of National Biography.* Electronic Edition 1.1. Oxford University Press, 1997. *Edgewood College, Wisconsin, An Anthology of Tudor and Elizabethan Poetry (Poets Born Before 1576)* (http://english.edgewood.edu/eng359/lyric_poetry.htm). *English Poetry: Author Search.* Chadwyck-Healey Ltd., 1995 (http://www.lib.utexas.edu:8080/search/epoetry/author.html). *The Columbia Granger's Index to Poetry.* 11th ed. *The Columbia Granger's World of Poetry,* Columbia University Press, 2005 (http://www.columbiagrangers.org). *The Scottish Collection of Verse to 1800.* Eileen Dunlop and Kamm Antony, eds. Richard Drew, 1985.

FRANCIS, MATTHEW (1956–)

Born in Gosport, Hampshire, he was educated at the City of London School and graduated B.A. and M.A. from Magdalene College, Cambridge University. From 1994 he studied the work of William Sydney Graham (see entry) at Southampton University and gained his Ph.D. in English in 1998. He received a Hawthornden Fellowship in 1998. In 1999 he moved to Cardiff to take up a post as lecturer in creative writing at the University of Glamorgan. He is now reader in creative writing at the University of Aberystwyth and teaches creative writing at undergraduate, M.A. and Ph.D. levels. His poem "The Ornamental Hermit" won the 2000 TLS/Blackwell's Prize. "City Autumn" won the national Gathering Swallows prize for the best poem by a published poet in response to John Keats' "To Autumn." He edited *New Collected Poems of W S Graham* in 2005. Some of his other poetry publications: *Blizzard,* 1996. *Dragons,* 2001. *Whereabouts,* 2005. Some of his other poems: "Interior Designers in the Forest," "Margin," "Museum of the Forest," "Nest of Devils," "Surface."

Sources: *Aberystwyth University,* Department of English (http://www.aber.ac.uk/english/staffinfo/mwf.html). *Biography and Works of Matthew Francis* (http://www.7greenhill.freeserve.co.uk/). *Biography of Matthew Francis, Poetry Book Society* (http://www.poetrybooks.co.uk/PBS/pbs_francis_matthew.asp). *Links to Poets* (http://www.pmpoetry.com/linkspb.shtml). Personal correspondence.

FRANKAU, GILBERT (1884–1952)

Born in London the son of a wholesale cigar merchant, his mother was a successful novelist, writing under the pen name of 'Frank Danby.' Although both his parents were Jewish, he was discouraged from identifying with Jews and Judaism and was baptized into the Anglican Church at the age of thirteen. He was educated at Eton College, then chose to work in the family business. He was commissioned into the 9th Battalion of the East Surrey Regiment in 1914. Later, in the Royal Field Artillery, he saw service at Loos, Ypres, and the Somme, and was released in February 1918, suffering from 'shell shock.' He wrote many novels, as well as popular fiction and short stories and an autobiography. Some of his novels were made into films; one was *Christopher Strong* (1933) starring Katharine Hepburn. He died at his home at Hove, Sussex. Some of his poetry publications: *Eton Echoes,* 1901. *The Guns,* 1916. *The City of Fear,* 1917. *The Judgement of Valhalla,* 1918. Some of his poems: "Ammunition Column," "Eyes in the Air," "Gun Teams," "Headquarters," "Signals," "The Deserter," "The Observers," "The Voice of the Slaves."

Sources: *Dictionary of National Biography.* Electronic Edition 1.1. Oxford University Press, 1997. *Lives of War Poets of the First World War* (http://www.warpoetry.co.uk/biogs99.htm#GILBERT). *Peace and War: A Collection of Poems.* Michael Harrison and Christopher Stuart-Clark, eds. Oxford University Press, 1989. *The Columbia Granger's Index to Poetry.* 11th ed. *The Columbia Granger's World of Poetry,* Columbia University Press, 2005 (http://www.columbiagrangers.org). *The Guns.* Gilbert Frankau. Chatto and Windus, 1916. *The Literary Encyclopedia* (www.LitEncyc.com). *The National Portrait Gallery* (www.npg.org.uk).

FRASER, GEORGE SUTHERLAND (1915–1980)

He was born in Glasgow but moved to Aberdeen when his father became town clerk. He was educated at Aberdeen grammar school and graduated in English and history from St. Andrews University in 1937. During the war he worked as a journalist at the public relations directorate in Cairo, then as editor in charge of the *Eritrean Daily News.* After the war he worked in London, scraping a living from articles in the *Times Literary Supplement, New States-man* and broadcasts on poetry for the BBC *Third Program*. In 1950 he became cultural adviser to the British Embassy in Japan and went there with his wife and daughter, a son being born not long after their arrival. He suffered a breakdown in health and the family returned to England. He was appointed in 1958 as a lecturer in English literature at Leicester University. He wrote several well-received books of literary criticism. Some of his poems: "A Bought Embrace," "Ballata II: Last Song: from Exile," "Christmas Letter Home," "Crises," "Home Town Elegy," "Lament," "Lean Street," "The Song of the Dogs," "The Traveller Has Regrets," "To a Scottish Poet."

Sources: *List of Reading University Library Special Collections* (http://www.library.rdg.ac.uk/colls/special/collsindex.html#f). *Poems from Italy.* William Jay Smith and Dana Gioia, eds. New Rivers, 1985. *The Columbia Granger's Index to Poetry.* 11th ed. *The Columbia Granger's World of Poetry,* Columbia University Press, 2005 (http://www.columbiagrangers.org). *The Oxford Book of Twentieth-Century English Verse.* Philip Larkin, ed. Oxford University Press, 1973. *The Oxford Companion to English Literature.* 6th edition. Margaret Drabble, ed. Oxford University Press, 2000. *The War Poets: An Anthology of the War Poetry of the 20th Century.* Oscar Williams, ed. John Day, 1945.

FRAUNCE, ABRAHAM (fl. 1587–1633)

Born in Shropshire, he was educated at Shrewsbury School. Sir Philip Sidney, a former pupil at Shrewsbury, sent him to St. John's College, Cambridge, from where he graduated M.A. in 1583. He was called to the bar at Gray's Inn and practiced in Wales. When Sidney died in 1586, Sidney's sister Mary, countess of Pembroke, took Fraunce under her patronage and to her he dedicated several of his works. He entered the service of John Egerton, first earl of Bridgewater, who became president of the council of Wales in 1631. Fraunce's earliest published work was the translation of Thomas Watson's (see entry) *Amyntas* (1585), which he entitled *The Lamentations of Amintas*; it is in the form of eleven eclogues, each called a "day." He contributed to Allot's *English Parnassus* (1600) and five songs at the close of Sir Philip Sidney's *Astrophel and Stella* (1591). His other major publications: *Victoria,* 1579, (a Latin comedy. *The Arcadian Rhetorike,* 1588. *The Lawiers Logike,* 1588. *The Countesse of Pembrokes Emanuel,* 1591. *The Countesse of Pembrokes Yuychurch,* 1591. *The Third part of the Countesse of Pembrokes Yuychurch,* 1592.

Sources: *Dictionary of National Biography.* Electronic Edition 1.1. Oxford University Press, 1997. *Encyclopædia Britannica Ultimate Reference Suite DVD,* 2006. *English Poetry: Author Search.* Chadwyck-Healey Ltd., 1995

(http://www.lib.utexas.edu:8080/search/epoetry/author.html). *Great Books Online* (www.bartleby.com). *Stanford University Libraries and Academic Information Resources* (http://library.stanford.edu). *The Oxford Companion to English Literature.* 6th edition. Margaret Drabble, ed. Oxford University Press, 2000. *Wikipedia, the Free Encyclopedia.* (http://en.wikipedia.org/wiki/Wikipedia).

FREEMAN, JOHN (1880–1929)

Born at Dalston, Middlesex, he suffered from ill health through the effects on the heart of scarlet fever at the age of three. At thirteen he started work as a clerk in the head office of the Liverpool Victoria Friendly Society and by the age of thirty-four he was chief executive of a multi-million dollar corporation. He was a critic for the *New Statesman* and the *London Mercury*. Among his earliest literary friends was Walter de la Mare (see entry). He wrote two dramas: *Prince Absalom* (1925) and *Solomon and Balkis* (1926), and several novels. He was awarded the Hawthornden prize in 1920. He died at Anerley, London, and was buried in the churchyard at Thursley, Surrey. Freeman is best known for his poems of nature, about which he was passionate. Some of his publications: *Twenty Poems,* 1909. *Fifty Poems,* 1911. *Memories of Childhood,* 1919. *Poems New and Old,* 1920. *Music,* 1921. *The Grove,* 1924. *Collected Poems* 1928. *Last Poems,* 1930. Some of his poems: "A Visit to Thomas Hardy," "English Hills," "The Grove," "The Pigeons," "The Stars in their Courses."

Sources: *101 Patriotic Poems.* Contemporary Books, 1986. *Collected Poems by John Freeman.* MacMillan and Co., 1928. *Dictionary of National Biography.* Electronic Edition 1.1. Oxford University Press, 1997. *The Columbia Granger's Index to Poetry.* 11th ed. *The Columbia Granger's World of Poetry,* Columbia University Press, 2005 (http://www.columbiagrangers.org). *The National Portrait Gallery* (www.npg.org.uk).

FREETH, JOHN (1731–1808)

Known as the "Birmingham poet," by trade he was an innkeeper, as well as political ballad writer. He earned the reputation of being one of the best political ballad writers in the kingdom. Nothing is known of his education or his early years, although he was probably an itinerant street singer. The Leicester Arms, Birmingham, or "Freeth's Coffee House," of which he was landlord from 1768 until his death, became renowned for entertainment. To draw attention to the hospitality he provided, Freeth issued printed invitation cards written in verse. He performed his own songs, written to popular tunes about local and national events, affairs of state and often of a radical nature; others were complimentary, jocular, and satirical. The words of nearly 400 songs appeared in several collections between 1766 and 1805. The most substantial of these collections is his *The Political Songster: Touch on the Times* (1790). Some of his poems: "Botany Bay," "Bunker's Hill, or the Soldier's Lamentation," "Cottager's Complaint," "Marble Playing," "On the Petitions for the Abolition of the Slave Trade," "The Colliers' March," "The New Navigation," "The Paviers."

Sources: *Dictionary of National Biography.* Electronic Edition 1.1. Oxford University Press, 1997. *Frontispiece of the Political Songster* (www.search.revolutionaryplayers. org.uk/). *Dictionary of National Biography.* Electronic Edition 1.1. Oxford University Press, 1997. *The New Oxford Book of Eighteenth Century Verse.* Roger Lonsdale, ed. Oxford University Press, 2003. *The Oxford Book of English Traditional Verse.* Frederick Woods, ed. Oxford University Press, 1983.

FRENCH, WILLIAM PERCY (1854–1920)

Born near Roscommon, Ireland, he graduated with a degree in civil engineering from Trinity College, Dublin, then worked on a government drainage scheme in County Cavan. At university he developed his remarkable talents for song writing, dramatics, banjo playing and watercolor painting. Through the medium of the Dublin comic weekly, *The Jarvey,* of which he was editor for two years, he promoted a series of concerts throughout Ireland under the name of "The Jarvey Concert Company." In 1891 he went into partnership with Houston Collisson, who wrote much of the music for the operas they produced, including "The Irish Girl." In 1900 he moved to London, where he became known as Percy French. They toured Canada, the USA and the West Indies in 1910, and the ski resorts of Switzerland, and visited Ireland every year. While performing in Glasgow in 1920 he was taken ill and died some days later in Formby, Lancashire. Some of his songs: "Abdul Abulbul Amir," "Come Back Paddy Reilly," "Mulligan's Masquerade," "Phil the Fluther's Ball," "The Emigrant's Letter," "The Mountains of Mourne," "The Oklahoma Rose," "When Erin Wakes."

Sources: *Boosey & Hawkes Opera* (http://www.boosey. com/pages/opera/moreDetails.asp?musicID=7494). *Biography of Percy French* (http://users2.evl.net/~smyth/liner notes/personel/FrenchPercy.htm), and at (http://www. pdevlinz.btinternet.co.uk/percyfrench.htm). *Oldpoetry* (www.oldpoetry.com). *The Columbia Granger's Index to Poetry.* 11th ed. *The Columbia Granger's World of Poetry,* Columbia University Press, 2005 (http://www.columbia-grangers.org). *The Contemplator's Very Short Biography of Percy French* (http://www.contemplator.com/history/pfrench.html). *The Copper Family, Coppersongs: The Irish Girl* (http://www.thecopperfamily.com/songs/copper songs/irish.html). *Wikipedia, the Free Encyclopedia* (http:// en.wikipedia.org/wiki/Wikipedia).

FULLER, ROY BROADBENT, and JOHN LEOPOLD (1912–)

Roy, the father, 1912–1991

Born in Lancashire, the son of a businessman, he was educated at Blackpool High School. From 1934 to 1969, with service in the Royal Navy from 1941 to 1945, he worked as a solicitor for the Woolwich Equitable Building Society. He was professor of poetry at Oxford University from 1968 to 1973; *Owls and Artificers* (1971) and *Professors and Gods* (1973) are collections of his Oxford lectures on poetry. He was made a commander of the Order of the British Empire in 1970. He wrote several novels, including *Image of a Society* (1956), as well as crime thrillers and juvenile fiction. His memoirs were published in four volumes from 1980 to 1991. Some of his publications: *Poems,* 1939. *Collected Poems,* 1962. *New poems,* 1968. *Off Course: Poems,* 1969. *An Ill-Governed Coast: Poems,* 1976. *The Individual and His Times: A Selection of the Poetry of Roy Fuller,* 1982. *New and Collected Poems,* 1934–1984, 1985. Some of his poems: "ABC of a Naval Trainee," "Autobiography of a Lungworm," "Autumn 1942," "Ghost Voice," "Mythological Sonnets," "The Cancer Hospital."

John Leopold, the son, 1937–

Born in Ashford, Kent, he was educated at New College, Oxford, where he won the Newdigate Prize in 1960 for his poem "A Dialogue Between Caliban and Ariel." He was visiting lecturer in English at the State University of New York at Buffalo (1962, 1963); assistant lecturer at Manchester University 1963–1966; and fellow and tutor at Magdalen College, Oxford, 1966–2002, where he is now emeritus professor. He has written many novels and stories for children. He collaborated with James Fenton (see entry) in writing *Partingtime Hall* (1987), a collection of satirical poems. His poetry collection *Epistles to Several Persons* won the Geoffrey Faber Memorial Prize in 1974; *The Illusionists* won Southern Arts Literature Prize in 1980; *Stones and Fires* won the Forward Poetry Prize, Best Poetry Collection of the Year, in 1996. He is a fellow of the Royal Society of Literature. Some of his poems: "Alex at the Barber's," "Band Music," "Concerto for Double Bass," "Creatures," "Fox-Trot," "God Bless America," "The Butterfly," "The Red Light District Nurse," "Valentine," "Wasp Nest."

Sources: *British Poetry Since 1945.* Edward Lucie-Smith, ed. Penguin Books, 1985. *Biography and Works of John Fuller* (http://www.contemporarywriters.com/authors/ ?p=auth182). *Encyclopædia Britannica Ultimate Reference Suite DVD,* 2006. *New Poets of England and America.* Donald Hall, and Robert Pack, ed. World, 1962. *Peace and War: A Collection of Poems.* Michael Harrison, and Christopher

Stuart-Clark, ed. Oxford University Press, 1989. *The Antaeus Anthology.* Daniel Halpern, ed. Bantam Books, 1986. *The Columbia Granger's Index to Poetry.* 11th ed. *The Columbia Granger's World of Poetry,* Columbia University Press, 2005 (http://www.columbiagrangers.org). *The National Portrait Gallery* (www.npg.org.uk). *The Oxford Book of Death.* D.J. Enright, ed. Oxford University Press, 1987. *The Oxford Companion to English Literature.* 6th edition. Margaret Drabble, ed. Oxford University Press, 2000. *The Penguin Book of Light Verse.* Gavin Ewart, ed. Penguin Books, 1980. *The Sonnet: An Anthology.* Robert M. Bender and Charles L. Squier, ed. Washington Square Press, 1987. *Who's Who.* London: A & C Black, 2005.

FURNESS, RICHARD (1791–1857)

The son of a small farmer, from Eyam, Derbyshire, the famous "plague village," he became an apprenticed leather worker at Chesterfield, Derbyshire. He turned out to be proficient in mathematics, French, music, and poetry, and became a Wesleyan Methodist local preacher. In 1812, he walked to London to enlist as a volunteer soldier and was invited to preach at the City Road Chapel. He left the Methodists, who criticized him for writing a patriotic song that was sung at a meeting in a public house. In 1821 he moved to the small village of Dore, Derbyshire, where it is recorded he wrote letters for people, calculated their taxes, pulled their teeth, educated their children, and represented the village on parish business. He was buried in Eyam Churchyard. Many of his miscellaneous poems were printed in the *Sheffield Iris,* and his *Poetical Works,* with a sketch of his life by Dr. G. Calvert Holland, was published in 1858. He left behind him the words of an Oratorio entitled *The Millennium.* Some of his poems: "Medicus-Magus," "Old Year's Funeral," "Rag Bag," "Sheffield," "To Anna in Heaven, from Her Father."

Sources: *Dictionary of National Biography.* Electronic Edition 1.1. Oxford University Press, 1997. *Eyam, Derbyshire, England, "The Plague Village."* (http://www.cressbrook.co.uk/eyam). Genuki: The History and Antiquities of Eyam, Derbyshire (http://www.genuki.org.uk/big/eng/DBY/Eyam/Wood/Minstrels.html). *The Columbia Granger's Index to Poetry.* 11th ed. *The Columbia Granger's World of Poetry,* Columbia University Press, 2005 (http://www.columbiagrangers.org).

GALVIN, PATRICK (1927–)

Galvin was born in Cork, though there is some doubt about his exact date of birth. Apparently his mother changed the date on his birth certificate so he could more easily find work. His early education was by the Christian Brothers and three years in prison in a reformatory outside Cork. His plays have been produced in Dublin, Belfast and London, and he lectured on Irish folk music, including in Eastern Germany. In the 1970s, through a Leverhulme Fellowship in Drama, many of his plays were staged at the Lyric Players Theatre in Belfast. His three-part autobiography *The Raggy Boy Trilogy* was published in 2002. *Song for a Raggy Boy* (part of the trilogy) was filmed in 2003, starring Aidan Quinn. He wrote *Irish Songs of Resistance: 1169–1923* (1962) and has recorded several collections of Irish ballads. Although he worked mainly with the ballad tradition, his poetry portrays his left-wing politics. Some of his poems: "My Father Spoke with Swans," "Plaisir d'Amour," "The Death of Art O'Leary," "The Madwoman of Cork," "Your Grave Disfigures Me."

Sources: *Bitter Harvest: An Anthology of Contemporary Irish Verse.* John Montague, ed. Scribner's, 1989. *Biography of Patrick Galvin* (http://www.irishwriters-online.com/patrickgalvin.html). *Patrick Galvin: An Inventory of His Papers at the Burns Library, Boston College, Massachusetts* (http://www.bc.edu/bc_org/avp/ulib/Burns/galvinb.html). *The Columbia Granger's Index to Poetry.* 11th ed. *The Columbia Granger's World of Poetry,* Columbia University Press, 2005 (http://www.columbiagrangers.org). *Wikipedia, the Free Encyclopedia* (http://en.wikipedia.org/wiki/Wikipedia).

GARIOCH, ROBERT (1909–1987)

Robert Garioch, born in Edinburgh, was educated at the Royal High School and Edinburgh University. His book *Two Men and a Blanket: Memoirs of Captivity* (1975) recount his wartime experiences of being a prisoner of war from 1942 to 1945. He taught in schools in London, Kent and Edinburgh, retired from teaching in 1964, then worked as lexicographer and transcriber in the School of Scottish Studies at Edinburgh University, where he held a writer's fellowship. He not only wrote in Scots, he translated from the French, Greek, and Latin, and translated 120 sonnets of Guiseppe Belli, a Roman poet of the nineteenth century. Some of his other publications: *17 poems for 6d,* 1940, with Sorley Maclean (see entry). *Chuckies on a Cairn,* 1949. *Jephthah,* 1959 *Poetical Works,* 1983. Some of his poems: "And They Were Richt," "At Robert Fergusson's Grave, October 1962," "Did Ye See Me?" "Heard in the Cougate," "In Princes Street Gairdens," "On Seein an Aik-Tree Sprent Wi Galls," "The Canny Hen,'" "The Anatomy of Winter" (translation from Hesiod).

Sources: *A Book of Scottish Verse.* Maurice Lindsay, and R.L. Mackie, ed. St. Martin's Press, 1983. *Biography of Robert Garioch* (http://www.nls.uk/writestuff/heads/wee-garioch.html). *Learning Journeys* (www.bbc.co.uk/scotland/arts/writingscotland/). *Scottish Authors* (http://www.slainte.org.uk/Scotauth/gariodsw.htm). *The Columbia Granger's Index to Poetry.* 11th ed. *The Columbia Granger's World of Poetry,* Columbia University Press, 2005 (http://www.columbiagrangers.org). *The Faber Book of War*

Poetry. Kenneth Baker, ed. Faber and Faber, 1996. *The Oxford Book of Comic Verse.* John Gross, ed. Oxford University Press, 1994. *The Oxford Companion to English Literature.* 6th edition. Margaret Drabble, ed. Oxford University Press, 2000.

GARNETT, RICHARD (1835–1906)

Soon after his birth, at Lichfield, Staffordshire, his father became assistant keeper of printed books at the British Museum in London. At the age of sixteen Richard became an assistant in the library of the British Museum, and eventually became chief keeper of the museum. He received an honorary LL.D. degree from Edinburgh in 1833 and was made commander of the Bath in 1895. His literary works include numerous translations from the Greek, German, Italian, Spanish, and Portuguese; several books of verse; the book of short stories *The Twilight of the Gods* (1888); biographies of Carlyle, Milton, Blake, and others; *The Age of Dryden* (1895); a *History of Italian Literature*; and many articles for encyclopedias and the *Dictionary of National Biography.* Some of his other publications: *Primula, a Book of Lyrics,* 1858. *Poems From the German,* 1862. *Idylls and Epigrams, Chiefly From the Greek Anthology,* 1869. *Iphigenia in Delphi,* 1891. *One Hundred and Twenty-four Sonnets from Dante, Petrarch, and Camoens,* 1896. *The Queen and Other Poems,* 1901. Some of his poems: "Bismarck and Moltke," "Io in Egypt," "Memorial Verses," "On Revisiting Lichfield Cathedral," "To America."

Sources: *Dictionary of National Biography.* Electronic Edition 1.1. Oxford University Press, 1997. *Encyclopædia Britannica Ultimate Reference Suite DVD,* 2006. *English Poetry: Author Search.* Chadwyck-Healey Ltd., 1995 (http://www.lib.utexas.edu:8080/search/epoetry/author.html). *Poems of Richard Garnett.* Elkin Mathews and John Lane, 1893. *The Columbia Granger's Index to Poetry.* 11th ed. *The Columbia Granger's World of Poetry,* Columbia University Press, 2005 (http://www.columbiagrangers.org). *The Home Book of Modern Verse.* Burton Egbert Stevenson, ed. Henry Holt, 1953. *The National Portrait Gallery* (www.npg.org.uk). *The Oxford Companion to English Literature.* 6th edition. Margaret Drabble, ed. Oxford University Press, 2000. *Wikipedia, the Free Encyclopedia* (http://en.wikipedia.org/wiki/Wikipedia).

GARTH, SIR SAMUEL (1661–1719)

The "dispensary poet" was born and educated in the West Riding of Yorkshire. He studied at Peterhouse, Cambridge, and at Leyden in the Netherlands, qualifying as doctor in 1691. He settled in London and was elected a fellow of the College of Physicians in 1693. His "The Dispensary, a Poem"—published in 1699, and which reached a tenth edition in 1741—describes the efforts to establish a dispensary where poor people could obtain advice and prescriptions from the best physicians. He was knighted (with the sword of Marlborough) by King George I on his accession and became physician in ordinary to the king and physician-general to the army. Some of his poems are included in Dryden's collections. He had a lucrative practice. He died after a brief illness and was buried beside his wife at Harrow. Some of his poems: "Claremont," "Death," "Designed for Tamerlane," "On Her Majesty's Statue," "On the King of Spain," "On the New Conspiracy, 1716," "To the Duke of Marlborough," "To the Lady Louisa Lenox," "To the Music-Meeting."

Sources: *Dictionary of National Biography.* Electronic Edition 1.1. Oxford University Press, 1997. *English Poetry: Author Search.* Chadwyck-Healey Ltd., 1995 (http://www.lib.utexas.edu:8080/search/epoetry/author.html). *The Columbia Granger's Index to Poetry.* 11th ed. *The Columbia Granger's World of Poetry,* Columbia University Press, 2005 (http://www.columbiagrangers.org). *The National Portrait Gallery* (www.npg.org.uk). *The Works of the British Poets V. 9 (Dryden and Garth).* J. Sharpe, 1808.

GASCOIGNE, GEORGE (?1525–1577)

The dates of his birth and death are uncertain; those given here are from the DNB. He came from a Bedfordshire family and was educated at Trinity College, Cambridge, but left without a degree. He became a lawyer at Gray's Inn in 1555 and spent some time in debtors' prison in 1570. He fought in the army in the Netherlands from 1572 to 1574 and was repatriated as a prisoner of war. In his time as court poet he wrote the play *Supposes,* presented before Queen Elizabeth at Kenilworth castle in 1575. His *Jocasta* (performed in 1566) was the first Greek tragedy to be presented on the English stage. His *Complete Works* appeared in two volumes in *Cambridge English Classics,* 1907–1908, edited by Prof. J.W. Cunliffe. He died at Bernack, near Stamford, Lincolnshire. Some of his other publications: *A Hundreth Sundrie Flowres,* 1573. *The Posies of George Gascoigne,* 1575. *The Steele Glas* 1576 (a satire). Some of his poems: "A Sonet Written in Prayse of the Browne Beautie," "De Profundis," "The Greene Knights Farewell to Fansie," "This Vaine Availe Which Thou By Mars Hast Woonne."

Sources: *Chapters into Verse. Vol. I: Genesis to Malachi.* Robert Atwan and Laurance Wieder, eds. Oxford University Press. 1993. *Dictionary of National Biography.* Electronic Edition 1.1. Oxford University Press, 1997. *Encyclopædia Britannica Ultimate Reference Suite DVD,* 2006. *English Poetry: Author Search.* Chadwyck-Healey Ltd., 1995 (http://www.lib.utexas.edu:8080/search/epoetry/author.html). *English Renaissance Poetry: A Collection of Shorter Poems from Skelton to Jonson.* John Williams, ed. University of Arkansas, 1990. *Life and Work of George Gascoigne* (http://www.luminarium.org/renlit/gascoigne.htm). *The Columbia Granger's Index to Poetry.* 11th ed. *The Columbia*

Granger's World of Poetry, Columbia University Press, 2005 (http://www.columbiagrangers.org). *The Oxford Book of War Poetry.* Jon Stallworthy, Oxford University Press, 1984. *The Oxford Companion to English Literature.* 6th edition. Margaret Drabble, ed. Oxford University Press, 2000.

GASCOYNE, DAVID EMERY (1916–2001)

Born in Harrow, Middlesex, he was educated at Salisbury Cathedral School and the Regent Street Polytechnic, London. His first collection of poetry, *Roman Balcony and Other Poems,* was published in 1932. He quickly established himself as a leading surrealist and was one of the organizers of the London International Surrealist Exhibition in 1936. He lived in France from 1937 to 1939, 1947 to 1948 and 1953 to 1964. He was a respected translator of Johann Christian Friedrich Hölderlin (1770–1843) and of the leading French surrealists. In 1996 he was made a *Chevalier dans l'Ordre des Arts et Lettres* by the French Ministry of Culture for his lifelong services to French literature. Some of his other publications: *A Short Survey of Surrealism,* 1935. *Man's Life is This Meat,* 1936. *Hoelderlin's Madness,* 1938. *Poems 1937–1942,* 1943. *A Vagrant and Other Poems,* 1950. *Night Thoughts,* 1956. *Collected Poems,* 1965. Some of his poems: "An Autumn Park," "And the Seventh Dream is the Dream of Isis," "De Profundis," "Miserere Salvador Dali," "The Cage," "The Uncertain Battle," "The Writer's Hand," "Tinian" (translation from Hölderlin).

Sources: *David Gascoyne's Home Page* (http://www.connectotel.com/gascoyne/index.html). *Encyclopædia Britannica Ultimate Reference Suite DVD,* 2006. *Poemhunter* (www.poemhunter.com). *Poetry of the World Wars.* Michael Foss, ed. Peter Bedrick Books, 1990. *Surrealist Poetry in English.* Edward B. Germain, ed. Penguin Books, 1978. *The Columbia Granger's Index to Poetry.* 11th ed. *The Columbia Granger's World of Poetry,* Columbia University Press, 2005 (http://www.columbiagrangers.org). *The National Portrait Gallery* (www.npg.org.uk). *The New British Poetry, 1968–88.* Gillian Allnutt, Fred D'Aguiar and Ken Edwards, eds. Grafton Books, 1989. *The Oxford Companion to English Literature.* 6th edition. Margaret Drabble, ed. Oxford University Press, 2000.

GAY, JOHN (1685–1732)

Born in Barnstaple, Devon, he lived most of is life in London. He was secretary to the Duchess of Monmouth and to Lord Clarendon, envoy to the court of Hanover. Although chiefly remembered as the author of *The Beggar's Opera* (1728) (which ran for 62 performances, not consecutively), he wrote many other dramas and poems. He lost most of his money through disastrous investment in the South Sea Bubble investment scheme. He was buried in Poets' Corner of Westminster Abbey. Some of his other publications: *Wine,* 1708 (a burlesque). *The Present State of Wit,* 1711 (a survey of contemporary periodical publications). *The Shepherd's Week,* 1711 (mock classical poems). *Rural Sports,* 1713. *Trivia: or, The Art of Walking the Streets of London,* 1716. *Three Hours After Marriage,* 1717. *Collected Poems,* 1720. *The Captives,* 1724. *Fables,* 1727. Some of his poems: "Poems From Gay's Chair," "Sweet William's Farewell to Black-ey'd Susan," "The Birth of the Squire; an Eclogue," "The Tea-Table, a Town Eclogue," "The Story of Arachne," "The Story of Cephisa," "Thought on Eternity."

Sources: *Dictionary of National Biography.* Electronic Edition, 1.1. *Encyclopædia Britannica.* Electronic Edition, 2005. *English Poetry: Author Search.* Chadwyck-Healey Ltd., 1995 (http://www.lib.utexas.edu:8080/search/epoetry/author.html). *Fellow Mortals: An Anthology of Animal Verse.* Roy Fuller, ed. Macdonald and Evans, 1981. *The Columbia Granger's Index to Poetry.* 11th ed. *The Columbia Granger's World of Poetry,* Columbia University Press, 2005 (http://www.columbiagrangers.org). *The Harper Anthology of Poetry.* John Frederick Nims, ed. Harper and Row, 1981. *The National Portrait Gallery* (www.npg.org.uk). *The Oxford Companion to English Literature.* 6th edition. Margaret Drabble, ed. Oxford University Press, 2000. *The Poetical Works of John Gay.* G.C. Faber, ed. Russell and Russell, 1926. *Westminster Abbey Official Guide* (no date).

GIBSON, WILFRID WILSON (1878–1962)

Born in Hexham, Northumberland, son of a chemist and amateur archaeologist. His half-sister, Elizabeth Cheyne Gibson, encouraged him to write poetry. In 1907 he published "The Stonefolds" and "On the Threshold," poems that in plain speech told of country folk in everyday life. Around 1912, he was associated with many of the Georgian poets of his day in London, including (Sir) Edward Marsh, who became his patron. Gibson contributed to Marsh's five volumes of *Georgian Poetry* (1912–22). His friendship with Rupert Brooke resulted his being made one of three benefactors of Brooke's will, which included the lucrative proceeds of his poems. He died at Weybridge in Surrey and was memorialized by a stone in Poets' Corner of Westminster Abbey along with other poets of the First World War. Some of his other publications: *Daily Bread,* 1910. *Fires,* 1912. *Borderlands,* 1914. *Livelihood,* 1917. *Krindlesyke,* 1922. *Kestrel Edge,* 1924. *Coming and Going,* 1938. *The Outpost,* 1944. *Within Four Walls,* 1950. Some of his poems: "Ambulance Train," "As Trout in the Amber Cool," "Breakfast," "Eagles and Isles," "Skye," "The Edinburgh Sisters," "Troopship: Mid-Atlantic."

Sources: *Dictionary of National Biography.* Electronic Edition 1.1. Oxford University Press, 1997. *Encyclopædia Britannica Ultimate Reference Suite DVD,* 2006. *Never Such Innocence: A New Anthology of Great War Verse.* Martin

Stephen, ed. Buchan and Enright, 1988. *The Columbia Granger's Index to Poetry.* 11th ed. *The Columbia Granger's World of Poetry,* Columbia University Press, 2005 (http://www.columbiagrangers.org). *The Golden Room: Poems, 1925–1927 of Wilfrid Gibson.* Macmillan and Co., Limited, 1928. *The Home Book of Modern Verse.* Burton Egbert Stevenson, ed. Henry Holt, 1953. *The Oxford Companion to English Literature.* 6th edition. Margaret Drabble, ed. Oxford University Press, 2000. *Westminster Abbey Official Guide* (no date).

GIFFORD, WILLIAM (1756–1826)

Born in Ashburton, Devon, the son of a glazier of South Molton, he became classical scholar and satirical poet. Orphaned at the age of twelve, he was sent to sea, then apprenticed to a shoemaker. William Cookesley, a surgeon who was impressed with Gifford's poetic potential, with the help of local residents bought out the remainder of the indentures and sent him to school, then to Exeter College, Oxford, from where he graduated in 1782. He became tutor to Lord Grosvenor's son and took up his previous task of translating *Juvenal,* which was published in 1802. A second edition of his *Juvenal* appeared in 1817, followed by a translation of *Persius* in 1821. Around 1798 he brought out his paper, *The Anti-Jacobin Review,* which he continued to edit until 1824. From 1809 to 1824 he was also editor of *The Quarterly Review,* founded by London publisher John Murray to combat the liberalism of *The Edinburgh Review.* A collection of "beauties" from Gifford's prose and verse, edited by A. Howard, came out in 1834. Some of his other publications: *Baviad,* 1794. *Mæviad,* 1795. *Epistle to Peter Pindar,* 1800.

Sources: *Dictionary of National Biography.* Electronic Edition 1.1. Oxford University Press, 1997. *Encyclopædia Britannica Ultimate Reference Suite DVD,* 2006. *English Poetry: Author Search.* Chadwyck-Healey Ltd., 1995 (http://www.lib.utexas.edu:8080/search/epoetry/author.html). *The Columbia Granger's Index to Poetry.* 11th ed. *The Columbia Granger's World of Poetry,* Columbia University Press, 2005 (http://www.columbiagrangers.org). *The National Portrait Gallery* (www.npg.org.uk). *The New Oxford Book of Romantic Period Verse.* Jerome J. McGann. Oxford University Press, 1993. *The Oxford Book of Verse in English Translation.* Charles Tomlinson, ed. Oxford University Press, 1980. *The Oxford Companion to English Literature.* 6th edition. Margaret Drabble, ed. Oxford University Press, 2000.

GILBERT, SIR WILLIAM SCHWENCK (1836–1911)

Born in London, the son of the novelist William Gilbert, he was educated at King's College, London, and graduated from London University in 1857. His name has become immortalized as the librettist of the duo Gilbert and Sullivan, a collaboration that began in 1875; together they wrote fourteen highly popular operettas. He also wrote scores of stage pieces, reviews, short stories, and a great many short poems. He built and owned the Garrick Theatre in Charing Cross Road, London, opened in 1889. When Sir Arthur Sullivan (knighted 1883) died in 1900, Gilbert wrote, "A Gilbert is no good without a Sullivan, and I can't find one." He was knighted in 1907 and died of heart failure as a result of trying to save a young woman from drowning. His ashes were buried at Great Stanmore Church, Middlesex. Some of his poems: "Annie Protheroe: A Legend of Stratford-Le-Bow," "Captain Reece," "Ellen M'Jones Aberdeen," "Gentle Alice Brown," "The Baffled Grumbler," "The British Tar," "The Duke and the Duchess," "The Fable of the Magnet and the Churn," "To a Little Maid — By a Policeman."

Sources: *Dictionary of National Biography.* Electronic Edition 1.1. Oxford University Press, 1997. *English Poetry: Author Search.* Chadwyck-Healey Ltd., 1995 (http://www.lib.utexas.edu:8080/search/epoetry/author.html). *Innocent Merriment: An Anthology of Light Verse.* Franklin P. Adams, ed. McGraw-Hill, 1942. *The Columbia Granger's Index to Poetry.* 11th ed. *The Columbia Granger's World of Poetry,* Columbia University Press, 2005 (http://www.columbiagrangers.org). *The National Portrait Gallery* (www.npg.org.uk). *The Norton Anthology of English Literature.* 5th ed. Vol. 2, M.H. Abrams, ed. W.W. Norton, 1986. *The Norton Anthology of English Literature.* 6th ed. Vol. 2, M.H. Abrams, ed. W.W. Norton, 1993. *The Oxford Companion to English Literature.* 6th edition. Margaret Drabble, ed. Oxford University Press, 2000.

GILFILLAN, ROBERT (1798–1850)

Born in Dunfermline, Fifeshire, Scotland, the son of a master weaver, he was influenced in poetry by his mother. He joined with other lads in "guising"— going around at Halloween entertaining householders with a poem or a song or telling jokes in return for nuts, apples, sweets or small coins. Young Robert made up his own poems; one of them being about the death of General Sir Ralph Abercromby, hero of the Napoleonic Wars. He began his seven year apprenticeship as a cooper at the age of thirteen at Leith. From 1818 he had various jobs, ending as collector of the police rates at Leith, a job he held until he died. His songs were circulated and sung all over Scotland. His *Original Songs* was published in 1831, with a new (enlarged) edition in 1835, marked by dinner at the Royal Exchange, Edinburgh, and the presentation of a massive silver cup. A third (enlarged) edition was published in 1839. A monument was erected to him in Leith. His best known poem, "The Exile's Song," tells the story of a young man leaving his loved one to emigrate to Canada.

Sources: *Dictionary of National Biography.* Electronic Edition 1.1. Oxford University Press, 1997. *Did You*

Know?— Halloween in Scotland (http://www.rampantscot-land.com/know/blknow_halloween.htm). *English Poetry: Author Search.* Chadwyck-Healey Ltd., 1995 (http://www.lib.utexas.edu:8080/search/epoetry/author.html). *Poems and Songs.* Fourth edition. *With Memoir of the Author, and Appendix of His Latest Pieces.* Sutherland and Knox, 1851. *The Columbia Granger's Index to Poetry.* 11th ed. *The Columbia Granger's World of Poetry,* Columbia University Press, 2005 (http://www.columbiagrangers.org). *Treasury of Favorite Poems.* Joseph H. Head, ed. Gramercy Books, 2000.

GLOVER, RICHARD (1712–1785)

He was born in London, the son of a Hamburg merchant. While at school in Cheam, Surrey, he published a poem "Upon Sir Isaac Newton" (1728) (it went through four editions) to the memory of Sir Isaac Newton. Dr. Pemberton appended this to his *View of Newton's Philosophy,* published in 1728. He entered his father's business in 1742 and was active in petitioning Parliament for more protection of British commerce. He was member of Parliament for Weymouth from 1761 to 1785. He died in London. Some of his publications: *Leonidas,* 1737 (poem in nine books; warmly commended by the Prince of Wales and his court, it passed through several editions, was enlarged to twelve books in 1770, and translated into French [1738] and German [1766]). *London, or the Progress of Commerce,* 1739 (poem). *Admiral Hosier's Ghost,* 1740 (ballad, included in Thomas Percy's *Reliques of Ancient English Poetry* [1765]). *Memoirs by a Distinguished Literary and Political Character,* 1742 (shortened title). *Boadicea,* 1753 (tragedy). *Medea,* 1761 (tragedy). *Athenaid,* 1788 (an epic poem in thirty books, published by his daughter). *Jason,* 1799 (tragedy).

Sources: *Dictionary of National Biography.* Electronic Edition 1.1. Oxford University Press, 1997. *English Poetry: Author Search.* Chadwyck-Healey Ltd., 1995 (http://www.lib.utexas.edu:8080/search/epoetry/author.html). *The Columbia Granger's Index to Poetry.* 11th ed. *The Columbia Granger's World of Poetry,* Columbia University Press, 2005 (http://www.columbiagrangers.org). *The National Portrait Gallery* (www.npg.org.uk). *The Oxford Companion to English Literature.* 6th edition. Margaret Drabble, ed. Oxford University Press, 2000. *Wikipedia, the Free Encyclopedia* (http://en.wikipedia.org/wiki/Wikipedia).

GODOLPHIN, SIDNEY (1610–1643)

Born into a wealthy family in Breage, Cornwall, he was educated at Exeter College, Oxford (1624–27) and at one of the Inns of Court, London. He was a member of Parliament several times, serving in both the Short and Long Parliaments of 1640. During the first Civil War he joined the Royalist forces of Sir Ralph Hopton and was killed in action while advancing into Devon. He was buried in the chancel of Okehampton Church. *The Passion of Dido for Aeneas,* a translation from Virgil's fourth book of the Aeneid, apparently unfinished at his death, was completed and published by his co-author Edmund Waller (see entry) in 1658, and was included in the fourth volume of Dryden's *Miscellany Poems* (1716). Thomas Hobbes eulogized him in *Leviathan* (1660). Some of his other poems: "A Dialogue Between a Lover and His Mistress," "Chloris, It Is Not Thy Disdain," "Elegy on John Donne," Epitaph Upon the Lady Rich," "Hymn" (for Christmas), "On Ben Jonson," "Song: Or Love Me Less, or Love Me More," "Song: No More Unto My Thoughts Appear."

Sources: *Ben Jonson and the Cavalier Poets.* Hugh MacLaen, ed. New York: W.W. Norton and Company, 1974. *Dictionary of National Biography.* Electronic Edition 1.1. Oxford University Press, 1997. *Encyclopædia Britannica Ultimate Reference Suite DVD,* 2006. *English Poetry: A Poetic Record from Chaucer to Yeats.* David Hopkins, ed. Routledge, 1990. *The Columbia Granger's Index to Poetry.* 11th ed. *The Columbia Granger's World of Poetry,* Columbia University Press, 2005 (http://www.columbiagrangers.org). *The Oxford Companion to English Literature.* 6th edition. Margaret Drabble, ed. Oxford University Press, 2000. *The Penguin Book of Renaissance Verse 1509–1659.* David Norbrook, ed. Penguin Books, 1992. *The Poems of Sidney Godolphin.* William Dighton, ed. Clarendon Press, 1931.

GOGARTY, OLIVER ST. JOHN (1878–1957)

Born in Dublin, the son and grandson of doctors, he received a Jesuit education, then went on to University College, Dublin, where he was a fellow student of James Joyce, who portrayed him as the character Buck Mulligan in *Ulysses.* He qualified in medicine from Trinity College, Dublin, in 1907 and built up a prosperous practice in Dublin as a throat surgeon; he was prominent in the early days of the Irish Free State. He moved to America in 1939 and died in New York. Seventeen of his poems were included in *The Oxford Book of Modern Verse* (1936), which he edited. Some of his publications: *An Offering of Swans* 1923, (poems). *As I Was Going Down Sackville Street,* 1937 (memoirs). *Tumbling in the Hay,* 1939 (memoirs). *Collected Poems,* 1951. *It Isn't This Time of Year at All,* 1954 (memoirs). Some of his poems: "After Galen," "Death May Be Very Gentle," "Elegy on the Archpoet William Butler Yeats Lately Dead," "Farrell O'Reilly," "The Airman's Breastplate," "The Crab Tree," "The Gallant Irish Yeoman," "The Plum Tree by the House."

Sources: *Dictionary of National Biography.* Electronic Edition 1.1. Oxford University Press, 1997. *Encyclopædia Britannica Ultimate Reference Suite DVD,* 2006. *Fifty Years of American Poetry. Anniversary Volume for the Academy of American Poets.* Harry N. Abrams, ed. American Academy of Poets, 1984. *Poems to Read Aloud*, Edward Hodnett, ed. W.W. Norton, 1967. *The Columbia Granger's Index to Poetry*. 11th ed. *The Columbia Granger's World of Poetry*, Columbia University Press, 2005 (http://www.columbia grangers.org). *The National Portrait Gallery* (www.npg. org.uk). *The Oxford Companion to English Literature*. 6th edition. Margaret Drabble, ed. Oxford University Press, 2000. *Treasury of Irish Religious Verse*. Patrick Murray, ed. Crossroad, 1986.

GOLDING, LOUIS (1895–1958)

English novelist, poet and essayist, was the son of Ukrainian Jewish immigrant parents from Cherkassy. Golding grew up in Manchester and attended Manchester Grammar School and Queen's College, Oxford. World War I — in which he fought in the Salonika campaign — interrupted his studies. After graduating from Oxford he traveled widely in the Mediterranean and the Middle East. His novel *Magnolia Street* (1932) — a story of working-class life among Jews and Gentiles in a Manchester back street — was produced as a play in 1934. His book *The Jewish Problem* (1938) was a study of anti-Semitism. A broadcaster and lecturer, he also wrote film scripts (he worked on the screenplay of the Paul Robeson 1940 film *The Proud Valley*), verse, short stories, and books on boxing. His five-volume series *Tales of the Silver Sisters*, also known as the *Doomington Saga* (1934–1954), are novels that examine twentieth-century Jewish life in Western Europe. His poetry publications: *Sorrow of War*, 1919. *Shepherd Singing Ragtime*, 1921. *Prophet and Fool*, 1923. Some of his poems: "Broken Bodies," "Doom-devoted," "Ploughman at the Plough," "Quarries in Syracuse," "Second Seeing."

Sources: *Encyclopædia Britannica Ultimate Reference Suite DVD*, 2006. *Louis Golding, Collection Description*. Washington University, St. Louis, Missouri, USA (http://library.wustl.edu/units/spec/manuscripts/mlc/golding/golding.html). *The National Portrait Gallery* (www.npg.org.uk). *Our Holidays in Poetry*. Mildred P. Harrington and Josephine H. Thomas, ed. H.W. Wilson, 1929. *Poetry of the First World War*. Edward Hudson, ed. Wayland Publishers Ltd., 1988. *Poets' Corner: Ploughman at the Plough by Louis Golding* (http://www.theotherpages.org/poems/golding1.html). *The Home Book of Modern Verse*. Burton Egbert Stevenson, ed. Henry Holt, 1953. *Wikipedia, the Free Encyclopedia* (http://en.wikipedia.org/wiki/Wikipedia).

GOLDSMITH, OLIVER (1728–1774)

Born in Ireland, the son of an Anglo-Irish clergyman, he graduated from Trinity College, Dublin, in 1749. After studying medicine at Edinburgh, though he took no degree, and at Leiden, he wandered Europe and arrived in London in 1756 almost destitute. He supported himself with doctoring and as a hack writer, where he was noticed for his grace-ful, lively, and readable style. His rise to fame started with *Enquiry into the Present State of Polite Learning in Europe* (1759). In 1764 he became one of the nine founder-members of the "Club" of famous people. He died after a short illness, burdened with debt, and is memorialized by a monument in Poets' Corner of Westminster Abbey. "The Deserted Village" is probably his finest poem. Several shorter pieces, including "When Lovely Woman Stoops to Folly" and "Elegy on the Death of a Mad Dog," appear in his novel *The Vicar of Wakefield* (1762). Some of his other poems: "Britain," "Epitaph on Dr. Parnell," "Retaliation," "Song: From the Oratorio of the Captivity," "Stanzas on the Taking of Quebec," "The Clown's Reply," "The Double Transformation," "The Hermit."

Sources: *Dictionary of National Biography*. Electronic Edition 1.1. Oxford University Press, 1997. *Encyclopædia Britannica Ultimate Reference Suite DVD*, 2006. *English Poetry: Author Search*. Chadwyck-Healey Ltd., 1995 (http://www.lib.utexas.edu:8080/search/epoetry/author.html). *Everyman's Book of English Verse*. John Wain, ed. J.M. Dent, 1981. *The Columbia Granger's Index to Poetry*. 11th ed. *The Columbia Granger's World of Poetry*, Columbia University Press, 2005 (http://www.columbiagrangers.org). *The National Portrait Gallery* (www.npg.org.uk). *The Oxford Companion to English Literature*. 6th edition. Margaret Drabble, ed. Oxford University Press, 2000. *The Poetical Works of Oliver Goldsmith*. Rev. J. Mitford, ed. William Pickering, 1851. *Westminster Abbey Official Guide* (no date).

GOOGE, BARNABE (1540–1594)

The son of Robert Googe, recorder of Lincoln, he was born at Alvingham in Lincolnshire on 11 June, St. Barnaby's Day (St. Barbabas). He studied at Christ's College, Cambridge, and at New College, Oxford, but does not appear to have taken a degree. He then became a retainer to his kinsman, Sir William Cecil 1st Lord Burghley (chief adviser to Queen Elizabeth), and in 1563 the queen appointed him one of her gentlemen-pensioners. In 1574 he was sent on service to Ireland, and in 1582 he was appointed provost marshal of the presidency court of Connaught, Ireland. Some of his publications (spelling original): *Eglogs, Epytaphes, and Sonettes*, 1563. *The Zodiake of Life*, 1565. *The Shippe of Safegarde*, 1569. *The Popish Kingdome*, 1570. *The Overthrovv of the Gout*, 1577. *The Prouerbes of Sir Iames Lopez de Mendoza*, 1579. *A Prophecie Lately Transcribed*, 1672. Some of his poems: "Egloga Septima," "The Popish Kingdome," "Egloga Tertia," "Commynge Home Warde Out of Spayne," "The Vnfortunate Choyse of His Ualentyne," "Two Lynes Shall Tell the Gryefs," "Ons Musynge as I Sat," "To Alexander Neuell."

Sources: *Dictionary of National Biography*. Electronic

Edition 1.1. Oxford University Press, 1997. *Eclogues, Epitaphs, and Sonnets of Barnabe Googe.* Judith M. Kennedy, ed. University of Toronto Press, 1989. *English Poetry, Second Edition Bibliography* (http://collections.chadwyck.co.uk/html/ep2/bibliography/d.htm). *English Poetry: Author Search.* Chadwyck-Healey Ltd., 1995 (http://www.lib.utexas.edu:8080/search/epoetry/author.html). *SETIS: The Scholarly Electronic Text and Image Service* (http://setis.library.usyd.edu.au). *The Columbia Granger's Index to Poetry.* 11th ed. *The Columbia Granger's World of Poetry,* Columbia University Press, 2005 (http://www.columbiagrangers.org). *The Oxford Companion to English Literature.* 6th edition. Margaret Drabble, ed. Oxford University Press, 2000.

GORE-BOOTH, EVA SELINA (1870–1926)

One of three daughters (and two sons) of Sir Henry Gore-Booth, fifth baronet, Anglo-Irish landlord and Arctic explorer. Josslyn introduced cooperatives to Sligo and became the first landlord in Ireland to sell his land to his tenants after the 1903 Land Act. Gore-Booth's sister Constance (later Countess) Markievicz became the "rebel countess" of the 1916 Irish rebellion. Recovering in Italy from suspected tuberculosis, in 1896 Eva met Esther Roper, an organizer for the North of England Society for Women's Suffrage. They fell in love and lived together in Manchester, where they edited the *Women's Labour News.* Eva devoted her life to social reform—trade unionism, suffrage, and adult education for women. She was at one time mentor of Christabel Pankhurst, but Eva proved not militant enough, and the friendship ended. Her health broke down after World War I and she and Esther retired to Hampstead. After her death, Esther collected many of her poems for publication and wrote a biographical introduction to them. Some of her poems: "A Heretic's Pilgrimage," "Crucifixion," "Harvest," "The Little Waves of Breffny," "The Sad Years," "The Travelers," "The Vision of Niamh."

Sources: *Dictionary of National Biography.* Electronic Edition 1.1. Oxford University Press, 1997. *Poems Between Women Four Centuries of Love, Romantic Friendship, and Desire.* Emma Donoghue, ed. Columbia University Press, 1997. *The Home Book of Modern Verse.* Burton Egbert Stevenson, ed. Henry Holt, 1953. *The National Portrait Gallery* (www.npg.org.uk). *The World's Great Religious Poetry.* Caroline Miles Hill, ed. Macmillan, 1954. *Treasury of Irish Religious Verse.* Patrick Murray, ed. Crossroad, 1986.

GORGES, SIR ARTHUR (1577–1625)

He was the third son of Sir William Gorges, vice-admiral of the fleet, and second cousin to Sir Walter Raleigh. Queen Elizabeth made him a gentleman-pensioner in 1582, and two years later he married Douglas Howard, one of the greatest heiresses of the day. Her death six years later is commemorated by Gorges' friend Spenser in the poem entitled "Daphnaida." In 1597 he commanded the *Wast Spite,* the ship in which Walter Raleigh sailed as vice-admiral under Robert Devereux, second earl of Essex, on the islands voyage. He, with eight others, was knighted in 1597. He was member of Parliament for four different constituencies between 1584 and 1691. He died in Chelsea and was buried in Sir Thomas More's chapel, Chelsea. Some of his publications: *The Olympian Catastrophe*; 1612. A translation of Lucan's *Pharsalia,* 1614. A translation of Bacon's *Wisedome of the Ancients,* 1619. A translation into French of Bacon's *Essays,* 1619. Some of his poems: "The Mayd So Trickt Her Selfe with Arte," "The Hungry Lionesse (With Sharpe Desire)," "Lvcans Pharsalia," "Let Doting Grandsires Knowe the Law," "My Lesbia, Let Vs Liue and Loue."

Sources: *Dictionary of National Biography.* Electronic Edition 1.1. Oxford University Press, 1997. *English Poetry: Author Search.* Chadwyck-Healey Ltd., 1995 (http://www.lib.utexas.edu:8080/search/epoetry/author.html). *The Columbia Granger's Index to Poetry.* 11th ed. *The Columbia Granger's World of Poetry,* Columbia University Press, 2005 (http://www.columbiagrangers.org). *The Gambit Book of Love Poems.* Geoffrey Grigson, ed. Gambit, 1973. *The New Oxford Book of Sixteenth Century Verse.* Emrys Jones, ed. Oxford University Press, 1991. *The Oxford Book of Sonnets.* John Fuller, ed. Oxford University Press, 2000. *The Oxford Companion to English Literature.* 6th edition. Margaret Drabble, ed. Oxford University Press, 2000.

GOSSE, SIR EDMUND WILLIAM (1849–1928)

Born in London, he was brought up in Devon by his father after his mother died. In his book *Father and Son* (1907) he describes the tension-ridden relationship with his father—a member of the Plymouth Brethren. He was liberated when Charles Kingsley, a friend of his father, secured his employment in the cataloguing section of the British Museum. He went on to translate three of Ibsen's plays and write literary histories, biographies, critical essays and many poems. From 1885 to 1890 he was Clark lecturer in English literature at Trinity College, Cambridge, and from 1904 to 1914, librarian to the House of Lords. He was made Commander of the Bath in 1912 and was knighted in 1925. From 1918 until his death he wrote a series of weekly articles in the *Sunday Times,* selections of which are included in his *Books on the Table* (1921), and *More Books on the Table* (1923). Some of his other publications: *Madrigals, Songs and Sonnets,* 1879. *New Poems,* 1879. *The Rose of Omar,* 1893. *Two Unpublished Poems,* 1929. Some of his poems: "An invitation," "Epithalamium," "Illusion," "Impression."

Sources: *Dictionary of National Biography.* Electronic Edition 1.1. Oxford University Press, 1997. *English Poetry:*

Author Search. Chadwyck-Healey Ltd., 1995 (http://www.lib.utexas.edu:8080/search/epoetry/author.html). *Poets' Corner, Sir Edmund William Gosse* (http://www.theotherpages.org/poems/poem-gh.html). *SETIS—English Poetry Collection* (http://setis.library.usyd.edu.au/poetry/browse/h-epdtoc.html). *The Columbia Granger's Index to Poetry*. 11th ed. *The Columbia Granger's World of Poetry*, Columbia University Press, 2005 (http://www.columbiagrangers.org). *The Home Book of Modern Verse*. Burton Egbert Stevenson, ed. Henry Holt, 1953. *The Making of a Poem: A Norton Anthology of Poetic Forms*. Mark Strand and Eavan Boland, ed. W.W. Norton, 2000. *The National Portrait Gallery* (www.npg.org.uk). *The Oxford Book of Victorian Verse*. Arthur Quiller-Couch, ed. Oxford University Press, 1971. *The Oxford Companion to English Literature*. 6th edition. Margaret Drabble, ed. Oxford University Press, 2000. *The Symbolist Poem: The Development of the English Tradition*. Edward Engelberg, ed. E.P. Dutton, 1967.

GOULD, ROBERT (d. ?1709)

What is known about this talented poet-playwright is that he was the protégé of John Oldham (see entry). He was a servant of Charles, Earl of Dorset and Middlesex, and of James, 1st Earl of Abingdon, at his country seat at Rycote in Oxfordshire. Some of his publications: *Love given over, or a Satyr against Woman*, 1680 (this attack against women evoked a torrent of replies from the pens of women for twenty years). *Presbytery rough-drawn, a Satyr: In contemplation of the late Rebellion*, 1683. *Poems chiefly consisting of Satyrs and Satyrical Epistles*, 1689. *The Corruption of the Times by Money, a Satyr*, 1693. *A Poem Most Humbly Offered to the Memory of Queen Mary*, 1695. *The Rival Sisters, or the Violence of Love*, 1696. *Works*, 1709 (2 volumes, published by his widow). *Innocence Distress'd, or the Royal Penitents*, 1737 (published by subscription for the benefit of his daughter, Hannah Gould). Some of his other poems: "Advice to a Fine Young Lady," "Fair, and Soft, and Gay, and Young," "Song: Wit and Beauty," "The Dream," "The Laureat."

Sources: *17. Cibber's the Careless Husband, page 31* (http://www.questia.com/PM.qst?a=oandd=96240127). *An Uninhibited Treasury of Erotic Poetry*. Louis Untermeyer, ed. Dial Press, 1963. *Dictionary of National Biography*. Electronic Edition 1.1. Oxford University Press, 1997. *English Poetry, Second Edition Bibliography* (http://collections.chadwyck.co.uk/html/ep2/bibliography/g.htm). *English Poetry: Author Search*. Chadwyck-Healey Ltd., 1995 (http://www.lib.utexas.edu:8080/search/epoetry/author.html). *Great Books Online* (www.bartleby.com). *Oldpoetry* (www.oldpoetry.com). *The Cavalier Poets*. Robin Skelton, ed. Oxford University Press, 1970. *The Columbia Granger's Index to Poetry*. 11th ed. *The Columbia Granger's World of Poetry*, Columbia University Press, 2005 (http://www.columbiagrangers.org).

GOWER, JOHN (?1325–1408)

The facts of this medieval poet's life are derived mainly from his poetry. He is thought to have owned land in Kent and in Yorkshire. He was blind from around 1400. He lived the latter part of his life as a layman in the priory of St. Mary Overie, Southwark, London, where he died, apparently. Some of Gower's stories are mirrored in Chaucer's *Canterbury Tales*. His two main French works are *Cinkante Balades*, written before 1374, and *Speculum Meditantis*, circa 1376–1368, in which he speaks of vices and virtues. His major Latin poem, *Vox clamantis*, in seven books, deals with the Peasants' Revolt of 1381, kingship, the state of England, and the need for spiritual and political reform. His two main English works are *In Praise of Peace*, in which he pleads urgently King Henry IV to avoid the horrors of war, and *Confessio amantis*, published in the 1390s, a collection in eight books of exemplary tales of love. Some of his other poems: "An Address to the King," "Concerning the Philosophers Stone," "This World Fares as a Fantasy."

Sources: *Dictionary of National Biography*. Electronic Edition 1.1. Oxford University Press, 1997. *Encyclopædia Britannica Ultimate Reference Suite DVD*, 2006. *English Poetry: Author Search*. Chadwyck-Healey Ltd., 1995 (http://www.lib.utexas.edu:8080/search/epoetry/author.html). *English Verse, 1300–1500: Longman Annotated Anthologies of English Verse. Vol. I*. John Burrow, ed. Longman, 1977. *Morality Plays, Interludes, and the Emergence of Mature Drama* (http://www.beyondbooks.com/leu11/2h.asp). *The Columbia Granger's Index to Poetry*. 11th ed. *The Columbia Granger's World of Poetry*, Columbia University Press, 2005 (http://www.columbiagrangers.org). *The Faber Book of English History in Verse*. Kenneth Baker, ed. Faber and Faber, 1988. *The John Gower Page* (http://faculty.arts.ubc.ca/sechard/gower.htm). *The National Portrait Gallery* (www.npg.org.uk). *The Oxford Companion to English Literature*. 6th edition. Margaret Drabble, ed. Oxford University Press, 2000.

GRAHAM, JAMES, MARQUIS OF MONTROSE (1612–1650)

He succeeded to the title in 1624 and was admitted to St. Andrews university in 1627. In 1638 he signed a covenant promising to defend Scotland's Presbyterian religion against attempts by Charles I to impose Anglican forms of worship. He was a brilliant general and won a series of spectacular victories in Scotland for King Charles I during the English Civil Wars. He was the scourge of the Covenanter army when it invaded England to fight for Parliament against the king in 1644. When the Royalist army was defeated at the Battle of Naseby in June 1645, Montrose's men melted away, the small force remaining was routed and Montrose fled with Charles to France. He returned in 1650 and was captured and hanged in the marketplace of Edinburgh. Some of his poems: "I'll Never Love Thee More," "In Praise of Women," "Montrose on His Own Condition,"

"My Dear and Only Love," "On Himself, Upon Hearing What Was His Sentence," "On the Faithlessness and Venality of the Times," "Sovereignty in Danger," "Speechless Grief," "Sympathy in Love."

Sources: *A Book of Scottish Verse.* Maurice Lindsay and R.L. Mackie, eds. St. Martin's Press, 1983. *Ben Jonson and the Cavalier Poets.* Hugh MacLaen, ed. New York: W.W. Norton and Company, 1974. *Dictionary of National Biography.* Electronic Edition 1.1. Oxford University Press, 1997. *Encyclopædia Britannica Ultimate Reference Suite DVD,* 2006. *English Poetry: Author Search.* Chadwyck-Healey Ltd., 1995 (http://www.lib.utexas.edu:8080/search/epoetry/author.html). *Poems of James Graham, Marquis of Montrose.* John Murray, 1938. *The Columbia Granger's Index to Poetry.* 11th ed. *The Columbia Granger's World of Poetry,* Columbia University Press, 2005 (http://www.columbiagrangers.org). *The National Portrait Gallery* (www.npg.org.uk).

GRAHAM, WILLIAM SYDNEY (1918–1986)

Born in Greenock, Scotland, where he was educated, he trained as an engineer and attended Newbattle Abbey College near Edinburgh. During World War II he worked in munitions in Glasgow and after the war he lived most of his life in Cornwall. He did a variety of jobs — copywriter, fisherman, and auxiliary coastguard — but his main concentration was on writing poetry. Many of his poems use the metaphor of fishing to explore his own inner life. Some of his work is spine-chilling. Over the years he lived frugally on the proceeds of his writing, the support of friends and patrons and small grants from the Arts Council. He was granted a civil list pension in 1974 and died after a long battle with cancer. Some of his publications: *Cage Without Grievance,* 1942. *The White Threshold,* 1949. *The Nightfishing,* 1955. *Malcolm Mooney's Land,* 1970. *Implements in their Places,* 1977. *Collected Poems 1942–1977,* 1979. *Selected Poems,* 1980. Some of his poems: "Beast in the Space," "Definition of My Brother," "Loch Thom," "The Children of Greenock," "The Conscript Goes," "The Dark Dialogues," "To Alexander Bell."

Sources: *Biography of W.S. Graham* (http://www.users. globalnet.co.uk/~crumey/w_s_graham.html). *The Columbia Granger's Index to Poetry.* 11th ed. *The Columbia Granger's World of Poetry,* Columbia University Press, 2005 (http://www.columbiagrangers.org). *The Faber Book of Twentieth Century Verse.* John Heath-Stubbs, and David Wright, ed. Faber and Faber, 1975. *The National Portrait Gallery* (www.npg.org.uk). *The Oxford Companion to English Literature.* 6th edition. Margaret Drabble, ed. Oxford University Press, 2000. *The Poetry Anthology, 1912–1977.* Daryl Hine and Joseph Parisi, eds. Houghton Mifflin, 1978. *Wikipedia, the Free Encyclopedia* (http://en.wikipedia.org/wiki/Wikipedia).

GRAHAME, JAMES (1765–1811)

Born in Glasgow, the son of a lawyer, he studied at Glasgow University, then trained as a lawyer and was called to the Scottish bar in 1795. He fulfilled his life-long ambition when he was ordained in the Church of England in 1809. He suffered from ill health for years and died in Scotland, leaving a widow with two sons and a daughter. His great-grand-nephew was Kenneth Grahame (see entry). Some of his publications: *Poems in English, Scotch and Latin,* 1794. *Wallace: A Tragedy,* 1799. *Mary Stewart, Queen of Scots,* 1801. *The Sabbath: A Poem,* 1804. *The Birds of Scotland,* 1806. *Thoughts on Trial by Jury in Civil Causes,* 1806. *Poems,* 1807 (2 volumes). *The Siege of Copenhagen,* 1808. *Africa Delivered,* 1809. *British Georgics,* 1809 (2nd edition, 1812). *Poems on the abolition of the slave trade,* 1809 (written with James Montgomery and E. Benger). Some of his other poems: "Biblical Pictures," "June," "Sunday Morning," "The Birds of Scotland," "The Cottars Lament," "The Rural Calendar," "The Thanksgiving Off Cape Trafalgar," "To a Redbreast."

Sources: *Dictionary of National Biography.* Electronic Edition 1.1. Oxford University Press, 1997. *English Poetry: Author Search.* Chadwyck-Healey Ltd., 1995 (http://www.lib.utexas.edu:8080/search/epoetry/author.html). *Island 8—Translations of Burns* (http://www.sc.edu/library/spcoll/britlit/burns/burns8.html). *Oldpoetry* (www.oldpoetry.com). *The Penguin Book of Bird Poetry.* Peggy Munsterberg, ed. 1984. *The Poetical Works of Henry Kirke White and James Grahame.* Nichol, 1856. *Wikipedia, the Free Encyclopedia* (http://en.wikipedia.org/wiki/Wikipedia).

GRAHAME, KENNETH (1859–1932)

Born in Edinburgh, the son of a lawyer, he was orphaned at an early age and was brought up by his grandmother in England, where he attended St. Edward's School, Oxford. He was employed at the Bank of England from 1879, working his way up from clerk to secretary, until he retired due to ill health in 1908. Acting on the advice of Frederick James Furnivall, scholar and founder of the *Early English Text Society,* he published essays, short stories, and sketches, and contributed articles to such journals as the *St. James Gazette* and the *Yellow Book,* but kept his job at the bank. He was shot and seriously wounded at the bank in 1903. He died suddenly at his home at Pangbourne, Berkshire. Some of his publications: *Pagan Papers,* 1893. *The Golden Age,* 1895. *Dream Days,* 1898. *The Wind in the Willows,* 1908 (dramatized by Mr. A.A. Milne [see entry] in 1929 as *Toad of Toad Hall*). Three of his *Wind in the Willows* poems: "Carol: Villagers all, this frosty tide," "Duck's Ditty," "The Song of Mr. Toad."

Sources: *Dictionary of National Biography.* Electronic

Edition 1.1. Oxford University Press, 1997. *Encyclopædia Britannica Ultimate Reference Suite DVD*, 2006. *Poems of Christmas*. Myra Cohn Livingston, ed. Atheneum, 1980. *The Columbia Granger's Index to Poetry*. 11th ed. *The Columbia Granger's World of Poetry*, Columbia University Press, 2005 (http://www.columbiagrangers.org). *The National Portrait Gallery* (www.npg.org.uk). *The Oxford Companion to English Literature*. 6th edition. Margaret Drabble, ed. Oxford University Press, 2000. *Who Has Seen the Wind? An Illustrated Collection of Poetry for Young People*. Kathryn Sky-Peck, ed. Museum of Fine Arts, Boston, 1991.

GRAINGER, JAMES (?1721–1766)

He was born in Dunse, Berwickshire, the son of an excise man who lost his lands in Cumberland for supporting the abortive Stuart uprising of 1715. Through the good offices of his half-brother, James studied medicine at Edinburgh University, then became an army surgeon and saw service in the 1745 rebellion and in Holland 1746–1748. After the 1748 peace of Aix-la-Chapelle, he returned to Scotland and graduated M.D. at Edinburgh in 1753. He settled in London and between 1756 and 1758 he wrote about poetry and drama in the *Monthly Review*. He also published *Essays Physical and Literary* (1756). In 1758 he translated *Leander to Hero* and *Hero to Leander* from Ovid's *Epistles*. In 1759 he left on a four year tour of the West Indies with John Bourryau, a former pupil and heir to property in the West Indies, where he practiced as a doctor. His main poetical work of that period is the mock heroic poem "Sugar Cane." He died at St. Christopher (St. Kitts and Nevis) of West Indian fever. Some of his poems: "Bryan and Pereene," "Elegies [Tibullus]," "Solitude: An Ode," "The Fate of Capua," "The Poems of Sulpicia [Tibullus]."

Sources: *Dictionary of National Biography*. Electronic Edition 1.1. Oxford University Press, 1997. *Eighteenth-Century English Verse*. Dennis Davison, ed. Penguin Books, 1988. *English Poetry: Author Search*. Chadwyck-Healey Ltd., 1995 (http://www.lib.utexas.edu:8080/search/epoetry/author.html). *The Columbia Granger's Index to Poetry*. 11th ed. *The Columbia Granger's World of Poetry*, Columbia University Press, 2005 (http://www.columbiagrangers.org). *The Oxford Book of Classical Verse in Translation*. Adrian Poole, and Jeremy Maule, ed. 1995. *The Oxford Companion to English Literature*. 6th edition. Margaret Drabble, ed. Oxford University Press, 2000. *The Penguin Book of Caribbean Verse in English*. Paula Burnett, ed. Penguin Books, 1986. *The Works of Tibullus*. Suttaby, Evance, and Fox, 1812.

GRANT, SIR ROBERT (1779–1838)

Born in India, the son of Charles Grant, the Indian philanthropist and statesman, he graduated M.A. from Magdalene College, Cambridge, in 1804 and was called to the bar in 1807. Several times member of Parliament, his major campaign in the House of Commons was the repeal of the civil disabilities of the Jews, a fight which was not won until 1858. He became judge advocate-general in 1832 and governor of Bombay in 1834, the same year in which he was knighted. He died at Dalpoorie in 1838 and was buried at St. Mary's Church in Poonah. His *Sacred Poems* was edited in 1839 by his brother, Charles, Lord Glenelg, and new editions appeared in 1844 and 1868. His poem "O Worship the King," based on Psalm 104, set to the tune "Hanover," is in most hymn books. Some of his other hymns/poems: "By Thy Birth, and by Thy Tears," "How Deep the Joy, Almighty Lord," "Lord of Earth, Thy Forming Hand," "Savior, When in Dust to Thee," "The Starry Firmament on High," "When Gathering Clouds Around I View," "Wherefore Do the Nations Rage."

Sources: *Dictionary of National Biography*. Electronic Edition 1.1. Oxford University Press, 1997. *English Poetry: Author Search*. Chadwyck-Healey Ltd., 1995 (http://www.lib.utexas.edu:8080/search/epoetry/author.html). *The Columbia Granger's Index to Poetry*. 11th ed. *The Columbia Granger's World of Poetry*, Columbia University Press, 2005 (http://www.columbiagrangers.org). *The National Portrait Gallery* (www.npg.org.uk). *The World's Great Religious Poetry*. Caroline Miles Hill, ed. Macmillan, 1954.

GRANVILLE, GEORGE, LORD LANSDOWNE (1667–1735)

Born in Yorkshire and educated in France, he graduated M.A. from Trinity College, Cambridge, in 1679. He was member of Parliament several times and succeeded Walpole as secretary of war in 1710. The following year he was created a peer of Great Britain with the title of Lord Lansdowne, Baron of Bideford, Devon. He fell out of favor when George I succeeded to the throne (1714) and, being suspected of having sympathies with the Jacobite cause, was imprisoned for two years in the Tower of London. Released in 1717, he settled at Longleat, Wiltshire. He died in London and was buried in a vault in the chancel of St. Clement Danes, London. His wife, who had died a few days before him, was buried in the same vault. His publications: translations of some of the orations of Demosthenes; several tragedies, comedies, and one opera, *The British Enchanters* (1706); *A Collection of Poems* (1701); and *Granville's Works* (1732). Some of his poems: "Poems to the King (James II)," "Beauty and Law, a Poetical Pleading," "To Myra, Loving at First Sight," "The Progress of Beauty," "Essay on Unnatural Flights in Poetry."

Sources: *Dictionary of National Biography*. Electronic Edition 1.1. Oxford University Press, 1997. *English Poetry: Author Search*. Chadwyck-Healey Ltd., 1995 (http://www.lib.utexas.edu:8080/search/epoetry/author.html). *Samuel Johnson's Lives of the English Poets*, 1779–1781 (http://www2.hn.psu.edu/Faculty/KKemmerer/poets/preface.htm). *The National Portrait Gallery* (www.npg.org.uk).

GRAVES, ALFRED PERCEVAL and ROBERT VAN RANKE (1846–1985)

Alfred Perceval, the father, 1846–1931

Graves was born in Dublin, son of Charles Graves, Bishop of Limerick, and educated at Windermere College and Trinity College, Dublin, where he studied classics, English literature, history, and language. From 1875 to 1910 he was inspector of schools in Lancashire, Yorkshire, Somerset and London. He pushed for the provision of playing fields for children in urban schools and the educational use of the cinema. He was a leading figure in the London Irish Literary Society. His autobiography, *To Return to All That* (1930), was in the nature of a reply to an autobiography by his son Robert, entitled *Good-bye to All That* (1929). He spent his last years at Harlech in North Wales and died there. Some of his other publications: *Songs of Killarney*, 1873. *Songs of Old Ireland*, 1892. *Songs of Erin*, 1892. Some of his songs/poems: "An Irish Lullaby," "Father O'Flynn," "Shamrock Leaves," "The Black '46," "The Fairy Host," "The Girl I Left Behind Me," "The Little Red Lark," "'Twas Pretty to Be in Ballinderry."

Robert Von Ranke, the son, 1895–1985.

Born in London, he started writing poetry while at Charterhouse School, London. He saw service in World War I, being twice mentioned in dispatches. In 1919 he began to read English at St. John's College, Oxford, but illness prevented him from graduating; he was awarded a B.Litt. in 1925. Apart from the war years he spent most of his life in Majorca, except when he gave the Clark lectures at Cambridge in 1954 and as professor of poetry at Oxford (1961–1966). St. John's College, Oxford, elected him an honorary fellow in 1971. He died in Majorca, and he is one of the poets of WWI memorialized in Poets' Corner of Westminster Abbey. Although a prolific poet, he was a versatile writer, covering many different genres, as well as being a literary critic, especially of poetry. Some of his best known works are: *I, Claudius* and *Claudius the God* (1934). *Greek Myths* (1955). Some of his poetry publications: *Over the Barzier*, 1916. *Collected Poems*, 1938. *Poetic Craft and Principle*, 1967. *On Poetry: Collected Talks and Essays*, 1969. *Poems 1968–1970*, 1970. Some of his poems: "Counting the Beats," "Country at War," "Grotesques," "The Avengers," "The Bards," "Two Fusiliers."

Sources: *An Anthology of Irish Verse: The Poetry of Ireland from Mythological Times to the Present.* Padraic Colum, ed. Liveright, 1948. *Chief Modern Poets of Britain and America.* 5th edition. Gerald DeWitt Sanders and John Herbert Nelson, eds., Macmillan, 1970. *Collected Poems,* 1975, *Robert Graves.* Oxford University Press, 1988. *Dictionary of National Biography.* Electronic Edition 1.1. Oxford University Press, 1997. *Encyclopædia Britannica Ultimate Reference Suite DVD,* 2006. *English Poetry: Author Search.* Chadwyck-Healey Ltd., 1995 (http://www.lib.utexas.edu:8080/search/epoetry/author.html). *Irish Songs and Ballads of Alfred Perceval Graves.* Alexander Ireland and Co., 1880. *Poemhunter* (www.poemhunter.com). *The Columbia Granger's Index to Poetry.* 11th ed. *The Columbia Granger's World of Poetry,* Columbia University Press, 2005 (http://www.columbiagrangers.org). *The Complete Poems of Robert Graves in One Volume.* Beryl Graves and Dunstan Ward, eds. Carcanet Press, 2000. *The Home Book of Modern Verse.* Burton Egbert Stevenson, ed. Henry Holt, 1953. *The Oxford Companion to English Literature.* 6th edition. Margaret Drabble, ed. Oxford University Press, 2000. *The Penguin Book of Irish Verse.* Brendan Kennelly, ed. Penguin Books, 1981. *Westminster Abbey Official Guide* (no date).

GRAVES, RICHARD (1715–1804)

Born at Mickleton, Gloucestershire, he was educated at the grammar school at Abingdon, Berkshire, and graduated from Pembroke College, Oxford, in 1736. He was later ordained into the Church of England, had various appointments in Berkshire and Somerset, and was appointed chaplain to the Countess of Chatham. He was zealous as a churchman and in politics; he was a Whig and he mixed in all shades of society. He died at Claverton, his home near Bath. His comic romance, *The Spiritual Quixote or the Summer's Ramble of Mr. Geoffey Wildgoose* (1772) ran into several editions. Some of his other publications: *The Festoon, A Collection of Epigrams,* 1766 and 1767. *Galateo, or A Treatise on Politeness,* 1774 (translated from the Italian of Giovanni della Casa, archbishop of Benevento). *The Love of Order* 1773 (a poetical essay, in three cantos). *Euphrosyne, or Amusements on the Road of Life,* 1776. *Columella, or the Distressed Anchoret, a Colloquial Tale,* 1779. *Eugenius, or Anecdotes of the Golden Vale,* 1785. *Fleurettes,* a translation of Fénelon's "Ode on Solitude," 1792. Three of his poems: "Maternal Despotism; or, The Rights of Infants," "Seven Beginnings," "Single Fare."

Sources: *Dictionary of National Biography.* Electronic Edition 1.1. Oxford University Press, 1997. *In the Grip of Strange Thoughts: Russian Poetry in a New Era.* J. Kates, ed. Zephyr Press, 1999. *The Columbia Granger's Index to Poetry.* 11th ed. *The Columbia Granger's World of Poetry,* Columbia University Press, 2005 (http://www.columbiagrangers.org). *The National Portrait Gallery* (www.npg.org.uk). *The New Oxford Book of Eighteenth Century Verse.* Roger Lonsdale, ed. Oxford University Press 2003. *The Oxford Companion to English Literature.* 6th edition. Margaret Drabble, ed. Oxford University Press, 2000.

GRAY, ALASDAIR (1934–)

Born in Glasgow, and while still a teenager, he wrote a version of one of Aesop's fables and read it, with some other poems, on a BBC children's program. After graduating in 1957 from Glasgow Art School—where he specialized in murals—he worked as a part-time art teacher, then as scene painter in the Glasgow Pavilion and Glasgow Citizens theatres. He was writer in residence at the Glasgow University from 1977 to 1979 and artist-recorder at Glasgow's People's Palace. With fellow Glaswegian poet Tom Leonard (see entry) he was part of the Phillip Hobsbaum (see entry) "Group." A prolific writer, he has written novels, short stories, plays, poems, pamphlets and literary criticism, and he designs and illustrates his own books and illustrates those of other writers. His two poetry publications are *Old Negatives* (1989) and *Sixteen Occasional Poems* (2000). Some of his poems: "Agamemnon's Return," "Bosnian Heads," "First of March 1990," "South Africa April 1994," "Tales from the Polish Woods," "Waiting in Galway."

Sources: *Alasdair Gray Books—Word Power* (www.word-power.co.uk/platform/Alasdair-Gray-Books). *Interview with Alasdair Gray* (http://homepage.ntlworld.com/dee.rimbaud/interviewsgray.html). *Poems of Alasdair Gray* (http://www.alasdairgray.co.uk/poetry/). *The Oxford Companion to English Literature.* 6th edition. Margaret Drabble, ed. Oxford University Press, 2000.

GRAY, SIR ALEXANDER (1882–1968)

Born near Dundee, he was educated at Dundee High School, where his father was art teacher, and graduated from Edinburgh University in 1902, winning a gold medal for mathematics. He gained a second degree in economic science at Edinburgh and was awarded the Gladstone memorial prize. He was in the Civil Service from 1905 to 1921, then was appointed to the Jaffrey chair of political economy at Aberdeen University. He held honorary degrees from four universities. He was made Commander of the Order of the British Empire in 1939 and knighted in 1947. He died in Edinburgh. His skill as a linguist was demonstrated in his book (from Dutch) *The Scottish Staple at Veere* (1909). His second major work was *Development of Economic Doctrine* (1931). Some of his poetry publications: *Songs and Ballads* 1920 (chiefly from Heinrich Heine [1797–1856]). *Any Man's Life,* 1924. *Gossip,* 1928. *Arrows* 1932 (German ballads). *Sir Halewyn,* 1949 (mainly from Dutch originals). *Four and Forty,* 1954 (Danish ballads into Scots). Some of his poems: "December Gloaming," "Epitaph on a Vagabond," "On a Cat Aging," "Scotland," "The Deil o' Bogie."

Sources: *A Book of Scottish Verse.* Maurice Lindsay and R.L. Mackie, eds. St. Martin's Press, 1983. *Dictionary of National Biography.* Electronic Edition 1.1. Oxford University Press, 1997. *The Columbia Granger's Index to Poetry.* 11th ed. *The Columbia Granger's World of Poetry,* Colum-

bia University Press, 2005 (http://www.columbiagrangers.org). *The Home Book of Modern Verse.* Burton Egbert Stevenson, ed. Henry Holt, 1953. *The National Portrait Gallery* (www.npg.org.uk).

GRAY, DAVID (1838–1861)

Born at Merkland near Kirkintilloch, Dumbartonshire, Scotland, the son of a hand-loom weaver, he became a pupil-teacher in Glasgow, then completed a course of four sessions at Glasgow University. He contributed poetry to *The Glasgow Citizen* and began his idyll on *The Luggie,* the little stream that ran through Merkland. Robert Buchanan (see entry) and Gray became friends and together they made for London in 1860, where Lord Houghton gave Gray some literary work. Gray contracted tuberculosis and Lord Houghton took him to Torquay, but his illness worsened and he returned to Merkland, where he died. He was buried in Kirkintilloch churchyard and Lord Houghton wrote the epitaph for the monument erected by friends in 1865. During his last year he wrote *In the Shadows,* a series of sonnets. The day before he died he saw the proofs of *The Luggie.* Robert Buchanan, who shared in his London hardships, tells of his brief life in *David Gray and Other Essays* (1868). Some of his other poems: "A Winter Ramble," "My Epitaph," "The Cross of Gold," "The Golden Wedding," "Where the Lilies Used to Spring."

Sources: *An American Anthology, 1787–1900.* Edmund Clarence Stedman, ed. Houghton Mifflin, 1900. *Dictionary of National Biography.* Electronic Edition 1.1. Oxford University Press, 1997. *English Poetry: Author Search.* Chadwyck-Healey Ltd., 1995 (http://www.lib.utexas.edu:8080/search/epoetry/author.html). *Gray, David (1838–1861), The Poetical Works.* Macmillan, 1874. *The Columbia Granger's Index to Poetry.* 11th ed. *The Columbia Granger's World of Poetry,* Columbia University Press, 2005 (http://www.columbiagrangers.org). *The Oxford Companion to English Literature.* 6th edition. Margaret Drabble, ed. Oxford University Press, 2000. *Wikipedia, the Free Encyclopedia* (http://en.wikipedia.org/wiki/Wikipedia).

GRAY, JOHN HENRY (1866–1934)

Born in Woolwich, London, to a Nonconformist family, he converted to the Roman Catholic Church and was ordained in 1901. For many years he was priest in charge of St. Peter's, Edinburgh. He was a voluminous writer of poetry; many of his poems have a religious theme. He also translated the French poets Paul Verlaine and Stéphane Mallarmé. Oscar Wilde encouraged him to publish his first volume of poetry, *Silverpoints,* in 1893. His long poem *The Flying Fish* was published in the *Dial* in 1896, and republished in *The Long Road* in 1926. His novel *Park: A Fantastic Story*—set in the future—was published in 1932. Some of his other poems: "Act of

Contrition," "And while the shepherds loitered, suddenly," "Adam of Saint Victor," "Fleurs: Imitated from the French of Stéphane Mallarmé," "Hymn to Saint Bernard," "Obedient to the Law, the Child is Brought," "On a Picture," "Parsifal Imitated from the French of Paul Verlaine," "The Barber," "The Emperor and the Bird," "The Long Road," "To Arthur Edmonds."

Sources: *English Poetry: Author Search*. Chadwyck-Healey Ltd., 1995 (http://www.lib.utexas.edu:8080/search/epoetry/author.html). *The Columbia Granger's Index to Poetry*. 11th ed. *The Columbia Granger's World of Poetry*, Columbia University Press, 2005 (http://www.columbiagrangers.org). *The Oxford Companion to English Literature*. 6th edition. Margaret Drabble, ed. Oxford University Press, 2000. *The Poems of John Gray*. Ian Fletcher, ed. ELT Press, 1988. *The Victorian Sonnet* (http://www.sonnets.org/victoria.htm).

GRAY, KATHRYN (1973–)

Welsh poet, born in Caerphilly, Glamorganshire, and raised in Swansea, she studied German and medievalism at the universities of Bristol and York; she currently lives in London, where she works as a freelance writer. She worked as a civil servant at the Wales Office in London, as assistant private secretary to Wales Office Minister Don Touhig. She received an Eric Gregory Award in 2001 and her poems have appeared in the *Times Literary Supplement, The Independent, Poetry Review, Poetry Wales* and other major journals. Her art, theatre and book reviews have also been published widely. Her first collection, *The Never-Never* (2004), was short listed for the prestigious Forward Prize for First Collection (2004), and for the T.S. Eliot Prize—the poetry equivalent of the Booker Prize for fiction. Her poems in this collection deal with joy riders in the rain-lashed back streets and housing estates of Wales, to London and in California; with love and loss, of friendship, exile and the distant promise of home. Some of her poems: "Saint Anthony of Padua," "The Book of Numbers," "The King's Head," "The Pocket Anglo-Welsh Canon," "The Storm," "The Wardrobe."

Sources: *Biography of Kathryn Gray* (http://kathrynlouisegray.blogspot.com/). *Kathryn Gray's delight at prize shortlist* (http://news.bbc.co.uk/2/hi/uk_news/wales/3993591.stm). *Poems by Kathryn Gray* (http://www.thepoem.co.uk/limelight/gray.htm). *Poems by Kathryn Gray* (http://www.transcript-review.org/sub.cfm?lan=enandid=2994).

GRAY, THOMAS (1716–1771)

Born in London into a prosperous family, he was a studious boy who disliked the sports ethos of Eton College, where he was educated from the age of eight. He was at Peterhouse College, Cambridge, between 1734–1738 but left without a degree and accompanied Horace Walpole on a grand tour of France, Switzerland, and Italy at Sir Robert Walpole's expense. By 1742 he had settled in Peterhouse, Cambridge, and in 1756, he moved to Pembroke College, Cambridge. His poems attracted little attention until "An Elegy Written in a Country Church Yard" was published in 1751. He buried himself in studying Celtic, Scandinavian, Gaelic and Welsh poetry. Upon the death of Colley Cibber in 1757, Gray declined the laureateship. He died at Cambridge and was buried in the country churchyard at Stoke Poges, Buckinghamshire, celebrated in his "Elegy." He is commemorated by a bust in Poet's Corner of Westminster Abbey. Some of his poems: "Bard," "The [A Pindaric Ode] Hymn to Adversity," "Ode on a Distant Prospect of Eton College," "The Candidate," "The Curse upon Edward," "The Death of Hoel," "The Descent of Odin."

Sources: *Cowboy Songs and Other Frontier Ballads*. Alan Lomax and John A. Lomax, eds. Macmillan, 1967. *Dictionary of National Biography*. Electronic Edition 1.1. Oxford University Press, 1997. *English Poetry: Author Search*. Chadwyck-Healey Ltd., 1995 (http://www.lib.utexas.edu:8080/search/epoetry/author.html). *Golden Treasury of the Best Songs and Lyrical Poems in the English Language*. Francis Turner Palgrave, ed. Oxford University Press (1964, Sixth edition, updated by John Press, 1994). *Gray's English Poems: Original and Translated from the Norse and the Welsh*. D.C. Tovey, ed. Reprint Services, 1922. *The Columbia Granger's Index to Poetry*. 11th ed. *The Columbia Granger's World of Poetry*, Columbia University Press, 2005 (http://www.columbiagrangers.org). *The New Oxford Book of English Verse, 1250–1950*. Helen Gardner, ed. Oxford University Press, 1972. *The Oxford Companion to English Literature*. 6th edition. Margaret Drabble, ed. Oxford University Press, 2000. *Westminster Abbey Official Guide* (no date).

GREACEN, ROBERT (1920–)

An Irish poet, born in Derry, he studied at the Methodist College, Belfast, and Trinity College, Dublin. He had a career in journalism and literary criticism in London, worked for the United Nations Association and was a lecturer in adult education. He has published several volumes of criticism and won bursaries from the Arts Council of Northern Ireland in 1971 and 1984. He is a member of Aosdána and lives in Dublin. In 1995, his *Collected Poems* won the Irish Times Literature Prize for Poetry. His autobiography, *Even Without Irene*, was published in 1969 and revised in 1995 with another volume, *The Sash My Father Wore* (1997). He published studies on C.P. Snow (1952) and on Noël Coward (1953). Some of his other publications: *The Bird*, 1941. *A Garland for Captain Fox*, 1975. *A Bright Mask*, 1985. *Carnival at the River*, 1990. *Ecstasy*, 1999. *Collected Poems, 1944–1994*, 1995. *Lunch at the Ivy*, 2002.

Some of his poems: "A Summer Day," "Father and Son," "Michael Walked in the Wood," "Old in Overijssel."

Sources: *Irish Contemporary Poets* (http://www.liunet. edu/cwis/cwp/library/sc/irish.htm). *Poets From The North of Ireland.* Frank Ormsby, ed. The Blackstaff Press, 1990. *Biography of Robert Greacen* (http://www.sarahferris. co.uk/pages/robertgreacen.htm). *The Columbia Granger's Index to Poetry.* 11th ed. *The Columbia Granger's World of Poetry,* Columbia University Press, 2005 (http://www.co lumbiagrangers.org). *Turning Tides: Modern Dutch and Flemish Verse in English Versions by Irish Poets.* Peter van de Kamp, ed. Story Line Press, 1994.

GREEN, MATTHEW (1696–1737)

While little is known of the life of this English poet, it appears he was born of Nonconformist parents (possibly Quaker) but did not follow their religion. He was employed in a custom house and died at a lodging in Nag's Head Court, Gracechurch Street, in the City of London. His wit and cheerfulness show through in his amusing poems. When an allowance for supplying the custom-house cats with milk was threatened by the authorities, he wrote a successful petition in their name. His poem "Spleen" appeared posthumously in 1737, with a preface by his friend, Richard Glover (see entry). It is an epistle to Mr. Cuthbert Jackson advocating cheerfulness, exercise and a quiet content as remedies for his spleen (depression). Both Alexander Pope and Thomas Gray expressed a warm admiration for the poem. Quotations from his poems are included in many books. Some of his other poems: "An Epigram," "Jove and Semele," "On Barclay's Apology for the Quakers," "The Grotto," "The Seeker," "The Sparrow and Diamond."

Sources: *Dictionary of National Biography.* Electronic Edition 1.1. Oxford University Press, 1997. *Eighteenth-Century English Verse.* Dennis Davison, ed. Penguin Books, 1988. *English Poetry: Author Search.* Chadwyck-Healey Ltd., 1995 (http://www.lib.utexas.edu:8080/search/epo etry/author.html). *Songs, Merry and Sad of John Charles McNeill.* Alan R. Light, ed. Stone, 1906. *The Columbia Granger's Index to Poetry.* 11th ed. *The Columbia Granger's World of Poetry,* Columbia University Press, 2005 (http:// www.columbiagrangers.org). *The Oxford Companion to English Literature.* 6th edition. Margaret Drabble, ed. Oxford University Press, 2000. *The Spleen and Other Poems by Matthew Green,* The Cayme Press, 1925.

GREENE, ROBERT (?1558–1592)

Born in Norwich, Norfolk (the date is disputed), he had degrees from both Cambridge (1575) and from Oxford (1588). He lived a dissolute life in London and deserted his wife and children. He lived in poverty and legend has it that he died after a dinner of pickled herrings and Rhenish wine, but it was more likely plague. He was buried in the New Churchyard near Bethlehem Hospital, London. He was a prominent prolific writer, renowned for his prose romances and dramas, and was one of the first professional writers and among the earliest English autobiographers. Many books were published in his name after his death. The best of his pastorals is *Pandosto* (1588), the direct source of Shakespeare's *The Winter's Tale.* Among his dramatic works are *The Scottish Historie of James the Fourth* (c. 1591) and *A Looking Glasse for London and England* (1588–1589). Some of his poems: "Against Enticing Cvrtizans," "Philomelaes Second Oade," "Philomelas Ode That Shee Svng in Her Arbovr," "Radagons Sonnet," "The Description of the Shepheard and His Wife," "The Hermites Exordivm," "The Shepheards Wives Song," "Verses Vnder a Pictvre of Fortvne."

Sources: *Dictionary of National Biography.* Electronic Edition 1.1. Oxford University Press, 1997. *English Poetry: Author Search.* Chadwyck-Healey Ltd., 1995 (http://www. lib.utexas.edu:8080/search/epoetry/author.html). *The Columbia Granger's Index to Poetry.* 11th ed. *The Columbia Granger's World of Poetry,* Columbia University Press, 2005 (http://www.columbiagrangers.org). *The New Oxford Book of Sixteenth Century Verse.* Emrys Jones, ed. Oxford University Press, 1991. *The Oxford Companion to English Literature.* 6th edition. Margaret Drabble, ed. Oxford University Press, 2000. *The Poetry of Robert Greene.* Tetsumaro Hayashi, ed. Ball State University, 1977.

GREENLAW, LAVINIA (1962–)

Born in London where she still lives, she has an M.A. in art history from the Courtauld Institute. A freelance writer since 1994, she has written dramas for the BBC, teaches in the creative writing M.A. program at Goldsmiths College, University of London, and has written a sequence of poems about the meaning of numbers for an *Equinox* BBC documentary. In the U.S. she has published in *The New Yorker, Paris Review, American Poet, Grand Street* and *Literary Imagination.* She was British Council Fellow in Writing at Amherst College Massachusetts in 1995 and held residencies in the Science Museum and the Royal Festival Hall, London. Her poetry publications: *Night Photograph,* 1993 (short listed for the Whitbread and Forward Poetry prizes). *A World Where News Traveled Slowly,* 1997 (won the Forward Prize for Best Single Poem). *Thoughts of a Night Sea,* 2002 (a series of meditations to illustrate Garry Fabian Miller's artistic work). *Minsk,* 2003 (short listed for the Forward Prize). Some of her poems: "Anchorage," "Hurting Small Animals," "Iron Lung," "Sex, Politics, and Religion," "The Chapel Snake," "The Gift of Life."

Sources: *ArtForum: Garry Fabian Miller — Rome — Thoughts of a Night Sea* (http://www.findarticles.com/p/ articles/mi_m0268/is_1_42/ai_108691829). *British Council Arts* (http://www.contemporarywriters.com). *Making* *for Planet Alice: New Women Poets.* Maura Dooley, ed. Bloodaxe Books, 1997. *New Women Poets.* Carol Rumens, ed. Bloodaxe Books, 1990. *The Columbia Granger's Index to Poetry.* 11th ed. *The Columbia Granger's World of Poetry,* Columbia University Press, 2005 (http://www.columbiagrangers.org). *The Oxford Companion to English Literature.* 6th edition. Margaret Drabble, ed. Oxford University Press, 2000.

GREENWELL, DORA (1821–1882)

Born at Greenwell Ford, near Lanchester, Lancashire, she was taught by a governess for five years, then taught herself, studying philosophy, political economy and languages. After the death of her mother she moved to London, and became friendly with Josephine Butler, the great Victorian campaigner, and Christina Rossetti (see entry). An evangelical Anglican, she was a woman of deep religious views, often expressed in her poems. Her essays were concerned with various social issues: child labor, women's education, the franchise, and education for those who at that time were called "imbeciles." She also wrote a memoir of the Quaker essayist John Woolman (1871). Some of her other publications: *Poems,* 1848, 1861, 1865, 1867. *Stories That Might Be True,* 1850. *Carmina Cruces,* 1868. *Songs of Salvation,* 1873. *The Soul's Legend,* 1873. *Camera Obscura,* 1876. Some of her poems: "A National Song," "Demeter and Cora," "Go and Come," "I Am Not Skilled to Understand" (hymn), "The Battle-Flag of Sigurd," "The Blade of Grass," "To Christina Rossetti," "To Elizabeth Barrett Browning, in 1851," "When the Night and Morning Meet."

Sources: *Dictionary of National Biography.* Electronic Edition 1.1. Oxford University Press, 1997. *English Poetry: Author Search.* Chadwyck-Healey Ltd., 1995 (http://www.lib.utexas.edu:8080/search/epoetry/author.html). *Poetry Archive* (www.poetry-archive.com). *Stanford University libraries and Academic Information Resources* (http://library.stanford.edu). *The Broadview Anthology of Victorian Poetry and Poetic Theory.* Thomas J. Collins and Vivienne Rundle, eds. Broadview, 1999. *The Columbia Granger's Index to Poetry.* 11th ed. *The Columbia Granger's World of Poetry,* Columbia University Press, 2005 (http://www.columbiagrangers.org). *The Oxford Book of Victorian Verse.* Arthur Quiller-Couch, ed. Oxford University Press, 1971. *The Oxford Companion to English Literature.* 6th edition. Margaret Drabble, ed. Oxford University Press, 2000. *Victorian Women Poets: An Anthology.* Angela Leighton and Margaret Reynolds, eds. Blackwell, 1991.

GREGORY, ISABELLA AUGUSTA, LADY GREGORY (1852–1932)

She was born Isabella Persse, the daughter a wealthy landowner of Roxborough, County Galway, Ireland. In 1880 she married a neighbor, Sir W.H. Gregory of Coole Park — former governor of Ceylon. She was widowed in 1892 and her son was killed in action as an airman in Italy 1918. She became heavily involved with W.B. Yeats in forming the Irish Literary Theatre, Dublin, which opened on 27 December 1904, and was a leading figure in the Irish Revival. Between 1903 and 1927 she wrote twenty-five plays and adapted four of Molière's, translating them into Irish country speech; she also wrote or translated nineteen other books and dozens of poems, many of which are taken from the Irish oral tradition. She wrote two plays of Irish folk (1912 and 1923). Some of her poems: "A Blessing on Patrick Sarsfield," "A Woman's Sonnets," "An Aran Maid's Wedding," "Credhe's Complaint at the Battle of the White Strand," "Forgaill's Praise of Columcille," "His Lament for O'Kelly," "The Army of the Sidhe," "The Call to Bran," "The Death of Osgar," "Yesterday Travelling Connacht."

Sources: *Dictionary of National Biography.* Electronic Edition 1.1. Oxford University Press, 1997. *Encyclopædia Britannica Ultimate Reference Suite DVD,* 2006. *Irish Poetry: An Interpretive Anthology from Before Swift to Yeats and After.* W.J. McCormack, ed. New York University Press, 2000. *Songs from the British Drama.* Edward Bliss Reed, ed. Yale University Press, 1925. *The Columbia Granger's Index to Poetry.* 11th ed. *The Columbia Granger's World of Poetry,* Columbia University Press, 2005 (http://www.columbiagrangers.org). *The Kiltartan Poetry Book by Lady Gregory.* G.P. Putnam's Sons, 1919 (http://digital.library.upenn.edu/women/gregory/poetry/poetry.html). *The National Portrait Gallery* (www.npg.org.uk). *The Oxford Companion to English Literature.* 6th edition. Margaret Drabble, ed. Oxford University Press, 2000. *Wikipedia, the Free Encyclopedia* (http://en.wikipedia.org/wiki/Wikipedia).

GREIG, ANDREW (1951–)

The unofficial poet laureate of the mountaineering community, he was born in Bannockburn (two miles South of Stirling), Scotland, and grew up in Anstruther, Fife. He lives between his homes in Orkney and South Queensferry, Edinburgh. He was educated at the University of Edinburgh and is a former Glasgow University Writing Fellow and Scottish Arts Council Scottish/Canadian Exchange Fellow. *Summit Fever: The Story of an Armchair Climber* (1985) is an account of the successful ascent of the Mustagh Tower in the Himalayas by previously little-known British climbers, of which he was one. His novel *The Return of John McNab* (1996) was short listed for the Romantic Novelists' Association Award and is being filmed for the BBC. His fifth novel, *In Another Light* (2004), won the 2004 Saltire Society Scottish Book of the Year Award. Some of his publications: *White Boats,* 1983. *Men on Ice,* 1977. *Surviving Passages,* 1982. *The Order of the Day,* 1990. *Into You,* 2001. Some of his poems: "In Galloway," "In the Tool-shed," "Interlude on Mustagh Tower,"

"Len's Poems," "The Glove," "The Maid and I," "Young Americans."

Sources: *A Book of Scottish Verse*. Maurice Lindsay and R.L. Mackie, eds. St. Martin's Press, 1983. *Poems of the Scottish Hills: An Anthology*. Hamish Brown, ed. Aberdeen University Press, 1982. *Poetry with an Edge*. Neil Astley, ed. Bloodaxe Books, 1988. *The Columbia Granger's Index to Poetry*. 11th ed. *The Columbia Granger's World of Poetry*, Columbia University Press, 2005 (http://www.columbia-grangers.org).

GRENFELL, JULIAN HENRY FRANCIS (1888–1915)

Born in London, the son of William Henry Grenfell, afterwards Baron Desborough, he was educated at Eton College and at Balliol College, Oxford. He was commissioned into the 1st (the Royal) Dragoons in 1910 and joined the regiment at Muttra, India. He served in France from 1914, was awarded the Distinguished Service Order, and was mentioned in dispatches. He was killed at Ypres and was buried in the military cemetery on the hills above Boulogne. At Eton he contributed to the *London World* and *Vanity Fair*; was one of the editors of the *Eton College Chronicle*, and edited a clever but short-lived periodical called *The Outsider*. His poem "Into Battle" appeared in *The Times* on the day his death was announced. The poet laureate Robert Bridges (see entry) included the poem in his anthology *The Spirit of Man* (1916). He is memorialized by a stone in Poets' Corner of Westminster Abbey along with other poets of the First World War. Some of his other poems: "Hymn to the Wild Boar," "Prayer for Those on the Staff," "The Hills," "To a Black Greyhound."

Sources: *Dictionary of National Biography*. Electronic Edition 1.1. Oxford University Press, 1997. *Men Who March Away: Poems of the First World War*. I.M. Parsons, ed. Viking Press, 1965. *Other Men's Flowers*. A.P. Wavell, ed. Jonathan Cape, 1990. *The Columbia Granger's Index to Poetry*. 11th ed. *The Columbia Granger's World of Poetry*, Columbia University Press, 2005 (http://www.columbiagrangers.org). *The Home Book of Modern Verse*. Burton Egbert Stevenson, ed. Henry Holt, 1953. *The Oxford Companion to English Literature*. 6th edition. Margaret Drabble, ed. Oxford University Press, 2000. *War and the Poet: An Anthology of Poetry Expressing Man's Attitudes to War from Ancient Times to the Present*. Richard Eberhart, and Selden Rodman, ed. Devin-Adair, 1945. *Westminster Abbey Official Guide* (no date).

GRENVILLE (GREYNVILE), SIR RICHARD (1542–1591)

The son of Sir Roger Greynvile, who commanded the *Mary Rose* and was lost when it sank in 1545. Sir Richard's single poem "In Praise of Seafaring Men, in Hopes (or hope) of Good Fortune" inspired Alfred, Lord Tennyson (see entry) to write "The Re-

venge: A Ballad of the Fleet." Sir Richard's exploits can be summarized: fought against the Turks in Hungary, 1566–1568; helped to suppress an uprising in Munster, Ireland, 1568–1569; developed plans to locate a northwest passage from England to China, 1573–1575 (the expedition was never made, but Sir Francis Drake adopted the plan for his circumnavigation voyage of 1577–1580); commanded the fleet that carried 100 English colonists to Roanoke Island, North Carolina, 1585; worked to establish a plantation in the Irish province of Munster, 1589–1591; was second in command of the *Revenge* in a squadron of about 15 vessels sent to intercept a Spanish treasure fleet off the Azores. After a long battle, the *Revenge* with all hands was captured. Grenville was wounded and died on board the Spanish flagship in 1591.

Sources: *Dictionary of National Biography*. Electronic Edition 1.1. Oxford University Press, 1997. *Encyclopædia Britannica Ultimate Reference Suite DVD*, 2006. *The Columbia Granger's Index to Poetry*. 11th ed. *The Columbia Granger's World of Poetry*, Columbia University Press, 2005 (http://www.columbiagrangers.org).

GREVILLE, SIR FULKE, FIRST BARON BROOKE (1554–1628)

Born at Beauchamp Court, Warwickshire, the son of Sir Fulke Greville, he was educated at Jesus College, Cambridge. He had a lifelong friendship with Philip Sidney, with whom he was a courtier. Greville was courtier for Elizabeth, James I and Charles I, and so much in Elizabeth's favor was he that she forbade him to travel abroad or to put himself in danger; when he did, he incurred her displeasure. As a member of Parliament he held various positions of government and was made a Knight of the Bath by James I, and a peer in 1621. Mystery surrounds his death; he was stabbed by a servant who then committed suicide. His works, chiefly published after his death, consist of tragedies and sonnets, and poems on political and moral subjects, including (1586) *Cælica*—109 sonnets composed of love poems as well as verses on religious and philosophical themes — and *The Life of the Rennowned Sir Philip Sidney* (1652.) Some of his other poems: "A Treatise of Monarchy," "Epitaph on Sir Philip Sidney," "Mustapha," "Myra," "Of Human Learning," "Under a throne I saw a virgin sit."

Sources: *Dictionary of National Biography*. Electronic Edition 1.1. Oxford University Press, 1997. *Encyclopædia Britannica Ultimate Reference Suite DVD*, 2006. *English Poetry: Author Search*. Chadwyck-Healey Ltd., 1995 (http://www.lib.utexas.edu:8080/search/epoetry/author.html). *English Renaissance Poetry: A Collection of Shorter Poems from Skelton to Jonson*. John Williams, ed. University of Arkansas, 1990. *The Columbia Granger's Index to Poetry*. 11th ed. *The Columbia Granger's World of Poetry*,

Columbia University Press, 2005 (http://www.columbia grangers.org). *The Faber Book of Political Verse.* Tom Paulin, ed. Faber and Faber, 1986. *The National Portrait Gallery* (www.npg.org.uk). *The Oxford Companion to English Literature.* 6th edition. Margaret Drabble, ed. Oxford University Press, 2000. *The Penguin Book of Renaissance Verse 1509–1659.* David Norbrook, ed. Penguin Books, 1992.

GRIERSON, CONSTANTIA (?1706–1733)

Irish poet whose name may have been Crawley before she married George Grierson, a printer for the government. She came from a poor family from County Kilkenny and went on to study midwifery under Dr. Van Lewen (see Pilkington, Laetitia), history, theology, philosophy, and mathematics, and she became expert in Greek, Latin, Hebrew and French. Like Laetitia Pilkington, she knew Jonathan Swift as well as other poets of the area. Mrs. Grierson edited Latin classics published by her husband. Of these the principal were *Terence* (1727), and *Tacitus* (1730), which was highly praised. Some of her other publications: *Poems,* 1735. *Poems by Mrs Grierson,* 1755. *The Art of Printing,* 1764. Some of her poems: "Prologue to Theodosius," "The Art of Printing," "The Speech of Cupid Upon Seeing Himself Painted," "To Miss Laetitia Van Lewen," "To the Hon. Mrs. Percival," "Verses Occasioned by Mrs. Barber's Son Speaking Latin."

Sources: *A Compendium of Irish Biography* (http://www.libraryireland.com/biography/biographyG.php). *Dictionary of National Biography.* Electronic Edition 1.1. Oxford University Press, 1997. *Eighteenth Century Women Poets an Oxford Anthology.* Roger Lonsdale, ed. Oxford University Press, 1989. *English Poetry: Author Search.* Chadwyck-Healey Ltd., 1995 (http://www.lib.utexas.edu:8080/search/epoetry/author.html). *Matilda Joslyn Gage Website: Biographical Dictionary of Women and Pro-Feminist Men* (http://www.pinn.net/~sunshine/gage/features/dict.html). *Poems by the Most Eminent Ladies of Great Britain and Ireland* (http://www.nku.edu/~issues/eminent_ladies/vol1/master_file_vol_1.html#grierson). *The Columbia Granger's Index to Poetry.* 11th ed. *The Columbia Granger's World of Poetry,* Columbia University Press, 2005 (http://www.columbiagrangers.org). *The Poetry of Laetitia Pilkington (1712–1750) and Constantia Grierson (1706–1733).* Bernard Tucker, ed. The Edwin Mellen Press, 1996.

GRIFFIN, BARTHOLOMEW (fl. 1596)

He was possibly from Northamptonshire or Coventry and may have been buried at Holy Trinity Church, Coventry, in 1602 (his will was proved in 1603). It is thought he might have been an attorney because of his sixty-two sonnets, *Fidessa, More Chaste Than Kinde,* published in 1596, his only known work. The frontispiece reads, "To the Gentlemen of the Inns of Court," and says that it is the first of his writing, which is dedicated to William Essex of Lamborne, Berkshire. He does go on to say that if his poem pleases, then in the next term he will submit a *Pastoral.* Sonnet 1 starts with a Latin tag: "It is said that fortune favors a winner." The poem is rich in imagery and symbolism. Some of his sonnets/poems: "Clip Not Sweet Love the Wings of My Desire," "For I Have Loved Long, I Crave Rewarded," "Grief Urging Guest, Great Cause Have I to Plain Me," "My Spotless Love That Never Yet Was Tainted," "Oh She Must Love My Sorrows to Assuage," "Well May My Soule Immortal and Divine," "When Silent Sleep Had Closed Up Mine Eyes."

Sources: *Dictionary of National Biography.* Electronic Edition 1.1. Oxford University Press, 1997. *Elizabethan Sonnets.* Maurice Evans, ed. J.M. Dent, 1977. *English Poetry: Author Search.* Chadwyck-Healey Ltd., 1995 (http://www.lib.utexas.edu:8080/search/epoetry/author.html). For the complete sonnets of Bartholomew Griffin see www.sonnets.org. *The Columbia Granger's Index to Poetry.* 11th ed. *The Columbia Granger's World of Poetry,* Columbia University Press, 2005 (http://www.columbiagrangers.org).

GRIFFIN, GERALD (1803–1840)

Born in Limerick, where his father was a brewer, he emigrated to Pennsylvania in 1820 with his parents but returned to London in 1823. Encouraged by John Banim (see entry) he had some work published in the *Literary Gazette* and other periodicals. His opera *The Noyades*— entirely in recitative — was produced by him in 1826 at the English opera house, London. He returned to Ireland in 1827 and became a member of the Catholic society of the Christian Brothers in 1838, a body devoted to teaching, a task he fulfilled until he died of a fever. His play *Gisippus*— a blank verse drama of classical times — was produced at Drury Lane in 1842. Dion Boucicault based his play *The Colleen Bawn: or the Brides of Garry-Owen* on Griffin's *The Collegians,* a dark novel (1820). Some of his other publications: *Tales of the Munster Festivals,* 1827. *Tales Illustrative of the Five Senses,* 1830. *Poetical Works,* 1851. Some of his poems: "Eileen Aroon," "I Love My Love in the Morning," "Maiden Eyes," "Brazil, the Isle of the Blest," "Old Times," "To a Seagull," "To the Blessed Virgin Mary."

Sources: *An Anthology of Catholic Poets.* Shane Leslie, ed. Macmillan, 1952. *Dictionary of National Biography.* Electronic Edition 1.1. Oxford University Press, 1997. *Online Encyclopedia: 11th Edition of Encyclopedia. Geralld Griffin* (http://encyclopedia.jrank.org/GRA_GUI/GRIFFIN_OGRIoBTA_OGREEVA_GERAL.html). *The Best Loved Poems of the American People.* Hazel Fellman, ed. Doubleday, 1936. *The Columbia Granger's Index to Poetry.* 11th ed. *The Columbia Granger's World of Poetry,* Columbia University Press, 2005 (http://www.columbiagrangers.org). *The*

Oxford Book of English Verse, 1250–1918. Sir Arthur Quiller-Couch, ed. (New edition, revised and enlarged), Oxford University Press, 1939. *The Oxford Companion to English Literature.* 6th edition. Margaret Drabble, ed. Oxford University Press, 2000.

GRIFFITHS, BILL (1948–)

Born in Kingsbury, Middlesex, he graduated from University College, London, in 1969 with a B.A. in history and gained a Ph.D. in Old English from King's College, London, in 1988. Since 1990, he has lived in Seaham on the Durham coast, where he has produced titles on local history, dialect and place-names. He has also published a number of editions and translations of Old English texts. He is an officer of the Durham and Tyneside Dialect Association and Story of Seaham heritage group. He runs his own publishing company, Amra Press, which publishes his poetry and books of local studies. His experiences as a teenage Hell's Angel provided material for many of his early poems. His first poems were published in *Poetry Review* and in *Writers Forum* circa 1971. Griffiths is a prolific poet and has published widely in Britain and the United States. Some of his publications: *Rousseau and the Wicked,* 1996. *Nomad Sense,* 1997. *A Book of Spilt Cities,* 1999. *Durham and Other Sequences,* 2002. Some of his poems: "Building: The New London Hospital," "Compass Poem," "For P — Celtic: found text from Machen," "Into Prison," "Terzetto: Brixton."

Sources: *Bill Griffiths' Home Page* (http://www.bgriffiths7.freeserve.co.uk/subindex.html). *The Columbia Granger's Index to Poetry.* 11th ed. *The Columbia Granger's World of Poetry,* Columbia University Press, 2005 (http://www.columbiagrangers.org). *The New British Poetry, 1968–88.* Gillian Allnutt, Fred D'Aguiar and Ken Edwards, eds. Grafton Books, 1989. *Wikipedia, the Free Encyclopedia* (http://en.wikipedia.org/wiki/Wikipedia).

GRIGSON, GEOFFREY EDWARD HARVEY (1905–1985)

Born in Pelynt, Cornwall, the son of the local vicar, his autobiography *The Crest on the Silver* (1950) describes his unhappy childhood and adolescence. He graduated from St. Edmund Hall, Oxford, in 1927. Three of his brothers were killed in World War I and three in World War II. He worked on the *Yorkshire Post,* then the *Morning Post,* where he became literary editor; he also founded the influential British poetry magazine *New Verse.* During the war he worked for the BBC, thereafter as a free lancer. In 1972 he received the Duff Cooper memorial prize for a volume of poems. Much of his poetry celebrates his native Cornwall. He made his home in Broad Town, Wiltshire, were he died and is buried. Some of his poetry publications: *Several Observations,* 1939. *Collected Poems 1924–1962,* 1963.

Angles and Circles and Other Poems, 1974. *Collected Poems 1963–1980,* 1984. Some of his poems: "Above the High," "An Administrator," "And Forgetful of Europe," "Bibliotheca Bodleiana," "Death of a Farmyard," "Hardy's Plymouth," "June in Wiltshire," "On a Lover of Books," "To Wystan Auden."

Sources: *Dictionary of National Biography.* Electronic Edition 1.1. Oxford University Press, 1997. *Encyclopædia Britannica Ultimate Reference Suite DVD,* 2006. *English Love Poems.* John Betjeman and Geoffrey Taylor, eds. Faber and Faber, 1957. *The Columbia Granger's Index to Poetry.* 11th ed (http://www.columbiagrangers.org). Index to Poetry, 11th ed (http://www.columbiagrangers.org). *The Faber Book of Epigrams and Epitaphs.* Geoffrey Grigson, ed. Faber and Faber, 1977. *The Gambit Book of Love Poems.* Geoffrey Grigson, ed. Gambit, 1973. *The National Portrait Gallery* (www.npg.org.uk). *The Oxford Companion to English Literature.* 6th edition. Margaret Drabble, ed. Oxford University Press, 2000. *Wikipedia, the Free Encyclopedia* (http://en.wikipedia.org/wiki/Wikipedia).

GRIMALD, NICHOLAS (1519–1562)

Born in Huntingdonshire, he attended both Cambridge and Oxford universities and became a lecturer in theology at Cambridge. He was licensed as a preacher in 1551–1552 and was chaplain to Nicholas Ridley, bishop of London. Ridley was executed in 1555 under the rule of the Catholic Queen Mary. Grimald was imprisoned in the Marshalsea but released, it is assumed because he recanted, but he returned to the Protestant faith when Elizabeth came to the throne in 1558. His friend Barnabe Googe (see entry) wrote an epitaph or elegy on Grimald, which was published in Googe's *Eclogs, Epytaphes, and Sonettes* (1563). Grimald contributed 40 poems to *Songes and Sonettes* (1557), known as *Tottel's Miscellany,* an anthology of contemporary poetry, which he may have edited. Some of his Latin dramas: *Christus Redivivus, Comedia Tragica Sacra,* 1543. *Archiropheta,* 1548 (a tragedy about John the Baptist). *M.T. Ciceroe's Three Bookes of Dueties,* 1553. Some of his poems: "Cleobulus The Lydians Riddle," "Concerning Virgils Eneids," "Description of Vertue," "Marcus Catoes Comparison of Mans Life with Yron," "Marcus Tullius Ciceroes Death," "Prayse of Measure-Kepyng."

Sources: *An Anthology of Renaissance Lyrics: Biography and Songs of Nicholas Grimald* (http://english.edgewood.edu/eng359/lyric_poetry2.htm). *Dictionary of National Biography.* Electronic Edition 1.1. Oxford University Press, 1997. *Elizabethan Lyrics.* Norman Ault, ed. William Sloane Associates, 1949. *Encyclopædia Britannica Ultimate Reference Suite DVD,* 2006. *English Poetry: Author Search.* Chadwyck-Healey Ltd., 1995 (http://www.lib.utexas.edu:8080/search/epoetry/author.html). *The Columbia Granger's Index to Poetry.* 11th ed. *The Columbia Granger's World of Poetry,* Columbia University Press, 2005 (http://www.columbiagrangers.org). *The Oxford Companion to English*

Literature. 6th edition. Margaret Drabble, ed. Oxford University Press, 2000. *The Penguin Book of Renaissance Verse 1509–1659.* David Norbrook, ed. Penguin Books, 1992.

GROARKE, VONA (1964–)

Irish poet, born in Edgeworthstown, County Longford, she is the author of three collections of acclaimed poetry. *Shale* (Gallery Press, 1994) won the Brendan Behan Memorial Award in 1995. *Other People's Houses* (Gallery Press, 1999) was received by the *Times Literary Supplement* as "a remarkable achievement." Her third collection, *Flight* (Gallery Press, 2002) features three substantial poems that received important prizes: "The Way It Goes," the inaugural Strokestown Poetry Prize (1999); "Or to Come," the Stand Magazine International Poetry Prize (2000); and "Imperial Measure," the inaugural Davoren Hanna Prize (2001). She has been writer-in-residence with the National University at Galway and at Maynooth, County Kildare, and with Cavan County Council. She was co-holder of the Heimbold Chair in Irish Studies at Villanova University, Pennsylvania (spring 2004). Some of her other poems: "Indoors," "The Family Photograph," "The History of My Father's House," "The Riverbed," "Trousseau."

Sources: *Biography of Verona Groark* (http://www.gallerypress.com/Authors/Vgroarke/vgroarke.html). *Flight, by Vona Groarke, Book Review.* The Gallery Press (http://www.gallerypress.com/Authors/Vgroarke/Books/vgf.html). *Indoors, Poem by Vona Groarke: Virtual Writer* (http://www.virtualwriter.net/vona-groarke.htm). *Making for Planet Alice: New Women Poets.* Maura Dooley, ed. Bloodaxe Books, 1997. *Virtual Writer* (http://www.virtualwriter.net/vona-groarke.htm).

GROSE, FRANCIS (?1731–1791)

Born in Middlesex, the eldest son of a prosperous jeweler, he chose to study art rather than go to university, and he went on to illustrate his own books. He served for more than twenty years in the army and is one of the period's greatest antiquarians. In character he was described as a sort of antiquarian Falstaff. Robert Burns wrote "Tam O' Shanter" so that Grose would include a drawing of Alloway Kirk in his *Antiquities of Scotland* (1789–1791). Burns wrote a poem, "On the late Captain Grose's Peregrinations." Grose died in Dublin and is buried in Drumcondra churchyard. Some of his publications: *The Antiquities of England and Wales,* 1772–1776. *Advice to the Officers of the British Army,* 1782. *A Guide to Health, Beauty, Riches, and Honor,* 1783. *A Classical Dictionary of the Vulgar Tongue,* 1785. *Military Antiquities,* 1786–1788. *A Provincial Glossary,* 1787. *Rules for Drawing Caricatures,* 1788. *Antiquities of Ireland,* 1791 (completed by his friend Dr. Edward Ledwich). Some of his poems: "On a Wife," "On One Munday, Who Hanged Himself," "Poetical Epistle to Mrs. Green."

Sources: *Dictionary of National Biography.* Electronic Edition 1.1. Oxford University Press, 1997. *Francis Grose (c. 1731–1791), The Antiquities of England and Wales* (http://www.antiquemapsandprints.com/GROSE.htm). *Great Books Online* (www.bartleby.com). *On Captain Francis Grose* (http://www.worldburnsclub.com/poems/translations/on_captain_francis_grose.htm). *The National Library of Ireland—Collections—Prints and Drawings* (http://www.nli.ie/co_print.htm).

GUNN, THOM (1929–2004)

Born in Gravesend, Kent, the son of a journalist and newspaper editor, his mother seems to have inspired his future career. After National Service he graduated from Trinity College, Cambridge, in 1953, then moved to America with Mike Kitay, with whom he remained a companion until his death. He was awarded a writing fellowship at Stanford University, where he became a student of the poet and critic Yvor Winters and taught at Berkeley. He made his home in San Francisco, where he could be more open about his sexuality, expressed in *The Passages of Joy* (1982). His awards have been many across the world. "He was particularly honored for his powerful work in *The Man with Night Sweats,* a collection of laments and elegies of the AIDS epidemic published in 1992" (*The San Francisco Chronicle,* April 29, 2004). Some of his other publications: *Selected Poems,* 1962. *Positives,* 1966. *Poems, 1950–1966,* 1967. *Selected Poems 1950–1975,* 1979. *The Occasion of Poetry,* 1982. Some of his poems: "Autobiography," "Cafeteria in Boston," "Jack Straw's Castle," "San Francisco Streets," "Talbot Road," "The Missing," "Transients and Residents."

Sources: *Biography of Thom Gunn* (http://www.interviews-with-poets.com/thom-gunn/gunn-note.html). *Collected Poems of Thom Gunn.* Faber and Faber, 1994. *The Columbia Granger's Index to Poetry.* 11th ed. *The Columbia Granger's World of Poetry,* Columbia University Press, 2005 (http://www.columbiagrangers.org). *The Oxford Companion to English Literature.* 6th edition. Margaret Drabble, ed. Oxford University Press, 2000. *Threepenny: Kitay, Thom Gunn* (http://www.threepennyreview.com/samples/kitay_su05.html).

GURNEY, IVOR BERTIE (1890–1937)

Born in Gloucester, England, the son of a tailor, he was educated as a chorister of Gloucester Cathedral. He began composing music at the age of 14 and won a scholarship to the Royal College of Music in 1911, studying under Sir Charles Stanford. He enlisted into the Gloucestershire Regiment in 1915, was wounded, and gassed during the third battle of Ypres. After the war he resumed his musical studies but was unable to concentrate. There is consensus that he suffered from some form of mental illness, and he did try several times to commit suicide. He spent the last years of his life at the City of London Mental Hospital, Dartford, Kent, where he died from tuberculosis. In addition to his songs, he wrote poetry; many of his poems celebrate the Gloucestershire countryside. He is one of the poets of World War I memorialized in Poets' Corner of Westminster Abbey. Two of his volumes of poetry are *Severn and Somme*, 1917, and *War's Embers*, 1919. Some of his poems: "Bach and the Sentry," "Cotswold Ways," "Sonnet — September 1922," "The Silent One," "Yesterday Lost," "Ypres — Minsterworth."

Sources: *Dictionary of National Biography.* Electronic Edition 1.1. Oxford University Press, 1997. *Ivor Gurney — Poet-Composer* (http://www.geneva.edu/~dksmith/gurney/index.html). *Selected Poems of Ivor Gurney.* P.J. Kavanagh, ed. Oxford University Press, 1990. *The Columbia Granger's Index to Poetry.* 11th ed. *The Columbia Granger's World of Poetry,* Columbia University Press, 2005 (http://www.columbiagrangers.org). *The Oxford Companion to English Literature.* 6th edition. Margaret Drabble, ed. Oxford University Press, 2000. *Westminster Abbey Official Guide* (no date). *Wikipedia, the Free Encyclopedia* (http://en.wikipedia.org/wiki/Wikipedia).

GUTTERIDGE, BERNARD (1916–1985)

Born in Southampton, he was educated at Cranleigh, Surrey. He wrote poems about the Spanish Civil War and about his experiences during World War II. He served in Madagascar, India and Burma in the 36th Division of the British Army. He and Alun Lewis (see entry) served together with Combined Operations until Lewis died. Gutteridge worked in advertising both before and after WWII, and his 1954 novel *The Agency Game* is set in the advertising world. Almost all the poems in *The Traveler's Eye* (1947) describe his experiences during military service in the Far East. Some of his other publications: *Spanish Earth*, 1939. *Dog Bites Grass*, 1949. *A Loathing of Cats*, 1952. *Old Damson-Face: Poems 1934 to 1974*, 1975. Some of his poems: "Burma Hills," "In September 1939," "Man into a Churchyard," "Namkwin Pul," "Patrol; Buonamary," "Rim of Red," "Shillong," "Sniper," "The Enemy Dead."

Sources: *Poetry of the World Wars.* Michael Foss, ed. Peter Bedrick Books, 1990. *The Columbia Granger's Index to Poetry.* 11th ed. *The Columbia Granger's World of Poetry,* Columbia University Press, 2005 (http://www.columbiagrangers.org). *The War Poets: An Anthology of the War Poetry of the 20th Century.* Oscar Williams, ed. John Day, 1945. *Wikipedia, the Free Encyclopedia* (http://en.wikipedia.org/wiki/Wikipedia).

HABINGTON, WILLIAM (1605–1654)

He was born at Hindlip, Worcestershire, and educated at the comparatively new Catholic College of St. Omer near Calais and also at Paris. At that time, when England was turning to Protestantism, Catholic education was forbidden. Some say he left France because of pressure to become a Jesuit. He married Lucy Herbert, daughter of William Herbert, first baron Powis, and his long poem *Castara* (1634) is a collection of poems in her praise with some elegies to his friends. Some of his other publications: *Queene of Arragon: A Tragi-Comedie*, 1640. *The History of Edward the Fourth, King of England*, 1640. *Observations upon Historie*, 1641. Some of his poems: "Against Them Who Lay Unchastity to the Sex of Women," "Elegie Upon the Death of Ben Johnson," "In Hymeneum Ingeniosissimiiacobi Shirley," "On Master John Fletchers Dramaticall Poems," "Purification," "The Compliment," "To My Friend the Author," "To My Friend, Will Davenant," "To Vaine Hope," "To Zephirus," "Welcome, Thou Safe Retreat!" "What Am I Who Dare," "When I Survey the Bright Celestial Sphere."

Sources: *A Treasury of Poems for Worship and Devotion.* Charles L. Wallis, ed. Harper, 1959. *Dictionary of National Biography.* Electronic Edition 1.1. Oxford University Press, 1997. *English Poetry: Author Search.* Chadwyck-Healey Ltd., 1995 (http://www.lib.utexas.edu:8080/search/epoetry/author.html). *Great Books Online* (www.bartleby.com). *The Columbia Granger's Index to Poetry.* 11th ed. *The Columbia Granger's World of Poetry,* Columbia University Press, 2005 (http://www.columbiagrangers.org). *The Oxford Companion to English Literature.* 6th edition. Margaret Drabble, ed. Oxford University Press, 2000. *The Poems of William Habington.* University Press of Liverpool, 1948.

HAGTHORPE, JOHN (?1585–?1630)

He had links with Chester-le-Street, County Durham, and Scarborough Castle, Yorkshire. Several bad land transactions reduced him to poverty and, fearing he might have to emigrate to Virginia, he appealed to James I for assistance to get his son into Charterhouse School. As Captain Hagthorpe he commanded one of His Majesty's ships protecting the Hull ships bound for Holland against the attacks from the French. He also took part in the Cadiz expedition of 1625. He was alive in January 1630, when he presented a petition to the admiralty. He wrote *Visiones Rerum* (The Visions of Things, 1623), which consists of four poems: "Principium and Mutabilitas Rerum. Or, The Beginning and Mutabilitie of All Things," "Cursus and Ordo Rerum. Or, Art and Nature," "Opineo and Ratio Rerum. Or, Wealth and Pouertie," "Malum and Finis Rerum. Or, Sinne and Vertue, concluding with the last Iudgement and end of all things." He also wrote: *Englands-Exchequer, or a Discourse of the Sea and Navigation, with Some Things — Concerning Plantations*, 1625. *Divine Meditations*, 1662.

Sources: *Dictionary of National Biography.* Electronic Edition 1.1. Oxford University Press, 1997. *English Poetry: Author Search.* Chadwyck-Healey Ltd., 1995 (http://www. lib.utexas.edu:8080/search/epoetry/author.html). *English Poetry: Author Search* (http://www.lib.utexas.edu:8080/ search/epoetry/author.html). *Oldpoetry* (www.oldpoetry. com). *SETIS: The Scholarly Electronic Text and Image Service, English Poetry Collection* (http://setis.library.usyd. edu.au/poetry/browse/h-epdtoc.html). *Stanford University libraries and Academic Information Resources* (http://li brary.stanford.edu).

HAKE, THOMAS GORDON (1809–1895)

Hake was born at Leeds, though the family lived in Devonshire. His mother, widowed when he was young, secured him a place at Christ's Hospital School, London. He graduated in medicine from Glasgow University and practiced in many different parts of the country, then settled at Roehampton, where he was physician to the West London Hospital and to the Countess of Ripon — to whom his mother was related — at Nocton Hall, Lincolnshire (the Hall was destroyed by fire on 24 October 2004). He became a close friend with Dante Rossetti (see entry) and helped him through the dark days of mental turmoil. His autobiography, *Memoirs of Eighty Years*, was published in 1892. He retired from medicine to concentrate on poetry and died at his home near St. John's Wood, London. Some of his publications: *Madeline: With Other Poems and Parables*, 1871. *The New Day*, 1890. *Parables and Tales*, 1872. *Poetic Lucubrations*, 1828. *Queen Victoria's Day*, 1892. Some of his poems: "The Blind Boy," "The Cripple," "The Golden Wedding," "The Infant Medusa," "The Sybil," "The Wedding Ring," "Venus Urania," "When I Think of Thee, Brother."

Sources: *Dictionary of National Biography.* Electronic Edition 1.1. Oxford University Press, 1997. *English Poetry: Author Search.* Chadwyck-Healey Ltd., 1995 (http://www. lib.utexas.edu:8080/search/epoetry/author.html). *Great Books Online* (www.bartleby.com). *SETIS: The Scholarly Electronic Text and Image Service, English Poetry Collection* (http://setis.library.usyd.edu.au/poetry/browse/h-epdtoc.html). *Sonnets of the Century* (http://www. sonnets.org/bibliogr.htm#sharp1). *The Columbia Granger's Index to Poetry.* 11th ed. *The Columbia Granger's World of Poetry*, Columbia University Press, 2005 (http://www. columbiagrangers.org). *The Poems of Thomas Gordon Hake.* Alice Meynell, ed. AMS Press, 1971.

HALL (HALLE), JOHN (?1529–?1566)

Hall's poems were mainly on religious themes. He was also a surgeon at Maidstone, Kent (his impossibly long titles have been paraphrased and translated into modern English). Some of his publications: *Certain Chapters from Proverbs the Psalms and Other Books of the Bible*, 1549. *A Metrical Version of Proverbs, Three Chapters of Ecclesiastes, and Certain Psalms*, 1550. *Commendatory English Verses Prefixed to Thomas Gale's "Manual of Surgery,"* 1563. *A Posy in Form of a Vision, Against Devilish Practices, Including Astrology*, 1563. *The Court of Virtue, Containing Many Holy or Spiritual Songs, Sonnets, Psalms, Ballads*, 1565. *A Most Excellent and Learned Work of Surgery*, 1565. *A Very Fruitful and Necessary Brief Work of Anatomy*, 1565. *An Historical Expostulation: Against the Beastly Abusers, Both of Surgery, and Physic, in Our Time: With a Goodly Doctrine and Instruction, Necessary to Be Marked and Followed, of All True Surgeons*, 1565. Some of his poems: "Job I," "Numbers 13," "Proverbs 30," "The Praise of Faith," "The Praise of Godly Love Out of 1 John 4."

Sources: *Chapters into Verse. Vol. I: Genesis to Malachi.* Robert Atwan and Laurance Wieder, eds. Oxford University Press. 1993. *Chapters into Verse. Vol. II: Gospels to Revelation.* Robert Atwan and Laurance Wieder, eds. Oxford University Press, 1993. *Dictionary of National Biography.* Electronic Edition 1.1. Oxford University Press, 1997. *English Poetry: Author Search.* Chadwyck-Healey Ltd., 1995 (http://www.lib.utexas.edu:8080/search/epoetry/author. html). *The Columbia Granger's Index to Poetry.* 11th ed. *The Columbia Granger's World of Poetry*, Columbia University Press, 2005 (http://www.columbiagrangers.org).

HALL, JOHN, OF DURHAM (1627–1656)

Poet and pamphleteer, born and educated at Durham. He studied at St. John's College, Cambridge, then at Gray's Inn, London. He accompanied Cromwell in 1650 to Scotland, where he wrote the pamphlet *The Grounds and Reasons of Monarchy*, with an appendix, *An Epitome of Scottish Affairs*. He was awarded a pension by Cromwell and the council for his pamphleteering services. He left work unfinished when he died. Some of his other publications: *Horæ Vacivæ, or Essays. Some Occasional Considerations*, 1646. *Commendatory Verses*, 1646. *Poems*, 1646–1647. *The Second Book of Divine Poems*, 1647. *A Satire against Presbytery*, 1648. *Answer to the Grand Politick Informer*, 1653. *A Letter from a Gentleman in the Country*, 1653. *A Treatise Discovering the Horrid Cruelties of the Dutch Upon Our People at Amboyna*, 1624. *Emblems with Elegant Figures, Newly Publishe*, 1658. *Hierocles Upon the Golden Verses of the Pythagoreans. Translated Immediately Out of the Greek into English*, 1682. Some of his poems: "A Pastoral Hymn," "An Epicurean Ode," "Home Travel," "Of Beauty," "On an Hour-Glass," "The Call."

Sources: *Dictionary of National Biography*, Electronic Edition, 1.1. *English Poetry: Author Search.* Chadwyck-Healey Ltd., 1995 (http://www.lib.utexas.edu:8080/ search/epoetry/author.html). *The Columbia Granger's Index to Poetry.* 11th ed. *The Columbia Granger's World of Poetry*, Columbia University Press, 2005 (http://www.

columbiagrangers.org). *The New Oxford Book of Seventeenth Century Verse*. Alastair Fowler, ed. Oxford University Press, 1991.

HALLAM, ARTHUR HENRY (1811–1833)

He was born in London, the son of the historian Henry Hallam (1777–1859), and was educated at Eton College. He graduated from Trinity College, Cambridge, in 1832, having won several prizes, one being for an essay upon the philosophical writings of Cicero. He was a member of the "Cambridge Apostles," which included Lord Tennyson (see entry) and their friendship is the subject of Tennyson's long poem "In Memoriam A.H.H.," written in 1849, in which he grieves over the loss of his friend who was in love with his sister, Emily. On a tour with his father in Austria, he suddenly died, having had some circulatory problem, which first showed at Cambridge. He was buried in the chancel of Clevedon Church, Somersetshire. For one who died so young, his output was prodigious. His *Remains* was edited by his father in 1834. Some of his poems: "A melancholy thought had laid me low," "Lady, I bid thee to a sunny dome," "Oh Poetry, Oh Rarest Spirit of All," "Still Here — Thou Hast Not Faded from My Sight," "To My Mother," "When gentle fingers cease to touch the string."

Sources: *Dictionary of National Biography*. Electronic Edition 1.1. Oxford University Press, 1997. *Sonnet Central* (www.sonnets.org). *The Columbia Granger's Index to Poetry*. 11th ed. *The Columbia Granger's World of Poetry,* Columbia University Press, 2005 (http://www.columbiagrangers.org). *The Oxford Book of Regency Verse 1798–1837*. H.S. Milford, ed. Oxford University Press, 1928. *The Oxford Companion to English Literature*. 6th edition. Margaret Drabble, ed. Oxford University Press, 2000. *The Victorian Web* (http://www.victorianweb.org/authors/hallam/bioov.html).

HALLORAN, LAWRENCE HYNES (1766–1831)

Born in Ireland, he was a schoolmaster at Alphington, near Exeter, Devon. He then became a chaplain in the royal navy on board the *Britannia*, the vessel which carried the flag of Admiral the Earl of Northesk at the battle of Trafalgar. He was afterwards appointed rector of the public grammar school, Cape Town, and chaplain to the forces in South Africa. For criticizing a high-ranking officer over a court-martial, a case was brought against him; he was found guilty and banished from South Africa. After that he led a wandering life and in 1818 was charged at the Old Bailey, London, with forgery, found guilty and transported to Australia for seven years. There he established and ran a successful school at Sydney, New South Wales, where he died.

Some of his publications (with shortened titles): *A Collection of Odes, Poems, and Translations*, 1789. *An Ode (Attempted in Sapphic Verse)*, 1789. *Poems on Various Occasions*, 1791. *Lachrymae Hibernicae, or the Genius of Erin's Complaint, a Ballad*, 1801. *The Battle of Trafalgar, a Poem, to Which is Added a Selection of Fugitive Pieces*, 1806.

Sources: *Bibliography of 19th-c. Irish Literature* (http://info.wlu.ca/~wwweng/faculty/jwright/irish/biblio-main.htm). *Deception: Forgery, Lawrence Halloran, 09 Sept. 1818* (http://www.oldbaileyonline.org/html_units/1810s/t18180909-4.html). *Dictionary of National Biography*. Electronic Edition 1.1. Oxford University Press, 1997. *The Columbia Granger's Index to Poetry*. 11th ed. *The Columbia Granger's World of Poetry,* Columbia University Press, 2005 (http://www.columbiagrangers.org). *The New Oxford Book of Eighteenth Century Verse*. Roger Lonsdale, ed. Oxford University Press, 2003.

HAMILTON, WILLIAM OF BANGOUR (1704–1754)

He was born at Bangour, near Linlithgow, son of a Scottish barrister, and succeed to the family estate in 1750. He supported the Stuart cause and after the Battle of Culloden (1746) was forced into hiding in the Highlands. He escaped to France an ill man and he died in Lyons of tuberculosis. His body was buried in the Abbey Church, Holyrood, Edinburgh. William Wordsworth and Sir Walter Scott were full of praise for Hamilton's work. An unauthorized collection, *Poems on Several Occasions*, was published by Foulis of Glasgow in 1748–1749 and reissued as *Hamilton of Bangour's Poems*. *The Poems and Songs of William Hamilton of Bangour* was published in 1850. Some of his poems: "A Soliloquy Wrote in June 1746," "Contemplation, or the Triumph of Love," "Episode of the Thistle," "Gladsmuir," "Seven Familiar Epistles," "The Braes of Yarrow," "The Faithful Few: An Ode," "The Parting of Hector and Andromache."

Sources: *Dictionary of National Biography*. Electronic Edition 1.1. Oxford University Press, 1997. *English Songs and Ballads*. T.W.H. Crosland, ed. Oxford University Press, 1918. *Oldpoetry* (www.oldpoetry.com). *The Columbia Granger's Index to Poetry*. 11th ed. *The Columbia Granger's World of Poetry*, Columbia University Press, 2005 (http://www.columbiagrangers.org). *The Oxford Companion to English Literature*. 6th edition. Margaret Drabble, ed. Oxford University Press, 2000. *The Poems of Allan Ramsay. Vol. 2*. T. Cadell and W. Davies, 1800.

HAMMOND, JAMES (1710–1742)

The son of Anthony Hammond of Somersham Place, Huntingdonshire, who, according to Samuel Johnson was "a man of note among the wits, poets, and parliamentary orators in the beginning of this century." James was educated at Westminster School but had no university education. He became a member of the clique that gathered around Frederick, Prince of Wales (father of George III) and in 1733 was made one of the equerries to the prince. His term of office as member of Parliament for Truro, Cornwall, in 1741 was short-lived. He died at Stowe in Buckinghamshire. He wrote fifteen love elegies, and of these, Johnson says, "He produces nothing but frigid pedantry. It would be hard to find in all his productions three stanzas that deserve to be remembered." Some of his poems: "Against Lovers Going to War," "An Elegy to a Young Lady," "He despairs that he shall ever possess Delia," "On Delia's Being in the Country," "On his Falling in Love with Neæra," "Prologue to Lillo's Elmerick," "Sonnet 57: Written in Netley Abbey, Near Southampton."

Sources: *Dictionary of National Biography.* Electronic Edition 1.1. Oxford University Press, 1997. *English Poetry: Author Search.* Chadwyck-Healey Ltd., 1995 (http://www.lib.utexas.edu:8080/search/epoetry/author.html). *Oldpoetry* (www.oldpoetry.com). *Samuel Johnson's Lives of the English Poets,* 1779–1781 (http://www2.hn.psu.edu/Faculty/KKemmerer/poets/preface.htm). *The Columbia Granger's Index to Poetry.* 11th ed. *The Columbia Granger's World of Poetry,* Columbia University Press, 2005 (http://www.columbiagrangers.org). *The Poetical Works of James Hammond.* Glasgow University, 1787.

HANMER, SIR JOHN, BARON HANMER (1809–1881)

The son of Thomas Hanmer, colonel of the royal Flints militia, descended from the Welsh family of Sir John de Hanmere, Constable of Carnarvon Castle in the time of Edward I. He was educated at Eton College and at Christ Church, Oxford, but did not proceed to a degree. His grandfather, Sir Thomas Hanmer, died in 1828, and John succeeded him as third baronet. He was member of Parliament for several different constituencies between 1832 and 1872 and was raised to the peerage as Baron Hanmer of Hanmer and Flint in 1872. He supported free trade and religious liberty and voted for the total repeal of the Corn Laws. He died at Knotley Hall, near Tunbridge Wells, and was buried at Bettisfield Park, Whitchurch, Shropshire. Some of his publications: *Proteus and Other Poems,* 1833. *Poems on Various Subjects,* 1836. *Fra Cipolla,* 1839. *Sonnets,* 1840. *A Memorial of the Parish,* 1877. Some of his poems: "Alexowitz," "Approach to Venice on a November Day," "Asmodeus Redivivus," "Enter Monks: From the Same," "Gondolier's Song: In an Unfinished Mask," "Pescara," "The Tricolor."

Sources: *Dictionary of National Biography.* Electronic Edition 1.1. Oxford University Press, 1997. *English Poetry: Author Search.* Chadwyck-Healey Ltd., 1995 (http://www.lib.utexas.edu:8080/search/epoetry/author.html). *Oldpoetry* (www.oldpoetry.com). *SETIS—English Poetry Collection* (http://setis.library.usyd.edu.au/poetry/browse/h-epdtoc.html). *The National Portrait Gallery* (www.npg.org.uk).

HANNAH, SOPHIE (1971–)

Born in Manchester, and now living in West Yorkshire, she studied English literature and Spanish at Manchester University. In 2004 she was named as one of the Poetry Book Society's "Next Generation" poets. She won the 1995 Eric Gregory Award and the 1996 Arts Council Writers' Award for her collection *Hotels Like Houses.* A regular contributor to BBC Radio, she also appears on poetry shows on television. Her career to date: writer-in-residence at the Portico Library, Manchester, 1994–1997; fellow commoner in creative arts, Trinity College, Cambridge, 1997–1999; fellow of Wolfson College, Oxford, 1999–2001; creative writing lecturer, Manchester Metropolitan University, 1998 to the present. Her poetry publications: *Early Bird Blues,* 1993. *Second Helping of Your Heart,* 1994. *The Hero and the Girl Next Door,* 1995. *Hotels Like Houses,* 1996. *Leaving and Leaving You,* 1999. *The Box Room,* 2001 (children). *First of the Last Chances,* 2003. *Selected Poems,* 2006. *Love Me Slender,* 2000. Some of her poems: "My Enemies," "Postcard from a Travel Snob," "The Good Loser," "Where is Talcott Parsons Now?" "Your Dad Did What?" "Your Street Again."

Sources: *British Council Arts* (http://www.contemporarywriters.com). *Biography of Sophie Hannah* (http://www.sophiehannah.com/biographical.html). *Making for Planet Alice: New Women Poets.* Maura Dooley, ed. Bloodaxe Books, 1997. *Poemhunter* (www.poemhunter.com). *The Columbia Granger's Index to Poetry.* 11th ed. *The Columbia Granger's World of Poetry,* Columbia University Press, 2005 (http://www.columbiagrangers.org). *The Harvill Book of Twentieth-Century Poetry in English.* Michael Schmidt, ed. The Harvill Press, 1999. *The New Exeter Book of Riddles.* Kevin Crossley-Holland and Lawrence Sail, ed. Enitharmon Press, 1999.

HANNAY, PATRICK (d. ?1629)

He was born at Sorbie Castle, Wigtown, Scotland, where the family had owned land for generations. Early in the reign of James I, Hannay and his cousin Robert came to the English court and were favorably noticed by Queen Anne. In 1620, the cousins were granted land in County Longford, Ireland. In 1627 Patrick became master of chancery in Ireland. At some time he was general of artillery in the army of Prince Fredericke, King of Bohemia, to whom he dedicated one of his sonnets. Robert was created a baronet of Nova Scotia in 1629. Patrick is said to have died at sea in 1629. He does not seem to have married. He wrote many sonnets. Some of his publications (shortened titles): *A Happy Husband, or Directions for a Maide to Choose Her Mate,*

1618–19. *Two Elegies on the Late Death of Our Soveraigne Queene Anne*, 1619. *Happy Husband* 1622, (a new edition, the elegies, with some new poems). His previous works include: *Philomela the Nightingale*, *Sheretine* and *Mariana*, and songs and sonnets, some of which have been set to music.

Sources: *Dictionary of National Biography.* Electronic Edition 1.1. Oxford University Press, 1997. *Dumfries and Galloway, Scotland—Ancestors Stories* (http://freepages.genealogy.rootsweb.com/~debbie/stories/dum.html. *English Poetry: Author Search* (http://www.lib.utexas.edu:8080/search/epoetry/author.html). *Great Books Online* (www.bartleby.com). *Oldpoetry* (www.oldpoetry.com). *Sorbie Village* (http://www.whithorn.info/community/sorbie.htm). *The Columbia Granger's Index to Poetry.* 11th ed. *The Columbia Granger's World of Poetry,* Columbia University Press, 2005 (http://www.columbiagrangers.org). *The Penguin Book of Bird Poetry.* Peggy Munsterberg, ed. 1984.

HARDY, THOMAS (1840–1928)

Hardy was born at Higher Bockhampton, a hamlet near Stinsford, Dorset, to a musical family who contributed to the life of the village and to the church services. He was educated locally and became a pupil of John Hicks, an ecclesiastical architect in Dorchester. He then worked as an architect under Sir Arthur William Blomfield in London. Ill health brought him home to Dorset in 1867, and over the next thirty years he published fourteen novels — based mainly around Wessex — and a number of short stories. From 1898 he produced eight volumes of poetry as well as an epic poetic drama, *The Dynasts*, published as a whole in 1910. His three major collections are: *Wessex Poems*, 1898. *Poems of Past and Present*, 1901. *Time's Laughingstocks*, 1909. He was appointed to the Order of Merit in 1910. His ashes are buried in Poets' Corner of Westminster Abbey; his heart is buried at Stinsford. Some of his poems: "Afternoon Service at Mellstock," "Last Week in October," "Logs on the Hearth," "The Beauty," "The Chapel-Organist," "The Death of Regret," "The Farm-Woman's Winter," "The Harvest-Supper."

Sources: *Chief Modern Poets of Britain and America.* 5th edition. Gerald DeWitt Sanders and John Herbert Nelson, eds. Macmillan, 1970. *Dictionary of National Biography.* Electronic Edition 1.1. Oxford University Press, 1997. *Encyclopædia Britannica Ultimate Reference Suite DVD,* 2006. *English Poetry: Author Search* (http://www.lib.utexas.edu:8080/search/epoetry/author.html). *The Columbia Granger's Index to Poetry.* 11th ed. *The Columbia Granger's World of Poetry,* Columbia University Press, 2005 (http://www.columbiagrangers.org). *The Complete Poems of Thomas Hardy.* James Gibson, ed. Macmillan, 1978. *The Faber Book of War Poetry.* Kenneth Baker, ed. Faber and Faber, 1996. *The Oxford Companion to English Literature.* 6th edition. Margaret Drabble, ed. Oxford University Press, 2000. *Westminster Abbey Official Guide* (no date).

HARINGTON, SIR JOHN (1561–1612)

Harrington was Queen Elizabeth's godson. Educated at Eton College, King's College, Cambridge (graduating M.A. in 1581), and Lincoln's Inn, London, he was knighted in 1599 for leading a military expedition to Ireland. The queen banished him from court from 1596–1598 for writing some innuendo about the Earl of Leicester. Back in favor, he accompanied Robert Devereux, earl of Essex (1567–1601) (see Essex, Robert Devereux), on his ill-fated expedition to Ireland, where he served as commander of horse under the Earl of Southampton. After James became king (1603), Harington's popularity waned, though he took some part in Prince Henry's education. He invented the flush lavatory and installed one for Queen Elizabeth in her palace at Richmond, Surrey. He translated Ariosto's epic poem *Orlando Furioso*, published in 1591. Some of his other poems: "A Groom of the Chamber's Religion in King Henry the Eighth's Time," "A Sonnet Made on Isabella Markham," "A Sonnet Written upon My Lord Admiral Seymour," "Elegy Wrote in the Tower, 1554," "Husband to Wife," "I See My Plaint," "Of the Wars in Ireland," "Sir John Raynsford's Confession," "To His Mother," "Wife to Husband."

Sources: *Dictionary of National Biography.* Electronic Edition 1.1. Oxford University Press, 1997. *Elizabethan Lyrics.* Norman Ault, ed. William Sloane Associates, 1949. *Encyclopædia Britannica Ultimate Reference Suite DVD,* 2006. *English Poetry: Author Search* (http://www.lib.utexas.edu:8080/search/epoetry/author.html). *The Columbia Granger's Index to Poetry.* 11th ed. *The Columbia Granger's World of Poetry,* Columbia University Press, 2005 (http://www.columbiagrangers.org). *The National Portrait Gallery* (www.npg.org.uk). *The Oxford Book of English Verse.* Christopher Ricks, ed. Oxford University Press, 1999. *The Oxford Companion to English Literature.* 6th edition. Margaret Drabble, ed. Oxford University Press, 2000.

HARRIS, JOHN (1820–1884)

Born to a miner at Six Chimneys Cottage, Bolennowe Hill, Camborne, Cornwall, he started working underground in Dolcoath mine with his father at the age of twelve. Mainly self-educated, he was encouraged by the rector of Camborne to write poetry. An industrious man, he built his own house and in 1845 he married. He was scripture reader in Falmouth and a Methodist local preacher. His *Lays from the Mine, the Moor, and the Mountain* was published in 1853, and from then on he published a volume nearly every year. In 1864 he won first prize for the Shakespeare tercentenary poem. He died at Falmouth and was buried at Treslothan. His *My Autobiography* was published in 1882. Some of his other publications: *The Land's End and Other Poems*, 1859. *The Mountain Prophet*, 1860. *Wayside Pictures*, 1874. *Walks with the Wild Flowers*, 1875. Some of his poems: "Elihu Burritt in Cornwall," "Out of Cornwall," "Sonnets to the Months," "The Avon," "The Cannon in the Lane," "The Fall of Slavery," "The Monument of Chatterton," "The Winding Wye."

Sources: *Dictionary of National Biography.* Electronic Edition 1.1. Oxford University Press, 1997. *Shakespeare's Shrine By John Harris.* Hamilton, Adams, and Co., 1866. *The Columbia Granger's Index to Poetry.* 11th ed. *The Columbia Granger's World of Poetry,* Columbia University Press, 2005 (http://www.columbiagrangers.org). *The Life of a Miner* (http://www.lynherparishes.co.uk/LYjohnharris.htm). *The Oxford Companion to English Literature.* 6th edition. Margaret Drabble, ed. Oxford University Press, 2000.

HARRISON, TONY (1937–)

Born in Leeds, he was educated at Leeds Grammar School and read classics at Leeds University. He traveled widely in West Africa, Europe, Russia and the USA. He is a a noted translator, dramatist, and librettist whose works have been performed by Britain's National Theatre and the New York Metropolitan Opera. He was made a fellow of the Royal Society of Literature in 1984. *Laureate's Block* (1953) relates to his refusal to be considered for the role of poet laureate. Attempts to block a film version of his poem *V* (1985) from being shown on television, because of its strong language, did not succeed. He has won several major prizes and awards. His poems reflect his background and his travels. Some of his other publications: *Earthworks,* 1964. *The Loiners,* 1970. *From the School of Eloquence and Other Poems,* 1978. *US Martial,* 1981. *Selected Poems,* 1995. *The Shadow of Hiroshima and Other Film/Poems,* 1995. *Under the Clock,* 2005. Some of his poems: "Art and Extinction," "Doomsday, the Mysteries," "Sentences," "The Bedbug," "The Eumenides," "The Zeg-Zeg Postcards."

Sources: *British Council Arts* (http://www.contemporarywriters.com). *The Literary Encyclopedia* (www.LitEncyc.com). *The Columbia Granger's Index to Poetry.* 11th ed. *The Columbia Granger's World of Poetry,* Columbia University Press, 2005 (http://www.columbiagrangers.org). *The Faber Book of Blue Verse.* John Whitworth, ed. Faber and Faber, 1990. *The Harvill Book of Twentieth-Century Poetry in English.* Michael Schmidt, ed. The Harvill Press, 1999. *The National Portrait Gallery* (www.npg.org.uk). *The Oxford Book of Classical Verse in Translation.* Adrian Poole and Jeremy Maule, eds. 1995. *The Oxford Companion to English Literature.* 6th edition. Margaret Drabble, ed. Oxford University Press, 2000. *Who's Who.* London: AandC Black, 2005. *Wikipedia, the Free Encyclopedia* (http://en.wikipedia.org/wiki/Wikipedia).

HARRISON, WILLIAM (1685–1713)

Born in the parish of St. Cross, Winchester, he entered Winchester College in 1698, gained a scholarship to New College, Oxford, in 1704 and was awarded a fellowship in 1706. Through his friend Joseph Addison (see entry) he secured the post of governor to the son of the Duke of Queensberry. Addison introduced him to Jonathan Swift, who found him a personable and likeable young man, not least because he was a Whig. Around 1711 he became secretary to Lord Raby, the ambassador extraordinary at the Hague. Harrison's job was to arrange a barrier treaty with France, which he did and returned in 1713. However, it appears he was very ill and heavily in debt because of this trip and only at the intervention of Lord Bolingbroke was he able to survive for a few weeks. Some of his poems: "In Praise of Laudanum," "The Medicine, a Tale," "To the Yacht Which Carried the Duke of Marlborough to Holland," "Woodstock Park."

Sources: *Dictionary of National Biography.* Electronic Edition 1.1. Oxford University Press, 1997. *Oldpoetry* (www.oldpoetry.com). *Stanford University Libraries and Academic Information Resources* (http://library.stanford.edu). *The Columbia Granger's Index to Poetry.* 11th ed. *The Columbia Granger's World of Poetry,* Columbia University Press, 2005 (http://www.columbiagrangers.org). *The New Oxford Book of Eighteenth Century Verse.* Roger Lonsdale, ed. Oxford University Press, 1984.

HARTNETT, MICHAEL (1944–1999)

He was born, brought up and educated in County Limerick, then worked as a tea boy on a London building site. His article "The Teaboy of the Western World," which appeared in one of the newspapers, brought him to the attention of John Jordan, professor of English in University College Dublin, who sponsored him for a year at the school. He and his family moved back to Ireland in 1968, where he worked in the telephone exchange. He was an occasional lecturer and taught creative writing at Thomond College, Limerick. He won several awards for his poetry, and in 1999, the documentary film on his life and work, *Michael Hartnett: Necklace of Wrens,* was shown on Irish television. He died from from the effects of alcoholism. His poetry is written in both English and Irish. Some of his other publications: *Anatomy of a Cliché,* 1968. *A Farewell to English,* 1975. *Inchicore Haiku,* 1985. *The Killing of Dreams,* 1992. *Selected and New Poems,* 1994. Some of his poems: "All That is Left," "Death of an Irishwoman," "For My Grandmother, Bridget Halpin," "Mountains, Fall on Us," "The Purge."

Sources: *Biography of Michael Hartnett* (http://www.irishcultureandcustoms.com/Poetry/Hartnett.html). *Contemporary Irish Poetry: An Anthology.* Anthony Bradley, ed. University of California Press. New and rev. ed., 1988. *The Columbia Granger's Index to Poetry.* 11th ed. *The Columbia Granger's World of Poetry,* Columbia University Press, 2005 (http://www.columbiagrangers.org). *Wikipedia, the Free Encyclopedia* (http://en.wikipedia.org/wiki/Wikipedia).

HARVEY, CHRISTOPHER (1597–1663)

Son of the Rev. Christopher Harvey of Bunbury in Cheshire, he graduated M.A. from Brasenose College, Oxford, in 1619–20. He was rector at Whitney, Herefordshire, then at Clifton Upon Dunsmore, Warwickshire, where he died and was buried. The *Synagogue* is a series of devotional poems appended anonymously to the 1640 edition of George Herbert's *Temple* and reprinted with most of the later editions. His friend Izaak Walton quoted the *Synagogue* in the 1655 edition of the *Compleat Angler* (1653–1655). Some of his other publications: *Faction Supplanted: or a Caveat against the ecclesiastical and secular Rebels*, 1645. *Schola Cordis, or the Heart of it Selfe gone away from God*, 1647. *The Right Rebel. A Treatise discovering the true Use of the Name by the Nature of Rebellion*, 1661. Some of his other poems: "Church Festivals," "Comfort in Extremity," "Forgetting God," "The Covetousness of the Heart," "The Hardness of the Heart," "The Oppression of the Heart," "Travels at Home," "Vows Broken and Rewarded."

Sources: *Dictionary of National Biography*. Electronic Edition 1.1. Oxford University Press, 1997. *English Poetry: Author Search*. Chadwyck-Healey Ltd., 1995 (http://www.lib.utexas.edu:8080/search/epoetry/author.html). *English Poetry: A Poetic Record, from Chaucer to Yeats*. David Hopkins, ed. Routledge, 1990. *The Columbia Granger's Index to Poetry*. 11th ed. *The Columbia Granger's World of Poetry*, Columbia University Press, 2005 (http://www.columbiagrangers.org). *The New Oxford Book of Seventeenth Century Verse*. Alastair Fowler, ed. Oxford University Press, 1991. *The Speaker's Treasury of 400 Quotable Poems*. Croft M. Pentz, ed. Zondervan, 1963.

HARVEY, GABRIEL (?1550–1631)

Born at Saffron Walden, Essex, the son of a master rope-maker, he graduated B.A. from Christ's College, Cambridge in 1569; he was elected a fellow of Pembroke Hall, Cambridge, in 1570, was granted an M.A. in 1573, and elected a fellow of Trinity Hall in 1578. He and Edmund Spenser (see entry) formed a friendship that lasted until Spenser died. Sir James Croft and the Earl of Oxford were much displeased at satirical allusions in some of his poems (printed, he alleged, without his permission), but friends interceded and he escaped punishment. He died at Saffron Walden and is buried there. Some Latin publications: *Rhetor sive*, 1577. *Ciceronianus sive*, 1577. *Dierum Oratio de Natura*, 1577. *Smithus, vel Musarum Lachrymæ pro Obitu honoratiss. Viri*, 1578. *Gratulationes Waldenses*, 1578 (composed for the visit of Queen Elizabeth to the Duke of Norfolk at Audley End, Essex, and presented to her majesty in person). His English publications: *The Story of Mercy Harvey*, 1574–1575. *Letters to and from Edmund Spenser*, 1579–1580. *Foure Letters and Certaine Sonnets*, 1592. *Precursor of Pierce's Supererogation*, 1593. *Pierce's Supererogation, or a new Prayse of the Olde Asse*, 1593.

Sources: *Dictionary of National Biography*. Electronic Edition 1.1. Oxford University Press, 1997. *Encyclopædia Britannica Ultimate Reference Suite DVD*, 2006. *Foure Letters and Certaine Sonnets, Gabriel Harvey*. Bodley Head Quartos, 1592. *The Columbia Granger's Index to Poetry*. 11th ed. *The Columbia Granger's World of Poetry*, Columbia University Press, 2005 (http://www.columbiagrangers.org). *The Oxford Companion to English Literature*. 6th edition. Margaret Drabble, ed. Oxford University Press, 2000.

HARWOOD, LEE (1939–)

He was born and grew up in Chertsey, Surrey, and studied English at Queen Mary College, University of London. He has lived many years in Brighton, Sussex, except for a few years spent in the USA and Greece. He has had several occupations: monumental mason, librarian, bookshop assistant, post office counter clerk, and railway man. His writing career started in the early 1960s and since then he has published over 20 volumes of poetry and prose, as well as translations of the Rumanian-born French poet Tristan Tzara. "He makes use of avant-garde poetic techniques not to dramatize a radical skepticism about language or meaning, but in order to recover for poetry the kinds of "directness" or expressive energy postmodernism has taught us to distrust" (Mark Ford, *The Guardian*, 18 September 2004). Some of his recent publications: *Monster Masks*, 1985. *Crossing the frozen river: selected poems*, 1988. *Rope boy to the rescue*, 1988. *Morning Light*, 1993. Slow Dancer Press, 1998. *Collected Poems, 1975–2000*, 2004. Some of his poems: "Czech Dream," "Salt Water," "Soft White," "The Blue Mosque," "The Words."

Sources: *Anthology of Twentieth-Century British and Irish Poetry*. Keith Tuma, ed. Oxford University Press, 2001. *British Electronic Poetry Centre* (http://www.soton.ac.uk/~bepc/index.htm). *Collected Poems with Wolf Tongue: Poems 1975–2000*. Shearsman Books, 2004. *The National Portrait Gallery* (www.npg.org.uk). *The Columbia Granger's Index to Poetry*. 11th ed. *The Columbia Granger's World of Poetry*, Columbia University Press, 2005 (http://www.columbiagrangers.org). *The New British Poetry, 1968–88*. Gillian Allnutt, Fred D'Aguiar and Ken Edwards, eds. Grafton Books, 1989. *The Penguin Book of Homosexual Verse*. Stephen Coote, ed. Penguin Books, 1983.

HASSALL, CHRISTOPHER VERNON (1912–1963)

London-born poet, biographer, playwright, and librettist, he entered Wadham College, Oxford, but owing to a family financial crisis had to leave without graduating. He formed a renowned musical partnership with the composer Ivor Novello. *Christ's Comet*, an Easter play, for which he also composed the music, was written for the 1938 Canterbury Cathedral Festival. *The Player King* was the Edinburgh Festival play of 1952. *Out of the Whirlwind* (1953) was the first secular play to be staged in Westminster Abbey since the Reformation. He also wrote the libretto for Sir William Walton's 1954 production of *Troilus and Cressida*. He died of a heart attack on a train and was buried at St. Nicholas church, Harbledown, Kent. His awards: the Hawthornden prize, for the poem *Penthesperon*, 1938; the A.C. Benson medal for *Crisis*, a sonnet sequence, 1939; and the James Tait Black memorial prize, for the biography *Edward Marsh: Patron of the Arts*, 1959. Some of his other publications: *The Slow Night*, 1949. *The Red Leaf*, 1957. *Bell Harry, and Other Poems*, 1963 (a sequence of forty sonnets in memory of his friend, the poet Frances Crofts Cornford, see entry).

Sources: *Dictionary of National Biography.* Electronic Edition 1.1. Oxford University Press, 1997. *The Columbia Granger's Index to Poetry.* 11th ed. *The Columbia Granger's World of Poetry,* Columbia University Press, 2005 (http://www.columbiagrangers.org). *The Oxford Book of Twentieth-Century English Verse.* Philip Larkin, ed. Oxford University Press, 1973. *The Oxford Companion to English Literature.* 6th edition. Margaret Drabble, ed. Oxford University Press, 2000.

HAVERGAL, WILLIAM HENRY and FRANCES RIDLEY (1793–1879)

William Henry, the father, 1793–1870

He was born at Chipping Wycombe, Buckinghamshire, and educated at Merchant Taylors School, London, and St. Edmund's Hall, Oxford. He was ordained a deacon in 1816 and priest in 1817 and was rector of three different churches in the Midlands. In 1844 he began to write hymns, sacred songs and carols for the periodical *Our Own Fireside*. He also wrote, harmonized and arranged vocal music. The proceeds from his setting of Reginald Heber's "From Greenland's Icy Mountains" he donated to the Church Missionary Society. He was buried at Astley, Worcestershire. In addition to his music compositions, he wrote sermons and doctrinal books. He wrote over 20 hymns, and although they have passed out of modern hymnbooks, some the titles are: "Blessed Jesus, Lord and Brother," "Forever and Forever, Lord," "In Doubt and Dread Dismay," "Our Faithful God Hath Sent Us," "To Praise Our Shepherd's Care."

Frances Ridley, the daughter, 1836–1879

She was born at her father's rectory at Astley, Worcestershire, and from an early age showed superior intellectual ability. Owing to a delicate constitution, she was discouraged from pursing intellectual studies. She began writing poetry from the age of seven, and her poems were soon being published in *Good Words* and other religious periodicals. In 1878, with both parents dead, she moved from Leamington to South Wales, near the Mumbles, where she died. She wrote over seventy hymns, many of which are used in current hymnbooks. *Her Autobiography Memorials of Frances Ridley Havergal, by her Sister, M.V.G. Havergal* was published in 1880. Some of her publications of hymns and poems: *The Ministry of Song* 1870 (5th edition, 1874). *Under the Surface,* 1874. *Loyal Responses,* 1878. *Life Chords,* 1880. *Life Echoes,* 1883. *Poetical Works,* 1884. *Coming to the King,* 1886. Some of her poems/hymns: "A Happy Christmas," "A New Year Wish," "A Teacher," "At the Portal, God Will Take Care of You," "Golden Harps Are Sounding," "I Am Trusting Thee, Lord Jesus," "I Gave My Life for Thee," "Life-Mosaic," "Master, Speak! Thy Servant Heareth," "Take My Life and Let It Be," "The One Reality," "The Thoughts of God," "Who Is on the Lord's Side?"

Sources: *A Sacrifice of Praise: An Anthology of Christian Poetry in English from Caedmon to the Mid-Twentieth Century.* James H. Trott, ed. Cumberland House Publishing, 1999. *A Treasury of Poems for Worship and Devotion.* Charles L. Wallis, ed. Harper, 1959. *Biography of William Henry Havergal: AIM25: Royal College of Music* (http://www.aim25.ac.uk/cgi-bin/frames/fulldesc?inst_id=25and coll_id=5684). *Dictionary of National Biography.* Electronic Edition 1.1. Oxford University Press, 1997. *English Poetry: Author Search* (http://www.lib.utexas.edu:8080/search/epoetry/author.html). *The Best Loved Religious Poems.* James Gilchrist Lawson, ed. Fleming H. Revell, 1933. *The Columbia Granger's Index to Poetry.* 11th ed. *The Columbia Granger's World of Poetry,* Columbia University Press, 2005 (http://www.columbiagrangers.org). *The Cyber Hymnal* (http://www.cyberhymnal.org/index.htm).

HAWES, STEPHEN (?1474/5–1523)

Not much is not known about this Tudor poet, who is thought to come from Suffolk (the dates are uncertain; those quoted are from the Columbia Granger's Index to Poetry.) Educated at Oxford University, he was groom of the chamber to Henry VII. Around 1506 he wrote and dedicated to the king *The Passetyme of Pleasure, or the History of Graunde Amoure and la Bel Pucel, conteining the Knowledge of the Seven Sciences and the Course of Man's Life in this World.* It is an allegory, rhyming a b a b b c c, of about 6000 lines, divided into forty-five chapters. Hawes marks the end of the Middle English (Chaucerian) and the Early Modern English or Renaissance periods. Another poem (1505–1506), *Here begynneth the boke called the example of vertu*—a simpler and shorter poem — is an allegory of life spent in the pursuit of purity. His other known publications: *A Joyfull medytacyon to all Englonde of the Coronacyon of Our Moost Naturall Souerayne Lorde Kynge*

Henry the Eyght, 1509. *The Couercyon of Swerers*, 1509. *The Comforte of Louers Made and Compyled by Steuen Hawes*, 1512.

Sources: *Dictionary of National Biography*. Electronic Edition 1.1. Oxford University Press, 1997. *Encyclopædia Britannica Ultimate Reference Suite DVD*, 2006. *English Poetry: Author Search*. Chadwyck-Healey Ltd., 1995 (http://www.lib.utexas.edu:8080/search/epoetry/author. html). *Poets of the English Language. Vol. I*. W.H. Auden, and Norman Holmes Pearson, ed. Viking Press, 1950. *The Columbia Granger's Index to Poetry*. 11th ed. *The Columbia Granger's World of Poetry*, Columbia University Press, 2005 (http://www.columbiagrangers.org). *The Oxford Companion to English Literature*. 6th edition. Margaret Drabble, ed. Oxford University Press, 2000. *Wikipedia, the Free Encyclopedia* (http://en.wikipedia.org/wiki/Wikipedia).

HAWKER, ROBERT STEPHEN (1803–1875)

Born in Plymouth, Devon, the son of a doctor, he was educated at Cheltenham grammar school and graduated M.A. from Magdalen Hall in 1836. Ordained in 1831, he was appointed in 1834 as vicar to the Cornish parish of Morwenstow, where he spent most of his life. Imprudent in money matters, he suffered acutely from poverty for many years before he died in Plymouth, where he was buried. His unfinished poem "The Quest of the Sangraal" shows his fondness for the romance of medieval stories. Several of his articles on Cornish legends are in *Footprints of Former Men in Far Cornwall* (1870), edited by C.E. Byles. Some of his other poetic publications: *Records of the Western Shore*, 1832, 1836. *Reeds Shaken with the Wind*, 1843, 1844. *Echoes from Old Cornwall*, 1846. *Cornish Ballads and Other Poems*, 1869. Some of his other poems: "A Rapture on the Cornish Hills," "Aishah Schechinah," "Aunt Mary," "Be of Good Cheer!" "King Arthur's Waes-hael," "Morwennæ Station," "Queen Guennivar's Round," "The Silent Tower of Bottreaux," "The Tamar Spring."

Sources: *Dictionary of National Biography*. Electronic Edition 1.1. Oxford University Press, 1997. *English Poetry: Author Search*. Chadwyck-Healey Ltd., 1995 (http://www. lib.utexas.edu:8080/search/epoetry/author.html). *Everyman's Book of Victorian Verse*. J.R. Watson, ed. J.M. Dent, 1982. *I Sing of a Maiden: The Mary Book of Verse*. Sister M. Therese, ed. Macmillan, 1947. *Selected Poems of Robert Stephen Hawker*. Cecil Woolf, ed. Cecil Woolf, 1975. *The Columbia Granger's Index to Poetry*. 11th ed. *The Columbia Granger's World of Poetry*, Columbia University Press, 2005 (http://www.columbiagrangers.org). *The Cyber Hymnal* (http://www.cyberhymnal.org/index.htm). *The Golden Book of Catholic Poetry*. Alfred Noyes, ed. J.B. Lippincott, 1946. *The Oxford Companion to English Literature*. 6th edition. Margaret Drabble, ed. Oxford University Press, 2000.

HAY, GEORGE CAMPBELL (1915–1984)

Scottish poet (Deòrsa Mac Iain Deòrsa) was born in Elderslie, Renfrewshire, where his father, John Macdougall Hay — author of *Gillespie* (1914), a brooding novel of Tarbert life — was the minister. He died when George was only four and the family returned to Argyll, where young George developed an intense admiration for the Loch Fyne ring-net fishermen. He was educated at Fettes College, Edinburgh, and Oxford University. His service in the British Army in North Africa during World War II is reflected in his poems about that region. After the war he lived mostly in Edinburgh, where he was a staunch supporter of Scottish nationalism. He was a frequent contributor to *Gairm* magazine and other Gaelic periodicals, and his best work appeared in that language. A gifted linguist, he translated poems from many European languages into Gaelic, but his own poems in Gaelic and Scots represent his most significant achievement. He was a significant figure in the renaissance of Gaelic poetry in the twentieth century. Some of his poems: "Atman," "Bizerta," "Flooer o the Gean," "Still Gyte [mad], Man?" "The Old Fisherman," "The Two Neighbours," "To a Loch Fyne Fisherman."

Sources: *A Book of Scottish Verse*. Maurice Lindsay, and R.L. Mackie, ed. St. Martin's Press, 1983. *Collected Poems and Songs of George Campbell Hay* (Deorsa Mac Iain Dheorsa) (two volumes), Michel Byrne, ed. Edinburgh University Press, 1999. *Columbia University Press, George Campbell Hay* (http://www.columbia.edu/cu/cup/catalog/data/074861/0748610634.HTM). *Biography of George Campbell Hay* (http://www.nls.uk/writestuff/heads/wee-hay.html). *Scottish Authors, George Campbell Hay* (http://www.slainte. org.uk/scotauth/hayjodsw.htm). *The New Penguin Book of Scottish Verse*. Robert Crawford and Mick Imlah, ed. Penguin Books, 2000. *Wikipedia, the Free Encyclopedia* (http://en.wikipedia.org/wiki/Wikipedia).

HAYLEY, WILLIAM (1745–1820)

Born in Chichester, West Sussex, he was educated at Eton College and Trinity College, Cambridge, but left in 1767 without graduating. "The Triumphs of Temper" (1781) and "The Triumphs of Music" (1804) though popular, were ridiculed by Lord Byron as being feeble. A friend of William Cowper, he published his biography, *Life of Cowper*, in 1803. William Blake (see entry) designed and engraved the prints of *Ballads by William Hayley* (1805). However, the friendship was soured by Hayley's attempts to curb Blake's visionary genius. He was offered the laureateship in 1790 but refused it. He died at Felpham, West Sussex. While at Cambridge, he wrote an "Ode on the Birth of the Prince of Wales," which was published in the *Cambridge Collection* and reprinted in the *Gentleman's Magazine* for January 1763. Some of his publications: *Poems and Plays*, 1788. *The national advocates, a poem*, 1795. *The Stanzas of an English Friend to the Patriots of Spain*, 1808. *Song for the Amicable Fraternity of Felpham*, 1817. Some of his poems: "An Essay on Epic Poetry," "Epistle to John Sargent, Esq.," "Epistle to Mrs. Hannah More," "Hymn for Christmas Day."

Sources: *Dictionary of National Biography*. Electronic Edition 1.1. Oxford University Press, 1997. *Encyclopædia Britannica Ultimate Reference Suite DVD*, 2006. *English Poetry, Second Edition Bibliography* (http://collections.chadwyck.co.uk/html/ep2/bibliography/g.htm). *English Poetry: Author Search*. Chadwyck-Healey Ltd., 1995 (http://www.lib.utexas.edu:8080/search/epoetry/author.html). *English Poetry: A Poetic Record, from Chaucer to Yeats*. David Hopkins, ed. Routledge, 1990. *The National Portrait Gallery* (www.npg.org.uk). *Poems on Serious and Sacred Subjects by William Hayley* (1818), Project Gutenberg. *The Columbia Granger's Index to Poetry*. 11th ed. *The Columbia Granger's World of Poetry*, Columbia University Press, 2005 (http://www.columbiagrangers.org). *The Oxford Companion to English Literature*. 6th edition. Margaret Drabble, ed. Oxford University Press, 2000.

HEADLEY, HENRY (1765–1788)

The son of Henry Headley, rector of Irstead, Norfolk, he was educated at Trinity College, Oxford. Part-way through he quit college and married. He returned to Oxford and graduated in 1786. Taken ill with tuberculosis, he died in Norwich and was buried at North Walsham, Norfolk. He contributed to the publication *The Lounger's Miscellany, or the Lucubrations of Abel Slug, Esq.*, which ran to twenty numbers in 1788 and 1789. He also published articles in the *Gentleman's Magazine* (*GM*), sometimes under the pseudonym of "C.T.O." Some of his other publications: *Fugitive Pieces*, 1785 (reissued with additions in 1786 as *Poems and Other Pieces by Henry Headley*). Account of Johnson's *Prayers*, 1785 (*GM*). Baron's *Cyprian Academy*, 1785 (*GM*). *Beggar's Dog*, 1785 (*GM*). *Instances of Poetical Imitations in Milton*, 1786 (*GM*). *Select Beauties of Ancient English Poetry. With Remarks*, 1787. Some of his poems: "A Parody on Gray's Elegy," "An Invocation to Melancholy," "Ode to the Memory of Chatterton," "Prostituted Honour, or Lothario, a Character," "To Cynthia, a Fragment," "Verses Written on a Winter's Night."

Sources: *Dictionary of National Biography*. Electronic Edition 1.1. Oxford University Press, 1997. *Eighteenth-Century English Verse*. Dennis Davison, ed. Penguin Books, 1988. *English Poetry: Author Search*. Chadwyck-Healey Ltd., 1995 (http://www.lib.utexas.edu:8080/search/epoetry/author.html). *Gentleman's Magazine* (http://www.bodley.ox.ac.uk/ilej/journals/srchgm.htm). *The Columbia Granger's Index to Poetry*. 11th ed. *The Columbia Granger's World of Poetry*, Columbia University Press, 2005 (http://www.columbiagrangers.org).

HEALY, RANDOLPH (1956–)

Born in Irvine, Scotland, the family moved to Dublin soon afterward. After leaving school at 14, he had various dead-end jobs, which he admits to not disliking. He returned to Ballymun Community School then went on to Trinity College, Dublin, where he studied mathematical sciences. He runs the publishing house Wild Honey Press of County Wicklow, Ireland, and works as a teacher of mathematics and science. Some of his publications: *25 Poems*, 1983. *Rana Rana!* 1997. *Arbor Vitae*, 1997. *Flame*, 1998. *Scales*, 1998. *Selected Poems*, 2000. *Daylight Saving Sex*, 2001. *Green 532*, 2002. Some of his poems: "Colonies of Belief," "Mutability Checkers," "Primula veris," "The Size of This Universe."

Sources: *Anthology of Twentieth-Century British and Irish Poetry*. Keith Tuma, ed. Oxford University Press, 2001. *Biography of Randolph Healy: Sound Eye* (http://indigo.ie/~tjac/Poets/Randolph_Healy/randolph_healy.htm). *The Columbia Granger's Index to Poetry*. 11th ed. *The Columbia Granger's World of Poetry*, Columbia University Press, 2005 (http://www.columbiagrangers.org). *Wikipedia, the Free Encyclopedia* (http://en.wikipedia.org/wiki/Wikipedia).

HEANEY, SEAMUS JUSTIN (1939–)

The eldest in a Catholic family of nine children, he grew up on his father's cattle farm near Castledawson, Londonderry, Northern Ireland. He attended St. Columb's College, Derry, and moved in 1957 to Belfast to continue his studies. He graduated from Queen's University, Belfast, in 1961, and trained as a teacher at St. Joseph's College of Education, where he was a lecturer for three years; then he was a lecturer at Queen's University, Belfast. He was professor of poetry at Oxford University from 1989 to 1994, and from 1982 to 1998 was visiting professor at Harvard. Since 1998 he has been Ralph Waldo Emerson Poet in Residence at Harvard. He was awarded the Nobel Prize for Literature in 1995. Some people rate him among the leading poets in the English-speaking world. Some of his publications: *Eleven Poems*, 1965. *Lough Neagh Sequence*, 1969. *Catherine's Poem*, 1970. *Bog Poems*, 1975. *Four Poems*, 1976. *Glanmore Sonnets*, 1977. *Selected Poems 1965–1975*, 1980. *New Selected Poems 1966–87*, 1990. *Beowulf*, 1999 (translation). Some of his poems: "Act of Union," "Blackberry-Picking," "Clearances," "Hercules and Antaeus," "Philoctetes," "Singing School," "Station Island," "Sweeney Redivivus," "Viking Dublin: Trial Pieces."

Sources: *Encyclopædia Britannica Ultimate Reference Suite DVD*, 2006. *Biography of Seamus Heaney* (http://www.kirjasto.sci.fi/heaney.htm). *The National Portrait Gallery* (www.npg.org.uk). *Opened Ground: Selected Poems 1966–1996 (Seamus Heaney)*. Farrar, Straus and Giroux (1998). *Poets from the North of Ireland*. Frank Ormsby, ed.

The Blackstaff Press, 1990. *The Columbia Granger's Index to Poetry*. 11th ed. *The Columbia Granger's World of Poetry*, Columbia University Press, 2005 (http://www.columbia-grangers.org). *The Oxford Companion to English Literature*. 6th edition. Margaret Drabble, ed. Oxford University Press, 2000. *Who's Who*. London: A & C Black, 2005.

HEARN, MARY ANNE (1834–1909)

Known as "Polly," she was born at Farningham, Kent, the daughter of Joseph Hearn, village postmaster (her pen name, Marianne Farningham, is a combination Mary Anne with Farningham). Her strict Baptist parents would not allow her to attend a secular school. Added to this, her mother died when she was twelve, so she became the housekeeper. By studying early morning and late at night she educated herself and was a schoolteacher from 1852 to 1866. After that she became editor of the *Sunday School Times* and joined the outside staff of the newly founded *Christian World*, for which she wrote regularly till her death at Barmouth, Wales. She became well-known as a hymn writer, poet and author, and a lecturer beloved by English Baptists. Some of her publications: *Lays and Lyrics of the Blessed Life*, 1861. *Poems*, 1865. *Morning and Evening Hymns for the Week*, 1870. *Songs of Sunshine*, 1875. *A Working Woman's Life*, 1907 (autobiography). Some of her poems/hymns: "A Blind Man's Story," "A Goodbye at the Door," "God Cares," "Jairus," "Last Hymn," "Rebekah," "The Burden."

Sources: *Dictionary of National Biography*. Electronic Edition 1.1. Oxford University Press, 1997. *Biography of Marianne Faringham Hearn* (http://website.lineone.net/~gsward/pages/mfarningham.html). *The National Portrait Gallery* (www.npg.org.uk). *The Best Loved Poems of the American People*. Hazel Felleman, ed. Doubleday, 1936. *The Best Loved Religious Poems*. James Gilchrist Lawson, ed. Fleming H. Revell, 1933. *The Columbia Granger's Index to Poetry*. 11th ed. *The Columbia Granger's World of Poetry*, Columbia University Press, 2005 (http://www.columbia grangers.org). *The Cyber Hymnal* (http://www.cyberhymnal.org/index.htm).

HEATH-STUBBS, JOHN FRANCIS ALEXANDER (1918–)

Born in London, he was educated at Worcester College for the Blind and at Queen's College, Oxford. He was lecturer in English literature at the College of St. Mark and St. John, Chelsea, London. From 1960 to 1961 he was visiting professor of English at the University of Michigan. He was made a fellow of the Royal Society of Literature in 1953 and president of the Poetry Society in 1993. In 1973 he was awarded the Gold Medal for Poetry, and in 1988 he received the Order of the British Empire. With Sidney Keyes and Michael Meyer, he edited the poetry anthology *Images of Tomorrow* (1953), co-ed-

ited *Eight Oxford Poets* (1941), and helped edit *Oxford Poetry* in (1942–1943). The inspiration for his poems come from Ancient Greece, Rome, Alexandria, classical myth, Christian legend and works of art. His most recent publications: *Galileo's Salad*, 1996. *The Sound of Light*, 1999. *The Return of the Cranes*, 2002. *Pigs Might Fly*, 2005. Some of his poems: "Footnote to Belloc's 'Tarantella,'" "Not Being Oedipus," "The Broom; or, The Flower of the Desert," "Virgin Martyrs," "Wishes for the Months."

Sources: *Carcanet press* (http://www.carcanet.co.uk). *The National Portrait Gallery* (www.npg.org.uk). *The Chatto Book of Modern Poetry 1915–1955*. Cecil Day Lewis, and John Lehmann, ed. Chatto and Windus, 1966. *The Columbia Granger's Index to Poetry*. 11th ed. *The Columbia Granger's World of Poetry*, Columbia University Press, 2005 (http://www.columbiagrangers.org). *The Oxford Book of Comic Verse*. John Gross, ed. Oxford University Press, 1994. *The Oxford Companion to English Literature*. 6th edition. Margaret Drabble, ed. Oxford University Press, 2000. *Who's Who*. London: A & C Black, 2005. *Wikipedia, the Free Encyclopedia* (http://en.wikipedia.org/wiki/Wikipedia). *World Poetry: An Anthology of Verse from Antiquity to Our Time*. Katharine Washburn and John S. Major, ed. Publisher, 1338, 1998.

HEBER, REGINALD (1773–1826)

Born at Malpas, Cheshire, to a prosperous family, he was educated at Whitchurch grammar school and Brasenose College, Oxford. There he won several prizes, including the 1803 prize for the English verse "Palestine," which was set to music by Dr. Crotch in 1812. He was elected fellow of All Souls' College, Oxford, in 1805. Ordained in 1807, he took over his father's living of Hodnet (he had died in 1804). Just after receiving the degree of doctor of divinity from Oxford University in 1823, he became bishop of Calcutta. He died at Trichinopoly and a statue of him was erected at Calcutta. In addition to *Poems and Translations* (1812) and *A Journey through India* (1828), he was a prolific poet and hymn writer. Four of his hymns are included in most current hymnbooks: "Brightest and Best of the Sons of the Morning," "By Cool Siloam's Shady Rill," "From Greenland's Icy Mountains," and "Holy, Holy, Holy." Some of his other poems: "Advent Sunday," "An Evening Walk in Bengal," "Epitaph on a Young Naval Officer," "Europe: Lines on the Present War," "Providence," "Sympathy," "Who Follows in His Train?"

Sources: *Dictionary of National Biography*. Electronic Edition 1.1. Oxford University Press, 1997. *English Poetry: Author Search*. Chadwyck-Healey Ltd., 1995 (http://www.lib.utexas.edu:8080/search/epoetry/author.html). *The Columbia Granger's Index to Poetry*. 11th ed. *The Columbia Granger's World of Poetry*, Columbia University Press, 2005 (http://www.columbiagrangers.org). *The Cyber Hymnal* (http://www.cyberhymnal.org/index.htm). *The Home Book of Modern Verse,* Burton Egbert Stevenson, ed. Henry Holt, 1953. *The New Oxford Book of Christian Verse*. Donald Davie, ed. Oxford University Press, 1981. *The Oxford Companion to English Literature*. 6th edition. Margaret Drabble, ed. Oxford University Press, 2000. *The Poetical Works of Crabbe, Heber, and Pollok,* Lippincott, Grambo, 1854.

HEGLEY, JOHN (1953–)

Born in Islington, London, he was brought up in Luton and Bristol and graduated B.S. in literature and sociology from Bradford University. He worked on Soapbox Children's Theatre in 1979, presented the TV poetry series *Word of Mouth* in 1990, and the BBC Radio series *Hearing with Hegley,* 1997–1999. He was BBC on-line poet in residence, 1998, and played Vernon Hines in *Pyjama Game,* 1999. His poems range from the surreal to the humorous to the personal and emotional. His stage act includes elements of poetry, music and comedy. In 2000 he received an honorary arts doctorate from Luton University. In addition to his poetry he has also released his own CD of songs and poetry, *Saint and Blurry* (2002). Some of his publications: *Poems for Pleasure,* 1989. *Glad to Wear Glasses,* 1990. *Can I Come Down Now Dad,* 1991. *Five Sugars Please,* 1993. *Beyond Our Kennel,* 1998. *Dog,* 2000. *My Dog is a Carrot,* 2002. *The Sound of Paint Drying,* 2003. Some of his poems: "Love Poem by My Dog," "Poetry in India," "The Death of a Scoutmaster," "Tuna Day (for the USA)."

Sources: *John Hegley* (http://www.contemporarywriters.com/authors/?p=auth02D4J450112627326). *The Columbia Granger's Index to Poetry.* 11th ed. *The Columbia Granger's World of Poetry,* Columbia University Press, 2005 (http://www.columbiagrangers.org). *The Kingfisher Book of Children's Poetry.* Michael Rosen, ed. Kingfisher Books, 1985. *The New Exeter Book of Riddles.* Kevin Crossley-Holland and Lawrence Sail, ed. Enitharmon Press, 1999. *The Oxford Companion to English Literature*. 6th edition. Margaret Drabble, ed. Oxford University Press, 2000. *Who's Who.* London: A & C Black, 2005. *Wikipedia, the Free Encyclopedia* (http://en.wikipedia.org/wiki/Wikipedia).

HEMANS, FELICIA DOROTHEA (1793–1835)

Dorothea Browne was from Liverpool, the daughter of a merchant whose business suffered as a result of the war with France. The family moved to Wales in 1800, and the father to Canada, where he died. Dororhea married Captain Alfred Hemans in 1812, but they separated in 1818 and she returned to Wales. She died in Ireland after a prolonged illness and was buried in St. Anne's Church, Dublin. *Poems* was published in 1808, followed in the same year by "England and Spain, or Valor and Patriotism," a poem inspired by the fighting of her two brothers in the Peninsular War. She published 12 volumes of poems and hymns, and her *Hymns for Childhood* was first published in America in 1827. Her sister, Mrs. Hughes, published *The Works of Mrs. Hemans, with a Memoir of her Life* (W. Blackwood and Sons, Edinburgh, 1839). Some of her poems: "Ancient Battle Song," "Song of Emigration," "The American Forest Girl," "The Cambrian in America," "The Homes of England," "The Landing of the Pilgrim Fathers," "The Stranger in Louisiana," "The Voice of Home to the Prodigal."

Sources: *Confucius to Cummings: An Anthology of Poetry.* Ezra Pound and Marcella Spann, ed. New Directions Publishing Corporation, 1964. *Dictionary of National Biography.* Electronic Edition 1.1. Oxford University Press, 1997. *English Poetry: Author Search* (http://www.lib.utexas.edu:8080/search/epoetry/author.html). *The Best Loved Poems of the American People.* Hazel Felleman, ed. Doubleday, 1936. *The Columbia Granger's Index to Poetry.* 11th ed. *The Columbia Granger's World of Poetry,* Columbia University Press, 2005 (http://www.columbiagrangers.org). *The Cyber Hymnal* (http://www.cyberhymnal.org/index.htm). *The Oxford Companion to English Literature*. 6th edition. Margaret Drabble, ed. Oxford University Press, 2000. *The Poetical Works of Mrs. Felicia Hemans.* Phillips and Sampson, 1848.

HENDERSON, HAMISH (1919–2002)

Born in Blairgowrie, Perthshire, he was introduced to folksong by his mother, who also taught him to speak Gaelic. He was educated locally, then at Dulwich College, London, and Downing College, Cambridge, where he studied modern languages. As a student in Germany he acted as a courier for a Quaker network which helped refugees to escape the Nazi regime; he left just before the outbreak of World War II. During the war he served as an intelligence officer in Europe and North Africa and was present at El Alamein. Out of his experiences he wrote the poem sequence *Elegies for the Dead in Cyrenaica,* for which he received the Somerset Maugham Award in 1947. He held several honorary degrees. In 1983 he refused an Order of the British Empire in protest of the nuclear arms policy of the Thatcher government. He was a staff member, and after his retirement an honorary fellow, of the School of Scottish Studies in Edinburgh. He died in Edinburgh. Some of his poems: "Ding Dong Dollar," "End of a Campaign," "Opening of an Offensive," "Seven Good Germans," "The Flyting o' Life and Daith," "We Show You That Death as a Dancer."

Sources: *An Album of Songs and Poems: A' The Bairns O Adam by Hamish Henderson* (http://www.footstompin.com/artists/hamish_henderson. *Folksinger's Wordbook.* Irwin Silber, and Fred Silber, ed. Oak Publications, 1973.

Poetry of the World Wars. Michael Foss, ed. Peter Bedrick Books, 1990. *The Columbia Granger's Index to Poetry.* 11th ed. *The Columbia Granger's World of Poetry,* Columbia University Press, 2005 (http://www.columbiagrangers. org). *The Living Tradition* (http://www.folkmusic.net/htmfiles/inart486.htm). *The Oxford Book of Scottish Verse,* John MacQueen and Tom Scott, ed. Oxford University Press, 1966.

HENDRY, JAMES FINDLAY
(1912–1986)

Born in Glasgow, he read modern languages at Glasgow University but did not graduate. During World War II he served in the Royal Artillery and the Intelligence Corps. After the war he worked as a translator for the United Nations and the International Labor Organization, then worked at the Institute of Soviet and East European Studies at Laurentian University, Sudbury, Ontario, before becoming its head of School of Translating and Interpreting. With Henry Treece (see entry) he edited the poetry anthology *The New Apocalypse* (1939) which gave its name to the "New Apocalyptics" poetic group. He died in Toronto and left his papers to Glasgow University. These consist mainly of press cutting reviews of his work, drafts of novels, notes and notebooks, and audio cassettes. Included are over 500 letters, many from other poets, artists and authors. Some of his other publications: *The White Horseman,* 1941 (poetry anthology with Henry Treece). *Bombed Happiness,* 1942. *Crown and Sickle,* 1944 (poetry anthology with Henry Treece). *Your Career as a Translator and Interpreter,* 1980. Some of his poems: "Inverberg," "Orpheus," "The Constant North," "The Ship," "Tir-Nan-Og."

Sources: *James Findlay Hendry Papers.* University of Glasgow, Special Collections (http://special.lib.gla.ac.uk/collection/hendry.html). *Nationmaster.com* (http://www.nationmaster.com/encyclopedia/J.-F.-Hendry). *Poetry and War* (http://perso.univ-lyon2.fr/~goethals/warpoet/WW2_menu.html). *The Columbia Granger's Index to Poetry.* 11th ed. *The Columbia Granger's World of Poetry,* Columbia University Press, 2005 (http://www.columbiagrangers.org). *The New British Poets: An Anthology.* Kenneth Rexroth, ed. New Directions, 1949. *The Oxford Book of Scottish Verse,* John MacQueen and Tom Scott, ed. Oxford University Press, 1966.

HENLEY, WILLIAM ERNEST
(1849–1903)

He was born and educated in Gloucester, where he was the pupil of Thomas Edward Brown (see entry). Tuberculosis necessitated the amputation of one foot in 1867, then in 1873 he underwent surgery at Edinburgh under Dr. Joseph Lister and was hospitalized for almost a year. Out of his experience he wrote *Invictus* (1875) and a series of poems, *Hospital Outlines* (1875). He and R.L. Stevenson (see entry) became friends and collaborated in writing four plays, none of which was successful. He worked on the staff of the *Encyclopædia Britannica* and edited the *Scots Observer of Edinburgh,* the *London,* the *Pen,* and *Magazine of Art.* In 1893 he received the degree of doctor of laws from St. Andrews University. He died at Woking, Surrey, and his ashes were taken to Cockayne Hatley, Bedfordshire. Some of his other publications: *A Book of Verses,* 1888. *The Song of the Sword and Other Verses,* 1892. *London Voluntaries,* 1893. *In Hospital,* 1903. Some of his poems: "Arabian Nights' Entertainments," "At Queensferry," "Attadale, West Highlands," "From a Window in Princes Street," "Over the Hills and Far Away," "To Robert Louis Stevenson."

Sources: *A Century of Humorous Verse, 1850–1950.* Roger Lancelyn Green, ed. E.P. Dutton (Everyman's Library), 1959. *Dictionary of National Biography.* Electronic Edition 1.1. Oxford University Press, 1997. *Encyclopædia Britannica Ultimate Reference Suite DVD,* 2006. *Poems of William Ernest Henley.* AMS Press, Inc., 1970. *The Columbia Granger's Index to Poetry.* 11th ed. *The Columbia Granger's World of Poetry,* Columbia University Press, 2005 (http://www.columbiagrangers.org).

HENRI, ADRIAN MAURICE
(1932–2000)

Born in Birkenhead, Merseyside, he graduated with an honors degree in fine art from Durham University in 1955. He settled in Liverpool where he, Roger McGough and Brian Patten (see entries) were known as the "Liverpool poets." He helped compile *Penguin Modern Poets 10* (1967), after which he became a performer with the multi-media poetry-rock group Liverpool Scene. He has been compared with the American beat poets and writers of the 1950s, such as Jack Kerouac and Allen Ginsberg. He was also a prolific artist, winning the 1992 John Moores Prize with pieces of his work becoming a part of a permanent collection in the Liverpool's Walker Art Gallery. He was awarded the Freedom of the City of Liverpool shortly before his death and received an honorary degree of doctor of letters from the city's university. Some of his other poetry publications: *Tonight at Noon,* 1968. *City,* 1969. *From the Loveless Motel,* 1980. *Penny Arcade,* 1983. *Collected Poems 1967–1985,* 1986. Some of his poems: "Adrian Henri's Talking After Christmas Blues," "Crowfield," "Drinking Song," "Early Spring," "Love Story."

Sources: *A Year Full of Poems.* Michael Harrison, and Christopher Stuart-Clark, ed. Oxford University Press, 1991. *All-Info About Poetry* (http://poetry.allinfo-about.com/features/adrian-henri.html). *Precinct, Honorary Degrees for Adrian Henri and John Peel* (http://www.liv.ac.uk/precinct/Jan2001/2.html). *The National Portrait Gallery* (www.npg.org.uk). *The Columbia Granger's Index to Poetry.* 11th ed. *The Columbia Granger's World of Poetry,*

Columbia University Press, 2005 (http://www.columbia grangers.org). *The Faber Book of Drink, Drinkers and Drinking.* Simon Rae, ed. Faber and Faber, 1991. *The Oxford Companion to English Literature.* 6th edition. Margaret Drabble, ed. Oxford University Press, 2000. *The Penguin Book of Light Verse.* Gavin Ewart, ed. Penguin Books, 1980. *Under All Silences: Shades of Love.* Ruth Gordon, ed. Harper and Row, 1987.

HENRY VIII, KING OF ENGLAND (1491–1547)

Henry was born at Greenwich, near London, the son of Henry VII, and succeeded to the throne of England in 1509. He presided over the beginnings of the English Renaissance and the English Reformation, and in 1521 Pope Leo X conferred on him the title "Defender of the Faith," which title every other British monarch holds. The fact that he had six wives and that he had two of them beheaded gives the impression of a cruel monarch. But he was educated in the classics, spoke and wrote several languages fluently, including Latin, studied philosophy and religion, and was a talented musician who made his court a center of musical culture. He wrote prose and romantic poetry and composed masses and ballads. He was buried in St. George's Chapel, Windsor. Some of his many poems; "Alas, What Shall I Do for Love?" "Green Groweth the Holly," "Oh My Heart," "Pastyme with Good Company," "Though That Men Do," "Call It Dotage to His Lady," "Whereto Should I Express," "Whoso That Will for Grace Sue," "Without Discord."

Sources: *Dictionary of National Biography.* Electronic Edition 1.1. Oxford University Press, 1997. *Encyclopædia Britannica Ultimate Reference Suite DVD,* 2006. *English Poetry: Author Search.* Chadwyck-Healey Ltd., 1995 (http://www.lib.utexas.edu:8080/search/epoetry/author.html). *Medieval English Lyrics: A Critical Anthology.* R.T. Davies, ed. Northwestern University Press, 1964. *The National Portrait Gallery* (www.npg.org.uk). *Oldpoetry* (www.oldpoetry.com). *The Columbia Granger's Index to Poetry.* 11th ed. *The Columbia Granger's World of Poetry,* Columbia University Press, 2005 (http://www.columbiagrangers.org). *The Music of Henry VIII* (http://tudors.crispen.org/music). *The New Oxford Book of Sixteenth Century Verse.* Emrys Jones, ed. Oxford University Press, 1991. *The Oxford Companion to English Literature.* 6th edition. Margaret Drabble, ed. Oxford University Press, 2000. *The Works of Henry VIII* (http://www.luminarium.org/renlit/tudorbib.htm).

HENRY THE MINSTREL (?1470–?1492)

Henry the Minstrel, or Blind Harry or Hary, a Scottish poet, was the author of the epic poem in 12 books *The Life of Sir William Wallace* around 1460; it was translated into modern English by William of Gilbertfield in 1722. Little is known about Henry, but it is thought he came from the Lothian area and

that he was blind from birth. The treasury accounts show that in 1490 he received a sum of money on the king's command and similar payments until 1492. William Dunbar (see entry) mentions him on line 69 of *Lament for the Makaris* (middle Scots for maker, composer, craftsman). From the level of the language it appears he had been educated in the school of some monastery. He collected tales about Wallace (who was hung, drawn and quartered in London in 1305) from various sources and wrote them in the Scots language, adding them to the work of John Blair, Wallace's chaplain. The poem inspired Burns to write "Scots Wha Hae," and Randall Wallace also read the poem before creating the Mel Gibson film *Braveheart* (1995). There are some historical inaccuracies; however, the poem makes stirring reading and had a strong influence on Scottish nationality.

Sources: *Dictionary of National Biography.* Electronic Edition 1.1. Oxford University Press, 1997. *Overview of Blind Harry* (http://www.geo.ed.ac.uk/scotgaz/people/famousfirst1079.html). *Scottish Poetry Selection — Life of Sir William Wallace, an extract of the poem by Blind Harry* (http://www.rampantscotland.com/poetry/blpoems_wallace.htm). *The Columbia Granger's Index to Poetry.* 11th ed. *The Columbia Granger's World of Poetry,* Columbia University Press, 2005 (http://www.columbiagrangers.org). *The Oxford Companion to English Literature.* 6th edition. Margaret Drabble, ed. Oxford University Press, 2000. *The Scottish Collection of Verse to 1800.* Eileen Dunlop and Kamm Antony, eds. Richard Drew, 1985.

HENRYSON (HENDERSON), ROBERT (?1430–?1506)

The details of his birth are sketchy, but it can be judged from his writings that he was a schoolmaster of Dunfermline, Fifeshire, possibly at the Benedictine school at Dunfermline Abbey. He appears among the dead poets in William Dunbar's *Lament for the Makaris* (see Henry the Minstrel). One of the "Scottish Chaucerian" school (he and Dunbar its most prominent members), he is considered to be one of the finest early writers of fables. The translation of Aesop's Fables — *The Morall Fabillis of Esope the Phrygian,* and the *Phrygian, Compylit in Eloquent and Ornate Scottis,* a version of 13 fables based mainly on John Lydgate (see entry) and William Caxton, are his early works. His other main work is *The Testament of Cresseid I* (1663) a sequel to Chaucer's *Troilus and Criseyde.* Some of his other poems (all written in early Scots): "Aganis Haisty Credence of Titlaris," "Orpheus and Eurydice," "Sum Practysis of Medecyne," "The Bludy Serk [shirt]," "The Garmont of Gud Ladeis," "The Prais of Aige," "The Ressoning betuix Deth and Man Deth," "The Thre Deid Pollis," "Want of Wyse Men."

Sources: *An Anthology of Catholic Poets.* Shane Leslie, ed.

Macmillan, 1952. *Dictionary of National Biography.* Electronic Edition 1.1. Oxford University Press, 1997. *Encyclopædia Britannica Ultimate Reference Suite DVD,* 2006. *English Poetry: Author Search.* Chadwyck-Healey Ltd., 1995 (http://www.lib.utexas.edu:8080/search/epoetry/author.html). *Everyman's Book of English Verse.* John Wain, ed. J.M. Dent, 1981. *Scottish Literature 1: What were/are the Middle Ages?* (http://www.englit.ed.ac.uk/studying/undergrd/scottish_lit_1/Handouts/sd_intro_middleages.htm). *The Columbia Granger's Index to Poetry.* 11th ed. *The Columbia Granger's World of Poetry,* Columbia University Press, 2005 (http://www.columbiagrangers.org). *The Oxford Companion to English Literature.* 6th edition. Margaret Drabble, ed. Oxford University Press, 2000. *The Poems and Fables of Robert Henryson.* H. Harvey Wood, ed. Barnes and Noble, 1968.

HERAUD, JOHN ABRAHAM
(1799–1887)

Of Huguenot descent, he was born in the parish of St. Andrews, Holborn, London. Educated privately and with a sound knowledge of German, he started writing for magazines in 1818, rather than go into business. An adherent of the philosopher Friedrich Wilhelm Joseph von Schelling (1775–1854), he was active in popularizing his ideas in England. His large circle of acquaintances included many poets and authors of the period. He was appointed a brother of the Carthusian Charterhouse, London, where he died. He contributed to, edited, or was critic for the following magazines: *Athenæum*; *Christian's Monthly Magazine*; *Fraser's Magazine*; *Illustrated London News*; *Monthly Magazine*; *Quarterly*; *The Sunbeam, A Journal devoted to Polite Literature.* Some of his poetry publications: *The Legend of St. Loy with Other Poems,* 1820. *Tottenham,* 1820. *An Oration on the Death of S.T. Coleridge,* 1834. *The Descent into Hell,* 1835. *Salvator, the Poor Man of Naples,* 1845. *The Judgement of the Flood,* 1857. *The Wreck of the London,* 1866. *The In-Gathering,* 1870. *The War of Ideas,* 1871.

Sources: *Dictionary of National Biography.* Electronic Edition 1.1. Oxford University Press, 1997. *English Poetry, Second Edition Bibliography* (http://collections.chadwyck.co.uk/html/ep2/bibliography/g.htm). *English Poetry: Author Search.* Chadwyck-Healey Ltd., 1995 (http://www.lib.utexas.edu:8080/search/epoetry/author.html). *The National Portrait Gallery* (www.npg.org.uk). *Stanford University libraries and Academic Information Resources* (http://library.stanford.edu). *Wikipedia, the Free Encyclopedia* (http://en.wikipedia.org/wiki/Wikipedia).

HERBERT, SIR ALAN PATRICK
(1890–1971)

Born in Ashtead, Surrey, and educated at Winchester College, he graduated in jurisprudence from New College, Oxford, in 1914. He was wounded in 1917 while serving in the Royal Naval Volunteer Reserve, and invalided home. He wrote regularly for *Punch* using the initials A.P.H., and wrote more than 50 books. He was famous for his witty championing of minority causes as well as revues, operettas, and a novel, *The Water Gypsies* (1930). The theme of his *The Secret Battle* (1919) is cowardice in war. His *Misleading Cases* (1927) drew attention to the anomalies within the law. As an independent member of Parliament for Oxford University (1935–1950), he introduced the Matrimonial Causes Bill, which was enacted in 1937. He was knighted in 1945. Queen's University, Kingston, Ontario, made him an honorary doctor of laws in 1957, and Oxford University, a doctor of civil law, 1958. He died in London and his death was marked by speeches of condolence in the House of Representatives, Washington, D.C. Some of his poems: "At the Theater," "Bacon and Eggs," "Mr. Churchill," "The Chameleon," "Triangular Legs," "'Twas at the Pictures, Child, We Met."

Sources: *Dictionary of National Biography.* Electronic Edition 1.1. Oxford University Press, 1997. *Encyclopædia Britannica Ultimate Reference Suite DVD,* 2006. *Favorite Poems Old and New.* Helen Ferris, ed. Doubleday, 1957. *The Columbia Granger's Index to Poetry.* 11th ed. *The Columbia Granger's World of Poetry,* Columbia University Press, 2005 (http://www.columbiagrangers.org). *The Faber Book of English History in Verse.* Kenneth Baker, ed. Faber and Faber, 1988. *The Fireside Book of Humorous Poetry.* William Cole, ed. Simon and Schuster, 1959. *The Oxford Companion to English Literature.* 6th edition. Margaret Drabble, ed. Oxford University Press, 2000. *What Cheer: An Anthology of American and British Humorous and Witty Verse.* David McCord, ed. Coward-McCann, 1945.

HERBERT, EDWARD, and GEORGE
(1583–1648)

Edward, 1st Baron Herbert of Cherbury, 1583–1648

The elder brother, who was called "the black Lord Herbert," on account of his good looks, dark hair and complexion, was born at Eyton-on-Severn, Shropshire, into one of the most influential families on the Welsh border. He married his cousin Mary, a wealthy heiress, in 1599. In his autobiography *Life*, not published until 1764, he represents himself mainly as a gay Lothario, but the book, and he, became a laughingstock of English aristocracy. He was a diplomat in the service of Elizabeth, James I, and Charles I. Devoted to his books, he surrendered Montgomery Castle to parliamentary forces in 1644 in order to save his vast library. On his directions, his body was buried at twelve o'clock midnight in the church of St. Giles's-in-the-Fields, London. His chief philosophical treatise, *De Veritate*, first published in Paris in 1624, is the earliest purely metaphysical treatise written by an Englishman. Some of his poems: "Elegy for Dr. Donne," "In a Glass-Window for Inconstancy," "Inconstancy's the Greatest of Sins," "October 14, 1644," "To His Friend Ben Johnson."

George, 1593–1633.

The younger brother was educated at Westminster School and at Trinity College, Cambridge, and graduated M.A. in 1616. He was orator of the university from 1620 to 1627 and also wrote on behalf of the university all official letters to the government. James I took a liking to him and had not the king died in 1625, Herbert might have attained a high position at court. Instead, in 1630, he took holy orders and Charles I presented Herbert to the rectory of Fugglestone with Bemerton, Wiltshire. He died of tuberculosis and was buried beneath the altar of his church; a window in Henry VII Chapel of Westminster Abbey commemorates his life. The *Temple,* containing nearly all his surviving English poems, was published in 1633, with many subsequent editions. Some of the hymns he wrote are still used in worship: "King of Glory," "King of Peace," "Let All the World in Every Corner Sing," "Teach Me, My God and King," "The God of Love My Shepherd Is." Some of his poems: "Good Friday," "Joseph's Coat," "The Bunch of Grapes," "The Church Militant," "The Pearl, Matthew 13:45," "To the Lady Elizabeth Queen of Bohemia."

Sources: *Dictionary of National Biography.* Electronic Edition 1.1. Oxford University Press, 1997. *Encyclopædia Britannica Ultimate Reference Suite DVD,* 2006. *English Poetry: Author Search.* Chadwyck-Healey Ltd., 1995 (http://www.lib.utexas.edu:8080/search/epoetry/author.html). *English Poetry: A Poetic Record, from Chaucer to Yeats.* David Hopkins, ed. Routledge, 1990. *Great Books Online* (www.bartleby.com). *The National Portrait Gallery* (www.npg.org.uk). *Seventeenth Century Poetry: The Schools of Donne and Jonson.* Hugh Kenner, ed. Holt, Rinehart and Winston, 1964. *The Anchor Anthology of Seventeenth-Century Verse, Vol. II.* Louis L. Martz and Richard S. Sylvester, ed. Doubleday Anchor Books, 1969. *The Columbia Encyclopedia,* Sixth Edition. 2001–05 (http://www.bartleby.com/65/). *The Columbia Granger's Index to Poetry.* 11th ed. *The Columbia Granger's World of Poetry,* Columbia University Press, 2005 (http://www.columbia grangers.org). *The Complete English Poems of George Herbert.* John Tobin, ed. Penguin Books, 1991. *The Cyber Hymnal* (http://www.cyberhymnal.org/index.htm). *The Oxford Companion to English Literature.* 6th edition. Margaret Drabble, ed. Oxford University Press, 2000. *Westminster Abbey Official Guide* (no date).

HERBERT, MARY SIDNEY, COUNTESS OF PEMBROKE (1561–1621)

She was born at Ticknall Place, Bewdley, Worcestershire, the sister of the poets Sir Philip and Sir Robert Sidney (see entries). Her education in French, Italian, Latin, Greek, and music was mainly at Ludlow Castle, Shropshire. Queen Elizabeth invited her to court in 1575, and in the autumn of 1575, with her mother and brother Philip, she accompanied Elizabeth on a progress through Staffordshire and Worcestershire. In 1577 she married Henry Herbert, 2nd Earl of Pembroke, of Wilton House, near Salisbury, Wiltshire. Her home became a haven for such poets, musicians, and artists as Edmund Spenser, Michael Drayton, Sir John Davies, and Samuel Daniel (see entries). When Philip died in 1586, she devoted her life to completing his poetic works, particularly *Arcadia* (?1590), and the verse translation for the *Psalms.* She died in London and was buried beside her husband in Salisbury Cathedral. She was the first English woman to achieve a significant literary reputation. Some of her poems: "Dialogue between two shepherds," "To the Angell Spirit of the Most Excellent Sir Philip Sidney," "To the Thrice-Sacred Queen Elizabeth," "Triumph of Death" (Translation from Petrarch, 1304–74).

Sources: *A Sacrifice of Praise: An Anthology of Christian Poetry in English from Caedmon to the Mid–Twentieth Century.* James H. Trott, ed. Cumberland House Publishing, 1999. *Dictionary of National Biography.* Electronic Edition 1.1. Oxford University Press, 1997. *English Poetry: Author Search.* Chadwyck-Healey Ltd., 1995 (http://www.lib.utexas.edu:8080/search/epoetry/author.html). *Life and Works of Mary Sidney Herbert* (http://www.luminarium.org/renlit/mary.htm). *The National Portrait Gallery* (www.npg.org.uk). *The Collected Works of Mary Sidney Herbert: Volume I.* Margaret Hannay, Noel Kinnamon, and Michael Brennan, eds. Clarendon Press, 1998. *The Columbia Granger's Index to Poetry.* 11th ed. *The Columbia Granger's World of Poetry,* Columbia University Press, 2005 (http://www.columbiagrangers.org). *The Oxford Companion to English Literature.* 6th edition. Margaret Drabble, ed. Oxford University Press, 2000. *The Penguin Book of Renaissance Verse 1509–1659.* David Norbrook, ed. Penguin Books, 1992.

HERBERT, W.N. (1961–)

Born in Dundee, Scotland, he was educated at Brasenose College, Oxford. His doctorate on the work of Hugh MacDiarmid was published as *To Circumjack MacDiarmid* (1992). Herbert was Northern Arts Literary Fellow at Newcastle and Durham Universities from 1994 to 1996, and has also held residencies in Dumfries and Galloway (1993) and Moray Libraries (1993–1994), as well as for the Cumbria Arts' Skylines education project in 1997 and the Wordsworth Trust's Dove Cottage in Grasmere (1997–1998). He teaches creative writing at Lancaster University and lives in a converted lighthouse in North Shields. He won awards for *Forked Tongue, Cabaret McGonagall,* and *The Laurelude.* Some of his poetry publications: *Sterts and Stobies:*

Poems in Scots, 1985. *Sharawaggi: Poems in Scots,* 1990 (with Robert Crawford, see entry). *Dundee Doldrums,* 1991. *The Testament of the Reverend Thomas Dick,* 1994. *Forked Tongue,* 1994. *The Laurelude,* 1998. Some of his poems: "Praise of Italian Chip-Shops," "The Anxiety of Information," "The Baby Poem Industry," "The Black Wet," "The Postcards of Scotland," "The Socialist Manifesto for East Balgillo," "To a Mousse."

Sources: *Anthology of Twentieth-Century British and Irish Poetry.* Keith Tuma, ed. Oxford University Press, 2001. *British Council Arts* (http://www.contemporarywriters.com). *National Poetry Day—Thursday 9 October 2003, Dundee: Ode to the Old Tay Bridge by W.N. Herbert* (http://www.bbc.co.uk/radio4/arts/natpoetday/2003_dundee.shtml). *New Blood,* Neil Astley, ed. Bloodaxe Books, 1999. *Poetry with an Edge.* Neil Astley, ed. Bloodaxe Books, 1988. *The Faber Book of Twentieth Century Scottish Poetry.* Douglas Dunn, ed. Faber and Faber, 1992. *The New Penguin Book of Scottish Verse.* Robert Crawford and Mick Imlah, ed. Penguin Books, 2000. *The Penguin Book of Poetry from Britain and Ireland Since 1945.* Robert Crawford, and Simon Armitage, ed. Penguin Books, 1998.

HERBERT, WILLIAM (1778–1847)

The son of Henry Herbert, first earl of Caernarvon, he was educated at Eton College and Oxford University. He was a member of Parliament, practiced at the bar, and was ordained in 1814 after which he was rector of Sofforth, West Riding of Yorkshire, until 1840, when he became dean of Manchester. He died suddenly in London. He was a classical scholar, a linguist, and a naturalist, and discovered the bulb *Nerine humilis.* An annual medal is awarded in his name, the highest honor the International Bulb Society can bestow upon a person for meritorious achievement in advancing the knowledge of bulbous plants. Some of his poetry publications: *Ossiani Darthula,* 1801 (a small volume of Greek and Latin poetry). *Select Icelandic Poetry,* 1804 and 1806 (translated from the originals). *Helga,* 1815 (a poem in seven cantos). *Hedin, or the Spectre of the Tomb,* 1820 (a tale in verse from Danish history). *Wizard Wanderer of Jutland,* 1820–1821. *Attila, or the Triumph of Christianity,* 1838 (in twelve books). *The Christian,* 1846 (a collection of poems). Some of his poems: "Ode to Despair," "The Kiss; A Riddle," "The Morning Song," "The Song of Vala," "The Waterfall."

Sources: *Dictionary of National Biography.* Electronic Edition 1.1. Oxford University Press, 1997. *English Poetry: Author Search.* Chadwyck-Healey Ltd., 1995 (http://www.lib.utexas.edu:8080/search/epoetry/author.html).

HERBERT, WILLIAM, 3RD EARL OF PEMBROKE (1580–1630)

Born at Wilton House, near Salisbury, Wiltshire, he spent two years at New College, Oxford, and later gave his name to Pembroke College, Oxford. He spent a month in the Fleet prison and was banished from court in 1601 when he produced an illegitimate son to one of the ladies of the court. James I reinstated him and, then an earl, he was made a knight of the Garter in 1603; he entertained the king at Wilton House the same year. He was active in establishing an English foothold in New England and in the West Indies and was a member of the East India Company. He died at his London house and was buried in the family vault in Salisbury Cathedral. In 1660 the younger John Donne edited and published Herbert's *Poems* (shortened title), which included poems by several of Herbert's contemporaries. The whole volume was reprinted by Sir S.E. Brydges in 1817. A religious work, *Of the Internal and Eternal Nature of Man in Christ* (1654), is attributed to him. Some of his other poems: "A Paradox," "Disdain Me Still," "Song," "Urania."

Sources: *Dictionary of National Biography.* Electronic Edition 1.1. Oxford University Press, 1997. *Elizabethan Lyrics.* Norman Ault, ed. William Sloane Associates, 1949. *The Anchor Anthology of Seventeenth-Century Verse, Vol. II.* Louis L. Martz and Richard S. Sylvester, ed. Doubleday Anchor Books, 1969. *The Columbia Granger's Index to Poetry.* 11th ed. *The Columbia Granger's World of Poetry,* Columbia University Press, 2005 (http://www.columbiagrangers.org).

HERBISON, DAVID (1800–1880)

The "Bard of Dunclug" was born at Ballymena in County Antrim, where his father was an innkeeper. Blind for four years as a child, his education was scant, and at fourteen, he started learning linen weaving. In 1827, after his father died, he and his elder brother sailed for Canada and escaped a shipwreck in the St. Lawrence. The Quebec climate didn't suit David so he returned to Ireland in 1830 to resume his trade and his earlier interest in poetry. He was soon having his poems published in the Belfast and Dublin newspapers. He became the most famous of the "weaver poets" of Ireland—artisans, independent thinkers, very often self-employed, chiefly in the linen weaving industry, who published their poems in newspapers and in books which were paid for by subscription. He died in his cottage at Dunclug, near Ballymena, and a monument to his memory was erected by public subscription. Some of his publications: *The Fate of McQuillan and O'Neill's Daughter, a Legend of Dunluce, with Other Poems,* 1841. *Midnight Musings,* 1848. *Woodland Wanderings,* 1858. *The Snow-Wreath,* 1869. *The Children of the Year,* 1876.

Sources: *Dictionary of National Biography.* Electronic Edition 1.1. Oxford University Press, 1997. *Dunluce Castle Website, County Antrim, Ireland* (http://www.

northantrim.com/dunlucecastle.htm). *BBC, Northern Ireland Learning: Weaver Poets: The Bard of Dunclug* (http://www.bbc.co.uk/northernireland/schools/4_11/today/english/spr2000/index.shtml).

HERRICK, ROBERT (1591–1674)

When he was one year of age, his father, a London goldsmith, died, and the children were put in the care of his uncle, Sir William Hericke, also a goldsmith. He graduated M.A. from Trinity Hall, Cambridge, in 1620, was ordained in 1623, and took the living of Dean Prior, near Ashburton, Devonshire, in 1629. A royalist supporter, he lost his living in 1647 and retired to London; it was restored to him in 1662. He died and was buried at Dean Prior; he is one of the poets memorialized in Poets' Corner Window (above Chaucer's tomb) in the South Transept of Westminster Abbey. His only book, *Hesperides,* was published in 1648, comprising some 1400 poems, some quite short. "Gather Ye Rosebuds While Ye May" and "Cherry Ripe" are his best known. The English composer Henry Lawes and others wrote the music for some of poems. Some of his other poems: "A Bachanalian Verse," "A Canticle to Apollo," "All Things Decay and Die," "Ceremonies for Christmas," "Songs of New London," "The Deluge," "The Fairies," "The Good-Night, or Blessing," "The Wounded Heart."

Sources: *An Anthology of Revolutionary Poetry.* Marcus Graham, ed. The Active Press, 1929. *Dictionary of National Biography.* Electronic Edition 1.1. Oxford University Press, 1997. *Encyclopædia Britannica Ultimate Reference Suite DVD,* 2006. *English Poetry: Author Search.* Chadwyck-Healey Ltd., 1995 (http://www.lib.utexas.edu:8080/search/epoetry/author.html). *The Cavalier Poets.* Robin Skelton, ed. Oxford University Press, 1970. *The Columbia Granger's Index to Poetry.* 11th ed. *The Columbia Granger's World of Poetry,* Columbia University Press, 2005 (http://www.columbiagrangers.org). *The Oxford Companion to English Literature.* 6th edition. Margaret Drabble, ed. Oxford University Press, 2000. *The Poems of Robert Herrick.* L.C. Martin, ed. Oxford University Press, 1965. *Westminster Abbey Official Guide* (no date).

HERSCHEL, SIR JOHN FREDERICK WILLIAM (1792–1871)

Born in Slough, Buckinghamshire, he was the son of Sir William Herschel, the celebrated astronomer who discovered the planet Uranus. John graduated from St. John's College, Cambridge, in 1813, was immediately elected to a fellowship, and gained his M.A. in 1816. The Royal Society elected him a fellow in 1813; he received the Copley Medal in 1821, became president of the Royal Astronomical Society in 1827, and was knighted in 1831. He followed his father into the study of astronomy and spent 1834–1838 at the Cape of Good Hope cataloging double stars and nebulae of the southern hemisphere and studying Halley's comet. His major works were *Preliminary Discourse on the Study of Natural Philosophy* (1830) and *A Treatise on Astronomy* (1833), later revised into one of the most celebrated scientific treatises ever published, *Outlines of Astronomy* (1849). He is buried in the North Aisle of the Nave of Westminster Abbey. Three of his known poems: "On Burning a Parcel of Old MSS," "The Child to his Mother, Absent," "Tick! Tick! Tick!"

Sources: *Dictionary of National Biography.* Electronic Edition 1.1. Oxford University Press, 1997. *Encyclopædia Britannica Ultimate Reference Suite DVD,* 2006. *Encyclopedia of Britain.* Bamber Gascoigne. London: Macmillan, 1994. *The National Portrait Gallery* (www.npg.org.uk). *Westminster Abbey Official Guide* (no date).

HERVEY, THOMAS KIBBLE (1799–1859)

Born in Paisley, Scotland, but brought to Manchester at the age of four when his father changed jobs, he was educated at Manchester Grammar School, then at Trinity College, Cambridge, from 1818 to 1820, but left to concentrate on writing. He wrote for the *Dublin Review* and the *Art Journal*, was editor for *Friendship's Offering* and the *Amaranth,* and was sole editor of *Athenæum* from 1846 to 1853, when ill-health forced his retirement. His contributions to the *Athenæum* covered poetry and novels, history (particularly that of Nelson, Wellington and Napoleon), love and marriage, social conditions, travel, gift books, anthologies and almanacs, and galleries and museums. He died at Kentish Town, London, and was buried at Highgate Cemetery. In 1866 his widow collected his poems and published them, with memoir and portrait, at Boston, USA. Some of his publications: *The Poetical Sketch-Book*, 1829. *Prose and illustrative Poetry*, 1834. *The Book of Christmas*, 1836. *The English Helicon of the Nineteenth Century*, 1841. Some of his poems: "Australia," "Dead Trumpeter," "I Know Thou Art Gone," "The Convict Ship," "The Devil's Progress."

Sources: *Athenaeum Index: Contributor Record* (http://web.soi.city.ac.uk/~asp/v2/contributors/contributorfiles/HERVEY,ThomasKibble.html). *Dictionary of National Biography.* Electronic Edition 1.1. Oxford University Press, 1997. *Great Books Online* (www.bartleby.com).

HESKETH, PHOEBE (1909–2005)

Phoebe Rayner was born in Preston, Lancashire. Her father was pioneer radiologist A.E. Rayner; her mother was a violinist in the Hallé Orchestra. Educated at Cheltenham Ladies' College, Gloucestershire, she left at the age of 17 to care for her ill mother. She married Aubrey Hesketh in 1931. During World War II she worked as a reporter for the *Bolton Evening News*, then was a freelance lecturer, poetry teacher and journalist, producing many articles for journals and scripts for the BBC. The Royal Society of Literature elected her a fellow in 1956. She describes the Lancashire countryside in many of her poems and in her prose books *Rivington* (1972) and *Village of the Mountain Ash* (1990). She died in a nursing home in Lancashire. Some of her other poetry publications: *Lean Forward Spring*, 1948. *A Song of Sunlight*, 1974 (children). *Sundowner*, 1989. *Collected Poems*, 1989. *Netting the Sun*, 1989. *Six of the Best*, 1989 (children). *A Box of Silver Birch*, 1997. Some of her poems: "After Verlaine," "Academic," "Analyst," "Winter Daffodils," "Wordsworth's Old Age," "Yew Tree Guest House."

Sources: *Guardian Unlimited Obituary, Phoebe Hesketh* (http://www.guardian.co.uk/obituaries/). *The Columbia Granger's Index to Poetry*. 11th ed. *The Columbia Granger's World of Poetry*, Columbia University Press, 2005 (http://www.columbiagrangers.org). *The Leave Train: New and Selected Poems of Phoebe Hesketh*. Enitharmon Press, 1994. *Wikipedia, the Free Encyclopedia* (http://en.wikipedia.org/wiki/Wikipedia).

HEWITT, JOHN HAROLD (1907–1987)

Born in Belfast, the son of parents who were both teachers, he graduated B.A. in 1930 and was awarded an M.A. for his thesis on *Ulster Poets, 1800–1870* from the Queen's University, Belfast, in 1951. By 1943 he had established himself as a writer and art critic. Between 1943 and 1956 he was on the Arts Advisory Committee of the Arts Council of Northern Ireland, serving as chairman for a number of years. In 1974 he received the honorary degree of doctor of letters from the University of Ulster. From 1976 to 1979 he was writer in residence at Queen's University, Belfast. He was made a freeman of the City of Belfast in 1983. He was a voluminous writer from a young age and composed nearly 5000 poems and produced 20 collections and pamphlets of verse. Some of his publications: *No Rebel Word*, 1948. *Collected Poems 1932–1967*, 1968. *The Day of the Corncrake*, 1969. *The Planter and the Gael*, 1970. Some of his poems: "Bangor, Spring 1916," "Colonial Consequence," "Freehold," "Sonnets for Roberta (1954)," "The Anglo-Irish Accord," "The Bombed Public House," "The Volunteer," "Young Womanhood."

Sources: *The Collected Poems of John Hewitt*. Frank Ormsby, ed. Blackstaff Press, 1992. *The Columbia Granger's Index to Poetry*. 11th ed. *The Columbia Granger's World of Poetry*, Columbia University Press, 2005 (http://www.columbiagrangers.org). *The John Hewitt Papers, D/3838. Public Record Office of Northern Ireland* (http://www.proni.gov.uk/records/private/hewitt.htm).

HEWLETT, MAURICE HENRY (1861–1923)

He was born at Weybridge, Surrey, of French descent; his family were possibly Huguenot refugees. His father had the appointment of keeper of His Majesty's land revenue records. Called to the bar in 1890, he too became keeper of land revenue records, from 1897 to 1901. The success of his romantic novel of the Middle Ages, *The Forest Lovers* (1898), made him famous and he left law to concentrate on writing. He joined the Fabian Society in 1917 and worked on a report on wages for the Board of Agriculture. He died at Broadchalke, Salisbury. His writing career is in three phases: 1898–1904, mainly Italian and historical romances; 1904–1914, Regency novels and stories of modern life; 1914–1923, essays and poetry. Some of his poetry publications: *The Masque of Dead Florentines*, 1895. *Artemision*, 1909. *The Song of the Plow*, 1916. *The Village Wife's Lament*, 1918. Some of his poems: "Ariadne Forsaken," "Ballad of Clytié," "Canzone of Hymnia's Coronation," "Eros Narcissus," "Ode to the Dawn of Italy," "Prometheus," "Shakespeare in Church," "The Cretan Ode," "War-Songs for the English," "White Flowers."

Sources: *Dictionary of National Biography*. Electronic Edition 1.1. Oxford University Press, 1997. *Songs and Meditations by Maurice Hewlett*. Archibald Constable and Co., 1896. *The Columbia Granger's Index to Poetry*. 11th ed. *The Columbia Granger's World of Poetry*, Columbia University Press, 2005 (http://www.columbiagrangers.org). *The National Portrait Gallery* (www.npg.org.uk). *The Oxford Companion to English Literature*. 6th edition. Margaret Drabble, ed. Oxford University Press, 2000. *Wikipedia, the Free Encyclopedia* (http://en.wikipedia.org/wiki/Wikipedia).

HEYRICK, THOMAS (1649–1694)

Born at Market Harborough, Leicestershire, he was educated at Peterhouse, Cambridge, from where he graduated M.A. in 1675. In 1671 he was among the contributors to the collection of Cambridge verses on the death of Anne, Duchess of York. He was appointed curate of Market Harborough, Leicestershire, and died and was buried there. In 1685 he published *The Character of a Rebel: A Sermon preached on the Day of Thanksgiving for His Majesties Victory over the Rebels*, with a dedication to Edward Griffin, Esq., treasurer of the Great Chamber. His *Miscellany Poems* was published in 1691 with a dedication to the Countess of Rutland. Many of his poems relate to animals. *The New Atlantis: A Poem, in Three Books, With Some Reflections Upon the Hind and the Panther* was published in 1694. Some of his other publications: Some of his poems: "Martial," "On a Peacock," "On a Sunbeam," "On an Indian Tomineos, the Least of Birds," "On the Crocodile,"

"On the Death of a Monkey," "The Submarine Voyage."

Sources: *Dictionary of National Biography.* Electronic Edition 1.1. Oxford University Press, 1997. *English Poetry, Second Edition Bibliography* (http://collections.chadwyck.co.uk/html/ep2/bibliography/g.htm). *English Poetry: Author Search.* Chadwyck-Healey Ltd., 1995 (http://www.lib.utexas.edu:8080/search/epoetry/author.html). *Fellow Mortals: An Anthology of Animal Verse.* Roy Fuller, ed. Macdonald and Evans, 1981. *On Wings of Song: Poems about Birds.* J.D. McClatchy, ed. Alfred A. Knopf, 2000. *The Cavalier Poets.* Robin Skelton, ed. Oxford University Press, 1970. *The Columbia Granger's Index to Poetry.* 11th ed. *The Columbia Granger's World of Poetry,* Columbia University Press, 2005 (http://www.columbiagrangers.org). *The Metaphysical Poets.* Helen Gardner, ed. Penguin Books, 1969. *The Poetical Works of Robert Herrick:* F.W. Moorman, ed. Oxford: The Clarendon Press, 1815.

HEYWOOD, JOHN and JASPER (?1497–1598)

John, the father, ?1497–?1580

Thought to have come from either St. Albans, Hertfordshire, or London, he was a chorister of the Chapel Royal and is said to have been educated at Broadgates Hall (now Pembroke College), Oxford. His singing and virginal playing made him a favorite both with Henry VIII and Queen Mary. He was accused of denying the king's supremacy over the church (Edward VI) and in 1554 was forced to publicly recant. Under Elizabeth, refusing to renounce his Catholicism, he fled to Belgium, where it is thought he died. Heywood wrote interludes — short plays performed separately, or preceding or following a play, or between the acts. Some of his publications: *The Pardoner and the Frere,* 1533. *Johan the Husbande, Tyb the Wife, and Syr Jh_n the Preest,* 1533. *The Play of the Wether,* 1533. *The Four P.P.,* ?1534. *The Spider and the Flie,* 1556. Some of his poems: "A Ballad on the Marriage of Philip and Mary," "A Rose and a Nettle," "Cardinal Fisher," "Epygrams," "Of Birds and Birders," "The Cock and the Hen," "The Woodcock and the Daw," "A Ballad of the Green Willow," "A Praise of His Lady."

Jasper, the son, 1535–1598

Born in London, he was one of the boy pages of honor to Princess Elizabeth. He graduated M.A. from Merton College, Oxford, in 1558, and resigned his fellowship in 1558 on account of several misdemeanors. Seven months later he was elected a fellow of All Souls' College, and again he was forced to resign on account of non-compliance with certain religious changes. Already an ordained priest, he was admitted to the Society of Jesus in Rome in 1562 and became professor of moral theology and controversy at the Jesuit college at Dillingen in Bavaria.

He was there for seventeen years and took the degree of doctor of divinity and became a professed father of the society in 1570. In England, in 1580, he was arrested for being a priest, imprisoned first in the Clink prison, London, then in the Tower, and although others were executed he was deported to France. He eventually settled at Naples, where he died. He published his translation of Seneca's ten tragedies in 1581. One other poem is recorded, "Look or You Leap."

Sources: *A New Canon of English Poetry.* James Reeves, and Martin Seymour-Smith, ed. Barnes and Noble, 1967. *An Anthology of Catholic Poets.* Shane Leslie, ed. Macmillan, 1952. *Dictionary of National Biography.* Electronic Edition 1.1. Oxford University Press, 1997. *Elizabethan Lyrics.* Norman Ault, ed. William Sloane Associates, 1949. *Encyclopædia Britannica Ultimate Reference Suite DVD,* 2006. *English Poetry: Author Search.* Chadwyck-Healey Ltd., 1995 (http://www.lib.utexas.edu:8080/search/epoetry/author.html). *Poet's Corner Bookshelf, Olney Hymns by William Cowper* (http://www.theotherpages.org/poems/olney.html). *The Columbia Granger's Index to Poetry.* 11th ed. *The Columbia Granger's World of Poetry,* Columbia University Press, 2005 (http://www.columbiagrangers.org). *The Faber Book of Epigrams and Epitaphs.* Geoffrey Grigson, ed. Faber and Faber, 1977. *The National Portrait Gallery* (www.npg.org.uk). *The Oxford Book of Verse in English Translation.* Charles Tomlinson, ed. Oxford University Press, 1980. *The Oxford Companion to English Literature.* 6th edition. Margaret Drabble, ed. Oxford University Press, 2000. *The Penguin Book of Renaissance Verse 1509–1659.* David Norbrook, ed. . Penguin Books, 1992.

HEYWOOD, THOMAS (?1575–1650)

Born in Lincolnshire, he studied at Cambridge University. His career as actor-playwright spans the peak periods of Elizabethan and Jacobean drama. He joined Philip Henslowe's theatrical company, the Admiral's Men, in 1596, and was afterwards a member of the company belonging to Edward Somerset, fourth earl of Worcester. He was one of the players at the funeral of Queen Anne, wife of James I, in 1619. Heywood translated the works of various Greek and Latin writers, wrote or contributed to over 200 plays, and wrote seven lord mayor's shows (see John Tatham). His *Troia Britannica,* or *Great Britain's Troy* (1609), is a poem in seventeen cantos — a mixture of poetical tales and a chronicle from the creation until "the present time." Some of his other publications: *A Woman Killed with Kindness,* 1607. *The Rape of Lucrece,* 1608. *The Golden Age,* 1611. *The Silver Age,* 1612. *An Apology for Actors,* 1612. *Love's Mistress,* 1636. *The Brazen Age,* 1613. *The Iron Age,* 1632. Some of his poems: "From Mostellaria [from Plautus Titus Maccius (c. 250–184 B.C.)]," "Hierarchie of the Blessed Angels," "Pack Clouds, Away," "Ye Little Birds That Sit and Sing."

Sources: *Dictionary of National Biography.* Electronic

Edition 1.1. Oxford University Press, 1997. *English Poetry: Author Search*. Chadwyck-Healey Ltd., 1995 (http://www. lib.utexas.edu:8080/search/epoetry/author.html). *English Songs and Ballads*. T.W.H. Crosland, ed. Oxford University Press, 1918. *Songs from the British Drama*. Edward Bliss Reed, ed. Yale University Press, 1925. *The Columbia Granger's Index to Poetry*. 11th ed. *The Columbia Granger's World of Poetry*, Columbia University Press, 2005 (http://www.columbiagrangers.org). *The Oxford Book of Classical Verse in Translation*. Adrian Poole and Jeremy Maule, eds. 1995. *The Oxford Companion to English Literature*. 6th edition. Margaret Drabble, ed. Oxford University Press, 2000. *The World's Great Religious Poetry*. Caroline Miles Hill, ed. Macmillan, 1954.

HILL, AARON (1685–1750)

The son of a Wiltshire country gentleman, he was born in London and educated at Westminster School. In 1700 he went to Istanbul, where his relative, Lord Paget, the ambassador, sent him touring in the east with a tutor. In 1709 he published *Full Account of the Ottoman Empire*, and in the same year he addressed a complimentary poem, "Camillus," to Lord Peterborough. In 1711 he translated Rossi's libretto for Handel's opera *Rinaldo*. His attempts at being an entrepreneur failed and cost him, and others, a great deal of money. Alexander Pope satirized him in *The Duncaid* (1728), to which Hill responded in *The Progress of Wit* (1730). In 1724 he launched the bi-weekly *Plain Dealer* and co-coauthored the theatrical periodical *Promoter* (1734–1736). Seventeen plays are credited to him, some of them adaptations. Some of his poems: "Alone, in an Inn, at Southampton," "Apology for Death," "May-Day," "Modesty," "On a Lady, Preached into the Colic, by One of Her Lovers," "The Garden Window," "The Lord's Prayer in Verse," "The Recollected Complainer," "To Mr. Thomson," "Whitehall Stairs," "Written on a Window."

Sources: *Dictionary of National Biography*. Electronic Edition 1.1. Oxford University Press, 1997. *English Poetry: Author Search*. Chadwyck-Healey Ltd., 1995 (http://www. lib.utexas.edu:8080/search/epoetry/author.html). *Poets' Corner — Index of Poets* (http://www.theotherpages.org/ poems/poem-gh.html). *The Columbia Granger's Index to Poetry*. 11th ed. *The Columbia Granger's World of Poetry*, Columbia University Press, 2005 (http://www.columbia grangers.org). *The Faber Book of Useful Verse*. Simon Brett, ed. Faber and Faber, 1981. *The National Portrait Gallery* (www.npg.org.uk). *The New Oxford Book of Eighteenth Century Verse*. Roger Lonsdale, ed. Oxford University Press, 2003. *The Oxford Book of Garden Verse*. John Dixon Hunt, ed. Oxford University Press, 1993. *The Oxford Companion to English Literature*. 6th edition. Margaret Drabble, ed. Oxford University Press, 2000. *Wikipedia, the Free Encyclopedia* (http://en.wikipedia.org/wiki/Wikipedia).

HILL, GEOFFREY WILLIAM (1932–)

Born in Worcestershire, and after graduating in English from Keble College, Oxford, he taught at Leeds University from 1954 until 1980. From 1981 until 1988 — after a year at Bristol University on a Churchill Scholarship — he became a teaching fellow at Emmanuel College, Cambridge. Leeds University awarded him doctor of literature in 1988, when he became university professor and professor of literature and religion at Boston University, USA, a post he still holds. He was made a fellow of the Royal Society of Literature in 1972 and a fellow of the American Academy of Arts and Sciences in 1996. The power and beauty of poetry was awakened through reading William Palgrave's anthology *The Golden Treasury* (1964). He has written two books on literary criticism, *The Lords of Limit* (1984) and *The Enemy's Country* (1991). Some of his recent poetry publications: *New and Collected Poems*, 1994. *The Triumph of Love*, 1998. *The Orchards of Syon*, 2002. *Scenes from Comus*, 2005. Some of his poems: "Churchill's Funeral," "Ovid in the Third Reich," "Requiem for the Plantagenet Kings," "Scenes with Harlequins," "The Bidden Guest," "The White Ship."

Sources: *A Web Guide to Geoffrey Hill* (http://www.lit eraryhistory.com/20thC/HillG.htm). *Literary Heritage, West Midlands* (http://www3.shropshire-cc.gov.uk/ hillgeo.htm). *The National Portrait Gallery* (www.npg. org.uk). *New and Collected Poems, 1952–1992, of Geoffrey Hill*. Houghton Mifflin, 1994. *The Columbia Granger's Index to Poetry*. 11th ed. *The Columbia Granger's World of Poetry*, Columbia University Press, 2005 (http://www. columbiagrangers.org). *The Oxford Companion to English Literature*. 6th edition. Margaret Drabble, ed. Oxford University Press, 2000. *Who's Who*. London: A & C Black, 2005.

HILL, SELIMA (1945–)

Born in Hampstead, London, into a family of painters and writers, she now lives by the sea in Dorset. She read moral sciences at Cambridge University (1965–1967), married a painter, and had a family before publishing her first collection, *Saying Hello at the Station* (1984). She has known tragedy in her life, being badly burned when she was a baby and then later spending time in a psychiatric hospital. She has worked on multimedia projects with the Royal Ballet, Welsh National Opera and BBC Bristol. She is a tutor at the Poetry School in London, has taught creative writing in hospitals and prisons, and works for the Poetry Library in London. Some of her other poetry publications: *The Accumulation of Small Acts of Kindness*, 1989 (won first prize in the Arvon Foundation/Observer International Poetry Competition). *Violet*, 1997. *Bunny*, 2001 (won the Whitbread Poetry Award). *Portrait of My Lover as a Horse*, 2002. *Lou-Lou*, 2004. *Red Roses*, 2006. Some of her poems: "A Voice in the Garden," "Being a

Wife," "Crossing the Desert in a Pram," "Diving Archaeologists," "Looking for Camels."

Sources: *British Council Arts* (http://www.contemporarywriters.com). *Emergency Kit: Poems for Strange Times.* Jo Shapcott and Matthew Sweeney, ed. Faber and Faber, 1996. *The Bloodaxe Book of 20th Century Poetry, from Britain and Ireland.* Edna Longley, ed. Bloodaxe Books, 2000. *The Columbia Granger's Index to Poetry.* 11th ed. *The Columbia Granger's World of Poetry,* Columbia University Press, 2005 (http://www.columbiagrangers.org). *The Faber Book of 20th Century Women's Poetry.* Fleur Adcock, ed. Faber and Faber, 1987. *The New British Poetry, 1968–88.* Gillian Allnutt, Fred D'Aguiar and Ken Edwards, eds. Grafton Books, 1989. *The New Exeter Book of Riddles.* Kevin Crossley-Holland and Lawrence Sail, eds. Enitharmon Press, 1999. *The Oxford Companion to English Literature.* 6th edition. Margaret Drabble, ed. Oxford University Press, 2000.

HILL, TOBIAS (1970–)

Poet and novelist, born in London, he read English at Sussex University, then spent two years teaching in Japan. His 1997 collection of short stories, *Skin*, won the PEN/Macmillan Silver Pen Award. Adaptations of his poetry and short stories have been broadcast on BBC Radio 4. He has also worked as rock critic for the *Sunday Telegraph*, London, and as the poetry editor of the *Richmond Review*. His novel *The Love of Stones* (2001) has been published in seven languages and in 11 countries and is being developed as a film by Granada Films. He lives in London and is Royal Society of Literature Fellow at Sussex University. In 2004, he was named as one of the Poetry Book Society's "Next Generation" poets. Some of his publications: *Year of the Dog*, 1995. *Midnight in the City of Clocks*, 1996 (influenced by his experiences living in Japan). *Zoo*, 1998. *Nocturne in Chrome and Sunset Yellow*, 2006. Some of his poems: "A Bowl of Green Fruit," "Hiroshima Midnight," "Horse Chestnuts," "London Pastoral," "Nine in the Morning in the Station Bar," "One Day in Hiroshima," "Nocturne."

Sources: *British Council Arts* (http://www.contemporarywriters.com). *Guardian Unlimited Obituary, Tobia Hill* (http://www.guardian.co.uk/obituaries/). *Poems of Tobias Hill* (http://themargins.net/anth/1990–1999/hillhiroshima.html). *Review of Nocturne in Chrome and Sunset Yellow* (http://www.saltpublishing.com/books/smp/1844712621.htm).

HINKSON, KATHARINE (TYNAN) (1861–1931)

Born in Dublin, the daughter of a farmer, she is better known by her maiden name of Katherine Tynan. A studious child with poor eyesight due to measles, her schooling at a convent school in Drogheda was shortened. Catholicism and Irish patriotism dominated her work as a poet and novelist.

Her father paid for the publication of her first book of verse, *Louise de la Vallière* (1885). She went on to write more than 100 romantic novels and many poems. She married Albert Hinkson, a barrister and novelist, in 1883; she was widowed in 1919. She wrote the well-known song "All in The April Evening" popularized by the Glasgow Orpheus Choir. She died at Wimbledon, Surrey. Her autobiographical publications: *Twenty-five Years*, 1923. *The Middle Years*, 1917. *The Years of the Shadow*, 1919. *The Wandering Years*, 1922. *Memories*, 1924. Some of her other poetry publications: *Ballads and Lyrics*, 1891. *Irish Love-Songs*, 1892. *Cuckoo Songs*, 1984. *Poems*, 1901. *Innocencies*, 1905. *Collected Poems*, 1930. Some of her poems: "Assumpta Est Maria," "Chanticleer," "Joining the Colours," "Shamrock Song," "The Angel of the Annunciation."

Sources: *A Sacrifice of Praise: An Anthology of Christian Poetry in English from Caedmon to the Mid–Twentieth Century.* James H. Trott, ed. Cumberland House Publishing, 1999. *Carmina Mariana: An English Anthology in Verse in Honour of or in Relation to The Blessed Virgin Mary.* Orby Shipley, ed. Burns and Oates, 1894. *Dictionary of National Biography.* Electronic Edition 1.1. Oxford University Press, 1997. *Encyclopædia Britannica Ultimate Reference Suite DVD,* 2006. *The Columbia Granger's Index to Poetry.* 11th ed. *The Columbia Granger's World of Poetry,* Columbia University Press, 2005 (http://www.columbiagrangers.org). *The Home Book of Modern Verse.* Burton Egbert Stevenson, ed. Henry Holt, 1953. *The Oxford Companion to English Literature.* 6th edition. Margaret Drabble, ed. Oxford University Press, 2000. *Wikipedia, the Free Encyclopedia* (http://en.wikipedia.org/wiki/Wikipedia).

HOBSBAUM, PHILIP DENNIS (1932–2005)

Hobsbaum was born in London of orthodox Jewish parents but lived in Yorkshire from the age of five. He read English at Downing College, Cambridge, and in 1955 he moved to London, briefly worked in television, then taught in various schools until 1959, when he worked for his Ph.D. at Sheffield University, which resulted in *A Theory of Communication* (1969). He was lecturer at Queen's University, Belfast, reader in English literature at Glasgow University from 1965 and full professor in 1985. He was the founder of the "Group" along with like-minded poets such as Edward Lucie-Smith, Peter Redgrove and George Macbeth (see respective entries). Groups were formed in Cambridge, London, Belfast, and Glasgow. "Hobsbaum believed that criticism provided a solid basis for creative endeavor, and himself nurtured the talents of many well-known writers through a famous series of private critical 'groups'" (Alan Brownjohn, Thursday, July 7, 2005, *The Guardian*). Some of his poetry publications: *The Place's Fault*, 1964. *In Retreat*, 1966.

Coming Out Fighting, 1969. *Women and Animals*, 1972. Some of his poems: "A Credential," "A Lesson in Love," "Last Memo," "Timon Speaks to a Dog."

Sources: *Guardian Unlimited Obituary of Philip Dennis Hobsbaum* (http://www.guardian.co.uk/obituaries/). *P.E.N. New Poetry I.* Robert Nye, ed. Quartet Books, 1986. *The Columbia Granger's Index to Poetry.* 11th ed. *The Columbia Granger's World of Poetry,* Columbia University Press, 2005 (http://www.columbiagrangers.org). *The Oxford Book of Twentieth-Century English Verse.* Philip Larkin, ed. Oxford University Press, 1973. *The Oxford Companion to English Literature.* 6th edition. Margaret Drabble, ed. Oxford University Press, 2000. *Tygers of Wrath: Poems of Hate, Anger, and Invective.* X.J. Kennedy, ed. University of Georgia Press, 1981. *Wikipedia, the Free Encyclopedia* (http://en.wikipedia.org/wiki/Wikipedia).

HODGSON, RALPH EDWIN
(1871–1962)

He was born in, Darlington, County Durham, and brought up in Gatton, Surrey. In 1913 he founded *The Sign of the Flying Fame*, a journal that made an important contribution to printing design. He contributed to and edited *Fry's*, a magazine of sporting life, and throughout his life his name was associated with boxing, billiards, and especially dogs. The Plumage Act of 1921 was inspired by his campaign to end the trafficking in birds' feathers for women's apparel. He lectured in Japan from 1924 to 1938 and was awarded the Insignia of the Rising Sun. He then settled in Ohio, USA, and received an award for distinguished achievement from the American Academy and National Institute of Arts and Letters in 1946 and the Queen's gold medal for poetry in 1954. His first published poem, "The Storm Thrush," appeared in the *Saturday Review* in 1904. *Poems* (1917) contains "The Song of Honour," for which he had been awarded the Polignac prize in 1914. Some of his poems: "Babylon," "Flying Scrolls," "Hymn to Moloch," "Silver Wedding," "The Bells of Heaven," "The Birdcatcher," "The Bull," "Time, You Old Gypsy Man."

Sources: *British Poetry 1880–1920: Edwardian Voices.* Paul L. Wiley and Harold Orel, eds. Appleton-Century-Crofts, 1969. *Dictionary of National Biography.* Electronic Edition 1.1. Oxford University Press, 1997. *Encyclopædia Britannica Ultimate Reference Suite DVD,* 2006. *The Columbia Granger's Index to Poetry.* 11th ed. *The Columbia Granger's World of Poetry,* Columbia University Press, 2005 (http://www.columbiagrangers.org). *The Faber Book of Twentieth Century Verse.* John Heath-Stubbs, and David Wright, ed. Faber and Faber, 1975. *The New Oxford Book of English Verse, 1250–1950.* Helen Gardner, ed. Oxford University Press, 1972. *The Oxford Companion to English Literature.* 6th edition. Margaret Drabble, ed. Oxford University Press, 2000.

HODGSON, WILLIAM NOEL
(1893–1916)

The son of the vicar of the Devonshire village of Thornbury, later the Right Reverend Henry Hodgson, the first Bishop of Saint Edmundsbury and Ipswich, he graduated in classics from Christ Church College, Oxford, in 1913. The following year he was commissioned as bombing officer of the 9th Battalion the Devonshire Regiment. He was mentioned in dispatches and at Vermelles in 1915 was awarded the Military Cross, when he and a small party held a captured trench for 36 hours without food or reinforcements. In 1916, he began writing stories, poems, and essays about the front under the pseudonym "Edward Melbourne." He was killed on 1 July 1916, the first day of the Battle of the Somme, while taking a supply of bombs to his men in newly captured trenches near Mametz. His body, with his batman lying at his side, was found among 159 men, and that is where they were buried. He is immortalized in his last poem, "Before Action," written just before he was killed. Some of his poems: "Back to Rest," "England to Her Sons," "Glimpse," "Release," "Reverie," "To a Friend Killed in Action."

Sources: *Devonshire Cemetery, Mametz, Somme* (www.silentcities.co.uk/). For pictures of the Devonshire Cemetery see (http://www.webmatters.net/cwgc/devonshire.htm). *Oldpoetry* (www.oldpoetry.com). *Peace and War: A Collection of Poems.* Michael Harrison and Christopher Stuart-Clark, eds. Oxford University Press, 1989. *Poetry of the First World War.* Edward Hudson, ed. Wayland Publishers Ltd., 1988. *The Columbia Granger's Index to Poetry.* 11th ed. *The Columbia Granger's World of Poetry,* Columbia University Press, 2005 (http://www.columbiagrangers.org).

HOFMANN, MICHAEL (1957–)

Born in Freiburg, West Germany, son of the German novelist Gert Hofmann (1931–1993), he grew up in the U.K. and now lives in London. His translation of his father's novel — *The Film Explainer* — won the Independent Foreign Fiction Prize in 1995. He was educated in Edinburgh and Winchester, Magdalene College, Oxford (where he read English literature and classics), Trinity College, Cambridge and at the University of Regensburg, Bavaria. Since 1983 he has worked as a freelance writer, translator and reviewer. Also since 1993, he has held a half-time position at the University of Florida in Gainesville, USA, and in 1994, he was visiting associate professor at the University of Michigan, Ann Arbor. He has won nine literary awards, five for his translations. He has published more than thirty poetry translations. Some of his original publications: *Nights in the Iron Hotel*, 1983. *Acrimony*, 1986. *Corona, Corona*, 1993. *Approximately Nowhere*, 1999.

Some of his poems: "1967–1971," "Ancient Evenings," "By Forced Marches," "First Night," "Myopia in Rupert Brooke Country," "Postcard from Cuernavaca," "The Austrians After Sadowa (1866)."

Sources: *Ashes for Breakfast: Selected Poems of Durs Grunbein.* Michael Hofmann, translator. Farrar Straus Giroux, 2005. *British Council Arts* (http://www.contemporarywriters.com). *Emergency Kit: Poems for Strange Times.* Jo Shapcott and Matthew Sweeney, ed. Faber and Faber, 1996. *Penguin Modern Poets, Book 9.* John Burnside, Robert Crawford, and Kathleen Jamie, eds. Penguin Books, 1996. *Some Contemporary Poets of Britain and Ireland: An Anthology.* Michael Schmidt, ed. Carcanet Press, 1983. *The Chatto Book of Love Poetry.* John Fuller, ed. Chatto and Windus, 1990. *The Columbia Granger's Index to Poetry.* 11th ed. *The Columbia Granger's World of Poetry,* Columbia University Press, 2005 (http://www.columbiagrangers.org). *The Faber Book of 20th Century German Poems.* Michael Hofmann, Faber and Faber, 2005. *The Harvill Book of Twentieth-Century Poetry in English.* Michael Schmidt, ed. The Harvill Press, 1999. *The Oxford Companion to English Literature.* 6th edition. Margaret Drabble, ed. Oxford University Press, 2000.

HOGG, JAMES, "THE ETTRICK SHEPHERD" (1770–1835)

Hogg spent most of his youth and early manhood as a shepherd in Ettrick Forest in the Scottish Borders. He was almost entirely self-educated, but was able to read the Bible and the catechism. Sir Walter Scott included some poems from Hogg's family in *The Minstrelsy of the Scottish Border* (1802–1803). In 1810 Hogg went to Edinburgh, where he met Lord Byron, Robert Southey, and William Wordsworth (see entries), and became friends with publisher John Murray, who published the rest of his poems. In 1817 he assisted at the inauguration of *Blackwood's Magazine.* His patron, the Duchess of Buccleuch, left instructions in her will that he should be given Eltrive Lake farm in Yarrow at a nominal rate. He was buried in Ettrick churchyard and a monument was erected to him overlooking St. Mary's Loch. Some of his publications: *Scottish Pastorals,* 1801. *The Mountain Bard,* 1807. *The Forest Minstrel,* 1810. *The Queen's Wake,* 1813. *The Pilgrims of the Sun,* 1815. *The Poetic Mirror,* 1816. *The Jacobite Relics of Scotland,* 1891–1821. Some of his poems: "A Boy's Song," "Charlie is My Darling," "The Skylark," "When the Kye Comes Hame."

Sources: *Come Hither.* Walter de la Mare, ed. Knopf, 1957; Dover Publications, 1995. *Dictionary of National Biography.* Electronic Edition 1.1. Oxford University Press, 1997. *Encyclopædia Britannica Ultimate Reference Suite DVD,* 2006. *English Poetry: Author Search.* Chadwyck-Healey Ltd., 1995 (http://www.lib.utexas.edu:8080/search/epoetry/author.html). *James Hogg Society* (http://www.cc.gla.ac.uk/hogg/). *The National Portrait Gallery* (www.npg.org.uk). *Parodies: An Anthology from Chaucer to Beerbohm — and After.* Dwight Macdonald, ed. Modern Library, 1960. *The Columbia Granger's Index to Poetry.* 11th ed. *The Columbia Granger's World of Poetry,* Columbia University Press, 2005 (http://www.columbiagrangers.org). *The New Penguin Book of Scottish Verse.* Robert Crawford and Mick Imlah, eds. Penguin Books, 2000. *The Oxford Companion to English Literature.* 6th edition. Margaret Drabble, ed. Oxford University Press, 2000.

HOLLAND, HUGH (?1569–?1635)

A native of Denbigh, Wales, he was educated at Westminster School and Trinity College, Cambridge, where he became a fellow. He is known to have been in Jerusalem and that he embraced the Roman Catholic faith; it is thought that he was made a knight of the Sepulcher. Disgruntled at not being given some high office, he seems to have turned to poetry. As a poet he was patronized by George Villiers, duke of Buckingham. Holland was one of the poets who met at the Mermaid Tavern, Broad Street, London, and is likely to have been personally acquainted with Shakespeare. Some of his publications: *Pancharis,* 1603. *Seianus: His Fall,* 1605. *The Elements of Armories,* 1610. *Coryats Crudities,* 1611. *The Odcombian Banquet, or Laugh and be Fat,* 1611. *A Cypres Garland,* 1625. *Odes of Horace,* 1625. Some of his poems: "A parallel betweene Don Vlysses of Ithaca and Don Coryate of Odcombe," "Epitaph on Prince Henry," "Owen Tudor," "This man doth praise thy totterd ragged shirt," "Vpon the Lines and Life of the Famous Scenicke Poet, Master VVilliam Shakespeare."

Sources: *Anglo-Welsh Poetry, 1480–1980.* Raymond Garlick and Roland Mathias, ed. Poetry Wales Press, 1984. *Dictionary of National Biography.* Electronic Edition 1.1. Oxford University Press, 1997. *English Poetry, Second Edition Bibliography* (http://collections.chadwyck.co.uk/html/ep2/bibliography/g.htm). *English Poetry: Author Search.* Chadwyck-Healey Ltd., 1995 (http://www.lib.utexas.edu:8080/search/epoetry/author.html). *Preface to Shakespeare's First Folio* (http://shakespeare.palomar.edu/Folio1.htm). *Stanford University Libraries and Academic Information Resources* (http://library.stanford.edu). *The Columbia Granger's Index to Poetry.* 11th ed. *The Columbia Granger's World of Poetry,* Columbia University Press, 2005 (http://www.columbiagrangers.org). *The Faber Book of Epigrams and Epitaphs.* Geoffrey Grigson, ed. Faber and Faber, 1977. *The Oxford Book of Welsh Verse in English.* Gwyn Jones, ed. Oxford University Press, 1977.

HOLLAND, SIR RICHARD (?1420–?1485)

Nothing is known about the early life of this Scottish poet. He was secretary or chaplain to the earl of Moray (1450) and had some connection with the cathedral of Norway. The reign of James II of Scotland (1437–60) was a period of great upheaval, rivalry and struggle for power, and Holland supported the powerful Douglas clan. After the defeat of Arkinholm (now Langholm, Dumfriesshire) in 1455, which marked the fall of the Douglases, James, earl of Douglas, and his followers, including Holland, fled to England. James III promised a pardon to those who swore allegiance to him. Holland, however, sided with Edward IV in his attempt to rouse the Western Isles to resurrect Douglas power again. James banished him and he retired to Orkney and later to Shetland. His poem *The Buke of the Howlat,* written between 1442 and 1452, extending to 1001 lines, is a bird allegory and shows his devotion to the house of Douglas; he depicts his patrons, the earl and countess of Moray, as doves. Blind Harry (see Henry the Minstrel) refers to the poem and William Dunbar (see entry) names him in his *Lament for the Makaris.*

Sources: *Britain in Print: Henryson's Testament of Cresseid in Context, The Buke of the Howlat Discussed* (http://www.britaininprint.net/learning/studytools_4.php) . *Dictionary of National Biography.* Electronic Edition 1.1. Oxford University Press, 1997. *The Columbia Granger's Index to Poetry.* 11th ed. *The Columbia Granger's World of Poetry,* Columbia University Press, 2005 (http://www.columbiagrangers.org). *The Oxford Book of Late Medieval Verse and Prose.* Douglas Gray, ed. Clarendon Press, 1985. *The Oxford Book of Scottish Verse,* John MacQueen and Tom Scott, eds. Oxford University Press, 1966.

HOLLAND, ROBERT (1557–?1622)

Welsh clergyman-poet born at Conway, Caernarvonshire, where his family, over generations, had come to own most of the town, including the castle, as well as of good estates in the neighborhood. He studied at Clare College, Cambridge, Magdalene College, Cambridge, and Jesus College, Cambridge, and graduated M.A. in 1581. He is known to have made a paraphrase of the Gospels, although there is no date given. From 1591 until his death he was rector of several parishes in Pembrokeshire and Carmarthenshire. Some of his publications (shortened titles): *The Holy History of Our Lord and Saviour Issus Christ's nativity, life, acts, miracles, doctrine, death, passion, resurrection and ascension,* 1594. *Darmerth, neu Arlwy Gweddi,* 1600 (a prayer, preparation, or feast). *Dav Cymro yn taring yn Bell o'u Gwlad, ac ymgyffwrdd ar fynydd* (no date given) (stories told by two Welshmen meeting on a mountain, about all they had seen and heard with regard to conjurers, wizards, and the like). Two of his other poems: "Eve in Old Age," "The Fisherman Casts His Line into the Sea."

Sources: *Anthology of Magazine Verse and Yearbook of American Poetry.* Alan F. Pater, ed. Monitor Book Company, 1980. *Dictionary of National Biography.* Electronic Edition 1.1. Oxford University Press, 1997. *English Poetry:*
Author Search. Chadwyck-Healey Ltd., 1995 (http://www.lib.utexas.edu:8080/search/epoetry/author.html). *Stanford University Libraries and Academic Information Resources* (http://library.stanford.edu). *The Columbia Granger's Index to Poetry.* 11th ed. *The Columbia Granger's World of Poetry,* Columbia University Press, 2005 (http://www.columbiagrangers.org). *The Norton Introduction to Poetry.* 2nd ed., J. Paul Hunter, ed. W.W. Norton, 1981.

HOLLIS, MATTHEW (1971–)

Born in 1971 in Norwich, Norfolk, he studied at Edinburgh University and York University. He published a pamphlet, *The Boy on the Edge of Happiness* (1996), then went on to win an Eric Gregory Award in 1999. His first collection of poems, *Ground Water* (2004), is a Poetry Book Society Recommendation and was short listed for the 2004 Guardian First Book Award, the Whitbread Poetry Award and the Forward Poetry Prize (Best First Collection). He also edited *101 Poems Against War* (2003) with Paul Keegan (poetry editor at Faber and Faber), and *Strong Words: Modern Poets on Modern Poetry* (2000) with W.N. Herbert (see entry). In 2001 he took part in the Arts Council "First Lines" U.K. poetry tour and was selected by the British Council to participate in *Write On!* touring Croatia (2001) and Hungary in 2004. He is a tutor for the Poetry School in London and has taught creative writing in schools and universities. He lives in London, where he works as an editor at Faber and Faber.

Sources: *British Council Arts* (http://www.contemporarywriters.com).

HOLLOWAY, JOHN (1920–1999)

Brought up in south London, he won an open scholarship in history to New College, Oxford, where he graduated with a First in Modern Greats. After the war, in which he saw service in the Artillery and Intelligence Corps, he had several lecturing appointments in philosophy and English. He was a fellow at Queens' College, Cambridge, from 1955, and professor of modern English from 1959 until his death. He taught English in Greece, India, Ceylon, Pakistan, Hong Kong, New Zealand, Tunisia, and Japan. Some of his publications: *The Victorian Sage: Studies in Argument,* 1953 (reissued 1965). *The Charted Mirror: Literary and critical essays,* 1960. *The Story of the Night: Studies in Shakespeare's Major Tragedies,* 1961. *Blake's Lyric Poetry (Study in English Literature),* 1968. *Proud Knowledge: Poetry, Insight and the Self, 1620–1920,* 1977. *Planet of Winds,* 1977. *Later English Broadside Ballads,* 1979 (with Joan Black, his wife). Some of his poems: "Elegy for an Estrangement," "Family Poem," "Journey through the Night," "London, Greater London (After Satire III)," "The Brothers," "The Light," "Ulysses," "Warning to a Guest."

Sources: *New Poets of England and America.* Donald Hall, and Robert Pack, ed. World, 1962. *Obituary of Professor John Holloway, Fellow 1955–1999. Queens' College Cambridge Record, 2000* (http://www.quns.cam.ac.uk/Queens/Record/2000/Society/Holloway.html). *The Columbia Granger's Index to Poetry.* 11th ed. *The Columbia Granger's World of Poetry,* Columbia University Press, 2005 (http://www.columbiagrangers.org). *The Oxford Book of Local Verses.* John Holloway, ed. Oxford University Press, 1987.

HOME, JOHN (1722–1808)

Scottish soldier, playwright and clergyman, he was born in Leith, Edinburgh, and educated at Edinburgh University around 1742. He fought with the government army (he held the rank of lieutenant) at the time of the Jacobite Rebellion (1745). Captured at the Battle of Falkirk (1746), he made a daring escape from Doune Castle, Perthshire. He was minister at Athelstaneford, East Lothian, from 1747 to 1757. His play *Douglas* was produced in Edinburgh in 1756. David Garrick produced *Douglas* in 1759 and two other of Home's plays, *Fatal Discovery* (1769) and *Alonzo* (1773). *Douglas* was a great success, but it caused offense to the Church authorities, so he resigned. He became private secretary to John Stuart, 3rd Earl of Bute, and private tutor to the Prince of Wales (later King George III). With a generous pension from the king, he settled in Edinburgh (1779), where he died. *The History of the Rebellion of 1745* was published in 1802. Some of his poems: "Epistle to the Earl of Eglintoun," "Gill Morice, an Ancient Scottish Poem," "In Imitation of Gill Moris," "Prologue on the Birthday of the Prince of Wales," "The Fate of Caesar," "Verses upon Inveraray."

Sources: *Dictionary of National Biography.* Electronic Edition 1.1. Oxford University Press, 1997. *Encyclopædia Britannica Ultimate Reference Suite DVD,* 2006. *English Poetry: Author Search.* Chadwyck-Healey Ltd., 1995 (http://www.lib.utexas.edu:8080/search/epoetry/author.html). *The National Portrait Gallery* (www.npg.org.uk). *Online Classic Encyclopedia—LoveToKnow* (http://www.1911encyclopedia.org). *The Oxford Companion to English Literature.* 6th edition. Margaret Drabble, ed. Oxford University Press, 2000.

HOOD, THOMAS THE ELDER and YOUNGER (1799–1874)

Thomas, the father, 1799–1845

Born in London, the son of a bookseller, he spent the years 1815–1818 with his father's relatives in Dundee, Scotland, recuperating from what could have been rheumatic fever. Being apprenticed to an engraver proved too much for his constitution so he turned to writing, and he became famous for his humorous writing and punning. He was the assistant editor of the *London Magazine* and later edited other literary periodicals: *The Gem, Comic Annual, The New Monthly Magazine,* and *Hood's Magazine.* He was buried in Kensal Green cemetery, West London, where in 1854 a public monument was erected to him. Many of his poems, such as "The Song of the Shirt," "The Lay of the Labourer," and "The Bridge of Sighs" are moving protests against sweated labour, unemployment, and double sexual standards. Some of his publications: *Odes and Addresses to Great People,* 1825. *The Plea of the Midsummer Fairies,* 1827. *Hood's Own,* 1838. *Up the Rhine,* 1839. Some of his other poems: "A Lay of Real Life," "An Address to the Steam Washing Company," "Domestic Poems," "The Wee Man," "The Workhouse Clock," "Written in the Workhouse."

Thomas, the son, 1835–1874

Known as Tom Hood, he was born at Wanstead, Essex, and studied at Pembroke College, Oxford, with a view to reading for the church, but left without graduating. While living in Cornwall, he started working for *Liskeard Gazette* in 1856 and was editor during 1858–1859. He worked in the accountant-general's department of the war office from 1860 to 1865 and developed his skill as a caricaturist, then became editor of *Fun,* the comic newspaper founded in 1861. He wrote for the paper and drew and engraved many of its illustrations. With his sister, Frances Freeling Broderip, he illustrated and wrote many children's books. His first poem, "Farewell to the Swallows," was published in *Sharpe's Magazine,* 1853. He died at Peckham Rye, Surrey. Some of his publications: *Pen and Pencil Pictures,* 1857. *Captain Masters's Children,* 1865 (three volumes). *Tom Hood's Comic Annual,* 1867. *Rules of Rhyme, a Guide to English Versification,* 1869. Some of his poems: "His First Book," "A Catch," "All in the Downs," "Confounded Nonsense," "Poets and Linnets," "The Ballad of the Basking Shark," "The Cannibal Flea," "The Little Tigers are at Rest."

Sources: *A Century of Humorous Verse, 1850–1950.* Roger Lancelyn Green, ed. E.P. Dutton (Everyman's Library), 1959. *Dictionary of National Biography.* Electronic Edition 1.1. Oxford University Press, 1997. *Encyclopædia Britannica Ultimate Reference Suite DVD,* 2006. *English Poetry: Author Search.* Chadwyck-Healey Ltd., 1995 (http://www.lib.utexas.edu:8080/search/epoetry/author.html). *Fellow Mortals: An Anthology of Animal Verse.* Roy Fuller, ed. Macdonald and Evans, 1981. *Speak Roughly to Your Little Boy.* Myra Cohn Livingston, ed. Harcourt Brace Jovanovich, 1971. *The Chatto Book of Nonsense Poetry.* Hugh Haughton, ed. Chatto and Windus, 1988. *The Columbia Granger's Index to Poetry.* 11th ed. *The Columbia Granger's World of Poetry,* Columbia University Press, 2005 (http://www.columbiagrangers.org). *The Faber Book of Comic Verse.* Michael Roberts and Janet Adam Smith, eds.

Faber and Faber, 1978. *The Oxford Companion to English Literature.* 6th edition. Margaret Drabble, ed. Oxford University Press, 2000. *The Poetical Works of Thomas Hood V. 2.* Little, Brown and Co., 1857.

HOPE, CHRISTOPHER (1944–)

Born in Johannesburg, he grew up in Pretoria, was educated at the universities of Witwatersrand and Natal, and worked as a journalist. He came to London in 1975 and worked as a teacher before becoming a full-time writer and broadcaster. His first novel, *A Separate Development* (1980), won the David Higham Prize for Fiction. Many of his novels relate to the political and cultural situation in South Africa. *The Love Songs of Nathan J. Swirsky* (1993), a collection of short stories written for BBC Radio, describes childhood on a small 1950s housing estate in the Transvaal. *White Boy Running* (1988) is his autobiography. He has written about post–Cold War Russia in *Moscow! Moscow!* (1990), about the United Kingdom in *Darkest England* (1996), and about Languedoc (south France) in *Signs of the Heart* (1999). He has won seven major literary awards. His book of poems *Cape Drives* (1974) received the Cholmondeley Award. Some of his poems: "Lines on a Boer War Pin-up Girl Seen in the Falcon Hotel, Bude," "The Country of the Black Pig," "The Flight of the White South Africans," "Englishmen" (dramatized and broadcast by the BBC [1986]).

Sources: *British Council Arts* (http://www.contemporarywriters.com). *Emergency Kit: Poems for Strange Times.* Jo Shapcott and Matthew Sweeney, ed. Faber and Faber, 1996. *Microsoft Encarta* 2006 (DVD). Microsoft Corporation, 2006. *The Columbia Granger's Index to Poetry.* 11th ed. *The Columbia Granger's World of Poetry,* Columbia University Press, 2005 (http://www.columbiagrangers.org). *The Oxford Companion to English Literature.* 6th edition. Margaret Drabble, ed. Oxford University Press, 2000. *The Penguin Book of Southern African Verse.* Stephen Gray, ed. Penguin Books, 1989.

HOPKINS, CHARLES and JOHN (1664–?1700)

Charles, the elder brother, 1664–1700

The elder son of Ezekiel Hopkins, bishop of Londonderry, was born about 1664 at Exeter and was taken early to Ireland. He was educated at Trinity College, Dublin, and afterwards at Queen's College, Cambridge, where he graduated B.A. (1688). He subsequently settled in England and gained a reputation as a writer of poems and plays, and counted among his friends many poets, including John Dryden and William Congreve (see entry). His life of excesses led to an early death. He published four plays: *Pyrrhus, King of Epirus,* 1695; *Neglected Virtue,* 1696; *Boadicea, Queen of Britain,* 1697; and *Friend-*

ship Improved, or The Female Warrior, 1700. His poetry publications: *Epistolary Poems: On Several Occasions: With Several of the Choicest Stories of Ovid's Metamorphoses and Tibullus's Elegies,* 1694. *The History of Love. A Poem: In a Letter to a Lady,* 1695 (a selection of fables from Ovid's *Metamorphoses*). *Whitehall: or the Court of England. A Poem,* 1698.

John, the younger brother, 1675–?

He graduated B.A. (1693) and M.A. (1698) from Jesus College, Cambridge. In 1698 he published two Pindaric poems: "The Triumphs of Peace, or the Glories of Nassau" (written at the time of his Grace the Duke of Ormond's entrance into Dublin) and "The Victory of Death; or the Fall of Beauty." In 1869 he published *Milton's Paradise Lost Imitated in Rhyme;* the Fourth Book contained "The Primitive Loves"; the Sixth Book, "The Battel of the Angels"; and the Ninth Book, "The Fall of Man." His last work —*Amasia, or the Works of the Muses*— was a collection in three volumes of love-verses and translations (from Ovid) (1700). He also translated many of the Psalms into English. There is no evidence of the date of his death. Some of his other poems, most of which dealt with characters from Greek mythology: "Alphæus and Arethusa," "Boreas and Orythia," "Cephalus and Procris," "Hippomenes and Atalanta," "Jupiter and Calisto," "Phæbus and Leucothoe," "Pigmalion and his Iv'ry Statue," "Pluto and Proserpina," "Salmacis and Hermaphroditus," "Tereus and Philomela."

Sources: *Dictionary of National Biography.* Electronic Edition 1.1. Oxford University Press, 1997. *English Poetry: Author Search.* Chadwyck-Healey Ltd., 1995 (http://www.lib.utexas.edu:8080/search/epoetry/author.html), for most of Hopkins's poems. *Great Books Online* (www.bartleby.com). *Select Collection of Poems: With Notes, Biographical and Historical, by J. Nichols. The Second Volume* (http://www.orgs.muohio.edu/anthologies/nichol2.htm).

HOPKINS, GERARD MANLEY (1844–1889)

Born into a prosperous family in Stratford, Essex, he was brought up in Hampstead. At school he won the headmaster's poetry prize with his poem "The Escorial" in (1860). In 1866, while at Balliol College, Oxford, he converted to the Roman Catholic Church and in the following year completed his degree in *literae humaniores.* He joined the Society of Jesus and was ordained in 1877, then spent his life teaching. In 1884 he was appointed professor of Greek and Latin at University College, Dublin. He died in Dublin of typhoid fever and was buried in the common plot of the Jesuits at Glasnevin cemetery, near Dublin. He is one of the poets memorialized in Poets' Corner of Westminster Abbey. Before joining the Jesuits he symbolically burned all his poetry; Robert Bridges, to whom Hopkins sent copies, published a nearly complete edition of Hopkins' poems in 1918. Some of his poems: "A Vision of the Mermaids," "Duns Scotus's Oxford," "Songs from Shakespeare, in Latin and Greek," "Spring," "The Child is Father to the Man," "The Loss of the Eurydice," "The Windhover," "The Wreck of the Deutschland."

Sources: *Dictionary of National Biography.* Electronic Edition 1.1. Oxford University Press, 1997. *Encyclopædia Britannica Ultimate Reference Suite DVD,* 2006. *English Poetry: Author Search.* Chadwyck-Healey Ltd., 1995 (http://www.lib.utexas.edu:8080/search/epoetry/author. html). *Gerard Manley Hopkins.* Catherine Phillips, ed. Oxford University Press, 1986. *The Columbia Granger's Index to Poetry.* 11th ed. *The Columbia Granger's World of Poetry,* Columbia University Press, 2005 (http://www.columbia grangers.org). *The Oxford Companion to English Literature.* 6th edition. Margaret Drabble, ed. Oxford University Press, 2000. *Westminster Abbey Official Guide* (no date).

HOROVITZ, MICHAEL (1935–)

One of the Revival poets, he was born in Frankfurt and emigrated to England with his family as a child. He was educated at Brasenose College, Oxford, and is known as a performance artist and poet. Poetry for Horwitz is part of showbiz, part of everyday life, of every activity. An early champion of oral and jazz poetry, and he performed on both sides of the Atlantic. He founded *New Departures* publications and *Live New Departures* (1959); *Jazz Poetry Super-Jam Bandwagons* (1970); and the *Poetry Olympics Festivals* (1980). Some of his publications: *New Departures Anthology,* 1970 (editor). *Love Poems,* 1971. *Nineteen poems of love, lust and spirit,* 1971. *Growing Up: Selected Poems and Pictures, 1951–79,* 1979. *Midsummer Morning Jog Log,* 1986. *Grandchildren of Albion: An Illustrated Anthology of Voices and Visions of Younger Poets in Britain,* 1991 (editor). *Wordsounds and Sightlines: New and Selected,* 1994. *The POM! [Poetry Olympics Marathon] Anthology,* 2001 (editor). Some of his poems: "And the Ignorant Armies," "For Leon Bismarck Beiderbecke (1903–1931)," "ParadiCe," "West London Breakfast Morning."

Sources: *BBC — Radio 4 — Poetry Please,* with Micheal Horrovitz (http://www.bbc.co.uk/radio4/arts/poetry please_20050109.shtml). *Biography of Michael Horovitz* (http://www.connectotel.com/PoetryOlympics/horovitz. htm). *Gargoyle Magazine* (http://www.atticusbooks. com/gargoyle/index_poetry.htm). *P.E.N. New Poetry I.* Robert Nye, ed. Quartet Books, 1986. *The National Portrait Gallery* (www.npg.org.uk). *The Oxford Companion to English Literature.* 6th edition. Margaret Drabble, ed. Oxford University Press, 2000.

HOUSMAN, ALFRED EDWARD and LAURENCE (1859–1959)

Alfred Edward, the elder brother, 1859–1936

Born in Fockbury, Shropshire, he was educated at Bromsgrove School and St. John's College, Oxford, where he gained first class honors in classics in 1879. He failed to obtain honors in *literae humaniores;* some say it was because of his romantic attachment to another student, Moses Jackson. Working in the London Patent Office he found time for classical study and contributed to several learned journals. He was professor of Latin at University College, London, from 1892 until 1911, when he became Kennedy Professor of Latin at Trinity College, Cambridge, where he lived until his death. His ashes were buried at St. Lawrence's Church, Ludlow, and a statue of him was erected in Bromsgrove High Street in 1985. He is one of the poets memorialized in the Poets' Window of Westminster Abbey. Some of his poetry publications: *A Shropshire Lad,* 1896. *Last Poems,* 1922. *More Poems,* 1936 (published by his brother). Some of his other poems: "Amelia Mixed the Mustard," "As Through the Wild Green Hills of Wyre," "Aunts and Nieces or Time and Space," "The African Lion," "The Deserter," "When I Was One-and-Twenty."

Laurence, the younger brother, 1865–1959

He was educated at Bromsgrove, did not go to university but studied art in London. During his early years he lived with his sister Clemence, an author and wood-engraver whose book *The Were-Wolf* (1896) he illustrated. He was art critic on the *Manchester Guardian* from 1895 to 1911, and while there he tried his hand at writing plays. His first, *Bethlehem,* was banned in 1902, and when run privately it cost him a lot of money. Several other plays were banned. *Prunella, or Love in a Dutch Garden,* escaped the censor and was moderately successful, as were *Angels and Ministers* (1921) and *The Little Plays of St. Francis* (1922). He wrote several successful novels and many stories for both children and adults, and published his autobiography, *The Unexpected Years* (1937). Some of his poetry publications: *Green Arras,* 1896. *Spikenard,* 1898. *An Englishwoman's Love-Letters,* 1900. Some of his poems: "A Dead Warrior," "All Fellows," "Comrades," "Farewell to Town," "The City of Sleep," "The Continuing City," "The Settlers," "The Two Loves."

Sources: *Chief Modern Poets of Britain and America.* 5th edition. Gerald DeWitt Sanders and John Herbert Nelson, eds., Macmillan, 1970. *Dictionary of National Biography.* Electronic Edition 1.1. Oxford University Press, 1997.

Encyclopædia Britannica Ultimate Reference Suite DVD, 2006. The Housman Society (http://www.housman-society.co.uk/). *The National Portrait Gallery* (www.npg.org.uk). *The Chatto Book of Nonsense Poetry.* Hugh Haughton, ed. Chatto and Windus, 1988. *The Collected Poems of A.E. Housman.* Henry Holt, 1965. *The Columbia Granger's Index to Poetry.* 11th ed. *The Columbia Granger's World of Poetry,* Columbia University Press, 2005 (http://www.columbiagrangers.org). *The Home Book of Modern Verse.* Burton Egbert Stevenson, ed. Henry Holt, 1953. *The World's Great Religious Poetry.* Caroline Miles Hill, ed. Macmillan, 1954. *What Cheer: An Anthology of American and British Humorous and Witty Verse.* David McCord, ed. Coward-McCann, 1945.

HOVELL-THURLOW, EDWARD, 2nd BARON THURLOW (1781–1829)

Born in London, the son of Thomas Thurlow, Bishop of Durham, he was educated at the Charterhouse, London, and Magdalen College, Oxford, from where he graduated M.A. in 1801. He succeeded to the barony in 1806 on the death of his uncle, who was Lord-chancellor from 1778 to 1792. One of the posts to which he was elected in 1788 was "clerk of the custodies of idiots and lunatics." He died at Brighton, Sussex, and was succeeded by his son, Edward Thomas. He edited for private circulation in 1810 Sir Philip Sidney's *Defence of Poesy,* to which he attached some of his own sonnets. His contributions to the *Gentleman's Magazine:* Vol. 83-i (1813): pp. 357, 462. V; Vol. 83-ii (1813): pp. 469–470, 589, 664. V; Vol. 89-i (1819): pp. 254, 352 V. Some of his poems: *Poems on Several Occasions,* 1813; (1) *Moonlight*; (2) *The Doge's Daughter*; (3) *Ariadne*; (4) *Carmen Britannicum, or The Song of Britain*; (5) *Angelica, or The Rape of Proteus,* 1814; *Select Poems of Edward Hovel Thurlow,* 1821. Some of his poems: "May," "The Heron," "When in the Woods I Wander All Alone."

Sources: *Dictionary of National Biography.* Electronic Edition 1.1. Oxford University Press, 1997. *Encyclopædia Britannica Ultimate Reference Suite DVD, 2006. English Poetry: Author Search.* Chadwyck-Healey Ltd., 1995 (http://www.lib.utexas.edu:8080/search/epoetry/author.html). *Gentleman's Magazine* (http://etext.lib.virginia.edu/etcbin/browse-gm2?id=2GM1736). *The Columbia Granger's Index to Poetry.* 11th ed. *The Columbia Granger's World of Poetry,* Columbia University Press, 2005 (http://www.columbiagrangers.org). *The Home Book of Modern Verse.* Burton Egbert Stevenson, ed. Henry Holt, 1953. *The Home Book of Verse for Young Folks.* Burton Egbert Stevenson, ed. Holt, Rinehart and Winston, 1929. *The Oxford Companion to English Literature.* 6th edition. Margaret Drabble, ed. Oxford University Press, 2000.

HOWARD, HENRY, EARL OF SURREY (?1517–1547)

He took the title of Earl of Surrey in 1524 when his father, Thomas Howard, succeeded as 3rd Duke of Norfolk. He studied classical and modern literature and showed promise as a poet, and he could translate Latin, Italian, and Spanish with ease. He spent much of his young years at Windsor Castle as companion to Henry Fitzroy, Duke of Richmond, Henry VIII's natural son. He accompanied Henry VIII to France, was knighted in 1541, and served in Scotland, France, and Flanders. In 1546, he was condemned and beheaded on Tower Hill on the trumped-up charge of treasonably quartering the royal arms and advising his sister to become the king's mistress. He translated books 2 and 4 of Virgil's *Aeneid* in blank verse, and translated many of the Psalms and other books of the Bible. His sonnet form was later used by Shakespeare. Forty of his poems were published by Richard Tottell in *Miscellany* (1557). Some of his poems: "A Complaint by Night," "Complaint of a Lover Rebuked," "Reflections from the Tower," "Prison in Windsor Castle," "The Frailty and Hurtfulness of Beauty," "The Golden Mean."

Sources: *Chapters into Verse. Vol. I: Genesis to Malachi.* Robert Atwan and Laurance Wieder, eds. Oxford University Press, 1993. *Dictionary of National Biography.* Electronic Edition 1.1. Oxford University Press, 1997. *Encyclopædia Britannica Ultimate Reference Suite DVD, 2006. English Poetry: Author Search.* Chadwyck-Healey Ltd., 1995 (http://www.lib.utexas.edu:8080/search/epoetry/author.html). *The Genealogy Tree, Henry Howard, Earl of Surrey* (http://www.thegenealogytree.com/photo-gallery/henry-howard-earl-of-surrey.htm). *The National Portrait Gallery* (www.npg.org.uk). *Poems—Fourth Edition: The Wadsworth Handbook and Anthology.* C.F. Main and Peter J. Seng, ed. Wadsworth Publishing Company, 1978. *Silver Poets of the Sixteenth Century.* Gerald Bullett, ed. J.M. Dent, 1947. *The Columbia Granger's Index to Poetry.* 11th ed. *The Columbia Granger's World of Poetry,* Columbia University Press, 2005 (http://www.columbiagrangers.org). *The New Penguin Book of English Verse.* Paul Keegan, ed. Penguin Books, 2000. *The Oxford Companion to English Literature.* 6th edition. Margaret Drabble, ed. Oxford University Press, 2000.

HOWARD, PHILIP, 1ST EARL OF ARUNDEL (1557–1595)

He was the eldest son of Thomas Howard, 4th Duke of Norfolk, who was executed for high treason in 1572 (see also Howard, Henry). On the death of his maternal grandfather, the 12th earl, in 1580 he became Earl of Arundel (Arundel Castle is in West Sussex). At Cambridge University he did little work, but was awarded an M.A. in 1576. He led a merry life at the court of Queen Elizabeth but was never the Queen's favorite. Received into the Roman Catholic faith in 1584, in 1585 he was apprehended, tried on the charge of being a Romanist and attempting to leave England without the queen's consent. He was imprisoned in the Tower of London for the rest of his life while his wife lived in poverty. He was refused permission to see his wife and son unless he recanted, which he refused. He was buried in the chapel of the Tower; his remains were later conveyed to Arundel. His known publications: *An Epistle of Jesus Christ to the Faithful Soule*, 1595. *A Foure-Fould Meditation*, 1605. *In the Wrackes of Walsingham*, 1868.

Sources: *An Anthology of Catholic Poets*. Shane Leslie, ed. Macmillan, 1952. *Dictionary of National Biography*. Electronic Edition 1.1. Oxford University Press, 1997. *English Poetry: Author Search*. Chadwyck-Healey Ltd., 1995 (http://www.lib.utexas.edu:8080/search/epoetry/author. html). *SETIS—English Poetry Collection* (http://setis.li brary.usyd.edu.au/poetry/browse/h-epdtoc.html). *The Columbia Granger's Index to Poetry*. 11th ed. *The Columbia Granger's World of Poetry*, Columbia University Press, 2005 (http://www.columbiagrangers.org). *The Feast of Our Lady of Walsingham: Quenta Nârwenion, Pittsburgh, Pennsylvania, United States* (http://quenta-narwen.blogspot. com/2003/09/feast-of-our-lady-of-walsingham-is.html).

HOWARD, SIR ROBERT (1626–1698)

The son of Thomas Howard, first earl of Berkshire, he was educated either at Magdalen College, Oxford, or Magdalene College, Cambridge. He supported the king in the Civil War, and in 1644 was knighted on the field near Newbury for bravery. Imprisoned in Windsor Castle by the Parliamentarians, at the Restoration he became member of Parliament for Stockbridge, Hampshire, and was made a knight of the Bath. He became a member of the privy council in 1688 and held the lucrative post of auditor of the exchequer from 1677 until his death. He was buried in the Chapel of St. John the Baptist, Westminster Abbey. He will be remembered chiefly for his dispute with his brother-in-law, John Dryden, on the use of rhymed verse in drama. Some of his publications: *Poems*, 1660. *Foure New Plays*: (1) *Surprisal*; (2) *Committee*; (3) *Vestal Virgin*; (4) *Indian Queen*, 1665; *Great Favorite: or the Duke of Lerma*, 1688. Some of his poems: "Poor mortals that are clogged with earth below (Fairy Queen)," "The Achilleid," "To the Unconstant Cynthia."

Sources: *The English Civil War, Cropredy Bridge, 1644* (http://www.theteacher99.btinternet.co.uk/ecivil/cro predy.htm). *Dictionary of National Biography*. Electronic Edition 1.1. Oxford University Press, 1997. *Encyclopædia Britannica Ultimate Reference Suite DVD*, 2006. *The National Portrait Gallery* (www.npg.org.uk). *The Columbia Granger's Index to Poetry*. 11th ed. *The Columbia Granger's World of Poetry*, Columbia University Press, 2005 (http://www.columbiagrangers.org). *The Oxford Book of Classical Verse in Translation*. Adrian Poole, and Jeremy Maule, ed. 1995. *The Treasury of English Poetry*. Mark Caldwell and Walter Kendrick, ed. Doubleday, 1984. *Westminster Abbey Official Guide* (no date).

HOWELL, THOMAS (fl. 1568)

Born in Dunster in Somerset, when he was employed in the household of the Earl of Shrewsbury, he published *The Arbor of Amitie, Wherein Is Comprised Pleasant Poems and Pretie Poesies, Set Foorth by Thomas Howell, Gentleman* (1568). *Newe Sonets and Pretie* was licensed for publication in 1567–1568. Several of his poems are addressed to John Keeper (a Somerset man), and some of Keeper's own poems are included among Howell's *Newe Sonets*. Some of his poems: "Admonition to His Friend," "All of Greene Lawrell," "All of Greene Willow," "Another Way," "Being Burdened to Fayne His Good Will," "Being Charged with Finenesse, He Answereth Thus," "The Best Natures, Soonest Abused," "The Lover Deceived Writes to His Lady," "The Rose," "Where Abilitie Fayleth, Wyll Suffyceth."

Sources: *A Child's Treasury of Verse*. Eleanor Doan, ed. Zondervan Corporation, 1977. *Dictionary of National Biography*. Electronic Edition 1.1. Oxford University Press, 1997. *Elizabethan Lyrics*. Norman Ault, ed. William Sloane Associates, 1949. *English Poetry: Author Search*. Chadwyck-Healey Ltd., 1995 (http://www.lib.utexas.edu:8080/ search/epoetry/author.html). *Great Books Online* (www. bartleby.com). *Howell's Devises by Thomas Howell*. Oxford University Press, 1906. *Poems One Line and Longer*. William Cole, ed. Grossman, 1973. *The Columbia Granger's Index to Poetry*. 11th ed. *The Columbia Granger's World of Poetry*, Columbia University Press, 2005 (http:// www.columbiagrangers.org). *The Oxford Companion to English Literature*. 6th edition. Margaret Drabble, ed. Oxford University Press, 2000.

HOWITT, MARY and WILLIAM (1792–1888)

Mary, 1799–1888

Mary Botham was born in Coleford, Gloucestershire, to a Quaker family and was educated at home. She married William Howitt in 1821 and lived in Staffordshire, where they began a career of joint authorship. Their poems were published chiefly in periodicals, and their first selection, *The Desolation of Eyam and Other Poems*, was published in 1827. When living in Esher, Surrey (1837), she began her successful series of tales for children. While living in Heidelberg in 1840, she learned Swedish and Danish, translated Fredrika Bremer's 18 novels (1842–1863) into English, and translated many of Hans Andersen's tales. Among her other works is the *Popular History of the United States* (1859). She joined the church of Rome and was one of the English deputation who was received by the pope on 10 January 1888. She died in Rome. She authored, edited, or translated more than a hundred works. Some of her poems: "America. A Story of the Indian War," "Birds and Flowers," "Marien's Pilgrimage," "The Blind

Boy and his Sister," "The Sale of the Pet Lamb," "The Soldier's Story," "The Spider and the Fly."

William, 1792–1879

William was born at Heanor, Derbyshire, of Quaker parents. His poem "An Address to Spring," written when he was thirteen, was published in the *Monthly Magazine*. Although he studied chemistry and natural philosophy at school, his main education came from private reading and a natural aptitude for acquiring foreign languages. He wrote several books on Australia based on his travels and practical experience of working in a gold field (1852–1854). Between 1856 and 1862 he wrote five large volumes of a *Popular History of England* (from the reign of Edward II). He died in Rome and was buried in the Protestant cemetery. Some of his other publications: *Book of the Seasons, or Calendar of Nature*, 1831. *Pantika, or Traditions of the Most Ancient Times*, 1835 (2 volumes). *The Boys' Country Book*, 1838. *Visits to Remarkable Places*, 1839 (a series). *Homes and Haunts of the Most Eminent British Poets*, 1847. *The Year-Book of the Country*, 1850. *The Mad War-Planet, and Other Poems*, 1871. Some of his poems: "The Migration of the Grey Squirrels," "The Wind in a Frolic," "Invitation," "Summer and the Poet," "The Departure of the Swallow."

Sources: *Best Loved Story Poems*. Walter E. Thwing, ed. Garden City, 1941. *Dictionary of National Biography*. Electronic Edition 1.1. Oxford University Press, 1997. *English Poetry: Author Search*. Chadwyck-Healey Ltd., 1995 (http://www.lib.utexas.edu:8080/search/epoetry/author.html). *Moon is Shining Bright as Day: An Anthology of Good-humoured Verse*. Ogden Nash, ed. J.B. Lippincott, 1953. *Oldpoetry* (www.oldpoetry.com). *The Columbia Granger's Index to Poetry*. 11th ed. *The Columbia Granger's World of Poetry*, Columbia University Press, 2005 (http://www.columbiagrangers.org). *The Forest Minstrel and Other Poems of William and Mary Howitt*. Baldwin, Cradock, and Joy, 1823. *The Home Book of Modern Verse*. Burton Egbert Stevenson, ed. Henry Holt, 1953. *The Oxford Book of Children's Verse*. Iona Opie, and Peter Opie, ed. Oxford University Press, 1973. *The Poetical Works of Mary Howitt, Eliza Cook, and L.E.L.* Phillips, Sampson, and Company, 1857.

HOYLAND, FRANCIS (fl. 1763)

Born in Castle Howard, Yorkshire, he was educated in Halifax, Yorkshire, and graduated from Magdalene College, Cambridge, in 1748. He is known to have taken holy orders. Suffering from ill health, he traveled in the West Indies to recover and his health prevented him from accepting a living in South Carolina. The date of his death is uncertain. His poems were reprinted in Vol. 41 of *British Poets* (editor Thomas Park) (1808) and in *British Poets* (1822), Vol. 43. His main publications: *Poems and Translations by Francis Hoyland*, 1763 (containing three metrical versions of psalms by J. Caley). *Poems by the Reverend Mr. Hoyland*, 1769. *Odes. By the Rev. F. Hoyland*, 1783. Some of his poems: "An Autumnal Ode," "On Rural Happiness," "On The Death of a Notorious Bawd," "The 104th Psalm," "To a Dove," "To a Nightingale," "To His Guardian Angel," "To Sleep."

Sources: *Dictionary of National Biography*. Electronic Edition 1.1. Oxford University Press, 1997. *English Poetry, Second Edition Bibliography* (http://collections.chadwyck.co.uk/html/ep2/bibliography/g.htm). *English Poetry: Author Search*. Chadwyck-Healey Ltd., 1995 (http://www.lib.utexas.edu:8080/search/epoetry/author.html).

HUBERT, SIR FRANCIS (?1568 or ?1569–1629)

Although the information about this poet is scant, it can be gleaned that he was the son of Edward Hubert, a law clerk in London, and that he himself was a clerk in the chancery in 1601. His burial is recorded at St. Andrew's, Church, Holborn, on 13 December 1629. In 1629 he wrote *The Historie of Edward the Second, Surnamed Carnarvon, One of Our English Kings: Together with the Fatall Downfall of His Two Vnfortunate Favorites, Gaveston and Spencer*. The poem was completed during the reign of Elizabeth, but permission to print it was refused, on account of Hubert's treatment of the king's favorites. A rogue edition appeared in 1628; the authentic edition followed in 1629, with other editions in 1631 and 1721, with a portrait of the author. His *Egypt's Favorite. The Historie of Joseph, Divided into Foure Parts—Together with Old Israels Progresse into the Land of Goshen* was published in 1631. Some of his poems: "Jacobs Progresse," "The Chaste Covrtier," "The Innocent Prisoner," "The Life and Death of Edvvard the Second," "The Noble Favourite," "The Unfortunate Brother."

Sources: *Dictionary of National Biography*. Electronic Edition 1.1. Oxford University Press, 1997. *English Poetry: Author Search*. Chadwyck-Healey Ltd., 1995 (http://www.lib.utexas.edu:8080/search/epoetry/author.html). *The Columbia Granger's Index to Poetry*. 11th ed. *The Columbia Granger's World of Poetry*, Columbia University Press, 2005 (http://www.columbiagrangers.org). *The New Oxford Book of Seventeenth Century Verse*. Alastair Fowler, ed. Oxford University Press, 1991.

HUDDESFORD, GEORGE (1749–1809)

The youngest son of George Huddesford, doctor of divinity, president of Trinity College, Oxford, he was educated at Winchester College and graduated M.A. from New College, Oxford, in 1780. A pupil of Sir Joshua Reynolds, he had exhibited three pictures at the Academy. He took holy orders and had two livings: Loxley in Warwickshire (1803), and Sir George Wheler's Chapel, Spital Square, London, where he died. He contributed several articles to

Gentleman's Magazine in 1771 and 1806. His known publications: *Warley: A Satire*, 1778. *The Second Part of Warley, A Satire*, 1778. *The poems of George Huddesford*, 1801. *The Scum uppermost when the Middlesex Porridge-Pot Boils Over!* 1802. *Bonaparte, an Heroic Ballad*, 1803. *Wiccamical Chaplet*, 1804 (a collection of poems written by his contemporaries at Winchester). *Wood and stone*, or *a dialogue between a wooden duke and a stone lion*, 1804. *Les champignons du diable*, or, *Imperial mushrooms*, 1805 (a mock-heroic poem, in five cantos). Some of his poems: "Another Ode to Stella," "Bubble and Squeak," "Crambe Repetita," "Salmagundi," "The Plagiarism of the Poet-Laureate Detected," "Topsy-Turvy."

Sources: *Dictionary of National Biography*. Electronic Edition 1.1. Oxford University Press, 1997. *English Poetry, Second Edition Bibliography* (http://collections.chadwyck.co.uk/html/ep2/bibliography/g.htm). *Gentleman's Magazine* (http://www.bodley.ox.ac.uk/ilej/journals/srchgm.htm). *Stanford University libraries and Academic Information Resources* (http://library.stanford.edu). *The National Portrait Gallery* (www.npg.org.uk).

HUGGARDE (HOGGARDE), MILES (fl. 1548–1557)

Thought to have been a London shoemaker or hosier. He was one of the first lay people to write against Protestantism and for the Catholic cause. The fact that he lived in Pudding Lane caused much amusement to other people who were fond of making puns and disparaging remarks. He was a loyal servant of Queen Mary and dedicated some of his poems to her. As a leading opponent of the Reformation he incurred the displeasure of many notable Protestants of the day, and some of the Catholics were none too pleased either, that someone without "proper" education should be so much in the news. Some of his publications (shortened titles): *The Abuse of the blessed sacrament of the aultare*, 1548. *Treatise of three Weddings*, 1550. *The Pathwaye to the Towre of Perfection*, 1554. *The assault of the sacrament of the Altar*, 1554. *A treatise declaring howe Christ was banished*, 1554. *A mirrour of loue*, 1555. *A Short Treatise in Meter upon Psalm 129*, 1556. *The Displaying of the Protestants*, 1556. *A newe ABC*, 1557. *A Myrrovre of myserie*, 1557.

Sources: *Dictionary of National Biography*. Electronic Edition 1.1. Oxford University Press, 1997. *Stanford University Libraries and Academic Information Resources* (http://library.stanford.edu).

HUGHES, JOHN (1677–1720)

Born at Marlborough, Wiltshire, he was educated at a dissenting academy in Little Britain, in the center of London, where he was the contemporary of Isaac Watts (see entry). In spite of never being in good health, in 1717 he was appointed as secretary in the chancery, a post he held until he died. He contributed to the *Tatler*, *Spectator*, and the *Guardian*, and with Sir Richard Blackmore (see entry) he wrote *The Lay Monk*, a series of forty essays, 1713–1714. The periodical *The Monthly Amusement* published a number of his translations. Several of his cantatas were set to music by various composers including Handel, and other composers set some of his poems to music. His *Poems on Several Occasions, with some Select Essays in Prose* was published posthumously in 1735. Some of his poems: "A Thought in a Garden," "Advice to Mr. Pope, on His Intended Translation of Homer's Iliad," "An Ode in Praise of Musick," "An Ode to the Creator of the World," "The House of Nassau," "The Triumph of Peace," "To Mr. Addison, on His Tragedy of Cato," "To the Memory of Mr. Milton."

Sources: *Dictionary of National Biography*. Electronic Edition 1.1. Oxford University Press, 1997. *Eighteenth-Century English Verse*. Dennis Davison, ed. Penguin Books, 1988. *English Poetry: Author Search*. Chadwyck-Healey Ltd., 1995 (http://www.lib.utexas.edu:8080/search/epoetry/author.html). *Texts of John Hughes set to music* (http://www.recmusic.org/lieder/h/jhughes/). *The National Portrait Gallery* (www.npg.org.uk). *Samuel Johnson's Lives of the English Poets*, 1779–1781 (http://www2.hn.psu.edu/Faculty/KKemmerer/poets/preface.htm). *The Columbia Granger's Index to Poetry*. 11th ed. *The Columbia Granger's World of Poetry*, Columbia University Press, 2005 (http://www.columbiagrangers.org). *Turning Tides: Modern Dutch and Flemish Verse in English Versions by Irish Poets*. Peter van de Kamp, ed. Story Line Press, 1994.

HUGHES, JOHN CEIRIOG (1832–1887)

He was orn in Penbryn, Llanarmon-Dyffryn Ceiriog, Denbighshire, North Wales, from where he took his bardic name. The family could trace their lineage to Bleddyn ab Cynvyn, prince of Gwynedd and Powys in 1072. After several jobs, he settled in Manchester as a clerk. He remained there for sixteen years, leaving in 1865, after which he worked on the railway in Wales. His first prize for poetry was in 1853, and thereafter he published several volumes of verse, the first being *Oriau'r Hwyr* (*Evening Hours*, 1860). He investigated the history of old Welsh airs and of the harpists with whom the tunes were identified, and many of his lyrics were set to original music by various composers. In 1861 he won seven prizes at the Merthyr Eisteddfod for seven temperance songs. His remains were interred in the parish churchyard of Llanwnog, two miles from Caersws, Montgomeryshire. Some of his songs and poems: "All Through the Night (Ar Hyd Y Nos)," "David of the White Rock (Dafydd y Garreg Wen)," "Epilogue to Alun Mabon," "The Bells of Aberdyfi (Clychau Aberdyfi)," "The Court of Neptune," "The Mountain Stream."

Sources: *Dictionary of National Biography*. Electronic Edition 1.1. Oxford University Press, 1997. *Encyclopædia Britannica Ultimate Reference Suite DVD*, 2006. *Men of Harlech, the Song* (http://www.deutschegrammophon. com/brynterfel.welshalbum/album/texts/tr_04.html). *The Columbia Granger's Index to Poetry*. 11th ed. *The Columbia Granger's World of Poetry*, Columbia University Press, 2005 (http://www.columbiagrangers.org). *The Eternal Sea: An Anthology of Sea Poetry*. W.M. Williamson, ed. Coward-McCann, 1946. *The Oxford Book of Welsh Verse in English*. Gwyn Jones, ed. Oxford University Press, 1977. *Wales Online, John Ceiriog Hughes* (http://www.walesonline. com/info/literature/jchughes.shtml).

HUGHES, RICHARD ARTHUR WARREN (1900–1976)

Of Welsh descent, he was born in Weybridge, Surrey, educated at Charterhouse School, Godalming, Surrey, and graduated from Oriel College, Oxford, in 1922. Hughes lived most of his life in Wales. He was vice president of the Welsh National Theatre from 1924 to 1936. During World War II he worked for the Admiralty and, with J.D. Scott, wrote *The Administration of War Production* (1955). He was a fellow of the Royal Society of Literature, was appointed to the Order of the British Empire in 1946, and in 1956 received an honorary doctor of letters from the University of Wales. He was Gresham professor of rhetoric at Gresham College, London, from 1954 to 1957. His radio play *Danger*, believed to be the first radio play, was broadcast by the BBC in 1924. His 1929 novel *A High Wind in Jamaica* was filmed in 1965 starring Anthony Quinn, James Coburn, Dennis Price and Nigel Davenport. *Gipsy Night: And Other Poems* was published in 1922 while Huges was still at university. Some of his poems: "Burial of the Spirit of a Young Poet," "Explanation, on Coming Home Late," "Felo de Se," "Invocation to the Muse," "Old Cat Care," "Winter."

Sources: *Dictionary of National Biography*. Electronic Edition 1.1. Oxford University Press, 1997. *Eight Lines and Under: An Anthology of Short, Short Poems*. William Cole, ed. Macmillan, 1967. *Fantastic Fiction* (http://www.fantas ticfiction.co.uk/authors/Richard_Hughes.htm). *Modern British Poetry*. 7th rev. ed. Louis Untermeyer, ed. Harcourt, Brace, 1962. *The Columbia Granger's Index to Poetry*. 11th ed. *The Columbia Granger's World of Poetry*, Columbia University Press, 2005 (http://www.columbiagrangers. org). *The Oxford Book of Welsh Verse in English*. Gwyn Jones, ed. Oxford University Press, 1977. *The Oxford Companion to English Literature*. 6th edition. Margaret Drabble, ed. Oxford University Press, 2000.

HUGHES, TED (1930–1998)

Born at Mytholmroyd, West Yorkshire, the son of a carpenter, he was educated at Mexborough Grammar school and Pembroke College, Cambridge. He met Sylvia Plath there and they married in 1956. Plath committed suicide in 1963, as did Hughes' lover, Assia Wevill, in 1969. Hughes was married to Carol Orchard from 1970 until he died. From 1965 he was co-editor of the magazine *Modern Poetry in Translation in London*. Altogether he published fourteen volumes of poetry (the first being *The Hawk in the Rain* in 1957), prose, children's books and several anthologies. His *Remains of Elmet* (1979) gives an insight into his childhood. He was made poet laureate in 1984. *The Birthday Letters* (1998) was an homage and, in some ways, an explanation of his marriage to Plath. The couple lived latterly in Devon where he died, and his ashes were scattered on Dartmoor, close to the source of the River Taw. Some of his poems: "And the Phoenix Has Come," "Astrological Conundrums," "Bayonet Charge," "Hawk Roosting," "Prometheus on His Crag," "Scapegoats and Rabies," "Seven Dungeon Songs," "Skylarks," "St. Matthew," "The Dogs Are Eating Your Mother."

Sources: *Encyclopædia Britannica Ultimate Reference Suite DVD*, 2006. *Funeral service for Ted Hughes* (http:// www.poetsgraves.co.uk/hughes.htm). *The National Portrait Gallery* (www.npg.org.uk). *New Selected Poems 1957– 1994 of Ted Hughes*. Faber and Faber, 1995. *Selected Poems 1957–1981 of Ted Hughes*. Faber and Faber, 1982. *The Antaeus Anthology*. Daniel Halpern, ed. Bantam Books, 1986. *The Columbia Granger's Index to Poetry*. 11th ed. *The Columbia Granger's World of Poetry*, Columbia University Press, 2005 (http://www.columbiagrangers.org). *The Oxford Companion to English Literature*. 6th edition. Margaret Drabble, ed. Oxford University Press, 2000. *Wikipedia, the Free Encyclopedia* (http://en.wikipedia. org/wiki/Wikipedia).

HULME, THOMAS ERNEST (1883–1917)

He was born at Endon, Staffordshire, the eldest son of a wealthy family of landowners, and educated at Newcastle-under-Lyme grammar school where, in the school debating society he was known as "the Whip." He went on to St. John's College, Cambridge, to read mathematics, but in 1904 was expelled for repeated unruly behavior. He enrolled at University College, London, in October 1904 to read biology and physics, and continued to spend much time in Cambridge attending undergraduate lectures in philosophy. In 1906, he withdrew from his studies altogether and spent a year traveling in Canada, then he went to Belgium to improve his French and taught English in Brussels. He enlisted into the Army soon after the outbreak of war in 1914 and later transferred to the Royal Marines Artillery. He was killed manning a gun on the Belgian coast. He is one of the members of the Imagist School. Much of his work survived only in notebooks. Some of his poems: "Above the Dock," "As a Fowl,"

"Autumn," "Conversion," "Embankment," "Fragments," "Image," "Trenches: St Eloi."

Sources: *Anthology of Twentieth-Century British and Irish Poetry.* Keith Tuma, ed. Oxford University Press, 2001. *Encyclopædia Britannica Ultimate Reference Suite DVD,* 2006. *The Literary Encyclopedia* (www.LitEncyc. com). *Oldpoetry* (www.oldpoetry.com). *The Collected Writings of T.E. Hulme.* Karen Csengeri, ed. Clarendon Press, Oxford, 1994. *The Columbia Granger's Index to Poetry.* 11th ed. *The Columbia Granger's World of Poetry,* Columbia University Press, 2005 (http://www.columbiagrangers. org). *The Oxford Companion to English Literature.* 6th edition. Margaret Drabble, ed. Oxford University Press, 2000. *The Penguin Book of First World War Poetry.* Jon Silkin, ed. Penguin Books, 1979.

HUME (HOME), ALEXANDER (?1560–1609)

Scottish poet, born at Polwarth, Berwickshire, the son of Patrick Hume, fifth baron of Polwarth. A graduate of St. Andrews University, he studied law in Paris. Disappointed at not obtaining a suitable law appointment in Edinburgh, he became a minister of Logie Church, near Stirling, where he stayed until he died. His ardent Puritanism is expressed in *Hymns and Sacred Songs, accompanied by an Address to the Youth of Scotland* (1599), in which he exhorts young people to abstain from "profane sonnets and vain ballads of love...." all of which were anathema to devout Protestants. Some of his poems were published in Sibbald's *Chronicle of Scottish Poetry* (1802); in Leyden's *Scottish Descriptive Poetry* (1803); and in Campbell's *Specimens of the British Poets* (1819). Some of his other publications: *A Description of the Day Estivall*, 1588. *The Triumph of the Lord after the Manner of Men: Alluding to the Defait of the Spanish Navie,* 1588. *Of the Felicitie of the World to come,* 1594. Some of his poems: "Thankes for Deliverance of the Sicke," "To His Sorrowfull Saull, Consolation," "Of Gods Benefites Bestowed Vpon Man," "Happie Death."

Sources: *Dictionary of National Biography.* Electronic Edition 1.1. Oxford University Press, 1997. *English Poetry: Author Search.* Chadwyck-Healey Ltd., 1995 (http://www. lib.utexas.edu:8080/search/epoetry/author.html). *The Columbia Granger's Index to Poetry.* 11th ed (http://www.columbiagrangers.org). *The New Penguin Book of Scottish Verse.* Robert Crawford and Mick Imlah, eds. Penguin Books, 2000. *The Scottish Collection of Verse to 1800.* Eileen Dunlop and Kamm Antony, eds. Richard Drew, 1985.

HUMPHREYS, EMYR (1919–)

Welsh novelist, short-story writer, poet and dramatist from Flintshire, he read history at the University College of Wales, Aberystwyth. A conscientious objector in World War II, he was sent to work on the land in Pembrokeshire, then from 1944 to 1946 he served with Save the Children Fund under the aegis of the United Nations Organization in the Middle East and Italy. After teaching, from 1955 to 1965, he worked for BBC Wales as a drama producer, then lecturer in drama at the University College of North Wales, Bangor, until 1972, when he became a full-time writer. Five of his poems about Anglesey have been set to music by Alun Hoddinott and have formed part of a recital program sung by Stuart Burrows, the operatic tenor, in Vienna, Tokyo and New York. North Wales University made him honorary professor of English in 1988 and the University of Wales made him honorary doctor of letters in 1990. His four poetry collections: *Ancestor Worship*, 1970. *Landscapes*, 1976. *The Kingdom of Brân*, 1979. *Pwyll a Riannon*, 1980. Some of his poems: "An Apple Tree and a Pig," "From Father to Son," "Nant y Benglog."

Sources: *Anglo-Welsh Poetry, 1480–1980.* Raymond Garlick and Roland Mathias, eds. Poetry Wales Press, 1984. *Anglo-Welsh Poetry, 1480–1990,* Raymond Garlick and Roland Mathias, eds. Poetry Wales Press (1993). *CREW Welsh Writers Online* (http://www.swan.ac.uk/english/ crew/welshwriters/gclarke.htm). *The Collected Poems of Emyr Humphreys.* University of Wales Press, 1999. *The Columbia Granger's Index to Poetry.* 11th ed. *The Columbia Granger's World of Poetry,* Columbia University Press, 2005 (http://www.columbiagrangers.org). *The Oxford Book of Welsh Verse in English.* Gwyn Jones, ed. Oxford University Press, 1977. *The Oxford Companion to English Literature.* 6th edition. Margaret Drabble, ed. Oxford University Press, 2000. *Twentieth Century Anglo-Welsh Poetry.* Dannie Abse, ed. Seren Books / Dufour Editions, 1997. *Who's Who.* London: A & C Black, 2005.

HUNNIS, WILLIAM (d. 1597)

English musician and poet who in 1549 was in the service of William Herbert, afterwards earl of Pembroke, and was appointed by Edward VI (1547–1553) as gentleman of the Chapel Royal. A staunch Protestant, in 1555 he was involved in an abortive plot to dethrone the Catholic Queen "Bloody" Mary and to and install Elizabeth. For his attempt to rob the treasury, he was he was imprisoned in the Tower of London, but escaped execution. Elizabeth restored him to his position as gentleman of the Chapel Royal and appointed him supervisor of the Queen's Gardens at Greenwich, and in 1566, Master of the Children of the Chapel Royal. Two pieces by him appear in *England's Helicon,* 1600. Some of his publications (shortened titles): *Certayne Psalmes chosen out of the Psalter of David,* 1549. *A Hyve full of Hunnye, contayning the firste booke of Moses, called Genesis,* 1578. *Seven Sobs of a Sorrowfull Soule for Sinne,* 1583. *Hunnies' Recreations, conteining foure godlie and compendious discourses,* 1588. Some of his poems: "But Deliuer Vs from Euill," "The Songe of the Thre Children," "Our Father Which Art in Heauen."

Sources: *Dictionary of National Biography*. Electronic Edition 1.1. Oxford University Press, 1997. *Elizabethan Lyrics*. Norman Ault, ed. William Sloane Associates, 1949. *English Poetry: Author Search*. Chadwyck-Healey Ltd., 1995 (http://www.lib.utexas.edu:8080/search/epoetry/author.html). *Texts of William Hunnis set to music* (http://www.recmusic.org/lieder/h/hunnis/). *Online Classic Encyclopedia — Love to Know* (http://www.19.1911encyclopedia.org). *Poets' Corner* (http://www.theotherpages.org/poems/golding1.html). *The Columbia Granger's Index to Poetry*. 11th ed. *The Columbia Granger's World of Poetry*, Columbia University Press, 2005 (http://www.columbiagrangers.org). *William Hunnis: Certayne Psalmes* (http://newmedia.alma.edu/ottenhoff/psalm51/hunnis.htm).

HUNT, JAMES HENRY LEIGH (1784–1859)

English essayist, critic, journalist, and prolific poet, he was born in Southgate, Middlesex. His father, Isaac Hunt, an American lawyer turned Unitarian minister, and his mother were liberal in their politics and brought up their children to be free-thinkers. He was educated Christ's Hospital, the Bluecoat School, but did not attend university. In 1808 he and his brother John (1775–1848) launched the weekly *Examiner*, which advocated abolition of the slave trade, Catholic emancipation, the reform of Parliament and the elimination of prison sentences for debt. For their attacks on the unpopular prince regent, the brothers were imprisoned in 1813 for two years. He was buried in Kensal Green cemetery, West London. *Juvenilia*, published in 1801—which reached a fourth edition in 1804 — shows his love for Italian literature. His *Autobiography* was published in 1852. Some of his poems: "A Legend of Florence," "Abou Ben Adhem," "An ABC for Grown Gentlemen," "Ballads of Robin Hood," "Blue-Stocking Revels; or, The Feast of the Violets," "Idylls," "The Fish, the Man, and the Spirit," "The Nymphs," "To the Grasshopper and the Cricket," "Wallace and Fawdon."

Sources: *A Biographical Sketch by Blupete: Leigh Hunt* (http://www.blupete.com/Literature/Biographies). *Dictionary of National Biography*. Electronic Edition 1.1. Oxford University Press, 1997. *Encyclopædia Britannica Ultimate Reference Suite DVD*, 2006. *English Poetry: Author Search*. Chadwyck-Healey Ltd., 1995 (http://www.lib.utexas.edu:8080/search/epoetry/author.html). *Gladly Learn and Gladly Teach: Poems of the School Experience*. Helen Plotz, ed. Greenwillow Books, 1981. *The Wallace by Nigel Tranter* (http://www.scottishradiance.com/bookreviews/wallrev.htm). *The Columbia Granger's Index to Poetry*. 11th ed. *The Columbia Granger's World of Poetry*, Columbia University Press, 2005 (http://www.columbiagrangers.org). *The New Penguin Book of English Verse*. Paul Keegan, ed. Penguin Books, 2000. *The Oxford Companion to English Literature*. 6th edition. Margaret Drabble, ed. Oxford University Press, 2000. *The Poetical Works of Leigh Hunt*. H.S. Milford, ed. Oxford University Press, 1923.

HURDIS, JAMES (1763–1801)

Born at Bishopstone in East Sussex, he was educated at Chichester and St. Mary Hall, Oxford, and graduated from Magdalen College. From 1785 to 1791 he was curate of Burwash in East Sussex. In 1791, through the interest of the Earl of Chichester, to whose son he had been tutor, he was appointed to the living of Bishopstone. He was professor of poetry at Magdalen College, Oxford, from 1793 until his death at Buckland in Berkshire, while staying at the house of his friend Dr. Rathbone. Some of his publications: *Poems: By the Author of the Village Curate, and Adriano*, 1790. *The Tragedy of Sir Thomas More*, 1792. *Tears of Affliction*. 1794 (on the death of his sister Catharine). *A poem, written towards the close of the year 1794, Upon a prospect of the Marriage of the Prince of Wales*, 1795. *Poems: By the Rev. James Hurdis*, 1808. *The Relapse*, 1810. *The Favourite Village*, 1810. *The Village Curate, and Other Poems*, 1810. Some of his poems: "Adriano; or, The First of June," "Peasants at Work," "The Student."

Sources: *Dictionary of National Biography*. Electronic Edition 1.1. Oxford University Press, 1997. *English Poetry, Second Edition Bibliography* (http://collections.chadwyck.co.uk/html/ep2/bibliography/g.htm). *English Poetry: Author Search*. Chadwyck-Healey Ltd., 1995 (http://www.lib.utexas.edu:8080/search/epoetry/author.html). *Oxford Professors of Poetry, James Hurdis* (http://www.people.vcu.edu/~dlatane/pop.html). *Professorships Held by the Inklings* (http://home.earthlink.net/~dbratman/profs.html). *Stanford University Libraries and Academic Information Resources* (http://library.stanford.edu). *The Columbia Granger's Index to Poetry*. 11th ed. *The Columbia Granger's World of Poetry*, Columbia University Press, 2005 (http://www.columbiagrangers.org). *The Oxford Companion to English Literature*. 6th edition. Margaret Drabble, ed. Oxford University Press, 2000. *The Penguin Book of Bird Poetry*. Peggy Munsterberg, ed. 1984.

HUTCHINSON, PEARSE (1927–)

Born in Glasgow of Irish parents and reared in Dublin since 1932, he was educated at the Christian Brothers School, Synge Street, Dublin, and University College, Dublin. He lived in Spain for almost ten years in the 1950s and '60s and writes in many different languages. He now lives in Dublin and is a member of Aosdána. Among his translations is *Old Irish Poetry. Done into English,* a collection of translations — notably from Catalan and Gallico-Portugeuse — was published in 2003. Some of his other poetry publications: *Tongue Without Hands*, 1963. *Faoistin Bhacach*, 1968. *Watching the Morning Grow*, 1972. *Expansions*, 1969. *Selected Poems*, 1980. *Climbing the Light*, 1985. *The Soul that Kissed the Body*, 1990 (poems in Irish with translations into English). *Le Cead na Gréine*, 1992. *Barnsley Main Seam*, 1995. *Collected Poems*, 2002 (to celebrate his

75th birthday). Some of his poems: "Amhrán na mBréag," "Be Born a Saint," "Boxing the Foxa," "Bright after Dark," "Fleadh Cheoil," "Gaeltacht," "Look, No Hands," "The True Story Ending in False Hope."

Sources: *Contemporary Irish Poetry: An Anthology.* Anthony Bradley, ed. University of California Press. New and rev. ed., 1988. *Biography of Pearse Hutchinson* (http://www.irishwriters-online.com/pearsehutchinson.html). *Modern Irish Poetry.* Patrick Crotty, ed. The Blackstaff Press, 1995. *The Book of Irish Verse: An Anthology of Irish Poetry from the Sixth Century to the Present.* John Montague, ed. Macmillan, 1974. *The Faber Book of Drink, Drinkers and Drinking.* Simon Rae, ed. Faber and Faber, 1991. *The Penguin Book of Contemporary Irish Poetry.* Peter Fallon and Derek Mahon, eds. Penguin Books, 1990.

HUXLEY, ALDOUS LEONARD (1894–1963)

Born near Godalming, Surrey, he started at Eton College in 1908, and two years later a severe eye infection, which caused near-blindness, forced him to leave. He taught himself to read Braille and he graduated with a first in English literature from Balliol College, Oxford, in 1916. He worked on the periodical *Athenaeum* from 1919 to 1921. He spent much time in Italy until the late 1930s, when he settled in California and started using Dr. W.H. Bates' method for improving eyesight. By the middle of 1939 he said he was able to read and write without spectacles, and in 1942 he published his conclusions in *The Art of Seeing.* He died in Los Angeles; in 1971 his ashes were buried in his parents' grave at Compton cemetery, Surrey. He was an ardent supporter of the Peace Pledge Union, for which he lectured and wrote pamphlets. He wrote novels, essays, short stories, nonfiction and poetry anthologies. Some of his poems: "Antic Hay," "Armour," "Doors of the Temple," "Fifth Philosopher's Song," "Jonah," "September," "The Burning Wheel," "The Canal," "Villiers de l'Isle-Adam."

Sources: *Chapters into Verse. Vol. I: Genesis to Malachi.* Robert Atwan and Laurance Wieder, eds. Oxford University Press. 1993. *Collected Poetry of Aldous Huxley.* Donald Watt, ed. Chatto, 1971. *Dictionary of National Biography.* Electronic Edition 1.1. Oxford University Press, 1997. *Encyclopædia Britannica Ultimate Reference Suite DVD,* 2006. *Fantastic Fiction* (http://www.fantasticfiction.co.uk/authors/Aldous_Huxley.htm). *The National Portrait Gallery* (www.npg.org.uk). *The Columbia Granger's Index to Poetry.* 11th ed. *The Columbia Granger's World of Poetry,* Columbia University Press, 2005 (http://www.columbiagrangers.org). *The Complete Works of Aldous Huxley* (http://somaweb.org/w/huxworks.html). *The Oxford Book of Comic Verse.* John Gross, ed. Oxford University Press, 1994. *The Oxford Book of Sonnets.* John Fuller, ed. Oxford University Press, 2000.

HYDE, DOUGLAS (1860–1949)

Born at Castlerea, County Roscommon, Ireland, the son of clergyman, he was to become a distinguished Gaelic scholar and writer and first president of the Republic of Ireland (Éire) from 1938 to 1945. His Irish name is Dubhighlas de Hide and his pseudonym was an Craoibhin Aoibhinn. He studied ancient Gaelic at Trinity College, Dublin and graduated in law in 1884. He was the first professor of modern Irish at University College, Dublin, in 1909 and held the chair until his retirement in 1932. Languages were his forte — Latin, Greek, Hebrew, French, German and Irish. He was one of the founding members of the Gaelic League in 1893 and was president until 1915. His verse translations have been included in many anthologies of English verse. He died at Phoenix Park, Dublin. His *Love Songs of Connacht* was published in 1893. Some of his poems: "Columcille cecinit (Columba)," "Farewell to Ireland; I Am Raftery," "I Shall Not Die for Thee," "My Grief on the Sea," "My Love, Oh, She is My Love," "Nelly of the Top-Knots," "The Breedyeen," "The Cooleen," "The Song of Fionn."

Sources: *An Anthology of Irish Verse: The Poetry of Ireland from Mythological Times to the Present.* Padraic Colum, ed. Liveright, 1948. *Dictionary of National Biography.* Electronic Edition 1.1. Oxford University Press, 1997. *Lyra Celtica: An Anthology of Representative Celtic Poetry.* E.A. Sharp and J. Matthay, ed. John Grant, 1924. *Poemhunter* (www.poemhunter.com). *The Columbia Granger's Index to Poetry.* 11th ed. *The Columbia Granger's World of Poetry,* Columbia University Press, 2005 (http://www.columbiagrangers.org). *The Gaelic League* (http://www.usna.edu/EnglishDept/ilv/gaelic.htm). *The Oxford Book of Modern Verse, 1892–1935.* William Butler Yeats, ed. Oxford University Press, 1936. *The Oxford Companion to English Literature.* 6th edition. Margaret Drabble, ed. Oxford University Press, 2000. *University College Dublin* (http://www.ucd.ie/).

HYSLOP, JAMES (1798–1827)

Scottish poet and shepherd of Nether Wellwood farm, in the parish of Muirkirk, he was born at Damhead, parish of Kirkconnel, Dumfriesshire. He taught himself English, Latin, French, mathematics, and algebra. His early verses were published in the *Greenock Advertiser* and other newspapers, frequently signed "The Muirkirk Shepherd;" his later works could be found in the *Edinburgh Magazine.* He had several jobs: running a school in Greenock; three years as tutor on board his majesty's ship *Doris*; as a reporter in London (1826); and as tutor on board his majesty's ship *Tweed.* He died off the Cape Verde Islands, in the Atlantic, and he was buried at sea with full military honors. He wrote a good deal in prose, chiefly upon the persecution of the covenanters. His poem "The Cameronian Dream," written while he was a shepherd, tells the story of the murder of the Scottish covenanter Richard Cameron (see William Cleland). Two essays in the *Edinburgh Magazine* (1820) are "A Defence of Modern Scottish Poetry" and "An Account of an Apparition in Airsmoss." Four of his poems: "Scottish Verses," "The Child's Dream," "The Scottish National Melody," "The Scottish Sacramental Sabbath," "The Untombed Mariners."

Sources: *A Cloud of Witnesses: Mr. Richard Cameron* (http://www.truecovenanter.com/reformedpresbyterian/cloud/cloud_appendix_cameron_richard.html). *Dictionary of National Biography.* Electronic Edition 1.1. Oxford University Press, 1997. *Stanford University libraries and Academic Information Resources* (http://library.stanford.edu). *The Cameronian's Dream* (http://www.covenanter.org/Poems/cameroniandream.htm).

HYWEL AB OWAIN GWYNEDD (d. 1170)

Welsh warrior poet, the illegitimate son of Owain ab Gruffydd ab Cynan, prince of North Wales, and Pyvog, the daughter of an Irish noble. In 1143, taking advantage of a quarrel between his father and his uncle, Cadwaladr (died 1172), Hywel seized some part of Ceredigion (West Wales) and burned his uncle's castle of Aberystwyth. His exploits continued until 1150 when he suffered a reversal of fortunes. And in 1157, he fought against Henry II, whose aim was to subjugate the Welsh rebels. Hywel succeed his father in 1169 and soon afterward, when in Ireland — seeking his rightful lands, through his mother — his brother David rose against him in rebellion. Hywel was seriously injured in the ensuing battle, and according to some, taken to Ireland where he died. Of his poetical works the only known remains are eight odes printed in *Myvyrian Archæology,* 1197–9. His poetry is unique among the twelfth- and thirteenth-century court poets in that it consists very largely of love poetry which has been compared to that of the troubadours. Two of his poems: "Exultation," "The Poet's Loves."

Sources: *Project 1: Publications: The Poets of the Princes Series, Volume II: Centre for Advanced Welsh and Celtic Studies* (http://www.wales.ac.uk/newpages/external/E4154.asp). *School of Celtic Studies — Tionól 2005, Abstracts* (http://www.celt.dias.ie/gaeilge/tionol/achoim05.html). *The Columbia Granger's Index to Poetry.* 11th ed. *The Columbia Granger's World of Poetry,* Columbia University Press, 2005 (http://www.columbiagrangers.org). *The Oxford Book of Welsh Verse in English.* Gwyn Jones, ed. Oxford University Press, 1977.

INGELOW, JEAN (1820–1897)

Born at Boston, Lincolnshire, daughter of a banker of Scottish origin, she was educated at home. Her early life was spent in Lincolnshire and in the fen district of Suffolk — apparent in her poetry — and in 1863 she moved to London, where she spent the rest of her life. There she was acquainted with most of the poets, painters, and writers of her time. She died at Kensington and was buried at Brompton cemetery. Her compilation of short stories, *The Studies for Stories,* was published in 1864. Between *Stories told to a Child* in 1865 and 1871 she wrote numerous other children's stories. One of her novels, *Off the Skelligs,* was published in four volumes in 1872. Some of her poetry publications: *A Rhyming Chronicle of Incidents and Feelings,* 1850. *Poems,* 1863, 1876, 1885. *Mopsa, the Fairy,* 1869. Some of her poems: "A Cottage in a Chine," "About the Fairies," "Afternoon at a Parsonage," "Brothers, and a Sermon," "High Tide on the Coast of Lincolnshire, 1571," "Like a Laverock in the Lift," "Songs of Seven," "Supper at the Mill," "The Long White Seam," "Wedding Song."

Sources: *A Sacrifice of Praise: An Anthology of Christian Poetry in English from Caedmon to the Mid–Twentieth Century.* James H. Trott, ed. Cumberland House Publishing, 1999. *Dictionary of National Biography.* Electronic Edition 1.1. Oxford University Press, 1997. *English Poetry: Author Search.* Chadwyck-Healey Ltd., 1995 (http://www.lib.utexas.edu:8080/search/epoetry/author.html). *High Tide on the Coast of Lincolnshire, 1571.* Great Books Online (www.bartleby.com). *Poems by Jean Ingelow.* Roberts Brothers, 1864. *The Book of a Thousand Poems: A Family Treasury.* J. Murray Macbain, ed. Peter Bedrick Books, 1983. *The Columbia Granger's Index to Poetry.* 11th ed. *The Columbia Granger's World of Poetry,* Columbia University Press, 2005 (http://www.columbiagrangers.org). *The High Tides of Lincolnshire* (http://www.enderbymuseum.ca/thepast/geog/hightides.htm). *The Oxford Companion to English Literature.* 6th edition. Margaret Drabble, ed. Oxford University Press, 2000. *Wikipedia, the Free Encyclopedia* (http://en.wikipedia.org/wiki/Wikipedia).

INGRAM, JOHN KELLS (1823–1907)

Ingram was born at the rectory of Temple Carne, County Donegal, Ireland, and graduated from Trinity College in Dublin in 1843, showing considerable promise in both mathematics and classics and as a poet. He helped to found the Dublin Philosophical Society in 1842 and the Dublin Statistical Society in 1847, and was elected a member of the Royal Irish Academy in 1847. His early economic writings dealt mainly with the woefully inadequate Poor Law, which did little to alleviate the distress of Irish people. His writings on economy include *Present Position and Prospects of Political Economy* (1878) and *A History of Political Economy* (1888). From 1875 until he died he was a trustee of the National Library of Ireland and was Regius Professor of Greek at Trinity College, Dublin, from 1866 to 1877. He died in Dublin and was buried in Mount Jerome Cemetery. He wrote books on a wide range of topics and had poems published from an early age. His poem "The Memory of the Dead" (the Rebellion of 1798) became the anthem of Irish nationalism. *Sonnets and Other Poems By John K. Ingram* was published in 1900.

Sources: *Dictionary of National Biography.* Electronic Edition 1.1. Oxford University Press, 1997. *English Poetry, Second Edition Bibliography* (http://collections.chadwyck.co.uk/html/ep2/bibliography/g.htm). *English Poetry: Author Search.* Chadwyck-Healey Ltd., 1995 (http://www.lib.utexas.edu:8080/search/epoetry/author.html). *Great Books Online* (www.bartleby.com). *Ireland in Poetry.* Charles Sullivan, ed. Harry N. Abrams, 1990. *The Columbia Granger's Index to Poetry.* 11th ed. *The Columbia Granger's World of Poetry,* Columbia University Press, 2005 (http://www.columbiagrangers.org). *Wikipedia, the Free Encyclopedia* (http://en.wikipedia.org/wiki/Wikipedia).

IREMONGER, VALENTIN (1918–1991)

Irish poet born in Dublin, he was educated at the Christian Brothers' at Mhuire, County Longford, and at the Abbey Theatre School of Acting, Dublin. From 1940 to 1946 he was actor and producer at Abbey and Gate theatres. From 1946 and for nearly 20 years he was in the Irish diplomatic service in 1946, and was Ambassador to Sweden, Norway, Finland, India, Luxembourg and Portugal. He was poetry editor of *Envoy* (1949–1951) and with Samuel Beckett and Brian Coffey (see entries) he is credited with introducing modernism to Irish poetry. In 1945 he won the Æ (George William Russell) Memorial Prize for a manuscript collection of poems. He died in Dublin. Some of his poetry publications: *One Recent Evening,* 1944. *On the Barricades,* 1944. *Reservations,* 1950. *Horan's Field and Other Reservations,* 1972. *Sandymount Dublin: New and Selected Poems,* 1988. Some of his poems: "Clear View in Summer," "Evening in Summer," "Going Down the Mountain," "Hector," "Icarus," "The Toy Horse," "These Apple Trees," "This Houre Her Vigill."

Sources: *An Anthology of Irish Verse: The Poetry of Ireland from Mythological Times to the Present.* Padraic Colum, ed. Liveright, 1948. *Contemporary Irish Poetry: An Anthology.* Anthony Bradley, ed. University of California Press. New and rev. ed., 1988. *Biography of Valentin Iremonger* (http://archiver.rootsweb.com/th/read/IrelandGenWeb/2002–07/1025887586). *Modern Irish Poetry.* Patrick Crotty, ed. The Blackstaff Press, 1995. *New Irish Poets.* Devin A. Garrity, ed. Devin-Adair, 1948. *The Columbia Granger's Index to Poetry.* 11th ed. *The Columbia Granger's World of Poetry,* Columbia University Press, 2005 (http://www.columbiagrangers.org). *The Oxford Book of Irish Verse: XVIIth Century–XXth Century.* Donagh MacDonagh and Leenox Robinson, eds. Oxford University Press, 1958.

JACOB, HILDEBRAND (1693–1739)

He was the only son of Colonel Sir John Jacob, 3rd Baronet, of Bromley, Kent; his mother was Lady Catherine Barry, daughter of the second Earl of Barrymore. He died the year before his father, leaving a widow and two children. His son, also Hildebrand, succeeded to his grandfather's title in 1740. Few other details of his life are recorded. Some of his poetry publications: *The Curious Maid,* 1720–1721 (a poem that was frequently imitated and parodied). *Bedlam: A Poem,* 1732. *Chiron to Achilles: A Poem,* 1732. *Hymn to the Goddess of Silence,* 1734. *Brutus the Trojan: Founder of the British Empire,* 1735 (an epic poem). *The Works of Hildebrand Jacob ... Containing Poems on Various Subjects, and Occasions,* 1735. Some of his poems: "Here Delia's buried at fourscore," "Swain, give o'er your fond pretension," "The Alarm," "The Judgment of Tiresias," "The Writer," "To Cloe," "To Geron."

Sources: *Dictionary of National Biography.* Electronic Edition 1.1. Oxford University Press, 1997. *English Poetry, Second Edition Bibliography* (http://collections.chadwyck.co.uk/html/ep2/bibliography/g.htm). *English Poetry: Author Search.* Chadwyck-Healey Ltd., 1995 (http://www.lib.utexas.edu:8080/search/epoetry/author.html). *The National Portrait Gallery* (www.npg.org.uk). *Stanford University Libraries and Academic Information Resources* (http://library.stanford.edu). *The Columbia Granger's Index to Poetry.* 11th ed. *The Columbia Granger's World of Poetry,* Columbia University Press, 2005 (http://www.columbiagrangers.org). *The Faber Book of Comic Verse.* Michael Roberts and Janet Adam Smith, eds. Faber and Faber, 1978. *The Faber Book of Epigrams and Epitaphs.* Geoffrey Grigson, ed. Faber and Faber, 1977. *The New Oxford Book of Eighteenth Century Verse.* Roger Lonsdale, ed. Oxford University Press, 2003.

JAGO, RICHARD (1715–1781)

The son of a clergyman, of Cornish stock, he was born at Beaudesert, Warwickshire, and educated at Solihull, West Midlands. He graduated from University College, Oxford, in 1736, was ordained in 1737 and soon had three livings in Warwickshire, which he retained until 1771, when he moved to the more valuable rectory of Kimcote in Leicestershire. He died at Snitherfield, Warwickshire, and was buried in a vault which he had constructed for his family under the middle aisle of the church. He published several sermons and *Labor and Genius: A Fable* (1768). Two of his poetry publications: *The Blackbirds,* 1753 (an elegy, which was set to music by the organist of Worcester Cathedral), and *Edge Hill, or the Rural Prospect delineated and moralized,* 1767 (a poem in four books). Some of his poems: "Absence," "Adam; an Oratorio," (compiled from *Paradise Lost*), "Elegy on the Goldfinches," "Female Empire. A True History," "Hamlet's Soliloquy Imitated," "Labour, and Genius: Or, the Mill-Stream, and the Cascade," "The Scavengers. A Town Eclogue," "The Swallows," "Valentine's Day."

Sources: *Dictionary of National Biography.* Electronic Edition 1.1. Oxford University Press, 1997. *English Poetry: Author Search.* Chadwyck-Healey Ltd., 1995 (http://www.lib.utexas.edu:8080/search/epoetry/author.html). *The Columbia Granger's Index to Poetry.* 11th ed. *The Columbia Granger's World of Poetry,* Columbia University Press, 2005 (http://www.columbiagrangers.org). *The Oxford Book of English Verse, 1250–1918.* Sir Arthur Quiller-Couch, ed (New edition, revised and enlarged, Oxford University Press, 1939. *The Oxford Companion to English Literature.* 6th edition. Margaret Drabble, ed. Oxford University Press, 2000. *The Penguin Book of Bird Poetry.* Peggy Munsterberg, ed. 1984.

JAMES I, KING OF ENGLAND (VI OF SCOTLAND) (1566–1625)

Born at Edinburgh Castle, the son of Mary Queen of Scots and Henry Stewart, Lord Darnley, he succeeded Elizabeth in 1603 as "King of Great Britain, France, and Ireland" (Henry VII was their common ancestor). His insistence on the divine right of kings, or absolutism, brought him into conflict with Parliament and set the scene for the Revolution and the execution of his son, Charles I. *The True Lawe of Free Monarchies* (1598) expounded his views on the divine right of kings. James died at his country palace, Theobalds, Hertfordshire, on 27 March 1625, and his funeral took place on 5 May. His tomb is in the Chapel of Henry VII in Westminster Abbey. The King James Bible was published in 1611. *The Poems of James VI of Scotland,* 2 volumes, was edited by James Craigie (1955–1958). One of his sonnets was written with the poet Sir William Alexander (see entry). Some of his poems: "Admonition to Montgomerie," "An Epitaph on Sir Philip Sidney," "First Ioue, as greatest God aboue the rest," "Lady Cicely Wemyss," "The azur'd vault, the crystal circles bright."

Sources: *Dictionary of National Biography.* Electronic Edition 1.1. Oxford University Press, 1997. *Elizabethan Lyrics.* Norman Ault, ed. William Sloane Associates, 1949. *Encyclopædia Britannica Ultimate Reference Suite DVD,* 2006. *Golden Treasury of the Best Songs and Lyrical Poems in the English Language.* Francis Turner Palgrave, ed. Oxford University Press (1964, Sixth edition, updated by John Press, 1994). *The Columbia Granger's Index to Poetry.* 11th ed. *The Columbia Granger's World of Poetry,* Columbia University Press, 2005 (http://www.columbiagrangers. org). *The Oxford Companion to English Literature.* 6th edition. Margaret Drabble, ed. Oxford University Press, 2000. *The Sonnet: An Anthology.* Robert M. Bender and Charles L. Squier, ed. Washington Square Press, 1987. *Westminster Abbey Official Guide* (no date).

JAMES I, KING OF SCOTLAND (1394–1437)

The son and heir of King Robert III (reigned 1390–1406) was born in Dunfermline and educated at St. Andrews University. Fearing for his son's safety from rebel lords, the king sent James to France in 1404-5, but on the way, the ship was intercepted by an English ship. James spent eighteen comfortable years in strict custody by courtesy of Henry IV. James married Lady Jane Beaufort, the daughter of the Earl of Somerset, in 1424 and was restored to his kingdom. He immediately had many of the rebel lords executed and confiscated their property and improved the administration of justice for common people. On the night of 20 February 1437, in Perth, a group of conspirators assassinated him; his widow had the conspirators captured and executed. He was buried at the Convent of the Carthusians in the Holy Land. While in prison he wrote the vernacular poem *The Kingis Quair* (*The King's Book*), inspired by Jane; it was published in 1783. Some of his poems: "Christis Kirk on the Green," "Peblis to the Play," "Spring Song of the Birds," "The Ballad of the Good Counsel."

Sources: *An Anthology of Catholic Poets.* Shane Leslie, ed. Macmillan, 1952. *Dictionary of National Biography.* Electronic Edition 1.1. Oxford University Press, 1997. *Encyclopædia Britannica Ultimate Reference Suite DVD,* 2006. *Encyclopedia of Britain.* Bamber Gascoigne. London: Macmillan, 1994. *The National Portrait Gallery* (www.npg.org.uk). *Poemhunter* (www.poemhunter.com). *The Columbia Granger's Index to Poetry.* 11th ed. *The Columbia Granger's World of Poetry,* Columbia University Press, 2005 (http://www.columbiagrangers.org). *The Oxford Companion to English Literature.* 6th edition. Margaret Drabble, ed. Oxford University Press, 2000. *The Scottish Collection of Verse to 1800.* Eileen Dunlop and Kamm Antony, eds. Richard Drew, 1985.

JAMES V, KING OF SCOTLAND (1512–1542)

Born at the Linlithgow Palace, West Lothian, he succeeded his father, who was killed at the Battle of Flodden (near Berwick-on-Tweed) in 1513. Scotland then became caught in the grip of a power struggle between the pro-French regent, John Stewart, 2nd Duke of Albany, and the head of the English party, Archibald Douglas, 6th Earl of Angus, who had married James' mother, Margaret Tudor, sister of Henry VIII. Angus kept James a virtual prisoner until he escaped in 1528, forcing Angus to flee to England. In 1538 James married the French noblewoman Marie de Guise and allied with France against England. He died at Falkland Palace, Fife, a week after the birth of Mary Stuart (Mary, Queen of Scots), his only surviving legitimate child. He was a cruel man who instituted in his later years a near reign of terror in Scotland. However, he is said to have wandered anonymously among his people in beggar's disguise and was known as the "Gaberlunzie Man" (a tinker or traveling beggar, and an enduring figure in Scottish folklore), upon which experiences rest his poem "The Jolly Beggar."

Sources: *An Adventure in the Life of King James V of Scotland by William Topaz McGonagall* (see entry) (http://www.poemhunter.com/p/m/poem.asp?poet=6601and poem=26761). *Dictionary of National Biography.* Electronic Edition 1.1. Oxford University Press, 1997. *Encyclopædia Britannica Ultimate Reference Suite DVD,* 2006. *Biography of James V, King of Scots ("The Gaberlunzie Man")* (http://www.users.globalnet.co.uk/~crumey/james_v.html). *The Columbia Granger's Index to Poetry.* 11th ed. *The Columbia Granger's World of Poetry,* Columbia University Press, 2005 (http://www.columbiagrangers.org). *The Common Muse, an Anthology of Popular British Ballad Poetry, XVth–XXth Century.* Vivian de Sola Pinto and Allan Edwin Rodway, eds. Philosophical Library, 1957. *The Gaberlunzie Man* (http://ingeb.org/songs/oabeggar.html). *The Gaberlunzie Man* (http://www.contemplator.com/child/gaberlunz.html). *The Jolly Beggar* (http://mysongbook.de/msb/songs/r_clarke/jollybeg.htm).

JAMIE, KATHLEEN (1962–)

Scottish poet born in Renfrewshire, she graduated M.A. in philosophy from Edinburgh University and now lives in Fifeshire. In 1999 she was appointed lecturer in creative writing at St. Andrews University. She has received several prestigious awards for her poetry, including a Somerset Maugham Award, a Forward Poetry Prize (Best Single Poem), a Paul Hamlyn Award and a Creative Scotland Award, and has twice won the Geoffrey Faber Memorial Prize. Her collection *Mr. and Mrs. Scotland Are Dead* (2002)—which contains much of her work written before 1994—was short listed for the Griffin Poetry Prize. *The Tree House* (2004) won the 2004 Forward Poetry Prize (Best Poetry Collection of the Year) and the 2005 Scottish Arts Council Book of the Year Award. Some of her other poetry publications: *Black Spiders,* 1982. *A Flame in Your Heart,* 1986 (with Andrew Greig, see entry). *The Way We Live,* 1987. *The Autonomous Region: Poems and Photographs from Tibet,* 1993 (with the photographer Sean Mayne Smith). *Findings,* 2005. Some of her poems: "Arraheids," "Aunt Janet's Museum," "Flower-sellers, Budapest," "Julian of Norwich," "Katie's Poems," "Ultrasound," "War Widow."

Sources: *British Council Arts* (http://www.contemporarywriters.com). *Penguin Modern Poets, Book 9.* John Burnside, Robert Crawford, and Kathleen Jamie, eds. Penguin Books, 1996. *Poetry with an Edge.* Neil Astley, ed. Bloodaxe Books, 1988. *The Bloodaxe Book of 20th Century Poetry, from Britain and Ireland.* Edna Longley, ed. Bloodaxe Books, 2000. *The New Penguin Book of Scottish Verse.* Robert Crawford and Mick Imlah, ed. Penguin Books, 2000. *The Oxford Companion to English Literature.* 6th edition. Margaret Drabble, ed. Oxford University Press, 2000. *The Virago Book of Love Poetry.* Wendy Mulford, ed. Virago Press, 1990. *Wikipedia, the Free Encyclopedia* (http://en.wikipedia.org/wiki/Wikipedia).

JEFFREY, FRANCIS, LORD (1773–1850)

Born in Edinburgh, he was educated at the universities of Glasgow, Edinburgh, and Queen's College, Oxford, and was admitted to the Scottish bar in 1794. He joined with Sydney Smith and others to establish *The Edinburgh Review*—a liberal critical periodical that supported the Whig Party—and was editor from 1803 until 1829. He took part in the foundation of the Edinburgh Academy (1824) and was afterwards a director. When the Whig Party came into office in 1830, Jeffrey, who had built up a reputation as an advocate, was appointed lord advocate and introduced the Scottish Reform Bill in 1831. In 1834 he was made a judge and assumed the title of Lord Jeffrey. He wrote a great quantity of verse and two plays, and was severely critical of the "Lake Poets" (a group of Romantic poets—Samuel Taylor Coleridge, Robert Southey, and William Wordsworth—who lived in the "Lake District" in northwestern England). He was buried very quietly in the Dean Cemetery near Edinburgh. Some of his poems: "Epitaph on Richard Hind," "In Christ Church, Bristol, on Thomas Turner," "On Peter Robinson."

Sources: *Dictionary of National Biography.* Electronic Edition 1.1. Oxford University Press, 1997. *Encyclopædia Britannica Ultimate Reference Suite DVD,* 2006. *The National Portrait Gallery* (www.npg.org.uk). *The Columbia Granger's Index to Poetry.* 11th ed. *The Columbia Granger's World of Poetry,* Columbia University Press, 2005 (http://www.columbiagrangers.org). *The Faber Book of Epigrams and Epitaphs.* Geoffrey Grigson, ed. Faber and Faber, 1977. *The Norton Book of Light Verse.* Russell Baker, ed. W.W. Norton, 1986. *The Oxford Companion to English Literature.* 6th edition. Margaret Drabble, ed. Oxford University Press, 2000. *What Cheer: An Anthology of American and British Humorous and Witty Verse.* David McCord, ed. Coward-McCann, 1945.

JENKINS, NIGEL (1949–)

Born at Gorseinon, Glamorgan, he was educated at Essex University. A former journalist, he now lives in Swansea and is a free-lance writer, lecturer and broadcaster. His early work can be found, with that of Tony Curtis and Duncan Bush (see entries), in *Three Young Anglo-Welsh Poets* (1974). He has published plays, a monograph on John Tripp in the *Writers of Wales* series, and *Gwalia in Khasia* (1995), a book on the influence of Welsh missionaries in northeast India. He co-edited the anthology *Glas-Nos: Poems for Peace/Cerddi Dros Heddwch* (1987) and *Thirteen Ways of Looking at Tony Conran* (see entry) (1995). *Footsore on the Frontier* (2001) is a selection of his essays and articles. He has won two Welsh Arts Council bursaries and five literary awards. Some of his poetry publications: *Song and*

Dance, 1981. *Practical Dreams*, 1983. *Acts of Union: Selected Poems*, 1990. *Ambush*, 1998. *A Body of Questions*, 2002. Some of his poems: "Ainadamar," "Castration," "Land of Song," "Shirts," "Wild Cherry," "Yr Iaith [the language/diction]."

Sources: *Anglo-Welsh Poetry, 1480–1980.* Raymond Garlick and Roland Mathias, eds. Poetry Wales Press, 1984. *Anglo-Welsh Poetry, 1480–1990.* Raymond Garlick and Roland Mathias, eds. Poetry Wales Press, 1993. *Biography of Nigel Jenkins* (http://www.swan.ac.uk/english/crew/nigel_jenkins.htm). *The Columbia Granger's Index to Poetry.* 11th ed. *The Columbia Granger's World of Poetry,* Columbia University Press, 2005 (http://www.columbiagrangers.org). *The Welsh Academy Encyclopedia of Wales.* Nigel Jenkins, ed. University of Wales Press, 2006. *Twentieth Century Anglo-Welsh Poetry.* Dannie Abse, ed. Seren Books / Dufour Editions, 1997.

JENNER, CHARLES (1736–1774)

Novelist and poet clergyman, the eldest son of Charles Jenner, also a clergyman, he was educated at Pembroke Hall, Cambridge, and Sidney Sussex College, Cambridge. He had the livings of Claybrook in Leicestershire and of Craneford St. John, Northamptonshire. His first volume of poems was published in 1766 and republished in 1767. He published another volume of poems in 1773 and 1773, *Town Eclogues.* His only novel, *The Placid Man, or Memoirs of Sir Charles Beville,* was published in 1770 and republished in 1773. In 1767 he published *Letters from Altamont to his Friend in the Country* and essays, and in 1771, *Letters from Lothario to Penelope,* miscellaneous papers, which included two dramas, *Lucinda,* and *The Man of Family.* He composed and published a song, "The Syren," and in his novel and other of his writings, he showed much knowledge of music and musical literature. He died at St. Omer, France, and a monument was erected to his memory in Claybrook Church by Lady Craven, with commemorative verses of her own. Some of his other poems: "Elegy to the Memory of Lord Lyttelton," "The Destruction of Nineveh," "The Gift of Tongues."

Sources: *An Anthology of World Poetry.* Mark Van Doren, ed. Reynal and Hitchcock, Inc., 1936. *Dictionary of National Biography.* Electronic Edition 1.1. Oxford University Press, 1997. *Gentleman's Magazine* (http://www.bodley.ox.ac.uk/ilej/journals/srchgm.htm). *The Columbia Granger's Index to Poetry.* 11th ed. *The Columbia Granger's World of Poetry,* Columbia University Press, 2005 (http://www.columbiagrangers.org). *The New Oxford Book of Eighteenth Century Verse.* Roger Lonsdale, ed. Oxford University Press, 2003.

JENNER, EDWARD (1749–1823)

Born at Berkeley, Gloucestershire, the son of a clergyman, he became famous as the surgeon who discovered vaccination for smallpox in 1796. He was educated at a grammar school, then for eight years, from the age of 13, he was apprenticed to a surgeon. From 1770 to 1773 he was a pupil of the brilliant surgeon John Hunter at St. George's Hospital, London. It was from Hunter that he received advice to the effect that thinking or speculating should not replace experiment. Jenner was a countryman at heart who enjoyed all things of nature, joining in local events, playing the violin and singing. He observed that people infected with cowpox did not catch smallpox, and from his experiments he wrote a slender book entitled *An Inquiry into the Causes and Effects of the Variolae Vaccinae* (1798) and many other medical treatises. Vaccination rapidly proved its value and the procedure spread quickly around the world. The Edward Jenner Institute for Vaccine Research is based at Compton, Newbury, Berkshire. He died at Berkeley. Only two of Jenner's poems are recorded: "Sent to a Patient, with the Present of a Couple of Ducks," "Signs of Rain."

Sources: *Dictionary of National Biography.* Electronic Edition 1.1. Oxford University Press, 1997. *Encyclopædia Britannica Ultimate Reference Suite DVD,* 2006. *The National Portrait Gallery* (www.npg.org.uk). *The Best Loved Poems of the American People.* Hazel Felleman, ed. Doubleday, 1936. *The Faber Book of Useful Verse.* Simon Brett, ed. Faber and Faber, 1981.

JENNINGS, ELIZABETH (1926–2001)

Born in Boston, Lincolnshire, where her father was chief medical officer, the family moved to Oxford when she was six years old. Educated at Oxford High School, she graduated M.A. from St. Anne's College, Oxford, in 1949, after which she became a librarian at Oxford city library. She became associated with the "Movement" when her work was included in Robert Conquest's (see entry) *New Lines Anthology* (1956). She won a Somerset Maugham Award for *A Way of Looking* (1955), which enabled her to visit Italy. Her poetry often reflects her devout Roman Catholicism and her love of Italy. She was made Commander of the Order of the British Empire in 1992. Some of her other publications: *Poems,* 1953. *A Sense of the World,* 1958. *Song for a Birth or a Death,* 1961. *Recoveries,* 1964. *The Mind Has Mountains,* 1966. *Lucidities,* 1970. *Relationships,* 1972. *Growing-Pains,* 1975. *Familiar Spirits,* 1994. *Praises,* 1988. Some of her poems: "Christ Seen by Flemish Painters," "Father to Son," "In Praise of Creation," "The Rabbit's Advice," "The Second World War," "The Sonnets of Michelangelo," "The Young Ones."

Sources: *Encyclopædia Britannica Ultimate Reference Suite DVD,* 2006. *Going Over to Your Place: Poems for Each Other.* Paul B. Janeczko, ed. Bradbury Press, 1987. *Poemhunter* (www.poemhunter.com). *The Columbia Granger's*

Index to Poetry. 11th ed. *The Columbia Granger's World of Poetry,* Columbia University Press, 2005 (http://www.columbiagrangers.org). *The Harvill Book of Twentieth-Century Poetry in English.* Michael Schmidt, ed. The Harvill Press, 1999. *The Oxford Companion to English Literature.* 6th edition. Margaret Drabble, ed. Oxford University Press, 2000. *Tongues of Fire: An Anthology of Religious and Poetic Experience.* Karen Armstrong, ed. Penguin Books, 1987.

JERNINGHAM, EDWARD (1727–1812)

The son of Sir George Jerningham of Costessey, Norfolk, he was educated at the English College at Douay in France, and in Paris, and became proficient in Greek, Latin, French and Italian. Although brought up as Catholic and with the influence at Douay, he turned Protestant. The Prince Regent (later George IV) invited him to arrange his library at the Brighton Pavilion. Jerningham died in London. He wrote two dramas, *The Welch Heiress* (1795) and *The Peckham Frolic* (1799). Some of his poetry publications: *Amabella,* 1768. *Andromache to Pyrrhus,* 1761. *An Elegy Written Among the Tombs in Westminster Abbey,* 1762. *An Elegy Written Among the Ruins of an Abbey,* 1765. *Faldoni and Teresa,* 1773. *The Rise and Progress of the Scandinavian Poetry,* 1784. *The African Boy,* 1788 (an anti-slavery poem). *Lines on a Late Resignation,* 1790. *Stone Henge,* 1792. *The Old Bard's Farewell,* 1812. *Poems,* 1806 (9th ed.). Some of his poems: "The Deserter," "The Fall of Mexico," "The Nunnery," "The Old Bard's Farewell," "The Rookery," "The Shakespeare Gallery," "Tintern Abbey."

Sources: *Dictionary of National Biography.* Electronic Edition 1.1. Oxford University Press, 1997. *English Poetry: Author Search.* Chadwyck-Healey Ltd., 1995 (http://www.lib.utexas.edu:8080/search/epoetry/author.html). *English Prose Drama: Bibliography* (http://www.lib.uchicago.edu/efts/EPD/EPD.bib.html). *Gentleman's Magazine* (http://www.bodley.ox.ac.uk/ilej/journals/srchgm.htm). *Great Books Online* (www.bartleby.com). *Jerningham, "The African Boy."* (http://www2.bc.edu/~richarad/asp/ejab.html). *Stanford University Libraries and Academic Information Resources* (http://library.stanford.edu).

JEWSBURY, MARIA JANE (1800–1833)

The daughter of a cotton merchant, she was born at Measham, on the Derbyshire/Leicestershire border, and was educated at Shenstone, Staffordshire, but ill health forced her to leave school at fourteen. The family moved to Manchester and when Maria was 18, her mother died, leaving her to care for three brothers and six year old Geraldine, who later became a successful novelist. In 1832 she married William Kew Fletcher, a chaplain with the East India Company, with whom she sailed for Bombay (Mumbai). She died at Poonah (Pune) from cholera (see *Lancashire Worthies,* by Francis Espinasse, Abel Heywood and Son, 1874, for extracts from her journal of her voyage to and residence in India.) She dedicated to William Wordsworth *Phantasmagoria, or Sketches of Life and Character* (1825)—a collection of verse and prose. He in return addressed his poem "Liberty" to her in 1829. Much of her best writing appeared from 1830 to 1832 in the *Athenæum.* Some of her poems: "A Farewell to the Muse," "A Summer Eve's Vision," "My Heart's in the Kitchen, My Heart is Not Here," "Partings," "To a Young Brother," "To My Own Heart."

Sources: *Dictionary of National Biography.* Electronic Edition 1.1. Oxford University Press, 1997. *Selections from the Letters of Geraldine Endsor Jewsbury to Jane Welsh Carlyle,* 1892 (http://digital.library.upenn.edu/women/jewsbury/letters/gej.html). *The National Portrait Gallery* (www.npg.org.uk). *The Columbia Granger's Index to Poetry.* 11th ed. *The Columbia Granger's World of Poetry,* Columbia University Press, 2005 (http://www.columbiagrangers.org). *The Oxford Book of Children's Verse.* Iona Opie and Peter Opie, eds. Oxford University Press, 1973. *The Oxford Companion to English Literature.* 6th edition. Margaret Drabble, ed. Oxford University Press, 2000. *Victorian Women Poets: An Anthology.* Angela Leighton and Margaret Reynolds, eds. Blackwell, 1991.

JOHNSON, BRYAN STANLEY WILLIAM (1933–1973)

B.S. Johnson was born in London and graduated B.A. (with honors in English) from King's College, London, in 1959. His obituary from *The Times,* London, 15 November 1973 says Johnson, "who was found dead at his home in Islington on November 13, 1973, was one of the most naturally gifted writers of his generation. He was also one of the very small number to commit himself whole-heartedly to the experimental presentation of fiction." He won the Gregory award for *Traveling People and Poems* (1963) and several other awards for his novels. In his short life he wrote 8 novels, 7 plays, 5 screenplays and several collections of short stories as well as being a writer and director for television. Some of his poetry publications: *Poems,* 1964. *Poems Two,* 1972. *Hafod a Hendref,* 1972 (poem sequence). *A Dublin Unicorn,* 1973. *Penguin Modern Poets 25,* 1975. Some of his poems: "All This Sunday Long," "Great Man," "The Poet Holds His Future in His Hand," "Why Do We Lie," "Blaney's Last Directions," "Evening: Barents Sea," "Nine Stages Towards Knowing," "Porth Ceiriad Bay."

Sources: *Biography of BS Johnson* (http://www.bsjohnson.info). *Eight Lines and Under: An Anthology of Short, Short Poems.* William Cole, ed. Macmillan, 1967. *Poemhunter* (www.poemhunter.com). *The Faber Book of Blue Verse.* John Whitworth, ed. Faber and Faber, 1990. *The Oxford Companion to English Literature.* 6th edition. Margaret Drabble, ed. Oxford University Press, 2000.

JOHNSON, LINTON KWESI (1952–)

Born in Jamaica, LKJ joined his mother in England in 1963, was educated at Tulse Hill secondary school, then studied sociology at Goldsmiths College, University of London. On being awarded a Cecil Day-Lewis Fellowship, he became the writer in residence for the London Borough of Lambeth for 1977. He worked as the library resources and education officer at the Keskidee Centre, North London, the first home of black theatre and art, and from 1985 to 1988 was a reporter on TV Channel 4's *The Bandung File*. He is an associate fellow of Warwick University (1985), an honorary fellow of Wolverhampton Polytechnic (1987); honorary fellow of Goldsmiths College (2003), and in 2004 became honorary visiting professor of Middlesex University, London. He was awarded a silver Musgrave Medal from the Institute of Jamaica in 2005 for distinguished eminence in the field of poetry. Some of his poetry publications: *Voices of the Living and the Dead*, 1974. *Inglan' is a Bitch*, 1980. *Tings An' Times*, 1991 (selected poems). *Selected Poems*, 2006. Some of his poems: "Bass Culture," "Beacon of Hope," "Five Nights of Bleeding," "Mi Revalueshanary Fren," "Reggae Sounds," "Youtman."

Sources: *Anthology of Twentieth-Century British and Irish Poetry*. Keith Tuma, ed. Oxford University Press, 2001. *Caribbean Poetry Now*. Stewart Brown, ed. Edward Arnold, 1992. *Biography of Linton Kwesi Johnson* (http://lister.ultrakohl.com/Homepage/LKJ/lkj.htm). *The works of Linton Kwesi Johnson* (http://www.lkjrecords.com/lkj.html). *The National Portrait Gallery* (www.npg.org.uk). *The Columbia Granger's Index to Poetry*. 11th ed. *The Columbia Granger's World of Poetry*, Columbia University Press, 2005 (http://www.columbiagrangers.org). *The Faber Book of Political Verse*. Tom Paulin, ed. Faber and Faber, 1986. *The Heinemann Book of Caribbean Poetry*. Stewart Brown and Ian McDonald, eds. Heinemann, 1992. *The Oxford Companion to English Literature*. 6th edition. Margaret Drabble, ed. Oxford University Press, 2000. *The Penguin Book of Caribbean Verse in English*. Paula Burnett, ed. Penguin Books, 1986. *Wheel and Come Again: An Anthology of Reggae Poetry*. Kwame Dawes, ed. Goose Lane Editions, 1998.

JOHNSON, LIONEL PIGOT (1867–1902)

The son of an army officer, he was born at Broadstairs, Kent, but the family settled at Windsor Forest, Berkshire. He was educated at Winchester College, where he edited *The Wykehamist*, the school magazine, and won prizes for poetry and essay writing, one essay being "Fools of Shakespeare" published in *Noctes Shakesperianæ* (1887). After graduating *literæ humaniores* from New College, Oxford, in 1886, he became a review journalist for the *Academy*, *Anti-Jacobin*, *National Observer*, *Daily Chronicle*, and *Pall Mall Gazette*. *The Art of Thomas Hardy* was published in 1894 and *Ireland and Other Poems* in 1897. He died in St. Bartholomew's Hospital from a fall in Fleet Street and was buried at Kensal Green Cemetery, West London. His poems were published in *Century Guild Hobby-Horse* and in the first and second *Book of the Rhymers' Club* (1892–1894), and selections were published in the *Vigo Cabinet* series, 1908. Some of his poems: "Bagley Wood," "Dead," "In Memory," "July," "Oxford," "Poems from the Henn Manuscript," "The Age of a Dream," "The Dark Angel," "The Destroyer of a Soul," "The Precept of Silence."

Sources: *British Poetry 1880–1920: Edwardian Voices*. Paul L. Wiley and Harold Orel, eds. Appleton-Century-Crofts, 1969. *Dictionary of National Biography*. Electronic Edition 1.1. Oxford University Press, 1997. *English Poetry: Author Search*. Chadwyck-Healey Ltd., 1995 (http://www.lib.utexas.edu:8080/search/epoetry/author.html). *Oldpoetry* (www.oldpoetry.com). *Poets' Corner—Index of Poets* (http://www.theotherpages.org/poems/poem-gh.html). *The Columbia Granger's Index to Poetry*. 11th ed. *The Columbia Granger's World of Poetry*, Columbia University Press, 2005 (http://www.columbiagrangers.org). *The Complete Poems of Lionel Johnson*. Iain Fletcher, ed. The Unicorn Press, 1953. *Victorian Literature: Poetry*. Donald Gray and G.B. Tennyson, eds. Macmillan, 1976.

JOHNSON, SAMUEL (1709–1784)

The son of a poor bookseller of Lichfield, Staffordshire, he was educated at the local grammar school and from 1728 to 1731 at Pembroke College, Oxford, but poverty forced him to leave without graduating. He started working for *Gentleman's Magazine* in London in 1733. His renowned *Dictionary of the English Language*—which took him nine years to complete—was published in 1755. He started a series of bi-weekly moral and religious essays under the title *The Rambler* in 1750. In 1763 he met James Boswell, his future biographer (see entry). Trinity College, Dublin, awarded him an honorary doctorate in 1765, followed in 1775 with one from Oxford. His *Lives of the English Poets*—a project commissioned by a consortium of London booksellers—was published in 1779–1781. He was buried in Poets' Corner of Westminster Abbey. Some of his poems: "Anacreon's Dove," "Charade on Dr. Thomas Barnard," "Drury-lane Prologue Spoken by Mr. Garrick," "Epigram on Colley Cibber," "London: A Poem in Imitation of the Third Satire of Juvenal," "On Losing the Power of Speech," "The Vanity of Human Wishes" (excerpts), "The Winter's Walk."

Sources: *An American Anthology, 1787–1900*. Edmund Clarence Stedman, ed. Houghton Mifflin, 1900. *Dictionary of National Biography*. Electronic Edition 1.1. Oxford University Press, 1997. *Encyclopædia Britannica Ultimate Ref-*

erence Suite DVD, 2006. English Poetry: Author Search. Chadwyck-Healey Ltd., 1995 (http://www.lib.utexas.edu: 8080/search/epoetry/author.html). *Gentleman's Magazine* (http://www.bodley.ox.ac.uk/ilej/journals/srchgm.htm). *Poemhunter* (www.poemhunter.com). *Samuel Johnson's Lives of the English Poets, 1779–1781* (http://www2.hn.psu. edu/Faculty/KKemmerer/poets/preface.htm). *The Columbia Granger's Index to Poetry.* 11th ed. *The Columbia Granger's World of Poetry,* Columbia University Press, 2005 (http://www.columbiagrangers.org). *The Complete English Poems of Samuel Johnson.* J.D. Fleeman, ed. Penguin Books, 1971. *The Golden Treasury of Longer Poems.* Ernest Rhys, ed. E.P. Dutton, 1949. *The Oxford Companion to English Literature.* 6th edition. Margaret Drabble, ed. Oxford University Press, 2000. *Westminster Abbey Official Guide* (no date). *Wikipedia, the Free Encyclopedia* (http://en. wikipedia.org/wiki/Wikipedia).

JOHNSTON, ARTHUR (1587–1641)

He was born at Caskieben, Aberdeenshire, the son of Laird Johnston of Johnston and Caskieben, and on his mother's side a grandson of the seventh Lord Forbes. He was probably a student at King's College, Old Aberdeen — of which he became rector in 1637 — and qualified as a doctor in Padua, Northern Italy, in 1610. He wrote entirely in Latin. His first volume of epigrams was published in 1619 while working in Paris, and a second at Aberdeen in 1632. In 1625 he published an elegy on the death of James I. He died at Oxford while traveling to London. His sacred poems, which had appeared in the *Opera* (1642), were reprinted by William Lauder in his *Poetarum Scolorum musae sacrae* (1739) (DNB). Johnston left more than ten works, all in Latin; the two main ones, published in 1637, are the full version of the Psalms, *Psalmorum Davidis paraphrasis poetica et canticorum evangelicorum,* Aberdeen, and his anthology of contemporary Latin verse by Scottish poets, *Deliciae poetarum Scotorum huius aevi illustrium,* Amsterdam.

Sources: *Dictionary of National Biography.* Electronic Edition 1.1. Oxford University Press, 1997. *Biography of Arthur Johnston.* Freepedia (http://en.freepedia.org/Arthur_ Johnston.html). *The Columbia Granger's Index to Poetry.* 11th ed. *The Columbia Granger's World of Poetry,* Columbia University Press, 2005 (http://www.columbiagrangers. org). *The New Penguin Book of Scottish Verse.* Robert Crawford and Mick Imlah, eds. Penguin Books, 2000.

JONES, DAVID MICHAEL (1895–1974)

He was born in Brockley, Kent, of a Welsh father. From 1910 to 1914 he was a student at the Camberwell School of Art, London. In January 1915 he enlisted in the Welch Fusiliers, was wounded in 1916 in the attack on Mametz Wood on the Somme, and was evacuated from France with severe trench fever (a disease caused by lice) in February 1918. From 1919 to 1921 he worked at the Westminster School of Art and was commissioned to paint the lettering of the war memorial at New College, Oxford. His long poem *In Parenthesis* (1937) — which has its climax at Mametz in World War I — won the 1938 Hawthornden prize. He was appointed Commander of the Order of the British Empire in 1955, Companion of Honor in 1974, and received an honorary doctor of letters from the University of Wales in 1960. He died at Harrow, Middlesex, and is memorialized by a stone in Poets' Corner of Westminster Abbey along with other poets of the First World War. Some of his poems: "Mabinog's Liturgy," "The Anathemata," "The Sleeping Lord," "The Tribune's Visitation," "The Tutelar of the Place," "The Wall."

Sources: *Dictionary of National Biography.* Electronic Edition 1.1. Oxford University Press, 1997. *Everyman's Book of English Verse.* John Wain, ed. J.M. Dent, 1981. *The Columbia Granger's Index to Poetry.* 11th ed. *The Columbia Granger's World of Poetry,* Columbia University Press, 2005 (http://www.columbiagrangers.org). *The Oxford Companion to English Literature.* 6th edition. Margaret Drabble, ed. Oxford University Press, 2000. *The Poetry Anthology, 1912–1977.* Daryl Hine and Joseph Parisi, eds. Houghton Mifflin, 1978. *Twentieth Century Anglo-Welsh Poetry.* Dannie Abse, ed. Seren Books / Dufour Editions, 1997.

JONES, EBENEZER (1820–1860)

Born in Islington, London, into a strict Calvinistic family of Welsh extraction, the family found itself removed from its comfortable life when the father died. At seventeen Ebenezer was employed as a clerk in a city firm connected with the tea trade, exposed to long working hours. Fired by the desire to be a poet, he devoted his time and meager income in trying to get his poems published. *Sensation and Event* was published in 1843 and *Studies of Sensation and Event* in 1879. The indifference by which his poems were received threw him into despair and he destroyed his unfinished poems, then earned his living as an accountant and as a journalist. He died of tuberculosis and his work was saved from obscurity by Dante Rossetti in *Notes and Queries* (1870) and mention in the *Athenæum* in 1878. Some of his other poems: "A Development of Idiocy," "A Warning," "A Winter Hymn — to the Snow," "Eyeing the Eyes of One's Mistress," "Feminine Goodness," "Feminine Spite," "High Summer," "The Hand," "Ways of Regard," "When the World is Burning," "Whimper of Awakening Passion."

Sources: *Dictionary of National Biography.* Electronic Edition 1.1. Oxford University Press, 1997. *English Poetry: Author Search* (http://www.lib.utexas.edu:8080/search/ epoetry/author.html). *Lyra Celtica: An Anthology of Representative Celtic Poetry.* E.A. Sharp and J. Matthay, eds. John Grant, 1924. *Stanford University Libraries and Academic Information Resources* (http://library.stanford.edu). *The Columbia Granger's Index to Poetry.* 11th ed. *The*

Columbia Granger's World of Poetry, Columbia University Press, 2005 (http://www.columbiagrangers.org). *The New Oxford Book of Victorian Verse*. Christopher Ricks, ed. Oxford University Press, 1987. *The Oxford Book of Nineteenth-Century English Verse*. John Hayward, ed. Oxford University Press, 1964; reprinted, with corrections, 1965.

JONES, GLYN (1905–1995)

Poet, short-story writer and novelist, he was born in Merthyr Tydfil, Glamorganshire, and was educated at Cyfarthfa Castle Grammar School. He was deeply affected by the poverty he saw as a teacher in the slums of Cardiff in the 1920s and 1930s, something he later wrote about in his novel *The Learning Lark* (1960). Although dismissed from his post as a conscientious objector in the Second World War, from 1952 until his retirement in 1965 he taught at Glantaf County School, Cardiff. He became a fluent writer and speaker of Welsh, but felt constrained composing poetry in Welsh, as it was not his mother tongue. Nevertheless, he did translate Welsh poetry into English and collaborated with other Welsh translators. *The Dream of Jake Hopkins* (1954) was dramatized for radio. The first chapter of his novel *The Dragon Has Two Tongues* (1968) is biographical. His *Selected Poems* (1975) collects much of his later work and his *Collected Poems* was published posthumously in 1996. Some of his poems: "Again," "Dafydd's Seagull and the West Wind," "Esyllt," "Merthyr," "Swifts," "The Common Path," "Where All Were Good to Me, God Knows."

Sources: *Dylan Thomas's Choice: An Anthology of Verse Spoken by Dylan Thomas*. Ralph Maud and Aneirin Talfan Davies, eds. New Directions, 1963. *The Columbia Granger's Index to Poetry*. 11th ed. *The Columbia Granger's World of Poetry*, Columbia University Press, 2005 (http://www.columbiagrangers.org). *The Oxford Book of Welsh Verse in English*. Gwyn Jones, ed. Oxford University Press, 1977. *The Oxford Companion to English Literature*. 6th edition. Margaret Drabble, ed. Oxford University Press, 2000. *Twentieth Century Anglo-Welsh Poetry*. Dannie Abse, ed. Seren Books / Dufour Editions, 1997.

JONES, HENRY (1721–1770)

A self-educated Irish poet who was born at Beaulieu, near Drogheda, County Louth, he was employed as a bricklayer in the repair of Parliament House, Dublin, when Lord Chesterfield was appointed Lord-lieutenant of Ireland in 1745. Lord Chesterfield patronized the young poet who accompanied him to England in 1748 and helped his protégé publish *Poems on Several Occasions* (1749). His tragedy *The Earl of Essex* was played at Covent Garden in 1753 with Spranger Barry (1719–1777) in the title role. Jones died in the workhouse, his life ruined by success and drunkenness. Some of his other poetry publications: *An Epistle to the Right Honorable*

the Earl of Orrery, 1751. *Fortitude*, 1751. *Merit*, 1753. *The Relief, or, Day Thoughts*, 1754. *Verses to His Grace the Duke of Newcastle*, 1754. *The Invention of Letters*, 1755. *An Address to Britain*, 1758. *The Royal Vision*, 1763. *Kew Garden: A Poem in Two Cantos*, 1767. *Inoculation, or Beauty's Triumph*, 1768. *Shrewsbury Quarry*, 1769. *Clifton: A Poem in Two Cantos*, 1778. *Vectis, The Isle of Wight: A Poem in Three Cantos*, 1782.

Sources: *Dictionary of National Biography*. Electronic Edition 1.1. Oxford University Press, 1997. *English Poetry, Second Edition Bibliography* (http://collections.chadwyck.co.uk/html/ep2/bibliography/g.htm). *English Poetry: Author Search*. Chadwyck-Healey Ltd., 1995 (http://www.lib.utexas.edu:8080/search/epoetry/author.html). *The Columbia Granger's Index to Poetry*. 11th ed. *The Columbia Granger's World of Poetry*, Columbia University Press, 2005 (http://www.columbiagrangers.org).

JONES, MARY (1707–1778)

The second of four children of Oliver Jones, barrel maker of St. Aldates, Oxford, she was an accomplished linguist. It is thought that she was a governess and that this brought her into friendship with Martha, daughter of John Lovelace, fourth Baron of Hurley. Martha was maid of honor to Queen Caroline and later housekeeper of Windsor Castle. Mary visited Martha and her husband, Lord Henry Beauclerk (they married in 1739), at their home in Windsor Forest, Berkshire. Her ballad "The Lass of the Hill" was published in 1742, and in 1750 her *Miscellanies in Prose and Verse* was published by subscription in Oxford. Many of her poems were published in the *London Magazine*, and "her gentle satires on the lot of talented women, who lacked means, are among the most accomplished poems written by women in the eighteenth century" (DNB). She lived all of her life in Oxford and was postmistress when she died. Some of her other poems: "After the Small Pox," "An Epistle to Lady Bowyer," "Epistle from Fern Hill," "Soliloquy on an Empty Purse," "Stella's Epitaph."

Sources: *Dictionary of National Biography*. Electronic Edition 1.1. Oxford University Press, 1997. *Eighteenth Century Women Poets: An Oxford Anthology*. Roger Lonsdale, ed. Oxford University Press, 1989. *Poetry by English Women: Elizabethan to Victorian*, R.E. Pritchard, ed. Continuum, 1990. *The Columbia Granger's Index to Poetry*. 11th ed. *The Columbia Granger's World of Poetry*, Columbia University Press, 2005 (http://www.columbiagrangers.org).

JONES, SAMUEL (d. 1732)

Thought to have been the natural child of Hugh Machell of Crackenthorpe Hall, Appleby, Cumbria. He started as a clerk and from 1709 to 1731 was queen's searcher in the custom house of Whitby,

North Yorkshire. His *Poetical Miscellanies* were published in 1714. *Whitby: A Poem Occasioned by Mr. Andrew Long's Recovery from the Jaundice by Drinking of Whitby Spaw* [spa] *Waters* was published in 1718. Jones died at his house in Grape Lane, Whitby, and was buried in the parish church of St. Mary. Some of his other poems: "Poverty, in Imitation of Milton," "The Force of Love," "The Ploughman, in Imitation of Milton."

Sources: *Dictionary of National Biography.* Electronic Edition 1.1. Oxford University Press, 1997. *The Columbia Granger's Index to Poetry.* 11th ed. *The Columbia Granger's World of Poetry,* Columbia University Press, 2005 (http:// www.columbiagrangers.org). *The New Oxford Book of Eighteenth Century Verse.* Roger Lonsdale, ed. Oxford University Press, 1984.

JONES, SIR WILLIAM (1746–1794)

Born in London of Welsh parentage, the youngest child of William Jones, he was educated at Harrow School and graduated M.A. from University College, Oxford, in 1773. A language prodigy, by the end of his life he had learned 28 languages, including Chinese, often by teaching himself. After several years in translating and scholarship, for financial reasons, he turned to the study of law and was called to the bar in 1774. He was knighted in 1783 and took up his appointment as judge of the supreme court in Calcutta. His reputation as an Oriental scholar rests on his *Grammar of the Persian Language* (1771) and similar works, including *The Moallakat, or the Seven Arabian Poems which were suspended on the Temple at Mecca,* published in 1783. He died in Calcutta and was buried there. Some of his (in English) poems: "A Chinese Ode Paraphrased," "A Hymn to Indra," "An Ode in Imitation of Callistratus," "Epigram," "From the Persian Poem of Hatifi," "Laura, an Elegy from Petrarch," "Sonnet, to G. Hardynge Esq.," "The First Nemean Ode of Pindar," "The Muse Recalled."

Sources: *Dictionary of National Biography.* Electronic Edition 1.1. Oxford University Press, 1997. *Encyclopædia Britannica Ultimate Reference Suite DVD, 2006. English Poetry: Author Search.* Chadwyck-Healey Ltd., 1995 (http://www.lib.utexas.edu:8080/search/epoetry/author. html). *The National Portrait Gallery* (www.npg.org.uk). *The Columbia Granger's Index to Poetry.* 11th ed. *The Columbia Granger's World of Poetry,* Columbia University Press, 2005 (http://www.columbiagrangers.org). *The Oxford Companion to English Literature.* 6th edition. Margaret Drabble, ed. Oxford University Press, 2000. *The Poetical Works of Sir William Jones.* Thomas Park, ed. J. Sharpe, 1808.

JONSON, BEN (1572–1637)

Benjamin Jonson is generally regarded as the second most important English dramatist, after William Shakespeare, during the reign of James I. His bricklayer stepfather managed to send Ben to Westminster School for a time, after which he followed his stepfather's trade. He fought with the English forces in the Netherlands before becoming a strolling player and by 1597 he was writing plays for Philip Henslowe, the leading impresario for the public theatre. Although he wrote tragedies and masques, he is better know for his comedies; the best known are: *Every Man in His Humor* (1598), *Volpone* (1606), *The Alchemist* (1610), and *Bartholomew Fair* (1614). He was made poet laureate in 1619. Never careful with money and, in spite of gifts from the king, he died in great poverty in a house between Westminster Abbey and St. Margaret's church. He is buried in the nave and commemorated in Poets' Corner of Westminster Abbey. Some of his poems: "Author ad Librum," "Ben Jonson's Grace before King James," "Ben Jonson's Sociable Rules for the Apollo," "Charles Cavendish to His Posterity," "Come, My Celia," "The Witches' Song," "To True Soldiers."

Sources: *Dictionary of National Biography.* Electronic Edition 1.1. Oxford University Press, 1997. *Encyclopædia Britannica Ultimate Reference Suite DVD, 2006. English Poetry: Author Search.* Chadwyck-Healey Ltd., 1995 (http://www.lib.utexas.edu:8080/search/epoetry/author. html). *The National Portrait Gallery* (www.npg.org.uk). *Selected Poems of Ben Jonson.* Ian Donaldson, ed. Oxford University Press, 1995. *The Columbia Granger's Index to Poetry.* 11th ed. *The Columbia Granger's World of Poetry,* Columbia University Press, 2005 (http://www.columbia grangers.org). *The Complete Poems of Ben Jonson.* George Parfitt, ed. Penguin Books, 1988. *The Oxford Companion to English Literature.* 6th edition. Margaret Drabble, ed. Oxford University Press, 2000. *Westminster Abbey Official Guide* (no date).

JORDAN, THOMAS (?1612–1685)

Born in London, he was a boy player at the Red Bull Theatre, Clerkenwell. While in His Majesty's Revels Company in 1640, he performed the part of Lepida in the play *Messalin*. In 1639 he recited one of his poems before Charles I and continued to write poetry when, in 1642, all stage plays were banned. After the Restoration, Jordan wrote dedications, commendatory verses, panegyric broadsides in support of General Monck, and several pamphlets. He resumed his drama and acting, playing the part of Captain Penniless in his own plays *Money is an Ass,* produced in 1668. He was poet of the Corporation of London from 1671 until he died. Some of his poetry publications: *Poeticall Varieties or Variety of Fancies,* 1637. *Piety and Poetry,* 1646. *A Royal Arbour of Loyall Poesie, consisting of Poems and Songs,* 1664. *Wit in a Wildernesse of Promiscuous Poetrie,* 1664. *Pictures of Passions, Fancies, and Affections,* 1665. Some of his poems: "A Defence for Musick," "A Double Acrostic on Mrs. Susanna Blunt," "An Elegy of his

Mistress Fidelia," "Pyms Anarchy," "The Careless Gallant."

Sources: *Dictionary of National Biography.* Electronic Edition 1.1. Oxford University Press, 1997. *English Poetry: Author Search.* Chadwyck-Healey Ltd., 1995 (http://www.lib.utexas.edu:8080/search/epoetry/author.html). *Poetry for Pleasure: A Choice of Poetry and Verse on a Variety of Themes.* Ian Parsons, ed. W.W. Norton, 1977. *The Cambridge History of English and American Literature in 18 Volumes,* 1907–21. New York: Putnam, 1907–1921. *The Columbia Granger's Index to Poetry.* 11th ed. *The Columbia Granger's World of Poetry,* Columbia University Press, 2005 (http://www.columbiagrangers.org). *The New Penguin Book of English Verse.* Paul Keegan, ed. Penguin Books, 2000. *The Oxford Book of Seventeenth Century Verse.* H.J.C. Grierson and G. Bullough, eds. Oxford University Press, 1934.

JOSEPH, JENNY (1932–)

One of Britain's foremost living poets, she was born in Birmingham and read English literature at St. Hilda's College, Oxford. She has done various jobs; journalism in England and 18 months in Johannesburg, South Africa, working for *Drum Publications*; lecturing in English literature and language; and being a pub landlady. Her first book, *The Unlooked-for Season* (1960), won her a Gregory Award, and for *Rose in the Afternoon* (1974) she won a Cholmondeley Award. Many more awards followed. *All the Things I See* (2000) is a poetry selection for children. Her book, *Led by the Nose: A Garden of Smells* (2004), is a month-by-month memoir in which she captures the smells and senses of her Gloucestershire garden. Her witty poem "Warning"— about growing old — was the inspiration for the "Red Hat Society" founded in 1998 by Sue Ellen Cooper of Fullerton, California. A BBC poll found "Warning" to be the most popular 20th Century poem. Some of her other poems: "Abstract Study — Circles," "Against the Personality Cult," "An Animal Story," "An Exile in Devon," "Dawn Walkers," "Fables," "The Road from Glastonbury," "Zenith."

Sources: *Cambium Gardening* (http://www.cambiumgardening.com/books/bonsai/). *Biography of Jenny Joseph* (http://www.wheniamanoldwoman.com/pages/348545/). *Poetry with an Edge.* Neil Astley, ed. Bloodaxe Books, 1988. *Selected Poems of Jenny Joseph.* Bloodaxe Books, 1992. *The Columbia Granger's Index to Poetry.* 11th ed. *The Columbia Granger's World of Poetry,* Columbia University Press, 2005 (http://www.columbiagrangers.org). *The Oxford Companion to English Literature.* 6th edition. Margaret Drabble, ed. Oxford University Press, 2000. *Wikipedia, the Free Encyclopedia* (http://en.wikipedia.org/wiki/Wikipedia).

JOSEPH OF EXETER (fl. 1190)

Medieval Latin poet whose Latin name is Josephus Iscanus, and in his poems he says he a native of Exeter, Devon, and the fellow-townsman and lifelong friend of Baldwin, archbishop of Canterbury.

While he was studying in France, in 1188, Archbishop Baldwin invited Joseph to join him on the Third Crusade to the Holy Land (he had parted with King Richard at Marseilles.) The bishop died in the Holy Land and Joseph returned home. Nothing more is known of his life but he goes down in history as one of the best of medieval Latin poets. Although he is probably best known for his *De Bello Trojano* (c. 1184) — an epic poem in six books, written in the style of Virgil — his adventures in the Crusade were recounted in *Antiocheis.* His poems: "Panegyricus ad Henricum," "De Institutione Cyri," "Nugæ Amatoriæ," "Epigrammata," "Diversi generis Carmina."

Sources: *Dictionary of National Biography.* Electronic Edition 1.1. Oxford University Press, 1997. *Great Books Online* (www.bartleby.com).

JOYCE, JAMES AUGUSTINE (1882–1941)

Dublin-born novelist and poet, he was one of the significant figures in twentieth century English literature. Educated at Jesuit schools and Belvedere College, Dublin, he graduated from University College, Dublin, where he studied languages, in 1902. With his wife Nora and their family, he lived most of his life abroad. He is best known for his novel *Ulysses,* published in parts in *The Little Review* and *The Egoist,* and in book form in Paris in 1922. Its publication was banned in Britain as being obscene and for the same reason, until 1933, in the United States. His other great work is *Finnegans Wake* (1939). He died in Zürich after an operation for a perforated duodenal ulcer. The Joyce Museum, Dublin, contains pictures, papers, and first editions of Joyce's books. Some of his poetry publications: *Chamber Music,* 1907. *Poems Pennyeach,* 1927. *Collected Poems,* 1937. Some of his poems: "A Flower Given to My Daughter," "An Advertisement for Finnegans Wake," "Bahnhofstrasse," "On the Beach at Fontana," "She Weeps over Rahoon," "Watching the Needleboats at San Sabba."

Sources: *Collected Poems of James Joyce.* Viking Press, 1946. *Dictionary of National Biography.* Electronic Edition 1.1. Oxford University Press, 1997. *Encyclopædia Britannica Ultimate Reference Suite DVD,* 2006. *First Lines, Poems Written in Youth, from Herbert to Heaney.* Jon Stallworthy, ed. Carcanet, 1987. *The National Portrait Gallery* (www.npg.org.uk). *Poems for the Millennium: The University of California Book of Modern and Postmodern Poetry. Vol. 2.* Jerome Rothenberg and Pierre Joris, eds. University of California Press, 1998. *The Columbia Granger's Index to Poetry.* 11th ed. *The Columbia Granger's World of Poetry,* Columbia University Press, 2005 (http://www.columbiagrangers.org). *The Oxford Companion to English Literature.* 6th edition. Margaret Drabble, ed. Oxford University Press, 2000.

JOYCE, TREVOR (1947–　)

Irish poet born in Dublin, he has lived in Cork since 1984. He read philosophy and English at University College, Dublin, and mathematical sciences at University College, Cork. In 1966 he co-founded New Writers' Press (NWP) in Dublin with Michael Smith, and was founding editor of NWP's journal, *The Lace Curtain*. In 1983 he visited the People's Republic of China as a poet at the invitation of the Chinese government. He has lectured and given public readings throughout Ireland, the U.K. and the U.S.A. He was the founder of the Cork International Poetry Festival in 1997 and its director since then. He is a member of Aosdána, the Irish affiliation of artists. Since January 2000 he has been a full-time writer. Some of his publications: *Sole Glum Trek*, 1967. *Watches*, 1969. *Pentahedron*, 1972. *The Poems of Sweeny Peregrine*, 1976. *Stone Floods*, 1995. *Syzygy*, 1998. *Without Asylum*, 1999. *With the First Dream of Fire They Hunt the Cold: A Body of Work 1966–2000*, 2001. Some of his poems: "Chimaera," "Cold Course," "Cry Help," "Parallax," "The Drift," "The Net," "The Turlough," "Tohu-bohu."

Sources: *Anthology of Twentieth-Century British and Irish Poetry*. Keith Tuma, ed. Oxford University Press, 2001. *Biography of Trevor Joyce* (http://www.irishwriters-online.com/trevorjoyce.html). *Sound Eye* (http://indigo.ie/~tjac/Poets/Randolph_Healy/randolph_healy.htm). *The Columbia Granger's Index to Poetry*. 11th ed. *The Columbia Granger's World of Poetry*, Columbia University Press, 2005 (http://www.columbiagrangers.org).

KAVANAGH, PATRICK JOSEPH (1904–1967)

Irish poet born near Inniskeen, County Monaghan, son of a shoemaker and farmer. He tried his hand at shoemaking, gave it up and spent the next 20 years working on the family farm, educating himself and writing poetry. He had some poems published in a local newspaper in the early 1930s and moved to Dublin in 1939, where he became a journalist. In spite of the fact that the Dublin literary people poked fun at "That Monaghan Boy," he was appointed to the faculty of English in University College, Dublin, in 1955. His epic poem *The Great Hunger* (1942) put him in the front rank of modern Irish poets. He lived with lung cancer from 1955 and died in Dublin of bronchitis. Some of his other poetry publications: *Ploughman and Other Poems*, 1936. *A Soul for Sale*, 1947. *Come Dance with Kitty Stobling*, 1960. *Collected Poems*, 1964. Some of his poems: "A Christmas Childhood," "Canal Bank Walk," "Father Mat," "If Ever You Go to Dublin Town," "Inniskeen Road: July Evening," "Lines Written on a Seat on the Grand Canal, Dublin," "Potato Spraying."

Sources: *Anthology of Twentieth-Century British and Irish Poetry*. Keith Tuma, ed. Oxford University Press, 2001. *Chief Modern Poets of Britain and America*. 5th edition. Gerald DeWitt Sanders, and John Herbert Nelson, ed., Macmillan, 1970. *Contemporary Irish Poetry: An Anthology*. Anthony Bradley, ed. University of California Press. New and rev. ed., 1988. *Encyclopædia Britannica Ultimate Reference Suite DVD*, 2006. *Ireland in Poetry* Charles Sullivan, ed. Harry N. Abrams, 1990. *Irish Poetry after Yeats: Seven Poets*. Maurice Harmon, ed. Little, Brown, 1979. *The National Portrait Gallery* (www.npg.org.uk). *Poemhunter* (www.poemhunter.com). *The Columbia Granger's Index to Poetry*. 11th ed. *The Columbia Granger's World of Poetry*, Columbia University Press, 2005 (http://www.columbiagrangers.org). *The Oxford Companion to English Literature*. 6th edition. Margaret Drabble, ed. Oxford University Press, 2000.

KAY, JACKIE (1961–　)

Born in Edinburgh, Scotland, to a Scottish mother and a Nigerian father, she was adopted by a Glasgow couple who were communists and took their children on anti-apartheid protests and peace rallies. She studied at the Royal Scottish Academy of Music and Drama and read English at Stirling University. In 1985, now in London, the Theatre of Black Women commissioned her to write a play; *Chiaroscuro* was performed in 1986 at the Soho Polytechnic, London. She now lives in Manchester, Lancashire. She has published short stories and novels. Her poetry publications: *The Adoption Papers*, 1991 (won two awards and a commendation by the Forward Poetry Prize judges in 1992). *Other Lovers*, 1993 (explores the search for identity grounded in the experience of slavery). *Off Color*, 1998 (explores themes of sickness, health and disease through personal experience and metaphor). *Life Mask*, 2005 (poems that show how appearances are deceptive, and how many faces we make up in one face). Some of her poems: "Baby Lazarus," "Bette Davis," "Dance of the Cherry Blossom," "Generations," "Photo in the Locket," "The Waiting Lists," "Twelve Bar Bessie," "What Jenny Knows."

Sources: *A Dangerous Knowing: Four Black Women Poets*: Barbara Burford, Gabriela Pearse, Grace Nichols, Jackie Kay. Grace Nichols, ed. Sheba, 1985. *British Council Arts* (http://www.contemporarywriters.com). *Chloe Plus Olivia: An Anthology of Lesbian Literature from the Seventeenth Century to the Present*. Lillian Faderman, ed. Viking Penguin, 1994. *Emergency Kit: Poems for Strange Times*. Jo Shapcott and Matthew Sweeney, ed. Faber and Faber, 1996. *Knitting Circle, Jackie Kay* (http://myweb.lsbu.ac.uk/~stafflag/jackiekay.html). *New Women Poets*. Carol Rumens, ed. Bloodaxe Books, 1990. *The Columbia Granger's Index to Poetry*. 11th ed. *The Columbia Granger's World of Poetry*, Columbia University Press, 2005 (http://www.columbiagrangers.org). *The New British Poetry, 1968–88*. Gillian Allnutt, Fred D'Aguiar and Ken Edwards, eds. Grafton Books, 1989. *The New Oxford Book of*

Children's Verse. Neil Philip, ed. Oxford University Press, 1996. *The Oxford Companion to English Literature.* 6th edition. Margaret Drabble, ed. Oxford University Press, 2000.

KEATS, JOHN (1795–1821)

Born into a working-class family, Keats by the age of 14 was an orphan and caring for his younger siblings. After education at Clark's School, Enfield, he was apprenticed to a surgeon and was licensed to practice as an apothecary in 1816. In the same year, his poem "O Solitude" was published by Leigh Hunt (see Hunt, James Henry Leigh) in the *Examiner*. He knew Wordsworth and Shelley (see entries) and began to participate in the activities of literary people in London. In 1818 his brother Tom died of tuberculosis, and within a year Keats too was stricken with the disease. In search of a better climate, he went to Italy, and died in Rome. He had asked that his epitaph read, *Here lies one whose name was writ in water.* He is memorialized by a tablet in Poets' Corner, Westminster Abbey. It is probable that Keats produced more great poetry at an earlier age than any other poet. Some of his other publications: *Sleep and Poetry*, 1816. *Hyperion*, 1818. *Lamia*, 1819. *Ode to a Nightingale*, 1819. *Ode to Psyche*, 1819. *The Eve of St. Agnes*, 1819. *To Autumn*, 1819.

Sources: *Dictionary of National Biography.* Electronic Edition 1.1. Oxford University Press, 1997. *Encyclopædia Britannica Ultimate Reference Suite DVD*, 2006. *English Poetry: Author Search.* Chadwyck-Healey Ltd., 1995 (http://www.lib.utexas.edu:8080/search/epoetry/author.html). *Biography and Works of John Keats* (http://www.john-keats.com). *The National Portrait Gallery* (www.npg.org.uk). *The Columbia Granger's Index to Poetry.* 11th ed. *The Columbia Granger's World of Poetry,* Columbia University Press, 2005 (http://www.columbiagrangers.org). *The Complete Poems of John Keats.* John Barnard, ed. Penguin Books, 1988. *The Oxford Companion to English Literature.* 6th edition. Margaret Drabble, ed. Oxford University Press, 2000. *Westminster Abbey Official Guide* (no date). *Wikipedia, the Free Encyclopedia* (http://en.wikipedia.org/wiki/Wikipedia).

KEBLE, JOHN (1792–1866)

Born at Fairford, Gloucestershire, the son of a clergyman, he graduated with a double first-class honors from Corpus Christi College, Oxford, in 1811. In the same year he was elected to a fellowship at Oriel and held several academic posts at Oxford. He was ordained in 1816 while still at Oxford and served at various parishes, including Hursley, near Winchester, Hampshire, from 1836 until he died. He was professor of poetry at Oxford from 1831 to 1841 and is the acknowledged leader of the Oxford Movement, also known as Tractarians, because they published their views of Anglo-Catholicism in *Tracts for the Times* (1833–1841). Among his books of verse

are: *The Psalter or Psalms of David* (1839) and the poems for childhood, *Lyra Innocentium* (1846). He also wrote numerous hymn lyrics, including "Sun of My Soul, Thou Savior Dear." Keble College, Oxford, was founded in his honor in 1869. He is buried at Hursley and is memorialized by a stone in Poets' Corner of Westminster Abbey. Some of his other poems: "Address to Poets," "Burial of the Dead," "Fairford Again," "Holy is the Sick Man's Room," "The Exe below Tiverton at Sunrise."

Sources: *A Sacrifice of Praise: An Anthology of Christian Poetry in English from Caedmon to the Mid–Twentieth Century.* James H. Trott, ed. Cumberland House Publishing, 1999. *Dictionary of National Biography.* Electronic Edition 1.1. Oxford University Press, 1997. *Encyclopædia Britannica Ultimate Reference Suite DVD*, 2006. *English Poetry: Author Search.* Chadwyck-Healey Ltd., 1995 (http://www.lib.utexas.edu:8080/search/epoetry/author.html). *Miscellaneous Poems of the Reverend J. Keble.* James Parker and Co., 1870. *The National Portrait Gallery* (www.npg.org.uk). *The Columbia Granger's Index to Poetry.* 11th ed. *The Columbia Granger's World of Poetry,* Columbia University Press, 2005 (http://www.columbiagrangers.org). *The Oxford Companion to English Literature.* 6th edition. Margaret Drabble, ed. Oxford University Press, 2000. *Westminster Abbey Official Guide* (no date).

KELLY, ISABELLA (?1759–1857)

She was born at Cairnburgh Castle (off the coast of Mull, Scotland), the daughter of William Fordyce, a military officer who was in the service of George III, though in time he fell from favor at court. In 1789, she married Robert Hawke Kelly, an officer of the East India Company in Madras. Apparently deserted by her husband, she turned to writing and published a total of sixteen books in her career. In 1816 she married Mr. Hedgeland, a wealthy merchant, who died four years later, leaving her well provided for. She died in London following an accident. Some of her publications: *A Collection of Poems and Fables*, 1794. *Madeline or, The Castle of Montgomery*, 1794 (novel). *Joscelina: or, The Rewards of Benevolence*, 1797 (novel). *The Baron's Daughter: A Gothic Romance*, 1802. *Poems and Fables on Several Occasions* 1805 and 1807. *The Child's French Grammar*, 1805. Some of her poems: "To a Brother, on Entering the Army," "To a Wandering Husband, from a Deserted Wife," "To an Unborn Infant" (an elegy on her dead son), "To the Memory of the Lamented Mr. Robert Hawke K–y" (an elegy).

Sources: *The Treshnish Isles and Cairnburgh Castle, Mull* (http://www.mull-historical-society.co.uk/cairnburgh-castle.htm). *Dictionary of National Biography.* Electronic Edition 1.1. Oxford University Press, 1997. *Eighteenth Century Women Poets: An Oxford Anthology.* Roger Lonsdale, ed. Oxford University Press, 1989. *English Poetry, Second Edition Bibliography* (http://collections.chadwyck.co.uk/html/ep2/bibliography/g.htm). *Scottish Women Poets of the*

Romantic Period (http://www.alexanderstreet2.com/SWRP Live/bios/S7032-D001.html). *The Columbia Granger's Index to Poetry.* 11th ed. *The Columbia Granger's World of Poetry,* Columbia University Press, 2005 (http://www.co lumbiagrangers.org).

KELLY, THOMAS (1769–1855)

Born in Kellyville, County Queens, Ireland, son of an Irish judge, he graduated with honors from Trinity College, Dublin, then pursued legal studies at the Temple Bar, London. While there he experienced a religious conversion through reading a Hebrew concordance of the Old Testament. He abandoned law and was ordained in the Anglican faith. His evangelical zeal caused the Church authorities to ban him from preaching in Anglican churches in the Dublin diocese, so he left the Church of England and founded the "Kellyites," whose meeting place was in Duke Street, Dublin. Further meeting places were opened in other towns. He died in Dublin. Between 1804 and 1838 he produced eight editions of his hymnals; the final edition contained 767 hymns, many of which are still used in worship. Some of his publications: *A Collection of Psalms and Hymns,* 1802. *Hymns on Various Passages of Scriptures,* 1804. *Hymns of Thomas Kelly, not before Published,* 1815. Some of his hymns/poems: "The Head That Once Was Crowned with Thorns," "Look, ye saints! The sight is glorious," "We sing praise of him who died," "The Lord is Risen Indeed!"

Sources: *A Sacrifice of Praise: An Anthology of Christian Poetry in English from Caedmon to the Mid–Twentieth Century.* James H. Trott, ed. Cumberland House Publishing, 1999. *Biography of Thomas Kelly; Christian History Institute* (http://chi.gospelcom.net/DAILYF/2002/07/daily-07-13-2002.shtml). *Biography of Thomas Kelly* (http://www.evangelical-times.org/articles/may05/may05a12.htm). *The Columbia Granger's Index to Poetry.* 11th ed (http://www.columbiagrangers.org). *The Cyber Hymnal* (http://www.cyberhymnal.org/index.htm). *The Treasury of Religious Verse.* Donald T. Kauffman, ed. Fleming H. Revell, 1962.

KEN, THOMAS (1637–1711)

The son of an attorney, he was born at Great, or at Little, Berkhampstead, Hertfordshire. He was educated at Winchester College and graduated B.A. (1661) and M.A. (1664) from New College, Oxford, and took the degree of doctor of divinity in 1679. He held a tutorship at New College, lecturing on logic and mathematics. From 1679 to 1680 he was chaplain at the Hague to Mary, wife of William II, Prince of Orange. He was one of the chaplains to Charles II and in 1685 was appointed bishop of Bath and Wells. In 1688 he, with five other bishops, was imprisoned in the Tower of London and tried for sedition (but were later acquitted) for refusing to publish in their dioceses the *Declaration of Indulgence* of James II (toward Roman Catholics). For refusing to swear allegiance to the new regime of William and Mary, Ken was deprived of his office in 1691 and spent the remaining 20 years of his life in retirement. Some of his hymns/poems: "An Anodyne," "An Evening Hymn," "Direct This Day," "Morning Hymn," "Praise God, from Whom all Blessings Flow (The Doxology)," "The Priest of Christ."

Sources: *A Sacrifice of Praise: An Anthology of Christian Poetry in English from Caedmon to the Mid–Twentieth Century.* James H. Trott, ed. Cumberland House Publishing, 1999. *Dictionary of National Biography.* Electronic Edition 1.1. Oxford University Press, 1997. *Encyclopædia Britannica Ultimate Reference Suite DVD,* 2006. *The Columbia Granger's Index to Poetry.* 11th ed. *The Columbia Granger's World of Poetry,* Columbia University Press, 2005 (http://www.columbiagrangers.org). *The Cyber Hymnal* (http://www.cyberhymnal.org/index.htm). *The Family Album of Favorite Poems.* Ernest P. Edward, ed. Grosset and Dunlap, 1959. *The Oxford Book of Children's Verse.* Iona Opie and Peter Opie, eds. Oxford University Press, 1973. *The Oxford Book of Christian Verse.* Lord David Cecil, ed. Oxford University Press, 1940. *The Oxford Companion to English Literature.* 6th edition. Margaret Drabble, ed. Oxford University Press, 2000. *The Treasury of Religious Verse.* Donald T. Kauffman, ed. Fleming H. Revell, 1962.

KENDALL, TIMOTHY (fl. 1577)

Born in North Aston, Oxfordshire, he was educated at Eton and Magdalen Hall, Oxford, but left without graduating and became a law student at Staple Inn, London. In 1577 he published *Flowers of Epigrammes* (see Sources for full title), a collection in which he lists all the names of authors. Some of his poems: "A Tyrant In Sleep, Naught Differeth from a Common Man," "Calimachus (From Lucianus [B.C. 125, D. After 180])," "To One Diuersly Conditioned," "An Epitaph Vpon the Death of His Deare Aunt Ellen Kendall: Which Died, and Lyes Buried at Bloxam," "Desire of Dominion," "Of a Good Prince and an Evil," "Of a Tiger and a Lion," "The Difference Between a King and a Tyrant," "Timothe Kendal to the Reader," "To His Cosen Ihon Kendall," "Upon the Grave of a Beggar."

Sources: *Dictionary of National Biography.* Electronic Edition 1.1. Oxford University Press, 1997. *English Poetry, Second Edition Bibliography* (http://collections.chadwyck.co.uk/html/ep2/bibliography/g.htm). *English Poetry: Author Search.* Chadwyck-Healey Ltd., 1995 (http://www.lib.utexas.edu:8080/search/epoetry/author.html). *Flovvers of Epigrammes, Ovt of sundrie the moste singular authours selected, as well auncient as late writers. Pleasant and profitable to the expert readers of quicke capacitie: By Timothe Kendall.* London: Imprinted. by Ihon Shepperd (1577). *The Columbia Granger's Index to Poetry.* 11th ed. *The Columbia Granger's World of Poetry,* Columbia University Press, 2005 (http://www.columbiagrangers.org). *The New Oxford Book of Sixteenth Century Verse.* Emrys Jones, ed. Oxford

University Press, 1991. *The Oxford Book of Classical Verse in Translation.* Adrian Poole and Jeremy Maule, eds. 1995.

KENNEDY, RANN (1772–1851)

Born at Shenstone, Staffordshire, the son of Benjamin Kennedy, a surgeon who died in 1784, he graduated M.A. from St. John's, Cambridge, in 1798, where he formed a lasting friendship with S.T. Coleridge. He took holy orders and spent the next 50 years at St. Paul's, Birmingham, including 38 years as a master at King Edward's School, Birmingham, only giving up when he inherited a small property called the *Fox Hollies* near Birmingham. He died at his son Charles's house in St. Paul's Square, Birmingham. He contributed notes to the Italian edition of Byron's poems published in 1842 and assisted his son, Charles Rann Kennedy, in the translation of *Virgil*, published in 1849. Some of his publications: *A Poem on the Death of the Princess Charlotte of Wales*, 1817. *A Church of England Psalm-Book*, 1821. *Thoughts on the Music and Words of Psalmody*, 1821 (6th edition 1827). *A Tribute in Verse to the Character of George Canning*, 1827. *Britain's Genius: A Mask, on Occasion of the Marriage of Victoria, Queen of Great Britain—To Which is Added the Reign of Youth, a Lyrical Poem*, 1840.

Sources: *Dictionary of National Biography.* Electronic Edition 1.1. Oxford University Press, 1997.

KENNEDY, WALTER (1460?–1508?)

One of the "Scottish Chaucerians," the third son of Gilbert, first lord Kennedy. The family was connected to King Robert III (reigned 1390–1406); Walter's uncle, James Kennedy, bishop of St. Andrews, was one of the regents during the minority of James III (1460–1488). The family held great estates in the west of Scotland, especially in Carrick, Ayrshire, one of the most important of the minor noble houses of Scotland. He graduated M.A. from Glasgow College in 1478. Kennedy and William Dunbar (see entry) were rivals in the *Flyting* [scolding or wrangling] *of Dunbar and Kennedie* (1508) in which the two poets alternate in heaping outrageous abuse on each another (though without rancor), a favorite sport of the 16th-century Scots poets. In Dunbar's eyes Kennedy was a half-barbarous Celt, who always wore highland dress, spoke the Gaelic dialect, and resembled a leper on account of his lean neck, shriveled throat, and dry yellow skin. Some of Kennedy's other poems: "Ane Agit Manis Invective against Mouth Thankless," "Ane Ballat in Praise of Our Lady," "Honour with Age," "Pious Counsale," "The Passioun of Christ."

Sources: *Dictionary of National Biography.* Electronic Edition 1.1. Oxford University Press, 1997. *Encyclopædia Britannica Ultimate Reference Suite DVD*, 2006. *English*

Poetry: Author Search. Chadwyck-Healey Ltd., 1995 (http://www.lib.utexas.edu:8080/search/epoetry/author.html). *First Scottish Books* (Chepman and Myller Prints)— Digital Library (http://www.nls.uk/digitallibrary/chepman/page.htm). *The Columbia Granger's Index to Poetry.* 11th ed. *The Columbia Granger's World of Poetry*, Columbia University Press, 2005 (http://www.columbiagrangers.org). *The Oxford Book of Scottish Verse*, John MacQueen and Tom Scott, eds. Oxford University Press, 1966. *The Oxford Companion to English Literature.* 6th edition. Margaret Drabble, ed. Oxford University Press, 2000.

KENNEDY, WILLIAM (1799–1871)

Born in Dublin, the son of a manufacturer, he studied journalism at Belfast College in 1819, then at Dr. Lawson's seminary for dissenting students at Selkirk, Scotland. He worked for William Motherwell (see entry) on *Paisley Magazine*. Moving to London in 1833, he became secretary to the Earl of Durham, whom he accompanied to Canada. In 1839 he traveled in Texas and the United States to study local government in principal cities. He became Texas consul in London and British consul in Galveston from 1842 until Texas gained independence from Mexico in 1836, to became the 28th state in 1845. He died in Paris. His poem, "Lines, Written after a Visit to the Grave of My Friend, William Motherwell, November" (1847), is a tribute to their long friendship. Many of Kennedy's lyrics are in *Whistle Binkie* (1890) by Alexander Abernethy Ritchie. Some of Kennedy's other publications: *Fitful Fancies*, 1827 (a collection of short poems). *The Arrow and the Rose, and Other Poems*, 1830. *The Continental Annual and Romantic Cabinet for 1832*, 1831. *The Siege of Antwerp*, 1838 (an historical play). *The Rise, Progress, and Prospects of the Republic of Texas*, 1841.

Sources: *Dictionary of National Biography.* Electronic Edition 1.1. Oxford University Press, 1997. *Handbook of Texas Online: Kennedy, William* (http://www.tsha.utexas.edu/handbook/online/articles/KK/fke25.html). *ScotsteXt! Roughs* (http://www.scotstext.org/roughs/whistlebinkie/whistlebinkie%20_prefaces.asp). *The Poetical Works of William Motherwell.* Alexander Gardner, 1881. *The Texas Historical Commission* (http://www.thc.state.tx.us/triviafun/trvdefault.html).

KENNISH, WILLIAM (1799–1862)

Poet and inventor, he was born into a humble family from Maughold, Isle of Man, and started his working life as ploughboy, speaking only his native language. He joined the Royal Navy as an ordinary seaman in 1821 and rose to be a warrant officer, learning English on the way. Some of his many inventions: warship cannon fire and surveying instrument; the theodolite; changing the way the broadside was set up and used; the use of warship cannon on land; grey paint for naval warships instead of black, to make them less visible; artificial horizon, to compensate for the ship's deviation from the stars; steam engines, how to replace sails with steam; screw type ship propeller; and the pneumatic tube for document transport. In June 1832 he received the gold Isis Medal from the Society of Arts. The Admiralty gave him little credit so he resigned around 1841, and in 1844, he published *Mona's Isle and Other Poems* about his homeland. He emigrated to America and became attached to the United States admiralty, for which body he made a survey of Central America — the Panama Canal. He died in New York of tropical fever.

Sources: *Biography of William Kennish* (http://kennish. com/william). *Dictionary of National Biography.* Electronic Edition 1.1. Oxford University Press, 1997. *William Kennish Poet, Inventor, Engineer, Explorer* (http://www.isle-of-man.com/manxnotebook/iomnhas/v062p181.htm).

KENYON, JOHN (1784–1856)

He was born in Trelawney, Jamaica, where his father owned extensive sugar plantations. Both parents died while he was at school in Bristol. After that his education was desultory — Charterhouse, and Peterhouse, Cambridge, from 1802–1808, though he did not graduate. He married and settled at Woodlands, between Alfoxden and Nether Stowey in Somerset, where he met Coleridge (see entry) and other poets. He was generous in his giving of his considerable wealth to charitable causes, particularly in supporting Coleridge's family. Robert Browning (see entry) dedicated *Dramatic Romances and Lyrics* (1845) to Kenyon, and Elizabeth Browning dedicated *Aurora Leigh* (1864) to him in grateful remembrance of their friendship. Kenyon married twice and inherited fortunes from both wives, although he gave most of it away. He died at Cowes, Isle of Wight, and was buried in in Lewisham (London) churchyard. Some of his publications: *A Day at Tivoli: With Other Verses*, 1849. *Poems: For the Most Part Occasional*, 1838. *Rhymed plea for tolerance. In Two Dialogues. With a Prefatory Dialogue*, 1839. Some of his poems: "Champagne Rosée," "Childhood," "Destiny," "Freedom," "Gipsy Carol," "On a Florentine Picture by Albertinelli."

Sources: *Carmina Mariana: An English Anthology in Verse in Honour of or in Relation to the Blessed Virgin Mary.* Orby Shipley, ed. Burns and Oates, 1894. *Dictionary of National Biography.* Electronic Edition 1.1. Oxford University Press, 1997. *English Poetry, Second Edition Bibliography* (http://collections.chadwyck.co.uk/html/ep2/bibliography/g.htm). *English Poetry: Author Search.* Chadwyck-Healey Ltd., 1995 (http://www.lib.utexas.edu:8080/search/epoetry/author.html). *The National Portrait Gallery* (www.npg.org.uk). *The Columbia Granger's Index to Poetry.* 11th ed. *The Columbia Granger's World of Poetry,* Columbia University Press, 2005 (http://www.columbiagrangers.

org). *The Oxford Book of English Verse, 1250–1918.* Sir Arthur Quiller-Couch, ed. New edition, revised and enlarged, Oxford University Press, 1939.

KER, PATRICK (fl. 1691)

A Scottish Episcopalian who migrated to London during the reign of Charles II. His publications: *An Elegy on the Deplorable, and Never Enough to Be Lamented Death, of the Illustrious, and Serene Charles the II*, 1685. *Flosculum Poeticum. Poems Divine and Humane, Panegyrical, Satyrical, Ironical*, 1684 (which includes an artistic impression of Charles II hiding in the oak, and a number of scurrilous rhymes and anagrams on Oliver Cromwell). *The Conquest of Eloquence: Containing Two Witty Orations, The First Spoke by Ajax: The Second by Ulysses*, 1690. *The Map of Man's Misery: or, The Poor Man's Pocket-Book: Being a Perpetual Almanack of Spiritual Meditations or Compleat Directory for One Endless Week*, 1690 (which includes the poem *The Glass of Vain Glory*). *The Mournful Mite: Or the True Subject's Sigh. On the Death of the Illustrious and Serene Charles II*, 1685. *Scotland's Loyalty, Or, Sorrowfull Sighs on the Death of Our Late Sovereign His Sacred Majesty, Charles II*, 1685. *A Poem on the Coronation of James the II. King of Great-Britain, France and Ireland, andc. Who Was Crowned at Westminster-Abbey the 23 of April, 1685*, 1685.

Sources: *Dictionary of National Biography.* Electronic Edition 1.1. Oxford University Press, 1997. *English Poetry, Second Edition Bibliography* (http://collections.chadwyck.co.uk/html/ep2/bibliography/g.htm). *English Poetry: Author Search.* Chadwyck-Healey Ltd., 1995 (http://www.lib.utexas.edu:8080/search/epoetry/author.html).

KEYES, SIDNEY ARTHUR (1922–1943)

Born in Dartford, Kent, the only child of an army officer, he was brought up mainly by his grandparents after his mother died when he was six weeks old. He pays tribute to his grandfather's influence in "Elegy" and several other poems. An introspective child, he created an imaginary world of his own and by the time he left Tonbridge School he had written more than seventy poems, discovered in a manuscript book shortly after the war. A history scholarship took him to Queen's College, Oxford, in 1940, where he formed a friendship with the poet John Heath-Stubbs (see entry). With Michael Meyer he edited *Eight Oxford Poets* (1941). His *The Iron Laurel* was published in 1942. Commissioned into the Queen's Own Royal West Kent Regiment in September 1942, he was killed in Tunisia seven months later. A posthumous collection of poems, *The Cruel Solstice*, was published in 1943 and won the Hawthornden prize. Some of his other poems: "Advice for a Journey," "Death and the Plowman," "Europe's Prisoners," "Moonlight Night on the Port," "The Anti-Symbolist," "The Wilderness," "William Wordsworth."

Sources: *A Little Treasury of British Poetry.* Oscar Williams, ed. Scribner's, 1951. *Collected Poems (Poetry Pleiade) of Sidney Keyes.* Carcanet Press, 2002. *Dictionary of National Biography.* Electronic Edition 1.1. Oxford University Press, 1997. *Modern Poetry: American and British.* Kimon Friar, and John Malcom Brinnin, ed. Appleton-Century-Crofts, 1951. *Poetry of the World Wars.* Michael Foss, ed. Peter Bedrick Books, 1990. *The Columbia Granger's Index to Poetry.* 11th ed. *The Columbia Granger's World of Poetry,* Columbia University Press, 2005 (http://www.columbia grangers.org). *The Oxford Book of War Poetry.* Jon Stallworthy, Oxford University Press, 1984. *The Oxford Companion to English Literature.* 6th edition. Margaret Drabble, ed. Oxford University Press, 2000. *The War Poets Association* (http://www.warpoets.org/conflicts/ww2/keyes/).

KHALVATI, MIMI (1944–)

Born in Tehran, Iran, she grew up on the Isle of Wight, England, and was educated at the University of Neuchâtel, Switzerland, and at the Drama Centre and the School of African and Oriental Studies, London. She has worked as an actor and director in both the U.K. and Iran, and is coordinator of the Poetry School, London. She is a tutor at the Arvon Foundation (with centers in various parts of Britain) and has taught creative writing at universities and colleges in the U.S. and England. Khalvati was poet in residence at the Royal Mail, London, and has given readings of her work at festivals in Britain and mainland Europe. She won the 1994 Arts Council Writers' Award for her collection *Mirrorwork* (Carcanet Press 1995). Some of her other publications: *Entries on Light,* 1997. *Selected Poems,* 2000. *Tying the Song: A First Anthology from the Poetry School 1997–2000,* 2000 (co-editor, Pascale Petit, see entry). *The Chine,* 2002. *Entering the Tapestry: A Second Anthology from the Poetry School,* 2003 (co-editor, Graham Fawcett). Some of her poems: "Baba Mostafa," "Love in an English August," "Overblown Roses," "Rubaiyat."

Sources: *British Council Arts* (http://www.contemporarywriters.com). *English Literary Linguistic Studies: Franks Casket, Poems That Keep Ringing* (http://dspace.dial.pipex.com/town/walk/xen19/reviews.htm). *Poems of Mimi Khalvati* (http://www.shu.ac.uk/schools/cs/english/sheaf/khalvati.htm). *Making for Planet Alice: New Women Poets.* Maura Dooley, ed. Bloodaxe Books, 1997. *New Women Poets.* Carol Rumens, ed. Bloodaxe Books, 1990. *Parents: An Anthology of Poems by Women Writers.* Myra Schneider and Dilys Wood, eds. Enitharmon Press, 2000. *Poetry to Calm Your Soul.* Mimi Khalvati, ed. MQ Publications, 2005. *The Columbia Granger's Index to Poetry.* 11th ed. *The Columbia Granger's World of Poetry,* Columbia University Press, 2005 (http://www.columbiagrangers.org). *The New Exeter Book of Riddles.* Kevin Crossley-Holland and Lawrence Sail, ed. Enitharmon Press, 1999.

KICKHAM, CHARLES JOSEPH (1826–1882)

The son of local draper, he was born at Mullinahone, in County Tipperary, where the Anner flows and the Slievenamon mountain rises not far away. Exploding gunpowder so damaged his young eyes and ears that his hopes of a medical career were dashed, so he became a journalist. He was active in the Young Ireland Movement and the Tenant Right League. He became a Fenian about 1860 and one of the writers for the *Irish People* newspaper. He was arrested, tried for treason, and in 1866 sentenced to fourteen years' penal servitude, but served only four years in prisons in England. He died at Blackrock, near Dublin, and was buried in the Tipperary graveyard. Some of his publications: *Sally Cavanagh, or the Untenanted Graves,* 1869 (novel, written in prison). *Knockagow, or the Homes of Tipperary,* 1879 (novel). *Poems, Sketches, and Narratives Illustrative of Irish Life,* 1879. *For the Old Land, a Tale of Twenty Years Ago,* 1886. Some of his poems: "Patrick Sheehan" (set to music by Andy Stewart), "Rory of the Hill," "She Lived Beside the Anner," "The Irish Peasant Girl," "The Priest and his People."

Sources: *An Anthology of Irish Verse: The Poetry of Ireland from Mythological Times to the Present.* Padraic Colum, ed. Liveright, 1948. *Andy M. Stewart: By the Hush* (http://andymstewart.com/by-the-hush.htm). *Dictionary of National Biography.* Electronic Edition 1.1. Oxford University Press, 1997. *English Poetry, Second Edition Bibliography* (http://collections.chadwyck.co.uk/html/ep2/bibliography/g.htm). *Knocknagow, the history of the house* (http://www.exclassics.com/knockngw/kn2.htm). *She Lived Beside the Anner* (http://sniff.numachi.com/~rickheit/dtrad/pages/tiLNDMNTN.html). *Catholic Encyclopedia* (http://www.newadvent.org). *The Columbia Granger's Index to Poetry.* 11th ed. *The Columbia Granger's World of Poetry,* Columbia University Press, 2005 (http://www.columbia grangers.org). *The Valley Near Slievenamon, A Kickham Anthology: The Poems, Letters, Memoirs, Essays, Diary, and Addresses of Charles J. Kickham.* James Maher Mullinahone, ed. James Maher, 1942.

KILLIGREW, ANNE (1660–1685)

Born in St. Martin's Lane, London, she was the daughter of Henry Killigrew, doctor of divinity, master of the Savoy Hospital in the Strand, and chaplain to the Duke of York. Anne became maid of honor to Mary of Modena, Duchess of York but died of smallpox in her father's rooms in the cloisters of Westminster Abbey. She was buried in the chancel of St. John the Baptist's Chapel in the Savoy. In 1686 John Dryden wrote an ode: "To the Pious Memory of the Accomplished Young Lady Mrs. Anne Killigrew." Samuel Johnson considered this ode to be the noblest in the English language. *Poems by Mrs. Anne Killigrew* was published in 1685. Some of her poems: "A Farewell to Worldly Joys," "An Invective against Gold," "Alexandreis," "Cloris' Charms Dissolved by Eudora," "On Death," "On the Birth-Day of Queen Katherine," "On the Soft and Gentle Motions of Eudora," "Pastoral Dialogue," "The Complaint of a Lover," "The Discontent," "To the Queen," "Upon the Saying That My Verses Were Made by Another."

Sources: *Dictionary of National Biography.* Electronic Edition 1.1. Oxford University Press, 1997. *Early Modern Women Poets (1520–1700).* Jane Stevenson and Peter Davidson, ed. Oxford University Press, 2001. *English Poetry, Second Edition Bibliography* (http://collections.chadwyck.co.uk/html/ep2/bibliography/g.htm). *English Poetry: Author Search.* Chadwyck-Healey Ltd., 1995 (http://www.lib.utexas.edu:8080/search/epoetry/author.html). *The National Portrait Gallery* (www.npg.org.uk). *Poemhunter* (www.poemhunter.com). *The Broadview Anthology of Victorian Poetry and Poetic Theory.* Thomas J. Collins and Vivienne Rundle, ed. Broadview, 1999. *The Columbia Granger's Index to Poetry.* 11th ed. *The Columbia Granger's World of Poetry,* Columbia University Press, 2005 (http://www.columbiagrangers.org). *The Norton Anthology of Poetry.* 4th ed. Margaret Ferguson, Mary Jo Salter and Jon Stal, eds. W.W. Norton, 1996.

KING, HENRY (1592–1669)

Born the eldest son of John King, bishop of London, he was baptized at Worminghall, Buckinghamshire, and educated at Westminster School and Christ Church, Oxford. After being ordained, he took up a position at St. Paul's Cathedral, then in 1617 became archdeacon of Colchester in 1617. Soon afterwards he was made rector of Fulham and one of the royal chaplains, and doctor of divinity in 1625. He developed a life-long friendship with Izaak Walton and friendships with many other poets, to whom he dedicated poems — Ben Jonson, George Sandys and John Donne being a few (see entries). He became bishop of Chichester in 1641–2. His palace was captured when Chichester surrendered to the Parliamentarians in 1643. King died at Chichester and was buried in the cathedral. Some of his publications: *An Elegy Upon King Charles I,* 1648. *A Groane at the Fvnerall,* 1649. *Poems, Elegies, Paradoxes and Sonets,* 1664. *The Psalmes of David,* 1651. Some of his poems: "A Contemplation upon Flowers," "An Elegy upon My Best Friend," "My Midnight Meditation," "The Anniverse; an Elegy," "The Boyes Answer to the Blackmoor," "The Vow-Breakers."

Sources: *Dictionary of National Biography.* Electronic Edition 1.1. Oxford University Press, 1997. *Encyclopædia Britannica Ultimate Reference Suite DVD,* 2006. *English Poetry: Author Search.* Chadwyck-Healey Ltd., 1995 (http://www.lib.utexas.edu:8080/search/epoetry/author.html). *Jacobean and Caroline Poetry: An Anthology.* T.G.S. Cain, ed. Methuen, 1981. *The Columbia Granger's Index to Poetry.* 11th ed. *The Columbia Granger's World of Poetry,*

Columbia University Press, 2005 (http://www.columbiagrangers.org). *The Harper Anthology of Poetry.* John Frederick Nims, ed. Harper and Row, 1981. *The Oxford Book of Seventeenth Century Verse.* H.J.C. Grierson and G. Bullough, eds. Oxford University Press, 1934. *The Oxford Companion to English Literature.* 6th edition. Margaret Drabble, ed. Oxford University Press, 2000.

KING, WILLIAM (1663–1712)

Born in London, the son of Ezekiel King, from whom he inherited a small estate in Middlesex. Educated at Westminster School, King graduated M.A. from Christ Church, Oxford, in 1688 and was made doctor of civil law in 1692. He was secretary to Princess Anne (who was queen from 1702 to 1714) and judge of the admiralty court in Ireland. He wrote the poem "Mully of Mountown" in 1704 (Mountown is near Dublin; Mully was the red cow that furnished him with milk). He is buried in the North Cloister of Westminster Abbey. He is noted for his humorous and satirical writings. Some of his publications: *Some Remarks on the Tale of a Tub,* 1704. *Miscellanies in Prose and Verse,* 1709. *Historical Account of the Heathen Gods and Heroes,* 1710. *Rufinus, or the Favourite,* 1712. *Britain's Palladium,* 1712 (poetry). Some of his poems: "Apple Pye," "Imitation of Horace," "Orpheus and Eurydice (the Fairy Feast)," "The Art of Cookery," "The Art of Love," "The Art of Making Puddings," "The Beggar Woman," "The Furmetory."

Sources: *Dictionary of National Biography.* Electronic Edition 1.1. Oxford University Press, 1997. *Eighteenth-Century English Verse.* Dennis Davison, ed. Penguin Books, 1988. *Encyclopedia.com* (http://www.encyclopedia.com/html). *English Poetry, Second Edition Bibliography* (http://collections.chadwyck.co.uk/html/ep2/bibliography/g.htm). *English Poetry: Author Search.* Chadwyck-Healey Ltd., 1995 (http://www.lib.utexas.edu:8080/search/epoetry/author.html). *Fellow Mortals: An Anthology of Animal Verse.* Roy Fuller, ed. Macdonald and Evans, 1981. *The National Portrait Gallery* (www.npg.org.uk). *Oldpoetry* (www.oldpoetry.com). *The Columbia Granger's Index to Poetry.* 11th ed. *The Columbia Granger's World of Poetry,* Columbia University Press, 2005 (http://www.columbiagrangers.org). *The Faber Book of Useful Verse.* Simon Brett, ed. Faber and Faber, 1981. *The Oxford Companion to English Literature.* 6th edition. Margaret Drabble, ed. Oxford University Press, 2000. *Mully of Mountown.* See Samuel Johnson's Lives of the English Poets, 1779–1781 (http://www2.hn.psu.edu/Faculty/KKemmerer/poets/preface.htm). *Westminster Abbey Official Guide* (no date).

KINGSLEY, CHARLES (1819–1875)

Son of a clergyman, he was born at Holne Vicarage, Devonshire. Educated at King's College, London, he graduated in classics from Magdalene College, Cambridge, in 1842. In the same year he was ordained as curate of Eversley — on the borders of Hampshire and Berkshire — and became rector in

1844. He wrote many sermons, scientific and historical essays, pamphlets on social issues, historical romances, poems, and children's books. His novels *Alton Locke* (1850) and *Yeast, a Problem* (1851) take up the suffering of the working classes. He became chaplain to Queen Victoria (1859), professor of modern history at Cambridge (1860–1869), and canon of Westminster (1873). He died at Eversley, where he was buried; he is commemorated by a bust in the nave of Westminster Abbey. Some of his other publications: *Westword Ho!*, 1855. *The Heroes*, 1856. *Andromeda, and Other Poems*, 1858. *The Water-Babies*, 1863. *Poems*, 1875 (includes *The Saint's Tragedy*). Some of his ballads/poems: "A Christmas Carol," "A New Forest Ballad," "Alton Locke's Song," "Down to the Mothers," "Frank Leigh's Song," "Killarney," "The Watchman," "The Sands of Dee," "The Three Fishers."

Sources: *Dictionary of National Biography.* Electronic Edition 1.1. Oxford University Press, 1997. *Encyclopædia Britannica Ultimate Reference Suite DVD*, 2006. *English Poetry: Author Search.* Chadwyck-Healey Ltd., 1995 (http://www.lib.utexas.edu:8080/search/epoetry/author.html). *Poems. Vol. 2 of Charles Kingsley.* Macmillan and Co., 1884. *The Columbia Granger's Index to Poetry.* 11th ed. *The Columbia Granger's World of Poetry,* Columbia University Press, 2005 (http://www.columbiagrangers.org). *The Oxford Companion to English Literature.* 6th edition. Margaret Drabble, ed. Oxford University Press, 2000.

KINSELLA, THOMAS (1928–)

Born in Inchicore, Dublin, he was educated in the Irish language. Leaving University College, Dublin, without graduating, he joined the Irish Civil Service, where he worked at both the Land Commission and the Department of Finance. As well as writing poetry, editing the works of other poets, and translating Gaelic poems into English, he continued his university studies. He left the civil service in 1965 to take a teaching position at the University of Southern Illinois, where he was professor of English from 1967 to 1970, then professor of English at Temple University, Philadelphia, from 1970 to 1990. Although he retired from teaching in 1990, he continued writing, published some twenty books of poetry, and founded his own publishing company, Peppercanister, in Dublin in 1972. Some of his more recent publications: *Nightwalker and Other Poems*, 1968. *Notes from the Dead and Other Poems*, 1973. *One and Other Poems*, 1979. *St. Catherine's Clock*, 1987. *Poems From City Centre*, 1990. *Madonna and Other Poems*, 1991. Some of his poems: "Anniversaries," "Faith," "Mirror in February," "Old Harry," "Settings," "Songs of the Psyche," "Westland Row."

Sources: *Biography.ms* (http://www.biography.ms). *Carcanet Press* (http://www.carcanet.co.uk). *Collected Poems 1956–1994 of Thomas Kinsella.* Oxford University Press, 1996. *Collected Poems of Thomas Kinsella.* Carcanet Press, 2002. *Encyclopædia Britannica Ultimate Reference Suite DVD*, 2006. *The Columbia Granger's Index to Poetry.* 11th ed. *The Columbia Granger's World of Poetry,* Columbia University Press, 2005 (http://www.columbiagrangers.org). *Who's Who.* London: A & C Black, 2005.

KIPLING, JOSEPH RUDYARD (1865–1936)

He was born in Bombay (Mumbai), India, where his father was curator of the Lahore museum. From the age of six to eleven he was fostered at Southsea, England, and his education was mainly at the United Services College at Westward Ho, north Devon. At seventeen he returned to India and worked for seven years as a journalist. From then on his output of novels, poems, and children's stories (usually about life in India) was prodigious. He returned to England in 1889, and his reputation was enhanced in 1892 by the publication of *Barrack-Room Ballads*. In 1922 he was elected lord rector of St. Andrews University; honors were heaped upon him by many universities in Britain and Europe; he received the Nobel Prize for Literature in 1907. He died of a perforated duodenum at Burwash, Sussex, and was buried in Poets' Corner, Westminster Abbey. Some of his other poetry publications: *Departmental Ditties*, 1896. *The Seven Seas*, 1896. *The Five Nations*, 1903. *The Years Between*, 1919. Some of his poems: "An American," "Cuckoo Song," "Fuzzy Wuzzy Was a Bear," "If," "The Absent-Minded Beggar," "The Outlaws," "Verses on Games."

Sources: *Dictionary of National Biography.* Electronic Edition 1.1. Oxford University Press, 1997. *Encyclopædia Britannica Ultimate Reference Suite DVD*, 2006. *English Poetry: Author Search.* Chadwyck-Healey Ltd., 1995 (http://www.lib.utexas.edu:8080/search/epoetry/author.html). *Rudyard Kipling: Complete Verse, Definitive Edition.* Doubleday, 1989. *The Columbia Granger's Index to Poetry.* 11th ed. *The Columbia Granger's World of Poetry,* Columbia University Press, 2005 (http://www.columbiagrangers.org). *The Oxford Companion to English Literature.* 6th edition. Margaret Drabble, ed. Oxford University Press, 2000. *Westminster Abbey Official Guide* (no date).

KIRKUP, JAMES (1918–)

Born in South Shields, England, he was educated at the local high school and at Durham University. He held academic posts at Leeds University and at Kyoto University, Japan, where he was professor of English literature. He has published about thirty books from various publishers in Britain and abroad. His 1977 gay poem, *The love that dares to speak its name*, resulted in the first prosecution for blasphemous libel in over 50 years, and a suspended a sentence for the editor of *Gay News*, which published the poem. He was awarded the Japan P.E.N. prize for

International Poetry and the Japan Festival Prize for *A Book of Tanka* (translation of Japanese poems into English) (1997). He currently resides in Andorra. Some of his poetry publications: *The Drowned Sailor,* 1947. *A Correct Compassion,* 1952. *The Descent into the Cave,* 1957. *Paper Windows,* 1968. *A Bewick Bestiary,* 1971. *Islands in the Sky,* 2004. *No More Hiroshimas,* 2004. Some of his poems: "Baby's Drinking Song," "Gay Boys," "Japanese Fan," "Sumo Wrestlers," "The Astronaut," "The Love of Older Men," "The Zen Archer."

Sources: *A Green Place: Modern Poems.* William Jay Smith, ed. Delacorte Press/Seymour Lawren, 1982. *A New Treasury of Children's Poetry,* Old Favorites and New Discoveries. Joanna Cole, ed. Doubleday, 1984. *Biography of James Kirkup* (http://www.brindin.com/biogjk.htm). *Knitting Circle, James Kirkup* (http://myweb.lsbu.ac.uk/~stafflag/jameskirkup.html). *Spaceways: An Anthology of Space Poems.* John Foster, ed. Oxford University Press, 1986. *The Columbia Granger's Index to Poetry.* 11th ed. *The Columbia Granger's World of Poetry,* Columbia University Press, 2005 (http://www.columbiagrangers.org). *The Oxford Companion to English Literature.* 6th edition. Margaret Drabble, ed. Oxford University Press, 2000. *The Penguin Book of Homosexual Verse.* Stephen Coote, ed. Penguin Books, 1983.

KNEVET, RALPH (1600–1671)

He was a native of Norfolk and seems to have been closely associated as tutor or chaplain with the family of Sir William Paston of Oxnead, Norfolk. He was rector of Lyng, Norfolk, from 1652 till his death and is buried in the chancel of his church. A collection of sacred poems (no date given) by Knevet, entitled *A Gallery to the Temple. Lyricall Poemes upon sacred occasions, by Ra. Kneuett,* is in the British Museum. *Stratisticon, A Discourse of Militarie Discipline,* 1628 (which can be found in *The Shorter Poems of Ralph Knevet*) is a plea to the military men who were training in Norfolk at the time to better prepare themselves for battle. Some of his other publications: *Rhodon and Iris, a Pastoral, as it was presented at the Florists' Feast in Norwich,* 1631; *Funerall Elegies consecrated to the Immortal Memory of the Right Hon. Lady Katherine Paston,* 1637. Some of his other poems: "Hypocrisie," "Sanctification," "Self-Love," "The Antiphon," "The Apologye," "The Apparition," "The Newyeares Gift," "The Tempest," "The Transmutation," "The World," "Weakness."

Sources: *Dictionary of National Biography.* Electronic Edition 1.1. Oxford University Press, 1997. *English Poetry, Second Edition Bibliography* (http://collections.chadwyck.co.uk/html/ep2/bibliography/g.htm). *English Poetry: Author Search.* Chadwyck-Healey Ltd., 1995 (http://www.lib.utexas.edu:8080/search/epoetry/author.html). *The Columbia Granger's Index to Poetry.* 11th ed. *The Columbia Granger's World of Poetry,* Columbia University Press, 2005 (http://www.columbiagrangers.org). *The Shorter Poems of*

Ralph Knevet: A Critical Edition. Amy M. Charles. Columbus, Ohio: Ohio State University Press, 1966.

KNOWLES, HERBERT (1798–1817)

He was born at Gomersal, near Leeds, and both his parents died when he was young. Rather than let him become a clerk in an office in Liverpool, three clergymen helped raise enough money to send him to Richmond grammar school, Yorkshire, with the hope of his gaining a scholarship to St. John's College, Cambridge. His brother, J.C. Knowles (subsequently Q.C.) sent a copy of Herbert's poem "The Three Tabernacles" (composed in 1816) to Robert Southey, who approached Earl Spencer and Samuel Rogers (see entry). They agreed to help finance Herbert, who died before he could even start at Cambridge. Several verses were published in the *Literary Gazette* for 1819 and 1824 and the *Literary Souvenir* for 1825 (reprinted in *Saturday Magazine,* Vol. 16.). "The Three Tabernacles" (better known as "Stanzas in Richmond Churchyard") had a large circulation on a separate sheet and first appeared in book form in Carlisle's *Endowed Grammar Schools.* The opinion of experts is that this poem heralded the rising of another poetic star, whose short life was only nineteen years.

Sources: *A Sacrifice of Praise: An Anthology of Christian Poetry in English from Caedmon to the Mid–Twentieth Century.* James H. Trott, ed. Cumberland House Publishing, 1999. *Dictionary of National Biography.* Electronic Edition 1.1. Oxford University Press, 1997. *The Columbia Granger's Index to Poetry.* 11th ed. *The Columbia Granger's World of Poetry,* Columbia University Press, 2005 (http://www.columbiagrangers.org).

KNOX, WILLIAM (1789–1825)

Scottish Border poet, born at Firth, in the parish of Lilliesleaf, Roxburghshire. His education was at the elementary level and he ran his own farm at Langholm, Dumfriesshire. According to Sir Walter Scott, Knox did not handle the responsibility of being his own master and ruined his prospects by overindulgence. In 1820 the family settled in Edinburgh, where Knox became a journalist and was befriended by Sir Walter Scott, who frequently helped him financially. He died at Edinburgh of paralysis and was buried in New Calton Cemetery, Edinburgh. Knox published *The Lonely Hearth, and Other Poems,* 1818; *The Songs of Israel,* 1824, which contained the poem "Morality" (based on Job 3 and Ecclesiastes 1); and *The Harp of Zion,* 1825. A legend is that President Abraham Lincoln liked Knox's "Mortality" and was reading it on the day of his assassination. A complete edition of Knox's poems was published in 1847.

Sources: *Americans Who Came from Scotland* (http://www.edinburgh.gov.uk/Libraries/History_Sphere/Amer

icanlinks/edinburgh.html). *Dictionary of National Biography*. Electronic Edition 1.1. Oxford University Press, 1997. For the poem "Mortality," see (http://www.a.ghinn. btinternet.co.uk/mortalit.htm). *Oldpoetry* (www.oldpoetry.com). *The Best Loved Poems of the American People*. Hazel Felleman, ed. Doubleday, 1936. *The Columbia Granger's Index to Poetry*. 11th ed. *The Columbia Granger's World of Poetry*, Columbia University Press, 2005 (http://www.columbiagrangers.org).

KYNEWULF, CYNEWULF (CYNWULF) (CIRCA 750)

An Anglo-Saxon poet who flourished in the eighth century and was active around 750. Further, it is thought he might be Kenulphus, abbot of Peterborough in 992 and bishop of Winchester in 1006. He appears to have been a professional minstrel, who wrote in Northumbrian dialect. In his poem "Elene" he relates that in his youth he enjoyed hunting, the bow, and the horse, was known in festive halls, and was rewarded for his song with golden gifts. As he became an old man he studied many books, and the mystery of the cross, over which he had often pondered, became clear to him. His four main works: *Elene*, a poem of 1,321 lines; *The Fates of the Apostles*, 122 lines; *Christ II*, a lyrical version of a homily on the Ascension written by Pope Gregory I the Great (?540–604); and *Juliana*, 731 lines, a retelling of a Latin prose life of St. Juliana. Some of his other poems: "A Dream of the Rood," "Guthlac," "Riddles," "The Nature of the Siren," "The Phoenix."

Sources: *A Sacrifice of Praise: An Anthology of Christian Poetry in English from Caedmon to the Mid–Twentieth Century*. James H. Trott, ed. Cumberland House Publishing, 1999. *An Anthology of Catholic Poets*. Shane Leslie, ed. Macmillan, 1952. *An Anthology of Old English Poetry*. Charles W. Kennedy, ed. Oxford University Press, 1960. *Dictionary of National Biography*. Electronic Edition 1.1. Oxford University Press, 1997. *Encyclopædia Britannica Ultimate Reference Suite DVD*, 2006. *Great Books Online* (www.bartleby.com). *The Anglo-Saxon World: An Anthology*. Kevin Crossley-Holland, ed. Oxford University Press, 1982. *The Columbia Granger's Index to Poetry*. 11th ed. *The Columbia Granger's World of Poetry*, Columbia University Press, 2005 (http://www.columbiagrangers.org). *World Poetry: An Anthology of Verse from Antiquity to Our Time*. Katharine Washburn and John S. Major, ed. Publisher, 1338, 1998.

LAMB, LADY CAROLINE (1785–1828)

The only daughter of Frederick Ponsonby, third earl of Bessborough, and granddaughter of John, first earl of Spencer, she married the Hon. William Lamb, afterwards Lord Melbourne, in 1805. Throughout her life her mental health was precarious. She met Lord Byron in 1812 and they had short-lived, very public, and passionate affair. When Byron broke it off Lady Caroline entered into what today would be a stalking relationship, and spent the next four years pursuing him. She and her husband separated three years before she died at Melbourne House, Whitehall. She was buried at Hatfield, Hertfordshire. Her first and most well-known dark novel, *Glenarvon*, was published anonymously in 1816. Her life was made into the film *Lady Caroline Lamb* in 1973, starring Sarah Miles, Richard Chamberlain, Margaret Leighton and Laurence Olivier. Some of her poems: "A New Canto," "Amidst the Flowers Rich and Gay," "As the Flower Early Gathered," "By Those Eyes Where Sweet Expression," "Duet," "Fugitive Pieces and Reminiscences," "If Thou Couldst Know What 'Tis to Weep," "Sing Not for Others, But for Me," "Would I Had Seen Thee Dead and Cold."

Sources: *Dictionary of National Biography*. Electronic Edition 1.1. Oxford University Press, 1997. *English Poetry: Author Search*. Chadwyck-Healey Ltd., 1995 (http://www.lib.utexas.edu:8080/search/epoetry/author.html). *The National Portrait Gallery* (www.npg.org.uk). *Regency Personalities, Lady Caroline Lamb* (http://homepages.ihug.co.nz/~awoodley/regency/caro.html). *Romantic Women Poets: An Anthology*. Duncan Wu, ed. Blackwell Publishers, 1997. *Romanticism*. Duncan Wu, ed. Blackwell, 1994. *The Columbia Granger's Index to Poetry*. 11th ed. *The Columbia Granger's World of Poetry*, Columbia University Press, 2005 (http://www.columbiagrangers.org). *The Oxford Companion to English Literature*. 6th edition. Margaret Drabble, ed. Oxford University Press, 2000.

LAMB, CHARLES and MARY (1764–1847)

Charles, the brother (1775–1834)

Born in London, the son of John Lamb, a clerk of the Inner Temple, he was educated at Christ's Hospital, where he became friends with Samuel Taylor Coleridge (see entry) and Leigh Hunt (see Hunt, James Henry Leigh). From the age of fourteen he was a clerk at the South Sea Company, then from 1792 to 1822, a clerk at India House. From 1799 to 1802 he wrote for various journals. Coleridge included four of Lamb's sonnets in *Poems on Various Subjects* 1796, second edition 1796. In 1820 Lamb wrote a series of essays (under the pseudonym Elia) in *London Magazine*. He died from a fall and was buried in Edmonton churchyard. Some of his poetry publications: *The Old Familiar Faces*, 1789. *Blank Verse by Charles Lloyd and Charles Lamb*, 1798. *John Woodvil*, 1802 (a poetic tragedy). *Specimens of English Dramatic Poets, with Notes by Charles Lamb*, 1808. *On an Infant Dying as Soon as It Was Born*, 1828. Some of Charles's poems: "As When a Child," "Epitaph on a Dog," "Satan in Search of a Wife," "The Boy and the Snake," "The Triumph of the Whale," "The Young Catechist," "To John Lamb, Esq. of the South-Sea House."

Mary, the sister (1764–1847)

Mary received little formal education, and from an early age she helped support the family and her invalid mother by doing needlework. Brother and sister both suffered bouts of mental illness; Mary killed their mother in 1796 and was cared for by Charles until he died. In 1807 Mary and Charles published *Tales from Shakespear*, a collection of prose adaptations of Shakespeare's plays, intended for children, of which Mary wrote the majority. In 1809 they published two collaborative works, *Mrs. Leicester's School*, a book of children's stories, for which she contributed the major part, and *Poetry for Children*. After Charles's death, Mary's mental health deteriorated, but she survived him by 13 years and was buried with Charles. Brother and sister co-operated in writing other books, and poems. Some of Mary's poems: "Dialogue Between a Mother and Child," "Helen; In Miss Westwood's Album," "Maternal Lady with the Virgin Grace," "Parental Recollections," "The Two Boys," "What is Love?" Poems by Charles and Mary: "Choosing a Name," "Cleanliness," "Envy," "Going into Breeches," "The First Tooth."

Sources: *Dictionary of National Biography*. Electronic Edition 1.1. Oxford University Press, 1997. *Encyclopædia Britannica Ultimate Reference Suite DVD*, 2006. *English Poetry: Author Search*. Chadwyck-Healey Ltd., 1995 (http://www.lib.utexas.edu:8080/search/epoetry/author.html). *Essays of Elia* (http://www.angelfire.com/nv/mf/lamb/contents.html). *I Sing of a Maiden: The Mary Book of Verse*. Sister M. Therese, ed. Macmillan, 1947. *Imagination's Other Place: Poems of Science and Mathematics*. Helen Plotz, ed. Thomas Y. Crowell, 1955. *The National Portrait Gallery* (www.npg.org.uk). *Romanticism*. Duncan Wu, ed. Blackwell, 1994. *The Brand-X Anthology of Poetry*. William Zaranka, ed. Apple-Wood Books, 1981. *The Columbia Granger's Index to Poetry*. 11th ed. *The Columbia Granger's World of Poetry*, Columbia University Press, 2005 (http://www.columbiagrangers.org). *The Home Book of Verse for Young Folks*. Burton Egbert Stevenson, ed. Holt, Rinehart and Winston, 1929. *The Oxford Anthology of English Literature Vol. I*. Frank Kermode, and John Hollander, ed. Oxford University Press, 1973. *The Oxford Book of Children's Verse*. Iona Opie, and Peter Opie, ed. Oxford University Press, 1973. *The Oxford Companion to English Literature*. 6th edition. Margaret Drabble, ed. Oxford University Press, 2000. *The Works of Charles and Mary Lamb V. 5*. G.P. Putnam's Sons, 1903.

LANDON, LETITIA ELIZABETH (1802–1838)

She was born in Chelsea at a time when her father — a partner in a firm supplying the British army — made money. After the war the family lived in "reduced circumstances." In June 1838 she married George MacLean, governor of Cape Coast Castle, West Africa. In October she was found dead, clutching a bottle of prussic acid, a medication she had been taking to treat fits. She published four novels and several plays, and also wrote of passionate love at a time when convention restricted what women could and could not write. Some of her poetry publications (written under the initials L.E.L.): *Rome*, 1820. *The Fate of Adelaide*, 1821. *The Improvisatrice*, 1824 (6th edition, 1825). *The Troubadour*, 1825. *The Golden Violet*, 1827. *The Venetian Bracelet*, 1829. Some of her poems: "A Legend of Tintagel Castle," "Age and Youth," "Cafés in Damascus," "Love, Hope, and Beauty," "Poetical Portraits," "Sir Walter Scott," "St. George's Hospital, Hyde-Park Corner," "Subjects for Pictures," "The African Prince," "The Covenanters," "The Female Convict," "What is Success?"

Sources: *Dictionary of National Biography*. Electronic Edition 1.1. Oxford University Press, 1997. *Encyclopædia Britannica Ultimate Reference Suite DVD*, 2006. *English Poetry: Author Search*. Chadwyck-Healey Ltd., 1995 (http://www.lib.utexas.edu:8080/search/epoetry/author.html). *The National Portrait Gallery* (www.npg.org.uk). *Poetical Works of Letitia Elizabeth Landon "L.E.L.,"* F.J. Sypher, ed. Scholars' Facsimiles and Reprint, 1900. *The Columbia Granger's Index to Poetry*. 11th ed. *The Columbia Granger's World of Poetry*, Columbia University Press, 2005 (http://www.columbiagrangers.org). *The Oxford Companion to English Literature*. 6th edition. Margaret Drabble, ed. Oxford University Press, 2000.

LANDOR, WALTER SAVAGE (1775–1864)

Born in Warwick, Warwickshire, the son of a doctor, he was educated at Rugby School and at Oxford University. Of an independent mind, he refused to compete for any Latin prize, even though his Latin was outstanding. He left Oxford after being disciplined for firing a gun at the window of a Tory. His father died in 1805 and Landor dedicated his life to wine, women and poetry. Seeking adventure, in 1808 he joined the Spaniards against the French and was rewarded by an honorary commission as colonel in the service of Ferdinand. Embroiled in a difficult lawsuit, he fled to Italy to live with Robert and Elizabeth Browning in Florence, where he died. Some of his publications: *Poems*, 1795 and 1802. *Guy's Porridge Pot*, 1808. *Imaginary Conversations*, 1824. *The Impious Feast*, 1828. *Last Fruit Off an Old Tree*, 1853. *Heroic Idylls*, 1863. Some of his other poems: "Advice to a Poet," "After Wellington," "Dante Aligheri," "Henry the Eighth and Anne Boleyn," "Ianthe," "The Crimean Heroes," "The Gardener and the Mole," "Written in England on the Battle of Aboukir," "Youth to Age."

Sources: *Dictionary of National Biography*. Electronic Edition 1.1. Oxford University Press, 1997. *Encyclopædia Britannica Ultimate Reference Suite DVD*, 2006. *English*

Poetry, Second Edition Bibliography (http://collections.chadwyck.co.uk/html/ep2/bibliography/g.htm). *English Poetry: Author Search.* Chadwyck-Healey Ltd., 1995 (http://www.lib.utexas.edu:8080/search/epoetry/author.html). *Poems for the People—Poems by the People* (http://www.netpoets.com/classic/biographies/038000.htm). *The National Portrait Gallery* (www.npg.org.uk). *Poems of Walter Savage Landor.* Geoffrey Grigson, ed. Centaur Press, 1964. *Selections From Robert Landor.* Eric Partridge, ed. the Fanfrolico Press, 1927. *The Columbia Granger's Index to Poetry.* 11th ed. *The Columbia Granger's World of Poetry,* Columbia University Press, 2005 (http://www.columbiagrangers.org). *The Faber Book of War Poetry.* Kenneth Baker, ed. Faber and Faber, 1996. *The New Oxford Book of Romantic Period Verse.* Jerome J. McGann. Oxford University Press, 1993. *The San Antonio College LitWeb Walter Savage Landor Page* (http://www.accd.edu/sac/english/bailey/landorws.htm).

LANE, JOHN (fl. 1620)

Lane's poems suggest that he was from Somerset and that he was without any academic education. Nothing else is known of him. His poem of 1600, *Tom Tel-troths Message and His Pens Complaint,* in 120 six-line stanzas, is dedicated to Master George Dowse and is a vigorous denunciation of the vices of Elizabethan society. Lane describes it as "the first fruit of my barren brain." It was reprinted by the New Shakespere Society in 1876. In 1603 he wrote *An Elegie vpon the Death of the High and Renowned Princesse Our Late Soueraigne Elizabeth.* In *Squire's Tale,* 1615, Lane completed in manuscript Chaucer's unfinished poem, adding ten cantos to the original two and carrying out the hints supplied by Chaucer with reference to the chief characters, Cambuscan, Camball, Algarsife, and Canace. Some of his poems: "Æolus Trumpet to His Foure Winds," "Alarum to Poets," "Lane's Fresh Dedication," "Poetries Complaint," "The Muse to the Fowre Windes," "To the Gentlemen Readers."

Sources: *Dictionary of National Biography.* Electronic Edition 1.1. Oxford University Press, 1997. *English Poetry: Author Search.* Chadwyck-Healey Ltd., 1995 (http://www.lib.utexas.edu:8080/search/epoetry/author.html).

LANG, ANDREW (1844–1912)

The eldest son of John Lang, sheriff-clerk of Selkirkshire, Scotland, he was educated at the local grammar school, Edinburgh Academy, and St. Andrews University, and graduated *literae humaniores* from Balliol College, Oxford, in 1868. He held an open fellowship at Merton College, Oxford, until 1875, when he moved to London, where he was a journalist for nearly forty years. He wrote history books (including Scottish themes), novels and biographies, published prose translations of *The Odyssey,* and earned special praise for his 12-volume collection of fairy tales written between 1889 and

1893. He published translations of the *Idylls* of Theocritus (1880) and of the *Homeric Hymns* (1899). He died of a heart condition at Banchory, Aberdeenshire, and is buried in the cathedral precincts at St. Andrews. Some of his poetry publications: *Ballads and Lyrics of Old France,* 1872. *Ballads in Blue China,* 1880. *Helen of Troy,* 1882. *Rhymes à la Mode,* 1884. *Grass of Parnassus,* 1888. *Ban and Arrière Ban,* 1894. Some of his poems: "Brahma," "Clevedon Church," "Epistle to Mr. Alexander Pope," "Scythe Song," "To Lord Byron," "To the Gentle Reader," "Zimbabwe."

Sources: *A Book of Scottish Verse.* Maurice Lindsay and R.L. Mackie, eds. St. Martin's Press, 1983. *Book-Song.* Gleeson White, ed. Elliot Stock, 1893. *Dictionary of National Biography.* Electronic Edition 1.1. Oxford University Press, 1997. *Encyclopædia Britannica Ultimate Reference Suite DVD,* 2006. *English Poetry: A Poetic Record, from Chaucer to Yeats.* David Hopkins, ed. Routledge, 1990. *Golden Numbers.* Kate Douglas Wiggin and Nora Archibald Smith, eds. Doubleday, Doran, 1902. *The National Portrait Gallery* (www.npg.org.uk). *Poems of South African History* A.D. *1497–1910.* A. Petrie, ed. Oxford University Press. 1918. *The Columbia Granger's Index to Poetry.* 11th ed. *The Columbia Granger's World of Poetry,* Columbia University Press, 2005 (http://www.columbiagrangers.org). *The Faber Book of Comic Verse.* Michael Roberts and Janet Adam Smith, eds. Faber and Faber, 1978. *The Home Book of Verse for Young Folks.* Burton Egbert Stevenson, ed. Holt, Rinehart and Winston, 1929. *The Home Book of Verse.* Burton Egbert Stevenson, ed. New York: Henry Holt and Company, 1953. *The Oxford Companion to English Literature.* 6th edition. Margaret Drabble, ed. Oxford University Press, 2000.

LANGHORNE, JOHN (1735–1779)

The younger son of the Rev. Joseph Langhorne of Winton in the parish of Kirkby Stephen, Westmoreland, he was private tutor to a family near Ripon. After a year at Clare Hall, Cambridge, he became a clergyman in London. During his time as tutor he started writing poetry and in 1764 he began writing for the *Monthly Review.* His *Genius and Valor: a Scotch Pastoral* was published in 1764, and in 1766 he published his *Poetical Works,* which included the dramatic poem *The Fatal Prophecy.* In the same year he became rector of Blagdon, Somerset, where he died and was buried. With his older brother William he published a translation of *Plutarch's Lives* in 1770. Some of his other publications: *The Death of Adonis,* 1759. *The Tears of Music,* 1760. *A Hymn to Hope,* 1761. *The Viceroy,* 1762. *The Visions of Fancy, in Four Elegies,* 1762. *The Origin of the Veil,* 1773. *Milton's Italian Poem,* 1778 (translated into Italian). Some of his other poems: "Autumnal Elegy," "Caesar's Dream, Before His Invasion of Britain," "Owen of Carron," "The Amiable King," "The Bee-Flower," "The Country Justice," "The Visions of Fancy."

Sources: *Dictionary of National Biography.* Electronic Edition 1.1. Oxford University Press, 1997. *Encyclopædia Britannica Ultimate Reference Suite DVD,* 2006. *English Poetry: Author Search.* Chadwyck-Healey Ltd., 1995 (http://www.lib.utexas.edu:8080/search/epoetry/author. html). *The Columbia Granger's Index to Poetry.* 11th ed. *The Columbia Granger's World of Poetry,* Columbia University Press, 2005 (http://www.columbiagrangers.org). *The Oxford Companion to English Literature.* 6th edition. Margaret Drabble, ed. Oxford University Press, 2000. *The Poetical Works of John Langhorne.* Thomas Park, ed. J. Sharpe, 1808.

LANGLAND, WILLIAM (?1330–?1400)

The dates given here are taken from the Dictionary of National Biography. Little is known of Langland's life; he could have been born somewhere in the region of the Malvern Hills, in Worcestershire, or at Ledbury near the Welsh marshes. He could have been educated at the Benedictine school in Great Malvern. References in his allegorical poem suggest that he knew London and Westminster as well as Shropshire, and that he was a cleric in minor order. In London he apparently eked out his living by singing masses and copying documents. *The Vision of William concerning Piers the Plowman* is second only in importance to Chaucer's *Canterbury Tales* among medieval literature. The poem — both a social satire and a vision of the simple Christian life — consists of three dream visions: in which Holy Church and Lady Meed (representing the temptation of riches) woo the dreamer; in which Piers leads a crowd of penitents in search of St. Truth; and the vision of Do-well (the practice of the virtues), Do-bet (in which Piers becomes the Good Samaritan practicing charity), and Do-best (in which the simple plowman is identified with Jesus himself).

Sources: *Dictionary of National Biography.* Electronic Edition 1.1. Oxford University Press, 1997. *Encyclopædia Britannica Ultimate Reference Suite DVD,* 2006. *English Poetry: Author Search.* Chadwyck-Healey Ltd., 1995 (http://www.lib.utexas.edu:8080/search/epoetry/author. html). *The Columbia Granger's Index to Poetry.* 11th ed. *The Columbia Granger's World of Poetry,* Columbia University Press, 2005 (http://www.columbiagrangers.org). *The Life and Work of William Langland* (http://www.luminarium. org/medlit/langland.htm). *The Oxford Companion to English Literature.* 6th edition. Margaret Drabble, ed. Oxford University Press, 2000.

LANIER (LANYER), EMILIA (AEMELIA) (1569–1645)

Born in London, the daughter of Giovanni Baptista Bassano. The family were Italian Jewish émigrés from Venice and musicians and instrument-makers at Edward VI's court in 1531. Emilia was brought up by the dowager Countess of Kent and was for several years the mistress of Queen Elizabeth's cousin, Henry Cary, Lord Hunsdon. When she became pregnant in 1592, she married court musician Alfonso Lanyer. Lord Hunsdon was the patron of William Shakespeare's theatre company and there was speculation that Emilia was the subject of Shakespeare's *Dark Lady*, the woman to whom Shakespeare composed a portion of his sonnets. Lanier died in London and was buried in St. James's, Clerkenwell, London. She has every right to claim the status of first English female professional writer. *Salve Deus Rex Judaeorum (Eve's Apology in Defense of Women)* was published in 1611 (see Behn, Aphra, whose first play was published in 1670). The poem is prefaced by eleven dedicatory works, all to women. The title poem on Christ's passion is narrated entirely from the point of view of women.

Sources: *Dictionary of National Biography.* Electronic Edition 1.1. Oxford University Press, 1997. *Biography of Aemilia Lanyer: Sunshine for Women* (http://www.pinn. net/~sunshine/march99/lanyer2.html). *Kissing the Rod: An Anthology of Seventeenth-Century Women's Verse.* Germaine Greer, Susan Hastings and Jeslyn Medo, eds. Farrar Straus Giroux, 1988. *Library of Congress Citations* (www.mala.bc. ca/~mcneil/cit/citlclanyer1.htm). *Nationmaster.com* (http:// www.nationmaster.com/encyclopedia/Emilia-Lanier). *The Columbia Granger's Index to Poetry.* 11th ed. *The Columbia Granger's World of Poetry,* Columbia University Press, 2005 (http://www.columbiagrangers.org). *The New Oxford Book of Seventeenth Century Verse.* Alastair Fowler, ed. Oxford University Press, 2004. *The Norton Anthology of Literature by Women: The Tradition in English.* Sandra M. Gilbert and Susan Guber, eds. W.W. Norton, 1985. *The Oxford Companion to English Literature.* 6th edition. Margaret Drabble, ed. Oxford University Press, 2000. *The Poems of Aemilia Lanyer, Salve Deus Rex Judaeorum.* Susanne Woods, ed. Oxford University Press, 1993.

LAPRAIK, JOHN (1727–1807)

Scottish poet, born at Laigh Dalquhram (Dalfram), near Muirkirk, Ayrshire, he succeeded his father to the considerable estate that had been in the family for generations. He also rented the lands and mill of Muirsmill, in the neighborhood. Lapraik was ruined by the collapse of the Douglas and Heron Bank in 1772, was forced to sell his estate and mill, and spent some time in the debtors' prison. Around 1796 he opened a public house at Muirkirk, conducting also the village post office on the same premises, where he died. He was buried in the churchyard at Kirkgreen and a ten-foot high cairn was erected from the stones of his house. The best source of information about John Lapraik is found in *The Contemporaries of Burns and the More Recent Poets of Ayrshire* (1840). Robert Burns and Lapraik became friends and Burns (a near neighbor) wrote *The Three Epistles* to his friend in 1785, subsequently published by Burns in 1786. Lapraik published *Poems on Several Occasions: Poems and Songs* in 1788.

Sources: *Dictionary of National Biography*. Electronic Edition 1.1. Oxford University Press, 1997.

LARKIN, PHILIP ARTHUR
(1922–1985)

Born in Coventry, he graduated in English language and literature from St. John's College, Oxford, in 1943, but poor eyesight barred him for war service. He worked as a librarian all his life, taking charge of the Brynmor Jones Library, University of Hull, in 1955. He edited *The Oxford Book of Twentieth-Century English Verse* (1973). He published two novels, *Jill* (1940) and *A Girl in Winter* (1947); and two collections of critical pieces, *All What Jazz: A Record Diary, 1961–1968* (1970) — some of his reviews of jazz records for the *Daily Telegraph* — and *Required Writing* (1983). With the onset of deafness in the 1970s Larkin gradually ceased writing poetry and jazz criticism. Academic and civil honors were heaped upon him in England and in America. He died in hospital in Hull and people crowded Westminster Abbey for his memorial service. His poetry publications: *The North Ship*, 1946. *The Less Deceived*, 1955. *The Whitsun Weddings*, 1964. *High Windows*, 1974. Some of his poems: "Absences," "An Arundel Tomb," "Annus Mirabilis," "Aubade," "Church Going," "Last Will and Testament," "Love, We Must Part Now," "Myxomatosis."

Sources: *100 Poems by 100 Poets: An Anthology*. Harold Pinter, Geoffrey Godbert and Anthony Astbury, eds. Grove Press, 1986. *Collected Poems of Philip Larkin*. Anthony Thwaite, ed. Farrar, Straus and Giroux, 1988. *Dictionary of National Biography*. Electronic Edition 1.1. Oxford University Press, 1997. *Encyclopædia Britannica Ultimate Reference Suite DVD*, 2006. *The National Portrait Gallery* (www.npg.org.uk). *The Columbia Granger's Index to Poetry*. 11th ed. *The Columbia Granger's World of Poetry*, Columbia University Press, 2005 (http://www.columbiagrangers.org). *The Norton Anthology of Poetry*. 4th ed. Margaret Ferguson, Mary Jo Salter and Jon Stal, eds. W.W. Norton, 1996. *The Oxford Companion to English Literature*. 6th edition. Margaret Drabble, ed. Oxford University Press, 2000.

LAUDER, GEORGE (?1600–1677)

Scottish poet who graduated M.A. from Edinburgh University in 1620, then entered the English army, where he reached the rank of colonel. In 1627 he accompanied the Duke of Buckingham on the expedition to the isle of Ré (a small island off the French coast, opposite La Rochelle). Letters from the Prince of Orange suggest that Lauder was also an officer in his army (1662–1667). Edinburgh publisher David Laing published *Fugitive Scottish Poetry of the Seventeenth Century* (1823–1825), in which he includes an "Epitaph on the Honorable Colonel George Lauder, by Alexander Wedderburne" (see entry for Wedderburn Brothers). Lauder's poem "Damon, or a Pastoral Elegy on the Death of his Honored Friend, William Drummond of Hawthornden," was prefixed to Drummond's *Poems*, in *Corser's Collectanea Anglo-Poetica* (1711). Some of Llauder's publications: *Lauderdale's Valedictory Address*, 1622. *The Anatomie of the Romane Clergie*, 1623. *The Souldier's Wish*, 1628. *The Scottish Souldier*, 1629. *Tears on the Death of Evander*, 1630. *Aretophel, a Memorial of the Second Lord Scott of Buccleuch*, ?1634. *A Horse*, 1646. *Mars Belgicus, or ye Funeral Elegy on Henry, Prince of Orange*, 1647. *Death of King Charles*, 1649. *Caledonias Covenant*, 1661.

Sources: *Dictionary of National Biography*. Electronic Edition 1.1. Oxford University Press, 1997. *English Poetry: Author Search*. Chadwyck-Healey Ltd., 1995 (http://www.lib.utexas.edu:8080/search/epoetry/author.html). Stanford University Libraries and Academic Information Resources (http://library.stanford.edu).

LAWRENCE, DAVID HERBERT
(1885–1930)

A coal miner's son, he was born at Eastwood, Nottinghamshire. He was never robust; his mother, a former schoolteacher, was the driving force behind his winning a scholarship at Nottingham high school, and a teacher training course at Nottingham University. His *Sons and Lovers* (1913) is largely autobiographical of his early years. In 1915, his novel *The Rainbow*, with his use of four-letter words, was the subject of a prosecution; it was declared obscene. Lawrence felt the disgrace keenly and, dismayed at his treatment, when the war was over he and his wife left England and lived in many different countries — including the United States and Mexico. They finally settled in Italy, where he wrote *Lady Chatterley's Lover* (1928); the furor it raised raged for many years. He died in Vence, France, of tuberculosis. Some of his poetry publications: *Love Poems and Others*, 1913. *Look! We Have Come Through!*, 1917. *Bay: A Book of Poems*, 1919. *Birds, Beasts and Flowers*, 1923. *Pansies*, 1929. Some of his poems: "Bavarian Gentians," "Eagle in New Mexico," "The American Eagle," "The Hands of God," "Welcome to Quetzalcoatl," "Winter in the Boulevard."

Sources: *Chapters into Verse, Vol. II: Gospels to Revelation*. Robert Atwan and Laurance Wieder, eds. Oxford University Press, 1993. *Dictionary of National Biography*. Electronic Edition 1.1. Oxford University Press, 1997. *Encyclopædia Britannica Ultimate Reference Suite DVD*, 2006. *Poemhunter* (www.poemhunter.com). *The Columbia Granger's Index to Poetry*. 11th ed. *The Columbia Granger's World of Poetry*, Columbia University Press, 2005 (http://www.columbiagrangers.org). *The Complete Poems of D.H. Lawrence*. Vivian de Sola Pinto and Warren Roberts, ed. Penguin Books, 1993. *The Oxford Companion to English*

Literature. 6th edition. Margaret Drabble, ed. Oxford University Press, 2000. *The Top 500 Poems.* William Harmon, ed. Columbia University Press, 1992. *Wikipedia, the Free Encyclopedia* (http://en.wikipedia.org/wiki/Wikipedia).

LE GALLIENNE, RICHARD THOMAS (1866–1947)

Born in Liverpool, of Channel Islands descent, he was educated at Liverpool College and started off in accountancy, then decided on a literary career. From 1888 to 1891, he was secretary to the London actor-manager Wilson Barrett, then he was employed as book reviewer for the *Star*, using the pseudonym "Log-roller." He became reader for Bodley Head when the firm published his *Volumes in Folio* in 1889. From 1901 to 1927 he lived in the United States, writing mainly for newspapers and magazines. He spent the last years of his life in the south of France, continuing to write for the American press, mainly about life in Paris, and died at Menton, where he is buried. Some of his other publications: *English Poems*, 1892. *Odes from the Divan of Hafiz,* 1903 (translation). *New Poems*, 1910. *The Lonely Dancer and Other Poems,* 1913. *The Silk-Hat Soldier and Other Poems in War Time,* 1915. Some of his poems: "A Ballad of London," "A Melton Mowbray Pork Pie," "Brooklyn Bridge at Dawn," "Death in a London Lodging," "Matthew Arnold," "The City in Moonlight."

Sources: *Aesthetes and Decadents of the 1890s.* Karl Beckson, ed. Academy Chicago Publishers, 1981. *Book-Song.* Gleeson White, ed. Elliot Stock, 1893. *Dictionary of National Biography.* Electronic Edition 1.1. Oxford University Press, 1997. *English Poems by Richard Le Galliene.* Bodley Head, 1892. *Parodies: An Anthology from Chaucer to Beerbohm—and After.* Dwight Macdonald, ed. Modern Library, 1960. *The Columbia Granger's Index to Poetry.* 11th ed. *The Columbia Granger's World of Poetry,* Columbia University Press, 2005 (http://www.columbiagrangers.org). *The Home Book of Verse for Young Folks.* Burton Egbert Stevenson, ed. Holt, Rinehart and Winston, 1929. *The Home Book of Modern Verse.* Burton Egbert Stevenson, ed. Henry Holt, 1953. *The Oxford Book of Victorian Verse.* Arthur Quiller-Couch, ed. Oxford University Press, 1971. *The Oxford Companion to English Literature.* 6th edition. Margaret Drabble, ed. Oxford University Press, 2000. *Wikipedia, the Free Encyclopedia* (http://en.wikipedia.org/wiki/Wikipedia).

LEAPOR, MARY (1722–1746)

Born in Northamptonshire, the daughter of a gardener, she was a cook-maid of little education who taught herself to read the works of John Dryden and Alexander Pope and imitated Pope in her poems. Her poetry came to the attention of Bridget Freemantle, a member of the local gentry who encouraged Leapor to publish her work, but she died of measles before the arrangements were completed. *Poems on Several Occasions*, edited by Isaac Hawkins Browne, was published in two volumes. The first, in 1748, includes "Essay on Friendship" and "Essay on Hope." The second, in 1751, includes a tragedy in blank verse, *The Unhappy Father.* A selection from her poems appears in Mrs. Barber's *Poems by Eminent Ladies*, 1755. "Leapor is one of many gifted poets, mainly women and laborers, whose work stands outside the traditional canon of eighteenth-century verse" (from the jacket of Richard Greene and Ann Messenger's book [see below]). Some of her poems: "Crumble-Hall," "Epistle to Artemisia," "Mira's Picture, a Pastoral," "Silvia and the Bee," "Strephon to Celia: A Modern Love Letter," "The Epistle of Deborah Dough."

Sources: *A Treasury of Minor British Poetry.* J. Churton Collins, ed. Edward Arnold, 1896. *Dictionary of National Biography.* Electronic Edition 1.1. Oxford University Press, 1997. *Eighteenth Century Women Poets: An Oxford Anthology.* Roger Lonsdale, ed. Oxford University Press, 1989. For the full works of Mary Leapor see (http://www.orgs.muohio.edu/womenpoets/leapor/). *Poems by Eminent Ladies, Particularly Mrs. Barber, Mrs. Behn, Miss Carter.* George Colman and Bonnell Thornton, eds. 2 vols. R. Baldwin, 1755. *Selected Bibliography: Mary Leapor (1722–1746)* by Laura Mandell, Miami University of Ohio (http://www.c18.rutgers.edu/biblio/leapor.html). *Poetry by English Women: Elizabethan to Victorian,* R.E. Pritchard, ed. Continuum, 1990. *Poets' Corner, Mary Leapor* (http://www.theotherpages.org/poems/poem-kl.html). *The Columbia Granger's Index to Poetry.* 11th ed. *The Columbia Granger's World of Poetry,* Columbia University Press, 2005 (http://www.columbiagrangers.org). *The Oxford Companion to English Literature.* 6th edition. Margaret Drabble, ed. Oxford University Press, 2000. *The Works of Mary Leapor,* Richard Greene and Ann Messenger, eds. Oxford University Press, 2003.

LEAR, EDWARD (1812–1888)

One of a large family, he was born in Highgate, London, the son of a stockbroker, and earned his living as a zoological draftsman and water colorist of the highest order. While making illustrations of the earl of Derby's private menagerie at Knowsley, Lancashire, he produced for the earl's grandchildren *A Book of Nonsense* (1846) for which he became famous. Although he suffered from epilepsy and depression, he traveled widely, making sketches all the way, turning them into carefully finished watercolors and large oil paintings. The last few years of his life were spent at San Remo, on the Italian Riviera, where he died and was buried. He published three volumes of bird and animal drawings, seven illustrated travel books and three more books of nonsense. Among his publications: *Nonsense Songs, Stories, Botany, and Alphabets,* 1871. *More Nonsense, Pictures, Rhymes, Botany, etc.,* 1872. *Laughable Lyrics,* 1877. *Queery Leary Nonsense,* 1911. Some of his poems: "Ribands and Pigs," "Rice and Mice," "The Owl and the Pussy Cat," "The Table and the Chair," "The Two Old Bachelors," "The Young Lady of Tyre," "Turkey Discipline."

Sources: *Dictionary of National Biography.* Electronic Edition 1.1. Oxford University Press, 1997. *Encyclopædia Britannica Ultimate Reference Suite DVD,* 2006. *The National Portrait Gallery* (www.npg.org.uk). *Shrieks at Midnight: Macabre Poems, Eerie and Humorous.* Sara Brewton and John E. Brewton, eds. Thomas Y. Crowell, 1969. *The Columbia Granger's Index to Poetry.* 11th ed. *The Columbia Granger's World of Poetry,* Columbia University Press, 2005 (http://www.columbiagrangers.org). *The Complete Verse and Other Nonsense of Edward Lear.* Vivien Noakes, ed. Penguin Books, 2001. *The Oxford Companion to English Literature.* 6th edition. Margaret Drabble, ed. Oxford University Press, 2000. *The Rattle Bag: An Anthology of Poetry.* Seamus Heaney and Ted Hughes, eds. Faber and Faber, 1982. *Westminster Abbey Official Guide* (no date).

LEATHAM, WILLIAM HENRY 1815–1889

Born at Wakefield, Yorkshire, the son of a Quaker banker and author of *Letters on the Currency* (1840), he was educated under a classical tutor in London and at nineteen he entered his father's bank at Wakefield. He was member of Parliament for Wakefield from 1865 to 1868. He married Priscilla Gurney in 1839, retired from politics and settled at Sandal, near Wakefield, and made the place the subject of a poem, "Sandal in the Olden Time." The couple converted to the Anglican Church and purchased Hemsworth Hall in 1851. He died suddenly at Carlton, near Pontefract, Yorkshire. Some of his poetry publications: *The Victim, a Tale of the Lake of the Four Cantons,* 1841. *The Siege of Granada,* 1841. *Strafford, a Tragedy,* 1842. *Henry Clifford and Margaret Percy, a Ballad of Bolton Abbey,* 1843. *Emilia Monteiro, a Ballad of the Old Hall, Heath,* 1843. *Cromwell, a Drama in Five Acts,* 1843. *The Widow and the Earl, a Tale of Sharlston Hall,* 1844. *Montezuma,* 1845. *Life Hath Many Mysteries,* 1847. *Selections from Lesser Poems.* 1855.

Sources: *Dictionary of National Biography.* Electronic Edition 1.1. Oxford University Press, 1997.

LEDWIDGE, FRANCIS (1891–1917)

The son of a farm laborer of Slane, County Meath, in the Boyne Valley, Ireland, he was known as Frank. He had a variety of jobs — groom, farmhand, copper miner overseer of roads for the Slane area. Lord Dunsany (see entry) saw some of his poems and introduced him to other poets. He remained an overseer, involved himself in the local community, and founded the Slane Drama Group in which he was both chief actor and producer. Although a strong nationalist, he joined the 5th bat-

talion Royal Inniskillings in 1914 to fight for the Boyne he loved. He saw action at Gallipoli (1915) and was killed in Belgium, where he was buried. Ledwidge has been called the Burns and the Clare of the Irish; his themes are blossoms, roses of the lane, roadside birds on the tops of dusty hedges, and especially the blackbird's song. His publications: *Songs of the Field,* 1915. *Songs of Peace,* 1916. *Last Songs,* 1918. *Complete Poems,* 1919. Some of his poems: "After Court Martial," "Behind the Closed Eye," "Fairy Music," "Home," "In France," "Ireland," "To a Sparrow," "To Lord Dunsany."

Sources: *Dictionary of National Biography.* Electronic Edition 1.1. Oxford University Press, 1997. *Francis Ledwidge Museum* (http://www.francisledwidge.com). *The Columbia Granger's Index to Poetry.* 11th ed. *The Columbia Granger's World of Poetry,* Columbia University Press, 2005 (http://www.columbiagrangers.org). *The Complete Poems of Francis Ledwidge.* Herbert Jenkins Limited, 1919. *The Oxford Companion to English Literature.* 6th edition. Margaret Drabble, ed. Oxford University Press, 2000.

LEE, LAURIE (1914–1997)

Born in Slad, near Stroud, Gloucestershire, he worked in an office and as a builder's laborer, then spent 1935–1939 traveling in Europe. Some sources say he fought against Franco's Nationalists in the Spanish Civil War (1936–39); others say this is fantasy. During and after World War II he was a journalist and a film-script writer, worked for the Ministry of Information, made several documentary films, and worked for the Ministry of Information Publications. From 1950 to 1951 he was caption-writer-in-chief for the Festival of Britain. He was made a member of the Order of the British Empire and received several literary awards. He wrote travel books, essays, a radio play and short stories. His autobiographical trilogy: *Cider with Rosie* (U.S. title *The Edge of Day*), 1959; *As I Walked Out One Midsummer Morning,* 1969; and *A Moment of War,* 1991. His poetry publications: *The Sun My Monument,* 1944. *The Bloom of Candles,* 1947. *My Many-Coated Man,* 1955. *Pocket Poems,* 1960. *Selected Poems,* 1983. Some of his poems: "April Rise," "Day of These Days," "Home From Abroad," "The Edge of Day," "The Long War," "Town Owl," "Village of Winter Carols."

Sources: *A Book of Nature Poems.* William Cole, ed. Viking Press, 1969. *Biography of Laurie Lee* (http://www. kirjasto.sci.fi/lauriele.htm). *Encyclopædia Britannica Ultimate Reference Suite DVD,* 2006. *Golden Treasury of the Best Songs and Lyrical Poems in the English Language.* Francis Turner Palgrave, ed. Oxford University Press, 1964, sixth edition, updated by John Press, 1994. *The Columbia Granger's Index to Poetry.* 11th ed. *The Columbia Granger's World of Poetry,* Columbia University Press, 2005 (http:// www.columbiagrangers.org). *The National Portrait Gallery* (www.npg.org.uk). *The New Yorker Book of Poems.* The New Yorker editors. Viking Press, 1969. *The Oxford Book of Christmas Poems.* Michael Harrison and Christopher Stuart-Clark, eds. Oxford University Press, 1983. *The Oxford Companion to English Literature.* 6th edition. Margaret Drabble, ed. Oxford University Press, 2000.

LEE-HAMILTON, EUGENE JACOB (1845–1907)

Born in London, he lived with his widowed mother in Pau, in the Aquitaine Region of France, then around 1854 they moved to Paris. He entered Oriel College, Oxford, in 1864 but left without graduating to follow a diplomatic career. He was at the embassy at Tours, Bordeaux, and Versailles during the Franco-German war (1870–1871) and was third secretary in Lisbon in 1873. For the next twenty years, although an invalid living with his mother in Florence, he was highly creative. The grief he experienced when his one-year-old daughter died in 1904 is expressed in *Mimma Bella* (1909), a volume of elegiac sonnets. He died of a stroke and was buried in the new Protestant cemetery outside the Porta Romana, Florence. Some of his other publications: *Poems and Transcripts,* 1878. *Imaginary Sonnets,* 1888. *The Fountain of Youth,* 1891. *Sonnets of the Wingless Hours,* 1894. *Forest Notes,* 1899. Some of his poems: "A Spanish Legend," "Alexander Selkirk to His Shadow," "Among the Firs," "Eagles of Tiberius," "James Watt to the Spirit of His Kettle," "Luther to a Blue-Bottle Fly," "Sunken Gold."

Sources: *Dictionary of National Biography.* Electronic Edition 1.1. Oxford University Press, 1997. *Selected Poems of Eugene Lee-Hamilton.* The Edwin Mellen Press, 2002. *Stanford University Libraries and Academic Information Resources* (http://library.stanford.edu). *The Columbia Granger's Index to Poetry.* 11th ed. *The Columbia Granger's World of Poetry,* Columbia University Press, 2005 (http://www.columbiagrangers.org). *The New Oxford Book of Victorian Verse.* Christopher Ricks, ed. Oxford University Press, 1987. *The Sonnet: An Anthology.* Robert M. Bender and Charles L. Squier, eds. Washington Square Press, 1987.

LEHMAN, RUDOLPH JOHN FREDERICK (1907–1987)

Known as John, he was born at Bourne End, Buckinghamshire, and educated at Eton College, then read English at Trinity College, Cambridge. When he returned to England after working as a journalist and poet in Vienna from 1932 to 1936, he founded and edited the book-periodical *New Writing.* It ran under various titles until 1950 and published, among others, the works of W.H. Auden (see entry) and Christopher Isherwood. Lehmann was general manager of the Hogarth Press from 1938 to 1946 and advisory editor of *The Geographical Magazine* from 1940 to 1945. He and his sister, the novelist Rosamond Lehmann, directed the publishing firm of John Lehmann Ltd. from 1946 to 1953. In 1954 he founded and edited (until 1961) *The London Magazine,* a literary review, publishing new works by authors such as Jean-Paul Sartre and discovering talents like Thom Gunn and Laurie Lee (see entries). His three-part autobiography was published in one volume in the United States in 1969 as *In My Own Time.* He died in London. Some of his poems: "A Death in Hospital," "The Ballad of Banners (1944)," "The Last Ascent," "The Sphere of Glass."

Sources: *A Little Book of Comfort.* Anthony Guest, ed. HarperCollins, 1993. *Collected Poems of John Lehmann.* Eyre and Spottiswoode, 1963. *Encyclopædia Britannica Ultimate Reference Suite DVD,* 2006. *Modern Ballads and Story Poems.* Charles Causley, ed. Franklin Watts, 1965. *The National Portrait Gallery* (www.npg.org.uk). *Portraits of Poets.* Sebastian Barker, ed. Carcanet, 1986. *The Chatto Book of Modern Poetry 1915–1955.* Cecil Day Lewis and John Lehmann, eds. Chatto and Windus, 1966. *The Columbia Granger's Index to Poetry.* 11th ed. *The Columbia Granger's World of Poetry,* Columbia University Press, 2005 (http://www.columbiagrangers.org). *The Modern Poets: An American-British Anthology.* John Malcom Brinnin and Bill Read, eds. McGraw-Hill, 1963.

LEIGHTON, ROBERT (1822–1869)

Scottish poet, born in Dundee and educated at the academy, he started working for his brother William, a Dundee ship owner, in 1837. In 1842–43 he sailed the world in one of his brother's ships, then worked for the London and North-Western Railway at Preston. He spent much of his life traveling at home and abroad on business for a seed merchant in Liverpool. Following an accident in 1867 near Youghal, County Cork, Ireland, he became a helpless invalid and died at Liverpool. Before 1843 he had contributed "Ye Three Voyces" to Jerrold's *Shilling Magazine,* and his popular song "Jenny Marshall's Candy, O," was said to improve the confectionery business of that lady. Some of his publications: *Poems by Robin,* 1861. *Scotch Words and the Bapteesement o' the Bairn,* 1868. *Poems,* 1869. *Reuben and Other Poems,* 1875. *Records and Other Poems,* 1880. Some of his other poems: "Abraham Lincoln," "The Guid Gray Cat: A Witch Story of the Sea," "My Mither's Grave," "The Auld Gaberlunzie is Dead and Awa'," "The Drunkard's Sonnet," "The Duke of Brunswick's Diamonds," "The Lonely Isle."

Sources: *Dictionary of National Biography.* Electronic Edition 1.1. Oxford University Press, 1997. *English Poetry, Second Edition Bibliography* (http://collections.chadwyck.co.uk/html/ep2/bibliography/g.htm). *Poems by Robert Leighton.* George Routledge and Sons (1869). *The Columbia Granger's Index to Poetry.* 11th ed. *The Columbia Granger's World of Poetry,* Columbia University Press, 2005 (http://www.columbiagrangers.org). *Stanford University Libraries and Academic Information Resources* (http://library.stanford.edu).

LEONARD, TOM (1944–)

Born in Glasgow, he was educated at Lourdes Secondary School and at Glasgow University. He was a member of Philip Hobsbaum's Glasgow writers' group. He has been writer in residence at Bell College of Technology, Renfrew District Libraries and the universities of Glasgow and Strathclyde; he was appointed professor of creative writing at Glasgow University. His collection *Intimate Voices: Selected Work 1965–1983* (1984) was banned from Central Region school libraries in the same year that it shared the Scottish Book of the Year Award. His poetry makes frequent use of Glaswegian vernacular speech. He edited *Radical Renfrew: Poetry from the French Revolution to the First World War* (1990). As well as publishing collections of poetry, he has performed sound poetry in festivals in Britain and abroad. Some of his other publications: *Six Glasgow Poems*, 1969. *Poems*, 1973. *Access to the Silence*, 1974. *Poems*, 1984. *Nora's Place and Other Poems 1965–1995*, 1996 (Spoken Word CD AKA006CD, AK Press). Some of his poems: "100 Differences Between Poetry and Prose," "Ghostie Men," "The Fair Cop," "The Proxy Badge of Victimhood," "Unrelated Incidents," "Wish You Were Here."

Sources: *Anthology of Twentieth-Century British and Irish Poetry*. Keith Tuma, ed. Oxford University Press, 2001. *Biography of Tom Leonard, BBC—Writing Scotland—Scotland's Languages* (http://www.bbc.co.uk/scotland/arts/writingscotland/learning_journeys/scotlands_languages/tom_leonard). *Other British and Irish Poetry Since 1970*. Richard Caddel and Peter Quartermain, eds. Wesleyan University Press, 1999. *The Columbia Granger's Index to Poetry*. 11th ed. *The Columbia Granger's World of Poetry*, Columbia University Press, 2005 (http://www.columbia grangers.org). *The New British Poetry, 1968–88*. Gillian Allnutt, Fred D'Aguiar and Ken Edwards, eds. Grafton Books, 1989. *The New Penguin Book of Scottish Verse*. Robert Crawford and Mick Imlah, eds. Penguin Books, 2000. *The Oxford Companion to English Literature*. 6th edition. Margaret Drabble, ed. Oxford University Press, 2000.

LETTS, WINIFRED MARY (1882–1971)

She was born in Manchester or Cheshire of an English father and Irish mother and educated in Bromley, Kent, and Alexandra College, Dublin. During World War I she worked as a nurse at various base hospitals. After her marriage to William Henry Foster Verschoyle, of Kilberry, County Kildare, in 1926, they lived in Dublin and County Kildare. When he died, she lived for many years in Faversham, Kent, returning to Killiney, Dublin, where she lived until the late 1960s. She died in the Tivoli Nursing Home, Dun Laoghaire, Dublin. Her novels, plays, children's fiction, and poetry have strong Irish connections, and some of her poems were set to music by C.V. Stanford. Some of her publications: *Songs of Leinster*, 1913. *Hallow-e'en and Poems of the War*, 1916. *The Spires of Oxford, and Other Poems*, 1917. *More Songs of Leinster*, 1926. Some of her poems: "Boys," "Casualty," "Irish Skies," "My Blessing Be on Waterford," "The Chapel on the Hill," "The Children's Ghosts," "The Connaught Rangers," "The Deserter," "The Harbour," "Tim, an Irish Terrier," "To a Soldier in Hospital."

Sources: *Oldpoetry* (www.oldpoetry.com). *Scars Upon My Heart: Women's Poetry and Verse of the First World War*. Catherine W Reilly, ed. Virago Press, 1981. *The Book of a Thousand Poems: A Family Treasury*. J. Murray Macbain, ed. Peter Bedrick Books, 1983. *The Columbia Granger's Index to Poetry*. 11th ed. *The Columbia Granger's World of Poetry*, Columbia University Press, 2005 (http://www.columbia grangers.org). *Treasury of Irish Religious Verse*. Patrick Murray, ed. Crossroad, 1986.

LEVER, CHARLES JAMES (1806–1872)

Of English parentage, he was born in Dublin and graduated from Trinity College, Dublin, in 1827. He studied medicine at Göttingen, Germany, and qualified at Trinity College in 1831. His medical practice did not support his lifestyle, so he turned to writing, and in 1837 began a series—"Harry Lorrequer"—in the *Dublin University Magazine*. However, just as success seemed assured, he left Ireland for Brussels, where he had a successful practice. "Charles O'Malley, The Irish Dragoon" appeared in the *Dublin Magazine* for 1840, and he was editor of the magazine from 1842 to 1845. Thackeray (see entry) visited Lever on his own Irish tour in 1842–43 and dedicated to him his *Irish Sketch Book* (1876). He moved back to the Continent and was appointed British consul at Spezia, Italy, and in 1867 was made consul of Trieste, where he died of heart failure, his wife having died before him. A collected edition of his works in thirty-three volumes was issued between 1876 and 1878. Some of his other poems: "Mary Draper," "Old Dublin City," "The Bivouac," "The Widow Malone."

Sources: *Dictionary of National Biography*. Electronic Edition 1.1. Oxford University Press, 1997. *Encyclopædia Britannica Ultimate Reference Suite DVD*, 2006. *Irish Poems and Blessings: Poems by Charles Lever* (http://freepages.genealogy.rootsweb.com/~irelandlist/poems.html#gloryto). *Literature on the Age of Napoleon: Fiction and Drama* (Digital Texts http://napoleonic-literature.com/AgeOf Napoleon/E-Texts/Fiction.html). *The Columbia Granger's Index to Poetry*. 11th ed. *The Columbia Granger's World of Poetry*, Columbia University Press, 2005 (http://www.columbiagrangers.org). *War Songs*. Christopher Stone, ed. Oxford University Press, 1908.

LEVY, AMY (1861–1889)

Born in London to a wealthy middle class Anglo-Jewish family and educated at Brighton High

School, she was the first Jewish student at Newnham College, Cambridge, though she left after four semesters. She contributed to the leading feminist and women's periodicals of her day, including Emily Faithfull's *Victoria Magazine* and Oscar Wilde's *Woman's World*. She wrote fiction and essays on the position of women within Judaism and showed a strong interest in socialism. Her novel *Reuben Sachs* (1999) was translated into German by Eleanor Marx, the daughter of Karl Marx. Levy suffered from severe depression since childhood, and this influenced her writing; she wrote more about the dark side of life. She committed suicide by inhaling charcoal fumes. Her poetry publications: *Xantippe and Other Poems*, 1881. *A Minor Poet and Other Verse*, 1884. *A London Plane Tree and Other Poems*, 1889. Some of her poems: "A Ballad of Religion and Marriage," "Alma Mater," "At a Dinner Party," "At Dawn," "In the Black Forest," "Oh, is It Love?" "Two Translations of Jehudah Halevi."

Sources: *Biography of Amy Levy* (http://www.womenof brighton.co.uk/amylevy.htm). *Bread and Roses: An Anthology of Nineteenth- and Twentieth-Century Poetry by Women Writers*. Diana Scott, ed. Virago Press, 1982. *Dictionary of National Biography*. Electronic Edition 1.1. Oxford University Press, 1997. *Poems Between Women: Four Centuries of Love, Romantic Friendship, and Desire*. Emma Donoghue, ed. Columbia University Press, 1997. *The Columbia Granger's Index to Poetry*. 11th ed. *The Columbia Granger's World of Poetry*, Columbia University Press, 2005 (http://www.columbiagrangers.org). *The Complete Novels and Selected Writings of Amy Levy*. Melvyn New, ed. University Press of Florida, 1993. *The Oxford Companion to English Literature*. 6th edition. Margaret Drabble, ed. Oxford University Press, 2000.

LEWIS, ALUN (1915–1944)

The son of a schoolteacher, he was born in a South Wales mining village. He had a grammar school education and graduated with a first-class degree in history from University College of Wales at Aberystwyth in 1935 and an M.A. from Manchester University in 1936, then trained as a teacher at Aberystwyth. Although a pacifist, he was commissioned into the Royal Engineers in 1940 and saw service in India and in Burma, where he died, it is said, killed by his own revolver. His two books of short stories are *The Last Inspection* (1942) and *Letters from India* (1946). "Some critics see him as the last of the great Romantic poets, a twentieth century Keats" (Alun Lewis Biography, http://pages.eidosnet.co.uk). His poetry publications: *Raiders' Dawn and Other Poems*, 1942. *Ha! Ha! Among the Trumpets*, 1945. *Selected Poetry and Prose*, 1966. Some of his poems: "A Troopship in the Tropics," "After Dunkirk," "Burma Casualty," "On the Welsh Mountains," "The Assault Convoy," "The Captivity,"

"The Mountain over Aberdare," "The Soldier," "Threnody for a Starry Night," "War Wedding," "Westminster Abbey."

Sources: *Collected Poems of Alun Lewis*. Cary Archard, ed. Poetry Wales Press, 1994. *Dictionary of National Biography*. Electronic Edition 1.1. Oxford University Press, 1997. *Encyclopædia Britannica Ultimate Reference Suite DVD*, 2006. *The National Portrait Gallery* (www.npg.org.uk). *The Columbia Granger's Index to Poetry*. 11th ed. *The Columbia Granger's World of Poetry*, Columbia University Press, 2005 (http://www.columbiagrangers.org). *The Faber Book of War Poetry*. Kenneth Baker, ed. Faber and Faber, 1996. *The Oxford Companion to English Literature*. 6th edition. Margaret Drabble, ed. Oxford University Press, 2000. *War Poets Association: The Life of Alun Lewis* (http://www.warpoets.org/conflicts/ww2/lewis/).

LEWIS, CLIVE STAPLES (1898–1963)

C.S. Lewis, born in Belfast, Ireland, the son of a solicitor, started at University College, Oxford, in 1917, then enlisted into the Somerset Light Infantry. Wounded in the battle of Arras in April 1918, he returned to Oxford in 1919 to read classics. In 1925 Magdalen College elected him as a fellow and tutor in English language and literature, a post he held for nearly thirty years. *The Screwtape Letters* (1942) were highly popular and through these and his broadcasts on Christian topics, which began in August 1941, he became internationally known. The *Narnia* series of children's tales, begun in 1948, revealed a new facet of his imaginative gifts. He was professor in English medieval and Renaissance literature at Cambridge. He married Helen Joy Davidman of New York and when she died in 1960 he published the profound *A Grief Observed* (1961). Lewis was buried at Holy Trinity Church, Headington, Oxford. The film *Shadowlands*, starring Anthony Hopkins, was based on an original stage and television play (1993). Some of his poems: "After Prayers, Lie Cold," "Ballade of Dead Gentlemen," "Grief's Circle," "Joys That Sting," "Stephen to Lazarus."

Sources: *A Little Book of Comfort*. Anthony Guest, ed. HarperCollins, 1993. *A Sacrifice of Praise: An Anthology of Christian Poetry in English from Caedmon to the Mid–Twentieth Century*. James H. Trott, ed. Cumberland House Publishing, 1999. *Art and Love: An Illustrated Anthology of Love Poetry*. Kate Farrell, ed. The Metropolitan Museum of Art, 1990. *Dictionary of National Biography*. Electronic Edition 1.1. Oxford University Press, 1997. *Everyman's Book of English Verse*. John Wain, ed. J.M. Dent, 1981. *The Columbia Granger's Index to Poetry*. 11th ed. *The Columbia Granger's World of Poetry*, Columbia University Press, 2005 (http://www.columbiagrangers.org). *The Oxford Book of Comic Verse*. John Gross, ed. Oxford University Press, 1994. *The Oxford Companion to English Literature*. 6th edition. Margaret Drabble, ed. Oxford University Press, 2000.

LEWIS, DAVID (?1683–1760)

Many of the facts are vague. He was Welsh, the son of Roger Lewis of Llandewi Velfrey, Pembrokeshire. He graduated B.A. from Jesus College, Oxford, in 1702, and taught at Westminster School. His *Miscellaneous Poems by Several Hands* (1726) contains translations from Martial, Horace, and Anacreon. It also contains John Dyer's "Grongar Hill" (1726, see entry), Alexander Pope's "Vital Spark of Heavenly Flame" (1712, see entry), and the poems "*Wedding Song,*" "*See the Springing Day From Far,*" and "*Away! Let Nought to Love Displeasing,*" which was reprinted in Thomas Percy's *Reliques of Ancient English Poetry* (1765, see entry). Lewis published *Philip of Macedon*, a tragedy in blank verse (1727) and a second *Collection of Miscellany Poems* (1730). Some of his verses addressed to Pope were published by Richard Savage (see entry) in a *Collection of Pieces on Occasion of the Dunciad* (1732). Lewis died at Low Leyton, Essex, and was buried in Leyton Church, where an inscription speaks of his "many excellent pieces of poetry sufficiently testifying" to the fact that he was "a great favorite of the Muses" (DNB).

Sources: *Dictionary of National Biography.* Electronic Edition 1.1. Oxford University Press, 1997. *The Columbia Granger's Index to Poetry.* 11th ed. *The Columbia Granger's World of Poetry,* Columbia University Press, 2005 (http://www.columbiagrangers.org). *The Oxford Book of Eighteenth Century Verse.* David Nichol Smith, ed. Oxford University Press, 1926.

LEWIS, GWYNETH (1959–)

Welsh poet, born in Cardiff, she was educated at Pontypridd, Glamorganshire, but Welsh is her first language. She studied English at Girton College, Cambridge University, and received a Ph.D. in English from Oxford; her thesis was on eighteenth-century literary forgery. She also studied at Harvard and Columbia Universities and worked as a freelance journalist in New York; on returning to Britain she worked on BBC television. She was appointed Wales's first national poet in April 2005 and is one of the Poetry Book Society's "Next Generation" poets. She has written an oratorio for six hundred voices, *The Most Beautiful Man from the Sea,* with music by Richard Chew and Orlando Gough. *Two in a Boat: A Marital Voyage* (2005) is an hilarious prose account of a slice of life with her husband. She has received six literary awards. Some of her poetry publications in English: *Parables and Faxes,* 1995. *Zero Gravity,* 1998. *Keeping Mum,* 2003. *Chaotic Angels: Collected Poems,* 2005. Some of her poems: "Herod's Palace," "Six Poems on Nothing," "Sunday Park," "The Bad Shepherd," "Walking with the God," "Welsh Espionage."

Sources: *Biography of Gwyneth Lewis* (http://www. gwynethlewis.com/). *British Council Arts* (http://www.contemporarywriters.com). *New Blood,* Neil Astley, ed. Bloodaxe Books, 1999. *New Women Poets.* Carol Rumens, ed. Bloodaxe Books, 1990. *The Columbia Granger's Index to Poetry.* 11th ed. *The Columbia Granger's World of Poetry,* Columbia University Press, 2005 (http://www.columbiagrangers.org). *The Harvill Book of Twentieth-Century Poetry in English.* Michael Schmidt, ed. The Harvill Press, 1999. *Twentieth Century Anglo-Welsh Poetry.* Dannie Abse, ed. Seren Books / Dufour Editions, 1997.

LEWIS, SAUNDERS (1893–1985)

Born into a Welsh family living in Cheshire, he was studying English and French at Liverpool University when the First World War broke out. After serving as an officer with the South Wales Borderers he returned to university to graduate in English. In 1922 he was appointed as a lecturer in Welsh at the University College of Wales, Swansea, and in 1925 he co-founded the Welsh National Party, now Plaid Cymru. A talk he was invited to give on BBC Radio in 1930—banned by BBC officials as likely to inflame Welsh national sympathies—was subsequently published by Plaid Genedlaethol Cymru in 1931. In 1936, along with two other activists, he was involved in an arson attack on an air force base near Pwllheli, North Wales, which resulted in a nine month prison sentence and the loss of his academic post. Until he was appointed senior lecturer in Welsh at Cardiff in 1952, he supported himself through journalism, farming and teaching in schools. Among his many works are books on literary criticism. Some of his poems: "Ascension Thursday," "Mary Magdalene," "The Deluge 1939," "The Pine," "To the Good Thief."

Sources: *Life and Works of Saunders Lewis* (http://www. absoluteastronomy.com/reference/saunders_lewis). *Microsoft Encarta* 2006 (DVD). Microsoft Corporation, 2006. Saunders Lewis, "*The Banned Wireless Talk on Welsh Nationalism.*" (http://www.gtj.org.uk/en/item1/14563). *Selected Poems of Saunders Lewis,* translated by Joseph P. Clancy. University of Wales Press, 1993. *The Columbia Granger's Index to Poetry.* 11th ed. *The Columbia Granger's World of Poetry,* Columbia University Press, 2005 (http://www.columbiagrangers.org). *The Oxford Book of Welsh Verse in English.* Gwyn Jones, ed. Oxford University Press, 1977. *Wikipedia, the Free Encyclopedia* (http://en.wikipedia.org/wiki/Wikipedia).

LEYDEN, JOHN (1775–1811)

Scottish poet, born in Denholm, Roxburghshire, a farmer's son who became a physician, and who by the end of his life knew some thirty languages. He went to Edinburgh University with the idea of entering the church, but turned to medicine. In 1803 he was appointed assistant surgeon in Madras, India, and he remained in the Far East for the rest of his life. In 1809 he became commissioner of the Court of Requests in Calcutta. He died in Java and is mentioned in Canto IV of Sir Walter Scott's *The Lord of the Isles*. He studied the grammars of the Malay and Pracrit tongues and undertook many translations. His poems on Border themes had considerable influence on the poetry of Sir Walter Scott, whom he assisted with *The Minstrelsy of the Scottish Border* (1802), and he contributed poems to many other collected works of the day. His *The Poetical Remains* was published in 1819. Some of his poems: "Address to My Malay Krees," "Christmas in Penang," "Lords of the Wilderness," "Ode on Visiting Flodden," "The Lay of the Ettercap," "The Wail of Alzira" (an anti-slavery poem).

Sources: *Dictionary of National Biography.* Electronic Edition 1.1. Oxford University Press, 1997. *English Poetry: Author Search.* Chadwyck-Healey Ltd., 1995 (http://www. lib.utexas.edu:8080/search/epoetry/author.html). *Folk Songs.* John Williamson Palmer, ed. Charles Scribner and Company, 1867. *Go Britannia! Scotland: Great Scots of Note* (http://www.britannia.com/celtic/scotland/greatscots/l1. html). *Leyden, "The Wail of Alzira." The poem* (http:// www2.bc.edu/~richarad/asp/jlwa.html). *Stanford University Libraries and Academic Information Resources* (http:// library.stanford.edu). *The Brand-X Anthology of Poetry.* William Zaranka, ed. Apple-Wood Books, 1981. *The Columbia Granger's Index to Poetry.* 11th ed. *The Columbia Granger's World of Poetry,* Columbia University Press, 2005 (http://www.columbiagrangers.org). *The Oxford Book of Regency Verse 1798–1837.* H.S. Milford, ed. Oxford University Press, 1928. *The Oxford Book of Travel Verse.* Kevin Crossley-Holland, ed. Oxford University Press, 1986. *The Oxford Companion to English Literature.* 6th edition. Margaret Drabble, ed. Oxford University Press, 2000.

LINCHE (LYNCHE), RICHARD (d. 1601)

The details of the life of this Elizabethan poet have been lost. However, it is assumed with some certainty that he is the author of a collection of thirty-nine sonnets under the title *Deilia*, along with the *Amorous Poeme of Dom Diego and Gineura* dated 1596. The *Story of Dom Diego* is taken from the *Tragicall Discourses* (1567) of Sir Geoffrey Fenton. Linche also wrote *The Fountaine of English Fiction*, which tells the stories of the ancient gods. Another work is *An Historical Treatise of the Travels of Noah into Europe*. It covers the kings, governors, and rulers up to the time of the first building of Troy by Dardanus (from whom Dardanelles is derived); though based on Greek mythology, it is thought to relate to real history. Linche is the subject of the sonnet *In Praise of Music and Poetry* by Richard Barnfield (see entry). Some of the sonnets from *Dielia*: "End This Enchantment, Love, of My Desires," "Love's Despair," "Soon as the Azure-Colored Gates of th' East," "Weary with Serving Where I Nought Could Get," "What Sugared Terms, What All-Persuading Art."

Sources: *Anno Mundi Books: From Noah to Dardanus,* by Richard Linche (http://www.annomundi.com/history/ noah_to_dardanus.htm). *Dictionary of National Biography.* Electronic Edition 1.1. Oxford University Press, 1997. *Elizabethan Lyrics.* Norman Ault, ed. William Sloane Associates, 1949. *The Anchor Anthology of Seventeenth-Century Verse, Vol. II.* Louis L. Martz and Richard S. Sylvester, ed. Doubleday Anchor Books, 1969. *The Columbia Granger's Index to Poetry.* 11th ed. *The Columbia Granger's World of Poetry,* Columbia University Press, 2005 (http:// www.columbiagrangers.org). *The Sonnet: An Anthology.* Robert M. Bender and Charles L. Squier, eds. Washington Square Press, 1987. *The Sonnet-Series: Page Seventeen by John Erskine, The Elizabethan Lyric.* Macmillan Company, 1903, reprinted by Columbia University Press, 1916. *The Sonnet Series, Richard Linche* (http://www.sonnets. org/erskineq.htm).

LINDSAY (LYNDSAY), SIR DAVID (?1486–1555)

A Scottish poet of the pre-Reformation period who satirized the corruption of the Roman Catholic Church and contemporary government. He was one of the company of gifted courtly poets (makaris) who flourished in the golden age of Scottish literature. Born in Fifeshire of an aristocratic family, he was attendant and companion to the infant Prince James (born 1512), the son of King James IV. During the period when the young King James V fell under the domination of the Scottish nobles, David was away from court, and returned when James took control in 1528. He was an influential diplomat to several European monarchs. He wrote the morality play the *Thrie Estaits*, performed in 1552. *The Dreme* (completed 1528) is a long allegory of the contemporary condition of Scotland. Some of his other poems: "Ane Supplication in Contemptioun of Syde Taillis," "So Young Ane King," "The Answer to the Kingis Flyting," "The Complaynt of Schir David Lindesay," "The Deploratioun of the Deith of Quene Magdalene," "The Devisioun of the Eirth," "The Historie of Squyer William Meldrum," "The Tragedie of the Cardinall."

Sources: *Dictionary of National Biography.* Electronic Edition 1.1. Oxford University Press, 1997. *Encyclopædia Britannica Ultimate Reference Suite DVD,* 2006. *English Poetry, Second Edition Bibliography* (http://collections. chadwyck.co.uk/html/ep2/bibliography/g.htm). *English Poetry: Author Search.* Chadwyck-Healey Ltd., 1995 (http://www.lib.utexas.edu:8080/search/epoetry/author. html). *Selected Poems of Sir David Lyndsay.* Janet Hadley Williams, ed. Association for Scottish Literary Studies, 2000. *The Columbia Granger's Index to Poetry.* 11th ed. *The Columbia Granger's World of Poetry,* Columbia University Press, 2005 (http://www.columbiagrangers.org). *The Golden Treasury of Scottish Poetry.* Hugh MacDiarmid, ed. Macmillan, 1941. *The New Penguin Book of Scottish Verse.* Robert Crawford and Mick Imlah, ed. Penguin Books, 2000. *The Oxford Companion to English Literature.* 6th edition. Margaret Drabble, ed. Oxford University Press, 2000. *The Works of Sir David Lindsay of the Moun.* Douglas Hamer, ed. Printed for The [Scottish Text] Society by William Blackwood and Sons, 1931–1936.

LINTON, WILLIAM JAMES (1812–1898)

Born in London and educated at Stratford (East London), he became a renowned wood engraver, poet, political agitator and reformer, a Chartist, and a professed republican. In 1839 he established the political journal *The National*, reprinting extracts from publications not readily accessible to working men. In 1845 he became editor of *The Illuminated Magazine*, which published contributions from writers of more merit than popularity, including "A Royal Progress," a poem by Sarah Flower Adams (see entry). In 1866 he went to the United States, where he mainly devoted the rest of his life to the regeneration of American wood-engraving, at Appledore, a farmhouse near New Haven, Connecticut, where he died. He wrote several books on wood engraving, including *The Masters of Wood Engraving* (1890). He produced several volumes of his own poems on his own press, and in 1882, he edited *Rare Poems of the Sixteenth and Seventeenth Centuries.* He also translated French lyrics. Some of his poems: "A Book," "Be Thyself," "Bob Thin; or, the Poorhouse Fugitive," "Epicurean," "Faint Heart," "Fair England," "Spring and Autumn," "The Gathering of the People."

Sources: *Book-Song.* Gleeson White, ed. Elliot Stock, 1893. *Dictionary of National Biography.* Electronic Edition 1.1. Oxford University Press, 1997. *Encyclopædia Britannica Ultimate Reference Suite DVD,* 2006. *England 5 poems — poems of the week learn English* (http://www.learnenglish.org.uk/stories/poem_act/england_poetry.html). *English Poetry: Author Search* (http://www.lib.utexas.edu:8080/search/epoetry/author.html). *One Hundred and One Classics of Victorian Verse.* Ellen J. Greenfield, ed. Contemporary Books, 1992. *The Columbia Granger's Index to Poetry.* 11th ed. *The Columbia Granger's World of Poetry,* Columbia University Press, 2005 (http://www.columbiagrangers.org). *The Oxford Book of Victorian Verse.* Arthur Quiller-Couch, ed. Oxford University Press, 1971.

LLOYD, CHARLES (1775–1839)

Born in Birmingham, the son of Charles Lloyd the Quaker banker and philanthropist, he was groomed to take over his father's bank but turned to literature. He was a close fiend of Samuel Taylor Coleridge (see entry), whose sonnet "To a Friend" on the birth of his son Hartley and his lines "To a Young Man of Fortune" are probably addressed to Lloyd. Suffering from some delusional mental illness, he was admitted to an asylum near York, possibly The Retreat (a Quaker hospital), from which he escaped about 1818 and made his way back to his home in Westmoreland. He and his wife died near Versailles and their nine children were scattered over the world. Some of his publications: *Poems on various subjects,* 1795. *Poems on The Death of Priscilla Farmer,* 1796. *Poems,* 1797. *Blank Verse by Charles Lloyd and Charles Lamb.* 1798. Translation of Ovid's *Metamorphoses,* 1811. *Nugae Canorae,* 1819. *Desultory Thoughts in London,* 1821. *Poetical essays on the character of Pope,* 1821. *Beritola,* 1822. *Poems,* 1823. Some of his poems: "Address to a Virginian Creeper," "Lines," "Metaphysical Sonnet," "Stanzas to Ennui," "Written at the Hotwells, Near Bristol."

Sources: *Dictionary of National Biography.* Electronic Edition 1.1. Oxford University Press, 1997. *English Poetry: Author Search.* Chadwyck-Healey Ltd., 1995 (http://www.lib.utexas.edu:8080/search/epoetry/author.html). *Poems of Charles Lloyd.* Hurst, Rees, Orme, and Brown, 1823. Stanford University Libraries and Academic Information Resources (http://library.stanford.edu). *The Columbia Granger's Index to Poetry.* 11th ed. *The Columbia Granger's World of Poetry,* Columbia University Press, 2005 (http://www.columbiagrangers.org). *The New Oxford Book of Romantic Period Verse.* Jerome J. McGann. Oxford University Press, 1993. *The Romantic Era, List of Poets* (http://www.sonnets.org/romantic.htm).

LLOYD, EVAN (1734–1776)

Born near Bala, North Wales, he graduated M.A. from Jesus College, Oxford, in 1757, after which he took holy orders. About 1762 he became vicar of Llanvair Dyffryn Clwyd in Denbighshire, where he devoted himself to writing satirical humor. *The Powers of the Pen: A poem addressed to John Curre, Esquire* (1765), attacked the poet Samuel Johnson (see entry). In another he satirizes William Warburton, Bishop of Gloucester, in a thinly veiled poem *The Bishop, The Curate: A poem, inscribed to all the Curates in England and Wales* (1766) which attacks the way curates are put upon by their higher-ups. *The Methodist: A Poem* (1766), which attacked a neighboring squire, resulted in a libel suit and a term of imprisonment, where Lloyd formed a firm friendship with another prisoner, John Wilkes, the political agitator. "The Conversation: A Poem" appeared in 1767. *Epistle to David Garrick, Esq.* (1773) resulted in a warm friendship with the actor. He died unmarried and was buried in the family vault at Llanycil Church, Merionethshire; his epitaph was written by Wilkes.

Sources: *Anglo-Welsh Poetry, 1480–1980.* Raymond Garlick and Roland Mathias, eds. Poetry Wales Press, 1984. *Anglo-Welsh Poetry, 1480–1990.* Raymond Garlick and Roland Mathias, eds. Poetry Wales Press, 1993. *Dictionary of National Biography.* Electronic Edition 1.1. Oxford University Press, 1997. *English Poetry: Author Search.* Chadwyck-Healey Ltd., 1995 (http://www.lib.utexas.edu:

8080/search/epoetry/author.html). Stanford University Libraries and Academic Information Resources (http://library.stanford.edu). *The Columbia Granger's Index to Poetry.* 11th ed. *The Columbia Granger's World of Poetry,* Columbia University Press, 2005 (http://www.columbia grangers.org). *The New Oxford Book of Eighteenth Century Verse.* Roger Lonsdale, ed. Oxford University Press, 2003. *The Oxford Book of Satirical Verse.* Geoffrey Grigson, ed. Oxford University Press, 1980.

LLOYD, ROBERT (1733–1764)

Born in London and educated at Westminster School — where his father, Pierson Lloyd, doctor of divinity, was master — and at Trinity College, Cambridge, from where he graduated M.A. in 1758. While at Cambridge he contributed five sets of verses to the *Connoisseur,* the university magazine. On leaving Cambridge he returned to Westminster School but soon resigned and entered "into a reckless career of dissipation" (DNB), endeavoring to support himself by writing. He published the popular poem "The Actor" (1760), which is said to have stimulated Charles Churchill to write the *Rosciad* (1761). In 1764, Lloyd published *The Capricious Lovers* (a comic opera) performed at Drury Lane in the same year. Lloyd was often in debt and apparently died in Fleet Prison shortly after the death of Charles Churchill (see entry), with whom he shared his dissolute life. Some of his other poems: "A Familiar Epistle to J.B., Esq.," "Cit's Country Box," "Ode to Obscurity," "Ode to Oblivion," "On Rhyme," "Sent to a Lady, with a Seal," "Shakespeare: An Epistle to David Garrick, Esq.," "The Actor," "The Poetry Professors."

Sources: *Dictionary of National Biography.* Electronic Edition 1.1. Oxford University Press, 1997. *Eighteenth-Century English Verse.* Dennis Davison, ed. Penguin Books, 1988. *English Poetry: A Poetic Record, from Chaucer to Yeats.* David Hopkins, ed. Routledge, 1990. *Biography of Robert Lloyd* (http://www.fzc.dk/Boswell/People/people.php?id= 85). *The Columbia Granger's Index to Poetry.* 11th ed. *The Columbia Granger's World of Poetry,* Columbia University Press, 2005 (http://www.columbiagrangers.org). *The Faber Book of Useful Verse.* Simon Brett, ed. Faber and Faber, 1981. *The New Oxford Book of Eighteenth Century Verse.* Roger Lonsdale, ed. Oxford University Press, 1984.

LLUELYN (LLUELLYN), MARTIN (1616–1682)

Poet, physician, and principal of St. Mary Hall, Oxford, he was born in London, educated at Westminster School, and graduated M.A. from Christ Church, Oxford, in 1643. During the Civil War he served with the royalist army. He practiced as a doctor in London from around 1648, was granted the degree of M.D. from Oxford in 1653, was made a fellow of the College of Physicians in 1659, and became physician to Charles II after the Restoration. He left Oxford in 1664 and settled in High Wycombe, Buckinghamshire, and was elected mayor of the borough in 1671. He was buried in the north aisle of High Wycombe Church. Several of his poems were included in *Wit's Recreations* (1640) (believed to be by Thomas May [see entry]). Some of his publications: *Men-Miracles: With Other Poemes,* 1646. *An Elegy on the Death of the most Illustrious Prince, Henry Duke of Gloucester,* 1660. *To the Kings most excellent majesty,* 1660. *Wickham Wakened,* or, *The Quakers Madrigall in Rime Dogrell,* 1672. Three of his other poems: "Cock-throwing," "Epithalamium: to Mistress M.A.," "Ode to Celia."

Sources: *Dictionary of National Biography.* Electronic Edition 1.1. Oxford University Press, 1997. *English Poetry: Author Search.* Chadwyck-Healey Ltd., 1995 (http://www.lib.utexas.edu:8080/search/epoetry/author.html). *The Shakespeare Mystery: Harvard Magazine Article × PBS* (http://www.pbs.org/wgbh/pages/frontline/shakespeare/debates/harvardmag.html). *The Columbia Granger's Index to Poetry.* 11th ed. *The Columbia Granger's World of Poetry,* Columbia University Press, 2005 (http://www.columbiagrangers.org). *The New Oxford Book of Seventeenth Century Verse.* Alastair Fowler, ed. Oxford University Press, 1991. *The Penguin Book of Bird Poetry.* Peggy Munsterberg, ed. 1984.

LLWYD, HUGH (HUW) (?1568–1630)

The DNB gives the date of his birth as 1533. The Countryside Council for Wales and *Granger's Index* give 1568, which seems more likely. Llwyd was a Welsh poet, born in the parish of Maentwrog, Merionethshire. He was well educated and for some time held a commission in the English army and saw service abroad. He settled at Cynfael, Merionethshire, and because he was the seventh son of a family of sons and was well-read, he acquired a reputation as a magician. He increased his knowledge of the black art by the study of magical books and learning charms. It is said that he had the power to make all female black witches harmless, but nothing suggests he had the same power over male black witches. He traveled Wales, lifting curses and curing people, including rendering harmless the cat witches of Betwsy-coed. He is said to have died at Cynfael and was buried at Maentwrog. Thomas Love Peacock (see entry), in his book *Headlong Hall* (1816) refers to Llwyd, whose only extant work is a "Poem on the Fox, or The Fox's Counsel."

Sources: *Dictionary of National Biography.* Electronic Edition 1.1. Oxford University Press, 1997. *Headlong Hall, by Thomas Love Peacock* (http://www.thomaslovepeacock. net/Headlong.html). *Huw's Magic Books* (http://www. angelfire.com/wizard/dragonslore/page32e.html). "Poem on the Fox, or The Fox's Counsel": See *The Columbia Granger's Index to Poetry.* 11th ed. *The Columbia Granger's World of Poetry.* Columbia University Press, 2005 (http:// www.columbiagrangers.org). *The Cat Witches* (http:// www.red4.co.uk/Folklore/fairytales/catwitches.htm).

LLWYD, MORGAN (1619–1659)

Welsh poet born in Maentwrog, Merionethshire. In the English Civil Wars he served as a chaplain in the Parliamentary army and is identified with the first Dissenting church in Wales. Toward the end of his life, owing to his strained relations with the Presbyterians, who were dominant in the parish, he ceased to be vicar of Wrexham. He was buried in the "Dissenters' Graveyard" in Rhos-ddu Road near Wrexham. *Llyfr y Tri Aderyn (The Book of the Three Birds*, 1653) is an important original 17th century Welsh classic in two parts, on the theory of government and on religious liberty. The book is in the form of a discourse conducted among the eagle (Oliver Cromwell, or the secular power), the raven (the Anglicans, or organized religion), and the dove (the Nonconformists, or the followers of the inner light). Some of his poems: "1648," "Awake, O Lord, Awake Thy Saints," "Charles, the last king of Britain," "Come Wisdome Sweet," "The Summer."

Sources: *Anglo-Welsh Poetry, 1480–1980.* Raymond Garlick and Roland Mathias, eds. Poetry Wales Press, 1984. *Anglo-Welsh Poetry, 1480–1990.* Raymond Garlick and Roland Mathias, eds. Poetry Wales Press, 1993. *Dictionary of National Biography.* Electronic Edition 1.1. Oxford University Press, 1997. *Encyclopædia Britannica Ultimate Reference Suite DVD,* 2006. *Llyfr Y Tri Aderyn.* M. Wynn Thomas, ed. University of Wales Press, 1983. *The Columbia Granger's Index to Poetry.* 11th ed (http://www.columbiagrangers.org). *The Penguin Book of Renaissance Verse 1509–1659.* David Norbrook, ed. Penguin Books, 1992.

LLWYD, RICHARD (1752–1835)

"The Bard of Snowdon" was born in Beaumaris, Anglesey, where his father, a small coast trader, died when Richard was young. He spent only nine months at the free school at Beaumaris, then at the age of twelve entered the domestic service of a local gentleman. He used all his spare time to educate himself and by 1780 he was steward and secretary to a Mr. Griffith of Caerhun, near Conway, the local magistrate. He finally acquired sufficient income to retire to Beaumaris. He died at Chester and was buried at St. John's Church. His notes show that he was well versed in heraldry, genealogy, and Welsh archaeology. Some of his publications: *Beaumaris Bay,* 1800 (with many historical and genealogical notes). *Gayton Wake, or Mary Dod, and Her List of Merits,* 1804. *Poems, Tales, Odes, Sonnets, Translations from the British,* 1804. Some of his poems: "Einion Lonydd," "Elegy on Evan the Thatcher," "Llwyd to the Bard of the Wreekin," "Owen of Llangoed," "The Address of the Bard of Snowdon to His Countrymen," "The Castle of Harlech," "The Vision of Taliesin," "To the Gwyneddigion Society."

Sources: *Dictionary of National Biography.* Electronic Edition, 1.1. *Portrait of William Jones, National Museum Wales, Art Collections On-line* (http://www.nmgw.ac.uk/www.php/art/online/?action=show_item&item=1158). *The Columbia Granger's Index to Poetry.* 11th ed (http://www.columbiagrangers.org). *The Poetical Works of Richard Lllwyd.* Whittaker and Co., 1837.

LOCHHEAD, LIZ (1947–)

Born in Motherwell, Scotland, she studied painting at the Glasgow School of Art (1965–70) and during the early seventies took part in a writing group co-coordinated by Philip Hobsbaum (see entry), then worked as an art teacher until she became a full-time writer in 1979. Her revue *Sugar and Spite* was staged in 1978 and in the same year she was awarded a Scottish Writers Exchange Fellowship to Canada. She was writer in residence at Edinburgh University (1986–1987) and writer in residence at the Royal Shakespeare Company in 1988. She has published several stage plays and her poetry has been published in a number of collections, including *Penguin Modern Poets* 4 (1995). She was awarded an honorary degree by Edinburgh University in 2000. Some of her poetry publications: *Memo for Spring,* 1972 (which won a Scottish Arts Council Book Award). *The Grim Sisters,* 1981. *Dreaming Frankenstein,* 1984. *Three Scottish Poets,* 1996. *The Color of Black and White: Poems,* 1984–2003. Some of her poems: "An Abortion," "Bagpipe Muzak, Glasgow 1990," "Heartbreak Hotel," "Mirror's Song," "My Mother's Suitors," "Riddle-Me-Ree," "The Furies," "The Hickie."

Sources: *100 Poems on the Underground.* Gerald Benson, Judith Cherniak and Cicely Herb, eds. Cassell, 1991. *Anthology of Twentieth-Century British and Irish Poetry.* Keith Tuma, ed. Oxford University Press, 2001. *Biography of Liz Lochhead* (http://www.contemporarywriters.com/authors/?p=auth154&state=index%3Dl). *Biography of Liz Lochhead* (http://members.tripod.com/~giggly/liz_lochhead.html). *Love's Witness: Five Centuries of Love Poetry by Women.* Jill Hollis, ed. Carroll and Graf, Inc., 1993. *The Columbia Anthology of British Poetry.* Carl Woodring and James Shapiro, eds. Columbia University Press, 1995. *The Columbia Granger's Index to Poetry.* 11th ed (http://www.columbiagrangers.org). *The Faber Book of Seductions.* Jenny Newman, ed. Faber and Faber, 1988. *The New British Poetry, 1968–88.* Gillian Allnutt, Fred D'Aguiar and Ken Edwards, eds. Grafton Books, 1989. *The Oxford Companion to English Literature.* 6th edition. Margaret Drabble, ed. Oxford University Press, 2000.

LOCHORE, ROBERT (1762–1852)

Scottish poet, born at Strathaven, Lanarkshire, he became a shoemaker at the age of thirteen and ultimately had a successful business in Glasgow, where he was well known for his philanthropy and generosity. He died in Glasgow, leaving unpublished an autobiography and various Scottish tales and poems. In 1795 he published *Willie's Vision* and *The Foppish Taylor*, two poetical tracts. About 1815 he published anonymously *Tales in Rhyme and Minor Pieces, in the Scottish Dialect*. His poem *Last Speech of the Auld Brig of Glasgow on Being Condemned to Be Taken Down*—circulated as a broadsheet in 1850—also appeared in the *Reformers' Gazette* of 1850. His poems are valuable illustrations of Scottish life and character, one of them being "Marriage and the Care o't."

Sources: *Dictionary of National Biography.* Electronic Edition 1.1. Oxford University Press, 1997. *The Columbia Granger's Index to Poetry.* 11th ed. *The Columbia Granger's World of Poetry,* Columbia University Press, 2005 (http:// www.columbiagrangers.org). *The Home Book of Verse for Young Folks.* Burton Egbert Stevenson, ed. Holt, Rinehart and Winston, 1929. *The Home Book of Verse.* Burton Egbert Stevenson, ed. New York: Henry Holt and Company, 1953.

LOCKER-LAMPSON, FREDERICK (1821–1895)

More often known as Frederick Locker, he was born at Greenwich Hospital (the Royal Naval Hospital for Seamen) where his father was civil commissioner. He held several clerking jobs and in 1842 he was transferred to the admiralty. Subsequently he became deputy reader and précis writer, until 1849, when his health broke down. In July 1850 he married Lady Charlotte Bruce, daughter of Thomas Bruce, seventh earl of Elgin, who brought the famous Elgin marbles to England. Chapman and Hall published his first collection of verse, *London Lyrics,* in 1857, and his anthology, *Lyra Elegantiarum,* was published in 1867. His wife died in 1872 and in 1874 he married Hannah Jane, only daughter of Sir Curtis Miranda Lampson, of Rowfant, Sussex, and took the name of Lampson. He died at Rowfant. Some of his poems: "A Garden Lyric," "A Nice Correspondent," "At Her Window," "Loulou and Her Cat," "Love, Time and Death," "My Mistress's Boots," "On an Old Muff," "St. James's Street," "The Cuckoo," "The Jester's Plea," "The Skeleton in the Cupboard," "The Widow's Mite," "To My Grandmother."

Sources: *101 Favorite Cat Poems.* Sara L. Whittier, ed. Contemporary Books, 1991. *Dictionary of National Biography.* Electronic Edition 1.1. Oxford University Press, 1997. *English Poetry: Author Search.* Chadwyck-Healey Ltd., 1995 (http://www.lib.utexas.edu:8080/search/epo etry/author.html). *The National Portrait Gallery.* (www. npg.org.uk). *The Columbia Granger's Index to Poetry.* 11th ed. *The Columbia Granger's World of Poetry,* Columbia University Press, 2005 (http://www.columbiagrangers. org). *The Home Book of Verse for Young Folks.* Burton Egbert Stevenson, ed. Holt, Rinehart and Winston, 1929. *The Home Book of Modern Verse.* Burton Egbert Stevenson, ed. Henry Holt, 1953. *The Oxford Book of Victorian Verse.* Arthur Quiller-Couch, ed. Oxford University Press, 1971. *The Oxford Companion to English Literature.* 6th edition. Margaret Drabble, ed. Oxford University Press, 2000.

LODGE, THOMAS (?1558–1625)

Born in London, the son of Sir Thomas Lodge, lord mayor of London (1562), he was educated at Merchant Taylors' School and Trinity College, Oxford, from where he graduated M.A. in 1580. He abandoned the study of law for literature, thus forfeiting a promised legacy from his mother (who died in 1579) if he continued his law studies. He later studied medicine at the University of Avignon in 1598 and was incorporated M.D. at Oxford in 1602, becoming a respected physician in London and Brussels. He died in London fighting the plague. Two of his plays are *The Wounds of Civil War* (1594) and *A Looking Glasse for London and England* (1594). *A Fig for Momus* (1595) is a collection of satirical poems. He is best remembered for the prose romance *Rosalynde* (1590)—the source of William Shakespeare's *As You Like It*—and for his poems scattered throughout his romances, such as *A Margarite of America*. Some of his poems: "Egloga Prima Demades Damon," "Montanus praise of his faire Phæbe," "Montanus Sonnet to his faire Phæbe," "Scillaes Metamorphosis," "The Barginet of Antimachus," "Thirsis Ægloga Secunda."

Sources: *An Antidote Against Melancholy.* Pratt Manufacturing Company, 1884. *Dictionary of National Biography.* Electronic Edition 1.1. Oxford University Press, 1997. *Poets of the English Language. Vol. I.* W.H. Auden and Norman Holmes Pearson, eds. Viking Press, 1950. *The Anchor Anthology of Seventeenth-Century Verse, Vol. II.* Louis L. Martz and Richard S. Sylvester, eds. Doubleday Anchor Books, 1969. *The Columbia Granger's Index to Poetry.* 11th ed. *The Columbia Granger's World of Poetry,* Columbia University Press, 2005 (http://www.columbiagrangers. org). *The Complete Works of Thomas Lodge: Volume 4.* Russell and Russell, 1963. *The New Oxford Book of Sixteenth Century Verse.* Emrys Jones, ed. Oxford University Press, 1991. *The Oxford Companion to English Literature.* 6th edition. Margaret Drabble, ed. Oxford University Press, 2000. *The Penguin Book of Renaissance Verse 1509–1659.* David Norbrook, ed. Penguin Books, 1992.

LOGAN, JOHN (1748–1788)

Born at Soutra, Fala, Midlothian, Scotland, the son of a farmer, he had a grammar school education, then went to Edinburgh University. After he completed his studies for the ministry of the Church of Scotland, he was tutor to the son of Mr. (later Sir) John Sinclair of Ulbster, Caithness-shire. He was licensed to preach in 1770 and ordained in 1773 to the parish of South Leith. In 1775, he was appointed by the general assembly to the committee charged with the revision and enlargement of the paraphrases and hymns for use in public worship. In 1781, he published *Poems, By the Rev. Mr. Logan, One of the Ministers of Leith,* which included the "Ode to the Cuckoo," which was praised by Edmund Burke. That poem and several others were claimed to have been written by Michael Bruce (see entry) and a lawsuit followed. Logan resigned and moved to London. In 1790 and 1791 two volumes of his sermons were published. He is the author of the popular poem "The Braes of Yarrow," and he recast the hymn "O God of Bethel, by Whose Hand" by Philip Doddridge (see entry).

Sources: *A Book of Scottish Verse.* Maurice Lindsay, and R.L. Mackie, ed. St. Martin's Press, 1983. *Dictionary of National Biography.* Electronic Edition 1.1. Oxford University Press, 1997. *English Poetry: Author Search.* Chadwyck-Healey Ltd., 1995 (http://www.lib.utexas.edu:8080/search/epoetry/author.html). *Stanford University Libraries and Academic Information Resources* (http://library.stanford.edu). *The Columbia Granger's Index to Poetry.* 11th ed. *The Columbia Granger's World of Poetry,* Columbia University Press, 2005 (http://www.columbiagrangers.org).

LOGUE, CHRISTOPHER (1926–)

Born in Portsmouth, Hampshire, he was educated at Portsmouth Grammar School and served in the British Army from 1944 to 1948. He is one of the leaders in the movement to bring poetry closer to the people and was an early pioneer in the jazz poetry movement. His long and varied list of works includes plays, screenplays, documentaries and numerous children's books, in addition to poetry and translation. He also acted in several television, movie, and stage roles. One of the films was *Moonlighting* (1982) starring Jeremy Irons. For years he has been engaged in rendering Homer's *Iliad* into English, publishing his work in a series of slim volumes, each representing two or three books of the original epic. Some of his poetry publications: *The Weakdream Sonnets,* 1955. *The Man Who Told His Love,* 1958. *Songs from the Lily-White Boys,* 1960. *Logue's A.B.C,* 1966. *New Numbers,* 1969. *London in Verse,* 1984. Some of his poems: "Chinese England," "For My Father," "Letters from an Irishman to a Rat," "Red Bird," "The Ass's Song," "The Isles of Jessamy," "The Song of the Dead Soldier," "War Music."

Sources: *24-Hour War. Is Christopher Logue a genius or a madman?* Jim Lewis, 2003 (http://slate.msn.com/id/2082824/). *A Book of Animal Poems.* William Cole, ed. Viking, 1973. *Encyclopædia Britannica Ultimate Reference Suite DVD,* 2006. *Griffin Poetry Prize, 2002. Logue's Home, War Music* (http://www.griffinpoetryprize.com/shortlist_2002.php?t=5#a50). *Logue's Books* (http://www.cas.sc.edu/engl/LitCheck/logue.htm). *Interview with Christopher Logue.* poetrymagazines.org.uk (http://www.poetrymagazines.org.uk/magazine/record.asp?id=5237). *Selected*

Poems of Christopher Logue. Christopher Reid, ed. Faber and Faber, 1996. *The Columbia Granger's Index to Poetry.* 11th ed. *The Columbia Granger's World of Poetry,* Columbia University Press, 2005 (http://www.columbiagrangers.org). *The Faber Book of War Poetry.* Kenneth Baker, ed. Faber and Faber, 1996. *The Oxford Companion to English Literature.* 6th edition. Margaret Drabble, ed. Oxford University Press, 2000. *Who's Who.* London: A & C Black, 2005. *Wikipedia, the Free Encyclopedia* (http://en.wikipedia.org/wiki/Wikipedia).

LOK (LOCK or LOCKE), HENRY (?1553–?1608)

He was born in London, where his father was a dealer in textiles. In 1550 his mother published *Sermons upon the Song that Ezechias [Hezekiah] made after he had been sick and afflicted by the Hand of God,* which included *A Meditation of a penitent Sinner, written in manner of a Paraphrase after the 51 Psalm of David.* Henry spent time at Oxford University but there is no record of him graduating; he then had some appointment at the court of Elizabeth. There is no record of his death. In 1591 he contributed a sonnet to the *Essayes of a Prentice* by James VI of Scotland. The Scottish clergyman and literary editor Dr. Alexander Balloch Grosart (1827–1899) reprinted Lok's sonnets, together with the one prefixed to James VI's volume, in his *Miscellanies of the Fuller Worthies' Library,* Vol. II, 1871. Lok paraphrased Psalms 27, 71, 119, 121, and 130. Some of his poems: "Adue to worlds vaine delight," "Ecclesiasticus, otherwise called the Preacher," "Lords Prayer," "Sundry Christian Passions Contained in Two Hundred," "These sacred words king Dauids son did preach," "To the virtuous Lady."

Sources: *Athenaeum Online System, Issue Number 2288: Poems of Henry Lok, Gentleman 1593–1597* (http://web.soi.city.ac.uk/~asp/v2/titles/issuefiles/2288.html). *Dictionary of National Biography.* Electronic Edition 1.1. Oxford University Press, 1997. *English Poetry: Author Search.* Chadwyck-Healey Ltd., 1995 (http://www.lib.utexas.edu:8080/search/epoetry/author.html). *The Columbia Granger's Index to Poetry.* 11th ed. *The Columbia Granger's World of Poetry,* Columbia University Press, 2005 (http://www.columbiagrangers.org). *The Development of the Sonnet: An Introduction.* Michael R.G. Spiller. Routledge, 1993. *The Sonnet: An Anthology.* Robert M. Bender and Charles L. Squier, eds. Washington Square Press, 1987.

LONGLEY, MICHAEL GEORGE (1939–)

Irish poet, born in Belfast of English parents, he was educated at the Royal Belfast Academical Institution. After reading classics at Trinity College, Dublin, he was a schoolteacher in Belfast, Dublin and London. He was combined arts director for the Arts Council of Northern Ireland from 1970 to 1991, when he became a full-time writer. He was writer fellow at Trinity College, Dublin, and has written scripts for BBC Radio. Queen's University Belfast (1985) and Trinity College Dublin (1999) made him honorary doctor of laws. From 1965 to 2004 his poetry has won eight major literary awards. His collection, *The Weather in Japan* (2000), won the Hawthornden Prize, the T.S. Eliot Prize and the Belfast Arts Award for Literature. He lives in Belfast with his wife, the critic Edna Longley. Some of his publications: *Poems 1963–1983*, 1991. *Birds and Flowers: Poems*, 1994. *The Ghost Orchid*, 1995. *Ship of the Wind*, 1997. *Broken Dishes*, 1998. *Selected Poems*, 1998. *Snow Water*, 2004. Some of his poems: "Ceasefire," "Desert Warfare," "Odyssey," "The Beech Tree," "The Civil Servant," "The Hebrides," "Wounds," "Wreathes."

Sources: *Bitter Harvest: An Anthology of Contemporary Irish Verse.* John Montague, ed. Scribner's, 1989. *Irish Poetry: An Interpretive Anthology from Before Swift to Yeats and After.* W.J. McCormack, ed. New York University Press, 2000. *Biography of Michael Longley* (http://www.contemporarywriters.com/authors/?p=auth199). *The National Portrait Gallery* (www.npg.org.uk). *The Faber Book of Contemporary Irish Poetry.* Paul Muldoon, ed. Faber and Faber, 1986. *The Oxford Book of Classical Verse in Translation.* Adrian Poole and Jeremy Maule, eds. 1995. *The Oxford Companion to English Literature.* 6th edition. Margaret Drabble, ed. Oxford University Press, 2000. *The Penguin Book of Contemporary Irish Poetry.* Peter Fallon and Derek Mahon, eds. Penguin Books, 1990. *Who's Who.* London: A & C Black, 2005.

LOVELACE, RICHARD (1618–1658)

The handsome son of a wealthy knight, he was the prototype of the ideal Cavalier. Lovelace was born in London or possibly in the Netherlands, where his father was in military service. He was educated at Charterhouse School and Gloucester Hall, Oxford. Around the age of 16 he wrote *The Scholar*, a comedy acted at Whitefriars, in the City of London. After Oxford he was a courtier but favored a soldier's life. A Royalist, he fought with Charles in Scotland (1639–1640) and lost everything when Charles was defeated. He was imprisoned in the Gatehouse, London, where he wrote "To Althea, from Prison," which contains the familiar lines "Stone walls do not a prison make / Nor iron bars a cage." He spent four years abroad and fought for the French against the Spaniards at Dunkerque in 1646. In 1648 he was again imprisoned, where he wrote *Lucasta* (1649). He died in London in misery and poverty. Some of his poems: "A Fly Caught in a Cobweb," "Against the Love of Great Ones," "Love Enthroned," "Paris's Second Judgement," "Sonnet. To Generall Goring," "The Ant," "The Faire Begger," "The Grasshopper," "The Toad and Spyder."

Sources: *Cavalier Poets: Selected Poems.* Thomas Clayton, ed. Oxford University Press, 1978. *Dictionary of National Biography.* Electronic Edition 1.1. Oxford University Press, 1997. *Encyclopædia Britannica Ultimate Reference Suite DVD*, 2006. *English Poetry: Author Search.* Chadwyck-Healey Ltd., 1995 (http://www.lib.utexas.edu:8080/search/epoetry/author.html). *The National Portrait Gallery* (www.npg.org.uk). *The Columbia Granger's Index to Poetry.* 11th ed. *The Columbia Granger's World of Poetry*, Columbia University Press, 2005 (http://www.columbiagrangers.org). *The Oxford Book of Friendship.* D.J. Enright and David Rawlinson, eds. Oxford University Press, 1991. *The Oxford Companion to English Literature.* 6th edition. Margaret Drabble, ed. Oxford University Press, 2000. *The Poems of Richard Lovelace.* C.H. Wilkinson, ed. Oxford University Press, 1930, reprinted 1953. *Through the Year with the Poets.* Oscar Fay Adams, ed. D. Lothrop and Company, 1886.

LOVER, SAMUEL (1797–1868)

Born and educated in Dublin, of great musical and artistic talent, he turned his back on his father's stock broking business and became a successful painter of portraits and miniatures both in Dublin and in London. In 1828 he was elected to the Royal Hibernian Academy. In 1832 he painted the miniature of the celebrated violinist Paganini, exhibited at the Dublin Academy. In London he branched out and wrote novels and musical dramas, but in 1844 failing eyesight forced him to abandon art. The "Irish Evening"— which he first performed at the Princess's Concert Rooms, London, and repeated in Canada and the USA—was a solo performance of monologues, songs, recitations, and stories, all written by him. He died in Dublin. Some of his poetry publications: *Rory O'More*, 1826 (ballad, later a novel and a play). *Songs and Ballads*, 1858. *Metrical Tales*, 1860. *Original Songs*, 1861. Some of his poems: "Father Land and Mother Tongue," "Father Molloy," "Live in My Heart and Pay No Rent," "Paddy O'Rafther," "The Birth of Saint Patrick," "The Low-backed Car," "The Quakers' Meeting," "The War Ship of Peace."

Sources: *Dictionary of National Biography.* Electronic Edition 1.1. Oxford University Press, 1997. *Encyclopædia Britannica Ultimate Reference Suite DVD*, 2006. *English Poetry: Author Search.* Chadwyck-Healey Ltd., 1995 (http://www.lib.utexas.edu:8080/search/epoetry/author.html). *The National Portrait Gallery* (www.npg.org.uk). *Old-poetry* (www.oldpoetry.com). *Poems for Seasons and Celebrations.* William Cole, ed. World, 1961. *Poems of American History.* Burton Egbert Stevenson, ed. Houghton Mifflin, 1922. *Second Treasury of the Familiar.* Ralph L. Woods, ed. Macmillan, 1950. *The Bride's Book of Poems.* Cary Yager, ed. Contemporary Books, 1995. *The Columbia Granger's Index to Poetry.* 11th ed. *The Columbia Granger's World of Poetry*, Columbia University Press, 2005 (http://www.columbiagrangers.org). *The Home Book of Verse for Young Folks.* Burton Egbert Stevenson, ed. Holt, Rinehart and Winston, 1929. *The Home Book of Modern Verse.* Burton Egbert Stevenson, ed. Henry Holt, 1953.

LOVIBOND, EDWARD (1724–1775)

Born at Hampton, Middlesex, the son of a director of the East India Company, he was educated at Kingston-upon-Thames and at Magdalen College, Oxford. In his "Ode to Youth" he talks of his fortune of having enough money to enjoy the pleasures of a rural life. His contributions to *World*, a weekly newspaper — started in 1753 — brought him recognition. His best-known "The Tears of Old May Day" appeared in many English anthologies and was said to be bettered only by Thomas Gray's (see entry) "Elegy Written in a Country Church-Yard." Lovibond seems to have drawn his inspiration from Alexander Pope. His *Poems on Several Occasions* was published by his brother in 1785. Some of his poems: "A Dream," "Address to the Thames," "Dedication of Julia's Letter," "Imitation From Ossian's Poems," "Inscription on a Fountain," "Ode to Captivity," "On Rural Sports," "The Complaint of Cambria," "The Tears of Old May-Day," "Verses Written at Brighthelmstone."

Sources: *Dictionary of National Biography.* Electronic Edition 1.1. Oxford University Press, 1997. *English Poetry: Author Search.* Chadwyck-Healey Ltd., 1995 (http://www.lib.utexas.edu:8080/search/epoetry/author.html). *Stanford University Libraries and Academic Information Resources* (http://library.stanford.edu). *The Columbia Granger's Index to Poetry.* 11th ed. *The Columbia Granger's World of Poetry,* Columbia University Press, 2005 (http://www.columbiagrangers.org). *The Works of the British Poets V. 9 (Dryden and Garth).* J Sharpe, 1808.

LOWBURY, EDWARD JOSEPH LISTER (1913–)

He graduated in medicine from University College, Oxford, in 1939, spent three years of World War II in the Royal Army Medical Corps in East Africa, then did further study at London Hospital to become a pathologist and bacteriologist. He received Newidgate Prize in 1934 for his poem "Fire." He has written many medical textbooks and poetry collections and edited anthologies. In 1998 he wrote *To Shirk No Idleness: Critical Biography of the Poet Andrew Young* (his father-in-law; see entry). Some of his other publications: *Thomas Campion* (see entry)*: Poet, Composer, Physician,* 1970. *Green Magic (Poets for the Young),* 1972. *Poetry and Paradox: An Essay with Nineteen Relevant Poems,* 1976. *Troika: Poems,* 1977. *Goldrush: Poems,* 1983. *Flowering Cypress: Three Poems,* 1986. *Apollo: Anthology of Poems by Doctor Poets,* 1990. *Selected and New Poems 1935–1989,* 1990. *First Light: Eleven Poems,* 1991. *Collected Poems (Salzburg Studies: Poetic Drama and Poetic Theory),* 1993. *Hallmarks of Poetry: Reflections on a Theme,* 1996. Some of his other poems: "Faces," "In the Old Jewish Cemetery, Prague, 1970," "Night Train,"

"Swan," "The Monster," "The Roc," "Tree of Knowledge."

Sources: *Amazing Monsters: Verses to Thrill and Chill.* Robert Fisher, ed. Faber and Faber, 1982. *Golden Treasury of the Best Songs and Lyrical Poems in the English Language.* Francis Turner Palgrave, ed. Oxford University Press, 1964, Sixth edition, updated by John Press, 1994. *Oxford Poetry: Appendix 2: The Newdigate Prize* (http://www.gnelson.demon.co.uk/oxpoetry/index/inewd.html). *The Columbia Granger's Index to Poetry.* 11th ed. *The Columbia Granger's World of Poetry,* Columbia University Press, 2005 (http://www.columbiagrangers.org). *The Oxford Book of Story Poems.* Michael Harrison and Christopher Stuart-Clark, ed. Oxford University Press, 1990. *Voices Within the Ark: The Modern Jewish Poets.* Howard Schwartz and Anthony Rudolf, eds. Avon Books, 1980.

LOWE, JOHN (1750–1798)

Son of a gardener, born at Kenmure, East Galloway, South Scotland, he started life as a weaver. With help he went to Edinburgh University in 1771 to prepare for the church, although there is no evidence that he was ever licensed as a preacher in Scotland. He was tutor to the family of a Mr. M'Ghie of Airds on the Dee, East Galloway, and formed a romantic attachment with one of the daughters. In 1773 he went to the United States as tutor to the family of George Washington's elder brother, then opened a school at Fredericksburg, Virginia, where he took holy orders and obtained a living as a clergyman of the Church of England. Distance and time no doubt put a strain on the romantic relationship back in Scotland, and Lowe married a Virginia lady. The marriage was unhappy and Lowe took to drink. He was buried near Fredericksburg under the shade of two palm trees. His fame rests entirely on the ballad "Mary's Dream," inspired by the tragic death of a gentleman named Sandy Miller, a surgeon at sea who was attached to the other M'Ghie sister.

Sources: *Dictionary of National Biography.* Electronic Edition 1.1. Oxford University Press, 1997. *Biography of John Lowe. Significant and Famous Scots* (http://www.electricscotland.com/history/other/lowe_john.htm). *Biography of John Lowe, Virtual American Biographies* (http://www.famousamericans.net/johnlowe).

LOWE, ROBERT, VISCOUNT SHERBROOKE (1811–1892)

Born in Bingham, Nottinghamshire, the son of a clergyman, he was educated at Winchester College and graduated M.A. from University College, Oxford, in 1836. He was for several years tutor at Oxford before being called to the bar in 1842. He then emigrated to Australia, where he played an active role in politics as the elected representative for the district of St. Vincent, Sydney. His opposition to tens of thousands of acres being in the hands of a few isolated squatters and his opposition to the renewal of convict transportation to the Australian colonies are recorded in *Fifty Years in the Making of Australian History* by Sir Henry Parkes (1892). On his return to England in 1850, he was leader writer for *The Times* and entered Parliament two years later, where he distinguished himself as a speaker in the Reform debates of 1866–1867. He was chancellor of the exchequer, 1868–1873, and home secretary, 1873–1874, in William Gladstone's first administration (1868–1874). He was created Viscount Sherbrooke in 1880. His opposition to the squatters is expressed in his poem "Songs of the Squatters."

Sources: *Song of the Squatters, Robert Lowe. Australian Bush Ballads* (http://www.geocities.com/yorligau/poems.htm#sots). *Dictionary of National Biography.* Electronic Edition 1.1. Oxford University Press, 1997. *Encyclopædia Britannica Ultimate Reference Suite DVD*, 2006. *The National Portrait Gallery* (www.npg.org.uk). *Poetry in Australia, Vol. I: From the Ballads to Brennan.* T. Inglis Moore, ed. University of California Press, 1965. *The Columbia Granger's Index to Poetry.* 11th ed. *The Columbia Granger's World of Poetry,* Columbia University Press, 2005 (http://www.columbiagrangers.org). *The New Oxford Book of Australian Verse.* Les A. Murray, ed. Oxford University Press, 1991 (enlarged edition). University of Sydney Library, *Fifty Years in the Making of Australian History* (http://setis.library.usyd.edu.au/ozlit/pdf/fed0024.pdf).

LOY, MINA (1882–1966)

Born Mina Gertrude Lowy in London, the daughter of a second-generation Hungarian Jewish father and an English Protestant mother, she studied art in London, Munich, and Paris, then moved to Florence in 1907. She was highly skilled in so many different fields that it is difficult to say which is predominant. In Florence she came into contact with the Futurists and by 1913 she was using Futurist theories in literature to advance feminist politics in her poetry. She was not afraid to use taboo subjects in her poetry — childbirth, sex, and disillusionment in marriage — subjects that challenged women to free themselves of emotional and physical dependence on men. She finally settled in New York in 1937, then moved to Aspen, Colorado, in 1953, where she died. "Love Songs" was published in the magazine *Others* in 1915. Some of her publications: *Lunar Baedeker*, 1923. *Anglo-Mongrels and the Rose*, 1923–1925. *Lunar Baedeker and Time Tables*, 1958. Some of her other poems: "Apology of Genius," "Brancusi's Golden Bird," "Gertrude Stein," "Italian Pictures," "Jules Pascin," "Omen of Victory," "On Third Avenue," "The Widow's Jazz," "Three Moments in Paris."

Sources: *American Poetry: The Twentieth Century, Vol. 1.* Robert Hass, John Hollander, Carolyn Kizer, et al., ed. Library of America, 2000. *Anthology of Twentieth-Century British and Irish Poetry.* Keith Tuma, ed. Oxford University Press, 2001. *Encyclopædia Britannica Ultimate Reference Suite DVD*, 2006. *The Life of Mina Loy. Modern American Poetry* (http://www.english.uiuc.edu/maps/poets/g_l/loy/loy.htm). *Quest for Reality: An Anthology of Short Poems in English.* Yvor Winters and Kenneth Fields, eds. Swallow Press, 1969. *The Columbia Granger's Index to Poetry.* 11th ed. *The Columbia Granger's World of Poetry,* Columbia University Press, 2005 (http://www.columbiagrangers.org). *The Jazz Poetry Anthology.* Sascha Feinstein and Yusef Komunyakaa, ed. Indiana University Press, 1991. *The Oxford Companion to English Literature.* 6th edition. Margaret Drabble, ed. Oxford University Press, 2000. *The Virago Book of Love Poetry.* Wendy Mulford, ed. Virago Press, 1990.

LUCAS, HENRY (?1740–1795)

Born at Dublin, the son of Dr. Charles Lucas, M.D., the Irish patriot, he graduated M.A. from Trinity College, Dublin, in 1762. He became a student at the Middle Temple but abandoned law for literature. Nothing else about him is known. His publications: *The Tears of Alnwick: A Pastoral Elegy on the Death of the Duchess of Northumberland*, 1777. *A Visit from the Shades, or Earl Chatham's Adieu to his Friend, Lord Camden: A Poem*, 1778. *Poems to Her Majesty*, 1779 (dedicated to Queen Charlotte, wife of George III, it contains "The Ejaculation," occasioned by seeing the royal children). *An Oblation: A Lyric Poem on Her Majesty's Happy Delivery of a Daughter, the now amiable Princess Sophia. The Earl of Somerset* (a tragedy in blank verse, literally founded on history). *The Cypress Wreath: A Poem to the Memory of Lord Robert Manners*, 1782. *A Pastoral Elegy in Memory of the Duke of Northumberland*, 1786 (Henry Percy, 3rd Duke (1785–1847), Lord Lieutenant of Ireland). *Celina, a Mask — commemorative of the Nuptials of their Royal Highnesses the Prince of Wales and Princess Caroline*, 1795.

Sources: *Dictionary of National Biography.* Electronic Edition 1.1. Oxford University Press, 1997. *The National Portrait Gallery* (www.npg.org.uk).

LUCIE-SMITH, JOHN EDWARD MCKENZIE (1933–)

British art critic, writer, poet, and photographer, born at Kingston, Jamaica, but lived in Britain since 1946. Educated at King's School, Canterbury, he graduated M.A. from Merton College, Oxford, where he read history. From 1954 to 1956 he was an education officer in the Royal Air Force, then worked for ten years in advertising, then as a freelance journalist and broadcaster. He was associated with "The Group," an informal association of writers, mostly poets, set up in London in 1955 by Philip Hobsbaum (see entry). He is a regular contributor to many newspapers and magazines. A prolific author, his books are mostly on art, but also biography; he has written a historical novel as well as poetry collections.

Some of his publications: *The Fantasy Poets*, 1954. *Tropical Childhood and Other Poems*, 1961. *French Poetry: The Last Fifteen Years* 1971 (with S.W. Taylor). *Group Anthology with Philip Hobsbaum*, 1973. *Changing Shape*, 2002. Some of his poems: "A Former Lover," "At the Roman Baths, Bath," "Imperialists in Retirement," "Seven Colors," "The Dodo," "The Giant Tortoise," "The Ladybirds," "Your Own Place."

Sources: *Biography of Edward Lucie-Smith, Knitting Circle.* (http://myweb.lsbu.ac.uk/~stafflag/edwardlucie-smith.html#Biography). *British Poetry Since 1945.* Edward Lucie-Smith, ed. Penguin Books, 1985. *The National Portrait Gallery* (www.npg.org.uk). *New Poets of England and America.* Donald Hall and Robert Pack, eds. World, 1962. *Poems One Line and Longer.* William Cole, ed. Grossman, 1973. *The Columbia Granger's Index to Poetry.* 11th ed. *The Columbia Granger's World of Poetry,* Columbia University Press, 2005 (http://www.columbiagrangers.org). *The Oxford Companion to English Literature.* 6th edition. Margaret Drabble, ed. Oxford University Press, 2000. *The Penguin Book of Homosexual Verse.* Stephen Coote, ed. Penguin Books, 1983. *Voices in the Gallery.* Dannie Abse and Joan Abse, eds. Tate Gallery, 1986. *Who's Who.* London: A & C Black, 2005.

LUKE, JEMIMA THOMPSON (1813–1906)

She was born at Islington, London, the daughter of Thomas Thompson, who was involved with the Bible Society, the Sunday School Union, and the Foreign Sailors' Society. In 1843 she married Samuel Luke, a congregational minister, and after his death in 1873 she lived at Newport, Isle of Wight. An ardent nonconformist, she was an active opponent of the Education Act of 1902 and was summoned among the Isle of Wight "passive resisters" in September 1904 — the oldest such resister in the country. The resisters objected to the act on the grounds that they would be taxed to pay for religious education. By 1906 over 170 Nonconformists had gone to prison for refusing to pay their school taxes. She published her autobiography, *Early Years of My Life,* in 1900. She is best known for her children's hymn "I Think When I Read that Sweet Story of Old," which first appeared in the *Sunday School Teachers' Magazine* (1841). In 1853 it appeared, anonymously, in *The Leeds Hymn Book*, and has since been included in all hymn books of repute. She died on the Isle of Wight.

Sources: *Biography of Jemima Luke, by Lynn Parr* (http://www.ensignmessage.com/archives/jemimaluke.htm l). *Dictionary of National Biography.* Electronic Edition 1.1. Oxford University Press, 1997. *Oxford Concise Dictionary of World Religions: Nonconformists* (http://www.spartacus. schoolnet.co.uk/REnonconformists.htm). *The Cyber Hymnal* (http://www.cyberhymnal.org/index.htm).

LUTTRELL, HENRY (?1765–1851)

The natural son of Henry, 2nd Earl Carhampton, was born at Woodstock, Oxfordshire. His father used his influence to obtain for him a seat for Clonmines, County Wexford, in the last Irish parliament (1798), and a post in the Irish government, which he subsequently commuted for a pension. He was introduced to London society through the Duchess of Devonshire and soon gained the reputation of being a most agreeable, accomplished, and entertaining wit and poet. He was friendly with Sir John Henry Moore (see entry) and it is said that they were "seldom apart, and always hating, abusing, and ridiculing each other" (DNB). He died at his house, No. 31 Brompton Square, London. Some of his publications: *Lines written at Ampthill Park in the autumn of 1818,* 1819. *Letters to Julia, in Rhyme,* 1822 (3rd edition). *A Rhymer in Rome,* 1826. *Crockford House,* 1827 (a satire). Some of his poems: "Appeal to Chemistry," "City Shower," "Death, Thy Certainty is Such," "Letters of a Dandy to a Dolly," "On a Man Run Over by an Omnibus," "The Description of a London Fog."

Sources: *Crockford-House (1827) Canto II, Henry Luttrell* (http://www.english.upenn.edu/Projects/knarf/EtAlia/luttrell.html). *Dictionary of National Biography.* Electronic Edition 1.1. Oxford University Press, 1997. *English Poetry: Author Search.* Chadwyck-Healey Ltd., 1995 (http://www.lib.utexas.edu:8080/search/epoetry/author.html). *The Columbia Granger's Index to Poetry.* 11th ed. *The Columbia Granger's World of Poetry,* Columbia University Press, 2005 (http://www.columbiagrangers.org). *The Faber Book of Epigrams and Epitaphs.* Geoffrey Grigson, ed. Faber and Faber, 1977. *The New Oxford Book of Romantic Period Verse.* Jerome J. McGann. Oxford University Press, 1993. *The Oxford Companion to English Literature.* 6th edition. Margaret Drabble, ed. Oxford University Press, 2000.

LYALL, SIR ALFRED COMYN (1835–1911)

Born at Coulsdon, Surrey, the son of a clergyman, he was educated at Eton College then at Haileybury College, Hertfordshire, the training ground for the Indian Civil Service, which he joined in 1856. He fought during the Mutiny of 1857–1858 and received the Mutiny Medal. Subsequently he held a number of high-ranking appointments; his final, in 1881, was lieutenant governor of the North-West Provinces. Between his return from India in 1887 and his death, he was one of the best-known and most distinguished men in English society and advised the government as a member of the India Council in London. He was made Knight Commander of the Bath (1881) and received honorary degrees from Oxford and Cambridge. He died from heart disease at Farringford in the Isle of Wight and was buried at Harbledown near Canterbury, Kent. Some of his poems: "A Sermon in Lower Bengal," "After the Skirmish," "Joab Speaketh," "Meditations of a Hindu Prince," "Rajpoot Rebels," "Studies at Delhi, 1876," "The Amir's Message," "The Amir's Soliloquy," "The Land of Regrets," "The Monk and the Bird," "Translations from Horace."

Sources: *Dictionary of National Biography.* Electronic Edition 1.1. Oxford University Press, 1997. *English Poetry: Author Search.* Chadwyck-Healey Ltd., 1995 (http://www.lib.utexas.edu:8080/search/epoetry/author.html). *The National Portrait Gallery* (www.npg.org.uk). *Poemhunter* (www.poemhunter.com). *The Columbia Granger's Index to Poetry.* 11th ed. *The Columbia Granger's World of Poetry,* Columbia University Press, 2005 (http://www.columbiagrangers.org). *The Oxford Book of Travel Verse.* Kevin Crossley-Holland, ed. Oxford University Press, 1986. *The World's Great Religious Poetry.* Caroline Miles Hill, ed. Macmillan, 1954. *Verses Written in India by Alfred Lyall.* Kegan Paul, 1890.

LYDGATE, JOHN (?1370–?1451)

He was born at Lidgate, Suffolk, and at fifteen was a novice in the Benedictine abbey of Bury St. Edmunds, where he became a priest in 1397. He knew Chaucer, who was his inspiration as a poet. That he knew what it was like to be poor in London is portrayed in his poem "London Lackpenny." He celebrated in verse Henry V's return to London after Agincourt in 1415 and was regularly court poet from 1422. In this last years he wrote his *Testament,* declaring his readiness for death. He died at Bury St. Edmunds while translating the *Secreta Secretorum (Secrets of Old Philosophers).* Most of his works have been produced by various publishers within the last two centuries. His vast output can be grouped thus: narrative or epic — 3; devotional — 6; hagiological — 5; philosophical and scientific — 3; allegories, fables, and moral romances —11; historical (political)— 3; and social satire — 3. Some of his poems: "A Kalendare," "Bycorne and Chychevache," "The Boy Serving at Table," "The Daunce of Machabree," "The Floure of Curtesy," "The Servant of Cupyde Forsaken."

Sources: *An Anthology of Catholic Poets.* Shane Leslie, ed. Macmillan, 1952. *Dictionary of National Biography.* Electronic Edition 1.1. Oxford University Press, 1997. *Encyclopædia Britannica Ultimate Reference Suite DVD,* 2006. *English Poetry: Author Search.* Chadwyck-Healey Ltd., 1995 (http://www.lib.utexas.edu:8080/search/epoetry/author.html). *English Poetry: A Poetic Record, from Chaucer to Yeats.* David Hopkins, ed. Routledge, 1990. *The Columbia Granger's Index to Poetry.* 11th ed. *The Columbia Granger's World of Poetry,* Columbia University Press, 2005 (http://www.columbiagrangers.org). *The Oxford Book of Children's Verse.* Iona Opie and Peter Opie, eds. Oxford University Press, 1973. *The Oxford Book of English Verse.* Christopher Ricks, ed. Oxford University Press, 1999. *The Oxford Book of Medieval English Verse.* Celia Sisam and Kenneth Sisam, eds. Oxford University Press, 1970. *The Oxford Compan-*

ion to English Literature. 6th edition. Margaret Drabble, ed. Oxford University Press, 2000. *The Palis of Honoure: Introduction.* Gavin Douglas and David Parkinson, eds. Kalamazoo, Mich.: Medieval Institute Publications, 1992 (http://www.lib.rochester.edu/camelot/teams/palisint.htm). *The Penguin Book of Bird Poetry.* Peggy Munsterberg, ed. 1984.

LYNCH, THOMAS TOKE (1818–1871)

Born at Dunmow, Essex, son of surgeon, he was educated at a school in Islington, London. He was pastor of Highgate Independent Church 1847–1849 and Mornington Church, in the Hampstead Road, although he labored at his task, was never a popular preacher, and was never in good health. Known as a hymn writer, he also wrote some hundred poems, not all with religious themes; however, some of his hymns — which expressed an admiration for nature — were criticized as being too theologically unsound to be suitable for public worship. He was a cultured musician and composed several tunes to his own hymns. He published several prose works, and he produced *Hymns for Heart and Voice: The Rivulet* in 1855 (third edition 1868), and *Songs Controversial* (issued under the pseudonym "Silent Long") in 1856. Some of his poems: "Chestnut Roasting," "Egg-Shell," "Sunshine," "The Poet Warned," "The Singer," "The Vine," "Trust." Some of his hymn/poems: "Christ in His Word Draws Near," "Gracious Spirit, Dwell with Me," "Lift Up Your Heads, Rejoice," "Lord, on Thy Returning Day," "My Faith, It is an Oaken Staff."

Sources: *Dictionary of National Biography.* Electronic Edition 1.1. Oxford University Press, 1997. *English Poetry: Author Search.* Chadwyck-Healey Ltd., 1995 (http://www.lib.utexas.edu:8080/search/epoetry/author.html). *The Best Loved Religious Poems.* James Gilchrist Lawson, ed. Fleming H. Revell, 1933. *The Columbia Granger's Index to Poetry.* 11th ed. *The Columbia Granger's World of Poetry,* Columbia University Press, 2005 (http://www.columbiagrangers.org). *The Cyber Hymnal* (http://www.cyberhymnal.org/index.htm). *The Oxford Book of Victorian Verse.* Arthur Quiller-Couch, ed. Oxford University Press, 1971. *The Treasury of Christian Poetry.* Lorraine Eitel, ed. Fleming H. Revell, 1982.

LYTE, HENRY FRANCIS (1793–1847)

Born at Ednam, near Kelso, Roxburghshire, Scotland, and orphaned young, he was educated at Portora (the royal school of Enniskillen) in Ireland, where he excelled in English poetry. He was ordained in 1818 and had two main curacies — Lymington, Hampshire, and All Saints Church, Lower Brixham, Devonshire, where he served for twenty-five years. Never robust, he made frequent trips abroad and died at Nice, where he is buried in the English cemetery. He is commemorated by a tablet in the nave of Westminster Abbey. Although chiefly known as a hymn writer, he was a prolific poet; most of his verse was written while at Lymington. His three publications: *Tales in Verse Illustrative of the Several Petitions of the Lord's Prayer*, 1829. *Miscellaneous Poems*, 1868. *Remains of the late Rev. Henry Francis Lyte*, 1850. Some of his poems: "A Lost Love," "Declining Days," "On a Naval Officer," "Stay Gentle Shadow of My Mother Stay," "The Poet's Plea." Some of His hymns/poems: "Abide with Me," "Pleasant Are Thy Courts Above," "Jesus, I My Cross Have Taken," "Praise, My Soul, the King of Heaven."

Sources: *Dictionary of National Biography.* Electronic Edition 1.1. Oxford University Press, 1997. *English Poetry: Author Search.* Chadwyck-Healey Ltd., 1995 (http://www.lib.utexas.edu:8080/search/epoetry/author.html). *English Poetry: L Bibliographic Entries.* The University of Texas at Austin General Libraries. (http://www.lib.utexas.edu:8080/search/epoetry/biblio-L.html). *Henry Francis Lyte— His Life and Times* (http://homepage.tinet.ie/~taghmon/histsoc/vol1/3lyte/3lyte.htm). *Invisible Light: Poems About God.* Diana Culbertson, ed. Columbia University Press, 2000. *The National Portrait Gallery* (www.npg.org.uk). *Poemhunter* (www.poemhunter.com). *The Columbia Granger's Index to Poetry.* 11th ed. *The Columbia Granger's World of Poetry,* Columbia University Press, 2005 (http://www.columbiagrangers.org). *The Cyber Hymnal* (http://www.cyberhymnal.org/index.htm). *The Treasury of Religious Verse.* Donald T. Kauffman, ed. Fleming H. Revell, 1962.

LYTTON, EDWARD GEORGE EARLE, FIRST BARRON OF LYTTON (1803–1873)

Born in London, the son of William Earle Bulwer of Heydon Hall, Norfolk. His tutor encouraged him to publish a collection of poems, *Ismael,* in 1820. He graduated M.A. from Trinity Hall in 1835 and received the honorary degree of doctor of laws from both Cambridge and Oxford. In Parliament his speech on the abolition of Negro apprenticeship— published by the Anti-Slavery Society—raised a furor. He was secretary for the colonies in Lord Derby's ministry (1858–1859) and was largely responsible for the reorganization of British Columbia (where a village is named for him) and for separating Queensland from New South Wales. He was created Baron Lytton of Knebworth in 1866 and died at Hagley, Worcestershire. He wrote historical novels, essays, romances, plays, and an epic poem, *King Arthur* (1848–1849), and in 1844 translated Schiller's ballads. Some of his other poetry publications: *Delmour, or the Tale of a Sylphid, and Other Poems,* 1823. *Weeds and Wild Flowers,* 1825. *Eva, the Ill-omened Marriage, and Other Tales and Poems,* 1842. *Letters to John Bull, Esq.,* 1851. *The Lost Tales of Miletus,* 1866. *The Odes and Epodes of Horace,* 1869.

Sources: *Dictionary of National Biography.* Electronic Edition 1.1. Oxford University Press, 1997. *Encyclopædia Britannica Ultimate Reference Suite DVD,* 2006. *The National Portrait Gallery* (www.npg.org.uk). *The Oxford Companion to English Literature.* 6th edition. Margaret Drabble, ed. Oxford University Press, 2000.

LYTTON, EDWARD ROBERT BULWER, FIRST EARL OF LYTTON (1831–1891)

Born in London, the son of the first Baron Lytton, he was educated privately in Bonn. From 1849 he was private secretary to his uncle, Lord Dalling, first in Washington, then in Florence; thereafter he followed a diplomatic career in Europe. In 1873 he became Baron Lytton on the death of his father and was viceroy of India from 1876 to 1880, but his reforms were not well received back in England. He was created Earl of Lytton and Viscount Knebworth in 1880, and was appointed ambassador to France in 1887. He died of an aortic aneurysm while he was writing poetry and was buried at Knebworth, Hertfordshire. His poems—under the pseudonym of Owen Meredith—are descriptive and marked by brilliancy of idea. Some of his publications: *Clytemnestra, and Other Poems,* 1855. *The Wanderer,* 1857. *Lucile,* 1860. *Chronicles and Characters,* 1868. *The Poems,* 1869. *Fables in Song,* 1874. *Glenaveril,* 1885. *After Paradise,* 1887. Some of his poems: "Irene," "King Solomon and the Mouse," "Last Lines," "Midges," "Since We Parted," "The Death of King Hacon," "The Siege of Constantinople," "The White Anemone."

Sources: *A Treasury of Poems for Worship and Devotion.* Charles L. Wallis, ed. Harper, 1959. *Dictionary of National Biography.* Electronic Edition 1.1. Oxford University Press, 1997. *Encyclopædia Britannica Ultimate Reference Suite DVD,* 2006. *English Poetry: Author Search* (http://www.lib.utexas.edu:8080/search/epoetry/author.html). *Golden Numbers.* Kate Douglas Wiggin and Nora Archibald Smith, eds. Doubleday, Doran, 1902. *Love in Verse.* Kathleen Blease, ed. Ballantine Publishing Group, 1998. *The National Portrait Gallery* (www.npg.org.uk). *Poems: Historical and Characteristic of Robert Lord Lytton.* Chapman and Hall, 1887. *Very Bad Poetry.* Kathryn Petras and Ross Petras, eds. Vintage Books, 1997.

MACAULAY, DAME EMILIE ROSE (1881–1958)

Born at Rugby, Warwickshire, she was the daughter of an assistant master at Rugby School (later a lecturer in English at Cambridge) and related to the historian Lord Macaulay (see entry). Educated mainly by her parents while they lived in Italy, she read history at Somerville College, Oxford. For nearly three years during World War II she served as a voluntary part-time ambulance driver in London.

Cambridge University conferred an honorary doctor of literature upon her in 1951 and in 1958 she was appointed Dame of the British Empire. Severe periods of depression colored her novels. She died in London. Her earliest published writings were poems entered for competitions in the *Westminster Gazette*. She was awarded the James Tait Black Memorial Prize for her novel *The Towers of Trebizond* (1956). In a writing career that covered the first fifty years of the twentieth century, she produced twenty-three novels, six books of criticism, four books of travel and history, as well as a large correspondence and two collections of poetry: *The Two Blind Countries* (1914) and *Three Days* (1919). Some of her poems: "Many Sisters to Many Brothers," "Picnic," "The Shadow."

Sources: *Biography of Dame Rose Macaulay, by Sarah La Fanue. Guardian Unlimited Books, Review* (http://books.guardian.co.uk/review/story/0,12084,975703,00.html). *Dictionary of National Biography.* Electronic Edition 1.1. Oxford University Press, 1997. *Encyclopædia Britannica Ultimate Reference Suite DVD,* 2006. *Never Such Innocence: A New Anthology of Great War Verse.* Martin Stephen, ed. Buchan and Enright, 1988. *Scars upon My Heart: Women's Poetry and Verse of the First World War.* Catherine W Reilly, ed. Virago Press, 1981. *The Columbia Granger's Index to Poetry.* 11th ed. *The Columbia Granger's World of Poetry,* Columbia University Press, 2005 (http://www.columbiagrangers.org). *The Oxford Companion to English Literature.* 6th edition. Margaret Drabble, ed. Oxford University Press, 2000.

MACAULAY, THOMAS BABINGTON, BARON MACAULAY (1800–1859)

Born at Rothley Temple, Leicestershire, son of the philanthropist Zachary Macaulay, he was educated at Trinity College, Cambridge, where he won the English prize for a poem in 1819 ("Pompeii") and in 1821 ("Evening"). Called to the bar in 1826, he entered Parliament in 1830 as a Whig and took an active part in the first Reform Act of 1832. In 1834 he was appointed to the Supreme Council of India, and the publication of his *Minutes on Law and Education* (1835) considerably influenced Indian society. He was buried at the foot of Joseph Addison's statue in Poets' Corner of Westminster Abbey. His *History of England* appeared between 1845 and 1855, and his collected *Essays Critical and Historical* was published in 1834. His *Lays of Ancient Rome*— a series of poems on leading figures in Roman history — was published in 1842. Some of his poems: "A Jacobite's Epitaph," "A Radical War Song," "An Election Ballad," "Epitaph on Henry Martyn," "Horatius," "Ivry," "Sermon in a Churchyard," "The Armada," "The Battle of Naseby," "The Battle of the Lake Regillus," "The Last Buccaneer."

Sources: *Dictionary of National Biography.* Electronic Edition 1.1. Oxford University Press, 1997. *Encyclopædia Britannica Ultimate Reference Suite DVD,* 2006. *Everyman's Book of Evergreen Verse.* David Herbert, ed. J.M. Dent, 1984. *The National Portrait Gallery* (www.npg.org.uk). *Oldpoetry* (*www.oldpoetry.com*). *Other Men's Flowers.* A.P. Wavell, ed. Jonathan Cape, 1990. *The Columbia Granger's Index to Poetry.* 11th ed. *The Columbia Granger's World of Poetry,* Columbia University Press, 2005 (http://www.columbiagrangers.org). *The Eternal Sea: An Anthology of Sea Poetry.* W.M. Williamson, ed. Coward-McCann, 1946. *The Oxford Book of War Poetry.* Jon Stallworthy, Oxford University Press, 1984. *The Oxford Companion to English Literature.* 6th edition. Margaret Drabble, ed. Oxford University Press, 2000. *Westminster Abbey Official Guide* (no date).

MacBETH, GEORGE MANN (1932–1992)

The son of a miner, he was born in Shotts, North Lanarkshire, Scotland, but brought up in Sheffield, and graduated from New College, Oxford, in 1955. In London during the 1950s he was an influential member of "The Group" formed by Philip Hobsbaum and Edward Lucie-Smith; *A Group Anthology* (1963) is about their work. He was a popular producer of programs for the BBC and wrote novels, books for children, and many anthologies, including *The Penguin Book of Sick Verse* (1963), *The Penguin Book of Animal Verse* (1965) and *The Penguin Book of Victorian Verse* (1969). His early work was experimental, innovative, and extravagant, concentrating on themes of sex, death, war and violence. His later work was simpler and more reflective. He suffered from motor neuron disease and died in Tuam, County Galway, Ireland. Some of his publications: *A Form of Words,* 1954. *The Broken Places,* 1963. *Poems of Love and Death,* 1983. *Trespassing: Poems from Ireland,* 1991. Some of his poems: "A Basket of Walnuts," "Ash," "The God of Love," "The Miner's Helmet," "The Renewal," "The Rumanian of Maria Banus," "When I Am Dead."

Sources: *Emergency Kit: Poems for Strange Times.* Jo Shapcott and Matthew Sweeney, ed. Faber and Faber, 1996. *Encyclopædia Britannica Ultimate Reference Suite DVD,* 2006. *Biography of George MacBeth* (http://nlc.oldedwardians.org.uk/personal/GeorgeMacBeth.html). *Holocaust Poetry.* Hilda Schiff, ed. HarperCollins, 1995. *The National Portrait Gallery* (www.npg.org.uk). *P.E.N. New Poetry I.* Robert Nye, ed. Quartet Books, 1986. *Portraits of Poets.* Sebastian Barker, ed. Carcanet, 1986. *The Columbia Granger's Index to Poetry.* 11th ed. *The Columbia Granger's World of Poetry,* Columbia University Press, 2005 (http://www.columbiagrangers.org). *The New Modern Poetry: British and American Poetry since World War II.* M.L. Rosenthal, ed. Macmillan, 1967. *The Oxford Companion to English Literature.* 6th edition. Margaret Drabble, ed. Oxford University Press, 2000.

MacCAIG, NORMAN ALEXANDER (1910–1996)

Born in Edinburgh, the son of a chemist, he was educated at the Royal High School, then studied classics at Edinburgh University. During the war he was a conscientious objector on humanitarian grounds. He became a primary school teacher then spent the next thirty-six years in teaching. He was fellow in creative writing at Edinburgh University (1967–69), and for eight years, from 1970, he lectured at Stirling University; he was awarded the Queen's Medal for Poetry in 1986. His Gaelic-speaking mother, from Scalpay in Harris, had a profound influence on his use of language in his poems, where every word is fresh and precise. He spent much of his holiday time at Assynt in the northwest of Scotland, to which he refers in many of his poems. Some other Scottish poets criticized him because he wrote only in standard English. He died in Edinburgh. Some of his sixteen volumes of poetry: *Far Cry,* 1943. *Measures,* 1965. *A Man in My Position,* 1969. *Selected Poems,* 1971. *Voice-over,* 1988. Some of his poems: "Above Inverkirkaig," "By Achmelvich Bridge," "Crofter's Kitchen, Evening," "Hogmanay," "Loch Sionascaig," "Wild Oats."

Sources: *Biography of Norman MacCaig, Answers.com* (http://www.answers.com/topic/norman-maccaig). *Biography of MacCaig, Norman Alexander* (http://www.users. globalnet.co.uk/~crumey/norman_maccaig.html). *Encyclopædia Britannica Ultimate Reference Suite DVD, 2006. Poems of the Scottish Hills: An Anthology.* Hamish Brown, ed. Aberdeen University Press, 1982. *The Columbia Granger's Index to Poetry.* 11th ed. *The Columbia Granger's World of Poetry,* Columbia University Press, 2005 (http://www.columbiagrangers.org). *The Faber Book of Drink, Drinkers and Drinking.* Simon Rae, ed. Faber and Faber, 1991. *The New Modern Poetry: British and American Poetry since World War II.* M.L. Rosenthal, ed. Macmillan, 1967. *The New Penguin Book of Scottish Verse.* Robert Crawford and Mick Imlah, eds. Penguin Books, 2000. *The Oxford Companion to English Literature.* 6th edition. Margaret Drabble, ed. Oxford University Press, 2000.

MacCARTHY, DENIS FLORENCE (1817–1882)

Born into a Roman Catholic family in Dublin, and although he considered the church and law, he turned to literature. He contributed his first poem — "My Wishes"— to the *Dublin Satirist* when he was seventeen, and in 1843, he started contributing a series of political verse to the *Nation,* with the pen name of "Desmond." He was energetic in supporting the cause for national reform and supported the Young Ireland party rally in 1845. He died at Blackrock, near Dublin. He edited *Poets and Dramatists of Ireland* (1864) and the *Book of Irish Ballads* (1869). In 1881 he received the medal of the Royal Academy of Spain for his translations of the Spanish dramatist Pedro Calderon De La Barca: *Justina,* 1848; *Dramas,* 1853; *Love, the Greatest Enchantment,* 1861; *Mysteries of Corpus Christi,* 1867; *The Two Lovers of Heaven,* 1870; and *The Wonder-working Magician,* 873. Some of his other publications: *The Bell-Founder, and Other Poems,* 1857. *The Book of Irish Ballads,* 1869. *The Centenary of Moore,* 1880. *Poems,* 1882. Some of his poems: "Home Sickness," "The Dead Tribune," "The Foray of Con O'Donnell," "The Pillar Towers of Ireland," "Youth and Age."

Sources: *An Anthology of Catholic Poets.* Shane Leslie, ed. Macmillan, 1952. *Ballads, Poems, and Lyrics of Denis Florence McCarthy.* James McGlashan, 1850. *Dictionary of National Biography.* Electronic Edition 1.1. Oxford University Press, 1997. *English Poetry: Author Search.* Chadwyck-Healey Ltd., 1995 (http://www.lib.utexas.edu: 8080/search/epoetry/author.html). *The Columbia Granger's Index to Poetry.* 11th ed. *The Columbia Granger's World of Poetry,* Columbia University Press, 2005 (http://www.columbiagrangers.org). *Underglimpses, and Other Poems of MacCarthy, Denis Florence.* David Bogue, 1857. *Wikipedia, the Free Encyclopedia* (http://en.wikipedia.org/wiki/Wikipedia).

MacDIARMID, HUGH (1892–1978)

Pseudonym of Christopher Murray Grieve. He was born in Langholm, Dumfrieshire, and educated at Langholm Academy. During his time as a pupil-teacher in Edinburgh, he joined the Edinburgh branches of the Independent Labor Party and the Fabian Society. He was a founder of the Scottish Nationalist Party in 1928. His nationalism is clearly seen in many of his poems. Before World War I, and after service in the Royal Army Medical Corps from 1915 to 1919, he was a journalist in Scotland and Wales and editor of several papers. He was the core figure in the revival of Scots as a poetic language. His early work was supported by John Buchan (see entry), who wrote the preface to his first volume of poetry, *Sangschaw* (1925). Some of his other publications: *Annals of the Five Senses,* 1923. *Penny Wheep,* 1926. *A Drunk Man Looks at the Thistle,* 1926. *At the Sign of the Thistle,* 1934. *More Collected Poems,* 1971. *Complete Poems,* 1978. Some of his poems: "A Vision of Scotland," "After Two Thousand Years," "England is Our Enemy," "I Heard Christ Sing," "Ode to All Rebels," "The Battle Continues," "The Covenanters," "The Innumerable Christ," "The War with England."

Sources: *Biography of Hugh MacDiaramid. Recommended site* (http://www.users.globalnet.co.uk/~crumey/hugh_macdiarmid.html). *Chapters into Verse. Vol. II: Gospels to Revelation.* Robert Atwan and Laurance Wieder, eds. Oxford University Press, 1993. *Dictionary of National Biography.* Electronic Edition 1.1. Oxford University Press, 1997. *Scottish Authors* (http://www.slainte.org.uk/scotauth/macdidsw.htm). *Selected Poetry of Hugh MacDiarmid.* Alan Riach and Michael Grieve, eds. New Directions, 1992. *The Columbia Granger's Index to Poetry.* 11th ed. *The Columbia Granger's World of Poetry,* Columbia University Press, 2005 (http://www.columbiagrangers.org). *The National Portrait Gallery* (www.npg.org.uk).

MacDONAGH, THOMAS and DONAGH (1878–1968)

Thomas, the father (1878–1916)

Born in Cloughjordan, County Tipperary, the son of schoolteachers, he was educated by the Holy Ghost Fathers. He graduated M.A. in literature from the National University, Dublin, where he became professor of English. He joined the Gaelic League and became friends with Pádraic Pearse, with whom he helped found St. Enda's School for boys in Rathfarnham, a suburb of Dublin. There, through the use of firearms and the medium of the Irish language, pupils were inspired to be "Gaelic and Free." In 1911 he helped found the *Irish Review* with Padraig Colum and David Houston. In 1913 MacDonagh joined the Irish Republican Army and put his name to the Proclamation of the Irish Republic. Following the 1916 Rising he was imprisoned in Kilmainham Gaol, Dublin, tried by field general court martial and executed by firing squad on May 3, 1916. Francis Ledwidge (see entry) wrote the "Lament for Thomas MacDonagh." Some of his poems: "Ideal," "John-John," "The Lifting of the Cloud," "The Man Upright," "The Night Hunt," "To Death," "Wishes for My Son."

Donagh, the son (1912–1968)

Born in Dublin, he graduated M.A. in English literature from University College, Dublin, and concurrently read for the bar at King's Inn in Dublin. He practiced law from 1936 to 1946 and was a district judge from 1946 to 1968. He was a leading Irish poet, playwright, ballad writer and prominent figure of lively Irish entertainment in the mid–20th century. He died in Dublin. His son writes, "His plays are all written in verse, but are hardly serious. Even the tragedy, *Lady Spider* (based on the story of Deirdre of the Sorrows) is as funny as it is tragic." (http://members.tripod.com/IrishBornMan/DMacD.html). Some of his publications: *Veterans and Other Poems,* 1941. *Happy as Larry,* 1946 (comedy). *God's Gentry,* 1951 (comedy). *Step-in-the-Hollow,* 1962 (comedy). *The Oxford Book of Irish Verse,* 1958 (editor, with E.S. Lennox Robinson). Some of his poems: "A Warning to Conquerors," "Ballade which Villon Made," "Charles Donnelly," "Dublin Made Me," "Galway," "Going to Mass Last Sunday," "Just an Old Sweet Song," "Love's Language," "On the Bridge of Athlone: A Prophecy," "The Hungry Grass."

Sources: *A Little Book of Irish Verse.* Chronicle Books, 1993. *An Anthology of Irish Verse: The Poetry of Ireland from Mythological Times to the Present.* Padraic Colum, ed. Liveright, 1948. *Biography and poetry of Donagh MacDonagh* (http://www.turlach.net/macdonagh/dmacd/dmacd.htm). *Contemporary Irish Poetry: An Anthology.* Anthony Bradley, ed. University of California Press. New and rev. ed., 1988.

Encyclopædia Britannica Ultimate Reference Suite DVD, 2006. *Ireland in Poetry.* Charles Sullivan, ed. Harry N. Abrams, 1990. *Lament for Thomas MacDonagh* (http://www.cs.rice.edu/~ssiyer/minstrels/poems/1608.html). *Lyra Celtica: An Anthology of Representative Celtic Poetry.* E.A. Sharp and J. Matthay, eds. John Grant, 1924. *New Irish Poets.* Devin A. Garrity, ed. Devin-Adair, 1948. *Searc's Web Guide to 20th Century Ireland—Thomas MacDonagh* (http://www.searcs-web.com/mcdonagh.html). *Songs Collected by Donagh MacDonagh* (http://songbook1.tripod.com/). *Stephen's Study Room: British Military & Criminal History in the period 1900 to 1999* (http://www.stephen-stratford.co.uk/thos_macdonagh.htm). *The 1916 Rebellion, Thomas MacDonagh* (http://www.1916rising.com/pic_tom_mcdonagh.html). *The Columbia Granger's Index to Poetry.* 11th ed. *The Columbia Granger's World of Poetry,* Columbia University Press, 2005 (http://www.columbiagrangers.org). *The Oxford Book of Irish Verse: XVIIth Century–XXth Century.* Donagh MacDonagh and Leenox Robinson, eds. Oxford University Press, 1958. *Treasury of Irish Religious Verse.* Patrick Murray, ed. Crossroad, 1986.

MacDONALD, ALEXANDER, ALASDAIR (?1700–?1780)

His Gaelic name is Alasdair MacMhaighstir Alasdair. He was born at Dalilea on Loch Shiel, Argyllshire, the son of the Episcopal clergyman of Ardnamurchan. He attended Glasgow University and was teacher in Ardnamurchan in the service of the Society for Propagating Christian Knowledge in the Highlands and Isles. He held a commission in the highland army under his cousin, Charles MacEachainn, and was active in the '45 Rebellion. When the battle was lost, his property was confiscated and he wandered the Highlands until the passing of the Act of Indemnity gave him again a settled home. He was buried in the cemetery of Kilmhoree, Arisaig. Some of his publications: *Gaelic and English Vocabulary,* 1741. *Incitement to the Highland Clans,* 1745 (a rallying call for Bonnie Prince Charlie in the '45 rebellion). *Resurrection of the Ancient Scottish Tongue,* 1751 (the first book of Gaelic Poetry). Some of his poems: "Clanranald's Galley," "Song of Summer," "The Birlinn of Clanranald," "The Manning of the Birlinn," "Oran Nam Fineachan Gaidhealach [The Gaelic Song of the Clans]."

Sources: *Alasdair MacMhaighstir Alasdair (c. 1695-c. 1770), Poet* (http://www.users.globalnet.co.uk/~crumey/alexander_macdonald.html). *Dictionary of National Biography.* Electronic Edition 1.1. Oxford University Press, 1997. *The Columbia Granger's Index to Poetry.* 11th ed. *The Columbia Granger's World of Poetry,* Columbia University Press, 2005 (http://www.columbiagrangers.org). *The Gaelic Song of the Clans* (http://chrsouchon.free.fr/oran nam.htm). *The New Penguin Book of Scottish Verse.* Robert Crawford and Mick Imlah, eds. Penguin Books, 2000. *The Poetry of Alasdair MacMhaighstir Alasdair.* Ronald Black, ed. Association for Scottish Literary Studies, 2005. *The*

Scottish Collection of Verse to 1800. Eileen Dunlop and Kamm Antony, eds. Richard Drew, 1985. *Who's Who in the Jacobite Camp* (http://homepage.ntlworld.com/stephen.lord2/Page%20Four.htm).

MacDONALD, GEORGE (1824–1905)

Born at Huntly, Aberdeenshire, he graduated M.A. from King's College, Aberdeen, in 1845, and in 1868 his university made him honorary doctor of laws. Ordained as a Congregational minister in 1850, he then became a free-lance preacher and lecturer and made literature his profession following the success of his poetic tragedy, *Within and Without* (1855). He lived mostly in London, but spent long spells in Bordighera, Italy. In 1872 he lectured to enthusiastic audience in America. His ashes were buried in the English cemetery at Bordighera. He was a novelist, hymn writer and author of children's stories, such as *At the Back of the North Wind* (1871), *Princess and the Goblin* (1872) and *The Princess and Curdie* (1873). Some of his other poetry publications: *Poems,* 1857. *The Disciple and Other Poems,* 1867. *A Threefold Cord: Poems by Three Friends,* 1883. *Scotch Songs and Ballads,* 1893. Some of his poems: "A Baby-Sermon," "A Christmas Carol," "At Aberdeen," "Diary of an Old Soul," "Father's Hymn for the Mother to Sing," "The Preacher's Prayer," "The Sheep and the Goat," "The Wind and the Moon."

Sources: *A Sacrifice of Praise: An Anthology of Christian Poetry in English from Caedmon to the Mid–Twentieth Century.* James H. Trott, ed. Cumberland House Publishing, 1999. *Biography of George Macdonald.* The Victorian Web (http://www.victorianweb.org/authors/gm/bio.html). *Dictionary of National Biography.* Electronic Edition 1.1. Oxford University Press, 1997. *Encyclopædia Britannica Ultimate Reference Suite DVD,* 2006. *The Columbia Granger's Index to Poetry.* 11th ed. *The Columbia Granger's World of Poetry,* Columbia University Press, 2005 (http://www.columbiagrangers.org). *The Cyber Hymnal* (http://www.cyberhymnal.org/index.htm). *The Faber Book of Comic Verse.* Michael Roberts and Janet Adam Smith, eds. Faber and Faber, 1978. *The Moon is Shining Bright as Day: An Anthology of Good-humoured Verse.* Ogden Nash, ed. J.B. Lippincott, 1953. *The Oxford Companion to English Literature.* 6th edition. Margaret Drabble, ed. Oxford University Press, 2000. *The Poetical Works of George MacDonald* (2 vols). IndyPublishing.com, U.S., 2005. *The Treasury of Christian Poetry.* Lorraine Eitel, ed. Fleming H. Revell, 1982. *Who Has Seen the Wind? An Illustrated Collection of Poetry for Young People.* Kathryn Sky-Peck, ed. Museum of Fine Arts, Boston, 1991.

MacFARLAN, JAMES (1832–1862)

Born in Glasgow, the son of a weaver and pedlar, he was largely self-educated, through the subscription library. By the age of twenty, his poetry had acquired the sort of reputation that secured him a post at the Glasgow Athenæum (which in 1968 became the Royal Scottish Academy for Music and Drama).

Possibly feeling hemmed in by the big city, he returned to the life of a peddler. Struggling against tuberculosis, poverty, and neglect, he found employment as a police-court reporter to the weekly Glasgow *Bulletin* and contributed short stories to the paper. Charles Dickens (see entry) printed several of Macfarlan's poems in *Household Words.* In 1859, William Makepeace Thackeray (see entry), on hearing Samuel Lover (see entry) recite Macfarlan's poem, *Lords of Labour,* likened him to Robert Burns. Macfarlan was buried in Cheapside Cemetery, Anderston, Glasgow, and a tombstone was erected by his admirers in 1885. He published a poetic tract *The Wanderers of the West* (no date). His poems were written in fluent English rather than in the Scots dialect. His other poetry publications: *Poems: Pictures of the Past,* 1854. *City Songs, and Other Poetical Pieces,* 1855. *Lyrics of Life,* 1856.

Sources: *Dictionary of National Biography.* Electronic Edition 1.1. Oxford University Press, 1997.

MacGREEVY, THOMAS (1893–1967)

Born in Tarbert, County Kerry, he worked for the Irish Land Commission, Dublin, from 1910 until World War I. He was an officer in the Royal Field Artillery and by Christmas 1917 he was fighting at the Somme. His war experiences clearly influenced his poems. After the war he read history and political science at Trinity College, Dublin. In 1924 he became assistant editor for *The Connoisseur* in London and wrote art and literature reviews for *The Times Literary Supplement, The Nation* and the *Athenaeum.* From 1927 to 1928, he was lecturer in English literature at the Ecole Normale Supérieure, Paris. Returning to London in 1933, he became chief art critic of *The Studio,* then was director of the National Gallery of Ireland from 1950 to 1963. He was awarded the Chevalier de l'ordre de la Légion d'honneur (1948), Officier de la Légion d'honneur (1962) and an honorary doctorate of letters from the National University of Ireland (1962). He died in Dublin from heart failure. Some of his poems: "Aodh Ruadh O'Domhnaill," "Crón Tráth na nDéithe" (the "cab" poem), "De Civitate Hominum," "Homage to Marcel Proust," "Recessional," "The Six Who Were Hanged."

Sources: *An Anthology of Irish Verse: The Poetry of Ireland from Mythological Times to the Present.* Padraic Colum, ed. Liveright, 1948. *Anthology of Twentieth-Century British and Irish Poetry.* Keith Tuma, ed. Oxford University Press, 2001. *Collected Poems of Thomas MacGreevy: An Annotated Edition.* Susan Schreibman, ed. Anna Livia Press, Dublin, 1991. *Contemporary Irish Poetry: An Anthology.* Anthony Bradley, ed. University of California Press. New and rev. ed., 1988. *Kennys Irish Bookshop* (http://www.kennysirishbookshop.ie/categories/irishwriters/macgreevythomas.shtml).

Poemhunter (www.poemhunter.com). The Columbia Granger's Index to Poetry. 11th ed. The Columbia Granger's World of Poetry, Columbia University Press, 2005 (http://www.columbiagrangers.org). The Oxford Book of Modern Verse, 1892–1935. William Butler Yeats, ed. Oxford University Press, 1936.

MacINTYRE, DUNCAN BAN (1724–1812)

Gaelic poet "Donnacha bàn nan Oran, fair-haired Duncan of the songs" was born of humble parents at Druimliaghart of Glenorchy, Argyllshire. Though he could not write, nor could he speak English, he could repeat all seven thousand verses of his poems. He fought for the Hanoverian army against Bonnie Prince Charlie and was present at the Battle of Falkirk on 17 January 1746, memorialized in some of his poems. He was a sergeant in the private regiment of the earl of Breadalbane from 1793 to 1799, and from 1806 until his death the bard lived on the earnings from his poetry. He died at Edinburgh and was buried in Greyfriars churchyard. In 1859 a monument was erected to him, under Celtic and Masonic auspices, on the Beacon Hill of Breadalbane, near Dalmally. Hugh MacDiarmid (see entry) translated MacIntyre's "Praise of Ben Doran." Some of his other poems: "Aoir Anna," "Final Farewell to the Bens [hills]," "Praise of Ben Doran," "Song of Edinburgh," "Song of the Battle of Falkirk," "Song to the Argyll Regiment," "The Author's Epitaph on Himself," "The Dark Maid of Rannoch," "Verses on Iona."

Sources: Dictionary of National Biography. Electronic Edition 1.1. Oxford University Press, 1997. The Columbia Granger's Index to Poetry. 11th ed. The Columbia Granger's World of Poetry, Columbia University Press, 2005 (http://www.columbiagrangers.org). The Songs of Duncan Ban Macintyre. Angus Macleod, ed. Scottish Gaelic Text Society, 1952. Poems of Duncan Ban Macintyre (http://www.electricscotland.com/poetry/macintyre/).

MacKAIL, JOHN WILLIAM (1859–1945)

Scottish poet, the son of Rev. John Mackail, a Free Church minister, he was born on the Isle of Bute, Scotland's jewel on the River Clyde. He graduated literae humaniores from Balliol College, Oxford, in 1881, and winning four major scholarships, he was reckoned the most brilliant undergraduate scholar of his time. From 1884 to 1919 he worked for the Education Department of the Privy Council, which later became the Board of Education, and was active in establishment of secondary education under the 1902 Education Act. From 1906 to 1911 he was professor of poetry at Oxford. He received honorary degrees from six universities in Britain and in Adelaide, Australia, and was appointed Order of Merit

in 1935. He died in London. In 1890 he published Select Epigrams from the Greek Anthology, and with Henry Beeching and Bowyer Nichols (see entries) he published Mensae Secundae, 1879. Some of his other publications: Love in Idleness, 1883. Love's Looking-glass, 1891. Some of his poems: "An Autumn Lily," "Confession of Faith," "Debate of the Heart and Soul," "Fate's Prisoner," "Mountain Echo," "Summer and Winter," "The Golden Book of Cupid and Psyche," "Within and Without."

Sources: Dictionary of National Biography. Electronic Edition 1.1. Oxford University Press, 1997. Love's Looking Glass, Beeching, Mackail, and Nichols, Percival and Co., 1891. The Columbia Granger's Index to Poetry. 11th ed. The Columbia Granger's World of Poetry, Columbia University Press, 2005 (http://www.columbiagrangers.org).

MACKAY, CHARLES (1814–1889)

Scottish poet born in Perth, the son of an army officer, he was educated at the Royal Caledonian Asylum at Caledonian Road, Holloway, Middlesex, a school for children of Scottish parentage. Fluent in several European languages, in 1830 he became private secretary to the inventor William Cockerill in Belgium. A journalist of renown, he edited several important papers of the day and in 1860 established the London Review. From 1862 to 1865 he was the special correspondent of the Times at New York during the Civil War. He was buried in Kensal Green cemetery, West London. He was a prolific author of poetry and many of his songs were set to music by his friends Henry Russell and Sir Henry Bishop. Some of his publications: The Hope of the World, 1840. Legends of the Isles, 1845. Voices from the Mountain, 1847. Collected Songs, 1859. Cavalier Songs and Ballads of England, 1863. A Thousand and One Gems of English Poetry, 1867. Some of his poems: "Children's Auction," "If I Were a Voice," "The Holly Bough," "The Poor Man's Sunday Walk," "The Three Preachers," "Tubal Cain," "Vixi."

Sources: A Treasury of the Familiar. Ralph L. Woods, ed. Macmillan, 1942. An Anthology of Revolutionary Poetry. Marcus Graham, ed. The Active Press, 1929. British Minstrelsie. T.C. and E.C. Jack, Grange Publishing works, Edinburgh (?1900). Dictionary of National Biography. Electronic Edition 1.1. Oxford University Press, 1997. English Poetry: Author Search (http://www.lib.utexas.edu:8080/search/epoetry/author.html). Virtual American Biographies. Charles Mackay (http://www.famousamericans.net/charlesmackay). Picture of the New Caedonian Asylum, London (http://www.londonancestor.com/views/vb-asylumcal.htm). The National Portrait Gallery (www.npg.org.uk). The Columbia Granger's Index to Poetry. 11th ed. The Columbia Granger's World of Poetry, Columbia University Press, 2005 (http://www.columbiagrangers.org). The Home Book of Verse for Young Folks. Burton Egbert Stevenson, ed. Holt, Rinehart and Winston, 1929. The Oxford Book of Victorian Verse. Arthur Quiller-Couch, ed. Oxford University Press, 1971. *The Lied and Art Song Texts Page* (http://www.recmusic.org/lieder/m/cmackay/). *Treasury of Favorite Poems.* Joseph H. Head, ed. Gramercy Books, 2000.

MACKINTOSH, EWART ALAN (1893–1917)

Born in Brighton, Sussex, of Highland parents, he was educated at St. Paul's School and read classics at Christ Church College, Oxford. Commissioned into the 5th Battalion Seaforth Highlanders in December 1914, he joined the Battalion at Laventie, France, in July 1915. He played the pipes, spoke Gaelic, and was loved by his men, who affectionately called him "Tosh." Within ten months he was awarded the Military Cross at the battle of the Somme for carrying wounded Private David Sutherland through 100 yards of German trenches, although the solider died. Wounded, gassed, and sent home for recuperation, Macintosh insisted on returning to France to join the 4th Battalion Seaforth Highlanders. He was killed in the village of Fantaine Notre-Dame during the Battle of Cambrai. Along with Charles Hamilton Sorley (see entry) he was regarded as one of Scotland's finest war poets. Some of his poems: "Before the Summer," "Cha Till Maccruimein [Departure of the 4th Camerons]" (thought to herald his own death), "Farewell," "In Memoriam R.M. Stalker, Missing, September 1916," "In Memoriam, Private D. Sutherland."

Sources: *A Little Book of Scottish Verse.* Chronicle Books, 1993. *Clan of the Cat: Ewart Alan Mackintosh* (http://a2fister2000.tripod.com/id66.htm). *Never Such Innocence: A New Anthology of Great War Verse.* Martin Stephen, ed. Buchan and Enright, 1988. *Poetry of the First World War: Scottish Poets. Ewart Alan Mackintosh* (http://www.scuttlebuttsmallchow.com/listscot.html). *The Columbia Granger's Index to Poetry.* 11th ed. *The Columbia Granger's World of Poetry,* Columbia University Press, 2005 (http://www.columbiagrangers.org). *The Overshadowed and Surprising* (http://www.lib.byu.edu/~english/WWI/over/over.html). *The Oxford Book of Friendship.* D.J. Enright and David Rawlinson, ed. Oxford University Press, 1991.

MacLEAN, SORLEY (1911–1996)

"Somhairle MacGill-Eain" was born at Osgaig on the island of Raasay in the Inner Hebrides into a family and community immersed in Gaelic language and culture, particularly song. Educated at Portree, Skye, he graduated with a first class honors in English from Edinburgh University in 1933. During World War II he was seriously wounded at El Alamein. He spent his working life as a schoolteacher, and for many years was head teacher at Plockton High School, Wester Ross. He was a founder of the School of Scottish Studies in Edinburgh and received the Queen's Gold Medal for po-

etry in 1990. He died at Raigmore Hospital, Inverness. Gaelic was his medium, although he translated many of his poems into English. The poem "Hallaig" is one of the lyrics included in Peter Maxwell-Davies' opera *The Jacobite Rising* (1997). From 1940 onward he published collections of his own and in collaboration with other Gaelic-speaking poets. A bilingual edition of his *Collected Poems* appeared in 1989. Some of his poems: "A Highland Woman," "Calvary," "Kinloch Ainort," "McIntyre and Ross," "My Een Are Nae on Calvary," "The Clan MacLean," "The Cry of Europe," "The Cuillin."

Sources: *Anthology of Magazine Verse and Yearbook of American Poetry.* Alan F. Pater, ed. Monitor Book Company, 1980. *Biography of Sorley Maclean: BBC—Writing Scotland—Scotland's Languages* (http://www.bbc.co.uk/scotland/arts/writingscotland/learning_journeys/scotlands_languages/sorley_maclean/). *Clan MacLean Articles, In Memory of Sorley, A Tribute, by Mary McLean Hoff.* (http://www.maclean.org/clan-maclean-articles/clan-maclean-tribute-to-sorley.htm). *Poems of the Scottish Hills: An Anthology.* Hamish Brown, ed. Aberdeen University Press, 1982. *Portraits of Poets.* Sebastian Barker, ed. Carcanet, 1986. *Sorley MacLean—An Obituary. The Capital Scot* (http://thecapitalscot.com/pastfeatures/smaclean.html). *The Columbia Granger's Index to Poetry.* 11th ed. *The Columbia Granger's World of Poetry,* Columbia University Press, 2005 (http://www.columbiagrangers.org). *The Faber Book of War Poetry.* Kenneth Baker, ed. Faber and Faber, 1996. *The Harvill Book of Twentieth-Century Poetry in English.* Michael Schmidt, ed. The Harvill Press, 1999. *The New Penguin Book of Scottish Verse.* Robert Crawford and Mick Imlah, eds. Penguin Books, 2000. *The Oxford Companion to English Literature.* 6th edition. Margaret Drabble, ed. Oxford University Press, 2000. *Wikipedia, the Free Encyclopedia* (http://en.wikipedia.org/wiki/Wikipedia).

MacLEOD, MARY (1569–1674)

Gaelic bard Màiri Nighean Alasdair Ruaidh was born at Rodel, Isle of Harris, and died at Dunvegan, Isle of Skye. Her poetry deals with the heroic exploits of the Macleod family and expresses her deep emotional attachment to the family. She spent most of her life at the Macleod household of Dunvegan Castle, acting as nurse to successive generations of chieftains. One of the finest poets in the language, she was reputed to have excused her poetry as mere lullabies for the children in her care. Legend also has it that she was buried face down at St. Clement's Church in Rodel, Harris, for daring to compose poetry—a fate usually reserved for those accused of witchcraft. Some of her poems: "A Satiric Song," "Blue Song," "Crònan an Taibh," "Dirge," "Jealousy," "Lament for MacLeod," "MacLeod's Lilt," "Song to Iain Son of Sir Norman," "The Croon," "The Wedding of MacLeod," "Tricky Margaret."

Sources: *Early Modern Women Poets (1520–1700).* Jane Stevenson and Peter Davidson, ed. Oxford University

Press, 2001. *Gaelic Song—An Introduction* (http://www.gaelicmusic.com/gaelicsong). *Gaelic Songs of Mary Macleod.* J. Carmichael Watson, ed. Blackie and Son Limited, 1934. *Microsoft Encarta* 2006 (DVD). Microsoft Corporation, 2006. *The Columbia Granger's Index to Poetry.* 11th ed. *The Columbia Granger's World of Poetry,* Columbia University Press, 2005 (http://www.columbiagrangers.org). *The New Penguin Book of Scottish Verse.* Robert Crawford and Mick Imlah, eds. Penguin Books, 2000.

MacNEICE, FREDERICK LOUIS (1907–1963)

He was born in Belfast, the son of the rector of Holy Trinity, later bishop of Down, Connor and Dromore. Educated at Sherborne School, Dorset, and Marlborough College, Wiltshire, he graduated *literae humaniores* from Merton College, Oxford, in 1930. In 1936 he was appointed lecturer in Greek at Bedford College, London, and also lectured at Cornel University, New York. Rejected for active service in World War II because of bad eyesight, he joined the BBC features department in May 1941 as writer-producer. In 1946 he produced *The Dark Tower,* a radio dramatic fantasy with music by Benjamin Britten. Queen's University, Belfast, awarded him an honorary doctorate in 1957, and in 1958 he was appointed Commander of the British Empire. He died of viral pneumonia in London. His autobiography, *The Strings Are False,* was published posthumously in 1965. Some of his publications: *Agamemnon,* 1936 (translation from Aeschylus). *Poems, 1925–1940,* 1940. *Springboard,* 1945. *Holes in the Sky,* 1948. *Ten Burnt Offerings,* 1952. *Solstices,* 1961. Some of his poems: "Bagpipe Music," "Cock o' the North," "Didymus," "Donegal Triptych," "Suite for Recorders," "The Stygian Banks."

Sources: *Chief Modern Poets of Britain and America.* 5th edition. Gerald DeWitt Sanders and John Herbert Nelson, eds., Macmillan, 1970. *Dictionary of National Biography.* Electronic Edition 1.1. Oxford University Press, 1997. *Encyclopædia Britannica Ultimate Reference Suite DVD,* 2006. *The National Portrait Gallery* (www.npg.org.uk). *Seven Centuries of Poetry: Chaucer to Dylan Thomas.* A.N. Jeffares, ed. Longmans, Green, 1955. *The Collected Poems of Louis MacNeice.* E.R. Dodds, ed. Faber and Faber, 1966. *The Columbia Granger's Index to Poetry.* 11th ed. *The Columbia Granger's World of Poetry,* Columbia University Press, 2005 (http://www.columbiagrangers.org). *The Oxford Anthology of English Poetry. Vol. II: Blake to Heaney.* John Wain, ed. Oxford University Press, 1990. *The Oxford Companion to English Literature.* 6th edition. Margaret Drabble, ed. Oxford University Press, 2000.

MACNEILL, HECTOR (1746–1818)

Scottish poet, the son of James Macneill, a retired captain of the 42nd Regiment, was born at Rosebank, near Roslin, Midlothian. Educated at Stirling Grammar School, he then worked as a sailor in the West Indies until around 1776. From 1780 to 1787 he was assistant secretary to Admiral Geary's flagship with the grand fleet, then to the flagship of Sir Richard Bickerton in Indian waters. His attempts to make his living by writing proved unsuccessful for a time and not until 1796 did his fortunes change. He achieved popularity when living in Edinburgh, where he died. A portrait by John Henning is in the National Portrait Gallery, Edinburgh. Some of his publications: *An Advice From an Old Lover,* 1798. *The Poetical Works,* 1806. *The Pastoral, or Lyric Muse of Scotland,* 1808. *Town Fashions or Modern Manners Delineated,* 1810. *Bygane Times and Late-come Changes,* 1811. Some of his poems: "Come under My Plaidie," "My Boy Tammy" (a song), "Scotland's Scaith, or the History of Will and Jean," "The Harp, a Legendary Tale," "The Links o' Forth, or a Parting Peep at the Carse of Stirling."

Sources: *Auld Scots Ballants.* Robert Ford, ed. Alexander Gardner, 1889. *Come Hither.* Walter de la Mare, ed. Knopf, 1957; Dover Publications, 1995. *Dictionary of National Biography.* Electronic Edition 1.1. Oxford University Press, 1997. *English Poetry: Author Search.* Chadwyck-Healey Ltd., 1995 (http://www.lib.utexas.edu:8080/search/epoetry/author.html). *Stanford University Libraries and Academic Information Resources* (http://library.stanford.edu). *The Columbia Granger's Index to Poetry.* 11th ed. *The Columbia Granger's World of Poetry,* Columbia University Press, 2005 (http://www.columbiagrangers.org). *The Scottish Collection of Verse to 1800.* Eileen Dunlop and Kamm Antony, eds. Richard Drew, 1985.

MACPHERSON, JAMES (1736–1796)

Scottish poet who was born into a poor family from Ruthven, Inverness-shire. He collected Gaelic manuscripts and transcribed orally transmitted Gaelic poems, published as *Fragments of Ancient Poetry ... Translated from the Gallic or Erse Language* (1760). From 1764 to 1766 he worked in some government capacity in West Florida. He grew rich in London defending (as his agent) Mohammed Ali, nabob of Arcot, against the East India Company. He was a member of Parliament for Camelford, Cornwall, from 1780 until he died in Inverness-shire; he is memorialized by a stone in Poets' Corner of Westminster Abbey. His poetic works are overshadowed by doubts about the authenticity of his *Ossian Poems* (1762); were they genuine translations from the 3rd-century Gaelic poet Ossian (as he claimed), or the product of his fertile imagination? Samuel Johnson denounced the poems as forgeries and campaigned vigorously against Macpherson. The decision was reached in the late 19th century that there was no hard evidence they were wholly genuine. Some of his other poems: "On the Death of Marshal Keith," "The Highlander," "The Hunter," "The Night-Song of the Bards," "The Songs of the Five Bards, & of the Chief."

Sources: *Dictionary of National Biography.* Electronic Edition 1.1. Oxford University Press, 1997. *Encyclopædia Britannica Ultimate Reference Suite DVD,* 2006. *English Poetry: Author Search.* Chadwyck-Healey Ltd., 1995 (http://www.lib.utexas.edu:8080/search/epoetry/author.html). *Lyra Celtica: An Anthology of Representative Celtic Poetry.* E.A. Sharp and J. Matthay, eds. John Grant, 1924. *Mark Akenside, James Macpherson, Edward Young.* S.H. Clark, ed. Fyfield Books, 1994. *The Columbia Granger's Index to Poetry.* 11th ed. *The Columbia Granger's World of Poetry,* Columbia University Press, 2005 (http://www.columbiagrangers.org). *The Oxford Companion to English Literature.* 6th edition. Margaret Drabble, ed. Oxford University Press, 2000. *The Poems of Ossian.* Nichol, 1765. *University of Delaware Library: Forging a Collection. James Macpherson and the Ossian Poems* (http://www.lib.udel.edu/ud/spec/exhibits/forgery/ossian.htm).

MacSWEENEY, BARRY (1948–2000)

Born in Newcastle upon Tyne and educated at Rutherford Grammar School, he spent many years as a journalist on a variety of provincial newspapers, as well as teaching journalism and creative writing. He was North of England correspondent for the insurance and shipping newspaper Lloyd's Lists, and ran adult literacy classes. He was a regular contributor at the Morden Tower, an enterprise set up by Tom Pickard (see entry) and his wife Connie, who organized readings by influential local, national and international poets. In 1970 MacSweeney established Blacksuede Boot Press. Much of his work appeared in local poetry magazines and pamphlets, or as contributions to poetry anthologies. His love for the city of Newcastle as well as the wild, open spaces of Northumberland is obvious in his poetry. Alcohol dependence and subsequent ill health led to his early death at Denton Burn, Newcastle upon Tyne. Some of his publications: *Brother Wolf,* 1972. *Fools Gold,* 1972. *Black Torch,* 1978. *Odes,* 1978. *Ranter,* 1985. *Finnbar's Lament,* 1997. *Letter to Dewey,* 1999. *Pearl in the Silver Morning,* 1999. *The Book of Demons,* 1997. Some of his poems: "Blackbird," "Far Cliff Babylon," "Flame Ode," "Ode Long Kesh," "Sunk in My Darkness."

Sources: *Anthology of Twentieth-Century British and Irish Poetry.* Keith Tuma, ed. Oxford University Press, 2001. *Nicholas Johnson, An Appreciation* by Barry MacSweeney (www.pores.bbk.ac.uk). *Other: British and Irish Poetry Since 1970.* Richard Caddel and Peter Quartermain, eds. Wesleyan University Press, 1999. *The Columbia Granger's Index to Poetry.* 11th ed. *The Columbia Granger's World of Poetry,* Columbia University Press, 2005 (http://www.columbiagrangers.org). *The New British Poetry, 1968–88.* Gillian Allnutt, Fred D'Aguiar and Ken Edwards, ed. Grafton Books, 1989. *Wolf Tongue: Selected Poems 1965–2000.* Barry MacSweeney. Bloodaxe Books, 2003.

McCARTHY, THOMAS (1954–)

Born in Cappoquin, County Waterford, Ireland, he was educated at University College Cork, has worked for Cork City Library and currently works for the Cork City Council. His awards include the Patrick Kavanagh Award (1977); the Alice Hunt Bartlett Prize (1981); the Annual Literary Award, American Irish Foundation (1984); and the O'Shaughnessy Poetry Award, Irish-American Cultural Institute, 1991. He is former editor of *The Cork Review* and *Poetry Ireland Review.* His work has been widely translated and has appeared in over thirty anthologies. Some of his poetry is primarily concerned with a detailed examination of the Republic of Ireland's failures and successes as an independent state. In addition to his novels and poetry, he published a memoir, *The Garden of Remembrance* (1998). Some of his recent poetry publications: *Seven Winters in Paris,* 1989. *The Lost Province,* 1996. *Mr. Dineen's Careful Parade,* 1999. *New and Selected Poems,* 1999. *Merchant Prince,* 2005. Some of his poems: "A Neutral State," "November in Boston," "Seven Orange Tulips," "The Canadian Diplomat, 1942," "The Dying Synagogue at South Terrace," "The Emigration Trains," "With Paul Engle at Fort Madison, 1978."

Sources: *Biography of Thomas McCarthy* (http://www.irishwriters-online.com/thomasmccarthy.html). *Bitter Harvest: An Anthology of Contemporary Irish Verse.* John Montague, ed. Scribner's, 1989. *Books by Thomas McCarthy* (http://www.munsterlit.ie/Conwriters/thomas_mccarthy.htm). *Contemporary Irish Poetry: An Anthology.* Anthony Bradley, ed. University of California Press. New and rev. ed., 1988. *My Life, by Thomas McCarthy.* http://www.laoisedcentre.ie/LENGLISH/engrwww/tom.html). *Review of Merchant Prince by Thomas McCarthy* (http://www.inpressbooks.co.uk/merchant_prince_by_mccarthy_thomas_i016276.aspx). *The Columbia Granger's Index to Poetry.* 11th ed. *The Columbia Granger's World of Poetry,* Columbia University Press, 2005 (http://www.columbiagrangers.org). *The Inherited Boundaries: Younger Poets of the Republic of Ireland.* Sebastian Barry, ed. The Dolmen Press, 1986. *The Penguin Book of Contemporary Irish Poetry.* Peter Fallon and Derek Mahon, ed. Penguin Books, 1990. *Wikipedia, the Free Encyclopedia* (http://en.wikipedia.org/wiki/Wikipedia).

McCHEYNE, ROBERT MURRAY (1813–1843)

Scottish clergyman "the saintly McCheyne" was born in Edinburgh, the son of a lawyer, studied at Edinburgh University and was licensed to preach in 1835. He had two appointments: Annan and Larbert, Stirlingshire, before his health broke down. He was appointed to St. Peter's Church, Dundee, in 1836, but two years later his health again gave way. In 1839 the general assembly of the Church of Scotland invited McCheyne to be a three-member deputation to Israel to investigate the condition of the Jews there and throughout Europe. In 1842 he helped set up the British Society for the Propagation of the Gospel among the Jews. While visiting sick people in the parish he was stricken with typhus fever and died after two weeks. He was buried at St. Peter's and over six thousand people attended the funeral. Some of hymn/poems: "Beneath Moriah's Rocky Side," "Fountain of Siloam," "I am a debtor..." "I Once Was a Stranger," "Oil in the Lamp," "The Barren Fig Tree," "The Covenanters," "The Sea of Galilee," "Thy Word is a Lamp Unto My Feet," "When This Passing World is Done."

Sources: *Biography of Robert Murray McCheyne* (http://web.ukonline.co.uk/d.haslam/m-cheyne.htm). *Biography of Robert Murray McCheyne.* St. Peter's Free Church, Dundee (http://www.stpeters-dundee.org.uk/history.htm). *Bonar, A. and McCheyne, Mission of Discovery: The Beginnings of Modern Jewish Evangelism.* Alan Harman, ed. Fearn, 1996. *Dictionary of National Biography.* Electronic Edition 1.1. Oxford University Press, 1997. *The Cyber Hymnal* (http://www.cyberhymnal.org/index.htm). *The Impact of Robert Murray McCheyne, by J. Harrison Hudson* (http://web.ukonline.co.uk/d.haslam/mccheyne/hudson/Impact_of_McCheyne.htm).

McGONAGALL, WILLIAM TOPAZ (1825–1902)

He has the reputation of being the writer of the worst poetry in the English language. He was born in Edinburgh of Irish parentage and for a while the family lived in South Ronaldsay, Orkney, where the father was a peddler. William was largely self-educated and took up loom weaving in Dundee. He started his career as working poet in 1877 and delighted and appalled large audiences across Scotland and beyond with his peculiar poetic style and dramatic entertainment. After Dundee and a short stay in Perth, he returned to Edinburgh, where the title of "Sir William Topaz McGonagall, Knight of the White Elephant of Burma" was bestowed upon him (by letter) by order of the King of Burma. Part of his obituary reads: "Many in Dundee will regret to hear of the death of the 'Grand Old Man'" (*Dundee Courier*, 30 September 1902). All his poems can be read at http://www.mcgonagall-online.org.uk/. Some of his poems: "Adventures of King Robert the Bruce," "An Adventure in the Life of King James V of Scotland," "The Hero of Khartoum," "The Pennsylvania Disaster [1889]," "The Royal Review," "The Tay Bridge Disaster [1879]."

Sources: *Dictionary of National Biography.* Electronic Edition 1.1. Oxford University Press, 1997. *Poetic Gems of William McGonagall.* G. Duckworth, 1954. *The Oxford Book of Death.* D.J. Enright, ed. Oxford University Press, 1987. *The Oxford Companion to English Literature.* 6th edition. Margaret Drabble, ed. Oxford University Press, 2000. *Unauthorized Versions: Poems and Their Parodies.* Kenneth Baker, ed. Faber and Faber, 1990.

McGOUGH, ROGER (1937–)

Born in Liverpool, he was educated at St. Mary's College, Crosby, Liverpool, and graduated from Hull University, then worked as a teacher in Liverpool. Between 1963 and 1973 he was a member of the pop music and poetry group "The Scaffold" and was one of the "Liverpool Poets" with Adrian Henri and Brian Patten (see entries). He was fellow of poetry at the University of Loughborough (1973–1975), and honorary professor at Thames Valley University (1993). He wrote the lyrics for an adaptation of *The Wind in the Willows*, first staged in Washington, D.C., in 1984 and transferring to Broadway in 1995. He has written for and presented programs on BBC Radio, including *Poetry Please* and *Home Truths*. His live poetry album, *Lively*, is on CD. He won British Academy of Film and Television Arts awards in 1985 and 1993 and poetry awards in 1984 and 1999; in 1997 he received the Order of the British Empire and was made Commander in 2004. Some of his poems: "First Day at School," "Mother the Wardrobe is Full of Infantrymen," "Noah's Ark," "Prayer to Saint Grobianus," "Summer with Monika," "The Kleptomaniac," "The Newly Pressed Suit."

Sources: *British Council Arts* (http://www.contemporarywriters.com). *Messages: A Thematic Anthology of Poetry.* X.J. Kennedy, ed. Little, Brown, 1973. *Splinters: A Book of Very Short Poems.* Michael Harrison, ed. Oxford University Press, 1989. *The Columbia Granger's Index to Poetry.* 11th ed. *The Columbia Granger's World of Poetry*, Columbia University Press, 2005 (http://www.columbiagrangers.org). *The Mersey Sound: Penguin Modern Poets 10 (Roger McGough, Adrian Henri and Brian Patten).* Penguin, revised edition, 1980. *The New Oxford Book of Children's Verse.* Neil Philip, ed. Oxford University Press, 1996. *The Oxford Book of Comic Verse.* John Gross, ed. Oxford University Press, 1994. *The Oxford Book of Story Poems.* Michael Harrison and Christopher Stuart-Clark, eds. Oxford University Press, 1990. *The Oxford Book of Twentieth-Century English Verse.* Philip Larkin, ed. Oxford University Press, 1973. *The Oxford Companion to English Literature.* 6th edition. Margaret Drabble, ed. Oxford University Press, 2000. *The Kingfisher Book of Children's Poetry.* Michael Rosen, ed. Kingfisher Books, 1985. *Who's Who.* London: A & C Black, 2005.

McGUCKIAN, MEDBH (1950–)

Medbh (pronounced "Maeve") is an Irish-born poet who still lives in Ireland. After graduating in English B.A. (1972) and M.A. (1974) from Queen's University, Belfast, she returned to teaching English at secondary school. She was the first woman writer in residence at Queen's University from 1985 to 1988. Her awards: National Poetry Competition, 1979; Eric Gregory Award, 1980; Ireland Arts Council Award, 1982; Rooney Prize for Irish Literature, 1982; Alice Hunt Bartlett Award, 1983; The Cheltenham Prize, 1989; Forward Poetry Prize, 2002.

Some of her publications: *The Flower Master*, 1982. *Venus and the Rain*, 1984. *On Ballycastle Beach*, 1988. *Selected Poems: 1978–1994*, 1997. *Drawing Ballerinas*, 2001. *The Face of the Earth*, 2002. *The Book of the Angel*, 2004. Some of her poems: "Coleridge," "Marconi's Castle," "Mr. McGregor's Garden," "The Albert Chain," "The Aphrodisiac," "The Flitting," "Waterford."

Sources: *Anthology of Twentieth-Century British and Irish Poetry*. Keith Tuma, ed. Oxford University Press, 2001. *Biography of Medbh Mcguckian* (http://www.english.emory.edu/Bahri/McGuckian.html). *British Council Arts* (http://www.contemporarywriters.com). *Contemporary Irish Poetry: An Anthology*. Anthony Bradley, ed. University of California Press. New and rev. ed., 1988. *Irish Poetry: An Interpretive Anthology from Before Swift to Yeats and After*. W.J. McCormack, ed. New York University Press, 2000. *The Bloodaxe Book of 20th Century Poetry, from Britain and Ireland*. Edna Longley, ed. Bloodaxe Books, 2000. *The Columbia Granger's Index to Poetry*. 11th ed. *The Columbia Granger's World of Poetry*, Columbia University Press, 2005 (http://www.columbiagrangers.org). *The Faber Book of Contemporary Irish Poetry*. Paul Muldoon ed. Faber and Faber, 1986. *The Penguin Book of Contemporary Irish Poetry*. Peter Fallon and Derek Mahon, ed. Penguin Books, 1990.

McKENDRICK, JAMIE (1955–)

Born in Liverpool, he studied at Nottingham University and taught at the University of Salerno, Italy. He lives in Oxford, teaches part-time and reviews poetry and the visual arts for a number of newspapers and magazines. He has held residencies at Hertford College, Oxford; Masaryk University, Brno, Czech Republic; the University of Gothenburg, and is writer-in-residence at University College, London. His poems have been published in Holland and Italy. His poetry publications: *The Sirocco Room*, 1991. *The Kiosk on the Brink*, 1993. *The Marble Fly*, 1997 (winner of the Forward Poetry Prize [Best Poetry Collection of the Year], a Poetry Book Society Choice, and T.S. Eliot Prize [shortlist]); *Sky Nails: Poems*, 1979–1997, 2000; *Ink Stone*, 2003 (shortlisted for the 2003 T.S. Eliot Prize and the 2003 Whitbread Poetry Award). His other prizes and awards: Eric Gregory Award, 1984; Guardian/ World Wild Life Poetry Competition, 1989; Arts Council Writers' Award, 1991; Southern Arts Literature Award. 1994; Society of Authors Travel Award, 2003. Some of his poems: "A Shortened History in Pictures," "Obelisk," "Oil and Blood," "Postcard," "The Conquest of Albania."

Sources: *Biography of Jamie McKendrick. The Arvon Foundation* (http://www.arvonfoundation.org/pages/content/index.asp?PageID=45). *British Council Arts* (http://www.contemporarywriters.com). *Poems by Jamie McKendrick* (http://www.thepoem.co.uk/poems/mckendrick.htm). *The Columbia Granger's Index to Poetry.* 11th ed. *The*

Columbia Granger's World of Poetry, Columbia University Press, 2005 (http://www.columbiagrangers.org). *The Faber Book of 20th-Century Italian Poems.* Jamie McKendrick, ed. Faber and Faber, 2004. *The National Portrait Gallery* (www.npg.org.uk). *The Oxford Book of Sonnets.* John Fuller, ed. Oxford University Press, 2000. *The Oxford Book of Sonnets.* John Fuller, ed. Oxford University Press, 2000. *The Oxford Companion to English Literature.* 6th edition. Margaret Drabble, ed. Oxford University Press, 2000.

MADGE, CHARLES (1912–1996)

The son of an army officer, he was educated at Winchester College and Magdalene College, Cambridge, though he left without graduating. He worked as reporter on the *Daily Mirror* in 1935, which provided useful insights for his later work as a sociologist. In 1937, with Humphrey Jennings and Tom Harrison, he founded Mass-Observation — a United Kingdom social research organization. Although their work ended in the early 1950s, it was revived by the University of Sussex in 1981. The archives at Sussex University houses 22 boxes of papers which give an insight into Madge's aptitude for poetry. His life as a poet was gradually eclipsed by sociology, but was revived in later life. He was a friend of David Gascoyne (see entry); like Gascoyne he was generally classed as a surrealist poet. His first wife was Kathleen Raine (see entry). His other poetry publications: *The Disappearing Castle*, 1937. *The Father Found*, 1941. *Of Love, Time and Places*, 1993. Some of his poems: "At War," "Blocking the Pass," "Delusions," "In Conjunction," "Lusty Juventus," "Rumba of the Three Lost Souls," "Solar Creation," "The Birds of Tin," "To Make a Bridge."

Sources: *Anthology of Twentieth-Century British and Irish Poetry*. Keith Tuma, ed. Oxford University Press, 2001. *Archives Hub. Charles Madge Archive* (http://www.archiveshub.ac.uk/news/0402cm.html). *English and American Surrealist Poetry*. Edward B Germain, ed. Penguin Books, 1978. *The National Portrait Gallery* (www.npg.org.uk). *The Columbia Granger's Index to Poetry.* 11th ed. *The Columbia Granger's World of Poetry*, Columbia University Press, 2005 (http://www.columbiagrangers.org). *The Faber Book of Modern Verse.* 4th ed., revised by Peter Porter. Michael Roberts, ed. Faber and Faber, 1982. *The New British Poets: An Anthology.* Kenneth Rexroth, ed. New Directions, 1949. *The Oxford Companion to English Literature.* 6th edition. Margaret Drabble, ed. Oxford University Press, 2000. University of Sussex Library Special Collections: Charles Madge (http://www.sussex.ac.uk/library/speccoll/collection_introductions/madge.html).

MAGINN, WILLIAM (1793–1842)

Born in Cork, the son of a schoolmaster, he graduated in 1811 and gained a doctor of laws in 1819, both from Trinity College, Dublin. He contributed to Blackwood's magazine in Edinburgh and in 1824 moved to London, where he wrote extensively for periodicals, often under the pseudonym of "Ensign

Morgan O'Doharty." He was assistant editor of the *Evening Standard* and founding editor of *Fraser's Magazine*, 1830. Thackeray used him as the model for Charley Shandon in his serialized novel *Pendennis* (1848–1850). Maginn parodied many famous poets and politicians, and his 1836 attack on the novel *Berkeley Castle* by the Hon. Grantley Berkeley led to a duel between the two men, although neither was hurt. His brilliance was overshadowed by his reckless, intemperate character, yet his writings were humorous and entertaining, when they were not biting and caustic. He ended his life in desperate circumstances; a year in debtors' prison ruined his health and he died of tuberculosis at Walton-on-Thames, Surrey. Some of his poems: "I Give My Soldier-Boy a Blade," "St. Patrick of Ireland, My Dear!" "The Irishman and the Lady," "The Rime of the Auncient Waggonere," "The Storming of Magdeburgh."

Sources: *Biography of William Magin and engraving of the Fraserians* (http://www.munsterlit.ie/literarycork/fraser.html). *Dictionary of National Biography.* Electronic Edition 1.1. Oxford University Press, 1997. *English Poetry: Author Search* (http://www.lib.utexas.edu:8080/search/epoetry/author.html). *Folk Songs.* John Williamson Palmer, ed. Charles Scribner and Company, 1867. *Innocent Merriment: An Anthology of Light Verse.* Franklin P. Adams, ed. McGraw-Hill, 1942. *The Classic Hundred: All-Time Favorite Poems.* William Harmon, ed. Columbia University Press, 1990. *The Columbia Granger's Index to Poetry.* 11th ed. *The Columbia Granger's World of Poetry,* Columbia University Press, 2005 (http://www.columbiagrangers.org). *The Home Book of Verse.* Burton Egbert Stevenson, ed. New York: Henry Holt and Company, 1953. *The National Portrait Gallery* (www.npg.org.uk). *The Oxford Companion to English Literature.* 6th edition. Margaret Drabble, ed. Oxford University Press, 2000.

MAGUIRE, SARAH (1957–)

Born in West London (where she still lives), she trained as a gardener before attending university and then became a full-time poet and broadcaster. She is a creative writing tutor and is currently the writing fellow at the School of Oriental and African Studies at London University. The founder and director of the Poetry Translation Centre, she runs poetry translation workshops. She was the first writer to be sent to Palestine (1996) and to Yemen (1998) by the British Council. Since then she has been active in translating contemporary Arabic poetry into English. Her selected poems, *Haleeb Muraq*, translated by the leading Iraqi poet, Saadi Yousef, was published in Damascus in 2003. Some of her publications: *Spilt Milk*, 1991. *The Invisible Mender,* 1997. *A Green Thought in a Green Shade: Poetry in the Garden,* 2000. *Flora Poetica: The Chatto Book of Botanical Verse* (editor), 2001. *The Florist's at Mid-*

night, 2001. Some of her poems: "Communion," "Perfect Timing," "The Divorce Referendum," "The Fall." Her translated poems: "A Monkey at the Window," "At Thirty, the Party is Over," "Breathless," "Song," "Survivors."

Sources: *British Council Arts* (http://www.contemporarywriters.com). *Emergency Kit: Poems for Strange Times.* Jo Shapcott and Matthew Sweeney, eds. Faber and Faber, 1996. *Love's Witness: Five Centuries of Love Poetry by Women.* Jill Hollis, ed. Carroll and Graf, Inc., 1993. *Making for Planet Alice: New Women Poets.* Maura Dooley, ed. Bloodaxe Books, 1997. *Sarah Maguire, The Poetry Translation Centre* (http://www.poetrytranslation.soas.ac.uk/poets/index.cfm?type=3&poet=18). *The Columbia Granger's Index to Poetry.* 11th ed. *The Columbia Granger's World of Poetry,* Columbia University Press, 2005 (http://www.columbiagrangers.org).

MAHON, DEREK (1941–)

Born in Belfast — he now lives in Dublin — he was educated at the Royal Academical Institution and Trinity College, Dublin. In the 1960s, as one of the Northern Poets, he was associated with Seamus Heaney and Michael Longley (see entries). He has worked as a screenwriter, theatre critic, poetry editor, and features editor for *Vogue*; he contributes regularly to the *Irish Times*. In a survey conducted by the *Irish Times* in 1999, he was among the ten most popular writers (living and dead) in Ireland. He has received several major honors in Ireland and America, including a Lannan Foundation Award. He has translated several major poets and his screenplay *Summer Lightning* (based on Ivan Turgenev's *First Love*) was broadcast on Channel 4, 1985. Some of his other publications: *Night-Crossing*, 1968. *The Snow Party*, 1975. *Courtyards in Delft*, 1981. *The Hunt By Night*, 1982. *The Yaddo Letter*, 1992. *The Yellow Book*, 1997. *The Hudson Letter*, 1996. *Harbour Lights*, 2005. Some of his poems: "After the Titanic," "Afterlives," "Autobiographies," "Dawn at Saint Patrick's," "No Rest for the Wicked," "St. Patrick's Day," "Stanzas for Mary Stuart."

Sources: *Biography of Derek Mahon* (http://www.irishwriters-online.com/derekmahon.html). *Collected Poems of Derek Mahon.* The Gallery Press, 1999. *Selected Poems of Derek Mahon.* Viking, 1991. *The Columbia Granger's Index to Poetry.* 11th ed (http://www.columbiagrangers.org). *The Oxford Companion to English Literature.* 6th edition. Margaret Drabble, ed. Oxford University Press, 2000. *The Works of Derek Mahon* (http://www.infoplease.com/ipea/A0901434.html).

MAHONY, FRANCIS SYLVESTER (1804–1866)

Born in Camden Quay, Cork, his parents had a woolen business in Glanmire and subsequently in Blarney. He studied at the Jesuit College at Clongowes Wood, County Kildare, and at later in France and Italy, where for two years he studied philosophy. He excelled in ancient and modern languages and was ordained as a priest in 1832. Back in Cork he was hospital chaplain at the North Infirmary during the cholera outbreak of 1832. He moved to London, where he became a journalist, working for the *Daily News* and *The Globe*, and contributed a series to *Fraser's Magazine* called *Reliques of Father Prout*, the pseudonym he used for his poetry. He died in Paris and was buried in the Shadow of Shandon Steeple in Cork. His works can be found in the *Cornhill Magazine* and in the *Athenæum*. Some of his poems: "A Series of Modern Latin Poets," "Father Prout's Carousal," "The Attractions of a Fashionable Irish Watering-Place," "The Bells of Shandon," "The Rogueries of Tom Moore," "The Song of the Cossack," "The Songs of France," "The Songs of Italy."

Sources: *19th Century British Minor Poets.* W.H. Auden, ed. Delacorte Press, 1966. *Biography of Francis Sylvester Mahony (Father Prout)* (http://www.activate.ie/sites/cork citylib/ecclesiastical/stannesshandon/st_annes_father prout.htm). *Dictionary of National Biography.* Electronic Edition 1.1. Oxford University Press, 1997. *The Columbia Granger's Index to Poetry.* 11th ed. *The Columbia Granger's World of Poetry,* Columbia University Press, 2005 (http://www.columbiagrangers.org). *The Oxford Companion to English Literature.* 6th edition. Margaret Drabble, ed. Oxford University Press, 2000. *The Reliques of Father Prout (Francis Sylvester Mahony).* Oliver Yorke, ed. George Bell and Sons, 1889.

MAITLAND, SIR RICHARD, LORD LETHINGTON (1496–1586)

"Manly Maitland," as he was called in an epitaph, was the son of Sir William Maitland of Lethington, who was killed at Flodden (1513). In September 1549 Maitland's castle of Lethington was burned by the English, commemorated in his poem, "Againis the Theivis of Liddisdaill." He studied law at St. Andrews University and in Paris and was keeper of the Great Seal (1562–67) under Mary, Queen of Scots. He resigned the office in 1567 in favor of his son John, afterwards Lord Maitland of Thirlestane. Although he became blind about 1561, he remained active as a judge until 1584. The world of poetry owes him a debt for his collection of Scottish poetry, second only in importance to that by Bannatyne (1545–1608). A large selection, including Maitland's own poems, was published by John Pinkerton in two volumes in 1786 under the title *Ancient Scottish Poems never before in Print.* Some of his poems: "Ballat of the Creatioun of the World," "Lament for the Disorders of the Cuntrie," "Miseries of the Tyme," "Na Kyndes without Siller," "Satire on the Town Ladies," "The Satire of the Aige."

Sources: *Dictionary of National Biography.* Electronic

Edition 1.1. Oxford University Press, 1997. *Encyclopædia Britannica Ultimate Reference Suite DVD,* 2006. *English Poetry: Author Search.* Chadwyck-Healey Ltd., 1995 (http://www.lib.utexas.edu:8080/search/epoetry/author. html). For many of Sir Richard's poems, refer to *The Columbia Granger's Index to Poetry.* 11th ed. *The Columbia Granger's World of Poetry,* Columbia University Press, 2005 (http://www.columbiagrangers.org). *Great Books Online* (www.bartleby.com). *The Columbia Granger's Index to Poetry.* 11th ed. *The Columbia Granger's World of Poetry,* Columbia University Press, 2005 (http://www.columbia grangers.org). *The Golden Treasury of Scottish Poetry.* Hugh MacDiarmid, ed. Macmillan, 1941. *The Oxford Book of Scottish Verse.* John MacQueen and Tom Scott, eds. Oxford University Press, 1966. *The Scottish Collection of Verse to 1800.* Eileen Dunlop and Kamm Antony, eds. Richard Drew, 1985.

MALLET (ORIGINALLY MALLOCH), DAVID (?1705–1765)

Scottish poet born near Crieff, the son of a tenant farmer on Lord Drummond's Perthshire estate. From 1720 to 1723, he was tutor to the sons of Mr. Home of Dreghorn, Ayrshire, while studying at the same time at Edinburgh University. From 1723 to 1731 he was tutor to the sons of the Duke of Montrose at Shawford, near Winchester, Hampshire. While at Edinburgh he formed a friendship with James Thompson (see entry) his co-writer of several poems and masques, including *Alfred,* written to celebrate both the birthday of the Princess Augusta and the anniversary of George the First's accession (1714). Samuel Johnson thought that Mallet's poetry would remain alive as long as Mallet lived, and that was all. There was a long-running dispute as to whether Mallet or Thomson wrote the national ode of "Rule Britannia." *British Minstrelsie* (?1900) attributes the words to Thompson and the music to Dr. W.H.H. Arne. Mallet was buried in St. George's cemetery, South Audley Street, London. Some of his poems: "Cupid and Hymen," "Edwin and Emma," "Epigram, Written at Tunbridge Wells," "Of Verbal Criticism," "The Funeral Hymn," "To the Siege of Damascus."

Sources: *British Minstrelsie.* T.C. and E.C. Jack, Grange Publishing Works, Edinburgh (?1900). *Dictionary of National Biography.* Electronic Edition 1.1. Oxford University Press, 1997. *English Poetry: Author Search.* Chadwyck-Healey Ltd., 1995 (http://www.lib.utexas.edu:8080/search/epoetry/author.html). *English Poetry: A Poetic Record, from Chaucer to Yeats.* David Hopkins, ed. Routledge, 1990. *The Columbia Granger's Index to Poetry.* 11th ed. *The Columbia Granger's World of Poetry,* Columbia University Press, 2005 (http://www.columbiagrangers. org). *The Oxford Companion to English Literature.* 6th edition. Margaret Drabble, ed. Oxford University Press, 2000. *The Poetical Works of Edward Moore and David Mallet.* Thomas Park, ed. J. Sharpe, 1808.

MANGAN, JAMES CLARENCE (1803–1849)

Born in Dublin, the son of a grocer, at school he learned Latin, Spanish, French, and Italian. His work and personal life suffered from the effects of opium and alcoholism and finally reduced him to poverty and malnutrition. In 1834 he began submitting translations from German to the *Dublin University Magazine*. He wrote for various magazines associated with Irish political movements — the *Belfast Vindicator,* the *Nation* (the journal of the Young Ireland movement), and *United Irishman*. Some of his translations, which he claimed were of Irish or Eastern languages (which he did not know), were either much or all of his own work. When he died of cholera in Meath Hospital, Dublin, only two persons attended his funeral. Thirty of his ballads were issued in Hercules Ellis's *Romances and Ballads of Ireland* (1850). Some of his publications: *German Anthology,* 1845. *The Poets and Poetry of Munster,* 1849. *Irish and Other Poems,* 1886. Some of his poems: "Gone in the Wind," "Hymn for Pentecost," "Rest Only in the Grave," "St. Patrick's Hymn Before Tara," "The Fair Hills of Eiré," "The Irish Language," "The Karamanian Exile."

Sources: *1000 Years of Irish Poetry: The Gaelic and Anglo-Irish Poets from Pagan Times to the Present.* Kathleen Hoagland, ed. Devin-Adair, 1975. *Dictionary of National Biography.* Electronic Edition 1.1. Oxford University Press, 1997. *English Poetry: Author Search.* Chadwyck-Healey Ltd., 1995 (http://www.lib.utexas.edu:8080/search/epoetry/author.html). *English Romantic Poetry and Prose.* Russell Noyes, ed. Oxford University Press, 1956. *Lyra Celtica: An Anthology of Representative Celtic Poetry.* E.A. Sharp and J. Matthay, eds. John Grant, 1924. *The Columbia Granger's Index to Poetry.* 11th ed. *The Columbia Granger's World of Poetry,* Columbia University Press, 2005 (http://www.columbiagrangers.org). *The Golden Book of Catholic Poetry.* Alfred Noyes, ed. J.B. Lippincott, 1946. *The Oxford Book of Victorian Verse.* Arthur Quiller-Couch, ed. Oxford University Press, 1971. *The Oxford Companion to English Literature.* 6th edition. Margaret Drabble, ed. Oxford University Press, 2000.

MANNYNG, ROBERT (ROBERT DE BRUNNE) (?1288–?1338)

He came from Bourne in Lincolnshire and, in 1288, became a lay brother in the house of the Gilbertine canons at Sempringham, six miles from his birth place. He was at Cambridge University around 1300. One of his two main poems is *Handling Sin* (?1307), an adaptation in about 13,000 lines of the Manuel des Péchés (*Handbook of Sins*), which consists chiefly of a series of stories illustrating the commandments, the seven deadly sins, the sin of sacrilege and the Sacraments, the 12 requisites of confession, and the 12 graces of confession. It is a useful document of social history. The other is *Chronicle of England* (1338). The work falls into two parts. The first tells the story from the biblical Noah to the death of the British king Caedwalla in 689. In the second part, he takes the story to the death of Edward I (1307). He works into his narrative several topical songs, mainly on the Scottish wars of Edward's time. Some of his poems: "Meditations of the Supper of the Lord Jesus," "Praise of Women," "The Bishop's Harp," "The Round Table."

Sources: *An Anthology of Catholic Poets.* Shane Leslie, ed. Macmillan, 1952. *Catholic Encyclopedia* (http://www.newadvent.org/cathen). *Dictionary of National Biography.* Electronic Edition 1.1. Oxford University Press, 1997. *Encyclopædia Britannica Ultimate Reference Suite DVD,* 2006. *English Poetry: Author Search.* Chadwyck-Healey Ltd., 1995 (http://www.lib.utexas.edu:8080/search/epoetry/author.html). *Poetry in English: An Anthology.* M.L. Rosenthal, ed. Oxford University Press, 1987. *The Columbia Granger's Index to Poetry.* 11th ed. *The Columbia Granger's World of Poetry,* Columbia University Press, 2005 (http://www.columbiagrangers.org). *The Oxford Book of English Verse, 1250–1918.* Sir Arthur Quiller-Couch, ed., new edition, revised and enlarged, Oxford University Press, 1939. *The Oxford Companion to English Literature.* 6th edition. Margaret Drabble, ed. Oxford University Press, 2000.

MAPANGE, JACK (CURRENT)

Born in Kadango Village in southern Malawi, he was educated at a mission school, then at Zomba Catholic Secondary School. He has a B.A. degree and a diploma in education from the University of London. In 1975 he joined the staff of the Department of English at Chancellor College, University of Malawi, as a lecturer, then worked as a research student in linguistics at University College, London, in the early 1980s. Soon after his collection *Of Chameleons and Gods* (published in the U.K. in 1981) received the Rotterdam International Poetry Award in 1988, it was banned in Malawi. He was imprisoned without trial or charge by the Malawian government from 1987 to 1991. He lives in York and is currently teaching creative writing and literature of incarceration in the School of English, University of Newcastle-upon-Tyne. In 2002 he won the African Literature Association Fonlon-Nichols Award (USA). He has broadcast for the British Broadcasting Corporation (BBC) and acted as judge in BBC and commonwealth poetry competitions. Some of his other publications: *The Chattering Wagtails of Mikuyu Prison,* 1993. *Skipping Without Ropes,* 1998. *The Last of the Sweet Bananas: New and Selected Poems,* 2004.

Sources: *An African Thunderstorm and Other Poems.* Jack Mapange, ed. East African Publishing House (Nairobi), 2004. *British Council Arts* (http://www.contemporarywriters.com). *Gathering Seaweed: African Prison Writing.* Jack Mapange, ed. Heinemann International

(African Writers Series), 2002. *National Poetry Day, 2002. Jack Mapange* (http://www.bbc.co.uk/radio4/arts/natpo etday/jack_mapange.shtml). *Oral Poetry from Africa.* Jack Mapange, ed. Landeg White, Longman, 1983. *Summer Fires: New Poetry of Africa,* Jack Mapange, Angus Calder and Cosmo Pieterse, eds. African Writers Series, Heinemann Educational, 1983. *The African Writers' Handbook.* Jack Mapange and James Gibbs, eds. African Books Collective, 1999. *The International Poetry Festival in Medellín, 2004, Jack Mapange* (http://colombia.poetryinternational. org/cwolk/view/22148).

MARKHAM, E.A. (EDWARD ARCHIBALD) (1939–)

Poet, novelist and short-story writer, he was born on the Caribbean island of Montserrat, and after living in different parts of Europe he settled in Britain in 1956. He read English and philosophy at St. David's University College, Lampeter, Wales, and did further study at the University of East Anglia. From 1968 to 1970 he lectured at Kilburn Polytechnic in London, directed the Caribbean Theatre Workshop in the Eastern Caribbean (1970–1971), and lectured at the Abraham Moss Centre in Manchester (1976–1978). From 1983 to 1985, he worked as a media coordinator for the Enga Provincial government in Papua New Guinea, then was editor of the magazine *Artrage* from 1985 to 1987. He is currently professor of creative writing at Sheffield Hallam University. The government of Montserrat awarded him the Certificate of Honor in 1997. His most recent poetry collections are: *Misapprehensions* (1995) and *A Rough Climate* (2002), shortlisted for the T.S. Eliot Prize. Some of his poems: "An Old Thought for a New Couple," "Don't Talk to Me about Bread," "Grandfather's Sermon and Michael Smith," "Grandmotherpoem," "The Mother's Tale," "The Sea," "Towards the End of a Century."

Sources: *Anthology of Twentieth-Century British and Irish Poetry.* Keith Tuma, ed. Oxford University Press, 2001. *British Council Arts* (http://www.contemporarywriters.com). *Caribbean Poetry Now.* Stewart Brown, ed. Edward Arnold, 1992. *The Columbia Granger's Index to Poetry.* 11th ed. *The Columbia Granger's World of Poetry,* Columbia University Press, 2005 (http://www.columbiagrangers. org). *The Heinemann Book of Caribbean Poetry.* Stewart Brown and Ian McDonald, eds. Heinemann, 1992. *The Oxford Companion to English Literature.* 6th edition. Margaret Drabble, ed. Oxford University Press, 2000. *The Penguin Book of Caribbean Verse in English.* Paula Burnett, ed. Penguin Books, 1986.

MARKHAM, GERVASE (1568–1637)

The son of Sir Robert Markham of Gotham, Nottinghamshire, he was a soldier under the earl of Essex in Ireland. He knew Latin as well as several modern languages, was an authority on forestry and is credited with being the first breeder to import Arab horses. In 1593 he published *A Discourse of Horsemanshippe.* He also published *The English Hus-wife, Containing the Inward and Outward Virtues Which Ought to Be in a Complete Woman* (1615). He was buried at St. Giles's, Cripplegate, London. He wrote two plays, *The Dumb Knight* (1608) with Lewis Machin and *The True Tragedy of Herod and Antipater* (1622) with William Sampson. His poem (1595) *The Most Honorable Tragedie of Sir Richard Grenville, Knight* (see Grenville entry) commemorates the vice-admiral's death in 1591 when the *Revenge* was captured by the Spanish. Some of his other poems: "A Fragment," "Areteæ Lachrimæ," "Mary Magdalene's Laments in Seven Parts," "Rodomonths Infernall," "The Conclusion," "The Lamentable Complaint of Paulina the Famous Roman Curtezan," "The Poem of Poems, or, Sions Muse," "The Teares of the Beloued."

Sources: *Confucius to Cummings: An Anthology of Poetry.* Ezra Pound and Marcella Spann, eds. New Directions, 1964. *Dictionary of National Biography.* Electronic Edition 1.1. Oxford University Press, 1997. *Encyclopædia Britannica Ultimate Reference Suite DVD,* 2006. *English Poetry: Author Search.* Chadwyck-Healey Ltd., 1995 (http://www. lib.utexas.edu:8080/search/epoetry/author.html). *The Columbia Granger's Index to Poetry.* 11th ed (http://www. columbiagrangers.org). *The Oxford Companion to English Literature.* 6th edition. Margaret Drabble, ed. Oxford University Press, 2000. *Wikipedia, the Free Encyclopedia* (http://en.wikipedia.org/wiki/Wikipedia).

MARLOWE, CHRISTOPHER (1564–1593)

The son of a shoemaker, of Canterbury, Kent, he graduated B.A. in 1583–84 and M.A. in 1587 from Corpus Christi College, Cambridge. He went to London in 1587, where he became an actor and dramatist for the Lord Admiral's Company. As a dramatist only Shakespeare was greater than Marlowe. His death, at the age of twenty-nine, is still surrounded by mystery and myth. Some say he was assassinated as a spy, others that he was killed in a drunken brawl. Some of his tragedies (which contain rhyme and blank verse) and poetry publications: *Tamburlaine,* ?1590. *The First Book of Lucan's Pharsalia,* 1593. *Dido, Queen of Carthage,* 1594. *Edward II,* 1594. *Hero and Leander,* 1598. *The Jew of Malta,* ?1633. *Faustus,* 1694. *The Massacre of Paris,* unknown date. *All Ovid's Elegies* unknown date. Some (most of the titles are in Latin) of his other elgeies/poems: "Ad Cypassim Ancillam Corinna," "De Iunonis Festo," "Hero and Leander," "In Mortem Psittaci," "In Winter Woe Befell Me," "Quod Pro Gigantomachia Amores Scribere Sit Coactus," "The Atheist's Tragedy," "The Passionate Sheepheard to His Loue."

Sources: *A Treasury of Great Poems: English and American.* Louis Untermeyer, ed. Simon and Schuster, 1955. *Dictionary of National Biography.* Electronic Edition 1.1. Oxford University Press, 1997. *Encyclopædia Britannica Ultimate Reference Suite DVD,* 2006. *English Poetry: Author Search.* Chadwyck-Healey Ltd., 1995 (http://www.lib.utexas.edu:8080/search/epoetry/author.html). *Life and Works of Christopher Marlowe* (http://www.luminarium.org/renlit/marlowe.htm). *Silver Poets of the Sixteenth Century.* Gerald Bullett, ed. J.M. Dent, 1947. *The Cherry-Tree.* Geoffrey Grigson, ed. Phoenix House, 1959. *The Columbia Granger's Index to Poetry.* 11th ed. *The Columbia Granger's World of Poetry,* Columbia University Press, 2005 (http://www.columbiagrangers.org). *The Complete Poems and Translations of Christopher Marlowe.* Stephen Orgel, ed. Penguin Books, 1971. *The Complete Works of C.S. Calverley.* G. Bell and Sons, 1926 (for translations of some of Marlowe's Latin poems). *The Faber Book of English History in Verse.* Kenneth Baker, ed. Faber and Faber, 1988. *The Oxford Book of Classical Verse in Translation.* Adrian Poole and Jeremy Maule, eds., 1995. *The Oxford Book of Death.* D.J. Enright, ed. Oxford University Press, 1987. *The Oxford Companion to English Literature.* 6th edition. Margaret Drabble, ed. Oxford University Press, 2000. *The Penguin Book of Renaissance Verse 1509–1659.* David Norbrook, ed. Penguin Books, 1992.

MARRIOTT, JOHN (1780–1825)

The son of the rector of Cotesbach Church, Leicestershire, he was educated at Rugby School and graduated B.A. from Christ Church, Oxford, in 1802. From 1804 he was tutor to George Henry, Lord Scott, elder brother of the fifth Duke of Buccleuch, at Dalkeith, Scotland, until his pupil died in 1808. He was ordained priest on 1805, was granted an M.A. in 1806 and was latterly in charge of several churches in Devon. He died in London and was buried in Old St. Pancras Church. Sir Walter Scott addressed to him the second canto of "Marmion: A Tale of Flodden Field." Marriott contributed to Scott's *Minstrelsy of the Scottish Border* (1802) three poems: "The Feast of the Spurs," "On a Visit Paid to the Ruins of Melrose Abbey," and "Archie Armstrong's Aith [oath]." His "Marriage is Like a Devonshire Lane" was included in Joanna Baillie's *Collection of Poems* (1823) (see entry). Some of his hymns and poems: "A Devonshire Sketch," "A Saint! O Would That I Could Claim," "Grant to This Child the Inward Grace," "Let There Be Light," "Thou, Whose Almighty Word," "When Christ Our Human Form Did Bear."

Sources: *Dictionary of National Biography.* Electronic Edition 1.1. Oxford University Press, 1997. *Minstrelsy of the Scottish Border, Sir Walter Scott* (http://www.walterscott.lib.ed.ac.uk/works/poetry/minstrelsy.html). *Sir Walter Scott's Poem, Marmion.* (http://www.cs.rice.edu/~ssiyer/minstrels/poems/495.html). *St. Pancras Old Church, History of* (http://en.wikipedia.org/wiki/St_Pancras_Old_Church). *The Cyber Hymnal* (http://www.cyberhymnal.org/index.htm).

MARSTON, JOHN (1574–1634)

He was born possibly at Coventry, Warwickshire, and graduated from Brasenose College, Oxford, in 1594. He took orders around 1609 and was vicar of Christ Church, Hampshire, from which he resigned (possibly from ill health) in 1631. He died in Aldermanbury parish, London, and was buried in the Temple Church beside his father. Many of his poems relate to his plays; for example, "To Everlasting Oblivion" is taken from his play *The Scourge of Villainy* (1598) (burned by archiepiscopal order in 1599). Some of his other plays: *The Metamorphosis of Pigmalion's Image, and Certain Satyres,* 1598. *The Malcontent,* 1604. *Eastward Ho,* 1605 (for which he spent some time in prison for satirizing King James I). *Marston,* 1610. Written for the Children of Paul's Theatre Company: *The History of Antonio and Mellida,* 1602 (with its sequel *Antonio's Revenge* also in 1602). *What You Will,* 1607. Some of his poems: "Here's a toy to mock an Ape indeed," "Perfectioni Hymnus," "The Wonder of Women," "To euerlasting Obliuion," "To his Mistress," "Proemium in librum tertium," "A Cynicke Satyre," "To Detraction I Present My Poesie."

Sources: *Dictionary of National Biography.* Electronic Edition 1.1. Oxford University Press, 1997. *English Poetry: Author Search.* Chadwyck-Healey Ltd., 1995 (http://www.lib.utexas.edu:8080/search/epoetry/author.html). *Microsoft Encarta 2006* (DVD). Microsoft Corporation, 2006. *Poets of the English Language. Vol. I.* W.H. Auden and Norman Holmes Pearson, eds. Viking Press, 1950. *The Columbia Granger's Index to Poetry.* 11th ed. *The Columbia Granger's World of Poetry,* Columbia University Press, 2005 (http://www.columbiagrangers.org). *The New Oxford Book of Sixteenth Century Verse.* Emrys Jones, ed. Oxford University Press, 1991. *The Oxford Anthology of English Literature Vol. I.* Frank Kermode and John Hollander, eds. Oxford University Press. 1973. *The Oxford Companion to English Literature.* 6th edition. Margaret Drabble, ed. Oxford University Press, 2000. *The Penguin Book of Renaissance Verse 1509–1659.* David Norbrook, ed. Penguin Books, 1992. *The Poems of John Marston.* Arnold Davenport, ed. Liverpool University Press, 1961.

MARSTON, JOHN WESTLAND and PHILIP BOURKE (1819–1890)

John, the father, 1819–1890

Born at Boston, Lincolnshire, the son of a Baptist minister, his interest in literature took him away from his career in law. Interested in mysticism, he became editor of *The Psyche* magazine. He received the degree of doctor of laws from Glasgow University in 1863. In 1887 the actor Sir Henry Irving organized a benefit performance of Lord Byron's tragedy *Werner* (1822) for Marston at the Lyceum Theatre, London. He was buried with his wife and children in Highgate cemetery, London. His first play, the *Patrician's Daughter* (performed in 1842, with a prologue by Charles Dickens), is the idealization of his wife, whom he married in 1840. He contributed nearly 400 items to the *Athenaeum* magazine. Some of his other publications: *Gerald, a Dramatic Poem, and Other Poems,* 1842. *Strathmore,* 1849. *Philip of France,* 1850. *Anne Blake,* 1852. *A Life's Ransom,* 1857. *A Hard Struggle,* 1858. Some of his poems: "A Child in Heaven," "England, Written at the Time of the Revolt in India," "For a Silver Wedding," "Scenes in Normandy," "The Death-Ride, A Tale of the Light Brigade."

Philip, the son, 1850–1887

His godparents were Philip James Bailey and Dinah Maria Mulock Craik (see entries), and to him his godmother addressed her poem "Philip, My King." His later poetry is marked by deep sadness brought about by multiple bereavements, yet he retained the ability to paint word pictures that transport the reader into the world of trees waving in the wind, the setting sun, and the warmth of the fire in the hearth. His numerous short stories were collected by William Sharp in *For a Song's Sake and Other Stories* (1887). Louise Chandler Moulton, the American poet, published two collections of Philip's poems: *Garden Secrets* (1887) and *A Last Harvest* (1891). Philip suffered from poor eyesight and by 1878 he was almost totally blind. Father and son had a close relationship and it was while they were on holiday that Philip suffered from some sort of stroke and died. Some of his other publications: *Song-Tide and Other Poems,* 1871. *All in All,* 1875. *Wind Voices,* 1883. Some of his poems: "After," "A July Day," "After Summer," "At the Last," "If You Were Here," "Parted Lovers," "Wedded Memories."

Sources: *Athenaeum Index: Contributor Record* (http://web.soi.city.ac.uk/~asp/v2/contributors/contributorfiles/MARSTON, JohnWestland.html). *Dictionary of National Biography.* Electronic Edition 1.1. Oxford University Press, 1997. *English Poetry: Author Search.* Chadwyck-Healey Ltd., 1995 (http://www.lib.utexas.edu:8080/search/epoetry/author.html). *Stanford University Libraries and Academic Information Resources* (http://library.stanford.edu). *The Best Loved Poems of the American People.* Hazel Felleman, ed. Doubleday, 1936. *The Collected Poems of Philip Bourke Marston.* Mrs. Louise Chandler Moulton. Ward, Lock, Bowden and Co. 1892. *The Columbia Granger's Index to Poetry.* 11th ed. *The Columbia Granger's World of Poetry,* Columbia University Press, 2005 (http://www.columbiagrangers.org). *The Dramatic and Poetical Works of Westland Marston.* Chatto and Windus, 1876. *The Home Book of Verse.* Burton Egbert Stevenson, ed. New York: Henry Holt and Company, 1953. *The New Oxford Book of Victorian Verse.* Christopher Ricks, ed. Oxford University Press, 1987. *The Oxford Companion to English Literature.* 6th edition. Margaret Drabble, ed. Oxford University Press, 2000. *Through the Year with the Poets.* Oscar Fay Adams, ed. D. Lothrop and Company, 1886.

MARTIN, SIR THEODORE (1816–1909)

Born in Edinburgh and educated at Edinburgh University (1830–1833) he practiced law in Edinburgh and from 1846 in London, where he became head of the highly successful firm of Martin and Leslie, parliamentary agents. Edinburgh University awarded him and honorary doctor of laws in 1875. Queen Victoria made him Commander of the Bath (1878), Knight Commander of the Bath (1880), and Knight Commander Royal Victorian Order (1896). He died at Bryntysilio, near Llangollen, North Wales and was buried in Brompton cemetery, West London. He collaborated with W.E. Aytoun (see entry) in the writing of the humorous *Bon Gaultier Ballads* (1852). Martin translated many works from German, Latin, Danish and Italian and wrote a life of Prince Albert (5 volumes, 1875–1880) and *Queen Victoria as I knew her* (1902). Some of his other publications: *Madonna Pia,* 1894. *Poems,* 1863. *Introductory Poem to Queen Victoria,* 1908. Some of his poems: "Faust [Selections]," "I met a cracksman coming down the Strand," "The Dying Girl's Song," "The Monk's Dream," "The Thieves' Anthology," "To Miss Helen Faucit, As Rosalind," "Toll no sullen bell for me."

Sources: *Dictionary of National Biography.* Electronic Edition 1.1. Oxford University Press, 1997. *English Poetry: Author Search.* Chadwyck-Healey Ltd., 1995 (http://www.lib.utexas.edu:8080/search/epoetry/author.html). *The National Portrait Gallery* (www.npg.org.uk). *The Columbia Granger's Index to Poetry.* 11th ed. *The Columbia Granger's World of Poetry,* Columbia University Press, 2005 (http://www.columbiagrangers.org). *The Faber Book of Parodies.* Simon Brett, ed. Faber and Faber, 1984. *The Oxford Companion to English Literature.* 6th edition. Margaret Drabble, ed. Oxford University Press, 2000. *The Poems of Goethe.* Edgar Alfred Bowring, ed. George Bell and Sons, 1874. Stanford University Libraries and Academic Information Resources (http://library.stanford.edu). *Wikipedia, the Free Encyclopedia* (http://en.wikipedia.org/wiki/Wikipedia).

MARVELL, ANDREW (1621–1678)

He was born at Winestead in Holderness, Yorkshire, was educated under his father at the grammar school in Hull, graduated from Trinity College, Cambridge, in 1637, and left sometime before September 1641. He traveled in Europe, learning languages, then spent several years as tutor, first to Mary, the daughter of Thomas Fairfax, 3rd Baron (commander in chief of the Parliamentary army during the English Civil Wars), at Nun Appleton in Yorkshire, and to one of Oliver Cromwell's wards. In 1657 he was appointed Latin secretary to the Council of State, replacing his now totally blind friend John Milton (see entry). Marvell wrote a whole series of

Cromwellian poems around the period of the Commonwealth (1653–1658). In 1659 he was elected member of Parliament for Hull, an office he held until his death of a fever. He was buried in the church of St. Giles-in-the-Fields, London. Some of his poems: "Bermudas," "Blood and the Crown," "Clorinda and Damon," "On Mr. Milton's "Paradise Lost," "The Fair Singer," "The Gallery," "The Last Instructions to a Painter," "Upon Appleton House [To My Lord Fairfax]," "Young Love."

Sources: *Anthology of Poems on Affairs of State: Augustan Satirical Verse, 1660–1714.* George de F. Lord, ed. Yale University Press, 1975. *Dictionary of National Biography.* Electronic Edition 1.1. Oxford University Press, 1997. *Encyclopædia Britannica Ultimate Reference Suite DVD,* 2006. *English Poetry: Author Search.* Chadwyck-Healey Ltd., 1995 (http://www.lib.utexas.edu:8080/search/epoetry/author.html). *Jacobean and Caroline Poetry: An Anthology.* T.G.S. Cain, ed. *Methuen,* 1981. *The Columbia Granger's Index to Poetry.* 11th ed. *The Columbia Granger's World of Poetry,* Columbia University Press, 2005 (http://www.columbia grangers.org). *The Complete Poems of Andrew Marvell.* Elizabeth Story Donno, ed. Penguin Books, 1972, reprinted 1985. *The Oxford Book of English Verse, 1250–1918.* Sir Arthur Quiller-Couch, ed., new edition, revised and enlarged, Oxford University Press, 1939. *The Oxford Book of Satirical Verse.* Geoffrey Grigson, ed. Oxford University Press, 1980. *The Oxford Companion to English Literature.* 6th edition. Margaret Drabble, ed. Oxford University Press, 2000. *The Works of Andrew Marvell* (http://www.lu minarium.org/sevenlit/marvell/marvbib.htm).

MASEFIELD, JOHN EDWARD (1878–1967)

Born at The Knapp, Ledbury, Herefordshire, he was orphaned at a very early age and was brought up by relatives in Warwickshire. He was educated from 1891 to 1894 on board the HMS *Conway* on the River Mersey — the training ship for officers for the Merchant Navy. For several years he worked in a carpet mill in Yonkers, New York, and traveled around in America doing menial jobs. In 1907 he began to work on the *Manchester Guardian* newspaper. His first major poem, "The Everlasting Mercy" (1911), with its mixture of beauty and ugliness, and in places, language of the tap-room, shocked the literary world. He also wrote naval histories, novels, children's books and plays, and edited selections of the works of various poets and dramatists. He was appointed poet laureate in 1930 and received the Order of Merit in 1935, as well as honorary degrees from Oxford, Liverpool, and St. Andrews universities. He died at his home near Abingdon and his ashes are buried in Poets' Corner, Westminster Abbey. Some of his other poems: "August, 1914," "Dauber," "Reynard the Fox," "Sea Fever," "The Blacksmith," "The Daffodil Fields," "The Song of Roland."

Sources: *Ballads, 1903, Revised and Enlarged, 1910.* Cyder Press, 2004. *Dictionary of National Biography.* Electronic Edition 1.1. Oxford University Press, 1997. *Encyclopædia Britannica Ultimate Reference Suite DVD,* 2006. *Moods of the Sea: Masterworks of Sea Poetry.* George C. Solley and Eric Steinbaugh, eds. Naval Institute Press, 1981. *Introduction to HMS Conway: Cadets and Old Boys, Events and Daily Life, Closure.* (http://www.mersey-gateway.org/server.php?show=ConNarrative.73). *Salt Water Ballads,* John Masefield, 1902. Cyder Press, 2002. *The Collected Poems of John Masefield.* William Heinemann Ltd., 1923. *The Columbia Granger's Index to Poetry.* 11th ed. *The Columbia Granger's World of Poetry,* Columbia University Press, 2005 (http://www.columbiagrangers.org). *The Oxford Companion to English Literature.* 6th edition. Margaret Drabble, ed. Oxford University Press, 2000. *Westminster Abbey Official Guide* (no date).

MASON, JOHN (?1646–1694)

Born probably in Irchester, Northamptonshire, he graduated M.A. from Clare Hall, Cambridge, in 1668, and like his father was a clergyman in Northamptonshire. Increasingly drawn to interpreting apocalyptic passages of the Bible in the light of events of the time, he preached the personal reign of Christ on earth, which he announced was about to begin in his parish of Water Stratford. A crowd of followers camped out in a part of the village they called "Holy Ground." He died of a throat infection and was buried in the church of Water Stratford. Mason was one of the earliest writers of hymns used in congregational worship. His one poetry publication was *Spiritual Songs, or Songs of Praise* (1683, with the 16th edition in 1859). Some of his hymns/poems: "A Living Stream, as Crystal Clear," "A Song of Praise for Family-Prosperity," "A Song of Praise for Health," "A Song of Praise for the Morning," "Blest Be My God That I Was Born," "Blest Day of God, Most Calm, Most Bright," "Dives and Lazarus," "How Shall I Sing that Majesty," "I've Found the Pearl of Greatest Price."

Sources: *Dictionary of National Biography.* Electronic Edition 1.1. Oxford University Press, 1997. *English Poetry: Author Search.* Chadwyck-Healey Ltd., 1995 (http://www.lib.utexas.edu:8080/search/epoetry/author.html). Stanford University Libraries and Academic Information Resources (http://library.stanford.edu). *The Cyber Hymnal* (http://www.cyberhymnal.org/index.htm).

MASON, WILLIAM (1725–1797)

A clergyman poet, he was born at Kingston-upon-Hull, Humberside, and graduated M.A. from St. John's College, Cambridge, in 1749. Mason and Thomas Gray (see entry) became friends at Cambridge, and Mason published the *Life of Gray* in 1774, and his epitaph to Gray appears on their joint monument in Poets' Corner of Westminster Abbey. In 1749 Mason wrote an ode to Thomas Holles

Pelham, Duke of Newcastle, on his installation as chancellor of Cambridge University. From 1757 to 1773 he was one of the chaplains to George II, and then to George III. He died after what was a minor accident and was buried at Aston, Yorkshire. He also wrote poems under the pseudonym of Malcolm MacGregor. Some of his other publications: *An Heroic Epistle to Sir William Chambers,* 1774. *An Heroic Postscript to the Public,* 1774. *Ode to Mr. Pinchbeck,* 1776. *The Dean and the Squire,* 1782. *King Stephen's Watch,* 1782. Some of his other poems: "Anniversary," "Epistle to Sir Joshua Reynolds," "Ode to a Friend," "Ode to Memory," "Psalm 137," "Psalm 150," "The English Garden," "To a Gravel Walk."

Sources: *Dictionary of National Biography.* Electronic Edition 1.1. Oxford University Press, 1997. *English Poetry: Author Search.* Chadwyck-Healey Ltd., 1995 (http://www.lib.utexas.edu:8080/search/epoetry/author.html). *English Poetry: A Poetic Record, from Chaucer to Yeats.* David Hopkins, ed. Routledge, 1990. *Anniversary, poem by William Mason* (http://www.sonnets.org/mason.htm). Stanford University Libraries and Academic Information Resources (http://library.stanford.edu). *The Columbia Granger's Index to Poetry.* 11th ed. *The Columbia Granger's World of Poetry,* Columbia University Press, 2005 (http://www.columbia-grangers.org). *The Oxford Book of Eighteenth Century Verse.* David Nichol Smith, ed. Oxford University Press, 1926. *The Oxford Book of Garden Verse.* John Dixon Hunt, ed. Oxford University Press, 1993. *The Oxford Companion to English Literature.* 6th edition. Margaret Drabble, ed. Oxford University Press, 2000. *Westminster Abbey Official Guide* (no date).

MASSEY, GERALD (1828–1907)

A poet of the people, he was born into poverty, started work when he was eight, and learned to read at a "penny school." At 15 he worked as an errand boy in London and devoted his leisure to learning. His cheap journal *The Spirit of Freedom* started when he was 21 and, written by workingmen, aroused opposition, but he persisted. He used his pen to further the aims of the Chartists and wrote over 800 reviews for *Athenaeum* magazine. Between 1873 and 1888 he lectured on poetry in America, Australia and New Zealand. He died in London and was buried in Old Southgate cemetery, North London. His hymn "Surrounded by Unnumbered Foes" was set to music by William Shore. Some of his poetry publications: *Poems and Chansons,* 1848. *Voices of Freedom and Lyrics of Love,* 1850. *Robert Burns, a Song, and Other Lyrics,* 1859. *Havelock's March,* 1860. *A Tale of Eternity and Other Poems,* 1869. Some of his poems: "All's Right with the World," "Babe Christabel," "England," "His Banner over Me," "Robin Burns," "The Awakening of the People," "The Worker."

Sources: *Athenaeum Index: Contributor Record* (http://

web.soi.city.ac.uk/~asp/v2/contributors/contributorfiles/MASSEY,Gerald.html). *Dictionary of National Biography.* Electronic Edition 1.1. Oxford University Press, 1997. *English Poetry: Author Search.* Chadwyck-Healey Ltd., 1995 (http://www.lib.utexas.edu:8080/search/epoetry/author.html). *Everyman's Book of Victorian Verse.* J.R. Watson, ed. *J.M. Dent,* 1982. *The Columbia Granger's Index to Poetry.* 11th ed. *The Columbia Granger's World of Poetry,* Columbia University Press, 2005 (http://www.columbiagrangers.org). *The Cyber Hymnal* (http://www.cyberhymnal.org/index.htm). *The National Portrait Gallery* (www.npg.org.uk). *The Poorhouse Fugitives Self-Taught Poets and Poetry in Victorian Britain.* Brian Maidment, ed. Carcanet, 1987. *The World's Great Religious Poetry.* Caroline Miles Hill, ed. Macmillan, 1954. *Treasury of Favorite Poems.* Joseph H. Head, ed. Gramercy Books, 2000.

MASSINGER, PHILIP (1583–1640)

He was born near Salisbury, Wiltshire, the son of Arthur Massinger, the agent of Henry Herbert, second earl of Pembroke of Wilton House. Philip may have been a page in the Wilton household and the earl supported his attendance at St. Alban Hall, Oxford. However, on his conversion to Roman Catholicism he lost favor with his patron and left university in 1606 without graduating. In London he became a renowned playwright, writing plays for the theatrical manager Philip Henslowe. He collaborated with playwrights John Fletcher (see entry), Nathan Field, Thomas Dekker (see entry) to produce some 55 plays. In 1625 he succeeded Fletcher as the chief playwright of the King's Men and remained with the company until his death. He died suddenly in his house on the Bankside, Southwark, near the Globe Theatre, East London. His body was accompanied by a group of comedians to nearby St. Saviour's Church. Some of his poems: "Death Invoked," "Music Above, A Song of Pleasure," "Song by Pallas," "The Emperor of the East," "The Forest's Queen," "The Maid of Honour," "The Renegade," "The Virgins Character."

Sources: *An Anthology of Catholic Poets.* Shane Leslie, ed. Macmillan, 1952. *Dictionary of National Biography.* Electronic Edition 1.1. Oxford University Press, 1997. *Encyclopædia Britannica Ultimate Reference Suite DVD,* 2006. *Poetry Archive, Poems by Philip Massinger* (www.poetry-archive.com). *Songs from the British Drama.* Edward Bliss Reed, ed. Yale University Press, 1925. *The Columbia Granger's Index to Poetry.* 11th ed. *The Columbia Granger's World of Poetry,* Columbia University Press, 2005 (http://www.columbiagrangers.org). *The Golden Book of Catholic Poetry.* Alfred Noyes, ed. J.B. Lippincott, 1946. *The National Portrait Gallery* (www.npg.org.uk). *The Oxford Companion to English Literature.* 6th edition. Margaret Drabble, ed. Oxford University Press, 2000. *The Plays and Poems of Philip Massinger* (five volumes). Philip Edwards and Colin Gibson, eds. Clarendon Press, 1976. *The Poems of Philip Massinger, with Critical Notes.* Ball State University, Indiana, 1968.

MATHESON, GEORGE (1842–1906)

The eldest son of George Matheson, a prosperous Glasgow merchant, he was born with poor sight, and by the age of 17 he was totally blind. Notwithstanding, he learned Latin, Greek and several modern languages, graduated M.A. from Glasgow University in 1862, and became a Church of Scotland minister in 1867. It is said that he so memorized his sermons and entire sections of the Bible that strangers were not aware that he was blind. In 1874 he published *Aids to the Study of German Theology*, and he wrote many theological and devotional books and sacred poetry. Queen Victoria directed that the sermon Matheson preached at Balmoral in October 1885 be printed for private circulation. His *Sacred Songs* was published in 1890 and in the third edition (1904) he included "O Love that wilt not let me go," a hymn that is still in most hymn books. Edinburgh University made him doctor of divinity (1879) and Aberdeen University awarded him doctor of laws (1902). He was buried in the family vault in Glasgow, Necropolis. Two of his other hymns/poems: "Christian Freedom," "Make Me a Captive, Lord."

Sources: *A Sacrifice of Praise: An Anthology of Christian Poetry in English from Caedmon to the Mid–Twentieth Century.* James H. Trott, ed. Cumberland House Publishing, 1999. *A Treasury of Poems for Worship and Devotion.* Charles L. Wallis, ed. Harper, 1959. *Dictionary of National Biography.* Electronic Edition 1.1. Oxford University Press, 1997. *George Matheson, History of "O love that will not let me go."* (http://igracemusic.com/igracemusic/hymnbook/authors/george_matheson.html). *The Columbia Granger's Index to Poetry.* 11th ed. *The Columbia Granger's World of Poetry,* Columbia University Press, 2005 (http://www.columbiagrangers.org). *The Cyber Hymnal* (http://www.cyberhymnal.org/index.htm). *The Speaker's Treasury of 400 Quotable Poems.* Croft M. Pentz, ed. Zondervan, 1963.

MATHIAS, ROLAND (1915–)

Welsh poet, born at Talybont-on-Usk, Breconshire, the son of an army chaplain. He gained a first class honors in history from Jesus College, Oxford. His teaching career started in 1948 at Cowley Boys' Grammar School in Lancaster and ended in 1969 at King Edward VI Five Ways School in Birmingham, where he had been headmaster since 1964. On retiring to Brecon, he devoted his life to writing about Welsh culture and heritage. He contributed to *The Oxford Companion to the Literature of Wales* (1986). In 1985 Georgetown University in Washington, D.C., awarded him an honorary doctoral degree. The Roland Mathias Prize, a new literary prize for Welsh writing in English, was awarded for the first time in Brecon on 23 March 2005. Some of his poetry publications: *Days Enduring*, 1942. *Break in Harvest*, 1946. *The Roses of Tretower*, 1952. *Absalom in the Tree*, 1971. *Snipe's Castle*, 1979. *Burning Bram-*bles: Selected Poems 1944–1979, 1983. *A Field at Vallorcines*, 1996. Some of his poems: "Brechfa Chapel," "Cae Iago: May Day," "Craswall," "Departure in Middle Age," "Grasshoppers," "Sanderlings," "Tide-Reach."

Sources: *Anglo-Welsh Poetry, 1480–1980.* Raymond Garlick and Roland Mathias, ed. Poetry Wales Press, 1984. *Anglo-Welsh Poetry, 1480–1990.* Raymond Garlick and Roland Mathias, ed. Poetry Wales Press, 1993. *Biography of Ronald Mathias* (http://www.transcript-review.org/section.cfm?id=198&lan=en). *The Collected Poems of Roland Mathias.* University of Wales Press, 2002 (http://www.uwp.co.uk/book_desc/1760.html). *The Columbia Granger's Index to Poetry.* 11th ed (http://www.columbiagrangers.org). *The Oxford Book of Welsh Verse in English.* Gwyn Jones, ed. Oxford University Press, 1977. *The Roland Mathias Prize* (http://www.bbc.co.uk/wales/mid/sites/brecon_life/pages/roland_mathias_prize.shtml). *Twentieth Century Anglo-Welsh Poetry.* Dannie Abse, ed. Seren Books / Dufour Editions, 1997.

MAUDE, THOMAS (1718–1798)

He was born in Downing Street, Westminster, London, though from an ancient Yorkshire family. In 1755, he was appointed surgeon on board the *Barfleur*, commanded by Lord Harry Powlett. The admiral was court-martialed for breaking from the fleet and returning to port, on the advice of his carpenter who reported a loose stern-post, which proved to be exaggerated. Maude spoke on his defense and was later rewarded when Pawlett succeeded as sixth and last Duke of Bolton. From 1765 until the duke died in 1794, Maude was steward of the duke's Yorkshire estates. He retired to Burley Hall, near Otley, West Yorkshire, where he died and was buried in Wensley churchyard, North Yorkshire. Although a minor poet, his poems are highly descriptive of the Yorkshire dales. Francis Grose (see entry), in his description of Aysgarth Bridge, North Yorkshire, quotes from Maude's poem *Verbia*. His only recorded poetry publications: *Wensleydale, or Rural Contemplations*, 1772. *Verbeia, or Wharfedale*, 1782. *Viator, a Journey from London to Scarborough by way of York, a Poem, with notes historical and topographical*, 1782. *The Invitation, or Urbanity*, 1791.

Sources: *Dictionary of National Biography.* Electronic Edition 1.1. Oxford University Press, 1997. *Gentleman's Magazine* (http://www.bodley.ox.ac.uk/ilej/journals/srchgm.htm).

MAXWELL, GLYN (1962–)

Born in Welwyn Garden City, England, he read English at Worcester College, Oxford University (1982–1985), and poetry and drama at Boston University. He moved to the USA in 1996 (where he now lives) and taught at Amherst College, Massachusetts, Columbia University and the New School in New York City. In 1997 he was awarded the E.M.

Forster Award by the American Academy of Arts and Letters. In 2001 he was appointed poetry editor at the *New Republic*, Washington D.C., and is a fellow of the Royal Society of Literature. He has written a number of plays and libretti, and his radio play *Childminders* was broadcast on BBC Radio 3 in 2002. His verse drama one-person show, *Best Man's Speech*, was premiered in New York in 2005. His poetry publications: *Tale of the Mayor's Son*, 1990. *Rest for the Wicked*, 1995. *The World They Mean: A New Poem*, 1996. *The Breakage*, 1998. *The Boys at Twilight*, 2000. *Time's Fool*, 2000. *The Nerve*, 2002 (won the Geoffrey Faber Memorial Prize). *The Sugar Mile*, 2005. Some of his poems: "Mild Citizen," "Poisonfield," "Rumplestiltskin," "Stargazing."

Sources: *Biography of Glyn Maxwell* (http://www.glyn maxwell.com/index2.html). *British Council Arts* (http://www.contemporarywriters.com). *The Columbia Granger's Index to Poetry.* 11th ed. *The Columbia Granger's World of Poetry,* Columbia University Press, 2005 (http://www.co lumbiagrangers.org). *The Harvill Book of Twentieth-Century Poetry in English.* Michael Schmidt, ed. The Harvill Press, 1999. *The Oxford Book of Comic Verse.* John Gross, ed. Oxford University Press, 1994. *The Oxford Companion to English Literature.* 6th edition. Margaret Drabble, ed. Oxford University Press, 2000.

MAY, THOMAS (1595–1650)

The eldest son of Sir Thomas May of Mayfield, Sussex, he graduated from Sidney Sussex College, Cambridge, in 1612. May's writings include plays, poems, translations, and prose works. He produced his first play, *The Heir,* in 1620, with verses attached by Thomas Carew (see entry). His translations were Lucan's *Pharsalia* (1627), Virgil's *Georgics* (1628), Martial's *Epigrams* (1629), and a continuation of Lucan (1630) dedicated to Charles I. By the king's command, May wrote two narrative poems on the reign of Henry II (1633) and Edward III (1635). On the death of Ben Jonson (1637), despite being recommended by King Charles, the post of poet laureate went to Sir William D'Avenant (see entry). In his *Breviary of the History of the Parliament of England* (1650), May defended the Parliamentarians. His death was a mystery; the supposition was that he tied his nightcap too tightly and strangled himself. He is commemorated by a tablet in Poet's Corner of Westminster Abbey. Some of his other poems: "Dear, do not your fair beauty wrong," "Not he that knows how to acquire," "To My Deserving Friend Mr. James Shirley."

Sources: *Dictionary of National Biography.* Electronic Edition 1.1. Oxford University Press, 1997. *Encyclopædia Britannica Ultimate Reference Suite DVD,* 2006. *Songs from the British Drama.* Edward Bliss Reed, ed. Yale University Press, 1925. *The Dramatic Works and Poems of James Shirley Volume I.* Alexander Dyce and William Gifford, eds. Rus-

sell and Russell, 1966. *The National Portrait Gallery* (www.npg.org.uk). *The Oxford Book of Classical Verse in Translation.* Adrian Poole and Jeremy Maule, eds., 1995. *The Oxford Companion to English Literature.* 6th edition. Margaret Drabble, ed. Oxford University Press, 2000. *Westminster Abbey Official Guide* (no date).

MAYNE, JOHN (1759–1836)

Scottish poet, born at Dumfries, he was partly educated in the local grammar school, though he was largely self-educated. He was a printer on the *Dumfries Journal,* then in Glasgow, then in 1787 he settled in London, first as a printer, and then as proprietor and joint editor of the *Star.* From 1807–1817, he contributed poems to the *Gentleman's Magazine,* as well as to his own newspaper (he wrote in the Scots dialect). He died in London and was buried in his family vault at Paddington churchyard. The poem *The Siller Gun* was first published in *Ruddiman's Magazine* in 1780, and in its final form in 1836 Sir Walter Scott praised it, likening it to the poems of Robert Burns. Some of his other publications: *English, Scots and Irishmen,* 1803. *Glasgow,* 1803. *The Modern Scottish Minstrel,* 1855. Some of his other poems: "Apostrophe to the River Nith," "Bonaparte, o'er the sea," "Hallowe'en," "Helen of Kirkconnel," "Logan Braes," "My Johnnie" (air, *Johnnie's Gray Breeks*), "The King's Welcome to Scotland, Thursday, August 15, 1822," "The Winter Sat Lang," "The Troops Were Embarked."

Sources: *Biography of John Mayne, Significant Scots* (http://www.electricscotland.com/history/other/mayne_john.htm). *Dictionary of National Biography.* Electronic Edition 1.1. Oxford University Press, 1997. *English Poetry: Author Search.* Chadwyck-Healey Ltd., 1995 (http://www.lib.utexas.edu:8080/search/epoetry/author.html). *Stanford University Libraries and Academic Information Resources* (http://library.stanford.edu). *The Burns Encyclopedia: John Mayne* (http://robertburns.org/encyclopedia/MayneJohn 17591511836.597.shtml). *The Columbia Granger's Index to Poetry.* 11th ed. *The Columbia Granger's World of Poetry,* Columbia University Press, 2005 (http://www.columbia grangers.org). *The Home Book of Verse.* Burton Egbert Stevenson, ed. New York: Henry Holt and Company, 1953. *The Oxford Book of Scottish Verse.* John MacQueen and Tom Scott, eds. Oxford University Press, 1966. *The Scottish Collection of Verse to 1800.* Eileen Dunlop and Kamm Antony, eds. Richard Drew, 1985.

MEDLEY, SAMUEL (1738–1799)

He was born at Cheshunt, Hertfordshire, where his father ran a school, having previously been tutor to the Duke of Montague and attorney-general of the Island of St. Vincent. Medley, who had joined the Royal Navy in 1755, was wounded during the sea battle on 18 August 1759 off Cape Lagos, Portugal, between the flagship *Namur,* commanded by Admiral Edward Boscawen, and the defeated French ship *de la Clue*. He experienced a religious conversion and was ordained a Baptist minister in 1768 and took charge of Byrom Street church in Liverpool in 1772. He was immensely popular in Liverpool, particularly among the seamen of the port. He was a prolific writer of hymns, first printed in the *Gospel Magazine* and other publications. Some of his publications: *Hymns,* 1785. *Hymns on Select Portions of Scripture,* 1785. *Hymns,* 1794. *Original and Miscellaneous Poems,* 1807 (published by his daughter). Some of his hymns/poems: "Awake, My Soul, to Joyful Lays," "Father of Mercies, God of Love," "I Know That My Redeemer Lives," "Mortals Awake, with Angels Join," "Now, in a Song of Grateful Praise," "What Amazing Words of Grace."

Sources: *Dictionary of National Biography.* Electronic Edition 1.1. Oxford University Press, 1997. *The Cyber Hymnal* (http://www.cyberhymnal.org/index.htm).

MENDES, MOSES (d. 1758)

The only son of James Mendes, stockbroker, of Mitcham, Surrey, he spent some time at St. Mary Hall, Oxford, and was created M.A. from Oxford in 1750. He became a stockbroker, made a large fortune, and acquired St. Andrews, a fine estate at Old Buckenham, Norfolk, where he died and was buried. His poem "The Squire of Dames" appeared in James Dodsley's *Collection of Poems* (1782). His dramatic works, from which his poems are derived: *The Double Disappointment,* a ballad opera, first performed at Drury Lane in 1746, and at Covent Garden in 1759; *The Chaplet,* a musical entertainment with music by William Boyce (1710–1779), performed at Drury Lane in 1749; *Robin Hood,* a musical entertainment, with music by William Boyce, performed at Drury Lane in 1750; *The Shepherd's Lottery,* a musical entertainment, set to music by Charles Burney (1726–1814), acted at Drury Lane in 1751. His other poetical publications: *The Battiad,* 1751 (a satire in two cantos). *The Seasons, a Poem in Imitation of Spenser,* 1751.

Sources: *A Treasury of Jewish Poetry.* Nathan Ausubel, and Maryann Ausubel, ed. Crown, 1957. *Dictionary of National Biography.* Electronic Edition 1.1. Oxford University Press, 1997. *The National Portrait Gallery* (www.npg.org.uk). *The Columbia Granger's Index to Poetry.* 11th ed. *The Columbia Granger's World of Poetry,* Columbia University Press, 2005 (http://www.columbiagrangers.org).

MEREDITH, GEORGE (1828–1909)

Born in Portsmouth, Hampshire, he was educated at nearby Southsea and at the Moravian School at Neuwied, in present-day Germany. Although articled to a solicitor, he chose to support himself by journalism and met Charles Dickens, who included twenty-four of Meredith's earliest poems in *House-hold Words.* By his death Meredith had written 18 novels — the most famous of which are *The Ordeal of Richard Feverel* (1859) and *The Egoist* (1879) — and ten collections of poetry. From 1860 to 1894 he was reader for the publisher Chapman and Hall. He was awarded the Order of Merit in 1905. In 1867 he moved to Mickleham in Surrey, where he died, and his ashes were buried beside his wife in Dorking cemetery, Surrey. Some of his other poetry publications: *Poems and Lyrics of the Joy of Earth,* 1883. *A Reading of Earth,* 1888. *Odes in Contribution to the Song of French History,* 1898. *A Reading of Life, with Other Poems,* 1901. *Last Poems,* 1909. Some of his poems: "A Faith on Trial," "Modern Love," "The Young Princess," "Woodland Peace," "Young Reynard," "Youth in Memory."

Sources: *Dictionary of National Biography.* Electronic Edition 1.1. Oxford University Press, 1997. *How Does a Poem Mean?* 2nd edition. John Ciardi and Miller Williams, eds. Houghton Mifflin, 1975. *The National Portrait Gallery* (www.npg.org.uk). *The Columbia Granger's Index to Poetry.* 11th ed. *The Columbia Granger's World of Poetry,* Columbia University Press, 2005 (http://www.columbiagrangers.org). *The New Oxford Book of Victorian Verse.* Christopher Ricks, ed. Oxford University Press, 2002. *The Oxford Companion to English Literature.* 6th edition. Margaret Drabble, ed. Oxford University Press, 2000. *The Poems of George Meredith. Vol. 1.* Phyllis B. Bartlett, ed. Yale University Press, 1978. *Wikipedia, the Free Encyclopedia* (http://en.wikipedia.org/wiki/Wikipedia).

MERIVALE, HERMAN CHARLES (1839–1906)

The only son of Herman Merivale, permanent under-secretary of the India office, and grandson of John Herman Merivale (see entry), he was educated at Harrow School and graduated from Balliol College, Oxford, in 1861. Called to the bar in 1864, he was junior counsel for the government on Indian appeals and in 1867 boundary commissioner for North Wales under the Reform Act. From 1870 to 1880 he edited the *Annual Register* (a year-by-year record of world events, started in 1758). He died suddenly of heart failure and was buried in his father's grave in Brompton cemetery, Kensington, London. After his father's death in 1874 he gave up the law and devoted himself to literature, sometimes writing under the pseudonym of Felix Dale. He wrote farces, dramas, novels, a fairy tale for children, *Binko's Blues* (1884), *A Life of Thackeray* (1891), and *Bar, Stage and Platform, Autobiographic Memories* (1902). Some of his poems: "A Lost Morning," "A Sprig of Heather," "Aetate XIX," "Darwinity," "Ready, Ay, Ready," "The Lay of the Lifeboat," "The Storm," "The Heart of Midlothian," "Rorke's Drift," "Spinning-Wheel Song."

Sources: *A Nonsense Anthology.* Carolyn Wells, ed.

Scribner's; paperback edition, 1930. *Dictionary of National Biography*. Electronic Edition 1.1. Oxford University Press, 1997. *The Columbia Granger's Index to Poetry*. 11th ed. *The Columbia Granger's World of Poetry*, Columbia University Press, 2005 (http://www.columbiagrangers.org). *The Oxford Book of Victorian Verse*. Arthur Quiller-Couch, ed. Oxford University Press, 1971. *The Home Book of Verse*. Burton Egbert Stevenson, ed. New York: Henry Holt and Company, 1953. *Through the Year with the Poets*. Oscar Fay Adams, ed. D. Lothrop and Company, 1886.

MERIVALE, JOHN HERMAN (1779–1844)

Born in Exeter, Devon, he was educated at St. John's College, Cambridge, but left without graduating. He was called to the bar in 1804 and practiced in chancery and bankruptcy and sat on the Chancery Commission of 1824. In 1831 he was appointed to a commissionership in bankruptcy, which he held until his death. When past middle age he learned German, and shortly before his death he published, in 1840, translations of *The Minor Poems of Schiller of the Second and Third Periods*. Merivale was a friend of Byron, who warmly praised both his translations from the Greek and his *Orlando in Roncesvalles* (1814). He published *Collections from the Greek Anthology and from the Pastoral, Elegiac, and Dramatic Poets of Greece* (1813), and *Poems, Original and Translated* (1844). He was buried in the churchyard at Hampstead, northwest London. Some of his poems: "Almighty God! Before Thy Throne," "For the General Fast," "From the Lay of a Troubadour," "Invasion of Julius Cæsar," "Ode to a Son Entering College," "On Beauty," "The English Sailor and the King of Achen's Daughter," "The Wraith," "To My Mother, on Her Birth-Day."

Sources: *An Anthology of World Poetry*. Mark Van Doren, ed. Reynal and Hitchcock, Inc., 1936. *Dictionary of National Biography*. Electronic Edition 1.1. Oxford University Press, 1997. *English Poetry: Author Search*. Chadwyck-Healey Ltd., 1995 (http://www.lib.utexas.edu: 8080/search/epoetry/author.html). *Stanford University Libraries and Academic Information Resources* (http://library.stanford.edu). *The Columbia Granger's Index to Poetry*. 11th ed. *The Columbia Granger's World of Poetry*, Columbia University Press, 2005 (http://www.columbiagrangers.org).

MERRICK, JAMES (1720–1769)

Born and educated at Reading, Berkshire, he graduated M.A. from St. John's College, Oxford, in 1742. He was ordained in the English church and preached occasionally between 1747 and 1749, but ill-health prevented him from accepting any parish duties. He died after a long and painful illness and was buried near his parents in Caversham Church, Reading. He wrote several learned theses in Latin and Greek and was working on the compilation and amalgamation of indexes to the principal Greek authors. Some of his publications: *The Messiah, a Divine Essay*, 1734. *The Destruction of Troy*, 1739 (the sequel of the *Iliad*, translated from the Greek of Tryphiodorus, with notes). *Dissertation on Proverbs, Chap. 9: 1–6*, 1744. *Prayers for a Time of Earthquakes and Violent Floods*, 1756. *An Encouragement to a Good Life*, 1759. *Poems on Sacred Subjects*, 1763. *Three Dialogues of Plato*, 1771. *The Psalms Translated or Paraphrased in English Verse*, 1765. Some of his poems: "An Ode to Fancy," "Balaam's Blessing on Israel," "The Benedicite Paraphrased," "The Chameleon," "The Ignorance of Man," "The Song of Simeon Paraphrased," "The Trials of Virtue."

Sources: *A Collection of Poems in Six Volumes. By several hands*. Edited and published by Robert Dodsley, 1763. *Dictionary of National Biography*. Electronic Edition 1.1. Oxford University Press, 1997. *English Poetry: Author Search*. Chadwyck-Healey Ltd., 1995 (http://www.lib. utexas.edu:8080/search/epoetry/author.html). *The Columbia Granger's Index to Poetry*. 11th ed. *The Columbia Granger's World of Poetry*, Columbia University Press, 2005 (http://www.columbiagrangers.org). *The Home Book of Verse*. Burton Egbert Stevenson, ed. New York: Henry Holt and Company, 1953. *The Oxford Book of Christian Verse*. Lord David Cecil, ed. Oxford University Press, 1940.

MERRIMAN, BRIAN (1757–1805)

The Irish poet whose lasting reputation rests upon one poem. He was born in County Clare, the son of a journeyman stonemason and small farmer. It is probable that he was educated at one of the Hedge Schools: illegal schools run by Catholics during the time of the Irish Penal laws (forbidding Catholic teaching and legally binding until Catholic Emancipation in 1829). For some twenty years he was a schoolteacher and was also resident tutor to the families of the local gentry. A plaque honoring his memory was erected in Feakle churchyard, County Clare, and an obituary appeared in *The General Advertiser and Limerick Gazette* of the 27 July 1905. In 1780 he wrote his poem — in the form of a vision or aisling — of 1,026 lines, entitled *Cuirt an mheadhoin oidhche (The Midnight Court)*, divided into five parts: *Prologue, The Young Woman, The Old Man, The Young Woman Again*, and *The Judgment and Resolution*. The principal themes are the plight of young women who lack husbands, clerical celibacy, free love, and the misery of a young woman married to a withered old man. Cumann Merriman (Merriman Society) was founded in 1967 to promote the poet's work. They run an annual Merriman Summer School in Clare each August.

Sources: *Clare People: Brian Merriman* (http://www.clarelibrary.ie/eolas/coclare/people/merriman.htm). *Dictionary of National Biography*. Electronic Edition 1.1. Oxford University Press, 1997. *Hedge School Home Page* (http://hedgeschool.homestead.com/). *Irish Penal Laws* (http://www.law.umn.edu/irishlaw/). *Irishclans—The Penal Laws* (http://www.irishclans.com/articles/penallaws.html). *The Book of Irish Verse: An Anthology of Irish Poetry from the Sixth Century to the Present.* John Montague, ed. Macmillan, 1974. *The Columbia Granger's Index to Poetry.* 11th ed. *The Columbia Granger's World of Poetry,* Columbia University Press, 2005 (http://www.columbiagrangers.org). *The Cumann Merriman Website* (http://www.merriman.ie/). *The Midnight Court by Brian Merriman* (http://www.showhouse.com/prologue.html). *Wikipedia, the Free Encyclopedia* (http://en.wikipedia.org/wiki/Wikipedia).

MESTON, WILLIAM (?1688–1745)

Born in Aberdeenshire, the son of a blacksmith, and although poor, his parents sent him to Marischal College, Aberdeen. He was elected one of the doctors of Aberdeen high school, then, in 1715, professor of philosophy of Marischal College. He joined with Earl Marischal in fighting for James Stuart, the Old Pretender, and was rewarded by the governorship of Dunnottar Castle, Kincardineshire. After the battle of Sheriffmuir (November 1715) he, with many others, was forced into hiding in the hills. While in hiding he wrote verses called *Mother Grim's Tales,* published in Edinburgh in 1767. He died in Aberdeen and was buried in the Spittal churchyard in the old part of Aberdeen. Some of his other publications: *Phaethon, or the first Fable of the second Book of Ovid's Metamorphoses burlesqu'd,* 1720. *The Knight of the Kirk,* 1723. *Mob contra Mob, or the Rabblers Rabbled,* 1731. *The Poetical Works,* 1767. *The Wife of Auchtermuchty,* 1803. Some of his poems: "Cato's Ghost," "Holy Ode, From Mount Alexander," "Prologue to the Recruiting Officer," "The Publisher, to the Candid Reader," "To the Free-Masons."

Sources: *Biography of William Meston. Significant and Famous Scots* (http://www.electricscotland.com/history/other/meston_william.htm). *Dictionary of National Biography.* Electronic Edition 1.1. Oxford University Press, 1997. *English Poetry: Author Search.* Chadwyck-Healey Ltd., 1995 (http://www.lib.utexas.edu:8080/search/epoetry/author.html). *Stanford University Libraries and Academic Information Resources* (http://library.stanford.edu).

MEW, CHARLOTTE MARY (1869–1928)

Born in London, the daughter of a prosperous architect, she was educated privately and later attended lectures at University College, London. Her poems often express the sorrow of her life, where several of her siblings died young or were hospitalized with mental illness. She and her sister Anne made a pact to remain childless so as not to transmit what they believed to be a genetic disorder. After her father died in 1898, the family lived in genteel poverty. When Anne was diagnosed with cancer in 1926, Charlotte nursed her until she died the next year.

While hospitalized for minor surgery in 1928, Charlotte poisoned herself. Many of her poems, stories, essays, and studies were published in periodicals. She wrote around 60 poems and gained the patronage of several literary figures, among them Thomas Hardy and Siegfried Sassoon (see entries). Her poetry publications: *The Farmer's Bride,* 1915 (U.S. title, *Saturday Market*). *The Rambling Sailor,* 1929 (a collection of 32 previously uncollected poems). Some of her poems: "Afternoon Tea," "In Nunhead Cemetery," "Madeleine in Church," "My Heart is Lame," "On the Asylum Road," "To a Child in Death."

Sources: *Anthology of Twentieth-Century British and Irish Poetry.* Keith Tuma, ed. Oxford University Press, 2001. *Chloe Plus Olivia: An Anthology of Lesbian Literature from the Seventeenth Century to the Present.* Lillian Faderman, ed. Viking Penguin, 1994. *Collected Poems of Charlotte Mew.* Gerald Duckworth and Co., 1953. *Collected Poems and Selected Prose of Charlotte Mew.* Val Warner, ed. Fyfield Books, 2003. *Dictionary of National Biography.* Electronic Edition 1.1. Oxford University Press, 1997. *Encyclopædia Britannica Ultimate Reference Suite DVD,* 2006. *Salt and Bitter and Good: Three Centuries of English and American Women Poets.* Cora Kaplan, ed. Paddington Press, 1975. *The Columbia Granger's Index to Poetry.* 11th ed. *The Columbia Granger's World of Poetry,* Columbia University Press, 2005 (http://www.columbiagrangers.org). *The Faber Book of 20th Century Women's Poetry.* Fleur Adcock, ed. Faber and Faber, 1987. *The Oxford Companion to English Literature.* 6th edition. Margaret Drabble, ed. Oxford University Press, 2000.

MEYNELL, ALICE CHRISTIANA GERTRUDE (1847–1922)

Born Alice Thompson in Barnes, London, she spent several years in Italy and France. She converted to Catholicism in 1868 and married the journalist Wilfrid Meynell (also a convert to Catholicism) in 1877. From 1881 to 1898 they edited *The Weekly Register* and the monthly *Merry England.* Both magazines contain many of Alice's essays, as do several other periodicals in England, Scotland and Ireland. *The Rhythm of Life and Other Essays* (1891) ensured her place in the literary world. In 1894 she started writing a weekly article in the *Pall Mall Gazette.* She lectured on Dickens, the Brontës, and seventeenth-century poetry in the United States in 1901–1902. In addition to the poetry anthologies she edited, and her essays, she wrote *Holman Hunt* (1893), *Ruskin* (1900), *The Work of John S. Sargent* (1903), and *The Second Person Singular* (1921). She died in London. Her poetry publications: *Preludes,* 1875. *Poems,* 1893. *Later Poems,* 1902. *Last Poems,* 1923. Some of his poems: "Advent Meditation," "Beyond Knowledge," "Free Will," "In Honour of America, 1917," "Nurse Edith Cavell," "On Keats's Grave," "Renouncement," "Your Own Fair Youth."

Sources: *Chapters into Verse, Vol. I: Genesis to Malachi.* Robert Atwan and Laurance Wieder, eds. Oxford University Press, 1993. *Dictionary of National Biography.* Electronic Edition 1.1. Oxford University Press, 1997. *Encyclopædia Britannica Ultimate Reference Suite DVD,* 2006. *The Columbia Granger's Index to Poetry.* 11th ed. *The Columbia Granger's World of Poetry,* Columbia University Press, 2005 (http://www.columbiagrangers.org). *The National Portrait Gallery* (www.npg.org.uk). *The Oxford Companion to English Literature.* 6th edition. Margaret Drabble, ed. Oxford University Press, 2000. *The Poems of Alice Meynell at ELCore.Net* (http://poetry.elcore.net/Catholic Poets/Meynell/). *The Poems of Alice Meynell.* Oxford University Press, 1940. *The Poems of Thomas Gordon Hake.* Alice Meynell, ed. AMS Press, 1971. *Victorian Women Poets: An Anthology.* Angela Leighton and Margaret Reynolds, eds. Blackwell, 1991.

MICKLE, WILLIAM JULIUS (1735–1788)

Born at Langholm, Dumfriesshire, the son of the parish minister. He moved to London to concentrate on literature, having had his breakthrough when his poems "Knowledge, an Ode" and "A Night Piece" were published in *The Evergreen, Being a Collection of Scots Poems,* published by Alex Donaldson in 1761. He worked briefly as a corrector to the Clarendon Press, Oxford, from 1765, then left to concentrate on his translations. In need of funds, he took several different jobs, finishing as purser of HMS *Brilliant* (Vice-Admiral Sir Hyde Parker, 1739–1807), for which he was paid a handsome pension for life. He then married and settled at Wheatley, near Oxford, and died at his former home in Forest Hill, Oxford, where he is buried. Some of his poetry publications: *Providence,* 1762. *The Siege of Marseilles,* 1771. *The Lusiad,* 1776 (original author, the Portuguese poet, Luis de Camoëns, 1524–1580). *Poetical Works,* 1806. Some of his other poems: "Almada Hill: An Epistle from Lisbon," "Cumnor Hall," "The Spirit of the Cape," "There's Nae Luck about the House," "The Concubine," "The Sailor's Wife."

Sources: *Dictionary of National Biography.* Electronic Edition, 1.1. *English Poetry: Author Search* (http://www.lib.utexas.edu:8080/search/epoetry/author.html). *Golden Treasury of the Best Songs and Lyrical Poems in the English Language.* Francis Turner Palgrave, ed. Oxford University Press (1964, Sixth edition, updated by John Press, 1994). *The National Portrait Gallery* (www.npg.org.uk). *Poems of South African History* A.D. *1497–1910.* A. Petrie, ed. Oxford University Press. 1918. *The Columbia Granger's Index to Poetry.* 11th ed (http://www.columbiagrangers.org). *The Oxford Book of Ballads.* James Kinsley, ed. Oxford University Press, 1969. *The Oxford Book of Travel Verse.* Kevin Crossley-Holland, ed. Oxford University Press, 1986. *Stanford University Libraries and Academic Information Resources* (http://library.stanford.edu). *List of the Principal Collections of English and Scottish Ballads and Songs* (http://www.sacred-texts.com/neu/eng/child/chbib.htm).

MIDDLETON, THOMAS (?1570–1627)

He was born in London, the son of prosperous bricklayer, but there is confusion about his date of birth. The DNB and the National Portrait Gallery give 1570, while several others give 1580. He became renowned as a playwright and collaborated with Thomas Dekker (see entry), John Webster and others who wrote for the producer Philip Henslowe. He wrote and produced several lord mayor's pageants and other civic entertainments and in 1620 he was appointed city chronicler. His political satire (1625) *A Game at Chess* by the King's Players — in which Black King and his men, representing Spain and the Jesuits, are checkmated by the White Knight, Prince Charles (later Charles I) — offended the Spanish king. King James I suppressed further performances. Middleton was buried in the parish church of Newington Butts, Surrey. Some of his plays, from which his poems are derived: *Women Beware Women,* ?1621. *The Changeling,* 1622. *A Tricke to Catch the Old-one,* 1606. *The Revenger's Tragedie,* 1607. *In a Mad World, My Masters,* 1694. *A Chast Mayd in Cheape-side,* 1613. *The Honest Whore,* 1604 (with Dekker). *The Old Law,* 1618? (Philip Massinger [see entry] and William Rowley).

Sources: *Dictionary of National Biography.* Electronic Edition 1.1. Oxford University Press, 1997. *Elizabethan Lyrics.* Norman Ault, ed. William Sloane Associates, 1949. *Encyclopædia Britannica Ultimate Reference Suite DVD,* 2006. *English Poetry: Author Search.* Chadwyck-Healey Ltd., 1995 (http://www.lib.utexas.edu:8080/search/epoetry/author.html). *Poets of the English Language, Vol. II.* W.H. Auden and Norman Holmes Pearson, eds. Viking Press, 1950. *Songs from the British Drama.* Edward Bliss Reed, ed. Yale University Press, 1925. Stanford University Libraries and Academic Information Resources (http://library.stanford.edu). *The Columbia Granger's Index to Poetry.* 11th ed. *The Columbia Granger's World of Poetry,* Columbia University Press, 2005 (http://www.columbia-grangers.org). *The Oxford Book of Marriage.* Helge Rubenstein, ed. Oxford University Press, 1990. *The Oxford Companion to English Literature.* 6th edition. Margaret Drabble, ed. Oxford University Press, 2000. *Why Am I Grown So Cold? Poems of the Unknowable,* Myra Cohn Livingston, ed. Atheneum, 1982.

MIDLANE, ALBERT (1825–1909)

Born at Newport, Isle-of-Wight, he was a tinsmith and ironmonger. Reared as a Congregationalist, he later joined with the Plymouth Brethren and wrote over 800 hymns, used in many different hymnbooks. He died in Carisbrooke on the island and was buried in Carisbrooke Cemetery. As a child, and encouraged by his Sunday school teacher, he contributed verses to magazines under the pseudonym "Little Albert." He later wrote verses on national and historical prose and on local topics for the *Isle of Wight County Press* and other periodicals.

His first hymn—"Hark! in the presence of our God"—written at Carisbrook Castle—was published in the *Youth Magazine* when he was seventeen. Possibly his best-known hymn is "There's a Friend for Little Children" written in 1859. When it was included in *Hymns Ancient and Modern* (1868), it was to the tune "In Memoriam" by Sir John Stainer (1840–1901). "Revive Thy Work O Lord" is included in many modern hymnbooks. Some of his other publications: *Poetry Addressed to Sabbath School Teachers*, 1844. *Vecta Garland*, 1850. *Leaves from Olivet*, 1864. *Gospel Echoes*, 1865. *Above the Bright Blue Sky*, 1867. *Early Lispings*, 1880.

Sources: *Biography of Albert Midlane: Spiritual Songsters* (http://www.stempublishing.com/hymns/biographies/midlane.html). *Dictionary of National Biography.* Electronic Edition 1.1. Oxford University Press, 1997. *The Columbia Granger's Index to Poetry.* 11th ed. *The Columbia Granger's World of Poetry*, Columbia University Press, 2005 (http://www.columbiagrangers.org). *The Cyber Hymnal* (http://www.cyberhymnal.org/index.htm). *The Oxford Book of Children's Verse.* Iona Opie and Peter Opie, eds. Oxford University Press, 1973.

MILL (MILLE), HUMPHREY (fl. 1646)

The son of William Mille from Sussex, he was educated at Queen's College, Oxford. Nothing else is known of him. In 1638 he published *Poems Occasioned by a Melancholy Vision, Or a Melancholy Vision upon Divers Theames Enlarged*, which he describes as "the first fruits of his poore indeavours in this kinde," dedicated to Thomas, earl of Winchelsea. His second publication was *A Nights Search: Discovering the Nature and Condition of all sorts of Night-Walkers: with their Associates, As also the Life and Death of Many of Them* (1640), dedicated to the Earl of Essex. His final publications was *The Second Part of the Nights Search discovering the Condition of the various Fowles of Night. Or, the Second great Mystery of Iniquity Exactly Revealed* (1646), dedicated to Robert, earl of Warwick (*Fowles of Night* are not hens but people intent in mischief.) Some of his poems: "A Proeme to the Search," "Concerning Death," "Good Vse of Time," "Of Life," "The Allvring Sleights of Sin, and Promises," "The Resolutions of the Muse, in Her Pilgrimage," "To All Judges, Justices, Church-Wardens, Constables," "To the Fowles of Night."

Sources: *Dictionary of National Biography.* Electronic Edition 1.1. Oxford University Press, 1997. *English Poetry: Author Search.* Chadwyck-Healey Ltd., 1995 (http://www.lib.utexas.edu:8080/search/epoetry/author.html).

MILLER, LADY ANNA (1741–1781)

She was the daughter of Edward Riggs, a commissioner of customs in London. In 1765 Anna married John Miller, a member of a poor Irish family from Ballicasey, County Clare. She inherited great wealth from her grandfather, a privy councilor in Ireland, and after the couple built a grand house with gardens at Batheaston, near Bath, they toured Italy in 1770. In 1776 three volumes, *Letters from Italy, describing the Manners, Customs, Antiquities, Paintings, &c., of the Country, in 1770–1*, were published, with a second in 1777. Her husband was created an Irish baronet in 1778 and Lady Miller set up a literary salon in her villa. *Poetical Amusements at a Villa near Bath* (1775), a selection of the poems read, was published in 1775, with a fourth volume in 1781, the profits being donated to charity. Anna Seward (see entry) was one of the contributors. Lady Miller died at Bristol and was buried in the Abbey Church, Bath. Some of her poems: "Novelty: An Irregular Essay," "On the Pleasures of Society at Batheaston Villa," "On Trifles, and Triflers," "Subject, Painting, A Dream," "Subject, Dancing."

Sources: *Dictionary of National Biography.* Electronic Edition 1.1. Oxford University Press, 1997. *English Poetry: Author Search.* Chadwyck-Healey Ltd., 1995 (http://www.lib.utexas.edu:8080/search/epoetry/author.html).

MILLER, THOMAS (1807–1874)

"The basket-maker poet" was born at Gainsborough, Lincolnshire, the son of a wharf owner who disappeared when his son was three, leaving the family in poverty. His fortunes started to change on the publication of *Songs of the Sea Nymphs* (1832). He moved to London where, in 1838, some of his poems were printed in the magazine *Friendship's Offering*, for which he was paid. Around 1841 he set up business as a bookseller in Newgate Street and become acquainted with many of the literary figures of the day. He died at Kennington Park Road, London. He wrote novels, many children's books and a history of the *Anglo-Saxons from the Earliest Period to the Norman Conquest* (1848), which went to five editions. Some of his other poetry publications: *A Day in the Woods*, 1836. *Poems*, 1841. *Original Poems for My Children*, 1852. *The Poetical Language of Flowers*, 1855. *Original Songs*, 1861. *Birds, Bees, and Blossoms*, 1864. *Songs of the Seasons*, 1865. Some of his poems: "Evening," "Summer Morning," "The Alarm," "The Desolate Hall," "The Fountain," "The Sea-Deeps," "The Watercress Seller."

Sources: *A Child's Treasury of Poems.* Mark Daniel, ed. Dial / Penguin Books, 1986. *Dictionary of National Biography.* Electronic Edition 1.1. Oxford University Press, 1997. *English Poetry: Author Search.* Chadwyck-Healey Ltd., 1995 (http://www.lib.utexas.edu:8080/search/epoetry/author.html). Stanford University Libraries and Academic Information Resources (http://library.stanford.edu). *The Columbia Granger's Index to Poetry.* 11th ed. *The Columbia Granger's World of Poetry*, Columbia University Press, 2005 (http://www.columbiagrangers.org). *The Eternal Sea: An Anthology* *of Sea Poetry.* W.M. Williamson, ed. Coward-McCann, 1946. *The Poorhouse Fugitives: Self-Taught Poets and Poetry in Victorian Britain.* Brian Maidment, ed. Carcanet, 1987.

MILLER, WILLIAM (1810–1872)

A Scottish poet, "The Laureate of the Nursery" was born and lived most of his life in Glasgow. His desire to be a doctor was thwarted by ill health, so he became a wood turner and cabinetmaker, as well as an accomplished poet and songwriter. Ill and penniless, he died in Glasgow and was buried in the family plot at the Tollcross Burial Ground. A monument to him was erected by public subscription within the Glasgow Necropolis. Much of his early work — often written in the Scots dialect — was published in periodicals and his songs from 1832 to 1853 were published in *Whistle Binkie* (1890) by Alexander Abernethy Ritchie. His *Scottish Nursery Songs and Other Poems* was published in 1863 and *Willie Winkie and Other Songs and Poems* in 1902. Some of his other poems: "Chuckie [hen]," "Hogmanay," "Irish Love Song," "Lady Summer," "The Poet's Last Song," "The Sleepy Laddie," "The Wonderfu' Wean," "To My Dear Friend, James Ballantine, Esq."

Sources: *Dictionary of National Biography.* Electronic Edition 1.1. Oxford University Press, 1997. *English Poetry: Author Search.* Chadwyck-Healey Ltd., 1995 (http://www.lib.utexas.edu:8080/search/epoetry/author.html). *Folk Songs.* John Williamson Palmer, ed. Charles Scribner and Company, 1867. *Stanford University Libraries and Academic Information Resources* (http://library.stanford.edu). *The Columbia Granger's Index to Poetry.* 11th ed. *The Columbia Granger's World of Poetry,* Columbia University Press, 2005 (http://www.columbiagrangers.org). *The Real Mother Goose.* Blanche Fisher Wright, ed. Checkerboard Press, 1944.

MILLHOUSE, ROBERT (1788–1839)

The "weaver poet" of Nottingham earned his living from the age of six and at ten he was working at a stocking loom. It was at Sunday school where he learned to read and write; he also sang in the choir of St. Peter's Church. He obviously learned well, for he was an avid reader of the poets. During the period 1810–1814, his first verses were printed in the *Nottingham Review* while he was serving with the Nottinghamshire militia. When the regiment was disbanded he returned to the stocking frame, married and raised a family. To earn more money he took up writing again and received a pension from the Royal Literary Fund. He was buried in Nottingham cemetery. His long poem "The Park" tells of a Nottingham long gone and the park built on. Some of his other publications: *Vicissitude,* 1821 (a poem in four books). *Blossoms,* 1823 (sonnets). *The Song of the Patriot,* 1826 (sonnets and songs, with a brief memoir of the author). *Sherwood Forest, and Other Poems,* 1827. *The Destinies of Man,* 1832.

Sources: *Books by Robert Millhouse. Forget Me Not: A Hypertextual Archive* (http://www.orgs.muohio.edu/anthologies/FMN/Author_List.htm). *Dictionary of National Biography.* Electronic Edition 1.1. Oxford University Press, 1997. *Nineteenth-Century English Labouring-Class Poets (3 volumes).* John Goodridge, ed. Pickering and Chatto, 2005 (http://www.pickeringchatto.com/labouringpoets19.htm#Publication). *Robert Millhouse — St Peter's Church, Nottingham, England on-line* (http://www.stpetersnottingham.org/history/millhouse.html). *The Poets and the Poetry of the Nineteenth Century.* G. Routledge, 1906.

MILLIGAN, SPIKE (1918–2002)

Terence Alan Milligan was born in India, where his Irish father was a captain in the Royal Artillery; he finished his education at the South East London Polytechnic in Lewisham. Determined to be an entertainer, he learned to play the ukulele, guitar and trumpet, and won a Bing Crosby crooning competition at the Lewisham Hippodrome. His wartime experiences in the Royal Artillery provided material for several best selling novels. *The Goon Show* with Spike, Harry Secombe, Peter Sellers, and Michael Bentine —first broadcast in 1951— ran nine years on the BBC with 26 shows a year. He was a prolific writer and starred in five movies. In 2000, he was awarded an honorary knighthood, honorary because he was an Irish citizen. Plagued with manic depression for years, he died surrounded by his family. Some of his poetry publications: *Small Dreams of a Scorpion,* 1972. *Goblins,* 1978. *Silly Verse for Kids and Animals,* 1984. *Spike's Poems: Knees, Fleas, Hidden Elephants and Other Poems,* 1997. Some of his poems: "A Baby Sardine," "Cat Will Rhyme with Hat," "The Bongaloo," "You Must Never Bathe in an Irish Stew."

Sources: *Amazing Monsters: Verses to Thrill and Chill.* Robert Fisher, ed. Faber and Faber, 1982. *Prince Charles Leads Spike Milligan Tributes, Wednesday, 27 February, 2002: BBC News, TV and Radio* (http://news.bbc.co.uk/1/hi/entertainment/tv_and_radio/1843963.stm). *Cat Will Rhyme with Hat: A Book of Poems.* Jean Chapman, ed. Scribner's, 1986. *Once Upon a Rhyme: 101 Poems for Young Children.* Sara Corrin and Stephen Corrin, eds. Faber and Faber, 1982. *Poemhunter* (www.poemhunter.com). *The Columbia Granger's Index to Poetry.* 11th ed. *The Columbia Granger's World of Poetry,* Columbia University Press, 2005 (http://www.columbiagrangers.org). *The National Portrait Gallery* (www.npg.org.uk). *The New Oxford Book of Children's Verse.* Neil Philip, ed. Oxford University Press, 1996. *The Oxford Book of Christmas Poems.* Michael Harrison and Christopher Stuart-Clark, eds. Oxford University Press, 1983. *The Spike Milligan Tribute Site* (http://www.spikemilligan.co.uk/4680/index.html).

MILLIKIN, RICHARD ALFRED (1767–1815)

Irish poet born at Castlemartyr, County Cork, of Scottish parentage. Although employed as an attorney in Cork he devoted more time to painting, poetry, and music. He started contributing verse to the Cork *Monthly Miscellany* in 1795, and two years later, he and his sister, an historical novelist, started a monthly magazine called *The Casket*, which appeared until 1798 when he joined the Royal Cork volunteers at the outbreak of the Irish Rebellion. In 1807 he published "The Riverside," a blank-verse poem, and in 1810 a short tale, *The Slave of Surinam*. In 1815 he laid the foundation of a society for the promotion of the fine arts in Cork. He was buried with a public funeral at Douglas, near Cork. One of his songs is "The Groves of Blarney, They Look so Charming." Other of his lyrics, included in Irish anthologies, are the "Groves of de Pool" and "Had I the Tun Which Bacchus Used." Some of his other poems: "A Lover's Oath," "A Plea for Pilgrimages," "Ode to a Clock," "Ode to Love," "Sonnet to Spring," "The Dream of Napoleon," "The Fisherman's Boy," "The Rose," "To Cynthia."

Sources: *Dictionary of National Biography.* Electronic Edition 1.1. Oxford University Press, 1997. *English Poetry: Author Search.* Chadwyck-Healey Ltd., 1995 (http://www.lib.utexas.edu:8080/search/epoetry/author.html). *The Columbia Granger's Index to Poetry.* 11th ed. *The Columbia Granger's World of Poetry,* Columbia University Press, 2005 (http://www.columbiagrangers.org). *The Reliques of Father Prout (Francis Sylvester Mahony).* Oliver Yorke, ed. George Bell and Sons, 1889.

MILMAN, HENRY HART (1791–1868)

Born in London, the son of a physician, and educated at Eton College, he graduated M.A. from Brasenose College, Oxford, in 1816. He was awarded a doctor of divinity degree in 1849 and was made a fellow of Brasenose. He won the Newdigate prize in 1812 for his poem "Apollo" and in 1816 the chancellor's prize for his essay "A Comparative Estimate of Sculpture and Painting." From 1821 to 1831 he was professor of poetry at Oxford, then rector of St. Margaret's, Westminster, and canon of Westminster, and was made dean of St. Paul's in 1849. He was buried in St. Paul's Cathedral. A monument was erected in the south aisle of the choir. He wrote some major books on history and edited Edward Gibbon's *Decline and Fall of the Roman Empire* (1838). Some of his poetry publications: *Ode on the Arrival of the Potentates in Oxford,* 1814. *Fazio,* 1815. *The Fall of Jerusalem,* 1820. *The Martyr of Antioch,* 1822. *Belshazzar,* 1822. *Anne Boleyn* 1826. Some of his hymn/poems: "Ride On, Ride On, In Majesty!" "The Crucifixion," "The Holy Field," "Where the Wicked Cease from Troubling."

Sources: *A Sacrifice of Praise: An Anthology of Christian Poetry in English from Caedmon to the Mid–Twentieth Century.* James H. Trott, ed. Cumberland House Publishing, 1999. *Dictionary of National Biography.* Electronic Edition 1.1. Oxford University Press, 1997. *English Poetry: Author Search.* Chadwyck-Healey Ltd., 1995 (http://www.lib.utexas.edu:8080/search/epoetry/author.html). *Gentleman's Magazine, Founding of.* (http://www.spartacus.schoolnet.co.uk/Jgentleman.htm). *Great Books Online* (www.bartleby.com). *Milman's Poetical Works.* John Murray, 1840. *Stanford University Libraries and Academic Information Resources* (http://library.stanford.edu). *The Columbia Granger's Index to Poetry.* 11th ed. *The Columbia Granger's World of Poetry,* Columbia University Press, 2005 (http://www.columbiagrangers.org). *The Cyber Hymnal* (http://www.cyberhymnal.org/index.htm). *The National Portrait Gallery* (www.npg.org.uk). *The Oxford Book of Christian Verse.* Lord David Cecil, ed. Oxford University Press, 1940. *The Oxford Companion to English Literature.* 6th edition. Margaret Drabble, ed. Oxford University Press, 2000. *Wikipedia, the Free Encyclopedia* (http://en.wikipedia.org/wiki/Wikipedia).

MILNE, ALAN ALEXANDER (1882–1956)

Born in London, he was educated at Westminster School and graduated from Trinity College, Cambridge, in 1903. In 1906, he became assistant editor of *Punch*, where his humorous verse and whimsical essays attracted a large readership. He left *Punch* in 1919 to devote his time to stage comedy and he had many successes, including the stage adaptation of Kenneth Grahame's (see entry) *Wind in the Willows* (1929). His first play, *Wurzel-Flummery,* was staged in 1917, followed by *Mr. Pim Passes By* (1920), *The Dover Road* (1921), *The Truth About Blayds* (1922), and *Michael and Mary* (1930). He also wrote *The Red House Mystery*, a detective story (1922), two novels and many essays. He died at his home at Hartfield, Sussex. His poetry publications: *When We Were Very Young,* 1924 (a series of verses for children dedicated to his son, Christopher Robin, then aged 4). *Winnie-the-Pooh,* 1926. *Now We Are Six,* 1927. *The House at Pooh Corner,* 1928. Some of his poems: "At the Zoo," "Buckingham Palace," "Furry Bear," "King Hilary and the Beggarman," "Sneezles," "The Emperor's Rhyme," "Vespers," "Wind on the Hill."

Sources: *Dictionary of National Biography.* Electronic Edition 1.1. Oxford University Press, 1997. *Encyclopædia Britannica Ultimate Reference Suite DVD,* 2006. *Favorite Poems Old and New.* Helen Ferris, ed. Doubleday, 1957. *The National Portrait Gallery* (www.npg.org.uk). *Piping Down the Valley Wild: Poetry for the Young of All Ages,* Nancy Larrick, ed. Delacorte Press, 1968. *Sing a Song of Popcorn: Every Child's Book of Poems.* Beatrice Schenck De Regniers and others, eds. Scholastic, 1988. *The Columbia Granger's Index to Poetry.* 11th ed. *The Columbia Granger's World of Poetry,* Columbia University Press, 2005 (http://www.columbiagrangers.org). *The Oxford Companion to English Literature.* 6th edition. Margaret Drabble, ed. Oxford University Press, 2000. *Unauthorized Versions: Poems* *and Their Parodies.* Kenneth Baker, ed. Faber and Faber, 1990.

MILNES, RICHARD MONCKTON, 1ST BARON HOUGHTON (1809–1885)

Born in London, he graduated M.A. from Trinity College, Cambridge, in 1831, where he was one of the "Apostles" (see Rupert Brooke). He became Conservative member of Parliament for the Yorkshire constituency of Pontefract in 1837 and worked for several reforms, including the protection of copyright. He supported many poets by securing pensions for them; Tennyson is one. In 1848 he published *Life and Letters of Keats* and in 1855, in *The Times*, a poem on the English graves at Scutari. He was made a baron in the House of Lords in 1863 and supported the reform of the franchise. In 1869 he represented the Royal Geographical Society at the opening of the Suez Canal. Oxford, Cambridge and Edinburgh universities awarded him honorary degrees. He died at Vichy, Southern France, and was buried at Fryston, North Yorkshire. His *Poetical Works* was published in 1876. Some of his poems: "Columbus and the Mayflower," "Corfu," "England and America, 1863," "The Brookside," "The Burden of Egypt," "The Funeral of Napoleon," "The Ionian Islands," "Crimean Invalid Soldiers Reaping at Aldershot," "Good Night and Good Morning."

Sources: *A Second Treasury of the Familiar.* Ralph L. Woods, ed. Macmillan, 1950. *Dictionary of National Biography.* Electronic Edition 1.1. Oxford University Press, 1997. *English Poetry: Author Search.* Chadwyck-Healey Ltd., 1995 (http://www.lib.utexas.edu:8080/search/epoetry/author.html). *Poems of American History.* Burton Egbert Stevenson, ed. Houghton Mifflin, 1922. *The Book of a Thousand Poems: A Family Treasury.* J. Murray Macbain, ed. Peter Bedrick Books, 1983. *The Columbia Granger's Index to Poetry.* 11th ed. *The Columbia Granger's World of Poetry,* Columbia University Press, 2005 (http://www.columbiagrangers.org). *The Home Book of Verse.* Burton Egbert Stevenson, ed. New York: Henry Holt and Company, 1953. *The Oxford Book of Travel Verse.* Kevin Crossley-Holland, ed. Oxford University Press, 1986. *The Oxford Companion to English Literature.* 6th edition. Margaret Drabble, ed. Oxford University Press, 2000.

MILTON, JOHN (1608–1674)

Born in London, he was educated St. Paul's School and graduated M.A. from Christ's College, Cambridge, in 1632. He aligned himself with the Parliamentarians and for ten years he was Latin secretary to Cromwell's Council of State (Andrew Marvell [see entry] was his assistant for part of this time). At the Restoration in 1660 he was forced into hiding, but was arrested and fined for his part in the Commonwealth and for his controversial writings

on political, social and religious subjects. He lost a fortune, but got off with lighter punishment than many others of his party. By 1663 he was blind. He was buried at St. Giles's, Cripplegate, London, and a monument was erected in Poets' Corner, Westminister Abbey, in 1737. He was among the first to advocate freedom of the press (in the pamphlet *Areopagitica*). His three main publications: *Paradise Lost,* 1667. *Paradise Regained,* 1671. *Samson Agonistes,* 1671. Some of his poems: "That Nature Does Not Grow Old," "To Leonora Singing at Rome," "To My Father," "Upon the Circumcision," "When the Assault Was Intended to the City," "Woman."

Sources: *Dictionary of National Biography.* Electronic Edition 1.1. Oxford University Press, 1997. *Encyclopædia Britannica Ultimate Reference Suite DVD,* 2006. *English Poetry: Author Search.* Chadwyck-Healey Ltd., 1995 (http://www.lib.utexas.edu:8080/search/epoetry/author.html). *Invisible Light: Poems about God.* Diana Culbertson, ed. Columbia University Press, 2000. *The Columbia Granger's Index to Poetry.* 11th ed. *The Columbia Granger's World of Poetry,* Columbia University Press, 2005 (http://www.columbiagrangers.org). *The Complete Poetry of John Milton.* John T. Shawcross, ed. Doubleday, 1971. *The Oxford Companion to English Literature.* 6th edition. Margaret Drabble, ed. Oxford University Press, 2000. *The Penguin Book of English Christian Verse.* Peter Levi, ed. Penguin Books, 1984. *Westminster Abbey Official Guide* (no date).

MINHINNICK, ROBERT (1952–)

Born in Neath, South Wales, he studied at the universities of Aberystwyth and Cardiff, then after working as an environmentalist, co-founded Friends of the Earth (Cymru) and became the organization's joint coordinator for some years. He is advisor to the charity "Sustainable Wales" and edits the international quarterly *Poetry Wales.* He has published *Watching the Fire Eater* (1992), winner of the 1993 Arts Council of Wales Book of the Year Award, and *Badlands* (1996), essays about post-communist Albania, California, and the state of Wales and England. He has also edited *Green Agenda,* essays on the environment of Wales (1994). He lives in Porthcawl, South Wales. Some of his poetry publications: *A Thread in the Maze,* 1978. *Native Ground,* 1979. *Life Sentences,* 1983. *The Dinosaur Park,* 1985. *The Looters,* 1989. *Hey Fatman,* 1994. *Selected Poems,* 1999. *The Adulterer's Tongue: An Anthology of Welsh Poetry in Translation,* 2003. Some of his poems: "After a Friendship," "Catching My Breath," "Grandfather in the Garden," "The Ariel," "The Boathouse," "The Children," "The Drinking Art," "The Looters," "Twenty-Five Laments for Iraq."

Sources: *Anglo-Welsh Poetry, 1480–1980.* Raymond Garlick and Roland Mathias, eds. Poetry Wales Press, 1984. *Anglo-Welsh Poetry, 1480–1990.* Raymond Garlick and

Roland Mathias, eds. Poetry Wales Press, 1993. *British Council Arts* (http://www.contemporarywriters.com). *The Columbia Granger's Index to Poetry.* 11th ed. *The Columbia Granger's World of Poetry,* Columbia University Press, 2005 (http://www.columbiagrangers.org). *The Harvill Book of Twentieth-Century Poetry in English.* Michael Schmidt, ed. The Harvill Press, 1999. *The Oxford Book of Garden Verse.* John Dixon Hunt, ed. Oxford University Press, 1993. *Twentieth Century Anglo-Welsh Poetry.* Dannie Abse, ed. Seren Books / Dufour Editions, 1997.

MINOT, LAURENCE (?1300-?1352)

What is known of Minot has been gleaned from his poems. The belief that he was born and bred in the northeast midlands of England is supported by the dialect he uses and his frequent reference of certain people in Yorkshire. Even his name is deduced from one poem, which starts, "Now Laurence Minot will begin...." The DNB states that the name Minot was a widely well-known Yorkshire and Norfolk name in the fourteenth century. Judging from the many spirited and patriotic war songs and poems of the English against the Scots and the French during the reign of Edward III, it can be safely assumed he was a soldier, or someone closely connected to the English army, possibly a minstrel. Some of his poems: "Bannockburn Avenged" (1333; the Battle of Bannockburn, 1314, was where Robert Bruce beat the English under Edward II, the father of Edward III), "Burgesses of Calais," "Sir Dauid Had of His Men Grete Loss," "The Battle of Halidon Hill" (1333), "The Battle of Neville's Cross" (1346), "The Siege of Calais" (1347), "The Taking of Guines" (1352).

Sources: *An Anthology of Catholic Poets.* Shane Leslie, ed. Macmillan, 1952. *Dictionary of National Biography.* Electronic Edition 1.1. Oxford University Press, 1997. *English Poetry: Author Search.* Chadwyck-Healey Ltd., 1995 (http://www.lib.utexas.edu:8080/search/epoetry/author.html). *The Columbia Granger's Index to Poetry.* 11th ed. *The Columbia Granger's World of Poetry,* Columbia University Press, 2005 (http://www.columbiagrangers.org). *The Oxford Book of Medieval English Verse.* Celia Sisam and Kenneth Sisam, eds. Oxford University Press, 1970. *The Oxford Companion to English Literature.* 6th edition. Margaret Drabble, ed. Oxford University Press, 2000. *The Poems of Laurence Minot.* Richard H. Osberg, ed. Western Michigan University, 1996. *The Poems of Laurence Minot.* Second Edition. Clarendon Press, 1897. *The Works of Laurence Minot* (http://online.northumbria.ac.uk/faculties/art/humanities/cns/m-minot.html).

MITCHELL, ADRIAN (1932–)

Born in London, his schooling was interrupted by national service in the Royal Air Force from 1951 to 1952. He graduated with a degree in English from Christ Church College, Oxford, in 1955, then worked as a journalist in Oxford and for several London newspapers and magazines. In 1965 he was in-

volved in the International Festival of Poetry at the Albert Hall, and it was around this time that he emerged as a playwright and poet of substance, writing for adult and children. From his first writers workshop, University of Iowa (1963–1967), he has held fellowships in Britain, America, and Singapore. He was awarded the Gold Medal of the Theatre of Poetry, Varna, Bulgaria, and was awarded an honorary doctor of arts, North London University, 1997. Some of his poetry publications: *Poems,* 1964. *For Beauty Douglas, Collected Poems 1953–1979,* 1982. *Strawberry Drums,* 1984. *Heart on the Left (Collected Poems 1953–85),* 1997. *All Shook Up: Poems 1996–2000,* 2000. *The Shadow Knows: Poems 2000–2004,* 2004. Some of his poems: "A Tourist Guide to England," "Another Prince is Born," "Remember Suez?" "To a Russian Soldier in Prague."

Sources: *Biography and Works of Adrian Mitchell* (http://www.rippingyarns.co.uk/adrian/). *I Have No Gun But I Can Spit: An Anthology of Satirical and Abusive Verse.* Kenneth Baker, ed. Faber and Faber, 1980. *The Columbia Granger's Index to Poetry.* 11th ed. *The Columbia Granger's World of Poetry,* Columbia University Press, 2005 (http://www.columbiagrangers.org). *The Gambit Book of Love Poems.* Geoffrey Grigson, ed. Gambit, 1973. *The Kingfisher Book of Children's Poetry.* Michael Rosen, ed. Kingfisher Books, 1985. *The Naked Astronaut: Poems on Birth and Birthdays.* Ren Graziani, ed. Faber and Faber, 1983. *The New Yorker Book of Poems.* The New Yorker editors. Viking Press, 1969. *The Oxford Companion to English Literature.* 6th edition. Margaret Drabble, ed. Oxford University Press, 2000. *Who's Who.* London: A & C Black, 2005.

MITCHISON, LADY NAOMI (1897–1999)

She was born in Edinburgh, the daughter of a physiologist, John Scott Haldane. Her mother was a suffragist and Naomi grew up as a freethinking feminist. She studied science at Oxford University but left in 1915 to become a Voluntary Aid Detachment nurse, and in 1916 she married the barrister Gilbert Mitchison (1890–1970). He was the Labor member of Parliament for Kettering Division, Northants, from 1945 to 1964, and was created a life peer in 1964. Mitchison visited the USA in the 1930s to see how the working class, poor and minorities were faring. She was adopted as adviser and Mmarona (mother) of the Bakgatha tribe of Botswana in the sixties. During her life she published over 70 historical novels and short-stories. Her novel *We Have Been Warned* (1935), which dealt with abortion and birth control, was censored. She was created Commander of the British Empire in 1985. From 1937 she lived at Carradale in Kintyre, Scotland, where she died. Some of her poems: "1943," "Dick and Colin at the Salmon Nets," "My True Love Hath My Heart," "Tennessee Snow,"

"The Boar of Badenoch and the Sow of Atholl," "The Farm Woman: 1942," "Woman Alone."

Sources: *Biography of Lady Naomi Mitchison* (http://www.spartacus.schoolnet.co.uk/Wmitchison.htm). *Chaos of the Night: Women's Poetry and Verse of the Second World War.* Catherine W. Reilly, ed. Virago Press, 1984. *Love's Witness: Five Centuries of Love Poetry by Women.* Jill Hollis, ed. Carroll and Graf, Inc., 1993. *Naomi Mitchison—a queen, a saint and a shaman* (http://www.guardian.co.uk/Columnists/Column/0,5673,320853,00.html). *Papers of Lady Naomi Mitchison* (http://www.archiveshub.ac.uk/news/0501mitchison.html). *Poems of the Scottish Hills: An Anthology.* Hamish Brown, ed. Aberdeen University Press, 1982. *The Oxford Companion to English Literature.* 6th edition. Margaret Drabble, ed. Oxford University Press, 2000. *Women's Poetry of the 1930s: A Critical Anthology.* Jane Dowson, ed. Routledge, 1966.

MOIR, DAVID MACBETH (1798–1851)

One of the Scottish doctor poets, he was born at Musselburgh, East Lothian, and practiced there for most of his life. Using the pseudonym "Delta," he was a regular contributor to *Constable's Edinburgh Magazine* and to *Blackwood's Magazine, Fraser* and the *Edinburgh Literary Gazette.* His first professional publication was *Outlines of the Ancient History of Medicine* (1831). After an outbreak of cholera in the town he published several works on cholera. In 1851, he published *Antiquities of the Parish of Inveresk.* Following an accident, he died at Dumfries and was buried at Inveresk, East Lothian. A statue was erected in 1854 on the bank of the Esk, within Musselburgh. Some of his poetry publications: *The Bombardment of Algiers, and Other Poems,* 1818. *The Legend of Genevieve, with Other Tales and Poems,* 1824. *Domestic Verses,* 1843 (a volume of elegies prompted by the deaths of three of his children). *The Poetical Literature of the Past Half Century,* 1851. Some of his poems: "Eventide," "Flodden Field," "Hawthornden" (see Drummond, William of Hawthornden), "Spring Hymn," "The Dying Spaniel," "The Lost Lamb," "The Soldier's Grave."

Sources: *Biography of David Moir. Significant and Famous Scots* (http://www.electricscotland.com/history/other/moir_david.htm). *Dictionary of National Biography.* Electronic Edition 1.1. Oxford University Press, 1997. *English Poetry: Author Search.* Chadwyck-Healey Ltd., 1995 (http://www.lib.utexas.edu:8080/search/epoetry/author.html). *The Oxford Companion to English Literature.* 6th edition. Margaret Drabble, ed. Oxford University Press, 2000.

MONKHOUSE, WILLIAM COSMO (1840–1901)

Born in London, the son of a solicitor and a mother of Huguenot descent, he was educated at St. Paul's School. In his career at the Board of Trade, he worked his way up to assistant secretary of the finance department. From 1894 to 1896 he was a member of the committee on the Mercantile Marine Fund. In 1869 he published *Masterpieces of English Art* and in 1877 a *Handbook of Précis Writing.* "As a critic he had the happy faculty of conveying a well-considered and weighty opinion without suggesting superiority or patronage" (DNB). He wrote many poems, including limericks. He died at Skegness, Lincolnshire. Some of his poetry publications: *A Dream of Idleness, and Other Poems,* 1865. *Corn and Poppies,* 1890. *The Christ Upon the Hill: A Ballad,* 1895. *Nonsense Rhymes,* 1901. *Pasiteles the Elder and Other Poems,* 1901. Some of his limerick/poems: "A Lady There was of Antigua," "The Poor Benighted Hindoo," "There Once was a Girl of New York," "There was a Young Girl of Lahore," "There Was a Young Lady of Niger," "There was a Young Lady of Riga," "There were Three Young Women of Birmingham."

Sources: *A Century of Humorous Verse, 1850–1950.* Roger Lancelyn Green, ed. E.P. Dutton (Everyman's Library), 1959. *Book-Song.* Gleeson White, ed. Elliot Stock, 1893. *Dictionary of National Biography.* Electronic Edition 1.1. Oxford University Press, 1997. *Invitation to Poetry: A Round of Poems from John Skelton to Dylan Thomas.* Lloyd Frankenberg, Doubleday, 1956. *The National Portrait Gallery* (www.npg.org.uk). *The Columbia Granger's Index to Poetry.* 11th ed. *The Columbia Granger's World of Poetry,* Columbia University Press, 2005 (http://www.columbiagrangers.org). *The Home Book of Verse.* Burton Egbert Stevenson, ed. New York: Henry Holt and Company, 1953. *The New Oxford Book of Victorian Verse.* Christopher Ricks, ed. Oxford University Press, 1987.

MONRO, HAROLD EDWARD (1879–1932)

Born in Belgium, the son of a Scottish civil engineer, he was educated at Radley College, Oxfordshire, then graduated in medieval and modern languages from Gonville and Caius College, Cambridge, in 1901. He passed the fist part of his law exams, but gave up law in 1903 to marry. Thereafter he was a poultry farmer in Ireland, a publisher in Surrey, and a mill-owner in Switzerland. On the outbreak of World War I he became an officer in an anti-aircraft battery, but was later drafted for duty in the War Office. In 1913 he founded the Poetry Bookshop in London and started a series of readings by poets of their own works or of their favorite poets, which continued up to the time of his death. He published Sir Edward Marsh's five volumes of *Georgian Poetry* (1911–1922) and various other volumes of poetry. Crippled by increasing ill health and pain in his last two years of his life, he died at Broadstairs, Kent. Some of his poems: "Midnight Lamentation," "Milk for the Cat," "Officers' Mess," "Strange Meetings," "The Bird at Dawn," "The Nightingale Near the House," "Youth in Arms."

Sources: *101 Favorite Cat Poems*. Sara L. Whittier, ed. Contemporary Books, 1991. *British Poetry 1880–1920: Edwardian Voices*. Paul L. Wiley and Harold Orel, eds. Appleton-Century-Crofts, 1969. *Dictionary of National Biography*. Electronic Edition 1.1. Oxford University Press, 1997. *Biography of Harold Munro* (http://www.infoplease.com/ce6/people/A0833767.html). *Modern British Poetry*. 7th rev. ed. Louis Untermeyer, ed. Harcourt, Brace, 1962. *Strange Meetings by Monro, Harold*. The Poetry Bookshop, 1921. *The Columbia Granger's Index to Poetry*. 11th ed. *The Columbia Granger's World of Poetry*, Columbia University Press, 2005 (http://www.columbiagrangers.org). *The Oxford Book of Modern Verse, 1892–1935*. William Butler Yeats, ed. Oxford University Press, 1936. *The Oxford Companion to English Literature*. 6th edition. Margaret Drabble, ed. Oxford University Press, 2000.

MONSELL, JOHN SAMUEL BEWLEY (1811–1875)

Irish clergyman, the son of Thomas Bewley Monsell, Archdeacon of Londonderry, was born at St. Colombs, Londonderry, and graduated doctor of laws from Trinity College, Dublin, in 1856. He was ordained in 1834 and served as a minister in Ireland and in England. He was Rector of St. Nicholas, Guildford, and died after falling from the roof of his church while repairing it. He was a prolific hymnwriter; several of his books ran to many editions and his hymns have been included in many hymnbooks. Some of his 11 volumes of hymns and poetry publications: *Hymns and Miscellaneous Poems*, 1837. *Parish Musings, or Devotional Poems*, 1850. *Hymns of Love and Praise for the Church's Year*, 1863. *The Passing Bell, and Other Poems*, 1869. *Nursery Carols*, 1873. *The Parish Hymnal*, 1873. *Simon the Cyrenian, and Other Poems*, 1876. Some of his hymn/poems: "Daughter of Christian England" (a poem on Miss Nightingale's mission to Scutari), "Fight the Good Fight with All Thy Might," "O Worship the Lord in the Beauty of Holiness," "Rest of the Weary," "Sing to the Lord of Harvest."

Sources: *A Treasury of Poems for Worship and Devotion*. Charles L. Wallis, ed. Harper, 1959. *Biography of J.S.B. Monsell* (http://www.stempublishing.com/hymns/authors/monsell). *Dictionary of National Biography*. Electronic Edition, 1.1. *The Columbia Granger's Index to Poetry*. 11th ed. *The Columbia Granger's World of Poetry*, Columbia University Press, 2005 (http://www.columbiagrangers.org). *The Cyber Hymnal* (http://www.cyberhymnal.org/index.htm).

MONTAGU, CHARLES, EARL OF HALIFAX (1661–1715)

Born at Horton, Northamptonshire, he was the son of George Montagu and grandson of the first Earl of Manchester. Educated at Westminster School and Trinity College, Cambridge, where he formed a lifelong friendship with Isaac Newton and from where he graduated M.A. sometime before 1684. He was a member of Parliament for Maldon from 1689 to 1695, and in 1689 became one of the clerks of the Privy Council. He established the Bank of England in 1694, was appointed Chancellor of the Exchequer, and in 1697 became first lord of the treasury and leader of the House of Commons. In 1714 he was created an earl, but died after only seven months in office. He was buried in the Chapel of Henry VII, Westminster Abbey, in the vault of General Monck (1608–1670). Some of his poems: "An Epistle to the Right Honourable Charles Earl of Dorset and Middlesex," "Ode on the Marriage of Her Royal Highness The Princess Anne, and Prince George of Denmark," "On the Death of His Most Sacred Majesty King Charles II," "The Fable of the Pot and the Kettle," "The Man of Honour."

Sources: *Anthology of Poems on Affairs of State: Augustan Satirical Verse, 1660–1714*. George de F. Lord, ed. Yale University Press, 1975. *Dictionary of National Biography*. Electronic Edition 1.1. Oxford University Press, 1997. *Encyclopædia Britannica Ultimate Reference Suite DVD*, 2006. *English Poetry: Author Search*. Chadwyck-Healey Ltd., 1995 (http://www.lib.utexas.edu:8080/search/epoetry/author.html). *The National Portrait Gallery* (www.npg.org.uk). *Westminster Abbey Official Guide* (no date).

MONTAGU, LADY MARY WORTLEY (1689–1762)

She was born in London to Evelyn Pierrepont, the wealthy Earl of Kingston, where she became a friend of Mary Astell, the defender of woman's rights (see entry). In 1712, she secretly married Edward Worley Montagu, a Whig member of Parliament. When Alexander Pope (see entry) professed his love for her and she rejected him, Pope satirized her in several poems, and she responded equally acrimoniously. From around 1736 — her marriage having broken down — she lived in France and Italy and when her husband died in 1761, she returned to London where, within months, she died of breast cancer. A cenotaph was erected to her memory in Lichfield Cathedral, Staffordshire, commemorating her introduction of inoculation for smallpox, which she had seen used in Turkey, where her husband had been ambassador in 1716. Her three main publications: *Encheiridion*, (a translation of 1710, Epictetus from the Latin). *Town Eclogues*, 1716. *Letters from the East*, 1763. Some of her poems: "Cease, fond shepherd — cease desiring," "Epistle from Mrs. Yonge to Her Husband," "Farewell to Bath," "The Lady's Resolve," "Tho' I never get possession," "To a Lady Making Love."

Sources: *A Treasury of Minor British Poetry*. J. Churton Collins, ed. Edward Arnold, 1896. *Dictionary of National Biography*. Electronic Edition 1.1. Oxford University Press, 1997. *Eighteenth-Century English Verse*. Dennis Davison, ed. Penguin Books, 1988. *Encyclopædia Britannica Ultimate Reference Suite DVD*, 2006. *The National Portrait Gallery* (www.npg.org.uk). *The Columbia Granger's Index to Poetry.* 11th ed. *The Columbia Granger's World of Poetry,* Columbia University Press, 2005 (http://www.columbiagrangers.org). *The Norton Anthology of Poetry.* 4th ed. Margaret Ferguson, Mary Jo Salter and Jon Stal, eds. W.W. Norton, 1996. *The Oxford Companion to English Literature.* 6th edition. Margaret Drabble, ed. Oxford University Press, 2000. *The Treasury of English Poetry.* Mark Caldwell and Walter Kendrick, eds. Doubleday, 1984. *The Women Poets in English: An Anthology.* Ann Stanford, ed. McGraw-Hill, 1972.

MONTAGUE, JOHN (1929–)

Born in Brooklyn, New York, the son of an exiled Ulster Catholic Irish volunteer who fled Ireland after involvement in ambushes and house-burning, John was sent to Ireland in 1933 to be raised by his aunts in Garvaghey (near Fivemiletown), County Tyrone. He was educated at St. Patrick's College, Armagh, and University College Dublin. In 1953, he left Ireland for Yale on a Fulbright Fellowship and returned in 1956 to work at the Irish Tourist Office, then was Paris correspondent for the *Irish Times.* He has taught in Berkeley, New York, Paris, and Ireland. In 1987, New York's governor, Mario Cuomo, presented Montague with a citation for his literary achievements and contributions to the people of New York, and in 1998 he was elected the first Ireland Professor of Poetry. Some of his poetry publications: *Mount Eagle,* 1989. *The Love Poems,* 1992. *Time in Armagh,* 1993. *Collected Poems,* 1995. Some of his poems: "A Chosen Light," "Border Sick Call," "Ó Riada's Farewell," "The Cave of Night," "The Dead Kingdom," "The Hag of Beare," "Time in Armagh," "Wild Sports of the West."

Sources: *Arts Council of Northern Ireland. Appointment of John Montague, on May 14, 1998, as the first Ireland Professor of Poetry.* (http://www.albany.edu/writers-inst/jmaward.html). *Bitter Harvest: An Anthology of Contemporary Irish Verse.* John Montague, ed. Scribner's, 1989. *The Book of Irish Verse: An Anthology of Irish Poetry from the Sixth Century to the Present.* John Montague, ed. Macmillan, 1974. *John Montague—Poetry Irish culture and customs—World Cultures* (http://www.irishcultureandcustoms.com/Poetry/Montague.html). *Modern Irish Poetry.* Patrick Crotty, ed. The Blackstaff Press, 1995. *Poemhunter* (www.poemhunter.com). *The Book of Irish Verse: An Anthology of Irish Poetry from the Sixth Century to the Present.* John Montague, ed. Macmillan, 1974. *The Columbia Granger's Index to Poetry.* 11th ed. *The Columbia Granger's World of Poetry,* Columbia University Press, 2005 (http://www.columbiagrangers.org). *The Faber Book of Contemporary Irish Poetry.* Paul Muldoon ed. Faber and Faber, 1986. *The New Penguin Book of English Verse.* Paul Keegan, ed. Penguin Books, 2000.

MONTGOMERIE, ALEXANDER (?1556–?1610)

The dates of this Scottish poet, the son of Hugh Montgomerie of Hazelhead Castle, Ayrshire, are ob-

scure; those given are from the DNB. He was the laureate of the court of James VI around 1577. In 1586 he was given royal permission to leave Scotland to visit France, Flanders, Spain, and other countries. However, somewhere between Gravesend and the Netherlands his ship was captured and he spent some time in prison, possibly in Holland. His popular poem "The Cherrie and the Slae" secured him a place in the literature of Scotland. With 114 stanzas, it is a moral allegory, in which Virtue is represented by the cherry and Vice by the sloe. His sonnets throw light on the poet's life and character, although some are marred by their obsequious flattery. Some of his other poems: "A Lang Guidnicht," "Adieu to His Mistress," "Against the God of Love," "An Admonition to Young Lassies," "Ane Dreame," "Away Vane World," "Psalm 128," "Psalm 2," "Psalm 23," "The Commendatione of Love," "The Song of Simeon," "To His Majestie," "To the Blessed Trinity."

Sources: *Alexander Montgomerie and the Netherlands, 1586–89* (http://www2.arts.gla.ac.uk/SESLL/STELLA/COMET/glasgrev/issue1/lyall.htm). *Alexander Montgomerie: A Selection From His Songs and Poems.* Helena M. Shire, ed. The Saltire Society, 1960. *Dictionary of National Biography.* Electronic Edition 1.1. Oxford University Press, 1997. *Encyclopædia Britannica Ultimate Reference Suite DVD,* 2006. *The Cherrie and the Slae by Alexander Montgomerie.* H Harvey Wood, ed. Faber and Faber Ltd., 1937. First printed by Robert Waldegrave, 1597. For the whole poem see (http://www.scotstext.org/makars/alexander_montgomerie/). *The Columbia Granger's Index to Poetry.* 11th ed. *The Columbia Granger's World of Poetry,* Columbia University Press, 2005 (http://www.columbiagrangers.org). *The Golden Treasury of Scottish Poetry.* Hugh MacDiarmid, ed. Macmillan, 1941. *The Oxford Companion to English Literature.* 6th edition. Margaret Drabble, ed. Oxford University Press, 2000.

MONTGOMERY, JAMES (1771–1854)

He was born at Irvine in Ayrshire, where his father was pastor of the only Moravian congregation in Scotland. In 1783, his parents went as missionaries to the West Indies leaving James at the Moravian school at Fulneck, near Leeds; by 1791 both his parents were dead. In 1792 he began work as a clerk and bookkeeper for the *Sheffield Register.* He quickly became the editor, then in 1795, the owner, the name having been changed to the *Sheffield Iris.* He endured two short terms of imprisonment for indiscreet articles in the paper. Much of his life was devoted to religious and philanthropic undertakings, and he was honored by a public funeral. A monument was erected over his grave in the Sheffield cemetery. He was a prolific writer of both hymns and poems. Many of his hymns can be found in modern hymnbooks. Some of his publications:

Prison Amusements, 1797. *The Wanderer of Switzerland*, 1806. *Greenland and Other Poems*, 1819. *The Christian Psalmist*, 1825. Some of his hymn/poems: "Angels from the Realms of Glory," "Forever with the Lord," "The Ages of Man," "The Daisy in India."

Sources: *Dictionary of National Biography*. Electronic Edition 1.1. Oxford University Press, 1997. *Encyclopædia Britannica Ultimate Reference Suite DVD*, 2006. *English Poetry: Author Search*. Chadwyck-Healey Ltd., 1995 (http://www.lib.utexas.edu:8080/search/epoetry/author.html). *The National Portrait Gallery* (www.npg.org.uk). *Prison Amusement by James Mongomery* (http://freespace.virgin.net/cade.york/castle/prison5.htm). *The Columbia Granger's Index to Poetry*. 11th ed. *The Columbia Granger's World of Poetry*, Columbia University Press, 2005 (http://www.columbiagrangers.org). *The Cyber Hymnal* (http://www.cyberhymnal.org/index.htm). *The Home Book of Verse*. Burton Egbert Stevenson, ed. New York: Henry Holt and Company, 1953. *The New Oxford Book of Romantic Period Verse*. Jerome J. McGann. Oxford University Press, 1993. *The Poetical Works of James Montgomery, Vol. 2*. Longman, Orme, Brown, Green, 1841. *The Poetical Works of James Montgomery, Vol. 3*. Longman, Orme, Brown, Green, 1841.

MOORE, EDWARD (1712–1757)

He was born at Abingdon, Oxfordshire; when his clergyman father died, he was brought up by his uncle, John Moore, a schoolmaster at Bridgwater, Somerset. Edward eventually owned his own textile business in London and wrote poetry in his spare time. He was editor of the weekly *The World* from 1753 until it closed in 1757. The paper, whose contributors were well known society figures, satirized the vices and follies of fashionable society. He died in poverty and was buried in the South Lambeth parish graveyard without even a stone to mark the spot. He published several plays; *The Foundling* was staged at the Theatre Royal, Drury Lane, on 13 February 1747. His major poetical works are *Fables for the Female Sex* (1744) and *Poems, Fables, and Plays* (1756). Some of his poems: "Envy and Fortune," "Love and Vanity," "The Colt and the Farmer," "The Eagle and the Assembly of Birds," "The Farmer, the Spaniel, and the Cat," "The Goose and the Swans," "The Nightingale and Glow-Worm," "The Owl and the Nightingale," "The Poet and His Patron," "The Young Lion and the Ape."

Sources: *Eighteenth-Century English Verse*. Dennis Davison, ed. Penguin Books, 1988. *English Poetry: Author Search*. Chadwyck-Healey Ltd., 1995 (http://www.lib.utexas.edu:8080/search/epoetry/author.html). *The Columbia Granger's Index to Poetry*. 11th ed. *The Columbia Granger's World of Poetry*, Columbia University Press, 2005 (http://www.columbiagrangers.org). *The Oxford Companion to English Literature*. 6th edition. Margaret Drabble, ed. Oxford University Press, 2000. *The Penguin Book of Bird Poetry*. Peggy Munsterberg, ed. 1984. *The Poetical Works of*

Edward Moore and David Mallet. Thomas Park, ed. J. Sharpe, 1808.

MOORE, SIR JOHN HENRY (1756–1780)

Born in Jamaica, the son of Sir Henry Moore, he succeeded to the title in 1769 while still at Eton. He graduated M.A. from Emmanuel College, Cambridge, in 1776. Moore spent much of his time at Bath, Somerset, and died unmarried at Taplow, Buckinghamshire, when the title became extinct. His first volume of poetry, *The New Paradise of Dainty Devices* (1777), published anonymously, was sneered at in the *Critical Review* (43, 233). Moore retaliates in the poem "Palinode to the Reviewers." His book was reissued in 1778 as *Poetical Trifles*, and a third edition appeared in 1783, edited by his friend Edward Jerningham (see entry). His poem "Elegy Written in a College Library" is a parody of Thomas Gray's "Elegy Written in a Country Church-Yard" and "Hastings" commemorates the famous battle of 1066. Some of his other poems: "Absence, An Elegy," "Indeed, My Caelia, 'Tis in Vain," "The Chelsea Pensioner," "The Cock and the Horses, A Fable," "The Duke of Benevento."

Sources: *Dictionary of National Biography*. Electronic Edition 1.1. Oxford University Press, 1997. *English Poetry: Author Search*. Chadwyck-Healey Ltd., 1995 (http://www.lib.utexas.edu:8080/search/epoetry/author.html). *Stanford University Libraries and Academic Information Resources* (http://library.stanford.edu). *The Columbia Granger's Index to Poetry*. 11th ed. *The Columbia Granger's World of Poetry*, Columbia University Press, 2005 (http://www.columbiagrangers.org). *The Oxford Book of Eighteenth Century Verse*. David Nichol Smith, ed. Oxford University Press, 1926.

MOORE, NICHOLAS (1918–1986)

Born in Cambridge, the son of George Edward Moore 1873–1958, Cambridge philosopher, he studied classics at St. Andrews University and Trinity College, Cambridge. Most of his verse was published during World War II, in which he was a conscientious objector. He is one of the "New Apocalypse" English poets of the 1940s who reacted against the preoccupation with social and political issues of the 1930s by turning toward romanticism. *The Glass Tower*, a selected poems collection from 1944, appeared with illustrations by Lucien Freud. He edited poetry magazines in London, then in the 1950s, experiencing difficulty getting published, dropped out for a while. He turned his attention to horticulture and published a gardening book, *The Tall Bearded Iris* (1956). In 1968 he entered a competition for the *Sunday Times* with 31 different translations of Baudelaire's poem *Paris Spleen*. The resulting book, *Spleen*, is available online. Some of his poems: "Act of Love," "Alcestis in Ely," "Fred Apollus at Fava's,"

"Ideas of Disorder at Torquay," "Incidents in Play-fair House," "The Hair's-Breadth," "The Island and the Cattle," "The Phallic Symbol," "Winter and Red Berries."

Sources: *Anthology of Twentieth-Century British and Irish Poetry.* Keith Tuma, ed. Oxford University Press, 2001. *Encyclopædia Britannica Ultimate Reference Suite DVD,* 2006. *Erotic Poetry: The Lyrics, Ballads, Idylls, and Epics of Love—Classical to Contemporary.* William Cole, ed. Random House, 1963. *The New British Poets: An Anthology.* Kenneth Rexroth, ed. New Directions, 1949. *The Poetry Anthology, 1912–1977.* Daryl Hine, and Joseph Parisi, ed. Houghton Mifflin, 1978. *Wikipedia, the Free Encyclopedia* (http://en.wikipedia.org/wiki/Wikipedia).

MOORE, THOMAS (1779–1852)

Ireland's national poet was born in Dublin, the son of a grocer and wine merchant. Educated at Trinity College, Dublin, he studied law in London. Appointed admiralty registrar at Bermuda in 1803, he left his deputy in charge and set off on a tour of the United States and Canada. The deputy embezzled a large sum of money, resulting in Moore's falling into debt, which took years to pay back. He was a good musician and skillful writer of highly popular and often patriotic songs. He died in Wiltshire. His long romance, *Lalla Rookh* (1817), earned him the distinction of being paid the highest sum to date for a single poem. He wrote close to 1000 poems, songs, and hymns. Some of his publications: *Odes and Epistles,* 1806. *Irish Melodies,* 1807 to 1834 (with music by Sir John Stevenson). *The Twopenny Post Bag,* 1813. *Letters and Journals of Lord Byron,* 1830. Some of his song/poems: "'Tis the Last Rose of Summer," "Believe Me, If All Those Endearing Young Charms," "Oft in the Stilly Night," "The Harp That Once Through Tara's Halls," "The Minstrel Boy."

Sources: *British Minstrelsie.* T.C. and E.C. Jack, Grange Publishing Works, Edinburgh (?1900). *Dictionary of National Biography.* Electronic Edition 1.1. Oxford University Press, 1997. *Encyclopædia Britannica Ultimate Reference Suite DVD,* 2006. *English Poetry: Author Search.* Chadwyck-Healey Ltd., 1995 (http://www.lib.utexas.edu:8080/search/epoetry/author.html). *Biography of Thomas Moore* (http://www.kirjasto.sci.fi/tmoore.htm). *The Best Loved Poems of the American People.* Hazel Felleman, ed. Doubleday, 1936. *The Book of Irish Verse: An Anthology of Irish Poetry from the Sixth Century to the Present.* John Montague, ed. Macmillan, 1974. *The Columbia Granger's Index to Poetry.* 11th ed. *The Columbia Granger's World of Poetry,* Columbia University Press, 2005 (http://www.columbiagrangers.org). *The Complete Poems of Sir Thomas Moore.* William M. Rossetti, ed. A.L. Burt Company, 1910. *The Cyber Hymnal* (http://www.cyberhymnal.org/index.htm). *The New Oxford Book of Irish Verse.* Thomas Kinsella, ed. Oxford University Press, 1986. *The World's Great Religious Poetry.* Caroline Miles Hill, ed. Macmillan, 1954.

MORE, DAME GERTRUDE (1606–1633)

Born Helen, she was the daughter of Cresacre More and granddaughter of Sir Thomas More "The Blessed" (1478–1535), lord chancellor of England. In 1625 Helen pronounced her vows as a Benedictine nun of the English Congregation of Our Ladies of Comfort in Cambray, France, and changed her name to Gertrude. She died of smallpox. *The Spiritual Exercises of the Most Virtuous and Religious D. Gertrude More* were published from her manuscripts in Paris in 1658 and in London in 1873. She is known to have written only two poems: "A Dittie to the Same Subject," in which she dwells upon the Cruxifiction; and "A Short Oblation of This Smal Work by the Writer Gatherer Thereof to Our Most Sweet and Merciful God," in which she dedicates herself to God, possibly written when she took her vows.

Sources: *Dictionary of National Biography.* Electronic Edition 1.1. Oxford University Press, 1997. *Early Modern Women Poets (1520–1700).* Jane Stevenson and Peter Davidson, ed. Oxford University Press, 2001. *The Columbia Granger's Index to Poetry.* 11th ed. *The Columbia Granger's World of Poetry,* Columbia University Press, 2005 (http://www.columbiagrangers.org).

MORE, HANNAH (1745–1833)

Born at Stapleton, Gloucestershire, she was educated at home and at her sisters' school in Bristol, where she acquired mathematics, Italian, Spanish, and Latin. In 1773, she published *The Inflexible Captive*—a translation from Metastasio's *Regulus,* and in 1762, a pastoral drama, *The Search after Happiness.* In London she was friendly with many prominent figures, including Dr. Johnson, David and Mrs. Garrick, and all the Blue Stocking ladies. Her poem "Sir Eldred of the Bower" (1776) earned her a substantial fee. One of her plays, *Percy,* produced at Covent Garden in December 1777, resulted in the charge of plagiarism by Hannah Cowley (see entry). She went on to write many more plays and serious works often of a religious, moral or political nature and was involved in setting up Sunday schools. She died at Bristol. Some of her poems: "A Christmas Hymn," "Faith and Works, A Tale," "Ode to Charity," "Patient Joe; or, The Newcastle Collier," "Resolution," "Slavery, a Poem," "The Bas Bleu; Or, Conversation," "The Gin-Shop; A Peep into Prison," "The Sorrows of Yamba, or the Negro Woman's Lamentation."

Sources: *Dictionary of National Biography.* Electronic Edition 1.1. Oxford University Press, 1997. *Eighteenth Century Women Poets: An Oxford Anthology.* Roger Lonsdale, ed. Oxford University Press, 1989. *Encyclopædia Britannica Ultimate Reference Suite DVD,* 2006. *English Poetry:*

Author Search (http://www.lib.utexas.edu:8080/search/epoetry/author.html). *The National Portrait Gallery* (www.npg.org.uk). *The Columbia Granger's Index to Poetry.* 11th ed. *The Columbia Granger's World of Poetry,* Columbia University Press, 2005 (http://www.columbiagrangers.org). *The Oxford Companion to English Literature.* 6th edition. Margaret Drabble, ed. Oxford University Press, 2000. *The Poetical Works of Hannah More.* Scott, Webster, and Geary, 1835.

MORE, HENRY (1614–1687)

Born into a strong Calvinist family from Grantham, Lincolnshire, he was educated at Eton College School and at Christ's College, Cambridge. He graduated M.A. in 1639, the same year as he was ordained and elected a fellow, then spent almost the whole of his life at Christ's College, preferring a life of solitude and contemplation and music. He was one of the Cambridge Platonists, a group of anti-Calvinist divines who strove to establish a strictly rational basis for ethics and religion based on Plato's philosophy. Although More shrank from political controversy, he did not hesitate to use the church liturgy both in public and private when during the Commonwealth it was a crime to do so. He wrote poetry, hymns, and deeply religious and philosophical works. He died at Cambridge and was buried in the Christ's College chapel. In 1647, he published *Philosophical Poems,* and his *Divine Hymns* were published in 1706. Some of his poems: "A Platonick Song of the Soul," "Charity and Humility," "Cupids Conflict," "Devotion," "Eternal Life," "Psychozoia, or, the Life of the Soul," "Resolution," "The Oracle."

Sources: *A Sacrifice of Praise: An Anthology of Christian Poetry in English from Caedmon to the Mid–Twentieth Century.* James H. Trott, ed. Cumberland House Publishing, 1999. *Dictionary of National Biography.* Electronic Edition 1.1. Oxford University Press, 1997. *English Poetry: Author Search.* Chadwyck-Healey Ltd., 1995 (http://www.lib.utexas.edu:8080/search/epoetry/author.html). *The National Portrait Gallery* (www.npg.org.uk). *Seventeenth-Century Verse and Prose, Vol. II: 1660–1700.* Helen C. White, et al., ed. Macmillan. 1951, 1952. *Stanford University Libraries and Academic Information Resources* (http://library.stanford.edu). *The Columbia Granger's Index to Poetry.* 11th ed. *The Columbia Granger's World of Poetry,* Columbia University Press, 2005 (http://www.columbiagrangers.org). *The New Oxford Book of Seventeenth Century Verse.* Alastair Fowler, ed. Oxford University Press, 1991. *The Oxford Book of Christian Verse.* Lord David Cecil, ed. Oxford University Press, 1940. *The Oxford Companion to English Literature.* 6th edition. Margaret Drabble, ed. Oxford University Press, 2000. *The Treasury of Religious Verse.* Donald T. Kauffman, ed. Fleming H. Revell, 1962.

MORGAN, EDWIN GEORGE (1920–)

Born in Glasgow, his time at Glasgow University was interrupted by wartime service in the Royal Army Medical Corps. He graduated in 1947 and became a lecturer at the university and was professor of English from 1975 until his retirement in 1980. In 1999, Morgan was made the first Glasgow Poet Laureate, and in 2004, the first Scottish National Poet. He was one of the "Big Seven"—George Mackay Brown, Robert Garioch, Norman MacCaig, Hugh MacDiarmid, Sorley MacLean and Iain Crichton Smith (see entries). His *A.D. A Trilogy of Plays on the Life of Jesus* (2000) led to controversy with church leaders. He has been awarded seven honorary degrees and the Order of Merit from Hungary. His other awards: PEN Memorial Medal (Hungary), 1972; Order of the British Empire, 1982; Soros Translation Award (New York), 1985; Stakis Prize for Scottish Writer of the Year, 1998. Some of his other publications: *The Vision of Cathkin Braes,* 1952. *A Second Life,* 1968. *From Glasgow to Saturn,* 1973. *Collected Poems,* 1990. Some of his poems: "From the Domain of Arnheim," "Sonnets from Scotland," "The Loch Ness Monster's Song."

Sources: *In Quest of the Miracle Stag: The Poetry of Hungary.* Adam Makkai, ed. Atlantic-Centaur, Corvina, 1996. *Poems for the Millennium: The University of California Book of Modern and Postmodern Poetry, Vol. 2.* Jerome Rothenberg and Pierre Joris, eds. University of California Press, 1998. *The Bloodaxe Book of 20th Century Poetry, from Britain and Ireland.* Edna Longley, ed. Bloodaxe Books, 2000. *The Columbia Granger's Index to Poetry.* 11th ed. *The Columbia Granger's World of Poetry,* Columbia University Press, 2005 (http://www.columbiagrangers.org). *The Oxford Book of Sonnets.* John Fuller, ed. Oxford University Press, 2000. *The Oxford Companion to English Literature.* 6th edition. Margaret Drabble, ed. Oxford University Press, 2000. *Who's Who.* London: A & C Black, 2005. *Wikipedia, the Free Encyclopedia* (http://en.wikipedia.org/wiki/Wikipedia).

MORLEY, THOMAS (?1557/58–1602)

Where he was born is uncertain, but he was one of England's great organists and composer of madrigals. He was a pupil of William Byrd (1540–1623) and possibly a chorister of St. Paul's Cathedral. He graduated bachelor of music from Oxford in 1588 and was organist at St. Giles, Cripplegate, then at St. Paul's in London. He was also master of the children at Norwich Cathedral and one of the gentleman of the Chapel Royal. In 1598 he was granted a patent, similar to that previously held by Byrd, by which he enjoyed the exclusive right of printing books of music and selling ruled paper. That he was an outstanding musician is not in doubt, but at the time he was accused of plagiarizing the works of other composers. Between 1593 and 1600 he published six major volumes of song or madrigals and edited many more. Some of his poems: "In Nets of Golden Wires," "Ladies, You See time Flieth," "No, No, Nigella!" "On a Fair Morning," "Sing We and

Chant It," "You Black Bright Stars," "See, See, Mine Own Sweet Jewel."

Sources: *Dictionary of National Biography.* Electronic Edition 1.1. Oxford University Press, 1997. *Encyclopædia Britannica Ultimate Reference Suite DVD,* 2006. *English Poetry: Author Search.* Chadwyck-Healey Ltd., 1995 (http://www.lib.utexas.edu:8080/search/epoetry/author. html). *English Renaissance Poetry: A Collection of Shorter Poems from Skelton to Jonson.* John Williams, ed. University of Arkansas, 1990. *Love in Verse.* Kathleen Blease, ed. Ballantine Publishing Group, 1998. *The Columbia Granger's Index to Poetry.* 11th ed. *The Columbia Granger's World of Poetry,* Columbia University Press, 2005 (http://www.columbiagrangers.org). *The Oxford Companion to English Literature.* 6th edition. Margaret Drabble, ed. Oxford University Press, 2000.

MORRIS, SIR LEWIS (1833–1907)

Welsh poet, born at Carmarthen, where his father — grandson of the poet Lewis Morys (see entry) — was a solicitor. He was educated at Queen Elizabeth's grammar school, Carmarthen, Cowbridge School, South Glamorgan, then at Sherborne College, Dorset. He graduated *literæ humaniores* in 1855 from Jesus College, Oxford, then M.A. in 1858. He was called to the bar in 1861, and practiced, chiefly in conveyance. He published the series, *Songs of Two Worlds* in 1871, with another in 1874, and a third in 1878. In 1878 he became one of the honorary secretaries to the University College of Wales, Aberystwyth, then treasurer, then vice president from 1896 until he died. In 1906 he was awarded the honorary degree of doctor of literature from the recently formed University of Wales, and was knighted in 1895. He died at Penbryn and was buried at Llangunnor, Carmarthan. Some of his poems: "A Heathen Hymn," "At a Country Wedding," "Christmas 1898," "From an American Sermon," "Llyn Y Morwynion," "Lydstep Caverns," "The Beginnings of Faith," "The Epic of Hades," "When I Am Dead."

Sources: *A Treasury of Poems for Worship and Devotion.* Charles L. Wallis, ed. Harper, 1959. *Anglo-Welsh Poetry, 1480–1980.* Raymond Garlick and Roland Mathias, ed. Poetry Wales Press, 1984. *Anglo-Welsh Poetry, 1480–1990.* Raymond Garlick and Roland Mathias, eds. Poetry Wales Press, 1993. *Dictionary of National Biography.* Electronic Edition 1.1. Oxford University Press, 1997. *English Poetry: Author Search.* Chadwyck-Healey Ltd., 1995 (http://www.lib.utexas.edu:8080/search/epoetry/author.html). *Selections from the Works of Sir Lewis Morris.* Kegan Paul, 1897. *The Columbia Granger's Index to Poetry.* 11th cd. *The Columbia Granger's World of Poetry,* Columbia University Press, 2005 (http://www.columbiagrangers.org). *The Oxford Companion to English Literature.* 6th edition. Margaret Drabble, ed. Oxford University Press, 2000.

MORRIS, WILLIAM (1834–1896)

Born to a wealthy family from Walthamstow, Northeast London, he was educated at Marlborough College and Exeter College, Oxford, and was elected fellow in 1883. He was one of the founding members of the firm of Morris, Marshal, Faulkener and Co., producing expensive printed textiles, wallpaper and furniture; the designs of William Morris are still popular more than a century later. In 1877 he founded the Society for the Protection of Ancient Buildings and in 1879 he became treasurer of the National Liberal League. He published many socialist tracts and pamphlets, and his interest in socialism resulted in at least one arrest, though he was released without charge. He died at Hammersmith, London. Some of his poetry publications: *The Defence of Guenevere and Other Poems,* 1858. *The Life and Death of Jason,* 1867. *Books of Verse,* 1879. *Poems by the Way,* 1891. Some of his poems: "Golden Wings," "Love is Enough," "Shameful Death," "The Haystack in the Floods," "The Man Who Never Laughed Again," "The Sweet Valley of Deep Grass," "Two Red Roses across the Moon."

Sources: *Biography and Works of William Morris* (http://www.kirjasto.sci.fi/wmorris.htm). *Dictionary of National Biography.* Electronic Edition 1.1. Oxford University Press, 1997. *Encyclopædia Britannica Ultimate Reference Suite DVD,* 2006. *English Poetry: Author Search.* Chadwyck-Healey Ltd., 1995 (http://www.lib.utexas.edu:8080/search/epoetry/author.html). *Poems of Christmas.* Myra Cohn Livingston, ed. Atheneum, 1980. *Seven Centuries of Poetry: Chaucer to Dylan Thomas.* A.N. Jeffares, ed. Longmans, Green, 1955. *The Collected Works of William Morris* (24 vols). May Morris, ed. Longmans, Green and Company, 1910–1915. *The Columbia Granger's Index to Poetry.* 11th ed. *The Columbia Granger's World of Poetry,* Columbia University Press, 2005 (http://www.columbiagrangers.org). *The Earthly Paradise: A Poem by William Morris.* Longmans, Green, and Co., 1896. *The Oxford Companion to English Literature.* 6th edition. Margaret Drabble, ed. Oxford University Press, 2000. *The Victorian Web* (http://www.victorianweb.org/authors/morris/wmbio.html).

MORRIS-JONES, SIR JOHN (1864–1929)

John Jones was born at Trefor, Llandrygarn, Anglesey, and when he was knighted in 1918, he started styling himself Morris-Jones, after his father. Through a scholarship he went to Jesus College, Oxford, in 1883. He graduated with a third class in the final school of mathematics in 1887, mathematics having given place to Welsh literature. In 1886, Jones and six others founded the Dafydd ap Gwilym Society in Oxford for the discussion of Welsh problems. He was appointed lecturer in Welsh at Bangor University College in 1889, then professor of Welsh in 1895, a post he held until his death. His ode "Cymru Fu, Cymru Fydd," published in 1892, demonstrates his own skill in the ancient technique of the bards and revolutionized Welsh literature by raising the standard of the Welsh language of Eisteddfod poetry. He was given honorary degrees from Glasgow University and from the National University of Ireland. He died after a brief illness at his home at Llanfairpwll, Anglesey, North Wales. In 1928, he published *The Art of Poetry Orgraff yr Iaith Gymraeg*. Some of his poems: "The North Star," "Old Age," "The Wind's Lament."

Sources: *Dictionary of National Biography*. Electronic Edition 1.1. Oxford University Press, 1997. *Encyclopædia Britannica Ultimate Reference Suite DVD*, 2006. *The Columbia Granger's Index to Poetry*. 11th ed. *The Columbia Granger's World of Poetry*, Columbia University Press, 2005 (http://www.columbiagrangers.org). *The Oxford Book of Welsh Verse in English*. Gwyn Jones, ed. Oxford University Press, 1977.

MORRISEY, SINEAD (1972–)

Born in Portadown, Ireland, she read English and German at Trinity College, Dublin, and was awarded her Ph.D. in 2003. In 1990 she received the Patrick Kavanagh Award for Poetry. She lived and worked in Japan and New Zealand and now lives in Northern Ireland. In 2002 she was the Poetry International Writer in Residence at the Royal Festival Hall, London. The British Council selected her to take part in the Writers' Train Project in China in 2003. In 2005, she was awarded the Michael Hartnett Award for Poetry, and in 2006 she was appointed writer in residence at Queen's University, Belfast. Her poetry publications: *There was Fire in Vancouver*, 1996 (for which she won an Eric Gregory Award); *Between Here and There*, 2002 (which was short listed for the T.S. Eliot Award); *The State of the Prisons*, 2005 (this was a Poetry Book Society Recommendation). Some of her poems: "Awaiting Burial," "China," "Driving Alone on a Snowy Evening," "Lullaby," "Monteverdi Vespers," "The Inheriting Meek," "The Yellow Emperor's Classic."

Sources: *British Council Arts* (http://www.contemporarywriters.com). Carcanet Press (http://www.carcanet.co.uk). The Seamus Heaney Centre for Poetry, at the School of English, Queen's University Belfast. *Poems by Sinead Morrissey* (http://www.qub.ac.uk/heaneycentre/research/sinead-listofpoems.htm).

MORUS, HUW (1622–1709)

Welsh poet, was born at Pont y Meibion, in the valley of the Ceiriog, Denbighshire. For most of his life he worked on the family farm and was a warden of the Llansilin parish church, Powys. He won a great reputation as a composer of ballads, carols, and occasional verse. Next to the love poems the most familiar are those on political subjects. A staunch Royalist and a supporter of the Church of England, he satirised the roundhead preachers and soldiers, sometimes in allegory and sometimes without any disguise. In 1660 he wrote "Elegy upon Oliver's Men" and "Welcome to General Monk." He supported William of Orange over James II. He died unmarried and was buried at Llansilin. Poems by Huw Morus were included in the collection of songs printed for Foulk Owens in 1686 and reprinted (as *Carolau a Dyriau Duwiol*) in 1696 and 1729. The Rev. Walter Davies (Gwallter Mechain) published *Eos Ceiriog* (1823) in two volumes, which included 147 poems by Morus. Some of his poems: "Death-Bed Confession," "In Praise of a Girl," "Quick, Death!" "Thick Snow."

Sources: *British Literature to the Restoration* (http://www.tcnj.edu/~graham/LIT251fall05.htm). *Dictionary of National Biography*. Electronic Edition 1.1. Oxford University Press, 1997. *Encyclopædia Britannica Ultimate Reference Suite DVD*, 2006. *George Borrow: Wild Wales*, *CHAPTER XX, Huw Morus* (http://etext.library.adelaide.edu.au/b/borrow/george/wild/chapter20.html). *The Columbia Granger's Index to Poetry*. 11th ed. *The Columbia Granger's World of Poetry*, Columbia University Press, 2005 (http://www.columbiagrangers.org). *The Oxford Book of Welsh Verse in English*. Gwyn Jones, ed. Oxford University Press, 1977. *The Project Gutenberg eBook, A Celtic Psaltery*, by Alfred Perceval, eBook (http://www.gutenberg.org/files/14232/14232.txt).

MORYS, LEWIS (1700–1765)

He was the eldest of the three brothers known as "Morrisiaid Môn" (the Morrises of Anglesey), sons of Richard Morys and grandfather of Sir Lewis Morris (see entry). He was born at Tyddyn Melus in the parish of Llanfihangel, Monmouthshire, but was brought up in Penrhos Llugwy, Anglesey, where education was ordinary and English was a foreign language. He worked as a land surveyor and pioneered a survey of the ports and coastline of Wales. His *Plans of Harbors, Bars, Bays and Roads in St. George's Channel*, which included 25 detailed maps, was published in 1748. In Holyhead, he set up the first printing press in North Wales for the purpose of printing Welsh books and popularizing Welsh literature. He was an authority on the Welsh language and when he died at his home in Goginan, Dyfed, he was working on a new edition of John Davies's (Welsh) *Dictionarium Duplex* (1632) and a collection of Welsh proverbs. He was the author of a large body of light-hearted prose and poetry. Some of his poems: "Poem of the Frost and Snow," "Soul-Music," "The Fishing Lass of Hakin," "The Miner's Ballad."

Sources: *Anglo-Welsh Poetry, 1480–1980*. Raymond Garlick and Roland Mathias, eds. Poetry Wales Press, 1984. *Anglo-Welsh Poetry, 1480–1990*. Raymond Garlick and Roland Mathias, eds. Poetry Wales Press, 1993. *Dictionary of National Biography*. Electronic Edition 1.1. Oxford University Press, 1997. *Lewis Morris, "Tlysau yr Hen Oesoedd."* (http://www.gtj.org.uk/en/item1/14571). *Selections from the Works of Sir Lewis Morris*. Kegan Paul, 1897. *The*

Columbia Granger's Index to Poetry. 11th ed. *The Columbia Granger's World of Poetry*, Columbia University Press, 2005 (http://www.columbiagrangers.org). *The Oxford Book of Welsh Verse in English*. Gwyn Jones, ed. Oxford University Press, 1977.

MOSS, THOMAS (1740–1808)

Not much is known of this poet but that he graduated B.A. in 1761 from Emmanuel College, Cambridge, and after taking holy orders he was a minister in several parishes in Staffordshire and Worcestershire. In 1769 he published *Poems on Several Occasions*. The first poem is the heart-wrenching and popular "Beggar's Petition" to which Jane Austen refers in Chapter 1 of *Northanger Abbey*. Of Catherine Morland, Austen says, "Her mother was three months in teaching her only to repeat the "Beggar's Petition"; and after all, her next sister, Sally, could say it better than she did." The 26 stanzas written in 1766 tell the tale of bereavement and near-starvation. The beggar appeals to William Pitt (the Elder, the Earl of Chatham), who became prime minister in 1766, to alleviate the burden of the poor.

Sources: *Dictionary of National Biography*. Electronic Edition 1.1. Oxford University Press, 1997. *The Beggar's Petition (poem) by Thomas Moss* (http://www.pemberley.com/litcomp/beggar.html). *The Columbia Granger's Index to Poetry*. 11th ed. *The Columbia Granger's World of Poetry*, Columbia University Press, 2005 (http://www.columbiagrangers.org). *The New Oxford Book of Eighteenth Century Verse*. Roger Lonsdale, ed. Oxford University Press, 1984. *The New Oxford Book of Seventeenth Century Verse*. Alastair Fowler, ed. Oxford University Press, 1991.

MOTHERWELL, WILLIAM (1797–1835)

Born in Glasgow, the son of an ironmonger, he was educated in Edinburgh and in Paisley, Renfrewshire. He started work in the office of the sheriff-clerk at Paisley when he was fifteen, then studied classics for a year at Glasgow University. At some stage he was a trooper in the Renfrewshire yeomanry cavalry. From 1919 to 1929 he was deputy sheriff-clerk of Renfrewshire, then editor of the *Paisley Advertiser* before becoming editor of the Orange-Tory paper *Glasgow Courier* in 1830. He was summoned to a special committee in London to give information on Orangeism. He was taken ill at the meeting and died of a stroke soon afterward. Some of his publications: *The Harp of Renfrewshire*, 1819. *Renfrewshire Characters and Scenery*, 1824. *Minstrelsy Ancient and Modern*, 1827. *Poems, Narrative and Lyrical*, 1835 (supplemented and re-edited by William Kennedy [see entry] in 1848). Some of his poems: "And Hae Ye Seen My Ain True Luve?" "Facts From Fairyland," "Jeanie Morrison," "My Ain Countrie," "The Cavalier's Song," "The Covenanter's Battle Chant," "The Trooper's Ditty," "What is This World to Me?"

Sources: *Dictionary of National Biography*. Electronic Edition 1.1. Oxford University Press, 1997. *English Poetry: Author Search*. Chadwyck-Healey Ltd., 1995 (http://www.lib.utexas.edu:8080/search/epoetry/author.html). For information on Orangeism see http://www.findarticles.com/p/articles/mi_m0FKX/is_1–2_39/ai_n6150068. *Golden Numbers*. Kate Douglas Wiggin and Nora Archibald Smith, eds. Doubleday, Doran, 1902. *The Columbia Granger's Index to Poetry*. 11th ed. *The Columbia Granger's World of Poetry*, Columbia University Press, 2005 (http://www.columbiagrangers.org). *The Oxford Companion to English Literature*. 6th edition. Margaret Drabble, ed. Oxford University Press, 2000. *The Poetical Works of William Motherwell*. Alexander Gardner, 1881. *William Motherwell's Cultural Politics* By Mary Ellen Brown. University Press of Kentucky (http://www.kentuckypress.com/viewbook.cfm?Group=13&ID=387). *Wikipedia, the Free Encyclopedia* (http://en.wikipedia.org/wiki/Wikipedia).

MOTION, ANDREW PETER (1952–)

Born in London and educated at Radley College, Oxfordshire, he graduated master of literature in 1977 from University College, Oxford, where he was a student of poet John Fuller (see entry). He taught English at Hull University (1976 to 1981), was editor of *Poetry Review* (1981–83) and poetry editor and editorial director at Chatto and Windus (1983–89). He became professor of creative writing at Royal Holloway, University of London (2003) and poet laureate in (1999). Five universities have awarded him with honorary degrees, and he has received many literary awards. He has edited several anthologies and written biographies and fiction. Some of his poetry publications: *The Poetry of Edward Thomas*, 1980. *Dangerous Play: Poems 1974–1984*, 1984. *Two Poems*, 1988. *Selected Poems by Thomas Hardy*. 1994 (editor). *Selected Poems 1976–1997*, 1998. *101 Poems Against War*, 2003. Some of his poems: "An Elegy on the Death of HM Queen Elizabeth, The Queen Mother," "Anne Frank Huis," "Leaving Belfast," "No News from the Old Country," "Reading the Elephant," "Spring Wedding" (in honor of the wedding of the Prince of Wales and Camilla Parker Bowles).

Sources: *Encyclopædia Britannica Ultimate Reference Suite DVD*, 2006. *Golden Treasury of the Best Songs and Lyrical Poems in the English Language*. Francis Turner Palgrave, ed. Oxford University Press, 1964, xixth edition, updated by John Press, 1994. *The National Portrait Gallery* (www.npg.org.uk). *Some Contemporary Poets of Britain and Ireland: An Anthology*. Michael Schmidt, ed. Carcanet Press, 1983. *The Columbia Granger's Index to Poetry*. 11th ed. *The Columbia Granger's World of Poetry*, Columbia University Press, 2005 (http://www.columbiagrangers.org). *The Direction of Poetry: An Anthology of Rhymed and Metered Verse Written in the English Language since 1975*. Robert Richman, ed. Houghton Mifflin, 1988. *The Harvill Book* of *Twentieth-Century Poetry in English*. Michael Schmidt, ed. The Harvill Press, 1999. *The Oxford Companion to English Literature*. 6th edition. Margaret Drabble, ed. Oxford University Press, 2000. *Who's Who*. London: A & C Black, 2005. *Wikipedia, the Free Encyclopedia* (http://en.wikipedia.org/wiki/Wikipedia).

MOTTRAM, ERIC NOEL WILLIAM (1924–1995)

Born in London, he served in the Royal Navy from 1943 to 1947 and graduated from Pembroke College, Cambridge, in 1950. For the next ten years he taught at schools in Europe and the Far East and in 1960 was appointed lecturer in English and American literature at King's College, London University. In 1963 he co-founded the Institute of United States Studies, which merged with the Institute of Latin American Studies and is now the Institute for the Study of the Americas. He was appointed professor of English and American literature in 1982. His contacts in America with, for example, William Burroughs, and his biography, *William Burroughs: The Algebra of Need* (1971, British edition 1977), helped to introduce the "Beat" writers to British audiences. He retired in 1990 as professor emeritus of English and American literature; he died in London. He published some 35 collections of poetry; the first was *Inside the Whale* (1970) and the last was *Limits of Self-regard* (1998). Some of his poems: "Brief Novel (3)," "Elegy 11: Ford," "Meet in the Corpse," "Peace Project (5)," "Smell of Canyon Rain Storm," "Zuni Dancers."

Sources: *Obituary of Eric Mottram* (http://wings.buffalo.edu/epc/documents/obits/mottram). *Eric Mottram Catalogue, Appendix 2: A Checklist of His Published Poems* (http://www.kcl.ac.uk/kis/archives/mottram/mopoems.htm). Biography of Eric Mottram (http://www.kcl.ac.uk/kis/archives/mottram/motttxt.htm#MOT1). *King's College London College Archives, Eric Mottram Collection* (http://www.kcl.ac.uk/kis/archives/mottram/motttxt.htm#MOT1). *The National Portrait Gallery* (www.npg.org.uk). *Other: British and Irish Poetry since 1970*. Richard Caddel and Peter Quartermain, eds. Wesleyan University Press, 1999. *The New British Poetry, 1968–88*. Gillian Allnutt, Fred D'Aguiar and Ken Edwards, eds. Grafton Books, 1989. *Wikipedia, the Free Encyclopedia* (http://en.wikipedia.org/wiki/Wikipedia).

MOULTRIE, JOHN and GERARD (1799–1885)

John, the father, 1799–1874

Born in London, he was the son of George Moultrie, Shropshire clergyman, and grandson of Governor John Moultrie of Charleston, South Carolina. His great uncle William fought in the War of Independence and features in Thackeray's *Virginians* (1857). In 1776 his successful defense of the fort guarding Charleston harbor against a British fleet made him a national hero, but he was a prisoner of the British from 1780 to 1782. John was educated at Eton College and graduated M.A. from Trinity College, Cambridge, in 1822. He was ordained in 1825 and took the parsonage at Rugby, at the same time as Thomas Arnold was made headmaster. He died at Rugby and was buried in the parish church, to which an aisle was added in his memory. He published non-fiction books and wrote several hymns as well as poems. Some of his poetry publications: *Dream of Life, Lays of the English Church*, 1843. *Psalms and Hymns as Sung in the Parish Church, Rugby*, 1851. *Altars, Hearths, and Graves*, 1854. Some of his poems: "The Fairy Maimounè," "Forget Thee?" "My Brother," "The Three Sons," "To Margaret in Heaven," "Violets."

Gerard, the son, 1829–1885

He was educated at Rugby School and graduated M.A. from Exeter College, Oxford, in 1856. When he took holy orders he became third master and chaplain in Shrewsbury School; chaplain to the Dowager Marchioness of Londonderry (1855–59); curate of Brightwaltham, Berkshire (1859) and of Brinfield, Berkshire (1860); chaplain of Barrow Gurney, Bristol (1864); vicar of Southleigh, Devon (1869); and warden of St. James' College, Southleigh, where he died. The author of a great number of hymns, he also translated many Greek, Latin, and German hymns. Some of his publications: *Cantica Sanctorum, or Hymns for the Black Letter Saints Days in the English and Scottish Calendars*, 1850. *Hymns from the Post Reformation Editions*, 1864. *Hymns and Lyrics for the Seasons and Saints' Days of the Church*, 1867. *The Espousals of Saint Dorothea and Other Verses*, 1870. Some of his poems: "I Know That My Redeemer Liveth," "Let all mortal flesh keep silence," "Mary at Cana of Galilee," "Shadow of the Star," "St. George, Patron Saint of England," "The Loss of the London."

Sources: *A Sacrifice of Praise: An Anthology of Christian Poetry in English from Caedmon to the Mid–Twentieth Century*. James H. Trott, ed. Cumberland House Publishing, 1999. *Biography of Gerard Moultrie: Stone Campbell Archives* (http://www.bible.acu.edu/s-c/Default.asp?Bookmark=13416). *Carmina Mariana: An English Anthology in Verse in Honour of or in Relation to the Blessed Virgin Mary*. Orby Shipley, ed. Burns and Oates, 1894. *Dictionary of National Biography*. Electronic Edition 1.1. Oxford University Press, 1997. *English Poetry: Author Search*. Chadwyck-Healey Ltd., 1995 (http://www.lib.utexas.edu:8080/search/epoetry/author.html). *Folk Songs: John Williamson Palmer*, ed. Charles Scribner and Company, 1867. *Literary Heritage, West Midlands* (http://www3.shropshire-cc.gov.uk/extracts/E000088a.htm). *Poems that Touch the Heart*. A.L. Alexander, ed. Doubleday, 1956. *The Age of Revolution* (http://www.npg.si.edu/col/age/moultrie.htm). *The Best Loved Poems of the American People*. Hazel Felleman, ed. Doubleday, 1936. *The Book of a*

Thousand Poems: A Family Treasury. J. Murray Macbain, ed. Peter Bedrick Books, 1983. *The Columbia Granger's Index to Poetry.* 11th ed. *The Columbia Granger's World of Poetry,* Columbia University Press, 2005 (http://www.columbia grangers.org). *The Cyber Hymnal* (http://www.cyberhym nal.org/index.htm). *The New Oxford Book of Romantic Period Verse.* Jerome J. McGann. Oxford University Press, 1993. *The Patriot Resource: History — American Revolutionary Era (1775–1781)* (http://www.patriotresource.com/peo ple/moultrie.html).

MUIR, EDWIN (1887–1959)

The son of a farmer, he was born in Orkney, Scotland, and lived there until he was 14. The family moved to Glasgow, where he worked as office boy and clerk, and within five years, both his parents and two of his brothers had died. He married Willa Anderson in 1919 and from 1921 to 1924, they traveled throughout Europe while he supported them chiefly with literary reviews and teaching. He found peace within himself and started writing poetry in 1924–25 and wrote his best poems when over fifty. Between 1930 and 1952, the Muirs translated more than forty novels, and their close partnership continued until he died. He worked for the British Council in Edinburgh, Pargue, and Rome; was warden of Newbattle Abbey, an adult education college near Edinburgh (1950–55); and was Charles Eliot Norton professor, Harvard (1955–1956). He was appointed Commander of the British Empire in 1953 and received honorary degrees from five universities. He died in Cambridge. Some of his poems: "One Foot in Eden," "Robert the Bruce," "Salem, Massachusetts," "The Brothers," "The Enchanted Knight," "The Interrogation," "The Rider Victory," "The Wayside Station."

Sources: *Biography of Willa Muir, Writing Scotland: A Journey Through Scotland's Literature* (http://www.bbc. co.uk/scotland/arts/writingscotland/writers/willa_muir/. *Dictionary of National Biography.* Electronic Edition 1.1. Oxford University Press, 1997. *Edwin Muir, External Links and References* (http://muir.rhizomatics.org.uk/). *Encyclopædia Britannica Ultimate Reference Suite DVD,* 2006. *The Bloodaxe Book of 20th Century Poetry, from Britain and Ireland.* Edna Longley, ed. Bloodaxe Books, 2000. *The Columbia Granger's Index to Poetry.* 11th ed. *The Columbia Granger's World of Poetry,* Columbia University Press, 2005 (http://www.columbiagrangers.org). *The Complete Poems of Edwin Muir.* Peter Butter, ed. The Association for Scottish Literary Studies, 1991. *The Earth is the Lord's: Poems of the Spirit.* Helen Plotz, ed. Thomas Y. Crowell, 1965. *The Mentor Book of Major British Poets.* Oscar Williams, ed. New American Library, 1963. *The Oxford Companion to English Literature.* 6th edition. Margaret Drabble, ed. Oxford University Press, 2000.

MULDOON, PAUL (1951–)

Irish poet, born in Portadown, County Armagh, he read English at Queen's University, Belfast, where one of the lecturers was Seamus Heaney (see entry). He worked for the BBC in Belfast until 1986, and was writer in residence at Cambridge University, then moved to the USA in 1987 to teach at Columbia and Princeton universities. He is Howard G.B. Clark Professor of the Humanities and Creative Writing at Princeton University. He became professor of poetry at Oxford in 1999 and is president of the Poetry Society in London. His collection *Horse Latitudes* was due for publication in 2006. He won seven major literary awards in Britain and in the United States, where he lives with his wife, the novelist Jean Hanff Korelitz, and their two children. Some of his publications: *Selected Poems 1968–83,* 1986. *Selected Poems 1968–86,* 1987. *Madoc: A Mystery,* 1990. *The Annals of Chile,* 1994. *New Selected Poems 1968–94,* 1996. *Hay,* 1998. *Poems 1968–1998,* 2001. Some of his poems: "Armageddon, Armageddon," "At Master McGrath's Grave," "Hopewell Haiku," "The Princess and the Pea," "They That Wash on Thursday."

Sources: *Bitter Harvest: An Anthology of Contemporary Irish Verse.* John Montague, ed. Scribner's, 1989. *Paul Muldoon Home Page* (http://www.paulmuldoon.net/). *Poems, 1968–1998 of Paul Muldoon.* Farrar, Straus and Giroux, 2001. *The Columbia Granger's Index to Poetry.* 11th ed. *The Columbia Granger's World of Poetry,* Columbia University Press, 2005 (http://www.columbiagrangers.org). *The Faber Book of Contemporary Irish Poetry.* Paul Muldoon ed. Faber and Faber, 1986. *The Norton Anthology of Modern Poetry.* 2nd ed. Richard Ellmann and Robert O'Clair, eds. W.W. Norton, 1988. *The Oxford and Cambridge May Anthologies Poetry 2000.* Paul Muldoon, ed. Varsity/Cherwell, 2000. *The Oxford Companion to English Literature.* 6th edition. Margaret Drabble, ed. Oxford University Press, 2000. *Who's Who.* London: A & C Black, 2005.

MUNBY, ARTHUR JOSEPH (1828–1910)

Born in Clifton, North Yorkshire, where his father was a solicitor, he graduated M.A. from Trinity College, Cambridge, in 1856. Called to the bar in 1855, from 1858 he held a post in the ecclesiastical commissioners' office until he retired in 1888. He supported the London Working Men's College, where he taught Latin for three years. He died and was buried at Pyrford, near Ripley, Surrey. When his will was read, it came to light that in 1873 he had married his servant, Hannah Cullwick, who had died the previous year. He bequeathed many of his books to Trinity College, Cambridge, and to the British Museum two deed boxes containing photographs, manuscripts, diaries and other documents on the condition they were not to be opened or examined before 1 January 1950. Some of his publications: *Benoni,* 1852. *Elegiacs Dorothy,* 1859. *Verses New and Old,* 1865. *Vestigia Retrorsum,* 1891. *Susan,* 1893. *Ann*

Morgan's Love, 1896. *Poems*, 1901. *Relicta*, 1909. Some of his poems: "Bethesda," "Doris: A Pastoral," "In Retirement," "Magdalen," "The Milkwoman," "Then and Now — The North Downs," "When Autumn Returns."

Sources: *Dictionary of National Biography*. Electronic Edition 1.1. Oxford University Press, 1997. *English Poetry: Author Search*. Chadwyck-Healey Ltd., 1995 (http://www.lib.utexas.edu:8080/search/epoetry/author.html). *Munby: Man of Two Words, Derek Hudson*. John Murray, 1972. *Poems, Chiefly Lyric and Elegiac of Arthur Munby*. Kegan Paul, 1901. *Stanford University Libraries and Academic Information Resources* (http://library.stanford.edu). *The Columbia Granger's Index to Poetry*. 11th ed. *The Columbia Granger's World of Poetry*, Columbia University Press, 2005 (http://www.columbiagrangers.org). *The Faber Book of Poems and Places*. Geoffrey Grigson, ed. Faber and Faber, 1980. *The Home Book of Verse*. Burton Egbert Stevenson, ed. New York: Henry Holt and Company, 1953. *The Oxford Companion to English Literature*. 6th edition. Margaret Drabble, ed. Oxford University Press, 2000. *Working Women in Victorian Britain, 1850–1910: The Diaries and Letters of Arthur J. Munby (1828–1910) and Hannah Cullwick (1833–1909) from Trinity College, Cambridge*. Marlborough, Wiltshire: Adam Matthew Publications, 1993. 32 reels (http://www.library.utoronto.ca/robarts/microtext/collection/pages/workwomn.html).

MUNDAY, ANTHONY (1553–1633)

At the end of his apprenticeship to a London stationer around 1573, he spent some time at the English seminary in Rome, entertained by the rector who had been a friend of his father. Back in London he was an actor and wrote some plays, among them *John a Kent and John a Cumber* (?1595). He translated *Balladine of England* (1588) and *Amadis of Gaul* (?1590). His time at the English College in Rome provided material for *The English Romayne Lyfe* (1582). His many ballads were often satirized by Samuel Johnson. He died in London and was buried in the Church of St. Stephen, Coleman Street, within the City of London. Some of his other publications: *The Mirrour of Mutabilitie*, 1579. *To All Curteous and Freendly Readers*, 1579. *The paine of pleasure*, 1580. *The true reporte of the prosperous successe*, 1581. *A Banqvet of Daintie Conceits*, 1588. *Poems from Englands Helicon*, 1600. *Zelavto, The Fovntaine of Fame*, 1689. Some of his poems: "Jf euer Cæsar Had Such Gallant Fame," "The Sheepheards Sunne," "The Wood-mans Walke," "Who Wayeth Well Each Point of This Discourse."

Sources: *Dictionary of National Biography*. Electronic Edition 1.1. Oxford University Press, 1997. *English Poetry: Author Search*. Chadwyck-Healey Ltd., 1995 (http://www.lib.utexas.edu:8080/search/epoetry/author.html). *Songs from the British Drama*. Edward Bliss Reed, ed. Yale University Press, 1925. *The Columbia Granger's Index to Poetry*. 11th ed. *The Columbia Granger's World of Poetry*, Columbia University Press, 2005 (http://www.columbia

grangers.org). *The New Oxford Book of English Verse, 1250–1950*. Helen Gardner, ed. Oxford University Press, 1972. *The Oxford Book of Sixteenth Century Verse*. E.K. Chambers, ed. Oxford University Press, 1932. *The Oxford Companion to English Literature*. 6th edition. Margaret Drabble, ed. Oxford University Press, 2000.

MURDOCH, DAME JEAN IRIS (1919–1999)

Born in Dublin, she read classics, ancient history, and philosophy at Somerville College, Oxford, and philosophy as a postgraduate at Newnham College, Cambridge. Between 1942 and 1944 she worked in the British Treasury and then for two years as an administrative officer with the United Nations Relief and Rehabilitation Administration. In 1948 she became a fellow of St. Anne's College, Oxford. She married the novelist John Bayley, whom she met at Oxford. In addition to her 34 novels, she wrote plays, verse, and works of philosophy and literary criticism. In 1987, she was made a Dame Commander of the Order of the British Empire. She began to suffer the early effects of Alzheimer's disease in 1995, which she at first attributed to writer's block. Her life was made into a film, *Iris*, in 2001, with Judy Dench and John Broadbent in the lead roles. Her only two collections of verse are *A Year of Birds* (1978; revised edition, 1984), 12 engravings accompanying Murdoch's twelve poems, one for each month; and *Poems by Iris Murdoch* (1997).

Sources: *Dictionary of National Biography*. Electronic Edition 1.1. Oxford University Press, 1997. *The Oxford Companion to English Literature*. 6th edition. Margaret Drabble, ed. Oxford University Press, 2000. *Wikipedia, the Free Encyclopedia* (http://en.wikipedia.org/wiki/Wikipedia).

MURE, SIR WILLIAM (1594–1657)

This Scottish poet was the third successive owner of Rowallan, Ayrshire, with the same name and title. His mother was Elizabeth Montgomerie, sister of Alexander Montgomerie (see entry). Probably educated at Glasgow University, he became a member of the Scottish parliament in 1643 and fought with the Royalists against the Parliamentarians. He was wounded at the Battle of Marston Moore just outside York in July 1644, but by August he was at Newcastle. The title became extinct in 1700. His piety found expression in his poetry and in particular, his paraphrase of many of the Psalms. A complete edition of his works was edited by William Tough for the Scottish Text Society in 1898 and is held in the special editions section at Edinburgh University. He was also an accomplished lute player. Some of his poems: "A Spiritual Hymn," "Dido and Aeneas," "Doomsday Containing Hells Horror and Heavens Happiness," "Sonnet. To the Blessed Trinity," "The

Cry of Blood, and of a Broken Covenant," "The Power of Beauty," "The True Crucifix for True Catholics," "To the Royal Majesty of King Charles the II."

Sources: *Dictionary of National Biography.* Electronic Edition 1.1. Oxford University Press, 1997. *English Poetry: Author Search.* Chadwyck-Healey Ltd., 1995 (http://www.lib.utexas.edu:8080/search/epoetry/author.html). *Encyclopedia of Britain.* Bamber Gascoigne. London: Macmillan, 1994. Sir William Mure's lute nook is held in the special collections section of Edinburgh University. *The Columbia Granger's Index to Poetry.* 11th ed. *The Columbia Granger's World of Poetry,* Columbia University Press, 2005 (http://www.columbiagrangers.org). *The Oxford Companion to Scottish History.* Michael Lynch, ed. Oxford University Press, 2001. *The Penguin Book of Renaissance Verse 1509–1659.* David Norbrook, ed. Penguin Books, 1992. *Tours of Scotland, My Native Homeland, Biography of Sir William Mure* (http://www.fife.50megs.com/sir-william-mure.htm).

MURPHY, JERRY (1952–)

He was born in Cork, where he still lives. His experience includes spending 1975 to 1976 in a kibbutz in Israel, one year at University College Cork studying English and history, and work as a lifeguard at Mayfield swimming pool, Cork. The American playwright Roger Gregg produced a stage adaptation of Murphy's poetry in the Triskel Arts Centre, Cork, 1897. Some of his poetry publications: *A Small Fat Boy Walking Backwards,* 1985. *A Cartoon History of the Spanish Civil War,* 1991. *Rio de la Plata and All That,* 1993. *The Empty Quarter,* 1996. *Extracts from the Lost Log Book of Christopher Columbus,* 1999. *Torso of an Ex-Girlfriend,* 2002. Some of his poems: "As for Dante," "Clean Exit," "Honey," "Kissing Maura O'Keeffe," *The O'Neill Suite* ([i] "Wood Sprite," [ii] "Caherlag," [iii] "Bemused," [iv] "Balancing Act," [v] "Relative Densities," [vi] "Birdsong," [vii] "Be Fruitful and Multiply").

Sources: *Biography of Gerry Murphy* (http://www.dedaluspress.com/poets/murphy.html). *Kissing Maura O'Keeffe by Gerry Murphy* (http://www.munsterlit.ie/South wordnew/poetry1.html). *The O'Neill Suite by Gerry Murphy* (http://www.munsterlit.ie/Southword3/Poetry/Gerry_Murphy/gerry_murphy.html). *Works of Gerry Murphy* (http://www.munsterlit.ie/Conwriters/gerry_murphy.htm).

MURPHY, RICHARD (1927–)

Irish poet, born in County Mayo on the west of Ireland, he spent his early childhood years in Sri Lanka. His father was the last British mayor of Colombo and later replaced the Duke of Windsor as governor of the Bahamas. His education was in Ireland and England, and he was a chorister in Canterbury Cathedral. At Oxford University he studied English under C.S. Lewis, who sparked his desire to be a poet. He began reviewing poetry for the *Spec-* *tator* in 1950. Much of his poetry is inspired by the west of Ireland. Since 1971 he has taught creative writing and modern poetry as a visiting poet at Princeton and eight other American universities. He has received six major literary awards. He lives in Dublin. Some of his publications: *The Battle of Aughrim,* 1968. *High Island,* 1974. *New and Selected Poems,* 1975. *New Selected Poems,* 1989. *The Mirror Wall,* 1989. *Collected Poems,* 2000. Some of his poems: "Sailing to an Island," "Seals at High Island," "The Archaeology of Love," "The Philosopher and the Birds," "The Price of Stone," "Woman of the House."

Sources: *Biography of Richard Murphy* (http://www.cca.ukzn.ac.za/images/pa/PA2004/poets/murphy.htm). *Contemporary Irish Poetry: An Anthology.* Anthony Bradley, ed. University of California Press. New and rev. ed., 1988. *English Love Poems.* John Betjeman and Geoffrey Taylor, eds. Faber and Faber, 1957. *Irish Poetry after Yeats: Seven Poets.* Maurice Harmon, ed. Little, Brown, 1979. *Modern Irish Poetry.* Patrick Crotty, ed. The Blackstaff Press, 1995. *The Columbia Granger's Index to Poetry.* 11th ed. *The Columbia Granger's World of Poetry,* Columbia University Press, 2005 (http://www.columbiagrangers.org). *The Oxford Companion to English Literature.* 6th edition. Margaret Drabble, ed. Oxford University Press, 2000. *Works of Richard Murphy* (http://www.irishwriters-online.com/richardmurphy.html).

MURRAY, SIR DAVID OF GORTHY (1567–1629)

The son of Robert Murray of Abercairny, Perthshire, he was an officer in the household to James VI of Scotland and I of Great Britain. He also served Prince Henry. Charles I bestowed upon him the estate of Gorthy, Perthshire, but he died soon afterward without an heir. He wrote 22 sonnets as well as some other poems. Some of his poems: "A Paraphrase of the 104 Psalme," "Caelia. Containing Certaine Sonets," "Epitaph on the death of his deare cousin," "Gazing from out the windowes of mine eyes," "The Complaint of the Shepheard Harpalus," "The Tragicall Death of Sophonisba."

Sources: *Dictionary of National Biography.* Electronic Edition 1.1. Oxford University Press, 1997. *English Poetry: Author Search.* Chadwyck-Healey Ltd., 1995 (http://www.lib.utexas.edu:8080/search/epoetry/author.html). *Poems by Sir David Murray of Gorthy.* James Ballantyne and Co., 1823. *The Columbia Granger's Index to Poetry.* 11th ed. *The Columbia Granger's World of Poetry,* Columbia University Press, 2005 (http://www.columbiagrangers.org).

MYERS, FREDERIC WILLIAM and ERNEST JAMES (1843–1921)

Frederic William Henry, the elder brother, 1843–1901

He was born at Keswick, the Lake District, the elder son of a clergyman, and when his father died in 1851 the family moved to Cheltenham, Gloucestershire. Frederic was educated at Cheltenham College and graduated from Trinity College, Cambridge, in 1864. He took a year out traveling in Europe, the USA and Canada, where he swam across the Niagra River below the falls. From 1865 to 1869 he was he was classical lecturer in Trinity College, Cambridge, but teaching was not his forte, and from 1872 until his death he was a schools inspector. In addition to literature, his other passion was investigating the paranormal in connection with the Society for Psychical Research, which he helped found in 1882. He was also active in promoting education for women. He died at Rome and was buried at Keswick. Many of his poems appeared first in magazines and were afterwards collected and reissued with additions. Some of his poems: "Brighton," "Harold at Two Years Old," "God, How Many Years Ago," "Saint Paul," "Surrender to Christ," "When Summer Even Softly Dies," "Wind, Moon, and Tides."

Ernest James, the younger brother (1844–1921)

Educated at Cheltenham College, he graduated from Balliol College, Oxford, in 1865, and was fellow and lecturer at Wadham College, Oxford, from 1868 to 1871. Although called to the bar in 1874, he never practiced. He published several prose works and a biography of Viscount Althorp (1890). His essay on Aeschylus, included in the collection entitled *Hellenica*, was edited by Evelyn Abbott (1880). From 1876 to 1882 he was secretary to the London Society for the Extension of University Teaching, and he was on the council of the Hellenic Society from its foundation in 1879. He was also on the Society for the Protection of Women and Children and was on the central administrative committee of the Charity Organization Society until he left London to live in Kent. He died at Fontridge, Etchingham, Sussex. Some of his other publications: *Gathered Poems*, 1904. *The Judgment of Prometheus*, 1886. *The Puritans*, 1869. *Poems*, 1877. *The Defence of Rome*, 1880. Some of his poems: "A Garden Fable," "Achilles," "Could Ye Not Watch One Hour?" "The Lost Shepherd," "The Wreck of the *Birkenhead*," "To the Army in Africa."

Sources: *A Sacrifice of Praise: An Anthology of Christian Poetry in English from Caedmon to the Mid–Twentieth Century.* James H. Trott, ed. Cumberland House Publishing, 1999. *Collected Poems of Frederic William Henry Myers.* Macmillan, 1921. *Dictionary of National Biography.* Electronic Edition 1.1. Oxford University Press, 1997. *English Poetry: Author Search.* Chadwyck-Healey Ltd., 1995 (http://www.lib.utexas.edu:8080/search/epoetry/author.html). *The National Portrait Gallery* (www.npg.org.uk). *Stanford University Libraries and Academic Information Resources* (http://library.stanford.edu). *The Home Book of Verse.* Burton Egbert Stevenson, ed. New York: Henry Holt and Company, 1953. *The Oxford Book of Victorian Verse.* Arthur Quiller-Couch, ed. Oxford University Press, 1971. *The World's Great Religious Poetry.* Caroline Miles Hill, ed. Macmillan, 1954.

NAIRNE, CAROLINA OLIPHANT, BARONESS (1766–1845)

Born at Gask, Perthshire, the daughter of Laurence Oliphant, she was known as "The Flower of Strathearn." She married her cousin, Major William Murray Nairne, assistant inspector of barracks, in 1806. Under the dispensation afforded to Jacobite supporters, her husband was raised to the peerage in 1824, the fifth Lord Nairne of Nairne, Perthshire. When Lord Nairne died in 1829, Lady Nairne with her son left Edinburgh and spent several years moving around England, Ireland, and the Continent, trying to find a climate to suit his delicate health, but after an attack of influenza the young Lord Nairne died at Brussels in 1837. After two years of poor health, Lady Nairne died at Cask and was buried within the chapel there. Her *Lays From Strathearn* were published in 1846, with a new edition in 1886. Some of her song/poems: "Caller Herrin'," "Charlie is My Darling," "Farewell to Edinburgh," "The Auld House," "The Banks of the Earn," "The Hundred Pipers," "The Laird o' Cockpen," "The Land o' the Leal," "The Lass o' Gowrie," "The Rowan Tree."

Sources: *Dictionary of National Biography.* Electronic Edition 1.1. Oxford University Press, 1997. *Encyclopædia Britannica Ultimate Reference Suite DVD*, 2006. *Life and Songs of the Baroness Nairne of Caroline Oliphant the Yonger.* John Grant, 1886. *The Columbia Granger's Index to Poetry.* 11th ed. *The Columbia Granger's World of Poetry*, Columbia University Press, 2005 (http://www.columbiagrangers.org). *The Faber Book of English History in Verse.* Kenneth Baker, ed. Faber and Faber, 1988. *The Home Book of Modern Verse.* Burton Egbert Stevenson, ed. Henry Holt, 1953. *The Oxford Companion to English Literature.* 6th edition. Margaret Drabble, ed. Oxford University Press, 2000. *The Scottish Collection of Verse to 1800.* Eileen Dunlop and Kamm Antony, eds. Richard Drew, 1985.

NASHE (NASH), THOMAS (1567–1601)

Born in Lowestoft, Suffolk, the son of clergyman, he graduated B.A. from St. John's College, Cambridge, in 1585–86 and by 1588 had settled in London, where he was one of the "University Wits." His burning hatred of Puritanism fueled his satirical pamphlets, written under the pseudonym of "Martin Mar-Prelate." For years he was involved in a feud with his bitter rival Gabriel Harvey (see entry). However, in 1593 he published *Christes Teares over Jerusalem*, in which he desires to live at peace with all men. This was aimed at Harvey, who rejected the overture; the feud picked up steam again and by

1596 Nashe was back at the attack. His play *The Isle of Dogs* (1597) attacked the state and so aroused the wrath of the Privy Council that Nashe spent several months in Fleet Prison. Some of his poems: "A Litany in Time of Plague," "Adieu, Farewell Earth's Bliss," "Autumn," "Fair Summer Droops," "In Time of Pestilence," "Spring, The Sweet Spring," "Thus Hath My Penne Presum'd to Please My Friend," "To the Right Honorable the Lord S."

Sources: *Dictionary of National Biography.* Electronic Edition 1.1. Oxford University Press, 1997. *Encyclopædia Britannica Ultimate Reference Suite DVD,* 2006. *English Poetry: Author Search.* Chadwyck-Healey Ltd., 1995 (http://www.lib.utexas.edu:8080/search/epoetry/author. html). *Poemhunter* (www.poemhunter.com). *The Columbia Granger's Index to Poetry.* 11th ed. *The Columbia Granger's World of Poetry,* Columbia University Press, 2005 (http://www.columbiagrangers.org). *The Faber Book of Blue Verse.* John Whitworth, ed. Faber and Faber, 1990. *The National Portrait Gallery* (www.npg.org.uk). *The Oxford Book of Death.* D.J. Enright, ed. Oxford University Press, 1987. *The Oxford Companion to English Literature.* 6th edition. Margaret Drabble, ed. Oxford University Press, 2000.

NEALE, JOHN MASON (1818–1866)

Born in London, the son of a clergyman, he won a scholarship to Trinity College, Cambridge, from where he graduated in 1840. Closely connected to the Oxford Movement — which later brought him into conflict with some of the Church hierarchy — he was one of the founders of the Cambridge Camden Society. For a while he was chaplain and assistant tutor at Downing College, Cambridge. Ordained in 1842, in 1846 he was appointed warden of Sackville College, East Grinstead, Sussex, where he died, leaving behind several charitable institutions for the care of children and women in distress. He was the author of the *History of the Holy Eastern Church* (1847–1873) and a respected translator of ancient Latin and Greek hymns. Many of his hymns are used in modern hymn books. Some of his hymn/poems: "All glory, laud and honor," "Good Christian men, rejoice," "Good King Wenceslas," "Hymn for Easter Morn," "Jerusalem the golden," "O come, O come, Emmanuel," "Of the Father's love begotten," "Oh, Give Us Back the Days of Old!" "The Guide from St. Stephen the Sabaite."

Sources: *A Sacrifice of Praise: An Anthology of Christian Poetry in English from Caedmon to the Mid–Twentieth Century.* James H. Trott, ed. Cumberland House Publishing, 1999. *Biographical Sketches of Memorable Christians of the Past:* John Mason Neale (http://justus.anglican.org/re sources/bio/220.html). *Dictionary of National Biography.* Electronic Edition 1.1. Oxford University Press, 1997. *Eerdman's Book of Christian Poetry.* Pat Alexander and Veronica Zundel, eds. William B. Eerdmans, 1981. *The Colum bia Granger's Index to Poetry.* 11th ed. *The Columbia Granger's World of Poetry,* Columbia University Press, 2005 (http://www.columbiagrangers.org). *The Cyber Hymnal* (http://www.cyberhymnal.org/index.htm). *The New Oxford Book of Christian Verse.* Donald Davie, ed. Oxford University Press, 1981. *The Oxford Companion to English Literature.* 6th edition. Margaret Drabble, ed. Oxford University Press, 2000.

NEAVES, CHARLES, LORD NEAVES (1800–1876)

Scottish poet, the son of solicitor, he was born in Edinburgh — where he received all his education — and was called to the Scottish bar in 1822 and had a distinguished career. From 1845 to 1852 he was sheriff of Orkney and Shetland then solicitor-general for Scotland. From 1853 to1858 he was a judge in the court of session, taking the title of Lord Neaves, then was a lord of justiciary until his death. He was renowned for his phenomenal memory in court and his literary reputation was just as great. Edinburgh University awarded him the degree of doctor of laws in 1860, and in 1872 he was elected lord rector of St. Andrews University. Many of his most brilliant satires were published in *Songs and Verses, Social and Scientific* (1868 and 1872). *The Greek Anthology* was published in Blackwood's *Ancient Classics* (1870). Some of his poems: "Don't Forget the Rich," "Flask of Rosy Wine," "Grimm's Law," "A New Song," "Let Us All Be Unhappy on Sunday," "Why Should a Woman Not Get a Degree?" "Old Noah's Invention," "The Leather Bottèl," "The Three R's."

Sources: *Dictionary of National Biography.* Electronic Edition 1.1. Oxford University Press, 1997. *English Poetry: Author Search.* Chadwyck-Healey Ltd., 1995 (http://www. lib.utexas.edu:8080/search/epoetry/author.html). *Scotland's Lawyer Poets* (http://www.wvu.edu/~lawfac/jelkins/ lp–2001/intro/scots.html). *The Columbia Granger's Index to Poetry.* 11th ed. *The Columbia Granger's World of Poetry,* Columbia University Press, 2005 (http://www.columbia grangers.org). *The Faber Book of Comic Verse.* Michael Roberts and Janet Adam Smith, eds. Faber and Faber, 1978.

NEELE, HENRY (1798–1828)

He was born in London, where his father was a map and heraldic engraver. After a private education, he became a solicitor and while he carried out his law practice, he devoted much time to literature. In 1817, he published — at his father's expense — *Odes, and Other Poems,* and in 1823 *Poems, Dramatic and Miscellaneous,* inscribed to Joanna Baillie (see entry). This publication was so successful he became a popular contributor to magazines such as *Monthly Magazine* and *Forget Me Not.* In 1827 he published *Romance of English History* in three volumes, a collection of tales illustrative of romantic passages in

English history. He was found dead in bed, having cut his throat. Although some of his poems are tinged with melancholy, apparently there was no real indication of insanity. Some of his poems: "An Incantation," "David Rizzio," "Fair Moon, thou travellest in thy silvery sky," "God Help Thee, Weary One, Thy Cheek is Pale," "Hope," "Moan, Moan, Ye Dying Gales," "Real Love," "Sacontala," "Song. Written at Dijon," "Wake, Harp of mine! some lofty ditty ring," "White Hairs."

Sources: *Dictionary of National Biography.* Electronic Edition 1.1. Oxford University Press, 1997. *Poems, Vols. 1 and 2 of Henry Neele.* Smith, Elder, and Co., 1827. *The Columbia Granger's Index to Poetry.* 11th ed. *The Columbia Granger's World of Poetry,* Columbia University Press, 2005 (http://www.columbiagrangers.org).

NEILSON, PETER (1795–1861)

Born in Glasgow, he was educated at the high school and Glasgow University, then joined his father in exporting cambric and cotton goods to America. From the information gathered during business dealing in America, between 1822 and 1828, he published *Six Years' Residence in America* (1828). The death of his wife turned his thoughts strongly towards religion and poems on scriptural themes; he published *The Millennium* and *Scripture Gems* in 1834. In 1841 Neilson settled in Kirkintilloch, Dumbartonshire, with his three daughters and one son. *The Life and Adventures of Zamba, an African King: And His Experiences of Slavery in South Carolina* was published by Smith, Elder (1847), which predates *Uncle Tom's Cabin* by Harriet Beecher Stowe (1852). He also contributed to the *Glasgow Herald* a series of practical articles on cotton supply for Britain. His invention for iron-plated ships was adapted, although he received no credit for it. He died of heart disease at Kirkintilloch and was buried in the grounds of Glasgow Cathedral. His *Poems,* edited by Dr. Whitelaw, appeared in 1870, and contains *David: A Drama* from the Bible.

Sources: *Dictionary of National Biography.* Electronic Edition 1.1. Oxford University Press, 1997. *Peter Neilson, 1795–1861. The Life and Adventures of Zamba, an African Negro King: And His Experience of Slavery in South Carolina. Written by Himself.* Corrected and Arranged by Peter Neilson. London: Smith, Elder, 1847 (http://docsouth. unc.edu/neh/neilson/menu.html).

NESBIT, EDITH (1858–1924)

She was born in London, the daughter of John Collis Nesbit, agricultural chemist. Following her father's death in 1862, the family lived in France and Germany until 1872. Soon she married the writer Hubert Bland in 1880; he contracted smallpox and in 1914 died. Edith supported her family by writing verses and painting pictures for greeting cards. Although a notable poet and political thinker (she was a member of the Fabian Society), she published novels and collections of poetry for adults, but is most remembered as a writer of children's books (she published more than 60). She died of heart disease and possibly of lung cancer. The ever-popular *The Story of the Treasure Seekers* (1899) and *The Railway Children* (1905) have both been made into films. She died at Jesson St. Mary's, New Romney, Kent. Some of her poetry publications: *The Dawn,* 1876. *Lays and Legends,* 1886. *The Star of Bethlehem,* 1894. *A Pomander of Verse,* 1895. Some of her poems: "Among His Books," "Baby Seed Song," "Child's Song in Spring," "Mr. Ody Met a Body," "Spring in War-Time," "Summer Song."

Sources: *A Century of Humorous Verse, 1850–1950.* Roger Lancelyn Green, ed. E.P. Dutton (Everyman's Library), 1959. *Dictionary of National Biography.* Electronic Edition 1.1. Oxford University Press, 1997. *Encyclopædia Britannica Ultimate Reference Suite DVD,* 2006. *English Poetry: Author Search.* Chadwyck-Healey Ltd., 1995 (http://www. lib.utexas.edu:8080/search/epoetry/author.html). *Poems for Seasons and Celebrations.* William Cole, ed. World, 1961. *Scars upon My Heart: Women's Poetry and Verse of the First World War.* Catherine W. Reilly, ed. Virago Press, 1981. Stanford University Libraries and Academic Information Resources (http://library.stanford.edu). *The Columbia Granger's Index to Poetry.* 11th ed. *The Columbia Granger's World of Poetry,* Columbia University Press, 2005 (http:// www.columbiagrangers.org). *The Home Book of Verse for Young Folks.* Burton Egbert Stevenson, ed. Holt, Rinehart and Winston, 1929. *The New Oxford Book of Victorian Verse.* Christopher Ricks, ed. Oxford University Press, 1987. *The Oxford Companion to English Literature.* 6th edition. Margaret Drabble, ed. Oxford University Press, 2000.

NEVAY, JOHN (1792–1870)

Scottish poet born in Forfar, Angus, he earned his living as a handloom weaver. He contributed prose tales to the *Edinburgh Literary Journal* and to other periodicals. Many of his poems reflect his love of the slopes and valleys of the neighboring Grampians the hills and countryside around. His works are described as spontaneous and tender. His published works are: *A Pamphlet of Rhymes,* 1818. *A Second Pamphlet,* 1821. *Emmanuel,* 1831, a sacred poem in nine cantos. *Mary of Avonbourne,* 1833. *The Peasant,* 1834. *The Yeldron,* 1835 (the yellowhammer bird). *The Child of Nature and Other Poems,* 1835. *Rosaline's Dream,* 1853. *The Fountain of the Rock,* 1855.

Sources: *Dictionary of National Biography.* Electronic Edition 1.1. Oxford University Press, 1997.

NEWBOLT, SIR HENRY JOHN (1862–1938)

Born in Bilston, Staffordshire, the son of a clergyman, he was educated at Clifton Theological College and graduated from Corpus Christi College, Oxford, in 1881. Called to the bar by Lincoln's Inn, in 1887 he practiced for twelve years, then concentrated on literature. He served at the Admiralty and the Foreign Office during World War I. In 1923, at the request of the Committee of Imperial Defense, he wrote volumes 4 and 5 of the official *History of the Great War: Naval Operations*. He was knighted in 1915, appointed Companion of Honor in 1922, and received honorary degrees from seven universities in Britain and Canada. He served on many commissions, councils, and committees, and he was a trustee of the National Portrait Gallery. He died in London. Some of his poetry publications: *A Fair Death*, 1888. *Mordred*, 1895, a tragedy in blank verse. *Poems*, 1921. *A Child is Born*, 1931. *A Perpetual Memory*, 1939. Some of his poems: "Admirals All," "Drake's Drum," "For a Trafalgar Cenotaph," "He Fell Among Thieves," "Hope the Hornblower," "The Moss-Rose," "Victoria Regina."

Sources: *Collected Poems 1897–1907 of Henry Newbolt.* Thomas Nelson and Sons, 1910. *Dictionary of National Biography.* Electronic Edition 1.1. Oxford University Press, 1997. *Encyclopædia Britannica Ultimate Reference Suite DVD*, 2006. *English Poetry: Author Search.* Chadwyck-Healey Ltd., 1995 (http://www.lib.utexas.edu:8080/search/epoetry/author.html). *Moods of the Sea: Masterworks of Sea Poetry.* George C. Solley and Eric Steinbaugh, eds. Naval Institute Press, 1981. Stanford University Libraries and Academic Information Resources (http://library.stanford.edu). *The Columbia Granger's Index to Poetry.* 11th ed. *The Columbia Granger's World of Poetry*, Columbia University Press, 2005 (http://www.columbiagrangers.org). *The Home Book of Modern Verse*. Burton Egbert Stevenson, ed. Henry Holt, 1953. *The National Portrait Gallery* (www.npg.org.uk). *The Oxford Companion to English Literature*. 6th edition. Margaret Drabble, ed. Oxford University Press, 2000. *Victorian Parlor Poetry: An Annotated Anthology.* Michael R. Turner, ed. Dover Publications, 1992.

NEWCOMB, THOMAS (?1682–1765)

The son of William Newcomb, clergyman either from Westbury, Shropshire, or from Herefordshire, he graduated from Corpus Christi College, Oxford, in 1704. He was chaplain to the Duke of Richmond, Goodwood, Sussex, then rector of several parishes in Sussex. In 1721 he published a translation of the *Roman History of Velleius Paterculus* (circa 19 B.C.–circa A.D. 31). In 1723 he published *The Last Judgment of Men and Angels, A Poem in Twelve Books.* In his old age he suffered from gout, rheumatism, and possibly kidney stones. The Duke of Richmond settled a life pension on him. He died at Hackney, London, and was buried there. Between 1727 and 1763 he published 11 odes to royalty and other prominent figures, as well 5 undated odes, including *The Latin Works of the Late Mr. Addison, in Prose and Verse,*

Translated into English, a Paraphrase on Some Select Psalms and *A Miscellaneous Collection of Original Poems.*

Sources: *Dictionary of National Biography.* Electronic Edition 1.1. Oxford University Press, 1997.

NEWMAN, JOHN HENRY (1801–1890)

His father was a London banker of Huguenot stock, and after a private education, John graduated without distinction from Trinity College, Oxford, in 1820. He was fellow of Oriel College from 1822 to 1832, when he was forced to resign on a conflict of doctrine. With John Keble (see entry) and Edward Pusey (1800–1882), he was one of the founders of the Oxford Movement, started in 1833 with the object of stressing the Catholic elements in the English religious tradition and of reforming the Church of England. He was an Anglican priest from 1824 to 1843, when he converted to the Roman Catholic faith. He became a priest in 1845 and founded the Oratory at Edgbaston Birmingham in 1848, and was created a cardinal, in Rome, in 1879. He died at Edgbaston and after lying in state at the Oratory, he was buried at Rednall Hill, Birmingham. Some of his hymn/poems: "Christmas Without Christ," "David and Jonathan," "Lead Kingly Light," "Paraphrase of Isaiah, Chap. 64," "Praise to the Holiest in the Height," "The Dream of Gerontius," "The Gift of Tongues," "The Good Samaritan," "Zeal and Patience."

Sources: *An Anthology of Catholic Poets.* Shane Leslie, ed. Macmillan, 1952. *Collected Poems of John Henry Newman.* Fisher Press, 1992. *Dictionary of National Biography.* Electronic Edition 1.1. Oxford University Press, 1997. *Encyclopædia Britannica Ultimate Reference Suite DVD*, 2006. *The Columbia Granger's Index to Poetry.* 11th ed. *The Columbia Granger's World of Poetry*, Columbia University Press, 2005 (http://www.columbiagrangers.org). *The National Portrait Gallery* (www.npg.org.uk). *The Oxford Companion to English Literature*. 6th edition. Margaret Drabble, ed. Oxford University Press, 2000.

NEWTON, JOHN (1725–1807)

Born in London, the son of an officer in the merchant service, he joined his father at sea at the age of 11. He was press-ganged aboard HMS *Harwich*, then subsequently worked in the slave trade. During a violent storm he experienced a profound religious conversion and retired from the sea in 1754. In 1764 he was ordained to the curacy of Olney, Buckinghamshire, where he published the account of his life — *The Authentic Narrative*. A friend of William Cowper (see entry), in 1779 Newton published the *Olney Hymns*, which contained sixty-eight pieces by Cowper and 280 by Newton. In 1780, he took on St. Mary Woolchurch, Lombard Street. In 1792 he was awarded the degree of doctor of divinity by the University of New Jersey. He continued to preach till the last year of his life, although he was too blind to see his text. He was buried at St. Mary Woolnoth Church, near the Bank of England. Some of his hymn/poems: "Amazing Grace," "Glorious Things of Thee Are Spoken," "In Evil Long I Took Delight," "In Sweet Communion," "The Name of Jesus," "Thou Art Coming to a King."

Sources: *A Sacrifice of Praise: An Anthology of Christian Poetry in English from Caedmon to the Mid–Twentieth Century.* James H. Trott, ed. Cumberland House Publishing, 1999. *Best Loved Songs of the American People.* Denes Agay, ed. Doubleday, 1975. *Dictionary of National Biography.* Electronic Edition 1.1. Oxford University Press, 1997. *The Columbia Granger's Index to Poetry.* 11th ed. *The Columbia Granger's World of Poetry,* Columbia University Press, 2005 (http://www.columbiagrangers.org). *The Cyber Hymnal* (http://www.cyberhymnal.org/index.htm). *The Oxford Companion to English Literature.* 6th edition. Margaret Drabble, ed. Oxford University Press, 2000. *The World's Great Religious Poetry.* Caroline Miles Hill, ed. Macmillan, 1954.

NICCOLS, RICHARD (1584–1616)

Born in London, at the age of 12 he accompanied the Earl of Nottingham on board the *Ark Raleigh Galleon* (later *Ark Royal*) in the battle against the Spanish at Cadiz. In several of his poems Niccols refers to that battle, when a dove rested on the main yard of the ship and did not leave it till the vessel arrived in London. He graduated B.A. from Magdalen Hall, Oxford, in 1602, and in 1614 he published two books of epigrams. Many of his longer works are dedicated to influential people or to commemorate significant events. *The Cuckow* (1607) is a narrative poem that tells the story of a contest between the cuckoo and nightingale for supremacy in song. In 1610 he published his version of the *Mirror for Magistrates*— which first appeared in 1559 — by George Ferrers and William Baldwin (see entries). Some of his publications: *The Beggers Ape,* 1627. *Expicedium,* 1603. *The Furies with Vertues Encomium,* 1614. *Londons Artillery,* 1616. *Monodia or Walthams Complaint,* 1615. *Sir Thomas Overbvries Vision,* 1616. *Three Precious Teares of Blood,* 1611. *The Three Sisters Teares,* 1613.

Sources: *Dictionary of National Biography.* Electronic Edition 1.1. Oxford University Press, 1997. *English Poetry: Author Search.* Chadwyck-Healey Ltd., 1995 (http://www.lib.utexas.edu:8080/search/epoetry/author.html). *Stanford University Libraries and Academic Information Resources* (http://library.stanford.edu). *The Oxford Companion to English Literature.* 6th edition. Margaret Drabble, ed. Oxford University Press, 2000.

NICHOLS, GRACE (1950–)

Born in Georgetown, Guyana, she gained a diploma in communications at the University of Guyana, then worked as a freelance journalist and reporter. She migrated to the U.K. in 1977, where she still lives with her partner, the poet John Agard (see entry). Her first poetry collection, *I Is a Long-Memoried Woman* (1983) won the Commonwealth Poetry Prize, and the film adaptation won a gold medal at the International Film and Television Festival, New York. The book was also dramatized for radio by the BBC. Her poetry collections for children include *Come on Into My Tropical Garden* (1988) and *Give Yourself a Hug* (1994). Some of her other poetry publications: *The Fat Black Woman's Poems,* 1984. *No Hickory, No Dickory, No Dock: A Collection of Caribbean Nursery Rhymes,* 1991 (with John Agard). *Asana and the Animals: A Book of Pet Poems,* 1997. *The Poet Cat,* 2000. *Mouth to Mouth,* 2004 (with John Agard). *Everybody Got a Gift: New and Selected Poems,* 2005. Some of her poems: "Alligator," "Caribbean Woman Prayer," "Invitation," "Like a Beacon," "My Black Triangle," "Praise Song for My Mother."

Sources: *A Dangerous Knowing: Four Black Women Poets:* Barbara Burford, Gabriela Pearse, Grace Nichols, Jackie Kay. Grace Nichols, ed. Sheba, 1985. *Anthology of Twentieth-Century British and Irish Poetry.* Keith Tuma, ed. Oxford University Press, 2001. *British Council Arts* (http://www.contemporarywriters.com). *Erotic Literature: Twenty-four Centuries of Sensual Writing.* Jane Mills, ed. HarperCollins, 1993. *Microsoft Encarta* 2006 (DVD). Microsoft Corporation, 2006. *Penguin Modern Poets, Book 9.* John Burnside, Robert Crawford, and Kathleen Jamie, eds. Penguin Books, 1996. *The Columbia Granger's Index to Poetry.* 11th ed. *The Columbia Granger's World of Poetry,* Columbia University Press, 2005 (http://www.columbiagrangers.org). *The National Portrait Gallery* (www.npg.org.uk). *The New British Poetry, 1968–88.* Gillian Allnutt, Fred D'Aguiar and Ken Edwards, eds. Grafton Books, 1989. *The Oxford Book of Animal Poems.* Michael Harrison and Christopher Stuart-Clark, eds. Oxford University Press, 1992. *The Oxford Companion to English Literature.* 6th edition. Margaret Drabble, ed. Oxford University Press, 2000.

NICHOLS, ROBERT MALISE BOWYER (1893–1944)

Born in Shanklin, Isle of Wight, and educated at Winchester College and at Trinity College, Oxford, he was commissioned into the 104th Brigade, Royal Field Artillery, in October 1914. Invalided home in August 1916 from the Battle of the Somme, suffering from shell-shock (now post-traumatic stress disorder) he spent several months in a hospital. From 1917 he worked for the Foreign Office and in 1918 he was part of the British mission sent to New York, where he lectured on poetry. From 1921 to 1924, he was professor of English at Tokyo Imperial University. In 1924 he went to Hollywood as adviser to Douglas Fairbanks, senior, in his filmmaking, and wrote plays, which were only moderately successful. He lived in England from 1926 and died at Cambridge. Some of his publications: *Invocation*, 1915. *Aurelia*, 1920. *A Spanish Triptych*, 1936. *Such was My Singing*, 1942. *Anthology of War Poetry, 1914–1918*, 1943. Some of his poems: "A Faun's Holiday," "Danaë: Mystery in Eight Poems," "Don Juan's Address to the Sunset," "The Aftermath," "The Burial in Flanders," "The Flower of Flame," "The Water-Lily."

Sources: *Ardors and Endurances by Robert Nichols.* Chatto and Windus, 1917. *Dictionary of National Biography.* Electronic Edition 1.1. Oxford University Press, 1997. *Poetry of the First World War: British Poets* (http://www.scuttlebuttsmallchow.com/listbri3.html). *Putting Poetry First: A Life of Robert Nichols, 1893–1944.* William and Anne Charlton, eds. Michael Russell (Publishing) Ltd., 2003. *The Columbia Granger's Index to Poetry.* 11th ed. *The Columbia Granger's World of Poetry,* Columbia University Press, 2005 (http://www.columbiagrangers.org). *The National Portrait Gallery* (www.npg.org.uk). *The Oxford Book of Modern Verse, 1892–1935.* William Butler Yeats, ed. Oxford University Press, 1936. *The Oxford Book of Satirical Verse.* Geoffrey Grigson, ed. Oxford University Press, 1980. *The Oxford Companion to English Literature.* 6th edition. Margaret Drabble, ed. Oxford University Press, 2000. *The Penguin Book of Homosexual Verse.* Stephen Coote, ed. Penguin Books, 1983.

NICHOLSON, JOHN (1790–1843)

Born at Weardley, near Harewood, Yorkshire, he received a grammar school education at Eldwick, near Bingley, Yorkshire, then worked as a woolsorter for all his working life except for intervals when he was hawking his poems. A heavy drinker, he turned to Methodism, and for a time was a local preacher, but failed to keep the "pledge" and he returned to drink. He is buried in Bingley churchyard. Nicholson's first published work was *The Siege of Bradford* (1821), a dramatic poem which, along with a three-act drama, *The Robber of the Alps*, was written for the Bradford old theater. The outstanding success of *Airedale in Ancient Times* (1825) secured him the title of "the Airedale poet." Some of his other publications: *The Airedale poet's walk*, 1826. *Lines on the Present Distress of the Country*, 1830. *Lines on the present state of the country*, 1826. *Lines, suggested by the near approach of the cholera*, 1831. *Poems*, 1859. *The Poetical Works*, 1876. Some of his poems: "On a Calm Summer's Night," "The Bible," "The Factory Child's Mother," "The Wish of the Drunkard's Family," "Wakening of the Poet's Harp."

Sources: *Dictionary of National Biography.* Electronic Edition 1.1. Oxford University Press, 1997. *English Love Poems.* John Betjeman and Geoffrey Taylor, eds. Faber and Faber, 1957. *English Poetry: Author Search.* Chadwyck-Healey Ltd., 1995 (http://www.lib.utexas.edu:8080/search/epoetry/author.html). *Stanford University Libraries and Academic Information Resources* (http://library.stan

ford.edu). *The Poorhouse Fugitives: Self-Taught Poets and Poetry in Victorian Britain.* Brian Maidment, ed. Carcanet, 1987.

NICHOLSON, NORMAN (1914–1987)

Born in Millom, Cumbria, on the edge of the Lake District, he lived most of his life in the same house, apart from a long spell in his teens in a sanatorium with tuberculosis. Millom was one of the busiest iron ore mining areas in Europe during the late 1800s, and the whole of South and West Cumbria was peppered with quarries, mines and furnaces for smelting the iron ore. All of this is reflected in Nicholson's poetry, as well as religion and faith. He was awarded the Queen's Gold Medal for Poetry in 1977 and the Order of the British Empire in 1981. A memorial, in the form of a specially commissioned stained glass window, was placed in St. Georges Church in Millom. Some of his publications: *Five Rivers*, 1944. *Rock Face*, 1948. *The Pot Geranium*, 1954. *A Local Habitation*, 1972. *Sea to the West*, 1981. Some of his poems: "Black Combe White," "Cleator Moor," "For the Bicentenary of Isaac Watts," "Halley's Comet," "Ravenglass Railway Station, Cumberland," "The Blackberry," "The Burning Bush," "The Tune the Old Cow Died Of."

Sources: *Golden Treasury of the Best Songs and Lyrical Poems in the English Language.* Francis Turner Palgrave, ed. Oxford University Press (1964, Sixth edition, updated by John Press, 1994. *Modern British Poetry.* 7th rev. ed. Louis Untermeyer, ed. Harcourt, Brace, 1962. *Open Directory—Arts: Literature: World Literature: British* (http://dmoz.org/Arts/Literature/World_Literature/British/20th_Century/). *The Columbia Granger's Index to Poetry.* 11th ed. *The Columbia Granger's World of Poetry,* Columbia University Press, 2005 (http://www.columbiagrangers.org). *The Earth is the Lord's: Poems of the Spirit.* Helen Plotz, ed. Thomas Y. Crowell, 1965. *The New Yorker Book of Poems.* The New Yorker editors. Viking Press, 1969. *The Norton Anthology of Poetry.* 4th ed. Margaret Ferguson, Mary Jo Salter and Jon Stal, eds. W.W. Norton, 1996. *The Oxford Companion to English Literature.* 6th edition. Margaret Drabble, ed. Oxford University Press, 2000. *Wikipedia, the Free Encyclopedia* (http://en.wikipedia.org/wiki/Wikipedia).

NÍ CHUILLEANÁIN, EILÉAN (1942–)

Educated in Cork and Oxford, since 1966 she has taught at Trinity College, Dublin, where she is now associate professor of English and dean of the Faculty of Arts (Letters). She won the Patrick Kavanagh Award for Acts and Monuments in 1973; *The Magdalene Sermon* (1989) was short-listed for The Irish Times-Aer Lingus Award in 1990, and she was nominated for the *European Literature Prize* in 1992. The Irish-American Cultural Institute awarded her the O'Shaughnessy Prize for Poetry in 1992. She is a founding editor of the literary review *Cyphers* and a member of Aosdána—an affiliation of Irish artists engaged in literature, music, and visual arts. She lives in Dublin and is married to Macdara Woods (see entry), with whom she has a son, Niall. Her other publications: *Acts and Monuments*, 1972. *Site of Ambush*, 1975. *The Second Voyage*, 1977 and 1986. *The Rose Geranium*, 1981. *The Brazen Serpent*, 1994. *Wake Forest*, 1995. *The Girl Who Married the Reindeer*, 2001. Some of her poems: "Deaths and Engines," "Fireman's Lift," "Saint Margaret of Cortona," "Swineherd," "Trinity New Library," "Wash."

Sources: *Biography of Eiléan Ní Chuilleanáin* (http://homepage.tinet.ie/~writing/052.ENC.html). *Contemporary Irish Poetry: An Anthology.* Anthony Bradley, ed. University of California Press. New and rev. ed., 1988. *Emergency Kit: Poems for Strange Times.* Jo Shapcott and Matthew Sweeney, eds. Faber and Faber, 1996. *Poetry Ireland, The Poets' Chair, Eiléan Ní Chuilleanáin* (http://www.poetryireland.ie/chair/poet.asp?poet_id=8). *Poetry with an Edge.* Neil Astley, ed. Bloodaxe Books, 1988. *The Columbia Granger's Index to Poetry.* 11th ed. *The Columbia Granger's World of Poetry,* Columbia University Press, 2005 (http://www.columbiagrangers.org). *The Oxford Companion to English Literature.* 6th edition. Margaret Drabble, ed. Oxford University Press, 2000. *Works of Eiléan Ní Chuilleanáin* (http://www.irishwriters-online.com/eilean nichuilleanain.html).

NICOLL, ROBERT (1814–1837)

Scottish poet, born in Auchtergaven, about halfway between Perth and Dunkeld. The son of a farmer in reduced circumstances, his formal education was scant. At sixteen he was apprenticed to a grocer and wine merchant in Perth, and by hard work he saved enough to enable his mother to open a shop. His indentures were cancelled owing to ill-health, but in 1836 he was appointed editor of the *Leeds Times.* His strength was so sapped by the enthusiasm for his new task that in 1837 he resigned and returned to Scotland, where he died a few months later. His songs and poems in the Scottish dialect with their simplicity, truth to nature, ardent feeling, pathos, and humor are reckoned to be far superior to his attempts to write in "correct English." That Scotland lost a poet at such a young age is tragedy, for it might have had another Robert Burns. Some of his poems: "The Grave of Burns," "The Heather of Scotland," "The Herd Lassie," "The Hero," "The Making O' The Hay," "The Mossy Stane," "The Puir Folk," "We Are Brethren A'," "We Are Lowly."

Sources: *Dictionary of National Biography.* Electronic Edition 1.1. Oxford University Press, 1997. *English Poetry: Author Search.* Chadwyck-Healey Ltd., 1995 (http://www.lib.utexas.edu:8080/search/epoetry/author.html). *Hay in Art: Hay Poets Born in the Early Nineteenth Century* (http://www.hayinart.com/001405.html#nicoll). *Poems of Robert Nicol.* Second edition: with numerous additions. Simp-kin, Marshall and Co., 1842. *Stanford University Libraries and Academic Information Resources* (http://library.stanford.edu). *The Columbia Granger's Index to Poetry.* 11th ed. *The Columbia Granger's World of Poetry,* Columbia University Press, 2005 (http://www.columbiagrangers.org). *The Home Book of Modern Verse.* Burton Egbert Stevenson, ed. Henry Holt, 1953. *The Poorhouse Fugitives: Self-Taught Poets and Poetry in Victorian Britain.* Brian Maidment, ed. Carcanet, 1987.

NICOLSON, ADELA (VIOLET) FLORENCE (1865–1904)

Born in Gloucestershire, she was educated in Richmond, Surrey. When she was sixteen she joined her parents at Lahore, where her father was in the Indian army, and spent most of her life there. She married Colonel (later General) Malcolm Hassels Nicolson, a Bengal army veteran, in 1889. Her first book of poems—written under the pseudonym "Laurence Hope" which remained her pen-name—*The Garden of Kama* (1901) was hugely successful. She committed suicide by poison two months after her husband died. Many of her translations are thought to be her own work, and some of her poems were set to music by Amy Woodforde-Finden. *Indian Love Lyrics* was the title of a 1933 movie based on Hope's work, with Catherine Calvert in the lead role. Her son published her *Last Poems* in 1922. Her other publications: *Stars of the Desert*, 1903. *Last Poems*, 1905. *India's Love Lyrics Including Garden of Kama*, 1919. Some of her poems: "Ashore," "I Shall Forget," "In the Early, Pearly Morning," "Less Then the Dust," "The Bride," "The Masters," "The Temple Bells," "Till I Awake."

Sources: *Dictionary of National Biography.* Electronic Edition 1.1. Oxford University Press, 1997. *Four Indian Love Lyrics From "The Garden of Kama"* (song book). Hope, Laurence and Finden, Amy Wooforde. Boosey and Co., New York, 1943. *India's Love Lyrics by Laurence Hope.* Dodd, Mead and Company, 1902. *The Home Book of Modern Verse.* Burton Egbert Stevenson, ed. Henry Holt, 1953. *The Indian Love Lyrics Review, The New York Times, Movies* (http://movies2.nytimes.com/gst/movies/movie.html?v_id=96522). *The Oxford Book of Sonnets.* John Fuller, ed. Oxford University Press, 2000.

NÍ DHOMHNAILL, NUALA (1952–)

One of Ireland's foremost women poets writing in Irish, she was born in Lancashire of Irish parents and grew up in the Irish-speaking areas of West Kerry and in Tipperary. She studied at University College, Cork, then lived in Holland and in Turkey with her Turkish husband. She returned to Ireland in 1980 and now lives in Dublin with her family. She has held the Burns Chair of Irish Studies at Boston College and the Humboldt Chair of Irish Studies at Villanova University, Pennsylvania. She was Ireland Professor of Poetry from 2002 to 2004, and has won numerous international awards for works which have been translated into many different languages. Some of her publications: *An Dealg Droighin*, 1981. *Féar Suaithinseach*, 1984. *Rogha Dánta/Selected Poems*, 1986, 1988 and 1990. *Feis*, 1991. *Cead Aighnis*, 1988. *Pharoah's Daughter*, 1990. *The Astrakhan Cloak*, 1992. *The Water Horse*, 1999. Some of her poems: "An Orphan at the Door," "Annunciations," "Aubade," "Cathleen," "I Cannot Lie Here Anymore," "Miraculous Grass," "The Broken Doll," "The Language Issue," "The Shannon Estuary Welcomes the Fish."

Sources: *Biography of Nuala Ní Dhomhnaill* (http://www.usna.edu/EnglishDept/ilv/nuala.htm). *Biography of Nuala Ní Dhomhnaill*; The Gallery Press (http://www.gallerypress.com/Authors/NNdhomhnaill/nndhom.html). *Bitter Harvest: An Anthology of Contemporary Irish Verse.* John Montague, ed. Scribner's, 1989. *Modern Irish Poetry.* Patrick Crotty, ed. The Blackstaff Press, 1995. *The Columbia Granger's Index to Poetry.* 11th ed. *The Columbia Granger's World of Poetry,* Columbia University Press, 2005 (http://www.columbiagrangers.org). *The Oxford Companion to English Literature.* 6th edition. Margaret Drabble, ed. Oxford University Press, 2000. *Works of Nuala Ní Dhomhnaill* (http://www.irishwriters-online.com/nualanidhomhnaill.html).

NOEL, RODEN BERKELEY WRIOTHESLEY (1834–1894)

The son of Charles Noel, Lord Barham, later first Earl of Gainsborough. He was god-child of Queen Victoria, educated at Harrow School, and after graduating M.A. in 1858 from Trinity College, Cambridge, where he was one of the Cambridge Apostles, he spent a year traveling in the Libyan desert. He turned to poetry and his practical philanthropy earned him the title of "The Children's Knight." Toward the end of his life, he frequently lectured on poets, donating the proceeds to the welfare of poor children. He died in the train station of Mainz, Germany, where he is buried. Some of his publications: *Behind the Veil, and Other Poems*, 1863. *Beatrice, and Other Poems*, 1868. *The Red Flag*, 1872. *Livingstone in Africa*, 1874. *Little Child's Monument*, 1881. *Songs of the Heights and Deeps*, 1885. *Poor People's Christmas*, 1890. *My Sea, and Other Poems*, 1896. Some of his poems: "A Vision of the Desert," "Ah! Love Ye One Another Well!" "Alpine Hunter's Song," "Byron's Grave," "The Nile, Africa, and Egypt," "The Slave-Trade," "The Water-Nymph and the Boy."

Sources: *Dictionary of National Biography.* Electronic Edition 1.1. Oxford University Press, 1997. *Lyra Celtica: An Anthology of Representative Celtic Poetry.* E.A. Sharp and J. Matthay, eds. John Grant, 1924. *Noel Roden, Paragon Review of a Legacy of Words* (http://www.hull.ac.uk/oldlib/archives/paragon/1998/noel.html). *Poems of the Hon.*

Roden Noel, A Selection. Walter Scott, 1892. *The Columbia Granger's Index to Poetry.* 11th ed. *The Columbia Granger's World of Poetry,* Columbia University Press, 2005 (http://www.columbiagrangers.org). *The Oxford Companion to English Literature.* 6th edition. Margaret Drabble, ed. Oxford University Press, 2000. *Wikipedia, the Free Encyclopedia* (http://en.wikipedia.org/wiki/Wikipedia).

NOEL, THOMAS (1799–1861)

He was born Kirkby-Mallory, Leicestershire, the son of a clergyman, and graduated B.A. from Merton College, Oxford, in 1824. In 1833 he published *The Cottage Muse*, a series of stanzas upon proverbs and scriptural texts. In 1841 he published two works, *Village Verse* and *Rymes and Roundelayes*. He lived for many years in great seclusion at Boyne Hill, near Maidenhead, then in 1858 he moved to Brighton, Sussex, where he died. The DNB states that he "wrote the words of the familiar song *Rocked in the Cradle of the Deep.*" This is an error. The words were written by the American educator Emma Hart Willard (1787–1870) and set to music by Joseph P. Knight (1812–1887). Some of his poems: "A Thames Voyage," "An Old Man's Idyll," "Old Winter," "Pauper's Drive" (set to music by Henry Russell in 1839), "Poor Voter's Song," "Rat-tower Legend," "Snowdrops."

Sources: *A Treasury of Minor British Poetry.* J. Churton Collins, ed. Edward Arnold, 1896. *British Minstrelsie.* T.C. and E.C. Jack, Grange Publishing Works, Edinburgh, ?1900. *Dictionary of National Biography.* Electronic Edition 1.1. Oxford University Press, 1997. *Great Books Online* (www.bartleby.com). *Parlor Poetry: A Casquet of Gems.* Michael R. Turner, ed. The Viking Press, 1969. *Poems for Seasons and Celebrations.* William Cole, ed. World, 1961. *The Columbia Granger's Index to Poetry.* 11th ed. *The Columbia Granger's World of Poetry,* Columbia University Press, 2005 (http://www.columbiagrangers.org). *The Cyber Hymnal* (http://www.cyberhymnal.org/index.htm).

NORRIS, JOHN (1657–1711)

Born Collingbourne-Kingston, Wiltshire, where his father was the rector, he was educated at Winchester College. He graduated M.A. from Exeter College, Oxford, in 1680, was ordained soon afterwards, and from 1692 he was rector of Bemerton, near Salisbury, where he died. He was the last of the "Cambridge Platonists" (see More, Henry) and his views brought him into controversy with other Christians, such as the Quakers. His *Essay Towards the Theory of an Ideal and Intelligible World* appeared in two parts in 1701 and 1704 and brought him recognition, but little profit. He wrote several learned texts including, in 1707, *Christian Blessedness*, later entitled *Practical Discourses on the Beatitudes*, the first of the four volumes. Some of his poetry publications: *Poems and Discourses Occasionally Written*, 1684. *Pastoral Poem on Death of Charles II*, 1685.

Miscellanies, 1687. Some of his poems: "Hymn to Darkness," "My Estate," "The Aspiration," "The Choice," "The Consummation," "The Discontent," "The Meditation," "The Parting," "The Retirement," "To Melancholy."

Sources: *Dictionary of National Biography.* Electronic Edition 1.1. Oxford University Press, 1997. *English Poetry: Author Search.* Chadwyck-Healey Ltd., 1995 (http://www.lib.utexas.edu:8080/search/epoetry/author.html). *The Cavalier Poets.* Robin Skelton, ed. Oxford University Press, 1970. *The Columbia Granger's Index to Poetry.* 11th ed. *The Columbia Granger's World of Poetry,* Columbia University Press, 2005 (http://www.columbiagrangers.org). *The London Book of English Verse.* Herbert Read and Barbara Dobree, eds. MacMillan, 1952. *The Oxford Book of Christian Verse.* Lord David Cecil, ed. Oxford University Press, 1940. *The Oxford Companion to English Literature.* 6th edition. Margaret Drabble, ed. Oxford University Press, 2000.

NORRIS, LESLIE (1921–2006)

One of the most important Welsh writers of the post-war period, he was born in Merthyr Tydfil, Glamorgan, and became a teacher and college lecturer in England and in Wales. Since 1974 he was a full-time writer of short stories, essays, reviews, translations, and poetry for children as well as adults. He was resident lecturer at academic institutions in the United Kingdom and in the USA, and did not live permanently in Wales since 1948. Since 1983 he was associated with Brigham Young University in Utah, where he was humanities professor of creative writing. He was awarded important literary prizes and was a fellow of the Royal Society of Literature. In 1994 he was awarded an honorary doctor of literature from the University of Glamorgan. Between his first collection, *Tongue of Beauty* (1941), and *Collected Poems* (1996), he published fourteen collections, including two for children: *Merlin and the Snake's Egg* (1978) and *Norris's Ark* (1988). Some of his poems: "Barn Owl," "Belonging," "Boy Flying," "Mice in the Hay," "The Ballad of Billy Rose," "The Thin Prison," "Tiger in the Zoo."

Sources: *Anglo-Welsh Poetry, 1480–1980.* Raymond Garlick and Roland Mathias, eds. Poetry Wales Press, 1984. *Anglo-Welsh Poetry, 1480–1990.* Raymond Garlick and Roland Mathias, eds. Poetry Wales Press, 1993. *CREW Welsh Writers Online: Leslie Norris* (http://www.swan.ac.uk/english/crew/index.htm). *I Like You, If You Like Me: Poems of Friendship.* Myra Cohn Livingston, ed. Macmillan, 1987. *Obituary, of Leslie Norris, Wales, U.K., 11 April 2006* (http://icwales.icnetwork.co.uk/). *Poems of Christmas.* Myra Cohn Livingston, ed. Atheneum, 1980. *The Columbia Granger's Index to Poetry.* 11th ed. *The Columbia Granger's World of Poetry,* Columbia University Press, 2005 (http://www.columbiagrangers.org). *The Kingfisher Book of Children's Poetry.* Michael Rosen, ed. Kingfisher Books, 1985. *This Same Sky: A Collection of Poems from Around the World.* Naomi Shihab Nye, ed. Four Winds Press, 1992.

Twentieth Century Anglo-Welsh Poetry. Dannie Abse, ed. Seren Books / Dufour Editions, 1997.

NORTON, CAROLINE (1808–1877)

(Pseudonym, Caroline Elizabeth Sarah Sheridan). Born in London, the daughter of Thomas Sheridan (see entry), her literary career took off in 1829 with *The Sorrows of Rosalie: A Tale, with Other Poems.* The fact that the work was praised by James Hogg, the "Ettrick Shepherd" (see entry) brought her great satisfaction. Her marriage to the Honorable George Chapple Norton lasted from 1827 to 1830 and ended in lawsuit and countersuit. Her husband refused her access to her children, and her vigorous campaign for legal protection for married women eventually led to the Marriage and Divorce Act of 1857. She went on to support her family by writing for periodicals, as well as novels and poetry. Norton died in 1875 and his widow married Sir William Stirling-Maxwell in 1877 and died within a few months. A gifted artist and musician, she successfully set some of her own lyrics to music. Some of her poems: "As When from Dreams Awaking," "I Do Not Love Thee," "Marriage and Love," "The Arab to His Favorite Steed," "The King of Denmark's Ride," "The Widow to Her Son's Betrothed," "Weep Not for Him That Dieth."

Sources: *Best Loved Story Poems.* Walter E. Thwing, ed. Garden City, 1941. *Bibliography: Works by Caroline Norton* (http://digital.library.upenn.edu/women/norton/nc-bibliography.html). *Dictionary of National Biography.* Electronic Edition 1.1. Oxford University Press, 1997. *Encyclopædia Britannica Ultimate Reference Suite DVD,* 2006. *English Poetry: Author Search.* Chadwyck-Healey Ltd., 1995 (http://www.lib.utexas.edu:8080/search/epoetry/author.html). *Romanticism.* Duncan Wu, ed. Blackwell, 1994. *The Columbia Granger's Index to Poetry.* 11th ed. *The Columbia Granger's World of Poetry,* Columbia University Press, 2005 (http://www.columbiagrangers.org). *The Dream and Other Poems of Caroline Norton.* Jonathan Wordsworth, ed. Woodstock Books, 2001. *The Home Book of Modern Verse.* Burton Egbert Stevenson, ed. Henry Holt, 1953. *The Oxford Companion to English Literature.* 6th edition. Margaret Drabble, ed. Oxford University Press, 2000. *Victorian Women Poets: An Anthology.* Angela Leighton and Margaret Reynolds, ed. Blackwell, 1991.

NORTON, THOMAS (1532–1584)

He was born in London of wealthy parents who owned the manor of Sharpenhoe, Bedfordshire. As a boy he entered the service of Edward Seymour, Duke of Somerset — "Protector Somerset" — as scribe, and later became a lawyer. He was a member of Parliament and was appointed to record the trial (1571–1572) of the Duke of Norfolk for his negotiations with Queen Mary Stuart, which ended in the duke's death. Norton was a rabid anti-Catholic and his torture of Catholics earned him the nickname of "Rackmaster-General." His Calvinist views were regarded as too extreme and he was imprisoned in the Tower of London and although released, he died soon afterward at Sharpenhoe. He collaborated on *Tragedy of Gorboduc* with Thomas Sackville (1561) and translated John Calvin's *Institutes of the Christian Religion* (originally published 1536; translated 1561). He contributed poetry to Tottel's *Miscellany* (1557) and translated many of the Psalms for a collection published in 1561. Some of his poems: "Dixit in Sipiens," "Eripeme," "Laudate Dominum," "Non Nobis Domine," "All Ye Nations of the Lord," "The Creed of Athanasius," "The Ordinal of Alchemy," "The Ten Commandments," "Thomas Norton to the Reader."

Sources: *A Sacrifice of Praise: An Anthology of Christian Poetry in English from Caedmon to the Mid–Twentieth Century.* James H. Trott, ed. Cumberland House Publishing, 1999. *Dictionary of National Biography.* Electronic Edition 1.1. Oxford University Press, 1997. *English Poetry: Author Search.* Chadwyck-Healey Ltd., 1995 (http://www.lib.utexas.edu:8080/search/epoetry/author.html). *Microsoft Encarta* 2006 (DVD). Microsoft Corporation, 2006. Stanford University Libraries and Academic Information Resources (http://library.stanford.edu). *The Columbia Granger's Index to Poetry.* 11th ed. *The Columbia Granger's World of Poetry,* Columbia University Press, 2005 (http://www.columbiagrangers.org).

NOYES, ALFRED (1880–1958)

Born in Wolverhampton (West Midlands), the son of a teacher, he was educated on the classics at schools in Aberystwyth, Wales, and at Exeter College, Oxford, though he did not graduate. In 1913 he gave the Lowell lectures at Boston, Massachusetts, on *The Sea in English Poetry,* and from 1914 to 1923 he held the chair of modern English literature at Princeton University. He was appointed Commander of the British Empire in 1918. He challenged the authenticity of the diaries of Roger Casement (see entry) and stopped the public auction of a copy of *Ulysses* by James Joyce (see entry). He lived in Canada during World War II and lectured in the United States. By the age of seventy he was blind and returned to his home on the Isle of Wight, where he died. He received honorary degrees from four universities, three in America. Between his first volume of poetry, *The Loom of Years* (1902) and his death he published ten collections. Some of his poems: "A Song of Sherwood," "Daddy Fell into the Pond," "Love's Rosary," "The Barrel-organ," "The Butterfly Garden," "The Highwayman," "The World's May-Queen."

Sources: *A Sacrifice of Praise: An Anthology of Christian Poetry in English from Caedmon to the Mid–Twentieth Century.* James H. Trott, ed. Cumberland House Publishing, 1999. *Biography of Alfred Noyes* (http://www3.shropshire-cc.gov.uk/noyes.htm). *Dictionary of National Biography.* Electronic Edition 1.1. Oxford University Press, 1997. *Encyclopædia Britannica Ultimate Reference Suite DVD,* 2006. *Piping Down the Valley Wild: Poetry for the Young of All Ages,* Nancy Larrick, ed. Delacorte Press, 1968. *The Columbia Granger's Index to Poetry.* 11th ed. *The Columbia Granger's World of Poetry,* Columbia University Press, 2005 (http://www.columbiagrangers.org). *The Family Book of Verse.* Lewis Gannett, ed. Harper and Row, 1961. *The Highwayman by Alfred Noyes* (http://www.imagesaustralia.com/poetryromantic.htm). *The National Portrait Gallery* (www.npg.org.uk). *The Oxford Book of English Verse, 1250–1918.* Sir Arthur Quiller-Couch, ed. New edition, revised and enlarged, Oxford University Press, 1939. *The Oxford Book of Villains.* John Mortimer, ed. Oxford University Press, 1992.

NUGENT, ROBERT, EARL NUGENT (1702–1788)

Irish poet, from Carlanstown, Count Westmeath, who on his death had amassed a huge fortune from marrying three rich widows. It was of him that Horace Walpole coined the word "Nugentize" to describe such adventurers. He was controller of the household of Frederick Prince of Wales (1707–1751) (son of George II, and father of George III) and ensured royal favor by loaning the prince large sums of money, debts which were never repaid. Nugent was raised to the Irish peerage as Viscount Clare and Baron Nugent in 1766, and promoted to Earl Nugent in 1776. He died in Dublin, where he received blessing from the Catholic Church, which he had earlier abandoned. Some of his poetry publications: *Essay on Justice,* 1737. *Essay on Happiness,* 1737. *Ode to Mrs. Pulteney,* 1739. *Odes and Epistles,* 1739. *Faith,* 1774. *The Genius of Ireland,* 1775. Some of his poems: "An Elegy," "An Ode to Bavius," "loved thee beautiful and kind," "My heart still hovering round about you," "Revenge," "To Clarissa," "To the Earl of Chesterfield, an Ode."

Sources: *Dictionary of National Biography.* Electronic Edition 1.1. Oxford University Press, 1997. *Dukes of Buckingham and Chandos: Robert Nugent* (http://www.dukesofbuckingham.org/people/family/nugent/robert_nugent.htm). *English Poetry: Author Search.* Chadwyck-Healey Ltd., 1995 (http://www.lib.utexas.edu:8080/search/epoetry/author.html). *Odes and Epistles of Robert Nugent.* R. Dodsley, 1739. *Pith and Vinegar: An Anthology of Short Humorous Poetry.* William Cole, ed. Simon and Schuster, 1969. *The Columbia Granger's Index to Poetry.* 11th ed. *The Columbia Granger's World of Poetry,* Columbia University Press, 2005 (http://www.columbiagrangers.org). *The National Portrait Gallery* (www.npg.org.uk). *The New Oxford Book of Eighteenth Century Verse.* Roger Lonsdale, ed. Oxford University Press, 1984.

NUTTALL, JEFF (1933–2004)

Born in Clitheroe, Lancashire, he grew up in Orcop, near the Herefordshire-Welsh border, where his father was the village schoolmaster. His education was at Hereford and Bath art schools (1949–1953), where he trained as a painter and began writing poetry in 1962. From 1956 to 1968 he was a secondary school art master, then for 16 years he worked at art colleges in Bradford, Leeds, and then as Liverpool polytechnic's head of fine art. He was one of the group of "underground" writers and performers from the late 1950s to the mid–1970s. He also acted in film and television. He was chairman of the National Poetry Society in 1975 and steered it through the differences between two opposing schools of modernism and neo-Georgians. His poems reflect the influence of his involvement with jazz rhythms and with Welsh poetry. He was the *Guardian*'s poetry critic from 1979 to 1981 and published some 40 books — poetry, plays, fiction, memoirs, essays, and verbal portraits. He lived and died in Crickhowell, Wales. Some of his poems: "Goodbye to Leeds (Regret)," "Return Trip," "Scenes and Dubs," "The Whore of Kilpeck," "Three Scenes: Todmorden."

Sources: *Bomb Culture, Jeff Nuttall.* MacGibbon and Kee, 1968. *Guardian Unlimited Obituary, Jeff Nuttall* (http://www.guardian.co.uk/obituaries/story/0,1120760,00.html). *Jeff Nuttall Selected Poems* (2003). Introduction by Roy Fisher. Salt Publishing, 2003 (http://www.saltpublishing.com/books/smp/1844710130.htm). *Jeff Nuttall Video Titles, Available from Movies Unlimited* (http://www.movies unlimited.com/musite/findresults_actor.asp?search=Jeff+ Nuttall). *Selected Poems by Jeff Nuttall* (2003). Review by James Wilkes, 2004 (http://terriblework.co.uk/jeff_nut tall.htm). *The New British Poetry, 1968–88.* Gillian Allnutt, Fred D'Aguiar and Ken Edwards, eds. Grafton Books, 1989.

NYE, ROBERT (1939–)

Born in London, he grew up in Southend-on-Sea. Around the time he left school at 16, his first poetry was published in *London Magazine*. He became a full-time writer in 1961 and moved to a remote cottage in North Wales. He has published collections of poetry, novels, juvenile fiction, and radio plays; has been poetry editor for *The Scotsman* and poetry critic for *The Times*; and has contributed reviews to *The Guardian*. He edited *A Choice of Sir Walter Raleigh's Verse* (Faber and Faber, 1972). From 1976 to 1977 he was writer in residence at Edinburgh University, during which time he received the *Guardian* fiction prize, followed by the Hawthornden Prize for his novel *Falstaff*. Nye's manuscripts are located at the University of Texas, Austin; Colgate University in Hamilton, New York; and the National Library of Scotland, Edinburgh. He now lives in County Cork, Ireland. Some of his poetry publications: *Juvenilia 1*, 1961. *Juvenilia 2*, 1963. *Darker Ends: Poems*, 1969. *Divisions on a Ground*,

1976. *A Collection of Poems 1955–1988*, 1989. *Poems*, 1995. *Collected Poems*, 1998. *The Rain and the Glass: 99 Poems, New and Selected*, 2005.

Sources: *Biography and Bibliography of Robert Nye* (http://www.bookhelpweb.com/authors/nye/nye.htm). *Books by Robert Nye* (http://www.fantasticfiction.co.uk/authors/ Robert_Nye.htm). *Robert Nye Papers* (http://www.hrc. utexas.edu/research/fa/nye.html). *Shades of Green.* Anne Harvey, ed. Greenwillow Books, 1991. *The Columbia Granger's Index to Poetry.* 11th ed. *The Columbia Granger's World of Poetry,* Columbia University Press, 2005 (http://www.columbia grangers.org). *The National Portrait Gallery* (www.npg. org.uk). *The Oxford Companion to English Literature.* 6th edition. Margaret Drabble, ed. Oxford University Press, 2000. *Who's Who.* London: A & C Black, 2005.

O'BRIEN SEAN (1952–)

Born in London, he grew up in Hull, East Riding of Yorkshire, was educated at Selwyn College, Cambridge, then studied for a postgraduate certificate in education. He taught at Beacon School, Crowborough, East Sussex, between 1981 and 1989 and was creative writing fellow at the University of Dundee from 1989 to 1990. He co-founded the literary magazine *The Printer's Devil*, a computer publishing company offering out-of-print books on CD. He contributes regularly to newspapers and magazines, broadcasts on radio and presented BBC Radio 4's *With Great Pleasure*, a selection of his favorite poems and prose. He has held fellowships at six universities in Britain and abroad and has won nine major literary awards, including the E.M. Forster Award by the American Academy of Arts and Letters in 1991. His works include drama, essays, literary criticism, nonfiction, and poetry. Some of his poetry publications: *The Indoor Park*, 1983. *The Frighteners*, 1987. *HMS Glasshouse*, 1981. *Ghost Train*, 1995. *Downriver*, 2001. *Cousin Coat: Selected Poems 1976–2001*, 2002. Some of his poems: "Before," "Cousin Coat," "In Residence: A Worst Case View," "Not Sending Cards This Year," "Ryan's Rebirth," "Song of the South," "Terra Nova."

Sources: *Emergency Kit: Poems for Strange Times.* Jo Shapcott and Matthew Sweeney, ed. Faber and Faber, 1996. *Contemporary Writers in the UK* (www.contempo rarywriters.com). *Poetry with an Edge.* Neil Astley, ed. Bloodaxe Books, 1988. *The Columbia Granger's Index to Poetry.* 11th ed. *The Columbia Granger's World of Poetry,* Columbia University Press, 2005 (http://www.columbia grangers.org). *The Oxford Book of Comic Verse.* John Gross, ed. Oxford University Press, 1994. *The Oxford Companion to English Literature.* 6th edition. Margaret Drabble, ed. Oxford University Press, 2000.

OCCLEVE, THOMAS (HOCCLEVE) (?1370–?1450)

Next to John Lydgate (see entry), he is the most significant English poet of the 15th century (both of them knew Chaucer). Little is known of his life, but for many years he was a clerk of the privy seal office in London. From around 1424 he lived at the priory of Southwick, Hampshire, and although he was given an annuity by Henry IV, Occleve constantly complains in his poems of his state of poverty. Toward the end of his life he was nearly blind but too proud to wear spectacles. Some of his publications: *The Letter of Cupid*, 1402 (a translation of Christine de Pisan's *L'Épistre au dieu d'amours*). *The Male Regle*, 1406 (a picture of the entertainments afforded to bachelors in the taverns of Westminster, possibly biographical). *The Regiment of Princes*, 1411 (of 5,488 lines, written for Henry, Prince of Wales). Some of his poems: "A Description of His Ugly Lady," "Balade and Roundel of Master Somer," "Balade to Edward, Duke of York," "Balade to My Maister Carpenter," "De Regimine Principum," "My Compleinte," "The Sleepless Night," "Three Roundels."

Sources: *Dictionary of National Biography*. Electronic Edition 1.1. Oxford University Press, 1997. *Encyclopædia Britannica Ultimate Reference Suite DVD*, 2006. *English Poetry: Author Search*. Chadwyck-Healey Ltd., 1995 (http://www.lib.utexas.edu:8080/search/epoetry/author.html). *English Poetry: A Poetic Record, from Chaucer to Yeats*. David Hopkins, ed. Routledge, 1990. *Everyman's Book of English Verse*. John Wain, ed. J.M. Dent, 1981. *Medieval English Lyrics: A Critical Anthology*. R.T. Davies, ed. Northwestern University Press, 1964. *My Compleinte and Other Poems of Thomas Hoccleve*. Roger Ellis, ed. University of Exeter Press, 2001. *Selections from Hoccleve*. M.C. Seymour, ed. Clarendon Press 1981. Stanford University Libraries and Academic Information Resources (http://library.stanford.edu). *The Columbia Granger's Index to Poetry*. 11th ed. *The Columbia Granger's World of Poetry*, Columbia University Press, 2005 (http://www.columbiagrangers.org). *The Minor Poems (I.)*, Asher and Co., 1892. *The Oxford Book of Late Medieval Verse and Prose*. Douglas Gray, ed. Clarendon Press, 1985. *The Regimen of Princes*, published for the Early English Text Society by Kegan Paul, Trench, Trübner and Co., 1897. *Works*, published for The English Text Society by Humphrey Milford, Oxford University Press (1925).

O'DONNELL, JOHN (1960–)

John O'Donnell was born in Ireland and was educated at Gonzaga College (a Catholic boys' secondary school in Ranelagh, Dublin), University College Dublin, King's Inns school of Law, Dublin, and Cambridge University, England. His poems have been published many newspapers and journals in Ireland, the U.K., America and Australia, and in anthologies. He has also given public readings in Ireland and England and has broadcast on Irish radio and local radio. In 1998 he won the Hennessy/Sunday Tribune New Irish Writing Award for Poetry, having previously been short listed in 1997 and 1991. He also won the Listowel Writers' Week Prize for

Poetry in 1998, for Best Individual Poem and Best Short Collection. In 1997 he was runner up for the Patrick Kavanagh Poetry Award. *Some Other Country*, his first collection, was published in 2002; also in 2002 he won the SeaCat Irish National Poetry Prize. His most recent collection of poems, *Icarus Sees His Father Fly*, was published in 2004.

Sources: *Biography of John O'Donnell* (http://www.dedaluspress.com/poets/odonnell.html).

O'DONNELL, JOHN FRANCIS (1837–1874)

Irish poet from Limerick, the son of a shopkeeper, he was educated by the Christian Brothers. He spent his life as a newspaper reporter: the *Munster News*, in Limerick, where he began publishing his verse; sub-editor on the *Tipperary*; and editor of *The* (Catholic) *Tablet* in London. Many of his poems were published in *Chambers's Journal*, and Charles Dickens included some of his verses in *All the Year Round*. Returning to Dublin in 1862, he joined the staff of the *Nation*, the revolutionary newspaper of the Young Ireland Party, and was editor of *Duffy's Hibernian Magazine*. Wherever he lived, O'Donnell championed the nationalist movement, and he contributed many nationalist poems to Dublin newspapers under the pseudonyms of "Caviare" and "Monkton West." He was London correspondent of the *Irish People*, the organ of the Fenian Movement, which was suppressed by the government in September 1865. He died in London and was buried at Kensal Green. His grave was marked by a Celtic cross. His two poetry publications: 1865, *The Emerald Wreath*; and 1871, *Memories of the Irish Franciscans*. Three of his poems: "A Spinning Song," "By the Turnstile," "Limerick Town."

Sources: *Dictionary of National Biography*. Electronic Edition 1.1. Oxford University Press, 1997. *English Poetry, Second Edition Bibliography: 19th Century British Minor Poets*. W.H. Auden, ed. Delacorte Press, 1966. *Lyra Celtica: An Anthology of Representative Celtic Poetry*. E.A. Sharp and J. Matthay, eds. John Grant, 1924. *Lyra Celtica, Contents* (http://www.sundown.pair.com/Sharp/Lyra%20Celtica/celtica_contents.htm). *O'Donnell Coat of Arms and Family History* (http://www.araltas.com/features/odonnell/). *Poems, By John Francis O'Donnell*. Introduction by Richard Dowling. Ward and Downey, 1891. *The Columbia Granger's Index to Poetry*. 11th ed. *The Columbia Granger's World of Poetry*, Columbia University Press, 2005 (http://www.columbiagrangers.org).

O'DONOGHUE, BERNARD (1945–)

Irish poet, born in County Cork, where his father was a farmer. His mother was from Manchester and spent some time there after his father died in 1962. He studied English at Lincoln College, Oxford, and graduated in 1968, then received a bachelor of philosophy in medieval English in 1971. He has spent most of his academic life at Oxford and is a fellow of Magdalen College, where he teaches medieval literature. In addition to his poetry, he is a critic of contemporary poetry, and his book *Seamus Heaney and the Language of Poetry* was published by Prentice Hall in 1994. Some of his poetry publications: *The Courtly Love Tradition*, 1982. *Razorblades and Pencils*, 1984. *The Weakness*, 1992. *Gunpowder*, 1995. *Here Nor There*, 1999. *Poaching Rights*, 1999. *Outliving*, 2003. Some of his poems: "A Nun Takes the Veil," "Granary," "In Millstreet Hospital," "O'Regan he Amateur Anatomist," "Passive Smoking," "The Apparition," "The Fool in the Graveyard," "The Humors of Shrone," "The State of the Nation."

Sources: *Biography of Bernard O'Donoghue* (http://www.irishwriters-online.com/bernardodonoghue.html). *Golden Treasury of the Best Songs and Lyrical Poems in the English Language*. Francis Turner Palgrave, ed. Oxford University Press, 1964, Sixth edition, updated by John Press, 1994. *Interview with Bernard O'Donoghue* (http://lidiavianu.scriptmania.com/bernard_o'donoghue.htm). *Lincoln College, Oxford — College News* (http://www.lincoln.ox.ac.uk/news/2004/11/16/). *Modern Irish Poetry*. Patrick Crotty, ed. The Blackstaff Press, 1995. *The Columbia Granger's Index to Poetry*. 11th ed. *The Columbia Granger's World of Poetry*, Columbia University Press, 2005 (http://www.columbiagrangers.org). *The Norton Anthology of Poetry*. 4th ed. Margaret Ferguson, Mary Jo Salter and Jon Stal, eds. W.W. Norton, 1996. *The Oxford Companion to English Literature*. 6th edition. Margaret Drabble, ed. Oxford University Press, 2000.

O'DONOGHUE, GREGORY (1951–2005)

Irish poet born in Cork, he studied at University College, Cork. After spending twenty years as a lecturer at Queens University, Kingston, Ontario, Canada, he moved to Lincolnshire, England, in 1980. For the next ten years he worked freight trains between South Derbyshire and King's Cross, Nottingham and Skegness, then moved back to Cork. To mark the Cork Year of Culture in 2005, he translated *A Visit to the Clockmaker* by Bulgarian poet Kristin Dimitrova (1963). He co-facilitated the Thursday workshops of the Munster Literature Centre with Patrick Galvin (see entry) and was poetry editor of the journal *Southword*. In 2004 he was a recipient of an artist's bursary from Cork City Council. He died in Cork. His publications: *Kicking*, 1975. *The Permanent Way*, 1996. *Making Tracks*, 2001. Some of his poems: "A Polish Girl Standing on a Chair," "Ash and Ocean," "Emily Jane Bronte," "Making Tracks," "The Web."

Sources: *Biography of Gregory O'Donoghue* (http://www.irishwriters-online.com/gregoryodonoghue.html). *Cork 2005 Translation Project. Bulgaria/Cork Poet: Greg-*ory O'Donoghue* (http://www.munsterlit.ie/Conwriters/Translation%20Project/gregory_o'donoghue.htm). *The Book of Irish Verse: An Anthology of Irish Poetry from the Sixth Century to the Present*. John Montague, ed. Macmillan, 1974. *The Columbia Granger's Index to Poetry*. 11th ed. *The Columbia Granger's World of Poetry,* Columbia University Press, 2005 (http://www.columbiagrangers.org). *Turning Tides: Modern Dutch and Flemish Verse in English Versions by Irish Poets*. Peter van de Kamp, ed. Story Line Press, 1994. Works of *Gregory O'Donoghue* (http://www.munsterlit.ie/Conwriters/gregory_o'donoghue.htm).

O'DRISCOLL, DENNIS (1954–)

Irish poet, born in Thurles, County Tipperary, he studied law at University College, Dublin, and has been a civil servant since 1970. He is one of Ireland's most widely published and respected critics of poetry. He has reviewed poetry for *Hibernia* and *The Crane Bag* (focusing mainly on contemporary European writing), *The Irish Times* and international journals. His poetry includes *The Bottom Line* (1994), a poem of 550 lines on subject of business and bureaucracy. The collection *Weather Permitting* (1999) won the Lannan Prize, 2000. A selection from *Pickings and Cuttings'* column of poetry quotations, *As the Poet Said*, edited by Tony Curtis (see entry), was published by *Poetry Ireland* in 1997. Some of his other publications: *Kist*, 1982. *Hidden Extras*, 1987. *Long Story Short*, 1993. *Quality Time*, 1997. *Exemplary Damages*, 2002. *New and Selected Poems*, 2004. Some of his translations: *Epiphany* (Christine D'Haen, b. 1923). *Friendship for a Woman of Grace* (J. Greshoff, 1888–1971). *No, No, Nanette* (K. Schippers, b. 1936). *Pentecost* (Gerrit Achterberg). *Rubbish Bags* (Victor Vroomkoning, b. 1938). *That April Morning* (Patricia Lasoen, b. 1948).

Sources: *Biography of Dennis O'Driscoll* (http://www.irishwriters-online.com/dennisodriscoll.html). *The Columbia Granger's Index to Poetry*. 11th ed. *The Columbia Granger's World of Poetry,* Columbia University Press, 2005 (http://www.columbiagrangers.org). *Turning Tides: Modern Dutch and Flemish Verse in English Versions by Irish Poets*. Peter van de Kamp, ed. Story Line Press, 1994.

OGILBY, JOHN (1600–1676)

Scottish poet born near Edinburgh, and although of little education, through hard work and good fortune on a lottery, he saved enough money to have his father released from debtors' prison. He became a renowned dancing master in London and, in 1633, the Earl of Strafford (lord-deputy of Ireland) employed him to teach his children and to transcribe his papers. During the Civil War he became destitute and was patronized by some students at Cambridge University, from whom he learned Latin. There he produced a rhyming version *Aesop's Fables* (1581). He also learned Greek and translated Homer's *Iliad*

(1660). Tragedy struck again in the Great Fire of London of 1666, when he lost everything. He turned his hand to producing maps and atlases, for which his name has endured. He wrote two heroic poems, "The Ephesian Matron" and "The Roman Slave," and an epic poem in twelve books, *Carolies*, in honor of Charles I. He died in London and was buried in St. Bride's Church, Fleet Street. Three of his poems: "The Character of a Trooper," "To His Worthy Friend the Author," "To My Much Honoured and Learned Friend, Mr. James Shirley."

Sources: *Dictionary of National Biography*. Electronic Edition 1.1. Oxford University Press, 1997. *The Columbia Granger's Index to Poetry*. 11th ed. *The Columbia Granger's World of Poetry*, Columbia University Press, 2005 (http://www.columbiagrangers.org). *The Dramatic Works and Poems of James Shirley, Volume I*. Alexander Dyce and William Gifford, ed. Russell and Russell, 1966. *The Oxford Book of Classical Verse in Translation*. Adrian Poole and Jeremy Maule, eds. 1995.

OGILVIE, JOHN (1733–1813)

Scottish poet born in Aberdeen, the son of a Presbyterian minister. When he graduated from Aberdeen University he, too, became a minister, in 1759 of Midmar, Aberdeenshire, where he remained until his death. He was made doctor of divinity by Aberdeen University in 1766 and was one of the committee for the revision of the *Scottish Translations and Paraphrases* (1775). He was a member of the Edinburgh Royal Society. Two of his hymns are "Begin, My Soul, the Exalted Lay" and "Lo, in the Last of Days Behold." He married in January 1771, had a family, and died at Aberdeen. His poems are long and show learning rather than poetic charm. His poetry publications: *The Day of Judgment*, 1753. *Poems on Several Subjects, with Essay on Lyric Poetry*, 1762. *Providence: an Allegorical Poem*, 1764. *Solitude, or the Elysium of the Poets*, 1765. *Paradise*, 1769. *Rona: A Poem in Seven Books, with Map of the Hebrides*, 1777. *Britannia: A National Epic Poem in Twenty Books*, 1801.

Sources: *Begin, My Soul, the Exalted Lay: Metrical Version of Psalm 148, by John Ogilvie* (http://www.oremus. org/hymnal/b/b048.html). *Dictionary of National Biography*. Electronic Edition, 1.1.

O'HUSSEY, EOCHAIDH (c. 1574–c. 1630)

He was an Irish poet (in Irish, Ua hEodhasa) who came from a long line hereditary poets and historians, of which the earliest famous member was Aenghus, who died in 1350. The family were chief poets to Clan Maguire of Fermanagh. Eochaidh started writing at a young age and his earliest poem — of 228 verses (1593) — is on the escape of Aedh ruadh O'Donnell from Dublin Castle in 1592.

He wrote four poems of 508 verses in all on Cuchonacht Maguire, Lord of Fermanagh, and seven poems on his son, Hugh Maguire, Lord of Fermanagh (died 1600). He also wrote two verses on Tadhg O'Rourke of Breifne; on Eoghan óg MacSweeny of Donegal; on Feidhlimidh O'Beirne, and on Richard de Burgo MacWilliam of Connaught. He wrote a poetic address of 152 verses to Hugh O'Neill, the great earl of Tyrone (?1540–1616), and one of forty-four verses to Rory O'Donnell, earl of Tyrconnel (1575–1608). Some of his poems: "A Change in Style," "Hugh Maguire," "Mag Uidhir's Winter Campaign," "O'Hussey's Ode to the Maguire," "O Man of Ill-health!"

Sources: *An Anthology of Irish Literature*. David H. Greene, ed. H. Modern Library, 1954. *An Anthology of Irish Verse: The Poetry of Ireland from Mythological Times to the Present*. Padraic Colum, ed. Liveright, 1948. *Clan Maguire* (http://www.cov44.freeserve.co.uk/clanmag.htm). *Dictionary of National Biography*. Electronic Edition 1.1. Oxford University Press, 1997. *The Columbia Granger's Index to Poetry*. 11th ed. *The Columbia Granger's World of Poetry*, Columbia University Press, 2005 (http://www. columbiagrangers.org). *The New Oxford Book of Irish Verse*. Thomas Kinsella, ed. Oxford University Press, 1986.

O'KEEFFE, JOHN and ADELAIDE (1747–?1855)

John, the father, 1747–1833

Irish dramatist and poet, born in Dublin, he was educated by the Jesuits, after which he studied art in the Dublin School of Design. Attracted to the stage, he wrote his first play, *The Gallant*, at 15. In 1773 his farce *Tony Lumpkin in Town*, based on Oliver Goldsmith's *She Stoops to Conquer*, was produced in Dublin and performed at the Haymarket Theatre, London, in 1778. He lived in London from around 1798. He produced more than 60 plays, confining himself to farces and comic operas, mainly for the Haymarket and Covent Garden Theatres. He was an actor for twelve years but by 36 he was completely blind and had to rely on scribes to take his dictation. In 1800, he was accorded a benefit at Covent Garden under the patronage of the Prince of Wales, and in 1820 he was granted a pension from the privy purse. He died in Southampton, Hampshire. Some of his poems: "Air," "Amo, Amas; I love a lass," "I am a Friar of Orders Grey," "I Want a Tenant" (a satire).

Adelaide, the daughter, 1776–?1855

Not much is written about his only daughter and third child, Adelaide, but that she was born in Dublin and cared for her father and remained with him all through his long years of blindness. She contributed thirty-four poems to the *Original Poems for Infant Minds by Several Young Persons* (1804, and

1805) (see entry for The Taylor Sisters). She published a collection of poems titled *A Trip to the Coast* in 1819. The book *Little Ann and Other Poems* contains poems by the Taylor sisters and Adelaide O'Keeffe. It was illustrated by Kate Greenaway (1846–1901) and published in 1883. Some of her poems: "Beasts and Birds," "Careless Matilda," "Frances Keeps Her Promise," "George and the Chimney-Sweep," "James and the Shoulder of Mutton," "Rather Too Good, Little Peggy!" "The Butterfly," "The Kite," "To George Pulling Buds."

Sources: *Dictionary of National Biography.* Electronic Edition 1.1. Oxford University Press, 1997. *Little Anne: Book by Adelaide O'Keefe* (http://digital.library.upenn.edu/women/taylor/little-ann/little-ann.html). *Oldpoetry* (www.oldpoetry.com). *Shades of Green.* Anne Harvey, ed. Greenwillow Books, 1991. *The Columbia Granger's Index to Poetry.* 11th ed. *The Columbia Granger's World of Poetry,* Columbia University Press, 2005 (http://www.columbiagrangers.org). *The Faber Book of Useful Verse.* Simon Brett, ed. Faber and Faber, 1981. *The Gambit Book of Love Poems.* Geoffrey Grigson, ed. Gambit, 1973. *The Home Book of Verse for Young Folks.* Burton Egbert Stevenson, ed. Holt, Rinehart and Winston, 1929. *The National Portrait Gallery* (www.npg.org.uk). *The New Oxford Book of Children's Verse.* Neil Philip, ed. Oxford University Press, 1996. *The New Oxford Book of Eighteenth Century Verse.* Roger Lonsdale, ed. Oxford University Press, 1984. *The Oxford Companion to English Literature.* 6th edition. Margaret Drabble, ed. Oxford University Press, 2000. *The Poolbeg Book of Children's Verse.* Sean McMahon, ed. Poolbeg Press, 1987.

OLDHAM, JOHN (1653–1683)

Born at Shipton-Moyne, near Tetbury in Gloucestershire, to a clergyman father, he graduated B.A. from St. Edmund Hall, Oxford, in 1674. He satirizes his years between 1675 and 1678 as under-master (usher) at Archbishop Whitgift's free school at Croydon, Surrey, in his poem "Grammar-Bridewell." He was then tutor to several influential families. He died of smallpox at Lord Kingston's seat, Holme-Pierrepoint, near Nottingham. The Earl of Rochester (see Rochester, John Wilmot) befriended Oldham, who wrote "A Pastoral, in Imitation of the Greek of *Moschus*; Bewailing The Death of the Earl of Rochester." Oldham is credited with being the pioneer of the imitation of classical satire in English. Some of his publications: *Upon the Marriage of the Prince of Orange,* 1677. *Upon the Author of a Play Call'd Sodom,* 1680. *Satires Upon the Jesuits,* 1681. *The Works,* 1684. *A Pastoral,* 1696. Some of his poems: "A Quiet Soul," "Advice to a Painter," "Character of a certain Ugly Old Priest," "Fragment of Petronius, Paraphras'd," "On the Death of King Charles I," "The Careless Good Fellow," "The Parting," "The Praise of Homer," "Upon the Works of Ben Jonson."

Sources: *Encyclopædia Britannica Ultimate Reference Suite DVD,* 2006. *English Poetry: Author Search.* Chadwyck-Healey Ltd., 1995 (http://www.lib.utexas.edu:8080/search/epoetry/author.html). *English Poetry: A Poetic Record, from Chaucer to Yeats.* David Hopkins, ed. Routledge, 1990. *The Columbia Granger's Index to Poetry.* 11th ed. *The Columbia Granger's World of Poetry,* Columbia University Press, 2005 (http://www.columbiagrangers.org). *The Oxford Book of English Verse, 1250–1918.* Sir Arthur Quiller-Couch, ed. New edition, revised and enlarged, Oxford University Press, 1939. *The Oxford Book of Satirical Verse.* Geoffrey Grigson, ed. Oxford University Press, 1980. *The Oxford Book of Seventeenth Century Verse.* H.J.C. Grierson and G. Bullough, eds. Oxford University Press, 1934. *The Oxford Book of Verse in English Translation.* Charles Tomlinson, ed. Oxford University Press, 1980. *The Oxford Companion to English Literature.* 6th edition. Margaret Drabble, ed. Oxford University Press, 2000. *The Poems of John Oldham.* Harold F. Brooks, ed. Clarendon Press, 1987.

OLDMIXON, JOHN (?1673–1742)

Little is written about his life except that he was born at Bridgwater, Somerset, and died at his house in Great Pulteney Street, London. He was a poet, pamphleteer, and historian, and was disappointed at not being appointed poet laureate. Although his greater work was history, he was also a substantial poet. His main history publications: *The British Empire in America,* 1708. *The Secret History of Europe,* 1712 to 1715. *Critical History of England,* 1724–1747. *The History of England during the Reigns of the Royal House of Stuart,* 1729. *The History of England during the Reigns of King William and Queen Mary, Queen Anne, King George I,* 1735. His major poetry publications: *Poems on Several Occasions,* 1696. *An Idyll on the Peace,* 1697. *A Funeral Idyll,* 1702. *Amores Britannici,* 1703. *A Pastoral Poem,* 1704. *Ovid's Epistles,* 1705. *Iberia Liberata,* 1706. *The Catholick Poet,* 1716. Some of his poems: "I Lately Vowed, But 'Twas in Haste," "Rosamund to King Henry the Second," "The Country Wit," "The Picture," "The Second Ode of Anacreon," "To Cleora."

Sources: *Dictionary of National Biography.* Electronic Edition 1.1. Oxford University Press, 1997. *English Poetry: Author Search.* Chadwyck-Healey Ltd., 1995 (http://www.lib.utexas.edu:8080/search/epoetry/author.html). *Stanford University Libraries and Academic Information Resources* (http://library.stanford.edu). *The Columbia Granger's Index to Poetry.* 11th ed. *The Columbia Granger's World of Poetry,* Columbia University Press, 2005 (http://www.columbiagrangers.org). *The Home Book of Modern Verse.* Burton Egbert Stevenson, ed. Henry Holt, 1953. *The Oxford Companion to English Literature.* 6th edition. Margaret Drabble, ed. Oxford University Press, 2000.

OLIVER, DOUGLAS (1937–2000)

Born in Southampton, Hampshire, he was brought up in Branksome, Dorset. After serving his

National Service in the Royal Air Force, he was a journalist in Coventry and on the *Cambridge Evening News*. Fluent in French, he worked as translator for *Agence France-Presse* in Paris. In 1972, he read for a B.A. in literature at Essex University and taught part-time for five years until 1982, then took a lectureship at the British Institute in Paris. In 1987, *Kind*, his collected poems, was published. It was dedicated to his son, Tom, born with Down Syndrome and who died before his second birthday in 1969. From 1987 to 1992 Oliver lived in America and worked as a computer programmer in a cancer hospital and as a contact tracer for HIV patients, then returned to the British Institute in Paris. Some of his poetry publications: *Kitchen Poems*, 1968. *O poetique*, 1969. *Penniless Politics*, 1991. *Arrondissements*, 2003. *Selected Poems*, 1996. *Whisper "Louise,"* 2005. Some of his poems: "Love in the Dark Valley," "Mongol in the Woods," "Snowdonia at a Distance," "The Infant and the Pearl," "When I Was in Bridgeport."

Sources: *A Various Art.* Andrew Crozier and Tim Longville, eds. Carcanet Press, 1987. *The Literary Encyclopedia* (www.LitEncyc.com). *Obituary of Douglas Oliver*, The Independent *(London), April 26, 2000, by Nicholas Johnson* (http://www.findarticles.com/p/articles/mi_qn4158/is_20000426/ai_n14307041). *Other: British and Irish Poetry Since 1970.* Richard Caddel and Peter Quartermain, eds. Wesleyan University Press, 1999. *The Columbia Granger's Index to Poetry.* 11th ed. *The Columbia Granger's World of Poetry,* Columbia University Press, 2005 (http://www.columbiagrangers.org). *The New British Poetry, 1968–88.* Gillian Allnutt, Fred D'Aguiar and Ken Edwards, eds. Grafton Books, 1989.

OLIVERS, THOMAS (1725–1799)

Welsh poet born at Tregynon, near Newtown Montgomeryshire, he was orphaned as a young child and lacked a proper education. He became a shoemaker and traveled through England in a wretched state. At Bristol he heard George Whitefield (1714–1770) preach from the text "Is not this a brand plucked out of the fire?" (Zechariah 3:2) and experienced a profound conversion that changed his life. He joined the Methodist Society at Bradford-on-Avon, Wiltshire, and John Wesley took him on as a preacher. From 1753 he was an evangelist in Cornwall. He died in London and was buried in Wesley's tomb in the City Road Chapel burying ground, London. He is most widely known for his hymns "The God of Abraham Praise," which is sung to the Jewish melody *Leoni*; "Come Immortal King of Glory"; "O Thou God of My Salvation" with music by the American Methodist Daniel B. Towner (1850–1919); and "Hymn of Praise to Christ." His elegy "On the Death of the late Reverend John Wesley" was published in 1791.

Sources: *A Sacrifice of Praise: An Anthology of Christian Poetry in English from Caedmon to the Mid–Twentieth Century.* James H. Trott, ed. Cumberland House Publishing, 1999. *Dictionary of National Biography.* Electronic Edition 1.1. Oxford University Press, 1997. *Enchiridion: Biographies* (http://www.canamus.org/Enchiridion/Biogs/bo.htm). *The Columbia Granger's Index to Poetry.* 11th ed. *The Columbia Granger's World of Poetry,* Columbia University Press, 2005 (http://www.columbiagrangers.org). *The Cyber Hymnal* (http://www.cyberhymnal.org/index.htm).

O'NEILL, MARY DEVENPORT (1879–1967)

Irish poet and dramatist who studied at the National College of Art in Dublin, she published two verse plays, *Bluebeard* (1933) and *Cain* (1945) and one collection of poetry, *Prometheus and Other Poems* (1929). She was also a regular contributor to *The Dublin Magazine*. The ballet *Bluebeard* was based on her play and was choreographed by Dame Ninette de Valois (1898–2001) as one of the final productions of the Abbey School of Ballet, Dublin (1926–1933). O'Neill's regular Thursday salon was attended by W.B. Yeats (see entry), AE (George William Russell) (see entry) and other prominent Irish writers. She had a reputation as a psychic and Yeats consulted her while he was working on his book *A Vision* (1925) dealing with the phenomenon of automatic writing. O'Neill's husband Joseph was permanent secretary of the Department of Education, from whom Yeats learned much about the Irish education system to help him in his role as a member of Seanad Éireann (Senate of Ireland). Some of her poems: "An Old Waterford Woman," "Dead in Wars and in Revolutions," "Galway," "Scene-Shifter Death," "The Tramp's Song."

Sources: *An Anthology of Irish Verse: The Poetry of Ireland from Mythological Times to the Present.* Padraic Colum, ed. Liveright, 1948. *Biography of Mary Devenport O'Neill* (http://www.absoluteastronomy.com/ref/mary_devenport_oneill1). *New Irish Poets.* Devin A. Garrity, ed. Devin-Adair, 1948. *The Columbia Granger's Index to Poetry.* 11th ed. *The Columbia Granger's World of Poetry,* Columbia University Press, 2005 (http://www.columbiagrangers.org). *The Oxford Book of Irish Verse: XVIIth Century–XXth Century.* Donagh MacDonagh and Leenox Robinson, eds. Oxford University Press, 1958. *Wikipedia, the Free Encyclopedia* (http://en.wikipedia.org/wiki/Wikipedia).

OPIE, AMELIA (1769–1853)

She was the daughter of James Alderson, a respected physician of Norwich, Norfolk, whose wife died in 1784. In 1798 she married the painter John Opie (1761–1807), who greatly encouraged her in her writing; her novel *Father and Daughter* was published in 1801. She was satirized by the novelist Thomas Love Peacock (1785–1866) as Miss Poppyseed in *Headlong Hall* (1816) as one who could never stop compounding novels. When her husband died she returned and lived with her father in Norwich until he died in 1825. Brought up a Unitarian, she became a Quaker in 1825 and gave up writing novels. She was buried in the same grave as her father, in the Friends' burying ground at Norwich. Some of her poetry publications: *Elegy to the Memory of the Late Duke of Bedford*, 1802. *The Warrior's Return*, 1808. *Poems*, 1811 (6th edition). *The Black Man's Lament*, 1826. *Lays for the Dead*, 1840. Some of her poems: "Address of a Felon to His Child on the Morning of His Execution," "Fatherless Fanny," "Symptoms of Love," "The Despairing Wanderer," "The Negro Boy's Tale," "To the Glow-Worm."

Sources: *Dictionary of National Biography.* Electronic Edition 1.1. Oxford University Press, 1997. *English Poetry: Author Search.* Chadwyck-Healey Ltd., 1995 (http://www.lib.utexas.edu:8080/search/epoetry/author.html). *Poems of Amelia Alderson Opie.* T.N. Longman, 1802. *Romanticism.* Duncan Wu, ed. Blackwell, 1994. Stanford University Libraries and Academic Information Resources (http://library.stanford.edu). *The Columbia Granger's Index to Poetry.* 11th ed. *The Columbia Granger's World of Poetry,* Columbia University Press, 2005 (http://www.columbiagrangers.org). *The National Portrait Gallery* (www.npg.org.uk). *The Oxford Companion to English Literature.* 6th edition. Margaret Drabble, ed. Oxford University Press, 2000.

ORD, JOHN WALKER (1811–1853)

He was the son of Richard Ord, a tanner and leather merchant from Guisborough, Yorkshire. While studying medicine at Edinburgh he made the acquaintance of James Hogg, the "Ettrick Shepherd" (see entry). He abandoned medicine and in 1836 became a journalist in London. In 1836 he published *Remarks on the sympathetic Condition existing between the Body and the Mind especially during Disease.* In 1843, he returned to Guisborough and spent the later years of working on the history and literature of the Cleveland area. *The History and Antiquities of Cleveland* appeared in twelve monthly parts during 1844. It was published in one volume during 1846 and reprinted in 1972. He died at Guisborough. Some of his poetry publications: *The Wandering Bard and Other Poems*, 1833. *England: a historical Poem*, 1834–1835 (2 volumes). *The Bard, and minor Poems*, 1841. *Rural Sketches and Poems, chiefly relating to Cleveland*, 1845. Prince Oswy, 1868. Some of his poems: "Queen Victoria at Windsor," "Song of Miriam," "The Alum Rocks," "The Beloved," "The Rose of Cleveland," "To a Girl of Fifteen," "To the Cuckoo," "Tynemouth Prior."

Sources: *Dictionary of National Biography.* Electronic Edition 1.1. Oxford University Press, 1997. *English Poetry: Author Search.* Chadwyck-Healey Ltd., 1995 (http://www.lib.utexas.edu:8080/search/epoetry/author.html). Stan-

ford University Libraries and Academic Information Resources (http://library.stanford.edu). *Teesonline: Outlet: Who's Who in Literary Cleveland* (http://www.teesonline.org.uk/?lid=2205).

ORMOND, JOHN (1923–1990)

Welsh poet born at Dunvant, near Swansea, he was educated at the University College of Swansea, then became staff writer of the London *Picture Post* in 1945. He returned to Swansea as sub-editor of the *South Wales Evening Post* before embarking on a career with the BBC in Wales, to become a renowned producer and director of documentary films, which, over the years, included studies of Welsh painters and writers. His early verses (under the name Ormond Thomas) appeared in the volume *Indications* (1943) with that of James Kirkup and John Bayliss (see entries). Discouraged at the advice from Vernon Watkins (see entry) not to publish any more until he was thirty, he did not publish any more for almost twenty years. A selection of his work, including eight uncollected poems, was included in *Penguin Modern Poets 27* (1978). His other publications: *Requiem and Celebration*, 1969. *Definition of a Waterfall*, 1973. *Selected Poems*, 1987. *Cathedral Builders*, 1991. Some of his poems: "Ancient Monuments," "At His Father's Grave," "Definition of a Waterfall," "Design for a Quilt," "Design for a Tomb," "My Grandfather and His Apple-Tree."

Sources: *Anglo-Welsh Poetry, 1480–1980.* Raymond Garlick and Roland Mathias, ed. Poetry Wales Press, 1984. *Anglo-Welsh Poetry, 1480–1990.* Raymond Garlick and Roland Mathias, ed. Poetry Wales Press, 1993. *CREW Welsh Writers Online* (http://www.swan.ac.uk/english/crew/index.htm). *The Columbia Granger's Index to Poetry.* 11th ed. *The Columbia Granger's World of Poetry,* Columbia University Press, 2005 (http://www.columbiagrangers.org). *The Oxford Book of Death.* D.J. Enright, ed. Oxford University Press, 1987. *Twentieth Century Anglo-Welsh Poetry.* Dannie Abse, ed. Seren Books / Dufour Editions, 1997.

ORMSBY, FRANK (1947–)

Born in Enniskillen, County Fermanagh, Northern Ireland, and educated at Queen's University, Belfast, he is head of English at the Royal Belfast Academical Institution. He has edited a number of anthologies, including *Thine in Storm and Calm: An Amanda McKittrick Ros Reader* (1988); *The Collected Poems of John Hewitt* (see entry) (1991); and *Northern Windows: An Anthology of Ulster Autobiography* (1987). He edited the *Honest Ulsterman* from 1969 to 1989; the *Poetry Ireland Review*; and *The Hip Flask: Short Poems from Ireland* (2001), a collection of Irish lyric poems including work by W.B. Yeats, J.M. Synge and Seamus Heaney (see entries). In 1992 he received the Cultural Traditions Award, given in memory of John Hewitt, and in 2002 the Lawrence O'Shaughnessy Award for Poetry from the University of St. Thomas at St. Paul, Minnesota. Some of his other publications: *Ripe for Company*, 1971. *A Store of Candles*, 1977. *The Ghost Train*, 1995. Some of his poems: "A Northern Spring," "At the Jaffé Memorial Fountain, Botanic Gardens," "The Padre," "The War Photographers," "Winter Offerings."

Sources: *Bitter Harvest: An Anthology of Contemporary Irish Verse*. John Montague, ed. Scribner's, 1989. *Contemporary Irish Poetry: An Anthology*. Anthony Bradley, ed. University of California Press. New and rev. ed., 1988. *Life and Works of Frank Ormsby* (http://www.contemporary writers.com/authors/?p=auth133). *Poets from the North of Ireland*. Frank Ormsby, ed. The Blackstaff Press, 1990. *The Columbia Granger's Index to Poetry*. 11th ed. *The Columbia Granger's World of Poetry,* Columbia University Press, 2005 (http://www.columbiagrangers.org).

ORR, JAMES (1770–1816)

"The Poet of Ballycarry" was born at Ferranshane, County Antrim, Ireland, the son of a weaver. Orr became one of the Rhyming Weavers of Ulster, who wrote in the Ulster Scot dialect — inspired by Robert Burns — and who published their work mainly in the local newspapers. He joined the United Irishmen, formed in 1791 by a group of Protestants, inspired by the French Revolution, whose aim was equal rights for Catholics and Protestants alike. The '98 rebellion was a mass protest for democratic rights and against English rule in Ireland. After the battle of Antrim on 7 June 1798, in which the United Irishmen took part, Orr escaped to America, and while there wrote for the press. Back in Ireland he published by subscription *Poems on Various Subjects* (1804). He took to drink, died at Ballycarry, and was buried in Templecorran churchyard, where a public monument was erected over his grave. Four of his poems remain firm favorites: "The Irishman"; "The Execution" (which memorializes the hanging of his brother William, in 1797, on a trumped-up charge of sedition); "The Hill at Donegore," "The Irish Cottier's Death and Burial."

Sources: *BBC—History—The 1798 Irish Rebellion* (http://www.bbc.co.uk/history/state/nations/irish_reb_02. shtml). *BBC—History—United Irishmen—up to 1798* (http://www.bbc.co.uk/history/timelines/ni/united_irish men.shtml). *Biography of James Orr* (http://www.ullans. com/culture/JamesOrr.shtml). *Country Rhymes of James Orr: The Bard of Ballycarry*. Pretani Press, 1992. *Dictionary of National Biography*. Electronic Edition, 1.1. *Rabbie Burns, The Weaver Poets. James Orr.* (http://www.bbc.co. uk/northernireland/winter/rabbie/weaver1.shtml).

ORRERY, ROGER BOYLE, 1ST EARL OF (1621–1679)

The son of Richard Boyle, first Earl of Cork, was born at Lismore, County Waterford, and educated at Trinity College, Dublin. He served with the Earl of Northumberland, then took part in the campaign against the Irish in the rebellion of 1641. Oliver Cromwell got wind of Boyles' plan to reinstate Charles II and seduced him by offering him a general's command against the Irish, which he accepted. He was in Cromwell's parliament in 1654, and in 1656 was made lord president of the council to Scotland and created Earl of Orrery in 1660. He was buried at Youghal, East Cork. Between 1655 and 1659 he published *Parthenissa*, a romance in six volumes, and in 1677, *Treatise of the Art of War*. He also wrote *Poems on Most of the Festivals of the Church* (1681) as well as several rhymed-verse tragedies. Some of his publications: *Henry V*, 1664. *Mustapha*, 1665. *The Black Prince*, 1669. *Tryphon*, 1672. *Herod the Great,* 1694. Some of his poems: "A Poem on the Death of Abraham Cowley," "On Christmas Day," "The Dream," "The Earl of Orrery to Mrs. Philips."

Sources: *Biography of Roger Boyle, 1st Earl of Orrery: Answer.Com* (http://www.answers.com/topic/roger-boyle-1st-earl-of-orrery). *Dictionary of National Biography*. Electronic Edition 1.1. Oxford University Press, 1997. *Encyclopædia Britannica Ultimate Reference Suite DVD,* 2006. *Results in Early English Prose Fiction.* (http://www. letrs.indiana.edu/eepf/browse.html). *The Columbia Granger's Index to Poetry*. 11th ed. *The Columbia Granger's World of Poetry,* Columbia University Press, 2005 (http:// www.columbiagrangers.org). *The Oxford Companion to English Literature*. 6th edition. Margaret Drabble, ed. Oxford University Press, 2000. *Treasury of Irish Religious Verse.* Patrick Murray, ed. Crossroad, 1986.

ORWELL, GEORGE (1903–1950)

George Orwell, the pen name of Eric Arthur Blair, was born in Motihari, Bengal, India, where his father, Richard Walmesley Blair, was a civil servant for the British government. After his education at Eton College, he served for five years in the Burma Imperial Police and resigned because of growing dislike of British imperialism, vocalized in his essays *Shooting an Elephant* (1950) and *A Hanging* (1931). In 1926 he returned to Europe and, to learn the facts of poverty first-hand, he worked as a dish washer in Paris and as a tramp in England, out of which he wrote *Down and Out in Paris and London* (1933). By 1933 he was a full-time writer, using his now famous pseudonym, and went on to publish many more novels, essays and poetry. His last two books were *Animal Farm* (1945) and *Nineteen Eighty-Four* (1949). He died in London after a long struggle against tuberculosis. Some of his poems: "A Dressed man and a naked man," "As One Non-Combatant to Another," "Ironic Poem About Prostitution," "Oh You Young Men," "On Money," "Poem From Burma," "The Italian Soldier Shook My Hand," "The Lesser Evil."

Sources: *Biography of George Orwell* (http://www.on line-literature.com/orwell/). *Dictionary of National Biography.* Electronic Edition 1.1. Oxford University Press, 1997. *Encyclopædia Britannica Ultimate Reference Suite DVD,* 2006. *Everyman's Book of English Verse.* John Wain, ed. J.M. Dent, 1981. *The Columbia Granger's Index to Poetry.* 11th ed. *The Columbia Granger's World of Poetry,* Columbia University Press, 2005 (http://www.columbia grangers.org). *The Oxford Book of Travel Verse.* Kevin Crossley-Holland, ed. Oxford University Press, 1986. *The Oxford Book of Twentieth-Century English Verse.* Philip Larkin, ed. Oxford University Press, 1973. *The Oxford Book of War Poetry.* Jon Stallworthy, Oxford University Press, 1984. *Wikipedia, the Free Encyclopedia* (http://en.wikipedia.org/wiki/Wikipedia).

O'SHAUGHNESSY, ARTHUR WILLIAM EDGAR (1844–1881)

Born in London, he was educated privately, and in 1861 he began working for the zoological department of the British Museum, although his appointment without much experience aroused resentment among other naturalists. He made the study of reptiles and amphibians his specialty and was an authority on the subject. In 1873 he married Eleanor, daughter of John Westland Marston (see entry), with whom he wrote *Toyland* (1875), a book of tales for children. His wife died in 1879, two years before him. The opinion of his poetry was that he was the Chopin of words and covered a wide range of themes and ideas. His poetry publications: *An Epic of Women,* 1870. *Lays of France,* 1872. *Music and Moonlight,* 1874. *Songs of a Worker,* 1881. Some of his poems: "A Whisper from the Grave," "Azure Islands," "Bisclavaret," "John the Baptist," "Palm Flowers," "The Cypress," "The Fair Maid and the Sun," "The Fountain of Tears," "Zuleika."

Sources: *Best Loved Story Poems.* Walter E. Thwing, ed. Garden City, 1941. *Dictionary of National Biography.* Electronic Edition 1.1. Oxford University Press, 1997. *Encyclopædia Britannica Ultimate Reference Suite DVD,* 2006. *English Poetry: Author Search.* Chadwyck-Healey Ltd., 1995 (http://www.lib.utexas.edu:8080/search/epoetry/author.html). *Poems of Arthur O'Shaughnessy.* William Alexander Percy, ed. Greenwood Press, 1923. *Stanford University Libraries and Academic Information Resources* (http://library.stanford.edu). *The Columbia Granger's Index to Poetry.* 11th ed. *The Columbia Granger's World of Poetry,* Columbia University Press, 2005 (http://www.columbiagrangers.org). *The Oxford Companion to English Literature.* 6th edition. Margaret Drabble, ed. Oxford University Press, 2000.

O'SULLIVAN, SEAMUS (1879–1958)

He was born James Sullivan Starkey, in Dublin, and spent most of his adult life in the affluent Dublin suburb of Rathgar, where his father, William Starkey (1836–1918), was a doctor. He edited *The Dublin Magazine* from August 1923 to August 1925 as a monthly and from January 1926 to June 1958 as a quarterly, ceasing publication on O'Sullivan's death. The magazine featured fiction, poetry, drama and reviews; contributors included almost every significant Irish writer of the period, including Samuel Beckett and Patrick Kavanagh (see entries). Some of his poems: "A Blessing on the Cows," "The Convent," "The Half Door," "Lament for Sean MacDermott," "The Sedges," "Splendid and Terrible," "The Starling Lake," "The Trains."

Sources: *A Book of Animal Poems.* William Cole, ed. Viking, 1973. *An Anthology of Irish Verse: The Poetry of Ireland from Mythological Times to the Present.* Padraic Colum, ed. Liveright, 1948. *Poems One Line and Longer.* William Cole, ed. Grossman, 1973. *Reference.com/Encyclopedia/The Dublin Magazine* (http://www.reference.com/browse/wiki/The_Dublin_Magazine). *The Book of a Thousand Poems: A Family Treasury.* J. Murray Macbain, ed. Peter Bedrick Books, 1983. *The Columbia Granger's Index to Poetry.* 11th ed. *The Columbia Granger's World of Poetry,* Columbia University Press, 2005 (http://www.columbia grangers.org). *The Home Book of Modern Verse.* Burton Egbert Stevenson, ed. Henry Holt, 1953. *Wikipedia, the Free Encyclopedia* (http://en.wikipedia.org/wiki/Wikipedia).

OSWALD, ALICE (1966–)

Oswald lives with her husband and two children at Dartington in Devon, where she works as a gardener on the Dartington Estate. To write her second collection of poetry, called simply *Dart* (2002), she spent three years collecting information about the river and talking to people who use the river in their daily lives. "They include a poacher, a ferryman, a sewage worker and milk worker, a forester, swimmers and canoeists — and are interlinked with historic and mythic voices, drowned voices, dreaming voices and marginal notes which act as markers along the way" (*The Times,* 27 July 2002). In 2004, Alice Oswald was named one of the Poetry Book Society's "Next Generation" poets. She has received several prizes and awards and has been short listed for other awards. She has also been called Ted Hughes' rightful heir. Some of her other publications: *The Thing in the Gap-Stone Stile,* 1996. *The Thunder Mutters: 101 Poems for the Planet,* 2005; *Woods,* 2005. Some of her poems: "Ballad of a Shadow," "Mountains," "Sea Sonnet," "The Melon Grower," "The Pilchard-Curing Song," "Wedding."

Sources: *BBC — Get Writing — A2997886 — Alice Oswald* (http://www.bbc.co.uk/dna/getwriting/oswald). *Making for Planet Alice: New Women Poets.* Maura Dooley, ed. Bloodaxe Books, 1997. *River Dart — Alice Oswald* (http://www.poetrysociety.org.uk/places/river.htm). *The Columbia Granger's Index to Poetry.* 11th ed. *The Columbia Granger's World of Poetry,* Columbia University Press, 2005 (http://www.columbiagrangers.org). *The Oxford Book of Sonnets.* John Fuller, ed. Oxford University Press, 2000.

OUTRAM, GEORGE (1805–1856)

One of Scotland's Lawyer (comic) Poets, he was born at the Clyde ironworks, near Glasgow, of which his father was manager, and was educated at the high school of Leith. He studied at the university of Edinburgh and in 1827 was admitted a member of the Scottish bar. Not being successful as an advocate, in 1837 he became editor of the *Glasgow Herald* and soon acquired a share as proprietor. He continued his journalistic work till his death, on the Holy Loch, Dunoon, Argyl and Bute, and was buried in Warriston cemetery, Edinburgh. *Lyrics, Legal and Miscellaneous* (1874) consisted of verses — most of them in the Scots dialect — written to be sung at festive gatherings in Edinburgh and Glasgow. Some of his poems: "A Linnet Warbled," "Bonnie Mary," "My Nannie," "On Hearing a Lady Praise a Certain Rev. Doctor's Eyes," "Strictures on the Economy of Nature," "The Annuity," "The Banks o' the Dee," "The Lawyer's Suit," "We Be Three Poor Barristers," "When This Old Wig Was New."

Sources: *A Third Treasury of the Familiar.* Ralph L. Woods, ed. Macmillan, 1970. *Dictionary of National Biography.* Electronic Edition 1.1. Oxford University Press, 1997. *English Poetry: Author Search.* Chadwyck-Healey Ltd., 1995 (http://www.lib.utexas.edu:8080/search/epoetry/author.html). *Everyman's Book of Victorian Verse.* J.R. Watson, ed. J.M. Dent, 1982. *Submarine Base, Holy Loch, Scotland* (http://holyloch.com). *SubRon 14, Holy Loch, Scotland, 1961 to 1992* (http://www.thistlegroup.net/holyloch/). *The Devil's Book of Verse: Masters of the Poison Pen from Ancient Times to the Present Day.* Richard Conniff, ed. Dodd, Mead, 1983. *The Faber Book of Comic Verse.* Michael Roberts and Janet Adam Smith, eds. Faber and Faber, 1978. *The Home Book of Modern Verse.* Burton Egbert Stevenson, ed. Henry Holt, 1953. *Victorian Verse.* George MacBeth, ed. Penguin Books, 1986.

OWEN, GORONWY (GRONOW) (1723–1769?)

The son of a tinker, he was born at Rhos Fawr, Anglesey. Given no encouragement from his drunken father, his education was left to his mother, and from 1737 to 1741 he was at Friars School, Bangor. He was ordained deacon in 1745 while at Jesus College, Oxford, but did not graduate. In 1748, now married, he took the mastership of a small endowed school at Donnington, Shropshire, and with it the curacy of the neighboring church of Uppington. His poor health was made worse by over-indulgence in alcohol. In 1758 he took charge of the school attached to William and Mary College, Williamsburg, Virginia. Around 1760 he became minister of St. Andrew's, Brunswick County, Virginia, where he died. His poems are written in Cywydd, the strict Welsh meter. Some of his Welsh poems: "Calendr y Carwr (The Lover's Calendar)," "Cywydd y Farn Fawr (Lay of the Last Judgment)," "Cywydd y Gem neu'r Maen Gwerthfawr (Cywydd of the Gem or the Precious Stone)," "Cywydd yn ateb Huw'r Bardd Coch o Fôn (Cywydd in Answer to Huw the Red Poet [Hugh Hughes])."

Sources: *Dictionary of National Biography.* Electronic Edition 1.1. Oxford University Press, 1997. *Encyclopædia Britannica Ultimate Reference Suite DVD*, 2006. *The Columbia Granger's Index to Poetry.* 11th ed. *The Columbia Granger's World of Poetry*, Columbia University Press, 2005 (http://www.columbiagrangers.org). *The Faber Book of Epigrams and Epitaphs.* Geoffrey Grigson, ed. Faber and Faber, 1977. *The Oxford Book of Welsh Verse in English.* Gwyn Jones, ed. Oxford University Press, 1977.

OWEN, WILFRED EDWARD SALTER (1893–1918)

He was born in Plas Wilmot, near Oswestry, Shropshire, the son of a railway clerk, but brought up in Birkenhead and educated at Shrewsbury Technical School until 1911. From 1911 to 1913 he was pupil and lay assistant to the Rev. Herbert Wigan, the vicar of Dunsden, near Reading. Appalled by the discrepancy between the Church and the poverty all around him, he left to become a teacher of English at the Berlitz school in Bordeaux, where he remained until 1915. He enlisted in September 1915, and in May 1917 he was diagnosed with neurasthenia (chronic mental fatigue) and sent to Craiglockhart War Hospital, Slateford, near Edinburgh, to recuperate. It was here that he met Siegfried Sassoon (see entry), who influenced his poetry. He returned to the front and was killed in action one week before the armistice and was awarded the Military Cross. He is memorialized by a stone in Poets' Corner of Westminster Abbey along with other poets of the First World War. Some of his poems: "Greater Love," "He Died Smiling," "Soldier's Dream," "The Next War," "The Sentry," "Wild with All Regrets," "Winter Song."

Sources: *Dictionary of National Biography.* Electronic Edition 1.1. Oxford University Press, 1997. *Encyclopædia Britannica Ultimate Reference Suite DVD*, 2006. *Peace and War: A Collection of Poems.* Michael Harrison, and Christopher Stuart-Clark, ed. Oxford University Press, 1989. *The Collected Poems of Wilfred Owen.* C. Day Lewis, ed. New Directions, 1963. *The Columbia Granger's Index to Poetry.* 11th ed. *The Columbia Granger's World of Poetry*, Columbia University Press, 2005 (http://www.columbiagrangers.org). *The Faber Book of War Poetry.* Kenneth Baker, ed. Faber and Faber, 1996. *The Mentor Book of Major British Poets.* Oscar Williams, ed. New American Library, 1963. *The Penguin Book of First World War Poetry.* Jon Silkin, ed. Penguin Books, 1979. *Westminster Abbey Official Guide* (no date).

OWENSON, SYDNEY, LADY MORGAN (?1783–1859)

Born in Dublin, the daughter of Robert Owenson, a roving Irish actor, she was governess in the family of Featherstone of Bracklin Castle, Westmeath, from 1798 to 1800. She collected a number of Irish tunes and wrote English words to them, which were subsequently published. Her first novel, *St. Clair, or The Heiress of Desmond* (1803), was such a success that she devoted herself entirely to writing. Her second novel *The Wild Irish Girl* (1806) — which went through several editions — brought her financial success. In England she came under the patronage of the Marquis and Marchioness of Abercorn, where she met the Englishman Charles Morgan, the Marquis' personal physician. Morgan was knighted prior to their marriage in 1812 and the couple moved to Dublin. Altogether she published ten novels, along with biography and memoirs, and from an early age she wrote poetry. She was buried in Brompton cemetery, Kensington, London. Some of her poems: "Kate Kearney," "Ode to Whim," "On My Birth-Day," "On the Death of a Favourite Lap-Dog," "The Hawthorn Tree," "The Recantation," "To a Thrush," "To Sleep," "Will of the Wisp."

Sources: *Best Loved Songs of the American People.* Anthology Editor, Denes Agay, Doubleday (1975). *Biography of Lady Morgan Sydney Owenson* (http://www.sydneyowenson.com/SydneyOwensonBio.html). *Dictionary of National Biography.* Electronic Edition 1.1. Oxford University Press, 1997. *English Poetry: Author Search.* Chadwyck-Healey Ltd., 1995 (http://www.lib.utexas.edu:8080/search/epoetry/author.html). *Poems Between Women: Four Centuries of Love, Romantic Friendship, and Desire.* Emma Donoghue, ed. Columbia University Press, 1997. *Romantic Women Poets: An Anthology.* Duncan Wu, ed. Blackwell Publishers, 1997. *Romanticism.* Duncan Wu, ed. Blackwell, 1994. *The Columbia Granger's Index to Poetry.* 11th ed. *The Columbia Granger's World of Poetry,* Columbia University Press, 2005 (http://www.columbiagrangers.org). *The National Portrait Gallery* (www.npg.org.uk). *The Oxford Companion to English Literature.* 6th edition. Margaret Drabble, ed. Oxford University Press, 2000.

PADEL, RUTH (1946–)

The great great-grand-daughter of Charles Darwin, she was born in London and educated at the Sorbonne, Paris, the Free University, Berlin, and Oxford University, where her Ph.D. was on a Greek tragedy. She taught Greek at Oxford, Cambridge, and Birkbeck College, London, and opera in the Modern Greek Department, Princeton University, New Jersey. She is a fellow of the Royal Society of Literature and chair of the U.K. Poetry Society. Her talks on opera, *Close Encounters,* were broadcast on BBC Radio 3. Her book *52 Ways of Looking at a Poem* (2002) is based on her *Sunday Poem* discussion column for *The Independent on Sunday.* Her other non-fiction includes two books which link mind, madness, tragedy, myth and religion in ancient Greece to anthropology, psychoanalysis and poetry. She won the National Poetry Competition in 1997 and the Cholmondeley Award in 2003. Some of her poetry publications: *Summer Snow,* 1990. *Angel,* 1993. *Fusewire,* 1996. *Rembrandt Would Have Loved You,* 1998. *Voodoo Shop,* 2002. *The Soho Leopard,* 2004. Some of her poems: "On the Line," "On the Venom Farm," "Tell Me About It," "Watercourse," "Yew Berries."

Sources: *British Council Arts* (http://www.contemporarywriters.com). *Emergency Kit: Poems for Strange Times.* Jo Shapcott and Matthew Sweeney, eds. Faber and Faber, 1996. *Making for Planet Alice: New Women Poets.* Maura Dooley, ed. Bloodaxe Books, 1997. *Ruth Padel's Official Website* (http://www.rpadel.dircon.co.uk/rp_main.htm). *The Columbia Granger's Index to Poetry.* 11th ed. *The Columbia Granger's World of Poetry,* Columbia University Press, 2005 (http://www.columbiagrangers.org). *The Oxford Companion to English Literature.* 6th edition. Margaret Drabble, ed. Oxford University Press, 2000.

PALGRAVE, FRANCIS TURNER (1824–1897)

Born at Great Yarmouth, Norfolk, he was educated at Charthouse School, London, graduated M.A. in classics from Balliol College, Oxford, in 1856, and was made fellow of Exeter College the same year. As an official of the education department from 1855 to 1884, he was involved in the training of elementary teachers. He wrote art reviews and critical essays dealing with art and literature for several newspapers. His anthology of poetry, *Golden Treasury* (1861), was an instant and long-lasting success. In 1878, he was made honorary doctor of laws of Edinburgh University, and in 1885 he was elected professor of poetry at Oxford. His last work before he died was *Landscape in Poetry* (1897). He lived for twenty years at Lyme Regis, and the Dorset countryside features in many of his poems. Some of his other publications: *Shakespeare's Poems,* 1865. *Lyrical Poems,* 1871. *The Children's Treasury of English Song,* 1875. *Tennyson's Select Lyrics,* 1885. Some of his poems: "A Dorset Idyl," "A Dorset Valley," "At Lyme Regis," "The Doom of Death," "The Linnet in November," "The Pilgrim and the Ploughman," "Trafalgar."

Sources: *Best Loved Story Poems.* Walter E. Thwing, ed. Garden City, 1941. *Dictionary of National Biography.* Electronic Edition 1.1. Oxford University Press, 1997. *Encyclopædia Britannica Ultimate Reference Suite DVD,* 2006. *Everyman's Book of Victorian Verse.* J.R. Watson, ed. J.M. Dent, 1982. *Palgrave: Selected Poems of Francis Turner Palgrave.* Brian Louis Pearce, ed. Brentham Press, 1985. *The Columbia Granger's Index to Poetry.* 11th ed. *The Columbia Granger's World of Poetry,* Columbia University Press, 2005 (http://www.columbiagrangers.org). *The Oxford Companion to English Literature.* 6th edition. Margaret Drabble, ed. Oxford University Press, 2000.

PARK, ANDREW (1807–1863)

Scottish poet born in Renfrew, he was educated at Glasgow University, and after several fruitless attempts at setting himself up in business in Scotland and in London, he devoted himself to literature. Following a tour of the East he published *Egypt and the East* (1856). He died in Glasgow and was buried in the Paisley Cemetery, where a monument, consisting of a bronze bust on a granite pedestal, was erected to his memory in 1867. In addition to the sonnet sequence *The Vision of Mankind*, published by John Hamilton in 1833, he published *Bridegroom and the Bride* (1834) and *Silent Love* (under the pseudonym "James Wilson") (1843). The poem was translated into French by the Chevalier de Chatelain and was very popular in America. His final poem, *Veritas*, which appeared in 1849, is autobiographical in character. Several of Park's lyrics have been set to music by various composers.

Sources: *Dictionary of National Biography.* Electronic Edition 1.1. Oxford University Press, 1997.

PARNELL, THOMAS (1679–1718)

Irish-English poet, born in Dublin, he graduated M.A. from Trinity College, Dublin, in 1700. He was ordained priest in 1703, installed minor canon of St. Patrick's, Dublin in 1704, and was made archdeacon of Clogher in 1706 and doctor of divinity by Dublin University in 1712. His *Homer's Battle of the Frogs and Mice* was published in 1717. He was taken ill at Chester, where he died and was buried in the churchyard of Holy Trinity Church. According to his friend Alexander Pope (see entry) Parnell was an amiable character but too fond of the drink. Pope, although younger, offered Parnell advice on his poems and in return relied on Parnell's scholarship in his translation of the *Iliad*. The best of Parnell's poems are "The Hermit, the Fairy Tale," "Hymn to Contentment," and "Hesiod, or the Rise of Woman." Parnell's "Night Piece on Death" is said to have influenced Thomas Gray's (see entry) "An Elegy Written in a Country Church Yard." Some of his other poems: "A Tavern Feast," "Hezekiah," "The Isle of Wight," "The Test of Poetry," "The Vigil of Venus," "To Mr. Pope."

Sources: *Chapters into Verse, Vol. I: Genesis to Malachi.* Robert Atwan and Laurance Wieder, eds. Oxford University Press, 1993. *Dictionary of National Biography.* Electronic Edition 1.1. Oxford University Press, 1997. *Encyclopædia Britannica Ultimate Reference Suite DVD,* 2006. *The National Portrait Gallery* (www.npg.org.uk). *Poems on Several Occasions of Thomas Parnell.* Alexander Pope, ed. H. Lintot, 1737. *Samuel Johnson's Lives of the English Poets,* 1779–1781 (http://www2.hn.psu.edu/Faculty/KKemmerer/poets/preface.htm). *The Columbia Granger's Index to Poetry.* 11th ed. *The Columbia Granger's World of Poetry,* Columbia University Press, 2005 (http://www.columbia

grangers.org). *The Oxford Companion to English Literature.* 6th edition. Margaret Drabble, ed. Oxford University Press, 2000.

PARRY-WILLIAMS, SIR THOMAS HERBERT (1887–1975)

Welsh poet born in Rhyd-ddu, Caernarvonshire, the son of a schoolmaster. Educated at Porthmadog Intermediate School, he graduated M.A. from the University of Wales and earned a bachelor of literature from Oxford and a Ph.D. from Freiburg University, Germany. In 1912, he won both the chair and the crown at the National Eisteddfod of Wales in Wrexham, and again in 1915 at the National Eisteddfod held in Bangor. From 1914 until his retirement in 1952 he was lecturer, then professor, of Welsh at the University College of Wales, Aberystwyth. His Freiburg Ph.D. dissertation on *Some Points of Similarity in the Phonology of Welsh and Breton* was published in 1913; *The English Element in Welsh* followed in 1923. He is considered by some to be the most eloquent of all 20th century Welsh poets. He was awarded honorary doctorates from three universities and was knighted in 1958. He died at his home in Aberystwyth. Three of his other publications: *Cerddi*, 1931 (poem). *Lloffion*, 1942 (gleanings). *Myfyrdodau*, 1957 (meditation). Three of his poems: "Christmas Carol," "Llyn y Gadair [the seat by the pond]," "These Bones."

Sources: *Deg Soned.* A book of 12 sonnets held by The University of London Library (http://www.ull.ac.uk/exhibitions/bookbeautiful.pdf). *Dictionary of National Biography.* Electronic Edition 1.1. Oxford University Press, 1997. *The National Portrait Gallery* (www.npg.org.uk). *The Columbia Granger's Index to Poetry.* 11th ed. *The Columbia Granger's World of Poetry,* Columbia University Press, 2005 (http://www.columbiagrangers.org). *The Oxford Book of Welsh Verse in English.* Gwyn Jones, ed. Oxford University Press, 1977.

PATERSON, DON (1963–)

Scottish poet and musician, born in Dundee, who during the 1980s toured widely with his music. He has written incidental music for his plays for radio and theatre, and his compositions have been recorded and performed by the Scottish classical guitarist Allan Neave. He lived in London from 1984 to 1989, then moved to Brighton, Sussex, and lived there from 1989 to 1993 before becoming writer in residence at Dundee University. From 1995 to the present he has been poetry editor at Picador, a division of the Macmillan publishing company. He lives in Kirriemuir, on the East Coast of Scotland. He has won ten major literary awards. His poetry publications: *Nil Nil*, 1993. *God's Gift to Women*, 1997. *Sonnets: From Shakespeare to Heaney*, 1999 (editor). *Last Words: New Poetry for the New Century*, 1999 (co-editor with Jo Shapcott). *The Eyes*, 1999. *Robert Burns: Poems Selected by Don Paterson*, 2001 (editor). *Landing Light*, 2003. *All the Poems You Need to Say Goodbye*, 2004 (editor). Some of his poems: "A Private Bottling," "Bedfellows," "Heliographer," "The Chartres of Gowrie," "The Ferryman's Arms," "Wind-Tunnel."

Sources: *Biography of Don Paterson* (http://www.st-andrews.ac.uk/~www_se/paterson/home.html). *British Council Arts* (http://www.contemporarywriters.com). *Don Paterson's Web Site* (http://www.donpaterson.com/). *The Bloodaxe Book of 20th Century Poetry, from Britain and Ireland*. Edna Longley, ed. Bloodaxe Books, 2000. *The New Penguin Book of Scottish Verse*. Robert Crawford and Mick Imlah, ed. Penguin Books, 2000. *The Oxford Companion to English Literature*. 6th edition. Margaret Drabble, ed. Oxford University Press, 2000.

PATMORE, COVENTRY KERSEY DIGHTON (1823–1896)

Born at Woodford, Essex, the son of the author P.G. Patmore, he grew up without any sense of direction. When his father lost his money in 1845 through faulty speculations, he was forced to earn a living, firstly by freelance journalism, then as assistant in the printed book department of the British Museum. In 1849 he became linked to the pre-Raphaelite group of artists and contributed an essay on *Macbeth*, as well as verses to their organ, *The Germ*. One of his long narrative poems was *The Angel in the House*, which appeared in parts from 1854 to 1863. The death of his wife in 1862 from tuberculosis found expression in his poem "The Victories of Love." From 1885 he became a frequent contributor of essays and reviews to *St. James's Gazette*. He was one of the small group of religious poets influenced by the Oxford Movement. He died at Lymington, Hampshire. Some of his publications: *Tamerton Church Tower*, 1853. *The Children's Garland*, 1862. *The Unknown Eros*, 1877. *Amelia*, 1878. Some of his poems: "Alexander and Lycon," "Dartmoor," "The Flesh-Fly and the Bee," "Venus and Death."

Sources: *A Child's Treasury of Poems*. Mark Daniel, ed. Dial / Penguin Books, 1986. *A Sacrifice of Praise: An Anthology of Christian Poetry in English from Caedmon to the Mid-Twentieth Century*. James H. Trott, ed. Cumberland House Publishing, 1999. *Dictionary of National Biography*. Electronic Edition 1.1. Oxford University Press, 1997. *Encyclopædia Britannica Ultimate Reference Suite DVD*, 2006. *English Poetry: Author Search*. Chadwyck-Healey Ltd., 1995 (http://www.lib.utexas.edu:8080/search/epoetry/author.html). *The National Portrait Gallery* (www.npg.org.uk). *The Columbia Granger's Index to Poetry*. 11th ed. *The Columbia Granger's World of Poetry*, Columbia University Press, 2005 (http://www.columbiagrangers.org). *The Faber Book of Epigrams and Epitaphs*. Geoffrey Grigson, ed. Faber and Faber, 1977. *The Oxford Companion to English Literature*. 6th edition. Margaret Drabble, ed. Oxford University Press, 2000. *The Poems of Coventry Patmore*. Frederick Page, ed. Oxford University Press, 1949.

PATRICK, SAINT (387–493)

Although his dates are uncertain, these have been taken from the *Catholic Encyclopedia*. Born at Kilpatrick, near Dumbarton, in Scotland, he was captured by pirates when he was sixteen and taken to Ireland, where he was sold as a slave. After six years of tending his master's sheep he escaped and made his way to France, to St. Martin's monastery at Tours. Pope St. Celestine I commissioned Patrick to convert the Irish from Druidism and around 433 he and his companions landed at the mouth of the Vantry River close by Wicklow Head. He is credited also with Christianization of the Picts and Anglo-Saxons. Patrick is known only from two short works, the *Confessio*, a spiritual autobiography, and his *Epistola*, a denunciation of British mistreatment of Irish Christians. The 17th of March is St. Patrick's day, when Irish people wear a sprig of shamrock, used by Patrick to symbolize the Holy Trinity. The Cross of St. Patrick is part of the national flag of Britain. Some of his poems: "At Tara today in this fateful hour," "Rune of St. Patrick," "St. Patrick's Breastplate," "The Deer's Cry."

Sources: *An Anthology of Irish Literature*. David H. Greene, ed. H. Modern Library, 1954. *Catholic Encyclopedia* (http://www.newadvent.org). *Dictionary of National Biography*. Electronic Edition 1.1. Oxford University Press, 1997. *Earth Prayers from Around the World: 365 Prayers, Poems, and Invocations for Honoring the Earth*. Elizabeth Roberts and Elais Amidon, eds. Harper Collins, 1991. *Lyra Celtica: An Anthology of Representative Celtic Poetry*. E.A. Sharp and J. Matthay, eds. John Grant, 1924. *Miniature Lives of the Saints*. Henry Sebastian Bowden, ed. Burns and Oates, 1949. *The Columbia Granger's Index to Poetry*. 11th ed. *The Columbia Granger's World of Poetry*, Columbia University Press, 2005 (http://www.columbiagrangers.org). *The Faber Book of Children's Verse*. Janet Adam Smith, ed. Faber and Faber, 1953.

PATTEN, BRIAN (1946–)

Born in Liverpool, he made his name in the 1960s as one of the "Liverpool Poets" longside Adrian Henri and Roger McGough (see entries). Their joint anthology, *The Mersey Sound* (1967), brought poetry to a new audience. His poems are a mix of seriousness and humor and have been translated into many European languages. He writes for adults and children and his children's novel, *Mr. Moon's Last Case* (1975), won an award from the Mystery Writers of America Guild. His collection for children, *The Blue and Green Ark: An Alphabet for Planet Earth* (1999), won a Cholmondeley Award in 2002. He edited *The Puffin Book of Twentieth-Century Chil-*

dren's Verse (1991). He splits his time between London and Devon and has been honored with the Freedom of the City of Liverpool. Some of his other poetry publications: *Little Johnny's Confession,* 1967. *Vanishing Trick,* 1976. *Love Poems,* 1981. *Storm Damage,* 1996. *Armada,* 1996. Some of his poems: "After Frost," "How the New Teacher Got Her Nickname," "The Beast," "The Complacent Tortoise," "What Happened to Miss Frugle," "Where Are You Now Superman?"

Sources: *Amazing Monsters: Verses to Thrill and Chill.* Robert Fisher, ed. Faber and Faber, 1982. *British Council Arts* (http://www.contemporarywriters.com). *Everyman's Book of English Verse.* John Wain, ed. J.M. Dent, 1981. *Fine Frenzy: Enduring Themes in Poetry.* Robert Baylor and Brenda Stokes, eds. McGraw-Hill, 1978. *The National Portrait Gallery* (www.npg.org.uk). *Poemhunter* (www.poemhunter.com). *The Columbia Granger's Index to Poetry.* 11th ed. *The Columbia Granger's World of Poetry,* Columbia University Press, 2005 (http://www.columbiagrangers.org). *The New Exeter Book of Riddles.* Kevin Crossley-Holland and Lawrence Sail, eds. Enitharmon Press, 1999. *The Oxford Book of Story Poems.* Michael Harrison and Christopher Stuart-Clark, eds. Oxford University Press, 1990. *The Oxford Companion to English Literature.* 6th edition. Margaret Drabble, ed. Oxford University Press, 2000. *The Oxford Treasury of Children's Poems.* Michael Harrison and Christopher Stuart-Clark, eds. Oxford University Press, 1988.

PATTISON, WILLIAM (1706–1727)

Born at Peasemarsh, near Rye, Sussex, he was the son of a small farmer on the estate of the Earl of Thanet, who saw him through his education at a local free school. He was encouraged in his study of the classics by a neighboring clergyman and schoolmaster of Kirkby Stephen. He was admitted to Sidney-Sussex College, Cambridge, in 1724 and left two years later, preferring to work as a writer in London. In spite of verbal support from some distinguished figures, his collection of poems did not materialize and he was reduced to poverty and having to pass the nights on a bench in St. James's Park. H. Curll, a bookseller, gave him shelter in his house. He died of smallpox in Curll's house and was buried in the churchyard of St. Clement Danes, Westminster, London. Some of his poems: "A Divine Poem," "A Session of the Cambridge Poets," "Ad Coelum," "An Epistle to Laura," "Orpheus and Eurydice," "The Cambridge Beauties," "The Hour-Glass," "The Nightingale and Shepherd," "Wrote in a Lady's Pocket-Book."

Sources: *Dictionary of National Biography.* Electronic Edition 1.1. Oxford University Press, 1997. *English Poetry: Author Search.* Chadwyck-Healey Ltd., 1995 (http://www.lib.utexas.edu:8080/search/epoetry/author.html). *The Columbia Granger's Index to Poetry.* 11th ed. *The Columbia Granger's World of Poetry,* Columbia University Press, 2005 (http://www.columbiagrangers.org). *The Poetical Works of Mr. William Pattison: Vol. I and II.* H. Curll, 1728.

PAULIN, THOMAS NEILSON (1949–)

Irish poet, born in Leeds, Yorkshire, and raised in Belfast, where his father was headmaster of a grammar school and his mother was a doctor. He was educated at Hull University and Lincoln College, Oxford. His career: lecturer in English at Nottingham University, 1972–1989; director of Field Day Theatre Company in Derry, Northern Ireland, 1989–1994; G.M. Young Lecturer in English at Oxford, 1994 to the present; and fellow of Hertford College, Oxford, 1994 to the present. He holds honorary degrees from Saskatchewan, Stafford and Hull. In 2002, an invitation to speak at Harvard University was withdrawn (later reinstated) "after he allegedly made anti-Israeli comments" (BBC News, Friday, 15 November 2002). He has won three literary awards and was short-listed for two others. He has written non-fiction, edited poetry anthologies and written several plays. Some of his recent poetry publications: *The Argument at Great Tew: A Poem,* 1985. *Fivemiletown,* 1987. *Selected Poems 1972–1990,* 1993. *Thomas Hardy: Poems Selected by Tom Paulin,* 2001. Some of his poems: "Ballywaire," "Evening Harbour," "Inishkeel Parish Church," "Off the Back of a Lorry," "Thinking of Iceland."

Sources: *Anthology of Magazine Verse and Yearbook of American Poetry.* Alan F. Pater, ed. Monitor Book Company, 1980. *British Council Arts* (http://www.contemporarywriters.com). *Harvard University's Withdrawal of a Speaking Invitation to the Poet Tom Paulin* (http://news.bbc.co.uk/1/hi/in_depth/uk/2000/newsmakers/2481623.stm). *The National Portrait Gallery* (www.npg.org.uk). *The Columbia Granger's Index to Poetry.* 11th ed. *The Columbia Granger's World of Poetry,* Columbia University Press, 2005 (http://www.columbiagrangers.org). *The Faber Book of Contemporary Irish Poetry.* Paul Muldoon, ed. Faber and Faber, 1986. *The Oxford Companion to English Literature.* 6th edition. Margaret Drabble, ed. Oxford University Press, 2000. *The Penguin Book of Contemporary Irish Poetry.* Peter Fallon and Derek Mahon, eds. Penguin Books, 1990. *Who's Who.* London: A & C Black, 2005.

PEACOCK, THOMAS LOVE (1785–1866)

Poet, novelist, and essayist, he was born at Weymouth, Dorset, and at sixteen he moved with his widowed mother to work in London, where he spent his spare time studying the classics and languages. Through his publisher he developed a lifelong friendship with Percy Bysshe Shelley (see entry) and his wife, and in 1816 he published *Headlong Hall,* a satirical novel. He was summoned to India House and offered an appointment as administrator of the East India Company and became a well-paid and trusted executive, representing the company on many parliamentary committees. He retired from the company in 1856 and died at his country residence at Lower Halliford, near Shepperton, Middlesex. Some of his poetry publications: *The Monks of St. Mark*, 1804. *Palmyra and Other Poems*, 1805. *The Genius of the Thames Palmyra and Other Poems*, 1812. *The Philosophy of Melancholy*, 1812. *Sir Proteus: A Satirical Ballad*, 1814. *The Round Table, or King Arthur's Feast*, 1817. *Rhododaphne, or the Thessalian Spirit*, 1818. *Paper Money Lyrics*, 1837. Some of his poems: "A Border Ballad," "Gryll Grange," "Newark Abbey," "Pindar on the Eclipse of the Sun."

Sources: *Dictionary of National Biography*. Electronic Edition 1.1. Oxford University Press, 1997. *English Poetry: Author Search*. Chadwyck-Healey Ltd., 1995 (http://www. lib.utexas.edu:8080/search/epoetry/author.html). *The Brand-X Anthology of Poetry*. William Zaranka, ed. Apple-Wood Books, 1981. *The Chatto Book of Nonsense Poetry*. Hugh Haughton, ed. Chatto and Windus, 1988. *The Columbia Granger's Index to Poetry*. 11th ed. *The Columbia Granger's World of Poetry*, Columbia University Press, 2005 (http://www.columbiagrangers.org). *The New Oxford Book of Romantic Period Verse*. Jerome J. McGann, ed. Oxford University Press, 1993. *The New Oxford Book of Victorian Verse*. Christopher Ricks, ed. Oxford University Press, 2002. *The Oxford Companion to English Literature*. 6th edition. Margaret Drabble, ed. Oxford University Press, 2000. *The Pleasure of Poetry: From His* Daily Mirror *Column*. Kingsley Amis, ed. Cassell Publishers, 1990.

PEAKE, MERVYN LAURENCE (1911–1968)

The author of the *Gormenghast* books, he was born at Kuling, China, the son of a missionary doctor. He studied art at the Royal Academy Schools, then spent two years in an artist's commune on the Channel Island of Sark. From 1935 to 1939 he taught life drawing at Westminster School of Art. During the war he was a sapper in bomb disposal, was invalided out in 1943, then employed in the Ministry of Information. In 1945 he went to Belsen Concentration Camp as a war artist to record the atrocities and conditions. After another three years on Sark with his family, he took a part-time teaching post at the Central School of Art, Holborn, London. He was often in demand as a book illustrator and as a portrait painter. By 1960 he gave up teaching, suffering from Parkinson's, and died at Burcot, Berkshire. His poetry collections published during his life: *The Rhyme of the Flying Bomb*, 1962. *Poems and Drawings*, 1965. *A Reverie of Bone and Other Poems*, 1967. Three of his poems: "I cannot give the reasons," "My Uncle Paul of Pimlico," "The Frivolous Cake."

Sources: *Dictionary of National Biography*. Electronic Edition 1.1. Oxford University Press, 1997. *Mervyn Peake's*

Official Website (http://www.mervynpeake.org/). *Once Upon a Rhyme: 101 Poems for Young Children*. Sara Corrin and Stephen Corrin, eds. Faber and Faber, 1982. *Splinters: A Book of Very Short Poems*. Michael Harrison, ed. Oxford University Press, 1989. *The Chatto Book of Nonsense Poetry*, Anthology Editor, Hugh Haughton, Chatto and Windus (1988). *The Columbia Granger's Index to Poetry*. 11th ed. *The Columbia Granger's World of Poetry*, Columbia University Press, 2005 (http://www.columbiagrangers. org). *The Faber Book of War Poetry*. Kenneth Baker, ed. Faber and Faber, 1996. *The National Portrait Gallery* (www. npg.org.uk). *The New Oxford Book of Children's Verse*. Neil Philip, ed. Oxford University Press, 1996. *The Oxford Companion to English Literature*. 6th edition. Margaret Drabble, ed. Oxford University Press, 2000. *Wikipedia, the Free Encyclopedia* (http://en.wikipedia.org/wiki/ Wikipedia).

PEARSE, PATRICK HENRY (1879–1916)

Pádraig Mac Piarais was born in Dublin, the son of a sculptor. He graduated B.A. from University College, Dublin, in 1901, then studied law at the same college. A member of the Gaelic League from the age of sixteen, from 1903 to 1909 he was editor of the league's weekly newspaper, *An Claidheamh Soluis* (*The Sword of Light*). The aim of the paper was to promote the Irish language as a weapon against British domination, and to his end in 1908 he founded St. Enda's College near Dublin. He was commander in chief of the Irish forces in the anti-British Easter Rising that began on Monday, April 24, 1916. The revolt was crushed; he surrendered to the British on the 29th; he was tried by court-martial, and shot by a firing squad at Kilmainham Jail, Dublin. More than any other man, Pearse was responsible for establishing the republican tradition in Ireland. Some of his poems: "Christmas 1915," "I Am Ireland," "Ideal," "Prayer to Mother Mary," "Tara is Green," "The Fool," "The Mother," "To Death."

Sources: *An Anthology of Irish Verse: The Poetry of Ireland from Mythological Times to the Present*. Padraic Colum, ed. Liveright, 1948. *Dictionary of National Biography*. Electronic Edition 1.1. Oxford University Press, 1997. *Ireland in Poetry*. Charles Sullivan, ed, Harry N. Abrams, 1990. *Lyra Celtica: An Anthology of Representative Celtic Poetry*. E.A. Sharp and J. Matthay, eds. John Grant, 1924. *The Columbia Granger's Index to Poetry*. 11th ed. *The Columbia Granger's World of Poetry*, Columbia University Press, 2005 (http://www.columbiagrangers.org). *The Penguin Book of Irish Verse*. Brendan Kennelly, ed. Penguin Books, 1981.

PEELE, GEORGE (?1558–?1596)

One of the most significant poets who was writing before Shakespeare. He was born probably in London and was educated at Christ's Hospital, the Bluecoat School, from 1565 to 1570, where his father was clerk. He graduated M.A. from Christ Church

College, Oxford, in 1579, then became a successful playwright and actor, working for both the Lord Admiral's Company of Players and, in 1589, for the Queen's Men. His lyrics were included in the anthologies *The Phenix Nest*, 1593; *England's Helicon* and *England's Parnassus* (1600); and *Belvidera, or the Garden of the Muses* (1610). His work is in the categories of plays (written in verse), pageants, and miscellaneous verse. Most of his poetry is taken from his plays, often in the form of songs. Some of his plays: *The Arraignment of Paris*, ?1581. *Tale of Troy*, 1589. *The Hunting of Cupid*, 1591. *The Famous Chronicle of King Edward I, surnamed Edward Longshanks*, 1593. *The Battle of Alcazar*, 1594. *Old Wives' Tale*, 1595. *The Love of King David and Fair Bethsabe*, 1599. Some of his poems: "Anglorum Feriae," "Coridon and Melampus' Song," "Edward the First," "Polyhymnia."

Sources: *Dictionary of National Biography.* Electronic Edition 1.1. Oxford University Press, 1997. *The Columbia Granger's Index to Poetry.* 11th ed. *The Columbia Granger's World of Poetry*, Columbia University Press, 2005 (http://www.columbiagrangers.org). *The Oxford Companion to English Literature.* 6th edition. Margaret Drabble, ed. Oxford University Press, 2000. *The Penguin Book of Renaissance Verse 1509–1659.* David Norbrook, ed. Penguin Books, 1992. *The Works of George Peele: Vols. I and II.* A.H. Bullen, ed. Kennikat Press, Inc., 1966. *Wikipedia, the Free Encyclopedia* (http://en.wikipedia.org/wiki/Wikipedia).

PENNECUIK, ALEXANDER (UNCLE), and ALEXANDER (NEPHEW) (1652–1730)

Alexander, the uncle, 1652–1722

Born in Edinburgh, he was the son of Alexander Pennecuik of Newhall, Edinburgh, who had been an army surgeon. In 1715, he published *A Geographical, Historical Description of the Shire of Tweeddale, with a Miscellany and Curious Collection of Select Scottish Poems.* He was a friend of Allan Ramsay (see entry), and it is thought that Newhall was the scene for Ramsay's *The Gentle Shepherd.* Pennecuik died in 1722 and was buried by his father's side in the churchyard at Newlands, Peebles-shire. Some of his publications: *Caledonia Triumphans*, 1699. *A Panegyric to the King*, 1699. *The Tragedy of Graybeard*, 1700. *Curious Scots Poems*, 1762. Some of his poems: "Address to His Majesty King George," "Against Passionate Love," "Ane Letter by Way of Challenge," "In Imitation of Anacreon," "Indifferent Robin to Coy Meg his Mistress," "Inscription for My Bee-House," "On a Glutton," "The City and Country Mouse," "To His Highness the Prince of Orange," "Two Ingenious Gentlemen."

Alexander, the nephew, ?–1730

Little is know of this Alexander, other than he, too, was a doctor and was interested in all things of the countryside. He is often confused with his uncle. In 1720, he published *Streams from Helicon, or Poems on Various Subjects, in three parts, by Alexander Pennecuik, Gent.* In 1726 he published *Flowers from Parnassus*, and before his death he appears to have begun a periodical, *Entertainment for the Curious.* He was buried in the Greyfriars churchyard, Edinburgh, described in the register as "Alexander Pencook, merchant." His life, so it seems, was characterized by overindulgence, which resulted in never having enough money. He was the unofficial poet laureate of Edinburgh. Several collections were published posthumously, including *A Collection of Scots Poems on several occasions, by the late Mr. Alexander Pennecuik, Gent, and Others* (1787). Some of his writings are marred by obscenity, but his satires, generally aimed against Whigs and Presbyterians, are witty. Some of his other publications: *A Pastoral Poem sacred to the Memory of Lord Basil Hamilton*, 1701. *Britannia Triumphans*, 1718. *Groans from the Grave*, 1725. Some of his poems: "The Lost Maidenhead," "The Self-Tormentor," "The Mourning Muse," "The Fair Maid of Dumblain," "Sabbath-Days Thoughts Upon the Love of Jesus."

Sources: *Dictionary of National Biography.* Electronic Edition 1.1. Oxford University Press, 1997. *Stanford University Libraries and Academic Information Resources* (http://library.stanford.edu). *The Columbia Granger's Index to Poetry.* 11th ed. *The Columbia Granger's World of Poetry*, Columbia University Press, 2005 (http://www.columbia grangers.org). *The New Oxford Book of Eighteenth Century Verse.* Roger Lonsdale, ed. Oxford University Press, 1984. *The Works of Alexander Pennecuik, Esq.* A. Allardice, 1815.

PENNEFATHER, WILLIAM (1816–1873) and CATHERINE (1818–1893)

Born in Dublin, the son of a judge, William was educated privately, then at Trinity College, Dublin, from where he graduated in 1840. Ordained in 1842, he served the community of Mellifont, near Drogheda during the famine of 1845. He married Catherine, daughter of rear-admiral Hon. James William King in 1847, and the following year the couple moved to England. In 1864 he took the living of St. Jude's, Mildmay Park, Islington. The conference hall at Mildmay became the center of many permanent organizations for home and foreign mission work. Pennefather was one of the signatories of a treaty of 1871 between Queen Victoria and the Chippewa and Swampy Cree tribes of Indians to open up areas of land for settlements. The treaty stated that no alcohol would be allowed on the reserves, that the British government would pay a certain sum of money to each family, and that a school would be built on each reserve. It was through the social care of this couple that the Mildmay mission was formed out of the London cholera epidemic of 1866. Then in 1892 the Mildmay Mission Hospital was founded, which in 2005 is dedicated to improving the lives of men, women and children challenged by HIV and AIDS. William was a preacher known all over England and was equally involved in both evangelistic and pastoral work. When he died, Catherine carried on the work of the Mildmay Mission. Both William and Catherine were hymnwriters. William published *Hymns, Original and Selected* in 1875 — which contained twenty-five of his compositions — and *Original Hymns and Thoughts in Verse,* also in 1875. Catherine published *Songs of the Pilgrim Land* (1886) and *Homeward Journey,* a selection of poems by herself and others (1888). Some of their hymn/poems: "God of Glorious Majesty," "Haste Thy Coming Kingdom," "Help Us, O Lord, to Praise," "Holy, Holy Father," "How Shall We Praise Thy Name," "I'm Journeying Through a Desert World," "Jesus, in Thy Blest Name," "Jesus, Stand Among Us," "Lord, with One Accord," "Not Now, My Child," "Praise God, Ye Seraphs Bright," "Savior! We Adore Thee," "Thousands and Thousands Stand," "Yon Shining Shore is Nearer."

Sources: *Dictionary of National Biography.* Electronic Edition 1.1. Oxford University Press, 1997. *Manitoba and Country Adjacent with Adhesions.* Queen's Printer and Controller of Stationery Ottawa, 1957 (http://collections.ic. gc.ca/aboriginaldocs/treaty/html/t-treaty1.htm) *The Cyber Hymnal* (http://www.cyberhymnal.org/index.htm). *The History of Mildmay* (http://www.mildmay.org.uk/ChristianEthos.html). *Treaties 1 and 2, Between Her Majesty the Queen and the Chippewa and Cree Indians of Manitoba and Country Adjacent with Adhesions, 1871* (http://collections.ic. gc.ca/aboriginaldocs/treaty/html/t-treaty1.htm).

PENROSE, THOMAS (1742–1779)

The son of Thomas Penrose, rector at Newbury, Berkshire, he started at Oxford University but, seeking adventure, he was part of a private expedition which set sail in 1762 to attack Buenos Ayres, under the command of Captain Macnamara. On the way they attacked the settlement of Nova Colonia de Sacramento in the River Plate, which had been seized by the Spanish. In the battle, Macnamara's ship was lost with many lives. *The Ambuscade,* in which Penrose served as a lieutenant of marines, escaped, and ultimately arrived at the Portuguese settlement of Rio Janeiro. Although wounded, he recovered and on returning to England, he settled at Oxford and graduated B.A. from Hertford College in 1766. He took holy orders and became curate to his father at Newbury, then around 1777 he was appointed the rector of Beckington-cum-Standerwick, near Frome in Somerset. He died at Bristol shortly

afterward and was buried at Clifton, Bristol, where a monument was erected in his memory. Some of his poems: "Address to the Genius of Britain," "Bagatelle," "Donnington Castle," "Early Grey Hairs," "The Hermit's Vision," "To My Dearest Wife, on Our Wedding Day, 1768."

Sources: *Dictionary of National Biography.* Electronic Edition 1.1. Oxford University Press, 1997. *Ships of the 18th Cent. Royal Navy* (http://www.cronab.demon.co.uk/18a. HTM). *The Columbia Granger's Index to Poetry.* 11th ed. *The Columbia Granger's World of Poetry,* Columbia University Press, 2005 (http://www.columbiagrangers.org). *The New Oxford Book of Eighteenth Century Verse.* Roger Lonsdale, ed. Oxford University Press, 1984. *The Works of the British Poets, Vol. 33* (*Blair, Glynn, Boyce, Shaw, Lovibond, and Penrose*). J. Sharpe, 1808.

PERCY, THOMAS (1729–1811)

The son of a grocer, he was born at Bridgnorth, Shropshire, graduated B.A from Christ Church, Oxford, in 1750, and was made doctor of divinity from Emmanuel College, Cambridge, in 1770. From 1753 to 1782 he was the vicar of Easton-Maudit, Northamptonshire, was appointed chaplain to King George III, and was made dean of Carlisle in 1778 and bishop of Dromore in Ireland in 1782. Around 1804 his eyesight began to fail. His wife of nearly fifty years died in 1806, and both were buried in the transept of his cathedral. Some of his poetry publications: *Hau Kiou Choaun, or the Pleasing History,* 1761 (a translation from the Portuguese of a Chinese novel, which contained a collection of Chinese proverbs and fragments of Chinese poetry). *Miscellaneous Pieces relating to the Chinese,* 1762. *Five Pieces of Runic Poetry, translated from the Islandic Language,* 1763. *Reliques of Ancient English Poetry,* 1768. *The Hermit of Warkworth,* 1771 (translated from the Hebrew and Spanish). Some of his poems: "Bosworth Feilde," "Chevy Chase," "Edward the Third," "Flodden Feilde," "When First I Sawe Her Face," "Will Stewart and John."

Sources: *Bishop Percy's Folio MS: Ballads and Romances. Vols. 1, 2 and 3.* John W. Hales and Frederick J. Furnivall, eds. N. Trübner and Co., 1868. *Dictionary of National Biography.* Electronic Edition 1.1. Oxford University Press, 1997. *Loose and Humorous Songs from Bishop Percy's Folio Manuscript.* John Greenway, ed. Folklore Associates, Inc., 1963. *The National Portrait Gallery* (www.npg.org.uk). *The Columbia Granger's Index to Poetry.* 11th ed. *The Columbia Granger's World of Poetry,* Columbia University Press, 2005 (http://www.columbiagrangers.org). *The Oxford Companion to English Literature.* 6th edition. Margaret Drabble, ed. Oxford University Press, 2000.

PERCY, WILLIAM (1575–1648)

The third son of Henry Percy, eighth earl of Northumberland, was probably born at Topcliffe, near Thirsk, Yorkshire, and was educated at

Gloucester Hall (afterwards Worcester College), Oxford. Percy formed a close relationship with Barnabe Barnes (see entry), who was at Oxford at the same time. In 1593 Barnes dedicated his collection of sonnets, *Parthenophil*, to his friend. The following year Percy published a collection titled *Sonnets to the fairest Celia*, which closed with a madrigal dedicated to Barnes. There is little remarkable about his life, though at one time he was in the Tower of London on a charge of homicide. He died in Oxford, having lived the last decade of his life in obscurity, and was buried in Christ Church Cathedral. Some of his poems: "A Mysterie," "Coelia," "Echo," "Faire Queene of Gnidos Come Adorn My Forehead," "If It Be Sin So Dearely for to Loue Thee," "Ivdg'd By My Goddesse Doome to Endlesse Paine," "Proue Her? Ah No, I Did It But to Loue Her," "Strike Vp, My Lute, and Ease My Heauie Cares," "To Polyxena."

Sources: *Dictionary of National Biography.* Electronic Edition 1.1. Oxford University Press, 1997. *Elizabethan Sonneteers, Including William Percy* (http://www.sonnets.org/eliz.htm). *Stanford University Libraries and Academic Information Resources* (http://library.stanford.edu). *The Columbia Granger's Index to Poetry.* 11th ed. *The Columbia Granger's World of Poetry,* Columbia University Press, 2005 (http://www.columbiagrangers.org). *The Sonnet: An Anthology.* Robert M. Bender and Charles L. Squier, eds. Washington Square Press, 1987.

PERRONET, EDWARD (1726–1792)

The son of Vincent Perronet (1693–1785) — of Huguenot stock — an Anglican vicar of Shoreham, Sussex, Edward became one of Wesley's itinerant preachers around 1749. He pushed for separation from the Anglican Church and for the right to administer the sacraments. Not able to settle his difference with the Wesleys, he joined the Countess of Huntingdon's Connexion, although he separated from her because of his violent outbursts aimed at the Anglican Church. He became minister of an independent chapel at Canterbury. He was buried in the south cloister of the Canterbury cathedral. His fame as a hymn-writer rests on one hymn — "All Hail the Power of Jesus' Name." It is often referred to as the "National Anthem of Christendom" and has been translated into almost every language where there are Christians. The hymn first appeared in the November 1779 issue of the *Gospel Magazine*, edited by Augustus Toplady (see entry), author of "Rock of Ages." His poetry publications: *Select Passages of the Old and New Testament versified*, 1756. *The Mitre, a sacred poem*, 1757. *Small Collection of Hymns*, 1782. *Occasional Verses, moral and sacred*, 1785.

Sources: *A Sacrifice of Praise: An Anthology of Christian Poetry in English from Caedmon to the Mid-Twentieth Cen-*tury. James H. Trott, ed. Cumberland House Publishing, 1999. *Dictionary of National Biography.* Electronic Edition 1.1. Oxford University Press, 1997. *Edward Perronet, Hymn Writer, Death reported January 2, 1792* (http://chi.gospelcom.net/DAILYF/2003/01/daily-01-02-2003.shtml). *The Columbia Granger's Index to Poetry.* 11th ed. *The Columbia Granger's World of Poetry,* Columbia University Press, 2005 (http://www.columbiagrangers.org). *The Countess of Huntingdon's Methodist Connexion* (http://www.oxfordscholarship.com/oso/public/content/religion/0198263694/toc.html). *The Cyber Hymnal* (http://www.cyberhymnal.org/index.htm). *The New Oxford Book of Christian Verse.* Donald Davie, ed. Oxford University Press, 1981.

PETIT, PASCALE (1953–)

Born in Paris, she grew up in France and Wales and trained as a sculptor, gaining an M.A. from the Royal College of Art. She has worked as an environmental artist in schools and has twice traveled to the Venezuelan Amazon. She was one of the founders of *Poetry London* and was its editor from 1990 to 2005. In 2001 she was one of ten poets commissioned by BBC Radio 4 to write a poem for National Poetry Day, and in 2004 she was selected as one of the "Next Generation poets." In 2001 she received a New London Writers' Award and an Arts Council of England Writers' Award. Her other poetry publications: *Icefall Climbing*, 1994. *Heart of a Deer*, 1998. *Tying the Song: A First Anthology from the Poetry School 1997–2000*, 2000 (editor). *The Zoo Father*, 2001 (short listed for the 2001 T.S. Eliot Prize). *The Huntress*, 2005. *The Wounded Deer: Fourteen Poems After Frida Kahlo*, 2005, (Mexican artist, 1907–1954). Some of her poems: "During the Eclipse," "Embrace of the Electric Eel," "My Father's Body," "My Father's Clothes," "My Mother's Clothes," "The Ant Glove," "The Strait-Jackets."

Sources: *Biography of Pascale Petit* (http://www.bbc.co.uk/education/beyond/factsheets/poet01_petit.shtml). *Biography of Pascale Petit; Poetry Book* Society (http://www.poetrybooks.co.uk/PBS/pbs_petit_pascale.asp). *Parents: An Anthology of Poems by Women Writers.* Myra Schneider and Dilys Wood, eds. Enitharmon Press, 2000. *Poems by Pascale Petit* (http://english.chass.ncsu.edu/freeverse/Archives/Spring_2003/Poetry/P_Petit.htm). *Poems by Pascale Petit* (http://www.poetrypf.co.uk/pascalepetitpoems.html#p4). *Poetry London* (Magazine) *Says Farewell to Pascale Petit, Spring 2005* (http://www.poetrylondon.co.uk/index.htm?edits/edit50.htm). *The Columbia Granger's Index to Poetry.* 11th ed. *The Columbia Granger's World of Poetry,* Columbia University Press, 2005 (http://www.columbiagrangers.org). *Wikipedia, the Free Encyclopedia* (http://en.wikipedia.org/wiki/Wikipedia).

PETRUCCI, MARIO (1958–)

Originally a natural sciences graduate with a Ph.D. in optoelectronics, he now works as a free-lance creative writing tutor, broadcaster and educator. Mario's poetry and prose have been published in the U.K., in Canada, Australia, USA and Italy (in translation). In 1999 he became the first resident poet at the Imperial War Museum, London. Some of his poems are on display there and at the new Imperial War Museum North, Manchester. He co-founded the award-winning collaborative performance poetry group ShadoWork, and won the London Writers Competition in 1993, 1998, 2004, and 2005. The BBC commissioned him as Radio 3's first poet-in-residence, and he is currently a Royal Literary Fund Fellow at Oxford Brookes University, Headington, Oxford. Some of his poetry publications: *Departures*, 1991. *Shrapnel and Sheets*, 1996. *Bosco*, 1999. *The Stamina of Sheep*, 2002. *Half Life: Poems for Chernobyl*, 2004. *Heavy Water: A Poem for Chernobyl*, 2004 (awarded the 2002 Arvon/Daily Telegraph International Poetry Prize, arguably the most coveted poetry prize in the UK). *Catullus*, 2006. Some of his poems: "Ambient," "Light," "Miss Muffet," "Negatives," "The Liberation of Berlin Zoo."

Sources: *British Council Arts* (http://www.contemporarywriters.com). *Mario Petrucci's Home Page* (http://mario petrucci.port5.com/index.htm). Personal correspondence. *ShadoWork* (http://mariopetrucci.port5.com/shadowork.htm).

PHILIPOT, THOMAS (?1616–1682)

The son of John Philipot, Somerset herald, of the College of Arms, London, he graduated M.A. from Clare Hall, Cambridge, in 1635 and was incorporated in that degree at Oxford in July 1640. He was buried at Greenwich, London. In his will he left some of his money to Clare Hall to establish two fellowships for Kentish men, and the rest to the Clothworkers' Company to establish six almshouses for four people from Eltham and two from Chislehurst (both in what is now Greater London). Some of his poetry publications: *A Congratulatory Elegie*, 1641. *Elegies*, 1641. *Englands Sorrow*, 1646. *Poems*, 1646. *An Elegie Offer'd Up to the Memory of His Excellencie Robert Earle of Essex*, 1646. *Æsop's Fables*, 1687 (in rhyme). Some of his poems: "On Christs Passion, a Descant," "On the Death of a Prince; a Meditation," "On the future burning of the World," "On the Nativity of Our Saviour," "On Thought of Our Resurrection," "The Old Lion," "The Wood and Clown," "To Sir Henry Newton."

Sources: *Dictionary of National Biography*. Electronic Edition 1.1. Oxford University Press, 1997. *Jacobean and Caroline Poetry: An Anthology*. T.G.S. Cain, ed. Methuen, 1981. *Stanford University Libraries and Academic Information Resources* (http://library.stanford.edu). *The Columbia Granger's Index to Poetry*. 11th ed. *The Columbia Granger's World of Poetry*, Columbia University Press, 2005 (http://www.columbiagrangers.org). *The New Oxford Book of Seventeenth Century Verse*. Alastair Fowler, ed. Oxford University Press, 1991.

PHILIPS, AMBROSE (?1675–1749)

He was educated at Shrewsbury, Shropshire, and graduated M.A. from St. John's College, Cambridge, in 1700, and was a fellow from 1699 to 1707. He seems to have been employed abroad in service for the government; some of his poems make reference to Utrecht (1703) and to Copenhagen in 1709 and 1710. In 1712 he published *The Distressed Mother*, a successful adaptation of Jean Racine's *Andromaque*. When this was praised by the press, Alexander Pope (see entry) — seemingly out of jealousy — wrote a comparison between his own performance and that of Philips. A bitter feud ensued which almost ended in a case of slander against Pope. After the accession of George I, Philips was made justice of the peace for Westminster and in 1717 a commissioner for the lottery. He was a member of Parliament for Armagh, Ireland. He died in London. Some of his poems: "A Bacchanalian Song," "A Winter-Piece," "From Holland to a Friend in England in the Year 1703," "In the Year 1714," "Lament for Queen Mary," "The Happy Swain," "The Olympian Odes (Pindar)," "The Tea-Pot; or, The Lady's Transformation."

Sources: *Dictionary of National Biography*. Electronic Edition 1.1. Oxford University Press, 1997. *The Bride's Book of Poems*. Cary Yager, ed. Contemporary Books, 1995. *The Columbia Granger's Index to Poetry*. 11th ed. *The Columbia Granger's World of Poetry*, Columbia University Press, 2005 (http://www.columbiagrangers.org). *The Oxford Book of Classical Verse in Translation*. Adrian Poole and Jeremy Maule, eds. 1995. *The Oxford Companion to English Literature*. 6th edition. Margaret Drabble, ed. Oxford University Press, 2000. *The Poems of Ambrose Philips*. M.G. Segar, ed. Blackwell, Oxford, 1937.

PHILIPS, JOHN (1676–1709)

He was born at Bampton, Oxfordshire, where his father was a clergyman. Educated at Winchester College and Christ Church College, Oxford, with the intention of becoming a doctor, he chose the path of literature. Samuel Johnson comments at length on the work of Philips, which is centered around three works. One was *The Splendid Shilling* (unauthorized 1771 and authorized 1775), a burlesque that was praised by Joseph Addison (see entry) as being one of the best poems in the British language. Another was *Blenheim* (1705), written to commemorate the Duke of Marlborough's famous victory over the French at Blenheim in 1704. The third was *Cyder* (1708), written in imitation of Virgil's Georgics and an exact account of the culture of the apple tree and of the manufacture of cider with many local allusions to Herefordshire. He died of tuberculosis, was buried in Hereford Cathedral and is one of the poets memorialized in Poets' Corner of Westminster Abbey. Some of his other poems: "Cerealia," "Ode to Henry St. John, Esq. 1706," "The Fall of Chloe's Jordan," "The Thirsty Poet," "War Poetry."

Sources: *Dictionary of National Biography.* Electronic Edition 1.1. Oxford University Press, 1997. *Samuel Johnson's Lives of the English Poets,* 1779–1781 (http://www2.hn.psu.edu/Faculty/KKemmerer/poets/preface.htm). *The Columbia Granger's Index to Poetry.* 11th ed. *The Columbia Granger's World of Poetry,* Columbia University Press, 2005 (http://www.columbiagrangers.org). *The Faber Book of Drink, Drinkers and Drinking.* Simon Rae, ed. Faber and Faber, 1991. *The Faber Book of Useful Verse.* Simon Brett, ed. Faber and Faber, 1981. *The New Oxford Book of Eighteenth Century Verse.* Roger Lonsdale, ed. Oxford University Press, 1984. *The Oxford Anthology of English Poetry. Vol. I: Spenser to Crabbe.* John Wain, ed. Oxford University Press, 1990. *The Oxford Companion to English Literature.* 6th edition. Margaret Drabble, ed. Oxford University Press, 2000. *The Poetical Works of Samuel Butler.* Thomas Park, ed. J. Sharpe, 1808. *Westminster Abbey Official Guide* (no date).

PHILIPS, KATHERINE (1631–1664)

Katherine Flower was born in London to a merchant class family, educated at boarding school and was married at age 16 to James Philips, a man of 54. She spent her time in London, while he stayed primarily at Cardigan on the Welsh coast. Katherine had two children, one of whom died in infancy. She formed an organization of women called "The Society of Friendship," where the members each assumed classical pseudonyms. She was known as Orinda and was often referred to as "The Matchless Orinda." While most of her poetry was about her women lovers and was sensual in nature, the poems were said to be expressions of platonic love rather than sexual love. In 1662, in Ireland, she was encouraged by Lord Roscommon and the Earl of Orrery to complete a translation of Corneille's *Pompée.* The play was produced in Dublin in 1662 and later in London. She died of smallpox and was buried in the church of St. Benet Sherehog, London. Some of her poems: "A Country Life," "A Farewell to Rosania," "Against Love," "Invitation to the Countrey," "On the Welsh Language," "The Irish Greyhound."

Sources: *A Book of Women Poets from Antiquity to Now.* Aliki Barnstone and Willis Barnstone, eds. Schocken Books, 1980. *Dictionary of National Biography.* Electronic Edition, 1.1. *Isle of Lesbos, the Biography of Katherine Philips* (http://www.sappho.com/poetry/k_philip.html). *Stanford University Libraries and Academic Information Resources* (http://library.stanford.edu). *The Broadview Anthology of Victorian Poetry and Poetic Theory.* Thomas J. Collins and Vivienne Rundle, eds. Broadview, 1999. *The Collected Works of Katherine Philips: Volume 1, 2 and 3.* Patrick Thomas, ed. Stump Cross Books, 1990. *The Columbia Granger's Index to Poetry.* 11th ed (http://www.columbiagrangers.org). *The Oxford Companion to English Literature.* 6th edition. Margaret Drabble, ed. Oxford Univer-

sity Press, 2000. *The Penguin Book of Homosexual Verse.* Stephen Coote, ed. Penguin Books, 1983.

PHILLIMORE, JOHN SWINNERTON (1873–1926)

Born at Boconnoc, Cornwall, the son of Vice-Admiral Sir Augustus Phillimore, he was educated at Westminster School, London, and Christ Church, Oxford, where he won several distinguished literary prizes. He became a lecturer and tutor at Christ Church and in 1899 was appointed professor of Greek at Glasgow University, and later professor of humanities. For several years he took an active part in liberal politics in the west of Scotland. He published rhymed translation of Sophocles, Propertius, Statius, Philostratus, and from 1912, he published many learned works on Greek and Roman literature. He received honorary degrees from St. Andrews University and Trinity College, Dublin. In 1902, he published *Poems* and in 1918, another collection, *Things New and Old.* He became a Catholic in 1906 and in 1926 published *The Hundred Best Latin Hymns.* He died at Shedfield, Hampshire. Some of his poems: "A Cathedral Voluntary," "Desiderium," "Elegy in Lanarkshire," "Mortalia," "Night in the Desert," "Rain at Naples," "The Funeral March," "Trieste to Alexandria," "Virgil's Statue at Pietole," "Zephyrus Vernus."

Sources: *Dictionary of National Biography.* Electronic Edition 1.1. Oxford University Press, 1997. *Poems of John Swinnerton Phillimore.* James MacLehose and Sons, 1902. *The Columbia Granger's Index to Poetry.* 11th ed. *The Columbia Granger's World of Poetry,* Columbia University Press, 2005 (http://www.columbiagrangers.org).

PHILLIPS, STEPHEN (1864–1915)

The son of a clergyman, he was born at Summertown, near Oxford, was educated at Trinity College School, Stratford-upon-Avon, and at King's School, Peterborough; then around 1885 he joined the F.R. Benson theatrical company. His attempts at writing plays met with brief success, so after seven years he took the job as tutor in history until the success of his *Poems* (1898) convinced him to concentrate on writing poetic drama. When *Paolo and Francesca* was performed (1902), Phillips was greeted as the successor of Sophocles and Shakespeare, and his royalties jumped dramatically. Affluence did not sit easily with his lack of business acumen and his over-generous nature. He died in poverty at Deal, Kent. Some of his poems/verse dramas: *Orestes,* 1884. *Eremus,* 1894. *Herod,* 1901. *Ulysses,* 1902. *The Sin of David,* 1904. *Nero,* 1906. *New Poems,* 1908. *The New Inferno,* 1911. *Lyrics and Dramas,* 1913. *Panama and Other Poems,* 1915. Some of his poems: "Beautiful Death," "By the Sea," "Faces at a Fire,"

"Lazarus," "Penelope to Ulysses," "The Apparition," "The Lily," "The Woman with the Dead Soul."

Sources: *Dictionary of National Biography.* Electronic Edition 1.1. Oxford University Press, 1997. *Poems of Stephen Phillips.* John Lane, 1901. *Stanford University Libraries and Academic Information Resources* (http://library.stanford.edu). *The Columbia Granger's Index to Poetry.* 11th ed. *The Columbia Granger's World of Poetry,* Columbia University Press, 2005 (http://www.columbiagrangers.org). *The Oxford Companion to English Literature.* 6th edition. Margaret Drabble, ed. Oxford University Press, 2000.

PICKARD, TOM (1946–)

One of the British poetry Revivalists, he was born in Gateshead, Newcastle upon Tyne. On leaving school at 14 he soon made his name as one of the emerging band of British "underground" poets, inspired by the Beat poetry coming out of America. From 1963 to 1972 Pickard ran the Morden Tower Book Room, Newcastle upon Tyne, where he organized a series of readings by British and American modernist tradition poets. Moving to London in 1973, he started writing radio and documentary film scripts. His film credits include *Jarrow March* (1976), *We Make Ships* (1988), *Birmingham is What I Think With* (1991) and *The Shadow and the Substance* (1994). He directed the last three of these films. In 1974, his television play *Squire* was broadcast by the BBC. Some of his poetry publications: *High on the Walls,* 1968. *The Order of Chance,* 1971. *Hero Dust: New and Selected Poems,* 1979. *Hole in the Wall: New and Selected Poems,* 2002. Some of his poems: "A History Lesson from My Son on Hadrian's Wall," "Dawn Raid on an Orchard," "Détente," "Gypsy Music in Krakow," "The Decadent Voyeurs."

Sources: *Anthology of Twentieth-Century British and Irish Poetry.* Keith Tuma, ed. Oxford University Press, 2001. *Biography of Tom Pickard: Woodland Pattern Book Centre* (http://www.woodlandpattern.org/poems/tom_pickard01.shtml). *I Have No Gun But I Can Spit: An Anthology of Satirical and Abusive Verse.* Kenneth Baker, ed. Faber and Faber, 1980. *Other: British and Irish Poetry since 1970.* Richard Caddel and Peter Quartermain, ed. Wesleyan University Press, 1999. *The Columbia Granger's Index to Poetry.* 11th ed. *The Columbia Granger's World of Poetry,* Columbia University Press, 2005 (http://www.columbiagrangers.org). *The National Portrait Gallery* (www.npg.org.uk). *The New British Poetry, 1968–88.* Gillian Allnutt, Fred D'Aguiar and Ken Edwards, eds. Grafton Books, 1989. *The Oxford Companion to English Literature.* 6th edition. Margaret Drabble, ed. Oxford University Press, 2000. *Tom Pickard interview published March 2002* (http://www.lindisfarne.de/interviews/ivtp0203.htm). *Wikipedia, the Free Encyclopedia* (http://en.wikipedia.org/wiki/Wikipedia).

PILKINGTON, MATTHEW (1701–1774) and LAETITIA (1712–1750)

Matthew, a watchmaker' son, was born at Ballyboy in County Offaly, Ireland, graduated B.A. from Trinity College, Dublin, in 1722, then was ordained in the established church. An impecunious curate, he married Laetitia Van Lewen, daughter of a Dublin physician in 1729 (see Grierson, Constantia). Soon afterward he became chaplain to Lady Charlemont. The couple were introduced to Jonathan Swift (see entry), who was amused by Laetitia's wit and humor, and for a time was one of his favorites. It said that he referred to Matthew as "the mighty Thomas Thumb" and to Laetitia as "her Serene Highness of Lilliput." The Pilkingtons had several children before the marriage ended in divorce in the spiritual court, on the grounds of the wife's adultery. Shortly after her father died in 1734, her husband found her entertaining a man in her bedroom. She sued for maintenance, which he could never pay. In London she was sued for debt and imprisoned in the Marshalsea. With the help of Colley Cibber she published her *Memoirs* (1748), an account of her relationships with various people, plus some of her poems. She died in Ireland. Matthew became the protégée of Swift, at least for a time, and then the relationship went sour, particularly over Pilkington's treatment of his wife. Nothing is known of his death. Some of Matthew's poems: "An Hymn to Sleep," "Cupid's Reply," "Happiness," "Mira and Colin: A Song," "The Bee," "The Candle," "The Constant Shepherd," "The Gift," "The Girdle," "The Lost Muse," "The Progress of Musick in Ireland," Some of Laetitia's poems: "An Invitation to a Gentleman," "Consolatory Verses to Her Husband," "Queen Mab to Pollio," "Sent with a Quill to Dr. Swift," "The Happy Pair," "To Colley Cibber Esq.," "Your Rosy Wine."

Sources: *Dictionary of National Biography.* Electronic Edition, 1.1. *Matthew Pilkington — Offaly History, Famous Offaly People* (http://www.offalyhistory.com/content/reading_resources/famous_people/pilkington_matthew.htm). *The Celebrated Mrs. Pilkington's Jests, or the Cabinet of Wit and Humour,* published in 1751 and republished by Ams Pr. Publishing in 1964. *The Columbia Granger's Index to Poetry.* 11th ed. *The Columbia Granger's World of Poetry,* Columbia University Press, 2005 (http://www.columbiagrangers.org). *The Oxford Companion to English Literature.* 6th edition. Margaret Drabble, ed. Oxford University Press, 2000. *The Poetry of Laetitia Pilkington (1712–1750) and Constantia Grierson (1706–1733).* Bernard Tucker, ed. The Edwin Mellen Press, 1996.

PINTER, HAROLD (1930–)

Born in Hackney — a working-class neighborhood in London's East End — the son of a Jewish tailor, he was educated at Hackney Downs Grammar School and spent two years at London's Royal Academy of Dramatic Arts. In 1950 he started publishing poems in *Poetry* under the name Harold Pinta and became a full-time actor, then started writing for the stage. *The Birthday Party* was first performed by Bristol University's drama department in 1957 and produced in 1958 in London's West End. Since then he has gone on to write ten more plays, adapted many of them for radio and television and has written the screenplays to five films. He was made a Commander of the British Empire in 1966 and Companion of Honor in 2002. He has a clutch of 23 major literary awards, including the Nobel Prize for Literature in 2005. His wife is the writer Lady Antonia Fraser and they in London. Some of his poems: "American Football," "Democracy," "God Bless America," "Message," "Restaurant," "The Bombs," "The Ventriloquists," "Weather Forecast."

Sources: *Biography of Harold Pinter* (http://www.kirjasto.sci.fi/hpinter.htm). *British Council Arts* (http://www.contemporarywriters.com). *Poemhunter* (www.poemhunter.com). *Red Pepper, Harold Pinter War Poetry* (http://www.redpepper.org.uk/arts/x-feb04-pinter.htm). *The Oxford Companion to English Literature*. 6th edition. Margaret Drabble, ed. Oxford University Press, 2000. *Who's Who*. London: A & C Black, 2005.

PITT, CHRISTOPHER (1699–1748)

Born at Blandford, Dorset, the son of a doctor, he was educated at Winchester College and graduated M.A. from New College, Oxford, in 1724. He was rector at Pimperne in Dorset from 1722 until he died; he was buried in Blandford Church. The literary influence of the family is strong. His father contributed the *Plague of Athens* to the well-known translation of *Lucretius* by Thomas Creech (1682) (see entry) and his elder brother, Robert, translated into Latin five books of Milton's *Paradise Lost*. His *Poem on the Death of the late Earl of Stanhope, Humbly inscribed to the Countess of Stanhope* was published in 1721 while he was still an undergraduate. Some of his other publications: *Vida's Art of Poetry*, 1725 (a verse translation of the *De Arte Poetica* of Marcus Hieronymus Vida, bishop of Alba, first published at Paris in 1534). *Poems and translations*, 1727. *The Æneid of Virgil*, 1753. *Poems*, 1756. Some of his poems: "On a Shadow," "On the Death of a Young Gentleman," "On the Masquerades," "The 8th Psalm Translated," "The Fable of the Young Man and His Cat."

Sources: *Dictionary of National Biography*. Electronic Edition 1.1. Oxford University Press, 1997. *Eighteenth-Century English Verse*. Dennis Davison, ed. Penguin Books, 1988. *English Poetry: A Poetic Record, from Chaucer to Yeats*. David Hopkins, ed. Routledge, 1990. *Gentleman's Magazine* (http://www.bodley.ox.ac.uk/ilej/journals/srchgm.htm). *The National Portrait Gallery* (www.npg.org.uk). *Samuel Johnson's Lives of the English Poets*, 1779–1781 (http://www2.hn.psu.edu/Faculty/KKemmerer/poets/preface.htm). *Stanford University Libraries and Academic Information Resources* (http://library.stanford.edu). *The Colum-*

bia Granger's Index to Poetry. 11th ed. *The Columbia Granger's World of Poetry*, Columbia University Press, 2005 (http://www.columbiagrangers.org).

PITTER, RUTH (1897–1992)

She was born at Ilford, Essex, to parents who were both teachers in London's East End. Living as she did on the edge of London, she found much to stimulate her early interest in poetry. Her education was at Coborn School for Girls, Bow Road, London. Hilaire Belloc helped to publish her *First Poems* in 1920, and she rapidly established a sound reputation on both sides of the Atlantic. In total she produced eighteen volumes of verse; her work was praised by many poets as being highly original. From 1956 to 1960 she appeared regularly on the BBC's *The Brains Trust*, one of the first television "talk" programs. Her awards include the Hawthornden Prize (1937) and the Heinemann Award for Literature (1954), and she was the first woman recipient of the Queen's Gold Medal for Poetry (1955). She was made a Companion of Literature (1974) and a Commander of the British Empire (1979). Some of her poems: "A Solemn Meditation," "An Old Woman Speaks of the Moon," "For Sleep, or Death," "Help, Good Shepherd," "The Bat," "The Beautiful Negress," "The Coffin-Worm," "The Viper," "Time's Fool."

Sources: *A Treasury of Poems for Worship and Devotion*, Charles L. Wallis, ed. Harper, 1959. Enitharmon Press (http://www.enitharmon.co.uk/authors/viewAuthor.asp?AID=39). *Fellow Mortals: An Anthology of Animal Verse*. Roy Fuller, ed. Macdonald and Evans, 1981. *Modern British Poetry*. 7th rev. ed. Louis Untermeyer, ed. Harcourt, Brace, 1962. *The Columbia Granger's Index to Poetry*. 11th ed (http://www.columbiagrangers.org). *The Oxford Book of Christian Verse*. Lord David Cecil, ed. Oxford University Press, 1940. *Women's Poetry of the 1930s: A Critical Anthology*. Jane Dowson, ed. Routledge, 1966.

PLATH, SYLVIA (1932–1963)

Claimed by both England and America, she was born in Boston, Massachusetts, the daughter of a German immigrant professor and entomologist. She graduated with honors from Smith College, Massachusetts, in 1955, then studied at Newnham College, Cambridge, on a Fulbright fellowship. She married the English poet Ted Hughes (see entry) in 1956 and the couple moved America for two years, where Plath taught English at Smith College. In 1959 they returned to London, where she had two children, Frieda (1960) and Nicholas (1962). Soon afterward she and Hughes separated and she moved with the children to a small flat. Plath had suffered from depression for years, resulting in being hospitalized. On 11 February 1963 she gassed herself in the flat. Her strongly autobiographical novel, *The Bell Jar*, was published in 1963 under the pseudonym

"Victoria Lucas." Many of her poems are concerned with the dark side of life. Her poetry publications: *The Colossus*, 1960. *Crossing the Water*, 1971. *Winter Trees*, 1971. Some of her poems: "Blackberrying," "The Applicant," "The Arrival of the Bee Box," "The Bed Book," "The Bee Meeting," "Winter Trees."

Sources: *Anthology of Modern American Poetry*. Cary Nelson, ed. Oxford University Press, 2000. *Dictionary of National Biography*. Electronic Edition 1.1. Oxford University Press, 1997. *Poems for Young Children*. Caroline Royds, ed. Doubleday, 1986. *The Collected Poems of Sylvia Plath*. Ted Hughes, ed. HarperCollins, 1981. *The Columbia Granger's Index to Poetry*. 11th ed. *The Columbia Granger's World of Poetry*, Columbia University Press, 2005 (http://www.columbiagrangers.org). *The Harvard Book of Contemporary American Poetry*. Helen Vendler, ed. Belknap Press, 1985. *The Oxford Companion to English Literature*. 6th edition. Margaret Drabble, ed. Oxford University Press, 2000.

PLOMER, WILLIAM CHARLES FRANKLYN (1903–1973)

Born of British parents at Pietersburg, Transvaal, South Africa, his education was split between South Africa and England. His novel *Turbott Wolfe* (1925)—with its anti-apartheid message—aroused a storm of protest from the white population. He spent three years teaching in Japan before coming to England in 1929, and between 1938 and 1940 he edited three volumes of the diaries of the Victorian clergyman Francis Kilvert. During World War II he served in Naval Intelligence, then was literary consultant to the publishing house of Jonathan Cape and brought Ian Fleming's *James Bond* novels to the firm. In 1968 he was made Commander of the Order of the British Empire. In his career he wrote novels, short stories, memoirs, and opera librettos. His *Collected Poems* (1960) was republished and enlarged in 1973. He died at his home in Sussex. The *Autobiography of William Plomer* was published in 1975. Some of his poems: "Anglo-Swiss, or a Day Among the Alps," "Armistice Day," "Azure, or Green, or Purple," "Ganymede," "The Boer War," "The Murder on the Downs," "The Playboy of the Demi-World" (1938).

Sources: *Dictionary of National Biography*. Electronic Edition 1.1. Oxford University Press, 1997. *I Have No Gun But I Can Spit: An Anthology of Satirical and Abusive Verse*. Kenneth Baker, ed. Faber and Faber, 1980. *Rhythm Road: Poems to Move To*. Lillian Morrison, ed. Lothrop, Lee and Shepard, 1988. *The Columbia Granger's Index to Poetry*. 11th ed. *The Columbia Granger's World of Poetry*, Columbia University Press, 2005 (http://www.columbiagrangers.org). *The Oxford Book of Villains*. John Mortimer, ed. Oxford University Press, 1992. *The Oxford Companion to English Literature*. 6th edition. Margaret Drabble, ed. Oxford University Press, 2000. *The Penguin Book of Homosexual Verse*. Stephen Coote, ed. Penguin Books, 1983. *The Penguin Book of Southern African Verse*. Stephen Gray, ed. Penguin Books, 1989.

PLOWMAN, MAX (1883–1941)

Born in Tottenham, London, he was educated at various private schools. By the outbreak of World War I he had established himself as journalist and a romantic poet, and although he considered the war insane, he felt it his duty to join up as his way of dealing with it. He enlisted in the Territorial Field Ambulance on Christmas Eve, 1914, then accepted a commission in an infantry regiment. In 1917 he suffered concussion from an exploding shell and was returned to Craiglockhart War Hospital, Edinburgh. His collection of poems, *A Lap Full of Seed*, in October 1917, contains only eight poems about the war, but all the poems are about individual responsibility. His other book, *The Right to Live*, was published anonymously in 1918. His request to be discharged from the Army on religious grounds was denied; he was court-martialed and discharged, although he escaped a prison sentence. He joined Dick Sheppard's Peace Pledge Union after the war and became its secretary in 1937–38. He was buried in Langham churchyard, Essex. Some of his poems: "Her Beauty," "The Dead Soldiers," "When It's Over."

Sources: *Biography of Max Plowman by Michele Fry* (http://www.sassoonery.demon.co.uk/plowman.htm). *Oldpoetry* (www.oldpoetry.com). *Plowman (Max) Papers at University College, London. AIM25: University College London: Plowman Papers* (http://www.aim25.ac.uk/cgi-bin/frames/fulldesc?inst_id=13&coll_id=1650). *Poetry of the World Wars*. Michael Foss, ed. Peter Bedrick Books, 1990. *Subaltern on the Somme: Max Plowman*. Naval and Military Press, 2001. *The Columbia Granger's Index to Poetry*. 11th ed. *The Columbia Granger's World of Poetry*, Columbia University Press, 2005 (http://www.columbiagrangers.org). *The Home Book of Verse*. Burton Egbert Stevenson, ed. New York: Henry Holt and Company, 1953.

PLUNKETT, JOSEPH MARY (1887–1916)

Leader of the 1916 Irish Easter Rising, he was educated at the English Jesuit School at Stonyhurst, Lancashire, and was a member of the Gaelic League, the Irish Volunteers and the Irish Republican Brotherhood (IRB). During World War I he recruited his father—curator of the National Museum—who allowed his property in Kimmage, south Dublin, to be used as a training camp for young men wishing to escape conscription in England. He was sent to Germany to meet with Sir Roger Casement (see entry) who was negotiating with the Germans to support an Irish uprising. His tuberculosis, from which he had suffered all his life, flared up and he attended the uprising with his neck swathed in bandages, having undergone surgery on his glands. Hours before his execution by firing squad, he was married in the prison chapel to his sweetheart, Grace Gifford. Some of his poems: "I Saw the Sun at Midnight, Rising Red," "I See His Blood upon the Rose," "Saint Augustine," "The Claim That Has the Canker on the Rose," "The Stars Sang in God's Garden," "White Dove of the Wild Dark Eyes."

Sources: *1000 Years of Irish Poetry: The Gaelic and Anglo-Irish Poets from Pagan Times to the Present.* Kathleen Hoagland, ed. Devin-Adair, 1975. *Selection of poems by Joseph Mary Plunkett, A Taste of Ireland's Poets* (http://www.rc.net/wcc/ireland/plunkett.htm). *The Columbia Granger's Index to Poetry.* 11th ed. *The Columbia Granger's World of Poetry,* Columbia University Press, 2005 (http://www.columbiagrangers.org). *The Oxford Book of Irish Verse: XVI-Ith Century–XXth Century.* Donagh MacDonagh and Leenox Robinson, eds. Oxford University Press, 1958. *The Poems of Joseph Mary Plunkett* (http://poetry.elcore.net/CatholicPoets/Plunkett/). *Treasury of Irish Religious Verse.* Patrick Murray, ed. Crossroad, 1986. *Wikipedia, the Free Encyclopedia* (http://en.wikipedia.org/wiki/Wikipedia).

POLLEY, JACOB (1975–)

Born in Carlisle, he grew up in Bowness-on-Solway and Burgh-by-Sands, both of which are on the line of Hadrian's Wall, Cumbria; he lives in Carlisle. He holds an English degree from Lancaster University and an M.A. in creative writing. He is visiting fellow commoner in the creative arts for 2005–2007 at Trinity College, Cambridge. His poems were originally published in Cumbria County Council pamphlets. He became artist in residence at his local newspaper, where he wrote and published a poem a day for three months, and later a weekly poem for *Cumberland News*. In 2002 he received the Arts Council of England/Radio 4 "First Verse" Award and an Eric Gregory Award from the Society of Authors. *Brink* (2003) is his first poetry collection. He was selected by a judging panel chaired by the Poet Laureate Andrew Motion as one of the "Next Generation poets" in 2004. Some of his poems: "A Jar of Honey," "April," "First Light," "Fish," "Leaf," "Room," "The Boast," "The Kingdom of Sediment."

Sources: *A Jar of Honey, by Jacob Polley. The Poetry Book Society* (http://www.poetrybooks.co.uk/PBS/pbs_polley_jacob.asp). *April, by Jacob Polley. Blinking Eye Publishing* (http://www.blinking-eye.co.uk/writer/polley.html). *Interview with Jacob Polley. National Poetry Day, 2002. BBC Radio 4* (http://www.bbc.co.uk/radio4/arts/natpoetday/jacob_polley.shtml). *The Brink by Jacob Polley: Poetry Book Review* (http://www.poetsgraves.co.uk/poetry_book_review.htm).

POLLOK, ROBERT (1798–1827)

He was a Scottish poet, the son of a small farmer, born at North Moorhouse in the parish of Eagle-

sham, Renfrewshire. His education was elementary but sound, and he graduated M.A. from Glasgow University in 1822, where he gained distinction in logic and moral philosophy. From 1822 to 1827 he studied theology, both at the United Secession Hall and at Glasgow University. In spite of bad health, he devoted his leisure to literature and in 1825 began the work which developed into the *Course of Time*—prompted by Lord Byron's "Darkness"—published in 1827. His preaching career was shortened by poor health. With the intention of traveling to Italy, he reached Southampton, but got no farther. With his sister he settled at Shirley Common (a suburb of the city) where he died and was buried at nearby Millbrook Church. *The Course of Time* is a poem of blank verse in ten books, concerned with the destiny of man, which reached its twenty-fifth edition in 1867. His other known poems: "Happiness," "Helen of the Glen," "Ocean," "Ralph Gemmell," "The Persecuted Family," "Thoughts on Man."

Sources: *Dictionary of National Biography.* Electronic Edition 1.1. Oxford University Press, 1997. *Great Books Online* (www.bartleby.com). *Significant and Famous Scots* (http://www.electricscotland.com/history/other/pollok_robert.htm). *The Columbia Granger's Index to Poetry.* 11th ed. *The Columbia Granger's World of Poetry,* Columbia University Press, 2005 (http://www.columbiagrangers.org). *The Course of Time by Pollok.* Robert, J., and B. Williams, 1836. *The Eternal Sea: An Anthology of Sea Poetry.* W.M. Williamson, ed. Coward-McCann, 1946. *Treasury of Favorite Poems.* Joseph H. Head, ed. Gramercy Books, 2000.

POMFRET, JOHN (1667–1702)

Born at Luton, Bedfordshire, the son of a clergyman, he had a grammar school education and graduated MA from Queens' College, Cambridge, in 1688. He took holy orders and held appointments in Bedfordshire. In 1700 "The Choice: a Poem Written by a Person of Quality" won him instant fame. The tenth edition of this poem of 167 lines appeared in 1736. Samuel Johnson included Pomfret and "The Choice" in his *Lives of English Poets* (1779). Pomfret died of smallpox at Maulden, Bedfordshire. "The Choice" aroused controversy within the Church over one part of line 157, where he says, "I'd have no wife." Johnson comments on the malicious reaction of some of Pomfret's critics who interpreted this as saying he would rather have a mistress, although by this time he was married with a son. Some of his publications: *The Sceptical Muse,* 1699. *A Prospect of Death: An Ode,* 1700. *Reason: A Poem,* 1700. *Quæ Rara, Chara,* 1707. *Poems upon Several Occasions,* 1724. Some of his poems: "An Epistle to Delia," "Cruelty and Lust," "Love Triumphant Over Reason," "No Barren Leaves," "The Fortunate Complaint," "Upon the Divine Attributes."

Sources: A copy of "The Choice" is on *Samuel Johnson's Lives of the English Poets, 1779–1781* (http://www2.hn.psu.edu/Faculty/KKemmerer/poets/preface.htm). *Dictionary of National Biography.* Electronic Edition 1.1. Oxford University Press, 1997. *Friendship Poems.* Peter Washington, ed. Alfred A. Knopf, 1995. *Garden Poems.* John Hollander, ed. Alfred A. Knopf, 1996. *Stanford University Libraries and Academic Information Resources* (http://library.stanford.edu). *The Columbia Granger's Index to Poetry.* 11th ed. *The Columbia Granger's World of Poetry,* Columbia University Press, 2005 (http://www.columbiagrangers.org). *The Oxford Book of Friendship.* D.J. Enright and David Rawlinson, eds. Oxford University Press, 1991. *The Oxford Companion to English Literature.* 6th edition. Margaret Drabble, ed. Oxford University Press, 2000.

POPE, ALEXANDER (1688–1744)

He was born in London, the son of a Roman Catholic linen merchant, and later lived at Binfield in Windsor Forest, Berkshire. As a Catholic, he was barred from a university education in England, so he was largely self-taught. He suffered from curvature of the spine, caused possibly by tuberculosis. He died at Twickenham, South-West London and was buried near his father and mother. He is commemorated in the Poets' Corner Window of the South Transept of Westminster Abbey. Pope — who wrote from an early age — is one the great Augustan poets (1667–1780). His "Pastorals" written when he was 16 was published in Jacob Tonson's *Miscellany* in 1709. He was a fierce satirist, particularly of other poets. Some of his major publications: *Essay on Criticism,* 1711. *The Rape of the Lock,* 1712. *Ode for Music on St. Cecelia's Day,* 1713. *Windsor Forest,* 1713. *The Iliad of Homer,* 1715. *The Odyssey of Homer,* 1725–1726. *The Dunciad,* 1743. Some of his poems: "An Essay on Man," "The Challenge: A Court Ballad," "A Farewell to London in the Year 1715," "The Garden," "Sandys's Ghost."

Sources: *Dictionary of National Biography.* Electronic Edition 1.1. Oxford University Press, 1997. *Five Hundred Years of English Poetry: Chaucer to Arnold.* Barbara Lloyd-Evans, ed. Peter Bedrick Books, 1989. *Poetical Works of Alexander Pope.* Herbert Davis, ed. Oxford University Press, 1978; repr. 1990. *Stanford University Libraries and Academic Information Resources* (http://library.stanford.edu). *The Columbia Granger's Index to Poetry.* 11th ed. *The Columbia Granger's World of Poetry,* Columbia University Press, 2005 (http://www.columbiagrangers.org). *The National Portrait Gallery* (www.npg.org.uk). *The New Oxford Book of Eighteenth Century Verse.* Roger Lonsdale, ed. Oxford University Press, 1984. *The Oxford Anthology of English Poetry. Vol. I: Spenser to Crabbe.* John Wain, ed. Oxford University Press, 1990. *The Oxford Companion to English Literature.* 6th edition. Margaret Drabble, ed. Oxford University Press, 2000. *Westminster Abbey Official Guide* (no date).

PORDAGE, SAMUEL (1633–?1691)

Born in London, he was educated at Merchant Taylors' School, London. In 1654 his father, a clergyman, was charged with heresy and mysticism and dismissed from the church, although he was reinstated at the Restoration to the parsonage of Bradfield, Berkshire (he died only ten years before his son). At one time Samuel was chief steward to Philip Herbert, fifth earl of Pembroke, Wilton House, Salisbury. In 1673 his *Herod and Mariamne,* a tragedy, was acted at the Duke's Theatre, London, as was *The Siege of Babylon,* in 1678. The exact date of his death is uncertain. Some of his publications: *Troades,* 1660. *Poems upon Several Occasions,* 1660. *Heroick Stanzas on His Maiesties Coronation,* 1661. *Mundorum Explicatio,* 1661. *Azaria and Hushai,* 1682. *The Medal Revers'd,* 1682. *The Loyal Incendiary,* 1684. Some of his poems: "Absence," "Acrostick," "Corydon's Complaint," "Invocation," "Proæmium," "To Lucia Playing on Her Lute."

Sources: *Dictionary of National Biography.* Electronic Edition 1.1. Oxford University Press, 1997. Stanford *University Libraries and Academic Information Resources* (http://library.stanford.edu). *The Cavalier Poets.* Robin Skelton, ed. Oxford University Press, 1970. *The Columbia Granger's Index to Poetry.* 11th ed (http://www.columbiagrangers.org). *The New Oxford Book of Seventeenth Century Verse.* Alastair Fowler, ed. Oxford University Press, 1991.

PORTER, PETER NEVILLE FREDERICK (1929–)

Born in Brisbane, Queensland, Australia, he left school at 18, then worked as a newspaper reporter and in a Brisbane warehouse before sailing for England in 1951. In England he worked in bookselling and advertising before becoming a freelance writer and broadcaster in 1968, working as poetry critic for *The Observer.* He was associated with poets in "The Group" (see entries for Martin Bell and Philip Hobsbaum). He has frequently returned to Australia, and in 2001 he traveled to Melbourne for the premiere of his *The Voice of Love,* a song cycle with music by the British composer Nicholas Maw. He is visiting professor of poetry at Nottingham Trent University. He has been awarded six major literary awards, including the Gold Medal for Australian Literature (1990) and Queen's Gold Medal for Poetry (2002). He holds honorary doctorates from four universities. Some of his publications: *Once Bitten, Twice Bitten,* 1961. *Poems, Ancient and Modern,* 1964. *The Last of England,* 1970. *The Chair of Babel,* 1992. *Afterburner,* 2004. Some of his poems: "An Australian Garden," "Annotations of Auschwitz," "Returning," "Rimbaud's Ostrich," "The Sanitized Sonnets."

Sources: *British Council Arts* (http://www.contemporarywriters.com). *Dr. Peter Porter, Poet—Alumni at the University of Queensland* (http://www.alumni.uq.edu.au/?page=17162&pid=273). *Jacket 16, Peter Porter, Two Poems* (http://jacketmagazine.com/16/porter-peter.html). *Portraits of Poets.* Sebastian Barker, ed. Carcanet, 1986. *The*

Bloodaxe Book of Modern Australian Poetry. John Tranter, and Philip Mead, ed. Bloodaxe Books, 1991, 1994. *The Columbia Granger's Index to Poetry.* 11th ed. *The Columbia Granger's World of Poetry,* Columbia University Press, 2005 (http://www.columbiagrangers.org). *The Faber Book of Modern Australian Verse.* Vincent Buckley, ed. Faber and Faber, 1991. *The Faber Book of Modern Verse.* 4th ed., revised by Peter Porter. Michael Roberts, ed. Faber and Faber, 1982. *The National Portrait Gallery* (www.npg.org. uk). *The Oxford Book of Comic Verse.* John Gross, ed. Oxford University Press, 1994. *The Oxford Book of Twentieth-Century English Verse.* Philip Larkin, ed. Oxford University Press, 1973. *The Oxford Companion to English Literature.* 6th edition. Margaret Drabble, ed. Oxford University Press, 2000. *The Penguin Book of Light Verse.* Gavin Ewart, ed. Penguin Books, 1980. *Who's Who.* London: A & C Black, 2005.

PRAED, WINTHROP MACKWORTH (1802–1839)

Born in London, he was educated at Eton College, where he founded the school journal, the *Etonian.* He read classics at Trinity College, Cambridge. There he won medals for Greek odes and for epigrams and the chancellor's medal for English poem "Australasia" (1823) and for "Athens" (1824). After graduating B.A. in 1825, he became private tutor at Eton to Lord Ernest Bruce, younger son of the Marquis of Ailesbury. He was elected fellow at Trinity in 1827 and was called to the bar in 1829. He was in Parliament on the Tory benches from 1830 to 1832 and from 1834 until he died of tuberculosis. He was buried at Kensal Green Cemetery, London. Many of his poems appeared in newspapers, periodicals and annuals. His *Poems,* with a memoir by his friend Derwent Coleridge, appeared in 1864. *Selections* (1866) and *Political and Occasional Poems* (1888) were published by Sir George Young. Some of his poems: "A Child's Grave," "Arminius," "Arrivals at a Watering-Place," "One More Quadrille," "The Chaunt of the Brazen Head," "The County Ball," "The Covenanter's Lament for Bothwell Brigg," "The Red Fisherman," "The Troubadour."

Sources: *Dictionary of National Biography.* Electronic Edition 1.1. Oxford University Press, 1997. *Select Poems of Winthrop Mackworth Praed.* Henry Frowde, 1909. *Stanford University Libraries and Academic Information Resources* (http://library.stanford.edu). *The Columbia Granger's Index to Poetry.* 11th ed. *The Columbia Granger's World of Poetry,* Columbia University Press, 2005 (http://www.columbia grangers.org). *The New Oxford Book of English Light Verse.* Kingsley Amis, ed. Oxford University Press, 1978. *The Oxford Book of Regency Verse 1798–1837.* H.S. Milford, ed. Oxford University Press, 1928. *The Oxford Companion to English Literature.* 6th edition. Margaret Drabble, ed. Oxford University Press, 2000.

PRATT, SAMUEL JACKSON (1749–1814)

Born at St. Ives, Huntingdonshire, the son of a brewer who twice served as high sheriff of that county, he was ordained in the English church. He was a popular preacher, but after a tangled love affair, of which his parents disapproved, he left the church. He became an actor using the name "Courtney Melmoth" and took the part of Marc Antony in *All for Love* in the theatre in Smock Alley, Dublin, in 1773. He next appeared at Covent Garden Theatre, London, but his acting was not a success. He and his wife then toured the country telling fortunes to make a living. He wrote several plays that were produced at Drury Lane, London. He died in Birmingham after falling from his horse. Some of his poetry publications: *Landscapes in verse,* 1785. *Cottage-Pictures,* 1803. *John and Dame, or, the loyal cottagers,* 1803. *Harvest-Home,* 1805. *The Poor, Or, Bread, A Poem,* 1892. Some of his poems: "Elegy of a Nightingale," "Epitaph on a Lap-Dog," "The Weavers," "To the Memory of David Garrick," "Triumph of Benevolence."

Sources: *Dictionary of National Biography.* Electronic Edition 1.1. Oxford University Press, 1997. *The National Portrait Gallery* (www.npg.org.uk). *Stanford University Libraries and Academic Information Resources* (http://library. stanford.edu). *The Columbia Granger's Index to Poetry.* 11th ed. *The Columbia Granger's World of Poetry,* Columbia University Press, 2005 (http://www.columbiagrangers. org). *The Oxford Book of Garden Verse.* John Dixon Hunt, ed. Oxford University Press, 1993. *The Oxford Companion to English Literature.* 6th edition. Margaret Drabble, ed. Oxford University Press, 2000.

PREWETT, FRANK (1893–1962)

Born near Mount Forest, Ontario, he was brought up on a farm near Kenilworth, Ontario, and was educated at the University of Toronto but left to enlist as a private in the Canadian Army. Commissioned into the British Army, in the Royal Field Artillery, he was present at the third Battle of Ypres in France. Invalided out in 1917, he was rehabilitated at Craiglockhart War Hospital, Edinburgh, where he met Siegfried Sassoon (see entry). After graduating B.A. (1922) and M.A. (1928) from Christchurch College, Oxford, he taught in the University School of Agriculture and Forestry in Oxford. During World War II he served in the Royal Air Force, staying on in the Air Ministry until 1954. Retiring because of poor health, he farmed near Abingdon until his death. He was the only Canadian poet represented in *Georgian Poetry* 1920–1922, edited by Edward Marsh and published by the Poetry Bookshop (1922). Some of his poems: "I Shall Take You in Rough Weather," "If I Love You," "Plea for Peace,"

"The Pack," "The Red Man in the Settlements," "The Red-man."

Sources: *An Anthology of Revolutionary Poetry*. Marcus Graham, ed. The Active Press, 1929. *Harper's Anthology of 20th Century Native American Poetry*. Duane Niatum, ed. Harper and Row, 1988. *Native American Authors Project; Frank Prewett* (http://www.ipl.org/div/natam/bin/browse.pl/A398). http://www.library.utoronto.ca/canpoetry/meyer/bio.html). *The National Portrait Gallery* (www.npg.org.uk). *The Columbia Granger's Index to Poetry*. 11th ed. *The Columbia Granger's World of Poetry*, Columbia University Press, 2005 (http://www.columbiagrangers.org). *The Selected Poems of Frank Prewett*. Bruce Meyer and Barry Callaghan, eds. Toronto: Exile Editions, 1987. *Wikipedia, the Free Encyclopedia* (http://en.wikipedia.org/wiki/Wikipedia).

PRICKET, ROBERT (fl. 1603–1645)

A little-known poet who was a soldier in the service of Queen Elizabeth, then lived precariously on his earnings as a writer and pamphleteer against the Catholics. In 1603 he published a prose tract dedicated to King James I in which he denounces the pope and papists. He went to prison for his praise of the Earl of Essex (see Essex, Robert), who was executed for treason in 1601. An appeal to the secretary of state, the Earl of Salisbury, secured Pricket's release. Around 1606 he took holy orders and in 1645 he was in Bath, where he wrote in verse "Newes from the King's Bath." Some of his other publications: *A Sovldiers Wish unto the Sovereign Lord King James*, 1603. *Times Anatomie*, 1606 (which rejoices in the deliverance from the Gunpowder Plot [treason] of 1605). *Honors Fame in Trivmph Riding*, 1604 (a tribute to the memory of the Earl of Essex). *The Jesuits Miracles*, 1607. Some of his poems: "A Song of Reioycing for Our Late Deliuerance," "Cœlestiall Graces Helpe My Muse," "Thrise Noble King the Wonder of Our Daies," "To the Reader."

Sources: *Dictionary of National Biography*. Electronic Edition 1.1. Oxford University Press, 1997.

PRINCE, FRANK TEMPLETON (1912–2003)

Born in Kimberley, South Africa, and educated there, he graduated B.Litt. with first-class honors in 1934 from Balliol College, Oxford. He was visiting fellow at Princeton University, New Jersey, and served in the British Army Intelligence Corps from 1940 to 1946. He joined the English department at Southampton University in 1946 and was professor from 1957 to 1974. He then taught in Jamaica, the United States and North Yemen, and from 1968 to 1969 was visiting fellow at All Souls College, Oxford. He delivered the Clark lectures in Cambridge (1972–73) and received the E.M. Forster award from the American Academy of Arts and Letters in 1982.

His poetry is more widely read in America than it is in Britain. His two autobiographical works are *Memoirs of Oxford* (1970) and *Walks in Rome* (1987). He died in Southampton. Some of his poetry publications: *Poems*, 1938. *Soldiers Bathing and Other Poems*, 1954. *The Doors of Stone: Poems, 1938–1962*, 1963. *Collected Poems, 1935–1992*, 1993. Some of his poems: "Afterword on Rupert Brooke," "At Beaulieu," "For Thieves and Beggars," "Memoirs in Oxford," "Yüan Chěn Variations."

Sources: *Collected Poems, 1935–1992, of F.T. Prince*. The Sheep Meadow Press, 1993. *Golden Treasury of the Best Songs and Lyrical Poems in the English Language*. Francis Turner Palgrave, ed. Oxford University Press, 1964, Sixth edition, updated by John Press, 1994. *Guardian Unlimited Obituary of F.T. Prince by Anthony Howell*. Friday, August 8, 2003 (http://www.guardian.co.uk/obituaries/story/0,3604,1014413,00.html). *The Columbia Granger's Index to Poetry*. 11th ed. *The Columbia Granger's World of Poetry*, Columbia University Press, 2005 (http://www.columbiagrangers.org). *The Oxford Companion to English Literature*. 6th edition. Margaret Drabble, ed. Oxford University Press, 2000.

PRINCE, JOHN CRITCHLEY (1808–1866)

Born at Wigan, Lancashire, he was the son of a poor reed-maker for weavers. He learned to read and write at a Baptist Sunday school. For ten years from age nine he worked for his father, then sought work in France in 1830, but the country was once again caught up in revolution and he found no work. When he returned, destitute and starving, he found his wife and children in the poorhouse. He worked as a shopkeeper in Manchester but lived mainly off the sale of his poems that were written in the Lancashire dialect. In 1842 he traveled on foot to London and recorded his experiences in a series of letters to *Bradshaw's Journal*. From 1845 to 1851 he was paid editor of the *Ancient Shepherd's Quarterly Magazine*, published at Ashton-under-Lyne, Lancashire. He died at Hyde, Manchester, and was buried at St. George's Church. His poetry publications: *Hours with the Muses*, 1842. *Dreams and Realities*, 1847. *The Poetic Rosary*, 1850. *Autumn Leaves*, 1856. *Miscellaneous Poems*, 1861. Some of his poems: "Abjuration," "Anti-Corn-Law Lyric," "At My Wife's Grave Side," "Lyrics for the People," "Temperance Song," "Written in Affliction."

Sources: *Dictionary of National Biography*. Electronic Edition 1.1. Oxford University Press, 1997. *Lancashire Dialect Poets and Poems, Authors, Writers and Poets* (http://www.manchester2002-uk.com/celebs/authors4.html). *Stanford University Libraries and Academic Information Resources* (http://library.stanford.edu). *The Columbia Granger's Index to Poetry*. 11th ed. *The Columbia Granger's World of Poetry*, Columbia University Press, 2005 (http://www.columbiagrangers.org). *The Poetical Works of John*

Critchley Prince, Vols. 1 and 2. Abel Heywood and Son, 1880. *The Poorhouse Fugitives: Self-Taught Poets and Poetry in Victorian Britain.* Brian Maidment, ed. Carcanet, 1987.

PRINGLE, THOMAS (1789–1834)

Scottish poet born at Blaiklaw, Teviotdale, Roxburghshire, he was educated at Edinburgh University. While at university, in spite of being lame and on crutches, he challenged a group who were protesting against the first night of Joanna Baillie's *Family Legend* (1810) (see entry). He worked as a copyist in the Register Office, Edinburgh, and devoted his leisure to poetry. *The Institute* (1811) is a satire of one of Edinburgh's learned societies. He was a friend of Sir Walter Scott and for a short time was editor of the *Edinburgh Monthly.* Between 1820 and 1826, he lived in South Africa and gained the reputation as the father of South African poetry. Many of the poems in his two verse collections *Ephemerides* (1828) and *African Sketches* (1834) deal with the people, wildlife, and landscape of Africa. In 1827 he became secretary to the Anti-Slavery Society. He died in London and was buried in the Dissenter Cemetery, Bunhill Fields, London. Some of his poems: "Afar in the Desert," "An Emigrant's Song," "Paraphrase of the Twenty-Third Psalm," "The Bechuana Boy," "The Bushman," "The Ghona Widow's Lullaby," "The Lion and Giraffe," "The Slave Dealer."

Sources: *African Poems of Thomas Pringle (Killie Campbell Africana Library Publications).* Ernest Pereira and Michael Chapman, ed. University of Natal Press, 1996. *Dictionary of National Biography.* Electronic Edition 1.1. Oxford University Press, 1997. *The National Portrait Gallery* (www.npg.org.uk). *Poems Illustrative of South Africa: Vol. I, by Thomas Pringle.* John Robert Wahl, ed. C. Struik (Pty.) Ltd., 1970. *Poems of South African History A.D. 1497–1910.* A. Petrie, ed. Oxford University Press, 1918. *Stanford University Libraries and Academic Information Resources* (http://library.stanford.edu). *The Columbia Granger's Index to Poetry.* 11th ed. *The Columbia Granger's World of Poetry,* Columbia University Press, 2005 (http://www.columbiagrangers.org). *The Home Book of Verse.* Burton Egbert Stevenson, ed. New York: Henry Holt and Company, 1953. *The Oxford Companion to English Literature.* 6th edition. Margaret Drabble, ed. Oxford University Press, 2000. *The Penguin Book of Southern African Verse.* Stephen Gray, ed. Penguin Books, 1989.

PRIOR, MATTHEW (1664–1721)

Thought to have been the son of a joiner from Wimborne, Dorset, he was educated at Westminster School and St. John's College, Cambridge, from where he graduated B.A. in 1686. Two years later was made a fellow there. A diplomat, he was present at the Hague during the negotiations for the Treaty of Ryswick, 1697, which settled the War of the Grand Alliance. In 1711, he was sent to Paris as a se-

cret agent at the time of the negotiation for the Treaty of Utrecht, which was dubbed "Matt's Peace." After the death of Queen Anne, he was impeached and spent a year in prison, but used his time to write poetry. He retired from the diplomatic service to Down Hall, not very far from Harlow, Essex. His monument is in Poets' Corner of Westminster Abbey. At his request he was buried at the feet of Edmund Spenser. "Solomon on the Vanity of the World" (1719) ridicules various systems of philosophy. Some of his other poems: "Advice to the Painter," "Cautious Alice," "Daphne and Apollo," "Pontius and Pontia," "The Advice of Venus," "The Chameleon," "The Wandering Pilgrim."

Sources: *Anthology of Poems on Affairs of State: Augustan Satirical Verse, 1660–1714.* George de F. Lord, ed. Yale University Press, 1975. *Dictionary of National Biography.* Electronic Edition 1.1. Oxford University Press, 1997. *Erotic Poetry: The Lyrics, Ballads, Idylls, and Epics of Love — Classical to Contemporary.* William Cole, ed. Random House, 1963. *Fellow Mortals: An Anthology of Animal Verse.* Roy Fuller, ed. Macdonald and Evans, 1981. *Poets of the English Language, Vol. III.* W.H. Auden and Norman Holmes Pearson, eds. Viking Press, 1950. *Selected Poems of Matthew Prior.* Austin Dobson, ed. Kegan Paul, Trench and Co., 1889. *Stanford University Libraries and Academic Information Resources* (http://library.stanford.edu). *The Columbia Granger's Index to Poetry.* 11th ed. *The Columbia Granger's World of Poetry,* Columbia University Press, 2005 (http://www.columbiagrangers.org). *The Oxford Companion to English Literature.* 6th edition. Margaret Drabble, ed. Oxford University Press, 2000. *The Poetical Works of Matthew Prior: Volume I and 2,* Little, Brown, and Company, 1854. *Wikipedia, the Free Encyclopedia* (http://en.wikipedia.org/wiki/Wikipedia).

PROCTER, BRYAN WALLER and ADELAIDE ANNE (1787–1874)

Bryan Waller (pseudonym, Barry Cornwall), the father, 1787–1874

Born at Leeds, Yorkshire, he was educated at Harrow School, then trained as a solicitor. He practiced law in London, acquiring a large and prosperous practice specializing in conveyance work. In 1832 he was made a metropolitan commissioner in lunacy. His tragedy *Mirandola* was staged at Covent Garden Theatre in 1821 with Charles Kemble (1775–1854) in the lead role. The success introduced him to a wide range of literary people and he wrote much poetry and many stories for annuals, and he composed many delightful songs. He published a biography of Charles Lamb in 1866. His main poetical publications: *Dramatic Scenes,* 1819. *Marcian Colonna,* 1820. *A Sicilian Story,* 1821. *The Flood in Thessaly,* 1823. *Effigies Poeticæ, or the Portraits of the British Poets,* 1824. *English Songs and Other Smaller Poems,* 1832. Some of his poems: "A Christmas Reminiscence," "A Drinking Song," "A Bacchanalian Song," "Babylon," "Dramatic Fragments," "Golden-Tressed Adelaide," "The Approach of Winter," "The Beggar's Song," "The Farewell of the Soldier."

Adelaide Anne, the daughter, 1825–1864

She was the eldest daughter and first child, to whom her father addressed his poem "Golden-Tressed Adelaide" (see above). Most of her poems, under the pseudonym Mary Berwick, were published by Charles Dickens (see entry) in *Household Words*; Dickens was unaware of her identity. Not only until 1854 did Adelaide reveal her secret. Her poems were published in two volumes, *Legends and Lyrics* (1858), with a tenth edition in 1866. A philanthropist, she committed herself to the cause of single, fallen and homeless women. She campaigned for the Society for Promoting the Employment of Women, and supported the Providence Row Hostel for homeless women and children in East London. She died of tuberculosis and was buried at Kensal Green Cemetery, London. She also wrote hymns, and *The Lost Chord*, set to music by Sir Arthur Sullivan (1877) has been popular with soloists of both sexes ever since. Her narrative poems "The Angel's Story," "Legend of Bregenz" and "Legend of Provence" show her ability to compose sustained poetry. Some of her other hymn/poems: "A Doubting Heart," "A Woman's Answer," "Cleansing Fires," "I Do Not Ask, O Lord," "My God, I Thank Thee," "Three Evenings in a Life," "Three Roses."

Sources: *A Sacrifice of Praise an Anthology of Christian Poetry in English from Caedmon to the Mid-Twentieth Century.* James H. Trott, ed. Cumberland House Publishing, 1999. *Complete Poetical Works of Adelaide Anne Proctor.* Thomas Y. Crowell, 1903. *Dictionary of National Biography.* Electronic Edition 1.1. Oxford University Press, 1997. *English Songs, and Other Small Poems of Barry Cornwall.* Edward Moxon, 1844. *Gilbert and Sullivan Archive.* "The Lost Chord," by Adelaide Procter (http://math.boisestate.edu/gas/other_sullivan/songs/lost_chord/chord.html). *Sound the Deep Waters: Women's Romantic Poetry in the Victorian Age.* Pamela Norris, ed. Little, Brown, 1991. *The Columbia Granger's Index to Poetry.* 11th ed. *The Columbia Granger's World of Poetry*, Columbia University Press, 2005 (http://www.columbiagrangers.org). *The Home Book of Verse.* Burton Egbert Stevenson, ed. New York: Henry Holt and Company, 1953. *The Life and Work of Adelaide Procter* (http://www.litencyc.com/php/adpage.php?id=2677). *The Life and Work of Adelaide Procter: Poetry, Feminism and Fathers.* Nineteenth Century Series. Gill Gregory. Ashgate Publishing, 1998. *The National Portrait Gallery* (www.npg.org.uk). *The Oxford Companion to English Literature.* 6th edition. Margaret Drabble, ed. Oxford University Press, 2000. *The Poetical Works of Adelaide A. Proctor.* A.L. Burt, ?1900. *The World's Great Religious Poetry.* Caroline Miles Hill, ed. Macmillan, 1954.

PROCTOR (PROCTER), THOMAS (fl. 1578–1584)

He was the son of John Proctor, a schoolmaster from Tunbridge Wells, Kent, and is described as stationer, anthologist, and poet. Nothing else is known of him apart from his poetry. *A Gorgeous Gallery of Gallant Inventions*, 1578, contains several of Proctor's poems, the longest of which is "The History of Pyramus and Thisbie Truely Translated." It has been suggested that this poem was in Shakespeare's mind when he wrote *Midsummer Night's Dream* (?1595). The book was reprinted several times. *The Triumph of Truth*, ?1585, contains the poems "Caesars Triumph," "Gretians Conquest" and "Desert of Dives." *Of the Knowledge and Conduct of Wars* was published in 1578 and *Commendatory Poem in News from the North* in 1585. Some of his other poems: "A Briefe Dialogue Between Sicknesse and Worldly Desire," "A Maze of Maydens," "A Mirror of Mortallity," "Beauty is a Pleasant Pathe to Distruction," "How to Choose a Faythfull Freende," "Of Three Things to Be Shunned," "Proctors Precepts," "Win Fame, and Keepe It."

Sources: *Dictionary of National Biography.* Electronic Edition 1.1. Oxford University Press, 1997. Stanford University Libraries and Academic Information Resources (http://library.stanford.edu). *The Columbia Granger's Index to Poetry.* 11th ed. *The Columbia Granger's World of Poetry*, Columbia University Press, 2005 (http://www.columbia grangers.org). *The Faber Book of Reflective Verse.* Geoffrey Grigson, ed. Faber & Faber, 1984. *The Oxford Book of Sixteenth Century Verse.* E.K. Chambers, ed. Oxford University Press, 1932. *Years work in the Humanities Research Centre, 2003–2004, Thomas Proctor, Sheffield Hallam University* (http://www.shu.ac.uk/research/hrc/work.html).

PUDNEY, JOHN SLEIGH (1909–1977)

Born in Langley, Buckinghamshire, he has been an estate agent, a journalist, and a writer-producer in the BBC from 1934 to 1937. Commissioned into the Royal Air Force as an intelligence officer in 1940, he joined the Air Ministry's Creative Writers Unit and was present at the victory march through Paris in 1945. His poem "For Johnny" was spoken by Michael Redgrave in the 1945 film *The Way to the Stars*. He was elected Labor member of Parliament for Sevenoaks, Kent, in the 1945 general election. He went on to write many novels, short stories and 16 collections of poetry. Addicted to alcohol, he underwent therapy and made a complete recovery. He told the world about that and his dying from cancer of the throat in his autobiography, *Thank Goodness for Cake* (1978). Some of his later poetry publications: *Collected Poems*, 1957. *Spill Out: Poems and Ballads*, 1967. *Spandrels Poems and Ballads*, 1969. *Take This Orange: Poems and Ballads*, 1971. *Selected*

Poems 1967–1973, 1973. *Living in a One-Sided House*, 1976. Some of his poems: "After Bombardment," "For Johnny," "Missing," "On Seeing My Birthplace from a Jet Aircraft," "To You Who Wait."

Sources: *Dictionary of National Biography.* Electronic Edition 1.1. Oxford University Press, 1997. *The National Portrait Gallery* (www.npg.org.uk). *The Columbia Granger's Index to Poetry.* 11th ed. *The Columbia Granger's World of Poetry,* Columbia University Press, 2005 (http://www.columbiagrangers.org). *The New Yorker Book of Poems.* The New Yorker editors. Viking Press, 1969. *The Oxford Book of Twentieth-Century English Verse.* Philip Larkin, ed. Oxford University Press, 1973. *The Oxford Companion to English Literature.* 6th edition. Margaret Drabble, ed. Oxford University Press, 2000. *The War Poets: An Anthology of the War Poetry of the 20th Century.* Oscar Williams, ed. John Day, 1945.

PUGH, SHEENAGH (1950–)

Born in Birmingham, she graduated B.A. with honors from Bristol University, where she read ancient Greek, German and Russian. She moved to Wales in 1971 and now lives in Cardiff with her husband, two children and two cats. She is senior lecturer in creative writing at the University of Glamorgan. Her interests are language, history, and northern landscapes from Shetland to the Arctic. She has published nine collections of poetry along with translations and two novels. She won the Welsh Arts Council's Poem for Today competition in 1987 and the Cardiff International Poetry Prize in 1988 and 1994. Her work has been translated into several different languages and some have been set to music. Some of her publications: *Crowded by Shadows,* 1977. *What a Place to Grow Flowers,* 1980. *Earth Studies and Other Voyages,* 1983. *Beware Falling Tortoises,* 1987. *Selected Poems,* 1990. *Sing for the Taxman,* 1993. *Id's Hospit,* 1997. *Stonelight,* 1999. Some of her poems: "Allegiance," "King Billy on the Walls," "King Sigurd and King Eystein," "The Craft I Left in was Called Esau," "The Frozen Field," "The Guest," "The Woodcarver of Stendal."

Sources: *Anglo-Welsh Poetry, 1480–1980.* Raymond Garlick and Roland Mathias, eds. Poetry Wales Press, 1984. *Anglo-Welsh Poetry, 1480–1990.* Raymond Garlick and Roland Mathias, eds. Poetry Wales Press, 1993. *Biography of Sheenagh Pugh* (http://www.swan.ac.uk/english/Subpages/Pugh.htm). *Spaceways: An Anthology of Space Poems.* John Foster, ed. Oxford University Press, 1986. *The Columbia Granger's Index to Poetry.* 11th ed. *The Columbia Granger's World of Poetry,* Columbia University Press, 2005 (http://www.columbiagrangers.org). *The Oxford Companion to English Literature.* 6th edition. Margaret Drabble, ed. Oxford University Press, 2000. *Twentieth Century Anglo-Welsh Poetry.* Dannie Abse, ed. Seren Books / Dufour Editions, 1997. *University of Glamorgan, Staff Pages* (http://www.glam.ac.uk/hassschool/staff/personal_pages). *Wales on the Web: Poetry* (http://www.walesontheweb.org/cayw/index/en/821/all).

PUTTENHAM, GEORGE (?1529–1591)

He was the nephew of Sir Thomas Elyot (?1490–1546), diplomat and author of the *Boke Named the Governour* (1531), a treatise on education and politics. On account of his being a Catholic, Puttenham and his work came under Puritan persecution, so *The Arte of English Poesie* was published anonymously in 1589. He may fairly be regarded as the first English writer who attempted philosophical criticism of literature. There was doubt whether he or his brother Richard wrote it, but consensus now swings in favor of George. The book continues to exert a fascination. As recently as 2003 the scholar Charles Murray Willis published a book on Puttenham and Shakespeare (see Sources), in which he puts forward the view that some of the plays used by Shakespeare could have been written by Puttenham. For example, "The language displayed in the poems 'Venus and Adonis' and 'Lucrece' (1593–34) seems closely connected with Puttenham's 'Arte of English Poesie'" (Willis). Puttenham also wrote a collection of poems entitled *Partheniades,* consisting of seventeen poems in various meters. The *Posie* is in three books: *Of Poets and Posie*; *Of Proportion*; and *Of Ornament.*

Sources: *Elizabethan Lyrics.* Norman Ault, ed. William Sloane Associates, 1949. *Shakespeare and George Puttenham's The Arte of English Poesie.* UPSO (Universal Publishing Solutions Online) Ltd., 2003. *The Columbia Granger's Index to Poetry.* 11th ed. *The Columbia Granger's World of Poetry,* Columbia University Press, 2005 (http://www.columbiagrangers.org). *The Oxford Companion to English Literature.* 6th edition. Margaret Drabble, ed. Oxford University Press, 2000. *The Penguin Book of Renaissance Verse 1509–1659.* David Norbrook, ed. Penguin Books, 1992.

PYE, HENRY JAMES (1745–1813)

Born in London, the son of Henry Pye, a member of Parliament for Berkshire from 1746 until his death in 1766, he was created M.A. on 3 July 1766 and doctor of civil law in 1772. His father left huge debts, the family house burned down, and Henry was forced to sell the estate. He was a member of Parliament for a short while and a police magistrate for Westminster, and published a valued document, *Summary of the Duties of a Justice of the Peace out of Sessions,* in 1808. His appointment by William Pitt as poet laureate was scorned in 1790 by an unnamed author in "Epistle to the Poet Laureate." His epic poem in six books, *Alfred,* was published in 1801. Some of his other publications: *Verses on Several Subjects,* 1802. *Translation of the Hymns and Epigrams of Homer,* 1810. *The Siege of Meaux,* 1794 (drama, performed at Covent Garden). *Adelaide,* 1800 (tragedy, performed at Drury Lane). Some of his poems: "Bacchus; or,

The Pirates," "Ode on the Birth of the Prince of Wales," "On Midas," "The Myrtle and Bramble," "The Parsonage Improved," "The Snow-drop."

Sources: *Dictionary of National Biography*. Electronic Edition 1.1. Oxford University Press, 1997. *English Poetry: Author Search*. Chadwyck-Healey Ltd., 1995 (http://www.lib.utexas.edu:8080/search/epoetry/author.html). *The National Portrait Gallery* (www.npg.org.uk). *Poems on Various Subjects: Volume I of Henry James Pye*. John Stockdale, 1787. *The Batrachomuomachia: Or the Battle of the Frogs and Mice*. J. Sharpe, 1810. *The Columbia Granger's Index to Poetry*. 11th ed. *The Columbia Granger's World of Poetry*, Columbia University Press, 2005 (http://www.columbia grangers.org). *The Oxford Companion to English Literature*. 6th edition. Margaret Drabble, ed. Oxford University Press, 2000.

QUARLES, FRANCIS and JOHN (1592–1665)

Francis, the father, 1592–1644

Born near Romford, Essex, he graduated B.A. from Christ's College, Cambridge, in 1608, then studied law in London. In 1613 he was cup bearer to Princess Elizabeth on her marriage to the Frederick V Elector Palatine (Elizabeth, Queen of Bohemia, was the grandmother of George I; she is buried in Henry VII's chapel of Westminster Abbey.) In 1631 he wrote an epitaph on Michael Drayton, which was inscribed on the poet's tomb in Westminster Abbey. From around 1629 to 1633 he was private secretary to James Ussher, archbishop of Armagh. A staunch Royalist, he wrote a scathing attack on Oliver Cromwell, which resulted in his library being destroyed. He was buried in the church of St. Olave, Silver Street, London. Some of his publications: *Argalus and Parthenia*, 1629. *Divine Fancies*, 1632. *An Elegie Upon My Deare Brother*, 1637. *An Elegie on Sir Julius Cæsar*, 1636. *The Shepheards Oracles*, 1646. *Sighes At the Contemporary Deaths of Those Incomparable Sisters, The Countesse of Cleaveland, and Mistrisse Cicily Killegrve*, 1640. *Solomon's Recantation*, 1739. Some of his poems: "Buried in a New Tombe Hewen Out of a Rock," "On the Infancie of Our Saviour," "On Vsurers," "Tongues of Fire, and Sate Upon Each of Them," "The Sunne Was in a Totall Eclips, and Not As Naturally It Should Have Been in the Sign with the Moon."

John, the son, 1624–1665

John was educated under the care of Archbishop Ussher, then at Exeter College, Oxford, although he does not appear to have graduated. He supported the Royalist cause and was imprisoned and banished to Flanders. He lived in near-poverty, dependent on his writing for livelihood. He died of the plague in London. Some of his publications are: *Self-Conflict*, 1647. *Fons Lachrymarum*, 1648. *A Kingly Bed of Mis-*

erie, 1649. *Divine Meditations*, 1655. *Tarquin Banished*, 1655. *An Elegie on James Usher*, 1656. *The History of the Most Vile Dimagoras*, 1658. *Rebellion's Downfall*, 1662. *The Citizens' Flight*, 1665. *London's Disease, and Cure*, 1665. Some of his poems: "A Dialogue Between the Soul and Satan," "Lord, Help Me When My Griefs Doe Call," "Lord, Teach My Reins, That in the Night," "Lord, Thou That Hoord'st Thy Grace for Those," "My God, Full Tears Are All the Dyet."

Sources: *A Sacrifice of Praise: An Anthology of Christian Poetry in English from Caedmon to the Mid-Twentieth Century*. James H. Trott, ed. Cumberland House Publishing, 1999. *A Treasury of Poems for Worship and Devotion*. Charles L. Wallis, ed. Harper, 1959. *Chapters into Verse, Vol. I: Genesis to Malachi*. Robert Atwan and Laurance Wieder, eds. Oxford University Press, 1993. *Dictionary of National Biography*. Electronic Edition 1.1. Oxford University Press, 1997. *Stanford University Libraries and Academic Information Resources* (http://library.stanford.edu). *The Chatto Book of Cabbages and Kings: Lists in Literature*. Francis Spufford, ed. Chatto and Windus, 1989. *The Columbia Granger's Index to Poetry*. 11th ed. *The Columbia Granger's World of Poetry*, Columbia University Press, 2005 (http://www.columbiagrangers.org). *The Complete Works in Prose and Verse of Francis Quarles, Vol. 3* (No publisher listed), 1881. *The Oxford Book of Marriage*. Helge Rubenstein, ed. Oxford University Press, 1990. *The Oxford Companion to English Literature*. 6th edition. Margaret Drabble, ed. Oxford University Press, 2000. *The Penguin Book of Renaissance Verse 1509–1659*. David Norbrook, ed. Penguin Books, 1992. *Westminster Abbey Official Guide* (no date).

QUILLER-COUCH, SIR ARTHUR THOMAS (1863–1944)

Cornish poet who was a renowned novelist, literary critic, anthologist and writer of short stories for children and adults. He was born at Bodmin, the son of a physician, and graduated *literae humaniores* from Trinity College, Oxford, in 1886. He stayed on at Trinity as a lecturer in classics until 1887, then became a freelance journalist in London. At Oxford he started writing in the *Oxford Magazine* under the pseudonym "Q," which he continued to use. Plagued by ill health, he and his family moved to Fowey on the South Cornish coast. His first book was *The Oxford Book of English Verse* (1900). He was knighted in 1910 and in 1912 was appointed King Edward VII professor of English literature at Cambridge University. In 1926, he was made an honorary fellow of Trinity College, Oxford, and he has received honorary degrees from three universities. He was made the freeman of three Cornish towns, including Fowey, where he was mayor and where he died and was buried. Some of his poems: "Alma Mater," "De Tea Fabula," "Doom Ferry," "Sage Counsel," "The Harbour of Fowey," "The Splendid Spur," "The White Moth."

Sources: *A Century of Humorous Verse, 1850–1950.* Roger Lancelyn Green, ed. E.P. Dutton (Everyman's Library), 1959. *Dictionary of National Biography.* Electronic Edition 1.1. Oxford University Press, 1997. *Everyman's Book of Victorian Verse.* J.R. Watson, ed. J.M. Dent, 1982. *The National Portrait Gallery* (www.npg.org.uk). *Poemhunter* (www.poemhunter.com). *The Columbia Granger's Index to Poetry.* 11th ed. *The Columbia Granger's World of Poetry,* Columbia University Press, 2005 (http://www.columbia grangers.org). *The Home Book of Verse.* Burton Egbert Stevenson, ed. New York: Henry Holt and Company, 1953. *The Oxford Book of English Verse, 1250–1918.* Sir Arthur Quiller-Couch, ed. New edition, revised and enlarged, Oxford University Press, 1939. *The Oxford Book of Victorian Verse.* Arthur Quiller-Couch, ed. Oxford University Press, 1971. *The Oxford Companion to English Literature.* 6th edition. Margaret Drabble, ed. Oxford University Press, 2000. *What Cheer: An Anthology of American and British Humorous and Witty Verse.* David McCord, ed. Coward-McCann, 1945.

QUILLINAN, EDWARD (1791–1851)

He was born in Oporto, Portugal, the son of a prosperous Irish wine merchant. When France invaded Portugal in 1807, the father, now a widower, and his son fled to England. Edward became a cavalry officer in the Army and saw service in the Peninsular War (1808–1814) and in Ireland. He retired from the Army in 1821 and in the following year his wife died, leaving him with two young daughters. In grief he spent the next nineteen years roaming, until in 1841 he married Dorothy, William Wordsworth's daughter. In 1841 he published a three-volume novel, *The Conspirators,* an account of his military service in Spain and Portugal. In 1846 he contributed a valuable article to the *Quarterly* on Gil Vicente, the Portuguese dramatic poet. Dorothy died in 1847 and he died at Loughrig Holme, Ambleside and was buried in Grasmere churchyard. Some of his poetry publications: *Ball Room Votaries,* 1810. *Dunluce Castle,* 1814. *Elegiac Verses,* 1817. *Woodcuts and Verses,* 1820. *Poems,* 1853. Some of his poems: "Address to a Pony," "First Love," "Interior of Canterbury Cathedral," "The Rose-Wreathed Hour-Glass," "Val De Luz," "Zelinda."

Sources: *Dictionary of National Biography.* Electronic Edition 1.1. Oxford University Press, 1997. *The Columbia Granger's Index to Poetry.* 11th ed. *The Columbia Granger's World of Poetry,* Columbia University Press, 2005 (http:// www.columbiagrangers.org). *The New Oxford Book of Romantic Period Verse.* Jerome J. McGann. Oxford University Press, 1993. *The Oxford Book of Regency Verse 1798–1837.* H.S. Milford, ed. Oxford University Press, 1928.

RADCLIFFE, ANNE (1764–1823)

Ann Ward was born in London, where her father was a prosperous tradesman, and in 1787 she married William Radcliffe, editor and proprietor of the *English Chronicle,* who encouraged her in her writing. She published *The Castles of Athlin and Dunbayne* in 1789. It set the tone for the majority of her work, which tended to involve innocent but heroic young women who find themselves in gloomy, mysterious castles ruled by even more mysterious barons with dark pasts (Gothic fiction). Her 1794 novel, *The Mysteries of Udolpho*— a romance interspersed with some pieces of poetry — became a best-seller. She never visited the countries where the fearful happenings in her novels took place; her only journey abroad was to Holland and Germany. Sir Walter Scott considered her *A Sicilian Romance* to be the first modern English example of the poetical novel, and her work inspired many later writers. She was interred at the chapel of ease in Bayswater Road, London. Most taken from her novels, here are some of her poems: "A Sea View," "Night," "Rondeau," "Song of a Spirit," "The Mysteries of Udolpho," "To the Visions of Fancy."

Sources: *A Century of Sonnets: The Romantic-Era Revival 1750–1850.* Paula R. Feldman and Daniel Robinson, eds. Oxford University Press, 1999. *Dictionary of National Biography.* Electronic Edition 1.1. Oxford University Press, 1997. *Encyclopædia Britannica Ultimate Reference Suite DVD,* 2006. *English Poetry: Author Search.* Chadwyck-Healey Ltd., 1995 (http://www.lib.utexas.edu:8080/ search/epoetry/author.html). *Romantic Women Poets: An Anthology.* Duncan Wu, ed. Blackwell Publishers, 1997. *Romanticism.* Duncan Wu, ed. Blackwell, 1994. *The Columbia Granger's Index to Poetry.* 11th ed. *The Columbia Granger's World of Poetry,* Columbia University Press, 2005 (http://www.columbiagrangers.org). *The Oxford Companion to English Literature.* 6th edition. Margaret Drabble, ed. Oxford University Press, 2000. *The Women Poets in English: An Anthology.* Ann Stanford, ed. McGraw-Hill, 1972. *Wikipedia, the Free Encyclopedia* (http://en.wikipedia. org/wiki/Wikipedia).

RADCLYFFE-HALL, MARGUERITE ANTONIA (1880–1943)

Born at West Cliff, Bournemouth, Dorset, she was brought up mainly by governesses until she went to live in a stately house in Earls Court with her mother's third husband, Albert Visetti, a professor of singing at the Royal College of Music in London. She published collections of poems, seven novels, and a number of short stories. Her poem "The Blind Ploughman" was set to music by Conigsby Clarke. Her novels won her international fame. *Adam's Breed* (1926) won her several awards. *The Well of Loneliness* (1928), a courageous and serious novel about lesbianism, was prosecuted under the Obscene Publications Act of 1857, condemned as an obscene libel, all copies destroyed, and not republished in Britain until 1949. She shared her private life exclusively with women, notably with the socialite and beauty Mabel Veronica Batten. She was buried in the vault alongside Mabel Batten in Highgate Cemetery, North London. Her poetry publications: *Twixt Earth and Stars*, 1906. *A Sheaf of Verses*, 1908. *Poems of the Past and Present*, 1910. *Songs of Three Counties and Other Poems*, 1913. *The Forgotten Island*, 1915. *Rhymes and Rhythms*, 1948.

Sources: *Dictionary of National Biography.* Electronic Edition 1.1. Oxford University Press, 1997. *Encyclopædia Britannica Ultimate Reference Suite DVD*, 2006. *The Columbia Granger's Index to Poetry.* 11th ed. *The Columbia Granger's World of Poetry,* Columbia University Press, 2005 (http://www.columbiagrangers.org). *The Oxford Companion to English Literature.* 6th edition. Margaret Drabble, ed. Oxford University Press, 2000. *The Penguin Book of Homosexual Verse.* Stephen Coote, ed. Penguin Books, 1983.

RAFTERY, ANTHONY (1784–1835) (Ó REACHTABHRA, ANTOINE)

The son of a weaver from County Mayo, Ireland, he is often called the last of the wandering bards. An attack of smallpox at the age of five left him blind, and he earned his living by playing the fiddle and performing his songs and poems in the big houses of the West of Ireland. It is conjectured that he got his education from the "hedge schools," where he would have learned Irish, and from listening to the dinner time conversation and debate of visitors of the big houses. He died near Loughrea, County Galway, and in August 1900 a memorial stone was placed on his burial place by Lady Gregory who, with Thady Conlon, collected his poems and translated them into English around the turn of the 20th century. Most of his recitations were ballads describing real or imaginary events. Some of his poems: "Am Raftery (or Raferty)," "His Lament for O'Daly," "His Lament for O'Kelly," "His Repentance," "His Vision of Death," "I am Raifteiri, the poet, full of courage and love," "Raftery's Praise of Mary Hynes," "The County Mayo," "The Lass from Bally-na-Lee."

Sources: *An Anthology of Irish Literature.* David H. Greene, ed. H. Modern Library, 1954. *Anthony Raftery, Last of the Wandering Bards* (http://www.galwayonline. ie/history/history2/rafter.htm). *Biography of Anthony Rafferty* (http://www.cillaodain.ie/raftery.html). *Kings, Lords, and Commons.* Frank O'Connor, ed. Knopf, 1959. *The Book of Irish Verse: An Anthology of Irish Poetry from the Sixth Century to the Present.* John Montague, ed. Macmillan, 1974. *The Columbia Granger's Index to Poetry.* 11th ed. *The Columbia Granger's World of Poetry,* Columbia University Press, 2005 (http://www.columbiagrangers.org). *The Kiltartan Poetry Book by Lady Gregory.* G.P. Putnam's Sons, 1919 (http://digital.library.upenn.edu/women/gregory/poetry/poetry.html). *The New Oxford Book of Irish Verse.* Thomas Kinsella, ed. Oxford University Press, 1986. *Wikipedia, the Free Encyclopedia* (http://en.wikipedia.org/wiki/Wikipedia).

RAINE, CRAIG ANTHONY (1944–)

Born in Bishop Auckland, Durham, he read English at Exeter College, Oxford. He has lectured at Exeter College, Lincoln College, Oxford, and Christ Church, Oxford, and has been a fellow of New College, Oxford, since 1991. He has been book editor for *New Review* and *Quarto,* poetry editor at the *New Statesman,* poetry editor at the London publishers Faber and Faber since 1981, and is founder and editor of the literary magazine *Areté.* He has won four major literary awards. *A Martian Sends a Postcard Home* (1979) instigated the "Martian School" of poetry. He lives in Oxford. Some of his other publications: *The Onion, Memory*, 1978. *A Free Translation,* 1981. *Rich*, 1984. *History: The Home Movie,* 1994 (an epic poem that celebrates the history of his own family and that of his wife). *Collected Poems 1978–1999*, 1999. *A La Recherche Du Temps Perdu,* 2000 (an elegy to a former lover). Some of his poems: "An Attempt at Jealousy," "Anno Domini," "City Gent," "Dandelions," "In the Kalahari Desert," "Nature Study," "Sexual Couplets," "The Man Who Invented Pain."

Sources: *British Council Arts* (http://www.contemporarywriters.com). *Emergency Kit: Poems for Strange Times.* Jo Shapcott and Matthew Sweeney, eds. Faber and Faber, 1996. *Erotic Poems.* Peter Washington, ed. Alfred A. Knopf, 1994. *Literary Encyclopedia, Biography of Crain Raine* (http://www.litencyc.com/php/speople.php?rec=true&UID=5523). *The National Portrait Gallery* (www.npg.org. uk). *Poemhunter* (www.poemhunter.com). *The Columbia Granger's Index to Poetry.* 11th ed. *The Columbia Granger's World of Poetry,* Columbia University Press, 2005 (http://www.columbiagrangers.org). *The Faber Book of Blue Verse.* John Whitworth, ed. Faber and Faber, 1990. *The Norton Anthology of Modern Poetry.* 2nd ed. Richard Ellmann, and Robert O'Clair, eds. W.W. Norton, 1988. *The Norton Anthology of Poetry.* 3rd ed. Alexander W.Allison, ed. W.W. Norton, 1983. *The Oxford Companion to English Literature.* 6th edition. Margaret Drabble, ed. Oxford University Press, 2000. *Who's Who.* London: A & C Black, 2005. *Wikipedia, the Free Encyclopedia* (http://en.wikipedia.org/wiki/Wikipedia).

RAINE, KATHLEEN JESSIE (1908–2003)

Born in London of a Scottish mother and an English father from Northumberland, she studied psychology and the natural sciences at Girton College, Cambridge, and graduated M.A. in 1929. The Northumberland countryside and the landscapes of Wester Ross in the Scottish highlands have inspired her poetry. Under the patronage of Charles, Prince of Wales, Raine founded, in 1990, the Temenos Academy, a teaching institution that rejected the "secular materialism" of the current age; the *Temenos Academy Review* was created in 1999 and included lectures given at the academy. Raine was made a Commander of the British Empire in 2000. A professor at Cambridge and the author of a number of scholarly books, she was an expert on Coleridge, Blake, and Yeats. Some of her publications: *The Pythoness*, 1949. *The Hollow Hill*, 1965. *The Lost Country*, 1971. *The Oval Portrait*, 1977. *The Oracle in the Heart, and Other Poems, 1975–1978*, 1980. *Collected Poems*, 2000. Some of her poems: "Acacia Tree," "By the River Eden," "Childhood Memory," "Eileann Chanaidh," "My Mother's Birthday," "The Wilderness," "Three Poems of Incarnation," "Written in Exile."

Sources: *Encyclopædia Britannica Ultimate Reference Suite DVD*, 2006. *Poems of the Scottish Hills: An Anthology.* Hamish Brown, ed. Aberdeen University Press, 1982. *Selected Poems of Kathleen Raine.* Lindisfarne Press, 1988. *The Columbia Granger's Index to Poetry.* 11th ed. *The Columbia Granger's World of Poetry,* Columbia University Press, 2005 (http://www.columbiagrangers.org). *The New Yorker Book of Poems.* The New Yorker editors. Viking Press, 1969. *The Oxford Companion to English Literature.* 6th edition. Margaret Drabble, ed. Oxford University Press, 2000. *The Treasury of Christian Poetry.* Lorraine Eitel, ed. Fleming H. Revell, 1982. *The Women Poets in English: An Anthology.* Ann Stanford, ed. McGraw-Hill, 1972.

RALEGH (RALEIGH) SIR WALTER (1552–1618)

The military and naval commander and adventurer was born near Budleigh Salterton, South Devon. In 1569 he fought on the Huguenot side in the Wars of Religion in France and was later at Oriel College, Oxford (1572), and at the Middle Temple law college (1575). In 1580 he fought against the Irish in Munster, for which he was awarded vast estates there. He was in and out of favor with Queen Elizabeth; he was knighted in 1585 but committed to the Tower of London by the jealous queen in 1592 because he had secretly married one of the her maids of honor. He was governor of Jersey in the Channel Islands in 1600, imprisoned in 1603 by James I for suspected treason, released in 1616 to search for gold in South America — which failed — and was again arrested and died by execution. Some of his poems: "A Description of Love," "As Yee Came From the Holye Land," "But True Love is a Durable Fire," "My Body in the Walls Captived," "On the Cards and Dice," "The Advice," "The Arte of English Poesie," "The Excuse," "The Lie."

Sources: *A New Canon of English Poetry.* James Reeves and Martin Seymour-Smith, eds. Barnes and Noble, 1967. *Bishop Percy's Folio Ms: Ballads and Romances, Volume 3.* John W. Hales and Frederick J. Furnivall, eds. N. Trübner and Co., 1868. *Dictionary of National Biography.* Electronic Edition 1.1. Oxford University Press, 1997. *Encyclopædia Britannica Ultimate Reference Suite DVD*, 2006. *English Poetry: Author Search.* Chadwyck-Healey Ltd., 1995 (http://

www.lib.utexas.edu:8080/search/epoetry/author.html). *Silver Poets of the Sixteenth Century.* Gerald Bullett, ed. J.M. Dent, 1947. *The Columbia Granger's Index to Poetry.* 11th ed. *The Columbia Granger's World of Poetry,* Columbia University Press, 2005 (http://www.columbiagrangers.org). *The New Penguin Book of English Verse.* Paul Keegan, ed. Penguin Books, 2000. *The Oxford Companion to English Literature.* 6th edition. Margaret Drabble, ed. Oxford University Press, 2000. *The Poems of Sir Walter Ralegh* (Rudick Edition). Arizona Center for Medieval and Renaissance Studies, 1999 (http://www.asu.edu/clas/acmrs).

RALEIGH, SIR WALTER ALEXANDER (1861–1922)

Born in London, the son of a Congregationalist minister, his education was split between London and Edinburgh and he graduated B.A. from University College, London, in 1881. Although appointed the first professor of English literature in the Mohammedan Anglo-Oriental College, Aligarh, India, in 1885, he was invalided home in April 1887. After that he held the chairs at Liverpool and Glasgow. He was the first to hold the chair of English literature, Oxford University, from 1904, which in 1914 became the Merton chair of English literature. He was knighted in 1911. He died of typhoid fever contracted abroad and was buried at Ferry Hinksey, near Oxford. He published books on John Milton, Robert Louis Stevenson, William Shakespeare, Samuel Johnson, and English voyages of exploration in the sixteenth century. He wrote the first official volume of *The War in the Air* (1922). Some of his poems: "Attend My Words, My Gentle Knave," "How Far Is It to London?" "Johannesburg, New Year, 1896," "Ode to the Glasgow Ballad Club," "The Battle Hymn of Kensit's Men," "The Haunted House," "The Lie," "Wishes of an Elderly Man."

Sources: *A Sacrifice of Praise: An Anthology of Christian Poetry in English from Caedmon to the Mid-Twentieth Century.* James H. Trott, ed. Cumberland House Publishing, 1999. *Biography of Sir Walter Alexander Raleigh* (http://epona.lib.ed.ac.uk:1822/isaar/P0299.html). *Dictionary of National Biography.* Electronic Edition 1.1. Oxford University Press, 1997. *Encyclopædia Britannica Ultimate Reference Suite DVD*, 2006. *The Chatto Book of Love Poetry.* John Fuller, ed. Chatto and Windus, 1990. *The Cherry-Tree.* Geoffrey Grigson, ed. Phoenix House, 1959. *The Columbia Granger's Index to Poetry.* 11th ed. *The Columbia Granger's World of Poetry,* Columbia University Press, 2005 (http://www.columbiagrangers.org). *The Complete Works of C.S. Calverley.* G. Bell and Sons, 1926. *The Oxford Companion to English Literature.* 6th edition. Margaret Drabble, ed. Oxford University Press, 2000. *What Cheer: An Anthology of American and British Humorous and Witty Verse.* David McCord, ed. Coward-McCann, 1945.

RAMSAY, ALLAN (1686–1758)

A Scottish poet who wrote in the Scots tongue, he was born in Lanarkshire, where his father was manager of a lead mine. He spent most of his life as a prosperous wig maker in Edinburgh. He soon established himself as a poet and song writer, and children were sent out with a penny to buy sheets or half-sheets of "Ramsay's last piece." Between 1716 and 1718 he published *Chrysts-Kirke on the Greene*, a rollicking poem of several cantos, with a fifth edition in 1723. In 1726 he started the first circulating library in Scotland and his bookshop in Edinburgh attracted many men of letters. He died at Edinburgh and was buried in Old Greyfriars churchyard. Some of his other poetry publications: *Scots Songs*, 1719. *The Fair Assembly*, 1723. *The Tea-table Miscellany*, 1724–1727. *The Evergreen*, 1724–1727. *The Gentle Shepherd*, 1725 (pastoral drama, tenth edition, 1750). Some of his poems: "Allan Water," "Auld Lang Syne," "Eagle and the Robin Redbreast," "Horace to Virgil," "The Fox Turned Preacher," "The Highland Laddie," "The Yellow-haired Laddie," "Wine and Music," "Ye Watchful Guardians of the Fair."

Sources: *Dictionary of National Biography*. Electronic Edition 1.1. Oxford University Press, 1997. *Encyclopædia Britannica Ultimate Reference Suite DVD*, 2006. *English Poetry: Author Search*. Chadwyck-Healey Ltd., 1995 (http://www.lib.utexas.edu:8080/search/epoetry/author.html). *Seven Centuries of Poetry: Chaucer to Dylan Thomas*. A.N. Jeffares, ed. Longmans, Green, 1955. *The Columbia Granger's Index to Poetry*. 11th ed. *The Columbia Granger's World of Poetry*, Columbia University Press, 2005 (http://www.columbiagrangers.org). *The Oxford Book of Classical Verse in Translation*. Adrian Poole and Jeremy Maule, eds. 1995. *The Oxford Book of Scottish Verse*, John MacQueen and Tom Scott, eds. Oxford University Press, 1966. *The Oxford Companion to English Literature*. 6th edition. Margaret Drabble, ed. Oxford University Press, 2000. *The Poems of Allan Ramsay. Vols. 1 and 2*. T. Cadell and W. Davies, 1800. *The Scottish Collection of Verse to 1800*. Eileen Dunlop and Kamm Antony, eds. Richard Drew, 1985.

RANDOLPH, THOMAS (1605–1635)

The son of William Randolph, steward to Edward, Lord Zouch, he was born at Newnham-cum-Badby. Northamptonshire. At the age of nine or ten he wrote in verse the "History of the Incarnation of Our Savior." He was educated at Westminster School and graduated M.A. from Trinity College, Cambridge, in 1632, where he quickly assumed a reputation as a writer of English and Latin verse. In 1630 he published *Aristippus, or the Joviall Philosopher*, prose interspersed with verse in a satire on university education. In the same year he produced *The Muse's Looking-Glass*, followed by *The Jealous Lovers* (1634). *Hey for Honesty*, a comedy, was published posthumously in 1651. He died from smallpox. His volume *Poems, with the Muses' Looking-Glasse and Amyntas*, was published posthumously in 1638. Some of his poems: "A Devout Lover," "A Parley with His Empty Purse," "A Platonik Eligie," "In Praise of Women in General," "Maske for Lydia," "Necessary Observations," "On the Death of a Nightingale," "The Conceited Pedlar," "The Pedler," "The Song of Orpheus," "The Wedding Morne," "To a Painted Mistriss."

Sources: *Ben Jonson and the Cavalier Poets*. Hugh MacLaen, ed. New York: W.W. Norton and Company, 1974. *Dictionary of National Biography*. Electronic Edition 1.1. Oxford University Press, 1997. *Encyclopædia Britannica Ultimate Reference Suite DVD*, 2006. *English Poetry: Author Search*. Chadwyck-Healey Ltd., 1995 (http://www.lib.utexas.edu:8080/search/epoetry/author.html). *How Does a Poem Mean?* 2nd edition. John Ciardi and Miller Williams, eds. Houghton Mifflin, 1975. *Songs from the British Drama*. Edward Bliss Reed, ed. Yale University Press, 1925. *The Anchor Anthology of Seventeenth-Century Verse, Vol. II*. Louis L. Martz and Richard S. Sylvester, eds. Doubleday Anchor Books, 1969. *The Columbia Granger's Index to Poetry*. 11th ed. *The Columbia Granger's World of Poetry*, Columbia University Press, 2005 (http://www.columbiagrangers.org). *The Oxford Book of Classical Verse in Translation*. Adrian Poole and Jeremy Maule, eds. 1995. *The Oxford Book of Short Poems*. P.J. Kavanagh and James Michie, eds. Oxford University Press, 1985. *The Oxford Companion to English Literature*. 6th edition. Margaret Drabble, ed. Oxford University Press, 2000.

RANDS WILLIAM BRIGHTY (1823–1882)

"The laureate of the nursery" who also wrote under the pseudonyms of Henry Holbeach and Matthew Browne was born in Chelsea, London, the son of shopkeeper. His limited education was developed by reading from second-hand bookstalls. He taught himself shorthand and was employed as a reporter in the committee rooms of the House of Commons until ill health forced his resignation in 1875. He wrote for many periodicals, including *Illustrated London News*, *The Spectator*, *Good Words* and *Good Words for the Young*. He died at East Dulwich and was buried at Forest Hill (now in Greater London). His reputation was as a children's poet and writer of fairy tales, which he published every Christmas for many years. His poetry publications: *The Chain of Lilies, and Other Poems*, 1857. *Lilliput Levee*, 1864. *Little Ben Bute*, 1880 (with colored illustrations). *Lilliput Lyrics*, 1889. *Miss Hooper's Hoop*, 1949. Some of his poems: "Clean Clara," "Gipsy Jane," "Godfrey Gordon Gustavus Gore," "The Cat of Cats," "The Dream of a Boy Who Lived at Nine Elms," "The Pedlar's Caravan," "The Ship That Sailed into the Sun," "Topsy-turvy World."

Sources: *101 Favorite Cat Poems*. Sara L. Whittier, ed. Contemporary Books, 1991. *Dictionary of National Biography*. Electronic Edition 1.1. Oxford University Press, 1997. *English Poetry: Author Search*. Chadwyck-Healey Ltd., 1995 (http://www.lib.utexas.edu:8080/search/epo

etry/author.html). *Moon is Shining Bright as Day: An Anthology of Good-humoured Verse.* Ogden Nash, ed. J.B. Lippincott, 1953. *Stanford University Libraries and Academic Information Resources* (http://library.stanford.edu). *The Columbia Granger's Index to Poetry.* 11th ed. *The Columbia Granger's World of Poetry,* Columbia University Press, 2005 (http://www.columbiagrangers.org). *The Home Book of Verse for Young Folks.* Burton Egbert Stevenson, ed. Holt, Rinehart and Winston, 1929. *The Oxford Book of Children's Verse.* Iona Opie and Peter Opie, eds. Oxford University Press, 1973. *The Oxford Book of English Verse, 1250–1918.* Sir Arthur Quiller-Couch, ed. New edition, revised and enlarged, Oxford University Press, 1939. *The Oxford Companion to English Literature.* 6th edition. Margaret Drabble, ed. Oxford University Press, 2000. *The Penguin Book of Victorian Verse.* George Macbeth, ed. Penguin Classics, 1999. *The Writings of William Brighty Rands* (http://www.victorianweb.org/authors/rands/bibl. html).

RAWORTH, TOM (1938–)

Thomas Moore Raworth grew up in London, left school at 16, then during the 1960s made a major contribution to British interest in the new American poetry by publishing both English and American authors. In the 1970s, he taught at several universities in the United States and Mexico. He returned to England in 1977 and for a year was resident poet in King's College, Cambridge, where he still lives. He gives regular readings of his work in Europe and the U.S.A. He has made a number of recordings and has collaborated with musicians, other poets, and painters. In 1991, he was the first European writer in 30 years to be invited to teach at the University of Cape Town. His first collection was *The Relation Ship* (1966 and 1969). Some of his most recent publications: *Collected Poems,* 2003. *Tottering State,* 2000. *Landscaping the Future,* 2000. *Meadow,* 1999. *Clean and Well Lit,* 1996. Some of his poems: "Bolivia: Another End of Ace," "Eternal Sections," "My Face is My Own, I Thought," "Sentenced to Death," "South America," "The Empty Pain-Killer Bottles," "Wedding Day."

Sources: *Anthology of Twentieth-Century British and Irish Poetry.* Keith Tuma, ed. Oxford University Press, 2001. *English and American Surrealist Poetry.* Edward B Germain, ed. Penguin Books, 1978. *Poems for the Millennium: The University of California Book of Modern and Postmodern Poetry, Vol. 2.* Jerome Rothenberg and Pierre Joris, eds. University of California Press, 1998. *The Columbia Granger's Index to Poetry.* 11th ed. *The Columbia Granger's World of Poetry,* Columbia University Press, 2005 (http://www.columbiagrangers.org). *The New British Poetry, 1968–88.* Gillian Allnutt, Fred D'Aguiar and Ken Edwards, eds. Grafton Books, 1989. *The Tom Raworth Home Page* (http://tomraworth.com/biblio.html). *Wikipedia, the Free Encyclopedia* (http://en.wikipedia.org/wiki/Wikipedia).

READ, SIR HERBERT EDWARD (1893–1968)

Born in Yorkshire, he studied at Leeds University from 1911 to 1914, then was commissioned into the Green Howards regiment and won both the Military Cross and the Distinguished Service Order. He was assistant keeper at the Victoria and Albert Museum (1919–1922) and held several academic posts, including Watson Gordon professor of fine art in Edinburgh University, and Charles Eliot Norton professor of poetry at Harvard University. In 1947 he co-founded the Institute of Contemporary Arts and was a respected international authority on art. He was knighted in 1953. He died at Stonegrave, not far from where he was born. He published over sixty books on art, history and, with M. Foreman, edited the *Collected Works of C.J. Jung.* He is memorialized by a stone in Poets' Corner of Westminster Abbey along with other poets of the First World War. Some of his poetry publications: *Songs of Chaos,* 1915. *Poems, 1914–1934,* 1935. *Thirty-Five Poems,* 1940. *Collected Poems,* 1966. Some of his poems: "1945," "A Short Poem for Armistice Day," "Aeroplanes," "Bombing Casualties: Spain," "The Analysis of Love," "The Falcon and the Dove," "Ypres."

Sources: *Collected Poems of Herbert Read.* Sinclair-Stevenson, 1994. *Dictionary of National Biography.* Electronic Edition 1.1. Oxford University Press, 1997. *Encyclopædia Britannica Ultimate Reference Suite DVD,* 2006. *The National Portrait Gallery* (www.npg.org.uk). *Poems of Protest Old and New.* Arnold Kenseth, ed. MacMillan, 1968. *The Columbia Granger's Index to Poetry.* 11th ed. *The Columbia Granger's World of Poetry,* Columbia University Press, 2005 (http://www.columbiagrangers.org). *The Faber Book of Twentieth Century Verse.* John Heath-Stubbs and David Wright, eds. Faber and Faber, 1975. *The Oxford Companion to English Literature.* 6th edition. Margaret Drabble, ed. Oxford University Press, 2000. *Westminster Abbey Official Guide* (no date).

READING, PETER GRAY (1946–)

Born in Liverpool, he graduated B.A. in fine art and painting from the Liverpool College of Art, then worked as a school teacher in Liverpool (1967–1968) and at Liverpool College of Art, where he taught art history (1968–1970). He was writer in residence at Sunderland Polytechnic (1981–83). In 1997 he held the creative writing fellowship at the University of East Anglia. He is a fellow of the Royal Society of Literature and has lived in Shropshire since 1970. His awards: Cholmondeley, 1978; Dylan Thomas, 1983; Whitbread Poetry, 1986; Lannan Foundation, 1990 and 2004. Some of his poetry publications: *Water and Waste,* 1970. *The Prison Cell and Barrel Mystery,* 1976. *Nothing for Anyone,* 1977. *Diplopic,* 1983. *Ukelele Music,* 1985. *Stet,* 1986. *Final Demands,* 1988. *Work in Regress,* 1997. *Collected Poems, Poems*

1: 1970–1984, 1995. *Poems 2: 1985–1996*, 1996. *Poems 3: 1997–2003*, 2003. Some of his poems: "Ballad," "Carte Postale," "Correspondence," "Perduta Gente," "Travelogue," "Ye haue heard this yarn afore."

Sources: *Anthology of Twentieth-Century British and Irish Poetry*. Keith Tuma, ed. Oxford University Press, 2001. *Bloodaxe Books* (http://www.bloodaxebooks.com/personpage.asp?author=Peter+Reading). *British Council Arts* (http://www.contemporarywriters.com). *Emergency Kit: Poems for Strange Times*. Jo Shapcott and Matthew Sweeney, eds. Faber and Faber, 1996. *The Columbia Granger's Index to Poetry*. 11th ed. *The Columbia Granger's World of Poetry*, Columbia University Press, 2005 (http://www.columbiagrangers.org). *The Faber Book of Blue Verse*. John Whitworth, ed. Faber and Faber, 1990. *The Faber Book of Drink, Drinkers and Drinking*. Simon Rae, ed. Faber and Faber, 1991. *The Faber Book of Vernacular Verse*. Tom Paulin, Faber and Faber, 1990. *The Oxford Companion to English Literature*. 6th edition. Margaret Drabble, ed. Oxford University Press, 2000. *The Penguin Book of Light Verse*. Gavin Ewart, ed. Penguin Books, 1980. *Who's Who*. London: A & C Black, 2005.

REAVEY, GEORGE (1907–1976)

Born in Russia of an Irish father and a Russian mother, he lived there until his father was arrested in 1919 and his mother fled with him to Belfast. He was educated at the Royal Belfast Academical Institution and Gonville and Caius College, Cambridge, where he studied history and literature. He started a literary agency, the Bureau Littéraire Européen (based in Paris from 1932 to 1936, it became the European Literary Bureau, in London, from 1936 to 1939), and the Europa Press imprint, an important vehicle for Irish poets' work. To coincide with the opening of the International Surrealist Exhibition in 1936, Europa Press published *Thorns of Thunder*, the first collection of English translations of poems by Paul Eluard. During World War II Reavey served in Madrid and the Soviet Union with the Foreign Office, and in 1946 he moved to America to teach Russian literature, and lived the rest of his life there. Two of his collections are *Colors of Memory* (1955) and *Seven Seas* (1971). Some of his poems: "'How many fires,'" "Dismissing Progress and Its Progenitors," "Never," "The Bridge of Heraclitus."

Sources: *English and American Surrealist Poetry*. Edward B. Germain, ed. Penguin Books, 1978. *Surrealist Poetry in English*. Edward B. Germain, ed. Penguin Books, 1978. *The Book of Irish Verse: An Anthology of Irish Poetry from the Sixth Century to the Present*. John Montague, ed. Macmillan, 1974. *The Columbia Granger's Index to Poetry*. 11th ed. *The Columbia Granger's World of Poetry*, Columbia University Press, 2005 (http://www.columbiagrangers.org). *The Faber Book of Irish Verse*. John Montague, ed. Faber and Faber, 1978. *Wikipedia, the Free Encyclopedia* (http://en.wikipedia.org/wiki/Wikipedia).

REDGROVE, PETER WILLIAM (1932–2003)

Born Kingston-upon-Thames, Surrey, the son of an advertising copywriter, he was educated at Taunton School, Somerset, and at Queens' College, Cambridge, where he studied natural sciences, though he did not graduate. He worked as scientific journalist and copywriter. He was a founding member of "the Group." He had three periods of teaching at universities in America, then between 1962 and 1965 he was Gregory Fellow in Poetry at Leeds University, and from 1966 to 1983 he was lecturer in liberal studies at Falmouth School of Art, Cornwall. He was awarded the Queen's Gold Medal for Poetry in 1996 and an honorary doctorate of letters from Sheffield University. Redgrove published around 50 collections of verse, 27 plays, seven novels and a set of short stories. He married Penelope Shuttle (see entry) in 1980. Some of his more recent poetry publications: *The Moon Disposes: Poems 1954–1987*, 1987. *Poems 1954–1987*, 1989. *Under the Reservoir*, 1992. *Assembling a Ghost*, 1996. *From the Virgil Caverns*, 2002. Some of his poems: "Against Death," "Bedtime Story for My Son," "Required of You This Night," "The Apprentice at the Feast," "The Secretary."

Sources: *Biography of Peter William Redgrove* (http://www.tauntonschool.co.uk/alumni/obituaries/files/Redgrovep.html). *New Poets of England and America*. Donald Hall and Robert Pack, eds. World, 1962. *Obituary of Peter Redgrove*. *Telegraph News* (http://www.telegraph.co.uk/news/main.jhtml?xml=/news/2003/06/18/db1802.xml). *Obituary of Peter Redgrove: Queens' College Record 2004* (http://www.quns.cam.ac.uk/Queens/Record/2004/Old%20Members/Obituaries.html). *P.E.N. New Poetry I*. Robert Nye, ed. Quartet Books, 1986. *Philip Hobsbaum, 1932— Collection of Correspondence and Manuscripts of the Group, ca. 1955–1968* (http://www.hrc.utexas.edu/research/fa/hobsbaum.html). *The Columbia Granger's Index to Poetry*. 11th ed. *The Columbia Granger's World of Poetry*, Columbia University Press, 2005 (http://www.columbiagrangers.org). *The National Portrait Gallery* (www.npg.org.uk). *The New Modern Poetry: British and American Poetry since World War II*. M.L. Rosenthal, ed. Macmillan, 1967. *The Oxford Book of Twentieth-Century English Verse*. Philip Larkin, ed. Oxford University Press, 1973. *The Oxford Companion to English Literature*. 6th ed. Margaret Drabble, ed. Oxford University Press, 2000. *Wikipedia, the Free Encyclopedia* (http://en.wikipedia.org/wiki/Wikipedia).

REED, HENRY (1914–1986)

Born in Birmingham, the son of a master bricklayer, and educated at King Edward VI Grammar School, Birmingham, he won the Temperley Latin prize and a scholarship to Birmingham University. He graduated with a first-class degree (1934) and an M.A. for a thesis on the novels of Thomas Hardy (1936). He became a freelance writer and critic, then served for one year in the Army. Following severe pneumonia and convalescence he was transferred to the Government Code and Cipher School at Bletchley Park, where he was a cryptographer and Japanese translator. After the war he worked for the BBC as a radio broadcaster and playwright, where his most memorable set of productions was the *Hilda Tablet* series in the 1950s. His most famous poem, "Naming of Parts," is a witty parody of army basic training. It was published in 1946 in *A Map of Verona*, his only collection to be published within his lifetime. He died at St. Charles Hospital, Kensington. Some of his other poems: "Chard Whitlow," "Chrysothemis," "Lessons of the War," "Sailor's Harbor," "The Auction Sale," "The Château," "The Door and the Window."

Sources: *Modern British Poetry*. 7th rev. ed. Louis Untermeyer, ed. Harcourt, Brace, 1962. *Modern Verse in English, 1900–1950*. David Cecil and Allen Tate, eds. Macmillan, 1967. *Poemhunter* (www.poemhunter.com). *The Columbia Granger's Index to Poetry*. 11th ed. *The Columbia Granger's World of Poetry*, Columbia University Press, 2005 (http://www.columbiagrangers.org). *The Faber Book of Comic Verse*. Michael Roberts and Janet Adam Smith, eds. Faber and Faber, 1978. *The Harvill Book of Twentieth-Century Poetry in English*. Michael Schmidt, ed. The Harvill Press, 1999. *The Oxford Companion to English Literature*. 6th edition. Margaret Drabble, ed. Oxford University Press, 2000. *The Poetry of Henry Reed* (http://www.solearabiantree.net/namingofparts/home.html). *Wikipedia, the Free Encyclopedia* (http://en.wikipedia.org/wiki/Wikipedia).

REES-JONES, DERYN (1968–)

After reading English at the University College of North Wales, she did doctoral research at Birkbeck College on poetry by women writers. She now lives in Liverpool and lectures in literature at Liverpool University. The author of a monograph on the work of Carol Anne Duffy (1998), she was listed as one of the Poetry Book's "New Generation" poets in 2004. Her works include *The Memory Tray*, 1994, short listed for a Forward Prize in 1995 and winner of an Arts Council Writer's Award in 1996; *Signs Around a Dead Body*, 1999, Poetry Book Society Special Commendation; and *Quiver*, 2004, a book-length murder-mystery. She has also written: *Consorting with Angels: Essays on Modern Women Poets*, Bloodaxe Books (2005). *Modern Women Poets* (editor) Bloodaxe Books (2005). *Contemporary Women's Poetry: Reading/Writing/Practice*, with Alison Mark, Palgrave Macmillan (2000). Some of her poems: "And Please Do Not Presume," "I Know Exactly the Sort of Woman I'd Like to Fall in Love With," "It Will Not Do," "Largo," "Making for Planet Alice," "Service Wash," "The Great Mutando."

Sources: *Biography of Deryn Rees-Jones, BBC: Get Writing*, A3225386 (http://www.bbc.co.uk/dna/getwriting/ reesjones). *Making for Planet Alice: New Women Poets*. Maura Dooley, ed. Bloodaxe Books, 1997. *Meet the Next Generation Poets, Poetry Book Society* (http://www.poetry books.co.uk/PBS/pbs_next_generation.asp). *Summer by Deryn Rees-Jones* (http://www.poetrybooks.co.uk/PBS/ pbs_rees_jones_deryn.asp). *The Columbia Granger's Index to Poetry*. 11th ed. *The Columbia Granger's World of Poetry*, Columbia University Press, 2005 (http://www.columbia grangers.org). *The National Portrait Gallery* (www.npg. org.uk). *Twentieth Century Anglo-Welsh Poetry*. Dannie Abse, ed. Seren Books / Dufour Editions, 1997.

RELPH, JOSIAH (1712–1743)

Born at Churchtown, a small estate belonging to his father in the parish of Sebergham, Cumberland, he had a good education and went to Glasgow, presumably to the university, for on his return he became master of his local grammar school. He then took holy orders and became the priest of Sebergham, where he toiled in the education of the children of the parish. He died young, although there is no mention of how. His poetical works, *A Miscellany of Poems*, published in Glasgow in 1747, were edited by Thomas Sanderson, who supplied a life of the author and a pastoral elegy on his death. A second edition appeared at Carlisle in 1798, with the life of the author and engravings by Thomas Bewick. His *Songs and Poems* were published in Edinburgh in 1866. Relph's best verses are in the dialect of his native county; they show talent and appreciation of natural beauty. Some of his poems: "Hay-Time; Or, the Constant Lovers. A Pastoral," "Idylls [Of Theocritus]," "The Hour-Glass," "The Worm-Doctor," "Translated From Seneca," "The Husbandman and the Horse," "The Boy and the Sparrows."

Sources: *Dictionary of National Biography*. Electronic Edition 1.1. Oxford University Press, 1997. *English Poetry: Author Search*. Chadwyck-Healey Ltd., 1995 (http://www. lib.utexas.edu:8080/search/epoetry/author.html). *Stanford University Libraries and Academic Information Resources* (http://library.stanford.edu). *The Columbia Granger's Index to Poetry*. 11th ed. *The Columbia Granger's World of Poetry*, Columbia University Press, 2005 (http://www.columbia grangers.org). *The New Oxford Book of Eighteenth Century Verse*. Roger Lonsdale, ed. Oxford University Press, 1984. *The Oxford Book of Classical Verse in Translation*. Adrian Poole and Jeremy Maule, eds. 1995.

REYNOLDS, JOHN HAMILTON (1796–1852)

Born in Shrewsbury, Shropshire, the son of a master at Christ's Hospital School, he was educated at St. Paul's School, London. He started work for the Amicable Insurance Company, then took up law and became a partner of James Rice, a friend of John Keats. Under the pseudonym Edward Herbert he wrote reviews for the *London Magazine*, *Edinburgh*, *Westminster*, and *Retrospective*, and various items for the *Athenaeum*, of which he was one of the proprietors. Latterly he was clerk to the county court on the Isle of Wight, where he died. Possibly through his father's connections he became friendly with Leigh Hunt (see Hunt, James Henry Leigh) and John Keats (see entry), both Christ Hospital boys. Keats and Reynolds collaborated on a series of metrical versions of Boccaccio's tales (1818); Reynolds' contributions were "The Garden of Florence" and "The Ladye of Provence." Some of his publications: *The Eden of Imagination*, 1814. *The Naiad, With Other Poems*, 1816. *Peter Bell*, 1819. *The Garden of Florence*, 1821. *Odes and Addresses*, 1826. Some of his poems: "Farewell to the Muses," "Gallantly Within the Ring," "The Fairies," "To Keats," "To Spenser."

Sources: *Dictionary of National Biography.* Electronic Edition 1.1. Oxford University Press, 1997. *English Poetry: Author Search.* Chadwyck-Healey Ltd., 1995 (http://www.lib.utexas.edu:8080/search/epoetry/author.html). *Folk Songs.* John Williamson Palmer, ed. Charles Scribner and Company, 1867. *The National Portrait Gallery* (www.npg.org.uk). *Parodies: An Anthology from Chaucer to Beerbohm — and After.* Dwight Macdonald, ed. Modern Library, 1960. *Sprints and Distances: Sports in Poetry and the Poetry in Sport.* Lillian Morrison, ed. Thomas Y. Crowell, 1965. *Stanford University Libraries and Academic Information Resources* (http://library.stanford.edu). *The Columbia Granger's Index to Poetry.* 11th ed. *The Columbia Granger's World of Poetry,* Columbia University Press, 2005 (http://www.columbiagrangers.org). *The Oxford Book of Regency Verse 1798–1837.* H.S. Milford, ed. Oxford University Press, 1928. *The Oxford Companion to English Literature.* 6th edition. Margaret Drabble, ed. Oxford University Press, 2000. *The Sonnet: An Anthology.* Robert M. Bender and Charles L. Squier, eds. Washington Square Press, 1987.

RICHARDS, IVOR ARMSTRONG
(1893–1970)

Richards was born at Sandbach, Cheshire, the son of an engineer. He read moral sciences at Magdalene College, Cambridge, and graduated in 1915. His studies were interrupted by tuberculosis and a long period of recuperation. He lectured on English and moral sciences at Cambridge from 1922 to 1929 and co-authored *The Foundations of Aesthetics* (1922). He achieved great fame as an influential literary theorist of critical writing, with an emphasis on basic English and a new way of reading poetry; his *Principles of Literary Criticism* was published in 1925. He was visiting professor from 1929 to 1930 at Tsing Hua University in Peking and again from 1936 to 1938 at the Orthological Institute in Peking. He was a Harvard University professor of poetry from 1944 to 1963. He received honorary degrees from Cambridge and Harvard and was made a Companion of Honor in 1964. He died at Cambridge, England. His poetry publications: *Goodbye Earth, and Other*

Poems, 1958. *The Screens*, 1960. *Internal Colloquies*, 1972. Some of his poems: "End of a Course," "Nothing at All," "Spendthrift," "Trinity Brethren Attend," "Warhead Wakes," "Zarathustra."

Sources: *Contemporary Religious Poetry.* Paul Ramsey, ed. Paulist Press, 1987. *Dictionary of National Biography.* Electronic Edition 1.1. Oxford University Press, 1997. *Encyclopædia Britannica Ultimate Reference Suite DVD,* 2006. *Poetry for Pleasure: A Choice of Poetry and Verse on a Variety of Themes.* Ian Parsons, ed. W.W. Norton, 1977. *The Columbia Granger's Index to Poetry.* 11th ed. *The Columbia Granger's World of Poetry,* Columbia University Press, 2005 (http://www.columbiagrangers.org). *The Oxford Companion to English Literature.* 6th edition. Margaret Drabble, ed. Oxford University Press, 2000. *World Poetry: An Anthology of Verse from Antiquity to Our Time.* Katharine Washburn and John S. Major, eds. Publisher, 1338, 1998.

RICHARDSON, DAVID LESTER
(1801–1865)

Little is known of his background. He was an officer in the Bengal army and served on the staff of the governor-general, Lord William Bentinck, and in the education department at Calcutta. In 1827 he returned to England and founded the *London Weekly Review*, which afterwards became *Colburn's Court Journal*. In 1829 he returned to Calcutta and from 1830 to 1837 acted as editor of the *Bengal Annual*, then edited the *Calcutta Monthly Journal* and *The Calcutta Literary Gazette* (1834 to 1849). From 1836 he was professor of English literature of the Hindu College at Calcutta and from 1839, principal of the college. He returned to England in 1861 and became proprietor and editor of *The Court Circular* and editor of *Allen's Indian Mail*. He died at Clapham, London. Some of his publications: *Miscellaneous Poems*, 1822. *Sonnets and Other Poems*, 1825. *Selections from the British Poets*, 1840. *Literary Chit-chat, with Miscellaneous Poems*, 1848. Some of his poems: "Nature," "Sonnet on Autumn," "Sonnet Written at Netley Abbey," "Sonnet, Sunrise," "Sonnets from a British Indian Exile to his Distant Children," "Sounds at Sea," "The Soldier's Dream."

Sources: *Dictionary of National Biography.* Electronic Edition 1.1. Oxford University Press, 1997. *Publications by David Lester Richardson.* Forget Me Not: A Hypertextual Archive (http://www.orgs.muohio.edu/anthologies/FMN/Authors_GenD.htm#Richardson).

RICKWORD, JOHN EDGELL
(1898–1982)

Born in Colchester, Essex, he joined the Artists Rifles in 1916 and saw active service as an officer with the Royal Berkshire Regiment. He was invalided out of the army after the Armistice and was awarded the Military Cross. He went up to Pembroke College, Oxford in 1919, but stayed only four terms, reading

French literature, and leaving when he married. He became a reviewer for the *Times Literary Supplement* and the *New Statesman*. He founded the literary review *Calendar of Modern Letters*, which ran from 1925 to 1927. In the 1930s he joined the Communist Party of Great Britain and was politically active during the period of the Spanish Civil War. From 1944 to 1947 he was the editor of the Communist review *Our Time*. Some of his poetry publications: *Behind the Eyes*, 1921. *Rimbaud: The Boy and the Poet*, 1924. *Invocation to Angels*, 1928. *Collected Poems*, 1947. *Twittingpan and Some Others*, 1981. Some of his poems: "Complaint after Psycho-Analysis," "Cosmogony," "The Cascade," "The Contemporary Muse," "The Encounter," "The Handmaid of Religion," "The Soldier Addresses his Body," "Trench Poets," "Winter Warfare."

Sources: *Biography of Edgell Rickword* (http://encyclo pedie-en.snyke.com/articles/edgell_rickword.html). *Old-poetry* (www.oldpoetry.com). *Peace and War: A Collection of Poems*. Michael Harrison and Christopher Stuart-Clark, eds. Oxford University Press, 1989. *Poetry Nation: A Conversation with Edgell Rickword* (http://www.poetrymaga zines.org.uk/magazine/record.asp?id=1920). *Portraits of Poets*. Sebastian Barker, ed. Carcanet, 1986. *The Chatto Book of Modern Poetry 1915–1955*. Cecil Day Lewis and John Lehmann, eds. Chatto and Windus, 1966. *The Columbia Granger's Index to Poetry*. 11th ed. *The Columbia Granger's World of Poetry*, Columbia University Press, 2005 (http://www.columbiagrangers.org). *The Devil's Book of Verse: Masters of the Poison Pen from Ancient Times to the Present Day*. Richard Conniff, ed. Dodd, Mead, 1983. *The Faber Book of Twentieth Century Verse*. John Heath-Stubbs and David Wright, eds. Faber and Faber, 1975. *The Oxford Book of Satirical Verse*. Geoffrey Grigson, ed. Oxford University Press, 1980. *The Oxford Companion to English Literature*. 6th edition. Margaret Drabble, ed. Oxford University Press, 2000. *The Penguin Book of First World War Poetry*. Jon Silkin, ed. Penguin Books, 1979.

RIDDELL, HENRY SCOTT (1798–1870)

Scottish poet born at Sorbie, Dumfriesshire, the son of a shepherd; his education was mainly carried out during the winter months. Following his father's death in 1817, and after two years of formal education, he went on to Edinburgh University, which included a year at St. Andrews University, after which he became a licentiate of the church of Scotland. In 1833 he became minister of Caerlanrig Chapel, Roxburghshire. Mental illness overtook him and he spent the years between 1841 and 1844 in an asylum at Dumfries, possibly the Crichton Royal. Afterward he devoted himself to literary work and archaeology. Between 1855 and 1857 he translated St. Matthew and the Psalms of David into lowland Scots. He died at Teviothead and was buried in Caerlanrig churchyard. In 1831 he published a col-

lection of sacred songs, *Songs of the Ark;* his *Poems and Songs, and Miscellaneous Pieces* appeared in 1847. *The Poetical Works of Henry Scott Riddell*, edited, with a memoir, by Dr. Brydon, appeared in 1871. Four of his poems: "Ours is the Land of Gallant Hearts," "Scotland Yet," "The Crook and Plaid," "When the Glen All is Still."

Sources: *Dictionary of National Biography.* Electronic Edition 1.1. Oxford University Press, 1997. *Modern Asylums in Scotland* (http://www.dundeecity.gov.uk/liff/his tory5.html). *The Columbia Granger's Index to Poetry.* 11th ed. *The Columbia Granger's World of Poetry*, Columbia University Press, 2005 (http://www.columbiagrangers. org). *The Home Book of Verse*. Burton Egbert Stevenson, ed. New York: Henry Holt and Company, 1953."

RIDLER, ANNE (1912–2001)

Anne Barbara Bradby was born at Rugby, Warwickshire, where her father was a housemaster at Rugby School. After graduating in journalism from King's College, London, in 1932, she worked for Faber and Faber from 1935 to 1940, became the protégée of T.S. Eliot (see entry), and married Vivian Ridler in 1938. A few months before her death she received the Order of the British Empire. Her works include translations of libretti by Monteverdi, Cavalli and Mozart. Her version of *Cosi Fan Tutte* for Opera North in 1988 was televised by Channel 4. Her poetry dramas include: *Cain*, 1943. *The Trial of Thomas Cranmer*, 1956. *The Jesse Tree: A Masque in Verse*, 1970. *The Lambton Worm*, 1978. Her poems explore religious themes and celebrate human experience, notably marriage and motherhood. Her poetry publications include: *Poems*, 1939. *The New Bright Shiners*, 1945. *The Golden Bird*, 1951. *Some Time After*, 1972. *Collected Poems*, 1994. Some of her poems: "At Christmas," "At Parting," "Before Sleep," "For a Child Expected," "Poem for a Christmas Broadcast," "The Speech of the Dead," "Venetian Scene."

Sources: *A Sacrifice of Praise: An Anthology of Christian Poetry in English from Caedmon to the Mid-Twentieth Century.* James H. Trott, ed. Cumberland House Publishing, 1999. *Chaos of the Night: Women's Poetry and Verse of the Second World War.* Catherine W. Reilly, ed. Virago Press, 1984. *Encyclopædia Britannica Ultimate Reference Suite DVD*, 2006. *Guardian Unlimited, In Memoriam, Anne Ridler* (http://books.guardian.co.uk/departments/poetry/story/0, 6000,581905,00.html). *Oldpoetry* (www.oldpoetry.com). *Portraits of Poets*. Sebastian Barker, ed. Carcanet, 1986. *The Columbia Granger's Index to Poetry.* 11th ed. *The Columbia Granger's World of Poetry*, Columbia University Press, 2005 (http://www.columbiagrangers.org). *The Oxford Companion to English Literature*. 6th edition. Margaret Drabble, ed. Oxford University Press, 2000. *Women's Poetry of the 1930s: A Critical Anthology*. Jane Dowson, ed. Routledge, 1966.

RILEY, JOHN (1937–1978)

Born and raised in Leeds, Yorkshire, he served in the Royal Air Force from 1956 to 1958, graduated from Pembroke College, Cambridge, in 1961, then worked as a teacher in the Cambridge area. There he became associated with the Cambridge Group of the British Poetry Revival, with poets such as Andrew Crozier and Peter Riley (see entries). In 1968 he moved from Cambridge to teach near Oxford, and in the same year he co-founded the Grosseteste Press and started the magazine *Grosseteste Review*. He retired from teaching and returned to Leeds in 1970 to be a full-time writer. He was robbed and kicked to death at night near his home. Riley's poetry was influenced by the Black Mountain poets of North Carolina and by the Russian essayist and poet Osip Mandelshtam (1891–1938), whose poetry he translated into English. His *Collected Works* (1980) includes the first full printing of his important long poem *Czargrad*. Some of his poems: "A Sequence," "After the Music," "I shall not weary you with poems," "Pentecost," "Quiet, willows and primulas are growing," "Views of Where One Is," "Waves lap against rock."

Sources: *A Various Art.* Andrew Crozier and Tim Longville, eds. Carcanet Press, 1987. *Selected Poems of John Riley.* Michael Grant, ed. Carcanet Press, 1995. *The Columbia Granger's Index to Poetry.* 11th ed. *The Columbia Granger's World of Poetry,* Columbia University Press, 2005 (http://www.columbiagrangers.org). *The Yorkshire Post 28th October 1978* (John Riley's murder) (http://www.ypn.co.uk/). *Wikipedia, the Free Encyclopedia* (http://en.wikipedia.org/wiki/Wikipedia).

RILEY, PETER (1940–)

Born in Stockport, Cheshire, he studied at Pembroke College, Cambridge, and the universities of Keele and Sussex, and has taught at the University of Odense, Denmark. Since 1975 he has lived as a freelance writer, English teacher and book-seller, first in the Peak District of England and then in Cambridge. He is one of the Cambridge Group of the British Poetry Revival, with poets such as Andrew Crozier and John Riley (see entries). His poetry has appeared in ten principal collections. His long poem *Alstonefield* (2003) explores the small village on the Derbyshire side of Staffordshire. It is in the Peak District and specifically in the White Peak part of that district; it lies between the rivers Dove and Manifold and is largely a farming community. His other poetry collections: *Longings of the Acrobats,* 1990. *Lorand Gaspar,* 1993 (four long poems from French). *Snow Has Settled,* 1997. *Passing Measures,* 2000. Some of his poems: "Eight Preludes," "Excavations," "Lines on the Liver," "One Day," "Toy Instruments: A Song," "Window Piece."

Sources: *A Various Art.* Andrew Crozier and Tim Longville, eds. Carcanet Press, 1987. *Anthology of Twentieth-Century British and Irish Poetry.* Keith Tuma, ed. Oxford University Press, 2001. *Biography of Peter Riley* (http://au.geocities.com/masthead_2/issue6/biogs6.html). *Electronic Poetry Review #6 — Seven Transylvanian Songs* (http://www.epoetry.org/issues/issue6/text/cnotes/pr.htm). *Other: British and Irish Poetry since 1970.* Richard Caddel and Peter Quartermain, eds. Wesleyan University Press, 1999. *The Columbia Granger's Index to Poetry.* 11th ed. *The Columbia Granger's World of Poetry,* Columbia University Press, 2005 (http://www.columbiagrangers.org). Carcanet Press (http://www.carcanet.co.uk).

RIORDAN, MAURICE (1953–)

Born in Lisgoold, County Cork, Ireland, he was educated at University College, Cork, and McMaster University in Canada, and emigrated to England, where he now teaches at Goldsmiths College, London. He is the author of two books of poetry: *A Word from Loki* (1995), which was short listed for a T.S. Eliot Prize and was a Poetry Book Society Choice; and *Floods* (2000), short-listed for the Whitbread Prize. He edited, with science journalist Jon Turney, *A Quark for Mister Mark: 101 Poems about Science* (2000); and with John Burnside (see entry), *Wild Reckoning* (2004), an anthology of ecological poems to mark the fortieth anniversary of *Silent Spring* by Rachel Carson (American zoologist and biologist, 1907–1964). His *Confidential Reports,* translations of the Maltese poet Immanuel Mifsud, was published in 2005. *The Moon Has Written You a Poem: Poems to Read with Children on Moonlit Nights,* adapted from the Portuguese of José Letria, was also published in 2005. In 2004 he was selected as one of the Poetry Society's "Next Generation" poets and in 2005 he became poetry editor of *Poetry London.* Three of his poems: "Milk," "The January Birds," "Time Out."

Sources: *Biography of Maurice Riordan* (http://www.munsterlit.ie/Conwriters/Maurice%20Riordan.htm). *British Council Arts* (http://www.contemporarywriters.com). *Emergency Kit: Poems for Strange Times.* Jo Shapcott and Matthew Sweeney, eds. Faber and Faber, 1996. *Modern Irish Poetry.* Patrick Crotty, ed. The Blackstaff Press, 1995. *The January Birds by Maurice Riordan* (http://www.thepoem.co.uk/poems/riordan.htm).

RITSON, JOSEPH (1752–1803)

Born at Stockton-on-Tees, Cleveland, he trained as a solicitor, moved to London in 1775 and set up his own conveyancing practice in Grays Inn, then was called to the bar in 1789. On reading *Fable of the Bees* (1723) by Bernard de Mandeville (1670–1733), he became a vegetarian, existing solely on milk and vegetables. In 1772 he contributed to the *Newcastle Miscellany* verses addressed with some freedom to the ladies of Stockton. In 1782 he published *Obser-*

vations on the three first volumes of the History of English Poetry by Thomas Warton (see entry). His nit-picking criticism was offensive and created a literary storm; Sir Walter Scott engaged Ritson's help when he was compiling *Border Minstrelsy of the Scottish Border* (1802–1803). Ritson died insane; he barricaded himself in and set fire to his manuscripts. They buried him at Bunhill Fields, London. Some of his other publications: *Select Collection of English Songs*, 1783. *Ancient Songs from the time of King Henry the Third to the Revolution*, 1792. *English Anthology*, 1795. *Robin Hood, a Collection of all the Ancient Poems, Songs, and Ballads now extant relating to that celebrated English Outlaw*, 1795.

Sources: *History of Vegetarianism* (http://www.ivu.org/history/renaissance/mandeville.html). *Biography of Joseph Ritson* (http://online.northumbria.ac.uk/faculties/art/humanities/cns/m-ritson.html). *The Oxford Companion to English Literature*. 6th edition. Margaret Drabble, ed. Oxford University Press, 2000.

ROBERTS, LYNETTE (1909–1995)

Born Evelyn Beatrice in Buenos Aires, Argentina, of Welsh heritage parents, Spanish speaking Roberts came to Britain after the World War I. She was educated at the Central School of Art and then Constant Spry's School of Craft and Floristry. She married the journalist Keidrych Rhys in 1939, with Dylan Thomas as the best man. They settled in Llanybri, the small Carmarthenshire hamlet on the Laugharne side of the Llansteffan peninsular. The 1940s was a period of great creativity in painting and poetry, often during periods of ill heath. Rhys was called up during the war and the couple divorced in 1949, and there was an acrimonious battle for custody of the two children. Her final years were spent at a nursing home, where she died and was buried at Llanybri, Dyfed, Wales. Her three poetry publications: *Gods with stainless ears: an heroic poem*, 1951. *Poems*, 1944. *Collected Poems*, 2005. Some of her poems: "Low Tide," "Poem from Llanybri," "The Circle of C," "The Shadow Remains," "These Words I Write on Crinkled Tin," "To a Welsh Woman."

Sources: *Anglo-Welsh Poetry, 1480–1980*. Raymond Garlick and Roland Mathias, eds. Poetry Wales Press, 1984. *Anglo-Welsh Poetry, 1480–1990*. Raymond Garlick and Roland Mathias, eds. Poetry Wales Press, 1993. *The British Library* (http://www.bl.uk/collections/britirish/modbriroberts.html). *The Chatto Book of Modern Poetry 1915–1955*. Cecil Day Lewis and John Lehmann, eds. Chatto and Windus, 1966. *The Columbia Granger's Index to Poetry*. 11th ed. *The Columbia Granger's World of Poetry*, Columbia University Press, 2005 (http://www.columbiagrangers.org). *The New British Poets: An Anthology*. Kenneth Rexroth, ed. New Directions, 1949.

ROBERTS, MICHAEL SYMMONS (1963–)

Born in Preston, Lancashire, he read philosophy and theology at Oxford University, has worked as a producer and director of documentaries for the BBC, and still writes extensively for radio and television. His work for radio includes *Last Words*, commissioned by BBC Radio 4 to mark the first anniversary of 9/11. He regularly collaborates with composer James MacMillan as librettist on song cycles, choral works, music theatre pieces and operas, and he has worked with other composers, including James Whitbourn and John Harle. His first novel, *Patrick's Alphabet*, was published in 2006. His poetry publications: *Soft Keys*, 1993. *Raising Sparks*, 1999. *Burning Babylon*, 2001 (short listed for the T.S. Eliot Prize). *Corpus*, 2004 (short listed for the Best Poetry Collection of the Year; for the T.S. Eliot Prize, and for the Whitbread Poetry Award). Some of his poems: "Angel of the Perfumes," "Flesh," "Food for Risen Bodies," "Jairus."

Sources: *British Council Arts* (http://www.contemporarywriters.com). *Griffin Poetry Prize, 2005. Michael Symmons Roberts* (http://www.griffinpoetryprize.com/shortlist_2005.php?t=5). *Angel of the Perfumes, by Michael Symmons Roberts* (http://www.jeanettewinterson.com/pages/content/index.asp?PageID=230). *Jairus, by Michael Symmons Roberts*. http://www.poetryarchive.org/poetryarchive/singlePoem.do?poemId=3486.

ROBERTS, MICHAEL (WILLIAM EDWARD) (1902–1948)

Born in Bournemouth, Dorset, he lived on a farm in the New Forest, read chemistry at King's College, London, then mathematics at Trinity College, Cambridge, where he adopted the forename Michael. He graduated in 1925 and spent most of his working life teaching mathematics, physics and English literature at the Royal Grammar School in Newcastle-upon-Tyne. During World War II he worked for the BBC's European Service, organizing broadcasts to occupied countries. He returned to education in 1945 as principal of the College of St. Mark and St. John, an Anglican teacher-training college then based in London. In August of 1948 he was diagnosed with the leukemia that led to his death in December of that year. His poetry publications: *These Our Matins*, 1930. *Poems*, 1936. *Orion Marches*, 1939. The anthologies he edited: *New Signatures*, 1932. *New Countries*, 1933. *The Faber Book of Modern Verse*, 1936. *The Faber Book of Comic Verse*, 1942. Some of his poems: "H.M.S. Hero," "Hymn to the Sun," "In Our Time," "Midnight," "St. Gervais," "St. Ursanne," "The Caves," "The Green Lake."

Sources: *Collected Poems of Michael Roberts*. Faber and Faber, 1958. *The National Portrait Gallery* (www.npg.

org.uk). *The Chatto Book of Modern Poetry 1915–1955.* Cecil Day Lewis and John Lehmann, eds. Chatto and Windus, 1966. *The Columbia Granger's Index to Poetry.* 11th ed. *The Columbia Granger's World of Poetry,* Columbia University Press, 2005 (http://www.columbiagrangers.org). *The Faber Book of Children's Verse.* Janet Adam Smith, ed. Faber and Faber, 1953. *The Oxford Book of Twentieth-Century English Verse.* Philip Larkin, ed. Oxford University Press, 1973. *The Oxford Companion to English Literature.* 6th edition. Margaret Drabble, ed. Oxford University Press, 2000.

ROBERTS, MICHÈLE BRIGITTE (1949–)

Born in Hertfordshire, England, to a French Catholic mother and an English Protestant father, she studied at Somerville College, Oxford, and University College, London. She worked as a librarian for the British Council in Bangkok (1973–1974) and was poetry editor for *Spare Rib* (1974) and *City Limits* magazine (1981–1983). She was visiting fellow in creative writing at the University of East Anglia in 1992, where she is currently professor of creative writing and research fellow in writing (1995–96) at Nottingham Trent University (now visiting professor). She is chair of the British Council literature advisory panel and is a regular book reviewer and broadcaster. She is the author of ten novels, has written short stories and her play *The Journeyman* was first performed in 1988. Her literary awards includes Chevalier de l'Ordre des Arts et des Lettres (2000). She has published two collections of poetry: *The Mirror of the Mother: Selected Poems 1975–1985* (1986) and *All the Selves I Was: New and Selected Poems* (1995). Some of her poems: "After My Grandmother's Death," "Demeter Grieving," "Inconsistencies," "Madwoman at Rodmell," "Out of Chaos Out of Order Out," "The Spell."

Sources: *Ain't I a Woman! A Book of Women's Poetry from Around the World.* Illona Linthwaite, ed. Peter Bedrick Books, 1988. *Bread and Roses: An Anthology of Nineteenth- and Twentieth-Century Poetry by Women Writers.* Diana Scott, ed. Virago Press, 1982. *British Council Arts* (http://www.contemporarywriters.com). *The Columbia Granger's Index to Poetry.* 11th ed. *The Columbia Granger's World of Poetry,* Columbia University Press, 2005 (http://www.columbiagrangers.org). *The Light from Another Country: Poetry from American Prisons.* Joseph Bruchac, ed. The Greenfield Review Press, 1984. *The New British Poetry, 1968–88.* Gillian Allnutt, Fred D'Aguiar and Ken Edwards, eds. Grafton Books, 1989. *The New Exeter Book of Riddles.* Kevin Crossley-Holland and Lawrence Sail, eds. Enitharmon Press, 1999. *The Oxford Companion to English Literature.* 6th edition. Margaret Drabble, ed. Oxford University Press, 2000.

ROBERTS, WILLIAM HAYWARD (d. 1791)

Said to be of Gloucestershire origin, he was educated at Eton, graduated B.A. from King's College,

Cambridge, in 1757, and created doctor of divintiy at Cambridge in 1773. He was rector of two parishes: Everdon, Northamptonshire, and Farnham Royal, Buckinghamshire, before being appointed provost of Eton College in 1781 (where he died). He was also one of the chaplains to King George III. He had been twice married and at Eton he was said to have engaged in high and riotous living. His known poetry publications: *A Poetical Essay on the Existence, the Attributes, and the Providence of God,* 1771. *A Poetical Epistle to Christopher Anstey, Esq., on the English Poets, chiefly those who have written in Blank Verse,* 1773. *Poems,* 1774. *Judah Restored, a poem in six books and in blank verse,* 1774. Some of his poems: "Arimant and Tamira, An Eastern Tale," "The Poor Man's Prayer, Addressed to the Earl of Chatham," "To G.A.S., Esq. on His Leaving Eton School," "To Jacob Bryant, Esq.," "To the Jews," "To the Rev. Dr. Barnard, Provost of Eton College."

Sources: *Dictionary of National Biography.* Electronic Edition 1.1. Oxford University Press, 1997. *English Poetry: Author Search.* Chadwyck-Healey Ltd., 1995 (http://www.lib.utexas.edu:8080/search/epoetry/author.html). *Stanford University Libraries and Academic Information Resources* (http://library.stanford.edu).

ROBERTSON, ROBIN (1955–)

Raised on the northeast coast of Scotland, he now lives and works in London. In 2004, he was named by the Poetry Book Society as one of the "Next Generation" poets. He received the E.M. Forster Award from the American Academy of Arts and Letters. His poems have appeared in the *New Yorker,* the *Times Literary Supplement, Grand Street,* the *London Review of Books,* and other publications. He edited *Mortification: Writers' Stories of Their Public Shame,* published by Fourth Estate, 2003. More than eighty writers tell their stories, revealing their various foibles with humor rather than regret. Each new excerpt is prefaced by an apt quotation, a pithy addition to an already enjoyable sojourn through the embarrassment of others. Some of his poetry publications: *A Painted Field,* 1997 (won the Alderburgh Poetry Festival Prize and the Forward Poetry Prize [Best First Collection]; and the Saltire Society Scottish First Book of the Year Award). *Slow Air,* 2002. *Actaeon: The Early Years,* 2006. *Swithering,* 2006. Some of his poems: "Aberdeen," "At Dawn," "Crossing the Archipelago," "Feeding the Fire," "Trumpeter Swan," "Waves," "Wedding the Locksmith's Daughter."

Sources: *Biography of Robin Robertson* (http://www.griffinpoetryprize.com/trustees.php?t=6). *British Council Arts* (http://www.contemporarywriters.com). *Firebird 3: Writing Today.* Robin Robertson, ed. Penguin Books 1984. *Firebird 4: New Writing from Britain and Ireland.* Robin

Robertson, ed. Penguin Books 1985. *Penguin Modern Poets 13.* Robin Robertson, Michael Hofmann and Michael Longley, eds. Penguin Books, 1998. *Poetry 180: A Turning Back to Poetry.* Billy Collins, ed. Random House Trade Paperbacks, 2003. *The Columbia Granger's Index to Poetry.* 11th ed. *The Columbia Granger's World of Poetry,* Columbia University Press, 2005 (http://www.columbiagrangers. org). *The New Penguin Book of Scottish Verse.* Robert Crawford and Mick Imlah, eds. Penguin Books, 2000. *The New York Review of Books: Robin Robertson* (http://www.ny books.com/articles/article-preview?article_id=17314).

ROBINSON, MARY (1758–1800)

Mary Darby, of Irish descent, the daughter of a sea captain, was born at Bristol, and in 1774 she married Thomas Robinson. His promise of wealth was a fiction and the family spent ten months in debtors' prison. The poetry she wrote there gained her the patronage of the Duchess of Devonshire. From 1776 to 1780 she was on the stage and after her performance as Perdita in Shakespeare's *Winter's Tale* (1778) she became the mistress of the Prince of Wales (later George IV). He tired of her and she was left to support herself through an annuity granted by the Crown (in return for some letters written by the Prince). Thereafter she devoted herself to writing drama and poetry, some written under the pseudonyms of "Perdita" or "Horace Juvenal." She died, crippled and impoverished, in Surrey, and was buried in Old Windsor churchyard. Some of her publications: *Poems,* 1775. *The Songs, Chorusses, &c,* 1778. *Modern Manners,* 1793. *The Poetical Works,* 1806. Some of her poems: "Absence," "Horatian Ode," "Ode to the Nightingale," "The Haunted Beach," "The Progress of Liberty," "To the Muse of Poetry."

Sources: *Dictionary of National Biography.* Electronic Edition 1.1. Oxford University Press, 1997. *English Poetry: Author Search.* Chadwyck-Healey Ltd., 1995 (http://www. lib.utexas.edu:8080/search/epoetry/author.html). *Poems: 1791 of Mary Robinson.* Woodstock Books, 1994. *Romantic Women Poets: An Anthology.* Duncan Wu, ed. Blackwell Publishers, 1997. *Stanford University Libraries and Academic Information Resources* (http://library.stanford. edu). *The Columbia Granger's Index to Poetry.* 11th ed. *The Columbia Granger's World of Poetry,* Columbia University Press, 2005 (http://www.columbiagrangers.org). *The National Portrait Gallery* (www.npg.org.uk). *The New Oxford Book of Romantic Period Verse.* Jerome J. McGann. Oxford University Press, 1993. *The Oxford Companion to English Literature.* 6th edition. Margaret Drabble, ed. Oxford University Press, 2000.

ROBINSON, PETER (1953–)

The son of a vicar, he was born in Salford, Lancashire, and brought up mostly in Bootle and Garston, Liverpool. In 1996 he edited the anthology *Liverpool Accents: Seven Poets and a City,* in tribute to the place he still calls home. After graduating from York University in 1974, he edited the poetry

magazine *Perfect Bound,* helped organize several Cambridge International Poetry Festivals, and in 1988 was advisor to the *Poetry International* at the South Bank Centre, London. He taught for a while at the University of Wales, Aberystwyth, and at Cambridge University. He now lives with his family in Japan, where he teaches English literature and English as a second language at Tohoku University in Sendai. Some of his other poetry publications: *Overdrawn Account,* 1980. *This Other Life,* 1988. *Entertaining Fates,* 1992. *Leaf-viewing,* 1992. *Lost and Found,* 1997. *Anywhere You Like,* 2000. *About Time Too,* 2001. *Selected Poems,* 2003. Some of his poems: "Cleaning," "How He Changes," "Liverpool ... Of All Places," "Lost Objects," "More About the Weather," "Surfaces of Things," "The Happiness Plant," "'Their Fears,'" "Winter Interiors."

Sources: *Books by Peter Robinson* (http://charles.sal.to hoku.ac.jp/robinson/books.html). *Peter Robinson's Selected Poems, 2003* (http://charles.sal.tohoku.ac.jp/peternew book.htm). *The Poetry Kit Interviews Peter Robinson* (http://www.poetrykit.org/iv/robinson.htm). *Wikipedia, the Free Encyclopedia* (http://en.wikipedia.org/wiki/ Wikipedia). *Winter Interiors by Peter Robinson* (http:// www.webdelsol.com/Perihelion/robinsonpoetry.htm).

ROCHESTER, JOHN WILMOT 2ND EARL (1647–1680)

The son of Henry Wilmot, first earl of Rochester, he was born at Ditchley, Oxfordshire, and succeeded to the title in 1657. He was educated at Wadham College, Oxford, and created M.A. in 1661. He served with credit with Vice-Admiral Sir Thomas Teddeman on board HMS *Royal Katherine* and later under Admiral Sir Edward Spragge on the *Victory.* When he was 18 he abducted the heiress Elizabeth Malet, who later married him. At the court of Charles II he quickly gained the reputation of a philanderer and for drunken debauchery. Rochester wrote satires and lampooned just about everyone, yet is a witty and entertaining poet. His biting tongue spared neither Charles nor the royal mistresses, and he was frequently dismissed and reinstated. He patronized many poets (including John Dryden), but was scathingly critical of many others. He died young, after a deathbed conversion, and was buried in the north aisle of Spelsbury church in Oxfordshire. Some of his poems: "A Ramble in Saint James's Parke," "A Satire on Charles II," "Farewell to the Court," "Sodom; or the Quintessence of Debauchery," "The Bully," "The Mistress."

Sources: *Dictionary of National Biography.* Electronic Edition 1.1. Oxford University Press, 1997. *Invitation to Poetry: A Round of Poems from John Skelton to Dylan Thomas.* Lloyd Frankenberg, Doubleday, 1956. *The National Portrait Gallery* (www.npg.org.uk). *The Cavalier*

Poets. Robin Skelton, ed. Oxford University Press, 1970. *The Columbia Granger's Index to Poetry*. 11th ed. *The Columbia Granger's World of Poetry,* Columbia University Press, 2005 (http://www.columbiagrangers.org). *The New Oxford Book of Seventeenth Century Verse.* Alastair Fowler, ed. Oxford University Press, 1991. *The Oxford Book of Satirical Verse.* Geoffrey Grigson, ed. Oxford University Press, 1980. *The Oxford Book of Short Poems.* P.J. Kavanagh and James Michie, eds. Oxford University Press, 1985. *The Oxford Companion to English Literature.* 6th edition. Margaret Drabble, ed. Oxford University Press, 2000. *The Penguin Book of Homosexual Verse.* Stephen Coote, ed. Penguin Books, 1983. *The Poems of John Wilmot, Earl of Rochester.* Shakespeare Head Press, 1984.

RODD, SIR JAMES RENNELL, 1ST BARON RENNELL (1858–1941)

Born in London, the son of an officer in the Duke of Cornwall's Light Infantry, he graduated from Balliol College, Oxford, in 1880. A high-flyer in the diplomatic service, in 1884 he was attaché to Berlin and in 1885 third secretary. His biography *Frederick, Crown Prince and Emperor* (1888) created diplomatic ripples. He served in Athens, Rome, Paris, British East Africa, Egypt and Ethiopia. In 1899 he was made Knight Commander of the Order of St. Michael and St .George, and Knight Grand Cross of the Victorian Order in 1905. He retired from the diplomatic service in 1921 and in 1933 was raised to the peerage as Baron Rennell of Rodd, in the county of Hereford. He died at Ardath, Shamley Green, Surrey. Some of his poetry publications: *Raleigh,* 1880. *Songs in the South,* 1881. *Poems in Many Lands,* 1886. *The Unknown Madonna,* 1888. *Ballads of the Fleet,* 1901. *War Poems,* 1940. Some of his poems: "A Last Word," "A Roman Mirror," "A Song of Autumn," "In the Alps," "On the Border Hills," "Sea Pictures — France."

Sources: *Dictionary of National Biography.* Electronic Edition 1.1. Oxford University Press, 1997. *The National Portrait Gallery* (www.npg.org.uk). *Stanford University Libraries and Academic Information Resources* (http://library.stanford.edu). *The Columbia Granger's Index to Poetry.* 11th ed. *The Columbia Granger's World of Poetry,* Columbia University Press, 2005 (http://www.columbiagrangers.org). *The Home Book of Verse.* Burton Egbert Stevenson, ed. New York: Henry Holt and Company, 1953. *The Oxford Book of Victorian Verse.* Arthur Quiller-Couch, ed. Oxford University Press, 1971.

RODGER, ALEXANDER (1784–1846)

Scottish poet, born at Mid-Calder, Midlothian, the son of a farmer and inn-keeper in Mid-Calder. He became a handloom weaver in Glasgow in 1797. He married in 1806 and in 1819 joined the staff of the Glasgow weekly newspaper *The Spirit of the Union.* For its seditious tone the editor was transported for life; Rodger was imprisoned and used his time to write poetry and revolutionary songs. From 1821 to 1832 he was an inspector of the cloths used for printing and dyeing in Barrowfield print-works, Glasgow, then later he worked for the *Reformer's Gazette.* A public dinner was held in his honor in 1836, at which he was presented with a silver box filled with sovereigns. He was buried in Glasgow necropolis and a handsome monument was erected to him. Some of his publications: *A Word of Advice,* 1816. *Shaving Banks,* 1818. *Scotch Poetry,* 1821. *Peter Cornclips,* 1827. *Poems and Songs,* 1838. *The Devil's Visit to the Islands of Japan,* 1838. *Stray Leaves,* 1842. Some of his poems: "Here's to You Again," "Highland Politicians," "Dear is Our Hame," "Sanct Mungo," "The Twa Weavers," "The Waefu' Lamentation."

Sources: *Alexander Rodger: The Devil's Visit to the Islands of Japan: A Tale Translated from the Japanese, 1838* (http://themargins.net/anth/19thc/rodger.html). *Dictionary of National Biography.* Electronic Edition 1.1. Oxford University Press, 1997. *English Poetry,* Second Edition Bibliography (http://collections.chadwyck.co.uk/html/ep2/bibliography/r.htm). *English Poetry: Author Search.* Chadwyck-Healey Ltd., 1995 (http://www.lib.utexas.edu:8080/search/epoetry/author.html). *New Coasts and Strange Harbors: Discovering Poems.* Helen Hill and Agnes Perkins, eds. Thomas Y. Crowell Co., 1974. *Scottish Poetry Selection: Here's to You Again, Alexander Rogers* (http://www.rampantscotland.com/poetry/blpoems_toddle.htm). *Selected Work of Alexander Rodger* (http://quartet.cs.unb.ca/tapor/cgi-bin/view-works.cgi?c=rodgeral.1112&pos=3). *Stanford University Libraries and Academic Information Resources* (http://library.stanford.edu). *The Columbia Granger's Index to Poetry.* 11th ed. *The Columbia Granger's World of Poetry,* Columbia University Press, 2005 (http://www.columbiagrangers.org). *The Home Book of Verse.* Burton Egbert Stevenson, ed. New York: Henry Holt and Company, 1953. *The Poorhouse Fugitives: Self-Taught Poets and Poetry in Victorian Britain.* Brian Maidment, ed. Carcanet, 1987.

RODGERS, WILLIAM ROBERT (1909–1969)

Irish poet, prose essayist, book reviewer, radio broadcaster, script writer, lecturer and teacher, known as W.R., he was born in Belfast and ordained as a Presbyterian minister at Loughgall, County Armagh, in 1935. He resigned from the ministry in 1946 and joined the BBC in London, for whom he wrote radio programs about Ireland and the Irish poets. From 1966 to 1968, he was writer in residence at Pitzer College in Claremont, California, then moved to a similar position at California State Polytechnic College. He died in Los Angeles in 1969 and was buried at the site of his first ministry in Ireland. His *Collected Poems* appeared in 1971. Some of his poems: "Apollo and Daphne," "Beagles," "Resurrection: An Easter Sequence," "Scapegoat," "Stormy Night," "The Airman," "The Fountains," "The Train," "White Christmas."

Sources: *Awake! And Other Wartime Poems.* Harcourt Brace, 1942 (these poems, written between 1938 and 1940, were originally sent to press in London in 1940, and the first printing was entirely destroyed by German bombs.) (*Tomfolio.com: Poetry: Poets QZ*). *Contemporary Irish Poetry: An Anthology.* Anthony Bradley, ed. University of California Press. New and rev. ed., 1988. *Erotic Poetry: The Lyrics, Ballads, Idyls, and Epics of Love—Classical to Contemporary.* William Cole, ed. Random House, 1963. *Little Treasury of Modern Poetry: English and American.* 3d ed. Oscar Williams, ed. Scribner's, 1970. *Poets from the North of Ireland.* Frank Ormsby, ed. The Blackstaff Press, 1990. *Public Records Office of Northern Ireland* (http://www.proni.gov.uk/research/academic/strength.htm). *The Columbia Granger's Index to Poetry.* 11th ed. *The Columbia Granger's World of Poetry,* Columbia University Press, 2005 (http://www.columbiagrangers.org). *The War Poets: An Anthology of the War Poetry of the 20th Century.* Oscar Williams, ed. John Day, 1945. *William Robert Rodgers: The Susquehanna Quarterly.* (http://susquehannaquarterly.org/rodgers.htm).

ROGERS, SAMUEL (1763–1855)

Born at Stoke Newington, London, the son of a banker, when he inherited the family business in 1793, he became a major part of London society. His interest in Napoleon Bonaparte's Italian spoils in the Louvre made him a connoisseur. In 1803 he built a mansion in St. James's Street, Westminster, which became the meeting place for people of literature, many of whom he patronized, such as the young Sir Henry Taylor (see entry). In 1844 his bank was robbed of forty thousand pounds in notes and a thousand pounds in gold, although most of the notes were later recovered. He was buried in Hornsey churchyard with his brother Henry and his sister Sarah. Some of his publications: *An Ode to Superstition, with some Other Poems,* 1786. *The Pleasures of Memory,* 1792. *Epistle to a Friend,* 1798. *The Voyage of Columbus,* 1810. *Human Life,* 1819. *Italy,* 1822. Some of his poems: "An Epitaph on a Robin Redbreast," "Campagna of Rome," "The Alps at Day-Break," "The Brothers," "The Harper," "To the Gnat," "Written in the Highlands of Scotland."

Sources: *A Treasury of Minor British Poetry.* J. Churton Collins, ed. Edward Arnold, 1896. *Dictionary of National Biography.* Electronic Edition 1.1. Oxford University Press, 1997. *Encyclopædia Britannica Ultimate Reference Suite DVD,* 2006. *English Poetry: A Poetic Record, from Chaucer to Yeats.* David Hopkins, ed. Routledge, 1990. *Fellow Mortals: An Anthology of Animal Verse.* Roy Fuller, ed. Macdonald and Evans, 1981. *Poetical Works of Samuel Rogers.* Kessinger Publishing Co., 2004. *The Columbia Granger's Index to Poetry.* 11th ed. *The Columbia Granger's World of Poetry,* Columbia University Press, 2005 (http://www.columbiagrangers.org). *The Complete Poetical Works of Samuel Rogers.* Epes Sargent, ed. Phillips, Sampson, and Company, 1854. *The Oxford Companion to English Literature.* 6th edition. Margaret Drabble, ed. Oxford University Press, 2000.

ROGERSON, JOHN BOLTON (1809–1859)

Born in Manchester, Lancashire, from the age of thirteen he had several different jobs: solicitor, bookshop owner, and registrar of the North Manchester cemetery at Harpurhey. An amateur actor, he was president for some years of the Manchester Shakespearean Society and for a short time was on the staff of the Manchester Theatre Royal. He wrote *The Baron of Manchester,* a three-act play, and lectured on literary and educational subjects. Chronic rheumatism disabled him about 1855 from continuing his duties as registrar. He afterwards kept a tavern in Newton Street, Ancoats, Manchester, and in 1857 was master of a school at Accrington. In 1856 he was awarded a government pension, upon which he retired to the Isle of Man, where he died and was interred at Kirk Braddan, near Douglas. His verses were published in several Lancashire newspapers and magazines. His poetry publications: *Rhyme, Romance, and Revery,* 1852. *A Voice from the Town, and Other Poems,* 1843. *The Wandering Angel, and Other Poems,* 1844. *Poetical Works,* 1850. *Flowers for all Seasons,* 1854. *Musings in Many Moods,* 1859.

Sources: *Dictionary of National Biography.* Electronic Edition 1.1. Oxford University Press, 1997. *Harpurhey—Districts and Suburbs of Manchester, U.K.: John Bolton Rogerson* (http://www.manchester2002-uk.com/districts/harpurhey.html). *The Columbia Granger's Index to Poetry.* 11th ed. *The Columbia Granger's World of Poetry,* Columbia University Press, 2005 (http://www.columbiagrangers.org). *The Poorhouse Fugitives: Self-Taught Poets and Poetry in Victorian Britain.* Brian Maidment, ed. Carcanet, 1987.

ROLLAND, JOHN (fl. 1560)

Scottish poet who was possibly the son of John Rolland, sub-dean of Glasgow in 1481. He is known to have been a priest in Glasgow, to have been acting as a notary in Dalkeith, Midlothian, in 1555, and to have turned Protestant around 1560. His two major poems are *The Court of Venus,* in four books, thought to date from the reign of James V (1527–1542); and *The Seven Sages* (1560), which went through several reprints. One of the books contains 17,784 lines. Three of his other known poems: "The Author Says to the Book," "To the Reader," "The Prologue."

Sources: *Dictionary of National Biography.* Electronic Edition 1.1. Oxford University Press, 1997. *The Columbia Granger's Index to Poetry.* 11th ed. *The Columbia Granger's World of Poetry,* Columbia University Press, 2005 (http://www.columbiagrangers.org). *Wikipedia, the Free Encyclopedia* (http://en.wikipedia.org/wiki/Wikipedia).

ROLLE, RICHARD, OF HAMPOLE (?1300–1349)

Yorkshire-born mystical poet whose fees at Oxford University were paid by Thomas de Neville, archdeacon of Durham. He left Oxford at the age of nineteen and became a wandering hermit, finally settling at Hampole, near Doncaster, Yorkshire, near the Cistercian nunnery of St. Mary, founded by William de Clairefai in 1170. People flocked to his cell, and when he died they continued to visit his grave, where miracles were reported. He translated into English the Psalms and extracts from Job and Jeremiah. He wrote treatises in Latin and his English works were written in the Northumbrian dialect. His chief English work is the religious poem of nearly 10,000 lines, *Pricke of Conscience*, written in rhyming couplets, with many quotations from scripture and from the church fathers. His *Paraphrases of the Psalms and Canticles* was published at the Clarendon Press in 1884. Some of his poems: "A Charme for the Tethe-Werke," "Almyghty God in Trinite," "Fadir and Sone and Haly Gaste," "Hail Ihesu, My Creatowre, of Sorowyng Medicine," "Ihesu, Thi Swetnes Wha Moghte It Se," "Lorde Ihesu Cryste, Godd Almyghty," "My Trewest Tresowre Sa Trayturly Taken."

Sources: *A Sacrifice of Praise: An Anthology of Christian Poetry in English from Caedmon to the Mid-Twentieth Century.* James H. Trott, ed. Cumberland House Publishing, 1999. *Poets of the English Language. Vol. I,.* W.H. Auden and Norman Holmes Pearson, eds. Viking Press, 1950. *Richard Rolle, Translated by Rosamund Allen.* Paulist Press International, U.S., 1999. *The Columbia Granger's Index to Poetry.* 11th ed. *The Columbia Granger's World of Poetry,* Columbia University Press, 2005 (http://www.columbiagrangers.org). *The Harper Anthology of Poetry.* John Frederick Nims, ed. Harper and Row, 1981. *The Oxford Book of Christian Verse.* Lord David Cecil, ed. Oxford University Press, 1940. *The Oxford Companion to English Literature.* 6th edition. Margaret Drabble, ed. Oxford University Press, 2000.

ROSCOE, WILLIAM, WILLIAM STANLEY, and WILLIAM CALDWELL (1753–1859)

William, the father, 1753–1831

Lawyer, banker, book collector historian, botanist and benefactor, he was born Mount Pleasant, Liverpool, the son of a market-gardener. In October 1806 he was elected Whig member of Parliament for Liverpool, and his stand against the slave trade created many enemies. In 1816 the bank suspended trading and in 1820 he and the partners were declared bankrupt. In 1817 he was chosen the first president of the Liverpool Royal Institution, and in 1824 he was elected an honorary associate of the Royal Society of Literature, and was afterwards awarded its gold medal. He died from influenza and was buried in the ground attached to the chapel on Renshaw Street, Liverpool. Two of his historical books

are: *The Life of Lorenzo dé Medici* (1795) and *The Life of Leo X* (1805). In 1819 he published *Observations on Penal Jurisprudence*, advocating milder punishments as efficacious in reforming the criminal. His poetry publications: *Mount Pleasant*, a descriptive poem, 1777. *Ode on the Institution of a Society of Art in Liverpool*, 1777. *The Nurse*, 1804. *The Butterfly's Ball and the Grasshopper's Feast*, 1806 (set to music by Sir George Smart for the young princesses Elizabeth, Augusta, and Mary, daughters of George III). *The Wrongs of Africa*, 1787.

William Stanley, the son, 1782–1843

Educated at Peterhouse, Cambridge, he became a partner in his father's bank. When the bank failed, like his father he was bankrupt. In order to pay his creditors, the father sold off his priceless library, something his son portrays in "On Being Forced to Part with His Library." Like his father he studied languages, particularly Italian, literature and poetry. *Poems by William Stanley Roscoe* was published in 1834. He carried on his father's work against the slave trade and developed a passion for the cause of the Polish patriots, expressed in *On the Last Regiment of Polish Patriots Being Ordered by the French Government to Serve in the Island of St. Domingo* (1834) (Polish soldiers fought under Tadeusz Kosciuszko during the Polish Revolution of 1794, when 2/3 were killed.) In his latter years he was sergeant-at-mace to the court of passage at Liverpool (the mayor's attendant who is the only person entitled to touch the mace, carrying it before the civic head to and from meetings of the full council and other civic occasions). Some of his other poems: "A Dirge," "On the Death of an Infant Boy," "Sonnet to My Father," "The Camellia," "The Prisoner of War," "To a Favorite Myrtle," "To Spring: On the Banks of the Cam," "To the Harvest Moon."

William Caldwell, the grandson, 1823–1859

He was educated privately and graduated from University College, London, in 1843, and was called to the bar in 1850, but after two years relinquished practice, partly for health reasons and partly from doubts that law was his vocation. He married in 1855 and afterwards lived principally in Wales, where he was interested in slate quarries and devoted much of his time to literary pursuits. He died of typhoid fever at Richmond, Surrey. He published two tragedies, *Eliduc* (1846) and *Violenzia* (1851), a considerable amount of fugitive poetry, and numerous essays. His two poetry publications are *Poems* (1860) and *Poems* (1891). Some of his poems: "A Christmas Sonnet," "A Nightingale in Eastbury Woods," "After the Hungarian War," "Love's Creed," "Opportunity," "Parting," "Spiritual Love," "The Poetic Land."

Sources: *A Century of Sonnets: The Romantic-Era Revival, 1750–1850.* Paula R. Feldman and Daniel Robinson, eds. Oxford University Press, 1999. *Dictionary of National Biography.* Electronic Edition 1.1. Oxford University Press, 1997. *English Poetry: Author Search.* Chadwyck-Healey Ltd., 1995 (http://www.lib.utexas.edu:8080/search/epoetry/author.html). *Folk Songs.* John Williamson Palmer, ed. Charles Scribner and Company, 1867. *The National Portrait Gallery* (www.npg.org.uk). *Roscoe, "On the Last Regiment."* (http://www2.bc.edu/~richard/asp/wsrlr.html#int). *Stanford University Libraries and Academic Information Resources* (http://library.stanford.edu). *The Columbia Granger's Index to Poetry.* 11th ed. *The Columbia Granger's World of Poetry,* Columbia University Press, 2005 (http://www.columbiagrangers.org). *The Home Book of Verse.* Burton Egbert Stevenson, ed. New York: Henry Holt and Company, 1953. *The Oxford Book of Victorian Verse.* Arthur Quiller-Couch, ed. Oxford University Press, 1971. *The Oxford Companion to English Literature.* 6th edition. Margaret Drabble, ed. Oxford University Press, 2000.

ROSE, WILLIAM STEWART (1775–1843)

The son of the statesman George Rose (1744–1818), he was educated at Eton College, then from 1800 to 1924 he was clerk of the House of Lords and clerk of the private committees. In 1802 he published only the first volume of *A Naval History of the Late War,* seemingly written to please his father. In 1803 he published a rhymed version of the first three books of the *Amadis,* translated from Spanish into French by Herberay des Essarts (circa 1557). When Sir Walter Scott and Rose met in 1803 they became friends and Scott addressed his "Marion" to Rose. Rose's volume of poems, *The Crusade of St. Louis,* was published in 1810, and his translation of *Orlando Furioso,* by Ludovico Ariosto (1474–1533), was published in volumes between 1823 and 1831. On retirement through ill health he spent some time at Abbotsford, Sir Walter Scott's home, and at Brighton, Sussex. Some of his poems: "Edward the Martyr," "Gundimore," "Prologue," "Sonnet I, To a Pine-Tree," "The Court and Parliament of Beasts," "The Dean of Badajos," "The Talisman," "Thessalian Witcheries."

Sources: *Dictionary of National Biography.* Electronic Edition 1.1. Oxford University Press, 1997. *English Poetry: Author Search.* Chadwyck-Healey Ltd., 1995 (http://www.lib.utexas.edu:8080/search/epoetry/author.html). *Orlando Furioso, the Translation by William Stewart Rose* (http://omacl.org/Orlando).

ROSEN, MICHAEL WAYNE (1946–)

Born in Harrow, North London, of Jewish parents who were both teachers, he graduated in English from Wadham College, Oxford. In 1993, he gained an M.A. in children's literature from Reading University and a Ph.D. from University of London in 1997. He has worked for the BBC on *Play School,* schools TV and radio drama, and is now a freelance writer, broadcaster, lecturer and performer who has made a name for himself as a children's writer and as the presenter of BBC Radio 4's regular magazine program *Word of Mouth.* He was one of the first poets to visit schools throughout the U.K., as well as in Australia, Canada and Singapore, making poetry accessible to young people. He has won several children's poetry awards. Some of his publications: *Mind Your Own Business,* 1974. *We're Going on a Bear-Hunt,* 1989. *Walking on the Bridge of Your Nose,* 1997. *Lunch Boxes Don't Fly,* 1999. *Centrally Heated Knickers,* 2000. Some of his poems: "Chocolate Cake," "Down Behind the Dustbin," "Dear New Labour*," "From the Three Trains and the 30 Bus*," "Humpty Dumpty," "Three Songs of the Dead*." (*These three poems were written after the terrorist bombings in London on 7 July 2005.)

Sources: *Biography of Michael Rosen: Bloomsbury.com, Children's Authors* (http://www.bloomsbury.com/childrens/microsite.asp?id=635&section=3). *Classic Poetry: An Illustrated Collection.* Michael Rosen, ed. Paul Howard (Illustrator). Walker Books Ltd., 1998. *Michael Rosen: Three Songs of the Dead, 16Jul05, Socialist Worker* (http://www.socialistworker.co.uk/article.php4?article_id=6964). *Michael Rosen's Book of Very Silly Poems.* Puffin Books, 1996. *Microsoft Encarta* 2006 (DVD). Microsoft Corporation, 2006. *Poemhunter* (www.poemhunter.com). *Splinters: A Book of Very Short Poems.* Michael Harrison, ed. Oxford University Press, 1989. *The Columbia Granger's Index to Poetry.* 11th ed. *The Columbia Granger's World of Poetry,* Columbia University Press, 2005 (http://www.columbiagrangers.org). *The Kingfisher Book of Children's Poetry.* Michael Rosen, ed. Kingfisher Books, 1985. *The New Exeter Book of Riddles.* Kevin Crossley-Holland and Lawrence Sail, eds. Enitharmon Press, 1999. *Two poems by Michal Rosen* (http://www.thediagram.com/4_5/rosen.html). *Who's Who.* London: A & C Black, 2005. *Wikipedia, the Free Encyclopedia* (http://en.wikipedia.org/wiki/Wikipedia).

ROSENBERG, ISAAC (1890–1918)

He was born in Bristol to a Lithuanian Jewish couple, and when he was seven, the family moved to Whitechapel, London, where his father worked as a pedler and market dealer. Isaac served an apprenticeship as an engraver and studied painting at evening classes at Birkbeck College, London, and was inspired by reading the works of the great poets. In 1911 three Jewish women paid for him to attend the Slade School of Fine Art, London, where he won several prizes. In 1915 he enlisted in the Army; he was drafted into the King's Own Royal Lancaster Regiment and sailed for France in 1916. The anti–Semitism he experienced in the Army is expressed in several of his poems. He was killed on the western front and buried in an unmarked grave, and is memorialized by a stone in Poets' Corner of Westminster Abbey along with other poets of the First World War. His *Collected Works,* with a foreword by Siegfried Sassoon (see entry), was published in 1937. Some of his poems: "Break of Day in the Trenches," "Louse Hunting," "Moses," "Night and Day," "Returning, We Hear the Larks," "The Unicorn."

Sources: *A Treasury of Jewish Poetry.* Nathan Ausubel and Maryann Ausubel, eds. Crown, 1957. *Dictionary of National Biography.* Electronic Edition 1.1. Oxford University Press, 1997. *Encyclopædia Britannica Ultimate Reference Suite DVD,* 2006. *Golden Treasury of the Best Songs and Lyrical Poems in the English Language.* Francis Turner Palgrave, ed. Oxford University Press, 1964, Sixth edition, updated by John Press, 1994. *Selected Poems and Letters of Isaac Rosenberg.* Jean Liddiard, ed. Enitharmon Press, 2003. *The Columbia Granger's Index to Poetry.* 11th ed. *The Columbia Granger's World of Poetry,* Columbia University Press, 2005 (http://www.columbiagrangers.org). *The Norton Anthology of Poetry.* 4th ed. Margaret Ferguson, Mary Jo Salter and Jon Stal, eds. W.W. Norton, 1996. *The Oxford Companion to English Literature.* 6th edition. Margaret Drabble, ed. Oxford University Press, 2000. *The Penguin Book of First World War Poetry.* Jon Silkin, ed. Penguin Books, 1979. *Westminster Abbey Official Guide* (no date).

ROSENSTOCK, GABRIEL (1949–)

Irish poet born in Kilfinane, County Limerick, of an Irish mother and German father. He is the author or translator of over 100 books, mostly in Irish, and his translations include thousands of haiku poems of Japanense into Irish, as well as bhakti poems of India. He works as an assistant editor for the Irish-language publishing house *An Gúm.* He has given readings of his poetry and haiku in Wales, Scotland, England, Switzerland, Austria, Germany, Italy, USA, India, Australia and Japan. *Rogha Rosenstock* (1994) is a selection from ten volumes of poetry. His children's poetry was published as *Dánta Duitse* (1998). His most recent collection is *Krisnmurphy Ambaist'!* (2004). A member of many literary societies and organizations, he has been widely published abroad. He lives in Dublin and is a member of Aosdána. Some of his poems: "African Queen," "April Gusts," "Archaeological Find," "Baghdad," "Fata Morgana in Flanders," "Full Moon," "I Was a Beggar," "In a Transylvanian Mud-Bath," "Were I a Little Bird."

Sources: *Biography and Poems of Gabriel Rosenstock:* (http://www.poetry-chaikhana.com/R/RosenstockGa/). *The Columbia Granger's Index to Poetry.* 11th ed. *The Columbia Granger's World of Poetry,* Columbia University Press, 2005 (http://www.columbiagrangers.org). *Turning Tides: Modern Dutch and Flemish Verse in English Versions by Irish Poets.* Peter van de Kamp, ed. Story Line Press, 1994. *World Haiku Review (WHR) Photo-Haiku Gallery,* *Gabriel Rosenstock* (http://www.worldhaikureview.org/3–2/rosenstock-photohaiku/pages/biography.html).

ROSS, ALAN (1922–2001)

Born in Calcutta, where he spent the first seven years of his life, he was educated in Falmouth, Cornwall, then went up to St. John's College, Oxford, in 1940 to read modern languages; there he also represented the university at both cricket and squash. From 1941 to 1947, he was in the Royal Navy, saw service on the Russian convoys and ended as interpreter to the British Naval commander in chief, Germany. After the war he became a journalist and started writing travel books, and in 1949 he married Jennifer Fry, the heiress of the chocolate company. He was sports writer for *The Observer* in 1950, cricket correspondent in 1953, then editor of the *London Magazine* from 1961 until he died. *The Derelict Day, Poems from Germany* (1947) and *Something of the Sea: Poems 1942–52* (1954) reflect his experience of the war. *J.W. 51BA Convoy* celebrates the heroism and the exhilaration, as well as the horror, of a naval battle, and is considered the finest narrative poem of World War II. Some of his poems: "At Only That Moment," "Cricket at Oxford," "Destroyers in the Arctic," "Mess Deck Casualty," "Stanley Matthews," "Survivors," "The Boathouse."

Sources: *A Literature of Sports.* Tom Dodge, ed. D.C. Heath and Company, 1980. *Erotic Poetry: The Lyrics, Ballads, Idylls, and Epics of Love—Classical to Contemporary.* William Cole, ed. Random House, 1963. *Golden Treasury of the Best Songs and Lyrical Poems in the English Language.* Francis Turner Palgrave, ed. Oxford University Press, 1964, Sixth edition, updated by John Press, 1994. *Peace and War: A Collection of Poems.* Michael Harrison and Christopher Stuart-Clark, eds. Oxford University Press, 1989. *The Columbia Granger's Index to Poetry.* 11th ed. *The Columbia Granger's World of Poetry,* Columbia University Press, 2005 (http://www.columbiagrangers.org). *The New Yorker Book of Poems.* The New Yorker editors. Viking Press, 1969. *The Oxford Companion to English Literature.* 6th edition. Margaret Drabble, ed. Oxford University Press, 2000. *Wikipedia, the Free Encyclopedia* (http://en.wikipedia.org/wiki/Wikipedia).

ROSS, ALEXANDER (1591–1654)

Born at Aberdeen and educated at King's College, Aberdeen, around 1616 he became the headmaster of the free school at Southampton, Hampshire, England, and was vicar for twenty-six years at St. Mary's Church, Southampton (the church that inspired the ballad *The Bells of St. Mary,* words by Douglas Furber, music by Emmett Adams, 1917, and sung by Bing Crosby in the 1946 film by the same name). He became vicar of Carisbrooke on the Isle of Wight in 1642, and he died at Bramshill, Hampshire. In his will he left money to the poor householders of All Saints' parish, Southampton, to the parish of Carisbrooke for the poor; the universities of Aberdeen, Oxford and Cambridge also received legacies. It is said that after he died, a small fortune in gold was discovered among his books. Ross wrote many books, mostly very small, in English and Latin. His favorite subjects were theology, history, and philosophy, and he produced a considerable amount of verse. Some of his poems: "Ænæas," "Æsculapius," "Cyclops," "Endymeon," "Fortuna," "Ganimedes," "Gratiæ," "Three Decads of Divine Meditations."

Sources: *Dictionary of National Biography.* Electronic Edition 1.1. Oxford University Press, 1997. *English Poetry: Author Search.* Chadwyck-Healey Ltd., 1995 (http://www.lib.utexas.edu:8080/search/epoetry/author.html). *Stanford University Libraries and Academic Information Resources* (http://library.stanford.edu).

ROSS, ALEXANDER (1699–1784)

Born to a farmer from Aberdeenshire, he went on a bursary to Marischal College, Aberdeen, in 1714, and graduated M.A. in 1718. For some time afterwards he was tutor to the family of Sir William Forbes of Craigievar and Fintray, then taught in the schools at Aboyne, Aberdeenshire, and Laurencekirk, Kincardineshire. In 1732 he became schoolmaster at Lochlee, Forfarshire, where he spent the remainder of his life. He died at Lochlee and was buried there. Ross was a poetic disciple of Allan Ramsay (see entry), whose *The Gentle Shepherd* seems to have inspired Ross in his highly popular *Helenore, or The Fortunate Shepherdess*, a pastoral tale in three cantos — written in the Scottish dialect — which contains pleasant descriptions of country life and scenery. He also wrote witty songs, among them "The Rock and the Wee Pickle Tow, Wooed and Married and A" and "The Bridal O."

Sources: *Dictionary of National Biography.* Electronic Edition 1.1. Oxford University Press, 1997. *Significant and Famous Scots* (http://www.electricscotland.com/history/other/ross_alexander2.htm). *The Burns Encyclopedia, Alexander Ross* (http://www.robertburns.org/encyclopedia/index-r.shtml). *The Columbia Granger's Index to Poetry.* 11th ed. *The Columbia Granger's World of Poetry,* Columbia University Press, 2005 (http://www.columbiagrangers.org). *The Oxford Book of Scottish Verse,* John MacQueen and Tom Scott, eds. Oxford University Press, 1966. *The Oxford Companion to English Literature.* 6th edition. Margaret Drabble, ed. Oxford University Press, 2000.

ROSS, THOMAS (d. 1675)

A near relative of Alexander Ross (1591–1654), he was educated at Charterhouse School and graduated B.A. from Christ's College, Cambridge, in 1642–1643. An adherent of Charles II in his exile, he was involved in political intrigues of that period. About 1658 he became tutor to James Scott (afterwards

Duke of Monmouth), the king's natural son. His conspiracies worked against him, for at the Restoration, he was removed and given some sinecure. He was created M.A. at Oxford in 1663, and the following year he acted as secretary to Henry Coventry (1619–1686) when the latter was sent on an embassy to the court of Sweden. There is a reference in *Sailing Navies, 1650–1674* (http://www.sailingnavies.com/show_chronology.php?t=0) to one Thomas Ross, and a suggestion in the DNB that Ross was in the Navy. So it is possible that he died at sea. Some of his poems: "An Essay Upon the Third Punique War," "Silius Italicus of the Second Punick War," "The Phenix," "Theodosius His Advice to His Son," "To the Death of Hannibal," "To the King."

Sources: *Dictionary of National Biography.* Electronic Edition 1.1. Oxford University Press, 1997. *English Poetry: Author Search.* Chadwyck-Healey Ltd., 1995 (http://www.lib.utexas.edu:8080/search/epoetry/author.html). *Stanford University Libraries and Academic Information Resources* (http://library.stanford.edu). *The Oxford Book of Classical Verse in Translation.* Adrian Poole, and Jeremy Maule, ed. 1995.

ROSS, WILLIAM (1762–1790)

Born on the Island of Skye, his father, a peddler, ensured his son had a good education. Later the family moved Gairloch, Ross-shire, his mother's native place. In the course of traveling with his father, Thomas became proficient in the Gaelic dialects of the western highlands, and the scenes and the character of the highlands found expression in his poetry. He was an accomplished musician; he both sang well and played with skill on several instruments. He was appointed parish schoolmaster at Gairloch, where he was popular and successful. He died at 28, it is said, from a broken heart, after being rejected by Marion Ross of Stornoway, Isle of Lewis. His poem "Praise of the Highland Maid" was written in praise of his lost love. Two volumes of his Gaelic poems were published: Orain Ghae'lach' (1830) and *An dara clòbhualadh* (1834). Some of his other poems: "Conversation Between the Bard and Blaven," "Elegy for Prince Charlie," "The Bard's Advice to the Young Maidens," "The Bard's Lament for His Darling," "The Black Laddie," "The Braes of Glen Broom," "The Cuckoo of the Branches."

Sources: *Dictionary of National Biography.* Electronic Edition 1.1. Oxford University Press, 1997. *Gaelic Songs of William Ross.* Oliver and Boyd, 1937. *The Columbia Granger's Index to Poetry.* 11th ed. *The Columbia Granger's World of Poetry,* Columbia University Press, 2005 (http://www.columbiagrangers.org). *The New Penguin Book of Scottish Verse.* Robert Crawford and Mick Imlah, eds. Penguin Books, 2000.

ROSSETTI, DANTE GABRIEL and CHRISTINA GEORGINA (1828–1894)

Gabriel, the brother, 1828–1882

He was born in London, where his Italian father was a teacher of Italian, then professor of Italian in King's College, London. He studied art at the Royal Academy, and in 1848, with Holman Hunt and Sir John Everest Millais, founded the Pre-Raphaelite Brotherhood, whose members found their inspiration in the religious and scrupulously detailed art of Raphael (1483–1520). Rossetti's reputation as a poet overtook that of the painter and two of his best-known poems, "The Portrait" and "The Blessed Damozel" were written in 1842. *The Early Italian Poets* (1861) contains some of his own translations and works from other Italian writers. He married in 1860 Elizabeth Eleanor Siddal (see entry) the model for many of his paintings; she died two years later from an overdose of laudanum. In 1881 he published *Ballads and Sonnets*, which contained "Rose Mary," "The White Ship," "The King's Tragedy," and the sonnet sequence "The House of Life." Some of his other poems: "A Young Fir-Wood," "Antwerp and Bruges," "At the Sun-Rise in 1848," "La Vita Nuova," "The Bride's Prelude," "Youth's Spring-Tribute."

Christina Georgina, the sister, 1830–1894

Born in London, her first recorded verses were printed in 1842 at her grandfather's private press, with a second volume in 1847. Her early poetry was published under the pseudonym Ellen Alleyne in the *Germ*, a pre-Raphaelite journal, although she was not a member of the movement. A high Anglican and profoundly religious woman, she wrote several religious tracts. An invalid for many years, she died in London of cancer and was buried at Highgate Cemetery, North London. The majority of her poems were religious in nature and some have become well-known hymns. She also wrote ballads, sonnets, love lyrics, and nonsense rhymes as well as children's stories. Some of her publications: *Goblin Market and Other Poems*, 1862. *Sing-Song, A Nursery Rhyme Book*, 1872. *The Prince's Progress*, 1881. *A Pageant and Other Poems*, 1881. Some of her poems: "In the Bleak Mid-Winter," "Later Life: A Double Sonnet of Sonnets," "Love Came Down At Christmas," "None Other Lamb," "The Convent Threshold," "The Will of the Lord Be Done," "Within the Veil," "Yea, I Have a Goodly Heritage," "Yet a Little While," "Zara."

Sources: *A Child's Treasury of Verse.* Eleanor Doan, ed. Zondervan Corporation, 1977. *Bread and Roses: An An-thology of Nineteenth- and Twentieth-Century Poetry by Women Writers.* Diana Scott, ed. Virago Press, 1982. *Collected Writings of Dante Gabriel Rossetti.* Jan Marsh, ed. New Amsterdam Books, 2000. *Dictionary of National Biography.* Electronic Edition 1.1. Oxford University Press, 1997. *Encyclopædia Britannica Ultimate Reference Suite DVD,* 2006. *English Poetry: Author Search.* Chadwyck-Healey Ltd., 1995 (http://www.lib.utexas.edu:8080/search/epoetry/author.html). *Golden Numbers.* Kate Douglas Wiggin and Nora Archibald Smith, eds. Doubleday, Doran, 1902. *Microsoft Encarta* 2006 (DVD). Microsoft Corporation, 2006. *The National Portrait Gallery* (www.npg.org.uk). *Poemhunter* (www.poemhunter.com). *Poetry,* Jill P. Baumgaertner, ed. Harcourt, Brace, Jovanovich, 1990. *The Columbia Granger's Index to Poetry.* 11th ed. *The Columbia Granger's World of Poetry,* Columbia University Press, 2005 (http://www.columbiagrangers.org). *The Complete Poems of Christina Rossetti.* R.W. Crump, ed. Louisiana State University Press. Vol. 1, 1979; Vol. 2, 1986; Vol. 3, 1990. *The Cyber Hymnal* (http://www.cyberhymnal.org/index.htm). *The Early Italian Poets.* Sally Purcell, ed. Anvil Press Poetry, 1981. *The Oxford Companion to English Literature.* 6th edition. Margaret Drabble, ed. Oxford University Press, 2000. *Victorian Verse.* George MacBeth, ed. Penguin Books, 1986.

ROWE, NICHOLAS (1674–1718)

Born at Little Barford, Bedfordshire, the son of a London barrister, he was educated at Westminster School. He was called to the bar but disliked law, and when his father died in 1692, leaving him well provided for, he decided to follow his heart into literature. His first blank-verse tragedy, *The Ambitious Stepmother,* was produced at Lincoln's Inn Fields in 1700. His second tragedy, *Tamerlane,* was produced in 1702 and played annually at Drury Lane Theatre on 5 November until 1815. Sir Walter Scott criticized it; Samuel Johnson praised it. He went on to produce many more dramas; his one attempt at a comedy, *The Biter* (1704), was a flop. He published a six-volume edition of Shakespeare's works in 1709 and was appointed poet laureate in 1715. His poetical works include a famous translation (1718) of the Roman poet Lucan (A.D. 39–65). Rowe was buried in Poets' Corner, Westminster Abbey, where a monument was erected to him with an epitaph by Alexander Pope. Some of his poems: "Colin's Complaint," "Mecaenas," "Ode for the King's Birth-day, 1718," "On Contentment," "Song, Ah Willow," "The Contented Shepherd," "The Union."

Sources: *Dictionary of National Biography.* Electronic Edition 1.1. Oxford University Press, 1997. *Encyclopædia Britannica Ultimate Reference Suite DVD,* 2006. *English Poets Laureate: Nicholas Rowe* (http://www.mala.bc.ca/~lanes/english/laureate/rowe.htm). *The National Portrait Gallery* (www.npg.org.uk). *The Columbia Granger's Index to Poetry.* 11th ed. *The Columbia Granger's World of Poetry,* Columbia University Press, 2005 (http://www.columbiagrangers.org). *The Oxford Book of Verse in English Trans-*

lation. Charles Tomlinson, ed. Oxford University Press, 1980. *The Oxford Companion to English Literature.* 6th edition. Margaret Drabble, ed. Oxford University Press, 2000. *The Works of Nicholas Rowe, Esq. Vol. 2.* J. and R. Tonson and S. Draper, 1756. *Westminster Abbey Official Guide* (no date).

ROWLANDS, SAMUEL (?1570–?1630)

Nothing is known of this poet, other than he was a writer of tracts in prose and verse between 1598 and 1628, many of them of a religious nature. *The Betraying of Christ* (1598) was fervently religious. His second publication, *The Letting of Humours Blood in the Head-Vaine* (1600), secured his popularity. It consists of thirty-seven epigrams and seven satires on the abuses of contemporary society, and private persons are attacked under assumed Latin names. *A Mery Meeting, or 'tis Mery when Knaves mete* (1600) along with the previous one, were condemned as offensive; both pamphlets were burned and twenty-nine booksellers were fined for buying these books. Not deterred, Rowlands republished them under different titles. Many of his poems describe the low life of London — beggars, tipplers, thieves, and swaggering bully-boys. Some of his other publications: *Democritus,* 1607. *The Knave of Clubs,* 1611. *The Melancholie Knight,* 1615. *The Bride,* 1617. *Good Newes and Bad Newes,* 1622. *Hell's Broke Loose,* 1695. Some of his poems: "A Foole and His Money is Soone Parted," "A Pocket-Picker Most Exceeding Braue," "An Vnkind Man, Kills the Heart of a Woman."

Sources: *Dictionary of National Biography.* Electronic Edition 1.1. Oxford University Press, 1997. *Elizabethan Lyrics.* Norman Ault, ed. William Sloane Associates, 1949. *English Poetry: Author Search.* Chadwyck-Healey Ltd., 1995 (http://www.lib.utexas.edu:8080/search/epoetry/author.html). *Invitation to Poetry: A Round of Poems from John Skelton to Dylan Thomas.* Lloyd Frankenberg, Doubleday, 1956. *The Columbia Granger's Index to Poetry.* 11th ed. *The Columbia Granger's World of Poetry,* Columbia University Press, 2005 (http://www.columbiagrangers.org). *The New Oxford Book of Sixteenth Century Verse.* Emrys Jones, ed. Oxford University Press, 1991. *The Oxford Book of Comic Verse.* John Gross, ed. Oxford University Press, 1994.

ROYDON, MATTHEW (?1580–1622)

Roydon's fame rests on the 39 six-lined stanzas in "An Elegy, or Friend's Passion for His Astrophil Written upon the death of the right Honorable Sir Philip Sidney knight, Lord governor of Flushing." He is thought to be the Matthew Roydon who graduated M.A. from Oxford in 1580. He was a prominent member of the London's literary circle of Thomas Lodge, Sir Philip Sidney, Christopher Marlowe, and George Chapman (see entries). He commemorates his friendship with Sidney in the above poem, which was first published in the *Phenix Nest*

(1593), then was printed with Spenser's *Astrophel* in Spenser's *Colin Clout* (1595) and in all later editions of Spenser's works. The poem was praised by Thomas Nashe (see entry). Francis Meres, in his *Palladis Tamia,* (1598) describes Roydon as worthy of comparison with the great poets of Italy. George Chapman dedicated to him his *Shadow of Night* (1594) and Ovid's *Banquet of Sence* (1595). When he fell into poverty, Roydon was given a pension by Edward Alleyn, the actor and founder of Dulwich Hospital.

Sources: *Dictionary of National Biography.* Electronic Edition 1.1. Oxford University Press, 1997. *Elizabethan Lyrics.* Norman Ault, ed. William Sloane Associates, 1949. *The Columbia Granger's Index to Poetry.* 11th ed. *The Columbia Granger's World of Poetry,* Columbia University Press, 2005 (http://www.columbiagrangers.org). *The Penguin Book of Bird Poetry.* Peggy Munsterberg, ed. 1984. *The Phoenix Nest, Notes and Poem (1593)* (http://darkwing.uoregon.edu/~rbear/phoenix.html#Anelegiefor Astrophill).

RUSSELL, ARTHUR TOZER (1806–1874)

Clergyman and hymn-writer who translated many of Martin Luther's hymns, he was born at Northampton, the son of Thomas Russell, also a clergyman. He graduated bachelor of laws in 1830 from St. John's College, Cambridge, having been ordained a deacon in 1827. He was appointed vicar of Caxton, Cambridgeshire, in 1830, and his last appointment was rector of Southwick, Sussex, where he died. He contributed his first hymns to his father's *Collection of Hymns* (1813), which went through seventeen editions. In 1843 Russell published *Hymn Tunes, Original and Selected.* In all he produced about one hundred and forty original and one hundred and thirty translated hymns (some of which are in many current hymn books), as well as several sermons and essays. Many of his hymns were included in: *The Christian Life,* 1847. *Psalms and Hymns,* 1851. *The Choral Hymn-book,* 1861. *Book of Praise,* 1863 (by the Earl of Selborne, 1812–1895). Some of his hymn/poems: "The Lord Ascendeth Up on High," "In Thee Alone, O Christ, My Lord," "O Jesus We Adore Thee," "O Lamb of God Most Holy," "To Him Who for Our Sins Was Slain."

Sources: *Dictionary of National Biography.* Electronic Edition 1.1. Oxford University Press, 1997. *The Cyber Hymnal* (http://www.cyberhymnal.org/index.htm).

RUSSELL, THOMAS (1762–1788)

Born at Beaminster, Dorset, into a prosperous family of shipping merchants and ship-owners from Weymouth, he was educated at Winchester College, graduated B.A. from New College, Oxford, in 1784, and was ordained deacon in 1785 and priest in 1786.

His promising career was cut short by what was probably tuberculosis. He died at Bristol and was buried in the churchyard of Powerstock, Dorset. Russell was inspired by Edmund Spenser, John Milton, and John Dryden (see entries). *Sonnets and Miscellaneous Poems by the late Thomas Russell, Fellow of New College* was published in 1789. In this he wrote many sonnets and his work inspired many other poets. William Wordsworth (see entry) not only wrote with warm appreciation of Russell's genius as a sonneteer, but uses four lines from Russell to close his own sonnet "Iona." Some of his poems: "A Christian is a Man Who Feels," "Lay of Ancient Rome," "Ode to Work in Springtime," "The Names and Order of the Books of the Old Testament," "To a Violet," "To Delia," "To Silence," "To Zephyr."

Sources: *A Century of Sonnets: The Romantic-Era Revival 1750–1850.* Paula R. Feldman and Daniel Robinson, ed. Oxford University Press, 1999. *A Second Treasury of the Familiar.* Ralph L. Woods, ed. Macmillan, 1950. *Dictionary of National Biography.* Electronic Edition 1.1. Oxford University Press, 1997. *English Poetry: Author Search.* Chadwyck-Healey Ltd., 1995 (http://www.lib.utexas.edu: 8080/search/epoetry/author.html). *Innocent Merriment: An Anthology of Light Verse.* Franklin P. Adams, ed. McGraw-Hill, 1942. *The Columbia Granger's Index to Poetry.* 11th ed. *The Columbia Granger's World of Poetry,* Columbia University Press, 2005 (http://www.columbia grangers.org). *The Home Book of Modern Verse.* Burton Egbert Stevenson, ed. Henry Holt, 1953. *The Oxford Book of Eighteenth Century Verse.* David Nichol Smith, ed. Oxford University Press, 1926. *The Oxford Book of Sonnets.* John Fuller, ed. Oxford University Press, 2000. *The Penguin Book of the Sonnet: 500 Years of a Classic Tradition in English.* Phillis Levin, ed. Penguin Books, 2001. *What Cheer: An Anthology of American and British Humorous and Witty Verse.* David McCord, ed. Coward-McCann, 1945.

SACKVILLE, CHARLES, SIXTH EARL OF DORSET (1638–1706)

The son of the fifth earl (he succeeded to the title in 1677), he was elected to Parliament for East Grinstead, Sussex, in 1660. In 1662, he, with four others, was indicted for killing and robbing a tanner named Hoppy. Their defense was that they mistook him for a highwayman. He served under the Duke of York at the naval battle off Harwich, Essex, against the Dutch in 1665, and wrote the song "To All You Ladies Now at Land." Nell Gynne and he were friends and when she became the mistress of Charles II, Sackville was sent to France. William of Orange made him Lord Chamberlain (1689) and knight of the Garter (1692). He died at Bath and was interred in the family vault at Withyham, Sussex. His poems, together with those of Sir Charles Sedley (see entry), appeared in a *New Miscellany* (1701) and in *The Works of the Most Celebrated Minor Poets* (1749). Some of his other poems: "A Faithful Catalogue of

Our Most Eminent Ninnies," "A Song on Black Bess," "On the Countess of Dorchester," "The Duel of the Crabs."

Sources: *An Uninhibited Treasury of Erotic Poetry.* Louis Untermeyer, ed. Dial Press, 1963. *Anthology of Poems on Affairs of State: Augustan Satirical Verse, 1660–1714.* George de F. Lord, ed. Yale University Press, 1975. *Dictionary of National Biography.* Electronic Edition 1.1. Oxford University Press, 1997. *English Poetry: Author Search.* Chadwyck-Healey Ltd., 1995 (http://www.lib.utexas.edu:8080/ search/epoetry/author.html). *The National Portrait Gallery* (www.npg.org.uk). *Samuel Johnson's Lives of the English Poets,* 1779–1781 (http://www2.hn.psu.edu/Faculty/KKem merer/poets/preface.htm). *The Columbia Granger's Index to Poetry.* 11th ed. *The Columbia Granger's World of Poetry,* Columbia University Press, 2005 (http://www.columbia grangers.org). *The Faber Book of English History in Verse.* Kenneth Baker, ed. Faber and Faber, 1988. *The Faber Book of Useful Verse.* Simon Brett, ed. Faber and Faber, 1981. *The Oxford Companion to English Literature.* 6th edition. Margaret Drabble, ed. Oxford University Press, 2000. *The Poems of Sir George Etherege.* James Thorpe, ed. Princeton University Press, 1963. *Wikipedia, the Free Encyclopedia* (http://en.wikipedia.org/wiki/Wikipedia).

SACKVILLE, LADY MARGARET (1881–1936)

Although Lady Margaret Sackville was a popular and prolific writer during the first half of the twentieth century, details about her life are scant. She was the daughter of Reginald Windsor Sackville, 7th Earl De La Warr, and a protégée of Wilfrid Scawen Blunt (see entry). She is noted for her anti-war poems of World War I. Her work was collected in a slim volume of essays by her friend Georgina Somerville in *Harp Aeolian: Commentaries on the Works of Lady Margaret Sackville* (1953). Some say that she is no longer a popular poet because she was born either too early or too late, and that she was out of step with her age. She wrote fairy tales, dramas and short stories as well as poems. Some of her publications: *A Hymn to Dionysus and Other Poems,* 1905. *Bertrud and Other Dramatic Poems,* 1911. *Selected Poems,* 1919. *100 Little Poems,* 1928. *Collected Poems of Lady Margaret Sackville,* 1939. *Country Scenes and Country Verse,* 1945. *Quatrains and Other Poems,* 1960. Some of her poems: "A Memory," "A Sermon," "An Apple," "Epitaph," "Resurrection."

Sources: *Biography of Lady Margaret Sackville.* (http:// www.bookrags.com/biography-lady-margaret-sackville- dlb/). *Scars Upon My Heart: Women's Poetry and Verse of the First World War.* Catherine W. Reilly, ed. Virago Press, 1981. *The Columbia Granger's Index to Poetry.* 11th ed. *The Columbia Granger's World of Poetry,* Columbia University Press, 2005 (http://www.columbiagrangers.org). *The Home Book of Modern Verse.* Burton Egbert Stevenson, ed. Henry Holt, 1953. *The Oxford Book of Victorian Verse.* Arthur Quiller-Couch, ed. Oxford University Press, 1971.

SACKVILLE, THOMAS, 1ST EARL OF DORSET (1536–1608)

English statesman, poet, and dramatist, remembered largely for his share in the development of Elizabethan poetry and drama. The only son of Sir Richard Sackville, he was born at Buckhurst, Withyham, Sussex, and probably educated at Oxford. He settled in London around 1553 and in 1558 became a barrister of the Inner Temple, London, of which his father was governor. In 1566 his father died and he was created Baron Buckhurst in 1567 and earl of Dorset in 1604. He held several high positions: as member of the Privy Council he conveyed the death sentence to Mary, Queen of Scots, in 1586; chancellor of Oxford University; and Lord High Treasurer. He wrote *Complaint of Buckingham, for a Myrrour for Magistrates* (1563), and his *Induction*, the most famous part of the *Myrrour*, describes the poet's visit to the infernal regions, where he encounters figures representing forms of suffering and terror. He collaborated with Thomas Norton (see entry) in writing *the Tragedie of Gorboduc* (1561), the earliest known English drama in blank verse.

Sources: *Dictionary of National Biography.* Electronic Edition 1.1. Oxford University Press, 1997. *Encyclopædia Britannica Ultimate Reference Suite DVD,* 2006. The National Portrait Gallery (www.npg.org.uk). *The Anchor Anthology of Sixteenth Century Verse.* Richard Sylvester, ed. Doubleday/Anchor Books, 1974. *The Columbia Granger's Index to Poetry.* 11th ed. *The Columbia Granger's World of Poetry,* Columbia University Press, 2005 (http://www.co lumbiagrangers.org). *The Oxford Companion to English Literature.* 6th edition. Margaret Drabble, ed. Oxford University Press, 2000. *The Works of Thomas Sackville.* John Russell Smith, 1859.

SACKVILLE-WEST, VICTORIA MARY (1892–1962)

Related to Thomas Sackville (see entry) and known as Vita, she was born at Knole near Sevenoaks, Kent. Her father was created Baron Sackville in 1908. By the time she was eighteen, she had written eight novels (one in French) and five plays, all on historical themes. In 1913 she married Sir Harold Nicolson (Commander of the Order of St. Michael and St. George, 1920). One of her important books of the period leading up to the 1920s was *Knole and the Sackvilles* (1922), a history of her home and ancestors. She went on to write many more novels and biographies and two volumes of poetry, *Poems of West and East* (1917) and *Orchard and Vineyard* (1921). Her poems evoke the beauty of the English countryside and the rural year in Kent. Her love of gardening is legendary; she developed the famous gardens at her home, Sissinghurst Castle, which now belongs to the National Trust.

She was appointed Companion of Honor in 1948. She died of cancer. Some of her poems: "Absence," "Beechwoods at Knole," "Full Moon," "On the Lake," "September 1939," "The Aquarium, San Francisco," "The Garden."

Sources: *A New Treasury of Poetry.* Neil Philip, ed. Stewart, Tabori, and Chang, 1990. *Eerdman's Book of Christian Poetry.* Pat Alexander and Veronica Zundel, eds. William B. Eerdmans, 1981. *Microsoft Encarta 2006 (DVD).* Microsoft Corporation, 2006. *Moon is Shining Bright as Day: An Anthology of Good-humoured Verse.* Ogden Nash, ed. J.B. Lippincott, 1953. *The National Portrait Gallery* (www. npg.org.uk). *Poetry for Pleasure: A Choice of Poetry and Verse on a Variety of Themes.* Ian Parsons, ed. W.W. Norton, 1977. *Salt and Bitter and Good: Three Centuries of English and American Women Poets.* Cora Kaplan, ed. Paddington Press, 1975. *The Columbia Granger's Index to Poetry.* 11th ed. *The Columbia Granger's World of Poetry,* Columbia University Press, 2005 (http://www.columbia grangers.org). *The Oxford Companion to English Literature.* 6th edition. Margaret Drabble, ed. Oxford University Press, 2000. *Women's Poetry of the 1930s: A Critical Anthology.* Jane Dowson, ed. Routledge, 1966.

SALKELD, BLANAID (1880–1959)

Irish poet, dramatist, and actor, born in Chittagong, in what was then India but is now Pakistan, and grew up in Ireland. Salkeld's father, a doctor in the Indian Medical Service, introduced her to poetry at a young age, and when he was in India, she sent poems to him from Ireland; he had two volumes of these printed privately in Calcutta. Around 1908 she became an actor with the Abbey Players and played the lead role in George Fitzmaurice's three-act play *The Country Dressmaker* (1907). Her verse play *Scarecrow Over the Corn* was staged in 1941 at the Gate Theatre. She contributed numerous book reviews to *The Dublin Magazine,* reviewing a wide range of books. She focused especially on contemporary poetry and used her review writing to promote an interest in poetry by women, especially Irish women. Her poetry publications: *Hello, Eternity,* 1933. *The Fox's Covert,* 1935. *The Engine is Left Running,* 1937. *A Dubliner,* 1942. *Experiment in Error,* 1955. Some of her poems: "Anchises," "Evasion," "Leave Us Religion," "Men Walked To and Fro," "No Uneasy Refuge," "Now is Farewell," "Optimism," "Youth."

Sources: *A Celebration of Women Writers: Plays Produced by the Abbey Theatre Company* (http://digital.library.upenn. edu/women/gregory/theatre/appendix-I.html). *An Anthology of Irish Verse: The Poetry of Ireland from Mythological Times to the Present.* Padraic Colum, ed. Liveright, 1948. *New Irish Poets.* Devin A. Garrity, ed. Devin-Adair, 1948. *The Columbia Granger's Index to Poetry.* 11th ed. *The Columbia Granger's World of Poetry,* Columbia University Press, 2005 (http://www.columbiagrangers.org). *The Oxford Book of Irish Verse: XVIIth Century–XXth Century.* Donagh MacDonagh and Leenox Robinson, eds. Oxford

University Press, 1958. *Wikipedia, the Free Encyclopedia* (http://en.wikipedia.org/wiki/Wikipedia).

SANDYS, GEORGE (1578–1644)

The son of Edwin Sandys, archbishop of York, he was born at Bishopthorpe, Yorkshire, and educated at St. Mary Hall, Oxford University, but left without graduating. *The Relation of a Journey* (1615) is rich in description of his extensive journeys from 1610 to 1615. In 1621 he was appointed treasurer of the Virginian Company and sailed to America with the governor, Sir Francis Wyat. Sandys was twice member of the council, but seems to have been in conflict with his plantation neighbors and left Virginia around 1628 and joined the court of Charles I. He spent his last years at the home of a niece at Boxley Abbey, near Maidstone, where he died and was buried. His poetry prepared the way for the heroic couplet of Dryden and Alexander Pope. Some of his publications: *Christ's Passion*, 1640. *Ovid's Metamorphosis*, 1632. *A Paraphrase Upon the Divine Poems*, 1638. *A Paraphrase Upon the Song of Solomon*, 1641. Some of his other poems: "A Paraphrase Upon Job," "Hymn Written at the Holy Sepulchre in Jerusalem," "Judah in Exile Wanders," "To the King," "To the Queen," "Urania to the Queen."

Sources: *A Sacrifice of Praise: An Anthology of Christian Poetry in English from Caedmon to the Mid-Twentieth Century.* James H. Trott, ed. Cumberland House Publishing, 1999. *American Hymns Old and New. Vols. 1 and 2.* Albert Christ-Janer and Charles W. Hughes, eds. Columbia University Press, 1980. *Chapters into Verse, Vol. I: Genesis to Malachi.* Robert Atwan and Laurance Wieder, eds. Oxford University Press. 1993. *Dictionary of National Biography.* Electronic Edition 1.1. Oxford University Press, 1997. *Encyclopædia Britannica Ultimate Reference Suite DVD*, 2006. *English Poetry: Author Search* (http://www.lib.utexas.edu:8080/search/epoetry/author.html). *Microsoft Encarta 2006* (DVD). Microsoft Corporation, 2006. *Stanford University Libraries and Academic Information Resources* (http://library.stanford.edu). *The Oxford Companion to English Literature.* 6th edition. Margaret Drabble, ed. Oxford University Press, 2000. *The Poetical Works of Sandys, George, Volumes 1 and 2.* George Olms, 1968.

SASSOON, SIEGFRIED LORAINE (1886–1967)

Born in Kent, the son of a Jewish father and Anglican mother, he was educated at Marlborough College and Clare College, Cambridge University. He served in France in World War I and won the Military Cross for his part in the Battle of the Somme; he later threw his medal into the River Mersey. His public denunciation of the futility of war brought him into conflict with the authorities and he was admitted to Craiglockhart War Hospital in Edinburgh, suffering from shellshock, and invalided out in 1918. He was appointed Commander of the British Empire in 1951 and was awarded the Queen's medal for poetry (1957) and honorary doctor of literature at Oxford (1965). Between his first volume of poetry, the *Daffodil Murderer* (1913), and his last, *Collected Poems 1908–1956* (1961), he published twenty-one other volumes. He died at Heytesbury (Wiltshire) and was buried in Mells churchyard, Somerset, and memorialized by a stone in Poets' Corner of Westminster Abbey along with other poets of the First World War. Some of his poems: "An Absentee," "At the Cenotaph," "Battalion-Relief," "Christ and the Soldier," "Farewell to Youth," "The English Spirit," "Vigils."

Sources: *Chief Modern Poets of Britain and America.* 5th edition. Gerald DeWitt Sanders, and John Herbert Nelson, eds., Macmillan, 1970. *Collected Poems: 1908–1956 of Siegfried Sassoon.* Faber and Faber, 1984. *Dictionary of National Biography.* Electronic Edition, 1.1. *Encyclopædia Britannica.* Electronic Edition, 2006. *Microsoft Encarta 2006* (DVD). Microsoft Corporation, 2006. *Obituary of Siegfried Sassoon. The Times*, September 4, 1967. *Poems That Live Forever.* Hazel Felleman, ed. Doubleday, 1965. *The Book of a Thousand Poems: A Family Treasury.* J. Murray Macbain, ed. Peter Bedrick Books, 1983. *The Columbia Granger's Index to Poetry.* 11th ed. *The Columbia Granger's World of Poetry,* Columbia University Press, 2005 (http://www.columbiagrangers.org). *The National Portrait Gallery* (www.npg.org.uk). *The Norton Anthology of Poetry.* 4th ed. Margaret Ferguson, Mary Jo Salter and Jon Stal, eds. W.W. Norton, 1996. *The Oxford Companion to English Literature.* 6th edition. Margaret Drabble, ed. Oxford University Press, 2000. *Westminster Abbey Official Guide* (no date). *Wikipedia, the Free Encyclopedia* (http://en.wikipedia.org/wiki/Wikipedia).

SAVAGE, RICHARD (1697–1743)

Savage's claim to be the illegitimate son of Anne, Countess of Macclesfield, and Richard Savage, the 4th Earl of Rivers, was thought to be no more an over-imaginative mind. He claimed that his mother disowned him and had him apprenticed to a shoemaker, that he might be brought up in obscurity and forgotten. Samuel Johnson, in *Account of the Life of Mr. Richard Savage* (1744), says that Savage spent long, dark hours watching his mother's house 'in hopes of seeing her as she might come by accident to the window, or cross her apartment with a candle in her hand.' Savage published *Miscellaneous Poems and Translations by Several Hands* in 1726. In 1727 he was convicted for the murder of a man in a tavern brawl and only saved from the gallows by the intervention of Frances Thynne, countess of Hertford, who obtained his pardon the following year. He died poverty-stricken in a Bristol prison. Some of his poems: "Epistle to Damon and Delia," "On False Historians," "The Authors of the Town," "The Bastard," "The Genius of Liberty," "The Progress of a Divine," "The Wanderer," "Valentine's Day."

Sources: *Dictionary of National Biography.* Electronic Edition 1.1. Oxford University Press, 1997. *Encyclopædia Britannica Ultimate Reference Suite DVD,* 2006. *English Poetry: Author Search.* Chadwyck-Healey Ltd., 1995 (http://www.lib.utexas.edu:8080/search/epoetry/author. html). *Samuel Johnson's Lives of the English Poets,* 1779–1781 (http://www2.hn.psu.edu/Faculty/KKemmerer/poets/pref ace.htm). *The Columbia Granger's Index to Poetry.* 11th ed. *The Columbia Granger's World of Poetry,* Columbia University Press, 2005 (http://www.columbiagrangers.org). *The New Oxford Book of Eighteenth Century Verse.* Roger Lonsdale, ed. Oxford University Press, 1984. *The Oxford Book of Satirical Verse.* Geoffrey Grigson, ed. Oxford University Press, 1980. *The Oxford Companion to English Literature.* 6th edition. Margaret Drabble, ed. Oxford University Press, 2000. *The Poetical Works of Richard Savage.* John Bell, 1791.

SAVAGE-ARMSTRONG, GEORGE FRANCIS (1845–1906)

Irish poet, born at Rathfarnham, Dublin, he graduated B.A. from Trinity College, Dublin, in 1869, having won the vice-chancellor's prize for an English poem for *Circassia.* In 1870 he was appointed professor of history and English literature in Queen's College, Cork. Trinity College conferred upon him the honorary degree of M.A. in 1872. He was made a fellow of the Royal University (1881) and in 1891 received the honorary degree of doctor of literature from the Queen's University. He continued his duties as professor at Cork and as examiner at the Royal University in Dublin until 1905. His poems have none of the Celtic mysticism of the later Irish school. He died at Strangford, County Down. His poetry publications: *Poems, Lyrical and Dramatic,* 1869. *Tragedy of Israel,* 1872–1877. *Poetical Works of Edmund J. Armstrong,* 1877. *Garland from Greece,* 1882. *Victoria Regina et Imperatrix: A Jubilee Song from Ireland,* 1887. *Queen-Empress and Empire,* 1897. *Ballads of Down,* 1901. Some of his poems: "The Father," "Autumn Memories," "My Guide," "One in the Infinite," "The Mystery."

Sources: *Bibliography of 19th-c. Irish Literature* (http://irish-literature.english.dal.ca/biblio-main.htm). *Dictionary of National Biography.* Electronic Edition 1.1. Oxford University Press, 1997. *Extracts from "Ulster-Scots: A Grammar of the Traditional Written and Spoken Language"* by Philip Robinson (published for the Ulster-Scots Language Society by the Ullans Press, 1997) (http://www.ulsterscots agency.com/05-grammerbook.asp). *Index to Authors: Christina Georgina Rossetti to William Butler* (http://www. bartleby.com/246/index24.html).

SAYERS, DOROTHY LEIGH (1893–1957)

Born in Oxford, the daughter of a clergyman, she graduated with a first class honors degree in modern languages from Somerville College, Oxford, in 1915, and from 1916 to 1931 she worked as a copy writer in an advertising agency. Her *Opus 1* (1916) — a collection of poems — was followed by *Catholic Tales and Christian Songs* (1918). The first of her famous detective stories, *Whose Body?*, featuring the dashing, witty aristocrat-detective Lord Peter Wimsey, was published in 1923. Her anthology of the detective story, *Omnibus of Crime,* was published in 1929. Between 1949 to 1962 she published a translation, from the Italian of Dante's *The Divine Comedy,* and her copious notes make the reading of this classic invaluable. One of her several plays, *Man Born to Be King* (1941), with Christ speaking modern English, broadcast on children's radio, produced a storm of protest. She received an honorary doctor of literature from Durham University in 1950. She died at Witham, Essex, of heart failure. Some of her other poems: "Devil to Pay," "The English War," "The Song of Roland," "War Cat."

Sources: *Biography of Dorothy L. Sayers* (http://www. kirjasto.sci.fi/dlsayers.htm). *Dictionary of National Biography.* Electronic Edition 1.1. Oxford University Press, 1997. *Dorothy L Sayers, Writer and Theologian* (http://jus tus.anglican.org/resources/bio/19.html). *Dorothy L. Sayers: Her Opus 1* (http://digital.library.upenn.edu/women/ sayers/opi/dls-opi.html). *Encyclopædia Britannica Ultimate Reference Suite DVD,* 2006. *Microsoft Encarta* 2006 (DVD). Microsoft Corporation, 2006. *Other Men's Flowers.* A.P. Wavell, ed. Jonathan Cape, 1990. *The Columbia Granger's Index to Poetry.* 11th ed. *The Columbia Granger's World of Poetry,* Columbia University Press, 2005 (http://www.columbiagrangers.org). *The Faber Book of War Poetry.* Kenneth Baker, ed. Faber and Faber, 1996. *The Oxford Companion to English Literature.* 6th edition. Margaret Drabble, ed. Oxford University Press, 2000. *The Treasury of Christian Poetry.* Lorraine Eitel, ed. Fleming H. Revell, 1982. *The Triumphant Cat.* Walter Payne, ed. Carrol and Graf, 1993.

SAYERS, FRANK (1763–1817)

Born in London, he was educated at North Walsham, Norfolk, where he was a contemporary of Admiral Lord Nelson, and at Palgrave, Suffolk, where he made the acquaintance of his lifelong friend William Taylor (see entry). He studied medicine in London and Edinburgh, graduated M.D. from Harderwyck, Netherlands, and returned to Norwich at the end of 1789. He abandoned medicine and entered upon a literary career; in 1790 he published the poems *Dramatic Sketches of Northern Mythology* and the tragedies *Moina, Starno,* and *The Descent of Frea.* A later version included "Ode to Aurora, Pandora." In 1803 he published *Nugæ Poeticæ,* chiefly versifications of *Jack the Giant-Killer* and *Guy of Warwick.* He also published learned treatises on Saxon literature and early English history. He died at Norwich and a mural monument was erected to his memory in Norwich Cathedral. Some of his other poems: "Ode to Bacchus," "Ode to Morning," "The Constant Lover," "The Despairing Lover," "The Dying African," "The Jilted Lover," "The Song of Danae," "To Chaucer," "To Chloe Too Cold," "To Chloe Too Warm," "To the Grasshopper."

Sources: *Dictionary of National Biography.* Electronic Edition 1.1. Oxford University Press, 1997. *English Poetry: Author Search.* Chadwyck-Healey Ltd., 1995 (http://www.lib.utexas.edu:8080/search/epoetry/author.html). *Poetical Works of Frank Sayers.* W. Simpkin and R. Marshall, 1830. *Stanford University Libraries and Academic Information Resources* (http://library.stanford.edu).

SCANNELL, VERNON (1922–)

Born at Spilsby, Lincolnshire, he was brought up principally in Aylesbury, Buckinghamshire, and left school at 14. During World War II he served in the Gordon Highlanders in France and in Africa, and took part in the Normandy Landings. He was wounded, imprisoned for desertion and in 1945 he again deserted and was sent to a mental hospital. He wrote about these experiences in an *Argument of Kings* (1987). He worked as a boxer, was a school-teacher from 1945 to 1946, studied English literature at Leeds University from 1946 to 1947, and is now a freelance writer, poet and broadcaster. He was awarded a South Arts Writer's Fellowship (1975–1976) and was awarded a civil pension in 1981. His first volume of poetry, *Graves and Resurrections,* was published in 1948. Since then he has published six novels and his three-part autobiography: *The Tiger and the Rose* (1971); *Proper Gentleman* (1977); and *Drums of Morning—Growing Up in the Thirties* (1992). Some of his poems: "Act of Love," "Bayonet Training," "Moods of Rain," "Protest Poem," "Six Reasons for Drinking," "The Great War," "Walking Wounded," "Words and Monsters."

Sources: *A Book of Nature Poems.* William Cole, ed. Viking Press, 1969. *Erotic Poetry: The Lyrics, Ballads, Idylls, and Epics of Love—Classical to Contemporary.* William Cole, ed. Random House, 1963. *Not Without Glory: Poets of the Second World War.* Vernon Scannell. Routledge Falmer, 1976. *P.E.N. New Poetry I.* Robert Nye, ed. Quartet Books, 1986. *The Columbia Granger's Index to Poetry.* 11th ed. *The Columbia Granger's World of Poetry,* Columbia University Press, 2005 (http://www.columbiagrangers.org). *The Faber Book of War Poetry.* Kenneth Baker, ed. Faber and Faber, 1996. *The Oxford Companion to English Literature.* 6th edition. Margaret Drabble, ed. Oxford University Press, 2000. *Who's Who.* London: A & C Black, 2005. *Wikipedia, the Free Encyclopedia* (http://en.wikipedia.org/wiki/Wikipedia).

SCARFE, FRANCIS (1911–1986)

Born in South Shields, Tyneside, he was orphaned at the age of six and spent four years at an orphanage for the children of merchant seamen. He was educated at the Boys' High School in South Shields, Durham University, Fitzwilliam College, Cambridge, and at the Sorbonne, Paris. He taught at Glasgow University before he enlisted in the Army Education Corps in 1941. While on a posting to the Orkneys, he lodged with the family of young George Mackay Brown (see entry), on whom he was a major influence. After the war, Scarfe taught French poetry at Glasgow University and from 1959 to 1978 was director of the British Institute. In recognition of his contribution to Anglo-French cultural relations he was given three major French literary awards, including the Chevalier de la Légion d'Honneur (1978). Some of his poetry publications: *Inscapes,* 1940. *Forty Poems and Ballads,* 1941. *Underworlds,* 1950. *Complete Verse of Charles P. Baudelaire,* 1986 (translation). Some of his poems: "Cat's Eyes," "Cats," "Grenade," "Kitchen Poem," "Ode in Honour," "The Clock," "Tyne Dock."

Sources: *Biography of Francis Scarfe* (http://online.northumbria.ac.uk/faculties/art/humanities/cns/m-scarfe.html). *English and American Surrealist Poetry.* Edward B. Germain, ed. Penguin Books, 1978. *The Columbia Granger's Index to Poetry.* 11th ed. *The Columbia Granger's World of Poetry,* Columbia University Press, 2005 (http://www.columbiagrangers.org). *The Faber Book of War Poetry.* Kenneth Baker, ed. Faber and Faber, 1996. *The New British Poets: An Anthology.* Kenneth Rexroth, ed. New Directions, 1949. *Wikipedia, the Free Encyclopedia* (http://en.wikipedia.org/wiki/Wikipedia).

SCOTT, ALEXANDER (?1525–?1584)

Nothing certain is known of the life of this Scottish poet, though his father was linked with Chapel Royal, Stirling Castle. His poems, many of them written in the Scots metrical form, allude to his being in Edinburgh. Scott's works, consisting of thirty-six short pieces — the longest numbering a little over two hundred lines — are preserved in the *Manuscript of George Bannatyne* (1545–c. 1608) compiled in 1568 (Bannatyne's *Manuscript,* in two volumes, contains the work of 40 named, as well as many anonymous, authors). Scott's earliest poem was "The Lament of the Maister of Erskyn" (1547). "A New Yeir Gift to Quene Mary" (of Scots) (1562) throws light on the social life and lamentable condition at that time. Allan Ramsay (see entry) first printed seven of Scott's poems in *The Evergreen* (1724). In 1770, Lord Hailes published seven of Scott's poems from Bannatyne's *Manuscript* in *Ancient Scottish Poems.* Scott wrote many love lyrics as well as translating some of the Psalms. Some of his poems: "Coronach," "Glasgow," "My Heart is High Above," "Of May," "Return Thee, Heart," "The Justing at the Drum," "The First Psalm."

Sources: *A Book of Scottish Verse.* Maurice Lindsay and R.L. Mackie, eds. St. Martin's Press, 1983. *Chapel Royal, A Collegiate Church for the Scottish Royal Family* (http://

www.rosslyntemplars.org.uk/chapel_royal.htm). *Dictionary of National Biography.* Electronic Edition 1.1. Oxford University Press, 1997. *Encyclopædia Britannica Ultimate Reference Suite DVD,* 2006. *English Poetry: Author Search.* Chadwyck-Healey Ltd., 1995 (http://www.lib.utexas.edu:8080/search/epoetry/author.html). *Microsoft Encarta* 2006 (DVD). Microsoft Corporation, 2006. *The Bannatyne Manuscript Written in Time of Pest.* Johnson Reprint Corporation, 1988. *The Columbia Granger's Index to Poetry.* 11th ed. *The Columbia Granger's World of Poetry,* Columbia University Press, 2005 (http://www.columbiagrangers.org). *The New Penguin Book of Scottish Verse.* Robert Crawford and Mick Imlah, eds. Penguin Books, 2000. *The Oxford Book of Scottish Verse,* John MacQueen and Tom Scott, eds. Oxford University Press, 1966.

SCOTT, GEOFFREY (1883–1929)

Born in Hampstead, London, the son of Russell Scott, a prosperous businessman, he was educated at Rugby School and graduated *literae humaniores* from New College, Oxford, in 1907. From 1907 to 1909 he was secretary-librarian to Bernhard Berenson, the American art critic who lived in Italy. From about 1909, he worked with Cecil Pinsent, an English architect who designed and built Tuscan villas and gardens for the English speaking community in Tuscany. In 1914 Scott published *The Architecture of Humanism,* a work that influenced a whole generation of architects. He became honorary first secretary at the British embassy in Rome in 1915. In October 1927 he sailed to New York to begin the task of editing an important collection of James Boswell's papers that had been bought by Colonel R.H. Isham, an American. The eighteen volumes were published between 1928 and 1934. He died in New York and his ashes were placed in the cloisters at New College, Oxford. Some of his poems: "All Our Joy is Enough," "Boats of Cane," "The Singer in the Noon," "The Skaian Gate," "What Are the Ghosts of Trees?" "What Was Solomon's Mind?"

Sources: *Dictionary of National Biography.* Electronic Edition 1.1. Oxford University Press, 1997. *Poems of Geoffrey Scott.* Oxford University Press, 1931. *The Columbia Granger's Index to Poetry.* 11th ed. *The Columbia Granger's World of Poetry,* Columbia University Press, 2005 (http://www.columbiagrangers.org). *The Oxford Book of Modern Verse, 1892–1935.* William Butler Yeats, ed. Oxford University Press, 1936. *The Oxford Companion to English Literature.* 6th edition. Margaret Drabble, ed. Oxford University Press, 2000.

SCOTT, LADY JOHN (ALICIA ANN SPOTTISWOODE) (1810–1900)

Alicia Anne Spottiswoode was born at Westruther, Berwickshire, and in 1836 she married Lord John Scott, brother of the 5th Duke of Buccleuch, and was known as Lady John Scott. A collector of traditional songs, she wrote 69 of her own, often basing them on older pieces. One of her most well-known adaptations is "Annie Laurie." The poem — written about 1700 — was by William Douglas of Fingland, Kirkcudbrightshire, with the tune "Kempie Kaye." Lady John altered the words and melody and added a third verse. The song is now sung to her melody. Annie was one of four daughters of Sir Robert Laurie, first Baronet of Maxweltown, Dumfriesshire. Sadly, William Douglas did not get the hand of his Annie in marriage. Some of her other song/poems: "Durisdeer," "Ettrick," "Loch Lomond," "The Comin' o' the Spring."

Sources: *A Book of Scottish Verse.* Maurice Lindsay and R.L. Mackie, eds. St. Martin's Press, 1983. *British Minstrelsie.* T.C. and E.C. Jack, Grange Publishing works, Edinburgh (?1900). *Love's Witness: Five Centuries of Love Poetry by Women.* Jill Hollis, ed. Carroll and Graf, Inc., 1993. *Lyra Celtica: An Anthology of Representative Celtic Poetry.* E.A. Sharp and J. Matthay, ed. John Grant, 1924. *The Columbia Granger's Index to Poetry.* 11th ed. *The Columbia Granger's World of Poetry,* Columbia University Press, 2005 (http://www.columbiagrangers.org).

SCOTT, THOMAS (1705–1775)

The son of a dissenting clergyman, he was born at Hitchin, Hertfordshire, and probably educated by his father. For a time he took charge of a small boarding school at Wortwell in the parish of Redenhall, Norfolk, and once a month preached to the independent congregation at Harleston in the same parish. From 1733 to 1738 he was minister of the dissenting congregation at Lowestoft, Suffolk, dividing his time between that and St. Nicholas Street Chapel, Ipswich. His last position was the chapel at Hapton, Norfolk, where he died and was buried in the parish churchyard. He was better known as a hymn-writer; eleven of his hymns were first contributed to *Hymns for Public Worship* (1772). His poetry publications: *The Table of Cebes: or, the Picture of Human Life, in English Verse, with Notes,* 1754. *The Book of Job, in English Verse: Translated from the Original Hebrew, with Remarks, Historical, Critical, and Explanatory,* 1771 and 1773. Some of his hymns/poems: "Address to Jesus Christ," "Adversity," "Benefit of Early Piety," "Envy," "Humility," "Jewish and Christian Religion Compared," "The Agony of Jesus Christ," "The Penitent."

Sources: *American Hymns Old and New, Vols. 1 and 2.* Albert Christ-Janer and Charles W. Hughes, eds. Columbia University Press, 1980. *Dictionary of National Biography.* Electronic Edition 1.1. Oxford University Press, 1997. *Lyric Poems, Devotional and Moral of Thomas Scott.* James Buckland, 1773. *The Columbia Granger's Index to Poetry.* 11th ed. *The Columbia Granger's World of Poetry,* Columbia University Press, 2005 (http://www.columbiagrangers.org). *The Cyber Hymnal* (http://www.cyberhymnal.org/index.htm).

SCOTT, SIR WALTER (1771–1832).

Scottish poet born in Edinburgh. He was lame in his right leg from a young age (possibly from poliomyelitis). Educated at Edinburgh High School and at the university, he was called to the bar in 1792. From 1799 until his death he was sheriff deputy of the county of Selkirk as well as clerk to the Court of Session in Edinburgh, and was a partner the publishing firm owned by James Ballantyne and his brother John. He incurred debts in saving the company from bankruptcy, as well as building his house, Abbotsford, on the Scottish Borders. His novel *Waverly* was published in 1814 and altogether he wrote 28 novels and short stories. He is buried at Dryburgh Abbey, Scotland, and is memorialized by a stone in Poets' Corner of Westminster Abbey. Some of his poetry publications: *Minstrelsy of the Scottish Border*, 1802–1803. *The Lay of the Last Minstrel*, 1805. *Marmion*, 1808. *The Lady of the Lake*, 1810. *The Bridal of Triermain*, 1813. *The Lord of the Isles*, 1815. *Rob Roy*, 1817. Some of his other poems: "Hunting Song," "MacGregor's Gathering," "The Dreary Change," "The Eve of Saint John," "The Fire."

Sources: *A Book of Scottish Verse.* Maurice Lindsay and R.L. Mackie, eds. St. Martin's Press, 1983. *Dictionary of National Biography.* Electronic Edition 1.1. Oxford University Press, 1997. *Encyclopædia Britannica Ultimate Reference Suite DVD*, 2006. *Golden Treasury of the Best Songs and Lyrical Poems in the English Language.* Francis Turner Palgrave, ed. Oxford University Press, 1964, Sixth edition, updated by John Press, 1994. *Microsoft Encarta* 2006 (DVD). Microsoft Corporation, 2006. *Poets of the English Language. Vol. IV.* W.H. Auden and Norman Holmes Pearson, eds. Viking Press, 1950. *Selections from the Poems of Sir Walter Scott.* A. Hamilton Thompson, ed. Reprint Services 1921. *The Columbia Granger's Index to Poetry.* 11th ed. *The Columbia Granger's World of Poetry,* Columbia University Press, 2005 (http://www.columbiagrangers.org). *The Faber Book of War Poetry.* Kenneth Baker, ed. Faber and Faber, 1996. *The Oxford Book of Christmas Poems.* Michael Harrison and Christopher Stuart-Clark, eds. Oxford University Press, 1983. *The Oxford Companion to English Literature.* 6th edition. Margaret Drabble, ed. Oxford University Press, 2000. *Westminster Abbey Official Guide* (no date).

SCOTT, WILLIAM BELL (1811–1890)

Scottish poet and painter, who was born at St. Leonard's, Edinburgh, the son of Robert Scott the engraver (1777–1841). Educated at Edinburgh High School and at the Trustees' Academy, he then did some drawing at the British Museum, London. Thereafter he assisted his father's business in Parliament House Square, Edinburgh. In 1837 he moved to London and supported himself by etching, engraving, and painting. *The Old English Ballad Singer* was exhibited in 1838 at the British Institution.

Down to his last appearance at the academy in 1869, he exhibited twenty pictures in London. From 1844 to 1864 he worked in Newcastle-on-Tyne teaching design and organizing art schools under the department of science and art. He spent his latter years in London, where he died. His poetry is mystical and metaphysical rather than romantic. "Of Poetry" is an extensive work, where he addresses poets from ancient times to Burns, Byron, Dante, Shakespeare, Shelley, and many more. Some of his other poems: "A Lowland Witch Ballad," "Apple Gathering," "Before Marriage," "Continuity of Life," "End of Harvest," "Glenkindie," "The Apple Tree," "The Sickle; an Autumnal Ode."

Sources: *A Poet's Harvest Home: Poems of William Bell Scott.* Elkin Mathews and John Lane, 1893. *Dictionary of National Biography.* Electronic Edition 1.1. Oxford University Press, 1997. *The Columbia Granger's Index to Poetry.* 11th ed. *The Columbia Granger's World of Poetry,* Columbia University Press, 2005 (http://www.columbiagrangers.org). *The Home Book of Verse.* Burton Egbert Stevenson, ed. New York: Henry Holt and Company, 1953. *The Oxford Book of Sonnets.* John Fuller, ed. Oxford University Press, 2000. *The Oxford Companion to English Literature.* 6th edition. Margaret Drabble, ed. Oxford University Press, 2000.

SCOVELL, EDITH JOY (1907–1999)

Born in Sheffield, South Yorkshire, she was educated in Westmorland, England, and at Somerville College, Oxford. She married the ecologist Charles Sutherland Elton in 1937 and traveled with him through the West Indies and Central and South America. Most of her poetry deals with exotic places, paying meticulous attention to the flora and fauna of a given area. Her *Collected Poems* (1988) and *Selected Poems* (1991) were published by Carcanet Press. Her other publications: *Shadows of Chysanthemums*, 1944. *The Midsummer Meadow*, 1946. *The River Steamer*, 1956. Some of her poems: "A Wartime Story," "After Midsummer," "Bloody Cranesbill on the Dunes," "The First Year," "The Swan's Feet," "Water Images."

Sources: *Chaos of the Night: Women's Poetry and Verse of the Second World War.* Catherine W. Reilly, ed. Virago Press, 1984. *Washington University, St. Louis, University Libraries. Collection of Edith Joy Scovell* (http://library.wustl.edu/units/spec/manuscripts/mlc/scovell/scovell.html). *The Chatto Book of Modern Poetry 1915–1955.* Cecil Day Lewis and John Lehmann, eds. Chatto and Windus, 1966. *The Columbia Granger's Index to Poetry.* 11th ed. *The Columbia Granger's World of Poetry,* Columbia University Press, 2005 (http://www.columbiagrangers.org). *The Gambit Book of Love Poems.* Geoffrey Grigson, ed. Gambit, 1973. *The Harvill Book of Twentieth-Century Poetry in English.* Michael Schmidt, ed. The Harvill Press, 1999. *The Oxford Book of Twentieth-Century English Verse.* Philip Larkin, ed. Oxford University Press, 1973. *Wikipedia, the Free*

Encyclopedia (http://en.wikipedia.org/wiki/Wikipedia). *Women's Poetry of the 1930s: A Critical Anthology.* Jane Dowson, ed. Routledge, 1966.

SCROOPE (SCROPE), SIR CARR (1649–1680)

Born in Cockerington, Lincolnshire, he was created M.A. from Wadham College, Oxford (1666–1667), and took over the title when his father, Sir Adrian Scrope, was executed in 1667 for his part in the capture and execution of Charles I. In London Sir Carr was one of the companions of Charles II. Scroope's poem "In Defense of Satire" was an attack on John Wilmot (see Rochester, John Wilmot) who, so Scroope believed, had lampooned him in "Allusion to the Tenth Satire of the First Book of Horace." They then engaged in a war of words. He died at Tunbridge Wells, Kent, and was buried at St. Martin's-in-the-Fields; the baronetcy thereupon became extinct. At some stage he made a translation of the epistle of Sappho to Phaon, which was included in *Ovid's Epistles Translated by Various Hands,* of which numerous editions were published between 1681 and 1725. Two other poems are attributed to him: "Song: I cannot change as others do," "The Author's Reply."

Sources: *Anthology of Poems on Affairs of State: Augustan Satirical Verse, 1660–1714.* George de F. Lord, ed. Yale University Press, 1975. *Dictionary of National Biography.* Electronic Edition 1.1. Oxford University Press, 1997. *The Columbia Granger's Index to Poetry.* 11th ed. *The Columbia Granger's World of Poetry,* Columbia University Press, 2005 (http://www.columbiagrangers.org).

SCULLY, MAURICE (1952–)

Irish poet, born in Dublin and who works in what might be termed the modernist tradition. He was educated at Trinity College, Dublin, where he edited the student literary magazine, *Icarus.* After some years in Italy, Africa and the west of Ireland, he resettled with his wife and four children in Dublin, where he now teaches part-time at Dublin City University. He founded and edited two literary journals, the *Belle* and *The Beau,* and has also edited a number of influential magazines and chapbook series. Through the 1970s and 1980s he organized readings and literary events. Some of his publications: *Love Poems and Others,* 1981. *Five Freedoms of Movement,* 1987. *Steps,* 1998. *Livelihood,* 2004. Some of his poems: "Liking the Big Wheelbarrow," "Log," "Maturity," "Two Pages."

Sources: *Biography of Maurice Scully* (http://www.irishwriters-online.com/mauricescully.html). *Poems by Maurice Scully* (http://english.chass.ncsu.edu/freeverse/Archives/Spring_2002/poems/m_scully.html). *Wikipedia, the Free Encyclopedia* (http://en.wikipedia.org/wiki/Wikipedia).

SEAMAN, SIR OWEN (1861–1936)

Born in London, he was educated at Shrewsbury — a boys' boarding school on the banks of the River Severn and overlooking the ancient town — where he was captain. He graduated from Clare College, Cambridge, in 1883 and was successively a schoolmaster, professor of literature at Durham College of Science, Newcastle-upon-Tyne from 1890 to 1903, and a barrister of the Inner Temple (1897). He joined the staff of *Punch* and was editor from 1906 to 1932. He was elected an honorary fellow of Clare College in 1909, received honorary degrees from the universities of Durham (1906), Edinburgh (1924), and Oxford (1933), and was created a baronet in 1933. He died, unmarried, in London. Some of his publications: *Horace,* 1895. *In Cap and Bells,* 1899. *Borrowed Plumes,* 1902. *A Harvest of Chaff,* 1904. *War-Time,* 1915. *Made in England,* 1916. *From the Home Front,* 1918. Some of his poems: "A Birthday Ode to Mr. Alfred Austin," "A Nocturne at Danieli's," "Ballad of a Bun," "England's Alfred Abroad," "Of Baiting the Lion," "The Warrior's Lament," "Time's Revenges," "To Julia in Shooting Togs."

Sources: *A Century of Humorous Verse, 1850–1950.* Roger Lancelyn Green, ed. E.P. Dutton (Everyman's Library), 1959. *A Nonsense Anthology.* Carolyn Wells, ed. Scribner's; paperback edition, 1930. *Dictionary of National Biography.* Electronic Edition 1.1. Oxford University Press, 1997. *The National Portrait Gallery* (www.npg.org.uk). *The Columbia Granger's Index to Poetry.* 11th ed. *The Columbia Granger's World of Poetry,* Columbia University Press, 2005 (http://www.columbiagrangers.org). *The New Oxford Book of English Light Verse.* Kingsley Amis, ed. Oxford University Press, 1978. *Unauthorized Versions: Poems and Their Parodies.* Kenneth Baker, ed. Faber and Faber, 1990.

SEDLEY (SIDLEY) SIR CHARLES (?1639–1701)

Born at Aylesford in Kent, he was educated at Wadham College, Oxford, but did not graduate. After the Restoration he entered Parliament as one of the members (barons) for New Romney, Kent. He, with Lord Buckhurst (afterwards Earl of Dorset), and Sir Thomas Ogle soon gained a reputation of notoriety which brought them into disfavor with the Puritans and the authorities of the city of London. By his wit and conversational skill, however, Sedley gained the favor of Charles II. His one daughter became the favorite mistress of James, Duke of York, and was by him created Countess of Dorchester. The dramatists John Dryden and Thomas Shadwell were among his friends, and Dryden dedicated to Sedley "The Assignation" in an *Essay of Dramatic Poesy* (1673). Some of his verse publications: *Antony and Cleopatra,* 1677 (tragedy). *The*

Mulberry-garden, 1668 (comedy). *Bellamira, or the Mistress,* 1687 (comedy). Some of his poems: "Advice to the Old Beaux," "Get You Gone," "On a Cock at Rochester," "Song to Celia," "The Happy Pair," "Thyrsis, unjustly you complain," "To Nysus."

Sources: *Dictionary of National Biography.* Electronic Edition 1.1. Oxford University Press, 1997. *Encyclopædia Britannica Ultimate Reference Suite DVD,* 2006. *English Lyric Poems, 1500–1900.* C. Day Lewis, ed. Appleton-Century-Crofts, 1961. *English Poetry: Author Search.* Chadwyck-Healey Ltd., 1995 (http://www.lib.utexas.edu:8080/search/epoetry/author.html). *Golden Treasury of the Best Songs and Lyrical Poems in the English Language.* Francis Turner Palgrave, ed. Oxford University Press, 1964, Sixth edition, updated by John Press, 1994. *Seventeenth-Century Verse and Prose, Vol. II: 1660–1700.* Helen C. White, et al, ed. Macmillan. 1951, 1952. *Songs from the British Drama.* Edward Bliss Reed, ed. Yale University Press, 1925. *Stanford University Libraries and Academic Information Resources* (http://library.stanford.edu). *The Columbia Granger's Index to Poetry.* 11th ed. *The Columbia Granger's World of Poetry,* Columbia University Press, 2005 (http://www.columbiagrangers.org). *The Court Poets* (Great Books Online, www.bartleby.com). *The New Oxford Book of Seventeenth Century Verse.* Alastair Fowler, ed. Oxford University Press, 1991.

SERVICE, ROBERT WILLIAM (1874–1958)

Known as the "Canadian Kipling," he was born into a Scottish family from Preston, England. He was educated in Glasgow, emigrated to Canada in 1895 to work for the Canadian Bank of Commerce, and ended up in the Yukon. "The Shooting of Dan McGrew" and "The Cremation of Sam McGee" made him a fortune. These and other poems were published in Toronto as *Songs of a Sourdough* and in New York as *The Spell of the Yukon* (1907). *Ballads of a Cheechako* appeared in 1909. In 1912, he reported on the Balkan war for the *Toronto Star.* During World War I he served with the American ambulance unit and with Canadian army intelligence. After World War II, during which he lived in America, he moved to Brittany, where he died. He remained a British citizen and was honored on a Canadian postage stamp in 1976. Some of his poetry publications: *Rhymes of a Red-Cross Man,* 1916. *Ballads of a Bohemian,* 1921. *Bar-Room Ballads,* 1940. *Rhymes for My Rags,* 1956. Some of his other poems: "Little Moccasins," "The Call of the Wild," "The Law of the Yukon," "The Lure of Little Voices."

Sources: *Canadian Poetry in English.* Bliss Carman, Lorne Pierce and V.B. Rhodenize, eds. Ryerson Press, rev. and enl. ed., 1954. *Canadian Poets.* John W. Garvin, ed. McClelland, Goodchild and Stewart, 1916. *Dictionary of National Biography.* Electronic Edition 1.1. Oxford University Press, 1997. *Encyclopædia Britannica Ultimate Reference Suite DVD,* 2006. *Shrieks at Midnight: Macabre Poems, Eerie and Humorous.* Sara Brewton and John E. Brewton, eds. Thomas Y. Crowell, 1969. *The Columbia Granger's Index to Poetry.* 11th ed. *The Columbia Granger's World of Poetry,* Columbia University Press, 2005 (http://www.columbiagrangers.org). *The Complete Poems of Robert Service.* Dodd, Mead and Company, 1940. *The Oxford Companion to English Literature.* 6th edition. Margaret Drabble, ed. Oxford University Press, 2000. *Wikipedia, the Free Encyclopedia* (http://en.wikipedia.org/wiki/Wikipedia).

SETTLE, ELKANAH (1648–1724)

Born in Dunstable, Bedfordshire, he left Trinity College, Oxford, without graduating. The success of his rhymed verse tragedy, *Cambyses, King of Persia* (1666)—acted at Lincoln's Inn Fields—was used by Rochester (see Rochester, John Wilmot) as a weapon to humiliate his rival John Dryden. A state of war then existed between Settle and Dryden, who satirized Settle as Doeg in *Absalom and Achitophel* (1682), and Settle replied with *Absalom Senior* (1682). Several tragedies followed, which won him favor at the court of Charles II. His best-known drama, also in rhymed verse, was *The Empress of Morocco* (1673). He was appointed city poet of London in about 1691 where one of his functions was to prepare yearly pageants for the lord mayor's shows. His fierce Protestantism led to his unanimous election as organizer-in-chief of the pope-burning procession on Queen Elizabeth's birthday (17 November 1680). However, his promising career was wrecked by his jealous rivalry of Dryden and his switching sides from Whig to Tory and back again. He died in poor circumstances in the Charterhouse, London. Some of his poems: "A Satyr Against Persecution," "An Epistle," "Another Epistle," "Celia Sings," "The Medal Reversed."

Sources: *Anthology of Poems on Affairs of State: Augustan Satirical Verse, 1660–1714.* George de F. Lord, ed. Yale University Press, 1975. *Dictionary of National Biography.* Electronic Edition 1.1. Oxford University Press, 1997. *English Poetry: Author Search.* Chadwyck-Healey Ltd., 1995 (http://www.lib.utexas.edu:8080/search/epoetry/author.html). *Songs from the British Drama.* Edward Bliss Reed, ed. Yale University Press, 1925. *The Columbia Granger's Index to Poetry.* 11th ed. *The Columbia Granger's World of Poetry,* Columbia University Press, 2005 (http://www.columbiagrangers.org). *The Oxford Companion to English Literature.* 6th edition. Margaret Drabble, ed. Oxford University Press, 2000. *Wikipedia, the Free Encyclopedia* (http://en.wikipedia.org/wiki/Wikipedia).

SEWARD, ANNA (1742–1809)

Known as the "Swan of Lichfield," she was born at Eyam, Derbyshire, the daughter of the canon of Lichfield, where she lived out her life. She was a member there of a literary circle that included William Hayley and Erasmus Darwin (see entries).

A bright child who could repeat passages from John Milton's *L'Allegro* before she was three, in 1781 she published a "Monody on the unfortunate Major André," which was republished in 1817. *Louisa: A Poetical Novel*, which passed through five editions, was published in 1782. Her father died in 1790, leaving her well provided for, and she continued to live in her father's residence, the bishop's palace, Lichfield. One of her sonnets, *December Morning*, was admired by Leigh Hunt (see Hunt, James Henry Leigh). *Poem to the Memory of Lady Miller* (see entry), honored the lady who helped Seward's writing career. Seward died of scurvy and was buried in Lichfield Cathedral. Some of her poems: "Achilles, a Canzonet," "Blindness," "Colebrook Dale," "Eyam," "Lichfield, an Elegy," "Ode to Content," "Sonnets," "The Anniversary," "The Hay-Field," "Written December 1790."

Sources: *A Century of Sonnets: The Romantic-Era Revival, 1750–1850*. Paula R. Feldman and Daniel Robinson, eds. Oxford University Press, 1999. *Chloe Plus Olivia: An Anthology of Lesbian Literature from the Seventeenth Century to the Present*. Lillian Faderman, ed. Viking Penguin, 1994. *Dictionary of National Biography*. Electronic Edition 1.1. Oxford University Press, 1997. *Encyclopædia Britannica Ultimate Reference Suite DVD*, 2006. *English Poetry: Author Search*. Chadwyck-Healey Ltd., 1995 (http://www.lib.utexas.edu:8080/search/epoetry/author.html). *The National Portrait Gallery* (www.npg.org.uk). *The Columbia Granger's Index to Poetry*. 11th ed. *The Columbia Granger's World of Poetry*, Columbia University Press, 2005 (http://www.columbiagrangers.org). *The New Oxford Book of Eighteenth Century Verse*. Roger Lonsdale, ed. Oxford University Press, 1984. *The Poetical Works of Anna Seward: Volume I*. Walter Scott, ed. John Ballantyne and Co., 1810. *Visiting Emily: Poems Inspired by the Life and Work of Emily Dickinson*. Sheila Coghill and Thom Tammaro, eds. University of Iowa Press, 2000. *Women Romantic Poets, 1785–1832: An Anthology*. Jennifer Breen, ed. J.M. Dent and Sons, 1992.

SEWELL, GEORGE (?1690–1726)

Born at Windsor and educated at Eton College, he graduated B.A. from Peterhouse, Cambridge, in 1790. After studying medicine at Leyden, Holland, he graduated as a physician from Edinburgh in 1725. His London medical practice was not a success, so he became a booksellers' hack, publishing numerous poems, translations, and political and other pamphlets. He died of tuberculosis at Hampstead, London, in great poverty, and was given a pauper's funeral. His 1715 *True Account of the Life and Writings of Thomas Burnet* (?1635–1715) was a satirical attack on Burnet's book *Sacred Theory of the Earth* (1684). Sewell's best-known work of general literature was *Tragedy of Sir Walter Raleigh*, acted at the theater in Lincoln's Inn Fields in 1719. Several of his poems are in *Collection of Poems* (1709) by Matthew Prior (see entry). He contributed to *Miscellanies in Verse and Prose* (1725) by Joseph Addison (see entry). Some of his poems: "Anacreontic," "Apology for Loving a Wid," "Psalm the Sixth Paraphras'd," "Upon His Majesty's Accession," "The Character of Cato," "The Favourite," "The Patriot," "Verses to Her Royal Highness the Princess of Wales."

Sources: *Dictionary of National Biography*. Electronic Edition 1.1. Oxford University Press, 1997. *English Poetry: Author Search*. Chadwyck-Healey Ltd., 1995 (http://www.lib.utexas.edu:8080/search/epoetry/author.html). *Great Books Online* (www.bartleby.com). *Poems on Several Occasions by George Sewell*. E. Curll and J. Pemberton, 1719. *The Columbia Granger's Index to Poetry*. 11th ed. *The Columbia Granger's World of Poetry*, Columbia University Press, 2005 (http://www.columbiagrangers.org).

SHADWELL, THOMAS (?1642–1692)

Born at Weeting, Norfolk, he was educated at Caius College, Cambridge, but left without graduating, then entered law at the Middle Temple, London. The first of his seventeen plays, the *Sullen Lovers*, was performed at Lincoln's Inn Fields in 1668. His best known comedies are *Epsom Wells* (1672) and *The Squire of Alsatia* (1688). Shadwell and John Dryden (see entry) carried on a literary feud, and his satire *The Medal of John Bayes* (1682) attacks Dryden, who countered with *MacFlecknoe, or a Satire on the True Blue Protestant Poet, T.S* (1682). Shadwell succeeded Dryden as poet laureate and historiographer royal in 1689. He died of opium poisoning at Chelsea, where he is buried; he is memorialized by a stone in Poets' Corner of Westminster Abbey. Some of his poetry publications: *A Lenten Prologue*, 1683. *Ode to the King on His Return from Ireland*, 1690. *Ode on the Anniversary of the King's Birth*, 1690. *Votum Perenne*, 1692. Some of his poems: "A Song for St. Cecilia's Day, 1690," "Epilogue to the Loving Enemies," "Lovers lament, lament this fatal day," "Satyr to his Muse," "The Tory-Poets, A Satyr."

Sources: *Dictionary of National Biography*. Electronic Edition 1.1. Oxford University Press, 1997. *Encyclopædia Britannica Ultimate Reference Suite DVD*, 2006. *Microsoft Encarta* 2006 (DVD). Microsoft Corporation, 2006. *Songs from the British Drama*. Edward Bliss Reed, ed. Yale University Press, 1925. *The Columbia Granger's Index to Poetry*. 11th ed. *The Columbia Granger's World of Poetry*, Columbia University Press, 2005 (http://www.columbiagrangers.org). *The Complete Works of Thomas Shadwell V. 5*. The Fortune Press, 1927. *The Oxford Companion to English Literature*. 6th edition. Margaret Drabble, ed. Oxford University Press, 2000. *Westminster Abbey Official Guide* (no date).

SHAKESPEARE, WILLIAM (1564–1616)

It is believed that he was born on 23 April — which was also the date of his death — the son of a trader and leading citizen of Stratford Upon Avon, Warwickshire. He had a sound education at the local grammar school, where he would have studied Latin, as well as some of the classical historians, moralists, and poets. By the early 1590s he was making a name for himself in London as poet, playwright and actor. His first success was *Richard III*, 1592–93, and he went on to write over forty plays, as well as sonnets and many other poems; *The Tempest* (1611) is considered to be his last play. He was a leading member of the Chamberlain's Men theatrical company and owned a share in the Globe Theatre, built in 1599 on London's Bankside and destroyed by fire in 1613. He retired to Stratford, where he died and was buried in Holy Trinity Church. He is memorialized by a monument in Poets' Corner of Westminster Abbey. Some of his other publications: *Lvcrece*, 1594. *Venus and Adonis*, 1594. *The Passionate Pilgrim*, 1599. *The Phoenix and the Turtle*, 1601. *Sonnets,* 1609.

Sources: *Dictionary of National Biography.* Electronic Edition 1.1. Oxford University Press, 1997. *Encyclopædia Britannica Ultimate Reference Suite DVD, 2006. English Poetry: Author Search.* Chadwyck-Healey Ltd., 1995 (http://www.lib.utexas.edu:8080/search/epoetry/author.html). *Encyclopedia of Britain.* Bamber Gascoigne. London: Macmillan, 1994. *Moods of the Sea: Masterworks of Sea Poetry.* George C. Solley and Eric Steinbaugh, eds. Naval Institute Press, 1981. *Poetry for Pleasure: A Choice of Poetry and Verse on a Variety of Themes.* Ian Parsons, ed. W.W. Norton, 1977. *The Columbia Granger's Index to Poetry.* 11th ed. *The Columbia Granger's World of Poetry,* Columbia University Press, 2005 (http://www.columbiagrangers.org). *The Faber Book of Political Verse.* Tom Paulin, ed. Faber and Faber, 1986. *The Oxford Anthology of English Poetry, Vol. I: Spenser to Crabbe.* John Wain, ed. Oxford University Press, 1990. *The Oxford Companion to English Literature.* 6th edition. Margaret Drabble, ed. Oxford University Press, 2000. *Westminster Abbey Official Guide* (no date).

SHAPCOTT, JO (1953)

Born in London, she was educated at Trinity College, Dublin, Bristol University, and Harvard, on a Harkness Fellowship in English. She teaches on the M.A. in creative writing at Royal Holloway College, University of London, is visiting professor in poetry at the University of Newcastle and the University of the Arts, London, and is consulting editor for Arc Publications. With Matthew Sweeney (see entry) she edited *Emergency Kit for Strange Times* (1996) and edited *Penguin Modern Poetry 12* (1997). Her poems were set to music by composer Stephen Montague in *The Creatures Indoors*, premiered by the London Symphony Orchestra at the Barbican Centre in London in 1997. She has won six major literary awards and won the National Poetry Competition in 1985 and 1991. Some of her other publications: *Electroplating the Baby*, 1988. *Phrase Book*, 1992. *My Life Asleep*, 1998. *Last Words Poetry for the New Century*, 1999. *Her Book: Poems 1988–1998*, 2000. *Tender Taxes*, 2002. *Poet of the Periphery*, 2002. Some of her poems: "I'm Contemplated by a Portrait of a Divine," "Lies," "Lovebirds," "Mad Cow Dance," "Photograph: Sheepshearing," "Rattlesnake."

Sources: *Biography of Jo Shapcott: British Council Arts* (http://www.contemporarywriters.com). *Poetry with an Edge.* Neil Astley, ed. Bloodaxe Books, 1988. *The Bloodaxe Book of 20th Century Poetry, from Britain and Ireland.* Edna Longley, ed. Bloodaxe Books, 2000. *The Columbia Granger's Index to Poetry.* 11th ed. *The Columbia Granger's World of Poetry,* Columbia University Press, 2005 (http://www.columbiagrangers.org). *The New Exeter Book of Riddles.* Kevin Crossley-Holland and Lawrence Sail, eds. Enitharmon Press, 1999. *The Oxford Companion to English Literature.* 6th edition. Margaret Drabble, ed. Oxford University Press, 2000. *Who's Who.* London: A & C Black, 2005.

SHARP, WILLIAM (1855–1905)

Scottish poet born at Paisley, Strathclyde, he was educated at Glasgow University and spent a great deal of his life touring Australia, America, Germany, Italy, France and North Africa. Working in London, his poetry attracted the attention and encouragement of Gabriel Rossetti (see entry). In 1882 he published a short life of Rossetti, and in the same year he published "The Human Inheritance" which led to an invitation from the editor of *Harper's Magazine* for other poems. In 1884 he became editor of the *Canterbury Poets*, to which he contributed editions on sonnets and odes. From around 1890 he began writing mystical prose and verse under the pseudonym of "Fiona Macleod." He married his cousin Elizabeth Sharp in 1884, and they edited the 1896 edition of *Lyra Celtica*. He died at Castle Maniace, Sicily, and was buried in a woodland cemetery on the hillside. Some of his other publications: *Poems*, 1884. *Romantic Ballads*, 1889. *From the Hills of Dream*, 1897. *Poems and Dramas*, 1910. Some of his poems: "An Orange Grove," "Moonrise on the Antarctic," "Song of the Cornfields," "The Field Mouse," "The Wild Mare."

Sources: *Dictionary of National Biography.* Electronic Edition 1.1. Oxford University Press, 1997. *English Poetry: Author Search.* Chadwyck-Healey Ltd., 1995 (http://www.lib.utexas.edu:8080/search/epoetry/author.html). *Favorite Poems of Childhood.* Philip Smith, ed. Dover Publications, 1992. *Poems of William Sharp.* Mrs. William Sharp, ed. Duffield and Company, 1912. *Stanford University Libraries and Academic Information Resources* (http://library.stanford.edu). *The Columbia Granger's Index to Poetry.* 11th ed. *The Columbia Granger's World of Poetry,* Columbia University Press, 2005 (http://www.columbiagrangers.org).

SHAW, CUTHBERT (1739–1771)

Born at Ravensworth, near Richmond in Yorkshire, his first poem, *Liberty*, inscribed to the Earl of Darlington, was published in 1756. Feeling unappreciated in Yorkshire, he joined a company of comedians and in 1760 was at Bury St. Edmunds, where he published under the pseudonym of "W. Seymour" *Odes on the Four Seasons*. As an actor he had little to recommend him except his good looks, although he did appear at Covent Garden in 1761, and in a benefit performance for himself as Pierre in *Venice Preserved* (1762). During the last years of his life his contributions to *The Freeholder's Magazine* and other periodicals were noted for their caustic comments leveled at contemporary personalities and events. He died at Oxford. Some of his other publications: *An Elegy on the Death of Charles York*, 1770. *Monody to the Memory of a Young Lady*, 1770. *Poems on Different Occasions*, 1776. *The Race*, 1776. Some of his other poems: "Address to the Critics," "The Author, Being in Company with Emma," "Emma to Damon," "Evening Address to a Nightingale," "Invitation to Emma, After Marriage," "Song, to Emma," "To Emma, Doubting the Author's Sincerity."

Sources: *Dictionary of National Biography.* Electronic Edition 1.1. Oxford University Press, 1997. *English Poetry: Author Search.* Chadwyck-Healey Ltd., 1995 (http://www.lib.utexas.edu:8080/search/epoetry/author.html). *Stanford University Libraries and Academic Information Resources* (http://library.stanford.edu). *The Columbia Granger's Index to Poetry.* 11th ed. *The Columbia Granger's World of Poetry,* Columbia University Press, 2005 (http://www.columbia grangers.org). *The Works of the British Poets, Vol. 33 (Blair, Glynn, Boyce, Shaw, Lovibond, and Penrose).* J. Sharpe, 1808.

SHEERS, OWEN (1974–)

Born in Fiji, he was brought up in Abergavenny, South Wales, and educated at King Henry VIII comprehensive, Abergavenny, and New College, Oxford. He was the winner of an Eric Gregory Award and the 1999 *Vogue* Young Writer's Award. His first collection of poetry, the *Blue Book* (Seren, 2000) was short-listed for the Welsh Book of the Year and the Forward Prize Best First Collection 2001. His second collection of poetry, *Skirrid Hill,* was published by Seren in 2005. *The Dust Diaries* (Faber 2004), a travel memoir set in Zimbabwe, was short-listed for the Royal Society of Literature's Ondaatje Prize and won Welsh Book of the Year 2005. He has also written for radio, TV and newspapers and has toured extensively, most recently in New York, Croatia and Hungary. In 2004 he was writer in residence at the Wordsworth Trust and was selected as one of the Poetry Book Society's 20 "Next Generation" poets.

Sources: *Biography of Owen Sheers: The Blue Book* (http://www.owensheers.co.uk/back.htm). *Wikipedia, the Free Encyclopedia* (http://en.wikipedia.org/wiki/Wikipedia).

SHEFFIELD, JOHN (1648–1721)

He succeeded his father in 1658 as the third Earl of Mulgrave and later was created Duke of Buckingham and Normanby. He was gentleman of the bedchamber to Charles II and in 1680 he commanded an expedition for the relief of Tangier, besieged by the Moors. From 1682 to 1684 he was banished from court for making overtures to the future Queen Anne. He was in favor with James II, out of favor under William and Mary, in favor with Queen Anne and out of favor with George I, who removed him from all his posts. He was seen as a plotter, creating tensions between various people and heads of state. Samuel Johnson says of him: "His character is not to be proposed as worthy of imitation ... he was censured as covetous." He died at Buckingham House (now Buckingham Palace), St. James's Park, which he had built in 1703 on land granted by the crown. He is buried in the nave of Westminster Abbey. Some of his poems: "A Letter from Sea," "An Essay Upon Satire," "Essay on Poetry," "Love's Slavery," "The Nine," "The Rapture," "The Warning."

Sources: *Anthology of Poems on Affairs of State: Augustan Satirical Verse, 1660–1714.* George de F. Lord, ed. Yale University Press, 1975. *Dictionary of National Biography.* Electronic Edition 1.1. Oxford University Press, 1997. *English Poetry: Author Search.* Chadwyck-Healey Ltd., 1995 (http://www.lib.utexas.edu:8080/search/epoetry/author. html). *The National Portrait Gallery* (www.npg.org.uk). *Samuel Johnson's Lives of the English Poets,* 1779–1781 (http://www2.hn.psu.edu/Faculty/KKemmerer/poets/preface.htm). *Stanford University Libraries and Academic Information Resources* (http://library.stanford.edu). *The Columbia Granger's Index to Poetry.* 11th ed. *The Columbia Granger's World of Poetry,* Columbia University Press, 2005 (http://www.columbiagrangers.org). *The Home Book of Verse.* Burton Egbert Stevenson, ed. New York: Henry Holt and Company, 1953. *The Oxford Book of English Verse, 1250–1918.* Sir Arthur Quiller-Couch, ed. New edition, revised and enlarged, Oxford University Press, 1939. *The Oxford Companion to English Literature.* 6th edition. Margaret Drabble, ed. Oxford University Press, 2000. *The Poetical Works of Dryden.* George R. Noyes, ed. Houghton Mifflin Company. 1950. *Westminster Abbey Official Guide* (no date).

SHELLEY, PERCY BYSSHE and MARY WOLLSTONECRAFT (1792–1851)

Percy Bysshe, the husband, 1792–1822

Born at Field Place, Warnham, near Horsham, to a wealthy, aristocratic family, he was educated at Sion House Academy, Brentford, Essex, Eton College, and Oxford University, from which he was expelled in 1811 for co-writing *The Necessity of Atheism,* a pamphlet of which the university authorities disapproved. He married Harriet Westbrook soon afterward and moved to the Lake District of England.

In 1814, after separating from Harriet, he eloped with Mary Wollstonecraft Godwin to the Continent (she was seventeen), where they lived a bohemian lifestyle that included John Keats and Lord Byron (see entries). They married in 1816 soon after Harriet drowned herself in the Serpentine Lake in Kensington Gardens. Shelley drowned in a storm at sea off Italy; his body was washed ashore ten days later, and he was buried in the Protestant Cemetery at Rome. He is memorialized by a tablet in Poets' Corner of Westminster Abbey. Shelley has gone down in history as one of England's greatest poets for his sonnets, short, powerful poems, love lyrics, verse dramas and tragedies, as well as several prose works and translations. Some of his poems: "To a Skylark," "Ode to the West Wind," "The Cloud," "Peter Bell the Third," "The Boat on the Serchio," "To Mary Shelley," "To William Shelley," "Tribute to America," "Verses on a Cat."

Mary Wollstonecraft, the wife, 1797–1851

Mary's parents were the novelist and political philosopher William Godwin (1756–1836) and the author and feminist Mary Wollstonecraft (1759–1797), who died within days of Mary's birth. Following her first novel, *Frankenstein, or the Modern Prometheus* (1818) she went on to publish five more novels. She spent much time editing and annotating her late husband's work, but owing to father-in-law's opposition, she was unable to publish *Poetical Works* until 1839. To finance her son's private education, she wrote essays and short fiction for periodicals. Between 1835 and 1838 she produced a series of scholarly biographies. The death of her father-in-law, Sir Timothy Shelley, in 1844 provided financial security, and her son inherited the title. She died in Chester Square, London, and was interred in the churchyard at Bournemouth. Some of her poems: "Oh Listen While I Sing to Thee," "On Reading Wordsworth's Lines on Peele Castle," "Stanzas," "To the air of 'My Phillida, adieu, love!'"

Sources: *America in Poetry.* Charles Sullivan, ed. Harry N. Abrams, 1988. *Dictionary of National Biography.* Electronic Edition 1.1. Oxford University Press, 1997. *Encyclopædia Britannica.* Electronic Edition, 2006. *English Poetry: Author Search.* Chadwyck-Healey Ltd., 1995 (http://www.lib.utexas.edu:8080/search/epoetry/author.html). *Love's Witness: Five Centuries of Love Poetry by Women.* Jill Hollis, ed. Carroll and Graf, Inc., 1993. *Microsoft Encarta 2006* (DVD). Microsoft Corporation, 2006. *Poets of the English Language, Vol. IV.* W.H. Auden and Norman Holmes Pearson, eds. Viking Press, 1950. *Romanticism.* Duncan Wu, ed. Blackwell, 1994. *The Cherry-Tree.* Geoffrey Grigson, ed. Phoenix House, 1959. *The Columbia Granger's Index to Poetry.* 11th ed. *The Columbia Granger's World of Poetry,* Columbia University Press, 2005

(http://www.columbiagrangers.org). *The Complete Poems of Percy Bysshe Shelley.* Mary Shelley, ed. The Modern Library, 1994. *The Oxford Companion to English Literature.* 6th edition. Margaret Drabble, ed. Oxford University Press, 2000. *The Sophisticated Cat: A Gathering of Stories, Poems, and Miscellaneous Writings About Cats.* Joyce Oates, Carol and Daniel Halpern, eds. Penguin Books, 1992.

SHENSTONE, WILLIAM (1714–1763)

Born at Halesowen, Worcestershire, he was educated at the local grammar school and Pembroke College, Oxford — where he was a contemporary of Dr. Johnson — but did not graduate. The year 1745 saw the start of his life's work: the beautifying of the grounds of Leasowes, Halesowen, a property bought by his grandfather; and building a solid reputation in the history of English landscape-gardening. His theories, outlined in *Unconnected Thoughts on Gardening* (1764), involved the creation of winding waterways and walks and a series of picturesque views. He assisted Thomas Bishop Percy (see entry) in the compilation and editing of Percy's *Reliques of Ancient English Poetry* (1765). He died unmarried and was buried in Halesowen churchyard. His poetic works include elegies, songs, and ballads. Some of his other poetry publications: *Poems Upon Various Occasions,* 1737. *The Judgment of Hercules,* 1741. *The Schoolmistress,* 1742. *Pastoral Ballad,* 1743. *Works,* 1773. Some of his poems: "Epilogue to the Tragedy of Cleone," "Hint from Voiture," "Jemmy Dawson," "Love and Music," "On a Seat Under a Spreading Beech," "Progress of Taste," "The Progress of Advice."

Sources: *A Bundle of Ballads.* George Routledge and Sons, 1891. *Dictionary of National Biography.* Electronic Edition 1.1. Oxford University Press, 1997. *Encyclopædia Britannica Ultimate Reference Suite DVD,* 2006. *English Love Poems.* John Betjeman and Geoffrey Taylor, eds. Faber and Faber, 1957. *English Poetry: Author Search.* Chadwyck-Healey Ltd., 1995 (http://www.lib.utexas.edu:8080/search/epoetry/author.html). *The National Portrait Gallery* (www.npg.org.uk). *The Columbia Granger's Index to Poetry.* 11th ed. *The Columbia Granger's World of Poetry,* Columbia University Press, 2005 (http://www.columbiagrangers.org). *The Oxford Companion to English Literature.* 6th edition. Margaret Drabble, ed. Oxford University Press, 2000. *The Poetical Works of William Shenstone.* Charles Cowden Clarke, ed. James Nichol, 1854.

SHERBURNE, SIR EDWARD (1618–1702)

Born in London, he was educated at the school of Thomas Farnaby (see Fanshawe, Richard) and afterwards under Charles Aleyn (see entry), author of the *Historie of Henry the Seventh* (1638). On the outbreak of the Civil War, being a royalist and Roman Catholic, he was for some months in the custody of the usher of the black rod (senior official of the

House of Lords). On his release he joined with Charles I at Nottingham and was present at the (inconclusive) battle of Edgehill, Oxfordshire (1642). The king created him M.A. at Oxford soon after the battle. When Charles was ousted, Sherburne forfeited all his property and lived in near-poverty in London, where he dedicated himself to literature. He died unmarried and was buried in the chapel of the Tower of London. Some of his poetry publications: *Seneca's Answer to Lucilius*, 1648. *The Sphere of Marcus Manilius*, 1675. *The Tragedies of Seneca*, 1701. Some of his poems: "And She Washed His Feet with Her Tears," "And they laid him in a Manger," "Love's Arithmetic," "The Dream," "Violets in Thaumantia's Bosome," "Weeping and Kissing."

Sources: *An Anthology of Catholic Poets.* Shane Leslie, ed. Macmillan, 1952. *Dictionary of National Biography.* Electronic Edition 1.1. Oxford University Press, 1997. *English Poetry: Author Search.* Chadwyck-Healey Ltd., 1995 (http://www.lib.utexas.edu:8080/search/epoetry/author.html). *Metaphysical Lyrics and Poems of the Seventeenth Century: Donne to Butler.* Herbert J. Grierson, ed. Oxford University Press, 1921. *Stanford University Libraries and Academic Information Resources* (http://library.stanford.edu). *The Cavalier Poets.* Robin Skelton, ed. Oxford University Press, 1970. *The Columbia Granger's Index to Poetry.* 11th ed (http://www.columbiagrangers.org). *The New Oxford Book of Seventeenth Century Verse.* Alastair Fowler, ed. Oxford University Press, 1991. *The Oxford Book of Short Poems.* P.J. Kavanagh and James Michie, eds. Oxford University Press, 1985.

SHERIDAN, RICHARD BRINSLEY (1751–1816)

Born in Dublin, the grandson of Thomas Sheridan (see entry), he was educated at Harrow school, Middlesex. Living in Bath, in 1770, Sheridan fell in love with Eliza Linley, daughter of a music teacher, and the pair eloped to France and went through a form of marriage in Calais. Both fathers opposed the relationship, but Eliza's father withdrew his opposition and the couple were married in 1773. Sheridan's *Rivals* was performed at Covent Garden Theatre in 1775, and by 1776 he was manager of Drury Lane Theatre, in partnership with Eliza's father. His crowning triumph came in 1777 with *The School for Scandal*. He was elected to Parliament in 1780 and soon ranked highly among parliamentary orators, and fought for the freedom of the press. His funeral was a grand affair. He is memorialized by a stone in Poets' Corner of Westminster Abbey. Some of his poems: "An Address to the Prince Regent," "Drinking Song," "Epitaph on Brooks," "On the Death of Elizabeth Sheridan," "The Bath Picture," "The Duenna," "Think Not, My Love, When Secret Grief," "The Gentle Primrose," "The Swallows," "To Elizabeth Linley."

Sources: *Dictionary of National Biography.* Electronic Edition 1.1. Oxford University Press, 1997. *Encyclopædia Britannica Ultimate Reference Suite DVD,* 2006. *Life and Works of Richard Brinsley Sheridan* (http://www.rbsheridan.com/). *The National Portrait Gallery* (www.npg.org.uk). *The Columbia Granger's Index to Poetry.* 11th ed. *The Columbia Granger's World of Poetry,* Columbia University Press, 2005 (http://www.columbiagrangers.org). *The Faber Book of Drink, Drinkers and Drinking.* Simon Rae, ed. Faber and Faber, 1991. *The Oxford Anthology of English Poetry, Vol. I: Spenser to Crabbe.* John Wain, ed. Oxford University Press, 1990. *The Oxford Companion to English Literature.* 6th edition. Margaret Drabble, ed. Oxford University Press, 2000. *The Plays and Poems of Richard Brinsley Sheridan, 3 vols.* R. Crompton Rhodes, ed. Blackwell, 1928.

SHERIDAN, THOMAS (1687–1738)

Irish poet, grandfather of the dramatist Richard Brinsley Sheridan (see entry), he was born in the Ulster town of Cavan. Educated at Trinity College, Dublin, he graduated B.A. (1711); M.A. (1714); B.D. (1724); D.D. (1726), and around 1711 he opened a school in Dublin, which was attended by sons of the best families in Dublin. He and Jonathan Swift became friends when Swift (see entry) was appointed dean of St. Patrick's, Dublin. Sheridan had a number of different schools and when he was kept by illness from being present in his school, Swift took his place. A serious illness took Sheridan to stay with Swift just before he died at the dinner table in the house of a former pupil at Rathfarnham, Dublin. Some of his publications: *Prologue Spoken,* 1720. *The Blunderful Blunder of Blunders,* 1721. *The Philoctetes of Sophocles,* 1725. *A True and Faithful Inventory,* 1726. *Tom Punsibi's Letter to Dean Swift,* 1727. *An Answer to the Christmas-Box,* 1729. *The Simile,* 1748. Some of his poems: "Figures of Speech," "My Hens are Hatching," "Of the Genders of Nouns," "The Sick Lion and the Ass."

Sources: *Dictionary of National Biography.* Electronic Edition 1.1. Oxford University Press, 1997. *English Poetry: Author Search.* Chadwyck-Healey Ltd., 1995 (http://www.lib.utexas.edu:8080/search/epoetry/author.html). *Stanford University Libraries and Academic Information Resources* (http://library.stanford.edu). *The Columbia Granger's Index to Poetry.* 11th ed. *The Columbia Granger's World of Poetry,* Columbia University Press, 2005 (http://www.columbiagrangers.org). *The Poems of Thomas Sheridan.* Robert Hogan, ed. Associated University Presses, 1994.

SHIPMAN, THOMAS (1632–1680)

Royalist poet, born at Scarrington, near Newark, Northamptonshire, he entered St. John's College, Cambridge in 1651. There is a hint that he was an economist and that he lived in London. He knew Thomas Flatman (see entry), who praised some of Shipman's poems. He died at Scarrington. His wife was Margaret Traffford, who brought him an estate at Bulcote, Nottinghamshire, and survived him until about 1696. Their third son, William, settled at Mansfield, and was high sheriff of Nottinghamshire in 1730. Shipman produced two major collections. *Henry the Third of France, Stabbed by a Fryer, with the Fall of Guise*, 1678, was a rhymed tragedy that was performed at the Theatre Royal London. *Carolina, or Loyal Poems*, 1683, contains about two hundred poems, including a long piece on the Restoration, the *Hero* (1678), addressed to the Duke of Monmouth. Some of the poems criticize the morals of the Roundheads as well as their politics. Some of his poems: "Red Canary," "The Frost, 1654," "To Mr. W.L.," "The Heroine," "The Huffer," "The Kiss, 1656, To Mrs. C," "The Pick-Pocket," "Wit and Nature."

Sources: *Dictionary of National Biography.* Electronic Edition 1.1. Oxford University Press, 1997. *English Poetry: Author Search.* Chadwyck-Healey Ltd., 1995 (http://www.lib.utexas.edu:8080/search/epoetry/author.html). *Erotic Poetry: The Lyrics, Ballads, Idylls, and Epics of Love — Classical to Contemporary.* William Cole, ed. Random House, 1963. *The Columbia Granger's Index to Poetry.* 11th ed. *The Columbia Granger's World of Poetry,* Columbia University Press, 2005 (http://www.columbiagrangers.org). *The Gambit Book of Love Poems.* Geoffrey Grigson, ed. Gambit, 1973. *The New Oxford Book of Seventeenth Century Verse.* Alastair Fowler, ed. Oxford University Press, 1991.

SHIRLEY, JAMES (1596–1666)

Born in London, he was educated at Merchant Taylors' School, St. John's College, Oxford, and Catharine Hall, Cambridge. He took holy orders before becoming a schoolmaster in Hertfordshire; at sometime he converted to Roman Catholicism. He became a leading playwright and survived the closing of the theaters by the Puritan Parliament in 1642. *Love Tricks, with Complements* was acted at the Cockpit Theatre in 1625; he wrote 40 plays in all. In 1634 he provided the literary part of the Inns of Court masque *The Triumph of People.* Sometime during 1636–37 he went to Ireland, where he wrote more plays, and on his return to London in 1640 he became principal dramatist for the King's Players. Although he and his wife did not die in the Great Fire of 1666, they died together two months later and were buried in St. Giles's churchyard. Some of his poems: "Death the Leveller," "Death's Final Conquest," "Saint Patrick for Ireland," "The Contention of Ajax and Ulysses," "The Last Conqueror," "The Maid's Revenge," "To the People," "Victorious Men of Earth."

Sources: *Dictionary of National Biography.* Electronic Edition 1.1. Oxford University Press, 1997. *Encyclopædia Britannica Ultimate Reference Suite DVD,* 2006. *English Poetry: Author Search.* Chadwyck-Healey Ltd., 1995 (http://www.lib.utexas.edu:8080/search/epoetry/author.html).

Fine Frenzy: Enduring Themes in Poetry. Robert Baylor and Brenda Stokes, eds. McGraw-Hill, 1978. *Microsoft Encarta 2006 (DVD).* Microsoft Corporation, 2006. *The National Portrait Gallery* (www.npg.org.uk). *Songs from the British Drama.* Edward Bliss Reed, ed. Yale University Press, 1925. *Stanford University Libraries and Academic Information Resources* (http://library.stanford.edu). *The Columbia Granger's Index to Poetry.* 11th ed. *The Columbia Granger's World of Poetry,* Columbia University Press, 2005 (http://www.columbiagrangers.org). *The Dramatic Works and Poems of James Shirley, Vol. I.* Alexander Dyce and William Gifford, eds. Russell and Russell, 1966. *The Oxford Companion to English Literature.* 6th edition. Margaret Drabble, ed. Oxford University Press, 2000.

SHUKMAN, HENRY (1962–)

Born in Oxford, where he still lives, he has worked as a trombonist, a trawler man and a travel writer. The lyrical and deeply affecting, wryly funny or wildly imaginative poems in his first poetry collection, *In Doctor No's Garden* (2002), range across the globe, from Mexico to Japan, from the United States to Southern England. His prizes include: the Daily Telegraph Arvon (2000); a Times Literary Supplement (2002); the Aldeburgh Festival (2002); the Tabla and Peterloo prizes; writers' awards from the Arts Council of England; and short list for the 2002 Forward Prize for Best First Collection. He reviews for the *New York Times Book Review* and *Times Literary Supplement.* Until recently he was poet in residence at the Wordsworth Trust, Dove Cottage, Grasmere, Cumbria. *Darien Dogs* (2005), his first work of fiction, is about a banker getting into hot water while trying to close a deal to finance an oil pipeline across the isthmus of Panama. Some of his poems: "A Glass of Guinness," "Friday on the Wing," "Leaving," "Piano Solo," "'Schmaltz,'" "Snowy Morning," "Storm Lines."

Sources: *Leaving, Poem by Henry Shukman* (http://www.poetrybooks.co.uk/PBS/pbs_shukman_henry.asp). *Snowy Morning, Poem by Henry Shukman* (http://www.poem.co.uk/poems/shukman.htm). *Storm Lines, Poem by Henry Shukman* (http://www.tnr.com/directory/keyword.mhtml?kid=93). *The Independent Online, May 2004: Darien Dogs, by Henry Shukman* (http://enjoyment.independent.co.uk/books/news/article62061.ece). *William Wordsworth's Dove Cottage* (http://www.wordsworth.org.uk/).

SHUTTLE, PENELOPE (1947–)

Poet and novelist, she was born in Staines, Middlesex, and was married to Peter Redgrove (see entry) from 1980 until he died in 2003. She collaborated with Redgrove in writing two novels. Perhaps the best of them, *In the Country of the Skin* (1973), was influenced by his experiences while in the Army and by her novel *All the Usual Hours of Sleeping* (1969). She now lives in Cornwall and the Cornish countryside features very much in her poetry. Her poetry publications: *The Orchard Upstairs*, 1980. *The Child-Stealer*, 1983. *The Lion from Rio*, 1986. *Adventures with My Horse*, 1988. *Taxing the Rain*, 1992. *Building a City for Jamie*, 1996. *Selected Poems*, 1998. *A Leaf Out of His Book*, 1999. Some of her poems: "Early Pregnancy," "Expectant Mother," "Gone is the Sleepgiver," "Hide and Seek," "Mother and Child," "Passion," "The Flower-Press," "The Vision of the Blessed Gabriele."

Sources: *Ain't I a Woman! A Book of Women's Poetry from Around the World*. Illona Linthwaite, ed. Peter Bedrick Books, 1988. *Bread and Roses: An Anthology of Nineteenth- and Twentieth-Century Poetry by Women Writers*. Diana Scott, ed. Virago Press, 1982. *Love's Witness: Five Centuries of Love Poetry by Women*. Jill Hollis, ed. Carroll and Graf, Inc., 1993. *P.E.N. New Poetry I*. Robert Nye, ed. Quartet Books, 1986. *The Columbia Granger's Index to Poetry*. 11th ed. *The Columbia Granger's World of Poetry*, Columbia University Press, 2005 (http://www.columbiagrangers. org). *The New Exeter Book of Riddles*. Kevin Crossley-Holland and Lawrence Sail, eds. Enitharmon Press, 1999. *The Oxford Companion to English Literature*. 6th edition. Margaret Drabble, ed. Oxford University Press, 2000. *Who's Who*. London: A & C Black, 2005.

SIDDAL, ELIZABETH ELEANOR (1829–1862)

She was the daughter of a London ironmonger, and while working in a dressmaking and millinery shop she was noticed by Walter Deverell, one of the early pre–Raphaelites, and became the celebrated pre–Raphaelite artists' model. She sat for Deverell, William Holman Hunt, and John Everett Millais as the drowned Ophelia. Within a short time she was sitting only for Dante Gabriel Rossetti (see entry), whom she married in 1860. Her particular beauty was a strong influence on what beauty represented to the pre–Raphaelites. To please Rossetti, she dropped the second 'l' from her surname. She, herself, took up painting and did a self-portrait, and some of her designs were included in the 1857 pre–Raphaelite exhibition in London. Her paintings were often of the Arthurian legend and other idealized medieval themes. It is thought that she suffered from tuberculosis or depression and this was her reason for taking laudanum, which eventually killed her. She was buried with other members of the Rossetti family in Highgate Cemetery, North London. Some of her poems: "A Silent Wood," "At Last," "Dead Love," "Lord, May I Come?" "The Passing of Love," "Worn Out."

Sources: *Dictionary of National Biography*. Electronic Edition 1.1. Oxford University Press, 1997. *Love's Witness: Five Centuries of Love Poetry by Women*. Jill Hollis, ed. Carroll and Graf, Inc., 1993. *Poemhunter* (www.poemhunter. com). *Sound the Deep Waters: Women's Romantic Poetry in the Victorian Age*. Pamela Norris, ed. Little, Brown, 1991. *The Columbia Granger's Index to Poetry*. 11th ed. *The Columbia Granger's World of Poetry*, Columbia University Press, 2005 (http://www.columbiagrangers.org). *The New Oxford Book of Victorian Verse*. Christopher Ricks, ed. Oxford University Press, 1987. *The Oxford Companion to English Literature*. 6th edition. Margaret Drabble, ed. Oxford University Press, 2000. *Victorian Women Poets: An Anthology*. Angela Leighton and Margaret Reynolds, eds. Blackwell, 1991. *Wikipedia, the Free Encyclopedia* (http://en.wikipedia.org/wiki/Wikipedia).

SIDNEY, SIR PHILIP (1554–1586)

Born at Penshurst, Kent, the godson of Philip II of Spain, Queen Mary's husband, he was educated at Christ Church College, Oxford, but did not graduate. A favorite of Queen Elizabeth, he was sent on several diplomatic missions, was knighted in 1583, and appointed governor of Flushing in the Netherlands in 1585. In 1586 he joined an expedition sent to aid the Netherlands against Spain, where he died of wounds received in a raid on a Spanish convoy at Zutphen in the Netherlands. Legend has it that, when mortally wounded, Sidney gave his cup of water to another soldier, with the words "Thy need is greater than mine." He was buried in St. Pauls' Cathedral, London. His pastoral romance *Arcadia* (1590) became a model for later pastoral poetry; *Astrophel and Stella* (1591) was a sequence of 108 sonnets. *The Defence of Poesie* was published in 1595. Some of his poems: "Absence," "Dispraise of a Courtly Life," "He That Loves," "Leave Me O Love," "Love Me, O Love," "The Seven Wonders of England," "Thou Blind Man's Mark."

Sources: *Biography of Sir Philp Sidney* (http://www.luminarium.org/renlit/sidbio.htm). *Dictionary of National Biography*. Electronic Edition 1.1. Oxford University Press, 1997. *Encyclopædia Britannica Ultimate Reference Suite DVD*, 2006. *English Poetry: Author Search*. Chadwyck-Healey Ltd., 1995 (http://www.lib.utexas.edu:8080/search/epoetry/author.html). *Erotic Poetry: The Lyrics, Ballads, Idylls, and Epics of Love—Classical to Contemporary*. William Cole, ed. Random House, 1963. *Microsoft Encarta* 2006 (DVD). Microsoft Corporation, 2006. *Selected Poems of Sir Philip Sidney*. Catherine Bates, ed. Penguin Books, 1994. *Silver Poets of the Sixteenth Century*. Gerald Bullett, ed. J.M. Dent, 1947. *The Columbia Granger's Index to Poetry*. 11th ed. *The Columbia Granger's World of Poetry*, Columbia University Press, 2005 (http://www.columbiagrangers.org). *The Heath Introduction to Poetry*. 4th edition. Joseph DeRoche, ed. D.C. Heath, 1992. *The London Book of English Verse*. Herbert Read and Barbara Dobree, eds. MacMillan, 1952. *The National Portrait Gallery* (www.npg.org.uk). *The Oxford Companion to English Literature*. 6th edition. Margaret Drabble, ed. Oxford University Press, 2000.

SILKIN, JON (1930–1997)

Born in London, the son of Jewish solicitor, in 1958 he won a two-year Gregory Fellowship to Leeds

University teaching English to foreign students, then graduated B.A. as a mature student in the School of English in 1962. He lectured in the USA, the Far East, and Australia. From 1965 until he died he lived in Newcastle-upon-Tyne and in 1994 he was appointed senior fellow in poetry at the School of English there. He was founder and editor of the quarterly magazine *Stand* from 1952 until his death. His first poetry collection, the *Peaceable Kingdom,* was published in 1954. He edited several anthologies and books of criticism, most notably on the poets of the First World War. Some of his other publications: *The Portrait and Other Poems,* 1950. *New and Selected Poems,* 1966. *Three Poems,* 1969. *Out of Battle: The Poetry of the Great War,* 1972. *Selected Poems,* 1980. *Selected Poems,* 1993. Some of his poems: "A Daisy," "Caring for Animals," "Death of a Son," "Lilies of the Valley," "The Chisel Grows Heavy," "Word About Freedom and Identity in Tel Aviv."

Sources: *Anthology of Twentieth-Century British and Irish Poetry.* Keith Tuma, ed. Oxford University Press, 2001. *Fine Frenzy: Enduring Themes in Poetry.* Robert Baylor and Brenda Stokes, eds. McGraw-Hill, 1978. *New Poets of England and America.* Donald Hall and Robert Pack, eds. World, 1962. *Obituary of John Silkin: Reporter 412, 15 December 1997* (http://reporter.leeds.ac.uk/412/section9. htm). *Portraits of Poets.* Sebastian Barker, ed. Carcanet, 1986. *The Columbia Granger's Index to Poetry.* 11th ed. *The Columbia Granger's World of Poetry,* Columbia University Press, 2005 (http://www.columbiagrangers.org). *The Oxford Companion to English Literature.* 6th edition. Margaret Drabble, ed. Oxford University Press, 2000. *This Same Sky: A Collection of Poems from Around the World.* Naomi Shihab Nye, ed. Four Winds Press, 1992. *Voices Within the Ark: The Modern Jewish Poets.* Howard Schwartz and Anthony Rudolf, eds. Avon Books, 1980. *Wikipedia, the Free Encyclopedia* (http://en.wikipedia.org/wiki/Wikipedia).

SILLITOE, ALAN (1928–)

Born in Nottingham, the son of a laborer, he left school at 14 to work in the Raleigh Bicycle Factory, then as an air traffic control assistant. He served as a Royal Air Force wireless operator in Malaya; after demobilization he was hospitalized for 18 months with tuberculosis. He was visiting professor of English at De Montfort University, Leicester (1994–1997), is a fellow of the Royal Geographical Society and holds an honorary fellowship from Manchester Polytechnic (1977). He has also been awarded honorary doctorates by Nottingham Polytechnic (1990), Nottingham University (1994) and De Montfort University (1998). He shot to fame with his novel *Saturday Night and Sunday Morning* (1958), followed by *The Loneliness of the Long-Distance Runner* (1959), both made into films. He went on to write many more novels, short stories and plays. He married the poet Ruth Fainlight (see entry) in 1959. They divide

their time between London and Somerset. Some of his poetry publications: *Without Bread or Beer,* 1957. *The Rats and Other Poems,* 1960. *A Falling Out of Love and Other Poems,* 1964. *Storm and Other Poems,* 1974. *Three Poems,* 1988. *Collected Poems,* 1993.

Sources: *British Council Arts* (http://www.contempo rarywriters.com). *Encyclopædia Britannica Ultimate Reference Suite DVD,* 2006. *Holocaust Poetry.* Hilda Schiff, ed. HarperCollins, 1995. *Spaceways: An Anthology of Space Poems.* John Foster, ed. Oxford University Press, 1986. *The Columbia Granger's Index to Poetry.* 11th ed. *The Columbia Granger's World of Poetry,* Columbia University Press, 2005 (http://www.columbiagrangers.org). *The Oxford Book of Twentieth-Century English Verse.* Philip Larkin, ed. Oxford University Press, 1973. *The Oxford Companion to English Literature.* 6th edition. Margaret Drabble, ed. Oxford University Press, 2000. *Who's Who.* London: A & C Black, 2005.

SIMPSON, MATT (1936–)

He was born in Bootle, Lancashire, educated at Cambridge and Liverpool universities, and from 1966 to 1996 he was a senior lecturer in English at what is now Liverpool Hope University. He lives in Liverpool with his wife, former German actress Monika Weydert. With John Lucas he co-edited *Stoneland Harvest— Selected Poems of Dimitris Tsaloumas* (1999) and in 2003 *The Way You Say the World,* a *festschrift* for Anne Stevenson (see entry) on her 70th birthday. He has published a collection of literary essays, *Hugging the Shore,* and five commentaries on Shakespeare plays. His work — which appears in over a hundred anthologies — includes poetry for children. In 1995 he was poet in residence in Tasmania. His poetry publications: *Making Arrangements,* 1982. *An Elegy for the Galosherman — New and Selected Poems,* 1990. *Catching Up with History,* 1995. *The Pigs' Thermal Underwear,* 1995 (children). *Cutting the Clouds Towards,* 1998. *Getting There,* 2001. *In Deep,* 2006. Some of his poems: "Barbus Vulgaris," "Dead Ringer," "The Ghost of My Mother," "Homecoming," "Knowing Where to Look," "My Grandmother's African Grey."

Sources: *Greenwich Exchange Publishing: Matt Simpson.* (http://www.greenex.co.uk/search/search.cgi?Terms= simpson). *Matt (Simpson), Wes (Magee) 'n' Pete.* (Dixon, Macmillan Children's Books, 1995) republished under the title *Lost Property Box,* 1998. Personal correspondence. *The Columbia Granger's Index to Poetry.* 11th ed. *The Columbia Granger's World of Poetry,* Columbia University Press, 2005 (http://www.columbiagrangers.org). *The Windows Project, Poetry, Matt Simpson's Publications* (www.windowsproject. demon.co.uk/writers/simpson.htm).

SINCLAIR, IAIN (1943–)

Novelist, short story writer, non-fiction author, poet and film-maker, he was born in Cardiff, the son of a Welsh general medical practitioner. He studied at Trinity College, Dublin, at the Courtauld Institute of Art, London, and at the London School of Film Technique (now London Film School). Much of his early work was poetry, followed by mostly fiction, then non-fiction; much of his early work was self-published. His novel *Downriver* (1991) won the James Tait Memorial Prize and the 1992 Encore Prize. The book envisages the U.K. under the rule of the Widow, a grotesque version of Margaret Thatcher (British Conservative prime minister, 1979–1990). His 2002 non-fiction book *London Orbital* (with a documentary film of the same name and subject) describes the series of trips he took on foot, following the M25, London's outer-ring motorway. Some of his poetry publications: *Back Garden Poems*, 1970. *The Birth Rug*, 1973. *Lud Heat*, 1975. *Suicide Bridge*, 1979. *Flesh Eggs and Scalp Metal: Selected Poems 1970–1987*, 1987. *The Ebbing of the Kraft*, 1997. Some of his poems: "Autistic Poses," "Big Meal," "Crossing the Morning," "German Bite," "Kristallnacht," "World's Oldest Comedian is Dead."

Sources: *A Various Art.* Andrew Crozier and Tim Longville, eds. Carcanet Press, 1987. *Other: British and Irish Poetry Since 1970.* Richard Caddel and Peter Quartermain, eds. Wesleyan University Press, 1999. *The Columbia Granger's Index to Poetry.* 11th ed. *The Columbia Granger's World of Poetry,* Columbia University Press, 2005 (http://www.columbiagrangers.org). *The New British Poetry, 1968–88.* Gillian Allnutt, Fred D'Aguiar and Ken Edwards, eds. Grafton Books, 1989. *The Oxford Companion to English Literature.* 6th edition. Margaret Drabble, ed. Oxford University Press, 2000. *Wikipedia, the Free Encyclopedia* (http://en.wikipedia.org/wiki/Wikipedia).

SISSON, CHARLES HUBERT (1914–2003)

Born and brought up in Bristol, he read English and philosophy at Bristol University, then studied in Germany and France. He was in the civil service from 1936 until he retired in 1972 as director of Occupational Safety and Health in the Department of Employment, with the rank of undersecretary. During World War II he served in the British Army in India and recorded his military experiences in a satire, *Asiatic Romance* (1953). Sisson converted from Methodism to the Anglican Church and became a zealous defender of the Anglican traditions. His outspoken criticism of the civil service culminated in his *Spirit of British Administration*, a comparison with other European methods. *On the Look-Out: A Partial Autobiography* appeared in 1989. His writings about Anglicanism were collected together in *Is There a Church of England?* (1993). Sisson was a notable translator of, among others, Virgil, Catullus, Dante and Racine. He was appointed a Companion

of Honor in 1993. Some of his poems: "Adam and Eve," "Au Clair de la Lune," "Ellick Farm," "Marcus Aurelius," "Over the Wall: Berlin, May 1975," "The London Zoo," "The Regrets," "Waking."

Sources: *Anthology of Twentieth-Century British and Irish Poetry.* Keith Tuma, ed. Oxford University Press, 2001. Carcanet Press (http://www.carcanet.co.uk). *Collected Poems of C H Sissons.* Carcanet, 1984 and 1998. *The National Portrait Gallery* (www.npg.org.uk). *Obituary of Charles Sisson, News, Telegraph, Sept. 8, 2003* (http://www.telegraph.co.uk/news/main.jhtml?xml=/news/2003/09/08/db0801.xml). *Portraits of Poets.* Sebastian Barker, ed. Carcanet, 1986. *The Columbia Granger's Index to Poetry.* 11th ed. *The Columbia Granger's World of Poetry,* Columbia University Press, 2005 (http://www.columbiagrangers.org). *The Direction of Poetry: An Anthology of Rhymed and Metered Verse Written in the English Language Since 1975.* Robert Richman, ed. Houghton Mifflin, 1988. *The Faber Book of Twentieth Century Verse.* John Heath-Stubbs and David Wright, eds. Faber and Faber, 1975. *The Faber Book of War Poetry.* Kenneth Baker, ed. Faber and Faber, 1996. *The Naked Astronaut: Poems on Birth and Birthdays.* Ren Graziani, ed. Faber and Faber. 1983. *The Oxford Companion to English Literature.* 6th edition. Margaret Drabble, ed. Oxford University Press, 2000. *Wikipedia, the Free Encyclopedia* (http://en.wikipedia.org/wiki/Wikipedia).

SITWELL FAMILY, EDITH, OSBERT and SACHEVERELL (1887–1988)

The Sitwells were probably the most famous literary family of their time. They were the children of Sir George Reresby Sitwell 4th Baronet, and his wife, Lady Ida Emily Augusta Denison, daughter of the Earl of Londesborough. They were born and brought up in Renishaw Hall, on the Derbyshire heights not far from Chesterfield.

Dame Edith Louisa, 1887–1964

Her earliest known verses were published in the *Daily Mirror* in 1913, and from 1916 to 1921 she ran *Wheels*, an annual anthology of new poems, which, in 1919, published seven of Wilfred Owen's war poems (see entry). In 1923 she performed her long poem *Façade* at London's Aeolian Hall to music composed by William Walton. She was awarded honorary doctorates of letters by the universities of Oxford, Leeds, Durham, and Sheffield and was made a Dame of the British Empire in 1954. She died in London. During World War II, she wrote poems about the blitz and other war issues. *Still Falls the Rain* describes a London air raid. Some of her other publications: *The Mother and Other Poems*, 1915. *The Sleeping Beauty*, 1924. *Gold Coast Customs*, 1929. *Gardeners and Astronomers*, 1953. *Music and Ceremonies*, 1963. Some of her poems: "Elegy on Dead Fashion," "The King of China's Daughter," "The Madness of Saul," "Three Poems of the Atomic Bomb."

Sir Francis Osbert, 1892–1969

Born in London and educated at Eton College, he served as a Grenadier Guards officer in World War I. His first poem, *Babel,* was published in *The Times* on 11 May 1916. He succeeded as 5th baronet in 1943 and was appointed Commander of the British Empire (1956), Companion of Honor (1958), honorary doctor of laws of St. Andrews (1946), and honorary doctor of literature of Sheffield University (1951). He suffered from Parkinson's disease and died in London. He wrote short stories and several novels; his best is *Before the Bombardment* (1926), a satirical portrayal of the last phase of Victorian society in Scarborough, Yorkshire, just before World War I. His reputation rests more on his autobiographical series, *Left Hand! Right Hand!* (1944), *Scarlet Tree* (1946), *Great Morning!* (1947), *Laughter in the Next Room* (1948), and *Noble Essences* (1950), than on his poetry. Some of his poetry publications: *Mrs. Kimber,* 1937. *Selected Poems, Old and New,* 1943. *Wrack at Tidesend,* 1952. Some of his poems: "How Shall We Rise to Greet the Dawn?" "Hymn to Moloch," "In the Potting Shed," "Peace Celebration," "The Next War," "War-Horses."

Sir Sacheverell, 1897–1988

He became the 6th baronet on the death of his brother in 1969. Although also a poet, he is best known for his books on art, baroque architecture, and travel. He was educated at Eton College and Balliol College, Oxford, but did not graduate. During World War I he served in the Grenadier Guards. Constant Lambert set his poem *The Rio Grande* to music; it was performed and broadcast in 1929. Sitwell was justice of the peace, 1943, and high sheriff of Northamptonshire, 1948–1949. He also wrote biographies of several composers. He was made a Companion of Honor in 1984. Some of his poetry publications: *The People's Palace,* 1918. *Selected Poems,* 1938. *Tropicalia,* 1971. *Agamemnon's Tomb,* 1972. *A Notebook on My New Poems,* 1974. *An Indian Summer: 100 Recent Poems,* 1982. Some of his poems: "Derbyshire Bluebells," "Fountains," "Kingcups," "The River God," "The Venus of Bolsover Castle," "Tulip Tree."

Sources: *British Women Writers: An Anthology from the Fourteenth Century to the Present.* Dale Spender and Janet Todd, eds. Peter Bedrick Books, 1989. *Dictionary of National Biography.* Electronic Edition 1.1. Oxford University Press, 1997. *Encyclopædia Britannica Ultimate Reference Suite DVD,* 2006. *Men Who March Away: Poems of the First World War.* I.M. Parsons, ed. Viking Press, 1965. *Microsoft Encarta* 2006 (DVD). Microsoft Corporation, 2006. *Modern British Poetry.* 7th rev. ed. Louis Untermeyer, ed. Harcourt, Brace, 1962. *The National Portrait Gallery* (www.npg.org.uk). *Poetry of the World Wars.* Michael Foss, ed. Peter Bedrick Books, 1990. *The Chatto Book of Modern Poetry 1915–1955.* Cecil Day Lewis and John Lehmann, eds. Chatto and Windus, 1966. *The Collected Poems of Edith Sitwell.* The Vanguard Press, 1954. *The Collected Satires and Poems of Osbert Sitwell.* Duckworth, 1931. *The Columbia Granger's Index to Poetry.* 11th ed. *The Columbia Granger's World of Poetry,* Columbia University Press, 2005 (http://www.columbiagrangers.org). *The Earth is the Lord's: Poems of the Spirit.* Helen Plotz, ed. Thomas Y. Crowell, 1965. *The Oxford Book of Modern Verse, 1892–1935.* William Butler Yeats, ed. Oxford University Press, 1936. *The Oxford Companion to English Literature.* 6th edition. Margaret Drabble, ed. Oxford University Press, 2000. *Wikipedia, the Free Encyclopedia* (http://en.wikipedia.org/wiki/Wikipedia).

SKELTON, JOHN (?1460–1529)

Tudor poet whose poetic style of short rhyming lines, based on natural speech rhythms, has been given the name of Skeltonics. Possibly from Diss, Norfolk, he studied at the universities of Oxford and Cambridge and was academic poet laureate in rhetoric at both universities. He was court poet to Henry VII and tutor to the Duke of York, the future king. He was made rector of Diss in 1498, royal orator, and adviser to Henry VIII on church and public affairs. He died at Westminster and was buried in the chancel of St. Margaret's Church. His principal poems: *The Bowge of Courte,* a satire on the court of Henry VII; *Phyllyp Sparrowe,* possibly the origin of *Who Killed Cock Robin?; Ware the Hawke,* an angry attack on a priest who had flown his hawk into Skelton's church; *Ballad of the Scottysshe Kynge,* written in 1513 after the Battle of Flodden; and *Collyn Clout* (see also Spenser, Edmund). Some of his poems: "A Lytell Ragge of Rethorike," "Knolege, Aquayntance, Resort, Fauour with Grace," "Magnyfycence, a Goodly Interlude," "Though Ye Suppose All Jeperdys Ar Paste."

Sources: *Dictionary of National Biography.* Electronic Edition 1.1. Oxford University Press, 1997. *Encyclopædia Britannica Ultimate Reference Suite DVD,* 2006. *English Poetry: Author Search.* Chadwyck-Healey Ltd., 1995 (http://www.lib.utexas.edu:8080/search/epoetry/author.html). *English Renaissance Poetry: A Collection of Shorter Poems from Skelton to Jonson.* John Williams, ed. University of Arkansas, 1990. *The National Portrait Gallery* (www.npg.org.uk). *Stanford University Libraries and Academic Information Resources* (http://library.stanford.edu). *The Columbia Granger's Index to Poetry.* 11th ed. *The Columbia Granger's World of Poetry,* Columbia University Press, 2005 (http://www.columbiagrangers.org). *The Complete Poems of John Skelton.* Philip Henderson, ed. J.M. Dent and Sons, Ltd., 1948. *The New Oxford Book of Sixteenth Century Verse.* Emrys Jones, ed. Oxford University Press, 1991. *The Norton Anthology of English Literature.* 5th ed. Vol. 2, M.H. Abrams, ed. W.W. Norton, 1986. *The Oxford Book of English Verse, 1250–1918.* Sir Arthur Quiller-Couch, ed. New edition, revised and enlarged, Oxford University Press, 1939. *The Oxford Companion to English Literature.* 6th edition. Margaret Drabble, ed. Oxford University Press,

2000. *The Penguin Book of English Christian Verse.* Peter Levi, ed. Penguin Books, 1984.

SKINNER, JOHN (1721–1807)

Born at Balfour, Aberdeenshire, the son of a schoolmaster, he was educated at Marischal College, Aberdeen, then took orders in the Scottish Episcopal Church in 1742 and settled at Longside, Aberdenshire. At the 1745 Rebellion, Skinner's church was destroyed and he was imprisoned for six months because he preached to more than four people. Robert Burns secured several of Skinner's best songs for James Johnson's *Musical Museum* (1787). His second son, John, was Bishop of Aberdeen (1788) and while staying with him, the old man died, eight years after his wife, and was buried at Longside. He was the author of *Ecclesiastical History of Scotland* (1788), and his *Theological Works*, with a biography, were published by his son in 1809. *Amusements of Leisure Hours, or Poetical Pieces Chiefly in the Scottish Dialect* and *Miscellaneous Collection of Fugitive Pieces of Poetry* were both published in 1809. *Songs and Poems*, with a sketch of his life, was published in 1859. Some of his songs/poems: "An Auld Minister's Song," "Lizzy Liberty," "On Bruns' Address to a Louse," "The Monymusk Christmas Ba'ing [football]," "The Owl and the Ass," "Tullochgorum."

Sources: *Dictionary of National Biography.* Electronic Edition 1.1. Oxford University Press, 1997. *English Poetry: Author Search.* Chadwyck-Healey Ltd., 1995 (http://www.lib.utexas.edu:8080/search/epoetry/author.html). *Songs and Poems of John Skinner.* G Reid, 1859. *The Burns Encyclopedia, John Skinner* (http://www.robertburns.org/encyclopedia/CunninghamAllan17841511842.253.shtml). *The Columbia Granger's Index to Poetry.* 11th ed. *The Columbia Granger's World of Poetry,* Columbia University Press, 2005 (http://www.columbiagrangers.org).

SKIPSEY, JOSEPH (1832–1903)

"The Collier Poet," he was born at Percy, Tynemouth, Northumberland, and when he was an infant, his father was shot and killed in a disturbance between pitmen and special constables. Working in the mines from the age of seven, he had no schooling, but taught himself to read and write. Until the age of 15 the Bible was his only book, but he went on to read translations from Greek, Latin and German. He was secretary of the Newcastle Literary and Philosophical Society from 1837 to 1842. He was granted a pension from the civil list in 1880, and in 1889 — on the recommendation of several poets, including Robert Browning and Alfred Lord Tennyson — he and his wife were appointed custodians of Shakespeare's birthplace at Stratford-on-Avon. Wearied by the drudgery, he returned to the north and died at Gateshead, where he was buried, his wife having died the previous year. Some of his publica-

tions: *Poems, Songs, and Ballads,* 1862. *The Collier Lad, and Other Lyrics,* 1864. *Poems,* 1871. *A Book of Miscellaneous Lyrics,* 1878. *Carols from the Coalfields,* 1886. Some of his poems: "Alas!" "Annie Lee," "Bereaved," "The Fatal Errand," "Thistle and Nettle," "Uncle Bob," "Young Fanny."

Sources: *Dictionary of National Biography.* Electronic Edition 1.1. Oxford University Press, 1997. *Joseph Skipsey: Songs and Lyrics* (http://www.gerald-massey.org.uk/cop_skipsey_index.htm). *Selected Poems of Joseph Skipsey.* Ceolfrith Press, 1976. *The Columbia Granger's Index to Poetry.* 11th ed. *The Columbia Granger's World of Poetry,* Columbia University Press, 2005 (http://www.columbiagrangers.org). *The Newcastle Literary and Philosophical Soceity, Joseph Skipsey and Some Other Men of Note* (http://www.litandphil.org.uk/skipsey.htm). *The Poorhouse Fugitives: Self-Taught Poets and Poetry in Victorian Britain.* Brian Maidment, ed. Carcanet, 1987.

SMART, CHRISTOPHER (1722–1771)

Born in Kent, and educated at Durham, northeast England, he graduated M.A. from Pembroke Hall (now Pembroke College), Cambridge, in 1747 and was elected a fellow in 1745. In 1750 his poem "Hymn to the Supreme Being" won the Seatonian Prize, which helped him to pay his creditors. From 1751 until he died, he suffered from bouts of mental illness of a religious nature and spent many years in one hospital or another. Between 1751 and 1753, under the pseudonym "Mary Midnight," he ran a cheap journal, the *Midwife, or the Old Woman's Magazine,* where many of his compositions appeared under the pseudonym "Pentweazle." He died in the debtors' prison and was buried in St. Paul's Churchyard. Some of his publications: *Hannah: An Oratorio,* 1764. *Hymns for the Amusement of Children,* 1772. *Poems on Several Occasions,* 1763. *The Parables of Jesus Christ,* 1768. *A Song to David,* 1763. *The Works of Horace,* 1767. Some of his poems: "A Morning Hymn," "A Story of a Cock and a Bull," "Apollo and Daphne," "Inscriptions on an Aeolian Harp," "The Hop-Garden," "The Stars."

Sources: *A Sacrifice of Praise: An Anthology of Christian Poetry in English from Caedmon to the Mid-Twentieth Century.* James H. Trott, ed. Cumberland House Publishing, 1999. *Chapters into Verse, Vol. II: Gospels to Revelation.* Robert Atwan and Laurance Wieder, eds. Oxford University Press, 1993. *Christopher Smart: Selected Poems.* Karina Williamson and Marcus Walsh, eds. Penguin Books, 1990. *Dictionary of National Biography.* Electronic Edition 1.1. Oxford University Press, 1997. *Encyclopædia Britannica Ultimate Reference Suite DVD,* 2006. *English Poetry: Author Search.* Chadwyck-Healey Ltd., 1995 (http://www.lib.utexas.edu:8080/search/epoetry/author.html). *Microsoft Encarta 2006 (DVD).* Microsoft Corporation, 2006. *The National Portrait Gallery* (www.npg.org.uk). *Stanford University Libraries and Academic Information Resources* (http://library.stanford.edu). *The Cherry-Tree.* Geoffrey Grigson, ed. Phoenix House, 1959. *The Columbia*

Granger's Index to Poetry. 11th ed (http://www.columbia grangers.org). *The Oxford Book of Children's Verse.* Iona Opie and Peter Opie, eds. Oxford University Press, 1973. *The Oxford Companion to English Literature.* 6th edition. Margaret Drabble, ed. Oxford University Press, 2000.

SMITH, ALEXANDER (1829/30–1867)

Scottish poet, born in Kilmarnock, Ayrshire, he followed his father into becoming a lace-pattern designer, but encouraged by the publication of his poetry in the *Critic* and the *Eclectic Review* in 1851–1852, he gave up his trade. After editing the *Glasgow Miscellany* for a short time and doing other journalistic and literary work in Glasgow, in 1854 he was appointed secretary to Edinburgh University. In 1854 he made the acquaintance of Sydney Dobell (see entry), then living in Edinburgh, and they collaborated in a series titled *Sonnets on the Crimean War* (1855). In 1864 Smith spent six weeks exploring the island of Skye — his wife's home. "A Summer in Skye" is his magnificent prose poem celebrating the island and its people. In 1866 he edited John W.S. Howe's *Golden Leaves from the American Poets.* He died at Granton, Midlothian, and was buried in Warriston Cemetery, Edinburgh. Some of his publications are: *Life Drama and Other Poems,* 1853. *Poems,* 1856. *City Poems,* 1857. *Edwin of Deira,* 1861. *Last Leaves,* 1868. Some of his poems: "A Boy's Poem," "A Life Drama," "America," "An Evening at Home," "Barbara," "Blaavin," "Miss Nightingale."

Sources: *A Book of Scottish Verse.* Maurice Lindsay and R.L. Mackie, eds. St. Martin's Press, 1983. *A Summer in Skye, Alexander Smith, Word Power* (http://www.word-power.co.uk/catalogue/1874744386). *Dictionary of National Biography.* Electronic Edition 1.1. Oxford University Press, 1997. *English Poetry: Author Search.* Chadwyck-Healey Ltd., 1995 (http://www.lib.utexas.edu:8080/search/epoetry/author.html). *Poems, by Alexander Smith.* Ticknoe, Reed, and Fields, 1853. *The Columbia Granger's Index to Poetry.* 11th ed. *The Columbia Granger's World of Poetry,* Columbia University Press, 2005 (http://www.columbiagrangers.org). *The New Penguin Book of Scottish Verse.* Robert Crawford and Mick Imlah, eds. Penguin Books, 2000. *The Oxford Book of Victorian Verse.* Arthur Quiller-Couch, ed. Oxford University Press, 1971. *The Oxford Companion to English Literature.* 6th edition. Margaret Drabble, ed. Oxford University Press, 2000. *Victorian Verse.* George MacBeth, ed. Penguin Books, 1986.

SMITH, CHARLOTTE (1749–1806)

The daughter of Nicholas Turner of Stoke House, Surrey, and Bignor Park, Sussex, her mother died when she was three, and when her father remarried, Charlotte's aunt arranged for her to marry Benjamin Smith, son of Richard Smith, a West India merchant and director of the East India Company. On the death of his wife, her father-in-law married Charlotte's aunt. In 1782, following his father's compli-

cated will and lawsuit, the Hampshire estate was sold and Smith was imprisoned for debt and for seven months Charlotte shared his confinement. The couple lived for a time in France, but Charlotte separated from her husband about 1786 and returned to England. To support herself and her twelve children, she took up writing. Between 1788 and 1798 she wrote eleven novels. She died at Tilford, near Farnham, Surrey, and was buried at Stoke Church, near Guildford. In 1784 she published *Elegiac Sonnets and Other Essays.* Some of her poems: "Apostrophe to an Old Tree," "Ode to the Missel Thrush," "The Close of Summer," "The Dictatorial Owl," "The Emigrants," "The Forest Boy," "The Glow-Worm," "To a Nightingale."

Sources: *Dictionary of National Biography.* Electronic Edition 1.1. Oxford University Press, 1997. *English Poetry: Author Search.* Chadwyck-Healey Ltd., 1995 (http://www.lib.utexas.edu:8080/search/epoetry/author.html). *Fellow Mortals: An Anthology of Animal Verse.* Roy Fuller, ed. Macdonald and Evans, 1981. *Poetry by English Women: Elizabethan to Victorian,* R.E. Pritchard, ed. Continuum, 1990. *The Columbia Granger's Index to Poetry.* 11th ed. *The Columbia Granger's World of Poetry,* Columbia University Press, 2005 (http://www.columbiagrangers.org). *The Oxford Companion to English Literature.* 6th edition. Margaret Drabble, ed. Oxford University Press, 2000. *The Poems of Charlotte Smith.* Stuart Curran, ed. Oxford University Press, 1993.

SMITH, FLORENCE MARGARET ("STEVIE") (1902–1971)

Born in Hull, she moved with her mother to Palmers Green, London, when she was three, and lived almost all her life there in the care of an aunt after her mother died and her father remarried. From the age of five, she spent three years in a sanatorium suffering from tuberculosis. For thirty years she worked for Newnes-Pearson, the magazine publishers. Her first, largely biographical, book, *Novel on Yellow Paper* (1936), was an immediate success. She wrote two more novels as well as short stories, literary reviews, and essays, but is remembered chiefly for her poetry, which she frequently illustrated with captivating line drawings. In 1966 she received the Cholmondeley award and in 1969 the Queen's gold medal for poetry. She died at Ashburton Cottage Hospital in Devon from a brain tumor. The stage play *Stevie* (1977) by Hugh Whitemore, starring Glenda Jackson, was later made into a successful film. Some of her poems: "Alfred the Great," "Analysand," "Bag-Snatching in Dublin," "Cat Asks Mouse Out," "Death in the Rose Garden," "Tender Only to One," "The Abominable Lake," "When the Sparrow Flies."

Sources: *Collected Poems of Stevie Smith.* James MacGibbon, ed. New Directions, 1976. *Dictionary of National Bi-*

ography. Electronic Edition 1.1. Oxford University Press, 1997. *Encyclopædia Britannica Ultimate Reference Suite DVD,* 2006. *Microsoft Encarta* 2006 (DVD). Microsoft Corporation, 2006. *The Columbia Granger's Index to Poetry.* 11th ed. *The Columbia Granger's World of Poetry,* Columbia University Press, 2005 (http://www.columbia grangers.org). *The Oxford Book of Villains.* John Mortimer, ed. Oxford University Press, 1992. *The Oxford Companion to English Literature.* 6th edition. Margaret Drabble, ed. Oxford University Press, 2000. *The Women Poets in English: An Anthology.* Ann Stanford, ed. McGraw-Hill, 1972.

SMITH, HORATIO (1779–1849)

Born in London, the son of solicitor, he was educated at Chigwell School, Essex, and became a successful stockbroker, earning the praise of Percy Bysshe Shelley as one who could not only make money well and be generous with it, but was also a good poet. When the Drury Lane Theatre was to be rebuilt, the managers offered a prize for an address to be recited at he opening. He, with his brother James, wrote *The Rejected Addresses* (1812), parodies of eight poets, none of whom took offense at the clever accuracy of the parodies. Smith went on to become friends with many poets, including Shelley, with whom he participated in a sonnet writing competition. His poem was "On a Stupendous Leg of Granite." Shelley's was "Ozymandias"; both were published in 1818. After making his fortune, Smith published a series of six historical novels and three volumes of *Gaieties and Gravities.* He died at Tunbridge Wells, Kent. Some of his poems: "Address to a Mummy," "Birthday of the Spring," "Diamond Cut Diamond," "Invocation to the Cuckoo," "Lachrymose Writers," "Sonnet to My Own Nose," "Winter," "York Kidney Potatoes."

Sources: *Dictionary of National Biography.* Electronic Edition 1.1. Oxford University Press, 1997. *English Poetry: Author Search.* Chadwyck-Healey Ltd., 1995 (http://www.lib.utexas.edu:8080/search/epoetry/author.html). *Roofs of Gold: Poems to Read Aloud.* Padraic Colum, ed. Macmillan, 1964. *The Columbia Granger's Index to Poetry.* 11th ed. *The Columbia Granger's World of Poetry,* Columbia University Press, 2005 (http://www.columbiagrangers.org). *The Poetical Works of Horace Smith: Volume I & II.* Henry Colburn, 1846. *Wikipedia, the Free Encyclopedia* (http://en.wikipedia.org/wiki/Wikipedia).

SMITH, IAIN CRICHTON (1928–1998)

Although born in Glasgow, he was brought up on the Gaelic speaking Hebridean Island of Lewis, with English as his second language. After graduating in English from Aberdeen University in 1949, and following National Service, he taught English at various high schools until he retired in 1977 to become a full-time writer. He was awarded the Order of the British Empire in 1980 and won several literary prizes, awards and fellowships. Three Scottish uni-

versities awarded him honorary doctorates. He died at Oban, Argyllshire. He wrote in both English and Gaelic; a number of his poems explore the subject of the Highland Clearances, and one of his many novels, *Consider the Lilies* (1968), is an account of the eviction of an elderly woman during such times. Some of his publications: *Modern Gaelic Verse,* 1966. *Selected Poems,* 1970. *Love Poems and Elegies,* 1972. *Selected Poems 1955–1982,* 1982. *Selected Poems,* 1990. *Collected Poems,* 1992. Some of his poems: "Australia," "Culloden and After," "Deer on the High Hills: A Meditation," "Gaelic Songs," "Owl and Mouse," "Shall Gaelic Die?" "Towards the Stars."

Sources: *A Book of Scottish Verse.* Maurice Lindsay and R.L. Mackie, eds. St. Martin's Press, 1983. *Golden Treasury of the Best Songs and Lyrical Poems in the English Language.* Francis Turner Palgrave, ed. Oxford University Press, 1964, Sixth edition, updated by John Press, 1994. *The Columbia Granger's Index to Poetry.* 11th ed. *The Columbia Granger's World of Poetry,* Columbia University Press, 2005 (http://www.columbiagrangers.org). *The Harvill Book of Twentieth-Century Poetry in English.* Michael Schmidt, ed. The Harvill Press, 1999. *The New Penguin Book of Scottish Verse.* Robert Crawford and Mick Imlah, eds. Penguin Books, 2000. *The Oxford Book of Animal Poems.* Michael Harrison and Christopher Stuart-Clark, eds. Oxford University Press, 1992. *The Oxford Companion to English Literature.* 6th edition. Margaret Drabble, ed. Oxford University Press, 2000. *Wikipedia, the Free Encyclopedia* (http://en.wikipedia.org/wiki/Wikipedia).

SMITH, SYDNEY, GOODSIR (1915–1975)

He was born in Wellington, New Zealand, of a Scottish mother and a father who was an army medical officer and later professor of forensic medicine at Edinburgh. After Malvern College, England, rather than medicine, Smith studied history at Oriel College, Oxford. With Hugh MacDiarmid he was at the forefront of the Scottish Renaissance and quickly adopted Scots (Lallan) for his poetry. His first collection, *Skail Wind,* was published in 1941 and his novel *Carotid Cornucopius* (1947) draws a vivid picture of all aspects of Edinburgh low life. His play *Wallace* was performed at the Edinburgh Festival of 1960. *Under the Eildon Tree* (1948) was a twenty-four part poem celebrating romantic love. He was a dedicated amateur painter and a gifted translator, and for several years he was art critic for *The Scotsman.* He took his place in the Makers' Court, Edinburgh, the Scottish equivalent of Westminster Abbey's Poets' Corner, in July 2003. Some of his poems: "Can I Forget?" "El Alamein," "Hamewith," "Leander Stormbound," "Loch Leven," "Omens," "The Deevil's Waltz," "The Grace of God and the Meth-Drinker," "War in Fife."

Sources: *Biography of Sidney Goodsir Smith: Scottish Au-*

thors (http://www.slainte.org.uk/scotauth/smithdsw.htm). *Collected Poems of Sydney Goodsir Smith*. Calder Publications Ltd (1976). *Poets' Work Makes Court Appearance*. *Evening News, 24th July 2003* (http://news.scotsman.com/arts.cfm?id=801792003). *Seven Centuries of Poetry: Chaucer to Dylan Thomas*. A.N. Jeffares, ed. Longmans, Green, 1955. *The Columbia Granger's Index to Poetry*. 11th ed (http://www.columbiagrangers.org). *The Faber Book of Twentieth Century Verse*. John Heath-Stubbs and David Wright, eds. Faber and Faber, 1975. *The New Penguin Book of Scottish Verse*. Robert Crawford and Mick Imlah, eds. Penguin Books, 2000. *The New Zealand Edge: Media / Newzedge: Sydney Goodsir Smith* (http://www.nzedge.com/media/archives/archv-arts-writers.html). *The Oxford Book of Verse in English Translation*. Charles Tomlinson, ed. Oxford University Press, 1980. *The Oxford Companion to English Literature*. 6th edition. Margaret Drabble, ed. Oxford University Press, 2000.

SMITH, WALTER CHALMERS (1824–1908)

Scottish poet and hymn writer, born in Aberdeen, he graduated M.A. from Marischal College at the age of 17, studied and at New College, Edinburgh, and was ordained in 1850. A highly respected churchman, he had churches in London, Fifeshire, Glasgow and Edinburgh. In 1867, he was admonished by the General Assembly for his outspoken, liberal views on Sunday observance. When Professor Robertson Smith was charged with heresy for articles he had written in the *Encyclopædia Britannica* in 1875, Smith argued for him. From 1893 to 1894 he was moderator of the General Assembly; he received the degrees of doctor of divinity from Glasgow University (1869) and doctor of laws from the universities of Aberdeen (1876) and Edinburgh (1893). His poem "Immortal, Invisible, God Only Wise" set to the tune *St. Denio* is included in most hymnbooks. Some of his poetry publications: *The Bishop's*, 1861. *North Country Folk*, 1883. *Kildrostan, a Dramatic Poem*, 1884. *Thoughts and Fancies for Sunday Evening*, 1887. *A Heretic*, 1890. Some of his poems: "Glenaradale," "In Edinburgh Castle," "The Cameronian Regiment," "The Macgregors," "The Siege of the Bass."

Sources: *A Sacrifice of Praise: An Anthology of Christian Poetry in English from Caedmon to the Mid-Twentieth Century*. James H. Trott, ed. Cumberland House Publishing, 1999. *Dictionary of National Biography*. Electronic Edition 1.1. Oxford University Press, 1997. *English Poetry: Author Search*. Chadwyck-Healey Ltd., 1995 (http://www.lib.utexas.edu:8080/search/epoetry/author.html). *Poems of the Scottish Hills: An Anthology*. Hamish Brown, ed. Aberdeen University Press, 1982. *The Columbia Granger's Index to Poetry*. 11th ed. *The Columbia Granger's World of Poetry*, Columbia University Press, 2005 (http://www.columbiagrangers.org). *The Oxford Book of English Verse, 1250–1918*. Sir Arthur Quiller-Couch, ed. New edition, revised and enlarged, Oxford University Press, 1939.

SMOLLETT, TOBIAS GEORGE (1721–1771)

Scottish poet, the son of Sir James of Bonhill, Dumbartonshire, he attended Glasgow University and was an apprenticed surgeon. He left the university in 1739 without a degree and in 1740 was commissioned surgeon's second mate in the Royal Navy on HMS *Chichester* and saw action in the West Indies. In London he set up as a surgeon on Downing Street, Westminster, where he wrote his famous poem "The Tears of Scotland" memorializing the Battle of Culloden, 1746. In 1750 he obtained the degree of M.D. from Marischal College, Aberdeen. He died at his villa in Leghorn, Italy, where he was buried. His novels made him famous and financially secure. Two of them are *The Adventures of Roderick Random* (1748) and *The Adventures of Sir Launcelot Greaves* (1762), which was serialized in *The British Magazine,* of which Smollett became editor in 1760. He also wrote the *Complete History of England* (1757–1758) and *Travels Through France and Italy* (1766). Some of his poems: "A Pastoral Ballad," "Adieu, Ye Streams That Smoothly Flow," "Advice: A Satire," "Burlesque Ode," "Come, Listen Ye Students of Ev'ry Degree," "Independence," "Thy Fatal Shafts Unerring Move."

Sources: *Dictionary of National Biography*. Electronic Edition 1.1. Oxford University Press, 1997. *Encyclopædia Britannica Ultimate Reference Suite DVD*, 2006. *Microsoft Encarta 2006 (DVD)*. Microsoft Corporation, 2006. *The National Portrait Gallery* (www.npg.org.uk). *The Columbia Granger's Index to Poetry*. 11th ed. *The Columbia Granger's World of Poetry*, Columbia University Press, 2005 (http://www.columbiagrangers.org). *The Oxford Book of Eighteenth Century Verse*. David Nichol Smith, ed. Oxford University Press, 1926. *The Oxford Companion to English Literature*. 6th edition. Margaret Drabble, ed. Oxford University Press, 2000. *The Works of Tobias Smollett: Poems, Plays, and the Briton*. University of Georgia Press, 1993.

SMYTH, GERARD (1951–)

Born in Dublin, he has been publishing poetry in literary journals in Ireland, Britain and North America since the late 1960s. He lives in Dublin, where he is a journalist with *The Irish Times*. Some of his poetry publications: *World Without End*, 1977. *Loss and Gain*, 1981. *Painting the Pink Roses Black*, 1986. *Daytime Sleeper*, 2002. *A New Tenancy*, 2004. Some of his poems: "Portobello Bridge," "Mid-Century Sunday," "Sunday Morning in Romania," "The Calling Angel."

Sources: *Biography of Gerard Smyth and Three Poems* (http://www.dedaluspress.com/poets/smyth.html). *Biography of Gerard Smyth* (http://www.irishwriters-online.com/gerardsmyth.html).

SOMERVILLE, WILLIAM (1675–1742)

Born on the family estate, Edstone, Warwickshire, he went from Winchester College to New College, Oxford, where he obtained a fellowship in 1696 before training in law at the Middle Temple. When his father died in 1705 he retired to Edstone to spend the rest of his life as a country gentleman. He had a good reputation; he enjoyed the respect of his neighbors and he cared for his animals. His poems abound with references to field sports, but he roundly condemned hare coursing. He died at Edstone heavily laden with property debt. His wife died childless in 1731, and they are both buried in the chantry chapel of the church of Wootton-Wawen, Warwickshire. While his fame rests more on *The Chase*, a blank verse poem in four books, of 540 lines; *Field Sports* runs a close second, illustrated as it was by his brother Bewick. Some of his other poems: "A Padlock for the Mouth," "Advice to the Ladies," "Field Sports," "Hobbinol; or The Rural Games," "The Bowling Green," "The Coquette," "The Happy Lunatic," "The Wise Builder," "The Yeoman of Kent."

Sources: *Dictionary of National Biography.* Electronic Edition 1.1. Oxford University Press, 1997. *Eighteenth-Century English Verse.* Dennis Davison, ed. Penguin Books, 1988. *Encyclopædia Britannica Ultimate Reference Suite DVD,* 2006. *English Poetry: Author Search.* Chadwyck-Healey Ltd., 1995 (http://www.lib.utexas.edu:8080/search/epoetry/author.html). *The National Portrait Gallery* (www.npg.org.uk). *The Columbia Granger's Index to Poetry.* 11th ed. *The Columbia Granger's World of Poetry,* Columbia University Press, 2005 (http://www.columbiagrangers.org). *The Faber Book of Useful Verse.* Simon Brett, ed. Faber and Faber, 1981. *The New Oxford Book of Eighteenth Century Verse.* Roger Lonsdale, ed. Oxford University Press, 1984. *The Oxford Companion to English Literature.* 6th edition. Margaret Drabble, ed. Oxford University Press, 2000. *The Poetical Works of William Somervile.* Thomas, Park, ed. J. Sharpe, 1808.

SORLEY, CHARLES HAMILTON (1895–1915)

Born in Aberdeen, he was the son of William Ritchie Sorley, professor of moral philosophy at Aberdeen University, who later became Knightbridge professor of moral philosophy at Cambridge University and a fellow of King's College. Charles was educated at Marlborough College, Wiltshire, where he developed the passion for cross-country running. His poetry—which started when he published the poem "The Tempest" at the age of ten, influenced by the work of John Masefield (see entry) and the stunning Wiltshire countryside. One of his most accomplished schoolboy poems is "The River," based on an actual suicide. He enlisted in the Suffolk Regiment and was in France by May 1915. He was killed by a sniper's bullet and buried where he fell. He is memo-

rialized by a stone in Poets' Corner of Westminster Abbey along with other poets of the First World War. Some of his poems: "A Tale of Two Careers," "Autumn Dawn," "Rooks," "The Seekers," "The Song of the Ungirt Runners," "To Germany," "Two Songs from Ibsen's Dramatic Poems," "Two Sonnets," "Whom Therefore We Ignorantly Worship."

Sources: *Dictionary of National Biography.* Electronic Edition 1.1. Oxford University Press, 1997. *Marlborough and Other Poems of Charles Hamilton Sorley.* Cambridge University Press, 1916. *Never Such Innocence: A New Anthology of Great War Verse.* Martin Stephen, ed. Buchan and Enright, 1988. *The Columbia Granger's Index to Poetry.* 11th ed. *The Columbia Granger's World of Poetry,* Columbia University Press, 2005 (http://www.columbiagrangers.org). *The Home Book of Modern Verse.* Burton Egbert Stevenson, ed. Henry Holt, 1953. *The Oxford Companion to English Literature.* 6th edition. Margaret Drabble, ed. Oxford University Press, 2000. *Westminster Abbey Official Guide* (no date).

SOUTAR, WILLIAM (1898–1943)

Scottish poet, born in Perth, who joined the Royal Navy in 1916 and served in the Atlantic and the North Sea. In 1919 he started a medical degree at Edinburgh University, but transferred to English, and graduated in 1923. He suffered from an incurable spinal disease, which was operated on in 1930, and he was confined to bed for the rest of his life. His father adapted a downstairs room for William, overlooking the back garden, where he wrote poetry and an extensive journal and entertained several hundred friends in the course of a year. Many of his visitors were writers and his room became a center for the Scottish literary renaissance. Diagnosed with tuberculosis in July 1943, he began a new volume of his journal, which he entitled *The Diary of a Dying Man.* Some of his publications: *Seeds in the Wind,* 1933. *Poems in Scots,* 1935. *Brief Words,* 1935. *Riddles in Scots,* 1937. *The Expectant Silence,* 1944. Some of his poems: "A Hint o' Snow," "A Riddle," "An Alphabet for Caledonian Bairns," "Among High Hills," "The Auld House," "The Three Puddocks," "Wait for the Hour."

Sources: *Biograhy of William Soutar: BBC, Writing Scotland. Scotland's Languages* (http://www.bbc.co.uk/scotland/arts/writingscotland/writers/william_soutar/). *Encyclopædia Britannica Ultimate Reference Suite DVD,* 2006. *Oldpoetry* (www.oldpoetry.com). *Poems of the Scottish Hills: An Anthology.* Hamish Brown, ed. Aberdeen University Press, 1982. *Scottish Authors, William Soutar* (http://www.slainte.org.uk/scotauth/soutadsw.htm). *The Columbia Granger's Index to Poetry.* 11th ed. *The Columbia Granger's World of Poetry,* Columbia University Press, 2005 (http://www.columbiagrangers.org). *The Faber Book of Vernacular Verse.* Tom Paulin. Faber and Faber, 1990. *The New British Poets: An Anthology.* Kenneth Rexroth, ed. New Directions, 1949. *The Oxford Book of Scottish Verse,* John

MacQueen and Tom Scott, eds. Oxford University Press, 1966. *The Oxford Companion to English Literature.* 6th edition. Margaret Drabble, ed. Oxford University Press, 2000.

SOUTHEY, CAROLINE ANNE BOWLES (1786–1854)

Caroline Bowles was born at Buckland Cottage, Lymington, Hampshire, the daughter of an officer in the East India Company. After her parents died, and after suffering from dishonesty of her guardian, her home was saved by an annuity from a friend. Determined to support herself, she took to writing and sent the poem *Ellen Fitzarthur: A Metrical Tale* to Robert Southey (see entry). It was published in 1820, the year that Southey and Caroline met. He proposed a partnership on a poem titled *Robin Hood,* but the rhymeless stanza style did not suit Caroline. The friendship continued, and in 1839 Caroline married the ailing Southey and moved to Keswick, where she was detested by her step-children. When Southey died, she returned to Lymington and wrote nothing further. A crown pension was conferred upon her two years before she died. She was buried in Lymington. Some of her other publications: *The Widow's Tale, and Other Poems,* 1822. *Tales of the Factories,* 1823. *Chapters on Churchyards,* 1829. *The Birthday,* 1836. Some of her poems: "Abjuration," "Autumn Flowers," "Mariner's Hymn," "The Treaty," "The Welcome Home, 1820," "To Death," "To Little Mary."

Sources: *Dictionary of National Biography.* Electronic Edition 1.1. Oxford University Press, 1997. *The Columbia Granger's Index to Poetry.* 11th ed. *The Columbia Granger's World of Poetry,* Columbia University Press, 2005 (http://www.columbiagrangers.org). *The Floral Wreath of Autumn Flowers By Caroline Bowles Southey* (no publisher), 1838. *The Oxford Book of English Verse, 1250–1918.* Sir Arthur Quiller-Couch, ed. New edition, revised and enlarged, Oxford University Press, 1939. *Treasury of Favorite Poems.* Joseph H. Head, ed. Gramercy Books, 2000.

SOUTHEY, ROBERT (1774–1843)

Born at Bristol, Somerset, the son of a linen draper, he was educated at Westminster School, from which he was expelled for writing a protest in a school magazine against excessive flogging. He met Samuel Taylor Coleridge (see entry) while at Balliol College, Oxford, and a life-long friendship was formed. Later they married two sisters. In 1803 he settled with the Coleridge family at Greta Hall, Keswick, neighbors of William Wordsworth (see entry). They became known as the Lake Poets. For 30 years from 1808 he augmented his income by contributing over ninety-five articles, mostly on publications of the day, to the *Quarterly Review.* He was made poet laureate in 1813. His wife died in

1837, and two years later he married Caroline Bowles (see Southey, Caroline Ann Bowles). He is memorialized by a stone in Poets' Corner of Westminster Abbey. Some of his poetry publications: *Joan of Arc,* 1796. *Thalaba the Destroyer,* 1801. *Wat Tyler: A Dramatic Poem,* 1817. *The Curse of Kehama,* 1810. Some of his other poems: "A Vision of Judgement," "Cataract of Lodore," "Epitaph on King John," "The Battle of Blenheim," "The Inchcape Rock."

Sources: *Dictionary of National Biography.* Electronic Edition 1.1. Oxford University Press, 1997. *Encyclopædia Britannica Ultimate Reference Suite DVD,* 2006. *English Romantic Poetry and Prose.* Russell Noyes, ed. Oxford University Press. 1956. *The Columbia Granger's Index to Poetry.* 11th ed. *The Columbia Granger's World of Poetry,* Columbia University Press, 2005 (http://www.columbiagrangers.org). *The Complete Poetical Works of Robert Southey, LL.D.D.* Appleton and Company, 1850. *Westminster Abbey Official Guide* (no date).

SOUTHWELL, SAINT ROBERT (?1561–1595)

Born near Horsham St. Faith, Norfolk, in the early part of Queen Elizabeth's reign, when being a Roman Catholic was becoming dangerous, he was sent to the French Jesuit college at Douai, became a Jesuit novice in 1578 in Rome and was ordained a priest in 1584. While he was away, a law was passed that made it illegal for priests ordained abroad to enter England, so when he returned in 1586 he was a hunted man. He spent six years sheltering in various houses, including that of Anne Howard, Countess of Arundel, for whom he was chaplain. He was arrested in 1592 while serving mass, repeatedly tortured to betray his fellow priests, imprisoned in the Tower of London and hanged at Tyburn on February 21, 1595. Southwell was declared blessed by Pope Pius XI in 1929 and canonized by Pope Paul VI in 1970. Some of his poems: "At Fotheringay," "At Home in Heaven," "Fortune's Falsehoode," "Saint Peter's Complaint," "The Assumption of Our Lady," "The Burning Babe," "The Martyrdom of Mary, Queen of Scots," "Upon the Image of Death," "What Joy to Live."

Sources: *A New Canon of English Poetry.* James Reeves, and Martin Seymour-Smith, ed. Barnes and Noble, 1967. *An Anthology of Catholic Poets.* Shane Leslie, ed. Macmillan, 1952. *Dictionary of National Biography.* Electronic Edition 1.1. Oxford University Press, 1997. *Encyclopædia Britannica Ultimate Reference Suite DVD,* 2006. *English Poetry: Author Search.* Chadwyck-Healey Ltd., 1995 (http://www.lib.utexas.edu:8080/search/epoetry/author.html). *English Verse 1830–1890.* Bernie Richards, ed. Longman, 1980). *Microsoft Encarta* 2006 (DVD). Microsoft Corporation, 2006. *The Columbia Granger's Index to Poetry.* 11th ed. *The Columbia Granger's World of Poetry,* Columbia University Press, 2005 (http://www.columbiagrangers.org). *The Complete Poems of Robert Southwell.* Alexander B. Grosart, ed.

Reprint Services, 1872. *The Oxford Companion to English Literature*. 6th edition. Margaret Drabble, ed. Oxford University Press, 2000.

SPARK, MURIEL (1918–2006)

Born Muriel Sarah Camberg in Edinburgh to a Jewish Lithuanian father and an English Protestant mother, she was educated at the Edinburgh James Gillespie's School for Girls. It was possibly this experience that inspired her novel (later a film) *The Prime of Miss Jean Brodie* (1962). During the war she worked for the propaganda department of the British Foreign Office and after the war she edited *The Poetry Review*, wrote studies of several famous authors and published *The Fanfarlo and Other Verse* (1952). Her winning of the Observer Prize for short fiction inspired her to write fiction full-time, and between *The Comforters* (1957) and *The Finishing School* (2004) she wrote altogether 22 novels. Converting to Roman Catholicism in 1954 was a major transition in her life. She spent much of her life in Italy, where she died. She has received honors from six universities, received the David Cohen British Literature Prize for Lifetime Achievement, and was made a Dame of the British Empire and in 1997. Some of her poems: "Against the Transcendentalists," "Canaan," "Elegy in a Kensington Churchyard," "Faith and Works," "Kensington Gardens," "The She Wolf."

Sources: *All the Poems of Muriel Spark*. W.W. Norton and Co. Ltd., 2004. *All the Poems: Collected Poems of Muriel Spark*. Carcanet Press, 2004. *Biography of Muriel Spark* (http://www.bbc.co.uk/scotland/arts/writingscotland/writers/muriel_spark/). *Encyclopædia Britannica Ultimate Reference Suite DVD*, 2006. *Microsoft Encarta* 2006 (DVD). Microsoft Corporation, 2006. *Obituary of Muriel Spark, BBC News, 15th April 2006* (http://news.bbc.co.uk/1/hi/entertainment/3659703.stm). *The National Portrait Gallery* (www.npg.org.uk). *The Columbia Granger's Index to Poetry*. 11th ed. *The Columbia Granger's World of Poetry*, Columbia University Press, 2005 (http://www.columbiagrangers.org). *The New Yorker Book of Poems*. The New Yorker editors. Viking Press, 1969. *The Oxford Book of Garden Verse*. John Dixon Hunt, ed. Oxford University Press, 1993. *The Oxford Companion to English Literature*. 6th edition. Margaret Drabble, ed. Oxford University Press, 2000. *Who's Who*. London: A & C Black, 2005. *Wikipedia, the Free Encyclopedia* (http://en.wikipedia.org/wiki/Wikipedia).

SPENCER, CHARLES BERNARD (1909–1963)

Born in Madras, where his father, Sir Charles Gordon Spencer, was a High Court Judge, he was brought up in Hampshire and Oxfordshire. Educated at Marlborough College, he graduated from Oxford in 1932, then scratched a living from teaching and writing. In 1936 he married the actress Norah Gibbs. In 1939 he started working for the British Council and was transferred from Greece to Egypt in early 1941. His wife died of tuberculosis in 1947 and Bernard himself was treated for the disease in a Swiss clinic, and after a year's convalescence he was posted to Madrid in 1949. He found happiness again when he married Anne Marjoribanks in 1961. He was accidentally killed in Vienna. Some of his publications: *Aegean Islands and Other Poems*, 1946. *The Twist in the Plotting*, 1960. *With Luck Lasting*, 1963. Some of his poems: "Aegean Islands 1940–41," "Castanets," "Egyptian Dancer at Shubra," "Greek Excavations," "Olive Trees," "Part of Plenty," "The Empire Clock," "Yachts on the Nile."

Sources: *Collected Poems of Bernard Spencer*. Alan Ross, 1965. *Collected Poems of Bernard Spencer*. Roger Bowen, 1981. *Dance in Poetry: An International Anthology of Poems on Dance*. Alkis Raftis, ed. Princeton Book Company, 1991. *The Chatto Book of Modern Poetry 1915–1955*. Cecil Day Lewis and John Lehmann, eds. Chatto and Windus, 1966. *The Columbia Granger's Index to Poetry*. 11th ed. *The Columbia Granger's World of Poetry*, Columbia University Press, 2005 (http://www.columbiagrangers.org). *The New British Poets: An Anthology*. Kenneth Rexroth, ed. New Directions, 1949. *The Oxford Book of Travel Verse*. Kevin Crossley-Holland, ed. Oxford University Press, 1986. *University of Reading, Papers of Bernard Spencer* (http://www.library.rdg.ac.uk/colls/special/spencer.html). *Wikipedia, the Free Encyclopedia* (http://en.wikipedia.org/wiki/Wikipedia).

SPENCER, WILLIAM ROBERT (1770–1834)

The younger son of Lord Charles Spencer, second son of the third Duke of Marlborough, he was educated at Harrow School and Christ Church, Oxford, but took no degree, and his occupation was that of wit and poet. In 1796 he published a translation of Bürger's *Leonore*; in 1802 *Urania*, a burlesque of German ghost literature, successfully performed at Drury Lane; in 1804 *The Year of Sorrow*, in memory of his mother-in-law and other ladies; and in 1811 a volume of *Poems* (a new edition with corrections and additions, London, James Cochrane and Co., was issued in 1835). Byron was probably being polite when he said he thought Spencer's verses, just like his conversation, were aristocratic. Spencer died in ill health and poverty in Paris and was buried at Harrow. Some of his poems: "A Deux Amies," "Beth Gelert," "Parting Song," "The Nursing of True Love," "The Visionary," "To the Hon. Miss Crewe," "Too Late I Stayed," "Wife, Children, and Friends."

Sources: *Dictionary of National Biography*. Electronic Edition 1.1. Oxford University Press, 1997. *English Poetry: Author Search*. Chadwyck-Healey Ltd., 1995 (http://www.lib.utexas.edu:8080/search/epoetry/author.html). *Folk Songs*. John Williamson Palmer, ed. Charles Scribner and

Company, 1867. *Good Dog Poems*. William Cole, ed. Scribner's, 1981. *Poems of William R. Spencer*. James Cochrane and Co., 1835. *The Columbia Granger's Index to Poetry*. 11th ed. *The Columbia Granger's World of Poetry*, Columbia University Press, 2005 (http://www.columbiagrangers.org). *The Poetical Registry and Repository of Fugitive Poetry for 1802*. F. and C. Rivington, 1803.

SPENDER, SIR STEPHEN HAROLD (1909–1995)

The son of journalist, he was brought up in London and educated at University College School, London, and at University College, Oxford. His book *The Thirties and After* (1979) recalls the outspoken Oxford literary figures and others prominent in the arts and politics, and his *Journals 1939–1983*, published in 1986, is a detailed account of his times and contemporaries. He edited *Horizon* magazine from 1939 to 1941 and *Encounter* magazine from 1953 to 1967. During World War II Spender was a member of the National Fire Service. He taught at various U.S. institutions, accepting the Elliston Chair of Poetry at Cincinnati University in 1953, and was the first non-American to serve as poetry consultant to the Library of Congress, a position he held for one year. In 1970 he was appointed professor of English at University College, London, and professor emeritus in 1977. He was knighted in 1983. He published his autobiography, *World Within World,* in 1951. Some of his poetry publications: *Poems of Dedication*, 1936. *Collected Poems, 1928–1953*, 1955. *The Generous Days*, 1971. Some of his poems: "Abrupt and charming mover," "Auden's Funeral," "The Conscript."

Sources: *Collected Poems of Stephen Spender*. Faber and Faber, 1985. *Encyclopædia Britannica Ultimate Reference Suite DVD*, 2006. *Microsoft Encarta 2006 (DVD)*. Microsoft Corporation, 2006. *The National Portrait Gallery* (www.npg.org.uk). *The Antaeus Anthology*. Daniel Halpern, ed. Bantam Books, 1986. *The Columbia Anthology of Gay Literature*. Byrne R.S. Fone, ed. Columbia University Press, 1998. *The Columbia Granger's Index to Poetry*. 11th ed. *The Columbia Granger's World of Poetry*, Columbia University Press, 2005 (http://www.columbiagrangers.org). *The Oxford Companion to English Literature*. 6th edition. Margaret Drabble, ed. Oxford University Press, 2000. *Wikipedia, the Free Encyclopedia* (http://en.wikipedia.org/wiki/Wikipedia).

SPENSER, EDMUND (?1552–1599)

Born in London and educated at the Merchant Taylors' School, he graduated from Pembroke College, Cambridge University, in 1576. He fought in Ireland and was awarded lands in Cork, including Kilkolman Castle Cork. His pamphlet *View on the Present State of Ireland* (written in the 1590s) recommended complete subjugation of the Irish people, their language and customs and a scorched earth policy. Spenser was driven from his castle by Irish rebels during the Nine Years' War in 1598. The first of his major poems, *The Shepheardes Calender* (1579), is an allegory written from the point of view of various shepherds throughout the months of the year. *The Faerie Queene* (1580–1596) — dedicated to Queen Elizabeth — is an epic allegory of Christian virtues, tied into England's mythology of King Arthur. He died in London in a distressed financial state and his funeral expenses were borne by the Earl of Essex. He was buried near Chaucer in Westminster Abbey. Some of his other poems: "An Hymne of Heavenly Love," "I Saw Two Bears," "Lament for Daphnaida," "Prosopopoia: Or Mother Hubberds Tale," "Ruins of Rome," "The Teares of the Muses," "Virgils Gnat."

Sources: *Dictionary of National Biography*. Electronic Edition 1.1. Oxford University Press, 1997. *Encyclopædia Britannica Ultimate Reference Suite DVD*, 2006. *English Poetry: Author Search*. Chadwyck-Healey Ltd., 1995 (http://www.lib.utexas.edu:8080/search/epoetry/author.html). *The Columbia Granger's Index to Poetry*. 11th ed. *The Columbia Granger's World of Poetry*, Columbia University Press, 2005 (http://www.columbiagrangers.org). *The Complete Poetical Works of Spenser*. R.E. Neil Dodge, ed. Houghton Mifflin, 1936. *The Oxford Companion to English Literature*. 6th edition. Margaret Drabble, ed. Oxford University Press, 2000. *Westminster Abbey Official Guide* (no date). *Wikipedia, the Free Encyclopedia* (http://en.wikipedia.org/wiki/Wikipedia).

SPRACKLAND, JEAN (1962–)

Born and brought up in Burton-on-Trent, Staffordshire, she now lives in Southport, Merseyside. After studying English and philosophy at the University of Kent at Canterbury, she taught for a few years before beginning to write poetry at the age of 30. She has held residencies in schools and universities and is a tutor for the Arvon Foundation. She also works in education, training and consultancy for organizations including the Poetry Society and the Poetry Archive. In 2004 she was one of the judges of the Arvon International Poetry Competition. In 2004 she was named by the Poetry Book Society as one of the "Next Generation" poets. Her poetry publications: *Tattoos for Mothers Day*, 1997 (short listed for the 1998 Forward Poetry Prize, Best First Collection). *Hard Water*, 2003 (short listed for the 2003 T.S. Eliot Prize and the Whitbread Poetry Award). Some of her poems: "Sewing Fingertips," "Reading Leaves," "Note from the Outside," "No Man's Land" (with a series of photographs by David Walker), "The Hairdresser's Across the Street," "A Baby in the Filing Cabinet," "In the Planetarium."

Sources: *Biography of Jean Sprackland: British Council Arts* (http://www.contemporarywriters.com). *Hear Jean Sprackland's Poems on CD* (http://www.poetrybooks.co.

uk/book-template.asp?isbn=190555642X). *Sewing Fingers, by Jean Sprackland: The Poetry Book Society* (http://www.poetrybooks.co.uk/PBS/pbs_sprackland_jean.asp). *The Works of Jean Sprackland: The Poetry Archive* (http://www.poetryarchive.org/poetryarchive/singlePoet.do?poetId=456).

SPRAT, THOMAS (1635–1713)

Born at Beaminster, Dorset, the son of a clergyman, he was educated at Wadham College, Oxford, earning a B.A. (1654), M.A. (1657), and D.D. (1669), and was a fellow at Wadham until 1670. Wadham was the meeting place for scientific study out of which grew the Royal Society, and of which Sprat was an active member; he wrote a *History of the Royal Society of London* (1667). Later in his career he was bishop of Rochester and dean of Westminster, and as such he directed Christopher Wren's restoration of the abbey. He assisted at the coronation of William and Mary (1689) and was a member of King James II's ecclesiastical commission (1688). He died of a stroke and was buried in the nave of Westminster Abbey. His other prose works are *Observations Upon Monsieur de Sorbier's Voyage into England* (1665) and *Account of The Life of Mr. Abraham Cowley* (1667). His poetic reputation was gained by his poem "To the Happie Memory of the Most Renowned Prince Oliver, Lord Protector" (1659). Three other poems are recorded: "On His Mistress Drown'd," "The Plague of Athens," "To the Happy Memory of the Late Usurper, Oliver Cromwell."

Sources: *Dictionary of National Biography.* Electronic Edition 1.1. Oxford University Press, 1997. *English Love Poems.* John Betjeman and Geoffrey Taylor, eds. Faber and Faber, 1957. *English Poetry: Author Search.* Chadwyck-Healey Ltd., 1995 (http://www.lib.utexas.edu:8080/search/epoetry/author.html). *Samuel Johnson's Lives of the English Poets,* 1779–1781 (http://www2.hn.psu.edu/Faculty/KKemmerer/poets/preface.htm). *The Columbia Granger's Index to Poetry.* 11th ed. *The Columbia Granger's World of Poetry,* Columbia University Press, 2005 (http://www.columbiagrangers.org). *The Oxford Companion to English Literature.* 6th edition. Margaret Drabble, ed. Oxford University Press, 2000.

SQUIRE, SIR JOHN COLLINGS (1884–1958)

Born at Plymouth, the son of a veterinary surgeon, he graduated in history from St. John's College, Cambridge, in 1905. He worked as a journalist in Plymouth and in London and in 1913 became literary editor of the newly founded *New Statesman,* and as "Solomon Eagle" his critical essays were popular and were later published in three volumes titled *Books in General* (1918–1921). His *Collected Parodies* were published in 1921; his contributions to the *Sunday Observer* were published in *Sunday Mornings* (1930). His small book of poems *The Survival of the*

Fittest (1916) was probably the earliest poetic protest against the war to win much attention in England. In 1919 he established the monthly magazine *London Mercury,* encouraged by many poets. He edited *Book of Women's Verse* (1921), the *Comic Muse* (1925), *Cambridge Book of Lesser Poets* (1927). Between 1921 and 1934 he edited three volumes of *Selections from Modern Poets.* He died at Rushlake Green, East Sussex. Some of his poems: "1914," "Anarchy," "Approaching America," "Country Wooing," "Fen Landscape," "The Birds," "The Hands-across-the-Sea Poem," "The Swallow," "Wars and Rumours, 1920."

Sources: *An Anthology of Revolutionary Poetry.* Marcus Graham, ed. The Active Press, 1929. *Dictionary of National Biography.* Electronic Edition 1.1. Oxford University Press, 1997. *Encyclopædia Britannica Ultimate Reference Suite DVD,* 2006. *The National Portrait Gallery* (www.npg.org.uk). *Poems, Second Series by John Collings Squire.* William Heinemann Ltd., 1921. *The Brand-X Anthology of Poetry.* William Zaranka, ed. Apple-Wood Books, 1981. *The Columbia Granger's Index to Poetry.* 11th ed. *The Columbia Granger's World of Poetry,* Columbia University Press, 2005 (http://www.columbiagrangers.org). *The Faber Book of English History in Verse.* Kenneth Baker, ed. Faber and Faber, 1988. *The Oxford Companion to English Literature.* 6th edition. Margaret Drabble, ed. Oxford University Press, 2000. *The Penguin Book of Bird Poetry.* Peggy Munsterberg, ed. 1984.

STAGG, JOHN (1770–1823)

"The Blind Bard" was born at Burg-by-Sands, near Carlisle, where his father, a tailor, possessed a small property. Blind from a young age, he made his living by playing the fiddle and running a small library in the town of Wigton, Cumberland. He married at twenty, moved to Manchester, which was his base for the rest of his life, and died at Workington. He traveled the countryside gathering information and impressions to include in his poetry, and was patronized by many well-to-do people of Cumberland and academics of Oxford and Cambridge, who encouraged him to publish *Minstrel of the North* (1810). It included one of the earliest original vampire poems in English, the *Vampyre.* His other publications: *Miscellaneous Poems,* 1804. *Miscellaneous Poems,* 1897. *The Cumberland Minstrel,* 1821 (3 volumes). Some of his poems: "A Prayer to Jehovah," "Auld Lang Seyne," "Frederick and Eliza; or, the Shipwreck," "On Hope," "The Apparition," "The Bridewain," "The Disappointment," "The Messiah," "The Pleasures of Contemplation," "The Vision: From the Fourth Chapter of Job."

Sources: *Dictionary of National Biography.* Electronic Edition 1.1. Oxford University Press, 1997. *Miscellaneous Poems, Some of Which Are in the Cumberland and Scottish Dialects.* John Stagg (no publisher), 1807. *The Columbia Granger's Index to Poetry.* 11th ed. *The Columbia Granger's*

World of Poetry, Columbia University Press, 2005 (http://www.columbiagrangers.org). *The Literary Gothic, Works by John Stagg* (http://www.litgothic.com/Authors/stagg.html).

STAINER, PAULINE (1941–)

Born in Burslem, Stoke-on-Trent, she graduated in English from St. Anne's College, Oxford, and took an M.Phil. at Southampton University. Her poetry explores sacred myth, legend, history-in-landscape, and human feeling, with a strong influence from her industrial background. She was awarded a Hawthornden Fellowship in 1987, and came to public notice with her first volume, the *Honeycomb* (1989). *Sighting the Slave Ship* (1992) contains poems in homage to many prominent figures, including the illustrator and war artist Eric Ravilious, who died in 1942 when the Coastal Command airplane from Iceland on which he was traveling disappeared. She spent several years on the Orkney island of Rousay, from which came her book collection *Parable Island* (1999). She now lives in Hadleigh, Suffolk, England. Her other publications: *Little Egypt,* 1991. *The Ice-Pilot Speaks,* 1994. *The Wound-dresser's Dream,* 1996. *A Litany of High Waters,* 2002. *The Lady and the Hare: New and Selected Poems,* 2003. Some of her poems: "Bleaklow," "Sarcophagus," "The Figurehead," "The Gargoyles," "The Honeycomb," "The Seals."

Sources: *New Blood,* Neil Astley, ed. Bloodaxe Books, 1999. *Poetry with an Edge.* Neil Astley, ed. Bloodaxe Books, 1988. *The New Exeter Book of Riddles.* Kevin Crossley-Holland and Lawrence Sail, ed. Enitharmon Press, 1999. *The Oxford Companion to English Literature.* 6th edition. Margaret Drabble, ed. Oxford University Press, 2000. *Wikipedia, the Free Encyclopedia* (http://en.wikipedia.org/wiki/Wikipedia).

STALLWORTHY, JON (1935–)

Born in London to New Zealand parents, his father, Sir John Stallworthy, was Nuffield Professor of Obstetrics at Oxford University. Educated at Rugby School, he served in the Royal West African Frontier Force before continuing his education at Magdalen College, Oxford University (M.A. and B.Litt.). He joined Oxford University Press as poetry editor and became a deputy academic publisher until 1977. From 1977 to 1986 he was John Wendell Anderson Professor of English at Cornell University, New York, and from 1992 to 2000, professor of English literature at Oxford University, then emeritus senior research fellow, Wolfson College, Oxford. He is a noted translator of the works of Russian poet Aleksandr Aleksandrovich Blok (1880–1921). Some of his more recent publications: *The Apple Barrel: Selected Poems 1956–1963,* 1974. *A Familiar Tree,* 1978. *The Anzac Sonata: New and Selected Poems,* 1986.

The Guest from the Future, 1995. *Rounding the Horn: Collected Poems,* 1998. Some of his poems: "Epilogue to an Empire 1600–1900," "Here Comes Sir George," "Mother Tongue," "The Almond Tree," "Walking against the Wind," "War Story."

Sources: *Golden Treasury of the Best Songs and Lyrical Poems in the English Language.* Francis Turner Palgrave, ed. Oxford University Press, 1964, Sixth edition, updated by John Press, 1994. *Louis MacNeice (Biography).* Jon Stallworthy. Faber and Faber, 1996. *Microsoft Encarta 2006* (DVD). Microsoft Corporation, 2006. *Selected Poems of Aleksandr Blok.* Carcanet Press, 2000. *The Columbia Granger's Index to Poetry.* 11th ed. *The Columbia Granger's World of Poetry,* Columbia University Press, 2005 (http://www.columbiagrangers.org). *The Norton Anthology of Modern Poetry.* 2nd ed. Richard Ellmann and Robert O'Clair, eds. W.W. Norton, 1988. *The Norton Anthology of Poetry.* 3rd ed. Alexander W. Allison, ed. W.W. Norton, 1983. *The Oxford Book of Contemporary Verse, 1945–1980.* D.J. Enright, ed. Oxford University Press, 1980. *The Oxford Companion to English Literature.* 6th edition. Margaret Drabble, ed. Oxford University Press, 2000. *Twentieth Century Russian Poetry: Silver and Steel, an Anthology.* Doubleday, 1993. *War Poems of Wilfred Owen.* Wilfred Owen. Jon Stallworthy, ed. Chatto and Windus, 1994. *Who's Who.* London: A & C Black, 2005.

STANLEY, THOMAS (1625–1678)

Born at Cumberlow, Hertfordshire, he graduated M.A. from Pembroke Hall, Cambridge, in 1641, entered into a prosperous marriage, traveled in France and took up residence in the Middle Temple, there to concentrate on writing. He used his wealth to support his many literary friends, most of whom dedicated works to him. A student of Greek philosophy, between 1655 and 1662, he published four volumes of *History of Philosophy.* His edition of *Æschylus* was published in 1663, and revised and enlarged (1809–1816 in 4 volumes) by Samuel Butler (see entry). Some of Stanley's verses were set to music by John Gamble and published by him in his *Ayres and Dialogues* (1656). Stanley died at his lodgings in Suffolk Street, Strand, and was buried in the church of St. Martin-in-the-Fields. He produced four volumes of poetry, many of them translations: *Poems,* 1647. *Europa: Cupid Crucified,* 1649. *Poems,* (1647–1651). *Psalterium Carolinum,* 1657. Some of his poems: "Beauty," "Celia Singing," "On a Violet in Her Breast," "The Bracelet," "The Magnet," "The Relapse," "The Repulse."

Sources: *An Anthology of World Poetry.* Mark Van Doren, ed. Reynal and Hitchcock, Inc., 1936. *Ben Jonson and the Cavalier Poets.* Hugh MacLaen, ed. New York: W.W. Norton and Company, 1974. *Encyclopædia Britannica Ultimate Reference Suite DVD,* 2006. *Metaphysical Lyrics and Poems of the Seventeenth Century: Donne to Butler.* Herbert J. Grierson, ed. Oxford University Press, 1921. *The National Portrait Gallery* (www.npg.org.uk). *Stanford University Libraries and Academic Information Resources* (http://library.

stanford.edu). *The Columbia Granger's Index to Poetry*. 11th ed. *The Columbia Granger's World of Poetry,* Columbia University Press, 2005 (http://www.columbiagrangers.org). *The Faber Book of Epigrams and Epitaphs.* Geoffrey Grigson, ed. Faber and Faber, 1977. *The Oxford Book of Classical Verse in Translation.* Adrian Poole and Jeremy Maule, eds. 1995. *The Oxford Companion to English Literature.* 6th edition. Margaret Drabble, ed. Oxford University Press, 2000. *The Poems and Translations of Thomas Stanley.* Galbraith Miller Crump, ed. Oxford University Press, 1962.

STAPLETON (STAPYLTON), SIR ROBERT (d. 1669)

He was a Yorkshire poet who was educated in the Benedictine convent of St. Gregory at Douay, where he became a professed monk of the order in 1625. He converted to Protestantism and was appointed one of the gentlemen in ordinary of the privy chamber to Prince Charles (later Charles II). He was with Charles I at the battle of Edgehill (1642), was knighted at Nottingham, and made doctor of civil law at Oxford in the same year, and at the Restoration he was again brought into the royal household. He was buried near the vestry door of Westminster Abbey and is memorialized by a stone in Poets' Corner. His works include: *The Slighted Maid,* 1663 (a verse comedy). *The Step-Mother,* 1664 (a tragicomedy, in verse). *The Tragedie of Hero and Leander,* 1669 (in verse). *The Loves of Hero and Leander: A Greek Poem,* 1645. *Juvenal's Sixteen Satyrs,* 1669. Two of his poems: "The Bard's Song," "To My Friend, Mr. Shirley, Upon His Comedy."

Sources: *Dictionary of National Biography.* Electronic Edition 1.1. Oxford University Press, 1997. *Great Books Online* (www.bartleby.com). *Seven Centuries of Poetry: Chaucer to Dylan Thomas.* A.N. Jeffares, ed. Longmans, Green, 1955. *The Columbia Granger's Index to Poetry.* 11th ed. *The Columbia Granger's World of Poetry,* Columbia University Press, 2005 (http://www.columbiagrangers.org). *The Dramatic Works and Poems of James Shirley, Vol. I.* Alexander Dyce and William Gifford, eds. Russell and Russell, 1966. *The National Portrait Gallery* (www.npg.org.uk).

STEELE, ANNE (1717–1778)

The daughter of William Steele (1689–1769), timber merchant and lay Baptist preacher, was born at Broughton, Hampshire. Her mother died when Anne was just three, and an accident at 19 caused a hip injury that left her a semi-invalid. Her fiancé died in a drowning accident a few hours before the wedding; she never married and died at Broughton. She published many poems and hymns under the pseudonym "Theodosia." Her complete works were published in one volume in 1863 by the hymnologist Daniel Sedgwick (1814–1879) under the title *Hymns, Psalms, and Poems by Anne Steele, with Memoir by John Sheppard.* The collection includes 144 hymns, 34 metrical psalms, and about 50 poems on moral subjects. Her poems were reprinted in America in 1808, and her hymns were popular there and among Baptists elsewhere. Some of her hymns/poems: "Absence from God," "An Evening Hymn," "Aspiring Towards Heaven," "Bidding Adieu to Earthly Pleasures," "Christ Dying and Rising," "Life a Journey," "Messiah, an Ode," "On Children's Play," "The Absent Muse," "The Happy Man."

Sources: *Dictionary of National Biography.* Electronic Edition 1.1. Oxford University Press, 1997. *Miscellaneous Pieces, in Verse and Prose by Anne Steele.* 1780 (http://gandhara.usc.edu/data/a7f4/10/06/97/86/40.html). *Poems on Subjects Chiefly Devotional, Vol. 1, by Anne Steele* (No publisher), 1780. *The Columbia Granger's Index to Poetry.* 11th ed. *The Columbia Granger's World of Poetry,* Columbia University Press, 2005 (http://www.columbiagrangers.org). *The Cyber Hymnal* (http://www.cyberhymnal.org/index.htm).

STEELE, SIR RICHARD (1672–1729)

Born in Dublin, the son of wealthy attorney who died when his son was five years old, he was educated at Charterhouse School at the same time as Joseph Addison (see entry), with whom he developed a lifelong friendship. He left Merton College, Oxford, without taking a degree, and was in the Army from 1694 to 1705. He then engaged in producing and writing for several magazines and newspapers, including the *Tatler* and *The Spectator*, where the fictionalized life of Sir Roger de Coverley was popularized. He entered Parliament but because he supported the succession of George I in a pamphlet, the *Crisis*, he was expelled, only to be knighted in 1718 and appointed as manager of the Drury Lane Theatre. He seems to have lived perpetually in debt, which forced him to leave London to live in Wales, where he died. He wrote four comic dramas: *The Funeral,* 1701. *The Lying Lover,* 1703. *The Tender Husband,* 1705. *The Conscious Lovers,* 1722. Some of his poems: "Epigrams Adapted from Martial," "Lyric for Italian Music," "Tamerlane Revived," "The Procession," "Toasts for the Kit-Cat Club."

Sources: *Dictionary of National Biography.* Electronic Edition 1.1. Oxford University Press, 1997. *Encyclopædia Britannica Ultimate Reference Suite DVD,* 2006. *Microsoft Encarta* 2006 (DVD). Microsoft Corporation, 2006. *The Columbia Granger's Index to Poetry.* 11th ed. *The Columbia Granger's World of Poetry,* Columbia University Press, 2005 (http://www.columbiagrangers.org). *The Occasional Verse of Richard Steele.* Rae Blanchard, ed. Oxford University Press, 1952. *The Oxford Companion to English Literature.* 6th edition. Margaret Drabble, ed. Oxford University Press, 2000.

STEPHEN, JAMES KENNETH (1859–1892)

Born in London, the son of a judge, he was educated at Eton and graduated from King's College,

Cambridge, with firsts in history and law in 1881, and was elected a fellow in 1885. In 1883 for a short time he was tutor at Sandringham to Prince Edward of Wales, the future Duke of Clarence (who died in 1892). Although called to the bar in 1884, he devoted most of his energy to journalism and started a weekly paper, the *Reflector*, in 1888. He settled at Cambridge in 1891 to lecture on history and writing. His pamphlet *The Living Languages* (1891) was a defense of keeping Greek as an essential for a degree. In 1886 he suffered a head injury which affected his brain and he died in an asylum. He was buried at Kensal Green Cemetery. Both the Duke of Clarence and Stephen have been suggested as the possible identities of the serial killer Jack the Ripper. Some of his poems: "A Grievance," "After the Golden Wedding," "An Election Address," "Cynicus to W. Shakspere," "England and America," "My Education," "The Ballade of the Incompetent Ballade-Monger."

Sources: *19th Century British Minor Poets.* W.H. Auden, ed. Delacorte Press, 1966. *A Century of Humorous Verse, 1850–1950.* Roger Lancelyn Green, ed. E.P. Dutton (Everyman's Library), 1959. *Casebook: Jack the Ripper, James Kenneth Stephen* (http://www.casebook.org/suspects/jkstephen.html). *Dictionary of National Biography.* Electronic Edition 1.1. Oxford University Press, 1997. *Lapsus Calami and Other Verses, by James Kenneth Stephen.* Macmillan and Bowes, 1892. *The Columbia Granger's Index to Poetry.* 11th ed. *The Columbia Granger's World of Poetry,* Columbia University Press, 2005 (http://www.columbia grangers.org). *The Oxford Book of Marriage.* Helge Rubenstein, ed. Oxford University Press, 1990. *The Oxford Companion to English Literature.* 6th edition. Margaret Drabble, ed. Oxford University Press, 2000. *Victorian Literature: Poetry.* Donald Gray and G.B. Tennyson, eds. Macmillan, 1976.

STEPHENS, JAMES (1880–1950)

Irish poet, born in Dublin and largely self-educated, he became one of the leading figures of the Irish literary renaissance. His family roots are obscure, but he was raised in a Protestant orphanage from which he ran away and lived the life of a vagrant. He became a solicitor's clerk and later registrar of the National Gallery of Ireland. Among his many literary friends was James Joyce, and the Irish poet Æ (George William Russell) (see entry) encouraged him and helped him publish *Insurrections,* his first book of poetry, in 1909. His novel *The Crock of Gold* (1912), with its rich Celtic theme, established his fame. Stephens was active in the Irish nationalist movement. By 1940 he was living in London, where he was a frequent radio broadcaster of verse and stories. He was a founder-member of the Irish Academy of Letters and in 1942 he was awarded a civil list pension. He died in London. Some of his poems: "And It Was Windy Weather," "At the Edge of the Sea," "The Ancient Elf," "The Centaurs," "The Crown of Thorns," "The King of the Fairy Men," "Women Shapes."

Sources: *Amazing Monsters: Verses to Thrill and Chill.* Robert Fisher, ed. Faber and Faber, 1982. *Biography of James Stephens* (http://www.irishwriters-online.com/james stephens.html). *Collected Poems of James Stephens.* Macmillan, 1928. *Encyclopædia Britannica Ultimate Reference Suite DVD,* 2006. *Microsoft Encarta* 2006 (DVD). Microsoft Corporation, 2006. *Songs from the Clay by James Stephens.* The Macmillan Company, 1915. *The Columbia Granger's Index to Poetry.* 11th ed. *The Columbia Granger's World of Poetry,* Columbia University Press, 2005 (http://www.co lumbiagrangers.org). *The Oxford Companion to English Literature.* 6th edition. Margaret Drabble, ed. Oxford University Press, 2000. *The Poems of James Stephens.* Shirley Mulligan, ed. Colin Smythe Ltd., 2005.

STEPNEY, GEORGE (1663–1707)

Born in London and educated at Westminster School, he graduated M.A. from Trinity College, Cambridge, in 1689 and was made a fellow in 1687. He had a successful diplomatic career and between 1695 and 1697 was envoy to several important European negotiations. In 1697 he was appointed a commissioner of trade and plantations, a post which, in spite of his diplomatic work, he retained until his death. In Vienna, in 1705, a misunderstanding between him and the imperial minister caused Prince Eugène to insist upon his withdrawal. He died of dysentery and was buried in the nave of Westminster Abbey, the pall being carried by two dukes, two earls, and two barons. Stepney contributed a translation of Ovid's elegy on the death of Tibullus to Dryden's *Miscellany Poems* (1684). His other poetry publications: *Epistle to Charles Montague,* 1691. *Poems Dedicated to the Blessed Memory of Her Late Gracious Majesty Queen Mary,* 1695. *The Eighth Satyr of Juvenal,* 1693. Some of his poems: "On the Late Horrid Conspiracy," "The Audience," "The Austrian Eagle," "The Nature of Dreams," "Verses Imitated from the French of Monsieur Maynard, to Cardinal Richelieu."

Sources: *Anthology of Poems on Affairs of State: Augustan Satirical Verse, 1660–1714.* George de F. Lord, ed. Yale University Press, 1975. *Dictionary of National Biography.* Electronic Edition 1.1. Oxford University Press, 1997. *English Poetry: Author Search.* Chadwyck-Healey Ltd., 1995 (http://www.lib.utexas.edu:8080/search/epoetry/author.html). *The National Portrait Gallery* (www.npg.org.uk). *Samuel Johnson's Lives of the English Poets,* 1779–1781 (http://www2.hn.psu.edu/Faculty/KKemmerer/poets/preface.htm). *Stanford University Libraries and Academic Information Resources* (http://library.stanford.edu). *The Columbia Granger's Index to Poetry.* 11th ed. *The Columbia Granger's World of Poetry,* Columbia University Press, 2005 (http://www.columbiagrangers.org). *Westminster Abbey Official Guide* (no date).

STEVENSON, ANNE KATHARINE(1933–)

The daughter of the American philosopher C.L. Stevenson, she was born in Cambridge, England. She completed her education at the University of Michigan and returned in the 1960s where has remained, living high up in the County of Durham, and spending much time in Wales. During a varied career, she has worked as a teacher both in Britain and America, held the post of Compton Fellow in Creative Writing at the University of Dundee, and was Arts Council writer-in-residence at Reading. For two years she was an arts fellow at Oxford University and in 1981 became Northern Arts Literary Fellow. She is a member of the Arts Council literature panel. Her biography of Sylvia Plath, *Bitter Fame,* was published in 1989. Some of her poetry publications: *Living in America,* 1965. *Reversals,* 1970. *Enough of Green,* 1977. *The Fiction Makers,* 1985. *The Other House,* 1990. *The Collected Poems 1955–1995,* 1996. *Poems 1955–2005,* 2005. Some of her poems: "After Her Death," "Attitudes and Beliefs," "By the Boat House, Oxford," "North Sea off Carnoustie," "Poem to My Daughter," "Respectable House," "Willow Song."

Sources: *Anne Stevenson's Poetry: Guardian Unlimited Books, By Genre, Border Crossings* (http://books.guardian. co.uk/poetry/features/0,12887,1317578,00.html). *Early Ripening: American Women's Poetry Now.* Marge Piercy, ed. Pandora Press, 1987. *No More Masks.* 2nd Edition. Florence Howe, ed. HarperCollins Publishers, 1993. *The Columbia Granger's Index to Poetry.* 11th ed. *The Columbia Granger's World of Poetry,* Columbia University Press, 2005 (http://www.columbiagrangers.org). *The Faber Book of 20th Century Women's Poetry.* Fleur Adcock, ed. Faber and Faber, 1987. *The Hopwood Anthology: Five Decades of American Poetry.* Harry Thomas and Steven Lavine, eds. University of Michigan Press, 1981. *The Oxford Book of the Sea.* Jonathan Raban, ed. Oxford University Press, 1992. *The Oxford Companion to English Literature.* 6th edition. Margaret Drabble, ed. Oxford University Press, 2000. *Who's Who.* London: A & C Black, 2005.

STEVENSON, MATTHEW (?1654–1685)

Possibly from Yorkshire, he resided most of his life in Norfolk. He was known to have been in London after the Restoration, moving in a circle of poets who haunted the law courts. He has several known poetic publications. *Bellum Presbyteriale,* 1661, is a heroic poem that refers to the burning of the covenant by the common hangman on 22 May 1661. This was an act ordered by Charles II against the Presbyterian clergy of Scotland, effectively banning them; it led to severe persecution and mass migration to Ulster. *The Twelve Months,* 1661, covers all the activities of the year, as well as the various sports and occupations of the countryside. *Florus Britannicus,* 1662, is the history of England from William the Conqueror. Others include *Occasions Off-spring,* 1645; *Poems,* 1665; *Norfolk Drollery,* 1673; and *The Wits Paraphras'd,* 1680. Some of his poems: "An Elegy Upon Old Freeman," "John, King of England," "On the Gun-Powder Treason," "Stephen, King of England," "The Fleets," "The Weavers Memento Mori," "To a Faire Lady," "Upon a Great Windy Night," "Upon Yorkshire Ale."

Sources: *Dictionary of National Biography.* Electronic Edition 1.1. Oxford University Press, 1997. *English Poetry: Author Search.* Chadwyck-Healey Ltd., 1995 (http://www. lib.utexas.edu:8080/search/epoetry/author.html). *Stanford University Libraries and Academic Information Resources* (http://library.stanford.edu). *The Cavalier Poets.* Robin Skelton, ed. Oxford University Press, 1970. *The Columbia Granger's Index to Poetry.* 11th ed (http://www.columbia grangers.org). *The Covenanters by Brian Orr Part One* (http://www.tartans.com/articles/cov1.html). *The New Oxford Book of Seventeenth Century Verse.* Alastair Fowler, ed. Oxford University Press, 1991.

STEVENSON, ROBERT LOUIS (1850–1894)

He was a Scottish poet, born in Edinburgh, the son of a lighthouse engineer, who from about his eighteenth year dropped the use of his third Christian name, Balfour, and changed the spelling of Lewis to Louis. He was an imaginative child whose inner child never aged. In spite of suffering from tuberculosis he was a great traveler and attended classes at Edinburgh University when health permitted. After purchasing a plantation on Samoa, he became a kind of chief among the Samoans, who christened him "Tusitala," meaning "storyteller." He died of an apparent stroke. His novels of adventure, romance, and horror are of considerable psychological depth and have continued in popularity long after his death, both as books and as films. Two of his poems are "Requiem," which describes the place where he died in Samoa, and "Sing Me a Song of a Lad That is Gone," which records memories of sailing past the Hebrides, off western Scotland, in 1874. Some of his other poems: "Bright is the Ring of Words," "The Canoe Speaks," "The Light-Keeper," "The Swing," "To an Island Princess," "To Princess Kaiulani," "To the Stormy Petrel," "Winter."

Sources: *Complete Collection of Poems by Robert Louis Stevenson* (http://www.poetryloverspage.com/poets/steven son/stevenson.html). *Dictionary of National Biography.* Electronic Edition 1.1. Oxford University Press, 1997. *Encyclopædia Britannica Ultimate Reference Suite DVD,* 2006. *English Poetry: Author Search.* Chadwyck-Healey Ltd., 1995 (http://www.lib.utexas.edu:8080/search/epoetry/author. html). *Everyman's Book of Victorian Verse.* J.R. Watson, ed. J.M. Dent, 1982. *Microsoft Encarta* 2006 (DVD). Microsoft Corporation, 2006. *The National Portrait Gallery* (www.npg.org.uk). *Sprints and Distances: Sports in Poetry and the Poetry in Sport.* Lillian Morrison, ed. Thomas Y. Crowell, 1965. *The Columbia Granger's Index to Poetry.* 11th ed. *The Columbia Granger's World of Poetry,* Columbia University Press, 2005 (http://www.columbiagrangers.org). *The Oxford Companion to English Literature.* 6th edition. Margaret Drabble, ed. Oxford University Press, 2000. *The Works of Robert Louis Stevenson;* Vailima Edition (8 volumes). William Heinemann and Chatto W., 1922. *Wikipedia, the Free Encyclopedia* (http://en.wikipedia.org/wiki/Wikipedia).

STODDART, THOMAS TOD (1810–1880)

Scottish poet, born in Edinburgh, the son of Admiral Pringle Stoddart, he was educated at Edinburgh University and met such poets as Hartley Coleridge, James Hogg (the Ettrick Shepherd), and William Ayton (see entries). His papers on the *Art of Angling,* which appeared in *Chambers's Journal,* were published in 1835 in book form; it was the first treatise of its kind that appeared in Scotland. In 1847 he published his classic *The Angler's Companion to the Rivers and Lakes of Scotland.* He married in 1836 and settled in Kelso, where he found the surroundings so congenial for the practice of his art in the rivers Tweed and Teviot that it became his home for life, and where he died. Some of his poetry publications: *The Death-Wake or Lunacy,* 1831. *Songs and Poems,* 1839. *Songs of the Seasons,* 1873. *An Angler's Rambles,* 1866. Some of his poems: "A Loch Scene," "A Winter Landscape," "My Ain Wee Fisher Boy," "The Angler's Benediction," "The Angler's Complaint," "The Bonnie Tweed," "The Fairy Angler," "The Flee," "The Lamp," "To a Spirit."

Sources: *Angling Songs of Thomas Tod Stoddart.* William Blackwood and Sons, 1889. *Dictionary of National Biography.* Electronic Edition 1.1. Oxford University Press, 1997. *English Poetry: Author Search.* Chadwyck-Healey Ltd., 1995 (http://www.lib.utexas.edu:8080/search/epoetry/author.html). *The National Portrait Gallery* (www.npg.org.uk). *Stanford University Libraries and Academic Information Resources* (http://library.stanford.edu). *The Columbia Granger's Index to Poetry.* 11th ed. *The Columbia Granger's World of Poetry,* Columbia University Press, 2005 (http://www.columbiagrangers.org). *The New Oxford Book of Romantic Period Verse.* Jerome J. McGann. Oxford University Press, 1993.

STOKES, HENRY SEWELL (1808–1895)

"The Laureate for Cornwall" was born at Gibraltar, where his father was a government official. He was educated in England in a school of a young Baptist minister called William Giles at Chatham, where Charles Dickens was his companion. He became a solicitor and eventually settled at Truro, Cornwall, where, in 1883, he started the *Cornish Guardian and*

Western Chronicle and for three years was its editor. In 1856 he was elected mayor of Truro and in 1859 was appointed its town clerk; he was clerk of the peace for Cornwall from 1865 until his death in Bodmin. His poetry publications: *The Lay of the Desert,* 1830. *The Song of Albion: A Poem on the Reform Crisis,* 1831. *Discourses on Opinion,* 1831. *The Vale of Lanherne,* 1853. *Echoes of War,* 1855. *Scattered Leaves,* 1862. *Rhymes from Cornwall,* 1871 (reissued in 1884 as *Voyage of Arundel and Other Rhymes from Cornwall*). *Memories,* 1879. *Poems of Later Years,* 1873 (reissued in 1881 as *The Chantry Owl and Other Verses*). *Restormel: A Legend of Piers Gaveston,* 1875. *The Gate of Heaven: The Plaint of Morwenstow,* 1876.

Sources: *Dictionary of National Biography.* Electronic Edition 1.1. Oxford University Press, 1997.

STORY, ROBERT (1795–1860)

Northumberland poet, born at Wark, his education was at the local school. From 1810 he began to teach in various elementary schools and in 1820 he started a successful school at Gargrave, North Yorkshire, his home for over twenty years. About 1825 he made the acquaintance of John Nicholson (see entry), the "Airedale poet" who inspired his volume of poems *Craven Blossoms* (1826). His political views were at odds with the parents and many withdrew their children from school, creating financial strain. His poems brought him some income and for his support of the Conservatives he was given employment in the audit office. In 1854 he visited Paris and was presented to Napoleon III as a successor of Robert Burns. He died at Battersea, London, and was buried in Brompton Cemetery. Some of his other publications: *The Harvest,* 1816. *The Magic Fountain,* 1829. *The Outlaw,* 1839. *Songs and Poems,* 1849. *The Third Napoleon,* 1854. *The Poetical Works,* 1857. *Lyrical Poems,* 1861. Some of his poems: "Another Year," "Be Still, My Wild Heart," "Long Within the Danish Camp," "My Own Hills."

Sources: *Dictionary of National Biography.* Electronic Edition 1.1. Oxford University Press, 1997. *English Poetry: Author Search.* Chadwyck-Healey Ltd., 1995 (http://www.lib.utexas.edu:8080/search/epoetry/author.html). *Stanford University Libraries and Academic Information Resources* (http://library.stanford.edu). *The Columbia Granger's Index to Poetry.* 11th ed. *The Columbia Granger's World of Poetry,* Columbia University Press, 2005 (http://www.columbiagrangers.org). *The Poorhouse Fugitives: Self-Taught Poets and Poetry in Victorian Britain.* Brian Maidment, ed. Carcanet, 1987.

STRODE, WILLIAM (1602–1645)

Born near Plympton, Devonshire, he was educated at Westminster School and Christ Church, Oxford, with a B.A. (1621), M.A. (1624), B.D. (1631) and D.D. (1638). After taking holy orders, he became chaplain to Richard Corbet, bishop of Oxford, and in 1633 he became rector of East Bradenham, Norfolk, but continued to reside in Oxford University, where he was public orator. When Charles I and Queen Henrietta visited the university in 1636, Strode welcomed them at the gate of Christ Church with a Latin oration, and later the students performed a tragi-comedy by him called *The Floating Island*. The songs were set to music by Henry Lawes. He died at Christ Church and was buried in the divinity chapel of Christ Church Cathedral. Some of his poems: "A Devonshire Song," "Bracelets," "In Commendation of Music," "On Chloris Walking in the Snow," "On Westwall Downs," "Once Venus' cheeks, that shamed the morn," "Opposite to Melancholy," "The Nightingale."

Sources: *Dictionary of National Biography.* Electronic Edition 1.1. Oxford University Press, 1997. *English Lyric Poems, 1500–1900.* C. Day Lewis, ed. Appleton-Century-Crofts, 1961. *English Poetry: Author Search.* Chadwyck-Healey Ltd., 1995 (http://www.lib.utexas.edu:8080/search/epoetry/author.html). *Poets of the English Language, Vol. II.* W.H. Auden and Norman Holmes Pearson, eds. Viking Press, 1950. *Songs from the British Drama.* Edward Bliss Reed, ed. Yale University Press, 1925. *The Columbia Granger's Index to Poetry.* 11th ed. *The Columbia Granger's World of Poetry,* Columbia University Press, 2005 (http://www.columbiagrangers.org). *The New Oxford Book of Seventeenth Century Verse.* Alastair Fowler, ed. Oxford University Press, 1991. *The Oxford Companion to English Literature.* 6th edition. Margaret Drabble, ed. Oxford University Press, 2000.

STRONG, LEONARD ALFRED GEORGE (1896–1956)

He was born in Plymouth of a half-Irish father and Irish mother and was educated at Brighton College. A spinal complaint interrupted his education at Wadham College, Oxford, and kept him from active service in World War I. He became an assistant master at Summer Fields School, Oxford, returned to Wadham and graduated B.A. in 1920. He went back to Summer Fields and remained a master there until 1930, when he became a full-time writer. He published more than 20 novels as well as short stories, biographies and criticism, and collaborated with Cecil Day-Lewis (see entry) in compiling anthologies. He was a director of the publishers Methuen Ltd. from 1938. Some of his poems have been set to music by Arthur Bliss, and his novel, the *Brothers*, was filmed in 1947. When he died in Guildford, Surrey, he left a posthumous autobiography of his early life, *Green Memory* (1961). Some of his poetry publications: *Dublin Days,* 1921. *Difficult Love,* 1927. *Selected Poems,* 1931. *The Doll,* 1947. *The Body's Imperfection,* 1957. Some of his poems: "Coroner's Jury," "The Brewer's Man," "The Mad Woman of Punnet's Town," "Zeke."

Sources: *Collected Poems of L.A.G. Strong.* Methuen, 1957. *Dictionary of National Biography.* Electronic Edition 1.1. Oxford University Press, 1997. *Dylan Thomas's Choice: An Anthology of Verse Spoken by Dylan Thomas.* Ralph Maud and Aneirin Talfan Davies, ed. New Directions, 1963. *Modern British Poetry.* 7th rev. ed. Louis Untermeyer, ed. Harcourt, Brace, 1962. *Old Brightonian Association, Leonard Strong* (http://www.oldbrightonians.com/strong_01.htm). *The Columbia Granger's Index to Poetry.* 11th ed. *The Columbia Granger's World of Poetry,* Columbia University Press, 2005 (http://www.columbiagrangers.org). *The Oxford Book of Twentieth-Century English Verse.* Philip Larkin, ed. Oxford University Press, 1973. *The Oxford Companion to English Literature.* 6th edition. Margaret Drabble, ed. Oxford University Press, 2000. *What Cheer: An Anthology of American and British Humorous and Witty Verse.* David McCord, ed. Coward-McCann, 1945. *Wikipedia, the Free Encyclopedia* (http://en.wikipedia.org/wiki/Wikipedia).

STRUTHERS, JOHN (1776–1853)

The son of a shoemaker, he was born at Longcalderwood near East Kilbride, Lanarkshire. Joanna Baillie (see entry) and her mother and her sister, then living nearby, took an interest in young Struthers and encouraged him in his writing. He worked as a shoemaker in Glasgow until 1819, then worked as editorial reader to several publishing houses, including Fullerton. Joanna Baillie introduced him to Sir Walter Scott (see entry), who was much impressed with the young man. From 1833 to 1848 he was librarian of Stirling's public library, Glasgow. *The Harp of Caledonia* (3 volumes), a good collection of Scottish songs with an appended essay on Scottish song writers, was published in 1819, and a similar anthology, the *British Minstrel,* appeared in 1821. Struthers wrote many of the lives in Chambers' *Biographical Dictionary of Eminent Scotsmen,* and also contributed to the *Christian Instructor.* He died in Glasgow. Some of his other poetry publications: *Poems,* 1801. *Anticipation,* 1803. *The Poor Man's Sabbath* 1804. *Dychmont,* 1836. *Poetical Works,* 1850 (with autobiography; 2 volumes). Three of his poems: "House of Mourning," "Sonnet," "The Plough."

Sources: *Dictionary of National Biography.* Electronic Edition 1.1. Oxford University Press, 1997. *Great Books Online* (www.bartleby.com). *Significant and Famous Scots* (http://www.electricscotland.com/history/other/struthers_john.htm). *The Columbia Granger's Index to Poetry.* 11th ed. *The Columbia Granger's World of Poetry,* Columbia University Press, 2005 (http://www.columbiagrangers.org). *The Poetical Works of John Struthers: Vol. I.* A. Fullarton and Co., 1850.

STUDDERT KENNEDY, GEOFFREY ANKETELL (1883–1929)

Born in Leeds, Yorkshire, the son of a clergyman, he graduated in classics and divinity from Trinity

College, Dublin, in 1904, after which he taught for two years at a school in West Kirby in Liverpool. He was ordained in 1908 and served in several parishes until 1915, when he became an Army chaplain with the troops in France and Flanders. The nickname "Woodbine Willie" summed up his ministry — a packet of fags (cigarettes) and a heart full of love. He was awarded the Military Cross for his tending of the wounded under fire during the attack on the Messines Ridge (1917). He was appointed a chaplain to king George V in 1919. He died on a speaking tour in Liverpool working for the Industrial Christian Fellowship (ICF). His publications: *Rough Rymes of a Padre*, 1918. *More Rough Rhymes*, 1919. *Songs of Faith and Doubt*, 1922. *The Unutterable Beauty*, 1927. Some of his poems: "Awake, Awake to Love and Work!" "Indifference," "Is it a Dream?" "My Peace I Give unto You," "Roses in December," "The Lord of the World," "Woodbine Willie."

Sources: *Dictionary of National Biography.* Electronic Edition 1.1. Oxford University Press, 1997. *Eerdman's Book of Christian Poetry.* Pat Alexander and Veronica Zundel, eds. William B. Eerdmans, 1981. *Biography of Geoffrey Studdert Kennedy* (http://www.spartacus.schoolnet.co.uk/FWWstuddert.htm). *Poems for the Great Days.* Thomas Curtis Clark, and Robert Earle Clark, ed. Abingdon-Cokesbury Press, 1948. *Poems that Touch the Heart.* A.L. Alexander, ed. Doubleday, 1956. *The Columbia Granger's Index to Poetry.* 11th ed. *The Columbia Granger's World of Poetry,* Columbia University Press, 2005 (http://www.columbiagrangers.org). *The Treasury of Christian Poetry.* Lorraine Eitel, ed. Fleming H. Revell, 1982. *The Treasury of Religious Verse.* Donald T. Kauffman, ed. Fleming H. Revell, 1962. *The Unutterable Beauty. The Collected Poetry of G.A. Studdert Kennedy.* Hodder and Stoughton, 1927 (http://www.mun.ca/rels/restmov/texts/dasc/TUB.HTM).

SUCKLING, SIR JOHN (1609–1642)

Born in Twickenham, Middlesex, the son of Sir John Suckling, secretary of state and comptroller of the household under James I, he was educated at Westminster School and Trinity College, Cambridge, but did not graduate. His father's death in 1627 made him heir to rich estates in Suffolk, Lincolnshire, and Middlesex. He was knighted in 1630 and briefly became a soldier between 1631 and 1632, but his life seems to have been a round of entertainment; he is said to have invented the game of cribbage. Suckling took part as a Royalist in various military actions early in the Civil Wars, including the unsuccessful Scottish campaign of 1639 and the abortive plot to rescue the Earl of Strafford from the Tower of London. He fled to the Continent and soon, reduced to poverty and misery, died in Paris, by poison, so it is said. Two of his plays are the tragedy *Aglaura* (1637) and the comedy *The Goblins* (1638). Some of his poems: "A Barber," "A Barley-Break," "Brennoralt," "Love Turned to Hatred," "Proffered Love Rejected," "The Careless Lover," "The Goblins," "Upon Christ His Birth."

Sources: *A New Canon of English Poetry.* James Reeves and Martin Seymour-Smith, eds. Barnes and Noble, 1967. *Dictionary of National Biography.* Electronic Edition 1.1. Oxford University Press, 1997. *Encyclopædia Britannica Ultimate Reference Suite DVD,* 2006. *English Poetry: Author Search.* Chadwyck-Healey Ltd., 1995 (http://www.lib.utexas.edu:8080/search/epoetry/author.html). *English Poetry: A Poetic Record, from Chaucer to Yeats.* David Hopkins, ed. Routledge, 1990. *The National Portrait Gallery* (www.npg.org.uk). *The Columbia Granger's Index to Poetry.* 11th ed. *The Columbia Granger's World of Poetry,* Columbia University Press, 2005 (http://www.columbiagrangers.org). *The Oxford Companion to English Literature.* 6th edition. Margaret Drabble, ed. Oxford University Press, 2000. *The Works of Sir John Suckling in Prose and Verse.* A. Hamilton Thompson, ed. Reprint Services, 1910.

SWAIN, CHARLES (1801–1874)

Born in Manchester, Lancashire, he worked for 14 years as a clerk, then the rest of his working life in engraving and lithographing, which business he eventually bought. Any leisure he had he devoted to writing poetry, and his first poem was printed in a Manchester magazine, the *Iris*. Between that and his last publication, he acquired a solid reputation as poet and song writer; many of his poems were set to music. Of him, Robert Southey (see entry) is reported to have said that if any man was born to be a poet it was Swain. In 1846, he lectured on modern poets at Manchester Royal Institution and was made honorary professor of poetry. He died at his house, Prestwich Park, near Manchester, and was buried in Prestwich churchyard. Some of his publications: *Metrical Essays*, 1827. *Beauties of the Mind*, 1831. *Rhymes for Childhood*, 1846. *Dramatic Chapters*, 1847. *English Melodies*, 1849. *Poems*, 1857. *Art and Fashion*, 1863. *Songs and Ballads*, 1867. Some of his poems: "Be Kind to Each Other," "The Blind Boy Dying," "The Covenanter's Son," "Wreck of the Steam-Ship the 'President.'"

Sources: *British Minstrelsie.* T.C. and E.C. Jack, Grange Publishing works, Edinburgh (?1900). *Dictionary of National Biography.* Electronic Edition 1.1. Oxford University Press, 1997. *Dramatic Chapters, Poems and Songs of Charles Swain.* David Bogue, 1848. *English Poetry: Author Search.* Chadwyck-Healey Ltd., 1995 (http://www.lib.utexas.edu:8080/search/epoetry/author.html). *Index of Charles Swain's Contributions to British Literary Annuals: Forget Me Not: A Hypertextual Archive* (http://www.orgs.muohio.edu/anthologies/FMN/Authors_Swain.htm). *Stanford University Libraries and Academic Information Resources* (http://library.stanford.edu). *The Columbia Granger's Index to Poetry.* 11th ed. *The Columbia Granger's World of Poetry,* Columbia University Press, 2005 (http://www.columbiagrangers.org). *The National Portrait Gallery* (www.npg.org.uk). *The Poorhouse Fugitives: Self-Taught*

Poets and Poetry in Victorian Britain. Brian Maidment, ed. Carcanet, 1987.

SWEENEY, MATTHEW (1952–)

Irish poet, born in Donegal, he studied at the Polytechnic of North London and the University of Freiburg, Switzerland. He has held residencies at the University of East Anglia and the South Bank Centre in London, and was poet in residence at the National Library for the Blind as part of the "Poetry Places" scheme run by the Poetry Society in London. He gives regular poetry readings, works in schools and on radio and judges poetry competitions. He won a Cholmondeley Award in 1987 and an Arts Council Writers' Award in 1999. He is a member of Aosdána and spends much of his time in Romania. Some of his recent publications: *The Lame Waltzer*, 1985. *Blue Shoes*, 1989. *Cacti*, 1992. *The Flying Spring Onion*, 1992 (for children). *Fatso in the Red Suit*, 1995 (for children). *The Bridal Suite*, 1997. *A Smell of Fish*, 2000. *Up on the Roof: New and Selected Poems*, 2001 (for children). *Selected Poems*, 2002. *Sanctuary*, 2004. Some of his poems: "Alone with the Dawn," "New Year Party," "The Bats," "The Statue," "Where Fishermen Can't Swim."

Sources: *Anthology of Magazine Verse and Yearbook of American Poetry.* Alan F. Pater, ed. Monitor Book Company, 1980. *Bitter Harvest: An Anthology of Contemporary Irish Verse.* John Montague, ed. Scribner's, 1989. *British Council Arts* (http://www.contemporarywriters.com). *Life and Works of Matthew Sweeney* (http://www.writersartists. net/msweeney.htm). *National Library for the Blind* (http:// www.nlbuk.org/readon/poet/index.html). *The Columbia Granger's Index to Poetry.* 11th ed. *The Columbia Granger's World of Poetry,* Columbia University Press, 2005 (http:// www.columbiagrangers.org). *The Inherited Boundaries: Younger Poets of the Republic of Ireland.* Sebastian Barry, ed. The Dolmen Press, 1986. *The Oxford Companion to English Literature.* 6th edition. Margaret Drabble, ed. Oxford University Press, 2000.

SWIFT, JONATHAN (1667–1745)

Born in Dublin — his father was a lawyer whose family had gone to Ireland after the Restoration — he attended Trinity College and from 1689 to 1699 was secretary to Sir William Temple in Surrey. After Temple's death, Swift was ordained an Anglican priest and returned to Ireland, where he served as dean of St. Patrick's, Dublin, from 1713. He suffered from what is now believed to be Ménière's syndrome — a condition of vertigo, nausea, and deafness. In the autumn of 1739 a great celebration was held in his honor. Following a stroke in 1742 he was declared incapable of caring for himself and guardians were appointed. He was buried in St. Patrick's Cathedral beside Esther Johnson, his life-long friend. Swift was a prolific poet, and a brilliant

satirist. Besides the celebrated novel *Gulliver's Travels* (1726), he wrote such shorter works as a *Tale of a Tub* (1704) and *A Modest Proposal* (1729). Some of his poems: "Advice to a Parson," "Advice to the Grub Street Verse-Writers," "Apollo Outwitted," "Clever Tom Clinch Going to Be Hanged," "The Author's Manner of Living," "The Description of a Salamander," "The Fable of Midas."

Sources: *Anthology of Poems on Affairs of State: Augustan Satirical Verse, 1660–1714.* George de F. Lord, ed. Yale University Press, 1975. *Dictionary of National Biography.* Electronic Edition 1.1. Oxford University Press, 1997. *Encyclopædia Britannica Ultimate Reference Suite DVD,* 2006. *Microsoft Encarta* 2006 (DVD). Microsoft Corporation, 2006. *The National Portrait Gallery* (www.npg.org.uk). *The Columbia Granger's Index to Poetry.* 11th ed. *The Columbia Granger's World of Poetry,* Columbia University Press, 2005 (http://www.columbiagrangers.org). *The Complete Poems of Jonathan Swift.* Pat Rogers, ed. Penguin Books, 1983. *The Faber Book of 20th Century Women's Poetry.* Fleur Adcock, ed. Faber and Faber, 1987. *The New Oxford Book of Irish Verse.* Thomas Kinsella, ed. Oxford University Press, 1986. *The Oxford Book of Satirical Verse.* Geoffrey Grigson, ed. Oxford University Press, 1980. *The Oxford Companion to English Literature.* 6th edition. Margaret Drabble, ed. Oxford University Press, 2000.

SWINBURNE, ALGERNON CHARLES (1837–1909)

Born into an aristocratic London family, he was reared at Bonchurch on the Isle of Wight. After Eton College and Balliol College, Oxford (he did not graduate), he settled in London, where he became one of the pre-Raphaelites (see Dante Gabriel Rossetti). His first book, *The Queen Mother and Rosamond* (1860), was two blank verse plays. *Atalanta in Calydon* (1865), a poetic drama modeled on Greek tragedy, brought him fame. His poetry was highly controversial, much of it containing recurring themes of sadomasochism, death-wish, lesbianism and anti-Christian sentiments. He suffered from chronic epilepsy and alcoholism, and by 1878 he was near death. He was restored to health under the guardianship of Theodore Watts-Dunton (see entry) with whom he lived after 1879 at The Pines, Putney, until he died of influenza. He was buried at Bonchurch. Most of his creative work was done in the first half of his life. He wrote three related dramas on Mary, Queen of Scots: *Chasteland* (1865), *Bothwell* (1874) and *Mary Stuart* (1881). Some of his poems: "A Ballad of Dreamland," "After Death," "Evening by the Sea," "In Guernsey," "On the Downs," "The Oblation."

Sources: *A Treasury of Poems for Worship and Devotion.* Charles L. Wallis, ed. Harper, 1959. *Choice of Swinburne's Verse.* Robert Nye, ed. Faber and Faber, 1973. *Dictionary of National Biography.* Electronic Edition 1.1. Oxford University Press, 1997. *Encyclopædia Britannica Ultimate Ref-*

erence Suite DVD, 2006. *English Poetry: Author Search.* Chadwyck-Healey Ltd., 1995 (http://www.lib.utexas.edu:8080/search/epoetry/author.html). *First Lines, Poems Written in Youth, from Herbert to Heaney.* Jon Stallworthy, ed. Carcanet, 1987. *Microsoft Encarta* 2006 (DVD). Microsoft Corporation, 2006. *Poets of the English Language. Vols. I-V.* W.H. Auden and Norman Holmes Pearson, eds. Viking Press, 1950. *The Columbia Granger's Index to Poetry.* 11th ed. *The Columbia Granger's World of Poetry,* Columbia University Press, 2005 (http://www.columbiagrangers.org). *The Home Book of Verse.* Burton Egbert Stevenson, ed. New York: Henry Holt and Company, 1953. *The Oxford Companion to English Literature.* 6th edition. Margaret Drabble, ed. Oxford University Press, 2000. *The Symbolist Poem: The Development of the English Tradition.* Edward Engelberg, ed. E.P. Dutton, 1967. *Wikipedia, the Free Encyclopedia* (http://en.wikipedia.org/wiki/Wikipedia).

SWINGLER, RANDALL (1909–1967)

The son of a clergyman from an industrial background in the Midlands, he was educated at Winchester College and New College, Oxford University, and seemed at one point to be set for a career as a professional flautist. He joined the Communist Party of Great Britain (CPGB) in 1934, set up various newspapers for it, and left the CPGB in 1956. He was one of the organizers of the covert Writer's Group of the late 1930s, attempting to coordinate a "literary policy" of the left, and was also involved also in work for the Unity Theatre, London. He served with the British Army in Italy in World War II, joining as a private soldier, and was awarded the Military Medal. He was a founder of E.P. Thompson's *The New Reasoner* (from 1957). Having donated most of his inherited wealth to the Communist Party and the *Daily Worker,* he spent his later years in a state of chaotic poverty in Essex. He collapsed and died in Soho, London. Some of his poems: "Briefing for Invasion," "Letter I," "Letter VIII," "No Pity, No Poetry," "The Years of Anger," "They Live."

Sources: *Comrade Heart: A Life of Randall Swingler.* Andy Croft. Manchester University Press, 2003 (http://les.man.ac.uk/chnn/CHNN15ARS.html). *Selected Poems of Randall Swingler.* Andy Croft, ed. Trent Editions, 2000. *The Columbia Granger's Index to Poetry.* 11th ed. *The Columbia Granger's World of Poetry,* Columbia University Press, 2005 (http://www.columbiagrangers.org). *The Randall Swingler Archives* (http://www2.ntu.ac.uk/english/centrearchives/Randall%20Swingler%20Archive.html). *The War Poets: An Anthology of the War Poetry of the 20th-Century.* Oscar Williams, ed. John Day, 1945. *Wikipedia, the Free Encyclopedia* (http://en.wikipedia.org/wiki/Wikipedia).

SYLVESTER, JOSUAH (1563–1618)

Born in Kent and orphaned at a young age, he was raised by an uncle and educated at a school in Southampton, Hampshire, where not being fluent in French ensured wearing the dunce's cap. In 1606

Prince Henry made him a groom of his chamber and his first poet pensioner. When he became secretary of a Dutch trading company, he moved to Middelburg, the Netherlands, where he spent the last five years of his life, and where he died. Sylvester's major literary work was the translation of the scriptural epic — on the creation, the fall of man, and other early parts of Genesis — the *Divine Weekes and Workes,* translated from a French Protestant poet, Guillaume du Bartas (1544–90). It appeared in sections between 1592 and 1608, and was reprinted for the fifth time in 1641. The 1621 edition contained his "Lachrymae Lachrymarum" as well as John Donne's "Elegie upon the Untimely Death of the Incomparable Prince Henry." Some of his poems: "A Dialogve Vpon the Trovbles Past," "Autumnus," "The Mysterie of Mysteries," "The Qvadrains of Pibrac," "The Trivmph of Faith," "To Vertves Patterne, and Beavties Paragon."

Sources: *Dictionary of National Biography.* Electronic Edition 1.1. Oxford University Press, 1997. *Encyclopædia Britannica Ultimate Reference Suite DVD,* 2006. *English Poetry: Author Search.* Chadwyck-Healey Ltd., 1995 (http://www.lib.utexas.edu:8080/search/epoetry/author.html). *Great Books Online* (www.bartleby.com). *The National Portrait Gallery* (www.npg.org.uk). *The Columbia Granger's Index to Poetry.* 11th ed. *The Columbia Granger's World of Poetry,* Columbia University Press, 2005 (http://www.columbiagrangers.org). *The Complete Works of Joshuah Sylvester: Volume II.* Alexander B. Grosart, ed. Edinburgh University Press, 1880. *The Faber Book of Epigrams and Epitaphs.* Geoffrey Grigson, ed. Faber and Faber, 1977. *The Gift of Great Poetry.* Lucien Stryk, ed. Regnery Gateway, 1992. *The Oxford Companion to English Literature.* 6th edition. Margaret Drabble, ed. Oxford University Press, 2000.

SYMONS, ARTHUR WILLIAM (1865–1945)

Born at Milford Haven, Wales, the son of a Methodist minister from Cornwall, he was an introspective and self-absorbed child who found solace in literature. In 1884, he edited four volumes of the *Shakespeare Quarto Facsimiles* for the publisher F.J. Furnivall, and in 1886, published an *Introduction to the Study of Browning.* He became a member of the staff of the *Athenaeum* in 1891, and of the *Saturday Review* in 1894. His *Symbolist Movement in Literature* was published in 1899. He wrote plays, edited anthologies, and made translations from authors in six languages. He published his experiences of his suffering from manic depression (bi-polar disorder) in *Confessions: A Study in Pathology* (1930). He died at Wittersham in Kent. Some of his publications: *Days and Nights,* 1889. *London Nights,* 1895. *Images of Good and Evil,* 1899. *Poems,* 1902 (2 volumes). *A Book of Twenty Songs,* 1905. *Knave of*

Hearts, 1913. *Love's Cruelty*, 1923. *Jezebel Mort, and Other Poems*, 1931. Some of his poems: "During Music," "From an Old French Song-book," "Hallucination," "The Abandoned," "The Absinthe-Drinker," "The Blind Beggar."

Sources: *An Anthology of World Poetry.* Mark Van Doren, ed. Reynal and Hitchcock, Inc., 1936. *Dictionary of National Biography.* Electronic Edition 1.1. Oxford University Press, 1997. *Encyclopædia Britannica Ultimate Reference Suite DVD,* 2006. *Poems by Arthur Symons: Volume I.* William Heinemann, 1911. *The Columbia Granger's Index to Poetry.* 11th ed. *The Columbia Granger's World of Poetry,* Columbia University Press, 2005 (http://www.columbia grangers.org). *The Oxford Companion to English Literature.* 6th edition. Margaret Drabble, ed. Oxford University Press, 2000. *The Symbolist Poem: The Development of the English Tradition.* Edward Engelberg, ed. E.P. Dutton, 1967. *Victorian Verse.* George MacBeth, ed. Penguin Books, 1986.

SYNGE, EDMUND JOHN MILLINGTON (1871–1909)

Born in Rathfarnham, Dublin, the son of a Protestant barrister who died when Edmund was a year old. He graduated from Trinity College, Dublin, in 1892, then went to Germany to study music but chose literature instead, and lived in France and Italy, honing up his natural gift for languages. W.B. Yeats (see entry) suggested that Synge went to the Aran Islands in order to write about the culture there. After *The Aran Islands* was published in 1907, he we went on to write tragedies and comedies and translate the works of Francesco Petrarch (1304–1374), François Villon (1431–1465), and Walther (or Walter) von der Vogelweide (?1170–?1230). His last months of life were spent in writing and rewriting the unfinished three-act play *Deirdre of the Sorrows*, which was acted at the Abbey Theatre on 13 Janunary 1910. He died unmarried at a private nursing home in Dublin and was buried in a family tomb at the Protestant Mount Jerome general graveyard at Harold's Cross, Dublin. Some of his poems: "Beg-Innish," "I've Thirty Months," "On a Birthday," "The Curse," "To the Oaks of Glencree," "Winter."

Sources: *Biography and Works of J.M. Synge* (http://www.imagi-nation.com/moonstruck/clsc26.html). *Dictionary of National Biography.* Electronic Edition 1.1. Oxford University Press, 1997. *Irish Poetry: An Interpretive Anthology from Before Swift to Yeats and After.* W.J. McCormack, ed. New York University Press, 2000. *Poems and Translations of J.M. Synge.* John W. Luce and Company, 1911. *The Book of Irish Verse: An Anthology of Irish Poetry from the Sixth Century to the Present.* John Montague, ed. Macmillan, 1974. *The Columbia Granger's Index to Poetry.* 11th ed. *The Columbia Granger's World of Poetry,* Columbia University Press, 2005 (http://www.columbiagrangers. org). *The Faber Book of Epigrams and Epitaphs.* Geoffrey

Grigson, ed. Faber and Faber, 1977. *The National Portrait Gallery* (www.npg.org.uk). *The Oxford Companion to English Literature.* 6th edition. Margaret Drabble, ed. Oxford University Press, 2000.

TALFOURD, SIR THOMAS NOON (1795–1854)

Born at Reading, Berkshire, the son of a brewer, he was called to the bar in 1821 and became a judge in 1849. While he was member of Parliament for Reading, he introduced a copyright bill in 1837, but owing to the death of William IV in 1837, the bill took another seven years before it was passed. His tragedy *Ion* was produced at Covent Garden theatre in 1836, at Sadler's Wells Theatre in December 1861 and in America. Talfourd was a friend and executor of Charles Lamb and published his letters. The first part was in 1837 and the second in 1848; the two were brought together in 1892 as *Talfourd's Memoirs of Charles Lamb.* Charles Dickens dedicated *Pickwick Papers* (1837) to Talfourd, who died of a stroke while addressing the grand jury at Stafford. He was buried in Norwood cemetery, London. Some of his poems: "'Tis a Little Thing," "A Friend," "Hospitality," "Indian Tale," "Prologue to Cato," "On a Tear," "On the Education of the Poor," "On the Tomb of an Infant," "The Memory of the Poets," "The Westminster Play."

Sources: *Dictionary of National Biography.* Electronic Edition 1.1. Oxford University Press, 1997. *English Poetry: Author Search.* Chadwyck-Healey Ltd., 1995 (http://www.lib.utexas.edu:8080/search/epoetry/author.html). *The National Portrait Gallery.* (www.npg.org.uk). *Poems that Touch the Heart.* A.L. Alexander, ed. Doubleday, 1956. *Stanford University Libraries and Academic Information Resources* (http://library.stanford.edu). *The Columbia Granger's Index to Poetry.* 11th ed. *The Columbia Granger's World of Poetry,* Columbia University Press, 2005 (http://www.columbia grangers.org). *Treasury of Favorite Poems.* Joseph H. Head, ed. Gramercy Books, 2000.

TALIESIN (fl. 550)

Welsh bard, the popular rendering of whose name is "fair forehead," whose name is associated with the *Book of Taliesin,* a book of poems written down in the 10th century but which most scholars believe to date in large part from the 6th century. The manuscript, known as *Peniarth MS 2,* is kept at the National Library of Wales. He is believed to have been the chief bard in the courts of at least three British kings of that era. In legend he attained the status Chief Bard of Britain and as such would have been responsible for judging poetry competitions among all the royal bards of Britain. According to tradition, he was buried near his childhood home in Ceredigion and a village named after him in the 19th century now sits below the hillside at the site of his grave. Some of his poems: "A Song to the Wind," "Death Song for Owain ab Urien," "Elegy for Geraint," "Elegy for Owain," "Song of Taliesin," "The Battle of Argoed Llwyfain," "The Battle of Goddeu," "The Spoils of Annwfn," "Urien of Yrechwydd."

Sources: *Dictionary of National Biography.* Electronic Edition 1.1. Oxford University Press, 1997. *Encyclopædia Britannica Ultimate Reference Suite DVD*, 2006. *Lyra Celtica: An Anthology of Representative Celtic Poetry.* E.A. Sharp and J. Matthay, eds. John Grant, 1924. *Oldpoetry* (www.oldpoetry.com). *Ralph Waldo Emerson: Collected Poems and Translations.* Harold Bloom and Paul Kane, eds. The Library of America, 1994. *Taliesin Arts Centre, Swansea* (http://www.taliesinartscentre.co.uk/index.asp?id=1). *The Columbia Granger's Index to Poetry.* 11th ed. *The Columbia Granger's World of Poetry,* Columbia University Press, 2005 (http://www.columbiagrangers.org). *The Oxford Book of Welsh Verse in English.* Gwyn Jones, ed. Oxford University Press, 1977. *The Oxford Companion to English Literature.* 6th edition. Margaret Drabble, ed. Oxford University Press, 2000. *Wikipedia, the Free Encyclopedia.* (http://en.wikipedia.org/wiki/Wikipedia).

TANNAHILL, ROBERT (1774–1810)

The "Paisley Poet" was a Scottish silk-weaver, born into a weaving family from Paisley, and while at the loom he would be writing poetry in his head. Although he went elsewhere to work, he returned to Paisley to work with his mother in 1802 when his father died. His poems, set to music, soon gained in popularity and he was visited by James Hogg, the Ettrick Shepherd (see entry). He was active in setting up a library for working men in the town. Never a robust man, and falling into difficulties with some publishers, he drowned himself in the Paisley Canal and was interred in the West Relief burying-ground. In 1866 an obelisk monument was placed at his grave. The centenary of his birth was celebrated with elaborate ceremony on 3 June 1874. His reputation rests mainly on his sentimental Scottish songs, many of which were published in the Scottish periodicals such as *The Scots Magazine.* Some of his poems: "Bonny Winsome Mary," "Filial Duty," "Jessie, the Flower o' Dunblane," "Row Thee in My Highland Plaid," "The Ambitious Mite," "The Braes of Balquidder," "Will Ye Go Lassie, Go."

Sources: *British Minstrelsie.* T.C. and E.C. Jack, Grange Publishing Works, Edinburgh (?1900). *Dictionary of National Biography.* Electronic Edition 1.1. Oxford University Press, 1997. *English Poetry: Author Search.* Chadwyck-Healey Ltd., 1995 (http://www.lib.utexas.edu:8080/search/epoetry/author.html). *Poems and Songs, Chiefly in the Scottish Dialect, by Robert Tannahill.* John Cain, 1819. *Significant and Famous Scots* (http://www.electricscotland.com/history/men/tannahill_robert.htm). *The Columbia Granger's Index to Poetry.* 11th ed. *The Columbia Granger's World of Poetry,* Columbia University Press, 2005 (http://www.columbiagrangers.org). *The Home Book of Verse.* Burton Egbert Stevenson, ed. New York: Henry Holt and Company, 1953. *The Oxford Companion to English Literature.* 6th edition. Margaret Drabble, ed. Oxford University Press, 2000. *Wikipedia, the Free Encyclopedia.* (http://en.wikipedia.org/wiki/Wikipedia).

TASKER, WILLIAM (1740–1800)

The son of the rector of Iddesleigh, Devonshire, he was educated at Barnstaple and graduated B.A. from Exeter College, Oxford, in 1762. He was ordained in 1767 and took over Iddesleigh when his father died in 1772. He was rector there until he died and was buried near his father; his wife died the following year. Tasker met Samuel Johnson (see entry) and submitted poems to him for his opinion. At the time of his death, Tasker was employed on a history of physiognomy from Aristotle to Lavater, and many letters by him on this subject appeared in *Gentleman's Magazine* (vols. 67–69). Some of his publications: *Ode to the Warlike Genius of Great Britain,* 1778. *Carmen Seculare of Horace, Translated into English Verse,* 1779. *Congratulatory Ode to Admiral Keppell,* 1779. *Elegy on the Death of David Garrick,* 1779. *Ode to Memory of Bishop Wilson,* 1780. *Ode to Speculation,* 1780. *Select Odes of Pindar and Horace Translated,* 1780. *Annus Mirabilis, or the Eventful Year,* 1782, 1783, (possibly a reference to the closing stages of the American War of Independence and the Battle of Yorktown in April 1782).

Sources: *Dictionary of National Biography.* Electronic Edition 1.1. Oxford University Press, 1997. *Gentleman's Magazine* (http://www.bodley.ox.ac.uk/ilej/journals/srchgm.htm). *Wikipedia, the Free Encyclopedia.* (http://en.wikipedia.org/wiki/Wikipedia).

TATE, NAHUM (1652–1715)

He was an Irish playwright, the son of a Dublin clergyman, who graduated B.A. from Trinity College, Dublin, in 1672. Moving to London in 1677, he changed his name from Teate to Tate and began his literary career. He collaborated with John Dryden (see entry) to complete the second half of Dryden's epic poem *Absalom and Achitophel.* In his adaptation of Shakespeare's *King Lear,* Tate created a happy ending where Cordelia lives and marries Edgar and the fool is written out completely. The true version was not restored until the 19th century. He also wrote several hymns; the most well-known is the Christmas carol "While Shepherds Watched." On the death of Thomas Shadwell (1692), Tate was appointed poet laureate, then historiographer-royal, in 1702. With Nicholas Brady (see entry) he produced *New Version of the Psalms* in meter (1696). He was hiding from his creditors in the Mint when he died; he was buried in the neighboring church of St. George's. Some of his other poems: "As Pants the Hart," "Britannia's Prayer for the Queen," "Lord,

Who's the Happy Man," "Old England," "Song for the New-Year 1708," "The Speech of Ajax."

Sources: American Hymns Old and New, Vols. 1–2. Albert Christ-Janer and Charles W. Hughes, eds. Columbia University Press, 1980. *Anthology of Poems on Affairs of State: Augustan Satirical Verse, 1660–1714.* George de F. Lord, ed. Yale University Press, 1975. *Christmas Poems.* John Hollander and J.D. McClatchy, eds. Alfred A. Knopf, 1999. *Dictionary of National Biography.* Electronic Edition 1.1. Oxford University Press, 1997. *English Poetry: Author Search.* Chadwyck-Healey Ltd., 1995 (http://www.lib.utexas.edu:8080/search/epoetry/author.html). *Selected Writings of the Laureate Dunces, Nahum Tate, Laurence Eusden, and Colley Cibber.* The Edwin Mellen Press, 1999. *The Columbia Granger's Index to Poetry.* 11th ed. *The Columbia Granger's World of Poetry,* Columbia University Press, 2005 (http://www.columbiagrangers.org). *The Oxford Companion to English Literature.* 6th edition. Margaret Drabble, ed. Oxford University Press, 2000. *The Poems of John Dryden. Vol. 2, 1682–1685.* Paul Hammond, ed. Longman, 1995. *The Poetical Works of Dryden.* George R. Noyes, ed. Houghton Mifflin Company. 1950. *Treasury of Irish Religious Verse.* Patrick Murray, ed. Crossroad, 1986. *Wikipedia, the Free Encyclopedia.* (http://en.wikipedia.org/wiki/Wikipedia).

TATHAM, JOHN (fl 1632–1664)

Little is known of him other than his writings and that he succeeded John Taylor and Thomas Heywood (see entries) as city poet and laureate to the lord mayor's show between 1657 and 1664, and his successor was Thomas Jordan (see entry). His pastoral play *Love Crowns the End* was produced in 1652, then there was a gap of ten years, which suggests to scholars that some of his work has been lost. His hatred of the Scots is shown in his comedy *Scots Figgaries* [peculiar dress], *or a Knot of Knaves* (1652). His other plays are *The Distracted State, A Tragedy* (1641), and the comedy *Rump, or the Mirrour of the Late Times* (1660). There is no record of his death. Some of his poems: "A Frown," "A Smile," "I will follow through yon grove," "Ostella forth of Town: To My Heart," "Reason," "Song: Fortune Descending," "The Letter," "The Swallow," "To the Deceiving Mistress."

Sources: Dictionary of National Biography. Electronic Edition 1.1. Oxford University Press, 1997. *English Poetry: Author Search.* Chadwyck-Healey Ltd., 1995 (http://www.lib.utexas.edu:8080/search/epoetry/author.html). *The National Portrait Gallery.* (www.npg.org.uk). *Songs from the British Drama.* Edward Bliss Reed, ed. Yale University Press, 1925. *The Cavalier Poets.* Robin Skelton, ed. Oxford University Press, 1970. *The Columbia Granger's Index to Poetry.* 11th ed. *The Columbia Granger's World of Poetry,* Columbia University Press, 2005 (http://www.columbiagrangers.org). *The New Oxford Book of Seventeenth Century Verse.* Alastair Fowler, ed. Oxford University Press, 1991.

TAYLOR, SIR HENRY (1800–1886)

Born at Bishop-Middleham, Count Durham, the son of a farmer, he was educated mainly at home

until 1814. He was a midshipman for a year, but his health was not up to it, so he returned home to immerse himself in his father's well-stocked library. In 1817, two of his brothers died from typhus in London, but Henry survived and from 1824 until 1872 he worked for the colonial office, during which time he exercised considerable influence on the colonial policy of the British Empire. In 1872 he was made a Knight of the Order of Saint Michael and Saint George, and retired to Bournemouth, Dorset, where he died. Taylor wrote a romantic comedy and four verse tragedies. *Philip Van Artevelde* (1834) was set in Flanders in the 14th century. *The Statesman* (1836) was a satire on the civil service. He was a friend and literary executor of Robert Southey (see entry). Some of his poems: "Alabama!" "A Welcome," "Heroism in the Shade," "St. Clement's Eve," "Sonnet in the Mail Coach," "The Eve of the Conquest," "The Hero, the Poet, and the Girl," "Women Singing."

Sources: Dictionary of National Biography. Electronic Edition 1.1. Oxford University Press, 1997. *English Poetry: Author Search.* Chadwyck-Healey Ltd., 1995 (http://www.lib.utexas.edu:8080/search/epoetry/author.html). *The National Portrait Gallery.* (www.npg.org.uk). *The Columbia Granger's Index to Poetry.* 11th ed. *The Columbia Granger's World of Poetry,* Columbia University Press, 2005 (http://www.columbiagrangers.org). *The Oxford Book of Regency Verse 1798–1837.* H.S. Milford, ed. Oxford University Press, 1928. *The Oxford Book of Victorian Verse.* Arthur Quiller-Couch, ed. Oxford University Press, 1971. *The Oxford Companion to English Literature.* 6th edition. Margaret Drabble, ed. Oxford University Press, 2000. *The Routledge Anthology of Cross-Gendered Verse.* Alan Michael Parker and Mark Willhardt, eds. Routledge, 1996. *The Treasury of English Poetry.* Mark Caldwell and Walter Kendrick, eds. Doubleday, 1984.

TAYLOR, JOHN (1580–1623)

Born of humble parents from Gloucester, he saw service as a pressed man in the Navy at the siege of Cadiz (1596) and at Flores in the Azores (1597). He then spent many years on the River Thames and dubbed himself "The Water Poet." When the English Civil Wars began, Taylor moved to Oxford, where he wrote royalist pamphlets, and when Oxford surrendered (1645) he returned to London and kept a public house until his death. He was buried in the churchyard of St. Martin-in-the-Fields. He composed the water pageant on the Thames at the marriage of the Princess Elizabeth in 1613, later Queen of Bohemia, and the pageant with which Charles I was welcomed on his return from Scotland in 1641. He was active in writing about the watermen's disputes of the early 17th century. A prolific and colorful popular writer, he gives a unique picture of England from James I to the Civil War through the eyes of a London waterman. Some of his poems:

"My Defence Against Thy Offence," "Roses Gone Wild," "Taylor's Travels from London to Prague," "The Mill," "The Trumpet of Liberty," "To My Despiteful Foes."

Sources: *All the Workes of John Taylor, the Water Poet.* Scolar Press, 1973. *Dictionary of National Biography.* Electronic Edition 1.1. Oxford University Press, 1997. *English Poetry: Author Search.* Chadwyck-Healey Ltd., 1995 (http://www.lib.utexas.edu:8080/search/epoetry/author. html). *From A to Z: 200 Contemporary American Poets.* David Ray, ed. Ohio University Press, 1981. *The National Portrait Gallery.* (www.npg.org.uk). *Poems of the Old West: A Rocky Mountain Anthology.* Levette J. Davidson, ed. University of Denver Press, 1951. *The Chatto Book of Nonsense Poetry.* Hugh Haughton, ed. Chatto and Windus, 1988. *The Oxford Book of Travel Verse.* Kevin Crossley-Holland, ed. Oxford University Press, 1986. *The Oxford Companion to English Literature.* 6th edition. Margaret Drabble, ed. Oxford University Press, 2000. *Works of John Taylor, the Water Poet,* Spencer Society, 1869.

THE TAYLOR SISTERS, ANN (1782–1866) and JANE (1783–1824)

Ann and Jane Taylor were born in London, the daughters of Isaac Taylor "of Ongar," an engraver, and were raised in Lavenham in Suffolk, where their father was also pastor of a nonconformist chapel. Educated at home, the sisters helped their father at his engraving. Ann contributed the correct solution to a puzzle in the annual *Pocket Book* for 1799 and won first prize, thus starting off her literary career. Thereafter she was a regular contributor, helping with the family income. From a very early age the sisters began imagining stories and writing plays and verses, and soon they were writing for the publishers Darton and Harvey. Volumes of *Original Poems for Infant Minds* appeared in 1804 and 1805 and *Rhymes for the Nursery* in 1806. *Hymns for Infant Minds* followed in 1810 and went through nearly one hundred editions in England and America; it was translated into German, Dutch, and Russian. *Original Hymns for Sunday Schools* was published in 1812. The father was called to the congregation at Ongar, Essex, in 1811, where he remained for the rest of his life. The sisters' poems had to be snatched between short breaks from their engraving work. Jane never married and devoted her life to parish work. She died at Ongar and was buried in the chapel grounds. In 1813, Ann married a Congregational minister, the Rev. Joseph Gilbert, and lived in Yorkshire and in Nottingham, where her husband died in 1852, and where she lived on until she died. During her married life Ann published *The Convalescent, Twelve Letters on Recovery from Sickness* (1839) and in 1844 *Seven Blessings for Little Children.* She also contributed about a quarter of the whole number of hymns in Dr. Leifchild's collection of *Original Hymns* published in 1842. On her husband's death she wrote *Memoir of the Rev. Joseph Gilbert.* Some of the sisters' poems: "Air, Earth, Fire, Water," "Dirty Jim," "Greedy Richard," "Jane and Eliza," "My Mother," "Notorious Glutton," "That God Would Bless the Slave as He Hath Us," "The Blind Sailor," "The Cow and the Ass," "The Maniac's Song," "The Plum-Cake," "The Tumble," "There is a Path That Leads to God," "Twinkle, Twinkle, Little Star," "Two Little Kittens."

Sources: *A Celebration of Women Writers* (http:// digital.library.upenn.edu/women/taylor/autobiography/ autobiography.html). *Dictionary of National Biography.* Electronic Edition, 1.1. *Freedom's Lyre: or Psalms, Hymns, and Sacred Songs, for the Slave and His Friends.* Edwin F. Hatfield, ed. S.W. Benedict, 1840. *Little Anne: Book* (http://digital.library.upenn.edu/women/taylor/little-ann/little-ann.html). *The Autobiography and Other Memorials of Mrs. Gilbert, Formerly Ann Taylor,* by Ann Taylor, Vols. I and II. Josiah Gilbert, ed. Henry S. King and Co., 1874. *The Book of a Thousand Poems: A Family Treasury.* J. Murray Macbain, ed. Peter Bedrick Books, 1983 (http:// digital.library.upenn.edu/women/taylor/autobiography/autobiography.html). *The Columbia Granger's Index to Poetry.* 11th ed. *The Columbia Granger's World of Poetry,* Columbia University Press, 2005 (http://www.columbia grangers.org). *The Home Book of Verse for Young Folks.* Burton Egbert Stevenson, ed. Holt, Rinehart and Winston, 1929. *The National Portrait Gallery.* (www.npg.org.uk). *The New Oxford Book of Children's Verse.* Neil Philip, ed. Oxford University Press, 1996. *The New Oxford Book of Romantic Period Verse.* Jerome J. McGann. Oxford University Press, 1993. *Victorian Parlor Poetry: An Annotated Anthology.* Michael R. Turner, ed. Dover Publications, 1992. *Women Romantic Poets, 1785–1832: An Anthology.* Jennifer Breen, ed. J.M. Dent and Sons, 1992.

TAYLOR, WILLIAM (1765–1836)

Born in Norwich, where his father was an export manufacturer, he was educated at a school run by Anna Letitia Barbauld (see entry) and Rochemont Barbauld. Taylor treasured her friendship for many years, and at the school he formed a lifelong friendship with Frank Sayers (see entry). He traveled extensively in Europe and became a competent translator. His father retired from business in 1791, having made his fortune, and William devoted his life to literature and became a leading member of Norwich intelligentsia and a political radical who applauded the French Revolution. Goethe ordered his publisher to issue a special edition of Taylor's 1793 translation of his (Goethe's) *Iphigenie auf Tauris* (1790). Taylor died, unmarried, in Norwich, and was buried in the graveyard of the Unitarian Octagon chapel. In his time he wrote over 1,700 literary reviews to various journals. William Wordsworth's and Samuel Taylor Coleridge's *Lyrical Ballads* of 1798 arose out of Taylor's translations of German Romantic literature.

Some of his poems: "Absolution," "Ellenore," "Female Caution," "Hull Ale," "Penance," "The Dropsical Man," "The Mistake," "The Resurrection," "The Vision."

Sources: *Anthology of Magazine Verse and Yearbook of American Poetry*. Alan F. Pater, ed. Monitor Book Company, 1980. *Dictionary of National Biography*. Electronic Edition 1.1. Oxford University Press, 1997. *English Poetry: Author Search*. Chadwyck-Healey Ltd., 1995 (http://www.lib.utexas.edu:8080/search/epoetry/author.html). *The National Portrait Gallery*. (www.npg.org.uk). *The Columbia Granger's Index to Poetry*. 11th ed. *The Columbia Granger's World of Poetry*, Columbia University Press, 2005 (http://www.columbiagrangers.org). *The New Oxford Book of Romantic Period Verse*. Jerome J. McGann. Oxford University Press, 1993. *The Oxford Companion to English Literature*. 6th edition. Margaret Drabble, ed. Oxford University Press, 2000. *Wikipedia, the Free Encyclopedia*. (http://en.wikipedia.org/wiki/Wikipedia).

TENNANT, WILLIAM (1784–1848)

Scottish poet from Anstruther Easter, Fifeshire, who was lame in both feet and used crutches from childhood. He was at St. Andrews University from 1799 to 1800 and taught himself Hebrew, Arabic, Syriac, and Persian. He helped form the Anstruther Musomanik Society, the aim of which was to spin rhymes; Sir Walter Scott was pleased to be admitted as a member. From 1813 to 1819 he was schoolmaster, and from 1819 to 1834 he taught classical and Oriental languages at Dollar Academy, Clackmannanshire. From 1834 until ill health forced his retirement in 1848, he was professor of Hebrew and Oriental languages at St. Mary's College, St. Andrews. He died unmarried and was buried at Anstruther. The poem "Anster Fair" (1812)—based on the ballad of "Maggie Lauder"—brought Tennant instant greatness. *To the Scottish Christian Herald* of 1836–1837 he contributed five "Hebrew Idylls." He edited the *Poems* of Allan Ramsay, with a prefatory biography (1819). Some of his poems: "Papistry Storm'd," "Epitaph on David Barclay," "Tammy Little," "The Tangiers Giant," "Ode to Peace (1814)," "The Winter Day," "The Thane of Fife" (thane is a minor Scottish noble).

Sources: *Dictionary of National Biography*. Electronic Edition 1.1. Oxford University Press, 1997. *English Poetry: Author Search*. Chadwyck-Healey Ltd., 1995 (http://www.lib.utexas.edu:8080/search/epoetry/author.html). *Significant and Famous Scots* (http://www.electricscotland.com/history/men/tennant_william.htm). *The Columbia Granger's Index to Poetry*. 11th ed. *The Columbia Granger's World of Poetry*, Columbia University Press, 2005 (http://www.columbiagrangers.org). *The New Oxford Book of Romantic Period Verse*. Jerome J. McGann. Oxford University Press, 1993. *The New Penguin Book of Scottish Verse*. Robert Crawford and Mick Imlah, eds. Penguin Books, 2000. *The Oxford Companion to English Literature*. 6th edition. Margaret Drabble, ed. Oxford University Press, 2000.

THE TENNYSON BROTHERS (1807–1898), FREDERICK, TURNER CHARLES and LORD ALFRED

The three poet brothers were the sons of the Rev. Dr. George Clayton Tennyson, rector of Somersby, a village in North Lincolnshire, between Horncastle and Spilsby. Frederick, Charles (who later adopted the name Turner when he inherited a small property from a great-uncle), and Alfred contributed to *Poems by Two Brothers* (1827). Charles and Alfred married sisters Louisa and Emily Sellwood.

Frederick, 1807–1898

Educated at Eton College, he graduated B.A from Trinity College, Cambridge, in 1832, having gained the Browne medal for Greek verse; he then spent twenty years in Florence, Italy, in close companionship with Elizabeth and Robert Browning (see entries). Discouraged by the criticism of his poetry, he published no more until 1890, when *The Isles of Greece*, based upon a few surviving fragments of Sappho and Alcæus, was published. *Daphne* followed in 1891; he also published *Days and Hours* (1854) and *Poems of the Day and Year* (1895). He married Maria Giuliotti, daughter of the chief magistrate of Siena, in 1839, and remained in Italy until 1859, then lived in St. Ewold's, Jersey, until 1896. He died at his son's house in Kensington, London. Some of his other poems: "An Incident," "Glory of Nature," "Harvest Home," "Iona," "Old Age," "Poetical Happiness," "The Holy Tide," "The Skylark."

Turner Charles, 1808–1879

Educated at Louth Grammar School, then at home by his father, he entered Trinity College, Cambridge, on the same day as Frederick and won the Bell scholarship (open to the sons of clergymen) in 1829. He graduated B.A. from Trinity College in 1832 and was ordained in 1835. Poor health forced his resignation from his living at Grasby, Lincolnshire, and he died at Cheltenham. His nephew Hallam (the second Lord Tennyson), writing of his uncle in the year following his death, tells of the charm of his personality, his fondness for flowers, for dogs and horses, and all living things, and his sweetness and gentleness of character. Some of his poems: "After the School-Feast," "Beau Nash and the Roman," "Christ and Orpheus," "The Aeolian Harp," "The Steam Threshing-Machine," "The Transfiguration," "Wind on the Corn," "Wölf and the Casket."

Lord Alfred (1809–1892)

Educated at Louth Grammar School, he went on to Trinity College, Cambridge, with his two brothers, where he joined the "Cambridge Apostles." In

1829 he won the chancellor's medal for English verse on the subject of "Timbuctoo." He left Cambridge in 1831, without taking a degree, to care for his ill father, who died within a month. He and his mother lived on at Somersby until 1837, after which they moved to Essex. Tennyson succeeded William Wordsworth as poet laureate in 1850, in the same year as he produced his masterpiece "In Memoriam A.H.H.," dedicated to his friend and brother-in-law Arthur Hallam, who died in 1833. He was created Baron Tennyson of Aldworth in the County of Sussex and of Freshwater in the Isle of Wight; he was the first English writer raised to the peerage. His poem "Crossing the Bar" was set to music by Sir Frank Bridge and first sung at his funeral in Westminster Abbey, where he is buried in Poets' Corner, next to Robert Browning. Some of his other poems: "Audley Court," "Columbus," "Idylls of the King," "Locksley Hall," "Ode on the Death of the Duke of Wellington," "The Charge of the Light Brigade," "To Mary Boyle," "To the Queen," "To Ulysses."

Sources: *A Century of Sonnets: The Romantic-Era Revival 1750–1850.* Paula R. Feldman and Daniel Robinson, eds. Oxford University Press, 1999. *A Sacrifice of Praise: An Anthology of Christian Poetry in English from Caedmon to the Mid-Twentieth Century.* James H. Trott, ed. Cumberland House Publishing, 1999. *Collected Sonnets of Turner, Charles Tennyson.* Gregg International Publishers, 1880. *Dictionary of National Biography.* Electronic Edition 1.1. Oxford University Press, 1997. *Encyclopædia Britannica Ultimate Reference Suite DVD,* 2006. *English Poetry: Author Search.* Chadwyck-Healey Ltd., 1995 (http://www.lib.utexas.edu:8080/search/epoetry/author.html). *Everyman's Book of Victorian Verse.* J.R. Watson, ed. J.M. Dent, 1982. *Golden Numbers.* Kate Douglas Wiggin and Nora Archibald Smith, eds. Doubleday, Doran, 1902. *Immortal Poems of the English Language.* Oscar Williams, ed. Simon and Schuster, 1952. *Microsoft Encarta* 2006 (DVD). Microsoft Corporation, 2006. *O Frabjous Day: Poetry for Holidays and Special Occasions.* Myra Cohn Livingston, ed. Atheneum, 1977. *Poet's Graves, Alfred Lord Tennyson* (http://www.poetsgraves.co.uk/tennyson.htm). *Stanford University Libraries and Academic Information Resources* (http://library.stanford.edu). *Tennyson: A Selected Edition.* Christopher Ricks, ed. University of California Press, 1989. *The Columbia Granger's Index to Poetry.* 11th ed. *The Columbia Granger's World of Poetry,* Columbia University Press, 2005 (http://www.columbiagrangers.org). *The Faber Book of Vernacular Verse.* Tom Paulin, Faber and Faber, 1990. *The Golden Book of Catholic Poetry.* Alfred Noyes, ed. J.B. Lippincott, 1946. *The Harper Anthology of Poetry.* John Frederick Nims, ed. Harper and Row, 1981. *The Oxford Book of Nineteenth-Century English Verse.* John Hayward, ed. Oxford University Press, 1964; reprinted, with corrections, 1965. *The Oxford Book of Victorian Verse.* Arthur Quiller-Couch, ed. Oxford University Press, 1971. *Westminster Abbey Official Guide* (no date). *Wikipedia, the Free Encyclopedia.* (http://en.wikipedia.org/wiki/Wikipedia).

TESSIMOND, ARTHUR SEYMOUR JOHN (1902–1962)

Born in Birkenhead, Cheshire, and educated at Charterhouse School and Liverpool University, he worked in bookshops in London and then as an advertising copywriter. He was found to be medically unfit for service in World War II. He suffered from depression (for which he received electric shock treatment) and he spent a great deal of money on psychoanalysis. He died of a brain hemorrhage. Stylistically he was of the Imagist School, and his poems are about the ordinary and city stereotypes; some are conversation poems, often with a tendency toward the melancholic. *Walls of Glass* (1934), *Voices in a Giant City* (1947), and *Selections* (1958) were published during his lifetime. *Not Love Perhaps* was published in 1972. In the mid–1970s he was the subject of a radio program entitled *Portrait of a Romantic.* His *Daydream* and *Voices in a Giant City* were featured in 2004 on BBC Radio 4's program *Poetry Please.* Some of his poems: "Cats," "Daydream," "Middle-aged Conversation," "Not Love Perhaps," "Postscript to a Pettiness," "The British," "The Children Look at the Parents."

Sources: *Cats, Poem by A.S.J. Tessimond* (http://www.cs.rice.edu/~ssiyer/minstrels/poems/1010.html). *Poemhunter* (www.poemhunter.com). *Biography of A.S.J. Tessiond, and List of Poems* (http://www.poetryconnection.net/poets/A.S.J._Tessimond). *Seven Centuries of Poetry: Chaucer to Dylan Thomas.* A.N. Jeffares, ed. Longmans, Green, 1955. *The Chatto Book of Modern Poetry 1915–1955.* Cecil Day Lewis and John Lehmann, eds. Chatto and Windus, 1966. *The Columbia Granger's Index to Poetry.* 11th ed. *The Columbia Granger's World of Poetry,* Columbia University Press, 2005 (http://www.columbiagrangers.org). *The Oxford Book of Animal Poems.* Michael Harrison and Christopher Stuart-Clark, ed. Oxford University Press, 1992. *The Oxford Companion to English Literature.* 6th edition. Margaret Drabble, ed. Oxford University Press, 2000. *Wikipedia, the Free Encyclopedia.* (http://en.wikipedia.org/wiki/Wikipedia).

THACKERAY, WILLIAM MAKEPEACE (1811–1863)

Born in Calcutta, India, the son of a wealthy English officer of the East India Company, he was educated at Charterhouse School and Trinity College, Cambridge, but left without graduating. He was a journalist in Paris and in London, writing under a number of amusing pseudonyms: "Charles James Yellowplush, a footman"; "Michael Angelo Titmarsh"; and "George Savage Fitz-Boodle." He joined the staff of *Punch* in 1842 and published the *Irish Sketchbook* in 1843 and *Cornhill to Cairo* in 1847. He achieved fame with his novel *Vanity Fair,* published in parts during 1847–1848. He did two lecture tours of the United States during the 1850s.

He died of a brain hemorrhage, was buried at Kensal Green Cemetery, and is memorialized by a stone in Poets' Corner of Westminster Abbey. His novels are noted for their humor and ironic portrayals of the middle and upper classes of his time. Some of his poems: "Dr. Birch and His Young Friends," "King Canute," "Pocahontas," "The Age of Wisdom," "The Ballad of Bouillabaisse," "The Battle of Limerick," "The Chronicle of the Drum," "The Last Irish Grievance," "The Yankee Volunteers."

Sources: *America in Poetry.* Charles Sullivan, ed. Harry N. Abrams, 1988. *Ballads and Songs by William Makepeace Thackeray.* Cassell, 1896. *Dictionary of National Biography.* Electronic Edition 1.1. Oxford University Press, 1997. *Encyclopædia Britannica Ultimate Reference Suite DVD,* 2006. *Innocent Merriment: An Anthology of Light Verse.* Franklin P. Adams, ed. McGraw-Hill, 1942. *Microsoft Encarta* 2006 (DVD). Microsoft Corporation, 2006. *The Columbia Granger's Index to Poetry.* 11th ed. *The Columbia Granger's World of Poetry,* Columbia University Press, 2005 (http://www.columbiagrangers.org). *The Faber Book of English History in Verse.* Kenneth Baker, ed. Faber and Faber, 1988. *The Oxford Companion to English Literature.* 6th edition. Margaret Drabble, ed. Oxford University Press, 2000. *Wikipedia, the Free Encyclopedia.* (http://en.wikipedia.org/wiki/Wikipedia).

THOMAS, D(ONALD) M(ICHAEL) (1935–)

Born in Redruth, Cornwall, and educated at the University High School Melbourne, Australia, he graduated M.A. in English from New College, Oxford University, in 1961. From 1963 to 1977 he was lecturer in English at Hereford College of Education, eventually becoming head of the department. Having learned Russian during national service (1951–1953), his own work is significantly influenced by Russian literature and he has translated the work of Anna Akhmatova (1889–1966) and Alexander Pushkin (1799–1837). He appeared in *Penguin Modern Poets 11* (1968); his poem "Dreaming in Bronze" (1981) received a Cholmondely Award. His novel *The Flute-Player* (1979) won the Guardian/Gollancz Fantasy Prize. His third novel, the *White Hotel* (1981), is a fascinating story about psychoanalysis. His autobiography *Memories and Hallucinations* was published in 1988. He lives in Truro, Cornwall. Thomas's themes are universal — love, death, eroticism, sexuality, family relations — with a strong Cornish influence. Some of his poetry publications: *Two Voices,* 1968. *The Shaft,* 1973. *Love and Other Deaths,* 1975. *The Honeymoon Voyage,* 1978. *Selected Poems,* 1983. *The Puberty Tree,* 1992. Some of his poems: "Eden," "Poetry Reading," "Smile," "Tangier: Hotel Rif."

Sources: *Anthology of Magazine Verse and Yearbook of American Poetry.* Alan F. Pater, ed. Monitor Book Company, 1980. *Encyclopædia Britannica Ultimate Reference Suite DVD,* 2006. *Biography and Works of DM Thomas* (http://www.falpublications.co.uk/falhtm/dmthomas.htm). *Biography of DM Thomas: The Literary Encyclopedia.* (http://www.litencyc.com/php/speople.php?rec=true&UID=4370). *Microsoft Encarta* 2006 (DVD). Microsoft Corporation, 2006. *The National Portrait Gallery.* (www.npg.org.uk). *New Coasts & Strange Harbors: Discovering Poems.* Helen Hill and Agnes Perkins, eds. Thomas Y. Crowell Co., 1974. *The Columbia Granger's Index to Poetry.* 11th ed. *The Columbia Granger's World of Poetry,* Columbia University Press, 2005 (http://www.columbiagrangers.org). *The Oxford Book of Travel Verse.* Kevin Crossley-Holland, ed. Oxford University Press, 1986. *The Oxford Companion to English Literature.* 6th edition. Margaret Drabble, ed. Oxford University Press, 2000. *Who's Who.* London: A & C Black, 2005.

THOMAS, DYLAN MARLAIS (1914–1953)

Born in Swansea, Wales, where his father taught at the Swansea Grammar School, Dylan left school at 17 and spent a year as a reporter on the South Wales *Daily Post.* His first collection, *18 Poems,* was published in 1934, the year in which he moved to London and entered upon a lifestyle of heavy drinking that eventually killed him. Underlying his poetry is a deep sense of the religious, as in "This Bread I Break." He died while on his fourth lecture tour of America, was buried in the parish church of St. Martin, Laugharne, Dyfed, Wales, and is memorialized by a stone in Poets' Corner of Westminster Abbey. Thomas also published short stories, wrote film scripts, publicly performed his works and was broadcast regularly on the radio. *Under Milk Wood* was made into a radio play (1954) (See http://www.geocities.com/dylanwthomas/under_milk_wood.htm for the complete play.). His most famous poem is possibly *Do Not Go Gentle into that Good Night.* Some of his other poems: "A Child's Christmas in Wales," "And Death Shall Have No Dominion," "Altarwise by Owl-Light," "Love in the Asylum," "The Conversation of Prayer."

Sources: *Anglo-Welsh Poetry, 1480–1980.* Raymond Garlick and Roland Mathias, eds. Poetry Wales Press, 1984. *Anglo-Welsh Poetry, 1480–1990.* Raymond Garlick and Roland Mathias, eds. Poetry Wales Press, 1993. *Dictionary of National Biography.* Electronic Edition 1.1. Oxford University Press, 1997. *Encyclopædia Britannica Ultimate Reference Suite DVD,* 2006. *Golden Treasury of the Best Songs & Lyrical Poems in the English Language.* Francis Turner Palgrave, ed. Oxford University Press, 1964, Sixth edition, updated by John Press, 1994. *Poemhunter* (www.poemhunter.com). *The Collected Poems of Dylan Thomas, 1934–1952.* New Directions, 1953, rev. ed. 1956. *The Columbia Granger's Index to Poetry.* 11th ed. *The Columbia Granger's World of Poetry,* Columbia University Press, 2005 (http://www.columbiagrangers.org). *The Oxford Book of Twentieth-Century English Verse.* Philip Larkin, ed. Oxford University Press, 1973. *The Poetry Anthology, 1912–1977.* Daryl Hine and Joseph Parisi, eds. Houghton Mifflin, 1978. *The Times Obituary of Dylan Thomas, November 10, 1953.* Microsoft *Encarta* 2006 (DVD). Microsoft Corporation, 2006. *Westminster Abbey Official Guide* (no date).

THOMAS (PHILIP) EDWARD (1878–1917)

Born in Lambeth, London, the son of a clerk at the Board of Trade, he was educated at St. Paul's School and graduated B.A. in modern history from Lincoln College, Oxford, in 1900. He was a journalist before World War I and began writing poetry in 1912 under the pseudonym Edward Eastaway; he devoted himself fully to poetry in 1913 after a meeting with Robert Frost, the American poet, who was then living in England. Thomas joined the Artists' Rifles in 1915 as a private, despite being a mature married man who could have avoided enlisting, and was killed in action at Arras soon after he arrived in France as an officer. Most of his poems — often about the English countryside — were published posthumously, and few are about the war. One links the countryside with the war: "In Memoriam." In his brief 15-year career he produced over two dozen books and wrote many reviews, focusing on local history and literary figures. Some of his poems: "Adlestrop," "Bird's Nests," "Haymaking," "Sedge-Warblers," "The Brook," "The Cherry Tree," "The Sheiling," "Under the Woods."

Sources: *Come Hither.* Walter de la Mare, ed. Knopf, 1957; Dover Publications, 1995. *Dictionary of National Biography.* Electronic Edition 1.1. Oxford University Press, 1997. *Microsoft Encarta* 2006 (DVD). Microsoft Corporation, 2006. *On Wings of Song: Poems About Birds.* J.D. McClatchy, ed. Alfred A. Knopf, 2000. *Poetry for Pleasure: A Choice of Poetry and Verse on a Variety of Themes.* Ian Parsons, ed. W.W. Norton, 1977. *Splinters: A Book of Very Short Poems.* Michael Harrison, ed. Oxford University Press, 1989. *The Artist's Rifles, Edward Thomas* (http://en.wikipedia.org/wiki/Artists%27_Rifles). *The Collected Poems of Edward Thomas.* Oxford University Press, 1979. *The Columbia Granger's Index to Poetry.* 11th ed. *The Columbia Granger's World of Poetry,* Columbia University Press, 2005 (http://www.columbiagrangers.org). *The Faber Book of English History in Verse.* Kenneth Baker, ed. Faber and Faber, 1988. *The Oxford Companion to English Literature.* 6th edition. Margaret Drabble, ed. Oxford University Press, 2000.

THOMAS, R(ONALD) S(TUART) (1913–2000)

The Welsh poet R.S. Thomas was born in Cardiff and raised in Holyhead, Anglesey. After reading classics at University College, Bangor, he was ordained in the Church of Wales (1936), in which he held appointments in several remote parishes; he retired from the church in 1978. After Dylan Thomas he is the best-known poet of 20th-century Wales. He learned Welsh as an adult and thereafter identified passionately with Welsh language and culture; he voiced sometimes in militant terms his contempt of those forces that threatened its survival. In 1964 he won the Queen's Gold Medal for Poetry. He was a fierce advocate of Welsh nationalism, but believed that Plaid Cymru did not go far enough in their opposition to England. He was a supporter of the Campaign for Nuclear Disarmament and was a passionate supporter of the preservation of wildlife. In 1996 he was nominated for the Nobel Prize for Literature, but lost out to his friend Seamus Heaney (see entry), who read the eulogy at his memorial service held in Westminster Abbey. Some of his poems: "A Blackbird Singing," "After Jericho," "Alpine," "Farm Child," "Judgment Day," "Taliesin 1952," "Welsh Landscape."

Sources: *A Book of Nature Poems.* William Cole, ed. Viking Press, 1969. *Anglo-Welsh Poetry, 1480–1980.* Raymond Garlick and Roland Mathias, eds. Poetry Wales Press, 1984. *Anglo-Welsh Poetry, 1480–1990.* Raymond Garlick and Roland Mathias, eds. Poetry Wales Press, 1993. *Collected Later Poems: 1988–2000 of R.S. Thomas.* Bloodaxe Books, 2004. *Contemporary Religious Poetry.* Paul Ramsey, ed. Paulist Press, 1987. *Room for Me and a Mountain Lion: Poetry of Open Space.* Nancy Larrick, ed. M. Evans, 1974. *The Bloodaxe Book of 20th Century Poetry, from Britain and Ireland.* Edna Longley, ed. Bloodaxe Books, 2000. *The Columbia Granger's Index to Poetry.* 11th ed. *The Columbia Granger's World of Poetry,* Columbia University Press, 2005 (http://www.columbiagrangers.org). *The Oxford Book of Contemporary Verse, 1945–1980.* D.J. Enright, ed. Oxford University Press, 1980. *The Oxford Companion to English Literature.* 6th edition. Margaret Drabble, ed. Oxford University Press, 2000. *Wales Loses Its Most Sustained Lyric Voice, R.S. Thomas* (http://www.guardian.co.uk/uk_news/story/0,3604,373779,00.html). beg

THOMPSON, FRANCIS (1859–1907)

Born in Preston, Lancashire, the son of a homeopath, he was educated in the classics at the Catholic Ushaw College near Durham, then studied medicine at Owens College, Manchester. He never practiced medicine, choosing instead a career in literature in London, but was reduced to selling matches and newspapers for a living. He became addicted to opium, which he first took as a remedy for some health problem, and was rescued from starvation by Alice and Wilfrid Meynell (see Meynell, Alice) who took him in. They arranged for the publication of his first volume of *Poems* in 1893, which included his best-known work, "The Hound of Heaven." *New Poems* was published in 1897. He died in London from tuberculosis and was buried in the Catholic cemetery, Kensal Green, where his tomb was inscribed with his own words, *Look for Me in the Nurs-*

eries of Heaven. He is sometimes mentioned as a possible Jack the Ripper suspect (see also Stephen, James Kenneth). Some of his other poems: "A Judgment in Heaven," "An Arab Love-Song," "Beneath a Photograph," "Contemplation," "Grace of the Way," "The Veteran of Heaven," "Whereto art Thou Come?"

Sources: *Dictionary of National Biography.* Electronic Edition 1.1. Oxford University Press, 1997. *Encyclopædia Britannica Ultimate Reference Suite DVD,* 2006. *English Poetry: Author Search.* Chadwyck-Healey Ltd., 1995 (http://www.lib.utexas.edu:8080/search/epoetry/author.html). *I Sing of a Maiden: The Mary Book of Verse.* Sister M. Therese, ed. Macmillan, 1947. *Microsoft Encarta* 2006 (DVD). Microsoft Corporation, 2006. *Modern American and British Poetry.* Louis Untermeyer, Karl Shapiro and Richard Wil, eds. Harcourt, Brace, Rev., shorter ed., 1955. *Other Men's Flowers.* A.P. Wavell, ed. Jonathan Cape, 1990. *The Columbia Granger's Index to Poetry.* 11th ed. *The Columbia Granger's World of Poetry,* Columbia University Press, 2005 (http://www.columbiagrangers.org). *The National Portrait Gallery.* (www.npg.org.uk). *The Oxford Book of Nineteenth-Century English Verse.* John Hayward, ed. Oxford University Press, 1964; reprinted, with corrections, 1965. *The Oxford Companion to English Literature.* 6th edition. Margaret Drabble, ed. Oxford University Press, 2000. *The Works of Francis Thompson, Poems* (3 volumes). Wilfred Meynell, ed. Burns and Oats Ltd., 1913. *Wikipedia, the Free Encyclopedia.* (http://en.wikipedia.org/wiki/Wikipedia).

THOMPSON, WILLIAM (?1712–1766)

Born in Westmoreland, the son of Francis Thompson, vicar of Brough, he graduated M.A. from Queen's College, Oxford, in 1738–39 and was elected a fellow of Queen's, and became rector of Hampton Poyle with South Weston in Oxfordshire. In 1745 he published "Sickness, a Poem" a tribute to the memory of Alexander Pope and Jonathan Swift, both recently dead (see entries). The subject of his verse tragedy *Gondibert and Bertha* (1751) was taken from Sir William D'Avenant's (see entry) poem "Gondibert." In 1756, on the presentation to Oxford University of the Pomfret statues (which had been part of the Arundelian collection of marbles), he wrote *Gratitude,* a poem in honor of the donor, Henrietta Louisa Fermor, countess dowager of Pomfret. Some of his other poems: "An Hymn to May," "Beauty and Musick," "Cupid Mistaken," "The Bee," "The Bower," "The Magi," "The Nativity," "Written in the Holy Bible."

Sources: *Dictionary of National Biography.* Electronic Edition 1.1. Oxford University Press, 1997. *Eighteenth-Century English Verse.* Dennis Davison, ed. Penguin Books, 1988. *English Poetry: Author Search.* Chadwyck-Healey Ltd., 1995 (http://www.lib.utexas.edu:8080/search/epoetry/author.html). *Poems on Several Occasions by William Thompson.* Oxford, 1757. *The Columbia Granger's Index to Poetry.* 11th ed. *The Columbia Granger's World of Poetry,*

Columbia University Press, 2005 (http://www.columbiagrangers.org).

THOMSON, JAMES (1700–1748)

Scottish poet, the son of a minister, born and raised in Roxburghshire and educated at Jedburgh Grammar School and Edinburgh University, where three of his poems appeared in the *Edinburgh Miscellany* of 1720. He worked as tutor for several notable figures, including Sir Charles Talbot, then solicitor-general. His collected poetry was published as *The Seasons* in 1730. He quickly became successful and won favor with Frederick, Prince of Wales, whom he supported politically. He also wrote several plays, including *The Tragedy of Sophonisba* (1734) and collaborated with David Mallet (see entry) on the masque *Alfred,* which contained the song "Rule Britannia," first performed at Cliveden, the country home of the Prince and Princess of Wales. He was buried near the font in Richmond parish church, Surrey, and is memorialized by a stone in Poets' Corner of Westminster Abbey. Some of his poems: "For I must sing of all I feel and know," "Liberty," "On Beauty," "On Happiness," "Short is the Doubtful Empire of the Night," "Sunday Up the River," "The Castle of Indolence," "The Doom of a City," "To the Memory of Sir Isaac Newton."

Sources: *An Anthology of World Poetry.* Mark Van Doren, ed. Reynal and Hitchcock, Inc., 1936. *Dictionary of National Biography.* Electronic Edition 1.1. Oxford University Press, 1997. *Encyclopædia Britannica Ultimate Reference Suite DVD,* 2006. *English Poetry: Author Search.* Chadwyck-Healey Ltd., 1995 (http://www.lib.utexas.edu:8080/search/epoetry/author.html). *Microsoft Encarta* 2006 (DVD). Microsoft Corporation, 2006. *Poems of James Thomson.* Henry Holt and Company, 1927. *Poets of the English Language, Vols. I–V.* W.H. Auden and Norman Holmes Pearson, eds. Viking Press, 1950. *The Columbia Granger's Index to Poetry.* 11th ed. *The Columbia Granger's World of Poetry,* Columbia University Press, 2005 (http://www.columbiagrangers.org). *The Oxford Companion to English Literature.* 6th edition. Margaret Drabble, ed. Oxford University Press, 2000. *The Poetical Works of James Thomson.* Houghton, Mifflin (no date). *Through the Year with the Poets.* Oscar Fay Adams, ed. D. Lothrop and Company, 1886. *Westminster Abbey Official Guide* (no date).

THOMSON, JAMES (1834–1882)

Born at Port Glasgow, as an orphan of an officer in the merchant service he was educated at the Royal Caledonian Asylum, London (see MacKay, Charles). From 1851 to 1862, he was an Army schoolmaster where, in Ireland, he fell in love with beautiful Matilda Weller, whose sudden death in 1853 affected the rest of his life. He made friends with Charles Bradlaugh, the founder of the radical journal *National Reformer* (1860), for which paper Thomson became a journalist, writing under the pseudonyms "B.V." or "Bysshe Vanolis" (in honor of Shelley and the German poet known as Novalis). From 1866 his life degenerated into heavy drinking, poverty, loneliness, insomnia, and deep pessimism, living in a one-room lodging on Gower Street, London. During this period he wrote his masterpiece, *City of Dreadful Night* (1874), a great poem of massive structure and profound symbolism. He died in University College Hospital and was buried without any religious ceremony in Highgate Cemetery. Some of his other poems: "A Capstan Chorus," "Robert Burns," "Siren's Song," "Sunday at Hampstead," "The Cypress and the Roses," "The Jolly Veterans," "Withered Leaves."

Sources: *Dictionary of National Biography.* Electronic Edition 1.1. Oxford University Press, 1997. *Encyclopædia Britannica Ultimate Reference Suite DVD,* 2006. *English Poetry: Author Search.* Chadwyck-Healey Ltd., 1995 (http://www.lib.utexas.edu:8080/search/epoetry/author.html). *Microsoft Encarta* 2006 (DVD). Microsoft Corporation, 2006. *Poems and Some Letters of James Thomson.* Anne Ridler, ed. Southern Illinois Univ. Press, 1963. *The Columbia Granger's Index to Poetry.* 11th ed. *The Columbia Granger's World of Poetry,* Columbia University Press, 2005 (http://www.columbiagrangers.org). *The Oxford Book of Nineteenth-Century English Verse.* John Hayward, ed. Oxford University Press, 1964; reprinted, with corrections, 1965. *The Oxford Book of Victorian Verse.* Arthur Quiller-Couch, ed. Oxford University Press, 1971. *The Oxford Companion to English Literature.* 6th edition. Margaret Drabble, ed. Oxford University Press, 2000.

THWAITE, ANTHONY SIMON (1930–)

Born in Chester, he was evacuated during the Second World War to relations in the United States, and after the war, and National Service, he read English at Christ Church, Oxford. His career includes posts in Libya, Japan and Kuwait; Henfield Writing Fellow at the University of East Anglia; literary editor of the *Listener, New Statesman,* and co-editor of *Encounter*; and producer for BBC Radio. Together with Andrew Motion (see entry) he is literary executor of the literary estate of Philip Larkin (see entry) and is a former director of the London publishers André Deutsch. He was poet in residence at Vanderbilt University, Nashville, in 1992. Hull University awarded him an honorary doctorate in 1989, and he was awarded the Order of the British Empire in 1990. He lives in Norfolk, England, with his wife, Ann Thwaite, the biographer and children's book writer. Some of his recent poetry publications: *A Portion for Foxes,* 1977. *Victorian Voices,* 1980. *Poems 1953–1988,* 1989. *Selected Poems 1956–1996,* 1997. *A Different Country: New Poems,* 2000. Some of his poems: "Ali Ben Shufti," "Arabic Script," "At Birth," "Simple Poem," "Sunday Afternoon," "Switzerland."

Sources: *Biography of Anthony Simon Thwaite: British Council Arts* (http://www.contemporarywriters.com). *Modern Ballads and Story Poems.* Charles Causley, ed. Franklin Watts, 1965. *The National Portrait Gallery.* (www.npg.org.uk). *New Poets of England and America.* Donald Hall and Robert Pack, eds. World, 1962. *Poems–Fourth Edition: The Wadsworth Handbook and Anthology.* C.F. Main and Peter J. Seng, eds. Wadsworth Publishing Company, 1978. *The Columbia Granger's Index to Poetry.* 11th ed. *The Columbia Granger's World of Poetry,* Columbia University Press, 2005 (http://www.columbiagrangers.org). *The Oxford Book of Travel Verse.* Kevin Crossley-Holland, ed. Oxford University Press, 1986. *The Oxford Book of Twentieth-Century English Verse.* Philip Larkin, ed. Oxford University Press, 1973. *The Oxford Companion to English Literature.* 6th edition. Margaret Drabble, ed. Oxford University Press, 2000. *The Penguin Book of Japanese Verse.* Geoffrey Bownes and Anthony Thwaite, eds. Penguin Books, 1964. *Who's Who.* London: A & C Black, 2005.

TICKELL, THOMAS (1686–1740)

Born at Bridekirk, Cumberland, the son of a clergyman, he graduated M.A. from Queen's College, Oxford, in 1708–1709, was made a fellow in 1710, then became university reader or professor of poetry at Oxford, although the opinion was that he was not really up to it. When Joseph Addison (see entry) was appointed secretary of state (1717) he chose Tickell as undersecretary. Tickell was involved in a bitter quarrel in 1715 between Addison and Alexander Pope (see entry). Both Pope and Tickell had produced a translation of the first book of Homer's *Iliad.* Pope more or less claimed that Tickell, with the aid of Addison, had plagiarized his. From 1724 to his death, Tickell was secretary to the lords justices of Ireland. He was buried at Glasnevin, Dublin, where he had a house. Some of his poems: "A Description of the Phoenix," "A Fragment of a Poem on Hunting," "Apollo Making Love," "Colin and Lucy," "Kensington Gardens," "On the Prospect of Peace," "Secure of Fame and Justice in the Grave," "The Royal Progress," "To the Earl of Warwick, on the Death of Mr. Addison."

Sources: *A Treasury of Minor British Poetry.* J. Churton Collins, ed. Edward Arnold, 1896. *Dictionary of National Biography.* Electronic Edition 1.1. Oxford University Press, 1997. *Eighteenth-Century English Verse.* Dennis Davison, ed. Penguin Books, 1988. *Encyclopædia Britannica Ultimate Reference Suite DVD,* 2006. *The National Portrait Gallery.* (www.npg.org.uk). *Poemhunter* (www.poemhunter.com). *Samuel Johnson's Lives of the English Poets,* 1779–1781 (http://www2.hn.psu.edu/Faculty/KKemmerer/poets/preface.htm). *The Columbia Granger's Index to Poetry.* 11th ed. *The Columbia Granger's World of Poetry,* Columbia University Press, 2005 (http://www.columbiagrangers.org). *The Oxford Companion to English Literature.* 6th edition. Margaret Drabble, ed. Oxford University Press, 2000. *The Poetical Works of Joseph Addison.* John Bell. Apollo Press, 1778.

TIGHE, MARY BLACHFORD (1772–1810)

Mary Blachford was born in Dublin, the daughter of a clergyman who died when she was one year old. Her mother was one of the women who took a prominent part in the Methodist movement in Ireland. Mary married her cousin, Henry Tighe, in 1793, but the marriage was not a happy one. She began writing, and her poem *Psyche or the Legend of Love,* which was printed privately in 1805, had many admirers, receiving high praise in *The Quarterly Review,* and is believed to have influenced John Keats's (see entry) poem of the same name. Charlotte Yong, the Hampshire novelist (1823–1901), in the preface to *Love and Life: An Old Story in Eighteenth Century Costume* (1880) (the novel is a version of the Cupid and Psyche legend, set in eighteenth-century England) makes reference to Tighe's *Psyche.* She died of tuberculosis and was buried at Inistioge, County Kilkenny. Some of her other poems: "1802," "A Faithful Friend is the Medicine of Life," "Acrostics," "Address to My Harp," "Bryan Byrne, of Glenmalure," "Calm Delight," "The Eclipse, Jan. 24, 1804," "When the Bitter Source of Sorrow."

Sources: *A Century of Sonnets: The Romantic-Era Revival 1750–1850.* Paula R. Feldman and Daniel Robinson, eds. Oxford University Press, 1999. *Dictionary of National Biography.* Electronic Edition 1.1. Oxford University Press, 1997. *English Poetry: Author Search.* Chadwyck-Healey Ltd., 1995 (http://www.lib.utexas.edu:8080/search/epoetry/author.html). *The National Portrait Gallery* (www.npg.org.uk). *Oldpoetry* (www.oldpoetry.com). *Psyche: or, the Legend of Love, Mary Blachford Tighe* (http://web.nmsu.edu/~hlinkin/Psyche/). *The Collected Poems and Journals of Mary Tighe.* University Press of Kentucky, 2005. *The Columbia Granger's Index to Poetry.* 11th ed. *The Columbia Granger's World of Poetry,* Columbia University Press, 2005 (http://www.columbiagrangers.org).

TILLER, TERENCE ROGERS (1916–1987)

Born in Truro, Cornwall, he studied at Jesus College, Cambridge University, and stayed as a research scholar and eventually lecturer in medieval history until the outbreak of World War II. From 1939 to 1946 he taught English and English literature at Cairo University, and from 1946 to 1976 he was employed by the BBC as a radio writer and producer, first in the features department (1946–65) and then in the drama department (1965–76). Thereafter he was a free-lance writer and broadcaster. He produced the first radio adaptation of Tolkien's *Lord of the Rings* and translated *Piers Plowman* and Dante's *Divine Comedy.* In 1966, he edited *Chess Treasury of the Air* (Penguin, 1966, republished by Hardinge Simpole, 2002) He died in London. His poetry publications: *The Inward Animal,* 1943. *Unarm, Eros,* 1947. *Reading a Medal and Other Poems,* 1957. *Notes for a Myth and Other Poems,* 1968. Some of his poems: "Bathers," "Egyptian Dancer," "Egyptian Beggar," "Image in a Lilac Tree," "Killed in Action," "The End of the Story," "The Vase."

Sources: *Dance in Poetry: An International Anthology of Poems on Dance.* Alkis Raftis, ed. Princeton Book Company, 1991. *Encyclopædia Britannica Ultimate Reference Suite DVD,* 2006. *Notes for a Myth.* Terence Tiller, the Hogarth Press Ltd., 1968. *The Chatto Book of Modern Poetry 1915–1955.* Cecil Day Lewis and John Lehmann, eds. Chatto and Windus, 1966. *The Columbia Granger's Index to Poetry.* 11th ed. *The Columbia Granger's World of Poetry,* Columbia University Press, 2005 (http://www.columbiagrangers.org). *The New British Poets: An Anthology.* Kenneth Rexroth, ed. New Directions, 1949. *Wikipedia, the Free Encyclopedia.* (http://en.wikipedia.org/wiki/Wikipedia).

TODD, RUTHVEN (1914–1978)

Born in Edinburgh and educated at Fettes College and Edinburgh School of Art, he worked for a short time for his architect father, then as an agricultural laborer on the Isle of Mull, the Inner Hebrides, before moving into copy-writing and journalism. During World War II he was a conscientious objector, and in 1947 he moved to the United States, where he worked at the University of New York and where, during the 1950s, he ran a small press, the *Weekend Press.* He wrote books for children under the *Space Cats* series and edited the works of the poet and painter William Blake (see entry). He settled in Majorca in 1958, where he died. Some of his poetry publications: *Poems,* 1938. *Poets of Tomorrow,* 1939. *Ten Poems,* 1940. *Until Now,* 1942. *Poems for a Penny,* 1942. *The Planet in My Hand,* 1944. *Love Poems for the New Year,* 1951. *Garland for the Winter Solstice,* 1961. Some of his poems: "A Mantelpiece of Shells," "Joan Miró," "Of Moulds and Mushrooms," "The Lonely Month," "Upon This Rock," "Various Ends," "Watching You Walk."

Sources: *English and American Surrealist Poetry.* Edward B. Germain, ed. Penguin Books, 1978. *The Columbia Granger's Index to Poetry.* 11th ed. *The Columbia Granger's World of Poetry,* Columbia University Press, 2005 (http://www.columbiagrangers.org). *The New British Poets: An Anthology.* Kenneth Rexroth, ed. New Directions, 1949. *The New Penguin Book of Scottish Verse.* Robert Crawford and Mick Imlah, eds. Penguin Books, 2000. *The New Yorker Book of Poems.* The New Yorker editors. Viking Press, 1969. *Wikipedia, the Free Encyclopedia.* (http://en.wikipedia.org/wiki/Wikipedia).

TOFTE, ROBERT (d. 1620)

He is known to have traveled in France and Italy, and was in Naples in 1593. He was known familiarly among his friends as "Robin Redbreast" and his works contain frequent allusions to the name. He died in the house of a Mrs. Goodall in Holborn, near Barnard's Inn, London, and was buried on 24 January in the church of St. Andrew, Holborn (DNB). Some of his publications: *Two Tales, Translated out of Ariosto,* 1597 (the one dispraising men, the other praising women). *Laura, The Toys of a Traveler. Or, the Feast of Fancy*, 1597 (the poem was dedicated to the Lady Lucy Percy, and consists of a collection of short poems conceived in Italy and more than thirty sonnets). *Alba, The Months Mind of a Melancholy Lover.* 1598. *Ariosto's Satires, in Seven Famous Discourses*, 1608. *The Fruits of Jealousy*, 1615. Some of his other poems: "Loue Fare Thou Well, Liue Will I Now," "Nor Life, Nor Vertue Haue I, Lest I Die," "Now I Haue Lost the Deare Light of Mine Eyes," "O Death, Which Vnto Death My Griefes Doest Consecrate."

Sources: *Dictionary of National Biography.* Electronic Edition 1.1. Oxford University Press, 1997. *English Poetry: Author Search.* Chadwyck-Healey Ltd., 1995 (http://www.lib.utexas.edu:8080/search/epoetry/author.html). *The Columbia Granger's Index to Poetry.* 11th ed. *The Columbia Granger's World of Poetry,* Columbia University Press, 2005 (http://www.columbiagrangers.org). *The Poetry of Robert Tofte 1597–1620.* Jeffrey N. Nelson, ed. Garland Publishing, 1994.

TOLLET, ELIZABETH (1694–1754)

The daughter of George Tollet, commissioner of the Navy in the reigns of William III (1689–1702) and Anne (1702–1714). For much of her childhood her father lived in a house in the grounds of Tower of London, then later at Stratford and West Ham, London, where she died. Highly educated and accomplished, in 1755 she published *Poems on Several Occasions,* as well as *With Anne Boleyn to King Henry VIII, An Epistle.* In 1760, she produced *Susanna: or Innocence Preserved,* a musical drama. She paraphrased over 20 of the Psalms, as well as other passages from the Bible. Nothing else is known of her life. Some of her poems: "Hymn to the Paraclete," "Hypatia," "On a Death's Head," "On Loving Once and Loving Often," "On the Prospect from Westminster Bridge," "The Lord's Prayer," "The Rose," "The Three Children in the Fiery Furnace," "To Mr. Handel," "To My Brother at St. John's College in Cambridge," "Winter Song."

Sources: *Dictionary of National Biography.* Electronic Edition 1.1. Oxford University Press, 1997. *Eighteenth Century Women Poets: An Oxford Anthology.* Roger Lonsdale, ed. Oxford University Press, 1989. *Love's Witness: Five Centuries of Love Poetry by Women.* Jill Hollis, ed. Carroll and Graf, Inc., 1993. *The Columbia Granger's Index to Poetry.* 11th ed. *The Columbia Granger's World of Poetry,* Columbia University Press, 2005 (http://www.columbiagrangers.

org). *The New Oxford Book of Eighteenth Century Verse.* Roger Lonsdale, ed. Oxford University Press, 1984. *The Sources for Anne Finch's Translations, Adaptations, Imitations* (http://www.jimandellen.org/finch/tollete.html).

TOMLINSON (ALFRED) CHARLES (1927–)

Born in Stoke-on-Trent, he graduated from Queens College, Cambridge University, in 1948 and gained his master's degree from London University in 1954. He has had a brilliant academic career, being professor of English in various universities in Britain, the USA and Canada, and since 1996 has been emeritus senior research fellow at Bristol University. Although he began as a painter, he is known primarily as a poet. The words he uses to paint word pictures of the sea, air, earth, stones, seasons, light and shadow ensure that the reader sees exactly the detail in the pictures. His first book, *Relations and Contraries*, was published in 1951. Since then, he has published many more collections and several hundred poems. His series of lectures delivered at Trinity College, Cambridge, in 1982 was published in 1983 under the title *Poetry and Metamorphosis.* He was made a Commander of the British Empire in 2001. He lives in Gloucestershire. Some of his poems: "Above Manhattan," "Above the Rio Grande," "Albuquerque," "Ariadne and the Minotaur," "At the Trade Center," "Ute Mountain," "Valle de Oaxaca," "Winter Encounters," "Winter Journey," "Zipangu."

Sources: *Collected Poems of Charles Tomlinson.* Oxford University Press, 1985. *Encyclopædia Britannica Ultimate Reference Suite DVD,* 2006. *Microsoft Encarta* 2006 (DVD). Microsoft Corporation, 2006. *Selected Poems 1955–1997 of Charles Tomlinson.* New Directions, 1997. *Skywriting by Charles Tomlinson.* Carcanet Press 2003. *The Charles Tomlinson Resource Centre.* (http://www3.sympatico.ca/sylvia.paul/CharlesTomlinson_poetry.htm). *The Columbia Granger's Index to Poetry.* 11th ed. *The Columbia Granger's World of Poetry,* Columbia University Press, 2005 (http://www.columbiagrangers.org). *The New Exeter Book of Riddles.* Kevin Crossley-Holland and Lawrence Sail, eds. Enitharmon Press, 1999. *The Oxford Companion to English Literature.* 6th edition. Margaret Drabble, ed. Oxford University Press, 2000. *Who's Who.* London: A & C Black, 2005. *Wikipedia, the Free Encyclopedia.* (http://en.wikipedia.org/wiki/Wikipedia).

TOPLADY, AUGUSTUS MONTAGUE (1740–1778)

Born at Farnham, Surrey, the son of an Army major who died at the siege of Carthagena (1741), he was educated at Westminster School and graduated from Trinity College, Dublin, in 1760. Around 1756 he was converted under the ministry of a follower of John Wesley, changed to extreme Calvinism, was ordained in 1764, and from 1768 until 1775 was curate of Broad Hembury, Devon. For a short time in 1776, he edited the Calvinist *Gospel Magazine*, founded 1766. He used the magazine to hound Wesley over their differing views of the doctrine of election, and the ensuing war of words brought discredit to the Christian church. In 1775, suffering from tuberculosis, Toplady moved to London to minister in the French Calvinist reformed church on Orange Street, near the Embankment. He died, avowing that he would not retract anything he said about Wesley, and was buried in Tottenham Court Chapel. He was a poet and hymn-writer and his best-known hymn is "Rock of Ages." Some of his other hymns/poems: "Ah! Give Me, Lord, the Single Eye," "Deathless Principle, Arise," "Grace, 'Tis a Charming Sound," "Happiness Found," "The Year of Jubilee."

Sources: *A Sacrifice of Praise: An Anthology of Christian Poetry in English from Caedmon to the Mid-Twentieth Century.* James H. Trott, ed. Cumberland House Publishing, 1999. *A Treasury of Poems for Worship and Devotion.* Charles L. Wallis, ed. Harper, 1959. *Augustus Montague Toplady* (http://www.btinternet.com/~alan.s.flint/toplady/),. *Dictionary of National Biography.* Electronic Edition 1.1. Oxford University Press, 1997. *Freedom's Lyre: or Psalms, Hymns, and Sacred Songs, for the Slave and His Friends.* Edwin F. Hatfield, ed. S.W. Benedict, 1840. *The National Portrait Gallery.* (www.npg.org.uk). *The Best Loved Religious Poems.* James Gilchrist Lawson, ed. Fleming H. Revell, 1933. *The Columbia Granger's Index to Poetry.* 11th ed. *The Columbia Granger's World of Poetry,* Columbia University Press, 2005 (http://www.columbiagrangers.org). *The Cyber Hymnal* (http://www.cyberhymnal.org/index.htm). *The Oxford Book of Christian Verse.* Lord David Cecil, ed. Oxford University Press, 1940. *The Oxford Companion to English Literature.* 6th edition. Margaret Drabble, ed. Oxford University Press, 2000. *Wikipedia, the Free Encyclopedia.* (http://en.wikipedia.org/wiki/Wikipedia).

TOWNSEND, AURELIAN (?1583–1643)

He was the son of John Townshend of Dereham Abbey, Norfolk (the name is often spelled with an 'h'), who at one time was steward to Sir Robert Cecil, first earl of Salisbury. He had the reputation from an early age as a poet and was on intimate terms with Ben Jonson (see entry). He traveled on the Continent with Edward Herbert (afterwards first Lord Herbert of Cherbury), where his knowledge of French, Italian and Spanish was put to good use, and he accompanied Herbert on his visit to the court of Henry IV of France. He became a gentleman of the privy chamber under Charles I and in 1631 succeeded Jonson as composer of court masques. His first masque, *Albion's Triumph,* was presented by the king and his lords at Whitehall in 1632. He disappeared from sight during the Civil War. Many of his poems are scattered among various miscellanies. Some of his poems: "Come Not to Me for Scarfs," "In Praise of His Mistress," "Let not thy beauty make thee proud," "Pure Simple Love," "The Fugitive Favourite," "When we were parted," "Youth and Beauty."

Sources: *Aurelian Townshend's Poems and Masks.* E.K. Chambers, ed. Clarendon Press, 1912. *Dictionary of National Biography.* Electronic Edition 1.1. Oxford University Press, 1997. *English Poetry: Author Search.* Chadwyck-Healey Ltd., 1995 (http://www.lib.utexas.edu:8080/search/epoetry/author.html). *Jacobean and Caroline Poetry: An Anthology.* T.G.S. Cain, ed. Methuen, 1981. *Seventeenth Century Poetry: The Schools of Donne and Jonson.* Hugh Kenner, ed. Holt, Rinehart and Winston, 1964. *The Anchor Anthology of Seventeenth-Century Verse, Vol. II.* Louis L. Martz and Richard S. Sylvester, eds. Doubleday Anchor Books, 1969. *The Columbia Granger's Index to Poetry.* 11th ed. *The Columbia Granger's World of Poetry,* Columbia University Press, 2005 (http://www.columbiagrangers.org). *The Oxford Companion to English Literature.* 6th edition. Margaret Drabble, ed. Oxford University Press, 2000.

TRAHERNE, THOMAS (1637–1674)

Born in Herefordshire, near the Welsh border, the son of a shoemaker, he graduated B.A. from Brasenose College, Oxford (1656), M.A. 1661, and B.D. 1669, which was awarded on his prose work, *Roman Forgeries* (published in 1673). He was ordained in 1660 and was priest at Credenhill, Herefordshire, until he died at Teddington, Middlesex. He was buried under the reading-desk in the church. The chance discovery in 1896 in a London street bookstall of the manuscripts of Traherne's *Poetical Works* (published 1903) and his prose work *Centuries of Meditations* (published 1908) created a literary sensation. The first collection of Traherne's poetry to be published was a book of paraphrases and imitations of the Psalms (1699) now known under the title *Thanksgivings.* In his will he left five houses in Herefordshire for the poor of the All Saints Parish Church. Some of his poems: "Christian Ethics," "Hosanna," "In Salem Dwelt a Glorious King," "On Christmas-Day," "On Leaping over the Moon," "The Circulation," "The Resurrection," "The Third Century."

Sources: *A Sacrifice of Praise: An Anthology of Christian Poetry in English from Caedmon to the Mid-Twentieth Century.* James H. Trott, ed. Cumberland House Publishing, 1999. *Chapters into Verse. Vol. I: Genesis to Malachi.* Robert Atwan, and Laurance Wieder, ed. Oxford University Press. 1993. *Chapters into Verse. Vol. II: Gospels to Revelation.* Robert Atwan, and Laurance Wieder, ED. Oxford University Press, 1993. *Dictionary of National Biography.* Electronic Edition 1.1. Oxford University Press, 1997. *Encyclopædia Britannica Ultimate Reference Suite DVD,* 2006. *English Poetry: Author Search.* Chadwyck-Healey Ltd., 1995 (http://www.lib.utexas.edu:8080/search/epoetry/author.html). *The Broadview Anthology of Victorian Poetry and Poetic Theory.* Thomas J. Collins and Vivienne Rundle, eds. Broadview, 1999. *The Columbia Granger's Index to Poetry.* 11th ed. *The Columbia Granger's World of Poetry,* Columbia University Press, 2005 (http://www.columbiagrangers.org). *The Oxford Companion to English Literature.* 6th edition. Margaret Drabble, ed. Oxford University Press, 2000. *The Poetical Works of Thomas Traherne.* Bertram Dobell, ed. Self-published, 1906. *Untune the Sky: Poems of Music and Dance.* Helen Plotz, ed. Thomas Y. Crowell, 1957.

TRAILL, HENRY DUFF (1842–1900)

Born at Morden Hill, Blackheath, London, he was educated at Merchant Taylors' School and at St. John's College, Oxford, and was called to the bar of the Inner Temple in 1869. From 1873 until he died he was a distinguished journalist, with the *Pall Mall Gazette,* the *St. James's Gazette,* the *Saturday Review*— contributing political "leaders," literary reviews, essays and poems. He was chief political leader-writer for the *Daily Telegraph,* editor of the *Observer,* and first editor of *Literature.* He published books on a variety of historical, literary, and political subjects, as well as biographies, and was editor of the six volumes of *Social England* from 1893 to 1897. *England, Egypt, and the Sudan* was published posthumously in 1900. He died of a heart attack and was buried in the Paddington Cemetery, Kilburn. Some of his poetry publications: *Saturday Songs,* 1890. *Recaptured Rhymes,* 1882. *Number Twenty,* 1892. *The Baby of the Future,* 1911. Some of his poems: "A Manly Protest," "After Dilettante Concetti," "An Enfant Terrible," "Tea Without Toast," "The Ants' Nest," "The Passing of the Aged Psychopath," "The Puss and the Boots."

Sources: *A Century of Humorous Verse, 1850–1950.* Roger Lancelyn Green, ed. E.P. Dutton (Everyman's Library), 1959. *Dictionary of National Biography.* Electronic Edition 1.1. Oxford University Press, 1997. *English Poetry: Author Search.* Chadwyck-Healey Ltd., 1995 (http://www.lib.utexas.edu:8080/search/epoetry/author.html). *The National Portrait Gallery.* (www.npg.org.uk). *Parodies: An Anthology from Chaucer to Beerbohm—and After.* Dwight Macdonald, ed. Modern Library, 1960. *The Columbia Granger's Index to Poetry.* 11th ed. *The Columbia Granger's World of Poetry,* Columbia University Press, 2005 (http://www.columbiagrangers.org).

TRAPP, JOSEPH (1679–1747)

Born at Cherrington, Gloucestershire, the son of the local clergyman, he was educated at Wadham College, Oxford, and incorporated M.A. of Cambridge (1714). While at Oxford, he wrote poems on the deaths of the young Duke of Gloucester, King William, Prince George of Denmark, and Queen Anne, and has the honor being the first professor poetry at Oxford (1708–1718). Between 1711 and 1736 he published three volumes of *Prælectiones Poeticæ,* and an English translation by the Rev. William Clarke and William Bowyer was published in 1742. He wrote several tracts defending the Anglican Church against Methodism and the Church of Rome, for which Oxford made him a doctor of divinity (1727). Two volumes of his *Sermons on Moral and Practical Subjects* were published in 1752. He died at Harlington, Middlesex. Some of his other publications: *Ædes Badmintonianæ,* 1701. *A Prologue to the University of Oxford,* 1703. *Peace,* 1713. *The Works of Virgil,* 1731. *Thoughts Upon the Four Last Things,* 1745. Some of his other poems: "Dark to Futurity, in Doubt, and Fear," "Epigram to King George," "Paraphrase Upon Psalm 137," "Virgil's Georgicks," "Virgil's Tomb, Naples 1741."

Sources: *Dictionary of National Biography.* Electronic Edition 1.1. Oxford University Press, 1997. *English Poetry: Author Search.* Chadwyck-Healey Ltd., 1995 (http://www.lib.utexas.edu:8080/search/epoetry/author.html). *Oxford Professors of Poetry* (http://www.poetsgraves.co.uk/oxford_professors_of_poetry.htm). *Stanford University Libraries and Academic Information Resources* (http://library.stanford.edu). *The Columbia Granger's Index to Poetry.* 11th ed. *The Columbia Granger's World of Poetry,* Columbia University Press, 2005 (http://www.columbiagrangers.org). *The Faber Book of Comic Verse.* Michael Roberts and Janet Adam Smith, eds. Faber and Faber, 1978.

TREECE, HENRY (1911–1966)

Born at Wednesbury, Staffordshire, he was educated at Birmingham University before becoming a schoolteacher. He served as an intelligence officer in Bomber Command during World War II, and after the war he became a broadcaster, writer of poetry, drama, short stories, books for children and historical novels. Together with J.F. Hendry (see entry) he was a founder of the New Apocalypse movement— a reaction against the politically oriented, machine-age literature and realist poetry of the 1930s. He edited *Issues of Transformation, and a New Romantic Anthology* with Stefan Schimanski (1949), *Issues of Kingdom Come* (the magazine of war-time Oxford) with Schimanski and Alan Rook, and *War-Time Harvest, How I See Apocalypse* (1946). He died at Barton-upon-Humber, Lincolnshire. Some of his other publications: *38 Poems,* 1940. *Air Force Poetry,* 1944 (edited by J. Pudney [see entry]). *The Black Seasons,* 1945. *The Haunted Garden,* 1947. *Selected Poems of Algernon Charles Swinburne,* 1948 (editor). *The Exiles,* 1952. *Collected Poems,* 1963. Some of his poems: "Birdwatcher," "In the Third Year of War," "Lincolnshire Bomber Station," "Prayer in Time of War," "The Crimson Cherry Tree," "The Dyke-Builder."

Sources: *A Little Treasury of British Poetry.* Oscar Williams, ed. Scribner's, 1951. *Encyclopædia Britannica Ultimate Reference Suite DVD,* 2006. *The Columbia Granger's Index to Poetry.* 11th ed. *The Columbia Granger's World of Poetry,* Columbia University Press, 2005 (http://www.columbiagrangers.org). *The New British Poets: An Anthology.*

Kenneth Rexroth, ed. New Directions, 1949. *The Oxford Book of Welsh Verse in English.* Gwyn Jones, ed. Oxford University Press, 1977. *The War Poets: An Anthology of the War Poetry of the 20th Century.* Oscar Williams, ed. John Day, 1945. *Wikipedia, the Free Encyclopedia.* (http://en.wikipedia.org/wiki/Wikipedia).

TRENCH, FREDERIC HERBERT (1865–1923)

Irish poet, born at Avoncore, County Cork, he graduated in modern history from Keble College, Oxford, in 1888, and was elected fellow of All Souls College in 1889. From 1891 to 1900 he was examiner for the Board of Education, then artistic director at the Haymarket Theatre, London. In collaboration with Thomas Evelyn Scott-Ellis, 8th Baron Howard de Walden, he put on Maeterlinck's *The Blue Bird* (1909) and Ibsen's *The Pretenders* (1913). His four-act play *Napoleon* was produced by the Stage Society in 1919. The last ten years of his life were spent in Settignano, near Florence, and he died in hospital at Boulogne-sur-Mer. In 1908 an opera written by Joseph Holbrooke for Trench's poem "Apollo and the Seaman" was performed, under Thomas Beecham. Some other poems of his were set to music by Arnold Bax. Some of his poetry publications: *Deirdre Wed and Other Poems*, 1901. *New Poems*, 1907. *Lyrics and Narrative Poems*, 1911. *Ode from Italy in Time of War*, 1915. *Poems*, 1921. Some of his poems: "Advance on the Somme," "In the Roman Amphitheatre, Verona," "Song of the Vine," "The Queen of Gothland."

Sources: *Dictionary of National Biography.* Electronic Edition 1.1. Oxford University Press, 1997. *English Poetry: Author Search.* Chadwyck-Healey Ltd., 1995 (http://www.lib.utexas.edu:8080/search/epoetry/author.html). *Irish Poets of To-Day.* L. D'O. Walters, ed. T. Fisher Unwin, 1921. *The National Portrait Gallery.* (www.npg.org.uk). *Poems with Fables in Prose by Herbert Trench, 3 Volume.* Constable and Company, 1924. *The Columbia Granger's Index to Poetry.* 11th ed. *The Columbia Granger's World of Poetry,* Columbia University Press, 2005 (http://www.columbiagrangers.org). *The Oxford Book of English Verse, 1250–1918.* Sir Arthur Quiller-Couch, ed. New edition, revised and enlarged, Oxford University Press, 1939. *The Oxford Companion to English Literature.* 6th edition. Margaret Drabble, ed. Oxford University Press, 2000. *Wikipedia, the Free Encyclopedia.* (http://en.wikipedia.org/wiki/Wikipedia).

TURBERVILLE (TURBERVILE), GEORGE (?1540–?1610)

Born in Whitchurch, Dorset, he was educated at Winchester College and was a fellow of New College, Oxford. He belonged to an old Dorsetshire family, the D'Urbervilles of Thomas Hardy's (see entry) novel, *Tess of the d'Urbervilles*. In 1568 he was secretary to Thomas Randolph (1523–1590) when he was ambassador from Queen Elizabeth to the court of Ivan the Terrible in Moscow. Turberville published *Epitaphs, Epigrams, Songs, and Sonnets* in 1567, and *Poems Describing the Places and Manners of the Country and People of Russia* in 1568. He translated the works of several poets, including Ovid (43 B.C.–A.D. 18), Mantuan (1448–1516), and Giovanni Boccaccio (1313–1375). He was the first English poet to publish a book of verses to his lady, a genre that became popular in the Elizabethan age. Some of his original poems: "A Vow to serue faithfully," "An Epitaph of Maister Win Drowned in the Sea," "Of a Rich Miser," "Of Homer and His Birth," "Of One That Had a Great Nose," "The Louer Abused Renounceth Love," "The Louer Whose Mistress Feared a Mouse," "The Pine to the Mariner."

Sources: *A New Treasury of Poetry.* Neil Philip, ed. Stewart, Tabori, and Chang, 1990. *Dictionary of National Biography.* Electronic Edition 1.1. Oxford University Press, 1997. *Elizabethan Lyrics.* Norman Ault, ed. William Sloane Associates, 1949. *Encyclopædia Britannica Ultimate Reference Suite DVD,* 2006. *English Poetry: Author Search.* Chadwyck-Healey Ltd., 1995 (http://www.lib.utexas.edu:8080/search/epoetry/author.html). *English Renaissance Poetry: A Collection of Shorter Poems from Skelton to Jonson.* John Williams, ed. University of Arkansas, 1990. *The Columbia Granger's Index to Poetry.* 11th ed. *The Columbia Granger's World of Poetry,* Columbia University Press, 2005 (http://www.columbiagrangers.org). *The Faber Book of Epigrams and Epitaphs.* Geoffrey Grigson, ed. Faber and Faber, 1977. *The Oxford Companion to English Literature.* 6th edition. Margaret Drabble, ed. Oxford University Press, 2000. *Tragical Tales, and Other Poems: by George Turbervile* (no publisher) 1837.

TURNBULL, GAEL (1928–2004)

Born in Edinburgh, he was brought up in Jarrow, County Durham, and Blackpool, and on the outbreak of World War II the family emigrated to Winnipeg. He studied natural science at Christ's College, Cambridge University, and graduated in medicine from the University of Pennsylvania in 1951, after which he specialized in anesthesiology. After retiring from medical practice Turnbull moved to Edinburgh, where he continued to write poems of all shapes and sizes. He died on a visit to Herefordshire, of a brain hemorrhage, and a memorial "Gathering for Gael" was held in Greyfriars Kirk, Edinburgh. In 1957 he founded Migrant Press, an important British-based small publisher. He was truly a Transatlantic poet who forged links with French-speaking Canadian poets, Black Mountain poets, Beat poets, concrete poets, and exiled Scottish and English poets. Some of his publications: *A Gathering of Poems, 1950–1980*, 1983. *A Trampoline: Poems 1952–1964*, 1968. *Transmutations*, 1997. *A Rattle of Scree*, 1997. *Might a Shape of Words*, 2000. Some of his poems: "George Fox, from His Journals," "Residues: Thronging the Heart," "There Are Words," "They Have Taken," "Thighs Gripping," "Twenty Words, Twenty Days."

Sources: *Anthology of Twentieth-Century British and Irish Poetry.* Keith Tuma, ed. Oxford University Press, 2001. *Laurie Duggan, Recollections of the Lakes and the Lake Poets: Gael Turnbull* (http://jacketmagazine.com/25/turnb-dugg.html). *Obituary of Gael Turnbull: John Lucas, Monday July 12, 2004, the Guardian* (http://books.guardian.co.uk/obituaries/story/0,11617,1258918,00.html). *Other: British and Irish Poetry Since 1970.* Richard Caddel and Peter Quartermain. eds. Wesleyan University Press, 1999. *The Columbia Granger's Index to Poetry.* 11th ed. *The Columbia Granger's World of Poetry,* Columbia University Press, 2005 (http://www.columbiagrangers.org). *The Scottish Poetry Library, Gael Turnbull* (http://www.spl.org.uk/news/2004_0707.html). *The Scottish Poetry Library* (http://www.spl.org.uk/poets_a-z/turnbull.html). *The New British Poetry, 1968–88.* Gillian Allnutt, Fred D'Aguiar and Ken Edwards, eds. Grafton Books, 1989. *Wikipedia, the Free Encyclopedia.* (http://en.wikipedia.org/wiki/Wikipedia).

TURNER, WALTER JAMES REDFERN (1889–1946)

Born in Melbourne, Australia, where his father was the organist of St. Paul's Cathedral, he came to England in 1907 and spent several years traveling and working in Europe. He emerged from his service with the Royal Garrison Artillery during World War I as a recognized poet and member of the Georgian group, having published two volumes of poetry by 1918. Among his friends were Siegfried Sassoon and Ralph Hodgson, and later W.B .Yeats (see entries). He was music critic of the *New Statesman,* drama critic of the *London Mercury,* and literary editor of the *Daily Herald,* and of the *Spectator* from 1942 until his death, which occurred in his London home of cerebral hemorrhage. He wrote several novels and published a volume of poems every two or three years, several minor works of musical criticism, studies of Beethoven, Mozart, Wagner, and Berlioz, and a satirical comedy *The Man Who Ate the Popomack* (1922). Some of his poems: "Clapham Common (or 'The Cap of Liberty')," "Clerks on Holiday," "In the Caves of Auvergne," "Sunflowers," "Talking with Soldiers," "The Hunter," "The Seven Days of the Sun."

Sources: *AustLit: The Resource for Australian Literature. Archives for W.J. Turner.* (http://www.austlit.edu.au/run?ex=ShowAgent&agentId=AT7). *Dictionary of National Biography.* Electronic Edition 1.1. Oxford University Press, 1997. *The National Portrait Gallery.* (www.npg.org.uk). *The Chatto Book of Modern Poetry 1915–1955.* Cecil Day Lewis and John Lehmann, eds. Chatto and Windus, 1966. *The Columbia Granger's Index to Poetry.* 11th ed. *The Columbia Granger's World of Poetry,* Columbia University Press, 2005 (http://www.columbiagrangers.org). *The Dark Wind.* Walter James Turner. E.P. Dutton, 1920. *The Home Book of Modern Verse.* Burton Egbert Stevenson, ed. Henry Holt, 1953. *The Oxford Book of Modern Verse, 1892–1935.* William Butler Yeats, ed. Oxford University Press, 1936. *The Oxford Companion to English Literature.* 6th edition. Margaret Drabble, ed. Oxford University Press, 2000.

TUSSER, THOMAS (?1524–1580)

Born in Rivenhall, Essex, he was a chorister, firstly in the collegiate chapel of the castle of Wallingford, Berkshire, then at St. Paul's Cathedral. His education continued at Eton College, at King's College, and Trinity Hall, Cambridge, then for ten years he was musician in the service of William, 1st Baron Paget of Beaudesart (1505–1563), Secretary of State and Lord Privy Seal at Exeter Place, London. He married and settled as a farmer at Cattiwade, Suffolk, near the river Stour, where he wrote a *Hundreth Good Pointes of Husbandrie* (1557). Although this poem of 48 chapters, in rhyming couplets, is about the country year, it contains many proverbs, advice to husbands and wives, and is full of humor and wise maxims on conduct in general. He had to seek refuge in Trinity Hall from the Great Plague of 1572–1573, and died at Chesterton, Cambridgeshire. Some of his other poems: "A Sonnet to the Lady Paget," "Certain table lessons," "Of the omnipotence of God, and debility of man," "Posies for thine own bed chamber," "The Authors Life," "The Winds," "Upon the Author's First Seven Years' Service."

Sources: *City of Westminster Manors and Estates: Bishop of Exeter's Inn (Essex House).* (http://www.middlesexpast.net/wexeter.html). *Dictionary of National Biography.* Electronic Edition 1.1. Oxford University Press, 1997. *Elizabethan Lyrics.* Norman Ault, ed. William Sloane Associates, 1949. *English Poetry: Author Search.* Chadwyck-Healey Ltd., 1995 (http://www.lib.utexas.edu:8080/search/epoetry/author.html). *Five Hundred Points of Good Husbandry by Thomas Tusser* (Oxford Paperbacks) Oxford University Press, 1984. *The Columbia Granger's Index to Poetry.* 11th ed. *The Columbia Granger's World of Poetry,* Columbia University Press, 2005 (http://www.columbiagrangers.org). *The National Portrait Gallery* (www.npg.org.uk). *The New Oxford Book of Sixteenth Century Verse.* Emrys Jones, ed. Oxford University Press, 1991. *The Oxford Companion to English Literature.* 6th edition. Margaret Drabble, ed. Oxford University Press, 2000. *Wikipedia, the Free Encyclopedia.* (http://en.wikipedia.org/wiki/Wikipedia).

TUTTIETT, LAWRENCE (1825–1897)

Born at Cloyton, Devonshire, the son of a Royal Navy surgeon, he was educated at Christ's Hospital (1833–1840) and at King's College, London, He was ordained in 1849 and had several appointments, the last one being canon of St. Ninian's Cathedral, Perth, and he died at his residence at St. Andrews, Fife. Best known as a hymn-writer, he published *Hymns* for Churchmen (1861), *Hymns for the Children of the Church* (1862) and *Through the Clouds: Thoughts in Plain Verse* (1866). He also published devotional books, including *Meditations on the Book of Common Prayer* (1872). An active member of the Parent Society, he advocated the teaching of the catechism in all church-aided schools. Some of his hymns/poems: "As Calmly in the Glowing West," "Come, Our Father's Voice is Calling," "Go Forward, Christian Soldier," "Happy Christian Children," "Inconstancy," "Lo, Like a Bride in Pure Array," "Now, Eternal Father, Bless," "Quickly Come, Dread Judge of All," "Shepherd, Good and Gracious," "When the World is Brightest," "Who is This? The Long Expected."

Sources: *Dictionary of National Biography*. Electronic Edition, 1.1. *Oldblues.com. Community Information for Christ's Hospital Old Blues: Lawrence Tuttiet* (http://www.oldblues.com/ontheweb.htm). *Biography of Lawrence Tuttiet* (http://www.ccel.org/ccel/nutter/hymnwriters.TuttietL.html). *The Cyber Hymnal* (http://www.cyberhymnal.org/index.htm).

TYNAN, KATHARINE (1861–1931)

Born at Whitehall, Clondalkin, County Dublin, the daughter of a farmer, her education was curtailed by measles, which affected her eyes. Through her writing she supported the fight for Irish home rule in the 1880s. After her first collection of poems, *Louise de la Vallière: And Other Poems* (de la Vallière was the mistress to Louis XIV of France from 1661 to 1667) in 1885 she went on to publish seventeen more collections, more than one-hundred novels, five volumes of her autobiography, twelve collections of short stories, and three plays. She revised *The Cabinet of Irish Literature* (4 volumes, 1902–05), and added a predominantly women's volume. In 1883 she married Henry Albert Hinkson, a barrister and novelist, who died in 1919. She died at Wimbledon, London. Her poems are dominated by the combined influences of Catholicism and Irish patriotism. Some of her other poetry publications: *Irish Love-Songs*, 1891. *The Rhymed Life of St. Patrick*, 1907. *New Poems*, 1911. *Herb O'Grace*, 1918. *Collected Poems*, 1930. Some of her poems: "Ivy of Ireland," "All in the April Evening," "Joining the Colours," "Shamrock Song," "The Broken Soldier," "The Nightingale," "Winter Sunset."

Sources: *A Sacrifice of Praise: An Anthology of Christian Poetry in English from Caedmon to the Mid-Twentieth Century*. James H. Trott, ed. Cumberland House Publishing, 1999. *An Anthology of Irish Verse: The Poetry of Ireland from Mythological Times to the Present*. Padraic Colum, ed. Liveright, 1948. *Carmina Mariana: An English Anthology in Verse in Honour of or in Relation to The Blessed Virgin Mary*. Orby Shipley, ed. Burns and Oates, 1894. *Dictionary of National Biography*. Electronic Edition 1.1. Oxford University Press, 1997. *Encyclopædia Britannica Ultimate Reference Suite DVD*, 2006. *English Poetry: Author Search*. Chadwyck-Healey Ltd., 1995 (http://www.lib.utexas.edu:8080/search/epoetry/author.html). *Biography of Katharine Tynan* (http://www.irishwriters-online.com/katharinetynan.html). *Lyra Celtica: An Anthology of Representative Celtic Poetry*. E.A. Sharp and J. Matthay, eds. John Grant, 1924. *Scars Upon My Heart: Women's Poetry and Verse of the First World War*. Catherine W. Reilly, ed. Virago Press, 1981. *The Columbia Granger's Index to Poetry*. 11th ed. *The Columbia Granger's World of Poetry*, Columbia University Press, 2005 (http://www.columbiagrangers.org). *The Home Book of Modern Verse*. Burton Egbert Stevenson, ed. Henry Holt, 1953. *The Oxford Companion to English Literature*. 6th edition. Margaret Drabble, ed. Oxford University Press, 2000.

VAUGHAN, HENRY and THOMAS (1622–1695)

Twin brothers, Henry and Thomas were born at Newton-by-Usk in the parish of Llansaintffraed, Brecknockshire, a part of southeast Wales once inhabited by a tribe called the Silures (hence the geological "Silurian Age"). Henry styled himself a "Silurist." It is known that Thomas entered Jesus College, Oxford in 1638 (probably in company with his brother). Thomas graduated in 1642, but there is no mention of Henry having graduated.

Henry, 1622–1695

Henry started practicing law in London but turned to medicine, and on the outbreak of the Civil War in 1642 he returned to Breconshirel, began practicing as a doctor, and was surgeon in the Royalist army in 1645. Before 1650, his poetry was mostly secular — he translated Ovid and other ancient writers and wrote fashionable love poetry. After 1650 his poetry turned toward the spiritual. He was buried in Llansaintffraed churchyard, Breconshire. Some of his publications: *Poems, with the Tenth Satyre of Juvenal*, 1646 and 1647. *Silex Scintillans*, 1650 and 1655. *Olor Iscanus*, 1651 (The Swan of Usk: A Collection of Some Select Poems and Translations). *The Mount of Olives*, 1652. *Thalia Rediviva. 1678* (Thalia Revived). Some of his poems: "Ascension Hymn," "Cheerfulness," "The Ass," "The Brecon Beacons and the Black Mountains," "The Charnel-house," "The Daughter of Herodias," "The Hidden Treasure," "The Passion."

Thomas, 1622–1666

He was rector of Llansantfraed, from which he was evicted by the Puritan administration in 1650, charged with being a drunkard and having taken up arms against Parliament. He then resided in London, where he devoted himself to alchemical experiments and theory. Between 1650 and 1655 he published various treatises (also translated on the

Continent) under the name "Eugenius Philalethes." He was an active poet, as well as an author of prose; 24 of his Latin poems were included in *Thalia Rediviva*. In 1665, when the Royal Court fled London for fear of the plague, Vaughan accompanied it to Oxford. He died (so it is reported as a result of mercury poisoning, a consequence of his scientific experiments) at Albury, near Oxford. Some of his poems: "So Have I Spent on the Banks of Ysca Many a Serious Hour," "On the Death of an Oxford Proctor," "The Stone," "The Usk."

Sources: *Anglo-Welsh Poetry, 1480–1980*. Raymond Garlick and Roland Mathias, eds. Poetry Wales Press, 1984. *Anglo-Welsh Poetry, 1480–1990*. Raymond Garlick and Roland Mathias, eds. Poetry Wales Press, 1993. *Biography of Thomas Vahughan: The Literary Encyclopedia* (http://www.litencyc.com/php/speople.php?rec=true&UID=5473). *Dictionary of National Biography*. Electronic Edition 1.1. Oxford University Press, 1997. *Encyclopædia Britannica Ultimate Reference Suite DVD*, 2006. *Five Seventeenth-Century Poets: Donne, Herbert, Crashaw, Marvell, Vaughan*. Brijraj Singh, ed. Oxford University Press, 1992. *Life and Works of Henry Vaughan* (http://www.luminarium.org/sevenlit/vaughan/). *Microsoft Encarta* 2006 (DVD). Microsoft Corporation, 2006. *The Columbia Granger's Index to Poetry*. 11th ed. *The Columbia Granger's World of Poetry*, Columbia University Press, 2005 (http://www.columbiagrangers.org). *The Faber Book of Poems and Places*. Geoffrey Grigson, ed. Faber and Faber, 1980. *The Oxford Book of Death*. D.J. Enright, ed. Oxford University Press, 1987. *The Oxford Companion to English Literature*. 6th edition. Margaret Drabble, ed. Oxford University Press, 2000. *The Three Treatises of Philalethes, in the Hermetic Museum*, pp 227–269. Arthur Edward Waite, Samuel Weiser, Inc. York Beach, Maine, paperback edition 1991. *The Works of Henry Vaughan*. Clarendon Press, 1957. *Wikipedia, the Free Encyclopedia* (http://en.wikipedia.org/wiki/Wikipedia).

VAUX, THOMAS, 2nd BARON VAUX OF HARROWDEN (1510–1556)

He succeeded his father to the barony of Vaux of Harrowden, Northamptonshire, at the age of 13. Vaux attended Cardinal Wolsey on his embassy to France in 1527 and accompanied the king to Calais and Boulogne in 1532. He was created a Knight of the Bath at the coronation of Anne Boleyn (1533) and was captain of the Isle of Jersey until 1536. He was buried at Harrowden. Vaux was at the courts of Henry VIII and Edward VI and emulated the poet Sir Thomas Wyatt the elder (see entry). George Puttenham (see entry) included some of Vaux's poems in *Art of English Poesie* (1589). Vaux's two best-known poems, in Richard Tottel's *Miscellany* (1557), are "The Aged Lover Renounceth Love" and "The assault of Cupide upon the fort where the lovers hart lay wounded, and how he was taken." The *Paradyse of Daynty Devises* (1576) contains 13 poems signed by Vaux. Some of his poems: "A Louer Disdained,

"Complaineth," "Beyng Disdained, He Complainethtrie Before You Trust," "In Loue He Complainethbeyng," "In Sorrowe He Complainethno," "Of Sufferaunce Commeth Easebeyng," "Pleasure Without Some Paine."

Sources: *An Anthology of Catholic Poets*. Shane Leslie, ed. Macmillan, 1952. *Dictionary of National Biography*. Electronic Edition 1.1. Oxford University Press, 1997. *Elizabethan Lyrics*. Norman Ault, ed. William Sloane Associates, 1949. *Encyclopædia Britannica Ultimate Reference Suite DVD*, 2006. *English Poetry: Author Search*. Chadwyck-Healey Ltd., 1995 (http://www.lib.utexas.edu:8080/search/epoetry/author.html). *English Renaissance Poetry: A Collection of Shorter Poems from Skelton to Jonson*. John Williams, ed. University of Arkansas, 1990. *The National Portrait Gallery* (www.npg.org.uk). *The Columbia Granger's Index to Poetry*. 11th ed. *The Columbia Granger's World of Poetry*, Columbia University Press, 2005 (http://www.columbiagrangers.org). *The Oxford Companion to English Literature*. 6th edition. Margaret Drabble, ed. Oxford University Press, 2000. *The Poems of Lord Vaux*. Larry P. Vonalt, ed. Books of the Renaissance, 1960. *Wikipedia, the Free Encyclopedia* (http://en.wikipedia.org/wiki/Wikipedia).

VELEY, MARGARET (1843–1887)

The daughter of an ecclesiastical solicitor, she was born at Braintree, Essex; educated mainly at home, she became proficient in French literature. Although she began early to write both prose and verse, she published nothing until 1870, when her first poem, "Michaelmas Daisies," appeared in the *Spectator*. Her first short story, "Milly's First Love," appeared in *Blackwood's Magazine* (1870). Her most successful novel, *For Percival*, was serialized in *Cornhill* magazine (1878). Other stories were serialized in the *Cornhill*, *Macmillan's* and *English Illustrated* magazines. She died after a short illness and was buried at Braintree. Some of her poems: "A Japanese Fan," "A Town Garden," "Game of Piquet," "Sonnet," "The Level Land."

Sources: *19th Century British Minor Poets*. W.H. Auden, ed. Delacorte Press, 1966. *A Marriage of Shadows and Other Poems by Margaret Veley*. Smith, Elder, 1888. *Dictionary of National Biography*. Electronic Edition 1.1. Oxford University Press, 1997. *Harper's New Monthly Magazine. The Level Land, by Margaret Veley* (pp. 856–857) Volume 61, Issue 366 (http://cdl.library.cornell.edu/cgi-bin/moa/sgml/moa-idx?notisid=ABK4014–0061&byte=119475497). *Margaret Veley, A Japanese Fan. The Complete Poem* (http://themargins.net/anth/19thc/veley.html). *Nineteenth-Century Women Poets: An Oxford Anthology*. Isobel Armstrong and Joseph Bristow with Cath Sharrock, eds. Oxford University Press, 1996. *The Columbia Granger's Index to Poetry*. 11th ed. *The Columbia Granger's World of Poetry*, Columbia University Press, 2005 (http://www.columbiagrangers.org). *Victorian Women Poets: An Anthology*. Angela Leighton and Margaret Reynolds, eds. Blackwell, 1991.

VILLIERS, GEORGE, 2nd DUKE OF BUCKINGHAM (1628–1687)

After the assassination of Villiers' father when he was eight months old, Charles I reared George and his young brother, Francis, with his own children. They both went to Trinity College, Cambridge, and George graduated M.A. in 1642. He fought with the Royalist army during the English Civil War and later served the exiled Charles II as privy counsellor. He was imprisoned by Oliver Cromwell and escaped execution only through the intervention of his father-in-law, the former Parliamentary general Baron Fairfax. After the Restoration he became a gentleman of the bedchamber, a privy councilor and a leading member of King Charles II's inner circle of ministers. In 1674 Parliament had Buckingham dismissed from his posts for his intemperate behavior and alleged Catholic sympathies. He died while hunting at Kirkby Moorside, Yorkshire, and was buried in Henry VII's chapel, Westminster Abbey. He is Zimri in John Dryden's (see entry) *Absalom and Achitophel*. Villiers wrote satires and the farce the *Rehearsal* (1672). Some of his poems: "An Epitaph upon Thomas, Lord Fairfax," "Prayer," "The Battle of Sedgemoor," "The Cabin-Boy," "The Militant Couple," "To His Mistress."

Sources: *A Treasury of Poems for Worship and Devotion.* Charles L. Wallis, ed. Harper, 1959. *Anthology of Poems on Affairs of State: Augustan Satirical Verse, 1660–1714.* George de F. Lord, ed. Yale University Press, 1975. *Dictionary of National Biography.* Electronic Edition 1.1. Oxford University Press, 1997. *Encyclopædia Britannica Ultimate Reference Suite DVD,* 2006. *Microsoft Encarta* 2006 (DVD). Microsoft Corporation, 2006. *The National Portrait Gallery* (www.npg.org.uk). *The Cavalier Poets.* Robin Skelton, ed. Oxford University Press, 1970. *The Columbia Granger's Index to Poetry.* 11th ed. *The Columbia Granger's World of Poetry,* Columbia University Press, 2005 (http://www.columbiagrangers.org). *The Oxford Companion to English Literature.* 6th edition. Margaret Drabble, ed. Oxford University Press, 2000. *Westminster Abbey Official Guide* (no date).

WADE, THOMAS (1805–1875)

Born at Woodbridge, Suffolk, he came to London, but when is uncertain. His plays give a clue: *Woman's Love, or the Triumph of Patience,* later *Duke Andrea,* 1828 (performed at Covent Garden); *The Phrenologists,* 1830 (a farce); *The Jew of Arragon: or the Hebrew Queen,* 1830 (a verse tragedy). He was a frequent contributor of poetry to the *Monthly Repository,* and his contributions were among those that appeared in *Mundi et Cordis Carmina* (or *Songs of the Universe and of the Heart*) in 1837. He lived on Jersey, the Channel Island, for many years, where he ran the *British Press,* and where he died. He wrote a series of sonnets inspired by his wife, Lucy Eager, a

musician. Some of his poetry publications: *Tasso and the Sisters,* 1825. *The Shadow Seeker,* 1837. *Prothanasia,* 1839. Dante's *Inferno,* 1845. *Monologue of Konrad,* 1845 (in the *Illuminated Magazine*). *Poems,* 1895. Some of his poems: "Corfe Castle Ruins," "On a Human Heart," "Shelley," "The Nest," "The Nuptials of Juno," "The True Martyr," "The Winter Shore," "To Three Skulls."

Sources: *19th Century British Minor Poets.* W.H. Auden, ed. Delacorte Press, 1966. *Dictionary of National Biography.* Electronic Edition 1.1. Oxford University Press, 1997. *English Poetry: Author Search.* Chadwyck-Healey Ltd., 1995 (http://www.lib.utexas.edu:8080/search/epoetry/author.html). *English Poetry: A Poetic Record, from Chaucer to Yeats.* David Hopkins, ed. Routledge, 1990. *Stanford University Libraries and Academic Information Resources* (http://library.stanford.edu). *The Columbia Granger's Index to Poetry.* 11th ed. *The Columbia Granger's World of Poetry,* Columbia University Press, 2005 (http://www.columbiagrangers.org). *The Oxford Anthology of English Literature,* Vols. I–III. Frank Kermode and John Hollander, eds. Oxford University Press, 1973. *The Oxford Book of Victorian Verse.* Arthur Quiller-Couch, ed. Oxford University Press, 1971. *Wikipedia, the Free Encyclopedia* (http://en.wikipedia.org/wiki/Wikipedia).

WAIN, JOHN BARRINGON (1925–1994)

Born in Stoke-on-Trent, Staffordshire, he graduated M.A. in 1950 from St. John's College, Oxford. He was a lecturer in English literature at Reading University and professor of poetry at Oxford University; some of his lectures are collected in his book *Professing Poetry* (1979). Thereafter he worked as a freelance journalist and author, writing and reviewing for newspapers and the radio. He is grouped either with the "Angry Young Men" of the 1950s or with "The Movement," but more accurately, with "The New University Wits." In 1983 he was made a Companion of the Order of the British Empire. He died at Oxford. He published a biography of Samuel Johnson (1974, revised 1980), his autobiography, *Sprightly Running* (1962), as well as plays, short stories, literary criticisms, and novels. Some of his poetry publications: *A Word Carved on a Sill,* 1956. *Weep Before God,* 1961. *Wildtrack,* 1965. *Poems 1949–79,* 1980. *Poems for the Zodiac,* 1980. *The Twofold,* 1981. *Open Country,* 1987. Some of his poems: "Anecdote of 2 A.M.," "Anniversary," "Apology for Understatement," "Brooklyn Heights," "Feng," "Gentleman Aged Five before the Mirror."

Sources: *Encyclopædia Britannica Ultimate Reference Suite DVD,* 2006. *Gladly Learn and Gladly Teach: Poems of the School Experience.* Helen Plotz, ed. Greenwillow Books, 1981. *The National Portrait Gallery* (www.npg.org.uk). *Poems–Fourth Edition: The Wadsworth Handbook and Anthology.* C.F. Main and Peter J. Seng, eds. Wadsworth Publishing Company, 1978. *The Columbia Granger's Index to*

Poetry. 11th ed. *The Columbia Granger's World of Poetry,* Columbia University Press, 2005 (http://www.columbia grangers.org). *The New Modern Poetry: British and American Poetry Since World War II.* M.L. Rosenthal, ed. Macmillan, 1967. *The Oxford Anthology of English Poetry, Vol. I: Spenser to Crabbe.* John Wain, ed. Oxford University Press, 1990. *The Oxford Anthology of English Poetry. Vol. II: Blake to Heaney.* John Wain, ed. Oxford University Press, 1990. *The Oxford Companion to English Literature.* 6th edition. Margaret Drabble, ed. Oxford University Press, 2000. *Twentieth-Century Poetry: American and British (1900–1970).* John Malcolm Brinnin and Bill Read, eds. McGraw Hill, Rev. ed., 1970.

WAINWRIGHT, JEFFREY (1944–)

Born in Longton, one of the six towns of Stoke-on-Trent, Staffordshire, the only child of parents who both worked in the local pottery industry. He graduated B.A. with honors in English and M.A. in English and American literature from Leeds University. While there he edited *Poetry and Audience* (then a weekly magazine), which was also published in other student magazines. He has been lecturer in English and American studies at the University College of Wales, Aberystwyth; visiting assistant professor, Long Island University, Brooklyn, New York; lecturer in English at Manchester Metropolitan University; fellow in creative writing at Cambridge University; and since 1999, professor of English at Manchester Metropolitan University. He has translated plays, was northern theatre critic for *The Independent,* has contributed to BBC Radio arts programs and has been included in many poetry anthologies. He lives in Manchester with his wife. Some of his poetry publications: *The Important Man,* 1971. *Heart's Desire,* 1978. *Selected Poems,* 1985. *The Red-Headed Pupil,* 1994. *Out of the Air,* 1999. Some of his poems: "The Mad Talk of George III," "The Apparent Colonnades," "The Fierce Dream," "Sentimental Education," "1815."

Sources: *Biography of Jeffrey Wainwright* (http://www.jeffreywainwright.co.uk/about.shtml). *British Council Arts* (http://www.contemporarywriters.com). *Some Contemporary Poets of Britain and Ireland: An Anthology.* Michael Schmidt, ed. Carcanet Press, 1983. *The Columbia Granger's Index to Poetry.* 11th ed. *The Columbia Granger's World of Poetry,* Columbia University Press, 2005 (http://www.co lumbiagrangers.org). *The Direction of Poetry: An Anthology of Rhymed and Metered Verse Written in the English Language Since 1975.* Robert Richman, ed. Houghton Mifflin, 1988. *The English Research Institute: The Works of Prof. Jeffrey Wainwright* (http://www.eri.mmu.ac.uk/staff/profile.php?id=29). *The Harvill Book of Twentieth-Century Poetry in English.* Michael Schmidt, ed. The Harvill Press, 1999. *The New Penguin Book of English Verse.* Paul Keegan, ed. Penguin Books, 2000.

WALEY, ARTHUR DAVID (1889–1966)

Born at Tunbridge Wells, Kent, he was educated at Rugby School and graduated in classics from King's College, Cambridge, in 1910, but losing sight in one eye curtailed his studies. Rest and travel on the Continent saved the other eye and he became a fluent linguist. From 1913 to 1929 he was assistant keeper of Oriental prints and manuscripts at the British Museum, during which time he taught himself Chinese and Japanese, partly to help catalogue the paintings in the museum's collection. Thereafter he devoted his life to literature. His awards were: honorary fellow of King's College, Cambridge (1945); Commander of the Order of the British Empire (1952); the Queen's Medal for Poetry (1953); and Companion of Honor (1956). He died in London and was buried in Highgate Cemetery. Some of his prose and verse translations of Chinese and Japanese authors: *The Tale of Genji* (1921–1933); *The Pillow Book of Sei Shōnagon* (1928); *Monkey* (1942). Some of his poems: "Life-Parting," "Separation," "The Two Red Towers," "The Valley Wind," "The Waters of Lung-t'ou," "To a Portrait Painter Who Desired Him to Sit," "To His Wife," "Winter Night."

Sources: *Art and Nature: An Illustrated Anthology of Nature Poetry.* Kate Farrell, ed. The Metropolitan Museum of Art, 1992. *Chinese Poems.* Arthur Waley, ed. Unwin Paperbacks, 1946. *Dictionary of National Biography.* Electronic Edition 1.1. Oxford University Press, 1997. *Encyclopædia Britannica Ultimate Reference Suite DVD,* 2006. *Japanese Poetry: The 'Uta' by Arthur Waley.* Percy Lund, Humphries and Co., 1956. *Microsoft Encarta* 2006 (DVD). Microsoft Corporation, 2006. *One Hundred and Seventy Chinese Poems, Translated by Arthur Waley.* Constable and Co., 1962. *The Columbia Granger's Index to Poetry.* 11th ed. *The Columbia Granger's World of Poetry,* Columbia University Press, 2005 (http://www.columbia grangers.org). *The Oxford Companion to English Literature.* 6th edition. Margaret Drabble, ed. Oxford University Press, 2000. *Translation of Dao De Jing: The Way and Its Power, The Naturalist, Individualist and Politic Doctrine of Lao-tse Exhibited in 81 Poetic and Obscure Texts.* Tr. Waley (en), Lau (en), Julien (fr) and Wilhelm (de) (http://afpc.asso.fr/wengu/wg/wengu.php?l=Daodejing&no=6). *Wikipedia, the Free Encyclopedia* (http://en.wikipedia.org/wiki/Wikipedia).

WALLER, EDMUND (1606–1687)

Born in Coleshill near Amersham, Buckinghamshire, and educated at Eton College and Cambridge University, he entered Parliament at a young age and switched from opposition to the king to being a Royalist and fighting against the Parliamentarians. In 1643 he was involved in a Royalist conspiracy against Parliament known as "Waller's Plot." Captured and imprisoned in 1643, he informed on his associates and, possibly because he was a distant relative of Oliver Cromwell, was given lenient treatment; he was exiled to the Continent until 1651. At the Restoration he again sided with Charles II and survived when all around lost their land and wealth. He died at Beaconsfield, Buckinghamshire. One of his often quoted poems is "Go Lovely Rose," and his poetic style was praised by John Dryden and Alexander Pope (see entries). Some of his publications: *The Passion of Dido for Æneas*, 1658. *A Poem on the Present Assembly of Parliament*, 1686. *A Poem on the Present Assembling of the Parliament*, 1697. Some of his poems: "Of Loving at First Sight," "On the Duke of Monmouth's Expedition," "The Battle of the Summer Islands," "The Garden of Bermuda."

Sources: *Ben Jonson and the Cavalier Poets.* Hugh MacLaen, ed. New York: W.W. Norton and Company, 1974. *Dictionary of National Biography.* Electronic Edition 1.1. Oxford University Press, 1997. *Encyclopædia Britannica Ultimate Reference Suite DVD,* 2006. *Garden Poems.* John Hollander, ed. Alfred A. Knopf, 1996. *Microsoft Encarta 2006 (DVD).* Microsoft Corporation, 2006. *Seventeenth Century Poetry: The Schools of Donne and Jonson.* Hugh Kenner, ed. Holt, Rinehart and Winston, 1964. *Seventeenth-Century British Poetry: 1603–1660.* John P. Rumrich, ed. University of Texas, Austin and Gregory Chaplin, Bridgewater State University, W.W. Norton, 2005. *The Columbia Granger's Index to Poetry.* 11th ed. *The Columbia Granger's World of Poetry,* Columbia University Press, 2005 (http://www.columbiagrangers.org). *Stanford University Libraries and Academic Information Resources* (http://library.stanford.edu). *The New Oxford Book of Christian Verse.* Donald Davie, ed. Oxford University Press, 1981. *The Oxford Companion to English Literature.* 6th edition. Margaret Drabble, ed. Oxford University Press, 2000. *The Poems of Edmund Waller.* Greenwood Press, 1968.

WALPOLE, SAINT HENRY (1558–1595)

One of the Forty Martyrs of England and Wales, he was born at Docking, Norfolk, educated at St. Peter's College, Cambridge, and while a student lawyer at Gray's Inn, London, he witnessed the execution of his Jesuit friend Edmund Campion in 1581. Some of Campion's blood splashed on Walpole, which he took as a sign to carry on Campion's mission. His anonymous poem in praise of Campion caused the printer to have his ears cut off, but he did not betray Walpole. He went to the English College at Rome, was ordained a Jesuit priest in 1588, and returned to England on 4 December 1593 to minister to covert Catholics around York. He was immediately arrested for the crime of priesthood and imprisoned in York and in the Tower of London, being repeatedly racked before being hanged, drawn and quartered at York. He was beatified in 1929 by Pope Pius XI and canonized 25 October 1970 by Pope Paul VI. Some of his poems: "An Epistle from Florence," "Epilogue to Tamerlane," "Martyrdom of Father Campion," "The Beauties," "The Song of Mary the Mother of Christ."

Sources: *An Anthology of Catholic Poets.* Shane Leslie, ed. Macmillan, 1952. *The Catholic Encyclopedia.* (http://www.newadvent.org/cathen/16049b.htm). *Dictionary of National Biography.* Electronic Edition 1.1. Oxford University Press, 1997. *Forty Martyrs* (http://www.geocities.com/francischinchoy/fortymartyrs.html). *I Sing of a Maiden: The Mary Book of Verse.* Sister M. Therese, ed. Macmillan, 1947. *Patron Saints Index* (http://www.catholic-forum.com/saints/sainth97.htm). *The Columbia Granger's Index to Poetry.* 11th ed. *The Columbia Granger's World of Poetry,* Columbia University Press, 2005 (http://www.columbiagrangers.org). *The Golden Book of Catholic Poetry.* Alfred Noyes, ed. J.B. Lippincott, 1946. *Wikipedia, the Free Encyclopedia* (http://en.wikipedia.org/wiki/Wikipedia).

WALSH, CATHERINE (1964–)

Irish poet from Cork City who trained at the Samuel Beckett Drama Centre, Trinity College, Dublin. She won the Irish Times/ESB Best Actress of the Year Award 2002. More recently she appeared as Pegeen Mike in *Playboy of the Western World* and as Nora Burke in *The Shadow of the Glen* as part of Druid Theatre Company's acclaimed production *DruidSynge* for Galway Arts Festival and as part of Edinburgh International Festival 2005. She has appeared on the BBC TV, on Radio Telefís Éireann (RTE) and on BBC Radio. She co-edits hardPressed Poetry, an Irish poetry publishing and distributing company in Dublin, with Billy Mills. Her poetry publications: *Macula*, 1986. *The Ca Pater Pillar Thing and More Besides*, 1986. *Making Tents*, 1987. *Short Stories*, 1989. *Pitch*, 1994. *Idir Eatortha and Making Tents*, 1997. *City West*, 2005.

Sources: *Anthology of Twentieth-Century British and Irish Poetry.* Keith Tuma, ed. Oxford University Press, 2001. *Biography of Catherine Walsh* (http://www.irishwriters-online.com/catherinewalsh.html). *Biography of Catherine Walsh* (http://www.lisarichards.ie/actor_768.html). *Other: British and Irish Poetry Since 1970.* Richard Caddel and Peter Quartermain. ed. Wesleyan University Press, 1999. *The Columbia Granger's Index to Poetry.* 11th ed. *The Columbia Granger's World of Poetry,* Columbia University Press, 2005 (http://www.columbiagrangers.org).

WALSH, EDWARD (1805–1850)

Irish poet born in Derry, where he became a teacher. He was imprisoned during the Tithe War of the late 1830s (over a levy to assist the Anglican clergy, which led to violence and death; relief was not granted until 1836) and was dismissed from his teaching position for articles he wrote in *The Nation*. He published *Irish Jacobite Poetry* (1844) and *Irish Popular Songs* (1847), and collected songs and poems throughout Ireland, which he dedicated to the people of Ireland. Being unable to secure a regular teaching post, he accepted the post of schoolmaster to the junior convicts on Spike Island prison colony, County Cork. In 1848 he was imprisoned for speaking with John Mitchel, the Irish nationalist who was being held at Spike Island before his transportation to Tasmania (Mitchel escaped from Tasmania in 1853 and established the radical Irish nationalist newspaper *The Citizen* in New York). Walsh later became a teacher in the Cork Workhouse, where he died of tuberculosis in 1850. Some of his poems: "Aileen the Huntress," "Have You Been at Carrick?" "Kitty Bhan," "Lament," "The Dawning of the Day."

Sources: *A Tragic Troubadour: The Life and Collected Works of the Cork Folklorist, Poet and Translator, Edward Walsh (1805–1850).* John J. Ó Ríordáin CSSR, 2005. *An Anthology of Catholic Poets.* Shane Leslie, ed. Macmillan, 1952. *An Anthology of Irish Verse: The Poetry of Ireland from Mythological Times to the Present.* Padraic Colum, ed. Liveright, 1948. *Dictionary of National Biography.* Electronic Edition 1.1. Oxford University Press, 1997. *Aileen the Huntress, by Edward Walsh* (http://www.mindspring.com/~mccarthys/whiskey/pipaddy.htm). *The Book of Irish Verse: An Anthology of Irish Poetry from the Sixth Century to the Present.* John Montague, ed. Macmillan, 1974. *The Columbia Granger's Index to Poetry.* 11th ed. *The Columbia Granger's World of Poetry,* Columbia University Press, 2005 (http://www.columbiagrangers.org). *The Oxford Book of Victorian Verse.* Arthur Quiller-Couch, ed. Oxford University Press, 1971. *The Penguin Book of Irish Verse.* Brendan Kennelly, ed. Penguin Books, 1981.

WALSH, WILLIAM (1663–1708)

Born at Abberley, Worcestershire, he entered Wadham College, Oxford, but never graduated. He was twice Whig member of Parliament for Worcestershire and once for Richmond, Yorkshire. Under the Duke of Somerset, he was gentleman of the horse from the beginning of Queen Anne's reign (1702) till his death. Samuel Johnson reports that in the opinion of John Dryden, Shaw was one of the best critics in the nation. He was also a friend of Alexander Pope, who respected Walsh's opinion of his 1705 *Pastorals.* According to Johnson, Walsh was a man of fashion who had a heart of love toward women, but not enough to ever marry. In 1691 he wrote a *Dialogue Concerning Women, Being a Defence of the Sex,* and in 1692, *Letters and Poems, Amorous and Gallant.* Many of his poems are elegies, epigrams and love poems. Some of his other publications: *A Funeral Elegy,* 1695. *Ode for the Thanksgiving Day,* 1706. *Poems,* 1749. Some of his poems: "Against Marriage to His Mistress," "Cure of Jealousy," "Loving One I Never Saw," "The Antidote," "The Fair Mourner," "The Golden Age Restor'd," "The Retirement," "Upon a Favour Offered."

Sources: *Anthology of Poems on Affairs of State: Augustan Satirical Verse, 1660–1714.* George de F. Lord, ed. Yale University Press, 1975. *Dictionary of National Biography.* Electronic Edition 1.1. Oxford University Press, 1997. *English Poetry: Author Search.* Chadwyck-Healey Ltd., 1995 (http://www.lib.utexas.edu:8080/search/epoetry/author.

html). *The National Portrait Gallery* (www.npg.org.uk). *Samuel Johnson's Lives of the English Poets,* 1779–1781 (http://www2.hn.psu.edu/Faculty/KKemmerer/poets/preface.htm). *The Columbia Granger's Index to Poetry.* 11th ed. *The Columbia Granger's World of Poetry,* Columbia University Press, 2005 (http://www.columbiagrangers.org). *The Gift of Great Poetry.* Lucien Stryk, ed. Regnery Gateway, 1992. *The Home Book of Modern Verse.* Burton Egbert Stevenson, ed. Henry Holt, 1953. *The Oxford Companion to English Literature.* 6th edition. Margaret Drabble, ed. Oxford University Press, 2000. *The Poetical Works of William Walsh.* Cooke's Edition, London: Printed for C. Cooke, 1797.

WARBURTON (EGERTON-WARBURTON), ROWLAND EYLES EGERTON (AKA "RAMBLING RICHARD") (1804–1891)

Born at Moston, near Chester, he was educated at Eton College and Corpus Christi College, Oxford. His clergyman father married the heiress of Sir Peter Warburton, of Arley Hall, Cheshire. Warburton made his life's work the care of the huge estate and the rebuilding of Arley Hall. Known affectionately as "the poet laureate of the hunting field," many of his poems are about the countryside and fox hunting. For the last seventeen years of his life he was totally blind from glaucoma. He died at Arley Hall, which is the now the home of the 11th Viscount Ashbrook, a direct descendant. Some of his publications: *Poems,* 1833. *Hunting Songs and Miscellaneous Verses,* 1846 (eighth edition, 1887). *Epigrams and Humorous Verses,* 1867. *Poems, Epigrams and Sonnets,* 1877. *Songs and Verses on Sporting Subjects,* 1879. *Twenty-Two Sonnets,* 1883. *Counsel for Cottagers and a Looking-Glass for Landlords,* 1887. Some of his poems: "Farmer Dobbin," "Riding to Hounds," "The Blooming Evergreen," "The Mare and Her Master," "The Roebuck at Toft," "The Stranger's Story."

Sources: *Arley Hall and Gardens* (http://www.touruk.co.uk/houses/house-cheshire-arley-%20hall.htm). *Carmina Mariana: An English Anthology in Verse in Honour of or in Relation to the Blessed Virgin Mary.* Orby Shipley, ed. Burns and Oates, 1894. *Dictionary of National Biography.* Electronic Edition 1.1. Oxford University Press, 1997. *English Poetry,* Second Edition Bibliography. (http://collections.chadwyck.co.uk/html/ep2/bibliography/g.htm). *English Poetry: Author Search* (http://www.lib.utexas.edu:8080/search/epoetry/author.html). *Stanford University Libraries and Academic Information Resources* (http://library.stanford.edu). *The Columbia Granger's Index to Poetry.* 11th ed. *The Columbia Granger's World of Poetry,* Columbia University Press, 2005 (http://www.columbiagrangers.org). *The New Oxford Book of Victorian Verse.* Christopher Ricks, ed. Oxford University Press, 1987. *Welcome to the Home of Viscount and Viscountess Ashbrook: Arley Hall Website* (http://arleyhallandgardens.com/home.html).

WARING, ANNA LETITIA (1823–1910)

Born at Plas-y-Velin, Neath, Glamorganshire, into a Quaker family, she learned Hebrew for the study of the poetry of the Old Testament, and daily read the Hebrew Psalter. Feeling more inclined toward the Anglicans, and following the example of her uncle, Samuel Miller Waring (1792–1827), a hymn writer and author of *Sacred Melodies* (1826), she was baptized at St. Martin's Anglican Church, Winnall, Winchester, in 1842. She was deeply involved in philanthropic work, especially the Discharged Prisoners' Aid Society, and visiting prisoners in the Bristol jail. She died unmarried at Clifton, Bristol. Some of her hymns are in modern hymnbooks. Her publications: *Hymns and Meditations,* 1850 (17th edition, 1896, and several American reprints). *Additional Hymns,* 1858. *Days of Remembrance,* 1886 (calendar of Bible texts, not poems). Some of her hymns/poems: "Abiding in Love," "Daily Mercies," "Father, I Know That All My Life," "Fellowship," "Homeward Led," "In Heavenly Love Abiding," "My Heart is Resting, O My God," "The Entered Year," "The Lowly Heart."

Sources: *A Sacrifice of Praise: An Anthology of Christian Poetry in English from Caedmon to the Mid-Twentieth Century.* James H. Trott, ed. Cumberland House Publishing, 1999. *Dictionary of National Biography.* Electronic Edition 1.1. Oxford University Press, 1997. *Nineteenth-Century Women Poets: An Oxford Anthology.* Isobel Armstrong and Joseph Bristow with Cath Sharrock, eds. Oxford University Press, 1996. *Poetry Worth Remembering: An Anthology of Poetry.* Roy W. Watson, ed. Brunswick, 1986. *The Columbia Granger's Index to Poetry.* 11th ed. *The Columbia Granger's World of Poetry,* Columbia University Press, 2005 (http://www.columbiagrangers.org). *The Cyber Hymnal* (http://www.cyberhymnal.org/index.htm). *Unity Hymns and Chorals.* William Channing Gannett, ed. Unity Publishing Company, 1911.

WARNER, SYLVIA TOWNSEND (1893–1978)

Born in Harrow, the daughter of a schoolmaster at Harrow School, she was educated privately and worked in a munitions factory during World War I. From 1918 to 1928 she was a member of the editorial board of *Tudor Church Music* (Oxford University Press, 1923–1929) and was also a contributor to Grove's Dictionary of Music. In 1927, she became guest critic of the *New York Herald Tribune.* A committed writer of the left, she worked for the Red Cross in the Spanish Civil War alongside her lifelong partner, Valentine Ackland, who died in 1969. She published some 140 short stories in the *New Yorker* and published eight novels, the last, *Kingdoms of Elfin,* in 1977, and eight collections of short stories. In 1958 she translated *Contre Sainte-Beuve* by Marcel Proust (1871–1922). She died at Maldon Newton, Dorset. Some of her poetry publications: *The Espalier,* 1925. *Whether a Dove Or Seagull,* 1933 (with Valentine Ackland). *Collected Poems,* 1982. Some of her poems: "Astrophysics," "Journey to Barcelona," "Killing No Murder," "Song from the Bride of Smithfield," "The Absence," "Under the Sudden Blue."

Sources: *Dictionary of National Biography.* Electronic Edition 1.1. Oxford University Press, 1997. *Encyclopædia Britannica Ultimate Reference Suite DVD,* 2006. *Microsoft Encarta* 2006 (DVD). Microsoft Corporation, 2006. *Modern British Poetry.* 7th rev. ed. Louis Untermeyer, ed. Harcourt, Brace, 1962. *The National Portrait Gallery* (www.npg.org.uk). *Poems Between Women: Four Centuries of Love, Romantic Friendship, and Desire.* Emma Donoghue, ed. Columbia University Press, 1997. *The Columbia Granger's Index to Poetry.* 11th ed. *The Columbia Granger's World of Poetry,* Columbia University Press, 2005 (http://www.columbiagrangers.org). *The Oxford Book of Sonnets.* John Fuller, ed. Oxford University Press, 2000. *The Oxford Companion to English Literature.* 6th edition. Margaret Drabble, ed. Oxford University Press, 2000. *The Sylvia Townsend Warner Society Homepage* (http://www.townsendwarner.com/bibliography.htm). *Women's Poetry of the 1930s: A Critical Anthology.* Jane Dowson, ed. Routledge, 1966.

WARNER, WILLIAM (1558–1609)

Born in London, he was educated at Magdalen Hall, Oxford, but did not take a degree. As an attorney in London, he was friends with the poets Michael Drayton, Henry Carey, the first Baron Hunsdon (see entries) and Carey's son, George, the second Baron. Warner died unexpectedly at Amwell in Hertfordshire, and was buried there. He published *Pan, His Syrinx* (seven prose tales) in 1584, and it is thought that an English translation in 1580 of the *Novelle* of Bandello (the Italian short story writer of 1485–1561) was Warner's work. In 1595 he translated the *Menaechmi* of Titus Maccius Plaautus (c. 254–184 B.C.). His main poetical work (1586 to 1606) was *Albion's England Or Historical Map of the Same Island,* an epic poem of 14 books and 107 chapters from the time of Noah. Francis Meres (1565–1647) is reported to have referred to Warner as "our English Homer." Some of his other poems: "A Tale of the Beginning of Friars and Cloisterers," "Argentile and Curan," "My Mistress," "The Fate of Narcissus," "The Patient Countess," "To the Reader," "To the Right Honovrable Sir Edvvard Coke."

Sources: *Albion's England by William Warner,* for the complete poem, see *The Columbia Granger's Index to Poetry.* 11th ed. *The Columbia Granger's World of Poetry,* Columbia University Press, 2005 (http://www.columbiagrangers.org). *Dictionary of National Biography.* Electronic Edition 1.1. Oxford University Press, 1997. *Elizabethan Lyrics.* Norman Ault, ed. William Sloane Associates, 1949. *Microsoft Encarta* 2006 (DVD). Microsoft Corporation,

2006. *The Oxford Companion to English Literature.* 6th edition. Margaret Drabble, ed. Oxford University Press, 2000.

WARREN, JOHN BYRNE LEICESTER, 3rd BARON DE TABLEY (1835–1895)

Born at Tabley House, Cheshire, educated at Eton College and at Christ Church, Oxford, he tried the diplomatic service, law, and was an officer of the Cheshire yeomanry, but his heart seemed elsewhere. He wrote two tragedies: *Philoctetes* (1866) and *Orestes* (1868), which were moderately successful, however, not one copy of *The Soldier's Fortune* (1876) was sold. He was greatly encouraged when in 1891 *Poets of the Century,* by A.H. Miles, was published, which contained some of his poems. He never married and he succeeded to the title four years before he died and was buried at Little Peover, Cheshire. His *Flora of Cheshire* was published posthumously in 1899. He published poetry under his own name and also as George Preston and William Lancaster. Some of his publications: *Ballads and Metrical Sketches,* 1860. *Praeterita,* 1863. *Studies in Verse,* 1865. *Rehearsals,* 1870. *Searching the Net,* 1873. *Poems, Dramatic and Lyrical,* 1893. Some of his poems: "All-Hallow-E'en," "Anticipation," "Semele," "The Churchyard on the Sands," "The Minstrel," "The Study of a Spider," "The Wreck of a Life."

Sources: *Come Hither.* Walter de la Mare, ed. Knopf, 1957; Dover Publications, 1995. *Dictionary of National Biography.* Electronic Edition 1.1. Oxford University Press, 1997. *English Love Poems.* John Betjeman and Geoffrey Taylor, eds. Faber and Faber, 1957. *English Lyric Poems, 1500–1900.* C. Day Lewis, ed. Appleton-Century-Crofts, 1961. *English Poetry: Author Search.* Chadwyck-Healey Ltd., 1995 (http://www.lib.utexas.edu:8080/search/epo etry/author.html). *The Columbia Granger's Index to Poetry.* 11th ed. *The Columbia Granger's World of Poetry,* Columbia University Press, 2005 (http://www.columbiagrangers. org). *The Oxford Companion to English Literature.* 6th edition. Margaret Drabble, ed. Oxford University Press, 2000. *Victorian Verse.* George MacBeth, ed. Penguin Books, 1986.

WARREN, SIR THOMAS HERBERT (1853–1930)

Born near Bristol, he was educated at Balliol College, Oxford, where he was an outstanding student, winning several prizes and graduating *literae humaniores* (1876). He was elected tutor in classics in 1877 and was president of Magdalen College from 1885 to 1928. So high was the standing of the college that King George V in 1912 chose it for the Prince of Wales, later Edward VIII, who abdicated in 1937. Outside the university, Warren's services were employed on several government commissions and committees. He was Oxford professor of poetry from

1911 to 1916, and he received honorary doctorates from the universities of Oxford, Birmingham and Bristol, and was created Knight Commander of the Royal Victorian Order in 1914. He died in Oxford. In 1888 he published his edition of the first five books of Plato's *Republic* and two volumes of poems, *By Severn Sea and Other Poems* (1897) and *The Death of Virgil* (1907). Some of his poems: "A New Year's Greeting," "An Excuse," "Hesperides," "In Memoriam Alfred Lord Tennyson," "Lines for a Sundial," "May-Day on Magdalen Tower," "Natural Religion," "Richard of Chichester," "The Point of Spring."

Sources: *Dictionary of National Biography.* Electronic Edition 1.1. Oxford University Press, 1997. *The National Portrait Gallery* (www.npg.org.uk). *Stanford University Libraries and Academic Information Resources* (http://library. stanford.edu). *The Columbia Granger's Index to Poetry.* 11th ed. *The Columbia Granger's World of Poetry,* Columbia University Press, 2005 (http://www.columbiagrangers. org). *The Oxford Book of Victorian Verse.* Arthur Quiller-Couch, ed. Oxford University Press, 1971.

WARTON, THOMAS, THE ELDER; JOSEPH; and THOMAS, THE YOUNGER (1688–1800)

Thomas, the elder, the father, 1688–1745

The son of Antony Warton, vicar of Godalming, Surrey, he graduated, B.A. (1709–10), M.A. (1712), and B.D. (1725) from Magdalen College, Oxford. His Jacobite sympathies made him popular and he was elected professor of poetry at Oxford for two terms from 1718 to 1728. In 1717–1718 Warton circulated both in manuscript and in print a satire in verse on George I, entitled *The Turnip Hoer.* In 1723 he became vicar of Basingstoke, Hampshire, and master of the grammar school, where he remained until his death at Basingstoke. Among his pupils was the great naturalist Gilbert White (1720–1793). After his death his son Joseph issued, by subscription, *Poems on Several Occasions by the Rev. Thomas Warton* (1748). Some of his poems: "Against Dress," "A Farewell to Poetry," "A Paraphrase on the 13th Ode of the 3d Book of Horace," "An American Love-Ode," "Avaro, a Tale," "Cupid Acquitted, a Tale," "Ode to Sleep," "Paraphrase on the 13th Chap. of Isaiah."

Joseph, the elder son, 1722–1800

Born at his grandfather's vicarage in Dunsfold, Surrey, he was educated at his father's school at Basingstoke, then at Winchester College and graduated from Oriel College, Oxford. He took holy orders immediately afterwards and was his father's curate at Basingstoke until his father's death. He was second master, then headmaster at Winchester College from

1755 to 1793, when he resigned after the boys mutinied. Between 1759 and 1768, he was awarded the degrees of M.A., B.D., and D.D. from Oxford University. He died at Wickham, Hampshire, and was buried beside his first wife in the north aisle of Winchester Cathedral. His most important critical work is an *Essay on the Genius and Writings of Pope* (1756, 1782). He and his brother popularized the early Romantic conception of poetry with their enthusiastic use of nature and natural scenery. Some of his publications: *The Enthusiast, or The Lover of Nature,* 1744. *Odes on Various Subjects,* 1746. *An Ode, Occasioned by Reading Mr. West's Translation of Pindar,* 1749. *The Eclogues and Georgics of Virgil,* 1753. Some of his poems: "Against Despair," "On Shooting," "The Happy Life," "The Revenge of America," "To the Nightingale," "Verses Written at Montauban in France, 1750."

Thomas, the younger, 1728–1790

Born at Basingsoke, he graduated from Trinity College, Oxford, and was a don at Oxford throughout his life. In 1754 he published *Observations on the Faery Queen of Spenser,* which established his reputation as a critic of exceptional learning, and won unstinting praise from Dr. Johnson, which resulted in a long friendship between them. From 1757 to 1767 Warton was professor of poetry at Oxford. In 1770 from the Clarendon Press appeared Warton's book on Theocritus (c. 308–c. 240 B.C.). He was appointed poet laureate in 1785. He wrote odes, sonnets and light verse, and between 1774 and 1781 he published in three volumes *History of English Poetry.* In 1771 he took on the living of the small parish of Kiddington in Oxfordshire. He died at Oxford. Some of his other publications: *Five Pastoral Eclogues,* 1745. *Pleasures of Melancholy,* 1745. *The Triumph of Isis,* 1749. *Newmarket, a Satire,* 1751. *The Union,* or *Select Scotch and English Pieces,* 1753. Some of his poems: "Elegy on the Death of Frederic Prince of Wales," "For the New Year, 1786," "Job, Chapter 39," "The Castle Barber's Soliloquy," "The First of April," "The Grave of King Arthur."

Sources: *Dictionary of National Biography.* Electronic Edition 1.1. Oxford University Press, 1997. *Eighteenth-Century English Verse.* Dennis Davison, ed. Penguin Books, 1988. *Encyclopædia Britannica Ultimate Reference Suite DVD,* 2006. *English Poetry: Author Search.* Chadwyck-Healey Ltd., 1995 (http://www.lib.utexas.edu:8080/search/epoetry/author.html). *English Romantic Poetry and Prose.* Russell Noyes, ed. Oxford University Press. 1956. *Garden Poems.* John Hollander, ed. Alfred A. Knopf, 1996. *Microsoft Encarta 2006* (DVD). Microsoft Corporation, 2006. *The National Portrait Gallery* (www.npg.org.uk). *Odes on Various Subjects by Joseph Warton.* London: printed for R. Dodsley and sold by M. Cooper, 1746 (*Ximenes Rare Books Inc.* (http://www.polybiblio.com/ximenes/B3419.

html). *Stanford University Libraries and Academic Information Resources* (http://library.stanford.edu). *The Columbia Granger's Index to Poetry.* 11th ed. *The Columbia Granger's World of Poetry,* Columbia University Press, 2005 (http://www.columbiagrangers.com). *The New Oxford Book of Eighteenth Century Verse.* Roger Lonsdale, ed. Oxford University Press, 1984. *The Oxford Book of Travel Verse.* Kevin Crossley-Holland, ed. Oxford University Press, 1986. *The Oxford Companion to English Literature.* 6th edition. Margaret Drabble, ed. Oxford University Press, 2000. *The Penguin Book of Bird Poetry.* Peggy Munsterberg, ed. 1984. *The Poetical Works of John Scott and Thomas Warton.* Thomas Park, ed. J. Sharpe, 1808.

WATKINS, VERNON PHILLIPS (1906–1967)

English-speaking Welsh poet, born at Maesteg, Glamorgan, but brought up in Swansea, where his father was a bank manager. He was educated at Repton School, Derbyshire, and Magdalene College, Cambridge, where he read modern languages, developing an interest in French and German poetry. Except for military service in World War II — when he was at Bletchley Park as part of the cryptographic team — he worked in the St. Helen's branch of Lloyds Bank in Swansea. He lectured at the University College Swansea (Calouste Gulbenkin Fellow in Poetry), and won several major poetry prizes. He was a visiting professor of Poetry in America and died in Seattle. He was a major figure for the Anglo-Welsh poetry tradition; his poems were included in major anthologies, and he was being considered for poet laureate. Some of his publications: *Ballad of Mari Lwyd,* 1941. *The Lamp and the Veil,* 1945. *The Lady with the Unicorn,* 1948. *The Death Bell,* 1954. *Cypress and Acacia,* 1959. *Affinities,* 1962. Some of his poems: "Ballad of the Two Tapsters," "Fatherland in the Heights," "Returning to Goleufryn," "Taliesin and the Mockers," "The Collier."

Sources: *Anglo-Welsh Poetry, 1480–1980.* Raymond Garlick and Roland Mathias, ed. Poetry Wales Press, 1984. *Anglo-Welsh Poetry, 1480–1990.* Raymond Garlick and Roland Mathias, ed. Poetry Wales Press, 1993. *Archives Network Wales, Vernon Watkins* (http://www.archivesnetworkwales.info/cgi-bin/anw/fulldesc_nofr?inst_id=35&coll_id=11890&expand=). *Bloomsbury.com — Research Centre; Vernon Watkins* (http://www.bloomsburymagazine.com/ARC/detail.asp?entryid=109648). *Dylan Thomas's Choice: An Anthology of Verse Spoken by Dylan Thomas.* Ralph Maud and Aneirin Talfan Davies, eds. New Directions, 1963. *Encyclopædia Britannica Ultimate Reference Suite DVD,* 2006. *In Quest of the Miracle Stag: The Poetry of Hungary.* Adam Makkai, ed. Atlantic-Centaur, Corvina, 1996. *Modern Ballads and Story Poems.* Charles Causley, ed. Franklin Watts, 1965. *The Collected Poems of Vernon Watkins.* Brian Keeble, ed. Golgonooza Press, 2000. *The Columbia Granger's Index to Poetry.* 11th ed. *The Columbia Granger's World of Poetry,* Columbia University Press, 2005 (http://www.columbiagrangers.org). *The New Yorker Book* of Poems. The New Yorker editors. Viking Press, 1969. *The Oxford Companion to English Literature.* 6th edition. Margaret Drabble, ed. Oxford University Press, 2000. *Wikipedia, the Free Encyclopedia* (http://en.wikipedia.org/wiki/Wikipedia).

WATSON, SIR (JOHN) WILLIAM (1858–1935)

Born at Burley-in-Wharfedale, Yorkshire, the son of a grocer, he was educated at Southport, Lancashire. His first volume of verse, the *Prince's Quest*, published at his father's expense, appeared in 1880; this was followed by twenty-seven other works of poetry and songs. He attracted attention with the appearance of *Wordsworth's Grave and Other Poems* (1890), and he was one of the poets considered for the laureateship when Robert Bridges (see entry) was appointed in 1913. Watson lectured in the United States, and several of his poems show gratitude for recognition generously given to him there. His happy marriage is reflected in many of his poems. In 1917 he was knighted, and he died at Ditchling Common, Sussex. Some of his other publications: *Lachrymae Musarum,* 1892. *Lyric Love: An Anthology,* 1892. *The Father of the Forest and Other Poems,* 1895. *Ode on the Coronation of King Edward VII,* 1902. *The Superhuman Antagonists and Other Poems,* 1919. Some of his poems: "Abdication," "England and her Dominions," "Sonnets to Miranda," "The Bard-in-waiting," "The Cathedral Music," "The King's Daughter," "Wales: A Greeting," "Wordsworth's Grave."

Sources: *Dictionary of National Biography.* Electronic Edition 1.1. Oxford University Press, 1997. *Encyclopædia Britannica Ultimate Reference Suite DVD,* 2006. *I Was an English Poet: Biography of Sir William Watson.* Jean Moorcroft. Wilson, C. Woolf, 1982. *The National Portrait Gallery* (www.npg.org.uk). *The Columbia Granger's Index to Poetry.* 11th ed. *The Columbia Granger's World of Poetry,* Columbia University Press, 2005 (http://www.columbiagrangers.org). *The Family Book of Best Loved Poems.* David L. George, ed. Doubleday, 1952. *The Oxford Companion to English Literature.* 6th edition. Margaret Drabble, ed. Oxford University Press, 2000. *The Poems of Sir William Watson.* George G. Harrap and Co, 1936.

WATSON, THOMAS (1557?–1592)

Possibly educated at Oxford University, he became a law student and devoted his life to poetry. He wrote several Latin poems and translated into Latin the works of several Italian poets, including the sonnets of Petrarch (1304–1374). Some of his works were published posthumously, including the Latin pastoral *Amintae Gaudia* (1592); other works were included in *The Phoenix Nest* (1593) and in *England's Helicon* (1600 and 1614). He was mentioned as "Amynta" in Edmund Spenser's (see entry) *Colin Clouts Come Home Againe* (1589–1591). He was buried at the church of St. Bartholomew the Less, situated near St. Bartholomew's Hospital, London. Some of his other publications: *Antigone,* 1581 (a Latin translation from Sophocles). *Passionate Century of Love,* 1582. *Aminta,* 1585 (Latin translation from the Italian poet Torauato Tasso, 1544–1595). *An Eclogue Upon the Death of Sir Francis Walsingham,* 1590. *Italian Madrigals Englished,* 1590 (set to music by William Byrd). Some of his poems: "All Yee, That Greeue to Thinke My Death So Neere," "If Loue had lost his shaftes," "My Humble Sute Hath Set My Minde on Pride," "When Cupid is Content to Keepe the Skies."

Sources: *Davison's Poetical Rhapsody: Vol. II, of Francis Davison.* A.H. Bullen, ed. George Bell and Sons, 1891. *Dictionary of National Biography.* Electronic Edition 1.1. Oxford University Press, 1997. *English Poetry: Author Search.* Chadwyck-Healey Ltd., 1995 (http://www.lib.utexas.edu:8080/search/epoetry/author.html). *Stanford University Libraries and Academic Information Resources* (http://library.stanford.edu). *The Anchor Anthology of Sixteenth Century Verse.* Richard Sylvester, ed. Doubleday/Anchor Books, 1974. *The Columbia Granger's Index to Poetry.* 11th ed. *The Columbia Granger's World of Poetry,* Columbia University Press, 2005 (http://www.columbiagrangers.org). *The Oxford Companion to English Literature.* 6th edition. Margaret Drabble, ed. Oxford University Press, 2000. *The Penguin Book of Bird Poetry.* Peggy Munsterberg, ed. 1984. *The Sonnet: An Anthology.* Robert M. Bender and Charles L. Squier, eds. Washington Square Press, 1987.

WATTS, ALARIC ALEXANDER (1797–1864)

Born in London, he was a tutor to several families until 1818, when he returned to London to become sub-editor of *New Monthly Magazine.* His *Borrowings of Byron* in the *Literary Gazette* in 1821 led to his being appointed as editor of *Leeds Intelligencer* in 1822. For the next fifteen years he was editor of the *Literary Souvenir,* which focused on annuals and pocket-books, of which paper he became the proprietor in 1826. He helped found the *Standard* newspaper (1827), and in 1833 he founded the *United Service Gazette,* from which he retired in 1847. He was made bankrupt in 1850 and was granted a civil pension in 1854. He died at Notting Hill and was buried in Highgate Cemetery. Some of his publications: *Poetical Album,* 1828 (a collection of fugitive poems). *Poetical Sketches,* 1828 and 1829. *Lyrics of the Heart,* 1851. *The Laurel and the Lyre,* 1867. Some of his poems: "An Austrian Army," "Come, Let Us Banish Sorrow," "Forget Thee? No, Never!" "The Aeolian Harp," "The First-Born," "The Home of Taliessin," "'Tis Eve on the Ocean."

Sources: *Dictionary of National Biography.* Electronic Edition 1.1. Oxford University Press, 1997. *English Poetry:*

Author Search. Chadwyck-Healey Ltd., 1995 (http://www.lib.utexas.edu:8080/search/epoetry/author.html). *The National Portrait Gallery* (www.npg.org.uk). *Poetical Sketches: The Profession: The Broken Heart, Etc.* Hurst, Robinson and Co., 1824. *Stanford University Libraries and Academic Information Resources* (http://library.stanford.edu). *The Columbia Granger's Index to Poetry.* 11th ed. *The Columbia Granger's World of Poetry,* Columbia University Press, 2005 (http://www.columbiagrangers.org). *The Faber Book of Comic Verse.* Michael Roberts and Janet Adam Smith, eds. Faber and Faber, 1978.

WATTS, ISAAC (1674–1748)

Born in Southampton, Hampshire, the son of a tradesman, he was educated at a Nonconformist academy at Stoke Newington, London, and in 1702 he became minister of the Mark Lane Chapel, London. His health was undermined by long hours of study, and for several years he lived at the home of Sir Thomas and Lady Abney. In 1728, Edinburgh University awarded Watts a doctor of divinity degree. He was buried in Burnhill Fields Cemetery, London; a monument stands in the nave of Westminster Abbey in 1779, and another is in Watt's Park, Southampton. He wrote educational, scriptural, philosophical, and divinity books, and published four poetry collections: *Horæ Lyricæ* (1706); *Hymns and Spiritual Songs* (1707); *The Divine and Moral Songs for the Use of Children* (1715); and *The Psalms of David Imitated* (1719). A few of his 500 hymns are: "Jesus Shall Reign Where'er the Sun"; "When I Wurvey the Wondrous Cross"; "Joy to the World"; and "Our God, Our Help in Ages Past." Some of his poems: "A Cradle Hymn," "Few Happy Matches," "Kind Deeds," "Sincere Praise," "The Adventurous Muse," "The Golden Rule," "The Sluggard."

Sources: *A Treasury of Poems for Worship and Devotion.* Charles L. Wallis, ed. Harper, 1959. *Dictionary of National Biography.* Electronic Edition, 1.1. *Encyclopædia Britannica Ultimate Reference Suite DVD,* 2006. *English Poetry: Author Search.* Chadwyck-Healey Ltd., 1995 (http://www.lib.utexas.edu:8080/search/epoetry/author.html). *English Poetry: A Poetic Record, from Chaucer to Yeats.* David Hopkins, ed. Routledge, 1990. *Folksinger's Wordbook.* Irwin Silber and Fred Silber, eds. Oak Publications, 1973. *Freedom's Lyre: or Psalms, Hymns, and Sacred Songs, for the Slave and His Friends.* Edwin F. Hatfield, ed. S.W. Benedict, 1840. *Microsoft Encarta* 2006 (DVD). Microsoft Corporation, 2006. *Samuel Johnson's Lives of the English Poets,* 1779–1781 (http://www2.hn.psu.edu/Faculty/KKemmerer/poets/preface.htm). *The Book of a Thousand Poems: A Family Treasury.* J. Murray Macbain, ed. Peter Bedrick Books, 1983. *The Columbia Granger's Index to Poetry.* 11th ed. *The Columbia Granger's World of Poetry,* Columbia University Press, 2005 (http://www.columbiagrangers.org). *The Cyber Hymnal* (http://www.cyberhymnal.org/index.htm). *The Home Book of Modern Verse.* Burton Egbert Stevenson, ed. Henry Holt, 1953. *The New Oxford Book of Eighteenth Century Verse.* Roger Lonsdale, ed. Oxford University Press, 1984. *The Oxford Companion to English Literature.* 6th edition. Margaret Drabble, ed. Oxford University Press, 2000. *Unity Hymns and Chorals.* William Channing Gannett, ed. Unity Publishing Company, 1911. *Westminster Abbey Official Guide* (no date).

WATTS-DUNTON, WALTER THEODORE (1832–1914)

The eldest child of a solicitor, of St. Ives, Huntingdonshire, he went to school in Cambridge, then became a solicitor in London. From 1874 he worked for two years as literary critic for the *Examiner,* after which he joined the staff of the *Athenæum* as chief poetry reviewer. His wrote a critical essay for the 9th edition (1885) of the *Encyclopædia Britannica.* He supported Dante Gabriel Rossetti in his declining years, and Algernon Charles Swinburne (see entries), who would certainly have died much sooner had not Watts-Dunton taken him to live with him. In addition to his poetry, he is known for his work with gypsies, told in his romantic novel the *Coming of Love* (1898), and his best-known novel, *Aylwin* (1898). His memoir, *Old Familiar Faces* (1916), is a valuable record of his life and times. Two of his other poetry publications: *Jubilee Greeting at Spithead to the Men of Greater Britain,* 1897. *The Work of Cecil Rhodes: A Sonnet Sequence,* 1907. Some of his poems: "Coleridge," "For the Shelley Centenary," "Mother Carey's Chicken," "The Death of Marlowe," "The First Kiss," "The Sonnet's Voice."

Sources: *Book-Song.* Gleeson White, ed. Elliot Stock, 1893. *Dictionary of National Biography.* Electronic Edition 1.1. Oxford University Press, 1997. *Encyclopædia Britannica Ultimate Reference Suite DVD,* 2006. *English Poetry: Author Search.* Chadwyck-Healey Ltd., 1995 (http://www.lib.utexas.edu:8080/search/epoetry/author.html). *Great Sonnets.* Paul Negri, ed. Dover, 1994. *Microsoft Encarta* 2006 (DVD). Microsoft Corporation, 2006. *Poetry's Plea for Animals.* Frances E. Clarke, ed. Lothrop, Lee & Shepherd, 1927. *Stanford University Libraries and Academic Information Resources* (http://library.stanford.edu). *The Columbia Granger's Index to Poetry.* 11th ed. *The Columbia Granger's World of Poetry,* Columbia University Press, 2005 (http://www.columbiagrangers.org). *The Home Book of Modern Verse.* Burton Egbert Stevenson, ed. Henry Holt, 1953. *The Oxford Book of Victorian Verse.* Arthur Quiller-Couch, ed. Oxford University Press, 1971. *The Oxford Companion to English Literature.* 6th edition. Margaret Drabble, ed. Oxford University Press, 2000.

WAUGH, EDWIN (1817–1890)

The "Lancashire Burns" was born in Rochdale, the son of a shoemaker, and from the age of nine he helped at his widowed mother's stall at the Rochdale market. After serving his printing apprenticeship, he earned his living as a journeyman printer, and in 1847 he was appointed assistant secretary to the Lancashire Public School Association, Manchester, whose aim was provide education free from religious ties. His first books were *Sketches of Lancashire Life and Localities* (1855) and *Poems and Songs* (1859). He wrote prose and verse, songs, tales, and character sketches in the Lancashire dialect. In 1881 he was granted a civil-list pension. He died at New Brighton, a watering-place on the Lancashire coast, and was buried in Kersal Church, near Salford, Lancashire. Many of Waugh's songs have been set to music, and a list of them occupies several pages of the music catalogue of the British Museum Library. Some of his poems: "Cultivate Your Men," "Dule's i' This Bonnet o' Mine," "Fishwoman's Song," "I've Worn My Bits o' Shoon Away," "It's Time to be Joggin' Away," "Now's the Time to Remember the Poor," "The Man of the Time."

Sources: *Dictionary of National Biography*. Electronic Edition 1.1. Oxford University Press, 1997. *English Poetry: Author Search*. Chadwyck-Healey Ltd., 1995 (http://www. lib.utexas.edu:8080/search/epoetry/author.html). *The Columbia Granger's Index to Poetry*. 11th ed. *The Columbia Granger's World of Poetry*, Columbia University Press, 2005 (http://www.columbiagrangers.org). *The Poorhouse Fugitives: Self-Taught Poets and Poetry in Victorian Britain*. Brian Maidment, ed. Carcanet, 1987.

WEBB, MARY GLADYS (1881–1927)

The daughter of George Edward Meredith, a schoolmaster of Welsh descent, and a Scottish mother, she was born at Leighton-under-the-Wrekin, Shropshire, where she was brought up. In 1912 she married a schoolmaster, and after several years of living in different places they settled at Hampstead, London, in 1921. At the age of 20 she developed Graves' disease, a thyroid disorder that was the cause of ill health throughout her life. Between 1916 and 1927 she published five novels; *Precious Bane* (1924) (set after the Battle of Waterloo) won the Femina Vie Heureuse prize for the best English novel published in 1924–1925. She died at St. Leonards on Sea, Sussex. Stella Gibbons, in *Cold Comfort Farm* (1932), ridicules Webb's prose style. Her novel *Gone to Earth* was filmed in 1950 and re-released in 1985. *The Spring of Joy* (essays and poems) was published 1917. Richard Moult, artist and composer, has set many of Mary Webb's poems to music, including: "A Hawthorn Berry," "Foxgloves," "A Summer Day," "A Night Sky," "To a Poet in April," "The Ancient Gods." Some of her other poems: "Autumn, 1914," "Green Rain," "Market Day," "The Water-Ousel," "Why?"

Sources: *Come Hither*. Walter de la Mare, ed. Knopf, 1957; Dover Publications, 1995. *Dictionary of National Biography*. Electronic Edition 1.1. Oxford University Press, 1997. *Encyclopædia Britannica Ultimate Reference Suite DVD*, 2006. *Scars Upon My Heart: Women's Poetry and*

Verse of the First World War. Catherine W. Reilly, ed. Virago Press, 1981. *The Book of a Thousand Poems: A Family Treasury*. J. Murray Macbain, ed. Peter Bedrick Books, 1983. *The Columbia Granger's Index to Poetry*. 11th ed. *The Columbia Granger's World of Poetry*, Columbia University Press, 2005 (http://www.columbiagrangers.org). *The Mary Webb Society* (http://pers-www.wlv.ac.uk/~me1927/mwebb/index.html).

WEBSTER, AUGUSTA (1837–1894)

Julia Augusta Davies, the daughter of an admiral, was born at Poole, Dorset. She attended classes at the Cambridge school of art, and in 1863 married Thomas Webster, fellow and later law lecturer of Trinity College, Cambridge. In 1864, under the pseudonym Cecil Home, she published *Lesley's Guardians*, a novel in three volumes. She contributed two highly acclaimed essays to *Examiner: The Translation of Poetry* and *Transcript and a Transcription*. A keen educationalist, she twice served on the London school board and was a strong advocate of the introduction of technical instruction into elementary schools. She was also a supporter of woman's suffrage. Some of her other poetry publications: *Blanche Lisle, and Other Poems*, 1860. *Lilian Gray*, 1864. *The Prometheus Bound*, 1866 (translation into English verse from Æschylus, 525–456 B.C.). *Dramatic Studies*, 1866. *Medea*, 1868 (translated from Euripides, c.480–406 B.C.). *Portraits*, 1870. *A Book of Rhyme*, 1881 (in the form of Italian peasant songs). *Mother and Daughter*, 1895 (an uncompleted sonnet sequence). Some of her poems: "Abbess Ursula's Lecture," "The Castaway," "The Snow Waste," "With the Dead."

Sources: *A Treasury of Minor British Poetry*. J. Churton Collins, ed. Edward Arnold, 1896. *Bread and Roses: An Anthology of Nineteenth- and Twentieth-Century Poetry by Women Writers*. Diana Scott, ed. Virago Press, 1982. *Dictionary of National Biography*. Electronic Edition, 1.1. *Dramatic Studies of Augusta Webster*. Macmillan and Co., 1866. *The National Portrait Gallery* (www.npg.org.uk). *Poem hunter* (www.poemhunter.com). *The Columbia Granger's Index to Poetry*. 11th ed. *The Columbia Granger's World of Poetry*, Columbia University Press, 2005 (http://www.columbiagrangers.org). *The Home Book of Verse*. Burton Egbert Stevenson, ed. New York: Henry Holt and Company, 1953. *The Oxford Companion to English Literature*. 6th edition. Margaret Drabble, ed. Oxford University Press, 2000. *Victorian Women Poets: An Anthology*. Angela Leighton and Margaret Reynolds, eds. Blackwell, 1991.

WEDDERBURN BROTHERS, JAMES, JOHN and ROBERT (?1495–1557)

(See also Cannan, May Wedderburn)

The three brothers were all born in Dundee, the sons of James Wedderburn, a prosperous merchant, and Janet Barrie. Educated at St. Andrews University, they all became zealous Scottish religious reformers. On the death of James V (1542) the brothers published the *Compendious Book of Psalms and Spiritual Songs* (also known as *The Gude and Godlie Ballatis*, or *The Dundee Book*, or *The Dundee Psalms*). It has been said that after the Bible itself, this book did more for the spread of reformation doctrines than any other book published in Scotland. And next to Knox's *Historie of the Reformatioun*, is the most memorable literary monument of the period in vernacular Scots. It consists of a calendar and almanac, a catechism, hymns — many of them translations from the German, metrical versions of the Psalms — and a collection of ballads and satirical poems against the Catholic Church and clergy. The book aroused a storm of opposition; the brothers were accused of heresy and the publishers were fined.

James, ?1495–1553

He composed two plays: *The Beheading of Johne the Baptist*, and *The Historie of Dyonisius the Tyrant*, a morality play satirizing church abuses, both of which were performed in 1540 in the play-field of Dundee. A charge of heresy was brought against him for counterfeiting the conjuring of a ghost, but he escaped to France and established himself as a merchant at Rouen or Dieppe, where he lived unmolested until his death, although attempts were made by the Scottish community there to bring further charges against him.

John, ?1500–1556

He took priests' orders and appears to have held the chaplaincy of St. Matthews, Dundee, but in March 1539 he, too, was accused of heresy, for his part in the *The Gude and Godlie Ballatis*. He escaped to Wittenberg, Germany, where he received the teaching of the German reformers. He returned to Scotland with the hope that with the death of James V a more enlightened religious atmosphere would prevail. This hope was not realized, and he fled to England, where he died.

Robert, 1510–1557

He also took priests' orders and succeeded his uncle John Barry as vicar of Dundee. But before he came into actual possession he also was suspected of heresy, and was compelled to flee to France and Germany. He returned to Scotland in 1546 and was vicar of Dundee in 1552. It is not possible to clearly identify which brother wrote which poem (the poems have been reproduced in their Scottish vernacular, with translations of obscure words). Some of their poems: "All My Hart Ay This is My Sang," "Ane Sang of the Birth of Christ, with the Tune of Baw [hush] Lula Low," "Christ is the Onlie Sone of God,"

"De Profundis, Psalm 30," "Dominus Regit Me, Psalm 23," "Grievous is My Sorrow," "Christ Quhilk [Which] Art the Licht of Day," "Of the False Fyre of Purgatorie," "Pray God for Grace, My Lufe [Love] Maist Deir," "The Supper of the Lord, and Richt Use of It to Be Sung," "We Thank Our God Baith Kynde and Liberall," "Welcvm Lord Christ, Welcum Againe," "With Heuie Hart Full of Distres," "With Huntis Up, with Huntis Up" (name of a song and dance).

Sources: *Dictionary of National Biography*. Electronic Edition 1.1. Oxford University Press, 1997. *English Poetry: Author Search*. Chadwyck-Healey Ltd., 1995 (http://www.lib.utexas.edu:8080/search/epoetry/author.html). *Biography of the Wedderburn Brothers* (http://23.1911encyclopedia.org/W/WE/WEDDERBURN_JAMES_JOHN_AND_ROBERT.htm). *The history of Sir John Wedderburn, who was executed for his part in the 1745 Rebellion* (http://perso.wanadoo.fr/euroleader/wedderburn/sirjohn.htm). *The Columbia Granger's Index to Poetry*. 11th ed. *The Columbia Granger's World of Poetry*, Columbia University Press, 2005 (http://www.columbiagrangers.org). *The New Penguin Book of Scottish Verse*. Robert Crawford and Mick Imlah, eds. Penguin Books, 2000. *The Oxford Companion to English Literature*. 6th edition. Margaret Drabble, ed. Oxford University Press, 2000. *The Wedderburn Book*. Published privately by Alexander Wedderburn, 1898 (these two volumes give a detailed history of the Wedderburn family and include *The Gude and Godlie Ballatis*, Vol. 1 xxxi, *The Wedderburn Pages*, *The Gude and Godlie Ballatis*, and history of the Wedderburn family) (http://perso.wanadoo.fr/euroleader/wedderburn/gudeandgodlie.htm#Play%20on%20your%20lute).

WEELKES, THOMAS (?1576–1623)

English composer and organist from Elsted Sussex, one of the finest composers of English madrigals. In addition to madrigals, he wrote anthems and services, and he is noted for his word painting, lively rhythms, and highly developed sense of form and structure. He also wrote music for virginal, viol, and organ. He was appointed organist at Winchester College, Hampshire, in 1598, and in 1602, organist at Chichester Cathedral, Sussex, the same year in which he graduated with a B.Mus. degree from New College, Oxford University. He fell foul of the cathedral authorities at Chichester for drunkenness and bad language on numerous occasions and was briefly dismissed in 1617, but he managed to retain the post until his death at a friend's house in London. Some of his publications: *Madrigals for 3, 4, 5, and 6 Voices*, 1597. *Balletts and Madrigals to Five Voices*, 1598. *Madrigals of 5 and 6. Parts to Viols and Voices*, 1600. *Ayeres or Phantasticke Spirites for Viols and Voices*, 1608. Some of his songs/poems: "Fara Diddle Dyno," "Cease Sorrows Now," "Come Sirrah Jack Ho," "The Ape, the Monkey, and Baboon."

Sources: *Dictionary of National Biography*. Electronic

Edition 1.1. Oxford University Press, 1997. *Encyclopædia Britannica Ultimate Reference Suite DVD*, 2006. *English Poetry: Author Search*. Chadwyck-Healey Ltd., 1995 (http://www.lib.utexas.edu:8080/search/epoetry/author.html). *English Renaissance Poetry: A Collection of Shorter Poems from Skelton to Jonson*. John Williams, ed. University of Arkansas, 1990. *Faber Book of Nonsense Verse*. Geoffrey Grigson, ed. Faber and Faber, 1979. *Microsoft Encarta 2006 (DVD)*. Microsoft Corporation, 2006. *Poemhunter* (www.poemhunter.com). *The Chatto Book of Love Poetry*. John Fuller, ed. Chatto and Windus, 1990. *The Columbia Granger's Index to Poetry*. 11th ed. *The Columbia Granger's World of Poetry*, Columbia University Press, 2005 (http://www.columbiagrangers.org). *The Faber Book of Comic Verse*. Michael Roberts and Janet Adam Smith, eds. Faber and Faber, 1978. *The Oxford Book of Light Verse*. W.H. Auden, ed. Oxford University Press, 1938. *The Oxford Companion to English Literature*. 6th edition. Margaret Drabble, ed. Oxford University Press, 2000. *Wikipedia, the Free Encyclopedia* (http://en.wikipedia.org/wiki/Wikipedia).

WEEVER, JOHN (1576–1632)

Lancashire poet who left Queens College, Cambridge, without graduating. After touring the Continent, and settling in London, he became an authority on antiquitiesm. In 1631 he published a large volume titled *Ancient Funeral Monuments* (of Britain, Ireland and the Islands), dedicated to Charles I. Weever was buried in the church of St. James's, Clerkenwell, London. The majority of his poems are short epigrams with Latin titles. Epigram 22 in *Epigrammes in the Oldest Cut, and Newest Fashion* (1599) is a sonnet addressed to Shakespeare and was thought to have been a response to Shakespeare's *Romeo and Juliet*. He also wrote epigrams on Edmund Spenser's poverty and death, on Samuel Daniel, Michael Drayton, Ben Jonson, John Marston, and William Warner (see entries). Some of his other publications: *Faunus and Melliflora Or, the Original of Our English Satyres*, 1600 (a copy is held at Rutgers University Library, New Jersey). *The Mirror of Martyrs*, 1601 (a copy is held at Rutgers University Library, New Jersey). *The Whipping of the Satyre*, 1601. *Rochester Bridge*, 1887 (printed for the Kent Archæological Society by Mitchell and Hughes, London).

Sources: *Dictionary of National Biography*. Electronic Edition 1.1. Oxford University Press, 1997. *English Poetry: Author Search*. Chadwyck-Healey Ltd., 1995 (http://www.lib.utexas.edu:8080/search/epoetry/author.html). *The National Portrait Gallery* (www.npg.org.uk). *Stanford University Libraries and Academic Information Resources* (http://library.stanford.edu). *The Columbia Granger's Index to Poetry*. 11th ed. *The Columbia Granger's World of Poetry*, Columbia University Press, 2005 (http://www.columbiagrangers.org). *The Faber Book of Epigrams and Epitaphs*. Geoffrey Grigson, ed. Faber and Faber, 1977. *Wikipedia, the Free Encyclopedia* (http://en.wikipedia.org/wiki/Wikipedia).

WELLESLEY, DOROTHY VIOLET, DUCHESS OF WELLINGTON (1889–1956)

Born at White Waltham, near Maidenhead, Berkshire, the daughter of Robert Ashton, she was educated at home, and after her father's death her mother married in 1899 the tenth Earl of Scarbrough. Dorothy married Lord Gerald Wellesley (later 7th Duke of Wellington), in 1914. She was editor for Hogarth Press of the Hogarth *Living Poets* series, and was editor of *The Annual* in 1929. W.B. Yeats (see entry) greatly admired her work and he included many of her poems in the *Oxford Book of Modern Verse*. His *Letters on Poetry* to her were published in 1940, and one of his poems is "To Dorothy Wellesley." She lived much of her life at Sherfield Court (on the Hampshire-Berkshire border), then at Penns in the Rocks, Withyham, Sussex, where she died. She published more than ten books, including the biography of Sir George Goldie, founder of Nigeria (1934). Her autobiography, *Far Have I Traveled*, was published in 1952. Some of her poems: "April 1939," "As Lambs into the Pen," "Asian Desert," "Deserted House," "Lenin," "Maiden Castle," "Matrix," "Walled Garden."

Sources: *Dictionary of National Biography*. Electronic Edition 1.1. Oxford University Press, 1997. *Early Light: The Collected Poems of Dorothy Wellesley*. Hart-Davis, 1955. *The National Portrait Gallery* (www.npg.org.uk). *The Columbia Granger's Index to Poetry*. 11th ed. *The Columbia Granger's World of Poetry*, Columbia University Press, 2005 (http://www.columbiagrangers.org). *The Faber Book of Twentieth Century Verse*. John Heath-Stubbs and David Wright, eds. Faber and Faber, 1975. *The Oxford Book of Modern Verse, 1892–1935*. William Butler Yeats, ed. Oxford University Press, 1936. *The Oxford Companion to English Literature*. 6th edition. Margaret Drabble, ed. Oxford University Press, 2000. *Wikipedia, the Free Encyclopedia* (http://en.wikipedia.org/wiki/Wikipedia). *William Butler Yeats, "To Dorothy Wellesley"* (http://plagiarist.com/poetry/3440). *Women's Poetry of the 1930s: A Critical Anthology*. Jane Dowson, ed. Routledge, 1966.

WELLS, ROBERT (1947–)

(The information is from the Carcanet Press website.) Born in Oxford, he has worked as a woodman on Exmoor, a teacher in Italy and Iran, and in publishing. He now lives in France. *The Day and Other Poems* (2006) consists of short, highly wrought poems divided into four sections: the poet's experience as an Exmoor forester; a sequence set in the Sabine hills in central Italy; a theme of erotic friendship; and miscellany that mixes anecdote and satirical epigram with compacted memories of travel. His other publications: *The Winter's Task*, 1977. *Virgil's Georgics*, 1892. *Selected Poems*, 1986. *Theocritus's Idylls*, 1988. *Lusus*, 1999 (a collection of classical poems). Some of his poems: "After Haymaking," "The Alfred Jewel," "Derelict Landscape," "The Colonist," "Further on Down," "The Stream," "Sunrise."

Sources: *P.E.N. New Poetry I.* Robert Nye, ed. Quartet Books, 1986. *Some Contemporary Poets of Britain and Ireland: An Anthology.* Michael Schmidt, ed. Carcanet Press, 1983. *The Columbia Granger's Index to Poetry.* 11th ed. *The Columbia Granger's World of Poetry,* Columbia University Press, 2005 (http://www.columbiagrangers.org).

WELSTED, LEONARD (1688–1747)

Born at Abington, Northamptonshire, where his father was a clergyman, he was educated at Westminster School and at Trinity College, Cambridge, but left Cambridge without graduating to marry a daughter of Henry Purcell the musician (she died in 1724), and took a post in the office one of the secretaries of state. His second wife, Anna Maria, a remarkable beauty, was sister to Admiral Sir Hovenden Walker (who settled on a plantation in South Carolina). Welsted then worked as a government clerk and in 1731 was made one of the commissioners for managing the state lottery. He died at his official residence in the Tower of London. Welsted's first poem, "Apple-Pye," often wrongly attributed to William King (see entry), was written in 1704. Some of his publications: *The Duke of Marlborough's Arrival,* 1709. *An Ode on the Birth-Day of His Royal Highness the Prince of Wales,* 1716. *An Ode to the Honourable Major-General Wade,* 1726. *A Hymn to the Creator,* 1727. *The Works,* 1787. Some of his other poems: "Amintor and the Nightingale," "Of False Fame," "The Faultless Fair," "The Genius; an Ode," "To Zelinda."

Sources: *An Anthology of Eighteenth-century Satire: Grub Street.* Peter Heaney, ed. Edwin Mellen Press, 1995. *Dictionary of National Biography.* Electronic Edition, 1.1. *English Poetry: Author Search* (http://www.lib.utexas.edu:8080/search/epoetry/author.html). *Vietual American Biogrphies: Sir Hovenden Walker* (http://www.famousamericans.net/sirhovendenwalker/). *Stanford University Libraries and Academic Information Resources* (http://library.stanford.edu). *The Columbia Granger's Index to Poetry.* 11th ed. *The Columbia Granger's World of Poetry,* Columbia University Press, 2005 (http://www.columbiagrangers.org). *The New Oxford Book of Eighteenth Century Verse.* Roger Lonsdale, ed. Oxford University Press, 1984. *The New Oxford Book of Seventeenth Century Verse.* Alastair Fowler, ed. Oxford University Press, 1991.

THE WESLEY FAMILY, SAMUEL, SAMUEL, JOHN and CHARLES (1662–1791)

Samuel, 1662–1735

Born at Winterborn-Whitchurch, Dorset, the son of the vicar, he was educated at Newington Green, a private school where he was a friend of Daniel Defoe. He graduated B.A. from Exeter College, Oxford, in 1688, and was incorporated M.A. at Cambridge in 1694. While at Oxford he published a volume of verse, *Maggots: or, Poems on Several Subjects* (1685). Ordained as an Anglican priest, from 1695 until he died he was rector of Epworth in Lincolnshire. Most of his poetry and hymns were lost in a fire at the rectory in 1702. One hymn that survived, "Behold the Savior of Mankind," was set to music by Henry Purcell. He was buried in the churchyard at Epworth. Some of his poetry publications: *The Life of Our Blessed Lord and Savior Jesus Christ: An Heroic Poem,* 1693 (ten books). *Elegies,* 1695 (on the death of Mary Queen of England, and John Tillotson, late Archbishop of Canterbury). *An Epistle to a Friend Concerning Poetry,* 1700. *The History of the Old and New Testament, Attempted in Verse,* 1704. *Marlborough, or the Fate of Europe,* 1705. *Eupolis's Hymn to the Creator,* 1788.

Samuel the younger, 1691–1739

Born at Spitalfields, London, he was educated at Westminster school and graduated M.A. from Christ Church, Oxford, in 1718. He was a teacher at Westminster school, then master of Tiverton grammar school, Devonshire. He suffered from ill health, died suddenly at Tiverton and was buried in the churchyard. His *Poems on Several Occasions* (1736, enlarged edition, 1743, and reprinted 1808 and 1862) besides humorous pieces, contains several hymns of great beauty. His other publications: *The Song of the Three Children,* 1724. *The Battle of the Sexes,* 1724. *The Parish Priest,* 1732. *The Christian Poet,* 1735. *The Pig, and the Mastiff.* 1735. Some of his poems: "A Pindaricque on the Grunting of a Hog," "Epigram on Miltonicks," "From a Hint in the Minor Poets," "Hymn to God the Father," "On Two Soldiers Killing One Another for a Groat," "The Monument."

John, 1703–1791

He was born in Epworth Rectory, 1703, and was rescued from a fire there in 1709. He was admitted to Charterhouse School in London in 1714. He graduated B.A. from Christ Church, Oxford, in 1724 and M.A. in 1727; he was ordained a deacon in 1725 and elected fellow of Lincoln College, Oxford, 1726. He did missionary work with Samuel and Charles in Georgia 1735–1737. After a religious conversion at a Moravian meeting at Aldersgate Street, London, in 1738, he began outdoor preaching in 1739. The First Methodist Conference was held in 1744. He married Mary Vazeille in 1751 and they were separated in 1755. John traveled thousands of miles around Britain on horseback and by carriage, wrote or edited some 400 publications, and left behind a movement of about 70,000 members. He was buried in the churchyard of St. Giles, Camberwell, and a tablet in the Nave of Westminster Abbey commemorates John and Charles Wesley. He published 32 volumes of prose works; seven volumes of the *Methodist Book Concern*; 13 volumes of *The Poetical Works of John and Charles* (1868–1872); *Sermons and Notes* (in 20 parts) 1740–1789, and adapted the *Book of Common Prayer* for use by American Methodists. In his Watch Night service, he made use of a devotional prayer now generally known as the *Wesley Covenant Prayer,* perhaps his most famous contribution to Christian liturgy. He also translated many hymns from the German. Some of his original hymns/poems: "A Rule," "Courage," "Eternal Son, Eternal Love," "Father of All, Whose Powerful Voice," "How Happy is the Pilgrim's Lot!" "Servant of God, Well Done!" "The Acts of the Apostles," "The Comforter."

Charles 1707–1788

Born at Epworth, he was educated at Westminster school and Christ Church, Oxford, where he was one of the "Methodist" group of students. He graduated B.A. in 1730, M.A. in 1733, and was ordained in 1775 just before leaving with his brothers for Georgia. Like John, he experienced a profound religious conversion at the same Aldersgate meeting place, and like John, he traveled many miles on horseback, preaching the gospel. He was buried in the churchyard of St. Marylebone, London. Charles wrote more than 6000 hymns, of which 157 are included in the current *Methodist Hymns and Psalms.* His poetical works, including many not before published, are contained in 13 volumes, *Poetical Works of John and Charles Wesley,* edited by George Osborn (1868–1872). Some of his hymns/poems: "A Charge to Keep I Have," "Ah! Lovely Appearance of Death!" "Come, Thou Almighty King," "Easter Hymn," "For the Anniversary Day of One's Conversion," "Gentle Jesus Meek and Mild," "Jesus, Lover of My Soul," "Love Divine, All Loves Excelling," "The Horrible Decree."

Sources: *A Sacrifice of Praise: An Anthology of Christian Poetry in English from Caedmon to the Mid–Twentieth Century.* James H. Trott, ed. Cumberland House Publishing, 1999. *Encyclopædia Britannica Ultimate Reference Suite DVD,* 2006. *English Poetry: Author Search.* Chadwyck-Healey Ltd., 1995 (http://www.lib.utexas.edu:8080/search/epoetry/author.html). *Freedom's Lyre: or Psalms, Hymns, and Sacred Songs, for the Slave and His Friends.* Edwin F. Hatfield, ed. S.W. Benedict, 1840. *Hymns and Psalms: A Methodist and Ecumenical Hymn Book.* London: Methodist Publishing House, 1983. *John Wesley's 300th Anniversary. Key Dates* (http://www.wesley2003.org.uk/dates.htm). *Methodist Archives and Research Centre: Samuel Wesley, Father of the Wesleys* (http://gbgm-umc.org/UMW/Wesley/quiz/1b.stm). *Microsoft Encarta 2006* (DVD). Microsoft Corporation, 2006. *Poems One Line and Longer.* William Cole, ed. Grossman, 1973. *Stanford University Libraries and Academic Information Resources* (http://library.stanford.edu). *The Columbia Granger's Index to Poetry.* 11th ed. *The Columbia Granger's World of Poetry,* Columbia University Press, 2005 (http://www.columbia grangers.org). *The Cyber Hymnal* (http://www.cyberhymnal.org/index.htm). *The Home Book of Verse.* Burton Egbert Stevenson, ed. New York: Henry Holt and Company, 1953. *The Homes, Haunts and Friends of John Wesley. The Centenary Number of the Methodist Recorder.* London: Charles H Kelly, 1891. *The National Portrait Gallery* (www.npg.org.uk). *The New Oxford Book of Christian Verse.* Donald Davie, ed. Oxford University Press, 1981. *The New Oxford Book of Eighteenth Century Verse.* Roger Lonsdale, ed. Oxford University Press, 1984. *The Oxford Book of Children's Verse.* Iona Opie and Peter Opie, eds. Oxford University Press, 1973. *The Oxford Book of Christian Verse.* Lord David Cecil, ed. Oxford University Press, 1940. *The Oxford Book of Short Poems.* P.J. Kavanagh and James Michie, eds. Oxford University Press, 1985. *The Oxford Companion to English Literature.* 6th edition. Margaret Drabble, ed. Oxford University Press, 2000. *The Poetical Works of John and Charles Wesley* (12 volumes). G. Osborn, ed. Wesleyan-Methodist Conference, 1871. *The World's Great Religious Poetry.* Caroline Miles Hill, ed. Macmillan 1954. *Unity Hymns and Chorals.* William Channing Gannett, ed. Unity Publishing Company, 1911. *Very Bad Poetry.* Kathryn Petras and Ross Petras, ed. Vintage Books, 1997. *Wesley Centre Online, John Wesley's Christian Library.* Northwest Nazarene University, Nampa, Idaho, USA (http://wesley.nnu.edu/index.htm). *Wikipedia, the Free Encyclopedia* (http://en.wikipedia.org/wiki/Wikipedia) (See links at (http://www.raptureme.com/resource/wesley/john_wesley.html). *American Hymns Old and New. Vols. 1–2.* Albert Christ-Janer and Charles W. Hughes, eds. Columbia University Press, 1980. *Dictionary of National Biography.* Electronic Edition 1.1. Oxford University Press, 1997. "What's Left of Wesley's London." *Methodist Recorder* (pp. 9–12). Methodist Newspaper Co. Ltd., 122 Golden Lane, London, EC1Y 0TL. January 5, 2006.

WEST, ARTHUR GRAEME (1891–1917)

Born in Norfolk but raised in London, he was educated at Blundell's School, Tiverton, Devon, and at Baliol College, Oxford. He volunteered in 1915, but was rejected for a commission owing to poor eyesight. However, he enlisted in the ranks of the Public Schools Battalion in February in 1915, was sent to France in November, and was repeatedly in action. His poem "The Night Patrol," written in March 1916, makes him one of the early poets to write about front-line action from direct personal experience. He turned against the war and thought about deserting, but in August he was commissioned into the Oxfordshire and Buckinghamshire Light Infantry and rose to the rank of acting captain. His sadness at losing his religious faith is recorded in "The End of the Second Year." He was killed by a sniper's bullet near Bapaume, France. Some of his other poems: "'The Owl Abash'd,'" "God! How I hate you," "God! How I hate you, you young cheerful men!" "On reading ballads," "Seeing her off," "Spurned by the Gods," "Tea in the Garden," "The Last God," "The Night Patrol," "The Traveller."

Sources: *Men Who March Away: Poems of the First World War.* I.M. Parsons, ed. Viking Press, 1965. *Never Such Innocence: A New Anthology of Great War Verse.* Martin Stephen, ed. Buchan and Enright, 1988. *Poetry of the First World War.* Edward Hudson, ed. Wayland Publishers Ltd., 1988. *The Columbia Granger's Index to Poetry.* 11th ed. *The Columbia Granger's World of Poetry,* Columbia University Press, 2005 (http://www.columbiagrangers.org). *The Diary of a Dead Officer: Being the Posthumous Papers of Arthur Graeme West,* C.E.M. Joad, ed. Allen and Unwin, 1918. Reissued in 1991 by the Imperial War Museum with an introduction by Dominic Hibbard (http://eudaemonist. com/biblion/west/). *The Faber Book of War Poetry.* Kenneth Baker, ed. Faber and Faber, 1996. *The War Poets Association:, Arthur Graeme West* (http://www.warpoets.org/ conflicts/greatwar/west/).

WEST, VICTOR (1920–2002)

Born in Lambeth, and brought up in Whitstable, Kent, his interest in battles was sparked by a lecture he heard at the age of 10 on the catastrophic Gallipoli campaign of the First World War. He received a sound education at Simon Langton Grammar School, Canterbury. He enlisted in the King's Royal Rifle Corps in 1939, was captured in Crete, and spent the years from 1941 to 1945 in German prisoner-of-war camps. There he forged passes and ration books for escapers, gave anti-fascist pep talks, and began to write poetry, sometimes while restrained in handcuffs. He got into his stride as a poet in the late 1960s. His best work up to then was collected in his one full-length volume, *The Horses of Falaise* (1975 Salamander Imprint). Post-war, he taught at Bedfont Junior School, 400 yards away from Heathrow Airport's runway one. Some of his poems: "1926 — The General Strike," "Angk St — On the Run," "Easter at Howth —1939," "Joanna Southcott's Box," "Kossovo," "La Pneumonie," "Militancy," "Not Marked in History," "Noughts and Crosses," "Sign Here," "The Bateman Syndrome."

Sources: *Alan Brownjohn, Guardian Unlimited, Obituary. Monday March 25, 2002* (http://education.guardian. co.uk/obituary/story/0,12212,753444,00.html). *Liddel Hart Centre for Military Archives, King's College, London University* (http://www.kcl.ac.uk/lhcma/summary/we70- 001.shtml). *Victor West on the Poetry Express* (http://pages. britishlibrary.net/poetry.express/log/VW I.html).

WESTWOOD, THOMAS (1814–1888)

Born in Enfield, Middlesex, the son of Thomas Westwood, a respected businessman and a friend of

Charles Lamb (see entry), who introduced Thomas to many of his literary friends. From 1844, Westwood lived and worked in Belgium as director and secretary of the Tournay railway, spending leisure and money to the collection of a splendid library of works on angling. He was recognized in England as an authority, probably without rival, and published several major works on the subject. He died in Belgium. Some of his poetry publications: *Poems,* 1840. *Beads from a Rosary,* 1843. *The Burden of the Bell,* 1850. *Berries and Blossoms,* 1855. *Fishing Gossip,* 1865. *Foxglove Bells: A Book of Sonnets,* 1856. *The Sword of Kingship,* 1866. *The Quest of Sancgreall,* 1868 (the Holy Grail). *Gathered in the Gloaming,* 1881. *Twelve Sonnets and an Epilogue,* 1884. Some of his poems: "A Fireside Story," "Earth," "Little Bell," "Mine Host of The Golden Apple," "Night of Spring," "The Grief of the Loving," "The Quest of the Sancgreall," "The Voices at the Throne," "Under My Window."

Sources: *Dictionary of National Biography.* Electronic Edition 1.1. Oxford University Press, 1997. *English Poetry: Author Search.* Chadwyck-Healey Ltd., 1995 (http://www. lib.utexas.edu:8080/search/epoetry/author.html). *Golden Numbers.* Kate Douglas Wiggin and Nora Archibald Smith, eds. Doubleday, Doran, 1902. *King Arthur: History and Link.* (http://www.library.rochester.edu/camelot/ arthmenu.htm). *Our Holidays in Poetry.* Mildred P. Harrington and Josephine H. Thomas, eds. H.W. Wilson, 1929. *Sound and Sense: An Introduction to Poetry.* 6th edition. Harcourt Brace Jovanovich, 1982. *The Columbia Granger's Index to Poetry.* 11th ed. *The Columbia Granger's World of Poetry,* Columbia University Press, 2005 (http:// www.columbiagrangers.org). *The Home Book of Verse for Young Folks.* Burton Egbert Stevenson, ed. Holt, Rinehart and Winston, 1929. *Victorian Verse.* George MacBeth, ed. Penguin Books, 1986.

WHALLEY, THOMAS SEDGWICK (1746–1828)

Born at Cambridge, the son of John Whalley, doctor of divinity, master and regius professor of divinity of St. Peter's College, Cambridge, he graduated B.A. in 1767 and M.A. in 1774 from St. John's College, Cambridge. About 1770 he was ordained in the Anglican church. Edinburgh University created him doctor of divinity in 1808. He also held an appointment at Wells Cathedral, Somerset, though when he carried out his church duties is unclear. He lived for a time in the Crescent at Bath (one of the most sought-after localities in the city), where he entertained lavishly. He spent much of his time abroad, died at La Flèche in France, and was buried in the consecrated ground of the Roman Catholic Church. Anna Seward (see entry) addressed a poem to Sedgwick: *Alpine Scenery, A Poem, Addressed to the Rev. Thomas Sedgwick Whalley, During His Res-*

idence on the Continent, In 1785. His poetry publications: *Edwy and Edilda,* 1794. *Poems and Translations,* ?1797. *The Fatal Kiss,* 1781. *Kenneth and Fenella,* 1809. *Mont Blanc,* 1788. *Verses to Mrs. Siddons,* 1782.

Sources: *Dictionary of National Biography.* Electronic Edition 1.1. Oxford University Press, 1997. *English Poetry: Author Search.* Chadwyck-Healey Ltd., 1995 (http://www.lib.utexas.edu:8080/search/epoetry/author.html). *The National Portrait Gallery* (www.npg.org.uk). *Stanford University Libraries and Academic Information Resources* (http://library.stanford.edu).

WHETSTONE, GEORGE (?1544–?1587)

Probably born in London, he spent what money he had on the traditional wine, women and song, joined the Army in 1572, was commissioned to an English regiment and saw distinguished service in the war with Holland against Spain. In Holland he made the acquaintance of George Gascoigne and Thomas Churchyard (see entries), whose life experiences resembled his own. On his return to England, like his two friends, he turned to literature. In 1576 he collected his varied literary efforts into a volume which he entitled the *Rocke of Regard,* a vast poetical work divided into four parts (1) *The Castle of Delight,* described the wretched end of wanton and dissolute living; (2) *The Garden of Extravagance,* describing the many sweet flowers (or rather fancies) of honest love; (3) *The Arbour of Virtue,* where slander is highly punished, and virtuous ladies and gentlewomen worthily commended; (4) *The Orchard of Repentance,* describing the miseries that follow gambling and quarrelling and the fall of wasteful living. In 1585 he returned to the army in Holland and was present at the Battle of Zutphen in 1586. In 1578 he wrote *Promos and Cassandra,* a play in rhymed verse.

Sources: *Dictionary of National Biography.* Electronic Edition, 1.1. *English Poetry: Author Search* (http://www.lib.utexas.edu:8080/search/epoetry/author.html). *Whetstone's Rock of Regard.* George Whetstone. Collier Reprints, ?1870.

WHITE, GILBERT (1720–1793)

The son of a barrister, he was born at the parsonage of Selborne, Hampshire, where his grandfather was vicar. His education was at the grammar school at Basingstoke, then kept by Thomas Warton, the elder (see entry). He graduated B.A. from Oriel College, Oxford, in 1743, and was made fellow in 1744. He was ordained in 1751 and had a number of posts before becoming curate at Selborne, where he remained until he died. White's passion was natural history, and his *Calendar of Flora and the Garden* (1765) was followed by the *Naturalist's Journal* (1795). The *Natural History and Antiquities of Selborne* (1789) was the first work on natural history to attain the status of an English classic. His house in Selborne, the Wakes, now contains the Gilbert White Museum, as well as the Oates Memorial Museum, commemorating Lawrence Oates, the British Antarctic explorer. White was buried on the north side of the chancel of Selborne Church. Some of his poems: "A Shower of Cobwebs," "On the Dark, Still, Dry, Warm Weather," "The Naturalist's Summer-Evening Walk," "A Harvest Scene," "The Invitation to Selborne."

Sources: *Dictionary of National Biography.* Electronic Edition 1.1. Oxford University Press, 1997. *Encyclopædia Britannica Ultimate Reference Suite DVD,* 2006. *Microsoft Encarta* 2006 (DVD). Microsoft Corporation, 2006. *Poem hunter* (www.poemhunter.com). *The Columbia Granger's Index to Poetry.* 11th ed. *The Columbia Granger's World of Poetry,* Columbia University Press, 2005 (http://www.columbiagrangers.org). *The New Oxford Book of Eighteenth Century Verse.* Roger Lonsdale, ed. Oxford University Press, 1984. *The Oxford Companion to English Literature.* 6th edition. Margaret Drabble, ed. Oxford University Press, 2000.

WHITE, HENRY KIRKE (1785–1806)

Born in Nottingham, where his father was a butcher, he worked briefly as a stocking weaver before being articled to a lawyer. He had some poems published in the *Monthly Preceptor* and the *Monthly Mirror.* To raise money to go to university, in 1803 he published *Clifton Grove,* a sketch in verse, dedicated to the Duchess of Devonshire. Various people helped him and he entered St. John's College, Cambridge, in 1805 with the aim of becoming a priest. He distinguished himself in classics, being top at the general college examination at the end of the first term and first of his year at the end of the summer term of 1806. But his health was failing; consumption threatened and he died in his college rooms in October. Robert Southey (see entry) compiled *The Remains of Henry Kirke White—With an Account of His Life* into two volumes in 1807. Some of his poems: "A Hymn for Family Worship," "Addressed to H. Fuseli," "Christmas Day," "Solitude," "The Christiad: A Divine Poem," "The Wandering Boy," "To Contemplation," "To the Harvest Moon."

Sources: *Dictionary of National Biography.* Electronic Edition 1.1. Oxford University Press, 1997. *English Poetry: Author Search.* Chadwyck-Healey Ltd., 1995 (http://www.lib.utexas.edu:8080/search/epoetry/author.html). *Five Sonnets of Henry Kirke White: Sonnet Central* (http://www.sonnets.org/white.htm). *The Columbia Granger's Index to Poetry.* 11th ed. *The Columbia Granger's World of Poetry,* Columbia University Press, 2005 (http://www.columbiagrangers.org). *The National Portrait Gallery* (www.npg.org.uk). *The Oxford Companion to English Literature.* 6th edition. Margaret Drabble, ed. Oxford University Press, 2000. *The Poetical Works of Henry Kirke White and James Grahame.* Nichol, 1856.

WHITEHEAD, CHARLES (1804–1862)

The son of a wine merchant, he was born in London and began life as a clerk in a mercantile house, but soon adopted literature as his profession. In 1831 he published "The Solitary," a poem that won the approval of Professor Wilson in the magazine *Noctes Ambrosianæ*, and of other critics of eminence. *The Solitary and Other Poems* was published in 1849. He also wrote *Lives and Exploits of English Highwaymen* (1834), and *The Autobiography of Jack Ketch* (1834) (a burlesque biography of the Newgate hangman, who was, himself, was hanged in 1718 for murder); a blank-verse drama, and *The Cavalier*, produced at the Haymarket Theatre in 1836. He recommended Charles Dickens (see entry) to the publishers Chapman and Hall; *The Pickwick Papers* (1836–1837) was the result. He descended into drunkenness, went to Australia, where he had some success, but died miserably in a Melbourne hospital and was buried in a pauper's grave. Some of his poems: "A Summer Storm," "My Gentle Friend, Last Refuge of a Soul," "Night," "Oft When I Lie Me Down to Rest at Night," "The Lamp," "The Riddle of Life," "The Solitary."

Sources: *Dictionary of National Biography.* Electronic Edition 1.1. Oxford University Press, 1997. *English Poetry: Author Search.* Chadwyck-Healey Ltd., 1995 (http://www.lib.utexas.edu:8080/search/epoetry/author.html). *Great Books Online* (www.bartleby.com). *Stanford University Libraries and Academic Information Resources* (http://library.stanford.edu). *The Columbia Granger's Index to Poetry.* 11th ed. *The Columbia Granger's World of Poetry,* Columbia University Press, 2005 (http://www.columbiagrangers.org). *The Oxford Book of English Verse, 1250–1918.* Sir Arthur Quiller-Couch, ed. (New edition, revised and enlarged, Oxford University Press, 1939. *The Oxford Book of Regency Verse 1798–1837.* H.S. Milford, ed. Oxford University Press, 1928. *The Oxford Companion to English Literature.* 6th edition. Margaret Drabble, ed. Oxford University Press, 2000.

WHITEHEAD, WILLIAM (1715–1785)

Born at Cambridge, where his father was a baker, he was educated at Winchester College and Clare Hall, Cambridge, from where he gradated B.A. (1739) and M.A. (1743); he was elected a fellow in 1742. He became tutor to the young Viscount Villiers, son of the Earl of Jersey, abandoning his fellowship, which would have necessitated taking holy orders. From 1754 to 1756 he accompanied Lord Villiers and Lord Nuneham, the eldest son of the Earl of Harcourt, on a tour of the Continent. Whitehead succeeded playwright and poet Colley Cibber as poet laureate in 1757 after Thomas Gray declined the honor. He died in London. Several of his plays were performed at Drury Lane, with David Garrick in the lead role. His poetry publications: *The Dan-*

ger of Writing Verse, 1741. *Creusa, Queen of Athens,* 1754. *A Charge to the Poets,* 1762. *The School for Lovers,* 1762. *A Trip to Scotland,* 1770. Some of his poems: "Ann Boleyn to Henry the Eighth," "Fatal Constancy," "Hymn to Venus," "Inscription, For a Cold Bath," "The Answer," "The Youth and the Philosopher, A Fable," "To Mr. Garrick."

Sources: *Dictionary of National Biography.* Electronic Edition 1.1. Oxford University Press, 1997. *Encyclopædia Britannica Ultimate Reference Suite DVD,* 2006. *English Poetry: Author Search.* Chadwyck-Healey Ltd., 1995 (http://www.lib.utexas.edu:8080/search/epoetry/author.html). *Microsoft Encarta* 2006 (DVD). Microsoft Corporation, 2006. *The National Portrait Gallery* (www.npg.org.uk). *Plays and Poems, by William Whitehead,* 2 Volumes (no publisher), 1774. *The Columbia Granger's Index to Poetry.* 11th ed. *The Columbia Granger's World of Poetry,* Columbia University Press, 2005 (http://www.columbiagrangers.org). *The Oxford Book of Satirical Verse.* Geoffrey Grigson, ed. Oxford University Press, 1980. *The Oxford Companion to English Literature.* 6th edition. Margaret Drabble, ed. Oxford University Press, 2000.

WHITNEY, GEOFFREY and ISABELLA

Geoffrey, the brother, ?1548–?1601

Born at, or near, Nantwich, Cheshire, he was educated at the universities of Oxford and Cambridge, but appears not to have graduated. In 1580 he was under-bailiff of Great Yarmouth, but for how long is not certain. During this time he had contact with many scholars in the Netherlands, and when he left Yarmouth he moved to Leyden (Leiden) where, in 1586, he became a student in its newly founded university. In 1586 he published *Choice of Emblems,* a book of 248 poems generally one or more stanzas of six lines. Some are original, others are drawn from other poets. He died unmarried in Cheshire. His only other known works are: *An Account in Latin of a Visit to Scratby Island, off Great Yarmouth,* 1580, and some verses in Dousa's *Odæ Britannicæ,* Leyden, 1586. Some of his Latin-titled poems: "Desidiam Abiiciendam," "Homines Voluptatibus Transformantur," "Iudicium Paridis," "Mortui Diuitiæ," "Noli Altum Sapere," "Quod in Te Est, Prome," "Ridicula Ambitio."

Isabella, the sister, dates unknown

Isabella appears to have had another brother with the initials B.W. Although little is known of her life, she was probably born in the late 1540s and appears to have been in service in London. She is believed to be the first professional female poet in England and the first woman to publish a collection of original poetry. Whitney was a pioneering author, for she produced marketable poetry designed to appeal to public taste at a time when devotional literature and translations of men's work was considered to be the only proper literary work for women. Much of her poetry was quite risky for the times, as she often wrote about gender issues and the liberation of women from the power of male dominance. Her publications: *The Copy of a Letter, Lately Written in Meter by a Young Gentlewoman: To Her Unconstant Lover* (1567). *A Sweet Nosegay or Pleasant Posy: Containing a Hundred and Ten Philosophical Flowers* (1573). Some of her poems: "A Carefull Complaynt By the Vnfortunate Auctor," "A Farewell to the Reader," "A Soueraigne Receipt," "The Auctor to the Reader," "The Maner of Her Wyll, & What She Left to London," "To Her Brother B.W."

Sources: *Biography and Works of Isabella Whitney* (http://www.users.muohio.edu/clarkjd/harper98.html). *Dictionary of National Biography.* Electronic Edition 1.1. Oxford University Press, 1997. *Early Modern Women Poets (1520–1700).* Jane Stevenson and Peter Davidson, eds. Oxford University Press, 2001. *Elizabethan Lyrics.* Norman Ault, ed. William Sloane Associates, 1949. *English Poetry: Author Search.* Chadwyck-Healey Ltd., 1995 (http://www.lib.utexas.edu:8080/search/epoetry/author.html). *Geoffrey Whitney's Mottos* (http://www.mun.ca/alciato/whit/w001.html). *Isabella Whitney, a Sweet Nosegay* (http://ise.uvic.ca/Library/SLT/literature/whitney.html). Isabella Whitney, Mary Sidney and Amelia Lanyer: Renaissance Women Poets. Penguin Books Ltd. (Penguin Classics), 2001. *Life and Works of Isabella Whitney* (http://ise.uvic.ca/Library/SLT/literature/whitney.html). *The Columbia Granger's Index to Poetry.* 11th ed. *The Columbia Granger's World of Poetry,* Columbia University Press, 2005 (http://www.columbiagrangers.org). *The Penguin Book of Renaissance Verse 1509–1659.* David Norbrook, ed. Penguin Books, 1992. *To Her Cousin, F.W., Isabella Whitney.* Erin M. Harper, ed. (http://www.users.muohio.edu/clarkjd/harper98.html).

WHYTEHEAD, THOMAS (1815–1843)

He was born at Thormanby in the North Riding of Yorkshire, the son of a clergyman who died young. His education was at grammar school and at St. John's College, Cambridge, where he won several poetry prizes. He graduated B.A. in 1837 and M.A. in 1840. He was classical lecturer at Clare College, Oxford, from 1838, but was ordained in 1839 as curate of Freshwater in the Isle of Wight. During 1841 he composed an ode for the installation of the Duke of Northumberland as chancellor of Cambridge University, which was set to music by Thomas Attwood Walmisley. He set out as a missionary to New Zealand in 1841, but died soon after arrival. Almost his last act was to translate the hymn "Glory to Thee, My God This Night" into Maori rhyming verse (written by Ken, Thomas, see entry). His poetry publications: *The Death of the Duke of Gloucester*, 1835. *The Empire of the Sea*, 1836. *Latin and Greek Epigrams*, 1836. *Poems*, 1842. Some of his other poems: "Last of Creation's Days," "Resting from his work today," "Sabbath of the Saints of Old."

Sources: *Dictionary of National Biography.* Electronic Edition 1.1. Oxford University Press, 1997. *The Cyber Hymnal* (http://www.cyberhymnal.org/index.htm). *The Hymnal [of the Protestant Episcopal Church in the USA].* "Resting from his work today" by Thomas Whytehead. (http://www.ccel.org/ccel/anonymous/eh1916.h165.html).

WICKHAM, ANNA (1884–1947)

Edith Alice Mary Harper was born in Wimbledon, London, and brought up mostly in Brisbane and Sydney, Australia. Her pen name "Wickham" was after a Brisbane street; and "John Oland" (for her first collection) alludes to the Jenolan Caves in New South Wales. She returned to London in 1904 to study singing at what is now the Royal Academy of Dramatic Art, then was coached in Paris by Jean de Reszke, the Polish tenor. In 1906 she married Patrick Hepburn, a London solicitor and astronomer; he died in 1929. She wrote prolifically and her poetry was more popular in America and France than in Britain. Her poems reflect her struggle to combine being an artist with wife and mother. Some of her publications: *Songs of John Oland*, 1911. *The Contemplative Quarry*, 1915. *The Man with a Hammer*, 1916. *The Little Old House*, 1921. *Thirty-six New Poems*, 1936. *Selected Poems*, 1971. Some of her poems: "Abdication," "Divorce," "King Alfred and the Peasant Woman," "Meditation at Kew," "Reality," "Ship near Shoals," "The Affinity," "The Contemplative Quarry," "The Singer."

Sources: *Biography of Anna Wickham* (http://www.madpoetry.org/wickham.html). *The Columbia Granger's Index to Poetry.* 11th ed. *The Columbia Granger's World of Poetry,* Columbia University Press, 2005 (http://www.columbiagrangers.org). *The Contemplative Quarry and the Man with a Hammer by Anna Wickham.* Harcourt, Brace, and Company, 1921. *The Home Book of Modern Verse.* Burton Egbert Stevenson, ed. Henry Holt, 1953. *The Norton Anthology of Literature by Women: The Tradition in English.* Sandra M. Gilbert and Susan Guber, eds. W.W. Norton, 1985. *The Oxford Companion to English Literature.* 6th edition. Margaret Drabble, ed. Oxford University Press, 2000. *The Writings of Anna Wickham: Free Woman and Poet.* Virago Press Ltd., 1984. *Wikipedia, the Free Encyclopedia* (http://en.wikipedia.org/wiki/Wikipedia). *Women's Poetry of the 1930s: A Critical Anthology.* Jane Dowson, ed. Routledge, 1966.

WICKS, SUSAN (1947–)

Born in Kent, she read French at the Universities of Hull and Sussex, and wrote a Ph.D. thesis on André Gide (French writer, 1869–1951). She has lived and worked in France, Ireland and America and has taught at University College, Dublin, and the University of Kent. She was included in the Poetry Society's "New Generation Poets" promotion in 1994. Her short memoir, *Driving My Father,* (1995) is an account of her relationship with her increasingly dependent father following her mother's death in 1992. Her novels are *The Key* (1997), the story of a middle-aged woman haunted by the memory of a former lover, and *Little Thing* (1998), about a young woman living in France adjusting to life with a new baby. Her poetry publications: *Singing Underwater*, 1992 (which won the Aldeburgh Poetry Festival Prize). *Open Diagnosis*, 1994. *The Clever Daughter*, 1996 (short listed for both the T.S. Eliot and Forward prizes). *Night Toad: New and Selected Poems*, 2003. Some of her poems: "Buying Fish," "Joy," "Knot," "Moderato," "On Re-recording Mozart," "Protected Species," "Rain Dance," "Stiltwalker," "The Clever Daughter," "Voice."

Sources: *British Council Arts* (http://www.contemporarywriters.com). *Emergency Kit: Poems for Strange Times.* Jo Shapcott and Matthew Sweeney, eds. Faber and Faber, 1996. *Making for Planet Alice: New Women Poets.* Maura Dooley, ed. Bloodaxe Books, 1997. *Parents: An Anthology of Poems by Women Writers.* Myra Schneider and Dilys Wood, eds. Enitharmon Press, 2000. *The Columbia Granger's Index to Poetry.* 11th ed. *The Columbia Granger's World of Poetry,* Columbia University Press, 2005 (http://www.columbiagrangers.org). *The Oxford Book of Sonnets.* John Fuller, ed. Oxford University Press, 2000.

WILD (WYLDE), ROBERT (1609–1679)

Born in St. Ives, Huntingdonshire, where his father was a shoemaker, he graduated B.A. (1636), and M.A. (1639) from St. John's College, Cambridge, and B.D. (1642) and D.D. (1660) from Oxford University. He was inducted into the living of Aynhoe, Northamptonshire, in 1646, but his non-conformist theology caused him to be ejected from his living in 1662, after which he was supported by friends. He died of a stroke. He had the reputation of being a wit, and in 1689 he wrote the comedy the *Benefice.* He wrote about many subjects, including the terrible sport of cock fighting (1660). Some of his publications: *The Grateful Nonconformist*, 1665. *Iter Boreale*, 1668. *Upon the Rebuilding the City*, 1670. *Dr. Wild's Humble Thanks*, 1672. *Poetica Licentia*, 1672. *A Panegyrique Humbly Addrest to the Kings Most Excellent Majesty*, 1673. *Oliver Cromwell's Ghost*, 1678. *Exclamation Against Popery*, 1678. *Dr. Wild's Last Legacie*, 1679. *Dr. Wild's Poem*, 1679. Some of his poems: "Alas Poore Scholler, Whither Wilt Thou Goe," "An Epitaph for a Godly Man's Tomb," "On His Preaching," "Sonnet — To the Mocking-Bird."

Sources: *Anthology of Poems on Affairs of State: Augustan Satirical Verse, 1660–1714.* George de F. Lord, ed. Yale University Press, 1975. *Dictionary of National Biography.* Electronic Edition 1.1. Oxford University Press, 1997. *English Poetry: Author Search.* Chadwyck-Healey Ltd., 1995 (http://www.lib.utexas.edu:8080/search/epoetry/author.html). *Stanford University Libraries and Academic Information Resources* (http://library.stanford.edu). *The Colum-*

bia Granger's Index to Poetry. 11th ed. *The Columbia Granger's World of Poetry,* Columbia University Press, 2005 (http://www.columbiagrangers.org). *The Faber Book of Epigrams and Epitaphs.* Geoffrey Grigson, ed. Faber and Faber, 1977. *The Penguin Book of Renaissance Verse 1509–1659.* David Norbrook, ed. Penguin Books, 1992.

WILDE, LADY JANE and OSCAR (1826–1900)

Lady Jane, the mother, 1826–1896

Jane Francisca Elgee, the daughter of an Episcopalian clergyman, was born at Wexford, Ireland, and in 1851 she married Sir William Robert Wills Wilde (1815–1876), an English surgeon. Lady Jane contributed Irish patriotic prose and verse to the *Nation* under the pseudonym "Speranza" until its suppression for sedition in 1848. In 1879, following the death of her husband, Lady Jane left Dublin for London, where she was a central figure of the circle of Irish writers. She contributed poems and articles to periodicals, including *The Woman's World,* of which Oscar was the editor in 1887–1889. She died while her son was in prison and was buried in Kensal Green cemetery, London. Her contribution to Irish literature is enormous. She published books on myths and legends, charms and superstitions, and a book on social studies. Some of her poems: "A Lament for the Potato," "An Appeal to Ireland," "Dedication: To Ireland," "The Brothers," "The Faithless Shepherds," "The Famine Year," "Thekla: A Swedish Saga," "'Tis Not Upon Earth."

Oscar, the son, 1854–1900

Oscar O'Flahertie Wills Wilde, the younger son, was born in Dublin and educated at Portora royal school, Enniskillen, and at Trinity College, Dublin (1873–1874). There he won the Berkeley gold medal with an essay on the Greek comic poets. In 1878 he graduated B.A. from Magdalen College, Oxford, where he studied classics. In 1882 he toured the United States, lecturing two hundred times on "Æsthetic Philosophy" in New York, Boston, and Chicago. In the period between his marriage in 1884 and 1895, he wrote many plays, including *The Ideal Husband* (1895) and *The Importance of Being Ernest* (1895); a novel, *The Picture of Dorian Gray* (1891); and *Happy Prince and Other Tales* (1888), a book of fairy stories. His love relationship with Alfred Lord Douglas (see entry) resulted in his being convicted of homosexuality and sent to prison for two years in 1895. His experience inspired *The Ballad of Reading Gaol* (1898), written in France, where he died. His *De Profundus* (1905) was by way of a justification for his life. He is commemorated in the Rose Window of Westminster Abbey. Some of his poems: "Ballade De Marguerite," "Louis Napoleon," "Magdalen

Walks," "Ravenna," "The Dole of the King's Daughter," "The Grave of Shelley," "Wasted Days."

Sources: *An Anthology of World Poetry*. Mark Van Doren, ed. Reynal and Hitchcock, Inc., 1936. *Biography of Lady Jane Francesca Wilde*. http://home.arcor.de/oscar. wilde/biography/speranza.htm). *Complete Poetry of Oscar Wilde*. Isobel Murray, ed. Oxford University Press, 1997. *De Profundis by Oscar Wilde* (http://www.upword.com/ wilde/de_profundis.html). *Dictionary of National Biography*. Electronic Edition 1.1. Oxford University Press, 1997. *Encyclopædia Britannica Ultimate Reference Suite DVD*, 2006. *Microsoft Encarta* 2006 (DVD). Microsoft Corporation, 2006. *Modern British Poetry*. 7th rev. ed. Louis Untermeyer, ed. Harcourt, Brace, 1962. *Obituary of Oscar Wilde: The Times, December 1, 1900* (http://www.the-times.co.uk/). *Oscar Wilde's Last Stand*. Philip Hoare, Arcade Publishing, 1998. *Poems by Speranza (Lady Wilde)*. M.H. Gill and Son, Ltd., 1907. *The Columbia Granger's Index to Poetry*. 11th ed. *The Columbia Granger's World of Poetry*, Columbia University Press, 2005 (http://www. columbiagrangers.org). *The Columbia Granger's Index to Poetry*. 11th ed (http://www.columbiagrangers.org). *The Making of a Poem: A Norton Anthology of Poetic Forms*. Mark Strand and Eavan Boland, eds. W.W. Norton, 2000. *The National Portrait Gallery* (www.npg.org.uk). *Westminster Abbey Official Guide* (no date). *Words of a Woman: A Website for Poems by Women* (http://www.photoaspects. com/lilip/wilde.shtml).

WILKIE, WILLIAM (1721–1772)

The "Scottish Homer" was born at Echlin, parish of Dalmeny, Midlothian, the son of a farmer, and educated at the local parish school and Edinburgh University. Licensed as a preacher of the Church of Scotland in 1745, he became the incumbent of Ratho, Midlothian, in 1746. In 1759 he was appointed professor of natural philosophy at St. Andrews University, which conferred on him the honorary degree of D.D. in 1766. After settling in St. Andrews, he purchased some acres of land and resumed his farming occupation, in which he succeeded so well as to leave at his death at St. Andrews property to the amount of £3000. His two publications were *The Epigoniad* (1769), a poem in nine books, in the style of Homer's *Iliad*, dealing with the Epigoni, sons of the seven heroes who fought against Thebes; and a collection of sixteen *Moral Fables, in Verse, 1768*. Some of his fables/poems: "The Ape, the Parrot, and the Jackdaw," "The Boy and the Rainbow," "The Crow and the Other Birds," "The Grasshopper and the Glow-Worm," "The Lover and His Friend," "The Muse and the Shepherd."

Sources: *Dictionary of National Biography*. Electronic Edition 1.1. Oxford University Press, 1997. *English Poetry: Author Search*. Chadwyck-Healey Ltd., 1995 (http://www. lib.utexas.edu:8080/search/epoetry/author.html). *Significant and Famous Scots* (http://www.electricscotland. com/history/men/wilkie_william.htm). *Stanford University Libraries and Academic Information Resources* (http://li

brary.stanford.edu). *The Columbia Granger's Index to Poetry*. 11th ed. *The Columbia Granger's World of Poetry*, Columbia University Press, 2005 (http://www.columbia grangers.org). *The Oxford Companion to English Literature*. 6th edition. Margaret Drabble, ed. Oxford University Press, 2000.

WILLIAMS, SIR CHARLES HANBURY (1709–1757)

Born in Pontypool, Glamorganshire, Wales — where his father was the owner of an ironworks — he was educated at Eton College. After the grand tour and marriage to a wealthy heiress, he was elected member of Parliament for Monmouthshire upon the death of his father in 1734, and continued to represent the county to 1747. From 1742 to 1747 he was lord lieutenant of Herefordshire. he was created a Knight of the Bath in 1744, and from 1746 he was a diplomat and saw service in Italy and Germany. In Russia, the treaty he negotiated between England and Russia was revoked, on account of strong protests from Prussia. The disillusioned Williams retired to his estate at Coldbrook Park, Pontypool, where he committed suicide. Some of his poems: "A Lamentable Case," "An Ode on Miss Harriet Hanbury at Six Years Old," "An Ode to the Duke of Argyll," "Come, Chloe, and Give Me Sweet Kisses," "Isabella; or, the Morning," "Orpheus and Hecate, An Ode," "The Country Girl," "The Heroes: A New Ballad," "The Statesman."

Sources: *A Collection of Poems, Principally Consisting of the Most Celebrated Pieces of Sir Charles Hanbury Williams* (no publisher), 1763. *An Uninhibited Treasury of Erotic Poetry*. Louis Untermeyer, ed. Dial Press, 1963. *Dictionary of National Biography*. Electronic Edition 1.1. Oxford University Press, 1997. *English Poetry: Author Search*. Chadwyck-Healey Ltd., 1995 (http://www.lib.utexas.edu: 8080/search/epoetry/author.html). *The National Portrait Gallery* (www.npg.org.uk). *Stanford University Libraries and Academic Information Resources* (http://library.stan ford.edu). *The Columbia Granger's Index to Poetry*. 11th ed. *The Columbia Granger's World of Poetry*, Columbia University Press, 2005 (http://www.columbiagrangers.org). *The New Oxford Book of Eighteenth Century Verse*. Roger Lonsdale, ed. Oxford University Press, 1984. *The Poetical Works of Sir William Jones*. Thomas Park, ed. J. Sharpe, 1808.

WILLIAMS, CHARLES WALTER STANSBY (1886–1945)

Born in London, he was educated at St. Albans School and at University College, London, but, too poor to continue his studies, he left without graduating and became a proofreader at Oxford University Press from 1908 until his death at Oxford. In 1912 he published his first book of verse, *Silver Stair*, and went on to produce over thirty volumes of poetry, plays, literary criticism, fiction, biography, and theological argument. His fantasy novels include

War in Heaven (1930), the *Place of the Lion* (1931), *Descent into Hell* (1937), and *All Hallows' Eve* (1945). His Arthurian poems, particularly the volumes *Taliessin Through Logres* (1938) and *The Region of the Summer Stars* (1944), are considered his best poetic work. He belonged to the Order of the Golden Dawn (later the Fellowship of the Rosy Cross), a hermetic secret society which included members such as W.B. Yeats and Aleister Crowley (see entries). Some of his poems: "Arthur and the Pope," "From a Walking Song," "The Advent of Galahad," "The Return of Bors," "The Taking of Camelot," "The Throne and Councils of Arthur," "The Vision of the Empire."

Sources: *Charles Williams.* David Llewellyn Dodds, ed. The Boydell Press, 1991. *Dictionary of National Biography.* Electronic Edition 1.1. Oxford University Press, 1997. *The Book of a Thousand Poems: A Family Treasury.* J. Murray Macbain, ed. Peter Bedrick Books, 1983. *The Columbia Granger's Index to Poetry.* 11th ed. *The Columbia Granger's World of Poetry,* Columbia University Press, 2005 (http://www.columbiagrangers.org). *The Oxford Companion to English Literature.* 6th edition. Margaret Drabble, ed. Oxford University Press, 2000.

WILLIAMS, EDWARD (1747–1826)

Welsh bard, known as "Iolo Morgannwg" (Welsh for "Ned of Glamorgan") was born at Penon, Glamorganshire, the son of a stone mason. Poor health limited his education but with his mother's help he made up for his lack of schooling, and from 1770 to 1781 he was journeyman stone mason. On returning to Wales he married and took to land surveying, living at Flemingston in the vale of Glamorgan. From there he made long expeditions, always on foot, in search of manuscripts relating to Welsh history. He died at Flemingston and was buried there. He founded the first *Gorsedd* (community of bards) in 1792, at Primrose Hill, London. He also authored fairly substantial works (most of which are now considered forgeries) claiming that the ancient druidic tradition had survived intact in Wales, despite persecution from the Romans, Christianity, and Elizabeth Tudor. Among his writings was *Cyfrinach Beirdd Ynys Prydain,* or *The Mystery of the Bards of the Isle of Britain* (1829), a treatise on Welsh metrics. Some of his poems: "In the Welsh Manner," "My Pet Goldfish," "Stanzas Written in London in 1773," "The Happy Farmer," "The Poet's Arbour in the Birchwood."

Sources: *Anglo-Welsh Poetry, 1480–1980.* Raymond Garlick and Roland Mathias, eds. Poetry Wales Press, 1984. *Anglo-Welsh Poetry, 1480–1990.* Raymond Garlick and Roland Mathias, eds. Poetry Wales Press, 1993. *Biography of Edward Williams.* http://www.maryjones.us/jce/iolo.html). *Dictionary of National Biography.* Electronic Edition 1.1. Oxford University Press, 1997. *Druid's Prayer* (En-

glish translation) (http://en.wikipedia.org/wiki/Druid%27s_Prayer). *In the Welsh Manner by Edward William* (http://www.sonnets.org/williams.htm). *Pet Poems.* Robert Fisher, ed. Faber and Faber, 1989. *The Columbia Granger's Index to Poetry.* 11th ed. *The Columbia Granger's World of Poetry,* Columbia University Press, 2005 (http://www.columbiagrangers.org). *Wikipedia, the Free Encyclopedia* (http://en.wikipedia.org/wiki/Wikipedia).

WILLIAMS, HELEN MARIA (1762–1827)

Born in London of a Welsh army officer father (who died when Anna was a child) and a Scottish mother, she was brought up in Berwick-on-Tweed, Northumbria. In 1788 she went over to France and lived there for most of her life. During the Rein of Terror she and her family were confined in the Luxembourg prison, where she worked on translations of French language works into English. She died in Paris and was buried in Père-Lachaise. She wrote novels, volumes of letters, as well as translations and poetry. One of William Wordsworth's poems is "Sonnet on Seeing Miss Helen Maria Williams Weep at a Tale of Distress." Some of her publications: *Edwin and Eltruda, A Legendary Tale,* 1782. *Ode on the Peace,* 1783. *Poems,* 1786. *Poem on the Bill Lately Passed for Regulating the Slave Trade,* 1788. *The Bastille, A Vision,* 1790. *Poems on Various Subjects,* 1823. Some of her poems: "An Address to Poetry," "An American Tale," "An Epistle to Dr. Moore," "Euphelia; an Elegy," "My Steadfast Heart," "Paraphrases from Scripture," "Queen Mary's Complaint," "The Bastille, A Vision."

Sources: *Dictionary of National Biography.* Electronic Edition 1.1. Oxford University Press, 1997. *Helen Maria Williams: Poems, 1786.* Woodstock Books, 1994. *Romantic Women Poets: An Anthology.* Duncan Wu, ed. Blackwell Publishers, 1997. *The Columbia Granger's Index to Poetry.* 11th ed. *The Columbia Granger's World of Poetry,* Columbia University Press, 2005 (http://www.columbiagrangers.org). The National Portrait Gallery (www.npg.org.uk). *The New Oxford Book of Romantic Period Verse.* Jerome J. McGann. Oxford University Press, 1993. *The Oxford Companion to English Literature.* 6th edition. Margaret Drabble, ed. Oxford University Press, 2000. *Unity Hymns and Chorals.* William Channing Gannett, ed. Unity Publishing Company, 1911.

WILLIAMS, HUGO MORDUANT (1942–)

Born in Windsor, son of the actor and playwright Hugh Williams, he grew up in Sussex and was educated at Eton College. He has spent his working life in journalism: he worked on the *London Magazine* from 1961 to 1970; writes a column in the *Times Literary Supplement;* has been poetry editor and TV critic on the *New Statesman,* theatre critic on the *Sunday Correspondent,* film critic for *Harper's and*

Queen; and a writer on popular music for *Punch* magazine. He has been a freelance journalist since 1995 and lives in London. Soon after leaving Eton he traveled the world and wrote *All the Time in the World* (1966) and a second travel book, *No Particular Place to Go,* in 1981. Prizes and awards: Eric Gregory Award, 1966; Cholmondeley Award, 1971; Geoffrey Faber Memorial Prize, 1975; T.S. Eliot Prize, 1999. Between *Symptoms of Loss: Poems* (1965) and *Collected Poems* (2005) he published ten other collections of poems. Some of his poems: "Aborigine," "Broken Dreams," "Calling Your Name in the Zoo," "Some Kisses from the Kama Sutra," "The Butcher," "When I Grow Up."

Sources: *British Council Arts* (http://www.contemporarywriters.com). *Curtain Call: 101 Portraits in Verse.* Hugo Williams, ed. Faber and Faber, 2001. *P.E.N. New Poetry I.* Robert Nye, ed. Quartet Books, 1986. *Penguin Modern Poets, Bk. 11.* Michael Donaghy, Andrew Motion, Hugo Williams, eds. Penguin Books Ltd., 1997. *The Chatto Book of Love Poetry.* John Fuller, ed. Chatto and Windus, 1990. *The Columbia Granger's Index to Poetry. 11th ed* (http://www.columbiagrangers.org). *The Columbia Granger's Index to Poetry.* 11th ed. *The Columbia Granger's World of Poetry,* Columbia University Press, 2005 (http://www.columbiagrangers.org). *The Oxford Book of Travel Verse.* Kevin Crossley-Holland, ed. Oxford University Press, 1986. *The Oxford Book of Twentieth-Century English Verse.* Philip Larkin, ed. Oxford University Press, 1973. *The Oxford Companion to English Literature.* 6th edition. Margaret Drabble, ed. Oxford University Press, 2000. *Who's Who.* London: A & C Black, 2005.

WILLIAMS, ISAAC (1802–1865)

Born near Aberystwyth, Cardiganshire, the son of a London barrister, he was educated at Harrow School. A skilled Latin scholar, he went on to Trinity College, Oxford, where a serious illness nearly cost him his life, so his hopes of a double first were dashed. His academic history: B.A, 1826; M.A., fellow of Trinity and ordained priest, 1831; lecturer in philosophy, 1832; dean of Trinity, 1833; lecturer in rhetoric, 1834–1840; B.D., 1839; vice-president of Trinity, 1841–1842. He was one of the members of the Oxford Movement and contributed verses to the *British Magazine,* later published as *Lyra Apostolica* (1864). He was curate to John Keble at Dartington, Devon, from 1842 to 1848 when he retired to Stinchcombe, where he died. Some of his publications: *Hymns Translated from the Parisian Breviary,* 1839. *Sacred Verses,* 1845. *The Altar,* 1847. *The Christian Scholar,* 1849. *The Christian Seasons,* 1854. *The Baptistery,* 1858. Some of his poems: "Invitation," "King George III," "The Athanasian Creed," "The Church in Fear," "The Church in Wales," "The Lord's Prayer," "The Nicene Creed."

Sources: *Dictionary of National Biography.* Electronic Edition 1.1. Oxford University Press, 1997. *English Poetry: Author Search.* Chadwyck-Healey Ltd., 1995 (http://www.lib.utexas.edu:8080/search/epoetry/author.html). *Stanford University Libraries and Academic Information Resources* (http://library.stanford.edu). *The Cyber Hymnal* (http://www.cyberhymnal.org/index.htm). *The Oxford Companion to English Literature.* 6th edition. Margaret Drabble, ed. Oxford University Press, 2000.

WILLIAMS, WALDO (1904–1971)

Born in Haverfordwest, Pembrokeshire, the son of a schoolteacher, English was his first language; he only learned Welsh at the age of seven, when he changed schools. After graduating in English from the University of Wales, Aberystwyth, in 1926, he taught in various schools in Pembrokeshire and in England. His Baptist parents were pacifists and were strongly opposed to the First World War, and Williams was a conscientious objector during Word War II (he became a Quaker in 1953). From 1950 to 1963 (when compulsory military service ended), he was imprisoned on several occasions for non-payment of income tax, which he did to protest the Korean war and continuing National Service. He died in St. Thomas Hospital, Haverfordwest, and was buried in the cemetery in Blaenconnin Baptist Church, Llandissilio, Pembrokshire. *Dail Pren (The Leaves of the Tree),* 1956, was his only volume of poetry published during his lifetime. A new edition was published in 1991 by Gwasg Gomer. Some of his poems: "A Summer Cloud," "Daffodil," "In Two Fields," "Remembering," "The peacemakers," "What is it to be Human?"

Sources: *100 Welsh Heroes / 100 Arwyr Cymru.* (http://www.100welshheroes.com/en/biography/waldowilliams). *The Columbia Granger's Index to Poetry.* 11th ed. *The Columbia Granger's World of Poetry,* Columbia University Press, 2005 (http://www.columbiagrangers.org). *The Oxford Book of Welsh Verse in English.* Gwyn Jones, ed. Oxford University Press, 1977. *Waldo Williams.* Tony Conran, trans. Gomer Press, 1997.

WILLIAMS, WILLIAM (1717–1791)

He was a Welsh poet and hymn writer (bardic name, Pantycelyn), the son of Presbyterian parents, born at Pantycelyn, Carmarthenshire, and educated at a Nonconformist academy near Hay-on-Wye, Breconshire. While there, under the preaching of Howell Harris (principal founder of Welsh Calvinistic Methodism), he became a deacon and curate in the Anglican Church but was never ordained. He allied himself with the Methodists and spent the rest of his life in evangelistic tours as a Methodist preacher, traveling 95,900 miles bringing the Gospel to his country. He published religious poems, treatises, and more than 800 hymns, of which "Guide me, O Thou Great Jehovah" is probably his best known. *Pantheologia*, a Welsh history of the religions of the world, with geographical notes, appeared in installments from 1762 to 1774. He died at Pantycelyn. Some of his hymns/poems: "A View of Christ's Kingdom," "Can I Forget Bright Eden's Grace?" "I Gaze Across the Distant Hills," "Now the Shadows Flee and Vanish," "Ride On, Jesus, All Victorious," "What is the World, and What is Life?"

Sources: *A Sacrifice of Praise: An Anthology of Christian Poetry in English from Caedmon to the Mid-Twentieth Century.* James H. Trott, ed. Cumberland House Publishing, 1999. *Anglo-Welsh Poetry, 1480–1980.* Raymond Garlick and Roland Mathias, eds. Poetry Wales Press, 1984. *Anglo-Welsh Poetry, 1480–1990.* Raymond Garlick and Roland Mathias, eds. Poetry Wales Press, 1993. *Dictionary of National Biography.* Electronic Edition 1.1. Oxford University Press, 1997. *Encyclopædia Britannica Ultimate Reference Suite DVD*, 2006. *The Columbia Granger's Index to Poetry.* 11th ed. *The Columbia Granger's World of Poetry*, Columbia University Press, 2005 (http://www.columbia-grangers.org). *The Best Loved Religious Poems.* James Gilchrist Lawson, ed. Fleming H. Revell, 1933. *The Oxford Book of Welsh Verse in English.* Gwyn Jones, ed. Oxford University Press, 1977. *The World's Great Religious Poetry.* Caroline Miles Hill, ed. Macmillan, 1954. *Wikipedia, the Free Encyclopedia* (http://en.wikipedia.org/wiki/Wikipedia).

WITHER (WITHERS), GEORGE (1588–1667)

Born into a wealthy family at Bentworth, near Alton, Hampshire, he was educated at Magdalen College, Oxford, but did not graduate. About 1610 he settled in London in order to study law and was entered at Lincoln's Inn in 1615. *Abuses Stript and Whipt* (1613) landed him in Marshalsea prison in 1614. *Withers Motto* (1621) and *Scholar's Purgatory*, an attack on the patenting process (1624–1625), also earned him a prison sentence. He sided with Cromwell in the Civil War, and when captured by the Royalists, he was saved from execution only by the intervention of Sir John Denham (see entry), a royalist sympathizer. He died in London and was buried at the church of the Savoy Hospital in the Strand. Some of his other publications: *A Collection of Emblems*, 1635. *The Hymns and Songs of the Church*, 1623. *A Paraphrase on the Ten Commandments*, 1697. *Psalms of David*, 1632. *The Songs of the Old Testament*, 1621. Some of his poems: "A Prisoner's Lay," "For Scholars and Pupils," "Sleep, Baby, Sleep," "The Alchemy of Love," "The Prayer of Hezekiah," "The Tired Petitioner."

Sources: *A Sacrifice of Praise: An Anthology of Christian Poetry in English from Caedmon to the Mid-Twentieth Century.* James H. Trott, ed. Cumberland House Publishing, 1999. *A Treasury of Minor British Poetry.* J. Churton Collins, ed. Edward Arnold, 1896. *Dictionary of National Biography.* Electronic Edition 1.1. Oxford University Press, 1997. *Encyclopædia Britannica Ultimate Reference Suite DVD*, 2006. *English Poetry: Author Search.* Chadwyck-Healey Ltd., 1995 (http://www.lib.utexas.edu:8080/search/epoetry/author.html). *Microsoft Encarta* 2006 (DVD). Microsoft Corporation, 2006. *The National Portrait Gallery* (www.npg.org.uk). *Poems by George Wither.* Henry Morley, ed. George Routledge and Sons, 1891. *Seventeenth-Century Verse and Prose, Vol. II: 1660–1700.* Helen C. White, et al., ed. Macmillan. 1951, 1952. *Stanford University Libraries and Academic Information Resources* (http://library.stanford.edu). *The Columbia Granger's Index to Poetry.* 11th ed. *The Columbia Granger's World of Poetry*, Columbia University Press, 2005 (http://www.columbia-grangers.org). *The Oxford Companion to English Literature.* 6th edition. Margaret Drabble, ed. Oxford University Press, 2000. *The Penguin Book of Renaissance Verse 1509–1659.* David Norbrook, ed. Penguin Books, 1992.

WOLCOT, JOHN (1738–1819)

He used the pseudonyms "Philomath Wizard" and "Peter Pindar." Born at Dodbrooke, near Kingsbridge, Devon, the son of a surgeon, he graduated in medicine from Aberdeen in 1767, and from 1767 to 1769 was physician to Sir William Trelawny, governor of Jamaica. Ordained in 1769, he seems to have spent his time between his two vocations. On the death of Trelawny, he set up medical practice in Truro, Cornwall, where his unorthodox methods brought him into dispute with his medical colleagues. Abandoning medicine in 1781, he moved to London to concentrate on writing, from which he derived a reasonable income. By 1811, he was almost blind. He died in London and was buried St. Paul's Church, Covent Garden. Some of his publications: *Persian Love Elegies*, 1773. *The Captive King*, ?1793. *The Regent and the King*, 1814. *Royalty Fog-Bound*, 1814. *Epistle to the Emperor of China*, 1817. Some of his poems: "Pindariana: Ode to Two Mice in a Trap," "Resignation: an Ode to the Journeyman Shoemakers," "The Apple Dumplings and a King," "The Royal Tour, and Weymouth Amusements," "The Sorrows of Sunday, an Elegy."

Sources: *Dictionary of National Biography.* Electronic Edition 1.1. Oxford University Press, 1997. *Encyclopædia Britannica Ultimate Reference Suite DVD*, 2006. *English Poetry: Author Search.* Chadwyck-Healey Ltd., 1995 (http://www.lib.utexas.edu:8080/search/epoetry/author.html). *The National Portrait Gallery* (www.npg.org.uk). *Peter Pindar's Poems.* P.M. Zall, ed. University of South Carolina, 1972. *Stanford University Libraries and Academic Information Resources* (http://library.stanford.edu). *The Columbia Granger's Index to Poetry.* 11th ed. *The Columbia Granger's World of Poetry*, Columbia University Press, 2005 (http://www.columbiagrangers.org). *The Faber Book of English History in Verse.* Kenneth Baker, ed. Faber and Faber, 1988. *The New Oxford Book of Eighteenth Century Verse.* Roger Lonsdale, ed. Oxford University Press, 1984. *The Oxford Book of Satirical Verse.* Geoffrey Grigson, ed. Oxford University Press, 1980. *The Oxford Companion to*

English Literature. 6th edition. Margaret Drabble, ed. Oxford University Press, 2000. *The Works of Peter Pindar*. Printed for Walker and Edwards, London, 1816.

WOLFE, CHARLES (1791–1823)

Born at Blackhall, County Kildare, he was brought up in England by his widowed mother. Educated at various schools in England, he graduated B.A. from Trinity College, Dublin, in 1814, was ordained in 1817, and was minister of two churches. He died of tuberculosis at Cove of Cork and was buried in the ruined church of Clonmel outside the Cove of Cork. Some of his poems: "Battle of Busaco," "Burial of Sir John Moore," "Go, Forget Me," "On Hearing," "The Last Rose of Summer," "Rewell to Lough Bray," "The Frailty of Beauty," "The Raising of Lazarus," "To a Friend," "To Mary."

Sources: *1000 Years of Irish Poetry: The Gaelic and Anglo-Irish Poets from Pagan Times to the Present*. Kathleen Hoagland, ed. Devin-Adair, 1975. *Dictionary of National Biography*. Electronic Edition 1.1. Oxford University Press, 1997. *Encyclopædia Britannica Ultimate Reference Suite DVD*, 2006. *The Columbia Granger's Index to Poetry*. 11th ed. *The Columbia Granger's World of Poetry*, Columbia University Press, 2005 (http://www.columbiagrangers. org). *The Home Book of Verse*. Burton Egbert Stevenson, ed. New York: Henry Holt and Company, 1953. *The Oxford Anthology of English Poetry, Vol. II: Blake to Heaney*. John Wain, ed. Oxford University Press, 1990. *The Oxford Companion to English Literature*. 6th edition. Margaret Drabble, ed. Oxford University Press, 2000.

WOLFE, HUMBERT (1886–1940)

Born in Milan of Jewish parents but raised in Bradford, where his father was in the woolen business, he graduated in classics from Wadham College, Oxford, and was in the civil service from 1908 until he died. He was appointed Commander of the British Empire (1918) and Companion Order of the Bath in 1925. Leading up to World War II, so successful was he in managing the recruitment drive for civil defense, the Territorial Army, and the Auxiliary Fire Service, by the time war broke out in September more than 2,000,000 men and women had volunteered. His circulatory system, already vulnerable from high blood pressure and advanced arteriosclerosis, collapsed. He died on his birthday, 5 January 1940. Between his first collection of poetry, *London Sonnets* (1920), and his last, *Out of Great Tribulation* (1939), he wrote ten other collections, as well as essays, satires, textbooks, translations, a ballet and his autobiography, *Now a Stranger* (1933). Some of his poems: "After Battle," "Autumn," "Balder's Song," "Hilaire Belloc," "Sonnets to Helen," "The First Airman," "To Him Whom the Cap Fits."

Sources: *Dictionary of National Biography*. Electronic Edition 1.1. Oxford University Press, 1997. *I Like You, If You Like Me: Poems of Friendship*. Myra Cohn Livingston, ed. Macmillan, 1987. *Shylock Reasons with Mr. Chesterton, by Humbert Wolfe*. B. Blackwell, 1920. *The Columbia Granger's Index to Poetry*. 11th ed. *The Columbia Granger's World of Poetry*, Columbia University Press, 2005 (http:// www.columbiagrangers.org). *The Faber Book of Epigrams and Epitaphs*. Geoffrey Grigson, ed. Faber and Faber, 1977. *The National Portrait Gallery* (www.npg.org.uk). *The Oxford Companion to English Literature*. 6th edition. Margaret Drabble, ed. Oxford University Press, 2000. *World Poetry: An Anthology of Verse from Antiquity to Our Time*. Katharine Washburn and John S. Major, eds. Publisher, 1338, 1998.

WOODFORD, SAMUEL (1636–1700)

Born in London, he was educated at St. Paul's School and Wadham College, Oxford, from where he graduated B.A. in 1657. He started as a lawyer, then was ordained as a priest to Hartley-Mauduit, Hampshire. He was appointed canon of Chichester in 1676, where was made doctor of divinity in 1677 and appointed in 1680 canon of Winchester, where he remained until he died. His chief works were *The Paraphrase Upon the Psalms* (1667) and *The Paraphrase Upon the Canticles* (1679). Some of his poems: "A Madrigal," "An Hymn for Vespers," "In Sacred Memory of Dr. Beaumont," "Ode," "Solitude," "St. Paul Done By Titian," "The Metamorphosis," "The Song of the Angels," "The Voyage: Ode," "To Celia," "To Mr. Isaac Walton."

Sources: *Dictionary of National Biography*. Electronic Edition 1.1. Oxford University Press, 1997. *English Poetry: Author Search*. Chadwyck-Healey Ltd., 1995 (http://www. lib.utexas.edu:8080/search/epoetry/author.html). *Stanford University Libraries and Academic Information Resources* (http://library.stanford.edu). *The Columbia Granger's Index to Poetry*. 11th ed. *The Columbia Granger's World of Poetry*, Columbia University Press, 2005 (http://www.columbia-grangers.org). *The Complete Poems of Dr. Joseph Beaumont*. 2 Volumes, Alexander B. Grosart, ed. Edinburgh University Press, 1880.

WOODLEY, GEORGE (1786–1846)

Born at Dartmouth, Devon, and largely self-taught, he served in a British man-of-war and began writing poetry for the amusement of his messmates before he was twelve years old. From 1808 he was editor of the Truro *Royal Cornwall Gazette*, the Tory paper of the county. Ordained in 1820, he was missionary of the Society for Promoting Christian Knowledge, on the Scilly Isles, until 1842. From 1843 until his death he was curate of Martindale in Westmorland. He wrote several theological essays and books on the Scilly Isles. For his essay *Divinity of Christ Proved* (1819; 2nd edit. 1821) he won a monetary prize from the Society for Promoting Christian Knowledge. Some of his poetry publications:

Mount Edgcumbe, 1804. *The Churchyard and Other Poems*, 1808. *Britain's Bulwarks, Or the British Seaman*, 1811. *Portugal Delivered: A Poem in Five Books*, 1812. *Redemption: A Poem in Twenty Books*, 1816. *Cornubia: A Poem in Five Cantos*, 1819. *Devonia: A Poem in Five Cantos*, 1820. Some of his poems: "Music," "Saint Warna's Well," "The Lighthouse," "The Sea at Noon," "To a Butterfly," "To the Moon."

Sources: *Dictionary of National Biography.* Electronic Edition 1.1. Oxford University Press, 1997. *Forget Me Not, Volumes 1823–1830: List of Authors* (http://www.orgs.muohio.edu/anthologies/FMN/Author_List.htm).

WOODS, MACDARA (1942–)

Born in Dublin, he is married to Eiléan Ní Chuilleanáin, a member of Aosdána, and lives mostly in Dublin or in Umbria, Italy. He, his wife, Leland Bardwell and Pearse Hutchinson (see entries), are founding editors of the literary review *Cyphers*. He has translated from a number of languages and edited *The Kilkenny Anthology* (1991). He frequently works with musicians and has written a number of songs. In 2003 he completed *The Cello Suites* to accompany a performance of the six Bach cello suites on double bass by American musician Richard Hartshorne, most recently performed in St. Bartholomew's Cathedral, New York, 2004. Two books of his poems have been published in Italian, *Biglietto di Sola Andata* (1998) and *Con Pesaro ai Miei Piedi* (1999), which included an audio CD with readings by the author and music by the Italian group Militia. Some of his publications: *Stopping the Lights in Ranelagh*, 1987. *Miz Moon*, 1988. *The Hanged Man Was Not Surrendering*, 1990. *Notes from the Country of Blood-Red Flowers*, 1994. *Selected Poems*, 1996. *The Nightingale Water*, 2001. *Knowledge in the Blood, New and Selected Poems*, 2001.

Sources: *Aosdána—An Irish Affiliation of Artists* (http://www.artscouncil.ie/aosdana/biogs/literature/macdarawoods.html). *Biograoghy and Works of Macdara Woods* (http://homepage.eircom.net/~writing/051.MW.html). *The Aspect of the Russian Verb*, by Mardara Woods (http://www.voiceourconcern.org/poetry_macdara_woods.htm).

WOOLNER, THOMAS (1825–1892)

Born at Hadleigh, Suffolk, he studied under the sculptor William Behnes from the age of twelve, and in 1842, he entered the schools of the Royal Academy, continuing to be employed by Behnes in his spare time. His first work, *Eleanor Sucking the Poison from the Arm of Prince Edward,* was exhibited in 1843. He went on to become a sculptor of world renown and was a member of the Pre-Raphaelites. The struggling woolner sailed for Melbourne, Australia, in 1852 to seek his fortune in gold, but re-

turned two years later not much better off. The turning point was his execution of the bust of Tennyson (1857); from then on, commissions rolled in. He was elected an associate of the Royal Academy in 1871 and academician in 1874. He died suddenly and was buried in the churchyard of St. Mary's, Hendon. Some of his poetry publications: *My Beautiful Lady,* 1863 (third edition 1866). *Pygmalion*, 1881. *Silenus*, 1884. *Tiresias*, 1886. *Children*, 1887. *My Beautiful Lady,* 1887 (in 3 parts, 17 cantos in all; issued in 1887 as volume 82 of *Cassell's National Library*).

Sources: *Dictionary of National Biography.* Electronic Edition 1.1. Oxford University Press, 1997. *Love in Verse.* Kathleen Blease, ed. Ballantine Publishing Group, 1998. *The National Portrait Gallery* (www.npg.org.uk). *The Columbia Granger's Index to Poetry.* 11th ed. *The Columbia Granger's World of Poetry*, Columbia University Press, 2005 (http://www.columbiagrangers.org). *The Oxford Companion to English Literature.* 6th edition. Margaret Drabble, ed. Oxford University Press, 2000.

WORDSWORTH, WILLIAM (1770–1850) and DOROTHY (1771–1855)

Born in Cockermouth, Cumbria, William was the second son and Dorothy the only daughter of the five children of the lawyer and agent to Sir James Lowther (afterwards first Earl of Lonsdale). William was educated at the grammar school at Hawkshead, near Lake Windermere; Dorothy at a boarding school in Hipperholme, near Halifax, Yorkshire. William graduated B.A. from St. John's College, Cambridge University, in 1787, and apart from his time there and in France during the early stages of the Revolution, brother and sister were rarely separated. From 1794 Dorothy's life was devoted to helping William with his poetry and fostering his love of nature. The year 1795 saw the development of a close relationship between the Wordsworths and Samuel Taylor Coleridge (see entry), and the trio spent the winter of 1798–1799 touring Germany, where William spent much of his time writing poetry, and Wordsworth and Coleridge collaborated in producing *Lyrical Ballads* (1798). In 1799 brother and sister moved into Dove Cottage (now the Wordsworth Trust), in Grasmere, and with Coleridge and Robert Southey (see entry) living nearby, they formed the "Lake Poets." In 1802 William married Mary Hutchinson, who had been his schoolmate, and in 1813 he, Mary and their children, with Dorothy, finally settled at Rydal Mount, near Ambleside. From 1812 to 1842 William earned income from the job of distributor of stamps for the county of Westmoreland, which he handed on to his son William. Wordsworth succeeded Southey as poet laureate in 1843. He died a peaceful death and was buried in

Grasmere churchyard. He is memorialized by a stone in Poets' Corner of Westminster Abbey. In 1835 Dorothy succumbed to pre-senile dementia and for the last two decades of her life was confined to the house and terrace of Rydal Mount, in the care of her sister-in-law. In addition to her poems (the majority of which are untitled) Dorothy published many journals and letters. Some of William's poems: "A Wren's Nest," "Composed upon Westminster Bridge, September 3, 1802," "The Solitary Reaper," "We Are Seven," "Written in Very Early Youth." Some of Dorothy's poems: "A Cottage in Grasmere Vale," "A Winter's Ramble in Grasmere Vale," "Floating Island at Hawkshead," "Loving and Liking," "Peaceful Our Valley, Fair and Green," "Thoughts on My Sick-bed."

Sources: *A Sacrifice of Praise: An Anthology of Christian Poetry in English from Caedmon to the Mid-Twentieth Century.* James H. Trott, ed. Cumberland House Publishing, 1999. *Animal Poems.* John Hollander, ed. Alfred A. Knopf, 1994. *Dictionary of National Biography.* Electronic Edition 1.1. Oxford University Press, 1997. *Biography of Dorothy Wordsworth* (http://www.kirjasto.sci.fi/dwordsw.htm). *Encyclopædia Britannica Ultimate Reference Suite DVD,* 2006. *Golden Treasury of the Best Songs and Lyrical Poems in the English Language.* Francis Turner Palgrave, ed. Oxford University Press, 1964, Sixth edition, updated by John Press, 1994. *Poems by Dorothy Wordsworth* (http://www.umd.umich.edu/casl/hum/eng/classes/236/dwordsworth2.html). *Microsoft Encarta* 2006 (DVD). Microsoft Corporation, 2006. *The National Portrait Gallery* (www.npg.org.uk). *Poetry by English Women: Elizabethan to Victorian,* R.E. Pritchard, ed. Continuum, 1990. *Romanticism.* Duncan Wu, ed. Blackwell, 1994. *The Best Loved Poems of the American People.* Hazel Felleman, ed. Doubleday, 1936. *The Columbia Granger's Index to Poetry.* 11th ed. *The Columbia Granger's World of Poetry,* Columbia University Press, 2005 (http://www.columbiagrangers.org). *The Major Works of William Wordsworth.* Stephen Gill, ed. Oxford University Press, 2000. *The Norton Anthology of Literature by Women: The Tradition in English.* Sandra M. Gilbert and Susan Guber, eds. W.W. Norton, 1985. *The Oxford Book of Children's Verse.* Iona Opie and Peter Opie, eds. Oxford University Press, 1973. *The Oxford Companion to English Literature.* 6th edition. Margaret Drabble, ed. Oxford University Press, 2000. *The Poetry of Dorothy Wordsworth.* Hyman Eigerman, ed. Columbia University Press, 1940. *Westminster Abbey Official Guide* (no date).

WOTTON, SIR HENRY (1568–1639)

Born in Kent and educated at Winchester school, he graduated B.A. from Queen's College, Oxford, in 1588, then spent the next seven years traveling on the Continent. During 1594 he wrote the prose work *State of Christendom* (published in 1657), and became the trusted agent and secretary to Robert Devereux, second earl of Essex. He conveyed a letter from the Duke of Tuscany to James VI of Scotland, warning him of an assassination plot, and was re-warded by a knighthood by the grateful monarch, James I, in 1604. Wotton was ambassador to Venice from 1604 to 1623 and a member of Parliament in 1614 and 1625. In 1624 he became provost of Eton College and in 1627 he took holy orders. He died at Eton and was buried in the college chapel. His *Reliquiæ Wottonianæ* (1654) contains fifteen of his poems. Some of his poems: "A Dialogue Betwixt God and the Soul," "A Poem Written by Sir Henry Wotton, in His Youth," "On a Bank as I Sat a-Fishing; a Description of the Spring," "The Character of a Happy Life," "You Meaner Beauties of the Night."

Sources: *A Sacrifice of Praise: An Anthology of Christian Poetry in English from Caedmon to the Mid-Twentieth Century.* James H. Trott, ed. Cumberland House Publishing, 1999. *Americans' Favorite Poems: The Favorite Poem Project Anthology.* Robert Pinsky and Maggie Dietz, eds. W.W. Norton, 2000. *Dictionary of National Biography.* Electronic Edition 1.1. Oxford University Press, 1997. *Encyclopædia Britannica Ultimate Reference Suite DVD,* 2006. *Golden Treasury of the Best Songs & Lyrical Poems in the English Language.* Francis Turner Palgrave, ed. Oxford University Press, 1964, Sixth edition, updated by John Press, 1994. *Metaphysical Lyrics and Poems of the Seventeenth Century: Donne to Butler.* Herbert J. Grierson, ed. Oxford University Press, 1921. *The National Portrait Gallery* (www.npg.org.uk). *Poemhunter* (www.poemhunter.com). *Seventeenth Century Poetry: The Schools of Donne and Jonson.* Hugh Kenner, ed. Holt, Rinehart and Winston, 1964. *Stanford University Libraries and Academic Information Resources* (http://library.stanford.edu). *The Columbia Granger's Index to Poetry.* 11th ed. *The Columbia Granger's World of Poetry,* Columbia University Press, 2005 (http://www.columbiagrangers.org). *Westminster Abbey Official Guide* (no date).

WRIGHT, DAVID (1920–1994)

Born in Johannesburg, South Africa, he was profoundly deaf by the age of seven. At fourteen he came to England and was educated at Northampton School for the Deaf and at Oriel College, Oxford, graduating in 1942. He became a freelance writer in 1947 after working on *The Sunday Times* for five years. He co-founded and co-edited the quarterly literary review *X* from 1959 to 1962. *His Deafness: A Personal Account* (1969) was his autobiography. He edited *Longer Contemporary Poems* (1966), the *Penguin Book of English Romantic Verse* (1968) and the *Penguin Book of Everyday Verse* (1976). He also translated *Beowulf* (1957) and *The Canterbury Tales* (1964). He died of cancer at Waldron, East Sussex. Some of his other poetry publications: *Moral Stories,* 1954. *Monologue of a Deaf Man,* 1958. *Adam at Evening,* 1965. *To the Gods the Shades: New and Collected Poems,* 1976. *Metrical Observations,* 1980. *Selected Poems,* 1988. *Elegies,* 1990. Some of his poems: "A Funeral Oration," "A Peripatetic Letter to Isabella Fey," "An Anniversary Approaches; of the Birth of

God," "Seven South African Poems," "The Lakes," "Winter at Gurnard's Head."

Sources: *Archives Hub: The David Wright Collection of Norman Nicholson Papers* (http://www.archiveshub.ac.uk/news/03020403.html). Miles, M. 2005. *"Deaf People Living and Communicating in African Histories, c. 960s—1960s"* (http://www.independentliving.org/docs7/miles2005a.html). *The Columbia Granger's Index to Poetry.* 11th ed. *The Columbia Granger's World of Poetry,* Columbia University Press, 2005 (http://www.columbiagrangers.org). *The Modern Poets: An American-British Anthology.* John Malcom Brinnin and Bill Read, eds. McGraw-Hill, 1963. *The Naked Astronaut: Poems on Birth and Birthdays.* Ren Graziani, ed. Faber and Faber, 1983. *The New Lake Poets.* William Scammell, ed. Bloodaxe Books, 1991. *The Oxford Companion to English Literature.* 6th edition. Margaret Drabble, ed. Oxford University Press, 2000. *The Penguin Book of South African Verse.* Jack Cope and Uys Krige, eds. Penguin Books, 1968.

WRIGHT, KIT (1944)

Born in Kent (he now lives in London), he studied English at New College, Oxford, then taught in a South London comprehensive school. From 1967 to 1970 he taught English at Brock University, Ontario, Canada, then worked for the Poetry Society (England) as education officer until he became a freelance writer in 1975. From 1977 to 1980 he was creative writing Fellow at Trinity College, Cambridge. He was one of the first poets to make regular trips into schools and is one of the most acclaimed and adored of poets for children. Although best known for his comic verse, he is not limited to this genre. Among his awards and prizes are: Geoffrey Faber Memorial Prize, 1978; Poetry Society Alice Hunt Bartlett Prize, 1978; Arts Council Bursary, 1985. Some of his children's publications: *Arthur's Father*, 1978. *Arthur's Granny*, 1978. *Arthur's Sister*, 1978. *Arthur's Uncle*, 1978. *Poems for Ten Year Olds and Over*, 1984. *Poems for Nine Year Olds and Under*, 1985. Some of his poems: "Acorn Haiku," "Dad and the Cat and the Tree," "Sergeant Brown's Parrot," "The Bear Looked Over the Mountain," "Victorian Family Photograph."

Sources: *100 Poems on the Underground.* Gerald Benson, Judith Cherniak and Cicely Herb, eds. Cassell, 1991. *A Year Full of Poems.* Michael Harrison, and Christopher Stuart-Clark, ed. Oxford University Press, 1991. *British Council Arts* (http://www.contemporarywriters.com). *Hoping It Might Be So: Poems, 1974–2000.* Kit Wright. Leviathan, 2000. *The National Portrait Gallery* (www.npg.org.uk). *Once Upon a Rhyme: 101 Poems for Young Children.* Sara Corrin and Stephen Corrin, eds. Faber and Faber, 1982. *Penguin Authors* (http://www.penguin.co.uk/nf/Author/AuthorPage/0,0_1000051386,00.html). *Shades of Green.* Anne Harvey, ed. Greenwillow Books, 1991. *The Columbia Granger's Index to Poetry.* 11th ed. *The Columbia Granger's World of Poetry,* Columbia University Press, 2005 (http://www.columbiagrangers.org). *The New Exeter Book*

of Riddles. Kevin Crossley-Holland and Lawrence Sail, eds. Enitharmon Press, 1999. *The Oxford Book of Comic Verse.* John Gross, ed. Oxford University Press, 1994. *The Oxford Companion to English Literature.* 6th edition. Margaret Drabble, ed. Oxford University Press, 2000. *The Penguin Book of Light Verse.* Gavin Ewart, ed. Penguin Books, 1980.

WRIGHT, MEHETABEL WESLEY (1697–1750)

Born in Epworth, the seventh of nineteen surviving children of Samuel Wesley, she was sister to John and Charles Wesley (see entry, The Wesley Family). Hetty, as she was generally known, was educated at home and could read Greek at the age of eight. She fell in love with a lawyer, but her father objected to this match. She fell pregnant by an unknown lover and in 1725 was forced into marriage to William Wright, a plumber and glazier of Louth, Lincolnshire, but her baby daughter survived only eight months. John openly disagreed with his father's actions and preached a sermon on the lack of charity. Hetty's mother would only accept her if she "truly repented." The couple had several children, none of whom survived, possibly due to the lead pollution of her husband's trade. He was a heavy drinker and the marriage was not a happy one. She made up with her family, but went to her grave feeling she was a sinner. Some of her poems: "Address to Her Husband," "An Epitaph on Herself," "To an Infant Expiring the Second Day of Its Birth," "Wedlock; A Satire."

Sources: *Dictionary of National Biography.* Electronic Edition 1.1. Oxford University Press, 1997. *Eighteenth Century Women Poets: An Oxford Anthology.* Roger Lonsdale, ed. Oxford University Press, 1989. *The Columbia Granger's Index to Poetry.* 11th ed. *The Columbia Granger's World of Poetry,* Columbia University Press, 2005 (http://www.columbiagrangers.org). *The New Oxford Book of Eighteenth Century Verse.* Roger Lonsdale, ed. Oxford University Press, 1984. *The Oxford Companion to English Literature.* 6th edition. Margaret Drabble, ed. Oxford University Press, 2000.

WROTH, LADY MARY (?1587–?1651)

The eldest daughter of Robert Sidney, first earl of Leicester and niece of Sir Philip Sidney (see entry), in 1604 she married Sir Robert Wroth, who became very wealthy on his father's death in 1614. Lady Mary was often at court after her marriage and acted in Ben Jonson's *Masque of Blackness* (1605). In 1621, she published *The Countess of Montgomery's Urania*, a close imitation, in four books, of *Arcadia* by Sir Philip Sidney. The volume includes a collection of poems, some hundred sonnets and twenty songs. The same year she published *Pamphilia to Amphilanthus*, a poem of 1,675 lines, one section of which is *Crown of Sonnets Dedicated to Love.* The book caused some offense and Lady Mary withdrew it.

She created a scandal at court by having two illegitimate children by her first cousin William Herbert, third Earl of Pembroke. Some of her other poems: "Cupid Blessed Bee Thy Might," "Drowne Me Not You Cruell Teares," "Love Lett Mee Live, Ore Lett Mee Dye," "Love, and Reason Once Att War," "Silent Woods with Desarts Shade," "The Sunne Hath No Long Iourney Now to Goe."

Sources: *Dictionary of National Biography.* Electronic Edition 1.1. Oxford University Press, 1997. *English Poetry: Author Search.* Chadwyck-Healey Ltd., 1995 (http://www.lib.utexas.edu:8080/search/epoetry/author.html). *The Columbia Granger's Index to Poetry.* 11th ed. *The Columbia Granger's World of Poetry,* Columbia University Press, 2005 (http://www.columbiagrangers.org). *The Life of Lady Mary Wroth.* (http://www.luminarium.org/sevenlit/wroth/wroth bio.htm). *The Poems of Lady Mary Wroth.* Louisiana State University Press, 1883.

WYATT, SIR THOMAS (?1503–1542)

He was born at Allington Castle, Kent, the only son of Sir Henry Wyatt. He graduated B.A. (1518), and M.A. (1520) from St. John's College, Cambridge. Although he married at seventeen, he was the lover of Anne Boleyn before she married Henry VIII. He had a distinguished career: clerk of the king's jewels (1524); a diplomat in Italy, Spain, the Netherlands, and France; high marshal of Calais; knighted in 1536; sheriff of Kent. He was twice imprisoned in the Tower of London, mainly as a result of accusations of treason by his enemies, but he never lost the favor of the king. He died at Sherborn, Dorset. Wyatt was one of Henry VIII's court circle and was admired for his skill in music, languages, knowledge of foreign literature, and his composition of English verse. It was he who introduced the sonnet from Italy into England, a form that was developed by Henry Howard, earl of Surrey (see entry). Some of his poems: "All Hevy Myndes," "From Thes Hye Hilles as When a Spryng Doth Fall," "O Goodely Hand," "Tagus, Fare Well, That Westward with Thy Stremes," "You That in Love Finde Lucke and Habundance."

Sources: *A Book of Love Poetry.* Jon Stallworthy, ed. Oxford University Press, 1974. *A Treasury of Great Poems: English and American.* Louis Untermeyer, ed. Simon and Schuster, 1955. *Complete Poems of Sir Thomas Wyatt.* R.A. Rebholz, ed. Penguin Books, 1978. *Dictionary of National Biography.* Electronic Edition 1.1. Oxford University Press, 1997. *Moods of the Sea: Masterworks of Sea Poetry.* George C. Solley and Eric Steinbaugh, eds. Naval Institute Press, 1981. *Poetry in English: An Anthology.* M.L. Rosenthal, ed. Oxford University Press, 1987. *Silver Poets of the Sixteenth Century.* Gerald Bullett, ed. J.M. Dent, 1947. *The Columbia Granger's Index to Poetry.* 11th ed. *The Columbia Granger's World of Poetry,* Columbia University Press, 2005 (http://www.columbiagrangers.org). *The Oxford Companion to English Literature.* 6th edition. Margaret Drabble, ed. Oxford University Press, 2000.

WYLEY, ENDA (1966–)

Born in Glenageary, County Dublin, she received an M.A. in creative writing from Lancaster University, England. Her poems are in many anthologies, including *Field Day Anthology of Irish Writing* (2002) and *Irish Women's Writing and Tradition, Vols. 4 and 5* (2002). She was awarded bursaries in literature from the Arts Council of Ireland and Chomhairle Ealaíon in 1997 and 2001. She has twice been a winner in the British National Poetry Competition and was the inaugural recipient of the Vincent Buckley Poetry Prize. In 2003 she published *Boo and Bear,* a children's book illustrated by Greg Massardier. Some of her poetry publications: *Eating Baby Jesus,* 1994. *Socrates in the Garden,* 1998. *Poems for Breakfast,* 2004. Some of her poems: "Buzz of a Change," "New Bridge," "New Year, New Century," "Socrates in the Garden," "Two Women in Kosovo," "Wedding Gift."

Sources: *Three Short Love Poems by Edna Wyley* (http://www.brakkehond.be/76/wyleyle.html). *Biography of Edna Wyley* (http://www.dedaluspress.com/poets/wyley.html). *Three Poems by Edna Wyley* (http://www.dedaluspress.com/samples/wyley-poems.html).

YALDEN, THOMAS (1670–1736)

Born in Oxford and educated at Magdalen College school and Magdalen College, Oxford. His principal dates are: B.A., 1691; M.A., 1694; fellow, 1699–1713; vicar of Willoughby, Warwickshire 1700–1709; lecturer on moral philosophy, 1705–1713; B.D., 1706; chaplain to the Duke of Beaufort, 1706; bursar of Magdalen College, 1707; D.D., 1708; dean of divinity, 1709; chaplain of Bridewell Hospital, London (where he died and was buried), 1713–1736. Robert Anderson and John Dryden (see entry) both included poems by Yalden in their collections. Many of Yalden's poems are poetic versions of Aesop's *Fables.* Some of his publications: *Ode for St. Cecilia's Day,* 1693 (set to music by Daniel Purcell, 1660–1717). *On the Conquest of Namur,* 1695. *Æsop at Court,* 1702. *An Essay,* 1704. *Poems,* 1810. Some of his poems: "Advice to a Lover," "An Owl and the Sun," "Ovid's Art of Love," "The Fox and Bramble," "The Iliad (Selections)," "The Nightingale and Cuckow," "The Satyr's Address," "The Sun and the Wind," "To Sir Humphry Mackworth."

Sources: *Dictionary of National Biography.* Electronic Edition 1.1. Oxford University Press, 1997. *Eighteenth-Century English Verse.* Dennis Davison, ed. Penguin Books, 1988. *English Poetry: Author Search.* Chadwyck-Healey Ltd., 1995 (http://www.lib.utexas.edu:8080/search/epoetry/author.html). *The Columbia Granger's Index to Poetry.* 11th ed. *The Columbia Granger's World of Poetry,* Columbia University Press, 2005 (http://www.columbiagrangers.org). *The Oxford Book of Classical Verse in Translation.* Adrian Poole and Jeremy Maule, eds. 1995.

YEARSLEY, ANN (1752–1806)

Ann Cromartie was born of humble parents in Bristol and was taught to read and write by her brother. She married in 1774 and had several children. She was patronized by Hannah More (see entry), who revised Ann's poems. The money raised from *Poems on Several Occasions* (1785) was invested in a trust by More that excluded Ann from any control; the situation caused a breach between the two women and More withdrew her patronage. Nothing deterred, Anne started a circulating library in Bristol, and in 1789 her verse tragedy *Earl Goodwin* was performed at Bath and at Bristol. In 1795 she published *The Royal Captives,* a historical novel. She retired to Melksham, Wiltshire, where she died. Some of her other publications: *A Poem on the Slave Trade,* 1788. *Reflections on the Death of Louis XVI,* 1793. *An Elegy on Marie Antoinette,* 1795. *The Rural Lyre,* 1796. Some of her poems: "Absence, a Juvenile Piece," "Addressed to Sensibility," "Lucy, a Tale for the Ladies," "To Frederick Yearsley," "To Mira, on the Care of Her Infant," "To the Bristol Marine Society."

Sources: *Dictionary of National Biography.* Electronic Edition 1.1. Oxford University Press, 1997. *Eighteenth Century Women Poets: An Oxford Anthology.* Roger Lonsdale, ed. Oxford University Press, 1989. *English Poetry: Author Search.* Chadwyck-Healey Ltd., 1995 (http://www.lib. utexas.edu:8080/search/epoetry/author.html). *The National Portrait Gallery* (www.npg.org.uk). *Poems on Various Subjects of Ann Yearsley.* Woodstock Books, 1994. *Romantic Women Poets: An Anthology.* Duncan Wu, ed. Blackwell Publishers, 1997. *Stanford University Libraries and Academic Information Resources* (http://library.stanford.edu). *The Columbia Granger's Index to Poetry.* 11th ed. *The Columbia Granger's World of Poetry,* Columbia University Press, 2005 (http://www.columbiagrangers.org). *The Oxford Companion to English Literature.* 6th edition. Margaret Drabble, ed. Oxford University Press, 2000.

YEATS, WILLIAM BUTLER (1865–1939)

Born in Dublin, the son of an artist, he was educated in London, Dublin High School, then until 1886, at the Metropolitan School of Art, Dublin. Principal dates: founding member of the Irish Literature Society in London and Dublin, 1891–1892; senator of the Irish Free State, 1992–1928; honorary degree from Dublin University, 1922; Nobel Prize for literature, 1923; founding member of the Irish Academy of Letters, 1932; United States lecture tour, 1932; *In the Poet's Parlor, In the Poet's Pub* radio series, 1937; honorary degree, Oxford University, 1931; honorary degree, Cambridge University, 1933. He died and was buried at Roquebrune, France. In 1948 his remains were reburied at Drumcliffe, near Sligo, Ireland. He edited *The Oxford Book of Modern Verse* (1936) and published essays, plays, fairy tales and legends. Some of his poetry was influenced by his wife's mystic communications through "automatic writing." Some of his poems: "Adam's Curse," "Alfred: A Masque," "An Acre of Grass," "Before the World Was Made," "The Witch," "Two Songs of a Fool," "Under Ben Bulben," "Wisdom," "Young Man's Song."

Sources: *A Little Book of Irish Verse.* Chronicle Books, 1993. *An Anthology of Irish Verse: The Poetry of Ireland from Mythological Times to the Present.* Padraic Colum, ed. Liveright, 1948. *Chief Modern Poets of Britain and America.* 5th edition. Gerald DeWitt Sanders and John Herbert Nelson, eds., Macmillan, 1970. *Dictionary of National Biography.* Electronic Edition 1.1. Oxford University Press, 1997. *Encyclopædia Britannica Ultimate Reference Suite DVD,* 2006. *Microsoft Encarta* 2006 (DVD). Microsoft Corporation, 2006. *The National Portrait Gallery* (www.npg. org.uk). *The Collected Poems of W.B. Yeats.* Richard J. Finneran, ed. Macmillan, 1989. *The Columbia Granger's Index to Poetry.* 11th ed. *The Columbia Granger's World of Poetry,* Columbia University Press, 2005 (http://www.columbiagrangers.org). *The Oxford Companion to English Literature.* 6th edition. Margaret Drabble, ed. Oxford University Press, 2000.

YOUNG, ANDREW JOHN (1885–1971)

He was a Scottish poet and canon of Chichester Cathedral, born in Elgin and educated at Edinburgh University and New College, Edinburgh. Young was ordained a minister of the United Free Church of Scotland in 1912. After war service in France he become a Presbyterian minister at Hove in Sussex, was ordained in the Church of England in 1939 and was vicar of Stoneygate (Sussex) from 1941 until 1959. He was awarded the Queen's Medal for poetry in 1952. *A Prospect of Flowers* (1945) reflects his lifelong interest in botany, as do many of his poems. He retired to Yapton near Arundel, Sussex, where he died. Some of his poetry publications: *Songs of Night,* 1910. *Thirty One Poems,* 1922. *Collected Poems,* 1936. *Nicodemus,* 1937 (verse play). *The Green Man,* 1947. *Into Hades,* 1952. *Out of the World and Back,* 1958. *Burning as Light,* 1967. *Quiet as Moss,* 1967. Some of his poems: "At Oxford," "Ben More," "Castle Rocks," "Chorus from Jephthah," "Climbing in Glencoe," "Downland Shepherd," "In Balcombe Forest," "Memorial Verses," "The Ant-Hill," "The Dead Sparrow."

Sources: *The National Portrait Gallery* (www.npg. org.uk). *Sprints and Distances: Sports in Poetry and the Poetry in Sport.* Lillian Morrison, ed. Thomas Y. Crowell, 1965. *The Columbia Granger's Index to Poetry.* 11th ed. *The Columbia Granger's World of Poetry,* Columbia University Press, 2005 (http://www.columbiagrangers.org). *The Oxford Companion to English Literature.* 6th edition. Margaret Drabble, ed. Oxford University Press, 2000. *The Poetical Works of Andrew Young.* Secker and Warburg, 1985. *Wikipedia, the Free Encyclopedia* (http://en.wikipedia.org/wiki/Wikipedia).

YOUNG, DOUGLAS (1913–1973)

Soon after birth his mother took him from Edinburgh to India, where his father was employed by a Dundee jute firm. From the age of eight he was educated at Merchiston Castle School, Edinburgh, then at the universities of St. Andrews and Oxford. In 1938 he became assistant professor of Greek at Aberdeen University and taught classics at St. Andrews University. Deeply committed to Scottish nationalism (he was chairman of the Scottish National Party 1942–1945), he spent two terms in prison for refusing conscription, arguing that Westminster did not have the right to impose conscription on Scotland. His first collection of poems —*Antran Ballads* (1943)— contains translations of verse from ten languages into English and Scots, as well as translations from the Gaelic of Sorley Maclean and George Campbell Hay (see entries). In 1963 he accepted the chair of classics at McMaster University, Hamilton, Ontario, and from 1970 until his death he worked at the University of North Carolina, Chapel Hill. Some of his poems: "Last Lauch [laugh]," "The Ballant o' the Laird's Bath," "The Frogs," "The Kirkyaird by the Sea," "The Shepherd's Dochter," "Winter Homily on the Calton Hill."

Sources: *A Book of Scottish Verse.* Maurice Lindsay and R.L. Mackie, eds. St. Martin's Press, 1983. *Biography of Douglas Young: Literary Encyclopedia* (http://www.litencyc.com/php/speople.php?rec=true&UID=5481). *The National Portrait Gallery* (www.npg.org.uk). *The Columbia Granger's Index to Poetry.* 11th ed. *The Columbia Granger's World of Poetry,* Columbia University Press, 2005 (http://www.columbiagrangers.org). *The Oxford Book of Classical Verse in Translation.* Adrian Poole and Jeremy Maule, eds. 1995. *The Oxford Book of Verse in English Translation.* Charles Tomlinson, ed. Oxford University Press, 1980.

YOUNG, EDWARD (1683–1765)

Born at Upham, near Winchester, Hampshire, where his father was rector, he was educated at Winchester College and graduated bachelor of civil law (1714) and doctor of civil law (1719) from New College, Oxford. From 1730 until his death, Young was rector at Welwyn, Hertfordshire. There he wrote his masterpiece, *Complaint, or Night Thoughts on Life, Death, and Immortality* (1742–1745), a long, meditative essay in blank verse inspired by the successive deaths of his step-daughter (1736), her husband (1740), and Young's wife (1741); this work is an example of the graveyard genre. *The Complete Works, Poetry and Prose, of the Rev. Edward Young* appeared in 1854. Young's works were popular in Europe, augmented by the prose work, the *Conjectures on Original Composition* (1759). Some of his other publications: *The Last Day*, 1714. *Bursiris*, 1719 (tragedy). *Paraphrase on Part of the Book of Job*, 1719. *The Re-venge* (the naval ship), 1721. *The Universal Passion*, 1725–1728 (a series of satires). *The Sea-piece*, 1730. *Resignation*, 1762. Some of his poems: "Epistles to Mr. Pope," "Ode to the King," "The Foreign Address," "The Instalment," "The Lament of the Damned in Hell."

Sources: *Dictionary of National Biography.* Electronic Edition 1.1. Oxford University Press, 1997. *Encyclopædia Britannica Ultimate Reference Suite DVD*, 2006. *English Poetry: Author Search.* Chadwyck-Healey Ltd., 1995 (http://www.lib.utexas.edu:8080/search/epoetry/author.html). *English Romantic Poetry and Prose.* Russell Noyes, ed. Oxford University Press. 1956. *Mark Akenside, James Macpherson, Edward Young.* S.H. Clark, ed. Fyfield Books, 1994. *Microsoft Encarta* 2006 (DVD). Microsoft Corporation, 2006. *The National Portrait Gallery* (www.npg.org.uk). *Samuel Johnson's Lives of the English Poets,* 1779–1781 (http://www2.hn.psu.edu/Faculty/KKemmerer/poets/preface.htm). *The Columbia Granger's Index to Poetry.* 11th ed. *The Columbia Granger's World of Poetry,* Columbia University Press, 2005 (http://www.columbiagrangers.org). *The Faber Book of Comic Verse.* Michael Roberts and Janet Adam Smith, eds. Faber and Faber, 1978. *The Oxford Book of Christian Verse.* Lord David Cecil, ed. Oxford University Press, 1940. *The Oxford Book of Satirical Verse.* Geoffrey Grigson, ed. Oxford University Press, 1980. *The Oxford Companion to English Literature.* 6th edition. Margaret Drabble, ed. Oxford University Press, 2000.

YOUNG, FRANCIS BRETT (1884–1954)

He was born at Halesowen, Worcestershire, educated at Epsom College, Surrey, and qualified as a doctor at Birmingham in 1907. His experiences at school and university were the basis of his early novel *The Young Physician* (1919). His novel *Marching on Tanga* (1917) is based on his experiences as a doctor in the Royal Army Medical Corps. His later novel *My Brother Jonathan* (1928) was a huge success. The war affected his health so badly that he had to give up doctoring. He and his wife settled in Capri until 1929, where he continued to write. They traveled a great deal, settling back in Worcestershire, England, in 1932. After World War II they moved to Cape Town, South Africa, where he died; his ashes were buried in Worcester Cathedral. Birmingham University awarded him the honorary degree of D.Litt. in 1950. He is known for his novels, short stories and poetry. Some of his poems: "104° Fahrenheit," "A Farewell to Africa," "After Action," "Atlantic Charter, A.D. 1620–1942," "On a Subaltern Killed in Action," "Song at Santa Cruz," "The Dhows," "The Rain-Bird."

Sources: *America Forever New: A Book of Poems.* Sara Brewton and John E. Brewton, eds. Thomas Y. Crowell, 1968. *Dictionary of National Biography.* Electronic Edition 1.1. Oxford University Press, 1997. *Encyclopædia Britan-*

nica Ultimate Reference Suite DVD, 2006. *The National Portrait Gallery* (www.npg.org.uk). *Poems 1916–1918 of Francis Brett Young.* E.P. Dutton, 1920. *The Columbia Granger's Index to Poetry.* 11th ed. *The Columbia Granger's World of Poetry,* Columbia University Press, 2005 (http://www.columbiagrangers.org). *The Eternal Sea: An Anthology of Sea Poetry.* W.M. Williamson, ed. Coward-McCann, 1946. *The Home Book of Modern Verse.* Burton Egbert Stevenson, ed. Henry Holt, 1953. *The Oxford Companion to English Literature.* 6th edition. Margaret Drabble, ed. Oxford University Press, 2000. *Wikipedia, the Free Encyclopedia* (http://en.wikipedia.org/wiki/Wikipedia).

ZANGWILL, ISRAEL (1864–1926)

He was born in London's East End of refugee parents who escaped the severe decree of Jewish child-conscription instituted by Tsar Nicholas I of Russia. He was educated at the Jews' Free School at Spitalfields, London, and London University, after which he became a journalist. He accepted an invitation to write a Jewish novel for the newly founded *Jewish Publication Society* of America. *The Children of the Ghetto* (1892) was a work that established his reputation as a writer. In 1905 — a time of great persecution in Russia and elsewhere — he broke away from the Zionist movement and founded the Jewish Territorial Organization, which unsuccessfully sought land within the British Empire where Jews might settle. He rejoined the Zionists in 1917. He died of pneumonia at Midhurst, Sussex. He wrote several other novels about Jewish life, as well as stories, plays, essays, and poems. His best-known play is *The Melting Pot* (1908). A small volume of poems, *Blind Children,* appeared in 1903. Some of his poems: "At the Worst," "At the Zoo," "Despair and Hope," "In the City," "Israel," "Seder Night in London," "Yom Kippur."

Sources: *A Treasury of Jewish Poetry.* Nathan Ausubel and Maryann Ausubel, eds. Crown, 1957. *Anthology of Modern Jewish Poetry.* Philip M. Raskin, ed. Behrman's Jewish Book Shop, 1927. *Dictionary of National Biography.* Electronic Edition 1.1. Oxford University Press, 1997. *Encyclopædia Britannica Ultimate Reference Suite DVD,* 2006. *Microsoft Encarta* 2006 (DVD). Microsoft Corporation, 2006. *The National Portrait Gallery* (www.npg.org.uk). *The Oxford Companion to English Literature.* 6th edition. Margaret Drabble, ed. Oxford University Press, 2000. *The World's Great Religious Poetry.* Caroline Miles Hill, ed. Macmillan, 1954.

ZEPHANIAH, BENJAMIN OBADIAH IQBAL (1958–)

British poet, novelist and playwright, he was born in Handsworth, Birmingham, England, left school at 13, spent much of his early life in youth correction institutions, and moved to London in 1979. He has been writer in residence at the Africa Arts Collective in Liverpool and creative artist in residence at Cambridge University; he was a candidate for the post of professor of poetry at Oxford University. He holds honorary doctorates from two British universities and advises on the place of music and art in the schools' national curriculum. He has written plays and has appeared in films. Ealing Hospital, London, named a ward after him in 1988. He helps children by speaking to them on Child Line. Some of his poetry publications: *The Dread Affair: Collected Poems,* 1985. *Rasta Time in Palestine,* 1990. *City Psalms,* 1992. *Talking Turkeys,* 1994 (for children). *Funky Chickens,* 1996 (for children). *We Are Britain!* 2002. Some of his poems: "Bought and Sold" (written in rejection to his being offered the Order of the British Empire), "Money," "Speak," "The British," "The Sun," "What Stephen Lawrence Has Taught Us" (Stephen Lawrence was a black teenager murdered in London in 1993).

Sources: *Anthology of Twentieth-Century British and Irish Poetry.* Keith Tuma, ed. Oxford University Press, 2001. *Biography of Benjamin Zephania; 100 Great Black Britons* (http://www.100greatblackbritons.com/bios/benjamin_zephaniah.html). *British Council Arts* (http://www.contemporarywriters.com). *Child Line: A Short Conversation with Benjamin Zephania* (http://www.childline.org.uk/extra/benjaminzephaniah.asp). *Letter from Benjamin Zephania, Refusing to Accept an OBE. The Guardian,* Thursday, November 27, 2003 (http://www.guardian.co.uk/arts/features/story/0,11710,1094011,00.html). *Other: British and Irish Poetry Since 1970.* Richard Caddel and Peter Quartermain, eds. Wesleyan University Press, 1999. *Poemhunter* (www.poemhunter.com). *The Columbia Granger's Index to Poetry.* 11th ed. *The Columbia Granger's World of Poetry,* Columbia University Press, 2005 (http://www.columbiagrangers.org). *The New Oxford Book of Children's Verse.* Neil Philip, ed. Oxford University Press, 1996. *The Oxford Companion to English Literature.* 6th edition. Margaret Drabble, ed. Oxford University Press, 2000. *Who's Who.* London: A & C Black, 2005.

The Poets by Nation
(England, Ireland, Scotland, Wales)

England

Abbot, John B. D. (fl. 1623)
Abercrombie, Lascelles (1881–1938)
Ackroyd, Peter (1949–)
Adams, Sarah Flower (1805–1848)
Adcock, Karen Fleur (1934–) (New Zealand)
Addison, Joseph (1672–1719)
Agard, John (1949–) (Guyana)
Agbabi, Patience (1965–) (Nigeria)
Akenside, Mark (1721–1770)
Alabaster, William (1567–1640)
Aldington, Richard Edward Godfrey (1892–1962)
Aleyn, Charles (d. 1640)
Alfred (Aelfred), King of the West Saxons (849–899)
Alvarez, Alfred (1929–)
Alvi, Moniza (1954–) (Pakistan)
Amhurst, Nicholas (1697–1742)
Amis, Sir Kingsley (1922–1995)
Anstey, Christopher (1724–1805)
Armitage, Simon (1963–)
Arnold, Matthew (1822–1888)
Arnold, Sir Edwin (1832–1904)
Askew, Anne (1521–1546)
Askham, John (1825–1894)
Asquith, Herbert Ashley (1881–1947)
Astell, Mary (1666–1731)
Atherstone, Edwin (1788–1872)
Auden, Wystan Hugh (1907–1973)
Austen, Jane (1775–1817)
Austin, Alfred (1835–1913)
Ayres, Pam (1947–)
Bacon, Sir, Francis, Viscount St. Albans (1561–1626)
Bailey, Thomas and Philip James (1785–1902)
Baker, Henry (1698–1774)
Baker, Sir Henry Williams (1821–1877)
Bakewell, John (1721–1819)
Baldwin, William (c.1515–1563)
Bamford, Samuel (1788–1872)

Bampfylde, John Codrington (1754–1796)
Barbauld, Anna Letitia (1743–1825)
Barclay, Alexander (?1475–1552)
Baring, Maurice (1874–1945)
Baring-Gould, Sabine (1824–1924)
Barker, George Granville (1913–1991)
Barker, Jane (1652–?1727)
Barker, Les (1947–)
Barnes, Barnabe (?1569–1609)
Barnes William (1801–1886)
Barnfield, Richard (1574–1629)
Bayliss, John Clifford (1919–1978)
Bayly, Nathaniel Thomas Haynes (1797–1839)
Beaumont, Bothers, Sir John and Francis (1583 —1627)
Beaumont, Joseph (1616–1699)
Beddoes, Thomas Lovell (1803–1849)
Bede (Baeda or Beda) Saint, the Venerable (673–735)
Beeching, Henry Charles (1859–1919)
Beedome, Thomas (d. ?1641)
Beer, Patricia (1919–1999)
Behn, Aphra (1640–1689)
Bell, Martin (1918–1978)
Bellerby, Frances (1899–1975)
Belloc, Joseph Hilaire Pierre Rene (1870–1953)
Benson, Arthur Christopher (1862–1925)
Bentley, Edmund Clerihew (1875–1956)
Berridge, John (1716–1793)
Berry, James (1924–) (Jamaica)
Besant, Sir Walter (1836–1901)
Betjeman, Sir John (1906–1984)
Bewick, Elizabeth (1919–)
Bickersteth, Edward Henry (1825–1906)
Bigg, John Stanyan (1828–1865)
Binyon (Robert) Laurence (1869–1943)
Blackmore, Richard Doddridge (1825–1900)

Blackmore, Sir Richard (1654–1729)
Blake, William (1757–1827)
Blamire, Susanna (1747–1794)
Blanchard, Samuel Laman (1804–1845)
Blind, Mathilde (1841–1896) (Germany)
Bloom, Valerie (1956–) (Jamaica)
Blunden, Edmund Charles (1896–1974)
Blunt, Wilfrid Scawen (1840–1922)
Bold, Henry (1627–1683)
Bolton (or Boulton), Edmund (?1575–?1633)
Bottomley, Gordon (1874–1948)
Bourdillon. Francis William (1852–1921)
Bourne, Vincent (1695–1747)
Bowles, William Lisle (1762–1850)
Bowring, Sir John (1792–1872)
Bramston, James (?1694–1744)
Brathwaite, Richard (?1588–1673)
Breton, Nicholas (?1545–?1626)
Brett, Reginald Baliol, 2nd Viscount Esher 1852–1930
Bridges, Robert Seymour (1844–1930)
Brittain, Vera (1892–1970)
Brome, Alexander (1620–1666)
Brontë, Family: Charlotte, Emily, Anne (1816–1855)
Brooke, Rupert Chawner (1887–1915)
Broome, William (1689–1745) (Orkney)
Brown, Thomas Edward (1830–1897) (Isle of Man)
Brown, Thomas (Tom) (1663–1704)
Browne, Isaac Hawkins (1705–1760)
Browne, Sir Thomas (1605–1882)
Browne, Sir William (1692–1774)
Browne, William (1591–?1643)
Browning, Elizabeth Barrett and Robert (1806–1889)
Brownjohn, Alan Charles (1931–)
Brydges, Sir Samuel Egerton (1762–1837)

Buchanan, Robert Williams (1841–1901)

Bunting, Basil (1900–1985)

Bunyan, John (1628–1688)

Burnand, Sir Francis Cowley (1836–1917)

Burrell, Lady Sophia (?1750–1802)

Burton, Sir Richard Francis (1821–1890)

Butler, Samuel (1612–1680)

Butler, Samuel (1835–1902)

Byrom, John (1692–1763)

Byron, George Gordon, Sixth Lord (1788–1824)

Caedmon (fl. 658–680)

Calverley, Charles Stuart (1831–1884)

Campion, Thomas (1567–1620)

Cannan, May Wedderburn (1893–1973)

Canning, George (1770–1827)

Canton, William (1845–1926)

Carew, Richard (1555–1620)

Carew, Thomas (?1595–?1639)

Carey, Henry (?1693–1743)

Carkesse, James (fl 1679)

Carr, Sir John (1732–1807)

Carroll, Lewis (1832–1898)

Carter, Angela Olive (1940–1992)

Carter, Elizabeth (1717–1806)

Cartwright, William (1611–1643)

Cary, Elizabeth, Viscountess Falkland (Circa.1585–1639)

Caryll, Lord John (1625–1711)

Caswall, Edward (1814–1878)

Causley, Charles (1917–2003)

Cavendish, Margaret, Duchess of Newcastle (1623–1673)

Cawthorn, James (1719–1761)

Cennick, John (1718–1755)

Chalkhill, John (fl. 1600)

Chapman, George (1559?–1634)

Chatterton, Thomas (1752–1770)

Chaucer, Geoffrey (?1340–1400)

Chester, Sir Robert (?1566–?1640)

Chesterfield, Philip Dormer Stanhope, 4th Earl of (1694–1773)

Chesterton, Gilbert Keith (1874–1936)

Childish, Billy (1959–)

Chudleigh, Lady Mary (1656–1710)

Churchill, Charles (1731–1764)

Churchyard, Thomas (?1520–1604)

Cibber, Colley (1671–1757)

Clanvow, Sir John (Circa 1341–1391)

Clare, John (1793–1864)

Claris, John Chalk (?1797–1866)

Cleveland, John (1613–1658)

Clive, Caroline Archer (1801–1873)

Clough, Arthur Hugh (1819–1861)

Cluysenaar, Anne (1936–) (Belgium)

Cobbing, Bob (1920–2002)

Cokayne, Sir Aston (1608–1684)

Coleridge, Hartley (1796–1849)

Coleridge, Mary Elizabeth (1861–1907)

Coleridge, Samuel Taylor and Sara (1772–1852)

Coles, Vincent Stuckey Stratton (1845–1929)

Collier, Mary (1688–?1762)

Collins, John (?1742–1808)

Collins, William (1721–1759)

Colman, George (1762–1836)

Colman, Walter (d. 1645)

Comfort, Alex (1920–2000)

Conder, Josiah (1789–1855)

Congreve, William (1670–1729)

Conquest, (George) Robert (Acworth) (1917–)

Conran, Anthony (1931–)

Constable, Henry (1562–1613)

Constantine, David (1944–)

Cook, Eliza (1818–1889)

Cooper, Thomas (1805–1892)

Cope, Wendy (1945–)

Coppard, Alfred Edgar (1878–1957)

Corbet, Richard (1582–1635)

Cornford, Frances Crofts Darwin and (Rupert) John (1886–1960)

Cory, William Johnson (1823–1892)

Cotton, Charles (1630–1687)

Cotton, Nathaniel (1705–1788)

Cotton, Roger (?1550–1650)

Courthope, William John (1842–1917)

Cousin, Anne Ross (1824–1906)

Coward, Sir Noel Peirce (1899–1973)

Cowley, Abraham (1618–1667)

Cowley, Hannah (1743–1809)

Cowper, William (1731–1800)

Crabbe, George (1754–1832)

Craik, Mrs. Dinah Maria Mulock (1826–1887)

Crashaw, Richard (?1613–1649)

Creech, Thomas (1659–1700)

Crewdson, Jane (1809–1863)

Cripps, Arthur Shearly (1869–1952)

Cristall, Anne Batten (born 1769)

Crompton, Hugh (c 1657)

Crosland Thomas William Hodgson (1865–1924)

Crossley-Holland, Kevin (1941–)

Crossman, Samuel (?1624–1684)

Crowe, William (1745–1829)

Crowley, Edward Alexander (Aleister) (1875–1947)

Crozier, Andrew (1943–)

Curry, Neil (1937–)

Cutts, John, Baron Cutts of Gowran (1661–1707)

Dabydeen, David (1955–) (Guyana)

D'aguiar, Fred (1960–) (Guyana)

Dalton, Amanda (1957–)

Dalton, John (1709–1763)

Daniel, Samuel (1562–1619)

Darby, John Nelson (1800–1882)

Darwin, Erasmus (1731–1802)

Daryush, Elizabeth (1887–1977)

D'avenant, Sir William 1606–1668

Davie, Donald Alfred (1922–1995)

Davies, John of Hereford (?1565–1618)

Davies, Sir John (1569–1626)

Davies, Sneyd (1709–1769)

Davison, Francis (? 1575–?1619) and Walter (1581–1608?)

De La Mare, Walter John (1873–1956)

De Stein, Sir Edward Sinauer (1887–1965)

De Vere, Edward, 17th Earl of Oxford (1550–1604)

Deck, James George. (1807–1884)

Defoe, Daniel (1660–1731)

Dekker, Thomas (?1570–1632)

Diaper, William (1685–1717)

Dickens, Charles Huffham (1812–1870)

Dixon, Richard Watson (1833–1900)

Dobell, Sydney Thompson (1824–1874)

Dobson, Henry Austin (1840–1921)

Doddridge, Philip (1702–1751)

Dodsley, Robert 1703–1764

Dolben, Digby Augustus Stewart Mackworth (1848–1867) (Guernsey)

Domett, Alfred (1811–1887)

Donne, John (1573–1631)

Dooley, Maura (1957–)

Doughty, Charles Montagu (1843–1926)

Douglas, Keith Castellain (1920–1944)

Douglas, Lord Alfred Bruce (1870–1945)

Dowland, John (1563–1626)

Downman, Hugh (1740–1809)

Dowson, Ernest Christopher (1867–1900)

Doyle, Sir Francis Hastings Charles 1810–1888

Drane, (Mother) Augusta Theodosia (1823–1894)

Draycott, Jane (1954–)

Drayton, Michael (1563–1631)

Drinkwater, John (1882–1937)

Dryden, John (1631–1700)

Duck, Stephen (1705–1756)

Duke, Richard (1658–1711)

Dunmore, Helen (1952–)

Dunsany, Edward John Moreton Draz Plunkett, 18th Baron (1878–1957)

D'urfey, Thomas (1653–1723)

Durrell, Lawrence George (1912–1990)

Dyer, George (1755–1841)

Dyer, Sir Edward (1543–1607)

Edwards, Thomas (1699–1757)

Egerton, Sarah Fyge (1670–1723)

Eliot, George (1819–1880)

Eliot, T(homas) S(tearns) (1888–1965) (America)

Elizabeth I (1533–1603)

Ellerton, John (1826–1893)

Elliott, Charlotte (1789–1871)

Elliott, Ebenezer (1781–1849)

Elton, Sir Charles Abraham (1778–1853)

Elys, Edmund (fl. 1707)

Empson, Sir William (1906–1984)

Enright, Dennis Joseph (1920–2002)

Essex, Robert Devereux, 2d Earl of (1567–1601)

Etherege. Sir George (1635–1691)

Eusden, Laurence (1688–1730)

Ewart, Gavin Buchanan (1916–1995)

Fairfax of Cameron, Thomas Fairfax, 3rd Baron (1612–1671)

Fane, Julian Henry Charles (1827–1870)

Fane, Mildmay, 2nd Earl of Westmorland (1602–1665)
Fainlight, Ruth (1931–) (America)
Fanshawe, Catherine Maria (1765–1834)
Fanshawe, Sir Richard (1608–1666)
Fanthorpe, U(rsula) A(skham) (1929–)
Farjeon, Eleanor (1881–1965)
Farley, Paul (1965–)
Fawcett, John (1740–1817)
Fawkes, Francis (1720–1777)
Feaver, Vicki (1943–)
Feinstein, Elaine Barbara (1930–)
Fenton, Elijah (1683–1730)
Fenton, James Martin (1949–)
Ferrers, George 1500?–1579
Finch, Anne, Countess of Winchilsea (1661–1720)
Fisher, Allen (1944–)
Fisher, Roy (1930–)
Fitchett, John (1776–1838)
Fitzgerald, Edward (1809–1883)
Flatman, Thomas (1637–1688)
Flecker, Herman James Elroy (1884–1915)
Fletcher, Giles, and Sons (1549?–1650)
Fletcher, John (1579–1625)
Fletcher, Robert (fl. 1586)
Flower, Robin Ernest William (1881–1946)
Ford, John (?1586–1640)
Ford, Thomas (?1580–1648)
Forrest, William (fl. 1581)
Francis, Matthew (1956–)
Frankau, Gilbert (1884–1952)
Fraunce, Abraham (fl. 1587–1633
Freeman, John (1880–1929)
Freeth, John (1731–1808)
Fuller, Roy Broadbent and John Leopold (1912–)
Furness, Richard (1791–1857)
Garnett, Richard (1835–1906)
Garth, Sir Samuel (1661–1719)
Gascoigne, George (?1525–1577)
Gascoyne, David Emery (1916–2001)
Gay, John (1685–1732)
Gibson, Wilfrid Wilson (1878–1962)
Gifford, William (1756–1826)
Gilbert, Sir William Schwenck (1836–1911)
Glover, Richard (1712–1785)
Godolphin, Sidney (1610–1643)
Golding, Louis (1895–1958)
Googe, Barnabe (1540–1594)
Gorges, Sir Arthur (1577–1625)
Gosse, Sir Edmund William (1849–1928)
Gould, Robert (D. ?1709)
Gower, John (?1325–1408)
Grant, Sir Robert (1779–1838) (India)
Granville. George, Lord Lansdowne (1667–1735)
Graves, Richard (1715–1804)
Gray, John Henry (1866–1934)
Gray, Thomas (1716–1771)
Green, Matthew (1696–1737)
Greene, Robert (?1558–1592)
Greenlaw, Lavinia (1962–)

Greenwell, Dora (1821–1882)
Grenfell, Julian Henry Francis (1888–1915)
Grenville (or Greynvile), Sir Richard (1542–1591)
Greville, Sir Fulke, First Baron Brooke (1554–1628)
Griffin, Bartholomew (fl. 1596)
Griffiths, Bill (1948–)
Grigson, Geoffrey Edward Harvey (1905–1985)
Grimald, Nicholas (1519–1562)
Grose, Francis (?1731–1791)
Gunn, Thom (1929–2004)
Gurney, Ivor Bertie (1890–1937)
Gutteridge, Bernard (1916–1985)
Habington, William (1605–1654)
Hagthorpe, John (?1585–?1630)
Hake, Thomas Gordon (1809–1895)
Hall or Halle, John (?1529–?1566)
Hall, John, of Durham (1627–1656)
Hallam, Arthur Henry (1811–1833)
Hammond, James (1710–1742)
Hannah, Sophie (1971–)
Hardy, Thomas (1840–1928)
Harington, Sir John (1561–1612)
Harris, John (1820–1884)
Harrison, Tony (1937–)
Harrison, William (1685–1713)
Harvey, Christopher (1597–1663)
Harvey, Gabriel (?1550–1631)
Harwood, Lee (1939–)
Hassall, Christopher Vernon (1912–1963)
Havergal, William Henry and Frances Ridley (1793–1879)
Hawes, Stephen (?1474/5–1523)
Hawker, Robert Stephen (1803–1875)
Hayley, William (1745–1820)
Headley, Henry (1765–1788)
Hearn, Mary Anne (1834–1909)
Heath-Stubbs, John Francis Alexander (1918–)
Heber, Reginald (1773–1826)
Hegley, John (1953–)
Hemans, Felicia Dorothea (1793–1835)
Henley, William Ernest (1849–1903)
Henri, Adrian Maurice (1932–2000)
Henry Viii, King of England (1491–1547)
Heraud, John Abraham (1799–1887)
Herbert, Edward, and George (1583–1648)
Herbert, Mary Sidney, Countess of Pembroke (1561–1621)
Herbert, Sir Alan Patrick (1890–1971)
Herbert, William (1778–1847)
Herbert, William, 3rd Earl of Pembroke (1580–1630)
Herrick, Robert (1591–1674)
Herschel, Sir John Frederick William (1792–1871)
Hesketh, Phoebe (1909–2005)
Hewlett, Maurice Henry (1861–1923)
Heyrick, Thomas (1649–1694)
Heywood, John (?1497–?1580) and Jasper (1535–1598)
Heywood, Thomas (1575?–1650)
Hill, Aaron (1685–1750)

Hill, Geoffrey William (1932–)
Hill, Selima (1945–)
Hill, Tobias (1970–)
Hobsbaum, Philip Dennis (1932–2005)
Hodgson, Ralph Edwin (1871–1962)
Hodgson, William Noel (1893–1916)
Hofmann, Michael (1957–) (Germany)
Hollis, Matthew (1971–)
Holloway, John (1920–1999)
Hood, Thomas the Elder and Younger (1799–1874)
Hope, Christopher (1944–) (South Africa)
Hopkins, Gerard Manley (1844–1889)
Horovitz, Michael (1935–) (Germany)
Housman, Alfred Edward and Laurence (1859–1959)
Hovell-Thurlow, Edward, 2d Baron Thurlow (1781–1829)
Howard, Henry, Earl of Surrey (?1517–1547)
Howard, Philip, 1st Earl of Arundel (1557–1595)
Howard, Sir Robert (1626–1698)
Howell, Thomas (fl 1568)
Howitt, Mary and William (1792–1888)
Hoyland, Francis (fl. 1763)
Hubert, Sir Francis (?1568 or ?1569–1629
Huddesford, George (1749–1809)
Huggarde or Hoggarde, Miles (fl. 1548–1557)
Hughes, John (1677–1720)
Hughes, Richard Arthur Warren (1900–1976)
Hughes, Ted (1930–1998)
Hulme, Thomas Ernest (1883–1917)
Hunnis, William (d. 1597)
Hunt, James Henry Leigh (1784–1859)
Hurdis, James (1763–1801)
Huxley, Aldous Leonard (1894–1963)
Ingelow, Jean (1820–1897)
Jacob, Hildebrand (1693–1739)
Jago, Richard (1715–1781)
James I, King of England (VI of Scotland) (1566–1625)
Jenner, Charles (1736–1774)
Jenner, Edward (1749–1823)
Jennings, Elizabeth (1926–2001)
Jerningham, Edward (1727–1812)
Jewsbury, Maria Jane (1800–1833)
Johnson, Bryan Stanley William (1933–1973)
Johnson, Linton Kwesi (1952–) (Jamaica)
Johnson, Lionel Pigot (1867–1902)
Johnson, Samuel (1709–1784)
Jones, David Michael (1895–1974)
Jones, Ebenezer (1820–1860)
Jones, Mary (1707–1778)
Jones, Samuel (d. 1732)
Jones, Sir William (1746–1794)
Jonson, Ben (1572–1637)
Jordan, Thomas (?1612–1685)
Joseph of Exeter (fl. 1190)
Joseph, Jenny (1932–)

Keats, John (1795–1821)
Keble, John (1792–1866)
Ken, Thomas (1637–1711)
Kendall, Timothy (fl 1577)
Kennedy, Rann (1772–1851)
Kennish, William (1799–1862) (Isle of Man)
Kenyon, John (1784–1856) (Jamaica)
Keyes, Sidney Arthur (1922–1943)
Khalvati, Mimi (1944–) (Iran)
Killigrew, Anne (1660–1685)
King, Henry (1592–1669)
King, William (1663–1712)
Kingsley, Charles (1819–1875)
Kipling, Joseph Rudyard (1865–1936)
Kirkup, James (1918–)
Knevet, Ralph (1600–1671)
Knowles, Herbert (1798–1817)
Kynewulf, Cynewulf, or Cynwulf (Circa 750)
Lamb, Charles (1775–1834) and Mary (1764–1847)
Lamb, Lady Caroline (1785–1828)
Landon, Letitia Elizabeth (1802–1838)
Landor, Walter Savage and Robert Eyres (1775–1869)
Lane, John (fl. 1620)
Langhorne, John (1735–1779)
Langland, William (1330?–1400?)
Lanier, [or Lanyer], Emilia [or Aemelia] (1569–1645)
Larkin, Philip Arthur (1922–1985)
Lawrence, David Herbert (1885–1930)
Le Gallienne, Richard Thomas (1866–1947)
Leapor, Mary (1722–1746)
Lear, Edward (1812–1888)
Leatham, William Henry 1815–1889
Lee, Laurie (1914–1997)
Lee-Hamilton, Eugene Jacob (1845–1907)
Lehman, Rudolph John Frederick (1907–1987)
Letts, Winifred Mary (1882–1971)
Levy, Amy (1861–1889)
Lewis, Saunders (1893–1985)
Linche or Lynche, Richard (d. 1601)
Linton, William James (1812–1898)
Lloyd, Charles (1775–1839)
Lloyd, Robert (1733–1764)
Lluelyn or Lluellyn, Martin (1616–1682)
Locker-Lampson, Frederick (1821–1895)
Lodge, Thomas (?1558–1625)
Logue, Christopher (1926–)
Lok, Lock, or Locke, Henry (?1553–?1608)
Lovelace, Richard (1618–1658)
Lovibond, Edward (1724–1775)
Lowbury, Edward Joseph Lister (1913–)
Lowe, Robert, Viscount Sherbrooke (1811–1892)
Loy, Mina (1882–1966) (Hungary)
Lucie-Smith, John Edward Mckenzie (1933–) (Jamaica)
Luke, Mrs. Jemima Thompson (1813–1906)

Luttrell, Henry (?1765–1851)
Lyall, Sir Alfred Comyn (1835–1911)
Lydgate, John (?1370–?1451)
Lynch, Thomas Toke (1818–1871)
Lytton, Edward George Earle, First Barron Lytton (1803–1873)
Lytton, Edward Robert Bulwer, 1st Earl of Lytton (1831–1891)
Macaulay, Dame Emilie Rose (1881–1958)
Macaulay, Thomas Babington. Baron Macaulay (1800–1859)
Mcgough, Roger (1937–)
Mckendrick, Jamie (1955–)
Mackintosh, Ewart Alan (1893–1917)
Macsweeney, Barry (1948–2000)
Madge, Charles (1912–1996)
Maguire, Sarah (1957–)
Mannyng, Robert, or Robert De Brunne (?1288–?1338)
Mapange, Jack (Current) (Malawi)
Markham, E(dward) A(rchibald) (1939–) (Montserrat)
Markham, Gervase (1568–1637)
Marlowe, Christopher (1564–1593)
Marriott, John (1780–1825)
Marston, John (1574–1634)
Marston, John Westland and Philip Bourke (1819–1890)
Marvell, Andrew (1621–1678)
Masefield, John Edward (1878–1967)
Mason, John (?1646–1694)
Mason, William (1725–1797)
Massey, Gerald (1828–1907)
Massinger, Philip (1583–1640)
Maude, Thomas (1718–1798)
Maxwell, Glyn (1962–)
May, Thomas (1595–1650)
Mcgough, Roger (1937–)
Medley, Samuel (1738–1799)
Mendes, Moses (d. 1758)
Meredith, George (1828–1909)
Merivale, Herman Charles (1839–1906)
Merivale, John Herman (1779–1844)
Merrick, James (1720–1769)
Mew, Charlotte Mary (1869–1928)
Meynell, Alice Christiana Gertrude (1847–1922)
Middleton, Thomas (?1570–1627)
Midlane, Albert (1825–1909)
Mill or Mille, Humphrey (fl. 1646)
Miller, Thomas (1807–1874)
Millhouse, Robert (1788–1839)
Milligan, Spike (1918–2002)
Milman, Henry Hart (1791–1868)
Milne, Alan Alexander (1882–1956)
Milnes, Richard Monckton, 1st Baron Houghton (1809–1885)
Milton, John (1608–1674)
Minot, Laurence (?300–?1352)
Mitchell, Adrian (1932–)
Monkhouse, William Cosmo (1840–1901)
Monro, Harold Edward (1879–1932)
Montagu, Charles, Earl of Halifax (1661–1715)
Montagu, Lady Mary Wortley (1689–1762)
Moore. Edward (1712–1757)

Moore, Sir John Henry (1756–1780)
Moore, Nicholas (1818–1986)
More, Dame Gertrude (1606–1633)
More, Hannah (1745–1833)
More, Henry (1614–1687)
Morley, Thomas (1557/58–1602)
Morris, William (1834–1896)
Moss, Thomas (1740–1808)
Motion, Andrew Peter (1952–)
Mottram, Eric Noel William (1924–1995)
Moultrie, John and Gerard (1799–1885)
Munby, Arthur Joseph (1828–1910)
Munday, Anthony (1553–1633)
Myers, Frederic William and Ernest James (1843–1921)
Nashe, or Nash, Thomas (1567–1601)
Neale, John Mason (1818–1866)
Neele, Henry (1798–1828)
Nesbit, Edith (1858–1924)
Newbolt, Sir Henry John (1862–1938)
Newcomb, Thomas (1682?–1765)
Newman, John Henry (1801–1890)
Newton, John (1725–1807)
Niccols, Richard (1584–1616)
Nichols, Grace (1950–) (Guyana)
Nichols, Robert Malise Bowyer (1893–1944)
Nicholson, John (1790–1843)
Nicholson, Norman (1914–1987)
Nicolson, Adela (Violet) Florence (1865–1904)
Noel, Roden Berkeley Wriothesley (1834–1894)
Noel, Thomas (1799–1861)
Norris, John (1657–1711)
Norton, Caroline (1808–1877)
Norton, Thomas (1532–1584)
Noyes, Alfred (1880–1958)
Nuttall, Jeff (1933–2004)
Nye, Robert (1939–)
O'Brien, Sean (1952–)
Occleve, Thomas (or Hoccleve) (?1370–?1450)
Oldham, John (1653–1683)
Oldmixon, John (?1673–1742)
Oliver, Douglas (1937–2000)
Opie, Mrs. Amelia (1769–1853)
Ord, John Walker (1811–1853)
Orwell, George (1903–1950)
O'shaughnessy, Arthur William Edgar (1844–1881)
Oswald, Alice (1966–)
Owen, Wilfred Edward Salter (1893–1918)
Padel, Ruth (1946–)
Palgrave, Francis Turner (1824–1897)
Patmore, Coventry Kersey Dighton (1823–1896)
Patten, Brian (1946–)
Pattison, William (1706–1727)
Peacock, Thomas Love (1785–1866)
Peake, Mervyn Laurence (1911–1968)
Peele, George (?1558–?1596)
Penrose, Thomas (1742–1779)
Percy, Thomas (1729–1811)
Percy, William (1575–1648)
Perronet, Edward (1726–1792)

Petrucci, Mario (1958–)
Philipot, Thomas (?1616–1682)
Philips, Ambrose (?1675–1749)
Philips, John (1676–1709)
Philips, Katherine (1631–1664)
Phillimore, John Swinnerton (1873–1926)
Phillips, Stephen (1864–1915)
Pickard, Tom (1946–)
Pinter, Harold (1930–)
Pitt, Christopher (1699–1748)
Pitter, Ruth (1897–1992)
Plath, Sylvia (1932–1963) (America)
Plomer, William Charles Franklyn (1903–1973)
Plowman, Max (1883–1941)
Polley, Jacob (1975–)
Pomfret, John (1667–1702)
Pope, Alexander (1688–1744)
Pordage, Samuel (1633–?1691)
Porter, Peter Neville Frederick (1929–) (Australia)
Praed, Winthrop Mackworth (1802–1839)
Pratt, Samuel Jackson (1749–1814)
Prewett, Frank (1893–1962) (Canada)
Pricket, Robert (fl. 1603–1645)
Prince, Frank Templeton (1912–2003) (South Africa)
Prince, John Critchley (1808–1866)
Prior, Matthew (1664–1721)
Procter, Bryan Waller and Adelaide Anne (1787–1874)
Proctor, Thomas (fl. 1578–1584)
Pudney, John Sleigh (1909–1977)
Pugh, Sheenagh (1950–)
Puttenham, George (?1529–1591)
Pye, Henry James (1745–1813)
Quarles, Francis and John (1592–1665)
Quiller-Couch, Sir Arthur Thomas (1863–1944)
Quillinan, Edward (1791–1851) (Portugal)
Radcliffe, Anne (1764–1823)
Radclyffe-Hall, Marguerite Antonia (1880–1943)
Raine, Craig Anthony (1944–)
Raine, Kathleen Jessie (1908–2003)
Ralegh, (or Raleigh) Sir Walter (1552–1618)
Raleigh, Sir Walter Alexander (1861–1922)
Randolph, Thomas (1605–1635)
Rands William Brighty (1823–1882)
Raworth, Tom (1938–)
Read, Sir Herbert Edward (1893–1968)
Reading, Peter Gray (1946–)
Reavey, George (1907–1976) (Russia)
Redgrove, Peter William (1932–2003)
Reed Henry (1914–1986)
Relph, Josiah (1712–1743)
Reynolds, John Hamilton (1796–1852)
Richards Ivor Armstrong (1893–1970)
Richardson, David Lester (1801–1865)
Rickword, John Edgell (1898–1982)
Ridler, Anne (1912–2001)
Riley, John (1937–1978)

Riley, Peter (1940–)
Ritson, Joseph (1752–1803)
Roberts, Michael Symmons (1963–)
Roberts, Michael (William Edward) (1902–1948)
Roberts, Michèle Brigitte (1949–)
Roberts, William Hayward (d. 1791
Robinson, Mary (1758–1800)
Robinson, Peter (1953–)
Rochester, John Wilmot 2nd Earl (1647–1680)
Rodd, Sir James Rennell, 1st Baron Rennell (1858–1941)
Rogers, Samuel (1763–1855)
Rogerson, John Bolton (1809–1859)
Rolle, Richard, of Hampole (?1300–1349)
Roscoe, William, William Stanley, and William Caldwell (1753–1859)
Rose, William Stewart (1775–1843)
Rosen, Michael Wayne (1946–)
Rosenberg, Isaac (1890–1918)
Ross, Thomas (d. 1675)
Rossetti, Dante Gabriel and Christina Georgina (1828–1894)
Rowe, Nicholas (1674–1718)
Rowlands, Samuel (?1570–?1630)
Roydon, Matthew (?1580–1622)
Russell, Arthur Tozer (1806–1874)
Russell, Thomas (1762–1788)
Sackville, Charles, 6th Earl of Dorset (1638–1706)
Sackville, Lady Margaret (1881–1936)
Sackville, Thomas, 1st Earl of Dorset (1536–1608)
Sackville-West, Victoria Mary (1892–1962)
Sandys, George (1578–1644
Sassoon, Siegfried Loraine (1886–1967)
Savage, Richard (1697–1743)
Sayers, Dorothy Leigh (1893–1957)
Sayers, Frank (1763–1817)
Scannell, Vernon (1922–)
Scarfe, Francis (1911–1986)
Scott, Geoffrey (1883–1929)
Scott, Thomas (1705–1775)
Scovell, Edith Joy (1907–1999)
Scroope, (or Scrope) Sir Carr (1649–1680)
Seaman, Sir Owen (1861–1936)
Sedley, (or Sidley) Sir Charles (?1639–1701)
Settle, Elkanah (1648–1724)
Seward, Anna (1742–1809)
Sewell, George (?1690–1726)
Shadwell, Thomas (?1642–1692)
Shakespeare, William (1564–1616)
Shapcott, Jo (1953)
Shaw, Cuthbert (1739–1771)
Sheffield, John (1648–1721)
Shelley, Percy Bysshe and Mary Wollstonecraft (1792–1851)
Shenstone, William (1714–1763)
Sherburne, Sir Edward (1618–1702)
Shipman, Thomas (1632–1680)
Shirley, James (1596–1666)
Shukman, Henry (1962–)
Shuttle, Penelope (1947–)
Siddal, Elizabeth Eleanor (1829–1862)

Sidney, Sir Philip (1554–1586)
Silkin, Jon (1930–1997)
Sillitoe. Alan (1928–)
Simpson, Matt (1936–)
Sisson, Charles Hubert (1914–2003)
Sitwell Family: Edith; Francis; Sacheverell (1887–1988)
Skelton, John (?1460–1529)
Skipsey, Joseph (1832–1903)
Smart, Christopher (1722–1771)
Smith, Charlotte (1749–1806)
Smith, Florence Margaret ("Stevie") (1902–1971)
Smith, Horatio (1779–1849)
Smith, Sydney, Goodsir (1915–1975) (New Zealand)
Somerville, William (1675–1742)
Southey, Mrs. Caroline Anne Bowles (1786–1854)
Southey, Robert (1774–1843)
Southwell, Saint Robert (?1561–1595)
Spencer, William Robert (1770–1834)
Spender, Sir Stephen Harold (1909–1995)
Spenser, Edmund (?1552–1599),
Sprackland, Jean (1962–)
Sprat, Thomas (1635–1713)
Squire, Sir John Collings (1884–1958)
Stagg, John (1770–1823)
Stainer, Pauline (1941–)
Stallworthy, Jon (1935–)
Stanley, Thomas (1625–1678)
Stapleton or Stapylton, Sir Robert (d. 1669
Steele, Anne (1717–1778)
Stephen, James Kenneth (1859–1892)
Stepney, George (1663–1707)
Stevenson, Anne Katharine(1933–) (America)
Stevenson, Matthew (?1654–1685)
Stokes, Henry Sewell (1808–1895)
Story, Robert (1795–1860)
Strode, William (1602–1645)
Strong, Leonard Alfred George (1896–1956)
Studdert Kennedy, Geoffrey Anketell (1883–1929)
Suckling, Sir John (1609–1642)
Swain, Charles (1801–1874)
Swinburne, Algernon Charles (1837–1909)
Swingler, Randall (1909–1967)
Sylvester, Josuah (1563–1618)
Talfourd, Sir Thomas Noon (1795–1854)
Tasker, William (1740–1800)
Tatham, John (fl 1632–1664)
The Taylor Sisters, Ann (1782–1866) Jane (1783–1824)
Taylor, Sir Henry (1800–1886)
Taylor, John (1580–1623)
Taylor, William (1765–1836)
Tennyson Brothers (1807–1898)
Thackeray, William Makepeace (1811–1863)
Thomas, D(Onald) M(Ichael) (1935–)
Thomas, (Philip) Edward (1878–1917)
Thompson, Francis (1859–1907)
Thompson, William (?1712–1766)

Thwaite, Anthony Simon (1930–)
Tickell, Thomas (1686–1740)
Tiller, Terence Rogers (1916–1987)
Tofte, Robert (d. 1620)
Tollet, Elizabeth (1694–1754)
Tomlinson, (Alfred) Charles (1927–)
Toplady, Augustus Montague (1740–
    1778)
Townsend Traherne, Thomas (1637–
    1674)
Traill, Henry Duff (1842–1900)
Trapp, Joseph (1679–1747)
Treece, Henry (1911–1966)
Turberville or Turbervile, George
    (?1540–?1610)
Turner, Walter James Redfern
    (1889–1946) (Australia)
Tusser, Thomas (?1524–1580)
Tuttiett, Lawrence (1825–1897)
Vaux, Thomas, 2nd Baron Vaux of
    Harrowden (1510–1556)
Veley, Margaret (1843–1887)
Villiers, George, 2d Duke of Buck-
    ingham (1628–1687)
Wade, Thomas (1805–1875)
Wain, John Barringon (1925–1994)
Wainwright, Jeffrey (1944–)
Waley, Arthur David (1889–1966)
Waller, Edmund (1606–1687)
Walpole, Saint Henry (1558 1595)
Walsh, William (1663–1708)
Warburton, Rowland Eyles Egerton
    (1804–1891)
Warner, Sylvia Townsend (1893–
    1978)
Warner, William (1558–1609)
Warren, John Byrne Leicester, 3d
    Baron De Tabley (1835–1895)
Warren, Sir Thomas Herbert (1853–
    1930)
Warton, Thomas, the Elder; Joseph;
    and Thomas, the Younger (1688–
    1800)
Watson, Sir (John) William (1858–
    1935)
Watson, Thomas (1557?–1592)
Watts, Alaric Alexander (1797–1864)
Watts, Isaac (1674–1748)
Watts-Dunton, Walter Theodore
    (1832–1914)
Waugh, Edwin (1817–1890)
Webb, Mary Gladys (1881–1927)
Webster, Mrs. Augusta (1837–1894)
Weelkes, Thomas (?1576–1623)
Weever, John (1576–1632)
Wellesley, Dorothy Violet, Duchess of
    Wellington (1889–1956)
Wells, Robert (1947–)
Welsted, Leonard (1688–1747)
The Wesleys, Family (1662–1791)
West, Arthur Graeme (1891–1917)
West, Victor (1920–2002)
Westwood, Thomas (1814–1888)
Whalley, Thomas Sedgwick (1746–
    1828)
Whetstone, George (?1544–?1587)
White, Gilbert (1720–1793)
White, Henry Kirke (1785–1806)
Whitehead, Charles (1804–1862)
Whitehead, William (1715–1785)

Whitney, Geoffrey and Isabella
    (?1548–?1601)
Whytehead, Thomas (1815–1843)
Wickham, Anna (1884–1947)
Wicks, Susan (1947–)
Wild or Wylde, Robert (1609–1679)
Williams, Charles Walter Stansby
    (1886–1945)
Williams, Helen Maria (1762–1827)
Williams, Hugo Morduant (1942–)
Wither or Withers, George (1588–
    1667)
Wolcot, John (1738–1819)
Wolfe, Humbert (1886–1940) (Italy)
Woodford, Samuel (1636–1700)
Woodley, George (1786–1846)
Woolner, Thomas (1825–1892)
Wordsworth, William and Dorothy
    (1770–1855)
Wotton, Sir Henry (1568–1639)
Wright, David (1920–1994) (South
    Africa)
Wright, Kit (1944)
Wright, Mehetabel Wesley (1697–
    1750)
Wroth, Lady Mary (?1587–?1651)
Wyatt, Sir Thomas (?1503–1542)
Yalden, Thomas (1670–1736)
Yearsley, Ann (1752–1806)
Young, Edward (1683–1765)
Young, Francis Brett (1884–1954)
Zangwill, Israel (1864–1926)
Zephaniah, Benjamin Obadiah Iqbal
    (1958–)

Ireland

A E (George William Russell) (1867–
    1935)
Alexander, Cecil Frances Humphreys
    (1818–1895)
Arbuckle, James (1700–?1734)
Armstrong, Edmund John (1841–
    1865)
Ashe, Thomas (1836–1889)
Banim, Brothers, Michael and John
    (1796–1874)
Barber Mary (1690–1757)
Bardwell, Leland (1928–)
Barry, Sebastian (1955–)
Beckett, Samuel Barclay (1906–1989)
Bickerstaffe, Isaac (?1733–?1812)
Blackwood, Helen Selina, Countess of
    Dufferin (1807–1867)
Boland, Eavan Aisling (1944–)
Bourke, Eva (Current) (Germany)
Boyse, Samuel (1708–1749)
Brady, Nicholas (1659–1726)
Campbell, Joseph (1879–1944)
Carbery, Ethna (Anna Macmanus)
    (1866–1902)
Carson, Ciaran Gerard (1948–)
Casement, Sir Roger (1864–1916)
Castillo, John (1792–1845)
Clarke, Austin (1896–1974)
Clerke, Ellen Mary (1840–1906)
Coffey, Brian (1905–1995)
Colum, Padraic (1881–1972)

Columba, Saint (fl 543–615)
Cormac, King of Cashel (836–908)
Croly, George (1780–1860)
Curtis, Tony (1955–)
Darley, George (1795–1846)
Davis, Thomas Osborne (1814–1845)
Day-Lewis, Cecil (1904–1972)
De Vere, Sir Aubrey (1788–1846) and
    Aubrey Thomas (1814–1902)
Deane, Seamus (1940–)
Deeley, Patrick (1953–)
Delanty, Greg (1958–)
Denham, Sir John (1615–1669)
Denny, Sir Edward (1796–1889)
Dermody, Thomas (1775–1802)
Dillon, Wentworth, 4th Earl of
    Roscommon (1633–1685)
Dorgan, Theo (1953–)
Dowden, Edward (1843–1913)
Drennan, William (1754–1820)
Drummond, William Hamilton
    (1778–1865)
Duffy, Katherine (1962–)
Duhig, Ian (1954–)
Dunne, Seán (1956–1995)
Durcan, Paul (1944–)
Egan, Desmond (1936–)
Fallon, Padraic (1905–1974)
Ferguson, Sir Samuel (1810–1886)
Flecknoe, Richard (d. 1678?)
Flynn, Leontia (1974–)
French, William Percy (1854–1920)
Galvin, Patrick (1927–)
Gogarty, Oliver St John (1878–1957)
Goldsmith, Oliver (1728–1774)
Gore-Booth, Eva Selina (1870–1926)
Graves, Alfred Perceval and Robert
    Van Ranke (1846–1985)
Greacen, Robert (1920–)
Gregory, Isabella Augusta, Lady Greg-
    ory (1852–1932)
Grierson, Constantia (?1706–1733)
Griffin, Gerald (1803–1840)
Groarke, Vona (1964–)
Halloran, Lawrence Hynes (1766–
    1831)
Hartnett, Michael (1944–1999)
Heaney, Seamus Justin (1939–)
Herbison, David (1800–1880)
Hewitt, John Harold (1907–1987)
Hinkson, Katharine (Tynan) (1861–
    1931)
Hopkins, Charles and John (1664–
    ?1700)
Hyde, Douglas (1860–1949)
Ingram, John Kells (1823–1907)
Iremonger, Valentin (1918–1991)
Jones, Henry (1721–1770)
Joyce, James Augustine (1882–1941)
Joyce, Trevor (1947–)
Kavanagh, Patrick Joseph (1904–
    1967)
Kelly, Thomas (1769–1855)
Kennedy, William (1799–1871)
Kickham, Charles Joseph (1826–
    1882)
Kinsella, Thomas (1928–)
Ledwidge, Francis (1891–1917)
Lever, Charles James (1806–1872)
Lewis, Clive Staples (1898–1963)

Longley, Michael George (1939–)
Lover, Samuel (1797–1868)
Lucas, Henry (?1740–1795)
Mccarthy, Thomas (1954–)
Maccarthy, Denis Florence (1817–
    1882)
Macdonagh, Thomas, and Donagh
    (1878–1968)
Macgreevy, Thomas (1893–1967)
Mcguckian, Medbh (1950–)
Macneice, Frederick Louis (1907–
    1963)
Maginn, William (1793–1842)
Mahon, Derek (1941–)
Mahony, Francis Sylvester (1804–
    1866)
Mangan, James Clarence (1803–1849)
Merriman, Brian (1757–1805)
Miller, Lady Anna (1741–1781)
Millikin, Richard Alfred (1767–1815)
Monsell, John Samuel Bewley (1811–
    1875)
Montague, John (1929–) (America)
Moore, Thomas (1779–1852)
Morrisey, Sinead (1972–)
Muldoon, Paul (1951–)
Murdoch, Dame Jean Iris (1919–1999)
Murphy, Jerry (1952–)
Murphy, Richard (1927–)
Ní Chuilleanáin, Eiléan (1942–)
Ní Dhomhnaill, Nuala (1952–)
Nugent, Robert, Earl Nugent (1702–
    1788)
O'donnell, John (1960–)
O'donnell, John Francis (1837–1874)
O'donoghue, Bernard (1945–)
O'donoghue, Gregory (1951–2005)
O'driscoll, Dennis (1954–)
O'hussey, Eochaidh (c.1574–c.1630)
O'keeffe, John and Adelaide (1747–
    1833)
O'neill, Mary Devenport (1879–1967)
Ormsby, Frank (1947–)
Orr, James (1770–1816)
Orrery, Roger Boyle, 1st Earl of
    (1621–1679)
O'sullivan, Seamus (1879–1958)
Owenson, Sydney, Lady Morgan
    (?1783–1859)
Parnell, Thomas (1679–1718)
Patrick, Saint (387–493)
Paulin, Thomas Neilson (1949–)
Pearse, Patrick Henry (1879–1916)
Pennefather, William (1816–1873) and
    Catherine (1818–1893)
Pilkington, Matthew and Laetitia
    (1701–1774)
Plunkett, Joseph Mary (1887–1916)
Raftery, Anthony (1784–1835) (Ó
    Reachtabhra, Antoine)
Maurice Riordan (1953–)
Rodgers, William Robert (1909–1969)
Rosenstock, Gabriel (1949–)
Ross, Alan (1922–2001)
Salkeld, Blanaid (1880–1959)
Savage-Armstrong, George Francis
    (1845–1906)
Scully, Maurice (1952–)
Sheridan, Richard Brinsley (1751–
    1816)

Sheridan, Thomas (1687–1738)
Smyth, Gerard (1951–)
Steele, Sir Richard (1672–1729)
Stephens, James (1880–1950)
Sweeney, Matthew (1952–)
Swift, Jonathan (1667–1745)
Synge, Edmund John Millington
    (1871–1909)
Tate, Nahum (1652–1715)
Tighe, Mrs. Mary Blachford
    (1772–1810)
Trench, Frederic Herbert (1865–1923)
Tynan, Katharine (1861–1931)
Walsh, Catherine (1964–)
Walsh, Edward (1805–1850)
Wilde, Lady Jane and Oscar (1826–
    1900)
Wolfe, Charles (1791–1823)
Woods, Macdara (1942–)
Wyley, Enda (1966–)
Yeats, William Butler (1865–1939)

Scotland

Adamson, Henry (d. 1639)
Aird, Thomas (1802–1876)
Alexander, Sir William, Earl of Stir-
    ling (?1567–1640)
Alves, Robert (1745–1794)
Anderson, Alexander (1845–1909)
Annand James King (1908–1993)
Armstrong, John (1709–1779)
Ayton, or Aytoun, Sir Robert (1570–
    1638)
Aytoun, William Edmondstoune
    (1813–1865)
Baillie, Joanna (1762–1857 or 1762–
    1851)
Baillie, Lady Grisel (1665–1746)
Barbour, John (?1316–1395)
Beattie, George (1786–1823)
Beattie, James (1735–1803)
Bellenden, John (1533–?1587)
Bisset, James (1762–1832)
Blackie, John Stuart (1809–1895)
Blacklock, Thomas (1721–1791)
Blair, Robert (1699–1746)
Bonar, Horatius (1808–1889)
Boswell, James (1740–1795)
Brown, George Mackay (1917–1996)
Bruce, George (1909–2002)
Bruce, Michael (1746–1767)
Buchan, John, 1st Baron Tweedsmuir
    (1875–1940)
Buchanan, Dugald 1716–1768
Burns, James Drummond (1823–
    1864)
Burns, Robert (1759–1796)
Burnside, John (1955–)
Cameron, John Norman (1905–1953)
Campbell, Thomas (1774–1844)
Carnegie, James, 9th Earl of Southesk
    (1827–1905)
Clanchy, Kate (1965–)
Cleland, William (1661–1689)
Clerk, Sir John, of Penicuik (1676–
    1755)
Colvin, Ian Duncan (1877–1938)

Craig, Alexander (?1567–1627)
Crawford, Robert (1959–)
Cunningham, Allan (1784–1842)
Davidson, John (1857–1909)
Devlin, Denis (1908–1959)
Douglas, Gawin or Gavin (?1474–
    1522)
Douglas, Neil (1750–1823)
Doyle, Sir Arthur Ignatius Conan
    (1859–1930)
Drummond, William of Hawthorn-
    den (1585–1649)
Duffy, Carol Ann (1955–)
Dunbar, William (?1465–?1513)
Dunn, Douglas Eaglesham (1942–)
Elliot, Jane or Jean (1727–1805)
Erceldoune, Thomas of Learmont (fl.
    ?1207–?1297)
Erskine, Ralph (1685–1752)
Erskine, Thomas, 1st Baron Erskine
    (1750–1823)
Falconer, William (1732–1769)
Fergusson, Robert (1750–1774)
Finlay, Ian Hamilton (1925–)
    (Orkney)
Finlay, John (1782–1810)
Fowler, William (1560–1612)
Fraser, George Sutherland (1915–
    1980)
Garioch, Robert (1909–1987)
Gilfillan, Robert (1798–1850)
Graham, James, Marquis of Montrose
    (1612–1650)
Graham, William Sydney (1918–1986)
Grahame, James (1765–1811)
Grahame, Kenneth (1859–1932)
Grainger, James (?1721–1766)
Gray, Alasdair (1934–)
Gray, David (1838–1861)
Gray, Sir Alexander (1882–1968)
Greig, Andrew (1951–)
Hamilton, William of Bangour
    (1704–1754)
Hannay, Patrick (D. ?1629)
Hay, George Campbell (1915–1984)
Healy, Randolph (1956–)
Henderson, Hamish (1919–2002)
Hendry, James Findlay (1912–1986)
Henry the Minstrel (?1470–?1492)
Henryson or Henderson, Robert
    (?1430–?1506)
Herbert, W. N (1961–)
Hervey, Thomas Kibble (1799–1859)
Hogg, James, "The Ettrick Shepherd"
    (1770–1835)
Holland, Sir Richard (?1420–?1485)
Home, John (1722–1808)
Hume or Home, Alexander (?1560–
    1609)
Hutchinson, Pearse (1927–)
Hyslop, James (1798–1827)
James V, King of Scotland (1512–
    1542)
James I, King of Scotland (1394–
    1437)
Jamie, Kathleen (1962–)
Jeffrey, Francis, Lord Jeffrey (1773–
    1850)
Johnston, Arthur (1587–1641)
Kay, Jackie (1961–)

Kelly, Isabella (?1759–1857)
Kennedy, Walter (1460?–1508?)
Ker, Patrick (fl. 1691)
Knox, William (1789–1825)
Lang, Andrew (1844–1912)
Lapraik, John (1727–1807)
Lauder, George (?1600 1677)
Leighton, Robert (1822–1869)
Leonard, Tom (1944–)
Leyden, John (1775–1811)
Lindsay [or Lyndsay] Sir David (?1486–1555)
Lochhead, Liz (1947–)
Lochore, Robert (1762–1852)
Logan, John (1748–1788)
Lowe, John (1750–1798)
Lyte, Henry Francis (1793–1847)
Macbeth, George Mann (1932–1992)
Maccaig, Norman Alexander (1910–1996)
Macdiarmid Hugh (1892–1978)
Macdonald, Alexander, Alasdair (?1700–?1780)
Macdonald, George (1824–1905)
Macfarlan, James (1832–1862)
Macintyre, Duncan Ban (1724–1812)
Mackail, John William (1859–1945)
Mackay, Charles (1814–1889)
Maclean, Sorley (1911–1996)
Macleod, Mary (1569–1674)
Macneill, Hector (1746–1818)
Macpherson, James (1736–1796)
Maitland, Sir Richard, Lord Lethington (1496–1586)
Mallet, (Originally Malloch), David (?1705–1765)
Martin, Sir Theodore (1816–1909)
Matheson, George (1842–1906)
Mayne, John (1759–1836)
Mccheyne, Robert Murray (1813–1843)
Mcgonagall, William Topaz (1825–1902)
Meston, William (?1688–1745)
Mickle, William Julius (1735–1788)
Miller, William (1810–1872)
Mitchison, Lady Naomi (1897–1999)
Moir, David Macbeth (1798–1851)
Montgomerie, Alexander (?1556–?1610)
Montgomery, James (1771–1854)
Morgan, Edwin George (1920–)
Motherwell, William (1797–1835)
Muir, Edwin (1887–1959) (Orkney)
Mure, Sir William (1594–1657)
Murray, Sir David of Gorthy (1567–1629)
Nairne, Carolina Oliphant, Baroness (1766–1845)
Neaves, Charles, Lord Neaves (1800–1876)
Neilson, Peter (1795–1861)

Nevay, John (1792–1870)
Nicoll, Robert (1814–1837)
Ogilby, John (1600–1676)
Ogilvie, John (1733–1813)
Outram. George (1805–1856)
Park, Andrew (1807–1863)
Paterson, Don (1963–)
Pennecuik, Alexander. and Nephew (1652–1730)
Pollok, Robert (1798–1827)
Pringle, Thomas (1789–1834)
Ramsay, Allan (1686–1758)
Riddell, Henry Scott (1798–1870)
Robertson, Robin (1955–)
Rodger, Alexander (1784–1846)
Rolland, John (fl. 1560)
Ross, Alexander (1591–1654)
Ross, Alexander (1699–1784)
Ross, William (1762–1790)
Scott, Alexander (?1525–?1584)
Scott, Lady John (Alicia Ann Spottiswoode) (1810–1900)
Scott, Sir Walter (1771–1832)
Scott, William Bell (1811–1890)
Service, Robert William (1874–1958) (Canada)
Sharp, William (1855–1905)
Skinner, John (1721–1807)
Smith, Alexander (1829/30–1867)
Smith, Iain Crichton (1928–1998)
Smith, Walter Chalmers (1824–1908)
Smollett, Tobias George (1721–1771)
Sorley, Charles Hamilton (1895–1915)
Soutar, William (1898–1943)
Spark, Muriel (1918–2006) Stevenson, Robert Louis (1850–1894)
Stoddart, Thomas Tod (1810–1880)
Struthers, John (1776–1853)
Tannahill, Robert (1774–1810)
Tennant, William (1784–1848)
Tessimond, Arthur Seymour John (1902–1962)
Thomson, James (1700–1748)
Thomson, James (1834–1882)
Todd, Ruthven (1914–1978)
Turnbull, Gael (1928–2004)
Wedderburn Brothers (?1495–?1557)
Wilkie, William (1721–1772)
Young, Andrew John (1885–1971)
Young, Douglas (1913–1973)

Wales

Abse, Dannie (1923–)
Aled, Tudur (fl 1480–1525)
Allott, Kenneth (1912–1973)
Aneirin (6th Century)
Bush, Duncan (1946–)
Clarke, Gillian (1937–)
Curtis, Tony (1946–)

Cynddelw Brydydd Mawr (?1157–?1195)
Davies, Grahame (1964–)
Davies, Idris (1905–1953)
Davies, William Henry (1871–1940)
Davis, David (1745–1827)
Dyer, John (1699–1758)
Elfyn, Menna (1951–)
Evans, Ellis Humphrey (1887–1917)
Finch, Peter (1947–)
Gray, Kathryn (1973–)
Hanmer, Sir John, Baron Hanmer (1809–1881)
Holland, Hugh (?1569–?1635)
Holland, Robert (1557–?1622)
Hughes, John Ceyiriog (1832–1887)
Humphreys, Emyr (1919–)
Hywel Ab Owain Gwynedd (d. 1170)
Jenkins, Nigel (1949–)
Jones, Glyn (1905–1995)
Lewis, Alun (1915–1944)
Lewis, David (?1683–1760)
Lewis, Gwyneth (1959–)
Lloyd, Evan (1734–1776)
Llwyd, Hugh or Huw (?1568–1630)
Llwyd, Morgan (1619–1659)
Llwyd, Richard (1752–1835)
Mathias, Roland (1915–)
Minhinnick, Robert (1952–)
Morris, Sir Lewis (1833–1907)
Morris-Jones, Sir John (1864–1929)
Morus, Huw (1622–1709)
Morys, Lewis (1700–1765)
Norris, Leslie (1921–2006)
Olivers, Thomas (1725–1799)
Ormond, John (1923–1990)
Owen, Goronwy or Gronow (1723–1769?)
Parry-Williams, Sir Thomas Herbert (1887–1975)
Petit, Pascale (1953–) (France)
Rees-Jones, Deryn (1968–)
Roberts, Lynette (1909–1995) (Argentina)
Sheers, Owen (1974–)
Sinclair, Iain (1943–)
Symons, Arthur William (1865–1945)
Taliesin (fl 550)
Thomas, Dylan Marlais (1914–1953)
Thomas, R(onald) S(tuart) (1913–2000)
Vaughan, Henry and Thomas (1622–1695)
Waring, Anna Letitia (1823–1910)
Watkins, Vernon Phillips (1906–1967)
Williams, Edward (1747–1826)
Williams, Isaac (1802–1865)
Williams, Sir Charles Hanbury (1709–1757)
Williams, Waldo (1904–1971)
Williams, William (1717–1791)

Timeline of British and Irish Poets

Old English (449–1066)

Pre-11th century
387–493	Patrick, Saint
6th century	Aneirin
fl. c. 543–615	Columba, Saint
849–99	Alfred, King of England
fl. 550	Taliesin
fl. 658–680	Cædmon
fl. 750	Kynewulf, Cynewulf, or Cynwulf
673–735	Venerable Bede, The
fl. 9th cent.	Cormac, King of Cashel

Middle English (1066–1485)

13th century
fl. 1220?–1297?	Erceldoune, Thomas of Learmont
?1288–?1338	Mannyng, Robert, or Robert de Brunne

14th century
1300?–1352?	Minot, Laurence
1316?–1395	Barbour, John
1325?–1408	Gower, John
1330?–1400?	Langland, William
1340?–1400	Chaucer, Geoffrey
c. 1341–1391	Clanvow, Sir John
1368?–1450	Occleve, Thomas (or Hoccleve)
1370?–1451?	Lydgate, John
1394–1437	James I, King of Scotland

fl. 15th cent
?1420–?1485	Holland, Sir Richard
1430?–1506?	Henryson or Henderson, Robert
1460?–1529	Skelton, John
1460?–1508?	Kennedy, Walter
1465?–1513?	Dunbar, William
?1470–?1492	Henry the Minstrel
1474?–1522	Douglas, Gawin or Gavin
1475?–1552	Barclay, Alexander
?1474/5–1523	Hawes, Stephen
1480–1525fl	Aled, Tudur
?1486–1555	Lyndsay, or Lyndsay Sir David
1491–1547	Henry VIII, King of England
1495?–1553	Wedderburn, James
1496–1586	Maitland, Sir Richard, Lord Lethington

Renaissance (1485–1603)

1510–65	Forrest, William
d. 1595	Howard, Philip, 1st Earl of Arundel
d. 1597	Hunnis, William
fl. 1557	Huggarde or Hoggarde, Miles
1560–1612	Fowler, William
fl. 1560	Rolland, John
fl. 1578–1584	Proctor, Thomas
fl. 1595	Edwards, Thomas
fl. 1596	Cotton, Roger
fl. 1596	Griffin, Bartholomew
1500?–1579	Ferrers, George
1500?–1556	Wedderburn, John
1503?–1542	Wyatt, Sir Thomas
1510–55	Bowring, Sir John
1510–1556	Vaux, Thomas, Baron Vaux of Harrowden
1510?–1557?	Wedderburn, Robert
1513–1542	James V, King of Scotland
c. 1515–1563	Baldwin, William
1517?–1547	Howard, Henry, Earl of Surrey
1519–1562	Grimald, Nicholas
?1520–1604	Churchyard, Thomas
1521–1546	Askew, Anne
1524?–1580	Tusser, Thomas
1525?–1577	Gascoigne, George
1525?–1584?	Scott, Alexander
1529?–1566?	Hall or Halle, John
?1529–1591	Puttenham, George
1532–1584	Norton, Thomas
1533–1587 fl.	Bellenden, or Ballenden, or Ballentyne, John
1533–1603	Elizabeth I
?1568–1620	Llwyd, Hugh or Huw
1535–1598	Heywood, Jasper
1536–1608	Sackville, Thomas, 1st Earl of Dorset
1540–1594	Googe, Barnabe
1540?–1610?	Turberville or Turbervile, George
?1540 after 1580	Whitney, Isabella
1542–1591	Grenville, Sir Richard
1544?–1587?	Whetstone, George
1545?–1626?	Breton, Nicholas
1548?–1601?	Whitney, Geoffrey
1549?–1611	Fletcher, Giles
1550–1604	De Vere, Edward, 17th Earl of Oxford
1550?–1631	Harvey, Gabriel
1552–1618	Ralegh, Sir Walter
1552?–1599	Spenser, Edmund

1553?–1608?	Lok, Lock, or Locke, Henry
1553–1633	Munday, Anthony
1554–1628	Greville, Sir Fulke, first Baron Brooke
1554–1586	Sidney, Sir Philip
1555–1620	Carew, Richard
1556?–1610?	Montgomerie, Alexander
1557–1622?	Holland, Robert
1557/58–1602	Morley, Thomas
1557?–1592	Watson, Thomas
1558?–1592	Greene, Robert
1558–1625	Lodge, Thomas
1558–1596	Peele, George
1558 1595	Walpole, Henry
1558?–1609	Warner, William
1559?–1634	Chapman, George
1560–1612	Fowler, William
1560?–1609	Hume or Home, Alexander
1561–1626	Bacon, Sir Francis, Viscount St. Albans
1561–1612	Harington, Sir John
1561–1621	Herbert, Mary Sidney, Countess of Pembroke
1561?–1595	Southwell, Saint Robert
1562–1613	Constable, Henry
1562–1619	Daniel, Samuel
1562–1621	Pembroke, Mary Sidney Herbert, Countess of
1563–1626	Dowland, John
1563–1631	Drayton, Michael
1563–1618	Sylvester, Josuah
1564–1593	Marlowe, Christopher
1564–1616	Shakespeare, William
1565?–1618,	Davies, John of Hereford
1566?–1640?	Chester, Robert
1566–1625	James I, King of England
1567–1640	Alabaster, William
1567?–1640	Alexander, Sir William, Earl of Stirling
1567?–1627	Craig, Alexander
1567–1601	Essex, Robert Devereux, 2nd Earl of
1567–1629	Murray, Sir David of Gorthy
1567–1601	Nashe, Thomas
?1568 or ?1569–1629	Hubert, Sir Francis
1568–1637	Markham, Gervase
?1568–?1635	Holland, Hugh
1569?–1609	Barnes, Barnabe
1569–1626	Davies, Sir John
1569–1645	Lanier, Emilia
1569–1674	MacLeod, Mary
?1570–1632	Dekker, Thomas
1570–1638	Ayton, or Aytoun, Sir Robert
?1570–1627	Middleton, Thomas
1570–?1630	Rowlands, Samuel
1572–1637	Jonson, Ben
1573–1631	Donne, John
1574–1627	Barnfield, Richard
1574–1634	Marston, John
1575?–1633?	Bolton or Boulton, Edmund
1575?–1638	Fitzgeffrey, Charles
1575?–1650	Heywood, Thomas
1575–1648	Percy, William
1576?–1623	Weelkes, Thomas
1576–1632	Weever, John
1578–1644	Sandys, George
1579–1625	Fletcher, John
1580?–1648	Ford, Thomas
1580–1630	Herbert, William, 3rd Earl of Pembroke
fl. 1580–1622	Roydon, Matthew
1580?–1626	Scott, Thomas
1580–1653	Taylor, John
1580?–1632?	Webster, John

?1581–1627	Adamson, Henry
1581–1608?	Davison, Walter
1582–1635	Corbet, Richard
1583–1627	Beaumont, Sir John
1583–1648	Herbert, Edward, 1st Baron Herbert of Cherbury
1583–1640	Massinger, Philip
?1583–1601–1643	Townsend, Aurelian
1584–1616	Beaumont, Francis
1584–1616	Niccols, Richard
c. 1585–1639	Cary, Lady Elizabeth
1585–1649	Drummond, William of Hawthornden
1585?–1630?	Hagthorpe, John
1586–1640	Ford, John
1587–1641	Johnston, Arthur
fl. 1587–1633	Fraunce, Abraham
1587?–1651?	Wroth, Lay Mary
1588?–1623	Fletcher, Giles, the younger
1588–1667	Wither or Withers, George
1589–1639	Carey, Lady Elizabeth
1591–1643?	Browne, William
1591–1674	Herrick, Robert
1591–1654	Ross, Alexander
1592–1676	Cavendish, William, Duke of Newcastle
1592–1669	King, Henry
1592–1644	Quarles, Francis
1593–1633	Herbert, George
1594–1657	Mure, Sir William
1595–1650	May, Thomas
1595?–1639?	Carew, Thomas
1596–1666	Shirley, James
1597–1663	Harvey, Christopher

17th century

d. 1601	Linche or Lynche, Richard
d. 1607	Dyer, Sir Edward
d. 1620	Campion, Thomas
d. 1620	Tofte, Robert
d. 1625	Gorges, Sir Arthur
1629?	Hannay, Patrick
d. 1641?	Beedome, Thomas
d. 1645	Colman, Walter
d. 1669	Stapleton or Stapylton, Sir Robert
d. 1675	Ross, Thomas
d. 1678?	Flecknoe, Richard
d. 1682	Philipot, Thomas
d. 1694	Heyrick, Thomas
fl. 1600	Chalkhill, John
fl. 1602	Davison, Francis
fl. 1603–1645	Pricket, Robert
fl. 1620	Lane, John
fl. 1630	O'Hussey, Eochaidh
fl. 1646	Mill Or Mille, Humphrey
fl. 1657	Crompton, Hugh
fl. 1679	Carkesse, James
fl. 1691	Ker, Patrick
1600–1671	Knevet, Ralph
?1600–1677	Lauder, George
1600–1676	Ogilby, John
1602–1665	Fane, Mildmay, 2d Earl of Westmorland
1602–1645	Strode, William
1605–1882	Browne, Sir Thomas
1605–1654	Habington, William
1605–1635	Randolph, Thomas
1606–1668	D'Avenant, Sir William
1606–1633	More, Dame Gertrude
1606–1687	Waller, Edmund
1608–1674	Milton, John
1609–1642	Suckling, Sir John

1609–1679	Wild or Wylde, Robert
1610–1643	Godolphin, Sidney
1611–1643	Cartwright, William
1612–1680	Butler, Samuel
1612–1671	Fairfax of Cameron, Thomas Fairfax, Baron
1612–1650	Graham, James, Marquis of Montrose
1612?–1685	Jordan, Thomas
1613?–1649	Crashaw, Richard
1614–1687	More, Henry
1615–1669	Denham, Sir John
1616–1682	Lluelyn or Lluellyn, Martin
1618–1667	Cowley, Abraham
1618–1658	Lovelace, Richard
1618–1702	Sherburne, Sir Edward
1619–1659	Llwyd, Morgan
1621–1678	Marvel1, Andrew
1621–1679	Orrery, Robert Boyle, 1st Earl of
1622–1695	Vaughan, Henry
1622–1666	Vaughan, Thomas
1622–1709	Morus, Huw
1623–1673	Cavendish, Margaret Duchess of Newcastle
1624?–1684	Crossman, Samuel
1624–1665	Quarles, John
1625–1678	Stanley, Thomas
1626–98	Howard, Sir Robert
1627–1683	Bold, Henry
1627–1656	Hall, John, of Durham
1630–1687	Cotton, Charles
1631–1700	Dryden, John
1631–1664	Philips, Katherine
1632–1680	Shipman, Thomas
?1632–1664	Tatham, John
1633–1685	Dillon, Wentworth, Earl of Roscommon
1633–1691?	Pordage, Samuel
?1635–1691	Etherege, Sir George
1635–1713	Sprat, Thomas
1636–1700	Woodford, Samuel
1637–1688	Flatman, Thomas
1637–1711	Ken, Thomas
1637–16 74	Traherne, Thomas
1638–1706	Sackville, Charles, sixth Earl of Dorset
1639?–1701	Sedley, Sir Charles
1640–1689	Behn, Aphra
1642?–1692	Shadwell, Thomas
1646?–1694	Mason, John
1647–1680	Rochester, John Wilmot Earl
1648–1724	Settle, Elkanah
1648–1721	Sheffield, John
1649–1680	Scroope, Sir Carr
1652–1722	Pennecuik, Alexander
1652–1715	Tate, Nahum
1653–1723	D'Urfey, Thomas
1653–1683	Oldham, John
1654–1729	Blackmore, Sir Richard
fl. 1654–1685	Stevenson, Matthew
1656–1710	Chudleigh, Lady Mary
1657–1711	Norris, John
1658–1711	Duke, Richard
1659-1700	Creech, Thomas
1660–1731	Defoe, Daniel
1660–1685	Killigrew, Anne
1661–1707	Cutts, John, Baron Cutts
1661–1720	Finch, Anne, Countess of Winchilsea
1661–1719	Garth, Sir Samuel
1661–1715	Montague, Charles, Earl of Halifax
1662–1735	Wesley, Samuel
1663–1704	Brown, Tom
1663–1771	King, William
1663–1707	Stepney, George

1663–1708	Walsh, William
1664?–1735	Glanvill, John
1664–1700?	Hopkins, Charles and John
1664–1721	Prior, Matthew
1667–1735	Granville. George, Lord Lansdowne
1667–1702	Pomfret, John
1667–1745	Swift, Jonathan

Augustans (1667–1780)

1670–1729	Congreve, William
1670–1723	Egerton, Sarah Fyge
1670–1736	Yalden, Thomas
1673–1742	Oldmixon, John
1674–1718	Rowe, Nicholas
1674–1748	Watts, Isaac
1675?–1749	Philips, Ambrose
1675–1742	Somerville, William
1676–1709	Philips, John
1677–1720	Hughes, John
1679–1718	Parnell, Thomas
1679–1747	Trapp, Joseph
1682?–1765	Newcomb, Thomas
1683?–1760	Lewis, David
1683–1765	Young, Edward
1685–1717	Diaper, William
1685–1752	Erskine, Ralph
1685–1732	Gay, John
1685–1713	Harrison, William
1685–1750	Hill, Aaron
1686–1758	Ramsay, Allan
1686–1740	Tickell, Thomas
1687–1738	Sheridan, Thomas
1688–1730	Eusden, Laurence
1688?–1745	Meston, William
1688–1744	Pope, Alexander
1688–1745	Warton, Thomas, the Elder
1688–1747	Welsted, Leonard
1689–1745	Broome, William
1689–1762	Montagu, Lady Mary Wortley
?1690–1726	Sewell, George
1692–1774	Browne, Sir William
1692–1763	Byrom, John
1693–1739	Jacob, Hildebrand
1608–1684	Cokayne, Sir Aston
1613–1658	Cleveland, John
1616–1699	Beaumont, Joseph, D.D.
1620–1666	Brome, Alexander
fl. 1623	Abbot, John, B.D. fl
1625–1711	Caryl1, John, titular Lord Caryll
1628–1688	Bunyan, John
1628–1687	Villiers, George, 2d Duke of Buckingham
d. 1640	Aleyn, Charles
1652–1727?	Barker, Jane
1659–1726	Brady, Nicholas
1661?–1689	Cleland, William
1666–1731	Astell, Mary
1672–1719	Addison, Joseph
1676–1755	Clerk, Sir John, Of Penicuik
1683–1730	Fenton, Elijah
1688–c.1762	Collier, Mary
1691–1739	Wesley, Samuel, the Younger
1694?–1744	Bramston, James
1694–1773	Chesterfield, Philip Dormer Stanhope, 4th Earl of
1694–1754	Tollet, Elizabeth
1695–1747	Bourne, Vincent
1696–1737	Green, Matthew

1697–1742	Amhurst, Nicholas
1697–1743	Savage, Richard
1697–1750	Wright, Mehetabel Wesley
1698–1774	Baker, Henry
1699–1746	Blair, Robert
1699–1757	Edwards, Thomas
1699–1748	Pitt, Christopher
1699–1784	Ross, Alexander

18th century

b. 1769	Cristall, Anne Batten
d. 1709?	Gould, Robert
d. 1730	Pennecuik, Alexander
d. 1732	Jones, Samuel
d. 1758	Mendes, Moses
fl. 1707	Elys, Edmund
fl. 1763	Hoyland, Francis
1700–1734?	Arbuckle, James
1700?–1758	Dyer, John
1700–1780?	Macdonald, Alexander, Alasdair
1700–1765	Morys, Lewis
1700–1748	Thomson, James
1701–1774	Pilkington, Matthew
1702–1751	Doddridge, Philip
1702–1788	Nugent, Robert, Earl Nugent
1703–1764	Dodsley, Robert
1703–1791	Wesley, John
1704–1754	Hamilton, William
1705–1760	Browne, Isaac Hawkins, the elder
1705–1788	Cotton, Nathaniel
1705–1756	Duck, Stephen
1705?–1765	Mallet, originally Malloch, David
1706?–1733	Grierson, Constantia
1706–1727	Pattison, William
1707–1778	Jones, Mary
1707–1788	Wesley, Charles
1708–1749	Boyse, Samuel
1709–1779	Armstrong, John, M.D.
1709–1763	Dalton, John
1709–1769	Davies, Sneyd
1709–1784	Johnson, Samuel
1709–1757	Williams, Sir Charles Hanbury
1710–1742	Hammond, James
1712–1785	Glover, Richard
1712–1757	Moore, Edward
1712–1750	Pilkington, Laetitia
1712–1743	Relph, Josiah
1712?–1766?	Thompson, William
1714–1763	Shenstone, William
1715–1804	Graves, Richard
1715–1781	Jago, Richard
1715–1785	Whitehead, William
1716–1793	Berridge, John
1716–1768	Buchanan, Dugald
1716–1771	Gray, Thomas
1716–1778	Steele, Anne
1716–1742	West, Richard
1717–1806	Carter, Elizabeth
1717–1778	Steele, Anne
1717–1791	Williams, William
1718–1755	Cennick, John
1718–1798	Maude, Thomas
1719–1761	Cawthorn, James
1721–1770	Akenside, Mark
1721–1819	Bakewell, John
1721–1807	Skinner, John
1721–1771	Smollett, Tobias George
1720–1777	Fawkes, Francis
1720–1800	Maxwell, James
1720–1769	Merrick, James

1720–1793	White, Gilbert
1721–1791	Blacklock, Thomas
1721–1759	Collins, William
1721?–1766	Grainger, James, M.D.
1721–1770	Jones, Henry
1721–1772	Wilkie, William
1722–1808	Home, John
1722–1746	Leapor, Mary
1722–1771	Smart, Christopher
1722–1800	Warton, Joseph
1723–1769?	Owen, Goronwy or Gronow
1724–1805	Anstey, Christopher
1724–1775	Lovibond, Edward
1724–1812	Macintyre, Duncan Ban
1725–1797	Mason, William
1725–1807	Newton, John
1725–1799	Olivers, Thomas
1726–1792	Perronet, Edward
1727–1805	Elliot, Jane or Jean
1727–1812	Jerningham, Edward
1727–1807	Lapraik, John
1728–1774	Goldsmith, Oliver
1728–1790	Warton, Thomas, the younger
1729–1773	Cunningham, John
1729–1811	Percy, Thomas
1729–1797	Shrubsole, William
1731–1764	Churchill, Charles
1731–1800	Cowper, William
1731–1802	Darwin, Erasmus
1731–1808	Freeth, John
?1731–1791	Grose, Francis
1732–1807	Carr, Sir John
1732–1769	Falconer, William
1733–1764	Lloyd, Robert
1733–1813	Ogilvie, John
1734–1776	Lloyd, Evan
1735–1803	Beattie, James
1735–1812	Bickerstaffe, Isaac
1735–1779	Langhorne, John
1735–1788	Mickle, William Julius
1736–1774	Jenner, Charles
1736–1796	Macpherson, James
1738–1799	Medley, Samuel
1738–1819	Wolcot, John
1739–1771	Shaw, Cuthbert
1740–1795	Boswell, James
1740–1809	Downman, Hugh
1740–1817	Fawcett, John
?1740–1795	Lucas, Henry
1740–1808	Moss, Thomas
1740–1800	Tasker, William
1740–1778	Toplady, Augustus Montague
1741–1781	Miller, Lady Anna
1742–1779	Penrose, Thomas
1743–1825	Barbauld, Anna Letitia
1743–1809	Cowley, Hannah
1745–1794	Alves, Robert
1745–1829	Crowe, William
1745–1827	Davis, David
1745–1820	Hayley, William
1745–1833	More, Hannah
1745–1813	Pye, Henry James
1746–1767	Bruce, Michael
1746–1794	Jones, Sir William
1746–1818	Macneill, Hector
1746–1828	Whalley, Thomas Sedgwick
1747–1794	Blamire, Susanna
1747–1833	O'Keeffe, John
1747–1809	Seward, Anna
1747–1826	Williams, Edward

1748–1825	Hall, William
1748–1788	Logan, John
1748–1806	Smith, Charlotte
1749–1809	Huddesford, George
1749–1823	Jenner, Edward
1749–1814	Pratt, Samuel Jackson
1750?–1802	Burrell, Lady Sophia
1750–1823	Douglas, Neil
1750–1823	Erskine, Thomas, 1st Baron Erskine
1750–1774	Fergusson, Robert
1750–1798	Lowe, John
1751–1816	Sheridan, Richard Brinsley
1752–1770	Chatterton, Thomas
1752–1835	Llwyd, Richard
1752–1803	Ritson, Joseph
1752–1806	Yearsley, Ann
1753–1831	Roscoe, William
1754–1832	Crabbe, George
1754–1820	Drennan, William
1756–1780	Moore, Sir John Henry
1757–1827	Blake, William
1757–1805	Merriman, Brian
1758–1800	Robinson, Mary
1759–1796	Burns, Robert
?1759–1857	Kelly, Isabella
1760?–1822	Thomas, David
1762–1851	Baillie, Joanna
1762–1832	Bisset, James
1762–1850	Bowles, William Lisle
1762–1837	Brydges, Sir Samuel Egerton
1762–1836	Colman, George
1762–1852	Lochore, Robert
1762–1790	Ross, William
1762–1788	Russell, Thomas
1762–1827	Williams, Helen Maria
1763–1801	Hurdis, James
1763–1855	Rogers, Samuel
1763–1817	Sayers, Frank
1764–1823	Radcliffe, Anne
1765–1834	Fanshawe, Catherine Maria
1765–1836	Taylor William
1608–1666	Sir Richard Fanshawe
1765–1811	Grahame, James
1765–1788	Headley, Henry
1765?–1851	Luttrell, Henry
1767–1815	Millikin, Richard Alfred
1769–1855	Kelly, Thomas
1769–1853	Opie, Mrs. Amelia
1770–1827	Canning, George
1770–1835	Hogg, James
1770–1816	Orr, James
1770–1834	Spencer, William Robert
1770–1823	Stagg, John
1770–1850	Wordsworth, William
1771–1854	Montgomery, James
1771–1832	Scott, Sir Walter
1771–1855	Wordsworth, Dorothy
1772–1834	Coleridge, Samuel Taylor
1772–1851	Kennedy, Rann
1772–1810	Tighe, Mrs. Mary Blachford
1773–1826	Heber, Reginald
1773–1850	Jeffrey, Francis, Lord Jeffrey
1774–1843	Southey, Robert
1774–1810	Tannahill, Robert
1775–1817	Austen, Jane
1775–1834	Lamb, Charles
1775–1864	Landor, Walter Savage
1775–1811	Leyden, John, M.D.
1775–1843	Rose, William Stewart
1766–1845	Nairne, Carolina

1776–1853	Struthers, John
1775–1839	Lloyd, Charles
1776–1855?	O'Keeffe, Adelaide
1775–1836	Bulmer, Agnes
1775–1802	Dermody, Thomas
1776–1838	Fitchett, John
1777–1844	Campbell, Thomas
1778–1865	Drummond, William Hamilton
1778–1853	Elton, Sir Charles Abraham
1778–1847	Herbert, William
1779–1838	Grant, Sir Robert
1779–1844	Merivale, John Herman
1779–1852	Moore, Thomas
1779–1849	Smith, Horatio

Romantics (1780–1830)

1780–1860	Croly, George
1781–1849	Elliott, Ebenezer
1781–1829	Hovell-Thurlow, Edward, 2d Baron Thurlow
1782–1843	Roscoe, William Stanley
1782–1866	Taylor, Ann
1783?–1859	Owenson, Sydney, Lady Morgan
1783–1824	Taylor, Jane
1784–1842	Cunningham, Allan
1784–1859	Hunt, James Henry Leigh
1784–1835	Raftery, Anthony
1784–1846	Rodger, Alexander
1784–1848	Tennant, William
1785–1828	Lamb, Lady Caroline
1785–1866	Peacock, Thomas Love
1785–1806	White, Henry Kirke
1786–1854	Southey, Mrs. Caroline Anne Bowles
1786–1846	Woodley, George
1787–1874	Procter, Bryan Waller
1788–1872	Atherstone, Edwin
1788–1846	De Vere, Sir Aubrey
1788–1839	Millhouse, Robert
1789–1855	Conder, Josiah
1789–1871	Elliott, Charlotte
1789–1825	Knox, William
1789–1834	Pringle, Thomas
1790–1843	Nicholson, John
1791–1857	Furness, Richard
1791–1868	Milman, Henry Hart
1791–1851	Quillinan, Edward
1791–1823	Wolfe, Charles
1792–1871	Herschel, John Frederick William
1792–1879	Howitt, William
1792–1866	Keble, John
1792–1870	Nevay, John
1792–1822	Shelley, Percy Bysshe
1793–1864	Clare, John
1793–1870	Havergal, William Henry
1793–1835	Hemans, Felicia Dorothea
1793–1847	Lyte, Henry Francis
1793–1842	Maginn, William
1795–1821	Keats, John
1795–1861	Neilson, Peter
1795–1860	Story, Robert
1795–1854	Talfourd, Sir Thomas Noon
1796–1849	Coleridge, Hartley
1796–1852	Reynolds, John Hamilton
1797–1839	Bayly, Nathaniel Thomas Haynes
1797?–1866	Claris, John Chalk
1797–1868	Lover, Samuel
1797–1835	Motherwell, William

1797–1851	Shelley, Mary Wollstonecraft
1797–1864	Watts, Alaric Alexander
1798–1827	Hyslop, James
1798–1817	Knowles, Herbert
1798–1851	Moir, David Macbeth
1798–1828	Neele, Henry
1798–1827	Pollok, Robert
1798–1870	Riddell, Henry Scott
1799–1871	Kennedy, William
1799–1862	Kennish, William
1799–1874	Moultrie, John
1799–1861	Noel, Thomas
1780–1825	Marriott, John
1782–1810	Finlay, John
1784–1849	Barton, Bernard
1784–1856	Kenyon, John
1786–1823	Beattie, George
1754–1796	Bampfylde, John Codrington
1788–1824	Byron, George Gordon, sixth lord
1788–1872	Bamford, Samuel
1795–1856	Bailey, Thomas
1795–1846	Darley, George
1798–1842	Banim, John
1798–1850	Gilfillan, Robert
1799–1887	Heraud, John Abraham
1799–1859	Hervey, Thomas Kibble
1799–1845	Hood, Thomas, The Elder
1799–1888	Howitt, Mary

19th century

d. 1808	Collins, John
1800–1882	Darby, John Nelson
1800–1880	Herbison, David
1800–1833	Jewsbury, Maria Jane
1800–1859	Macaulay, Thomas Babington, Baron Macaulay
1800–1876	Neaves, Charles, Lord Neaves
1800–1886	Taylor, Sir Henry
1801–1886	Barnes William
1801–1873	Clive, Caroline
1801–1890	Newman, John Henry
1801–1865	Richardson, David Lester
1801–1900	Scott, Lady John (Alicia Ann Spottiswoode)
1801–1874	Swain, Charles
1802–1876	Aird, Thomas
1802–1852	Coleridge, Sara
1802–1838	Landon, Letitia Elizabeth
1802–1865	Williams, Isaac
1803–1849	Beddoes, Thomas Lovell
1803–1845	Blanchard, Laman
1803–1840	Griffin, Gerald
1803–1875	Hawker, Robert Stephen
1803–1873	Lytton, Edward George Earle
1803–1849	Mangan, James Clarence
1804–1866	Mahony, Francis Sylvester
1804–1891	Warburton, Rowland Eyles Egerton
1804–1862	Whitehead, Charles
1805–1848	Adams, Sarah Flower
1805–1856	Outram, George
1805–1875	Wade, Thomas
1805–1850	Walsh, Edward
1806–1861	Browning-Barrett, Elizabeth
1806–1872	Lever, Charles James
1807–1867	Blackwood, Helen Selina, Countess of Dufferin
1807–1884	Deck, James George
1807–1874	Miller, Thomas
1807–1898	Tennyson, Frederick
1808–1889	Bonar, Horatius

1808–1877	Norton, The Hon, Mrs Caroline
1808–1866	Prince, John Critchley
1808–1895	Stokes, Henry Sewell
1808–1879	Tennyson, Turner, Charles
1809–1895	Blackie, John Stuart
1809–1863	Crewdson, Jane
1809–1883	Fitzgerald, Edward
1809–1895	Hake, Thomas Gordon
1809–1881	Hanmer, Sir John, Baron Hanmer
1809–1885	Milnes, Richard Monckton, 1st Baron Houghton
1809–1859	Rogerson, John Bolton
1809–1892	Tennyson, Lord Afred
1810–1888	Doyle, Sir Francis Hastings Charles
1810–1886	Ferguson, Sir Samuel
1810–1872	Miller, William
1810–1880	Stoddart, Thomas Tod
1811–1887	Domett, Alfred
1811–1833	Hallam, Arthur Henry
1811–1892	Lowe, Robert, Viscount Sherbrooke
1811–1875	Monsell, John Samuel Bewley
1811–1853	Ord, John Walker
1811–1890	Scott, William Bell
1811–1863	Thackeray, William Makepeace
1812–1889	Browning, Robert
1812–1870	Dickens. Charles Huffam
1812–188	Lear, Edward
1812–1898	Linton, William James
1813–1865	Aytoun, William Edmondstoune
1813–1906	Luke, Mrs. Jemima Thompson
1813–1843	McCheyne, Robert Murray
1814–1878	Caswall, Edward
1814–1845	Davis, Thomas Osborne
1814–1902	De Vere, Aubrey Thomas
1814–1889	Mackay, Charles
1814–1837	Nicoll, Robert
1814–1888	Westwood, Thomas
1815–1889	Leatham, William Henry
1815–1843	Whytehead, Thomas
1816–1902	Bailey, Philip James
1816–1855	Brontë, Charlotte
1816–1909	Martin, Sir Theodore
1816–1873	Pennefather, William
1817–1882	MacCarthy, Denis Florence
1817–1890	Waugh, Edwin
1818–1895	Alexander, Cecil Frances Humphrey
1818–1848	Brontë, Emily Jane
1818–1889	Cook, Eliza
1818–1986	Moore, Nicholas
1818–1866	Neale, John Mason
1818–1893	Pennefather Catherine
1819–1861	Clough, Arthur Hugh
1819–1880	Eliot, George
1819–1875	Kingsley, Charles
1819–1890	Marston, John Westland
1820–1849	Brontë, Anne
1820–1884	Harris, John
1820–1897	Ingelow, Jean
1820–1860	Jones, Ebenezer
1821–1890	Burton, Sir Richard Francis
1821–1882	Greenwell, Dora
1821–1895	Locker-Lampson, Frederick
1822–1888	Arnold, Matthew
1822–1869	Leighton, Robert
1823–1864	Burns, James Drummond
1823–1882	Rands, William Brighty
1823–1892	Cory, William Johnson
1823–1894	Drane, Augusta Theodosia
1823–1907	Ingram, John Kells
1823–1896	Patmore, Coventry Kersey Dighton

1823–1859	Roscoe, William Caldwell
1823–1910	Waring, Anna Letitia
1824–1889	Allingham, William
1824–1924	Baring-Gould, Sabine
1824–1906	Cousin, Anne Ross
1824–1874	Dobell, Sydney Thompson
1824–1905	MacDonald, George
1824–1897	Palgrave, Francis Turner
1824–1908	Smith, Walter Chalmers
1825–1894	Askham, John
1825–1900	Blackmore, Richard Doddridge
1825–1868	McGee, Thomas D'Arcy
1825–1902	McGonagall, William Topaz
1825–1909	Midlane, Albert
1825–1864	Procter, Adelaide Anne
1825–1897	Tuttiett, Lawrence
1825–1892	Woolner, Thomas
1826–1887	Craik, Dinah Maria (Mullock)
1826–1893	Ellerton, John
1826–1882	Kickham, Charles Joseph
1826–1896	Wilde, Lady Jane
1827–1905	Carnegie, James, ninth Earl of Southesk
1827–1870	Fane, Julian Henry Charles
1827–1856	Gibson, David Cooke
1828–1865	Bigg, John Stanyan
1828–1907	Massey, Gerald
1828–1909	Meredith, George
1828–1910	Munby, Arthur Joseph
1828–1882	Rossetti, Dante Gabriel
1829–1885	Moultrie, Gerard
1829–1862	Siddall, Elizabeth Eleanor
1829/30–1867	Smith, Alexander
1830–1897	Brown, Thomas Edward
1830–1894	Rossetti, Christina Georgina (Ellen Al)
1831–1884	Calverley, Charles Stuart
1831–1891	Lytton, Edward Robert Bulwer, first Earl of Lytton
1832–1904	Arnold, Sir Edwin
1832–1898	Carroll, Lewis
1832–1887	Hughes, John Ceiriog
1832–1862	Macfarlan, James
1832–1903	Skipsey, Joseph
1832–1914	Watts-Dunton, Walter Theodore

Victorians (1833–1903)

1833–1900	Dixon, Richard Watson
1833–1907	Morris, Sir Lewis
1834–1909	Hearn, Mary Anne
1834–1896	Morris, William
1834–1894	Noel, Roden Berkeley Wriothesley
1834–1882	Thomson, James
1835–1913	Austin, Alfred
1835–1902	Butler, Samuel
1835–1906	Garnett, Richard
1835–1841	Hood, Thomas, the Younger
1835–1911	Lyall, Sir Alfred Comyn
1835–1895	Warren, John Byrne Leicester, Baron de Tabley
1836–1889	Ashe, Thomas
1836–1901	Besant, Sir Walter
1836–1917	Burnand, Sir Francis Cowley
1836–1911	Gilbert, Sir William Schwenck
1836–1879	Havergal, Frances Ridley
1837–1909	Swinburne, Algernon Charles
1837–1894	Webster, Mrs. Augusta
1838–1861	Gray, David
1839–1906	Merivale, Herman Charles

1840–1922	Blunt, Wilfrid Scawen
1840–1906	Clerke, Ellen Mary
1840–1921	Dobson, Henry Austin
1840–1928	Hardy, Thomas
1840–1901	Monkhouse, William Cosmo
1841–1865	Armstrong, Edmund John
1841–1896	Blind, Mathilde
1841–1901	Buchanan, Robert Williams
1842–1917	Courthope, William John
1842–1906	Matheson, George
1842–1900	Traill, Henry Duff
1843–1926	Doughty, Charles Montagu
1843–1913	Dowden, Edward
1843–1901	Myers, Frederic William Henry
1843–1887	Veley, Margaret
1844–1930	Bridges, Robert Seymour
1844–1889	Hopkins, Gerard Manley
1844–1912	Lang, Andrew
1844–1921	Myers, Ernest James
1844–1881	O'Shaughnessy, Arthur William Edgar
1845–1909	Anderson, Alexander
1845–1929	Coles, Vincent Stuckey Stratton
1845–1926	Canton, William
1845–1907	Lee-Hamilton, Eugene Jacob
1845–1906	Savage-Armstrong, George Francis
1846–1931	Graves, Alfred Perceval
1847–1922	Meynell, Alice Christiana Gertrude
1848–1867	Dolben, Digby Augustus Stewart Mackworth
1849–1928	Gosse, Sir Edmund William
1850–1887	Marston, Philip Bourke
1850–1894	Stevenson, Robert Louis
1852–1921	Bourdillon. Francis William
1852–1930	Brett, Reginald Baliol, 2d Viscount Esher
1852–1932	Gregory, Isabella Augusta, Lady Gregory
1853–1930	Warren, Sir Thomas Herbert
1854–1920	French, William Percy
1854–1900	Wilde, Oscar
1855–1905	Sharp, William
1857–1909	Davidson, John
1858–1924	Nesbit, Edith
1858–1941	Rodd, Sir James, 1st Baron Rennell
1858–1935	Watson, Sir (John) William
1859–1919	Beeching, Henry Charles
1859–1930	Doyle, Sir Arthur Conan
1859–1932	Grahame, Kenneth
1859–1936	Housman, Alfred Edward
1859–1945	Mackail, John William
1859–1892	Stephen, James Kenneth
1859–1907	Thompson, Francis
1860–1949	Hyde, Douglas
1861–1907	Coleridge, Mary Elizabeth
1861–1923	Hewlett, Maurice Henry
1861–1931	Hinkson, Katharine
1861–1889	Levy, Amy
1861–1922	Raleigh, Walter Alexander
1861–1936	Seaman, Sir Owen
1861–1931	Tynan, Katharine
1862–1925	Benson, Arthur Christopher
1862–1938	Newbolt, Sir Henry John
1864–1916	Casement, Sir Roger
1864–1929	Morris-Jones, Sir John
1864–1915	Phillips, Stephen
1864–1926	Zangwill, Israel
1865–1924	Crosland Thomas William Hodgson
1865–1949	Housman, Laurence
1865–1936	Kipling, Joseph Rudyard
1865–1904	Nicolson, Adela (Violet) Florence
1865–1945	Symons, Arthur William

1865–1923	Trench, Frederic Herbert
1865–1939	Yeats, William Butler
1866–1902	Carbery, Ethna (Anna MacManus)
1866–1934	Gray, John Henry
1867–1935	AE (George William Russell)
1867–1900	Dowson, Ernest Christopher
1867–1902	Johnson, Lionel Pigot
1869–1952	Cripps, Arthur Shearly
1869–1928	Mew, Charlotte Mary
1870–1953	Belloc, Joseph Hilaire Pierre Rene
1870–1945	Douglas, Lord Alfred Bruce
1870–1926	Gore-Booth, Eva Selina
1871–1940	Davies, William Henry
1871–1962	Hodgson, Ralph Edwin
1871–1909	Synge, John Millington
1873–1956	de La Mare, Walter John
1873–1926	Phillimore, John Swinnerton
1874–1945	Baring, Maurice
1874–1948	Bottomley, Gordon
1874–1936	Chesterton, Gilbert Keith
1874–1958	Service, Robert W.
1875–1950	Bentley, Edmund Clerihew
1875–1940	Buchan, John, 1st Baron Tweedsmuir
1877–1938	Colvin, Ian Duncan
1878–1957	Coppard, Alfred Edgar
1878–1957	Dunsany, Edward John Moreton Draz Plunkett, 18th Baron
1878–1962	Gibson, Wilfrid Wilson
1878–1957	Gogarty, Oliver St John
1878–1916	Macdonagh, Thomas
1878–1967	Masefield, John Edward
1878–1917	Thomas, Philip Edward
1879–1944	Campbell, Joseph
1879–1932	Monro, Harold Edward
1879–1967	O'Neill, Mary Devenport
1879–1958	O'Sullivan, Seamus
1879–1916	Pearse, Patrick Henry
1880–1929	Freeman, John
1880–1958	Noyes, Alfred
1880–1943	Radclyffe-Hall, Marguerite Antonia
1880–1959	Salkeld, Blanaid
1880–1950	Stephens, James
1881–1865	Farjeon, Eleanor
1881–1938	Abercrombie, Lascelles
1881–1947	Asquith, Herbert
1881–1972	Colum, Padraic
1881–1946	Flower, Robin Ernest William
1881–1958	Macaulay, Dame Emilie Rose
1881–1936	Sackville, Lady Margaret
1881–1927	Webb, Mary Gladys
1882–1937	Drinkwater, John
1882–1968	Gray, Sir Alexander
1882–1941	Joyce, James Augustine
1882–1971	Letts, Winifred Mary
1882–1966	Loy, Mina
1882–1956	Milne, Alan Alexander
1883–1917	Hulme, Thomas Ernest
1883–1929	Scott, Geoffrey
1885–1930	Lawrence, David Herbert
1863–1944	Quiller-Couch, Sir Arthur Thomas
1883–1941	Plowman, Max
1883–1929	Studdert Kennedy, Geoffrey Anketell
1884–1915	Flecker, Herman James Elroy
1884–1952	Frankau, Gilbert
1884–1958	Squire, Sir John Collings
1884–1947	Wickham, Anna
1884–1954	Young, Francis Brett
1885–1971	Young, Andrew John
1886–1960	Cornford, Frances Crofts
1886–1967	Sassoon, Siegfried Loraine

1886–1945	Williams, Charles Walter Stansby
1886–1940	Wolfe, Humbert
1887–1915	Brooke, Rupert Chawner
1887–1977	Daryush, Elizabeth
1887–1965	De Stein, Sir Edward
1887–1959	Muir, Edwin
1887–1975	Parry-Williams, Sir Thomas Herbert
1887–1916	Plunkett, Joseph Mary
1887–1964	Sitwell, Dame Edith Louisa
1888–1965	Eliot, Thomas Stearns
1888–1915	Grenfell, Julian Henry Francis
1889–1946	Turner, Walter James Redfern
1889–1996	Waley, Arthur David
1889–1956	Wellesley, Dorothy Violet, Duchess of Wellington
1890–1937	Gurney, Ivor Bertie
1890–1971	Herbert, Sir Alan Patrick
1890–1918	Rosenberg, Isaac
1891–1917	Ledwidge, Francis
1891–1917	West, Arthur Graeme
1892–1962	Aldington, Richard Edward Godfree
1892–1970	Brittain, Vera
1892–1978	Grieve, Christopher Murray
1892–1978	MacDiarmid, Hugh
1892–1962	Sackville-West, Victoria Mary
1892–1969	Sitwell, Sir Francis Osbert Sacheverell
1893–1973	Cannan, May Wedderburn
1893–1916	Hodgson, William Noel
1893–1985	Lewis, Saunders
1893–1967	MacGreevy, Thomas
1893–1917	Mackintosh, Ewart Alan
1893–1944	Nichols, Robert Malise Bowyer
1893–1918	Owen, Wilfred Edward Salter
1893–1962	Prewett, Frank
1893–1968	Read, Sir Herbert Edward
1893–1970	Richards Ivor Armstrong
1893–1957	Sayers, Dorothy Leigh
1893–1978	Warner, Sylvia Townsend
1894–1963	Huxley, Aldous Leonard
1895–1985	Graves, Robert von Ranke
1895–1974	Jones, David Michael
1895–1958	Golding, Louis
1895–1915	Sorley, Charles Hamilton
1896–1974	Clarke, Austin
1896–1974	Blunden, Edmund Charles
1896–1956	Strong, Leonard Alfred George
1887–1917	Evans, Ellis Humphrey
1897–1999	Mitchison, Lady Naomi
1897–1992	Pitter, Ruth
1897–1988	Sitwell, Sir Schaverell
1898–1963	Lewis, Clive Staples
1898–1982	Rickword, Edgell
1898–1943	Soutar, William
1899–1973	Coward, Sir Noel Peirce
1899–1975	Bellerby, Frances

20th century

1900–1985	Bunting, Basil
1900–1976	Hughes, Richard Arthur Warren
1900–1967	Swingler, Randall
1902–1948	Roberts, Michael William Edward
1902–1971	Smith, Florence Margaret ("Stevie")
1902–1962	Tessimond, Arthur Seymour John

Georgians (1903–20)

1903–1950	Orwell, George
1903–1973	Plomer, William Charles Franklyn

1904–1972	Day-Lewis, Cecil
1904–1967	Kavanagh, Patrick Joseph
1904–1971	Williams, Waldo
1905–1953	Cameron, Norman
1905–1995	Coffey, Brian
1905–1953	Davies, Idris
1905–1974	Fallon, Padraic
1905–1985	Grigson, Geoffrey Edward Harvey
1905–1995	Jones, Glyn
1906–1989	Beckett, Samuel Barclay
1906–1984	Betjeman, Sir John
1906–1984	Empson, Sir William
1806–1874	Russell, Arthur Tozer
1906–1967	Watkins, Vernon Phillips
1907–1973	Auden, Wystan Hugh
1907–1987	Hewitt, John Harold
1907–1987	Lehmann, Rudolph John Fredrick
1907–1963	MacNeice, Frederick Louis
1907–1976	Reavey, George
1907–1999	Scovell, Edith Joy
1908–1993	Annand James King
1908-1959	Devlin, Denis
1908–2003	Raine, Kathleen Jessie
1909–1987	Garioch, Robert
1909–2005	Hesketh, Phoebe
1909–1977	Pudney, John Sleigh
1909–1995	Roberts, Lynette
1909–1969	Rodgers, William Robert
1909–1963	Spencer, Charles Bernard
1909–1995	Spender, Sir Stephen Harold
1910–1996	MacCaig. Norman Alexander
1911–1968	Peake, Mervyn Laurence
1911–1996	MacLean, Sorley
1911–1986	Scarfe, Francis
1911–1966	Treece, Henry
1912–1973	Allott, Kenneth
1912–1990	Durrell, Lawrence George
1912–1991	Fuller, Roy Broadbent
1912–1963	Hassall, Christopher Vernon
1912–1996	Madge, Charles
1912–1968	MacDonagh, Donagh
1912–2003	Prince, Frank Templeton
1912–2001	Ridler, Anne
1913–1991	Barker, George Granville
1913–	Lowbury, Edward Joseph Lister
1913–2000	Thomas, Ronald Stuart
1914–1997	Lee, Laurie
1914–1987	Nicholson, Norman
1914–1986	Reed Henry
1914–2003	Sisson, Charles Hubert
1914–1953	Thomas, Dylan Marlais
1914–1978	Todd, Ruthven
1915–1936	Cornford, (Rupert) John
1915–1980	Fraser, George Sutherland
1915–1984	Hay, George Campbell
1915–1944	Lewis, Alun
1915–	Mathias, Roland
1915–1975	Smith, Sydney, Goodsir
1916–1995	Ewart, Gavin Buchanan
1916–2001	Gascoyne, David Emery
1916–1985	Gutteridge, Bernard
1916–1987	Tiller, Terence Rogers
1917–1996	Brown, George Mackay
1917–2003	Causley, Charles
1917–	Conquest, George Robert Acworth
1918–1978	Bell, Martin
1918–1986	Graham, William Sydney
1918–	Heath-Stubbs, John Francis Alexander
1918–1991	Iremonger, Valentin
1918–	Kirkup, James

1918–2002	Milligan, Spike
1918–	Spark, Muriel
1919–1978	Bayliss, John Clifford
1919–1999	Beer, Patricia
1919	Bewick, Elizabeth
1919–2002	Henderson, Hamish
1919	Humphreys, Emyr
1919–1999	Murdoch, Dame Jean Iris

Moderns (1920–60)

1920–2002	Cobbing, Bob
1920–2000	Comfort, Alex
1920–1944	Douglas, Keith Castellain
1920–2002	Enright, Dennis Joseph
1920	Greacen, Robert
1920–1999	Holloway, John
1920	Morgan, Edwin George
1920–2002	West, Victor
1920–1994	Wright, David
1921–2006	Norris, Leslie
1922–1995	Amis, Kingsley
1922–1995	Davie, Donald
1922–1943	Keyes, Sidney Arthur Kilworth
1922–1985	Larkin, Philip Arthur
1922–2001	Ross, Alan
1922	Scannell, Vernon
1923	Abse, Dannie
1923–1990	Ormond, John
1924	Berry, James
1924–1995	Mottram, Eric Noel William
1925	Finlay, Ian Hamilton
1925–1994	Wain, John Barrington
1926–2001	Jennings, Elizabeth
1926–	Logue, Christopher
1927–	Galvin, Patrick
1927–	Hutchinson, Pearse
1927–	Murphy, Richard
1927–	Tomlinson, Alfred Charles
1928–	Bardwell, Leland
1928–	Kinsella, Thomas
1928–	Sillitoe. Alan
1928–1998	Smith, Iain Crichton
1928–2004	Turnbull, Gael
1929–	Alvarez, Alfred
1929–2004	Gunn, Thom
1929–	Montague, John
1929–	Fanthorpe, U(rsula) .A(skham)
1930–	Feinstein, Elaine Barbara
1930–	Fisher, Roy
1930–1998	Hughes, Ted
1930–	Pinter, Harold
1930–1997	Silkin, Jon
1930–	Thwaite, Anthony Simon
1931–	Brownjohn, Alan Charles
1931–	Conran, Anthony
1931–	Fanelight, Ruth
1932–	Hill, Geoffrey William
1932–2000	Henri, Adrian
1932–2005	Hobsbaum, Philip Dennis
1932–	Joseph, Jenny
1932–	Mitchell, Adrian
1932–1963	Plath, Sylvia
1932–2003	Redgrove, Peter William
1933–1973	Johnson, Bryan Stanley William
1933–	Lucie-Smith, John Edward Mckenzie
1933–	Nuttall, Jeff
1933–	Stevenson, Anne

1934–	Adcock, Karen Fleur
1934–	Gray, Alasdair
1935–	Horovitz, Michael
1935–	Stallworthy, Jon
1935–	Thomas, Donald .Michael
1936–	Cluysenaar, Anne
1936–	Egan, Desmond
1936–	Simpson, Matthew
1937–	Clarke, Gillian
1937–	Curry, Neil
1937–	Fuller, John Leopold
1937–	Harrison, Tony
1937–	McGough, Roger
1937–2000	Oliver, Douglas
1937–1978	Riley, John
1938–	Raworth, Tom
1939–	Harwood, Lee
1939–	Heaney, Seamus Justin
1939–	Longley, Michael George
1939–	Markham, E(dward) A(rchibald)
1939–	Nye, Robert
1939–	Porter, Peter Neville Frederick
1940–1992	Carter, Angela
1940–	Deane, Seamus
1940–	Riley, Peter
1941–	Crossley-Holland, Kevin
1941–	Mahon, Derek
1941–	Stainer, Pauline
1942–	Dunn, Douglas Eaglesham
1942–	Ní Chuilleanáin, Eiléan
1942–	Woods, Macdara
1942–	Williams, Hugo
1943–	Crozier, Andrew
1943–	Feaver, Vicki
1943–	Sinclair, Iain
1944–	Boland, Eavan Aisling
1944–	Constantine, David
1944–	Durcan, Paul
1944–	Fisher, Allen
1944–1999	Hartnett, (Harnet) Michael
1944–	Hope, Christopher
1944–	Khalvati, Mimi
1944–	Leonard, Tom
1944–	Raine, Craig Anthony
1944–	Wainwright, Jeffrey
1944–	Wright, Kit
1945–	Cope, Wendy
1945–	Hill, Selima
1945–	O'Donoghue, Bernard
1946–	Bush, Duncan
1946–	Curtis, Tony
1946–	Padel, Ruth
1946–	Patten, Brian
1946–	Pickard, Tom
1946–	Reading, Peter Gray
1946–	Rosen, Michael Wayne
1947–	Ayres Pam
1947–	Barker, Les
1947–	Finch, Peter
1947–	Joyce, Trevor
1947–	Lochhead, Liz
1947–	Ormsby, Frank
1947–	Shuttle, Penelope
1947–	Wells, Robert
1947–	Wicks, Susan
1948–	Carson, Ciaran Gerard
1948–	Griffiths, Bill
1948–2000	MacSweeney Barry
1949–	Ackroyd, Peter
1949–	Agard, John

1949–	Fenton, James Martin
1949–	Jenkins, Nigel
1949–	Paulin, Thomas Neilson
1949–	Roberts, Michelle Brigitte
1949–	Rosenstock, Gabriel

The Beat Generation (1950–70)

1950–	McGuckian, Medbh
1950–	Nichols, Grace
1950–	Pugh, Sheenagh
1951–2005	O'Donoghue, Gregory
1951–	Elfyn, Menna
1951–	Greig, Andrew
1951–	Muldoon, Paul
1951–	Smyth, Gerard
1952–	Dunmore, Helen
1952–	Johnson, Linton Kwesi
1952–	Minhinnick, Robert
1952–	Motion, Andrew Peter
1952–	Murphy, Gerry
1952–	Ni Dhomhnaill, Nuala
1952–	Scully, Maurice
1952–	Sweeney, Matthew
1953–	Deeley, Patrick
1953–	Dorgan, Theo
1953–	Hegley, John
1953–	Petit, Pascale
1953–	Riordan, Maurice
1953–	Robinson, Peter
1953–	Shapcott, Jo
1954–	Alvi, Moniza
1954–	Draycott, Jane
1954–	Duhig, Ian
1954–	McCarthy, Thomas
1954–	O'Driscoll
1955–	Barry, Sebastian
1955–	Burnside, John
1955–	Curtis, Tony
1955–	Duffy, Carol Ann
1955–	McKendrick, Jamie
1955–	Robertson, Robin
1956–	Bloom, Valerie
1956–	Dabydeen, David
1956–1995	Dunne, Sean
1956–	Healy, Randolph
1957–	Dalton, Amanda
1957–	Dooley, Maura
1957–	Hofmann, Michael
1957–	Maguire, Sarah
1958–	Delanty, Greg
1958–	Petrucci, Mario
1958–	Zephaniah, Benjamin Obadiah Iqbal
1959–	Childish, Billy
1959–	Crawford, Robert

The Movement (1960–80)

1956–	Francis, Matthew
Current	Boourke, Eva
Current	Mapange, Jack
1960–	D'Aguiar, Fred
1960–	O'Donnell, John
1961–	Herbert, W N.
1961–	Kay, Jackie
1962–	Duffy, Katherine

1962–	Greenlaw, Lavinia	1966–	Wyley, Enda
1962–	Jamie, Kathleen	1968–	Rees-Jones, Deryn
1962–	Maxwell, Glyn	1970–	Hill, Tobias
1962–	Shukman, Henry	1971–	Hannah, Sophie
1962–	Sprackland, Jean	1971–	Hollis, Matthew
1963–	Armitage. Simon	1972–	Morrisey, Sinead
1963–	Paterson, Don	1973–	Gray, Kathryn
1963–	Roberts, Michael Symmons	1974–	Flynn, Leontia
1964–	Davies, Grahame	1974–	Sheers, Owen
1964–	Groarke, Vona	1975–	Polley, Jacob
1964–	Walsh, Catherine		
1965–	Agbabi, Patience		
1965–	Clanchy, Kate		
1965–	Farley, Paul		
1966–	Oswald, Alice		

Post Moderns (1980)

Bibliography

Aberdeen Studies in Scottish Philosophy (www.abdn.ac.uk).

The Academy of American Poets (http://www.poets.org/index.cfm).

An Adventure in the Life of King James V of Scotland by William Topaz McGonagall (see entry) (http://www.poemhunter.com/p/m/poem.asp?poet=6601&poem=26761).

Aesthetes and Decadents of the 1890's. Karl Beckson, ed. Academy Chicago Publishers, 1981.

African Poems of Thomas Pringle (Killie Campbell Africana Library Publications). Ernest Pereira & Michael Chapman, ed. University of Natal Press, 1996.

An African Thunderstorm & Other Poems. Jack Mapange, ed. Nairobi: East African Publishing House, 2004.

The African Writers' Handbook. Jack Mapange, and James Gibbs, ed. African Books Collective, 1999.

Against Forgetting: Twentieth-Century Poetry of Witness. Carolyn Forché, ed. W.W. Norton, 1993.

The Age of Revolution (http://www.npg.si.edu/col/age/moultrie.htm).

Aileen the Huntress, by Edward Walsh (http://www.mindspring.com/~mccarthys/whiskey/pipaddy.htm).

AIM25: Royal College of Music (http://www.aim25.ac.uk/cgi-bin/frames/fulldesc?inst_id=25&coll_id=5684).

Ain't I a Woman! A Book of Women's Poetry from Around the World. Illona Linthwaite, ed. Peter Bedrick Books, 1988.

Alan Brownjohn (An Interview) (http://lidianu.esential.ro/alan_brownjohn.htm).

Alan Brownjohn, Guardian Unlimited, Obituary. Monday March 25, 2002 (http://education.guardian.co.uk/obituary/story/0,12212,753444,00.html).

Alasdair Gray Books — Word Power (www.word-power.co.uk/platform/Alasdair-Gray-Books).

Alasdair MacMhaighstir Alasdair (c1695–c1770) Poet (http://www.users.globalnet.co.uk/~crumey/alexander_macdonald.html).

Albion's England by William Warner, for the complete poem, see *The Columbia Granger's Index to Poetry. 11th ed. The Columbia Granger's World of Poetry,* Columbia University Press, 2005 (http://www.columbiagrangers.org).

An Album of Songs and Poems: A' The Bairns O Adam by Hamish Henderson (http://www.footstompin.com/artists/hamish_henderson).

Aleister Crowley, Poems & Miscellaneous (http://www.poeforward.com/poetrycorner/crowley/poems.htm).

Alexander Anderson, Dundee Advertiser. 6th January, 1896. Dundee Public Library (http://www.dundeecity.gov.uk/library/main.htm).

Alexander Craig, Two Sonnets (www.sonnets.org/craig.htm).

Alexander Montgomerie and the Netherlands, 1586–89 (http://www2.arts.gla.ac.uk/SESLL/STELLA/COMET/glasgrev/issue1/lyall.htm).

Alexander Montgomerie: A Selection from His Songs and Poems. Helena M. Shire, ed. The Saltire Society, 1960.

Alexander Rodger: The Devil's Visit to the Islands of Japan: A Tale Translated from the Japanese, 1838 (http://themargins.net/anth/19thc/rodger.html).

All-Info About Poetry (http://poetry.allinfo-about.com/features/adrian-henri.html).

All the Poems: Collected Poems of Muriel Spark. Carcanet Press, 2004.

All the Poems of Muriel Spark. W.W. Norton & Co. Ltd., 2004.

All the Poems You Need to Say Hello by Kate Clanchy. Picador, 2004.

All the Workes of John Taylor, the Water Poet. Scolar Press, 1973.

Amada Dalton, Books: Special Reports. Guardian Unlimited (http://books.guardian.co.uk/nextgenerationpoets).

Amazing Monsters: Verses to Thrill and Chill. Robert Fisher, ed. Faber and Faber, 1982.

America Forever New: A Book of Poems. Sara Brewton, and John E. Brewton, ed. Thomas Y. Crowell, 1968.

America in Poetry. Charles Sullivan, ed. Harry N. Abrams, 1988.

An American Anthology, 1787–1900. Edmund Clarence Stedman, ed. Houghton Mifflin, 1900.

American Hymns Old and New. Vols. 1–2. Albert Christ-Janer, and Charles W. Hughes, ed. Columbia University Press, 1980.

American Poetry: The Twentieth Century, Vol. 1. Robert Hass, John Hollander, Carolyn Kizer, et al, ed. Library of America, 2000.

Americans' Favorite Poems: The Favorite Poem Project Anthology. Robert Pinsky and Maggie Dietz, ed. W.W. Norton, 2000.

Americans Who Came from Scotland (http://www.edinburgh.gov.uk/Libraries/History_Sphere/Americanlinks/edinburgh.html).

The Anchor Anthology of Seventeenth-Century Verse, Vol. II. Louis L. Martz and Richard S. Sylvester, ed. Doubleday Anchor Books, 1969.

The Anchor Anthology of Sixteenth Century Verse. Richard Sylvester, ed. Doubleday/Anchor Books, 1974.

Andrew Crozier, Writing by Numbers: A Preview (http://jacketmagazine.com/11/lopez-by-crozier.html).

Andy M. Stewart: By The Hush (http://andymstewart.com/by-the-hush.htm).

Angel of the Perfumes, by Michael Symmons Roberts (http://www.jeanettewinterson.com/pages/content/index.asp?PageID=230).

The Angela Carter Unofficial Web Site (http://perso.wanadoo.fr/andrew.milne/page%201.htm).

Angling Songs of Thomas Tod Stoddart. William Blackwood and Sons, 1889.

The Anglo-Saxon World: An Anthology. Kevin Crossley-Holland, ed. Oxford University Press, 1982.

Anglo-Saxonists — 20th Century (http://www.u.arizona.edu/~ctb/20ef.html#rflower).

Anglo-Welsh Poetry, 1480–1980. Raymond Garlick and Roland Mathias, ed. Poetry Wales Press, 1984.

Anglo-Welsh Poetry, 1480–1990. Raymond Garlick and Roland Mathias, ed. Poetry Wales Press, 1993.

Angus Authors, Angus Council (www.angus.gov.uk/history/features/authors.htm).

Animal Poems. John Hollander, ed. Alfred A. Knopf, 1994.

Anne Stevenson's Poetry: Guardian Unlimited Books, By genre, Border crossings (http://books.guardian.co.uk/poetry/features/0,12887,1317578,00.html).

Anniversary, Poem by William Mason (http://www.sonnets.org/mason.htm).

Anno Mundi Books. From Noah to Dardanus, by Richard Linche (http://www.annomundi.com/history/noah_to_dardanus.htm).

The Antaeus Anthology. Daniel Halpern, ed. Bantam Books, 1986.

An Anthology of Catholic Poets. Joyce Kilmer, ed. Fredonia Books, 2003.

An Anthology of Catholic Poets. Shane Leslie, ed. Macmillan, 1952.

An Anthology of Eighteenth-century Satire: Grub Street. Peter Heaney, ed. Edwin Mellen Press, 1995.

An Anthology of Irish Literature. David H. Greene, ed. H. Modern Library, 1954.

An Anthology of Irish Verse: The Poetry of Ireland from Mythological Times to the Present. Padraic Colum, ed. Liveright, 1948.

Anthology of Magazine Verse and Yearbook of American Poetry. Alan F. Pater, ed. Monitor Book Company, 1980.

Anthology of Modern American Poetry. Cary Nelson, ed. Oxford University Press, 2000.

Anthology of Modern Jewish Poetry. Philip M. Raskin, ed. Behrman's Jewish Book Shop, 1927.

An Anthology of Old English Poetry. Charles W. Kennedy, ed. Oxford University Press, 1960.

Anthology of Poems on Affairs of State: Augustan Satirical Verse, 1660–1714. George de F. Lord, ed. Yale University Press, 1975.

An Anthology of Renaissance Lyrics: Biography and Songs of Nicholas Grimald (http://english.edgewood.edu/eng359/lyric_poetry2.htm).

An Anthology of Revolutionary Poetry. Marcus Graham, ed. The Active Press, 1929.

Anthology of Twentieth-Century British and Irish Poetry. Keith Tuma, ed. Oxford University Press, 2001.

An Anthology of World Poetry. Mark Van Doren, ed. Reynal & Hitchcock, Inc., 1936.

Anthony Raftery, Last of the Wandering Bards (http://www.galwayonline.ie/history/history2/rafter.htm).

An Antidote Against Melancholy. Pratt Manufacturing Company, 1884.

Aosdána — an Irish affiliation of artists (http://www.irishwriters-online.com).

The Aphra Behn Page (www.lit-arts.net/Behn/begin-ab.htm).

April, by Jacob Polley. Blinking Eye Publishing (http://www.blinking-eye.co.uk/writer/polley.html).

Archives Hub. Charles Madge Archive (http://www.archiveshub.ac.uk/news/0402cm.html).

Archives Hub: The David Wright Collection of Norman Nicholson Papers (http://www.archiveshub.ac.uk/news/03020403.html).

Archives Network Wales (http://www.archivesnetworkwales.info/cgi-bin/anw/fulldesc_nofr?inst_id=35&coll_id=11890&expand=).

Ardors and Endurances by Robert Nichols. Chatto & Windus, 1917.

Arley Hall & Gardens (http://www.touruk.co.uk/house/house-cheshire-arley-%20hall.htm).

Around the World in 80 Poems. James Berry. Illustrated by Katherine Lucas. Macmillan Children's Books, 2004.

Art & Love: An Illustrated Anthology of Love Poetry. Kate Farrell, ed. The Metropolitan Museum of Art, 1990.

Art & Nature: An Illustrated Anthology of Nature Poetry. Kate Farrell, ed. The Metropolitan Museum of Art, 1992.

The Art of Noise: Peter Finch Sounds Off Claire Powell (http://www.peterfinch.co.uk/noise.htm).

ArtForum: Garry Fabian Miller — Rome —Thoughts of a Night Sea (http://www.findarticles.com/p/articles/mi_m0268/is_1_42/ai_108691829).

Arthur Conan Doyle: Poems (http://www.poetry-archive.com/d/doyle_arthur_conan.html).

The Artist's Rifles, Edward Thomas (http://en.wikipedia.org/wiki/Artists%27_Rifles).

Arts Council of Northern Ireland. Appointment of John Montague, on May 14,1998, as the first Ireland Professor of Poetry (http://www.albany.edu/writers-inst/jmaward.html).

Ashes for Breakfast: Selected Poems of Durs Grunbein. Michael Hofmann, translator. Farrar Straus Giroux, 2005.

The Aspect of the Russian Verb, by Mardara Woods (http://www.voiceourconcern.org/poetry_macdara_woods.htm).

Athenaeum Index: Contributor Record (http://web.soi.city.ac.uk/~asp/v2/contributors/contributorfiles/HERVEY,Thomas Kibble.html).

Athenaeum Index: Contributor Record (http://web.soi.city.ac.uk/~asp/v2/contributors/contributorfiles/MARSTON,John Westland.html).

Athenaeum Index: Contributor Record (http://web.soi.city.ac.uk/~asp/v2/contributors/contributorfiles/MASSEY,Gerald.html).

Athenaeum Online System: Issue Number 2288: Poems of Henry Lok, Gentleman 1593 —1597 (http://web.soi.city.ac.uk/~asp/v2/titles/issuefiles/2288.html).

Augustus Montague Toplady (http://www.btinternet.com/~alan.s.flint/toplady/).

Auld Scots Ballants. Robert Ford, ed. Alexander Gardner, 1889.

Aurelian Townshend's Poems and Masks. E.K. Chambers, ed. Clarendon Press, 1912.

Austin Clarke: His Life and Works. Austin Clarke. Humanities Press, 1974.

AustLit: The Resource for Australian Literature. Archives for W.J. Turner (http://www.austlit.edu.au/run?ex=ShowAgent&agentId=AT7).

The Autobiography and Other Memorials of Mrs Gilbert, Formerly Ann Taylor, by Ann Taylor. Volume I and Volume II. Josiah Gilbert, ed. Henry S. King & Co., 1874.

"Autobiography" of Lord Alfred Douglas. Reprint Services Corporation, 1994.

Awake! And Other Wartime Poems. Harcourt Brace, 1942 (These poems, written between 1938 and 1940, were originally sent to press in London in 1940, and the first printing was entirely destroyed by German bombs.) (*Tomfolio.com: Poetry: Poets QZ*).

The Ballad of Thomas the Rhymer (http://www.cowdenknowes.com/rhymer.htm).

Ballads, 1903, revised and enlarged 1910. Cyder Press, 2004.

Ballads and Songs by William Makepeace Thackeray. Cassell, 1896.

Ballads, Poems, and Lyrics of Denis Florence McCarthy. James McGlashan, 1850.

The Bannatyne Manuscript Written in Time of Pest. Johnson Reprint Corporation, 1988.

Basil Bunting Poetry Centre (www.dur.ac.uk/basil_bunting_poetry.centre).

The Batrachomuomachia: or the Battle of the Frogs and Mice. J. Sharpe, 1810.

The Battle of Dunkeld (http://www.clan-cameron.org/battles/1689_b.html).

BBC — Get Writing — A2997886 — Alice Oswald (http://www.bbc.co.uk/dna/getwriting/oswald).

BBC — Historic Figures — Aphra Ben (www.bbc.co.uk/history/historic_figures/behn_aphra.shtml).

BBC — History — Roger Casement: Secrets of the Black Diaries (http://www.bbc.co.uk/history/society_culture/protest_reform/casement_04.shtml).

BBC — History —The 1798 Irish Rebellion (http://www.bbc.co.uk/history/state/nations/irish_reb_02.shtml).

BBC — History — United Irishmen — up to 1798 (http://www.bbc.co.uk/history/timelines/ni/united_irishmen.shtml).

BBC, Northern Ireland Learning: Weaver Poets: The Bard of Dunclug (http://www.bbc.co.uk/northernireland/schools/4_11/today/english/spr2000/index.shtml).

BBC — Radio 4 The Heard — Poetry with John Hegley (http://www.bbc.co.uk/radio4/arts/heardallaboutit_poets1.shtml).

BBC — Radio 4 — Poetry Please, with Micheal Horrovitz (http://www.bbc.co.uk/radio4/arts/poetryplease_20050109.shtml).

BBC —Writing Scotland (www.bbc.co.uk/scotland/arts/writingscotland / learning_journeys/place/george_mackay_brown).

Beckett Shorts: Selected Poems, Calder Publications (www.calderpublications.com/books/0714543055.html).

The Beggar's Petition (poem) by Thomas Moss (http://www.pemberley.com/litcomp/beggar.html).

Begin, My Soul, the Exalted Lay: Metrical Version of Psalm 148, by John Ogilvie (http://www.oremus.org/hymnal/b/b048.html).

Ben Jonson and the Cavalier Poets. Hugh MacLaen, ed. New York: W.W. Norton & Company, 1974.

The Best Loved Poems of the American People. Hazel Felleman, ed. Doubleday, 1936.

The Best Loved Religious Poems. James Gilchrist Lawson, ed. Fleming H. Revell, 1933.

Best Loved Songs of the American People. Denes Agay, ed. Doubleday, 1975.

Best Loved Story Poems. Walter E. Thwing, ed. Garden City, 1941.

Bibliography of 19th-c. Irish Literature (http://info.wlu.ca/~www eng/faculty/jwright/irish/biblio-main.htm).

Bibliography: Works by Caroline Norton (http://digital.library. upenn.edu/women/norton/nc-bibliography.html).

Bill Griffiths' Home Page (http://www.bgriffiths7.freeserve.co.uk/ subindex.html).

The Billy Childish Home Page (http://www.theebillychildish. com/index.htm).

A Biographical Sketch by blupete: Leigh Hunt (http://www. blupete.com/Literature/Biographies).

Biographical Sketches of Memorable Christians of the Past (http:// justus.anglican.org/resources/bio/220.html).

Biography and Bibliography of Douglas Dunn (http://www.arlin do-correia.com/020305.html).

Biography and Bibliography of Robert Nye (http://www.bookhelp web.com/authors/nye/nye.htm).

The Biography and Burial of Charles Causley (www.poetsgraves. co.uk/causley.htm).

Biography and Poems of Amanda Dalton. The Poetry Book Society (http://www.poetrybooks.co.uk/PBS/pbs_dalton_amanda. asp).

Biography and Poems of Gabriel Rosenstock : (http://www.poetry-chaikhana.com/R/RosenstockGa/).

Biography and Poems of Jane Draycott, Poetry Workshop (http:// www.btinternet.com/~carpenter/clock11.htm).

Biography and Poetry of Donagh MacDonagh (http://www. turlach.net/macdonagh/dmacd/dmacd.htm).

Biography and Works of Adrian Mitchell (http://www.ripping yarns.co.uk/adrian/).

Biography and Works of Allen Fisher (http://epc.buffalo.edu/ authors/fisher/bio.html) and at (http://www.soton.ac.uk/~bepc/ poets/fisher.htm).

Biography and Works of Carol Ann Duffy (http://www.contempo rarywriters.com/authors/?p=auth104).

Biography and Works of D.M. Thomas (http://www.falpublications co.uk/falhtm/dmthomas.htm).

Biography and Works of Eva Bourke, Dedalus (http://www.dedalus press.com/poets/bourke.html).

Biography and Works of Isabella Whitney (http://www.users. muohio.edu/clarkjd/harper98.html).

Biography and Works of James Berry. C4— BookBox (http://www. channel4.com/learning/microsites/B/bookbox/authors/berry/).

Biography and Works of J.M. Synge (http://www.imagi-nation. com/moonstruck/clsc26.html).

Biography and Works of John Fuller (http://www.contemporary writers.com/authors/?p=auth182).

Biography and Works of John Keats (http://www.john-keats.com).

Biography and Works of Macdara Woods (http://homepage. eircom.net/~writing/051.html).

Biography and Works of Matthew Francis (http://www.7greenhill. freeserve.co.uk/).

Biography and Works of Peter Finch (http://www.peterfinch.co.uk/).

Biography and Works of William Morris (http://www.kirjasto. sci.fi/wmorris.htm).

Biography.ms (http://www.biography.ms).

Biography of Aemilia Lanyer: Sunshine for Women (http://www. pinn.net/~sunshine/march99/lanyer2.html).

Biography of Albert Midlane: Spiritual Songsters (http://www.stem publishing.com/hymns/biographies/midlane.html).

Biography of Aleister Crowley (http://skepdic.com/crowley.html).

Biography of Alfred Noyes (http://www3.shropshire-cc.gov.uk/ noyes.htm).

Biography of Amy Levy (http://www.womenofbrighton.co.uk/ amylevy.htm).

Biography of Anna Wickham (http://www.madpoetry.org/ wickham.html).

Biography of Anthony Rafterty (http://www.cillaodain.ie/raftery. html).

Biography of Anthony Simon Thwaite: British Council Arts (http:// www.contemporarywriters.com).

Biography of Arthur Johnston. Freepedia (http://en.freepedia.org/ Arthur_Johnston.html).

Biography of Arthur Shearly Cripps, Zimbabwe, Anglican priest (http://www.dacb.org/stories/zimbabwe/cripps_arthur.html).

Biography of ASJ Tessiond, and List of Poems (http://www. poetryconnection.net/poets/A.S.J._Tessimond).

Biography of Austin Clarke (http://homepage.eircom.net/~splash/ Clarke.html).

Biography of Benjamin Zephania: 100 Great Black Britons (http://www.100greatblackbritons.com/bios/benjamin_zepha niah.html).

Biography of Bernard O'Donoghue (http://www.irishwriters-online.com/bernardodonoghue.html).

Biography of Billy Childish: The Poets, Part 1, Billy Childish (http://www.bbc.co.uk/radio4/arts/heardallaboutit_poets1. shtml).

Biography of Bob Coffe, (http://www.answers.com/topic/brian coffey).

Biography of B.S. Johnson (http://www.bsjohnson.info).

Biography of Catherine Walsh (http://www.irishwriters-online. com/catherinewalsh.html).

Biography of Catherine Walsh (http://www.lisarichards.ie/ actor_768.html).

Biography of Dame Rose Macaualy, by Srah La Fanue. Guardian Unlimited Books × Review (http://books.guardian.co.uk/ review/story/0,12084,975703,00.html).

Biography of Daniel Defoe (http://www.spartacus.schoolnet. co.uk/Jdefoe.htm).

Biography of David Constantine, and His Poem Dominion Poetry Review (http://www.poetrysociety.org.uk/review/pr91–2/ constant.htm).

Biography of David Moir. Significant and Famous Scots (http:// www.electricscotland.com/history/other/moir_david.htm).

Biography of Denis Devlin (http://www.irishwriters-online. com/denisdevlin.html).

Biography of Dennis O'Driscoll (http://www.irishwriters-online. com/dennisodriscoll.html).

Biography of Derek Mahon (http://www.irishwriters-online. com/derekmahon.html).

Biography of Deryn Rees-Jones: BBC— Get Writing, A3225386 (http://www.bbc.co.uk/dna/getwriting/reesjones).

Biography of Desmond Egan (http://www.irishwriters-online. com/desmondegan.html).

Biography of D.M. Thomas: The Literary Encyclopedia (http://www. litencyc.com/php/speople.php?rec=true&UID=4370).

Biography of Don Paterson (http://www.st-andrews.ac.uk/ ~www_se/paterson/home.html).

Biography of Donald Alfred Davie. Talk Poetry (http://www.talk poetry.com/pages/brief/brief.php?id=9&PHPSESSID=).

Biography of Dorothy L. Sayers (http://www.kirjasto.sci.fi/ dlsayers.htm).

Biography of Dorothy Wordsworth (http://www.kirjasto.sci.fi/ dwordsw.htm).

Biography of Douglas Young: Literary Encyclopedia (http:// www.litencyc.com/php/speople.php?rec=true&UID=5481).

Biography of Edgell Rickword (http://encyclopedie-en.snyke. com/articles/edgell_rickword.html).

Biography of Edna Wyley (http://www.dedaluspress.com/poets/ wyley.html).

Biography of Edward Lucie-Smith. Knitting Circle (http://myweb. lsbu.ac.uk/~stafflag/edwardluciesmith.html#Biography).

Biography of Edward Williams. http://www.maryjones.us/jce/ iolo.html).

Biography of Eiléan Ní Chuilleanáin (http://homepage.tinet. ie/~writing/052.ENC.html).

Biography of Eric Mottram (http://www.kcl.ac.uk/kis/archives/ mottram/motttxt.htm#MOT1).

Biography of Eva Bourke, Aosdana (http://www.artscouncil.ie/aos dana/biogs/literature/evabourke.html).

Biography of Fleur Adcock (www.english.emory.edu/Bahri/ Adcock.html).

Biography of Francis Scarfe (http://online.northumbria.ac.uk/fac ulties/art/humanities/cns/m-scarfe.html).

Biography of Francis Sylvester Mahony (Father Prout) (*http://www. activate.ie/sites/corkcitylib/ecclesiastical/stannesshandon/st_annes_ fatherprout.ht).*

Biography of Fred D'aguiar (http://www.humboldt.edu/~me2/ engl240b/student_projects/daguiar/daguiarbio.htm).

Biography of Gavin Ewart (http://www.arlindo-correia.com/ 051100.html).

Biography of Geoffrey Studdert Kennedy (http://www.spartacus. schoolnet.co.uk/FWWstuddert.htm).

Biography of George Bruce (http://www.nls.uk/writestuff/heads-/wee-bruce.html)

Biography of George Campbell Hay (http://www.nls.uk/write stuff/heads/wee-hay.html).

Biography of George MacBeth (http://nlc.oldedwardians.org. uk/personal/GeorgeMacBeth.html).

Biography of George Macdonald. The Victorian Web (http://www. victorianweb.org/authors/gm/bio.html).

Biography of George Orwell (http://www.online-literature.com/ orwell/).

Biography of Gerard Moultrie: Stone Campbell Archives (http:// www.bible.acu.edu/s-c/Default.asp?Bookmark=13416)

Biography of Gerard Smyth (http://www.irishwriters-online.com/ gerardsmyth.html).

Biography of Gerard Smyth and Three Poems (http://www.dedalus press.com/poets/smyth.html).

Biography of Gerry Murphy (http://www.dedaluspress.com/poets/ murphy.html).

Biography of Glyn Maxwell (http://www.glynmaxwell.com/index2. html).

Biography of Greg Delanty (http://64.233.179.104/search?q= cache:zr8WCedIK4gJ:64.78.63.75/downloads/Greg_Delanty. doc+Greg+Delanty&hl=en&ct=clnk&cd=5).

Biography of Greg Delanty (http://www.irishwriters-online.com/ gregdelanty.html).

Biography of Gregory O'Donoghue (http://www.irishwriters-online. com/gregoryodonoghue.html).

Biography of Gwyneth Lewis (http://www.gwynethlewis.com/).

Biography of Harold Munro (http://www.infoplease.com/ce6/peo ple/A0833767.html).

Biography of Harold Pinter (http://www.kirjasto.sci.fi/hpinter. htm).

Biography of Hugh MacDiaramid. Recommended site (http://www. users.globalnet.co.uk/~crumey/hugh_macdiarmid.html).

Biography of James Fenton, with Links (http://www.bedfordstmar tins.com/litlinks/poetry/fenton.htm).

Biography of James George Deck. Dictionary of New Zealand (http://www.dnzb.govt.nz/dnzb/default.asp?Find_Quick.asp? PersonEssay=1D8).

Biography of James Kirkup (http://www.brindin.com/biogjk.htm).

Biography of James Orr (http://www.ullans.com/culture/James Orr.shtml).

Biography of James Stephens (http://www.irishwriters-online. com/jamesstephens.html).

Biography of James V, King of Scots ("The Gaberlunzie Man") (http://www.users.globalnet.co.uk/~crumey/james_v.html).

Biography of Jamie McKendrick. The Arvon Foundation (http:// www.arvonfoundation.org/pages/content/index.asp?PageID=45).

Biography of Jane Draycott, The Poetry Book Society, (http://www. poetrybooks.co.uk/PBS/pbs_draycott_jane.asp).

Biography of Jean Sprackland: British Council Arts (http://www.con temporarywriters.com).

Biography of Jeffrey Wainwright (http://www.jeffreywainwright. co.uk/about.shtml).

Biography of Jemima Luke, by Lynn Parr (http://www.ensignmes sage.com/archives/jemimaluke.html).

Biography of Jenny Joseph (http://www.wheniamanoldwoman. com/pages/348545/).

Biography of Jo Shapcott: British Council Arts (http://www.contem porarywriters.com).

Biography of John Buchan: John Buchan Society (www.john-buchansociety.co.uk).

Biography of John Burnside (http://www.nls.uk/writestuff/heads/ wee-burnside.html).

Biography of John Fawcett (Spiritual Songsters) (http://www.stem publishing.com/hymns/biographies/fawcett.html).

Biography of John Lowe. Significant and Famous Scots (http://www. electricscotland.com/history/other/lowe_john.htm).

Biography of John Lowe. Virtual American Biographies (http://www. famousamericans.net/johnlowe).

Biography of John Mayne. Significant Scots (http://www.electric scotland.com/history/other/mayne_john.htm).

Biography of John O'Donnell (http://www.dedaluspress.com/ poets/odonnell.html).

Biography of Joseph Campbell: Ulster History Circle (http://www.ul sterhistory.co.uk/josephcampbell.html).

Biography of Joseph Ritson (http://online.northumbria.ac.uk/fac ulties/art/humanities/cns/m-ritson.html).

Biography of JSB Monsell (http://www.stempublishing.com/ hymns/authors/monsell).

Biography of Katharine Tynan (http://www.irishwriters-online. com/katharinetynan.html).

Biography of Katherine Duffy, Dedalus (http://www.dedaluspress. com/poets/duffy.html).

Biography of Kathryn Gray (http://kathrynlouisegray.blogspot. com/).

Biography of Kenneth Allott: Wikipedia, the Free Encyclopedia (http://en.wikipedia.org/wiki/Wikipedia).

Biography of Kevin Crossley-Holland (http://www.ncbf.org.uk/03/ crossley-holland/crossley-holland.html).

Biography of Lady Jane Francesca Wilde. http://home.arcor.de/ oscar.wilde/biography/speranza.htm).

Biography of Lady Margaret Sackville (http://www.bookrags.com/ biography-lady-margaret-sackville-dlb/).

Biography of Lady Morgan Sydney Owenson (http://www.sydney owenson.com/SydneyOwensonBio.html).

Biography of Lady Naomi Mitchison (http://www.spartacus.school net.co.uk/Wmitchison.html).

Biography of Lascelles Abercrombie (http://www.paralumun.com/ bioabercrombie.htm).

Biography of Laurie Lee (http://www.kirjasto.sci.fi/lauriele.htm).

Biography of Lawrence Durrell (http://www.kirjasto.sci.fi/durrell. htm).

Biography of Lawrence Tuttiet (http://www.ccel.org/ccel/nutter/ hymnwriters.TuttietL.html).

Biography of Leontia Flynn, Results—enCompass Culture (http:// www.encompassculture.com/results?qs=Leontia%20Flynn).

Biography of Linton Kwesi Johnson (http://lister.ultrakohl.com/ Homepage/LKJ/lkj.htm)**.**

Biography of Liz Lochhead (http://members.tripod.com/~giggly/ liz_lochhead.html).

Biography of Liz Lochhead (http://www.contemporarywriters. com/authors/?p=auth154&state=index%3Dl).

Biography of Marianne Faringham Hearn (http://website.lineone. net/~gsward/pages/mfarningham.html).

Biography of Mary Devenport O'Neill (http://www.absoluteastron omy.com/ref/mary_devenport_oneill1).

Biography of Mary Lee Chudleigh: Sunshine for Women (http://www. pinn.net/~sunshine/march99/chudle.html).

Biography of Matthew Francis, Poetry Book Society (http://www.po etrybooks.co.uk/PBS/pbs_francis_matthew.asp).

Biography of Maurice Riordan (http://www.munsterlit.ie/Conwrit ers/Maurice%20Riordan.htm).

Biography of *Maurice Scully* (http://www.irishwriters-online. com/mauricescully.html).

Biography of Max Plowman by Michele Fry (http://www.sassoon ery.demon.co.uk/plowman.htm).

Biography of McCaig, Norman Alexander (http://www.users.global net.co.uk/~crumey/norman_maccaig.html).

Biography of Medbh Mcguckian (http://www.english.emory.edu/ Bahri/McGuckian.html).

Biography of Michael Bruce. LoveToKnow Online Classic Encyclope-dia (http://34.1911encyclopedia.org).

Biography of Michael Hartnett (http://www.irishcultureandcus toms.com/Poetry/Hartnett.html).

Biography of Michael Horovitz (http://www.connectotel.com/Po etryOlympics/horovitz.htm).

Biography of Michael Longley (http://www.contemporarywriters. com/authors/?p=auth199).

Biography of Michael Rosen: Bloomsbury.com — Children's Authors (http://www.bloomsbury.com/childrens/microsite.asp?id=635&section=3).

Biography of Miss Charlotte Elliott, 1789–1871 (Spiritual Songsters) (http://www.stempublishing.com/hymns/biographies/elliott.html).

Biography of Muriel Spark (http://www.bbc.co.uk/scotland/arts/writingscotland/writers/muriel_spark/).

Biography of Nicholas Amhurst: Online Classic Encyclopedia- Love to Know (http://www.19.1911encyclopedia.org).

Biography of Nigel Jenkins (http://www.swan.ac.uk/english/crew/nigel_jenkins.htm).

Biography of Noel Coward: The Knitting Circle: Theatre (http://myweb.lsbu.ac.uk/~stafflag/noelcoward.html).

Biography of Norman MacCaig, Answers.com (http://www.answers.com/topic/norman-maccaig).

Biography of Nuala Ní Dhomhnaill (http://www.usna.edu/English Dept/ilv/nuala.htm).

Biography of Nuala Ní Dhomhnaill: The Gallery Press (http://www.gallerypress.com/Authors/NNdhomhnaill/nndhom.html).

Biography of Owen Sheers: The Blue Book (http://www.owensheers.co.uk/back.htm).

Biography of Padraic Colum (http://www.irelandseye.com/aarticles/history/people/writers/pcolum.shtm).

Biography of Padraic Fallon (http://www.irishwriters-online.com/padraicfallon.html).

Biography of Pascale Petit (http://www.bbc.co.uk/education/beyond/factsheets/poet01_petit.shtml).

Biography of Pascale Petit: Poetry Book Society (http://www.poetrybooks.co.uk/PBS/pbs_petit_pascale.asp).

Biography of Patrick Deeley. Dedalus Press (http://www.dedaluspress.com/poets/deeley.html).

Biography of Paul Durcan (http://www.irishwriters-online.com/pauldurcan.html).

Biography of Pearse Hutchinson (http://www.irishwriters-online.com/pearsehutchinson.html).

Biography of Percy French (http://users2.evl.net/~smyth/linernotes/personel/FrenchPercy.htm), and at (http://www.pdevlinz.btinternet.co.uk/percyfrench.htm).

Biography of Peter Riley (http://au.geocities.com/masthead_2/issue6/biogs6.html).

Biography of Peter William Redgrove (http://www.tauntonschool.co.uk/alumni/obituaries/files/Redgrovep.html).

Biography of Randolph Healy: Sound Eye (http://indigo.ie/~tjac/Poets/Randolph_Healy/ randolph_healy.htm).

Biography of Richard Murphy (http://www.cca.ukzn.ac.za/images/pa/PA2004/poets/murphy.htm).

Biography of Robert Conquest (http://www.hoover.stanford.edu/bios/conquest.html).

Biography of Robert Dodsley, with Links. Infoplease (http://www.infoplease.com/ce6/people/A0815765.html).

Biography of Robert Garioch (http://www.nls.uk/writestuff/heads/wee-garioch.html).

Biography of Robert Greacen (http://www.sarahferris.co.uk/pages/robertgreacen.htm).

Biography of Robert Lloyd (http://www.fzc.dk/Boswell/People/people.php?id=85).

Biography of Robert Murray McCheyne (http://web.ukonline.co.uk/d.haslam/m-cheyne.htm).

Biography of Robert Murray McCheyne. St Peter's Free Church, Dundee (http://www.stpeters-dundee.org.uk/history.htm).

Biography of Robin Robertson (http://www.griffinpoetryprize.com/trustees.php?t=6).

Biography of Roger Boyle, 1st Earl of Orrery: Answer.Com (http://www.answers.com/topic/roger-boyle-1st-earl-of-orrery).

Biography of Ronald Mathias (http://www.transcript-review.org/section.cfm?id=198&lan=en).

Biography of Roy Fisher: Literary Heritage (http://www3.shropshire-cc.gov.uk/fisher.htm).

Biography of Ruth Fainlight (http://www.arlindo-correia.com/081004.html).

Biography of Seamus Deane, Reading Group Centre (http://www.randomhouse.com/vintage/read/reading/deane.html).

Biography of Seamus Heaney (http://www.kirjasto.sci.fi/heaney.htm).

Biography of Seán Dunne (http://www.gallerypress.com/Authors/Sdunne/sdunne.html).

Biography of Seán Dunne, Irish Writers Online (http://www.irishwriters-online.com/seandunne.html).

Biography of Sheenagh Pugh (http://www.swan.ac.uk/english/Subpages/Pugh.htm).

Biography of Sidney Goodsir Smith: Scottish Authors (http://www.slainte.org.uk/scotauth/smithdsw.htm).

Biography of Sir Edward Denny, 1796–1889 (Spiritual Songsters) (http://www.stempublishing.com/hymns/biographies/denny.html).

Biography of Sir John Clerk, Concerto Caledonia (http://www.concal.org/clerk.htm).

Biography of Sir John Clerk, Scotland's People (http://www.scotlandspeople.gov.uk/content/help/index.aspx?1089).

Biography of Sir Kingsley Amis (www.kirjasto.sci.fi/amis.htm).

Biography of Sir Philp Sidney (http://www.luminarium.org/renlit/sidbio.htm).

Biography of Sir Walter Alexander Raleigh (http://epona.lib.ed.ac.uk:1822/isaar/P0299.html).

Biography of Sophie Hannah (http://www.sophiehannah.com/biographical.html)

Biography of Sorley Maclean: BBC—Writing Scotland—Scotland's Languages (http://www.bbc.co.uk/scotland/arts/writingscotland/learning_journeys/scotlands_languages/sorley_maclean/).

Biography of the Wedderburn Brothers (http://23.1911encyclopedia.org/W/WE/WEDDERBURN_JAMES_JOHN_AND_ROBERT.htm), and the history of Sir John Wedderburn, who was executed for his part in the 1745 Rebellion (http://perso.wanadoo.fr/euroleader/wedderburn/sirjohn.htm).

Biography of Theo Dorgan (http://www.irishwriters-online.com/theodorgan.html).

Biography of Thom Gunn (http://www.interviews-with-poets.com/thom-gunn/gunn-note.html).

Biography of Thomas Creech (http://68.1911encyclopedia.org/C/CR/CREECH_THOMAS.htm).

Biography of Thomas Kelly (http://www.evangelical-times.org/articles/may05/may05a12.htm).

Biography of Thomas Kelly: Christian History Institute (http://chi.gospelcom.net/DAILYF/2002/07/daily-07-13-2002.shtml).

Biography of Thomas McCarthy (http://www.irishwriters-online.com/thomasmccarthy.html).

Biography of Thomas Moore (http://www.kirjasto.sci.fi/tmoore.htm)

Biography of Thomas Vaughan: The Literary Encyclopedia (http://www.litencyc.com/php/speople.php?rec=true&UID=5473).

Biography of Tom Leonard. BBC—Writing Scotland—Scotland's Languages (http://www.bbc.co.uk/scotland/arts/writingscotland/learning_journeys/scotlands_languages/tom_leonard).

Biography of Tom Pickard: Woodland Pattern Book Centre (http://www.woodlandpattern.org/poems/tom_pickard01.shtml).

Biography of Trevor Joyce (http://www.irishwriters-online.com/trevorjoyce.html).

Biography of Velentin Iremonger (http://archiver.rootsweb.com/th/read/IrelandGenWeb/2002-07/1025887586).

Biography of Vona Groark (http://www.gallerypress.com/Authors/Vgroarke/vgroarke.html).

Biography of Willa Muir. Writing Scotland: A journey through Scotland's Literature (http://www.bbc.co.uk/scotland/arts/writingscotland/writers/willa_muir/)

Biography of William Henry Havergal: AIM25: Royal College of Music (http://www.aim25.ac.uk/cgi-bin/frames/fulldesc?inst_id=25&coll_id=5684).

Biography of William Kennish (http://kennish.com/william).

Biography of William Magin and engraving of the Fraserians (http://www.munsterlit.ie/literarycork/fraser.html).

Biography of William Meston. Significant and Famous Scots (http://www.electricscotland.com/history/other/meston_william.htm).

Biography of William Soutar: BBC—Writing Scotland—Scotland's Languages (http://www.bbc.co.uk/scotland/arts/writingscotland/writers/william_soutar/)

Biography of W.S. Graham (http://www.users.globalnet.co.uk/~crumey/w_s_graham.html).

Biography, Poems and Picture of Aleister Crowley (http://www.lovepoems.me.uk/biography_crowley_aleister.htm).

Bishop Percy's Folio MS: Ballads and Romances. Volume 1, 2 & 3.

John W. Hales & Frederick J. Furnivall, ed. N. Trübner & Co., 1868.

Bitter Harvest: An Anthology of Contemporary Irish Verse. John Montague, ed. Scribner's, 1989.

The Bloodaxe Book of Modern Australian Poetry. John Tranter, and Philip Mead, ed. Bloodaxe Books, 1991, 1994.

The Bloodaxe Book of Modern Welsh Poetry. Menna Elfyn, & John Rowland, ed. Bloodaxe Books, 2003.

The Bloodaxe Book of 20th Century Poetry, from Britain and Ireland. Edna Longley, ed. Bloodaxe Books, 2000.

Bloodaxe Books (http://www.bloodaxebooks.com/personpage. asp?author=Peter+Reading).

Bloomsbury.com—Research centre: Vernon Watkins (http://www. bloomsburymagazine.com/ARC/detail.asp?entryid=109648).

The Bluestockings: Bibliography (http://bartleby.school.aol.com/ 221/1500.html).

Bob Cobbing Publications: Bob Cobbing Author Page (http:// wings.buffalo.edu/epc/authors/cobbing/cobbing-pub.html).

The Bodleian Library, Oxford (http://search.ox.ac.uk/).

The Body Electric: America's Best Poetry from The American Poetry Review. Stephen Berg, David Bonanno, and Arthur Vogelsang, ed. W.W. Norton, 2000.

Bomb Culture, Jeff Nuttall. MacGibbon & Kee, 1968.

Bonar, A. and McCheyne, Mission of Discovery: The Beginnings of Modern Jewish Evangelism. Alan Harman, ed. Fearn, 1996.

The Book of a Thousand Poems: A Family Treasury. J. Murray Macbain, ed. Peter Bedrick Books, 1983.

The Book of Aneurin (With English translation) (http://www. maryjones.us/ctexts/aindex.html).

A Book of Animal Poems. William Cole, ed. Viking, 1973.

The Book of Irish Verse: An Anthology of Irish Poetry from the Sixth Century to the Present. John Montague, ed. Macmillan, 1974.

A Book of Love Poetry. Jon Stallworthy, ed. Oxford University Press, 1974.

A Book of Nature Poems. William Cole, ed. Viking Press, 1969.

A Book of Scottish Verse. Maurice Lindsay, and R.L. Mackie, ed. St. Martin's Press, 1983.

The Book of the Law: Liber AL vel Legis, sub figura CCXX (http:// www.sacred-texts.com/oto/engccxx.htm).

A Book of Women Poets from Antiquity to Now. Aliki Barnstone, and Willis Barnstone, ed. Schocken Books, 1980.

Book-Song. Gleeson White, ed. Elliot Stock, 1893.

Books and Writers, Biography of Vera Brittain (http://www.kirjasto. sci.fi/britta.htm).

Books by Duncan Bush: Results—enCompass Culture (http://www. encompassculture.com/results/?qs=Duncan%20Bush).

Books by Peter Robinson (http://charles.sal.tohoku.ac.jp/robinson/ books.html).

Books by Robert Millhouse. Forget Me Not: A Hypertextual Archive (http://www.orgs.muohio.edu/anthologies/FMN/Author_List. htm).

Books by Robert Nye (http://www.fantasticfiction.co.uk/authors/ Robert_Nye.htm).

Books by Thomas McCarthy (http://www.munsterlit.ie/Conwriters/ thomas_mccarthy.htm).

Boosey & Hawkes Opera (http://www.boosey.com/pages/opera/ moreDetails.asp?musicID=7494).

Bowden, the village. The Scottish Borders (www.bowden.bordernet. co.uk).

The Brand-X Anthology of Poetry. William Zaranka, ed. Apple-Wood Books, 1981.

Bread and Roses: An Anthology of Nineteenth- and Twentieth-Century Poetry by Women Writers. Diana Scott, ed. Virago Press, 1982.

The Bride's Book of Poems. Cary Yager, ed. Contemporary Books, 1995.

A Brief History of Wales-Ch. 26-Continued Concern (http://www. peternwilliams.com/wales/wal26.html).

The Brink by Jacob Polley: Poetry Book Review (http://www.poets graves.co.uk/poetry_book_review.htm).

Britain in Print. Henryson's Testament of Cresseid in Context: The Buke of the Howlat discussed (http://www.britaininprint.net/ learning/studytools_4.php).

Britannia (http://www.britannia.com/history/monarchs/mon45. html).

Britannia Biographies (http://www.britannia.com/bios/rhymer. html).

British Council Arts (http://www.contemporarywriters.com).

British Electronic Poetry Centre (http://www.soton.ac.uk/~bepc/ index.htm).

The British Library (http://www.bl.uk/collections/britirish/mod brimoberts.html).

British Literature 1640–1789 (www.blackwellpublishing.com/con tents.asp?ref=063121769X).

British Literature to the Restoration (http://www.tcnj.edu/~graham/ LIT251fall05.htm).

British Minstrelsie. Edinburgh: T.C. & E.C. Jack, Grange Publishing works, ?1900.

British Poetry 1880–1920: Edwardian Voices. Paul L. Wiley, and Harold Orel, ed. Appleton-Century-Crofts, 1969.

British Poetry Since 1945. Edward Lucie-Smith, ed. Penguin Books, 1985.

British Women Writers: An Anthology from the Fourteenth Century to the Present. Dale Spender, and Janet Todd, ed. Peter Bedrick Books. 1989.

Broad Grins, My Nightgown and Slippers and other Humorous Works Prose and Poetical of George Colman the Younger. George B. Buckstone, ed. John Camden Hotten, 1872.

The Broadview Anthology of Victorian Poetry and Poetic Theory. Thomas J. Collins and Vivienne Rundle, ed. Broadview, 1999.

The Brontes (www.bronte-country.com/brontes.html).

A Bundle of Ballads. George Routledge & Sons, 1891.

The Burns Encyclopedia (www.robertburns.org/encyclopedia).

The Burns Encyclopedia, Alexander Ross (http://www.robertburns. org/encyclopedia/index-r.shtml).

The Burns Encyclopedia: John Mayne (http://robertburns.org/en cyclopedia/MayneJohn17591511836.597.shtml).

The Burns Encyclopedia, John Skinner (http://www.robertburns. org/encyclopedia/CunninghamAllan17841511842.253.shtml).

Cambium Gardening (http://www.cambiumgardening.com/ books/bonsai/).

The Cambridge History of English and American Literature in 18 Volumes, 1907–21. New York: Putnam, 1907–1921.

The Cameronian's Dream (http://www.covenanter.org/Poems/ cameroniandream.htm).

Canadian Poetry in English. Bliss Carman, Lorne Pierce and V.B. Rhodenize, ed. Ryerson Press (Rev. and enl. ed.), 1954.

Canadian Poets. John W. Garvin, ed. McClelland, Goodchild & Stewart, 1916.

Canongate Books Ltd (www.canongate.net).

Carcanet Press (http://www.Carcanet.Press.co.uk).

Caribbean Poetry Now. Stewart Brown, ed. Edward Arnold, 1992.

Carmina Mariana: An English Anthology in Verse in Honor of or in Relation to the Blessed Virgin Mary. Orby Shipley, ed. Burns and Oates, 1894.

The Carnegie Mellon Anthology of Poetry. Gerald Costanzo, and Jim Daniels, ed. Carnegie Mellon University Press, 1993.

Casebook: Jack the Ripper—James Kenneth Stephen (http://www. casebook.org/suspects/jkstephen.html).

Cat Will Rhyme with Hat: A Book of Poems. Jean Chapman, ed. Scribner's, 1986.

The Cat Witches (http://www.red4.co.uk/Folklore/fairytales/ catwitches.htm).

Catholic Encyclopedia (http://www.newadvent.org).

Cats, Poem by ASJ Tessimond (http://www.cs.rice.edu/~ssiyer/min strels/poems/1010.html).

The Cavalier Poets. Robin Skelton, ed. Oxford University Press, 1970.

The Cavalier Poets: An Anthology. Thomas Crofts, ed. Dover Publications, 1995.

Cavalier Poets: Selected Poems. Thomas Clayton, ed. Oxford University Press, 1978.

Cecil Frances Alexander—Hymn Writer (www.ulsterhistory.co.uk).

The Celebrated Mrs. Pilkington's Jests, Or the Cabinet of Wit and Humour, published in 1751, and republished by Ams Pr Publishing in 1964.

A Celebration of Women Writers: Mrs. Seumas Macmanus (Anna Johnston). http://digital.library.upenn.edu/women/carbery/ macmanus.html).

A Celebration of Women Writers: Plays Produced by the Abbey The-

atre Company (http://digital.library.upenn.edu/women/greg-ory/theatre/appendix-I.html).

A Century of Humorous Verse, 1850–1950. Roger Lancelyn Green, ed. E.P. Dutton (Everyman's Library), 1959.

A Century of Sonnets: The Romantic-Era Revival 1750–1850. Paula R. Feldman and Daniel Robinson, ed. Oxford University Press, 1999.

Chadwyck-Healey English Poetry Database: Jacobean and Caroline Poetry1603–1660 (http://library.stanford.edu/depts/hasrg/hdis/engpo.html).

Chaos of the Night: Women's Poetry and Verse of the Second World War. Catherine W. Reilly, ed. Virago Press, 1984.

Chapel Royal. A Collegiate Church for the Scottish Royal family (http://www.rosslyntemplars.org.uk/chapel_royal.htm).

Chapman's Homer: The Iliad. Steven Shankman, ed. Princeton University Press, 1956.

Chapters into Verse. Vol. I: Genesis to Malachi. Robert Atwan, and Laurance Wieder, ed. Oxford University Press. 1993.

Chapters into Verse. Vol. II: Gospels to Revelation. Robert Atwan, and Laurance Wieder, ed. Oxford University Press, 1993.

Charles Stuart Calverley, Martley's "Lost" Poet." (http://www.martley.org.uk/people/lostpoet.htm).

The Charles Tomlinson Resource Centre (http://www3.sympatico.ca/sylvia.paul/CharlesTomlinson_poetry.htm).

Charles Williams. David Llewellyn Dodds, ed. The Boydell Press, 1991.

The Chatto Book of Cabbages and Kings: Lists in Literature. Francis Spufford, ed. Chatto and Windus, 1989.

The Chatto Book of Love Poetry. John Fuller, ed. Chatto & Windus, 1990.

The Chatto Book of Modern Poetry 1915–1955. Cecil Day Lewis, and John Lehmann, ed. Chatto & Windus, 1966.

The Chatto Book of Nonsense Poetry. Hugh Haughton, ed. Chatto & Windus, 1988.

The Cherrie and the Slae by Alexander Montgomerie. H. Harvey Wood, ed. Faber and Faber Ltd. 1937. First printed by Robert Waldegrave, 1597. For the whole poem see (http://www.scotstext.org/makars/alexander_montgomerie/)

The Cherry-Tree. Geoffrey Grigson, ed. Phoenix House, 1959.

Chief Modern Poets of Britain and America. 5th edition. Gerald DeWitt Sanders, and John Herbert Nelson, ed. Macmillan, 1970.

Child Line (http://www.childline.org.uk/extra/benjaminzephaniah.asp).

A Child's Treasury of Poems. Mark Daniel, ed. Dial / Penguin Books, 1986.

A Child's Treasury of Verse. Eleanor Doan, ed. Zondervan Corporation, 1977.

Chinese Poems. Arthur Waley, ed. Unwin Paperbacks, 1946).

Chloe Plus Olivia: An Anthology of Lesbian Literature from the Seventeenth Century to the Present. Lillian Faderman, ed. Viking Penguin, 1994.

Choice of Swinburne's Verse. Robert Nye, ed. Faber and Faber, 1973.

Christian History Institute, Philip Doddridge (http://chi.gospelcom.net/DAILYF/2003/10/daily-10–26–2003.shtml).

Christmas Poems. John Hollander and J.D. McClatchy, ed. Alfred A. Knopf, 1999.

Christopher Smart: Selected Poems. Karina Williamson and Marcus Walsh, ed. Penguin Books, 1990.

City of Westminster Manors And Estates: Bishop of Exeter's Inn (Essex House) (http://www.middlesexpast.net/wexeter.html).

Clan Carnegie (http://www.electricscotland.com/webclans/atoc/carnegi2.html).

Clan MacLean Articles, In Memory of Sorley. A Tribute, by Mary McLean Hoff (http://www.maclean.org/clan-maclean-articles/clan-maclean-tribute-to-sorley.htm).

Clan Maguire (http://www.cov44.freeserve.co.uk/clanmag.htm).

Clan of the Cat. Ewart Alan Mackintosh (http://a2fister2000.tripod.com/id66.htm).

Clare People: Brian Merriman (http://www.clarelibrary.ie/eolas/coclare/people/merriman.htm).

The Classic Hundred: All-Time Favorite Poems. William Harmon, ed. Columbia University Press, 1990.

Classic Poetry: An Illustrated Collection. Michael Rosen, ed. Paul Howard (Illustrator). Walker Books Ltd., 1998.

A Cloud of Witnesses: Mr. Richard Cameron (http://www.truecovenanter.com/reformedpresbyterian/cloud/cloud_appendix_cameron_richard.html).

Collected Later Poems: 1988–2000 of R.S. Thomas. Bloodaxe Books, 2004.

The Collected Poems and Journals of Mary Tighe. University Press of Kentucky, 2005.

Collected Poems and Selected Prose of Charlotte Mew. Val Warner, ed. Fyfield Books, 2003.

Collected Poems and Songs of George Campbell Hay (Dheorsa Mac Iain Dheorsa).(two volumes). Michel Byrne, ed. Edinburgh University Press, 1999.

Collected Poems, by A.E. London: Macmillan, 1913 and 2001.

Collected Poems by John Freeman. MacMillan and Co., 1928.

Collected Poems by Samuel Beckett, 1930–1978. John Calder Pub. 1999.

Collected Poems 1897–1907 of Henry Newbolt. Thomas Nelson & Sons, 1910.

Collected Poems Laurence Binyon: Volume 2. Macmillan and Co., Limited, 1931.

Collected Poems, 1908–1956 of Siegfried Sassoon. Faber and Faber, 1984.

Collected Poems, 1909–1962 of T.S. Eliot. Harcourt Brace, 1963: reprinted. 1991.

Collected Poems, 1935–1992 of F.T. Prince. The Sheep Meadow Press, 1993.

Collected Poems, 1956–1994 of Thomas Kinsella. Oxford University Press, 1996.

Collected Poems, 1975, Robert Graves. Oxford University Press, 1988.

The Collected Poems of A.E. Housman. Henry Holt, 1965.

Collected Poems of Alun Lewis. Cary Archard, ed. Poetry Wales Press, 1994.

Collected Poems of Austin Clarke. Liam Miller, ed. The Dolmen Press, 1974.

Collected Poems of Bernard Spencer. Alan Ross, 1965.

Collected Poems of Bernard Spencer. Roger Bowen, 1981.

The Collected Poems of Canon Richard Watson Dixon (1833–1900). Peter Lang Publishing, 1989.

Collected Poems of C.H. Sissons. Carcanet Press, 1984 and 1998.

Collected Poems of Charles Tomlinson. Oxford University Press, 1985.

Collected Poems of Charlotte Mew. Gerald Duckworth & Co., 1953.

Collected Poems of Derek Mahon. The Gallery Press, 1999.

Collected Poems of Donald Davie. Neil Powell, ed. Carcanet Press, 2002.

The Collected Poems of Dylan Thomas, 1934–1952. New Directions, 1953, rev. ed. 1956.

The Collected Poems of Edith Sitwell. The Vanguard Press, 1954.

The Collected Poems of Edward Thomas. Oxford University Press, 1979.

The Collected Poems of Emyr Humphreys. University of Wales Press, 1999.

Collected Poems of Frederic William Henry Myers. Macmillan, 1921.

Collected Poems of George Eliot. Lucien Jenkins, ed. Skoob Books Publication Ltd., 1989.

Collected Poems of Herbert Read. Sinclair-Stevenson, 1994.

Collected Poems of James Joyce. Viking Press, 1946.

Collected Poems of James Stephens. Macmillan, 1928.

The Collected Poems of John Betjeman. Birkenhead, Earl of, ed. John Murray, 1979, reissued 1990.

The Collected Poems of John Drinkwater (1917–1922). Sidgwick and Jackson Limited, 1923.

Collected Poems of John Henry Newman. Fisher Press, 1992.

The Collected Poems of John Hewitt. Frank Ormsby, ed. Blackstaff Press, 1992.

Collected Poems of John Lehmann. Eyre & Spottiswoode, 1963.

The Collected Poems of John Masefield. William Heinemann Ltd, 1923.

Collected Poems of L.A.G. Strong. Methuen, 1957.

The Collected Poems of Louis MacNeice. E.R. Dodds, ed. Faber and Faber, 1966.

The Collected Poems of Mary Coleridge. Theresa Whistler. Rupert Hart-Davis, 1954.

Collected Poems of Michael Roberts. Faber and Faber, 1958.

The Collected Poems of Philip Bourke Marston. Mrs. Louise Chandler Moulton. Ward, Lock, Bowden and Co., 1892.

Collected Poems of Philip Larkin. Anthony Thwaite, ed. Farrar, Straus and Giroux, 1988.

The Collected Poems of Roland Mathias. University of Wales Press, 2002 (http://www.uwp.co.uk/book_desc/1760.html).

The Collected Poems of Rupert Brooke. Kessinger Publishing Co., 2005.

Collected Poems of Stephen Spender. Faber and Faber, 1985.

Collected Poems of Stevie Smith. James MacGibbon, ed. New Directions, 1976.

Collected Poems of Sydney Goodsir Smith. Calder Publications Ltd (1976).

The Collected Poems of Sylvia Plath. Ted Hughes, ed. Harper-Collins, 1981.

The Collected Poems of T.E. Brown, Macmillan & Co., Ltd., 1909

Collected Poems of Thom Gunn. Faber and Faber, 1994.

Collected Poems of Thomas Kinsella. Carcanet Press, 2002.

Collected Poems of Thomas MacGreevy: An Annotated Edition. Susan Schreibman, ed. Anna Livia Press, Dublin, 1991.

The Collected Poems of Vernon Watkins. Brian Keeble, ed. Golgonooza Press, 2000.

Collected Poems of Walter De La Mare. Henry Holt, 1941.

The Collected Poems of W.B. Yeats. Richard J. Finneran, ed. Macmillan, 1989.

The Collected Poems of Wilfred Owen. C. Day Lewis, ed. New Directions, 1963.

Collected Poems (Poetry Pleiade) of Sidney Keyes. Carcanet Press, 2002.

Collected Poems with Wolf Tongue: Poems 1975–2000. Shearsman Books, 2004.

Collected Poetry of Aldous Huxley. Donald Watt, ed. Chatto, 1971.

The Collected Satires and Poems of Osbert Sitwell. Duckworth, 1931.

Collected Sonnets of Turner, Charles Tennyson. Gregg International Publishers, 1880.

Collected Works of G.K. Chesterton. Aidan Mackey, ed. Ignatius, 1994.

The Collected Works of Katherine Philips: Volume 1, 2 & 3. Patrick Thomas, ed. Stump Cross Books, 1990.

The Collected Works of Mary Sidney Herbert: Volume 1. Margaret Hannay, Noel Kinnamon, & Michael Brennan, ed. Clarendon Press, 1998.

The Collected Works of William Morris (24 vols.). May Morris, ed. Longmans, Green and Company, 1910–1915.

Collected Writings of Dante Gabriel Rossetti. Jan Marsh, ed. New Amsterdam Books, 2000.

The Collected Writings of T.E. Hulme. Karen Csengeri, ed. Clarendon Press, Oxford, 1994.

A Collection of Poems in Six Volumes. by Several Hands. with Notes. London: Printed for J. Dodsley, 1782 (www.muohio.edu/anthologies/dodsley.htm).

A Collection of Poems, Principally Consisting of the Most Celebrated Pieces of Sir Charles Hanbury Williams (no publisher), 1763.

Colley Cibber, Texts Set to Music (http://www.recmusic.org/lieder/c/cibber).

The Columbia Anthology of British Poetry. Carl Woodring, and James Shapiro, ed. Columbia University Press, 1995.

The Columbia Anthology of Gay Literature. Byrne R.S. Fone, ed. Columbia University Press, 1998.

The Columbia Encyclopedia, Sixth Edition. 2001–05 (http://www.bartleby.com/65/).

The Columbia Granger's Index to Poetry. 11th ed. The Columbia Granger's World of Poetry, Columbia University Press, 2005 (http://www.columbiagrangers.org).

Come Hither. Walter de la Mare, ed. Knopf, 1957: Dover Publications, 1995.

The Common Muse, an Anthology of Popular British Ballad Poetry, XVth–XXth Century. Vivian de Sola Pinto, and Allan Edwin Rodway, ed. Philosophical Library, 1957.

A Compendium of Irish Biography (http://www.libraryireland.com/biography/biographyG.php).

Complete Collection of Poems by Robert Louis Stevenson (http://www.poetryloverspage.com/poets/stevenson/stevenson.html).

The Complete English Poems of George Herbert. John Tobin, ed. Penguin Books, 1991.

The Complete English Poems of John Donne. A.J. Smith, ed. Penguin Books, 1971.

The Complete English Poems of Samuel Johnson. J.D. Fleeman, ed. Penguin Books, 1971.

The Complete Life and Works of Samuel Daniel (http://www.luminarium.org/renlit/daniel.htm).

The Complete Novels and Selected Writings of Amy Levy. Melvyn New, ed. University Press of Florida, 1993.

The Complete Poems and Translations of Christopher Marlowe. Stephen Orgel, ed. Penguin Books, 1971.

The Complete Poems of Andrew Marvell. Elizabeth Story Donno, ed. Penguin Books, 1972, reprinted 1985.

The Complete Poems of Basil Bunting. Richard Caddel, ed. Oxford University Press, 1994.

The Complete Poems of Ben Jonson. George Parfitt, ed. Penguin Books, 1988.

The Complete Poems of Christina Rossetti. R.W. Crump, ed. Louisiana State University Press. Vol. 1, 1979: Vol. 2, 1986: Vol. 3, 1990.

The Complete Poems of D.H. Lawrence. Vivian de Sola Pinto and Warren Roberts, ed. Penguin Books, 1993.

The Complete Poems of Dr. Joseph Beaumont. 2 Volumes, Alexander B. Grosart, ed. Edinburgh University Press, 1880.

The Complete Poems of Edwin Muir. Peter Butter, ed. The Association for Scottish Literary Studies, 1991.

The Complete Poems of Francis Ledwidge. Herbert Jenkins Limited, 1919.

The Complete Poems of John Keats. John Barnard, ed. Penguin Books, 1988.

The Complete Poems of John Skelton. Philip Henderson, ed. J.M. Dent and Sons Ltd., 1948.

The Complete Poems of Jonathan Swift. Pat Rogers, ed. Penguin Books, 1983.

The Complete Poems of Keith Douglas. Introduction by Ted Hughes. Faber and Faber, 2000.

The Complete Poems of Lionel Johnson. Iain Fletcher, ed. The Unicorn Press, 1953.

The Complete Poems of Percy Bysshe Shelley. Mary Shelley, ed. The Modern Library, 1994.

The Complete Poems of Robert Graves in One Volume. Beryl Graves and Dunstan Ward, ed. Carcanet Press, 2000.

The Complete Poems of Robert Service. Dodd, Mead and Company, 1940.

The Complete Poems of Robert Southwell. Alexander B. Grosart, ed. Reprint Services, 1872.

The Complete Poems of Sir Thomas Moore. William M. Rossetti, ed. A.L. Burt Company, 1910.

Complete Poems of Sir Thomas Wyatt. R.A. Rebholz, ed. Penguin Books, 1978.

The Complete Poems of Thomas Hardy. James Gibson, ed. Macmillan, 1978.

The Complete Poems of William Blake. Alicia Ostriker, ed. Penguin Books, 1977.

Complete Poetical Works of Adelaide Anne Proctor. Thomas Y. Crowell, 1903.

The Complete Poetical Works of Mrs. Browning [Elizabeth Barrett Browning]. Harriet Waters Preston, ed. Houghton Mifflin, 1900.

The Complete Poetical Works of Robert Southey, LL. D.D. Appleton & Company, 1850.

The Complete Poetical Works of Samuel Rogers. Epes Sargent, ed. Phillips, Sampson, and Company, 1854.

The Complete Poetical Works of Spenser. R.E. Neil Dodge, ed. Houghton Mifflin, 1936.

The Complete Poetical Works of Thomas Campbell. J. Logie Robertson, ed. Oxford University Press, 1907.

The Complete Poetry of John Milton. John T. Shawcross, ed. Doubleday, 1971.

Complete Poetry of Oscar Wilde. Isobel Murray, ed. Oxford University Press, 1997.

The Complete Poetry of Richard Crashaw. George Walton Williams, ed. New York University Press, 1972.

The Complete Verse and Other Nonsense of Edward Lear. Vivien Noakes, ed. Penguin Books, 2001.

The Complete Works in Prose and Verse of Francis Quarles V. 3 (No publisher listed), 1881.

The Complete Works in Verse and Prose of Samuel Daniel. Alexander B. Grosart, ed. Russell & Russell, 1963.

The Complete Works of Aldous Huxley (http://somaweb.org/w/hux works.html).

The Complete Works of C.S. Calverley. G. Bell and Sons, 1926.

The Complete Works of Idris Davies. Daffyd Johnston, ed. University of Wales Press, 1994.

The Complete Works of John Davies of Hereford. AMS Press, 1967.

The Complete Works of Joshuah Sylvester: Volume II. Alexander B. Grosart, ed. Edinburgh University Press, 1880.

The Complete Works of Thomas Lodge: Volume 4. Russell & Russell, 1963.

The Complete Works of Thomas Shadwell V. 5. The Fortune Press, 1927.

Comrade Heart: A Life of Randall Swingler. Andy Croft. Manchester University Press, 2003 (http://les.man.ac.uk/chnn/CHNN15ARS.html).

Confucius to Cummings: An Anthology of Poetry. Ezra Pound and Marcella Spann, ed. New Directions Publishing Corporation, 1964.

The Contemplative Quarry and the Man with a Hammer by Anna Wickham. Harcourt, Brace, and Company, 1921.

The Contemplator's Short Biography of Thomas D'Urfey (http://www.contemplator.com/history/durfey.html).

The Contemplator's Very Short Biography of Percy French (http://www.contemplator.com/history/pfrench.html).

Contemporary Irish Poetry: An Anthology. Anthony Bradley, ed. University of California Press. New and rev. ed., 1988.

Contemporary Religious Poetry. Paul Ramsey, ed. Paulist Press, 1987.

Contemporary Writers in the UK (www.contemporarywriters.com).

The Copper Family, Coppersongs: The Irish Girl (http://www.the copperfamily.com/songs/coppersongs/irish.html).

Cork 2005 Translation Project. Bulgaria/Cork Poet: Gregory O'Donoghue (http://www.munsterlit.ie/Conwriters/Translation%20Project/gregory_o'donoghue.htm).

The Countess of Huntingdon's Methodist Connexion (http://www.oxfordscholarship.com/oso/public/content/religion/0198263694/toc.html).

Country Rhymes of James Orr: The Bard of Ballycarry. Pretani Press, 1992.

County Donegal on the Internet (www.dun-na-ngall.com).

County Roscommon, IrelandGenWeb Project (http://www.rootsweb.com/~irlrosco/).

The Course of Time by Pollok. Robert, J. and B. Williams, 1836.

The Court Poets (Great Books Online, www.bartleby.com).

The Covenanters by Brian Orr Part One (http://www.tartans.com/articles/cov1.html).

Cowboy Songs and Other Frontier Ballads. Alan Lomax and John A. Lomax, ed. Macmillan, 1967.

CREW Welsh Writers Online (http://www.swan.ac.uk/english/crew/index.htm).

Crockford-House (1827) Canto II, Henry Luttrell (http://www.english.upenn.edu/Projects/knarf/EtAlia/luttrell.html).

The Cumann Merriman Website (http://www.merriman.ie/).

Curry, Neil & Dine, Jim—The Bending of the Bow (http://www.inpressbooks.co.uk/bending_of_the_bow_the_by_curry_neil_dine_jim_i079.aspx).

Curtain Call: 101 Portraits in Verse. Hugo Williams, ed. Faber and Faber, 2001.

The Cyber Hymnal (http://www.cyberhymnal.org/index.htm).

Dance in Poetry: An International Anthology of Poems on Dance. Alkis Raftis, ed. Princeton Book Company, 1991.

A Dangerous Knowing: Four Black Women Poets: Barbara Burford, Gabriela Pearse, Grace Nichols, Jackie Kay. Grace Nichols, ed. Sheba, 1985.

Dannie Abse Selected Poems. Canto Publications. ISBN: 1903515009: Compact Disk.

The Dark Wind. Walter James Turner. E.P. Dutton, 1920.

David Gascoyne's Home Page (http://www.connectotel.com/gascoyne/index.html).

Davison's Poetical Rhapsody: Volume II, of Francis Davison. A.H. Bullen, ed. George Bell and Sons, 1891.

Deception: Forgery, Lawrence Halloran, 09 Sep 1818 (http://www.oldbaileyonline.org/html_units/1810s/t18180909-4.html)

Deg Soned. A book of 12 sonnets held by The University of London Library (http://www.ull.ac.uk/exhibitions/bookbeautiful.pdf).

Department of English, University of Notre Dame, Faculty Bios (http://www.nd.edu/~english/Faculty-Bios.html).

De Profundis by Oscar Wilde (http://www.upword.com/wilde/de_profundis.html).

The Development of the Sonnet: An Introduction. Michael R.G. Spiller. Routledge, 1993.

The Devil's Book of Verse: Masters of the Poison Pen from Ancient Times to the Present Day. Richard Conniff, ed. Dodd, Mead, 1983.

Devonshire Cemetery, Mametz, Somme (www.silentcities.co.uk/).

The Diary of a dead Officer: Being the posthumous papers of Arthur Graeme West, C.E.M. Joad, ed. Allen and Unwin. 1918. Reissued in 1991 by the Imperial War Museum with an introduction by Dominic Hibbard) (http://eudaemonist.com/biblion/west/).

A Dictionary of Irish Biography. Henry Boylan, ed. Gill & Macmillan, 1998.

Dictionary of National Biography. Electronic Edition, 1.1. Oxford University Press, 1997.

Dictionary of Unitarian & Universalist Biography (http://www.uua.org/uuhs/duub/).

Did You Know?— Halloween in Scotland (http://www.rampantscotland.com/know/blknow_halloween.htm).

Dinah Maria Mulock Craik, 18 Sonnets (www.sonnets.org/craik.htm).

The Direction of Poetry: An Anthology of Rhymed and Metered Verse Written in the English Language since 1975. Robert Richman, ed. Houghton Mifflin, 1988.

Don Paterson's Web Site (http://www.donpaterson.com/).

Don't Forget to Fly: A Cycle of Modern Poems. Paul B. Janeczko, ed. Bradbury Press, 1981.

Dorothy L. Sayers: Her Opus 1 (http://digital.library.upenn.edu/women/sayers/opi/dls-opi.html).

Dorothy L. Sayers, Writer and Theologian (http://justus.anglican.org/resources/bio/19.html).

The Dorset Page (www.thedorsetpage.com).

Dr. Peter Porter, Poet—Alumni at the University of Queensland (http://www.alumni.uq.edu.au/?page=17162&pid=273).

The Dramatic and Poetical Works of Westland Marston. Chatto and Windus, 1876.

Dramatic Chapters, Poems & Songs of Charles Swain. David Bogue, 1848.

Dramatic Studies of Augusta Webster. Macmillan and Co., 1866.

The Dramatic Works and Poems of James Shirley Volume I. Alexander Dyce and William Gifford, ed. Russell & Russell, 1966.

The Dream and Other Poems of Caroline Norton. Jonathan Wordsworth, ed. Woodstock Books, 2001.

Druid's Prayer (English translation) (http://en.wikipedia.org/wiki/Druid%27s_Prayer).

Dryden, Poems and Prose. Douglas Grant, ed. Penguin Books, 1955, repr. 1985.

Duck, Stephen. The Thresher's Labor/Stephen Duck and the Woman's Labor / Mary Collier, Introduction by Moira Ferguson. Los Angeles: Williams Andrews Clark Memorial Library, University of California. 1985.

Dukes of Buckingham and Chandos: Robert Nugent (http://www.dukesofbuckingham.org/people/family/nugent/robert_nugent.htm).

Dumfries & Galloway, Scotland—Ancestor's Stories (http://freepages.genealogy.rootsweb.com/~debbie/stories/dum.html).

Dunluce Castle Website, County Antrim, Ireland (http://www.northantrim.com/dunlucecastle.htm).

The Dust Diaries, Sheers, Owen. Houghton Mifflin, 2004 (http://www.houghtonmifflinbooks.com/booksellers/press_release/sheers/).

Dylan Thomas's Choice: An Anthology of Verse Spoken by Dylan Thomas. Ralph Maud, and Aneirin Talfan Davies, ed. New Directions, 1963.

Early English Books Online Text Creation Partnership (http://www.lib.umich.edu/tcp/eebo/texts/letterE.html).

The Early Italian Poets. Sally Purcell, ed. Anvil Press Poetry, 1981.

Early Light: The Collected Poems of Dorothy Wellesley. Hart-Davis, 1955.

Early Modern Literary Studies (http://www.shu.ac.uk/emls/09-1/mcraerev.html).

Early Modern Women Poets (1520–1700). Jane Stevenson and Peter Davidson, ed. Oxford University Press, 2001.

Early Ripening: American Women's Poetry Now. Marge Piercy, ed. Pandora Press, 1987.

The Earth Is the Lord's: Poems of the Spirit. Helen Plotz, ed. Thomas Y. Crowell, 1965.

Earth Prayers from Around the World: 365 Prayers, Poems, and Invocations for Honoring the Earth. Elizabeth Roberts, and Elais Amidon, ed. Harper Collins, 1991.

The Earthly Paradise: A Poem by William Morris. Longmans, Green, and Co., 1896.

Eclogues, Epitaphs, and Sonnets of Barnabe Googe. Judith M. Kennedy, ed. University of Toronto Press, 1989.

Edgewood College, Wisconsin, An Anthology of Tudor and Elizabethan Poetry: (Poets born before 1576) (http://english.edgewood.edu/eng359/lyric_poetry.htm).

Edward de Vere, Earl of Oxford (http://www.luminarium.org/renlit/devere.htm).

Edward Perronet, hymn writer, death reported January 2, 1792 (http://chi.gospelcom.net/DAILYF/2003/01/daily-01–02–2003.shtml).

Edwin Muir, External Links & References (http://muir.rhizomatics.org.uk/).

Eerdman's Book of Christian Poetry. Pat Alexander and Veronica Zundel, ed. William B. Eerdmans, 1981.

Eight Lines and Under: An Anthology of Short, Short Poems. William Cole, ed. Macmillan, 1967.

Eighteenth-Century English Verse. Dennis Davison, ed. Penguin Books, 1988.

Eighteenth Century Women Poets: An Oxford Anthology. Roger Lonsdale, ed. Oxford University Press, 1989.

The Elaine Feinstein Page (http://www.elainefeinstein.com/).

Electronic Poetry Review #6 — Seven Transylvanian Songs (http://www.epoetry.org/issues/issue6/text/cnotes/pr.htm).

Elegy, by Patrick Deeley (http://www.stingingfly.org/issue4/4deeley.htm).

Elizabethan Lyrics. Norman Ault, ed. William Sloane Associates, 1949.

The Elizabethan Sonnet (www.sonnets.org).

Elizabethan Sonnets. Maurice Evans, ed. J.M. Dent, 1977.

Emergency Kit: Poems for Strange Times. Jo Shapcott and Matthew Sweeney, ed. Faber and Faber, 1996.

Enchiridion: Biographies (http://www.canamus.org/Enchiridion/Biogs/bo.htm).

Encyclopedia Britannica Ultimate Reference Suite DVD, 2006.

Encyclopedia of Britain. Bamber Gascoigne. London: Macmillan, 1994.

England 5 Poems — Poems of the Week Learn English (http://www.learnenglish.org.uk/stories/poem_act/england_poetry.html).

England's Helicon (www.shakespeares-sonnets.com/Helicon.htm).

England's Thousand Best Churches. S. Jenkins. Allen Lane, 1999.

English and American Surrealist Poetry. Edward B. Germain, ed. Penguin Books, 1978.

The English Civil War, Cropredy Bridge, 1644 (http://www.theteacher99.btinternet.co.uk/ecivil/cropredy.htm).

English Literary Linguistic Studies: Franks Casket, Poems That Keep Ringing (http://dspace.dial.pipex.com/town/walk/xen19/reviews.htm).

English Love Poems. John Betjeman, and Geoffrey Taylor, ed. Faber and Faber, 1957.

English Lyric Poems, 1500–1900. C. Day Lewis, ed. Appleton-Century-Crofts, 1961.

English Poems by Richard Le Galliene. Bodley Head, 1892.

English Poetry: Author Search. Chadwyck-Healey Ltd., 1995 (http://www.lib.utexas.edu:8080/search/epoetry/author.html).

English Poetry Bibliography: Thomas Aird. The University of Chicago (www.lib.uchicago.edu/efts/EngPo/ENGPO.bib.html).

English Poetry: L Bibliographic Entries. The University of Texas at Austin General Libraries (http://www.lib.utexas.edu:8080/search/epoetry/biblio-L.html).

English Poetry: A Poetic Record, from Chaucer to Yeats. David Hopkins, ed. Routledge, 1990.

English Poetry, Second Edition Bibliography (http://collections.chadwyck.co.uk/html/ep2/bibliography/r.htm).

English Poets Laureate: Nicholas Rowe (http://www.mala.bc.ca/~lanes/english/laureate/rowe.htm).

English Prose Drama: Bibliography (http://www.lib.uchicago.edu/efts/EPD/EPD.bib.html).

English Renaissance Poetry: A Collection of Shorter Poems from Skelton to Jonson. John Williams, ed. University of Arkansas, 1990.

The English Research Institute: The Works of Prof. Jeffrey Wainwright. http://www.eri.mmu.ac.uk/staff/profile.php?id=29).

English Romantic Poetry and Prose. Russell Noyes, ed. Oxford University Press, 1956.

English Songs and Ballads. T.W.H. Crosland, ed. Oxford University Press, 1918.

English Songs, and Other Small Poems of Barry Cornwall. Edward Moxon, 1844.

English Verse, 1300–1500: Longman Annotated Anthologies of English Verse. Vol. I. John Burrow, ed. Longman, 1977.

English Verse 1830–1890. Bernie Richards, ed. Longman, 1980.

Enitharmon Press (http://www.enitharmon.co.uk.

Eric Mottram Catalogue, Appendix 2: A Checklist of His Published Poems (http://www.kcl.ac.uk/kis/archives/mottram/mopoems.htm).

Erotic Literature: Twenty-four Centuries of Sensual Writing. Jane Mills, ed. HarperCollins, 1993.

Erotic Poems. Peter Washington, ed. Alfred A. Knopf, 1994.

Erotic Poetry: The Lyrics, Ballads, Idylls, and Epics of Love — Classical to Contemporary. William Cole, ed. Random House, 1963.

Essays of Elia (http://www.angelfire.com/nv/mf/lamb/contents.html).

The Eternal Sea: An Anthology of Sea Poetry. W.M. Williamson, ed. Coward-McCann, 1946.

Every-day Book (http://www.uab.edu/english/hone/etexts/edb/day-pages/117–april27.html).

Everyman's Book of English Verse. John Wain, ed. J.M. Dent, 1981.

Everyman's Book of Evergreen Verse. David Herbert, ed. J.M. Dent, 1984.

Everyman's Book of Victorian Verse. J.R. Watson, ed. J.M. Dent, 1982.

Extracts from "Ulster-Scots: A Grammar of the Traditional Written and Spoken Language" by Philip Robinson (Published for The Ulster-Scots Language Society by The Ullans Press, 1997) (http://www.ulsterscotsagency.com/05-grammerbook.asp).

Eyam, Derbyshire, England, "the plague village." (http://www.cressbrook.co.uk/eyam).

The Faber Book of Blue Verse. John Whitworth, ed. Faber & Faber, 1990.

The Faber Book of Children's Verse. Janet Adam Smith, ed. Faber & Faber, 1953.

The Faber Book of Comic Verse. Michael Roberts, and Janet Adam Smith, ed. Faber & Faber, 1978.

The Faber Book of Contemporary Irish Poetry. Paul Muldoon, ed. Faber & Faber, 1986.

The Faber Book of Drink, Drinkers and Drinking. Simon Rae, ed. Faber & Faber, 1991.

The Faber Book of English History in Verse. Kenneth Baker, ed. Faber and Faber, 1988.

The Faber Book of English Verse. John Hayward, ed. Faber & Faber, 1958.

The Faber Book of Epigrams and Epitaphs. Geoffrey Grigson, ed. Faber & Faber, 1977.

The Faber Book of Irish Verse. John Montague, ed. Faber and Faber, 1978.

The Faber Book of Modern Australian Verse. Vincent Buckley, ed. Faber & Faber, 1991.

The Faber Book of Modern Verse. 4th ed., revised by Peter Porter. Michael Roberts, ed. Faber & Faber, 1982.

Faber Book of Nonsense Verse. Geoffrey Grigson, ed. Faber & Faber, 1979.

The Faber Book of Parodies. Simon Brett, ed. Faber & Faber, 1984.

The Faber Book of Poems and Places. Geoffrey Grigson, ed. Faber & Faber, 1980.

The Faber Book of Political Verse. Tom Paulin, ed. Faber & Faber, 1986.

The Faber Book of Reflective Verse. Geoffrey Grigson, ed. Faber & Faber, 1984.

The Faber Book of Seductions. Jenny Newman, ed. Faber & Faber, 1988.

The Faber Book of 20th Century German Poems. Michael Hofmann, Faber & Faber, 2005.

The Faber Book of Twentieth Century Scottish Poetry. Douglas Dunn, ed. Faber & Faber, 1992.

The Faber Book of Twentieth Century Verse. John Heath-Stubbs, and David Wright, ed. Faber & Faber, 1975.

The Faber Book of 20th Century Women's Poetry. Fleur Adcock, ed. Faber & Faber, 1987.

The Faber Book of Useful Verse. Simon Brett, ed. Faber & Faber, 1981.

The Faber Book of Vernacular Verse. Tom Paulin, Faber & Faber, 1990.

The Faber Book of War Poetry. Kenneth Baker, ed. Faber and Faber, 1996.

The Family Album of Favorite Poems. Ernest, P. Edward, ed. Grosset & Dunlap, 1959.

The Family Book of Best Loved Poems. David L. George, ed. Doubleday, 1952.

The Family Book of Verse. Lewis Gannett, ed. Harper & Row, 1961.

Family Trees of the Famous: Hedd Wyn (Ellis Humphrey Evans) (http://www.s4c.co.uk/helachau/e_family_humphrey.shtml).

Famous Irish Lives — Sir Samuel Ferguson (http://www.irelandseye.com/irish/people/famous/sfergson.shtm).

Fantastic Fiction (http://www.fantasticfiction.co.uk/authors/Aldous_Huxley.htm).

Fantastic Fiction (http://www.fantasticfiction.co.uk/authors/Richard_Hughes.htm).

Favorite Poems of Childhood. Philip Smith, ed. Dover Publications, 1992.

Favorite Poems Old and New. Helen Ferris, ed. Doubleday, 1957.

The Feast of Our Lady of Welsingham: Quenta Nârwenion, Pittsburgh, Pennsylvania, United States (http://quenta-narwen.blogspot.com/2003/09/feast-of-our-lady-of-walsingham-is.html).

Fellow Mortals: An Anthology of Animal Verse. Roy Fuller, ed. Macdonald and Evans, 1981.

The Field Day Anthology of Irish Writing. Seamus Deane, ed. Faber and Faber, 1991.

Fifty Years of American Poetry: Anniversary Volume for the Academy of American Poets. Harry N. Abrams, ed. American Academy of Poets, 1984.

Fine Frenzy: Enduring Themes in Poetry. Robert Baylor, and Brenda Stokes, ed. McGraw-Hill, 1978.

Firebird 3: Writing Today. Robin Robertson, ed. Penguin Books, 1984.

Firebird 4: New Writing from Britain and Ireland. Robin Robertson, ed. Penguin Books, 1985.

The Fireside Book of Humorous Poetry. William Cole, ed. Simon and Schuster, 1959.

First Lines, Poems Written in Youth, from Herbert to Heaney. Jon Stallworthy, ed. Carcanet Press, 1987.

First Scottish Books (Chepman & Myller Prints) — Digital Library (http://www.nls.uk/digitallibrary/chepman/page.htm).

First World War.com — Prose & Poetry — Hedd Wyn. http://www.firstworldwar.com/poetsandprose/wyn.htm).

First World War.com — Who's Who — Sir Roger Casement (http://www.firstworldwar.com/bio/casement.htm).

Five Cantos by Sir John Clerk, Musica Scotica (http://www.musicascotica.org.uk/fivecantatas.htm).

Five Hundred Points of Good Husbandry by Thomas Tusser (Oxford Paperbacks) Oxford University Press, 1984.

Five Hundred Years of English Poetry: Chaucer to Arnold. Barbara Lloyd-Evans, ed. Peter Bedrick Books, 1989.

Five Seventeenth-Century Poets: Donne, Herbert, Crashaw, Marvell, Vaughan. Brijraj Singh, ed. Oxford University Press, 1992.

Five Sonnets of Henry Kirke White: Sonnet Central (http://www.sonnets.org/white.htm).

The Flag in the Wind Features — Scots Language: YULE, by John K, Annand (www.scotsindependent.org/features/scots/yule.htm).

Fleur Adcock (www.contemporarywriters.com/authors/?p=auth161).

Flight, by Verona Groarke, book review. The Gallery Press (http://www.gallerypress.com/Authors/Vgroarke/Books/vgf.html).

The Floral Wreath of Autumn Flowers By Caroline Bowles Southey (no publisher), 1838.

Flovvers of Epigrammes, Ovt of sundrie the moste singular authours selected, as well auncient as late writers. Pleasant and profitable to the expert readers of quicke capacitie: By Timothe Kendall. London: Imprinted by Ihon Shepperd (1577).

Folk Songs. John Williamson Palmer, ed. Charles Scribner and Company, 1867.

Folksinger's Wordbook. Irwin Silber, and Fred Silber, ed. Oak Publications, 1973.

The Forest Minstrel and Other Poems of William and Mary Howitt. Baldwin, Cradock, and Joy, 1823.

Forget Me Not: A Hypertextual Archive (http://www.orgs.muohio.edu/anthologies/FMN/Authors_GenD.htm#Richardson).

Forget Me Not Volumes 1823–1830: List of Authors (http://www.orgs.muohio.edu/anthologies/FMN/Author_List.htm).

Forty Martyrs (http://www.geocities.com/francischinchoy/fortymartyrs.html).

Founding of New Scotland (Nova Scotia) (www.chebucto.ns.ca/Heritage).

Four Indian Love Lyrics From "The Garden Of Kama" (song book). Hope, Laurence & Finden, Amy Wooforde. Boosey & Co, New York, 1943.

Foure Letters & Certaine Sonnets, Gabriel Harvey. Bodley Head Quartos, 1592.

Francis Grose (c.1731–1791) The Antiquities Of England And Wales (http://www.antiquemapsandprints.com/GROSE.htm).

Francis Ledwidge Museum (http://www.francisledwidge.com).

Fred Beake: The Poetry of Brian Coffey (http://www.dgdclynx.plus.com/lynx/lynx14.html).

Freedom's Lyre: or Psalms, Hymns, and Sacred Songs, for the Slave and His Friends. Edwin F. Hatfield, ed. S.W. Benedict, 1840.

Friendship Poems. Peter Washington, ed. Alfred A. Knopf, 1995.

From A to Z: 200 Contemporary American Poets. David Ray, ed. Ohio University Press, 1981.

From Steele and Addison to Pope and Swift. Vol. 9 (http://www.bartleby.com/219/0700.html).

Frontispiece of The Political Songster (www.search.revolutionaryplayers.org.uk/).

Funeral Service for Ted Hughes (http://www.poetsgraves.co.uk/hughes.htm).

The Gaberlunyie Man (http://ingeb.org/songs/oabeggar.html).

The Gaberlunzie Man (http://www.contemplator.com/child/gaberlunz.html).

The Gaelic League (http://www.usna.edu/EnglishDept/ilv/gaelic.htm).

Gaelic Song — An Introduction (http://www.gaelicmusic.com/gaelicsong).

The Gaelic Song of the Clans, (http://chrsouchon.free.fr/orannam.htm).

Gaelic Songs of Mary Macleod. J. Carmichael Watson, ed. Blackie & Son Limited, 1934.

Gaelic Songs of William Ross. Oliver and Boyd, 1937.

The Gambit Book of Love Poems. Geoffrey Grigson, ed. Gambit, 1973.

Garden Poems. John Hollander, ed. Alfred A. Knopf, 1996.

Gargoyle Magazine (http://www.atticusbooks.com/gargoyle/index_poetry.htm).

Gathering Seaweed: African Prison Writing. Jack Mapange, ed. Heinemann International (African Writers Series), 2002.

The Genealogy Tree, Henry Howard, Earl of Surrey (http://www.thegenealogytree.com/photo-gallery/henry-howard-earl-of-surrey.html).

Gentleman's Magazine (http://www.bodley.ox.ac.uk/ilej/journals/srchgm.htm).

Gentleman's Magazine, Founding of (http://www.spartacus.schoolnet.co.uk/Jgentleman.htm).

GENUKI: The History and Antiquities of Eyam, Derbyshire (http://www.genuki.org.uk/big/eng/DBY/Eyam/Wood/Minstrels.html).

GENUKI: Theological Colleges in Wales (http://www.genuki.org.uk/big/wal/TheoColl.html).

Geoffrey Whitney's Mottos (http://www.mun.ca/alciato/whit/w001.html).

George Borrow: Wild Wales, CHAPTER XX (http://etext.library.adelaide.edu.au/b/borrow/george/wild/chapter20.html).

George Mackay Brown site index (www.georgemackaybrown.co.uk/gmb/siteindex.htm).

George Matheson, History of "O love that will not let me go." (http://igracemusic.com/igracemusic/hymnbook/authors/george_matheson.html).

The Georgian Poets: Abercrombie, Brooke, Drinkwater, Lascelles, Thomas (Writers & Their Works.). Rennie Parker. Northcote House Educational Publishers, Tavistock, England, 1998.

Gerard Manley Hopkins. Catherine Phillips, ed. Oxford University Press, 1986.

The Gift of Great Poetry. Lucien Stryk, ed. Regnery Gateway, 1992.

Gilbert and Sullivan Archive Arthur Sullivan Major Works (http://math.boisestate.edu/gas/other_sullivan/html/othersul. html).

Gilbert & Sullivan Archive. The Lost Chord, by Adelaide Procter (http://math.boisestate.edu/gas/other_sullivan/songs/lost_chord/chord. html).

Giles and Phineas Fletcher: Poetical Works. Frederick S. Boas. ed (Cambridge: Cambridge University Press, 1908.

Gillian Clarke Welcome Page (http://www.gillianclarke.co.uk).

Gladly Learn and Gladly Teach: Poems of the School Experience. Helen Plotz, ed. Greenwillow Books, 1981.

The Glasgow Story (www.theglasgowstory.com).

GO BRITANNIA! Scotland: Great Scots of Note (http://www.britannia.com/celtic/scotland/greatscots/l1.html).

Go Britannia! Wales: Welsh Literature — Poets of the Gentry (www.britannia.com).

GO BRITANNIA! Wales: Welsh Literature — 20th Century, Pt III (http://www.britannia.com/wales/lit/lit18.html).

Going Over to Your Place: Poems for Each Other. Paul B. Janeczko, ed. Bradbury Press, 1987.

The Golden Book of Catholic Poetry. Alfred Noyes, ed. J.B. Lippincott, 1946.

Golden Numbers. Kate Douglas Wiggin, and Nora Archibald Smith, ed. Doubleday, Doran, 1902.

The Golden Room: Poems, 1925–1927 of Wilfrid Gibson. Macmillan and Co., Ltd., 1928.

The Golden Treasury of Longer Poems. Ernest Rhys, ed. E.P. Dutton, 1949.

The Golden Treasury of Scottish Poetry. Hugh MacDiarmid, ed. Macmillan, 1941.

Golden Treasury of the Best Songs & Lyrical Poems in the English Language. Francis Turner Palgrave, ed. Oxford University Press, 1964, Sixth edition, updated by John Press, 1994.

Goldsmith's College, University of London, (http://www.goldsmiths. ac.uk/departments/english-comparative-literature/staff/ m-dooley.php).

Good Dog Poems. William Cole, ed. Scribner's, 1981.

Gray, David (1838–1861) The Poetical Works. Macmillan, 1874.

Gray's English Poems: Original and Translated from the Norse and the Welsh. D.C. Tovey, ed. Reprint Services, 1922.

The Great Book of Gaelic. Malcolm Maclean & Theo Dorgan, ed. Canongate Books, 2002.

Great Books Online (www.bartleby.com).

Great Sonnets. Paul Negri, ed. Dover, 1994.

The Greek Anthology and Other Ancient Epigrams. Peter Jay, ed. Penguin Books, 1981.

The Greek Poets. Nathan Haskell Dole, ed. Crowell, 1904.

A Green Place: Modern Poems. William Jay Smith, ed. Delacorte Press/Seymour Lawren, 1982.

Greenwich Exchange Publishing: Matt Simpson (http://www. greenex.co.uk/search/search.cgi?Terms=simpson).

Griffin Poetry Prize, 2002. Logue's Home, War Music (http://www. griffinpoetryprize.com/shortlist_2002.php?t=5#a50).

Griffin Poetry Prize, 2005. Michael Symmons Roberts (http://www. griffinpoetryprize.com/shortlist_2005.php?t=5).

The Grove Dictionary of Art (http://www.artnet.com/library/02/ 0283/T028352.asp).

Guardian Unlimited, In Memoriam Anne Ridler (http://books. guardian.co.uk/departments/poetry/story/0,6000,581905,00. html).

Guardian Unlimited Obituary of F.T. Prince by Anthony Howell. Friday August 8, 2003 (http://www.guardian.co.uk/obituaries/ story/0,3604,1014413,00.html)

Guardian Unlimited Obituary, Jeff Nuttall (http://www.guardian. co.uk/obituaries/story/0,,1120760,00.html).

Guardian Unlimited Obituary of Philip Dennis Hobsbaum (http://www.guardian.co.uk/obituaries/).

Guardian Unlimited Obituary, Phoebe Hesketh (http://www. guardian.co.uk/obituaries/).

Guardian Unlimited Obituary, Tobia Hill (http://www.guardian. co.uk/obituaries/).

The Guns. Gilbert Frankau. Chatto & Windus, 1916.

Gwaith Cynddelw Brydydd Mawr: Volume I. Nerys Ann Jones and Ann Parry Owen, ed. University of Wales Press, 1991. Volumes 2, 1995.

Handbook of Texas Online: Kennedy, William (http://www.tsha. utexas.edu/handbook/online/articles/KK/fke25.html).

The Harper Anthology of Poetry. John Frederick Nims, ed. Harper & Row, 1981.

Harper's Anthology of 20th Century Native American Poetry. Duane Niatum, ed. Harper & Row, 1988.

Harper's New Monthly Magazine. Volume 61, Issue 366 (http://cdl. library.cornell.edu/cgi-bin/moa/sgml/moa-idx?notisid= ABK4014-0061&byte=119475497).

Harpurhey — Districts & Suburbs of Manchester UK: John Bolton Rogerson (http://www.manchester2002-uk.com/districts/ harpurhey.html).

Hartley Coleridge (http://www.sonnets.org/coleridgeh.htm#010).

The Harvard Book of Contemporary American Poetry. Helen Vendler, ed. Belknap Press, 1985.

Harvard University's Withdrawal of a Speaking Invitation to the Poet Tom Paulin (http://news.bbc.co.uk/1/hi/in_depth/uk/ 2000/newsmakers/2481623.stm).

The Harvill Book of Twentieth-Century Poetry in English. Michael Schmidt, ed. The Harvill Press, 1999.

Hay in Art: Hay Poets Born in the Early Nineteenth Century (http://www.hayinart.com/001405.html#nicoll).

Headlong Hall, by Thomas Love Peacock (http://www.thomaslove peacock.net/Headlong.html).

Hear Jean Sprackland's Poems on CD (http://www.poetrybooks. co.uk/book-template.asp?isbn=190555642X).

Heartsease by Elizabeth Bewick (http://www.peterloopoets.com/ html/stocklist_18.html).

The Heath Introduction to Poetry. 4th edition. Joseph DeRoche, ed. D.C. Heath, 1992.

Hedd Wyn (Ellis Humphrey Evans) / 100 Welsh Heroes / 100 Arwyr Cymru (http://www.100welshheroes.com/en/biography/ heddwyn).

Hedge School Home Page (http://hedgeschool.homestead.com/).

The Heinemann Book of Caribbean Poetry. Stewart Brown, and Ian McDonald, ed. Heinemann, 1992.

Helen Maria Williams: Poems, 1786. Woodstock Books, 1994.

Hellfire Corner — The Great War — At the Going Down of the Sun (http://www.hellfire-corner.demon.co.uk/jacky4.htm).

Henry Francis Lyte — His Life And Times (http://homepage. tinet.ie/~taghmon/histsoc/vol1/3lyte/3lyte.htm).

Here of a Sunday Morning, HOASM: Thomas Ford (http://www. hoasm.org/IVM/Ford.html).

High Tide on the Coast of Lincolnshire, 1571. Great Books Online, (www.bartleby.com).

The High Tides of Lincolnshire (http://www.enderbymuseum. ca/thepast/geog/hightides.htm)

The Highwayman by Alfred Noyes (http://www.imagesaustralia. com/poetryromantic.htm).

Historical Perspective for Moffat (Dumfries and Galloway) (http:// www.geo.ed.ac.uk/scotgaz/towns/townhistory358.html).

The History of Mildmay (http://www.mildmay.org.uk/Chris tianEthos.html).

History of Vegetarianism (http://www.ivu.org/history/renaissance/ mandeville.html).

Holocaust Poetry. Hilda Schiff, ed. HarperCollins, 1995.

The Home Book of Modern Verse. Burton Egbert Stevenson, ed. Henry Holt, 1953.

The Home Book of Verse. Burton Egbert Stevenson, ed. New York: Henry Holt and Company, 1953.

The Home Book of Verse for Young Folks. Burton Egbert Stevenson, ed. Holt, Rinehart and Winston, 1929.

The Homes, Haunts and Friends of John Wesley. The Centenary Number of The Methodist Recorder. London: Charles H. Kelly, 1891.

The Honey Gatherers: An Anthology Of Love Poems. Maura Dooley, ed. Bloodaxe Books, 2003.

Hoping It Might Be So: Poems, 1974–2000. Kit Wright. Leviathan, 2000.

The Hopwood Anthology: Five Decades of American Poetry. Harry Thomas, and Steven Lavine, ed. University of Michigan Press, 1981.

Horses in Literature (http://www.aptt2.org.uk/w3d/macador/horselit.html).

The Housman Society (http://www.housman-society.co.uk/)

How Does a Poem Mean? 2nd edition. John Ciardi, and Miller Williams, ed. Houghton Mifflin, 1975.

Howell's Devises by Thomas Howell. Oxford University Press, 1906.

Hugh Downman, MD (1740–1809) of Exeter and His Poem on Infant Care (http://fn.bmjjournals.com/cgi/content/full/88/3/F253).

The Humorous Poetry of the English Language. J. Parton, ed. Mason Brothers, 1857.

The Humorous Verse of Lewis Carroll. Amereon Ltd., 1960.

Huw's Magic Books (http://www.angelfire.com/wizard/dragonslore/page32e.html).

Hymn Devotionals (http://our.homewithgod.com/ewerluvd/hymndevotionals/5_13.htm).

A Hymn of the Dawn. Part autobiographical book by Padraic Fallon. Published by the Lilliput Press (http://www.lilliputpress.ie/listbook.html?oid=2733039).

Hymn Writers of the Church (http://www.ccel.org/ccel/nutter/hymnwriters.html3).

The Hymnal [of the Protestant Episcopal Church in the USA], (http://www.ccel.org/ccel/anonymous/eh1916.h165.html).

Hymns Ancient and Modern New Standard, 1987.

Hymns and Psalms: A Methodist and Ecumenical Hymn Book. London: Methodist Publishing House, 1983.

Hymns by James George Deck (http://www.stempublishing.com/hymns/authors/deck).

I Have No Gun But I Can Spit: An Anthology of Satirical and Abusive Verse. Kenneth Baker, ed. Faber and Faber, 1980.

I Like You, If You Like Me: Poems of Friendship. Myra Cohn Livingston, ed. Macmillan, 1987.

I Saw Esau: The Schoolchild's Pocket Book. Iona Opie, and Peter Opie, ed. 1947: American reissue, Candlewick Press, 1992.

I Sing of a Maiden: The Mary Book of Verse. Sister M. Therese, ed. Macmillan, 1947.

I Was an English Poet: Biography of Sir William Watson. Jean Moorcroft. Wilson, C. Woolf, 1982.

Ian Hamilton Finlay Artist and Art: The-artists.org (http://www.the-artists.org/ArtistView.cfm?id=8A01F432-BBCF-11D4-A93500D0B7069B40).

Idris Davies: A Carol for the Coalfield (http://www.nhi.clara.net/bs0057.htm).

Imagination's Other Place: Poems of Science and Mathematics. Helen Plotz, ed. Thomas Y. Crowell, 1955.

Immortal Poems of the English Language. Oscar Williams, ed. Simon & Schuster, 1952.

The Impact of Robert Murray Mccheyne, by J. Harrison Hudson (http://web.ukonline.co.uk/d.haslam/mccheyne/hudson/Impact_of_McCheyne.htm).

In Quest of the Miracle Stag: The Poetry of Hungary. Adam Makkai, ed. Atlantic-Centaur, Corvina, 1996.

In the Grip of Strange Thoughts: Russian Poetry in a New Era. J. Kates, ed. Zephyr Press, 1999.

In the Welsh Manner by Edward William (http://www.sonnets.org/williams.htm).

The Independent Online, May 2004: Darien Dogs, by Henry Shukman (http://enjoyment.independent.co.uk/books/news/article62061.ece).

Index of Charles Swain's Contributions to British Literary Annuals: Forget Me Not: A Hypertextual Archive (http://www.orgs.muohio.edu/anthologies/FMN/Authors_Swain.htm).

Index to Authors: Christina Georgina Rossetti to William Butler (http://www.bartleby.com/246/index24.html).

The Indian Love Lyrics Review, The New York Times, Movies (http://movies2.nytimes.com/gst/movies/movie.html?v_id=96522).

India's Love Lyrics by Laurence Hope. Dodd, Mead & Company, 1902.

Indoors, Poem by Vona Groarke: Virtual Writer (http://www.virtualwriter.net/vona-groarke.htm).

The Inherited Boundaries: Younger Poets of the Republic of Ireland. Sebastian Barry, ed. The Dolmen Press, 1986.

Innocent Merriment: An Anthology of Light Verse. Franklin P. Adams, ed. McGraw-Hill, 1942.

The International Poetry Festival in Medellín, 2004, Jack Mapange (http://colombia.poetryinternational.org/cwolk/view/22148).

Interview with Alasdair Gray (http://homepage.ntlworld.com/dee.rimbaud/interviewsgray.html).

Interview with Bernard O'Donoghue (http://lidiavianu.scriptmania.com/bernard_o'donoghue.htm).

Interview with Christopher Logue. poetrymagazines.org.uk (http://www.poetrymagazines.org.uk/magazine/record.asp?id=5237).

An Interview with George Bruce, by Mallie Boman: August 21. 2001 (http://www.wooster.edu/artfuldodge/interviews/bruce.htm).

Interview with Jacob Polley. National Poetry Day, 2002. BBC Radio 4 (http://www.bbc.co.uk/radio4/arts/natpoetday/jacob_polley.shtml).

An Introduction — Crossing Borders (Menna Elfyn) (http://www.mennaelfyn.co.uk/pages/Erthyglau/Winter%20Words%20-%20Menna%20Elfyn.htm).

Introduction to HMS Conway: Cadets and old boys, Events and daily life, Closure (http://www.mersey-gateway.org/server.php?show=ConNarrative.73).

Invisible Light: Poems about God. Diana Culbertson, ed. Columbia University Press, 2000.

Invitation to Poetry: A Round of Poems from John Skelton to Dylan Thomas. Lloyd Frankenberg, Doubleday, 1956.

Iona: A history of the Island. M. McNeil. Blackie and Son Ltd., 1920, republished, 1973.

Ireland in Poetry. Charles Sullivan, ed. Harry N. Abrams, 1990.

Irish Contemporary Poets (http://www.liunet.edu/cwis/cwp/library/sc/irish.htm).

Irish Penal Laws (http://www.law.umn.edu/irishlaw/).

Irish Poems and Blessings: Poems by Charles Lever (http://freepages.genealogy.rootsweb.com/~irelandlist/poems.html#gloryto).

Irish Poetry After Yeats: Seven Poets. Maurice Harmon, ed. Little, Brown, 1979.

Irish Poetry: An Interpretive Anthology from Before Swift to Yeats and After. W.J. McCormack, ed. New York University Press, 2000.

The Irish Poets Library (http://www.irishcultureandcustoms.com/Poetry/1Libr3.html).

Irish Poets of To-Day. J.D'O. Walters, ed. T. Fisher Unwin, 1921.

Irish Songs and Ballads of Alfred Perceval Graves. Alexander Ireland and Co., 1880.

Irish Writers, Books by Leland Bardwell (http://www.kennysirishbookshop.ie/categories/irishwriters/bardwellleland.shtml).

Irishclans — The Penal Laws (http://www.irishclans.com/articles/penallaws.html).

Isabella Whitney, A Sweet Nosegay (http://ise.uvic.ca/Library/SLT/literature/whitney.html).

Isabella Whitney, Mary Sidney and Aemilia Lanyer: Renaissance Women Poets (Penguin Classics). Penguin Books, 2001.

Island 8 — Translations of Burns (http://www.sc.edu/library/spcoll/britlit/burns/burns8.html).

Isle of Iona, Scotland (http://www.isle-of-iona.com).

Isle of Lesbos, the Biography of Katherine Philips (http://www.sappho.com/poetry/k_philip.html).

Ivor Gurney — Poet-Composer (http://www.geneva.edu/~dksmith/gurney/index.html).

Jacket 16 — Peter Porter — Two Poems (http://jacketmagazine.com/16/porter-peter.html).

Jacobean and Caroline Poetry: An Anthology. T.G.S. Cain, ed. Methuen, 1981.

Jairus, by Michael Symmons Roberts (http://www.poetryarchive.org/poetryarchive/singlePoem.do?poemId=3486).

James Findlay Hendry Papers. University of Glasgow, Special Collections (http://special.lib.gla.ac.uk/collection/hendry.html).

James Hogg Society (http://www.cc.gla.ac.uk/hogg/).

The January Birds by Maurice Riordan (http://www.thepoem.co.uk/poems/riordan.htm).

Japanese Poetry: The 'Uta' By Arthur Waley. Percy Lund, Humphries & Co., 1956.

A Jar of Honey, by Jacob Polley. The Poetry Book Society (http://www.poetrybooks.co.uk/PBS/pbs_polley_jacob.asp).

The Jazz Poetry Anthology. Sascha Feinstein and Yusef Komunyakaa, ed. Indiana University Press, 1991.

Jeff Nuttall Selected Poems (2003). Introduction by Roy Fisher. Salt Publishing, 2003 (http://www.saltpublishing.com/books/smp/1844710130.htm).

Jeff Nuttall Video Titles, Available from Movies Unlimited (http://www.moviesunlimited.com/musite/findresults_actor.asp?search=Jeff+Nuttall).

Jerningham, "The African Boy." (http://www2.bc.edu/~richarad/asp/ejab.htm).

John Betjeman Home Page (www.johnbetjeman.com).

John Burns Library, Boston College, Massachusetts .(www.bc.edu/libraries/centers/burns).

John Cornford, A Letter from Aragon (1936) (http://www.spartacus.schoolnet.co.uk/SPcornford.htm).

The John Gower Page (http://faculty.arts.ubc.ca/sechard/GOWER.HTM).

John Hegley (http://www.contemporarywriters.com/authors/?p=auth02D4J450112627326).

The John Hewitt Papers, D/3838. Public Record Office of Northern Ireland (http://www.proni.gov.uk/records/private/hewitt.htm).

John Locke Bibliography—Name/Title Index—E (http://www.libraries.psu.edu/tas/locke/ne.html).

John Montague—Poetry Irish culture and customs—World Cultures (http://www.irishcultureandcustoms.com/Poetry/Montague.html).

John Wesley's 300th anniversary. Key dates (http://www.wesley2003.org.uk/dates.htm).

The Jolly Beggar (http://mysongbook.de/msb/songs/r_clarke/jollybeg.htm).

Joseph Skipsey: Songs and Lyrics (http://www.gerald-massey.org.uk/cop_skipsey_index.htm).

The Joy of Sex & the Joy of Cooking Compared (http://www.goodbyemag.com/mar00/comfort.html).

Kate Clanchy, Poem for a Man with No Sense of Smell (http://www.thepoem.co.uk/poems/clanchy.htm).

Kathryn Gray's delight at prize shortlist (http://news.bbc.co.uk/2/hi/uk_news/wales/3993591.stm).

Kennys Irish Bookshop (http://www.kennysirishbookshop.ie/categories/irishwriters/macgreevythomas.html).

The Kiltartan Poetry Book by Lady Gregory. G.P. Putnam's Sons, 1919 (http://digital.library.upenn.edu/women/gregory/poetry/poetry.html).

King Arthur. History and link (http://www.library.rochester.edu/camelot/arthmenu.htm).

The Kingfisher Book of Children's Poetry. Michael Rosen, ed. Kingfisher Books, 1985.

King's College London College Archives, ERIC MOTTRAM COLLECTION (http://www.kcl.ac.uk/kis/archives/mottram/motttxt.htm#MOT1).

Kings, Lords, and Commons. Frank O'Connor, ed. Knopf, 1959.

Kissing Maura O'Keeffe by Gerry Murphy (http://www.munsterlit.ie/Southwordnew/poetry1.html).

Kissing the Rod: An Anthology of Seventeenth-Century Women's Verse. Germaine Greer, Susan Hastings and Jeslyn Medo, ed. Farrar Straus Giroux, 1988.

Knitting Circle, Jackie Kay (http://myweb.lsbu.ac.uk/~stafflag/jackiekay.html).

Knitting Circle, James Kirkup (http://myweb.lsbu.ac.uk/~stafflag/jameskirkup.html).

Knocknagow, the history of the house (http://www.exclassics.com/knockngw/kn2.htm).

Lament for Thomas MacDonagh (http://www.cs.rice.edu/~ssiyer/minstrels/poems/1608.html).

Lancashire Dialect Poets and Poems, Authors, Writers and Poets (http://www.manchester2002-uk.com/celebs/authors4.html).

Lapsus Calami and other verses, by James Kenneth Stephen. Macmillan and Bowes, 1892.

Last Words, the Complete, the Sands of Time Are Sinking (http://www.puritansermons.com/poetry/ruth18.htm).

Laurie Duggan, Recollections of the Lakes and the Lake Poets: Gael Turnbull (http://jacketmagazine.com/25/turnb-dugg.html).

Lawrence Eusden and Colley Cibber, Poet Laureate, exhibition (http://www.library.otago.ac.nz/Exhibitions/poet_laureate/pl_eusdenandcibber.html).

Learning Journeys (www.bbc.co.uk/scotland/arts/writingscotland/).

The Leave Train: New and Selected Poems of Phoebe Hesketh. Enitharmon Press, 1994.

Leaving, Poem by Henry Shukman (http://www.poetrybooks.co.uk/PBS/pbs_shukman_henry.asp).

Legends: Paladins and Princes: The Tale of Aucassin and Nicolette. http://www.legends.dm.net/paladins/aucassin.html.

Les Barker Books (www.waterbug.com).

Letter from Benjamin Zephania, refusing to accept an OBE. The Guardian, Thursday, November 27, 2003 (http://www.guardian.co.uk/arts/features/story/0,11710,1094011,00.html).

Lewis Morris, "Tlysau yr Hen Oesoedd." (http://www.gtj.org.uk/en/item1/14571).

Leyden, "The Wail of Alzira." (http://www2.bc.edu/~richarad/asp/jlwa.html).

Library of Congress Citations (www.mala.bc.ca/~mcneil/cit/citlclanyer1.htm).

Liddel Hart Centre for Military Archives, King's College, London University (http://www.kcl.ac.uk/lhcma/summary/we70–001.shtml)

The Lied and Art Song Texts Page (http://www.recmusic.org/lieder/m/cmackay/).

The Life and Opinion of Tristram Shandy. Laurence Sterne. The Folio Society, 1995.

Life and Songs of the Baroness Nairne of Caroline Oliphant the Yonger. John Grant, 1886.

The Life and Work of Adelaide Procter (http://www.litencyc.com/php/adpage.php?id=2677).

The Life and Work of Adelaide Procter: Poetry, Feminism and Fathers (Nineteenth Century Series. Gill Gregory. Ashgate Publishing, 1998.

The Life and Work of Edwin Atherstone: The Corvey Poets Project at the University of Nebraska (http://www.unl.edu/Corvey/html/Projects/Corvey%20Poets/PoetsIndex.htm).

The Life and Work of George Barker: Poets graves (www.poetsgraves.co.uk/barker.htm).

Life and Work of George Gascoigne (http://www.luminarium.org/renlit/gascoigne.htm).

Life and Work of Grahame Davies (http://www.grahamedavies.com/english_about.shtml).

Life and Work of Greg Delanty (http://www.munsterlit.ie/Conwriters/greg_delanty.htm).

Life and Work of Paul Durcan (http://www.contemporarywriters.com/authors/?p=auth01J17P482412620204).

The Life and Work of Ruth Fainlight (http://www.writersartists.net/rf2.htm).

Life and Work of Thomas Dekker (http://www.luminarium.org/sevenlit/dekker/).

The Life and Work of William Langland (http://www.luminarium.org/medlit/langland.htm).

Life and Works of Carol Ann Duffy: Knitting Circle (http://myweb.lsbu.ac.uk/~stafflag/carolannduffy.html).

Life and Works of Charles Causley, (http://pedia.newsfilter.co.uk/wikipedia/c/ch/charles_causley.html).

Life and Works of Christopher Marlowe (http://www.luminarium.org/renlit/marlowe.htm).

The Life and Works of Francis Beaumont (www.luminarium.org/sevenlit/beaumont).

Life and Works of Frank Ormsby (http://www.contemporarywriters.com/authors/?p=auth133).

Life and Works of Henry Vaughan (http://www.luminarium.org/sevenlit/vaughan/).

Life and Works of Isabella Whitney (http://ise.uvic.ca/Library/SLT/literature/whitney.html).

Life and Works of Mary Sidney Herbert (http://www.luminarium.org/renlit/mary.htm).

Life and Works of Matthew Sweeney (http://www.writersartists.net/msweeney.htm).

Life and Works of Richard Brinsley Sheridan (http://www.rbsheridan.com/).

Life and Works of Saunders Lewis (http://www.absoluteastronomy.com/reference/saunders_lewis).

Life and Works of Seán Dunne (http://www.munsterlit.ie/Conwriters/sean_dunne.htm).

Life and Works of T.E. Brown (www.isle-of-man.com/manxnotebook/people/writers/teb.htm).

The Life of a Miner (http://www.lynherparishes.co.uk/LYjohnharris.htm).

The Life of Lady Mary Wroth (http://www.luminarium.org/seven lit/wroth/wrothbio.htm).

Life of Mildmay Fane, 2nd Earl of Westmorland (http://www.lumi narium.org/sevenlit/fane/fanebio.htm).

The Life of Mina Loy. Modern American Poetry (http://www.en glish.uiuc.edu/maps/poets/g_l/loy/loy.htm).

Life of William Diaper by John Nichols (http://athena.english. vt.edu/~drad/NereidesBio.html).

The Light from Another Country: Poetry from American Prisons. Joseph Bruchac, ed. The Greenfield Review Press, 1984.

Lincoln College — College News (http://www.lincoln.ox.ac.uk/ news/2004/11/16/).

Links to Poets (http://www.pmpoetry.com/linkspb.shtml).

List of Famous Old Etonians Born in the 19th century (http://www.1-electric.com/articles/List_of_famous_Old_Etonians_born_in_ the_19th_century).

List of Irish Poets and Dramatists (www.answers.com/topic/list-of-irish-dramatists).

List of Reading University Library Special Collections (http://www. library.rdg.ac.uk/colls/special/collsindex.html#f).

List of the Principal Collections of English and Scottish Ballads and Songs (http://www.sacred-texts.com/neu/eng/child/chbib.htm).

The Literary Encyclopedia (www.LitEncyc.com).

The Literary Gothic, Works by John Stagg (http://www.litgothic. com/Authors/stagg.html).

Literary Heritage, West Midlands (http://www3.shropshire-cc. gov.uk/extracts/E000088a.htm).

A Literature of Sports. Tom Dodge, ed. D.C. Heath and Company, 1980.

Literature on the Age of Napoleon: Fiction & Drama (Digital Texts) (http://napoleonic-literature.com/AgeOfNapoleon/E-Texts/ Fiction.html).

Little Anne: Book by Adelaide O'Keefe (http://digital.library.upenn. edu/women/taylor/little-ann/little-ann.html).

A Little Book of Comfort. Anthony Guest, ed. Harper Collins, 1993.

A Little Book of Irish Verse. Chronicle Books, 1993.

A Little Book of Scottish Verse. Chronicle Books, 1993.

A Little Treasury of British Poetry. Oscar Williams, ed. Scribner's, 1951.

Little Treasury of Modern Poetry: English and American. 3d ed. Oscar Williams, ed. Scribner's, 1970.

Lives of War Poets of the First World War (http://www.warpoetry. co.uk/biogs99.htm#GILBERT).

The Living Tradition (http://www.folkmusic.net/htmfiles/inart 486.htm).

Llyfr Y Tri Aderyn. M. Wynn Thomas, ed. University of Wales Press, 1983.

Logue's books (http://www.cas.sc.edu/engl/LitCheck/logue.htm).

The London Book of English Verse. Herbert Read, and Barbara Dobree, ed. MacMillan. 1952.

A Look in the Mirror and Other Poems. Padraic Fallon & Eavan Boland, ed. Carcanet Press, 2003.

Loose and Humorous Songs from Bishop Percy's Folio Manuscript. John Greenway, ed. Folklore Associates, Inc., 1963.

Louis Golding, Collection Description. Washington University, St. Louis, Missouri, USA (http://library.wustl.edu/units/spec/man uscripts/mlc/golding/golding.html).

Louis MacNeice (Biography). Jon Stallworthy. Faber and Faber, 1996.

Love in Verse. Kathleen Blease, ed. Ballantine Publishing Group, 1998.

Love's Looking Glass, Beeching, Mackail, & Nichols, Percival and Co., 1891.

Love's Witness: Five Centuries of Love Poetry by Women. Jill Hollis, ed. Carroll and Graf, Inc., 1993.

LovetoKnow Encyclopedia (http://www.1911encyclopedia.org/).

Lucida Intervalla by James Carkasse. The Augustan Reprint Society, 1679.

Lyra Celtica: An Anthology of Representative Celtic Poetry. E.A. Sharp & J. Matthay, ed. John Grant, 1924.

Lyra Celtica, Contents (http://www.sundown.pair.com/Sharp/ Lyra%20Celtica/celtica_contents.htm).

Lyra Elegantiarum. Frederick Locker Lampson. Ward, Lock & Co., 1867.

Lyric Poems, Devotional and Moral of Thomas Scott. James Buckland, 1773.

The Major Works of Samuel Taylor Coleridge. H.J. Jackson, ed. Oxford University Press, 2000.

The Major Works of William Wordsworth. Stephen Gill, ed. Oxford University Press, 2000.

Make 'Em Laugh (www.monologues.co.uk).

Making a Roux, Book by Elizabeth Bewick (http://www.peterloop ets.com/html/stocklist_17.html).

Making for Planet Alice: New Women Poets. Maura Dooley, ed. Bloodaxe Books, 1997.

The Making of a Poem: A Norton Anthology of Poetic Forms. Mark Strand and Eavan Boland, ed. W.W. Norton, 2000.

Manitoba and Country Adjacent with Adhesions. Queen's Printer and Controller of Stationery Ottawa, 1957 (http://collections.ic.gc. ca/aboriginaldocs/treaty/html/t-treaty1.htm)

Margaret Veley, A Japanese Fan (http://themargins.net/anth/ 19thc/veley.html).

Mario Petrucci's Home Page (http://mariopetrucci.port5.com/ index.htm).

Mark Akenside, James Macpherson, Edward Young. S.H. Clark. ed. Fyfield Books, 1994.

Marlborough and Other Poems of Charles Hamilton Sorley. Cambridge University Press, 1916.

A Marriage of Shadows and Other Poems by Margaret Veley. Smith, Elder, 1888.

The Martin Bell Papers. The University of Tulsa, McFarlin Library, Department of Special Collections (www.lib.utulsa.edu/ Speccoll/bellm00.htm).

Mary Collier (http://www.pinn.net/~sunshine/march99/collier html).

The Mary Webb Society (http://pers-www.wlv.ac.uk/~me1927/ mwebb/index.html).

Matilda Joslyn Gage Website: Biographical Dictionary of Women and Pro-Feminists Men (http://www.pinn.net/~sunshine/gage/fea tures/dict.html).

Matt (Simpson), Wes (Magee) 'n' Pete (Dixon, Macmillan Children's Books, 1995) republished under the title Lost Property Box, 1998.

Matthew Pilkington — Offaly History, Famous Offaly People (http://www.offalyhistory.com/content/reading_resources/fa mous_people/pilkington_matthew.htm).

Medieval English Lyrics: A Critical Anthology. R.T. Davies, ed. Northwestern University Press, 1964.

Medieval Sourcebook: Bede: Ecclesiastical History of England (English translation) (www.fordham.edu/halsall/basis/bede-book1.html).

Meet the Next Generation Poets. Poetry Book Society (http://www.po etrybooks.co.uk/PBS/pbs_next_generation.asp).

Memoir of Mother Francis Raphael, O.SD., Augusta Theodosia Drane. B. Wilberforce, O.P., London, 1895.

Men of Harlech, the Song (http://www.deutschegrammophon. com/brynterfel.welshalbum/album/texts/tr_04.html).

Men Who March Away: Poems of the First World War. I.M. Parsons, ed. Viking Press, 1965.

The Mentor Book of Major British Poets. Oscar Williams, ed. New American Library, 1963.

The Mersey Sound: Penguin Modern Poets 10 (Roger McGough, Adrian Henri and Brian Patten). Penguin, revised edition, 1980.

Mervyn Peake's Official Website (http://www.mervynpeake.org/).

Messages: A Thematic Anthology of Poetry. X.J. Kennedy, ed. Little, Brown, 1973.

Metaphysical Lyrics & Poems of the Seventeenth Century: Donne to Butler. Herbert J. Grierson, ed. Oxford University Press, 1921.

The Metaphysical Poets. Helen Gardner, ed. Penguin Books, 1969.

Methodist Archives and Research Centre: Samuel Wesley, father of the Wesleys (http://gbgm-umc.org/UMW/Wesley/quiz/1b.stm).

Methodist Hymns and Psalms. London: Methodist Publishing House, 1983.

Michael Rosen: Three Songs of the Dead, 16Jul05, Socialist Worker (http://www.socialistworker.co.uk/article.php4?article_id=6964)

Michael Rosen's Book of Very Silly Poems. Puffin Books, 1996.

Microsoft Encarta 2006 [DVD]. Microsoft Corporation, 2006.

The Midnight Court by Brian Merriman (http://www.showhouse. com/prologue.html).

Miles, M. 2005. "Deaf People Living and Communicating in African Histories, c. 960s—1960s" (http://www.independentliving.org/ docs7/miles2005a.html).

Milman's Poetical Works. John Murray, 1840.

Minds at War, The Poetry and Experience of the First World War. David Roberts. Saxon Books, 1999, 2003 (www.warpoetry.co.uk/minds_pl.html).

Miniature Lives of the Saints. Henry Sebastian Bowden, ed. Burns and Oates, 1949.

The Minor Poems (I.), Asher & Co., 1892.

Minstrelsy of the Scottish Border (http://www.walterscott.lib.ed.ac.uk/works/poetry/minstrelsy.html).

Miscellaneous Pieces, in Verse and Prose by Anne Steele. 1780 (See http://gandhara.usc.edu/data/a7f4/10/06/97/86/40.html).

Miscellaneous Poems of the Reverend J. Keble. James Parker and Co., 1870.

Miscellaneous Poems, Some of Which Are in the Cumberland and Scottish Dialects. John Stagg (no publisher), 1807.

The Missouri Sequence by Brian Coffey (http://indigo.ie/~tjac/Poets/Brian_Coffey/brian_coffey.htm).

Modern American & British Poetry. Louis Untermeyer, Karl Shapiro and Richard Wil, ed. Harcourt, Brace, rev., shorter ed., 1955.

Modern American Poetry (http://www.english.uiuc.edu/maps/index.htm).

Modern Asylums in Scotland (http://www.dundeecity.gov.uk/liff/history5.html).

Modern Ballads and Story Poems. Charles Causley, ed. Franklin Watts, 1965.

Modern British Poetry. 7th rev. ed. Louis Untermeyer, ed. Harcourt, Brace, 1962.

Modern History Sourcebook: Samuel Bamford (1788–1872): Passages in the Life of a Radical-on the Peterloo Massacre, 1819 (www.fordham.edu/halsall/mod/1819bamford.html).

Modern Irish Poetry. Patrick Crotty, ed. The Blackstaff Press, 1995.

Modern Poetry: American and British. Kimon Friar, and John Malcom Brinnin, ed. Appleton-Century-Crofts, 1951.

The Modern Poets: An American-British Anthology. John Malcom Brinnin, and Bill Read, ed. McGraw-Hill, 1963.

Modern Verse in English, 1900–1950. David Cecil, and Allen Tate, ed. Macmillan, 1967.

Moods of the Sea: Masterworks of Sea Poetry. George C. Solley, and Eric Steinbaugh, ed. Naval Institute Press, 1981.

The Moon Is Shining Bright as Day: An Anthology of Good-humored Verse. Ogden Nash, ed. J.B. Lippincott, 1953.

Morality Plays, Interludes, and the Emergence of Mature Drama (http://www.beyondbooks.com/leu11/2h.asp).

More Verse and Prose by the Cornlaw Rhymer, Ebenezer Elliot. Charles Fox, 1850.

Most Unfashionable Poet Alive: Charles Causley. A review by Dana Gioia (http://www.danagioia.net/essays/ecausley.htm).

Munby: Man Of Two Words, Derek Hudson. John Murray, 1972.

The Music of Henry VIII (http://tudors.crispen.org/music).

My Cat in Her First Spring: Sixties Press— Poetry (http://www.sixtiespress.co.uk/poetry.htm).

My Compleinte and Other Poems of Thomas Hoccleve. Roger Ellis, ed. University of Exeter Press, 2001.

My Life, by Thomas McCarthy. http://www.laoisedcentre.ie/LENGLISH/engrwww/tom.html).

The Naked Astronaut: Poems on Birth and Birthdays. Ren Graziani, ed. Faber and Faber, 1983.

Naming the Waves: Contemporary Lesbian Poetry. Christian McEwen, ed. The Crossing Press, 1989.

Naomi Mitchison— a queen, a saint and a shaman (http://www.guardian.co.uk/Columnists/Column/0,5673,320853,00.html).

National Library for the Blind (http://www.nlbuk.org/readon/poet/index.html).

The National Library of Ireland— Collections— Prints & Drawings (http://www.nli.ie/co_print.htm).

National Poetry Day—Thursday 9 October 2003, Dundee: Ode to the Old Tay Bridge by W.N. Herbert (http://www.bbc.co.uk/radio4/arts/natpoetday/2003_dundee.shtml).

National Poetry Day, 2002. Jack Mapange (http://www.bbc.co.uk/radio4/arts/natpoetday/jack_mapange.shtml).

The National Portrait Gallery (www.npg.org.uk).

Nationmaster.com (http://www.nationmaster.com/encyclopedia/Emilia-Lanier).

Nationmaster.com (http://www.nationmaster.com/encyclopedia/J.-F.-Hendry).

Native American Authors Project: Frank Prewett (http://www.ipl.org/div/natam/bin/browse.pl/A398). (http://www.library.utoronto.ca/canpoetry/meyer/bio.html)

The Nature and Purpose of Poetry: Nature (http://www.ourcivilisation.com/smartboard/shop/poetl8/nature.htm).

Never Such Innocence: A New Anthology of Great War Verse. Martin Stephen, ed. Buchan and Enright, 1988.

New & Collected Poems, 1952–1992 of Geoffrey Hill. Houghton Mifflin, 1994.

New Blood. Neil Astley, ed. Bloodaxe Books, 1999.

The New British Poetry, 1968–88. Gillian Allnutt, Fred D'Aguiar and Ken Edwards, ed. Grafton Books, 1989.

The New British Poets: An Anthology. Kenneth Rexroth, ed. New Directions, 1949.

A New Canon of English Poetry. James Reeves and Martin Seymour-Smith, ed. Barnes & Noble, 1967.

New Catholic Dictionary (www.catholic-forum.com/saints/ncd01507.htm).

New Catholic Dictionary: Ecclesiastical Titles Act (http://www.catholic-forum.com/saints/ncd02922.htm).

New Coasts & Strange Harbors: Discovering Poems. Helen Hill, and Agnes Perkins, ed. Thomas Y. Crowell Co., 1974.

The New Exeter Book of Riddles. Kevin Crossley-Holland and Lawrence Sail, ed. Enitharmon Press, 1999.

New Internationalist magazine on-line (www.newint.org/issue326/mix.htm).

New Irish Poets. Devin A. Garrity, ed. Devin-Adair, 1948.

The New Lake Poets. William Scammell, ed. Bloodaxe Books, 1991.

New Lines: Poets Of The 1950s: An Anthology. Robert Conquest, ed. Macmillan, 1956 (http://homepages.wmich.edu/~cooneys/tchg/wby/new-lines.html).

New Media and the Welsh Language (http://spruce.flint.umich.edu/~ellisjs/Grahame%20Davies.pdf).

The New Modern Poetry: British and American Poetry since World War II. M.L. Rosenthal, ed. Macmillan, 1967.

The New Oxford Book of Australian Verse. Les A. Murray, ed. Oxford University Press, 1991 (enlarged edition).

The New Oxford Book of Children's Verse. Neil Philip, ed. Oxford University Press, 1996.

The New Oxford Book of Christian Verse. Donald Davie, ed. Oxford University Press, 1981.

The New Oxford Book of Eighteenth Century Verse. Roger Lonsdale, ed. Oxford University Press, 1984.

The New Oxford Book of Eighteenth Century Verse. Roger Lonsdale, ed. Oxford University Press, 2003.

The New Oxford Book of English Light Verse. Kingsley Amis, ed. Oxford University Press, 1978.

The New Oxford Book of English Verse, 1250–1950. Helen Gardner, ed. Oxford University Press, 1972.

The New Oxford Book of Irish Verse. Thomas Kinsella, ed. Oxford University Press, 1986.

The New Oxford Book of Romantic Period Verse. Jerome J. McGann. Oxford University Press, 1993.

The New Oxford Book of Seventeenth Century Verse. Alastair Fowler, ed. Oxford University Press, 1991.

The New Oxford Book of Seventeenth Century Verse. Alastair Fowler, ed. Oxford University Press, 2004.

The New Oxford Book of Sixteenth Century Verse. Emrys Jones, ed. Oxford University Press, 1991.

The New Oxford Book of Sixteenth Century Verse. Emrys Jones, ed. Oxford University Press, 2002.

The New Oxford Book of Victorian Verse. Christopher Ricks, ed. Oxford University Press, 1987.

The New Oxford Book of Victorian Verse. Christopher Ricks, ed. Oxford University Press, 2002.

The New Penguin Book of English Verse. Paul Keegan, ed. Penguin Books, 2000.

The New Penguin Book of Scottish Verse. Robert Crawford and Mick Imlah, ed. Penguin Books, 2000.

New Poets of England and America. Donald Hall, and Robert Pack, ed. World, 1962.

New Selected Poems 1957–1994 of Ted Hughes. Faber and Faber, 1995.

A New Treasury of Children's Poetry, Old Favorites and New Discoveries. Joanna Cole, ed. Doubleday, 1984.

A New Treasury of Poetry. Neil Philip, ed. Stewart, Tabori, and Chang, 1990.

New Women Poets. Carol Rumens, ed. Bloodaxe Books, 1990.

The New York Review of Books: Robin Robertson (http://www.ny books.com/articles/article-preview?article_id=17314).

The New Yorker Book of Poems. The New Yorker editors. Viking Press, 1969.

The New Zealand Edge: Media / NEWZEDGE: Sydney Goodsir Smith (http://www.nzedge.com/media/archives/archv-arts-writers.html).

New Zealand Love Poems. Lauris Edmond, ed. Oxford University Press, 2000.

Newborn, by Kate Clanchy—Poems Covering Pregnancy, Birth and Caring for a New Baby. Picador, 2005.

The Newcastle Literary & Philosophical Society, Joseph Skipsey and some other men of note (http://www.litandphil.org.uk/skipsey. htm).

Next Generation Poets: Lancaster University News (http://domino. lancs.ac.uk/info/lunews.nsf/Tx/1219B3BD2A8CB66F80256EB A00374FBD).

Nicholas Johnson, An Appreciation by *Barry MacSweeney* (www. pores.bbk.ac.uk).

The 1916 Rebellion, Thomas MacDonagh (.http://www.1916rising. com/pic_tom_mcdonagh.html).

1996–1998 Broadway Premieres. The Steward of Christendom (http://www.infoplease.com/ipea/A0152816.html).

19th Century British and Irish Authors (http://www.lang.nagoya-u. ac.jp/~matsuoka/19th-authors.html).

19th Century British Minor Poets. W.H. Auden, ed. Delacorte Press, 1966.

Nineteenth-Century English Laboring-Class Poets (3 volumes). John Goodridge, ed. Pickering & Chatto. 2005.

Nineteenth-Century Women Poets: An Oxford Anthology. Isobel Armstrong and Joseph Bristow with Cath Sharrock, ed. Oxford University Press, 1996.

No More Masks. 2nd Edition. Florence Howe, ed. HarperCollins Publishers, 1993.

Noel Roden, Paragon Review of a Legacy of Words (http://www. hull.ac.uk/oldlib/archives/paragon/1998/noel.html).

A Nonsense Anthology. Carolyn Wells, ed. Scribner's: paperback edition, 1930.

Norman Cameron: His Life, Work and Letters (http://www.greenex. co.uk/cameron.html).

The Norton Anthology of English Literature. 5th ed. Vol. 2, M.H. Abrams, ed. W.W. Norton, 1986.

The Norton Anthology of English Literature. 6th ed. Vol. 2, M.H. Abrams, ed. W.W. Norton, 1993.

The Norton Anthology of English Literature. 7th ed. Vol. 2, M.H. Abrams, ed. W.W. Norton, 2000.

The Norton Anthology of Literature by Women: The Tradition in English. Sandra M. Gilbert and Susan Guber, ed. W.W. Norton, 1985.

The Norton Anthology of Modern Poetry. 2nd ed. Richard Ellmann, and Robert O'Clair, ed. W.W. Norton, 1988.

The Norton Anthology of Poetry. 3rd ed. Alexander W. Allison, ed. W.W. Norton, 1983.

The Norton Anthology of Poetry. 4th ed. Margaret Ferguson, Mary Jo Salter and Jon Stal, ed. W.W. Norton, 1996.

The Norton Book of Light Verse. Russell Baker, ed. W.W. Norton, 1986.

The Norton Introduction to Literature. 7th edition. Jerome Beaty and J. Paul Hunter, ed. W.W. Norton, 1998.

The Norton Introduction to Poetry. 2nd ed. J. Paul Hunter, ed. W.W. Norton, 1981.

Not Without Glory: Poets of the Second World War. Vernon Scannell. Routledge Falmer, 1976.

Notes for a Myth. Terence Tiller, The Hogarth Press Ltd., 1968.

Notes on the history of Mental Health Care (http://www.mind. org.uk/Information/Factsheets/History+of+mental+health/Notes +on+the+History+of+Mental+Health+Care.htm).

O Frabjous Day: Poetry for Holidays and Special Occasions. Myra Cohn Livingston, ed. Atheneum, 1977.

Obituary of Charles Causley: Telegraph × News × Charles Causley (www.opinion.telegraph.co.uk/).

Obituary of Charles Sisson, News. Telegraph, Sept. 8, 2003 (http://

www.telegraph.co.uk/news/main.jhtml?xml=/news/2003/09/08 /db0801.xml).

Obituary of Douglas Oliver. The Independent, (London), Apr 26, 2000 by Nicholas Johnson (http://www.findarticles.com/p/arti cles/mi_qn4158/is_20000426/ai_n14307041).

Obituary of Eric Mottram (http://wings.buffalo.edu/epc/docu ments/obits/mottram).

Obituary of Gael Turnbull: John Lucas, Monday July 12, 2004, The Guardian (http://books.guardian.co.uk/obituaries/story/ 0,11617,1258918,00.html).

Obituary of John Silkin: Reporter 412, 15 December 1997 (http:// reporter.leeds.ac.uk/412/section9.htm).

Obituary of Muriel Spark, BBC News, 15th April 2006 (http://news. bbc.co.uk/1/hi/entertainment/3659703.stm).

Obituary of Oscar Wilde: The Times, December 1, 1900 (http://www. the-times.co.uk/).

Obituary of Peter Redgrove: Queens' College Record 2004 (http:// www.quns.cam.ac.uk/Queens/Record/2004/Old%20Members/ Obituaries.html).

Obituary of Peter Redgrove. Telegraph News (http://www.telegraph. co.uk/news/main.jhtml?xml=/news/2003/06/18/db1802.xml).

Obituary of Professor John Holloway, Fellow 1955—1999: Queens' College Cambridge Record, 2000 (http://www.quns.cam.ac.uk/ Queens/Record/2000/Society/Holloway.html).

Obituary of Leslie Norris. Wales.co.uk. 11 April 2006 (http://icwales. icnetwork.co.uk/).

Obituary of Siegfried Sassoon. The Times, September 4, 1967.

The Occasional Verse of Richard Steele. Rae Blanchard, ed. Oxford University Press, 1952.

Odes and Epistles of Robert Nugent. R. Dodsley, 1739.

Odes on Various Subjects by Joseph Warton. London: printed for R. Dodsley: And sold by M. Cooper 1746 (*Ximenes Rare Books Inc* (http://www.polybiblio.com/ximenes/B3419.html).

O'Donnell Coat of Arms and Family History (http://www.araltas. com/features/odonnell/).

The Official Dunmow Flitch Trials Committee website. www.dun mowflitchtrials.co.uk).

Old Brightonian Association Leonard Strong (http://www.old brightonians.com/strong_01.htm).

Oldblues.com. Community information for Christ's Hospital Old Blues: Lawrence Tuttiet (http://www.oldblues.com/ontheweb. htm).

Oldpoetry (www.oldpoetry.com).

On Captain Francis Grose (http://www.worldburnsclub.com/ poems/translations/on_captain_francis_grose.htm).

On Wings of Song: Poems about Birds. J.D. McClatchy, ed. Alfred A. Knopf, 2000.

Once Upon a Rhyme: 101 Poems for Young Children. Sara Corrin, and Stephen Corrin, ed. Faber and Faber, 1982.

100 Poems by 100 Poets: An Anthology. Harold Pinter, Geoffrey Godbert and Anthony Astbury, ed. Grove Press, 1986.

100 Poems on the Underground. Gerald Benson, Judith Cherniak and Cicely Herb, ed. Cassell, 1991.

100 Welsh Heroes / 100 Arwyr Cymru. http://www.100welshheroes. com/en/biography/waldowilliams).

One Hundred and One Classics of Victorian Verse. Ellen J. Green-field, ed. Contemporary Books, 1992.

101 Favorite Cat Poems. Sara L. Whittier, ed. Contemporary Books, 1991.

101 Patriotic Poems. Contemporary Books, 1986.

One Hundred and Seventy Chinese Poems, Translated by Arthur Waley. Constable & Co., 1962.

One River, Many Creeks: Poems from All Around the World. Valerie Bloom, ed. Macmillan Children's Books, 2003.

1000 Years of Irish Poetry: The Gaelic and Anglo-Irish Poets from Pagan Times to the Present. Kathleen Hoagland, ed. Devin-Adair, 1975.

The O' Neill Suite by Gerry Murphy (http://www.munsterlit.ie/ Southword3/Poetry/Gerry_Murphy/gerry_murphy.html).

The Online Books Page (http://digital.library.upenn.edu/books).

Online Classic Encyclopedia- Love to Know (http://www.19.1911en cyclopedia.org).

Online Encyclopedia: 11th Edition of Encyclopedia. Gerald Griffin (http://encyclopedia.jrank.org/GRA_GUI/GRIFFIN_OGRI-oBTA_OGREEVA_GERAL.html).

Only One of Me: Selected Poems, of James Berry. Macmillan Children's Books, 2004.

Open Directory—Arts: Literature: World Literature: British (http://dmoz.org/Arts/Literature/World_Literature/British/20th_Century/).

Opened Ground: Selected Poems 1966–1996m of Seamus Heaney. Farrar, Straus and Giroux, 1998.

Oral Poetry from Africa. Jack Mapange, ed. Landeg White, Longman, 1983.

Oranges At Christmas Time by Elizabeth Bewick Oscar Wilde's Last Stand. Philip Hoare, Arcade Publishing, 1998.

Orlando Furioso, the translation by William Stewart Rose (http://omacl.org/Orlando).

Oscar Wilde's Last Stand. Philip Hoare. Arcade Publishing. 1998.

Other: British and Irish Poetry since 1970. Richard Caddel and Peter Quartermain. ed. Wesleyan University Press, 1999.

Other Men's Flowers. A.P. Wavell, ed. Jonathan Cape, 1990.

Our Holidays in Poetry. Mildred P. Harrington and Josephine H. Thomas, ed. H.W. Wilson, 1929.

Outsiders: Poems about Rebels, Exiles, and Renegades. Laure-Anne Bosselaar, ed. Milkweed Editions, 1999.

The Overshadowed and Surprising (http://www.lib.byu.edu/~english/WWI/over/over.html).

Overview of Rev. Robert Blair (http://www.geo.ed.ac.uk/scotgaz/people/famousfirst2017.html).

The Oxford and Cambridge May Anthologies Poetry 2000. Paul Muldoon, ed. Varsity/Cherwell, 2000.

The Oxford Anthology of English Literature Vol. I. Frank Kermode, and John Hollander, ed. Oxford University Press. 1973.

The Oxford Anthology of English Literature. Vol. I–III. Frank Kermode, and John Hollander, ed. Oxford University Press, 1973.

The Oxford Anthology of English Poetry. Vol. I: Spenser to Crabbe. John Wain, ed. Oxford University Press, 1990.

The Oxford Anthology of English Poetry. Vol. II: Blake to Heaney. John Wain, ed. Oxford University Press, 1990.

The Oxford Book of Animal Poems. Michael Harrison, and Christopher Stuart-Clark, ed. Oxford University Press, 1992.

The Oxford Book of Ballads. James Kinsley, ed. Oxford University Press, 1969.

The Oxford Book of Children's Verse. Iona Opie, and Peter Opie, ed. Oxford University Press, 1973.

The Oxford Book of Christian Verse. Lord David Cecil, ed. Oxford University Press, 1940.

The Oxford Book of Christmas Poems. Michael Harrison, and Christopher Stuart-Clark, ed. Oxford University Press, 1983.

The Oxford Book of Classical Verse in Translation. Adrian Poole, and Jeremy Maule, ed. 1995.

The Oxford Book of Comic Verse. John Gross, ed. Oxford University Press, 1994.

The Oxford Book of Contemporary Verse, 1945–1980. D.J. Enright, ed. Oxford University Press, 1980.

The Oxford Book of Death. D.J. Enright, ed. Oxford University Press, 1987.

The Oxford Book of Eighteenth Century Verse. David Nichol Smith, ed. Oxford University Press, 1926.

The Oxford Book of English Mystical Verse, 13th-20th Centuries. D.H.S. Nicholson and A.H. Lee, ed. Oxford University Press, 1916.

The Oxford Book of English Traditional Verse. Frederick Woods, ed. Oxford University Press, 1983.

The Oxford Book of English Verse. Christopher Ricks, ed. Oxford University Press, 1999.

The Oxford Book of English Verse, 1250–1918. Sir Arthur Quiller-Couch, ed (New edition, revised and enlarged, Oxford University Press, 1939.)

The Oxford Book of Friendship. D.J. Enright and David Rawlinson, ed. Oxford University Press, 1991.

The Oxford Book of Garden Verse. John Dixon Hunt, ed. Oxford University Press, 1993.

The Oxford Book of Irish Verse: XVIIth Century–XXth Century. Donagh MacDonagh, and Leenox Robinson, ed. Oxford University Press, 1958.

The Oxford Book of Late Medieval Verse and Prose. Douglas Gray, ed. Clarendon Press, 1985.

The Oxford Book of Light Verse. W.H. Auden, ed. Oxford University Press, 1938.

The Oxford Book of Local Verses. John Holloway, ed. Oxford University Press, 1987.

The Oxford Book of Marriage. Helge Rubenstein, ed. Oxford University Press, 1990.

The Oxford Book of Medieval English Verse. Celia Sisam, and Kenneth Sisam, ed. Oxford University Press, 1970.

The Oxford Book of Modern Verse, 1892–1935. William Butler Yeats, ed. Oxford University Press, 1936.

The Oxford Book of Nineteenth-Century English Verse. John Hayward, ed. Oxford University Press, 1964: reprinted, with corrections, 1965.

The Oxford Book of Regency Verse 1798–1837. H.S. Milford, ed. Oxford University Press, 1928.

The Oxford Book of Satirical Verse. Geoffrey Grigson, ed. Oxford University Press, 1980.

The Oxford Book of Scottish Verse. John MacQueen and Tom Scott, ed. Oxford University Press, 1966.

The Oxford Book of Seventeenth Century Verse. H.J.C. Grierson, and G. Bullough, ed. Oxford University Press, 1934.

The Oxford Book of Short Poems. P.J. Kavanagh, and James Michie, ed. Oxford University Press, 1985.

The Oxford Book of Sixteenth Century Verse. E.K. Chambers, ed. Oxford University Press, 1932.

The Oxford Book of Sonnets. John Fuller, ed. Oxford University Press, 2000.

The Oxford Book of Story Poems. Michael Harrison and Christopher Stuart-Clark, ed. Oxford University Press, 1990.

The Oxford Book of the Sea. Jonathan Raban, ed. Oxford University Press, 1992.

The Oxford Book of the Supernatural. D.J. Enright, ed. Oxford University Press, 1994.

The Oxford Book of Travel Verse. Kevin Crossley-Holland, ed. Oxford University Press, 1986.

The Oxford Book of Twentieth-Century English Verse. Philip Larkin, ed. Oxford University Press, 1973.

The Oxford Book of Verse in English Translation. Charles Tomlinson, ed. Oxford University Press, 1980.

The Oxford Book of Victorian Verse. Arthur Quiller-Couch, ed. Oxford University Press, 1971.

The Oxford Book of Villains. John Mortimer, ed. Oxford University Press, 1992.

The Oxford Book of War Poetry. Jon Stallworthy, Oxford University Press, 1984.

The Oxford Book of Welsh Verse in English. Gwyn Jones, ed. Oxford University Press, 1977.

The Oxford Companion to English Literature. 6th edition. Margaret Drabble, ed. Oxford University Press, 2000.

The Oxford Companion to Scottish History. Michael Lynch, ed. Oxford University Press, 2001.

The Oxford Nursery Rhyme Book. Iona Opie, and Peter Opie, ed. Oxford University Press, 1955.

Oxford Poetry: Appendix 2: The Newdigate Prize (http://www.gnelson.demon.co.uk/oxpoetry/index/inewd.html).

Oxford Professors of Poetry (http://www.poetsgraves.co.uk/oxford_professors_of_poetry.htm).

Oxford Professors of Poetry, James Hurdis (http://www.people.vcu.edu/~dlatane/pop.html).

The Oxford Treasury of Children's Poems. Michael Harrison, and Christopher Stuart-Clark. ed. Oxford University Press, 1988.

Palgrave: Selected Poems of Francis Turner Palgrave. Brian Louis Pearce, ed. Brentham Press, 1985.

The Palis of Honoure: Introduction. Gavin Douglas. David Parkinson, ed. Kalamazoo, Michigan: Medieval Institute Publications, 1992. (http://www.lib.rochester.edu/camelot/teams/palisint.htm).

Papers of John Cennick—Collection 150. (www.wheaton.edu/bgc/archives/GUIDES/150.htm).

Papers of Lady Naomi Mitchison (http://www.archiveshub.ac.uk/news/0501mitchison.html).

Parents: An Anthology of Poems by Women Writers. Myra Schneider and Dilys Wood, ed. Enitharmon Press, 2000.

Parlor Poetry: A Casquet of Gems. Michael R. Turner, ed. The Viking Press, 1969.

Parodies: An Anthology from Chaucer to Beerbohm—and After. Dwight Macdonald, ed. Mosdern Library, 1960.

Patrick Galvin: An Inventory of His Papers at the Burns Library, Boston College, Massachusetts (http://www.bc.edu/bc_org/avp/ulib/Burns/galvinb.html).

The Patriot Resource (http://www.patriotresource.com/people/moultrie.html).

Patriotic Poems America Loves. Jean Anne Vincent, ed. Doubleday, 1968.

Patron Saints Index (http://www.catholic-forum.com/saints/sainth97.htm).

Patterns of Madness in the Eighteenth Century: A Reader. Allan Ingram, ed. Liverpool University Press, 1998.

Paul Muldoon Home Page (http://www.paulmuldoon.net/).

Peace and War: A Collection of Poems. Michael Harrison, and Christopher Stuart-Clark, ed. Oxford University Press, 1989.

P.E.N. New Poetry I. Robert Nye, ed. Quartet Books, 1986.

Penguin Authors (http://www.penguin.co.uk/nf/Author/AuthorPage/0,,0_1000051386,00.html).

The Penguin Book of Bird Poetry. Peggy Munsterberg, ed. 1984.

The Penguin Book of Caribbean Verse in English. Paula Burnett, ed. Penguin Books, 1986.

The Penguin Book of Contemporary Irish Poetry. Peter Fallon and Derek Mahon, ed. Penguin Books, 1990.

The Penguin Book of English Christian Verse. Peter Levi, ed. Penguin Books, 1984.

The Penguin Book of First World War Poetry. Jon Silkin, ed. Penguin Books, 1979.

The Penguin Book of Homosexual Verse. Stephen Coote, ed. Penguin Books, 1983.

The Penguin Book of Irish Verse. Brendan Kennelly, ed. Penguin Books, 1981.

The Penguin Book of Japanese Verse. Geoffrey Bownes, and Anthony Thwaite, ed. Penguin Books, 1964.

The Penguin Book of Light Verse. Gavin Ewart, ed. Penguin Books, 1980.

The Penguin Book of New Zealand Verse. Ian Wedde and Harvey McQueen, ed. Penguin Books, 1985.

The Penguin Book of Poetry from Britain and Ireland Since 1945. Robert Crawford, and Simon Armitage, ed. Penguin Books, 1998.

The Penguin Book of Renaissance Verse 1509–1659. David Norbrook, ed. Penguin Books, 1992.

The Penguin Book of South African Verse. Jack Cope, and Uys Krige, ed. Penguin Books, 1968.

The Penguin Book of Southern African Verse. Stephen Gray. ed. Penguin Books, 1989.

The Penguin Book of the Sonnet: 500 Years of a Classic Tradition in English. Phillis Levin, ed. Penguin Books, 2001.

The Penguin Book of Victorian Verse. George Macbeth, ed. Penguin Classics, 1999.

The Penguin Book of Women Poets. Carol Cosman, Joan Keefe and Kathleen Weaver, ed. Penguin Books, 1978.

Penguin Modern Poets, Book 9. John Burnside, Robert Crawford, and Kathleen Jamie, ed. Penguin Books, 1996.

Penguin Modern Poets, Bk. 11. Michael Donaghy, Andrew Motion, Hugo Williams, ed. Penguin Books, 1997.

Penguin Modern Poets 13. Robin Robertson, Michael Hofmann, Michael Longley, ed. Penguin Books, 1998.

Penguin Poetry Anthologies (http://encyclopedia.thefreedictionary.com/Penguin%20poetry%20anthologies).

Pet Poems. Robert Fisher, ed. Faber and Faber, 1989.

Peter Neilson, 1795–1861. The Life and Adventures of Zamba, an African Negro King: And His Experience of Slavery in South Carolina. Written by Himself. Corrected and Arranged by Peter Neilson. London: Smith, Elder, 1847 (http://docsouth.unc.edu/neh/neilson/menu.html).

Peter Pindar's Poems. P.M. Zall, ed. University of South Carolina, 1972.

Peter Robinson's Selected Poems, 2003 (http://charles.sal.tohoku.ac.jp/peternewbook.htm).

Philip Hobsbaum, 1932– Collection of Correspondence and Manuscripts of The Group, ca. 1955–1968 (http://www.hrc.utexas.edu/research/fa/hobsbaum.html).

The Phoenix Nest, Notes and Poem (1593) (http://darkwing.uoregon.edu/~rbear/phoenix.html#AnelegieforAstrophill).

Picture of the New Caledonian Asylum, London (http://www.londonancestor.com/views/vb-asylumcal.htm).

Piping Down the Valley Wild: Poetry for the Young of All Ages, Nancy Larrick, ed. Delacorte Press, 1968.

Pith and Vinegar: An Anthology of Short Humorous Poetry. William Cole, ed. Simon & Schuster, 1969.

Plays and Poems, by William Whitehead, 2 Volumes (no publisher), 1774.

The Plays and Poems of Philip Massinger, (five volumes). Philip Edwards and Colin Gibson, ed. Clarendon Press, 1976.

The Plays and Poems of Richard Brinsley Sheridan. 3 vols. R. Crompton Rhodes, ed. Blackwell, 1928.

The Pleasure of Poetry: From His Daily Mirror Column. Kingsley Amis, ed. Cassell Publishers, 1990.

Plowman (Max)Papers at University College, London. AIM25: University College London: Plowman Papers (http://www.aim25.ac.uk/cgi-bin/frames/fulldesc?inst_id=13&coll_id=1650).

A Poem a Day, Karen McCosker, and Nicholas Albery, ed. Steer Forth Press, 1996.

Poem by Katherine Duffy (http://www.brakkehond.be/76/duffyle.html).

Poemhunter (www.poemhunter.com).

The Poems and Fables of Robert Henryson. H. Harvey Wood, ed. Barnes & Noble, 1968.

Poems and Plays of Gordon Bottomley. Claude Colleer Abbott, ed. The Bodley Head, 1953.

The Poems and Prose of Mary, Lady Chudleigh. Margaret J.M. Ezell, ed. Oxford University Press, 1993.

Poems and Some Letters of James Thomson. Anne Ridler, ed. Southern Illinois Univ. Press, 1963.

Poems and Songs, Chiefly in the Scottish Dialect by Robert Tannahill. John Cain, 1819.

Poems and Songs. Fourth Edition. With Memoir of the Author, and Appendix of His Latest Pieces. Sutherland and Knox, 1851.

Poems and Songs Gaelic and English. Mary Mackellar. Maclachlan & Stewart. 1880.

Poems and Translations of J.M. Synge. John W. Luce & Company, 1911.

The Poems and Translations of Thomas Stanley. Galbraith Miller Crump, ed. Oxford University Press, 1962.

The Poems and Verse of Charles Dickens. F.G. Kitton, ed. New York: Harper & Brothers, 1903.

Poems and Writings from Les Barker (www.blodtandsmidigt.com/LesBarker/LesBarker.html).

Poems Between Women: Four Centuries of Love, Romantic Friendship, and Desire. Emma Donoghue, ed. Columbia University Press, 1997.

Poems, by Alexander Smith. Ticknoe, Reed, and Fields, 1853.

Poems by Arthur Symons: Volume I. William Heinemann, 1911.

Poems by Augusta Theodosia Drane: Poetry Archive (www.poetryarchive.com).

Poems by Caroline Clive. Longmans, Green, and Co., 1872.

Poems by Dorothy Wordsworth (http://www.umd.umich.edu/casl/hum/eng/classes/236/dwordsworth2.html).

Poems by Duncan Bush: Transcript (English) (http://www.transcript-review.org/sub.cfm?lan=en&id=2991).

Poems by Edward Caswall. Thomas Richardson and Son, 1861.

Poems by Eminent Ladies, Particularly Mrs. Barber, Mrs. Behn, Miss Carter. 2 volumes. George Colman and Bonnell Thornton, ed. R. Baldwin, 1755.

Poems, by George Dyer. Longman and Rees, 1801.

Poems by George Wither. Henry Morley, ed. George Routledge & Sons, 1891.

Poems by Jamie McKendrick (http://www.thepoem.co.uk/poems/mckendrick.htm).

Poems by Jean Ingelow. Roberts Brothers, 1864.

Poems by John Drinkwater: Poets' Corner Bookshelf (http://www.theotherpages.org/poems/gp2_4a.html).

Poems. By John Francis O'Donnell. With Introduction by Richard Dowling. Ward & Downey, 1891.

Poems by Katherine Duffy (http://homepage.tinet.ie/~johndeane/page19.html).

Poems by Kathryn Gray (http://www.thepoem.co.uk/limelight/gray.htm).

Poems by Kathryn Gray (http://www.transcript-review.org/sub.cfm?lan=en&id=2994).

Poems by Maurice Scully (http://english.chass.ncsu.edu/freeverse/Archives/Spring_2002/poems/m_scully.html).

Poems by Pascale Petit (http://english.chass.ncsu.edu/freeverse/Archives/Spring_2003/Poetry/P_Petit.htm).

Poems by Pascale Petit (http://www.poetrypf.co.uk/pascalepetitpoems.html#p4).

Poems by Paul Farley (http://www.poetryarchive.org/poetryarchive/singlePoet.do?poetId=27).

Poems by Robert Leighton. George Routledge & Sons, 1869.

Poems by Sir David Murray of Gorthy. James Ballantyne and Co., 1823.

Poems by Speranza (Lady Wilde). M.H. Gill & Son, Ltd., 1907.

Poems, by the Author of "A Life for a Life" [Dinah Maria Mulock Craik]. Ticknor & Fields, 1860.

Poems by the Most Eminent Ladies of Great Britain and Ireland (http://www.nku.edu/~issues/eminent_ladies/vol1/master_file_vol_1.html#grierson).

Poems, Chiefly Lyric and Elegiac of Arthur Munby. Kegan Paul, 1901.

Poems, 1833 of (Coleridge, Hartley). Woodstock Books, 1990.

Poems, 1833 of Hartley Coleridge. Woodstock Books, 1990.

Poems for Seasons and Celebrations. William Cole, ed. World, 1961.

Poems for the Great Days. Thomas Curtis Clark, and Robert Earle Clark, ed. Abingdon-Cokesbury Press, 1948.

Poems for the Millennium: The University of California Book of Modern & Postmodern Poetry. Vol. 2. Jerome Rothenberg and Pierre Joris, ed. University of California Press, 1998.

Poems for the People — Poems by the People (http://www.netpoets.com/classic/biographies/038000.htm).

Poems for Young Children. Caroline Royds, ed. Doubleday, 1986.

Poems—Fourth Edition: The Wadsworth Handbook and Anthology. C.F. Main and Peter J. Seng, ed. Wadsworth Publishing Company, 1978.

Poems from Italy. William Jay Smith, and Dana Gioia, ed. New Rivers, 1985.

Poems: Historical and Characteristic of Robert Lord Lytton. Chapman & Hall, 1887.

Poems Illustrative of South Africa: Volume I by Thomas Pringle. John Robert Wahl, ed. C. Struik, Ltd., 1970.

Poems 1916–1918 of Francis Brett Young. E.P. Dutton, 1920.

Poems, 1955–1987 of Roy Fisher. Oxford University Press, 1988.

Poems, 1968–1998 of Paul Muldoon. Farrar, Straus and Giroux, 2001.

The Poems of Aemilia Lanyer, Salve Deus Rex Judaeorum. Susanne Woods, ed. Oxford University Press, 1993.

Poems of Alasdair Gray (http://www.alasdairgray.co.uk/poetry/).

The Poems of Alice Meynell. Oxford University Press, 1940.

The Poems of Alice Meynell @ ELCore.Net (http://poetry.elcore.net/CatholicPoets/Meynell/).

The Poems of Allan Ramsay. Vol. 1 & 2. T. Cadell and W. Davies, 1800.

The Poems of Ambrose Philips. M.G. Segar, ed. Blackwell, Oxford, 1937.

Poems of Amelia Alderson Opie. T.N. Longman, 1802.

Poems of American History. Burton Egbert Stevenson, ed. Houghton Mifflin, 1922.

The Poems of Anna Letitia Barbauld. William McCarthy and Elizabeth Kraft, ed. University of Georgia Press, 1994.

The Poems of Arthur Hugh Clough. H.F. Lowry, A.L.P. Norrington and F.L. Mulhauser, ed. Clarendon Press, 1951.

Poems of Arthur O'Shaughnessy. William Alexander Percy, ed. Greenwood Press, 1923.

The Poems of Byron. Paul E. More, ed. Houghton Mifflin, 1933.

Poems of Charles Churchill. Barnes and Noble, 1933.

Poems of Charles Lloyd. Hurst, Rees, Orme, and Brown, 1823.

The Poems of Charlotte Smith. Stuart Curran, ed. Oxford University Press, 1993.

Poems of Christmas. Myra Cohn Livingston, ed. Atheneum, 1980.

The Poems of Coventry Patmore. Frederick Page, ed. Oxford University Press, 1949.

Poems of Duncan Ban Macintyre (http://www.electricscotland.com/poetry/macintyre/).

The Poems of Edmund Blunden, 1914–1930. Cobden-Sanderson, 1930.

The Poems of Edmund Waller. Greenwood Press, 1968.

Poems of Edward Dowden (http://www.sonnets.org/dowden.htm).

The Poems of Ernest Dowson. Arthur Symons Dodd, ed. Mead and Company, 1922.

Poems of Geoffrey Scott. Oxford University Press, 1931.

The Poems of George Meredith. Vol. 1. Phyllis B. Bartlett, ed. Yale University Press, 1978.

The Poems of Goethe. Edgar Alfred Bowring, ed. George Bell and Sons, 1874.

Poems of James Graham Marquis of Montrose. John Murray, 1938.

The Poems of James Stephens. Shirley Mulligan, ed. Colin Smythe Ltd., 2005.

Poems of James Thomson. Henry Holt and Company, 1927.

The Poems of John Dryden. Vol. 2, 1682–1685. Paul Hammond, ed. Longman, 1995.

The Poems of John Gray. Ian Fletcher, ed. ELT Press, 1988.

The Poems of John Marston. Arnold Davenport, ed. Liverpool University Press, 1961.

The Poems of John Oldham. Harold F. Brooks, ed. Clarendon Press, 1987.

Poems of John Swinnerton Phillimore. James MacLehose and Sons, 1902.

The Poems of John Wilmot, Earl of Rochester. Shakespeare Head Press, 1984.

The Poems of Joseph Mary Plunkett (http://poetry.elcore.net/CatholicPoets/Plunkett/).

The Poems of Lady Mary Wroth. Louisiana State University Press, 1883.

The Poems of Laurence Minot. 2nd. Edition. Clarendon Press, 1897.

The Poems of Laurence Minot. Richard H. Osberg, ed. Western Michigan University, 1996.

The Poems of Lord Vaux. Larry P. Vonalt, ed. Books of the Renaissance, 1960.

Poems of Mimi Khalvati (http://www.shu.ac.uk/schools/cs/english/sheaf/khalvati.htm).

The Poems of Ossian. Nichol, 1765.

The Poems of Philip Massinger, With Critical Notes. Ball State University, Indiana, 1968.

Poems of Protest Old and New. Arnold Kenseth, ed. MacMillan, 1968.

Poems of Richard Garnett. Elkin Mathews & John Lane, 1893.

The Poems of Richard Lovelace. C.H. Wilkinson, ed. Oxford University Press, 1930, reprinted 1953.

The Poems of Robert Herrick. L.C. Martin, ed. Oxford University Press, 1965.

Poems of Robert Nicol. Second edition: with numerous additions. Simpkin, Marshall & Co., 1842.

The Poems of Sidney Godolphin. William Dighton, ed. Clarendon Press, 1931.

Poems of Sir Frances Bacon (www.shakespeare-oxford.com).

The Poems of Sir George Etherege. James Thorpe, ed. Princeton University Press, 1963.

The Poems of Sir Walter Ralegh. [Rudick Edition]. Arizona Center for Medieval and Renaissance Studies, 1999 (http://www.asu.edu/clas/acmrs)

The Poems of Sir William Watson. George G. Harrap & Co,. 1936.

Poems of South African History A.D. 1497–1910. A. Petrie, ed. Oxford University Press, 1918.

Poems of Stephen Phillips. John Lane, 1901.

Poems of the Hon. Noel Roden, A Selection. Walter Scott, 1892.

Poems of the Old West: A Rocky Mountain Anthology. Levette J. Davidson, ed. University of Denver Press, 1951.

Poems of the Scottish Hills: An Anthology. Hamish Brown, ed. Aberdeen University Press, 1982.

The Poems of Thomas Davis. D. & J. Sadlier & Co., 1866.

The Poems of Thomas Gordon Hake. Alice Meynell, ed. AMS Press, 1971.

The Poems of Thomas Sheridan. Robert Hogan, ed. Associated University Presses, 1994.

Poems of Tobias Hill (http://themargins.net/anth/1990–1999/hillhiroshima.html).

Poems of Walter Savage Landor. Geoffrey Grigson, ed. Centaur Press, 1964.

Poems of Wendy Cope (http://www.arlindo-correia.com/050900.html).

Poems of Wilfrid Scawen Blunt. Macmillan and Co., 1923.

Poems of William Browne. Gordon Goodwin, 1894.

The Poems of William Dunbar. 2 Vols. Priscilla Bawcutt, ed. Assoc. for Scottish Lit. Studies. 1998.

Poems of William Ernest Henley. AMS Press, Inc., 1970.

The Poems of William Habington. University Press of Liverpool, 1948.

Poems of William R. Spencer. James Cochrane and Co., 1835.

Poems of William Sharp. Mrs. William Sharp, ed. Duffield and Company, 1912.

Poems on Poetry: The Mirror's Garland. Robert Wallace, and James G. Taaffe, ed. E.P. Dutton, 1963.

Poems on Serious and Sacred Subjects by William Hayley (Project Gutenberg) 1818.

Poems on Several Occasions by George Sewell. E. Curll and J. Pemberton, 1719.

Poems on Several Occasions by William Thompson. Oxford, 1757.

Poems on Several Occasions of Thomas Parnell. Alexander Pope, ed. H. Lintot, 1737.

Poems on Subjects Chiefly Devotional, V. I by Anne Steele (No publisher), 1780.

Poems on Various Subjects: Volume I of Henry James Pye. John Stockdale, 1787.

Poems on Various Subjects of Ann Yearsley. Woodstock Books, 1994.

Poems One Line & Longer. William Cole, ed. Grossman, 1973.

Poems, Second Series by John Collings Squire. William Heinemann Ltd., 1921.

Poems: 1791 of Mary Robinson. Woodstock Books, 1994.

Poems That Live Forever. Hazel Felleman, ed. Doubleday, 1965.

Poems That Touch the Heart. A.L. Alexander, ed. Doubleday, 1956.

Poems to Read Aloud, Edward Hodnett, ed. W.W. Norton, 1967.

Poems, V. 1 & 2 of Henry Neele. Smith, Elder, and Co., 1827.

Poems. Vol. 2 of Charles Kingsley. Macmillan and Co., 1884.

Poems with Fables in Prose by Herbert Trench, 3 Volume. Constable and Company, 1924.

Poet with a Wry Line on Dissenters and Devon Poet's Corner Bookshelf (http://www.theotherpages.org/poems/olney.html).

Poetic Gems of William McGonagall. G. Duckworth, 1954.

A Poetical Rapsody (http://www.bartleby.com/214/0609.html).

The Poetical Registry and Repository of Fugitive Poetry for 1802. F. and C. Rivington, 1803.

Poetical Sketches of Anne Batten: All Her Poems (http://etext.lib.virginia.edu/toc/modeng/public/CriSket.html).

Poetical Sketches: The Profession: The Broken Heart, Etc. Hurst, Robinson and Co., 1824.

The Poetical Works of Adelaide A. Proctor. A.L. Burt, ? 1900.

Poetical Works of Alexander Pope. Herbert Davis, ed. Oxford University Press, 1978: repr. 1990.

The Poetical Works of Andrew Young. Secker & Warburg, 1985.

The Poetical Works of Anna Seward: Volume I. Walter Scott, ed. John Ballantyne and Co., 1810.

The Poetical Works of Crabbe, Heber, and Pollok. Lippincott, Grambo, 1854.

The Poetical Works of Dryden. George R. Noyes, ed. Houghton Mifflin Company. 1950.

The Poetical Works of Edward Moore and David Mallet. Thomas Park, ed. J. Sharpe, 1808.

Poetical Works of Frank Sayers. W. Simpkin and R. Marshall, 1830.

The Poetical Works of Gavin Douglas. John Small, ed. William Paterson Publisher, 1874.

The Poetical Works of George MacDonald (2 vols.). IndyPublishing.com, 2005.

The Poetical Works of Hannah More. Scott, Webster, & Geary, 1835.

The Poetical Works of Henry Kirke White and James Grahame. Nichol, 1856.

The Poetical Works of Horace Smith: Volume I & II. Henry Colburn, 1846.

The Poetical Works of James Hammond. Glasgow University, 1787.

The Poetical Works of James Montgomery V. 2. Longman, Orme, Brown, Green, 1841.

The Poetical Works of James Montgomery V. 3. Longman, Orme, Brown, Green, 1841.

The Poetical Works of James Thomson. Houghton, Mifflin (no date).

The Poetical Works of John and Charles Wesley (12 volumes). G. Osborn, ed. Wesleyan-Methodist Conference, 1871.

The Poetical Works of John Critchley Prince, V. 1 & 2. Abel Heywood & Son, 1880.

The Poetical Works of John Gay. G.C. Faber, ed. Russell & Russell, 1926.

The Poetical Works of John Langhorne. Thomas Park, ed. J. Sharpe, 1808.

The Poetical Works of John Scott and Thomas Warton. Thomas Park, ed. J. Sharpe, 1808.

The Poetical Works of John Struthers: Volume I. A. Fullarton and Co., 1850.

The Poetical Works of Joseph Addison. John Bell. Apollo Press, 1778.

The Poetical Works of Leigh Hunt. H.S. Milford, ed. Oxford University Press, 1923.

Poetical Works of Letitia Elizabeth Landon "L.E.L." F.J. Sypher, ed. Scholars' Facsimiles & Reprint, 1900.

The Poetical Works of Mark Akenside and John Dyer. Robert Aris Willmott, ed. George Routledge and Co., 1855.

The Poetical Works of Mary Howitt, Eliza Cook, and L.E.L., Phillips. Sampson, and Company, 1857.

The Poetical Works of Matthew Prior: Volume 1 & 2. Little, Brown, and Company, 1854.

The Poetical Works of Mr. William Pattison: Volume 1 &2. H. Curll, 1728.

The Poetical Works of Mrs. Felicia Hemans. Phillips & Sampson, 1848.

The Poetical Works of Oliver Goldsmith. Rev. J. Mitford, ed. William Pickering, 1851.

The Poetical Works of Richard Lllwyd. Whittaker & Co., 1837.

The Poetical Works of Richard Savage. John Bell, 1791.

The Poetical Works of Robert Fergusson. Chapman and Lang, 1800.

The Poetical Works of Robert Herrick: F.W. Moorman, ed. The Clarendon Press, 1815.

The Poetical Works of Samuel Butler. Thomas Park, ed. J. Sharpe, 1808.

Poetical Works of Samuel Rogers. Kessinger Publishing Co., 2004.

The Poetical Works of Sandys, George. Volumes 1 & 2. George Olms 1968.

The Poetical Works of Sir William Alexander Volume 2. Maurice Ogle & Co.,1872.

The Poetical Works of Sir William Jones. Thomas Park, ed. J. Sharpe, 1808.

The Poetical Works of Thomas Hood V. 2. Little, Brown and Co., 1857.

The Poetical Works of Thomas Traherne. Bertram Dobell, ed. Self-Published, 1906.

The Poetical Works of William Broome. C. Cooke, 1796.

The Poetical Works of William Cowper. 3rd edition. H.S. Milford, ed. Oxford University Press, 1926.

The Poetical Works of William Motherwell. Alexander Gardner, 1881.

The Poetical Works of William Shenstone. Charles Cowden Clarke, ed. James Nichol, 1854.

The Poetical Works of William Somervile. Thomas, Park, ed. J. Sharpe, 1808.

The Poetical Works of William Walsh. Cooke's Edition. Printed for C. Cooke, 1797.

Poetry. Jill P. Baumgaertner, ed. Harcourt, Brace, Jovanovich, 1990.

Poetry and War (http://perso.univ-lyon2.fr/~goethals/warpoet/WW2_menu.html).

The Poetry Anthology, 1912–1977. Daryl Hine, and Joseph Parisi, ed. Houghton Mifflin, 1978.

Poetry Archive, Poems by Philip Massinger (www.poetryarchive.com).

Poetry Archive, Willliam Allingham (www.poetry-archive.com).

Poetry by English Women: Elizabethan to Victorian. R.E. Pritchard, ed. Continuum, 1990.

Poetry by John Agard (http://www.humboldt.edu/~me2/engl240b/student_projects/agard/poetry.htm).

Poetry for Pleasure: A Choice of Poetry and Verse on a Variety of Themes. Ian Parsons, ed. W.W. Norton, 1977.

Poetry in Australia. Vol. I: From the Ballads to Brennan. T. Inglis Moore, ed. University of California Press, 1965.

Poetry in English: An Anthology. M.L. Rosenthal, ed. Oxford University Press, 1987.

Poetry in Revolt—Adrian Mitchell (http://www.angelfire.com/mn2/anarchistpoetry/mitchelldir/mitchell4.html).

Poetry London (Magazine) Says Farewell to Pascale Petit, Spring 2005 (http://www.poetrylondon.co.uk/index.htm?edits/edit50.htm).

The Poetry of Alasdair MacMhaighstir Alasdair. Ronald Black, ed. Association. for Scottish Literary Studies, 2005.

The Poetry of Cats. Samuel Carr, ed. Viking Press, 1974.

The Poetry of Dorothy Wordsworth. Hyman Eigerman, ed. Columbia University Press, 1940.

The Poetry of Henry Reed (http://www.solearabiantree.net/naming ofparts/home.html).

The Poetry of Laetitia Pilkington (1712–1750) and Constantia Grierson (1706–1733). Bernard Tucker, ed. The Edwin Mellen Press, 1996.

The Poetry of Mary Barber. Bernard Tucker, ed. The Edwin Mellen Press, 1992.

The Poetry of Mildmay Fane, Second Earl of Westmorland. Tom Cain, ed. Manchester University Press, 2001.

The Poetry of Robert Greene. Tetsumaro Hayashi, ed. Ball State University, 1977.

The Poetry of Robert Tofte 1597–1620. Jeffrey N. Nelson, ed. Garland Publishing, 1994.

Poetry of the Anti-Jacobin. William Gifford, ed. J. Wright, pub., 1801.

Poetry of the First World War. Edward Hudson, ed. Wayland Publishers Ltd., 1988.

Poetry of the First World War: British Poets (http://www.scuttle buttsmallchow.com/listbri3.html).

Poetry of the First World War: Scottish Poets, (http://www.scuttle buttsmallchow.com/listscot.html).

Poetry of the World Wars. Michael Foss, ed. Peter Bedrick Books, 1990.

Poetry 180: A Turning Back to Poetry. Billy Collins, ed. Random House Trade Paperbacks, 2003.

Poetry Page—Brydges (http://www.geocities.com/Athens/Olym pus/2601/brydges.html).

Poetry to Calm Your Soul. Mimi Khalvati, ed. MQ Publications, 2005.

Poetry with an Edge. Neil Astley, ed. Bloodaxe Books, 1988.

Poetry Worth Remembering: An Anthology of Poetry. Roy W. Watson, ed. Brunswick, 1986.

Poetrybooks.co.uk, (www.poetrybooks.co.uk).

PoetryConnection.net .(www.poetryconnection.net).

Poetry's Plea for Animals. Frances E. Clarke, ed. Lothrop, Lee & Shepherd, 1927.

The Poets and the Poetry of the Nineteenth Century. G. Routledge, 1906.

Poet's Corner Bookshelf (http://www.theotherpages.org/poems/ olney.html).

Poets' Corner—Index of Poets (http://www.theotherpages.org/ poems/poem-gh.html).

Poets' Corner, Mary Leapor (http://www.theotherpages.org/poems/ poem-kl.html).

Poets' Corner: Ploughman at the Plough by Louis Golding (http:// www.theotherpages.org/poems/golding1.html).

Poets' Corner, Sir Edmund William Gosse (http://www.theother pages.org/poems/poem-gh.html).

Poets from the North of Ireland. Frank Ormsby, ed. The Blackstaff Press, 1990.

Poet's Graves, Alfred Lord Tennyson (http://www.poetsgraves.co. uk/tennyson.htm).

A Poet's Harvest Home Poems of William Bell Scott. Elkin Mathews & John Lane, 1893.

Poets of the English Language. Volumes I–V. W.H. Auden, and Norman Holmes Pearson, ed. Viking Press, 1950.

Poets' Work Makes Court Appearance. Evening News, 24th July 2003 (http://news.scotsman.com/arts.cfm?id=801792003).

The Poolbeg Book of Children's Verse. Sean McMahon, ed. Poolbeg Press, 1987.

The Poorhouse Fugitives: Self-Taught Poets and Poetry in Victorian Britain. Brian Maidment, ed. Carcanet Press, 1987.

Portrait of William Jones "Bard of Snowden," National Museum Wales, Art Collections On-line (http://www.nmgw.ac.uk/www. php/art/online/?action=show_item&item=l158).

Portraits of Poets. Sebastian Barker, ed. Carcanet Press, 1986.

Precinct, Honorary degrees for Adrian Henri and John Peel (http:// www.liv.ac.uk/precinct/Jan2001/2.html).

Preface to Shakespeare's First Folio (http://shakespeare.palomar. edu/Folio1.htm).

Prince Charles leads Spike Milligan tributes, Wednesday, 27 February, 2002: BBC News × TV AND RADIO (http://news.bbc. co.uk/1/hi/entertainment/tv_and_radio/1843963.stm).

Prison Amusement by James Mongomery (http://freespace.virgin. net/cade.york/castle/prison5.htm).

Professor Robert Crawford (Head of School) (http://www.st-andrews. ac.uk/english/crawford/home.html).

Professorships Held by the Inklings (http://home.earthlink.net/ ~dbratman/profs.html).

The Project Gutenberg eBook, A Celtic Psaltery, by Alfred Perceval (http://www.gutenberg.org/files/14232/14232.txt).

Project 1: Publications: The Poets of the Princes Series, Volume II: Centre for Advanced Welsh & Celtic Studies (http://www.wales. ac.uk/newpages/external/E4154.asp).

Psyche: or, the Legend of Love, Mary Blachford Tighe (http://web. nmsu.edu/~hlinkin/Psyche/).

Public Records Office of Northern Ireland (http://www.proni.gov. uk/research/academic/strength.htm).

Publications by David Lester Richardson. Forget Me Not: A Hypertextual Archive (http://www.orgs.muohio.edu/anthologies/ FMN/Authors_GenD.htm#Richardson).

Putting Poetry First: A Life of Robert Nichols, 1893–1944. William and Anne Charlton. Michael Russell (Publishing) Ltd, 2003.

Quest for Reality: An Anthology of Short Poems in English. Yvor Winters and Kenneth Fields, ed. Swallow Press,1969.

Rabbie Burns, The Weaver Poets. James Orr (http://www.bbc.co. uk/northernireland/winter/rabbie/weaver1.shtml).

Ralph Erskine's Marvelous Ministry by G. Ella (http://www.puri tansermons.com/erskine/erskin19.htm).

Ralph Waldo Emerson: Collected Poems and Translations. Harold Bloom and Paul Kane, ed. The Library of America, 1994.

The Randall Swingler Archives (http://www1.ntu.ac.uk/english/ centrearchives/Randall%20Swinger%20Archive.html).

The Random House Book of Poetry for Children. Jack Prelutsky, ed. The Random House Group, 1983.

The Rattle Bag: An Anthology of Poetry. Seamus Heaney, and Ted Hughes, ed. Faber and Faber, 1982.

Reading Lyrics. Robert Gottlieb and Robert Kimball, ed. Pantheon Books, 2000.

The Real Mother Goose. Blanche Fisher Wright, ed. Checkerboard Press, 1944.

Red Pepper, Harold Pinter War Poetry (http://www.redpepper. org.uk/arts/x-feb04-pinter.htm).

Reference.com/Encyclopedia/The Dublin Magazine (http://www.ref erence.com/browse/wiki/The_Dublin_Magazine).

The Reformed University Fellowship (RUF) Hymnbook (http://igrace music.com/igracemusic/hymnbook).

Regency Personalities, Lady Caroline Lamb (http://homepages. ihug.co.nz/~awoodley/regency/caro.html).

The Regimen of Princes. Published for The Early English Text Society by Kegan Paul, Trench, Trübner & Co., 1897.

The Reliques of Father Prout (Francis Sylvester Mahony). Oliver Yorke, ed. George Bell and Sons, 1889.

The Remains of Mr. Tho. Brown, Serious and Comical, in Prose and Verse. Printed for Sam. Briscoe, 1720.

Results in Early English Prose Fiction (http://www.letrs.indiana. edu/eepf/browse.html).

Review of Merchant Prince by Thomas McCarthy (http://www. inpressbooks.co.uk/merchant_prince_by_mccarthy_thomas_ i016276.aspx).

Review of Nocturne in Chrome & Sunset Yellow (http://www.salt publishing.com/books/smp/1844712621.htm).

Rhythm Road: Poems to Move To. Lillian Morrison, ed. Lothrop, Lee & Shepard, 1988.

Richard Crashaw (http://www.luminarium.org/sevenlit/crashaw/).

Richard Rolle. Translated by Rosamund Allen. Paulist Press International, U.S., 1999.

River Dart—Alice Oswald (http://www.poetrysociety.org.uk/ places/river.htm).

The Riverside Chaucer. F.N. Robinson, ed. Houghton Mifflin, 1987.

Robert Conquest, Biography (http://www.spartacus.schoolnet. co.uk/HISconquest.htm),

Robert Dodsley—The Famous Bookseller and Publisher of London (http://www.fzc.dk/Boswell/People/people.php?id=30).

Robert Millhouse — St. Peter's Church, Nottingham, England on-line (http://www.stpetersnottingham.org/history/millhouse.html).

Robert Nye Papers (http://www.hrc.utexas.edu/research/fa/nye.html).

The Roland Mathias Prize (http://www.bbc.co.uk/wales/mid/sites/brecon_life/pages/roland_mathias_prize.shtml).

The Romantic Era, List of Poets (http://www.sonnets.org/romantic.htm).

Romantic Women Poets: An Anthology. Duncan Wu, ed. Blackwell Publishers, 1997.

Romanticism. Duncan Wu, ed. Blackwell, 1994.

Roofs of Gold: Poems to Read Aloud. Padraic Colum, ed. Macmillan, 1964.

Room for Me and a Mountain Lion: Poetry of Open Space. Nancy Larrick, ed. M. Evans, 1974.

Roscoe, "On the Last Regiment." (http://www2.bc.edu/~richarad/asp/wsrlr.html#int).

The Routledge Anthology of Cross-Gendered Verse. Alan Michael Parker, and Mark Willhardt, ed. Routledge, 1996.

The Royal Literary Fund (http://www.rlf.org.uk/fellowshipscheme/profile.cfm?fellow=24&menu=3).

Rudyard Kipling: Complete Verse: Definitive Edition. Doubleday, 1989.

Ruth Padel's Official Website (http://www.rpadel.dircon.co.uk/rp_main.htm).

Sabine Baring-Gould Biography and the folk songs of South-West England (www.btinternet.com/~greenjack).

A Sacrifice of Praise: An Anthology of Christian Poetry in English from Caedmon to the Mid-Twentieth Century. James H. Trott, ed. Cumberland House Publishing, 1999.

St. Pancras Old Church, history of (http://en.wikipedia.org/wiki/St_Pancras_Old_Church).

Salt and Bitter and Good: Three Centuries of English and American Women Poets. Cora Kaplan, ed. Paddington Press, 1975.

Salt Water Ballads, John Masefield, 1902. Cyder Press, 2002.

Samuel Johnson's Lives of the English Poets, 1779–1781 (http://www2.hn.psu.edu/Faculty/KKemmerer/poets/preface.htm).

The San Antonio College LitWeb Walter Savage Landor Page (http://www.accd.edu/sac/english/bailey/landorws.htm).

Sarah Fyge Field Egerton (http://www.pinn.net/~sunshine/whm2000/eger2.html).

Sarah Maguire, The Poetry Translation Centre (http://www.poetrytranslation.soas.ac.uk/poets/index.cfm?type=3&poet=18).

Saturday's Children: Poems of Work. Helen Plotz, ed. Greenwillow Books, 1982.

Saunders Lewis, "The Banned Wireless Talk on Welsh Nationalism." (http://www.gtj.org.uk/en/item1/14563).

Scars Upon My Heart: Women's Poetry and Verse of the First World War. Catherine W. Reilly, ed. Virago Press, 1981.

School of Celtic Studies — Tionól 2005, Abstracts (http://www.celt.dias.ie/gaeilge/tionol/achoim05.html).

Scotch Myth — Thomas the Rhymer (http://www.firstfoot.com/scotchmyth/thomastherhymer.htm).

Scotland's Lawyer Poets (http://www.wvu.edu/~lawfac/jelkins/lp-2001/intro/scots.html).

Scots Language Resource Centre (http://scotsyett.com/scotsoun.htm).

ScotseXt! Roughs (http://www.scotstext.org/roughs/whistlebinkie/whistlebinkie%20_prefaces.asp).

Scottish Authors, George Campbell Hay (http://www.slainte.org.uk/scotauth/hayjodsw.htm).

Scottish Authors, Hugh MacDiarmid (http://www.slainte.org.uk/scotauth/macdidsw.htm).

Scottish Authors, William Soutar (http://www.slainte.org.uk/scotauth/soutadsw.htm).

The Scottish Collection of Verse to 1800. Eileen Dunlop and Kamm Antony, ed. Richard Drew, 1985.

Scottish Literature 1: What were/are the Middle Ages?, (http://www.englit.ed.ac.uk/studying/undergrd/scottish_lit_1/Handouts/sd_intro_middleages.htm).

The Scottish Poetry Library, Gael Turnbull (http://www.spl.org.uk/news/2004_0707.html).

The Scottish Poetry Library, Leontia Flynn (http://www.spl.org.uk/poets_a-z/flynn.html).

Scottish Poetry Selection: Here's to You Again, Alexander Rodger (http://www.rampantscotland.com/poetry/blpoems_toddle.htm).

Scottish Poetry Selection — Life of Sir William Wallace, an Extract of the Poem by Blind Harry (http://www.rampantscotland.com/poetry/blpoems_wallace.htm).

Scottish Women Poets of the Romantic Period (http://www.alexanderstreet2.com/SWRPLive/bios/S7032-D001.html).

The Seamus Heaney Centre for Poetry, at the School of English, Queen's University Belfast. Poems by Sinead Morrissey (http://www.qub.ac.uk/heaneycentre/research/sinead-listofpoems.htm).

Searc's Web Guide to 20th Century Ireland — Thomas MacDonagh (http://www.searcs-web.com/mcdonagh.html).

Sebastian Barry (http://www.contemporarywriters.com/authors/?p=auth02B11P375512626533).

A Second Treasury of the Familiar. Ralph L. Woods, ed. Macmillan, 1950.

Select Collection of Poems: With Notes, Biographical and Historical, by J. Nichols. The Second Volume (http://www.orgs.muohio.edu/anthologies/nichol2.htm).

Select Poems of Winthrop Mackworth Praed. Henry Frowde, 1909.

Selected Bibliography: Mary Leapor (1722–1746) By Laura Mandell, Miami University of Ohio (http://www.c18.rutgers.edu/biblio/leapor.html).

Selected Poems and Letters of Isaac Rosenberg. Jean Liddiard, ed. Enitharmon Press, 2003.

Selected Poems by Jeff Nuttall (2003): Review by James Wilkes, 2004 (http://terriblework.co.uk/jeff_nuttall.htm).

Selected Poems by Robert Buchanan (www.victorianweb.org/authors/buchanan).

Selected Poems 1955–1997 of Charles Tomlinson. New Directions, 1997.

Selected Poems 1957–1981 of Ted Hughes. Faber and Faber, 1982.

Selected Poems of Aleksandr Blok. Carcanet Press, 2000.

Selected Poems of Anne Finch, Countess of Winchilsea. Denys Thompson, ed. Carcanet Press, 1987.

Selected Poems of Ben Jonson. Ian Donaldson, ed. Oxford University Press, 1995.

Selected Poems of Bronte Sisters (www.web-books.com/Classics/Poetry/Anthology/Bronte).

Selected Poems of Christopher Logue. Christopher Reid, ed. Faber and Faber, 1996.

Selected Poems of Derek Mahon. Viking, 1991.

Selected Poems of Desmond Egan (http://mek.oszk.hu/00200/00271/html/index_ir.htm).

Selected Poems of Eugene Lee-Hamilton. The Edwin Mellen Press, 2002.

The Selected Poems of Frank Prewett. Bruce Meyer and Barry Callaghan, ed. Toronto: Exile Editions, 1987.

Selected Poems of Ivor Gurney. P.J. Kavanagh, ed. Oxford University Press, 1990.

Selected Poems of Jenny Joseph. Bloodaxe Books, 1992.

Selected Poems of John Riley. Michael Grant, ed. Carcanet Press, 1995.

Selected Poems of Joseph Skipsey. Ceolfrith Press, 1976.

Selected Poems of Kathleen Raine. Lindisfarne Press, 1988.

Selected Poems of Marina Tsvetaeva. Elaine Feinstein, ed. Penguin Books, 1993.

Selected Poems of Matthew Prior. Austin Dobson, ed. Kegan Paul, Trench & Co., 1889.

Selected Poems of Randall Swingler. Andy Croft, ed. Trent Editions, 2000.

Selected Poems of Robert Browning. Daniel Karlin, ed. Penguin Books, 1989.

Selected Poems of Robert Stephen Hawker. Cecil Woolf, ed. Cecil Woolf, 1975.

Selected Poems of Saunders Lewis, Translated by Joseph P. Clancy. University Of Wales Press. 1993.

Selected Poems of Sir David Lyndsay. Janet Hadley Williams, ed. Association for Scottish Literary Studies, 2000.

Selected Poems of Sir Philip Sidney. Catherine Bates, ed. Penguin Books, 1994.

Selected Poems of Walter De La Mare. Faber and Faber, 1973.

Selected Poetry of Hugh MacDiarmid. Alan Riach and Michael Grieve, ed. New Directions, 1992.

Selected Work of Alexander Rodger (http://quartet.cs.unb.ca/tapor/cgi-bin/view-works.cgi?c=rodgeral.1112&pos=3).

Selected Writings of the Laureate Dunces, Nahum Tate, Laurence Eusden, and Colley Cibber. The Edwin Mellen Press, 1999.

Selection of Poems by Joseph Mary Plunkett. A Taste of Ireland's Poets (http://www.rc.net/wcc/ireland/plunkett.htm).

Selections from Hoccleve. M.C. Seymour, ed. Clarendon Press, 1981.

Selections from Robert Landor. Eric Partridge, ed. the Fanfrolico Press, 1927.

Selections from the Letters of Geraldine Endsor Jewsbury to Jane Welsh Carlyle, 1892 (http://digital.library.upenn.edu/women/jewsbury/letters/gej.html).

Selections from the Poems of Sir Walter Scott. A. Hamilton Thompson, ed. Reprint Services 1921.

Selections from the Works of Sir Lewis Morris. Kegan Paul, 1897.

Septuagesima, Poem by John Burnside (http://www.thepoem.co.uk/poems/burnside.htm).

SETIS: The Scholarly Electronic Text and Image Service — English Poetry Collection (http://setis.library.usyd.edu.au).

Seven Centuries of Poetry: Chaucer to Dylan Thomas. A.N. Jeffares, ed. Longmans, Green, 1955.

17. Cibber's the Careless Husband, page 31 (http://www.questia.com/PM.qst?a=o&d=96240127).

1798 Ireland: History and Links (http://homepages.iol.ie/~fagann/1798/).

Seventeenth and Early Eighteenth Century Sonnets (www.sonnets.org/edwards.htm).

Seventeenth-Century British Poetry: 1603–1660. John P. Rumrich, ed. University of Texas, Austin and Gregory Chaplin, Bridgewater State University, W.W. Norton, 2005.

Seventeenth Century Poetry: The Schools of Donne and Jonson. Hugh Kenner, ed. Holt, Rinehart and Winston, 1964.

Seventeenth-Century Verse and Prose. Vol. II: 1660–1700. Helen C. White, et al, ed. Macmillan. 1951, 1952.

Sewing Fingers, by Jean Sprackland: The Poetry Book Society (http://www.poetrybooks.co.uk/PBS/pbs_sprackland_jean.asp).

Shades of Green. Anne Harvey, ed. Greenwillow Books, 1991.

ShadoWork (http://mariopetrucci.port5.com/shadowork.htm).

Shakespeare and George Puttenham's The Arte of English Poesie. UPSO (Universal Publishing Solutions Online) Ltd., 2003.

The Shakespeare Mystery: Harvard Magazine Article × PBS (http://www.pbs.org/wgbh/pages/frontline/shakespeare/debates/harvardmag.html).

Shakespeare's Shrine By John Harris. Hamilton, Adams, and Co., 1866.

She Lived Beside the Anner (http://sniff.numachi.com/~rickheit/dtrad/pages/tiLNDMNTN.html).

Ships of the 18th Cent. Royal Navy (http://www.cronab.demon.co.uk/18a.HTM).

A Short Biographical Dictionary of English Literature (www.blackmask.com/thatway/books164c/shobio.htm).

Short Biography and Works of Leland Bardwell (http://www.artscouncil.ie/aosdana/biogs/literature/lelandbardwell.html).

The Shorter Poems of Gavin Douglas. 2nd edition. P. Bawcutt, ed. Scottish Text Society, 2003.

The Shorter Poems of Ralph Knevet. A Critical Edition. Amy M. Charles. Ohio State University Press, 1966.

Shrieks at Midnight: Macabre Poems, Eerie and Humorous. Sara Brewton, and John E. Brewton, ed. Thomas Y. Crowell, 1969.

Shylock Reasons with Mr. Chesterton by Humbert Wolfe. B. Blackwell, 1920.

Sidney Sussex College Cambridge (www.sid.cam.ac.uk).

Sieges of Limerick (http://members.tripod.com/Preachan/sieges1.html).

Significant and Famous Scots (http://www.electricscotland.com).

Silver Poets of the Sixteenth Century. Gerald Bullett, ed. J.M. Dent, 1947.

Sing a Song of Popcorn: Every Child's Book of Poems. Beatrice Schenck De Regniers, and others, ed. Scholastic, 1988.

Singing Brink: Anthology of Poetry from Lumb Bank. Maura Dooley & David Hunter, ed. Arvon Press, 1988.

The Sir Richard Burton Society (www.pages.drexel.edu/~garsonkw/burton.html).

Sir Walter Scott's Poem, Marmion. (http://www.cs.rice.edu/~ssiyer/minstrels/poems/495.html).

Skywriting by Charles Tomlinson. Carcanet Press, 2003.

Snowy Morning, Poem by Henry Shukman (http://www.thepoem.co.uk/poems/shukman.htm).

Some Contemporary Poets of Britain and Ireland: An Anthology. Michael Schmidt, ed. Carcanet Press, 1983.

Some Sidelights on Ralph Erskine by Alasdair B. Gordon (http://www.puritansermons.com/erskine/erskin16.htm).

Song of the Squatters, Robert Lowe. Australian Bush Ballads (http://www.geocities.com/yorligau/poems.htm#sots).

Songs and Meditations by Maurice Hewlett. Archibald Constable and Co., 1896.

Songs and Poems of John Skinner. G. Reid, 1859.

Songs Collected by Donagh MacDonagh (http://songbook1.tripod.com/)

Songs from the British Drama. Edward Bliss Reed, ed. Yale University Press, 1925.

Songs from the Clay by James Stephens. The Macmillan Company, 1915.

The Songs of Duncan Ban Macintyre. Angus Macleod, ed. Scottish Gaelic Text Society, 1952.

Songs, Merry and Sad of John Charles McNeill. Alan R. Light, ed. Stone, 1906.

The Sonnet: An Anthology. Robert M. Bender and Charles L. Squier, ed. Washington Square Press, 1987.

Sonnet Central (http://www.sonnets.org/white.htm).

The Sonnet-Series: Page Seventeen by John Erskine, The Elizabethan Lyric. Macmillan Company, 1903 reprinted by Columbia University Press, 1916.

The Sonnet Series, Richard Linche (http://www.sonnets.org/erskineq.htm).

Sonnets of the Century (http://www.sonnets.org/bibliogr.htm#sharp1).

The Sonnets of Thomas Edwards (1765, 1780). William Andrews Clark Memorial Library, University of California, 1974.

The Sophisticated Cat: A Gathering of Stories, Poems, and Miscellaneous Writings about Cats. Joyce Oates, Carol and Daniel Halpern, ed. Penguin Books, 1992.

Sorbie Village (http://www.whithorn.info/community/sorbie.htm).

Sorley MacLean—An Obituary. The Capital Scot (http://thecapitalscot.com/pastfeatures/smaclean.html).

Sound and Sense: An Introduction to Poetry. 6th edition. Harcourt Brace Jovanovich, 1982.

Sound Eye (http://indigo.ie/~tjac/Poets/Randolph_Healy/randolph_healy.htm).

Sound the Deep Waters: Women's Romantic Poetry in the Victorian Age. Pamela Norris, ed. Little, Brown, 1991.

The Sources for Anne Finch's Translations, Adaptations, Imitations (http://www.jimandellen.org/finch/tollete.html).

Spaceways: An Anthology of Space Poems. John Foster, ed. Oxford University Press, 1986.

Spanner (Magazine) Home Page, Allen Fisher (http://www.shadoof.net/spanner/).

Speak Roughly to Your Little Boy. Myra Cohn Livingston, ed. Harcourt Brace Jovanovich, 1971.

The Speaker's Treasury of 400 Quotable Poems. Croft M. Pentz, ed. Zondervan, 1963.

The Spike Milligan Tribute Site (http://www.spikemilligan.co.uk/4680/index.html).

The Spleen and Other Poems by Matthew Green, The Cayme Press, 1925.

Splinters: A Book of Very Short Poems. Michael Harrison, ed. Oxford University Press, 1989.

Sprints and Distances: Sports in Poetry and the Poetry in Sport. Lillian Morrison, ed. Thomas Y. Crowell, 1965.

Stanford University Libraries And Academic Information Resources (http://library.stanford.edu).

Stephen's Study Room: British Military & Criminal History in the period 1900 to 1999 (http://www.stephen-stratford.co.uk/thos_macdonagh.htm).

The Steward of Christendom, details of the play (http://www.glue.umd.edu/~sschreib/autumn_02/investigations/steward.html).

Storm Lines, Poem by Henry Shukman (http://www.tnr.com/directory/keyword.mhtml?kid=93).

Strange Meetings by Monro, Harold. The Poetry Bookshop, 1921.

Subaltern on the Somme. Max Plowman. Naval and Military Press, 2001.

Submarine Base, Holy Loch, Scotland (http://holyloch.com).

SubRon 14, Holy Loch, Scotland, 1961 to 1992 (http://www.thistle group.net/holyloch/).

Summer by Deryn Rees-Jones (http://www.poetrybooks.co.uk/ PBS/pbs_rees_jones_deryn.asp).

Summer Fires: New Poetry of Africa. Jack Mapange, Angus Calder and Cosmo Pieterse, ed. African Writers Series, Heinemann Educational, 1983.

A Summer in Skye, Alexander Smith—Word Power (http://www. word-power.co.uk/catalogue/1874744386).

Sung Under the Silver Umbrella. Association for Childhood Education International, ed. Macmillan, 1935.

The Superfluous Woman, Poem by Vera Brittain (1920) (http://www. aftermathww1.com/brittain.asp).

Surrealist Poetry in English. Edward B. Germain, ed. Penguin Books, 1978.

Sweet Little Anger, by Sir Samuel Egerton Brydges. Angelic Poetry (www.sarahsarchangels.com/poems/poems3.html).

The Sylvia Townsend Warner Society Homepage (http://www. townsendwarner.com/bibliography.htm).

The Symbolist Poem: The Development of the English Tradition. Edward Engelberg, ed. E.P. Dutton, 1967.

Taliesin Arts Centre, Swansea (http://www.taliesinartscentre. co.uk/index.asp?id=1).

Teesonline: Outlet: Who's Who in Literary Cleveland (http://www. teesonline.org.uk/?lid=2205).

Tennyson: A Selected Edition. Christopher Ricks, ed. University of California Press, 1989.

The Texas Historical Commission (http://www.thc.state.tx.us/triv iafun/trvdefault.html).

Text of Yr Eneiniog by Hedd Wyn (http://cy.wikisource.org/ wiki/Yr_Arwr).

Texts of John Hughes set to music (http://www.recmusic.org/ lieder/h/jhughes/).

Texts of William Hunnis set to music (http://www.recmusic. org/lieder/h/hunnis/).

Thelma Texts in The Internet Sacred Text Archive (http://www. sacred-texts.com/oto/index.htm).

A Third Treasury of the Familiar. Ralph L. Woods, ed. Macmillan, 1970.

Thirteen Ways of Looking at Tony Conran. Nigel Jenkins, ed. Welsh Union of Writers, 1995.

This Same Sky: A Collection of Poems from around the World. Naomi Shihab Nye, ed. Four Winds Press, 1992.

Thomas Durfey and the Restoration Drama: The Work of a Forgotten Writer. John McVeagh. Ashgate Publishing, Limited, 2000.

Thomas d'Urfey, Texts Set to Music (http://www.recmusic.org/ lieder/u/durfey/).

Three Poems by Billy Childish (http://www.3ammagazine.com/ poetry/2002_jun/three_poems.html).

Three Poems by Edna Wyley (http://www.dedaluspress.com/ samples/wyley-poems.html).

Three Short Love Poems by Edna Wyley (http://www.brakkehond. be/76/wyley1e.html).

The Three Treatises of Philalethes, in The Hermetic Museum. pp 227–269. Arthur Edward Waite, Samuel Weiser, Inc. York Beach, Maine, paperback edition, 1991.

Threepenny: Kitay, Thom Gunn (http://www.threepennyreview. com/samples/kitay_su05.html).

Through the Year with the Poets. Oscar Fay Adams, ed. D. Lothrop and Company, 1886.

The Times Obituary of Dylan Thomas November 10, 1953. Microsoft Encarta 2006 [DVD]. Microsoft Corporation, 2006.

To Her Cousin, F.W., Isabella Whitney. Erin M. Harper, ed (http://www.users.muohio.edu/clarkjd/harper98.html).

Tom Pickard Interview Published March 2002 (http://www.lindis farne.de/interviews/ivtp0203.htm).

The Tom Raworth Home Page (http://tomraworth.com/biblio. html).

Tongues of Fire: An Anthology of Religious and Poetic Experience. Karen Armstrong, ed. Penguin Books, 1987.

Tony Curtis in De Brakke Hond (http://www.brakkehond.be/ bio.asp?au=Tony+Curtis).

The Top 500 Poems. William Harmon, ed. Columbia University Press, 1992.

Tours of Scotland, My Native Homeland (http://www.fife.50megs. com/sir-william-mure.htm).

A Tragic Troubadour: The Life and Collected Works of the Cork Folklorist, Poet and Translator, Edward Walsh (1805–1850). John J. Ó Ríordáin, CSSR, 2005.

Tragical Tales, and Other Poems: By George Turbervile, (no publisher) 1837.

Translation of Dao De Jing: The Way and Its Power. The Naturalist, Individualist and Politic Doctrine of Lao-tse Exhibited in 81 Poetic and Obscure Texts. Tr. Waley (en), Lau (en), Julien (fr) and Wilhelm (de) (http://afpc.asso.fr/wengu/wg/wengu.php?l= Daodejing&no=6).

The Treasury of Christian Poetry. Lorraine Eitel, ed. Fleming H. Revell, 1982.

The Treasury of English Poetry. Mark Caldwell and Walter Kendrick, ed. Doubleday, 1984.

Treasury of Favorite Poems. Joseph H. Head, ed. Gramercy Books, 2000.

A Treasury of Great Poems: English and American. Louis Untermeyer, ed. Simon and Schuster, 1955.

Treasury of Irish Religious Verse. Patrick Murray, ed. Crossroad, 1986.

A Treasury of Jewish Poetry. Nathan Ausubel, and Maryann Ausubel, ed. Crown, 1957.

A Treasury of Minor British Poetry. J. Churton Collins, ed. Edward Arnold, 1896.

A Treasury of Poems for Worship and Devotion. Charles L. Wallis, ed. Harper, 1959.

The Treasury of Religious Verse. Donald T. Kauffman, ed. Fleming H. Revell, 1962.

A Treasury of the Familiar. Ralph L. Woods, ed. Macmillan, 1942.

A Treasury of War Poetry—The Fallen (www.geocities.com/ ~bblair/fallen_twp.htm).

Treaties 1 and 2, Between Her Majesty the Queen and the Chippewa and Cree Indians of Manitoba and Country Adjacent with Adhesions, 1871 (http://collections.ic.gc.ca/aboriginaldocs/treaty/ html/t-treaty1.htm).

The Treshnish Isles and Cairnburgh Castle, Mull (http://www.mull-historical-society.co.uk/cairnburgh-castle.htm).

Tristram Shandy Online (http://www.gifu-u.ac.jp/~masaru/TS/ contents.html).

The Triumphant Cat. Walter Payne, ed. Carrol and Graf, 1993.

Turning Tides: Modern Dutch and Flemish Verse in English Versions by Irish Poets. Peter van de Kamp, ed. Story Line Press, 1994.

Twentieth Century Anglo-Welsh Poetry. Dannie Abse, ed. Seren Books, Dufour Editions, 1997.

Twentieth-Century Poetry: American and British (1900–1970). John Malcolm Brinnin, and Bill Read, ed. McGraw Hill, Rev. ed., 1970.

Twentieth Century Russian Poetry: Silver and Steel, an Anthology. Doubleday, 1993.

24-Hour War. Is Christopher Logue a genius or a madman? Jim Lewis, 2003 (http://slate.msn.com/id/2082824/).

A Twist in the Tale. Valerie Bloom, ed. Macmillan Children's Books, 2005.

Two Poems by Michal Rosen (http://www.thediagram.com/4_5/ rosen.html).

Two Poems by Theo Dorgan (http://www.munsterlit.ie/Conwrit ers/poems_by_theo.htm).

Tygers of Wrath: Poems of Hate, Anger, and Invective. X.J. Kennedy, ed. University of Georgia Press, 1981.

Unauthorized Versions: Poems and Their Parodies. Kenneth Baker, ed. Faber and Faber, 1990.

Under All Silences: Shades of Love. Ruth Gordon, ed. Harper & Row, 1987.

Under Another Sky: An Anthology of Commonwealth Poetry Prize Winners. Alastair Niven, ed. Carcanet Press, 1987.

Underglimpses, and Other Poems of MacCarthy, Denis Florence. David Bogue, 1857.

An Uninhibited Treasury of Erotic Poetry. Louis Untermeyer, ed. Dial Press, 1963.

Unity Hymns and Chorals. William Channing Gannett, ed. Unity Publishing Company, 1911.

University College Dublin (http://www.ucd.ie/).

University College Dublin Archives, Denis Devlin (http://www.ucd. ie/archives/html/collections/devlin-dennis.html).

University of Delaware Library: Forging a Collection (http://www. lib.udel.edu/ud/spec/exhibits/forgery/ossian.htm).

University of Delaware: Special Collections Department. ARCHIVE OF THE PARK 1. Andrew Crozier (http://www.lib.udel.edu/ ud/spec/findaids/thepark.htm).

University of Exeter Library (http://www.library.ex.ac.uk/ special/guides/archives/081–90/082_01.html).

University of Glamorgan, Staff Pages (http://www.glam.ac.uk/ hassschool/staff/personal_pages).

University of Reading, Papers of Bernard Spencer (http://www. library.rdg.ac.uk/colls/special/spencer.html).

University of Sussex Library Special Collections: Charles Madge (http://www.sussex.ac.uk/library/speccoll/collection_introduc tions/madge.html).

University of Sydney Library: Fifty Years in the Making of Australian History (http://setis.library.usyd.edu.au/ozlit/pdf/fed0024.pdf).

University of Wales, Centre for Advanced Welsh & Celtic Studies (http://www.wales.ac.uk/newpages/EXTERNAL/E4156.asp).

The Unofficial Website of Lord Alfred "Bosie" Douglas (http:// www.geocities.com/starparty1/bosie/).

Untune the Sky: Poems of Music and Dance. Helen Plotz, ed. Thomas Y. Crowell, 1957.

The Unutterable Beauty. The Collected Poetry of G.A. Studdert Kennedy. Hodder and Stoughton, 1927 (http://www.mun. ca/rels/restmov/texts/dasc/TUB.HTM).

Valerie Bloom's Home Page (http://www.valbloom.co.uk/).

The Valley Near Slievenamon: A Kickham Anthology: The Poems: Letters: Memoirs: Essays: Diary: Addresses of Charles J. Kickham James Maher Mullinahone, ed. James Maher, 1942.

A Various Art. Andrew Crozier, and Tim Longville, ed. Carcanet Press, 1987.

Vasco Da Gama: 1498, North Park University (http://campus.north park.edu/history/WebChron/WestEurope/DaGama.html).

Verses Written in India by Alfred Lyall. Kegan Paul, 1890.

Very Bad Poetry. Kathryn Petras and Ross Petras, ed. Vintage Books, 1997.

Vicci Bentley interviews Vicki Feaver (http://www.poetrymagazines. org.uk/magazine/record.asp?id=3900).

Victor West on the Poetry Express (http://pages.britishlibrary.net/ poetry.express/log/VW I.html).

A Victorian Anthology, 1837–1895. Edmund Clarence Stedman, ed. Cambridge: Riverside Press, 1895.

Victorian Literature: Poetry. Donald Gray, and G.B. Tennyson, ed. Macmillan, 1976.

Victorian Parlor Poetry: An Annotated Anthology. Michael R. Turner, ed. Dover Publications, 1992.

The Victorian Sonnet (http://www.sonnets.org/victoria.htm).

Victorian Verse. George MacBeth, ed. Penguin Books, 1986.

The Victorian Web (http://www.victorianweb.org/authors/hallam/ bioov.html).

The Victorian Web (http://www.victorianweb.org/authors/morris/ wmbio.html).

Victorian Women Poets: An Anthology. Angela Leighton, and Margaret Reynolds, ed. Blackwell, 1991.

The Virago Book of Love Poetry. Wendy Mulford, ed. Virago Press, 1990.

Virtual American Biographies: Sir Hovenden Walker (http://www. famousamericans.net/sirhovendenwalker/).

Virtual Writer (http://www.virtualwriter.net/vona-groarke.htm).

Visiting Emily: Poems Inspired by the Life and Work of Emily Dickinson. Sheila Coghill and Thom Tammaro, ed. University of Iowa Press, 2000.

Voices in the Gallery. Dannie Abse and Joan Abse, ed. Tate Gallery, 1986.

Voices Within the Ark: The Modern Jewish Poets. Howard Schwartz, and Anthony Rudolf, ed. Avon Books, 1980.

Waldo Williams. Tony Conran (Translator). Gomer Press, 1997.

Wales Loses Its Most Sustained Lyric Voice, R.S. Thomas (http:// www.guardian.co.uk/uk_news/story/0,3604,373779,00.html)

Wales on the Web: Poetry (http://www.walesontheweb.org/cayw/ index/en/821/all).

Wales Online, John Ceiriog Hughes (http://www.walesonline.com/ info/literature/jchughes.shtml).

The Wallace by Nigel Tranter (http://www.scottishradiance.com/ bookreviews/wallrev.htm).

War and the Poet: An Anthology of Poetry Expressing Man's Attitudes to War from Ancient Times to the Present. Richard Eberhart, and Selden Rodman, ed. Devin-Adair, 1945.

War Poems of Wilfred Owen. Wilfred Owen. Jon Stallworthy, ed. Chatto and Windus, 1994.

The War Poets: An Anthology of the War Poetry of the 20thCentury. Oscar Williams, ed. John Day, 1945.

The War Poets Association (http://www.warpoets.org/conflicts/ ww2/keyes/).

The War Poets Association: Arthur Graeme West (http://www.war poets.org/conflicts/greatwar/west/).

War Poets Association. The Life of Alun Lewis (http://www.war poets.org/conflicts/ww2/lewis/).

War Songs. Christopher Stone, ed. Oxford University Press, 1908.

Washington University, St Louis, University Libraries. Collection of Edith Joy Scovell (http://library.wustl.edu/units/spec/manu scripts/mlc/scovell/scovell.html).

Watchers and Seekers: Creative Writing by Black Women in Britain. Rhonda Cobham, and Merle Collins, ed. Peter Bedrick Books, 1988.

A Web Guide to Geoffrey Hill (http://www.literaryhistory.com/ 20thC/HillG.htm).

The Wedderburn Book (Volume 1, p 317), published privately by Alexander Wedderburn, 1898.

The Wedderburn Pages. The Gude and Godlie Ballatis, and history of the Wedderburn family (http://perso.wanadoo.fr/euroleader/ wedderburn/gudeandgodlie.htm#Play%20on%20your%20lute).

The Welsh Academy Encyclopedia of Wales. Nigel Jenkins, ed. University of Wales Press, 2006.

A Welsh American Portfolio (http://www.wiu.edu/foliopress/welsh/ pages/pcurtis.htm 0).

Wesley Centre Online. John Wesley's Christian Library. Northwest Nazarene University, Nampa, USA (http://wesley.nnu.edu/ index.htm)

Westminster Abbey Official Guide (no date).

What Cheer: An Anthology of American and British Humorous and Witty Verse. David McCord, ed. Coward-McCann, 1945.

What's Left of Wesley's. London. Methodist Recorder pp 9–12). Methodist Newspaper Co. Ltd. 122 Golden Lane, London, ECIY 0TL. January 5, 2006,

Wheel and Come Again: An Anthology of Reggae Poetry. Kwame Dawes, ed. Goose Lane Editions, 1998.

Whetstone's Rock of Regard. George Whetstone. Collier Reprints, ?1870.

Whitbread Prize Book Awards 2005 (http://www.lmsbooks.co.uk/ WhitbreadPrize.htm).

Who Has Seen the Wind? An Illustrated Collection of Poetry for Young People. Kathryn Sky-Peck, ed. Museum of Fine Arts, Boston, 1991.

Who's Who. London: A & C Black, 2005.

Who's Who in the Jacobite Camp (http://homepage.ntlworld.com/ stephen.lord2/Page%20Four.htm).

Why Am I Grown So Cold? Poems of the Unknowable, Myra Cohn Livingston, ed. Atheneum, 1982.

Wikipedia, the Free Encyclopedia (http://en.wikipedia.org/wiki/ Wikipedia).

William Butler Yeats, "To Dorothy Wellesley" (http://plagiarist.com/ poetry/3440).

William Crowe, Lewesdon Hill, 1788 (http://www.arts.ualberta. ca/~dmiall/Tintern/Crowe.htm).

William Drummond of Hawthornden, Poems (http://www.sonnets. org/drummond.htm).

William Falconer's Dictionary of the Marine (http://southseas. nla.gov.au/refs/falc/title.html).

William Hunnis: Certayne Psalmes (http://newmedia.alma.edu/ ottenhoff/psalm51/hunnis.htm).

William Kennish Poet, Inventor, Engineer, Explorer (http://www.isle-of-man.com/manxnotebook/iomnhas/v062p181.htm).

William Motherwell's Cultural Politics by Mary Ellen Brown. University Press of Kentucky (http://www.kentuckypress.com/view book.cfm?Group=13&ID=387).

William Robert Rodgers: The Susquehanna Quarterly. (c) (http:// susquehannaquarterly.org/rodgers.htm).

William Wordsworth's Dove Cottage (http://www.wordsworth. org.uk/).

The Windows Project, Poetry. Matt Simpson's Publications (www.windowsproject.demon.co.uk/writers/simpson.htm).

Winter Interiors by Peter Robinson (http://www.webdelsol.com/Perihelion/robinsonpoetry.htm).

Wolf Tongue: Selected Poems 1965–2000. Barry MacSweeney. Bloodaxe Books, 2003.

The Women Poets in English: An Anthology. Ann Stanford, ed. McGraw-Hill, 1972.

Women Romantic Poets, 1785–1832: An Anthology. Jennifer Breen, ed. J.M. Dent & Sons, 1992.

Women Writing Before 1800: Elizabeth Carter (1717–1806) (http://www.18thcenturyarchive.org/women/Carter/default.htm).

Women's Poetry of the 1930's: A Critical Anthology. Jane Dowson, ed. Routledge, 1966.

Words of a Woman: A Website for Poems by Women (http://www.photoaspects.com/lilip/wilde.shtml).

Working Women in Victorian Britain, 1850–1910: The Diaries and Letters of Arthur J. Munby (1828–1910) and Hannah Cullwick (1833–1909) from Trinity College, Cambridge. Marlborough, Wiltshire: Adam Matthew Publications, 1993. 32 reels (http://www.library.utoronto.ca/robarts/microtext/collection/pages/workwomn.html).

The Works in Verse and Prose of Nicholas Breton. Rev. Alexander B. Grosart, ed. Edinburgh University Press, 1879.

The Works of Alexander Pennecuik, Esq. A. Allardice, 1815.

The Works of Andrew Marvell (http://www.luminarium.org/sevenlit/marvell/marvbib.htm).

The Works of Charles and Mary Lamb V. 5. G.P. Putnam's Sons, 1903.

The works of Derek Mahon (http://www.infoplease.com/ipea/A0901434.html).

Works of Eiléan Ní Chuilleanáin (http://www.irishwriters-online.com/eileannichuilleanain.html).

The Works of Francis Thompson Poems, (3 volumes). Wilfred Meynell, ed. Burns & Oats Ltd., 1913.

The Works of George Peele: Volumes the First & Second. A.H. Bullen, ed. Kennikat Press, Inc., 1966.

Works of Gerry Murphy (http://www.munsterlit.ie/Conwriters/gerry_murphy.htm).

Works of Gregory O'Donoghue (http://www.munsterlit.ie/Conwriters/gregory_o'donoghue.htm).

The Works of Henry Vaughan. Clarendon Press, 1957.

The Works of Henry VIII (http://www.luminarium.org/renlit/tudorbib.htm).

The Works of Jean Sprackland: The Poetry Archive (http://www.poetryarchive.org/poetryarchive/singlePoet.do?poetId=456).

The Works of John Dryden. NTC/Contemporary Publishing Company, 1999.

The Works of John Dryden (www.luminarium.org/eightlit/dryden/drydenbib.htm).

Works of John Taylor, The Water Poet, Spencer Society, 1869.

The Works of Laurence Minot (http://online.northumbria.ac.uk/faculties/art/humanities/cns/m-minot.html).

The works of Linton Kwesi Johnson (http://www.lkjrecords.com/lkj.html).

The Works of Mary Leapor, Richard Greene and Ann Messenger, ed. Oxford University Press, 2003.

The Works of Nicholas Rowe, Esq. Vol. 2. J. and R. Tonson and S. Draper, 1756.

Works of Nuala Ní Dhomhnaill (http://www.irishwriters-online.com/nualanidhomhnaill.html).

The Works of Peter Pindar. Printed for Walker and Edwards, London, 1816.

Works of Richard Murphy (http://www.irishwriters-online.com/richardmurphy.html).

The Works of Robert Louis Stevenson: Vailima Edition: (8 Volumes). William Heinemann and Chatto W, 1922.

The Works of Sir David Lindsay of the Moun. Douglas Hamer, ed. Printed for The Scottish Text Society by William Blackwood & Sons 1931–1936.

The Works of Sir John Suckling in Prose and Verse. A. Hamilton Thompson, ed. Reprint Services, 1910,

The Works of the British Poets V. 9 (*Dryden and Garth*). J. Sharpe, 1808.

Works of the British Poets, Vol. 6: The Poetical Works of Samuel Butler, Vol. 3, including the Poems of John Phillips. Thomas Park, ed. J. Sharpe, 1808.

The Works of the British Poets, Vol. 33 (*Blair, Glynn, Boyce, Shaw, Lovibond, and Penrose*). J. Sharpe, 1808.

The Works of Thomas Campion. Walter R. Davis, ed. W.W. Norton, 1969.

The Works of Thomas Sackville. John Russell Smith, 1859.

The Works of Tibullus. Suttaby, Evance, and Fox, 1812.

The Works of Tobias Smollett: Poems, Plays, and The Briton. University of Georgia Press, 1993.

World Haiku Review (WHR) Photo-Haiku Gallery, Gabriel Rosenstock (http://www.worldhaikureview.org/3–2/rosenstock-photohaiku/pages/biography.html).

World Poetry: An Anthology of Verse from Antiquity to Our Time. Katharine Washburn and John S. Major, ed. 1338, 1998.

A World Treasury of Oral Poetry. Ruth Finnegan, ed. Indiana University Press, 1978.

The World's Great Religious Poetry. Caroline Miles Hill, ed. Macmillan, 1954.

The Writings of Anna Wickham: Free Woman and Poet. Virago Press Ltd., 1984.

The Writings of William Brighty Rands (http://www.victorianweb.org/authors/rands/bibl.html).

A Year Full of Poems. Michael Harrison, and Christopher Stuart-Clark, ed. Oxford University Press, 1991.

Years Work in the Humanities Research Centre, 2003–2004, Thomas Proctor, Sheffield Hallam University (http://www.shu.ac.uk/research/hrc/work.html).

Yesterday, Today and Forever: A Poem, in Twelve Books. New York: Robert Carter and Brothers, 1875.

Yorkshire Dialect Poems edited by F.W. Moorman (http://www.hyphenologist.co.uk/songs/ydp.html).

The Yorkshire Post 28th October 1978 (John Riley's murder) (http://www.ypn.co.uk/).

Index